AF575205

REUTERS

THE STATE OF THE WORLD

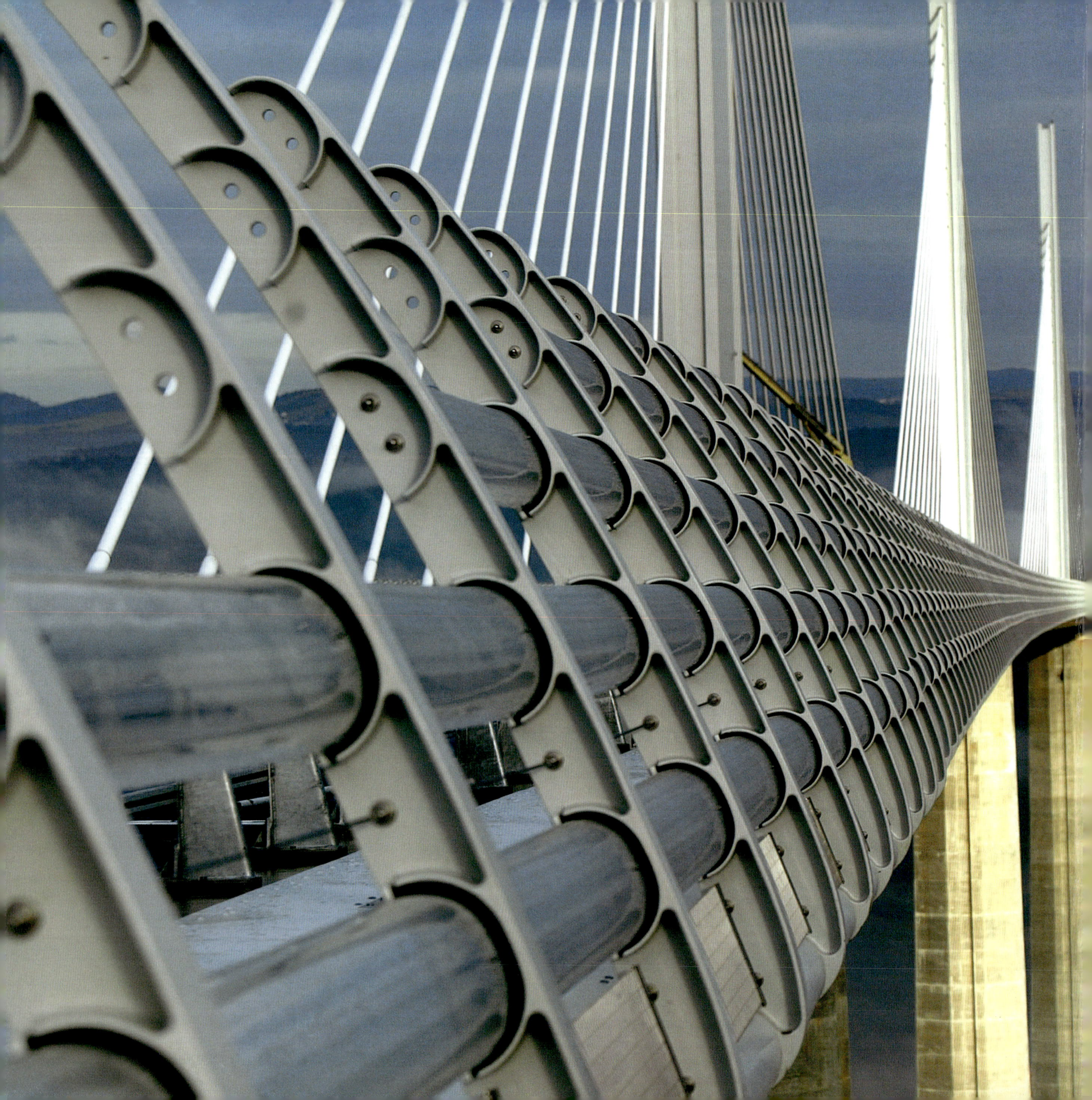

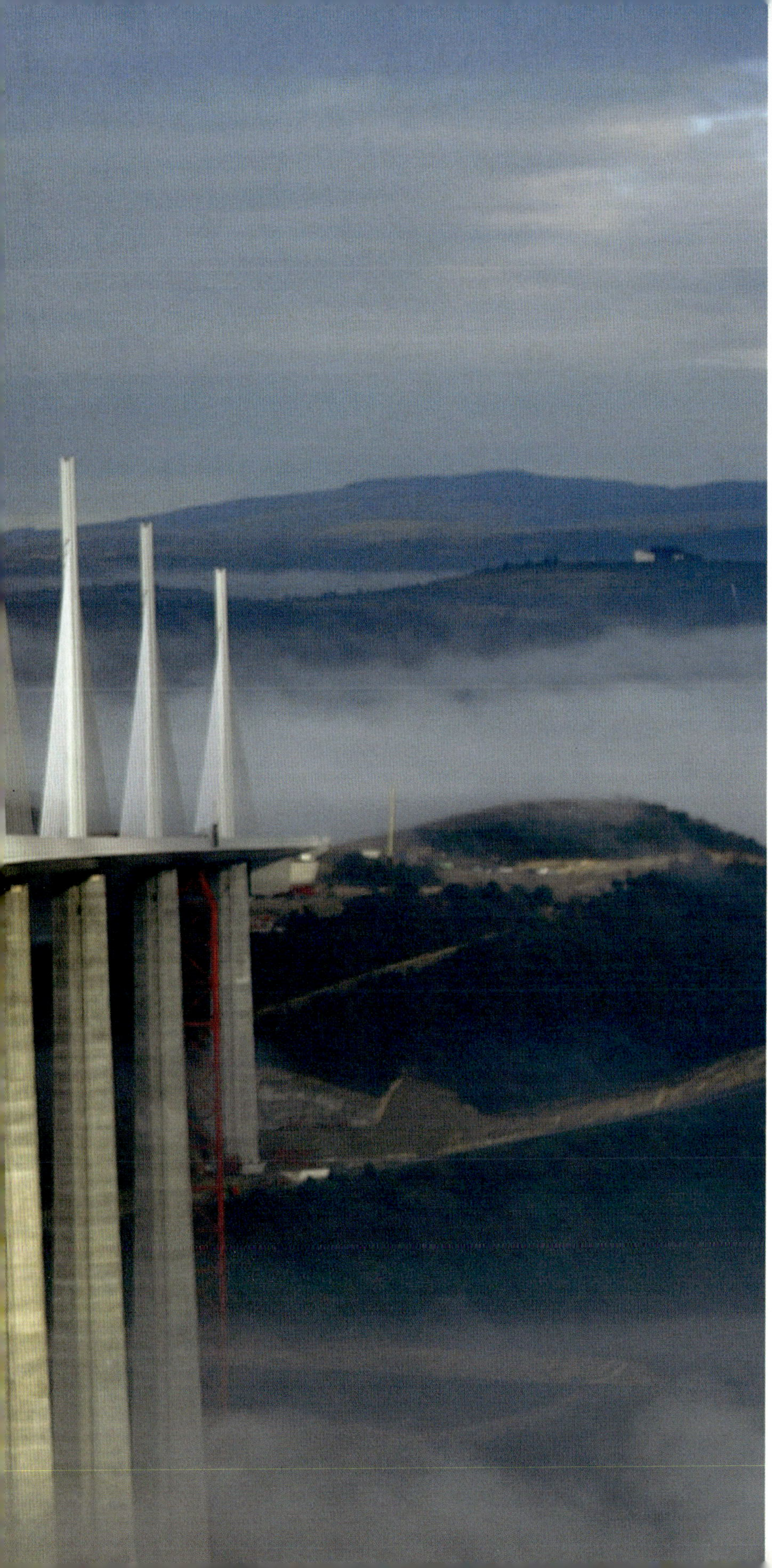

REUTERS

THE STATE OF THE WORLD

With 537 color illustrations

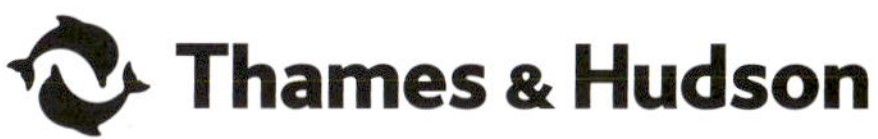

This book is dedicated to the *c.* 240 journalists killed in the course of reporting news in the first six years of the new century. We remember our Reuters colleagues:

Kurt Schork (2000, Sierra Leone)
Harry Burton (2001, Afghanistan)
Azizullah Haidari (2001, Afghanistan)
Taras Protsiuk (2003, Iraq)
Mazen Dana (2003, Iraq)
Adlan Khasanov (2004, Chechnya, Russia)
Dhia Najim (2004, Iraq)
Gene Boyd Lumawag (2004, Philippines)
Waleed Khaled (2005, Iraq)

Conceived, designed, edited and produced by
Thames & Hudson Ltd, London

For Reuters:
Executive director Monique Villa
Picture editor Ayperi Karabuda Ecer
Project director Jassim Ahmad

Art direction and design by Martin Andersen / Andersen M Studio

First published in 2006 in hardcover in the United States of America by Thames & Hudson Inc., 500 Fifth Avenue, New York, New York 10110

thamesandhudsonusa.com

Library of Congress Catalog Card Number 2006900830

ISBN-13: 978-0-500-54320-7
ISBN-10: 0-500-54320-8

Printed and bound in China by C&C Offset Printing Co. Ltd

CONTENTS

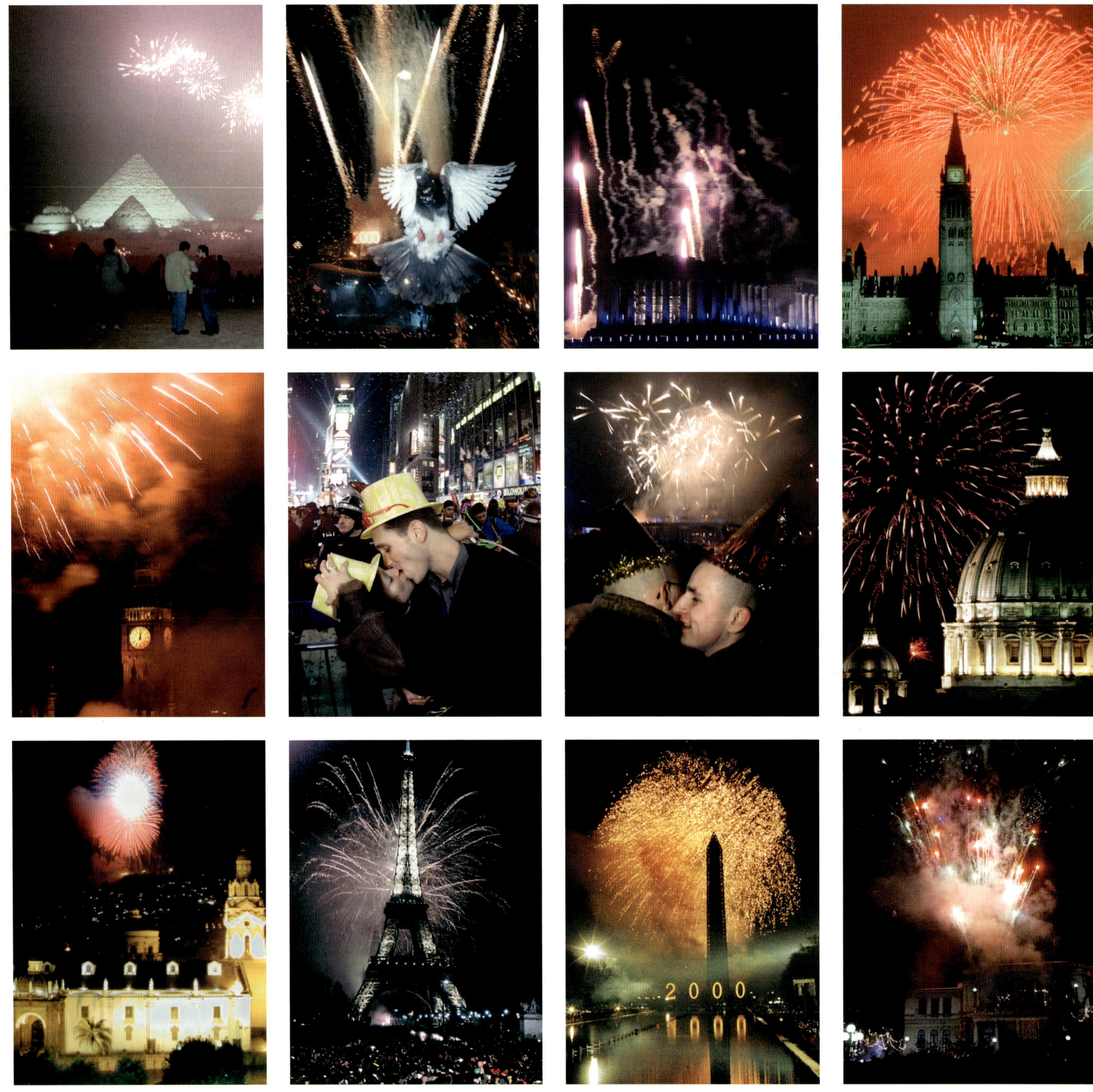
2000

INTRODUCTION

Life in the year 1000 was little different from what it had been a century before. By the year 2000, life in 1900 looked like a quaint bygone civilization. Now, even the turn of the third millennium is already starting to fade into history, such has been the accelerating pace of change in the few years since then.

Politics, economics, science, religion, the environment – almost everything has moved on since the world greeted the new epoch with parties, fireworks and messages of hope. For then it still seemed possible that with the Cold War over an era of peaceful coexistence was dawning. Those hopes vanished when airliners piloted by Islamic militants destroyed the World Trade Center in New York on September 11, 2001. That attack and the U.S.-led riposte in Afghanistan later the same year, and in Iraq in 2003, turned theories about a conflict of cultures into hard fact.

The twenty-first century has brought benefits for some. From Central Europe to China, liberalized economic systems are generating growing wealth. Rapidly advancing technology promises solutions to a host of problems. New drugs have brought hope to sufferers from cancer and AIDS. But, driven by short-term commercial logic, scientific progress remains uneven. Computing and communications have bounded ahead. Yet, despite the threat of global warming, no serious alternative to fossil fuels has so far been found as an energy source. And economic imbalances mean billions in the developing world are shut out from progress and prosperity, condemned to live in poverty at the mercy of natural disasters or corrupt rulers.

Few people have been better placed to chronicle the key events and trends of the opening years of the new century than the reporters and photographers of Reuters. Their job puts them in the front line wherever news is happening, sometimes at great danger, as the death of nine Reuters journalists in the first six years of the millennium testifies. This book is their first-hand take on the world's most recent history.

1 January 2000, WORLDWIDE

Opposite Millennium celebrations across the world. Top row (left to right): Cairo, Bethlehem, Athens, Ottawa. Middle row: London, New York, Warsaw, Vatican. Bottom row: Quito, Paris, Washington, DC, Sarajevo. See also page 380.

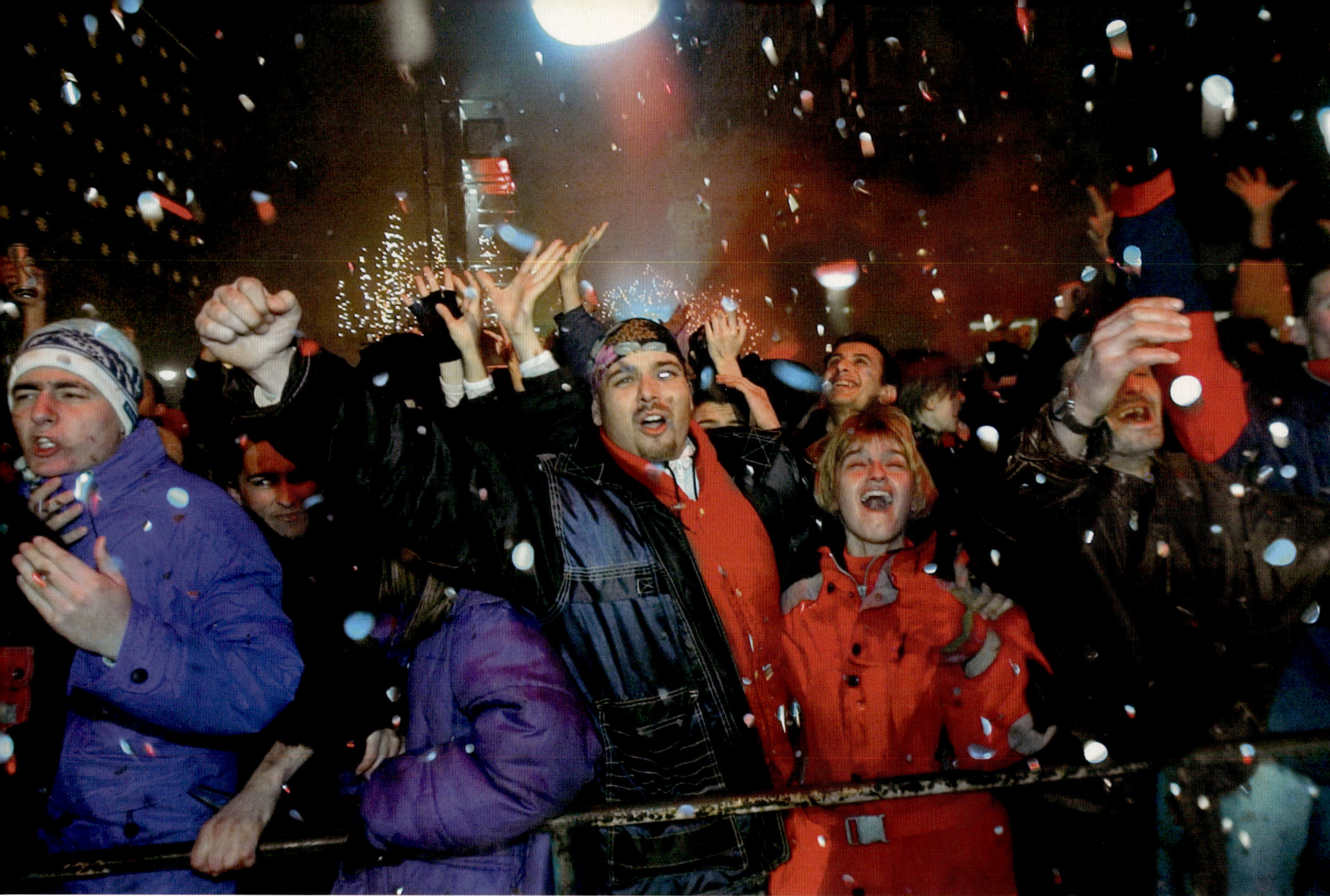

1 January 2000, BELGRADE, YUGOSLAVIA

Belgraders celebrate the arrival of the new Millennium in the city's main square.
Goran Tomasevic

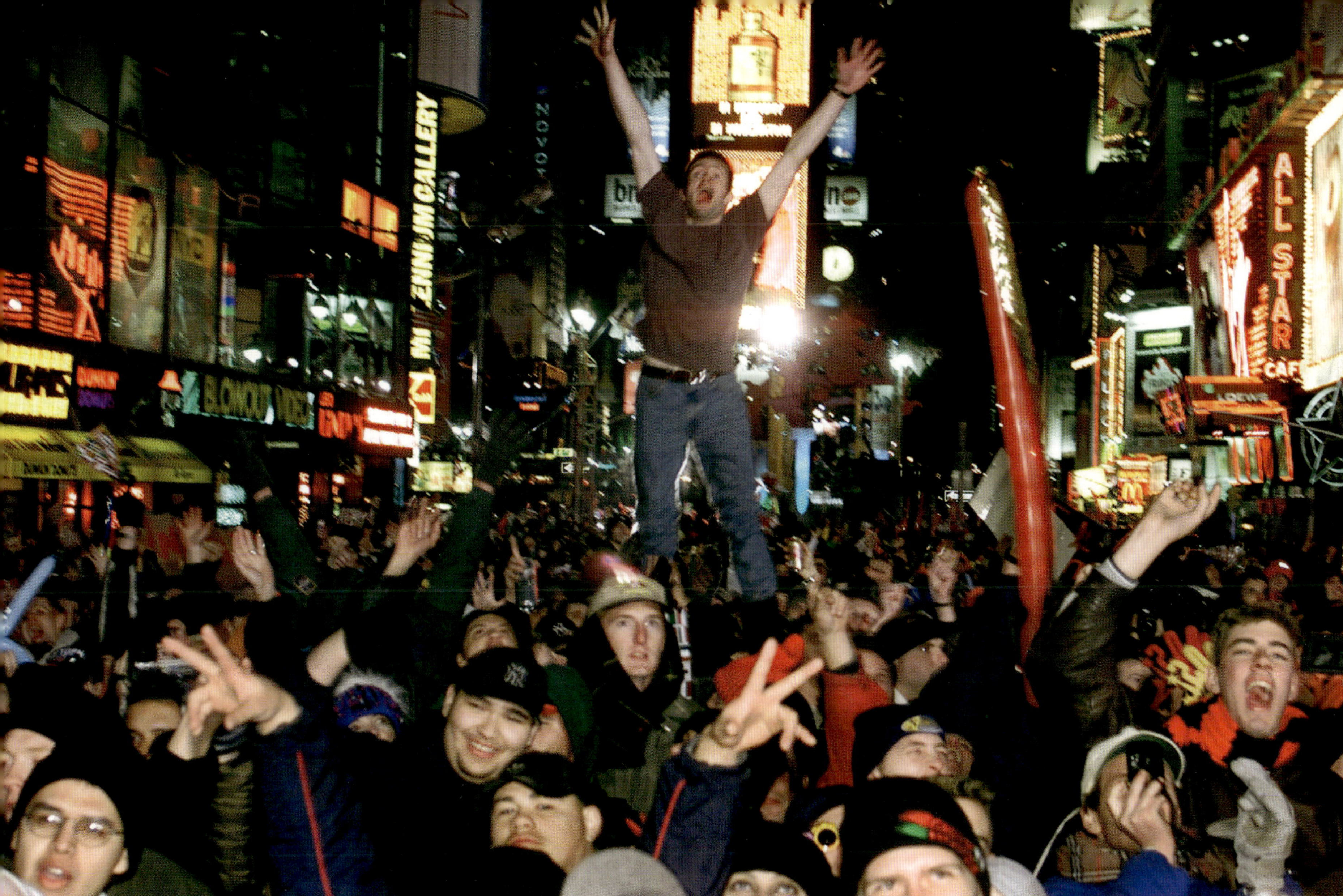

31 December 1999, NEW YORK, UNITED STATES

The crowd in Times Square celebrate the turn of the New Year in London and Greenwich Mean Time. Jim Bourg

Ease of travel and communication is creating an ever more globalized world, but so far in this new century we have come together as often in vulnerability as in strength. Terrorism and the war on terror have dramatically reshaped the world agenda in just a few years. The forces of nature have demonstrated their destructive might across continents. Yet global responses to global issues continue to prove elusive.

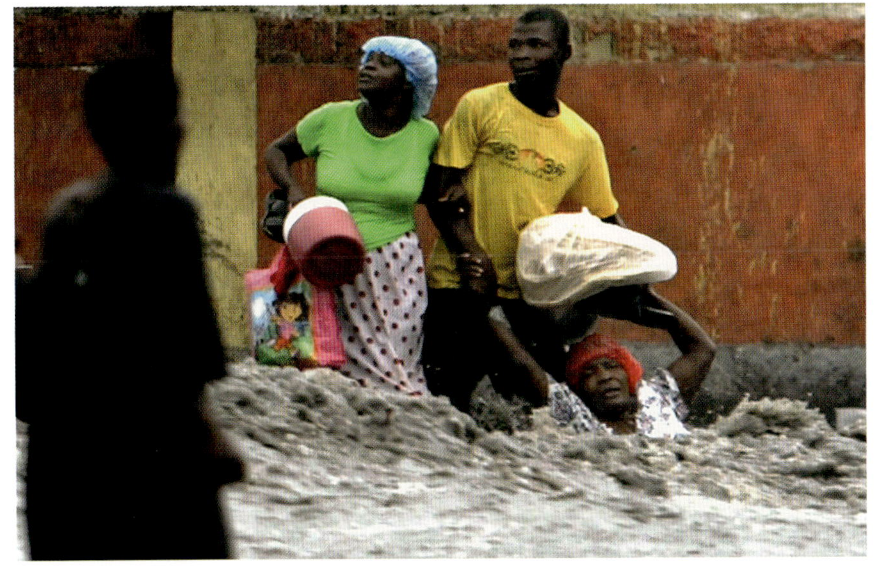

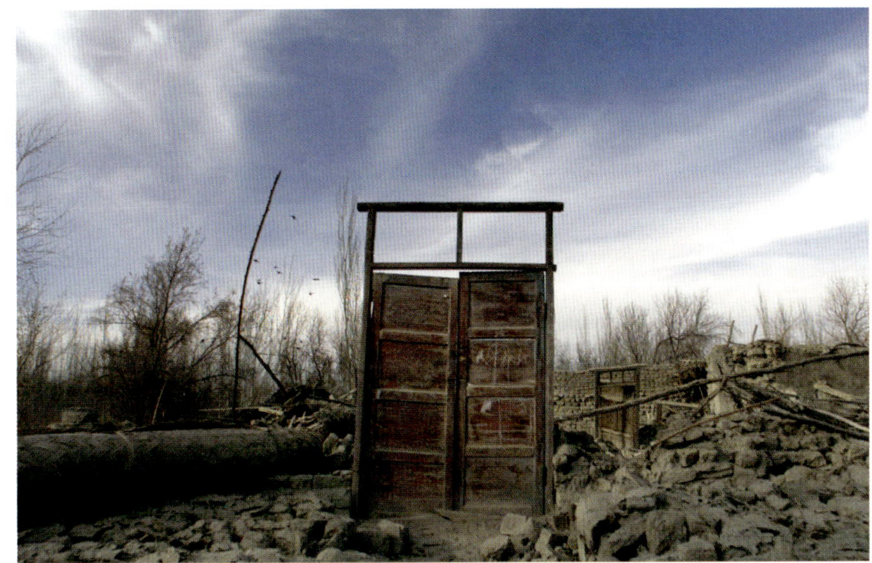

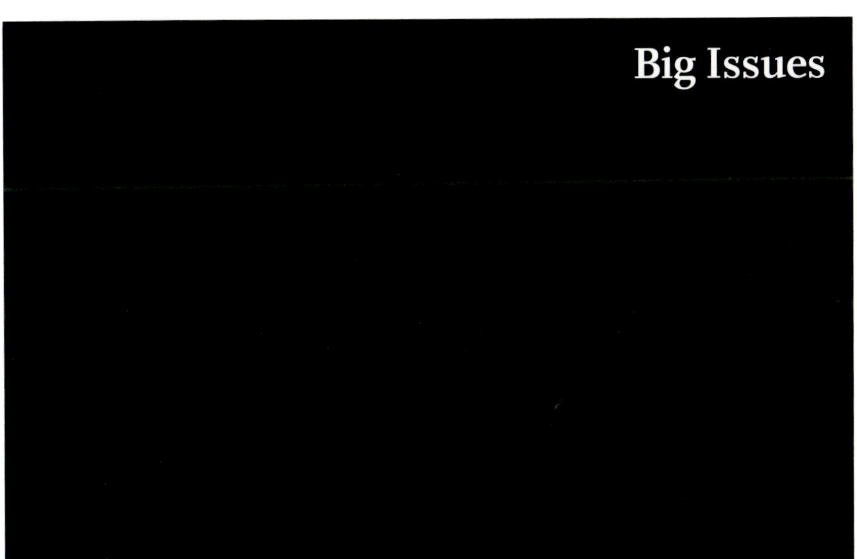

Big Issues

Terror / The Planet / Forces of Nature
Pollution / Climate / Population
Epidemics / Migration / Globalization

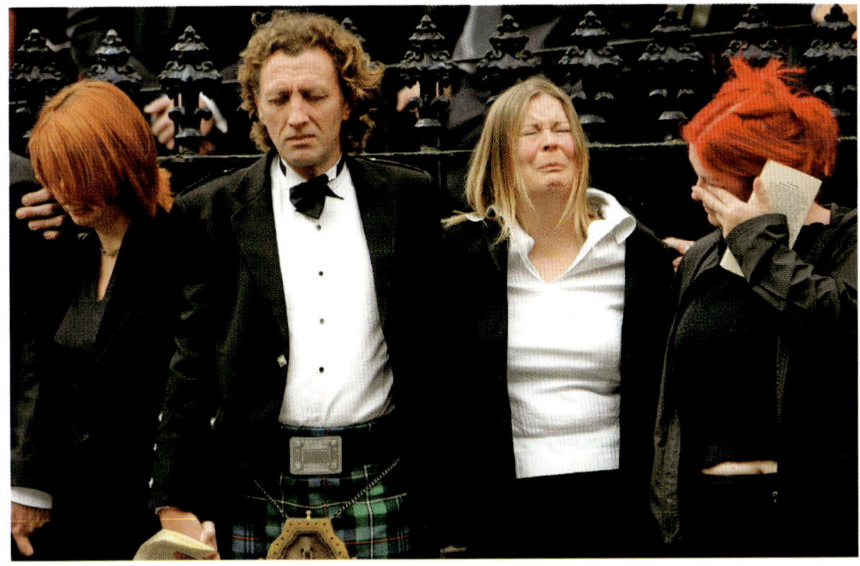

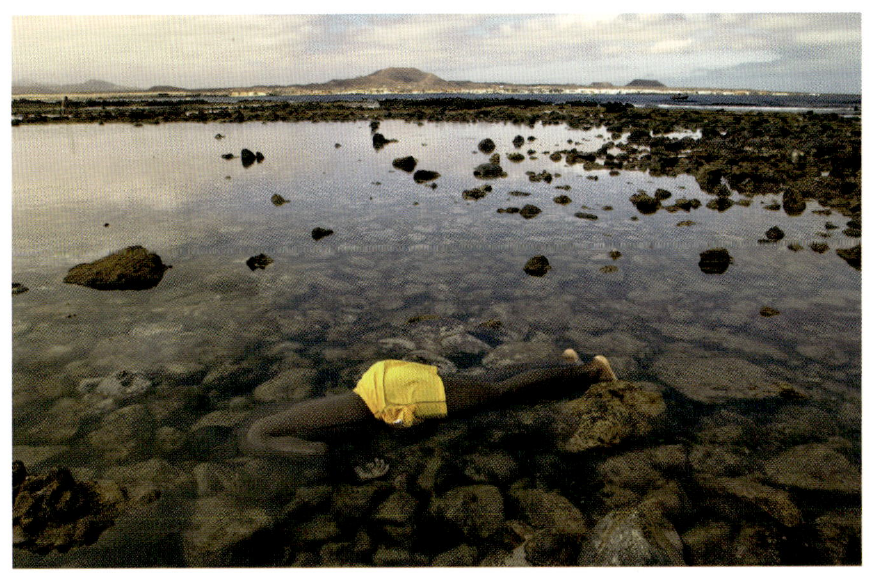

Big Issues

It was a girl.

Baby Astha, born in New Delhi's Safdarjang Hospital on 11 May 2000, was designated India's billionth citizen. Amid fussing officials and jostling journalists, her debut for a moment came to symbolize the entire world's hopes and fears for the new millennium. Hopes – her name means 'faith' in Hindi – for new life and a fresh start in the East, and for a global society based on peace, progress and technology after the appalling events of the twentieth century. Yet fears, too, that such prospects could be blighted by threats of overpopulation, pollution and competition for dwindling resources, even if the old threat of warring superpowers had finally gone away – and many doubted that.

Economists say the outlook is promising. World economic growth hit a 30-year record of 5.1 percent in 2004, led by China, Argentina and India – enough, surely, to feed those extra mouths? The trouble is that global wealth is so unevenly spread. One in every five people continues to survive on less than $1 a day. Astha's father himself earned little more – just $50 a month.

To overcome economic and other challenges, optimists put their trust in human ingenuity in devising new technologies. The dual potential of technology for good or ill, apparent since Stone Age man developed the axe, was put to its sternest test by the mastery of nuclear fission in the 1940s. Twentieth-century politicians passed the test – just. It was a close-run thing at times but in the end they always pulled back from a nuclear conflict that could have destroyed or seriously damaged the planet and its civilization. In the new millennium, the risk is that the same consequences could follow not from a bang but from a slower, more insidious process of climate change and resource depletion, caused more by greed and short-sightedness than by malice.

First, though, there is malice. Despite all the scientific advances of the past century, hopes of shaping a rational new world order from the ashes of the Cold War have been clouded by the revival of an ancient conflict of faiths that does not understand detente and deterrents. The struggle waged by al Qaeda against the 'Crusaders and Jews' whom it denounces as the enemies of Islam has confounded the sophisticated weaponry of the world's mightiest armies. It has led the world's most powerful nations to reconsider fundamental policies regarding security, and in doing so, frequently to encroach upon the liberty of ordinary individuals.

'The rules of the game are changing,' said British Prime Minister Tony Blair after bomb attacks on London in July 2005. Laws are being rewritten to extend police powers to track down potential terrorists, increase the surveillance of citizens and rein in freedom of speech in order to silence the supporters and mentors of the suicide bombers. Even in countries that opposed the war in Iraq, public opinion is hardening towards immigrants and asylum-seekers. A tough stance on terrorism was heavily stressed in the re-election campaigns of the U.S. and British leaders who led the Iraq war in defiance of widespread protests. Their political fortunes have been relatively unscathed by the war's military and civilian death toll, scandals over the abuse of Iraqi prisoners, and the failure to find the weapons of mass destruction that justified ousting Saddam Hussein in the first place.

Rescuing the early twenty-first century from a spiral of increasing violence and mistrust between the West and the Arab world will likely require more than just draconian police powers and an end to the armed resistance in Iraq. Government agencies are rushing to correct their ignorance of Islam – at home as well as abroad – and belatedly to assess the perils of a Middle East policy that has long played down democratic goals in favour of securing oil supplies and maintaining bulwarks of capitalism, such as Saudi Arabia, and secular rule, such as Egypt and Pakistan, in the Islamic world. Washington and its allies now emphasize democracy as the key to stability in the Middle East. That entails a risk in some Muslim states, as elsewhere, of bringing factions to power that may not always get along with the West. But Western politicians have pointed to Turkey, now aspiring to European Union membership, as an

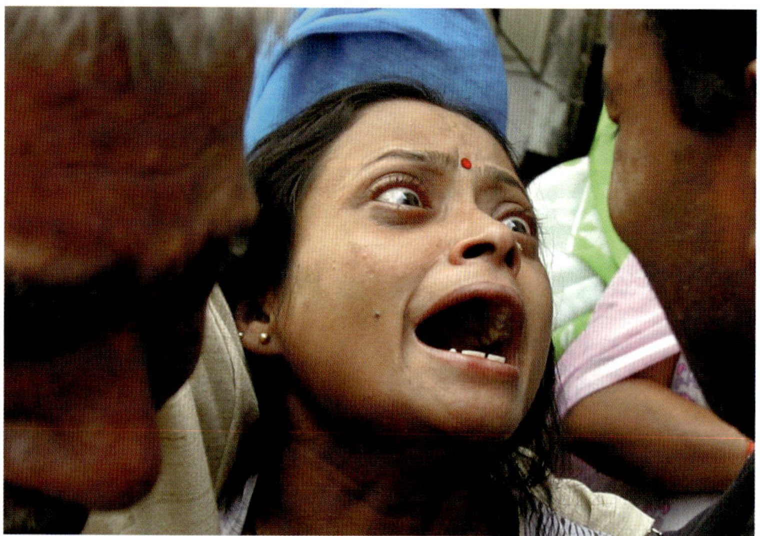

Sunita Devi cries after seeing the body of her daughter, Neha, one of 66 fatalities in the bomb blasts in New Delhi, India, on 29 October 2005, just days before major Hindu and Muslim festivals. An obscure Kashmiri militant group, Islami Inqilabi Mahaz (the Islamic Revolutionary Front) claimed responsibility for the attacks. Adnan Abidi.

example of a Muslim country where secular democracy can flourish even under a ruling party that is rooted in Islam.

There have been other hopeful signs too, from the West's point of view: Libya's renunciation of nuclear and chemical weapons; the resumption of nuclear disarmament talks with North Korea; the Irish Republican Army's announcement of the end of its armed campaign. But the otherwise dramatic decline in global security since the invasion of Iraq in March 2003 has underlined that the war on terror is now as much a matter of domestic politics as of security and foreign relations. Islam is the world's fastest-growing religion with well over a billion followers, including 3 million in the U.S. and 15 million in Europe. Al Qaeda's violence has made more urgent the

> This has been a period in which human and natural forces have conspired to sow fear, turning ordinary events – the train trip to work, a beach holiday, standing in a bread queue – into nightmares.

task of integrating the Islamic diaspora and tackling the poverty, unemployment and alienation that can make young Muslims in the West more susceptible to radicalization. Yet integration is more difficult than ever when the security crackdown focuses on Muslim communities, and when their non-Muslim fellow citizens find themselves on the front lines of a globalized Holy War.

Intensifying concerns for security and economic stability, global migration has hit an unprecedented level, as the world's population heads from almost 6.5 billion now to more than 9 billion by 2050, and as the birth rate in less developed countries stands nearly 10 times higher than in the rich world. Uprooted by hunger, poverty and unemployment, desperate people are undaunted by the difficulties of obtaining valid visas, by natural barriers such as the Mediterranean or the Rio Grande, or by man-made barriers such as the razor-wire fences separating the Spanish enclaves of Ceuta and Melilla from Morocco. U.S. border patrols are now arresting more than a million would-be illegal immigrants a year, most of them on the Mexican border.

The root causes are the huge global socio-economic inequalities that the United Nations' Millennium Development Goals aim to narrow. The facts are stark: 200 million Africans are underfed while rich nations complain of an epidemic of obesity. But while the initial response to the U.N.'s targets was lukewarm, tentative moves have been made to increase aid to the poorest countries, cancel their debts, and create fairer international trading conditions. Eventually such measures could reduce the need for so many to risk the hazards and humiliations of illegal migration.

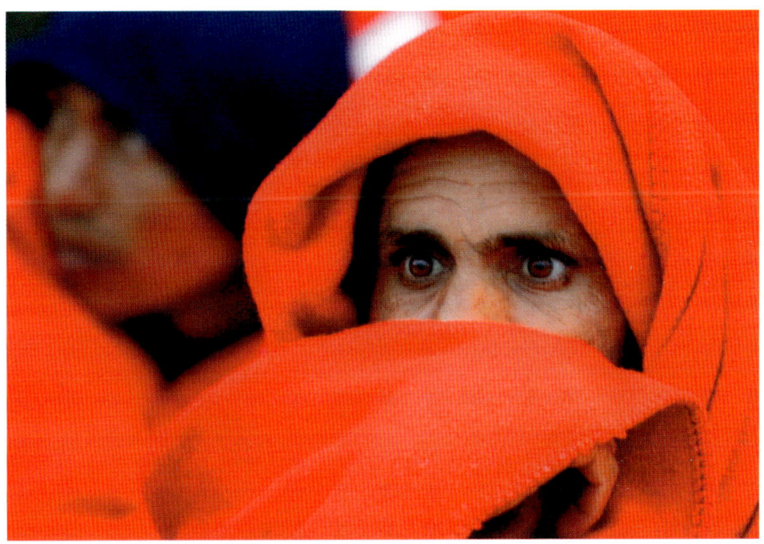

A would-be immigrant keeps warm in Tarifa, southern Spain, one of 75 people intercepted in the Strait of Gibraltar as they attempted to reach Spanish soil in fragile vessels on the night of 2 April 2005. Anton Meres.

In the European Union, expansion into the former Soviet bloc should eventually narrow the gap in earnings between east and west, though it will take time to overcome richer European nations' fears of their new partners poaching their industry and sending in floods of migrant workers. But with war in the Balkans still an open wound, expansion to the east and southeast appears the best way of guaranteeing stability in Europe, whose conflicts sparked two world wars last century.

The long-term benefits of migration are often less tangible than the immediate costs, and there is plenty of quick political capital to be made by playing up the alien threat to jobs, security, national culture and resources. Wealthier regions that attract migrants are struggling to find ways of successfully integrating those who are documented and legitimate, and keeping out, deporting or even legalizing those who are not. Poor countries worry about a drain of their most skilled workers and qualified professionals, but rely on remittances from emigrants. Japan and much of Europe fret about the future ability of a stagnant or shrinking working-age population to support a rising proportion of pensioners, whose life expectancy increases all the time. Yet for domestic political reasons they resist throwing open their labour markets to foreigners.

Where immigrants can settle, they often experience segregation into the second and third generation, raising questions about the merits of multiculturalism versus assimilation into the adopted culture and language. Even in the United States, most of whose people are descended from immigrants, many of the Hispanics who already form a tenth of the population and account for half of its growth have yet to overcome educational disadvantages to shake off the underclass label, and they remain under-represented in American politics. But those Arab-Americans who were unscathed by the anti-Muslim backlash following the September 11 attacks of 2001 are integrating into the U.S. economy well, especially in the auto industry hub around Detroit. In egalitarian France, also with 10 percent of immigrants, mainly Muslims from north and west Africa, discontent at the lack of equality and opportunity erupted in late 2005 in the worst disturbances for almost four decades. In China, internal migration is creating a nightmare of urban squalor, with one estimate that 99 million peasants have already uprooted to the booming cities.

It may soon be too late to reverse the damage to some natural habitats or the ecologically fragile farmlands that provide a subsistence living to many of the 70 percent of the world's poor who till the soil for their survival.

Today's global migration challenges pale into insignificance, however, compared to the refugee and migration crises that would be unleashed by the droughts, floods, diseases and famine that scientists warn with growing consensus could result from increasingly extreme global weather patterns. World temperatures are projected to rise by 1.4–5.8°C (2.5–10.5°F) by the end of the century and ocean levels could swell by as much as one metre in the same period. The Asian tsunami in December 2004, in which nearly a quarter of a million people died or went missing, was the most numbing of a long catalogue of natural disasters that have plagued the first years of the millennium: earthquakes in Iran, Algeria and Kashmir, floods in Bangladesh and Europe, typhoons in Japan, hurricanes in the Caribbean and southeast U.S., and locusts devouring crops in Africa.

It may soon be too late to reverse the damage to some natural habitats or the ecologically fragile farmlands that provide a subsistence living to many of the 70 percent of the world's poor who till the soil for their survival. Thousands of species are threatened with extinction by the middle of this century because of global warming, which is already melting the Greenland ice cap, the Siberian permafrost and many glaciers. Most developed nations have signed the Kyoto Protocol that commits them to cutting greenhouse gas emissions to below 1990 levels by 2012, though whether they will achieve that is by no means certain. The United States, the world's biggest polluter, pulled out of Kyoto in 2001 saying it would cost jobs in industry and that it wrongly excluded developing countries from the first round of clean-up targets. The U.S. has since forged an alternative global warming pact with Australia and the economic powerhouses of Asia, mainly China and India, which as they lure industrial, technological and service jobs away from the West and stamp their ownership on the new century, face increased pressure to take responsibility for controlling emissions. If they do not, Asia, which is home to more than half the world's people, risks lurching from one natural catastrophe to another as climate patterns shift. Already the ascent of 2.2 billion Chinese and Indians out of poverty is creating such an additional burden on the world's natural resources that the resulting rises in energy and commodity prices are straining the health of industrialized economies. Competition for resources also means more hardship for developing nations, which rely more than ever on the success of global free trade talks, floundering since 2001, to help their farm products compete with the subsidized agro-industry of the rich world. The World Bank believes that opening Western markets to Third World agricultural products could help rescue hundreds of millions from penury.

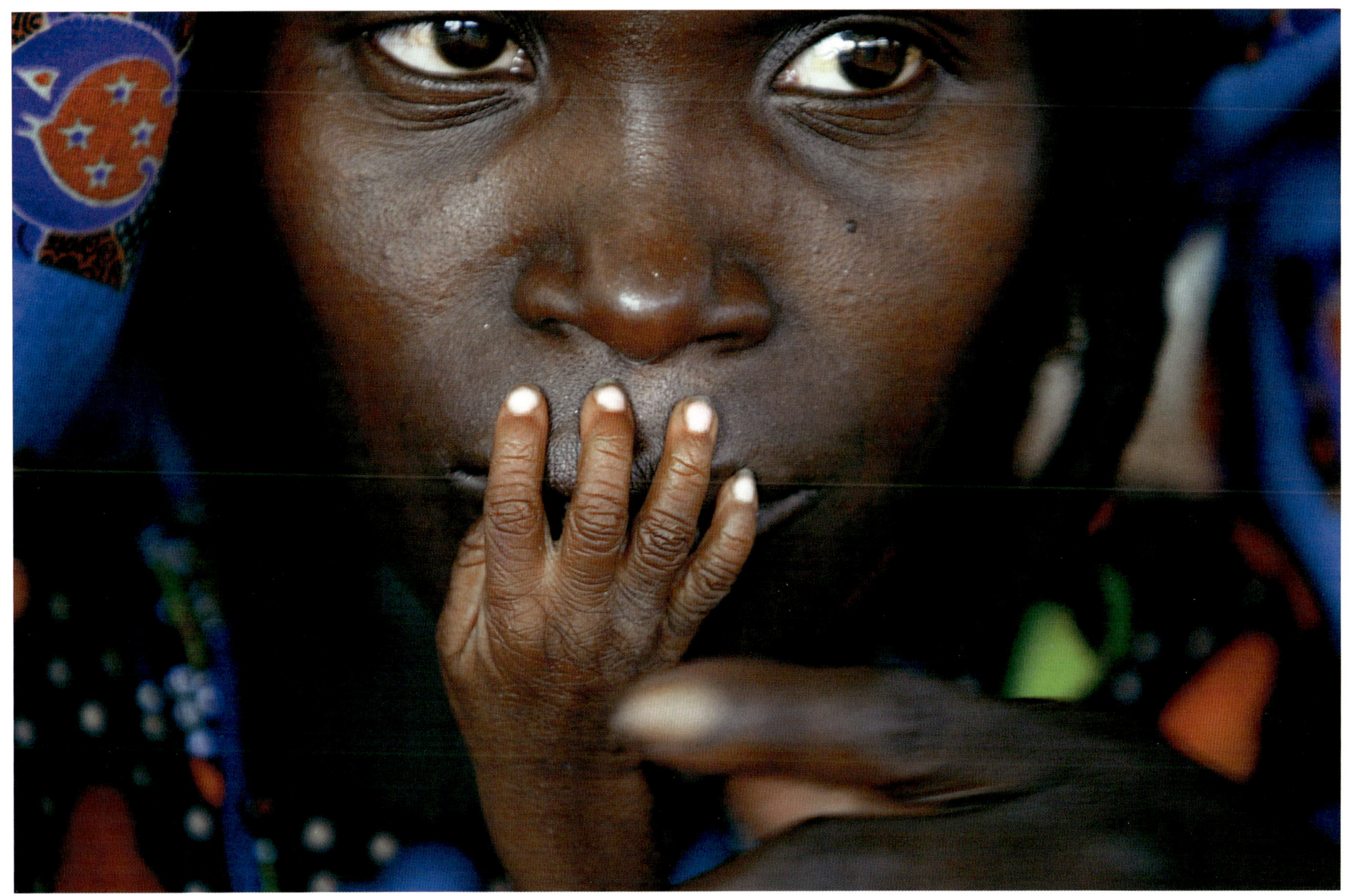

1 August 2005, TAHOUA, NIGER

The fingers of malnourished one-year-old Alassa Galisou are pressed against the lips of his mother Fatou Ousseini at an emergency feeding clinic in the town of Tahoua in northwestern Niger. One of Niger's worst droughts in living memory destroyed much of the crop that should have been harvested in October 2004, leaving an estimated 3.6 million people short of food, including tens of thousands of starving children. World Press Photo of the Year 2005. Finbarr O'Reilly

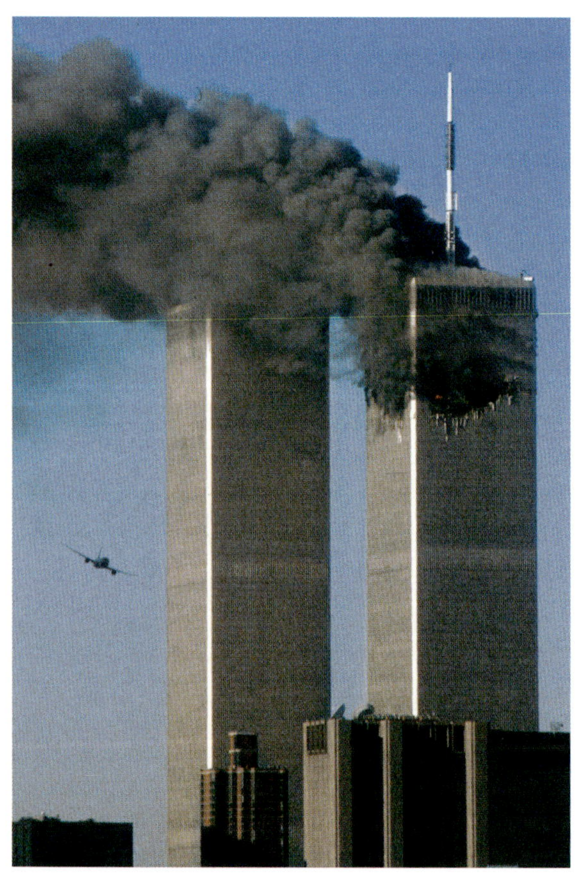
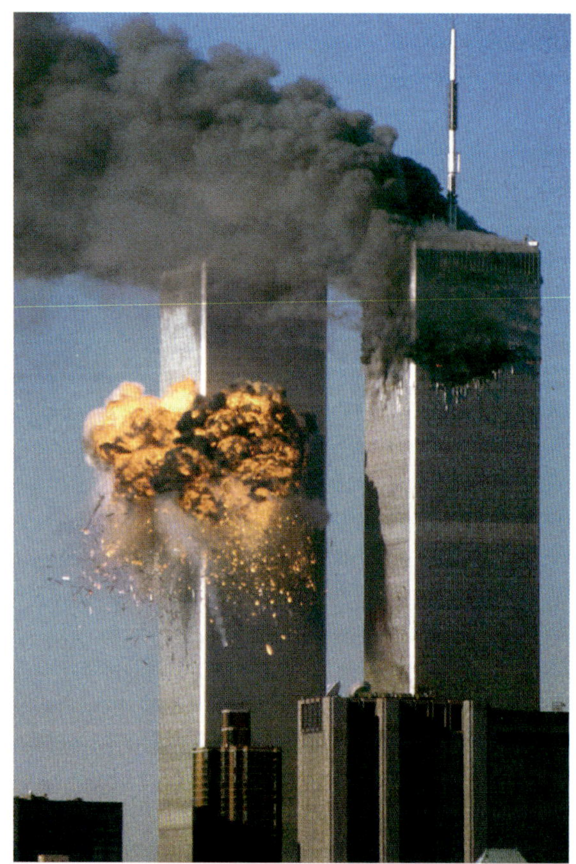
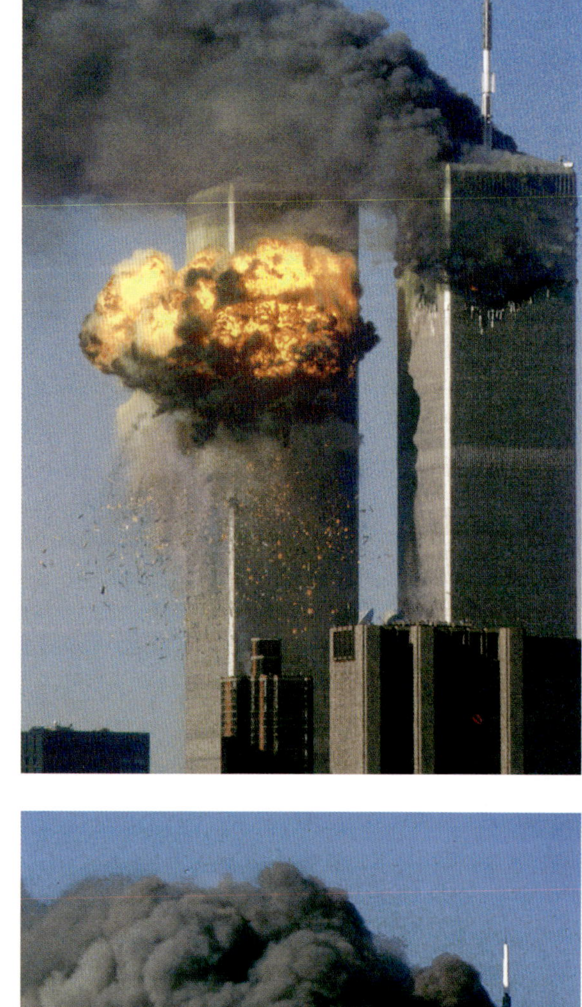
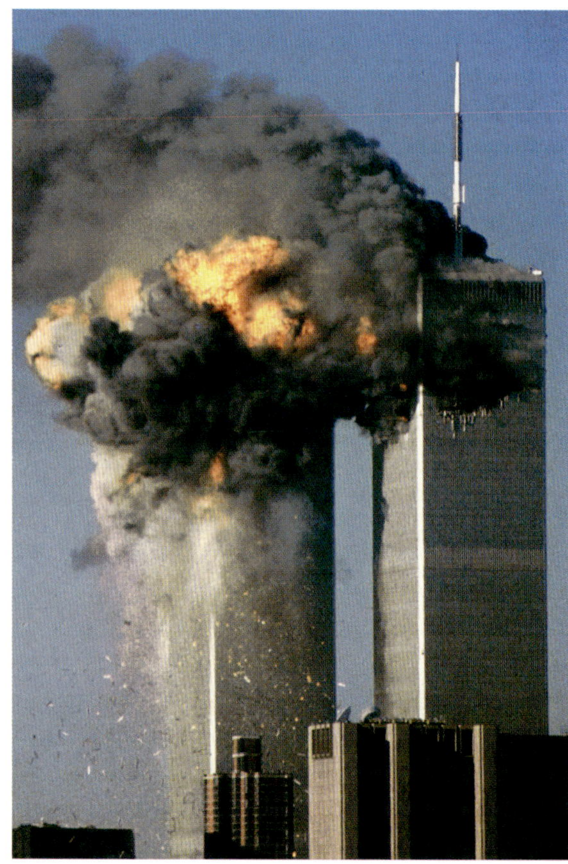
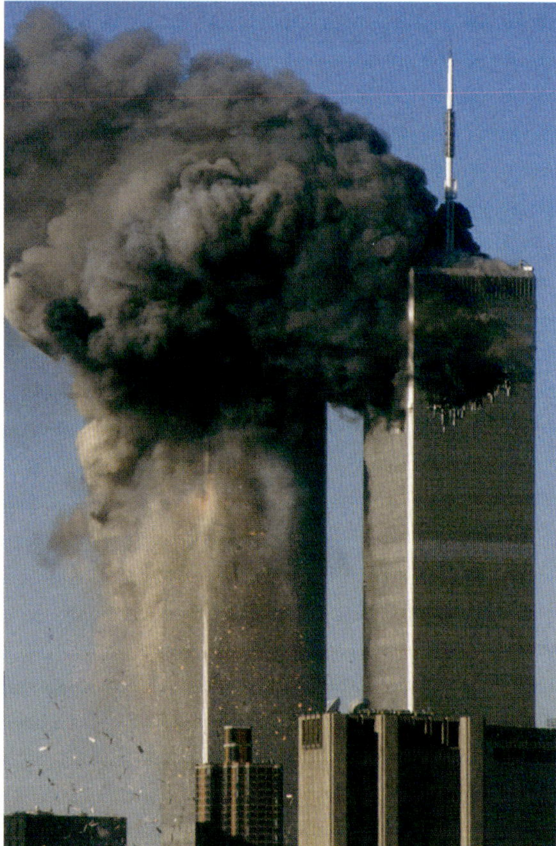
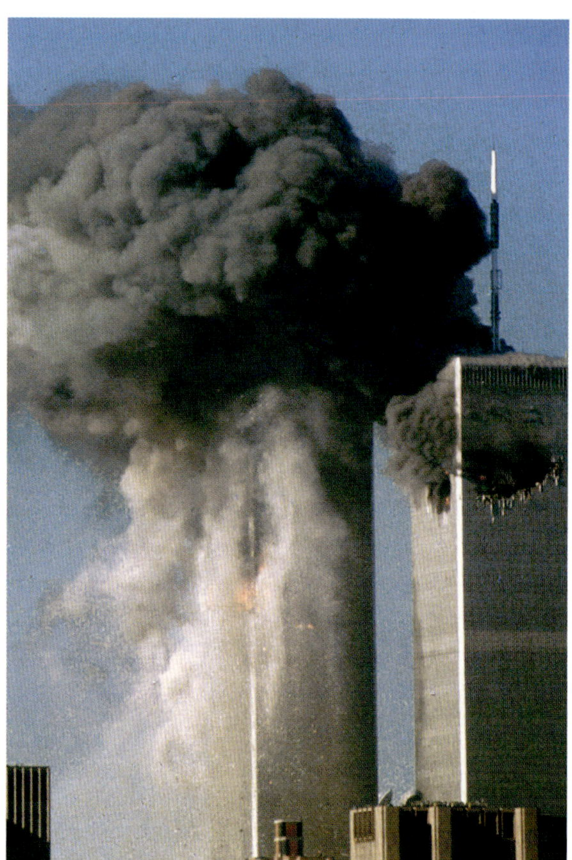

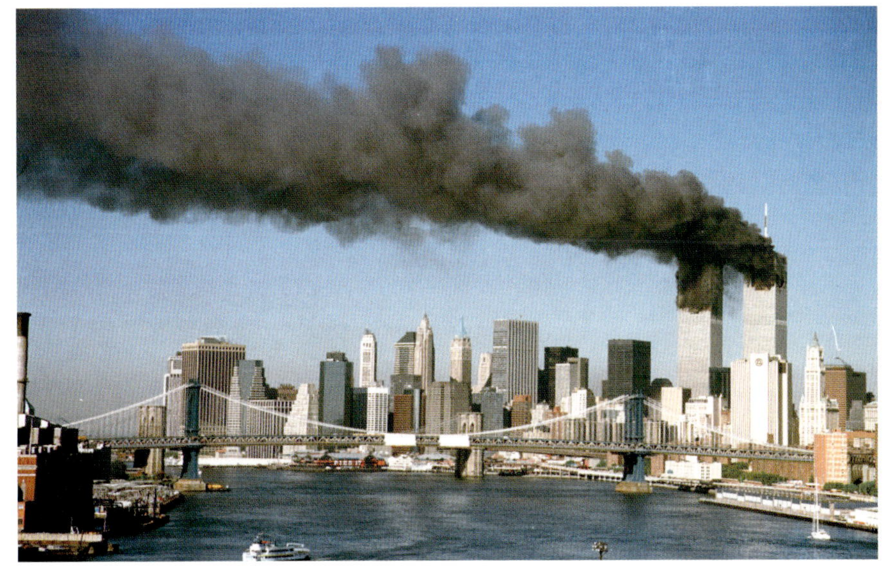

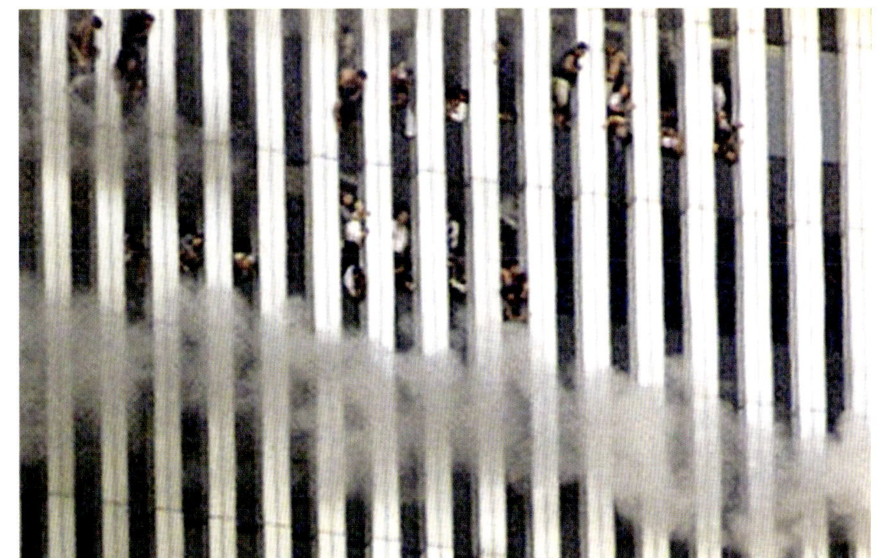

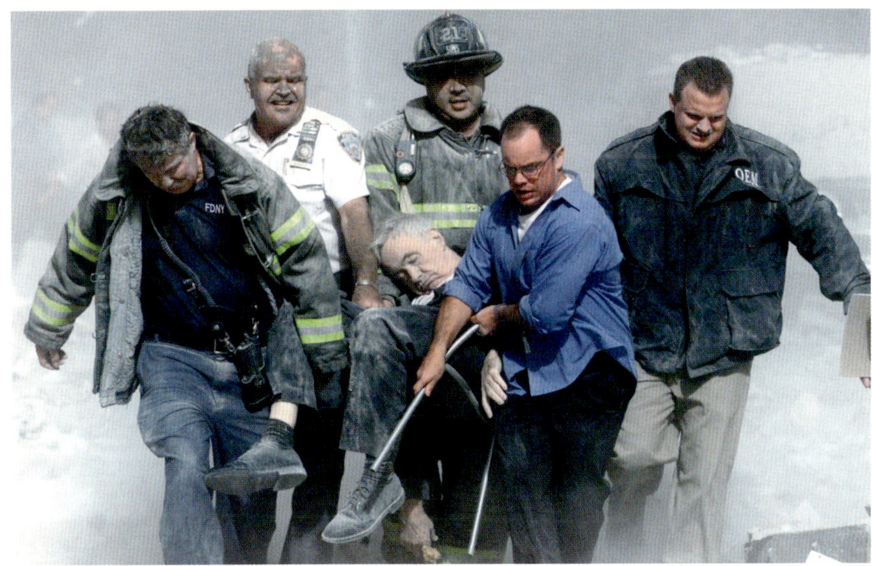
FDNY
OEM

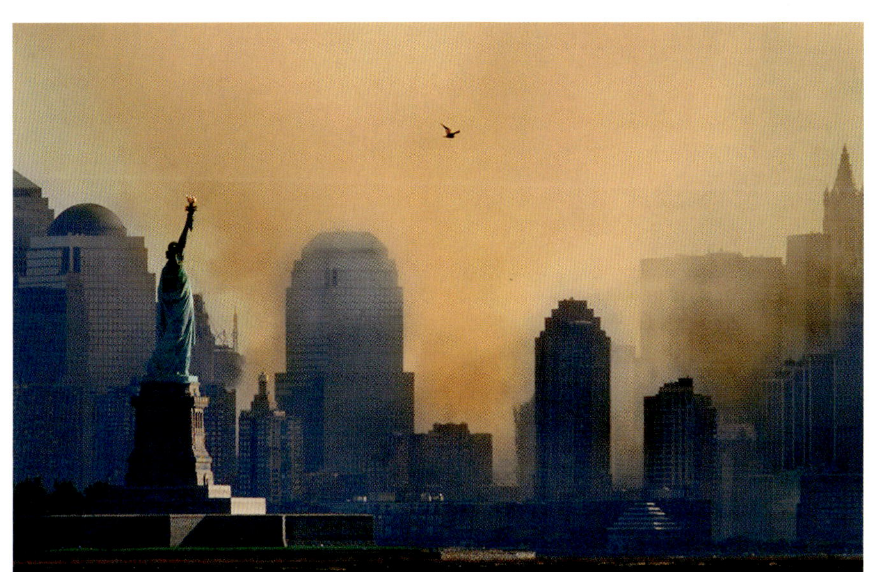

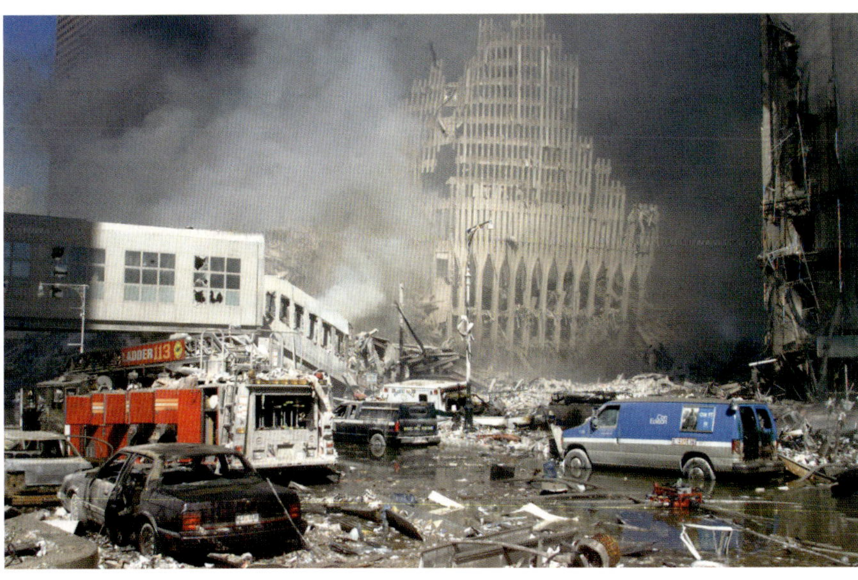
LADDER 113

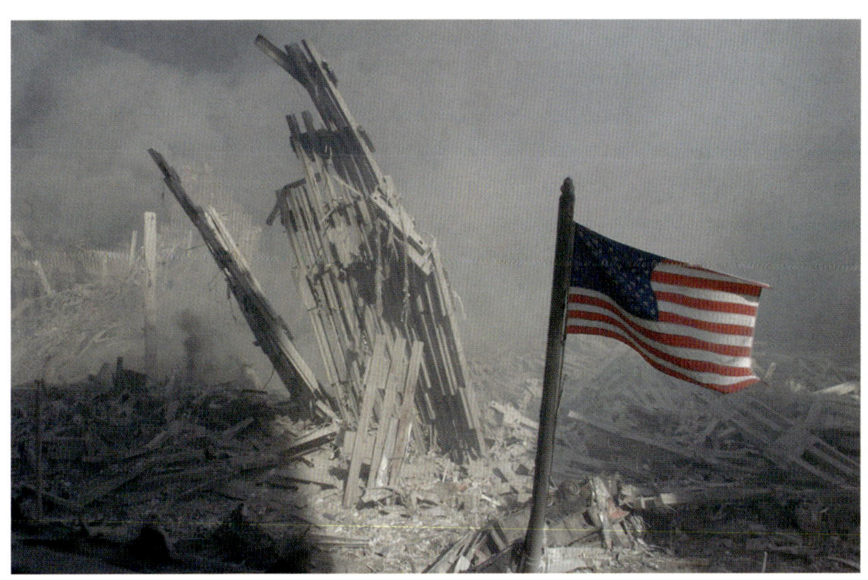

While Third World poverty and trade inequalities continue to provide 'globalphobics' with arguments for protectionism, the globalization of technology and communications proved its worth when Asia's tsunami struck: compassion spread around the globe to yield public and private emergency relief donations exceeding $12 billion. Television, newspapers and the Internet were dominated by the shaky camera phone images emailed by frightened tourists from the shores of the Indian Ocean to relatives, friends and the media back home. At last it seemed that people could feel the full force of human suffering across national, ethnic or religious boundaries and provide prompt assistance to match the scale of tragedy. The response to famine in Niger and neighbouring West

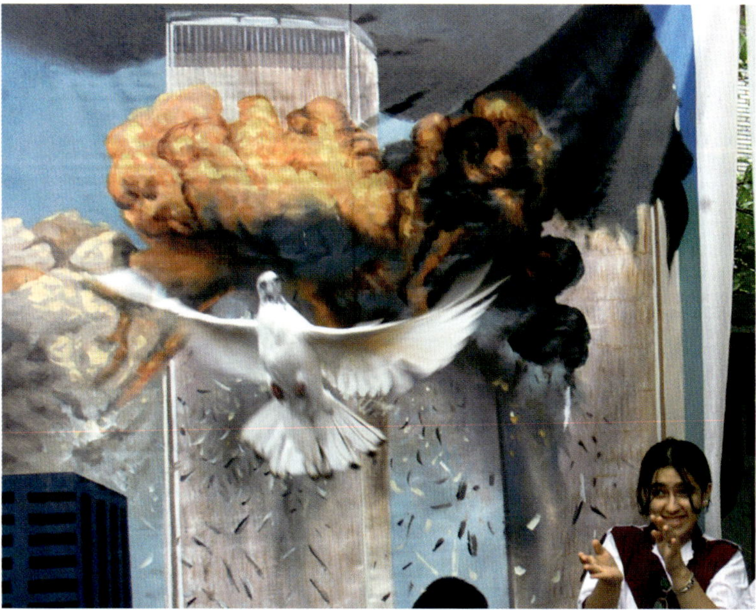

In Islamabad, a Pakistani supporter of the World Minorities Alliance releases a dove as a symbol of peace in front of a mural depicting the 2001 attacks on the World Trade Center in New York. 11 September 2002, Mian Khursheed.

African countries, where images of starving babies in 2005 hauntingly recalled those from Biafra 40 years ago and Ethiopia 20 years ago, will demonstrate if this cross-border compassion has staying power. Our addiction to fossil fuels, plus the devastation wreaked by HIV/AIDS and the threat of an impending influenza pandemic will mean plenty more opportunities for the global village's capacity for charity.

If the natural environment seems to be spinning out of control, such chaos often appears mirrored in the manmade virtual environment of cyberspace. Beset by piracy, hackers and worms, harbouring hate sites, fanatics, bomb-makers and paedophiles, the Internet remains an ethical quagmire, and all attempts to govern it have so far hardly touched its one billion users. If at the end of the twentieth century the Internet seemed to promise limitless opportunities to make us wiser and richer, it was fitting that the third millennium opened with the dot-com collapse, in which hundreds of over-valued and under-performing Internet-trading companies went bust.

In its anarchic way, however, the Internet also provides an unrivalled platform for transparency, freedom of information and free speech that largely defies national censors. Independent blogs and discussion forums bypass the established media to circulate breaking news stories and analyses of political and social trends. The Web gives ordinary consumers and voters a powerful tool to pursue their interests and defend their rights: prices can be compared and bank queues avoided – though accounts can also be emptied by fraudulent practices such as 'phishing'; books can be bought, sold or even published; religions can proselytize across the globe; clubs can recruit and so can cults; medical advice can be sought; and businesses can reach consumers direct, be they multinational giants or a small African village marketing hand-made furniture to Europe. The Internet was invented for the Pentagon as a Cold War weapon, and al Qaeda has demonstrated dramatically its potential for harm; but charities collecting for the starving in Darfur and the tsunami victims in Asia benefited from its capacity for good.

Geographic and social inequalities in access to information technology constitute a 'knowledge gap' that risks increasing rather than reducing the differences between rich and poor. But overcome this gap and humanity may respond more effectively to the challenges of war, natural disaster, disease, poverty and overcrowding that the twenty-first century will almost certainly bring.

Stephen Brown has worked for Reuters since 1987. He has spent most of his career in Latin America, covering politics and unrest in South America. He was bureau chief in 2001 during the political collapse of Argentina, and was the first reporter to confirm the resignation of Argentinean president Fernando de la Rua. Stephen is currently bureau chief of the Nordic and Baltic region.

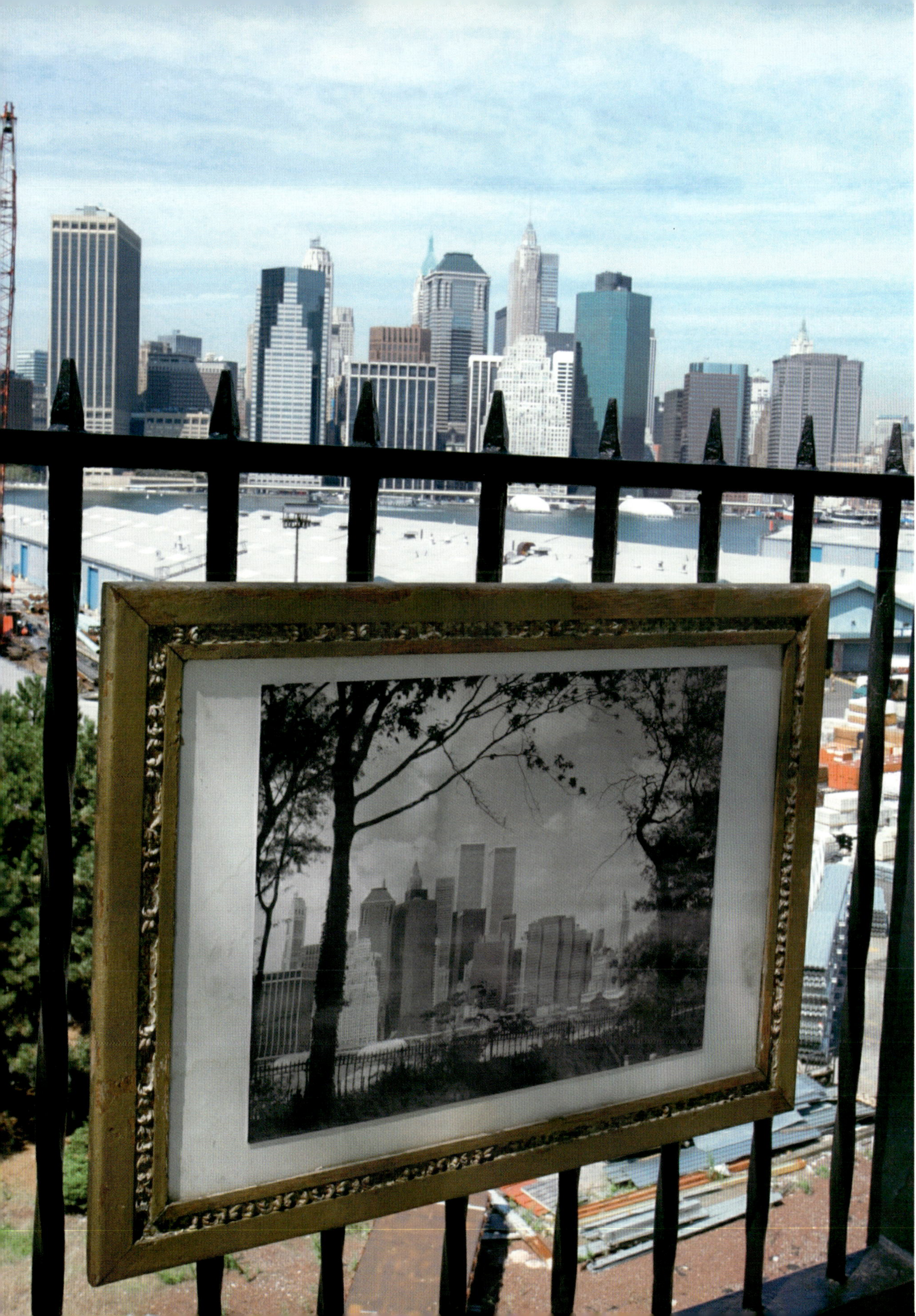

11 September 2001, NEW YORK, UNITED STATES

Previous pages, left-hand page Hijacked United Airlines Flight 175 approaches and hits the World Trade Center's South Tower, bursting into flames and raining a hail of debris on lower Manhattan. Sean Adair

Previous pages, right-hand page, clockwise from top left Smoke pours from the World Trade Center towers shortly after they were struck. Brad Rickerby. People look out of the burning North Tower. Jeff Christensen. Smoke shrouds lower Manhattan as a lone seagull flies overhead. Ray Stubblebine. An American flag flies near the base of the destroyed World Trade Center. Peter Morgan. Fire trucks sit amid the rubble. Peter Morgan. Rescue workers carry the fatally injured New York City Fire Department chaplain, the Reverend Mychal Judge, who was crushed to death by falling debris while giving a man last rites. Shannon Stapleton

10 September 2002, NEW YORK, UNITED STATES

Left A framed picture of the Manhattan skyline taken before attacks of 2001 hangs from the Brooklyn Heights Promenade. Shaun Best

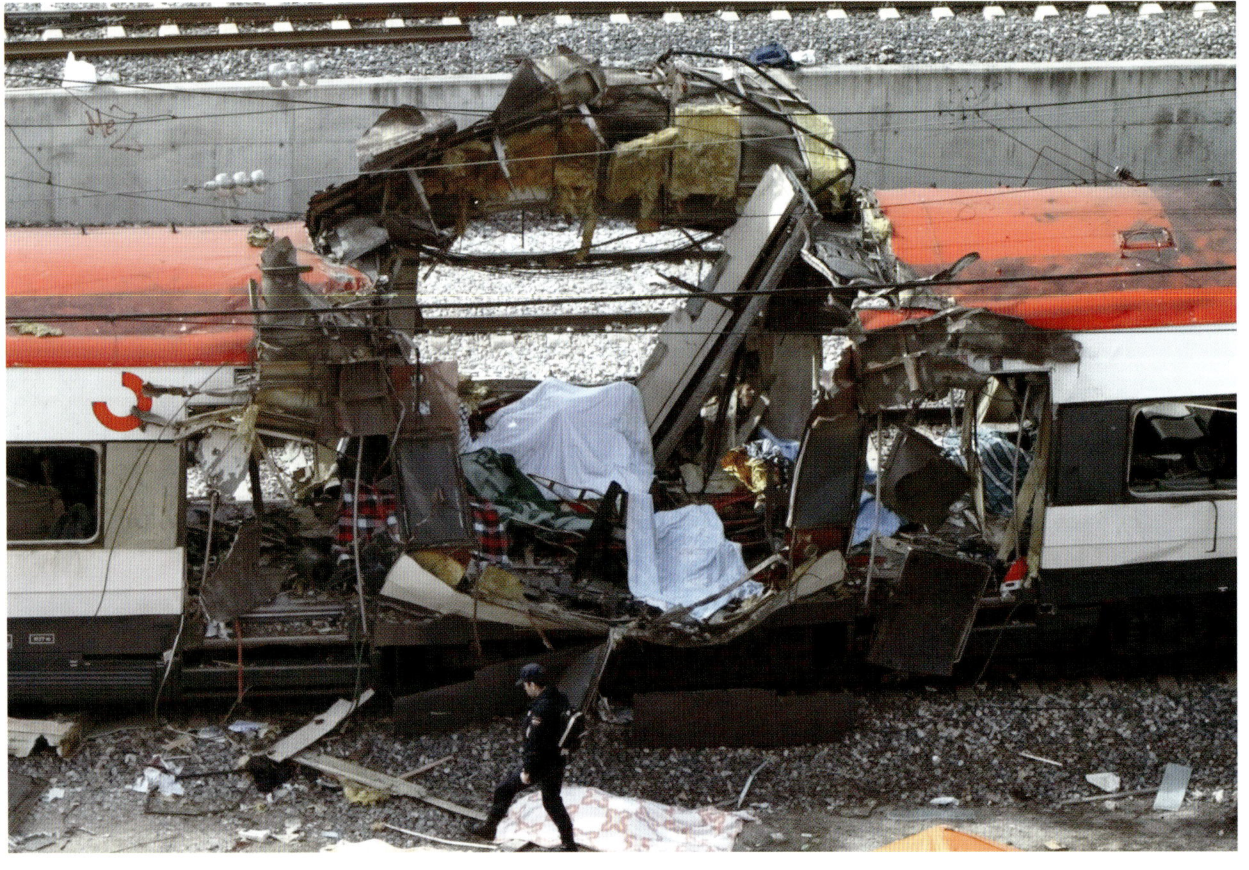

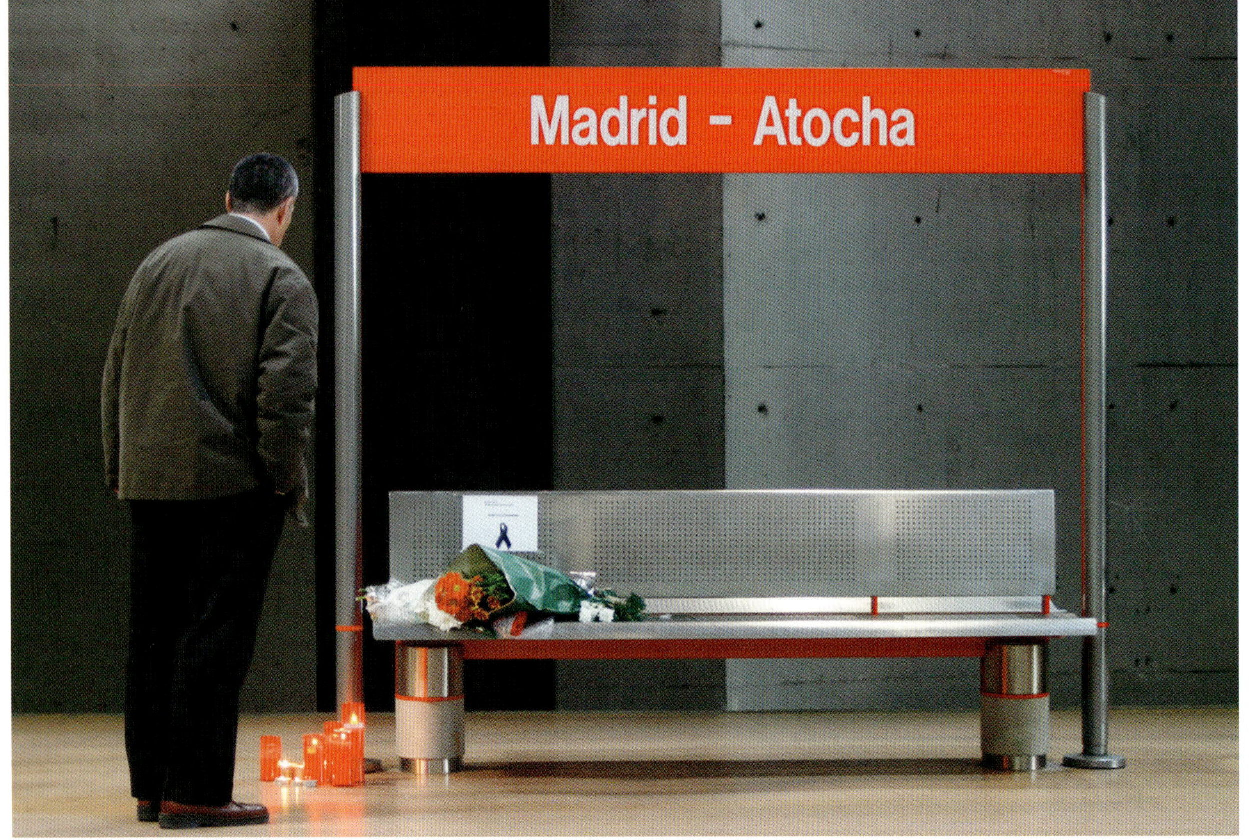

11 March 2004, MADRID, SPAIN

Left A Spanish policeman walks past part of a train destroyed in an explosion at Madrid's Atocha station, one of four simultaneous bomb attacks in packed rush-hour trains that killed 191 people and wounded over 1,800 on 11 March 2004. Islamist militants later claimed responsibility in the name of al Qaeda.
Andrea Comas

11 March 2005, MADRID, SPAIN

Left below A year on from the Madrid bomb attacks, a man pays his respects at a memorial site on one of the platforms at Atocha station. Spain solemnly commemorated the first anniversary of the train bombings, al Qaeda's worst attack in Europe, with church bells and silent tributes to the people who died.
Susana Vera

8 July 2005, LONDON, UNITED KINGDOM

Opposite above The wreckage of the number 30 double-decker bus that was destroyed by a suicide bomber in Tavistock Square in central London on 7 July 2005. A total of 52 people were killed by four suicide bombers who targeted London's transport system as G8 leaders were meeting in Scotland. In September 2005 al Qaeda said it carried out the attacks to strike at 'British arrogance'.
Dylan Martinez

14 July 2005, LONDON, UNITED KINGDOM

Opposite below A Muslim woman is one of thousands of mourners who attended a vigil in Trafalgar Square in central London to remember the victims of the bomb attacks a week earlier. Dylan Martinez

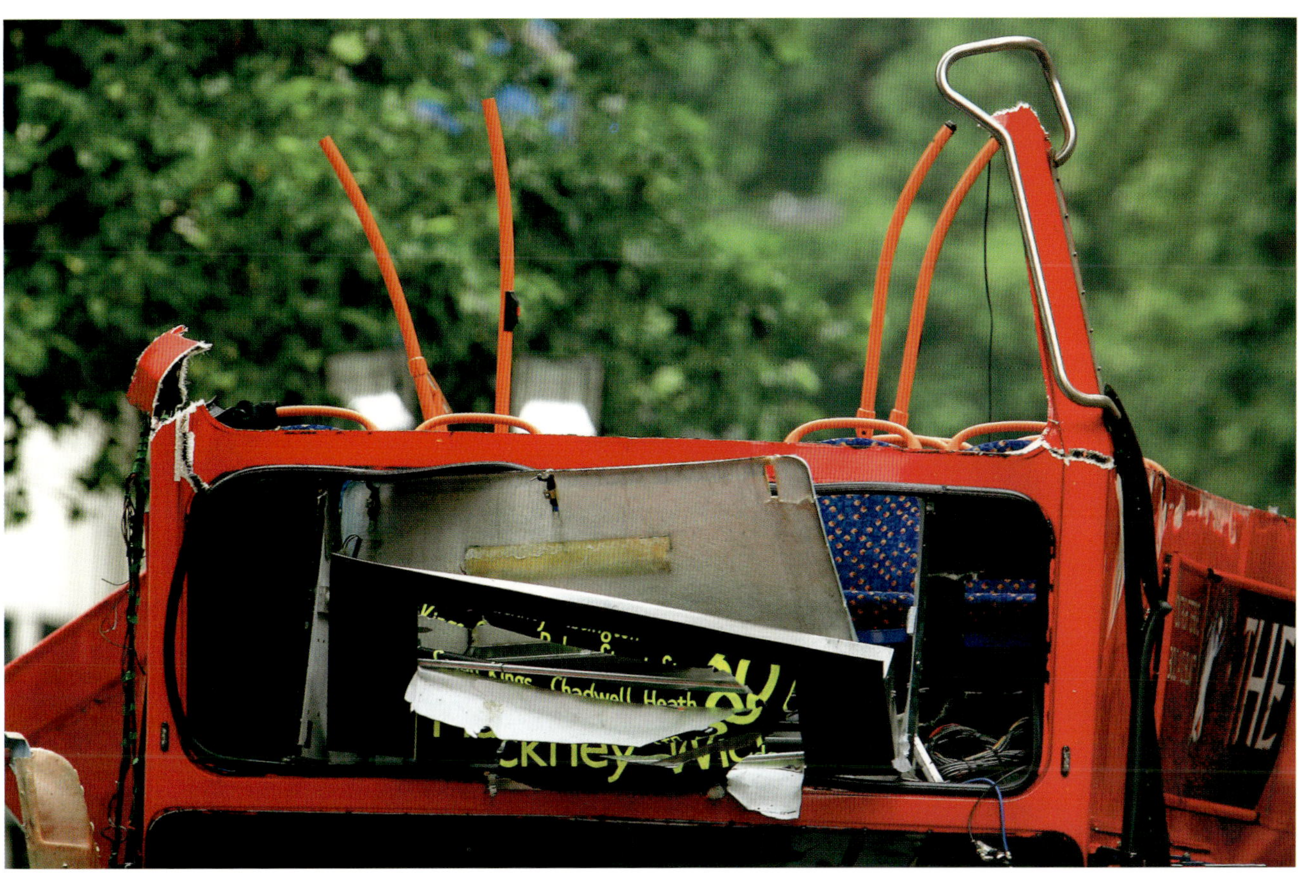
Chadwell Heath

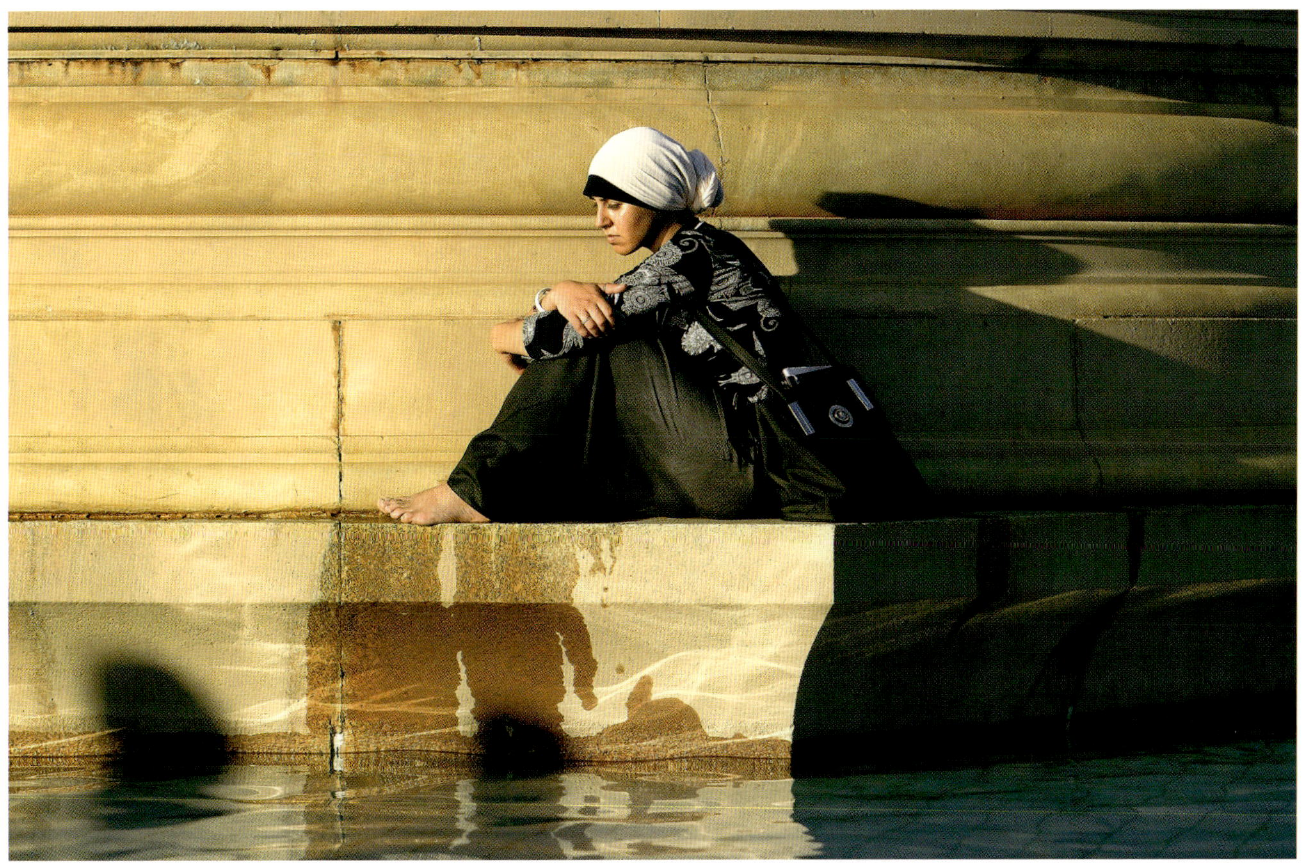

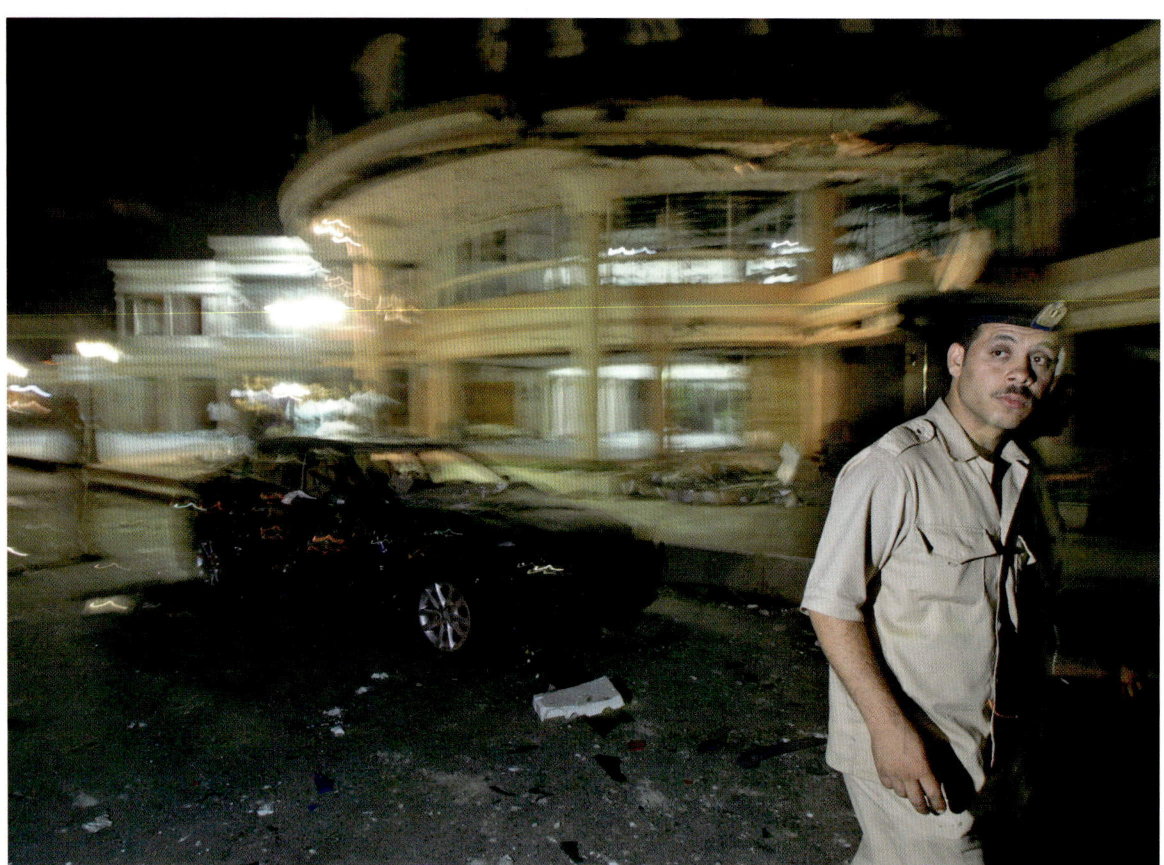

24 July 2005, SHARM EL-SHEIKH, EGYPT

An Egyptian policeman walks past a damaged car in the Red Sea resort of Sharm el-Sheikh the day after two car bombs and a suitcase bomb ripped through hotels and shopping areas, killing 67 and wounding more than 200. Nir Elias

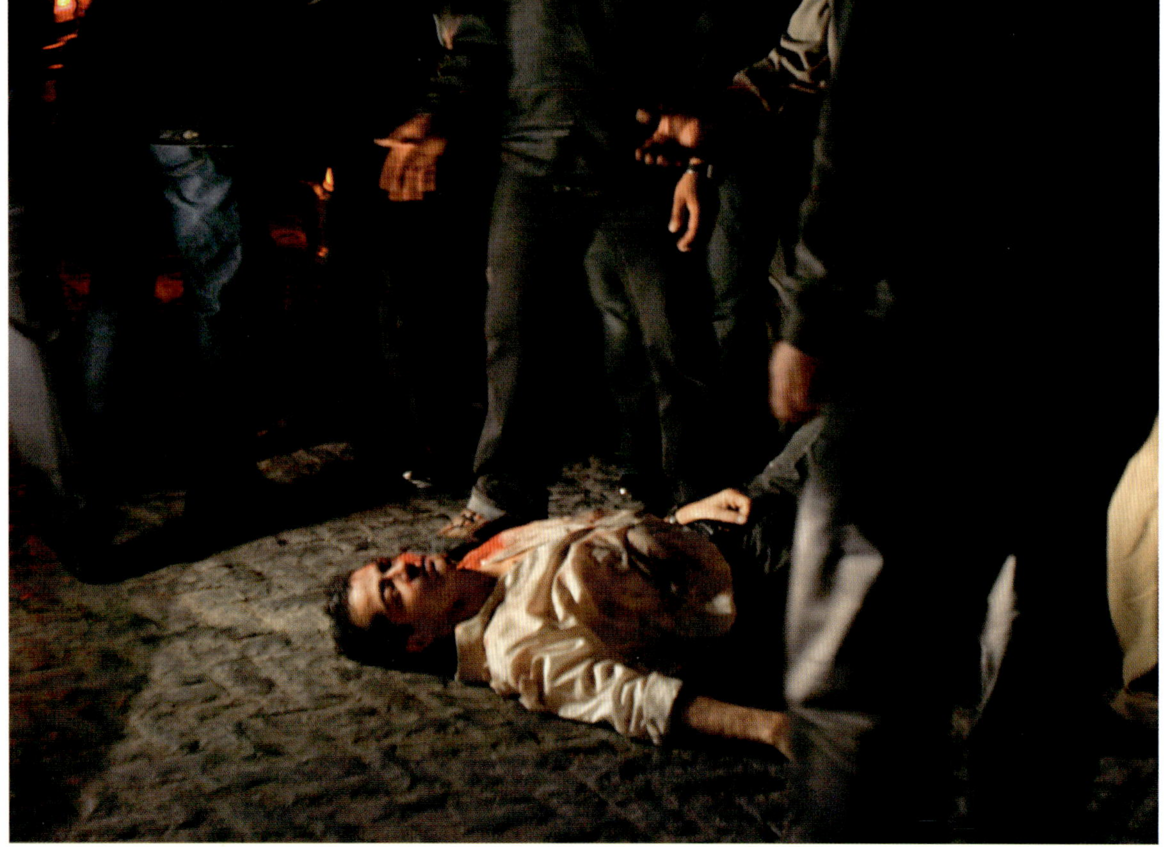

9 November 2005, AMMAN, JORDAN

Jordanians stand over the body of a victim of a suicide bomber who struck the Grand Hyatt hotel in central Amman, one of three bombers who blew themselves up in Amman hotels, killing 57 people, including guests at two separate wedding parties. Iraq's al Qaeda later claimed responsibility. Ali Jarekji

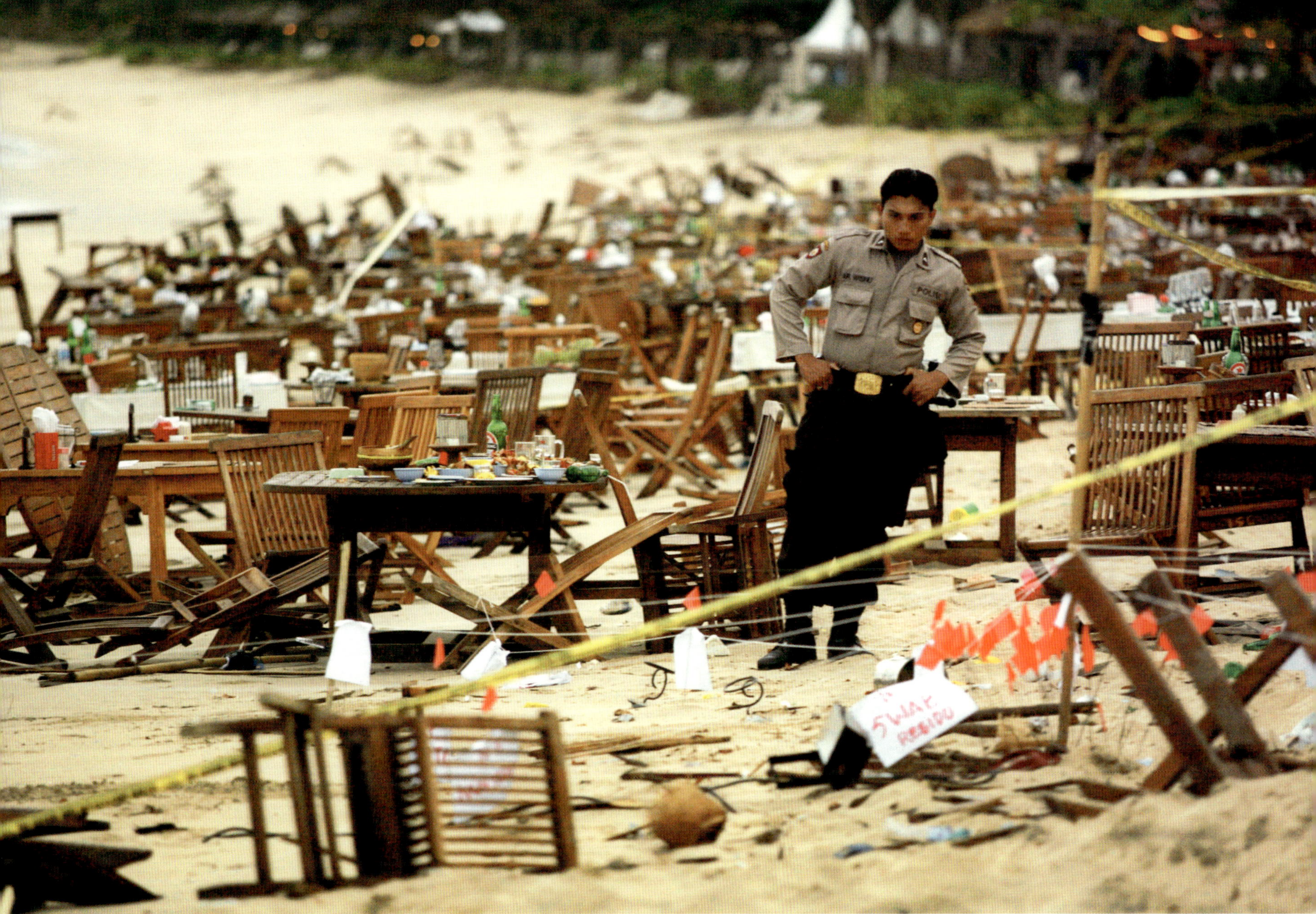

3 October 2005, BALI, INDONESIA

Two days after suicide bombers struck, a police officer looks at one of two blast sites marked with red flags in Jimbaran Beach on the resort island of Bali. A third bomber attacked a restaurant in Kuta Beach. In total 20 people were killed and around 150 wounded. Bomb attacks in Bali's Kuta Beach nightclub district three years earlier, on 12 October 2002, killed 202 people. Adrees Latif

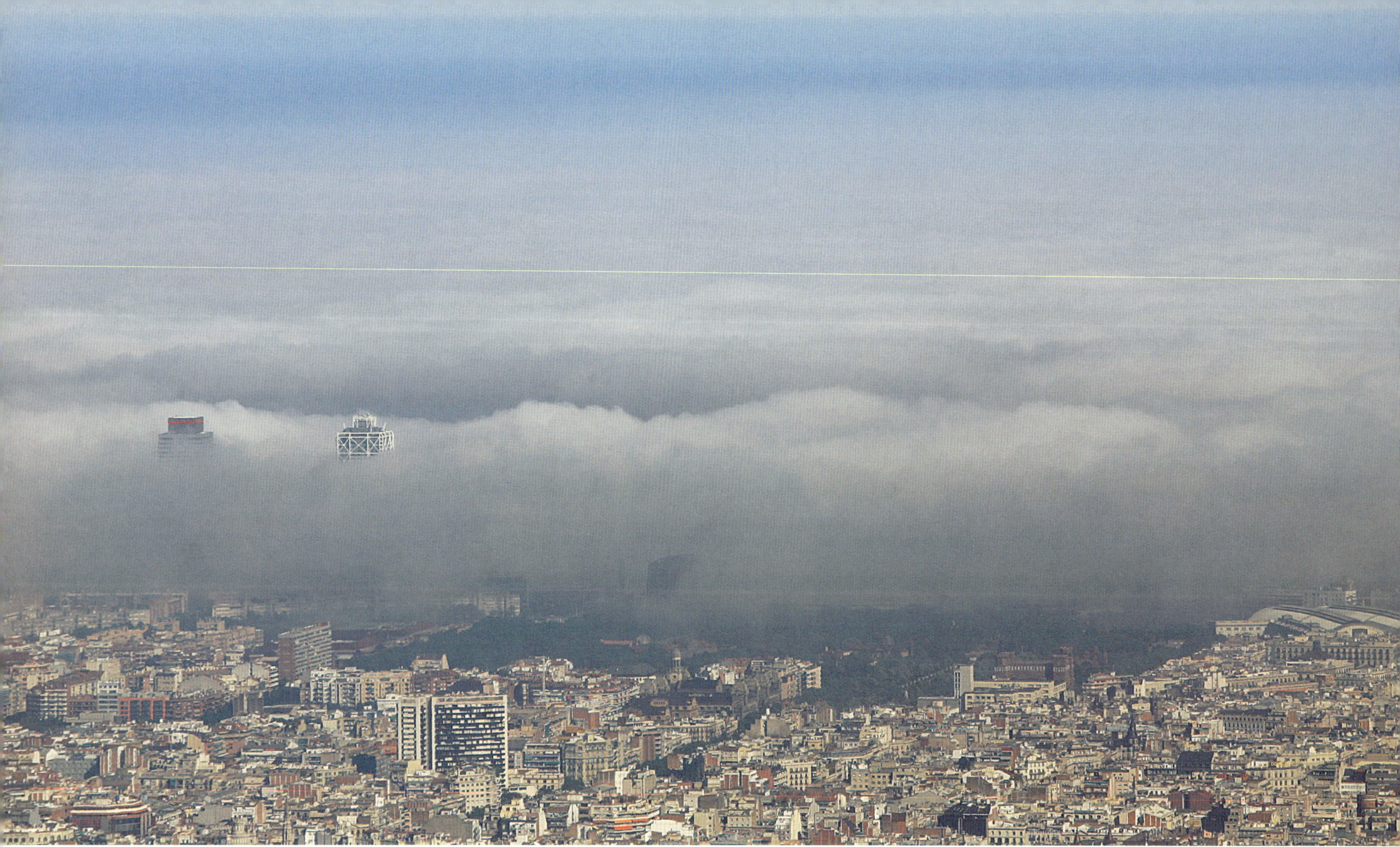

26 May 2005, BARCELONA, SPAIN

Dense fog settles over Barcelona's city coastline. The condition was caused by an unusually great difference in temperature between the sea and the air. Albert Gea

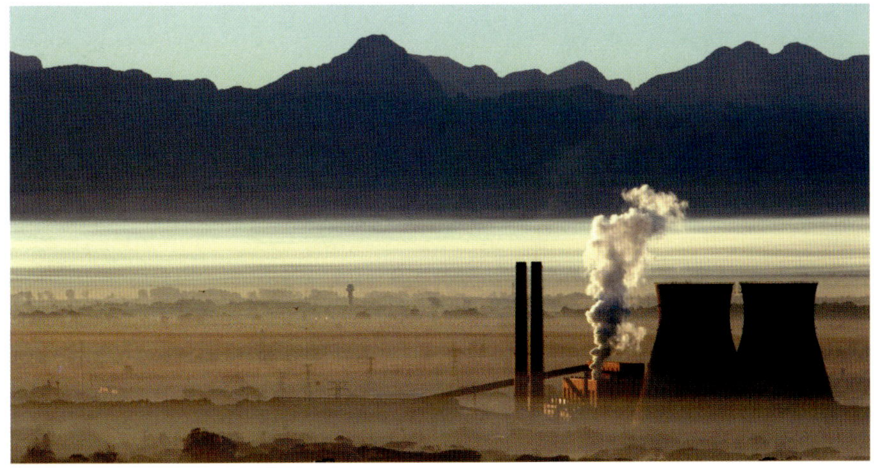

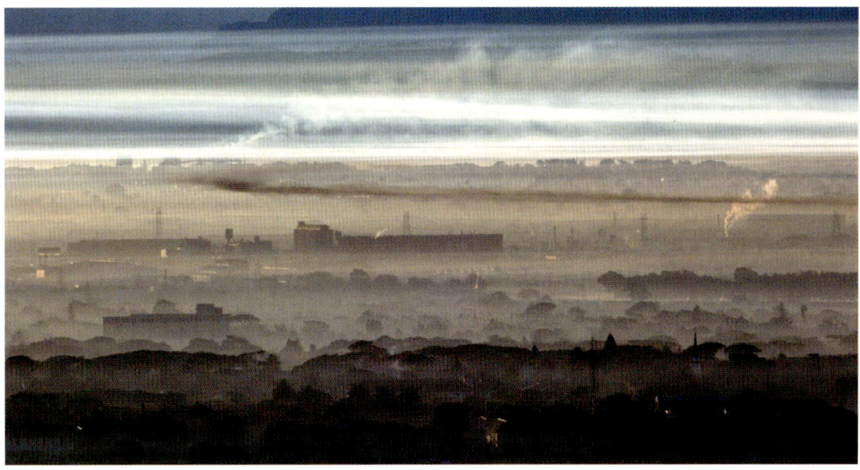

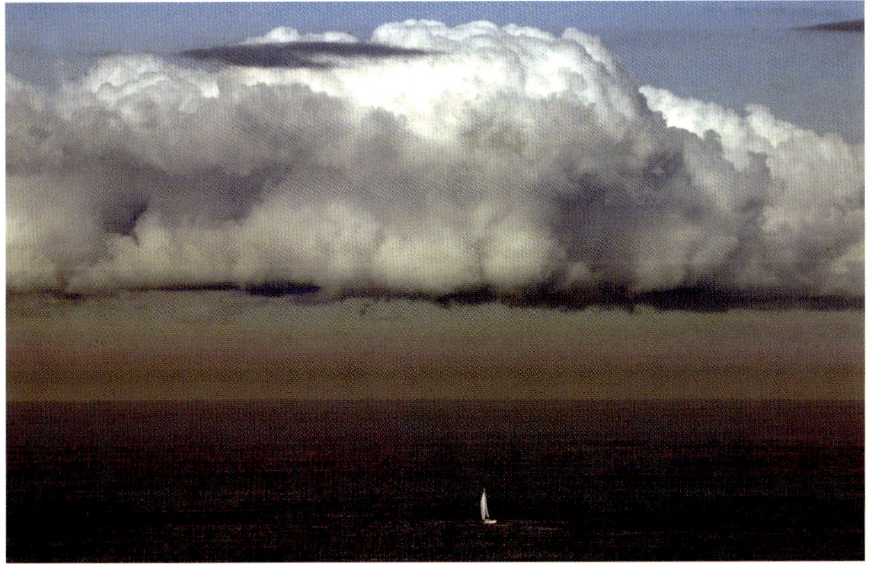

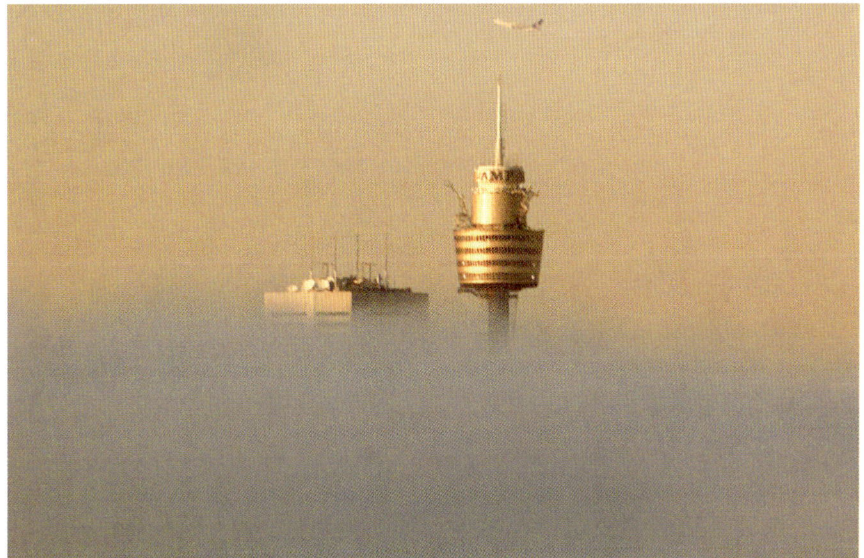

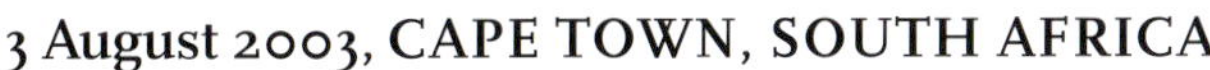

3 August 2003, CAPE TOWN, SOUTH AFRICA

Early morning smog hangs over Cape Town, the product of smoke and fumes from fires, factories and automobiles. Mike Hutchings

3 August 2003, CAPE TOWN, SOUTH AFRICA

Cape Town's seasonal smog or 'brown haze'. Mike Hutchings

26 June 2003, SYDNEY, AUSTRALIA

A small sailing boat heads out to sea as a pollution haze hangs beneath a massive storm cloud east of Sydney Harbour's headlands. David Gray

13 July 2001, SYDNEY, AUSTRALIA

A plane rises over Centrepoint Tower, Sydney's tallest building, as thick fog envelopes the city. David Gray

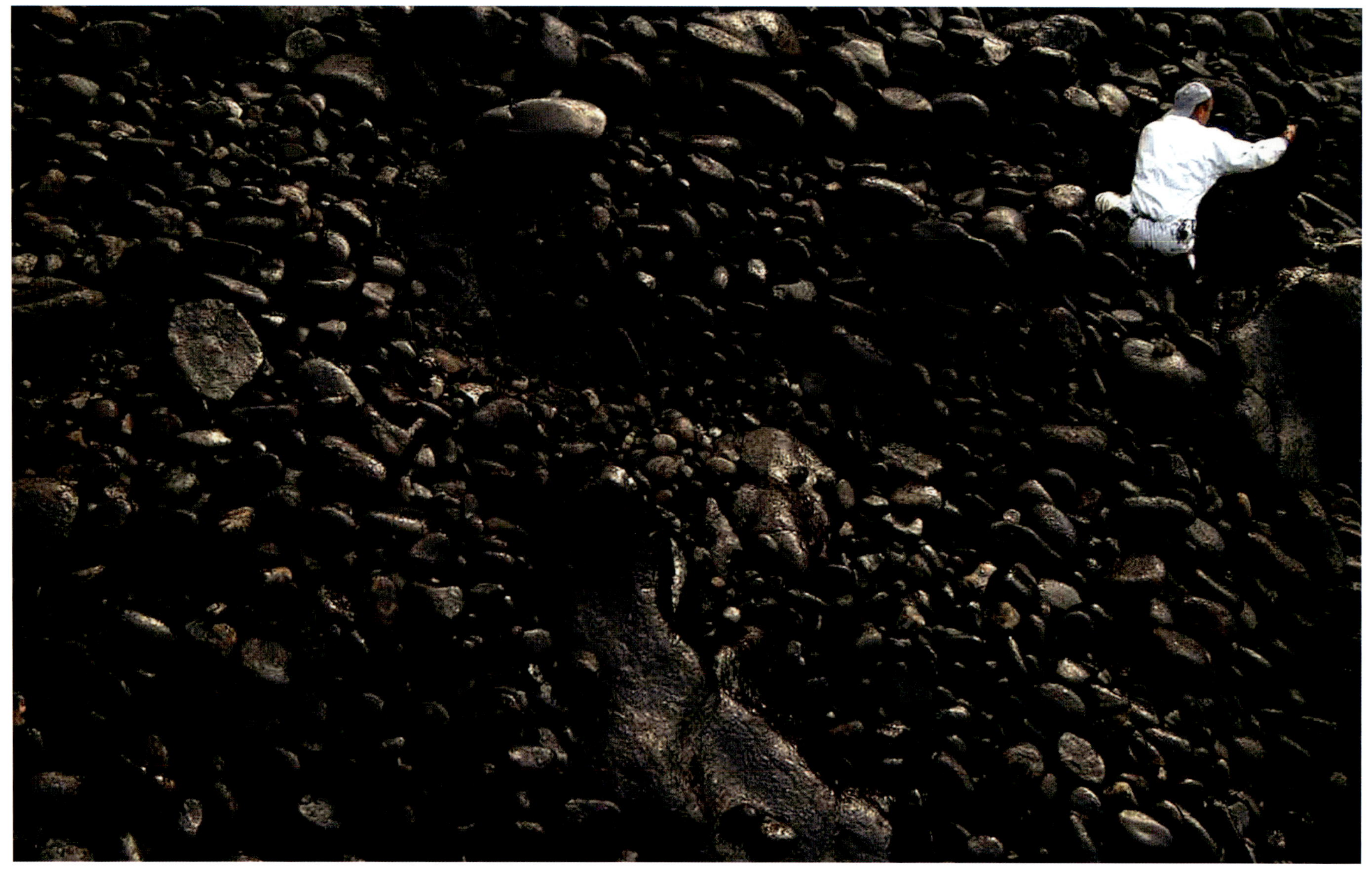

10 February 2003, MUXIA, SPAIN

A volunteer cleans up spilled oil from stained rocks on a beach in the village of Muxia after the Prestige, a Bahamanian-registered single-hull tanker carrying over 75,000 tonnes of fuel oil, broke in two and sank some 270 km (165 miles) off the coast of northwestern Spain in November 2002. The accident shut down Europe's largest fishing industry and blackened the rugged shores of Galicia with thousands of tonnes of oil, the worst pollution ever to hit Spain's coastline.
Miguel Vidal

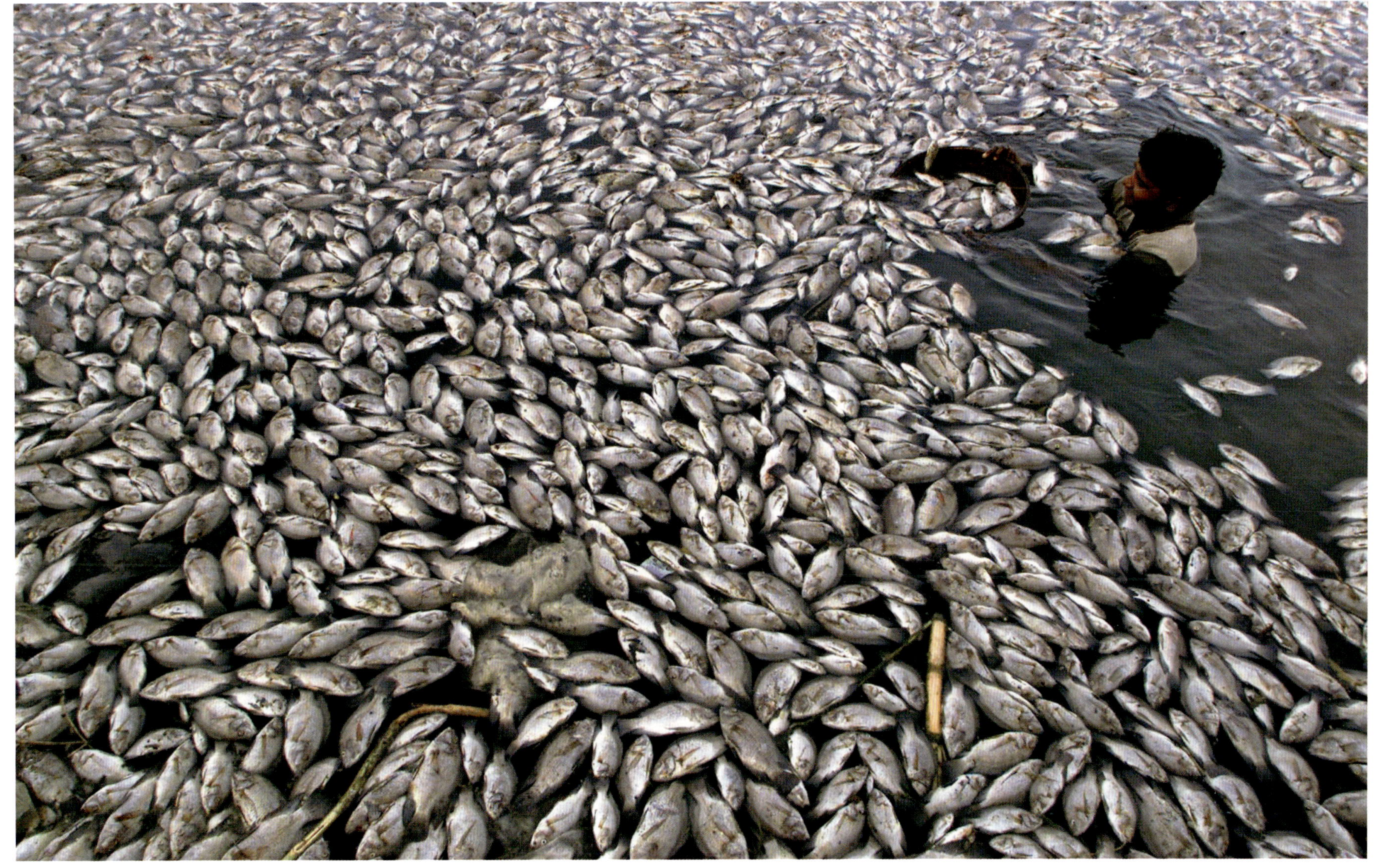

12 October 2004, AHMEDABAD, INDIA

A worker collects dead fish from Kankaria Lake in the western Indian city of Ahmedabad. According to local meteorologists, the mass death of the fish was caused by a decline in oxygen levels in the lake. Amit Dave

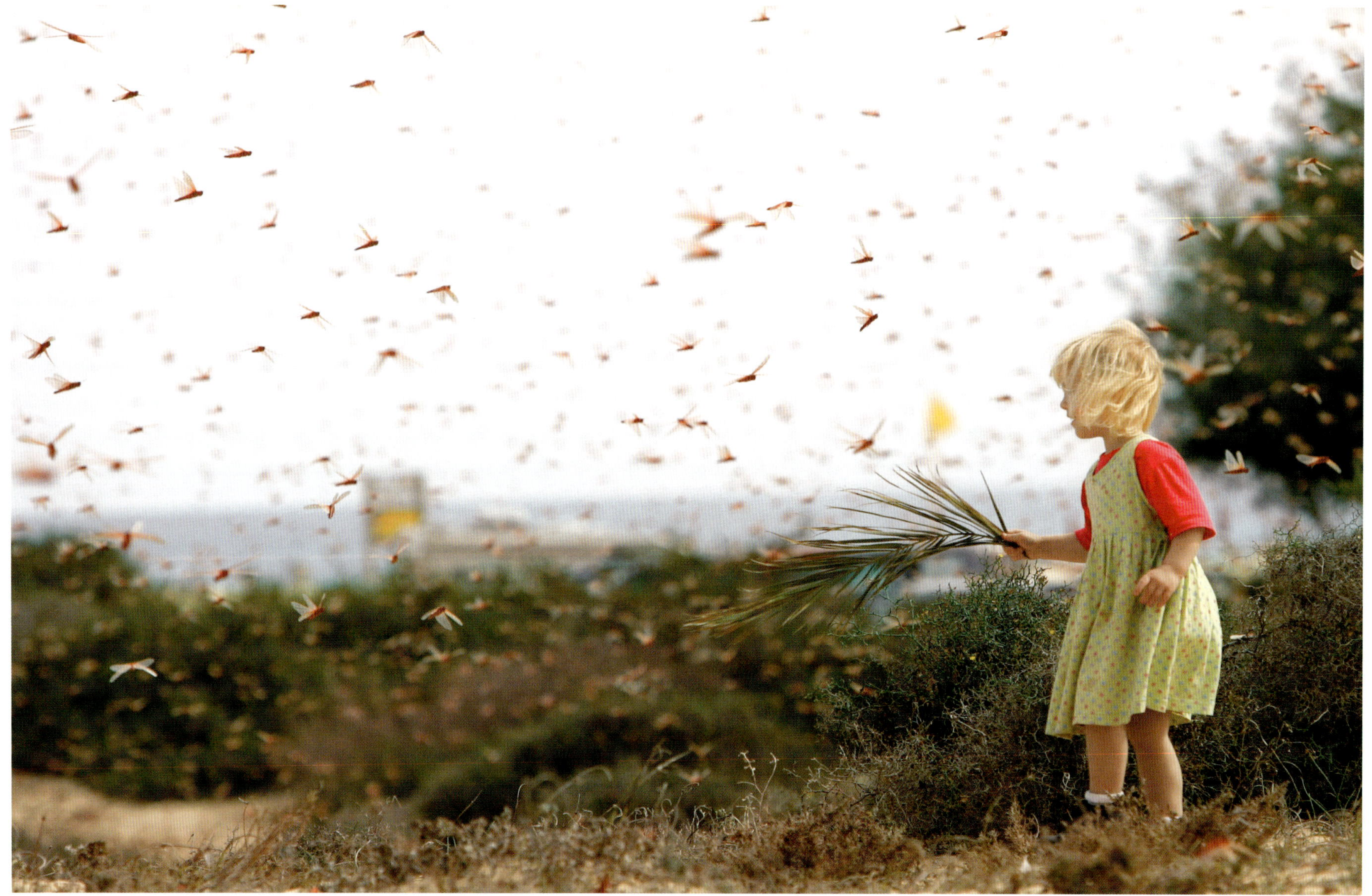

29 November 2004, FUERTEVENTURA, SPAIN

A girl plays on a beach as a swarm of pink locusts flies overhead near Corralejo on the Spanish Canary Island of Fuerteventura. More than 100 million of the insects reached Fuerteventura from west Africa, just 150 kms (95 miles) away. The swarm was soon killed off by heavy winds and rain, but the infestation, the worst in over a decade, had already inflicted major damage on cereal crops across several African countries. Juan Medina

1 September 2004, DAKAR, SENEGAL

Opposite West and central African countries affected by the locust infestation of 2004 included Senegal, Gambia, Niger, Mali, Chad, Burkina Faso and Mauritania. In some places locusts are eaten as a delicacy, fried and dusted with spices. But the long-term consequences of such a large-scale infestation can be devastating food-shortages and hunger. Pierre Holtz

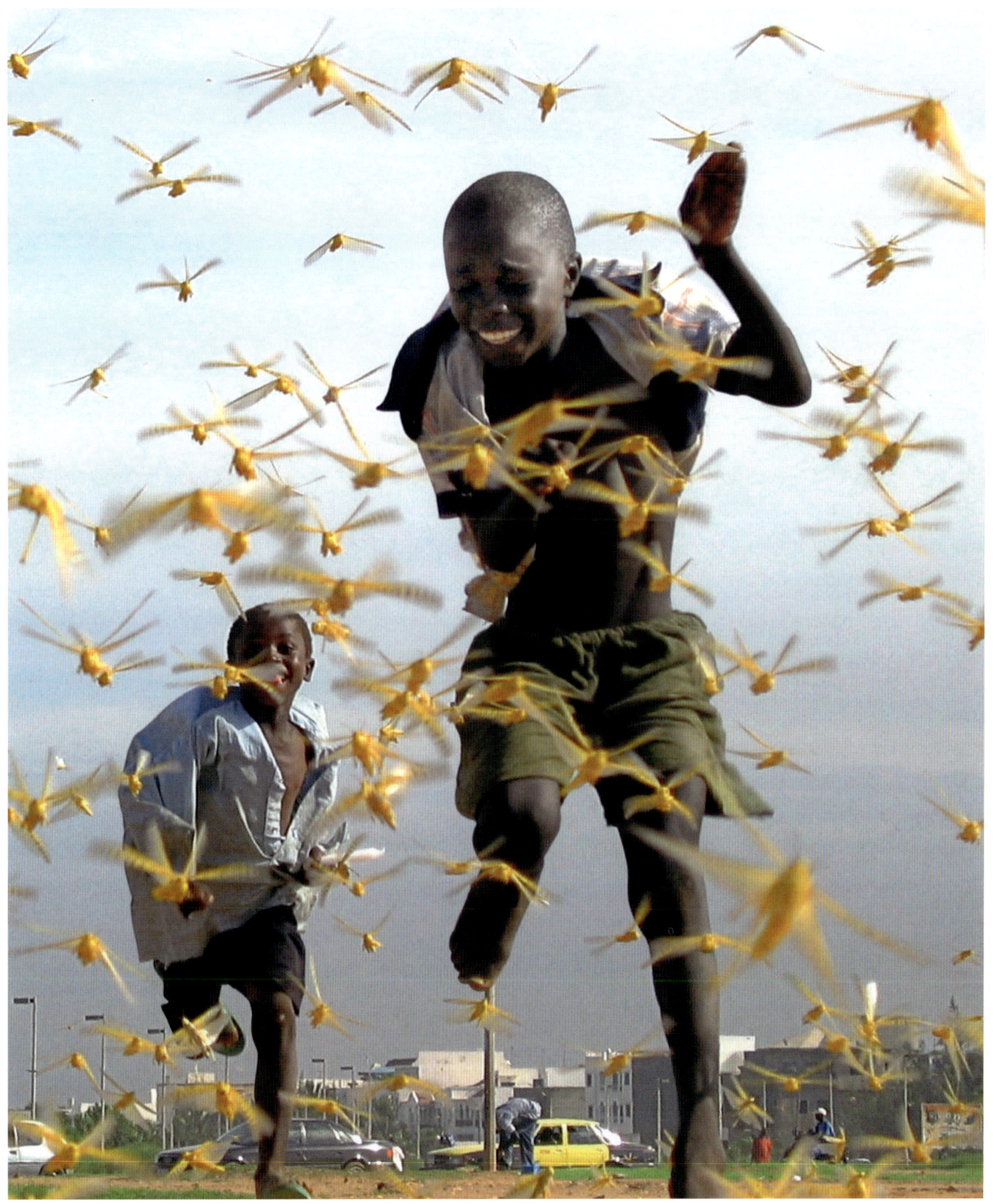

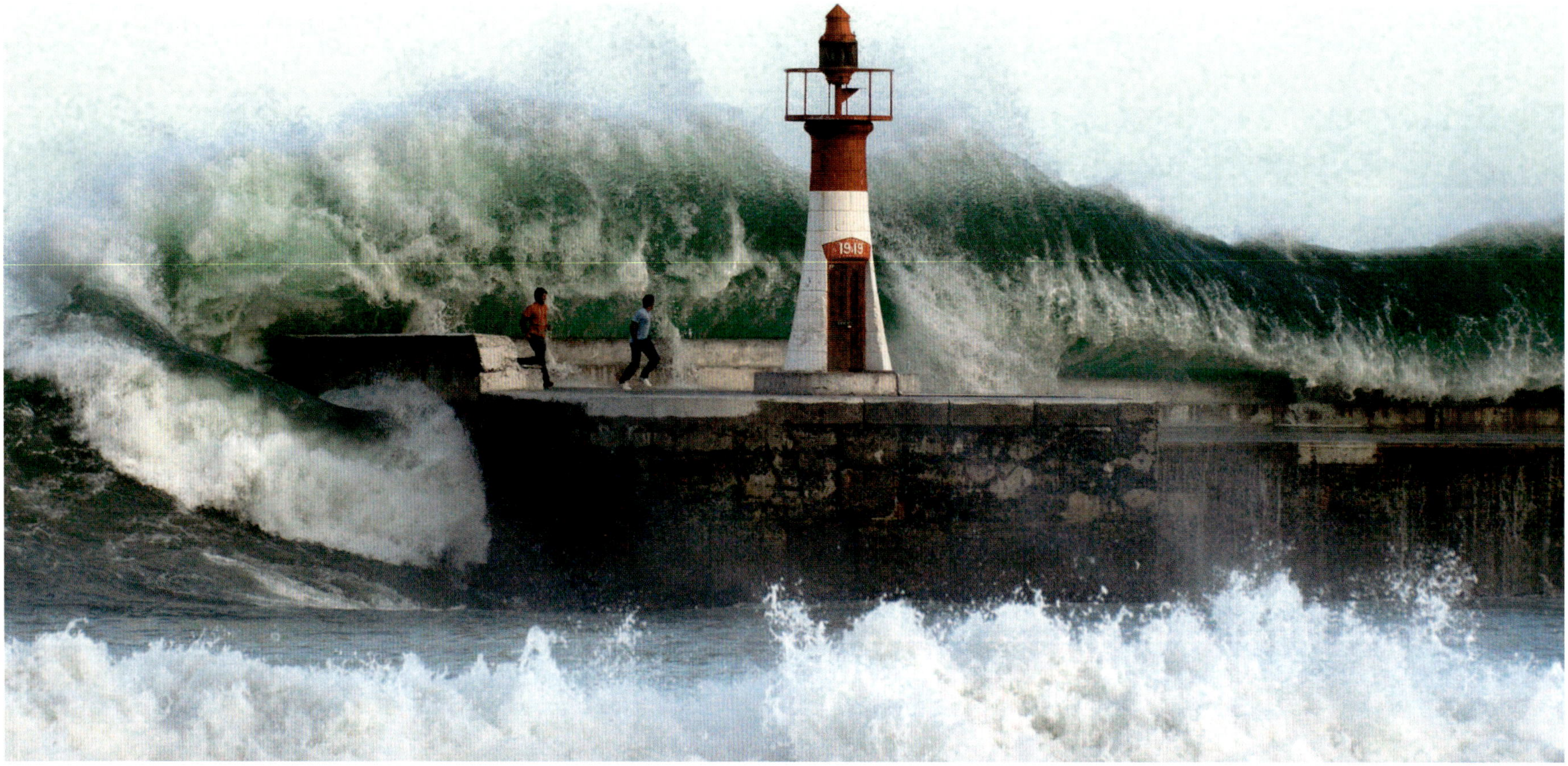

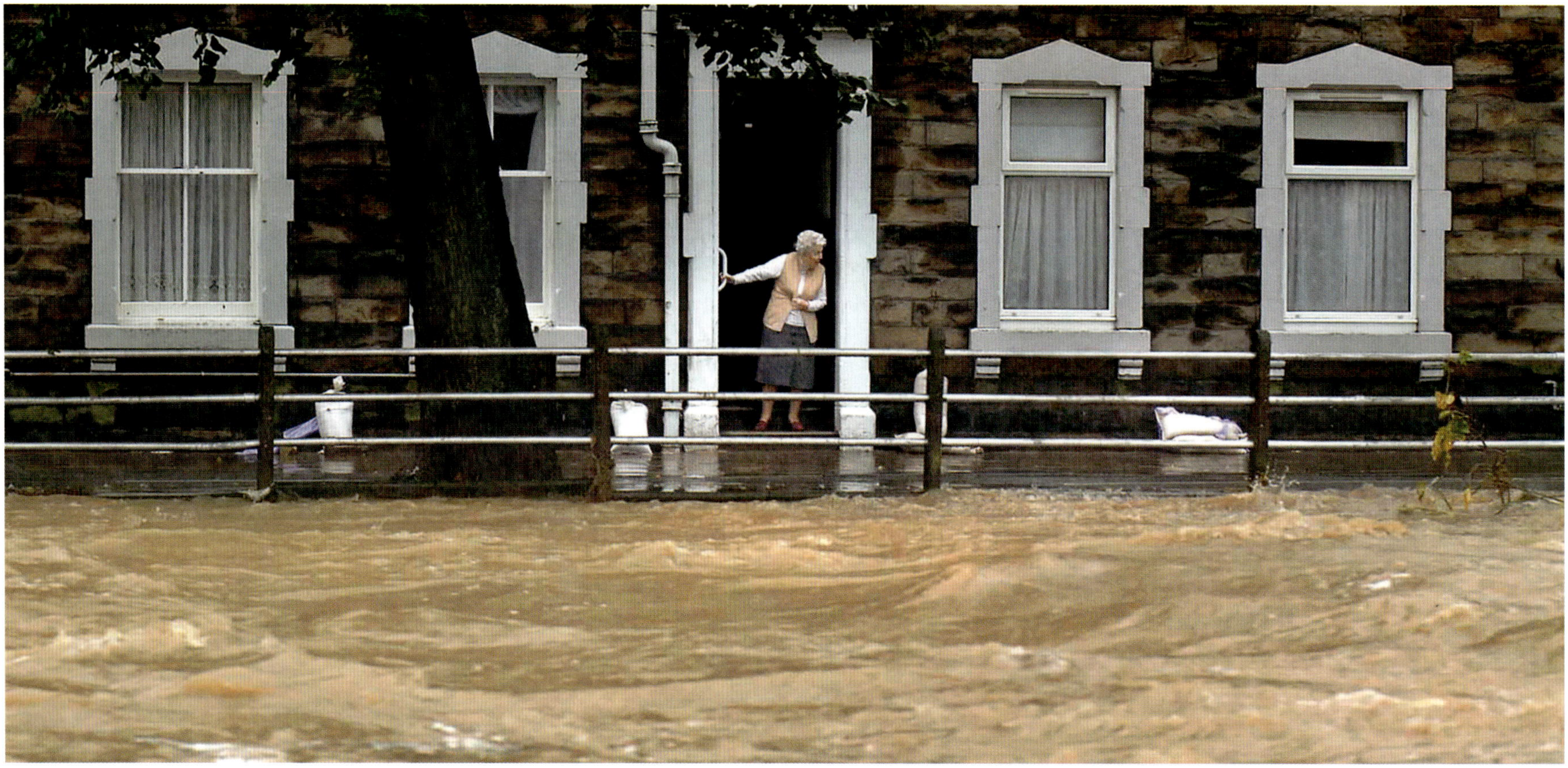

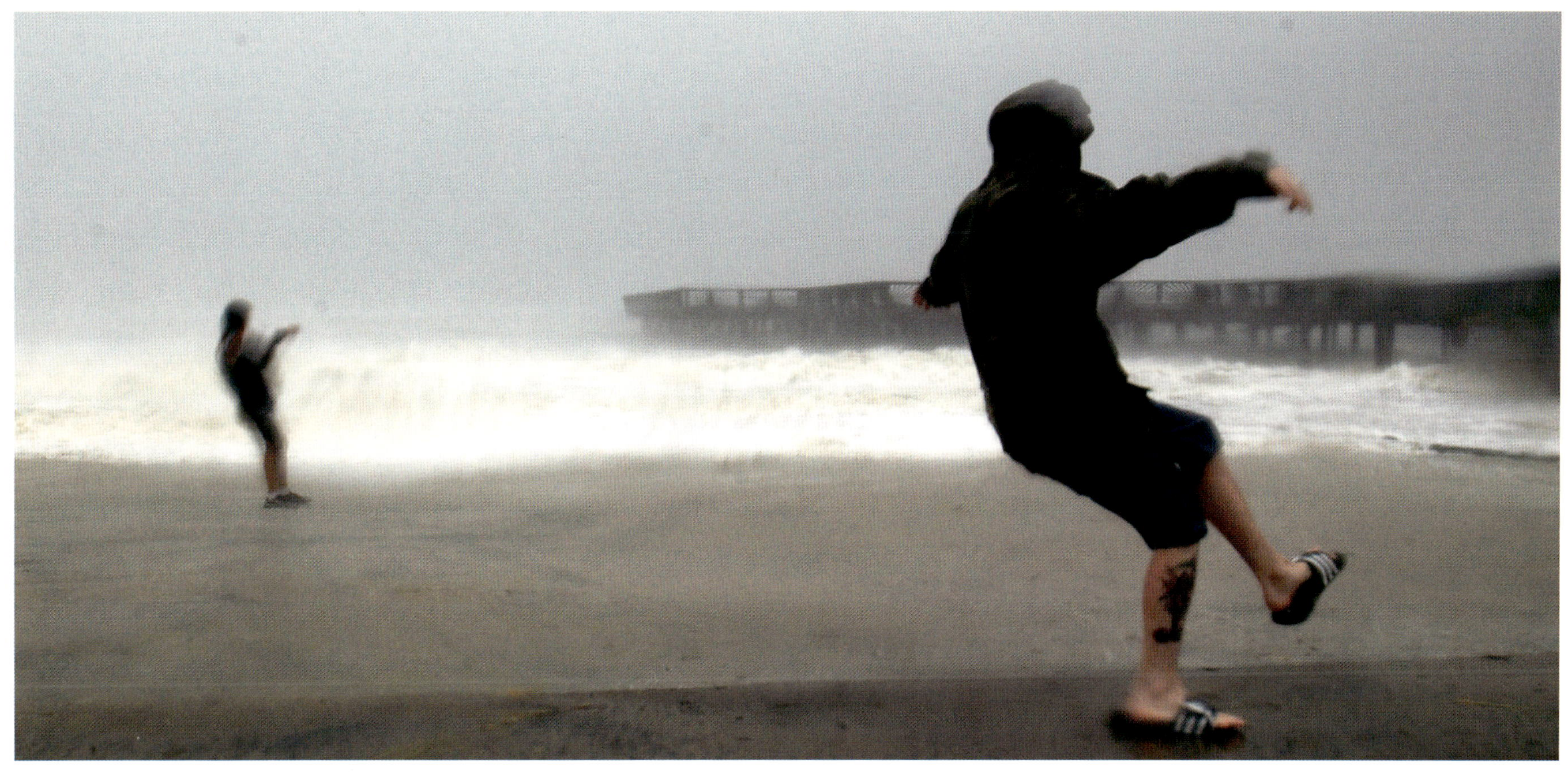

27 August 2005, CAPE TOWN, SOUTH AFRICA

Opposite above Giant waves crash over onlookers on the sea wall of Cape Town's Kalk Bay harbour. The two men were later rescued as storms created waves of an estimated 9 metres (30 feet). Philip Massie

12 October 2005, HAWICK, UNITED KINGDOM

Opposite below The River Teviot in southern Scotland bursts its banks, leaving parts of the town of Hawick under 1.2 metres (4 feet) of water. Chris Watt

18 September 2003, VIRGINIA, UNITED STATES

Above People brave the wind and rain in Hampton, Virginia, as Hurricane Isabel arrives on the U.S. east coast. Chip East

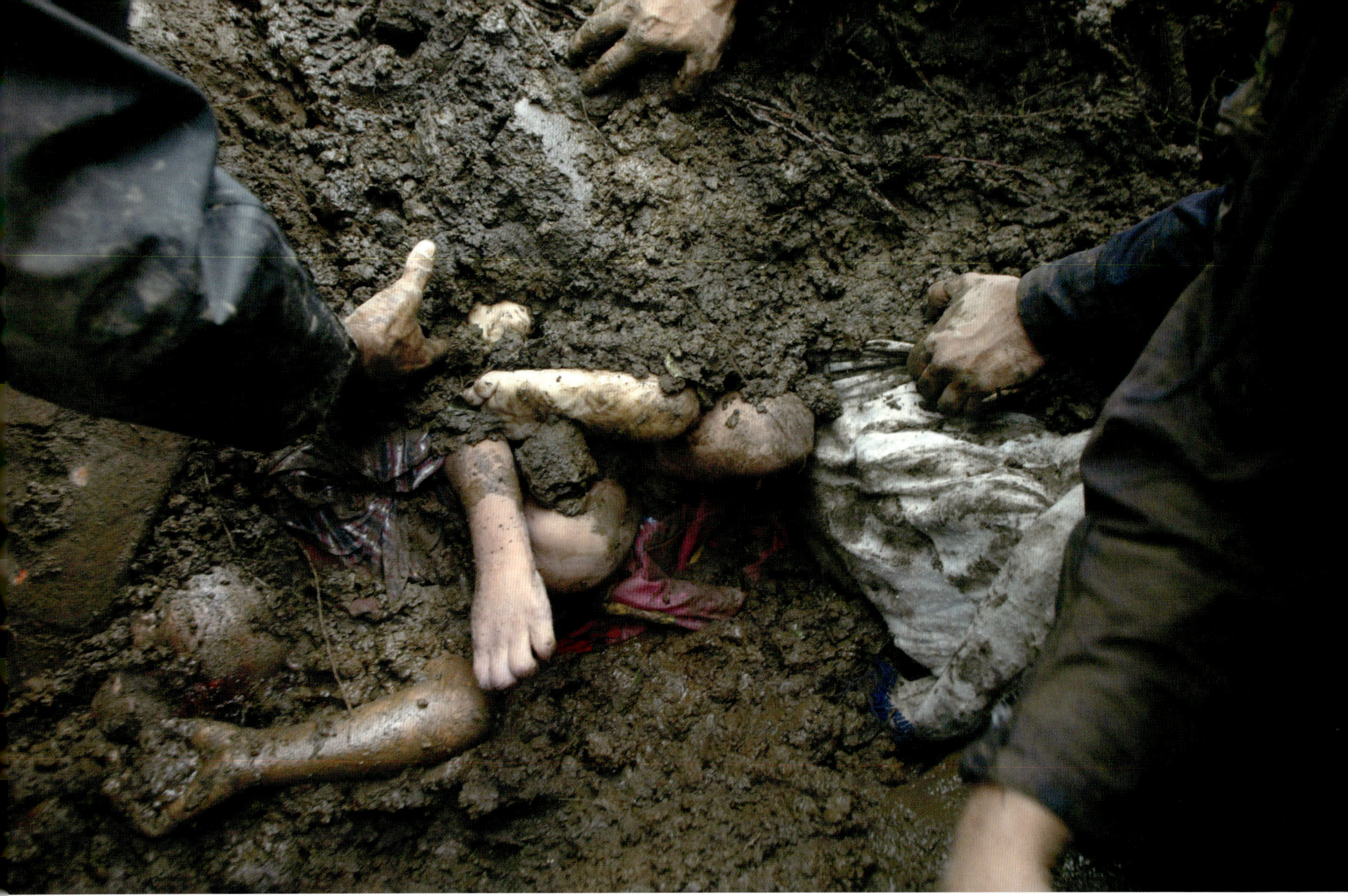

3 October 2005, LOURDES COLON, EL SALVADOR

Salvadoran soldiers dig out one of five people killed by a mudslide in Lourdes Colon about 20 km (12 miles) west of San Salvador. Torrential rains in the path of Hurricane Stan killed more than 1,000 people in Central America as collapsing hillsides buried homes and rivers burst their banks. Luis Galdamez

6 October 2005, CHIMALTENANGO, GUATEMALA

Opposite above A young Guatemalan boy looks at a river that has burst its banks, damaging houses and dragging away a truck, in the heavy rainfall associated with Hurricane Stan. Carlos Duarte

26 July 2004, NARAYANGANJ, BANGLADESH

Opposite below A girl swims with a jar to collect drinking water through a flooded residential area of Narayanganj town, 20 km (13 miles) from the Bangladeshi capital Dhaka, where up to 100,000 of the city's 10 million population were obliged to cram into shelters after floods inundated large parts of the city and boats replaced rickshaws as the primary means of transport. Rafiqur Rahman

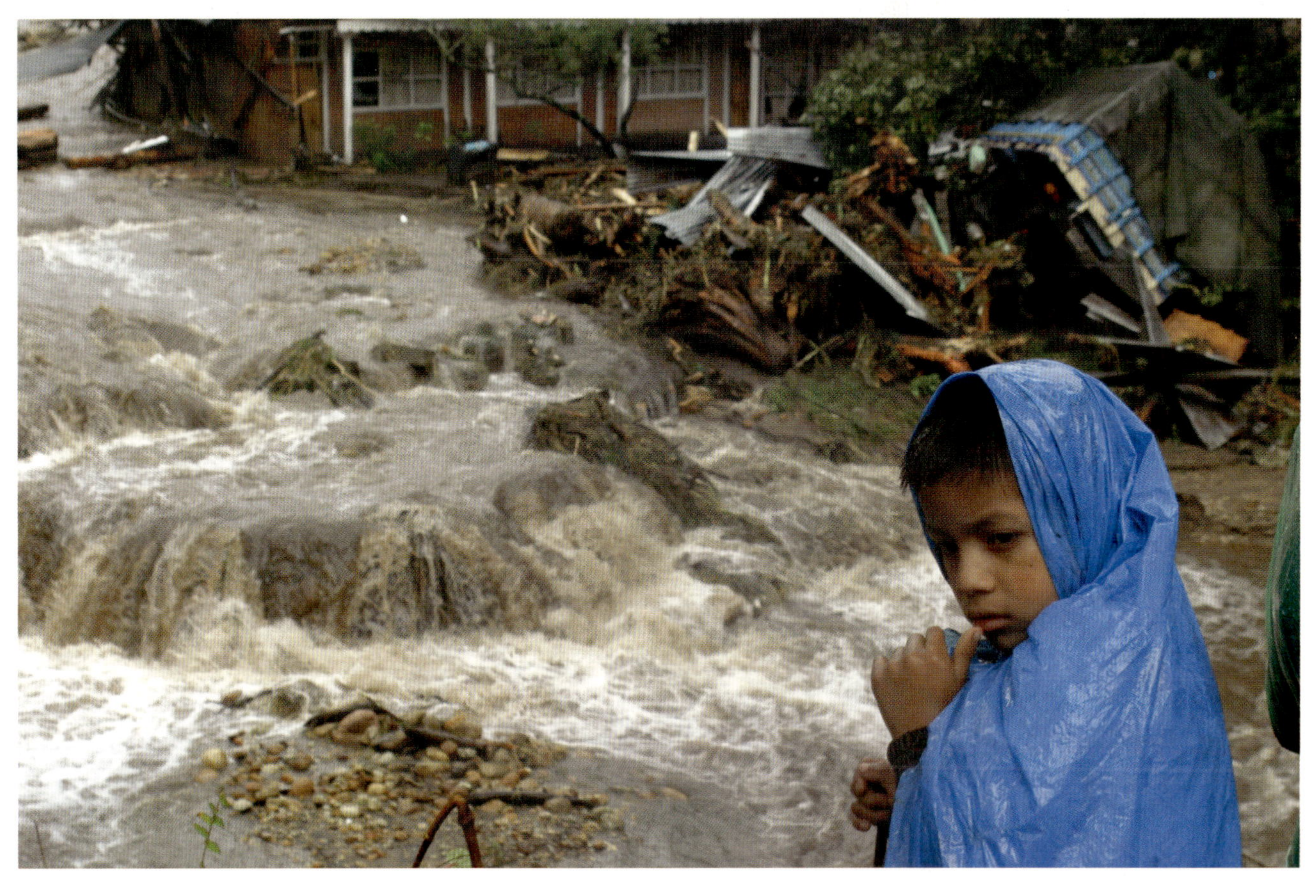

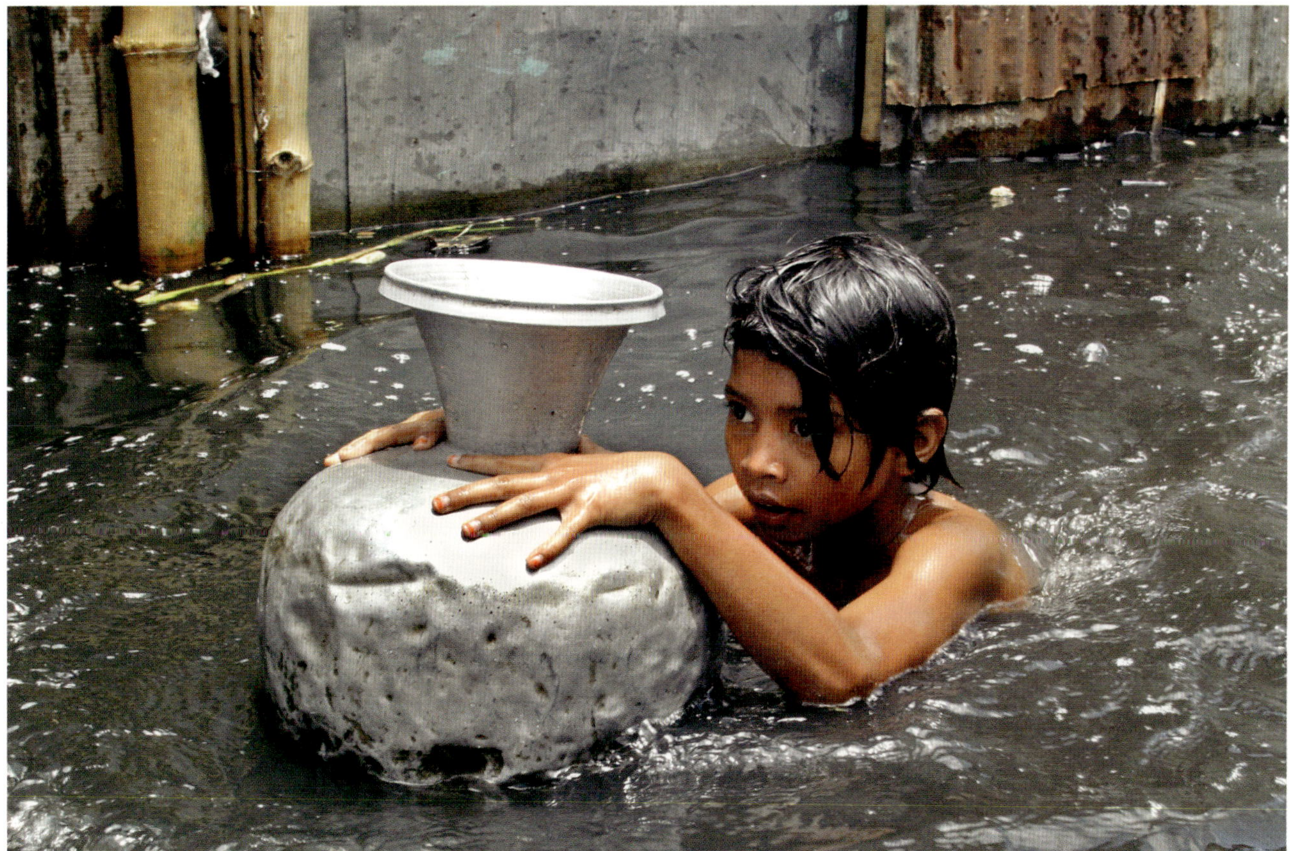

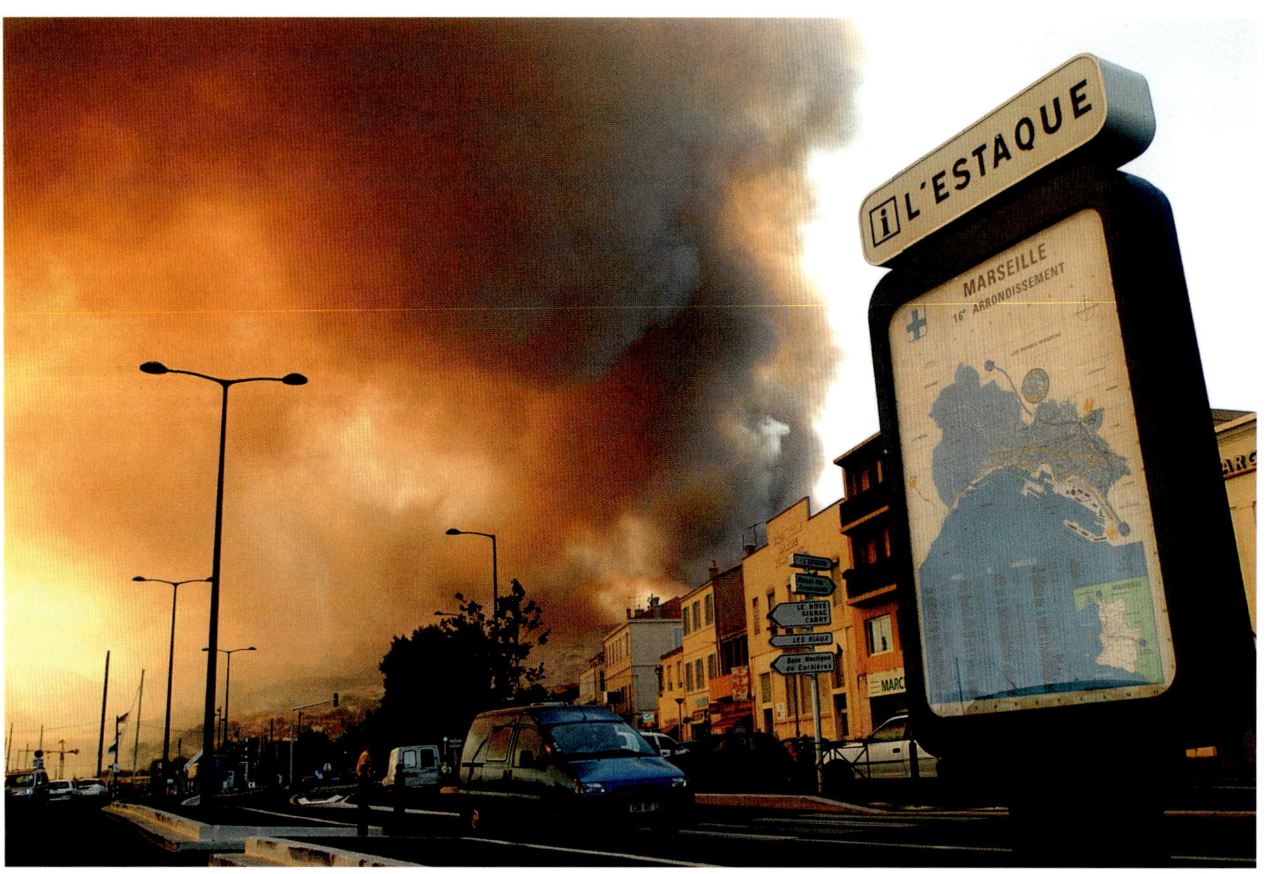

24 July 2004, MARSEILLE, FRANCE

Dense smoke rises into the sky as winds drive wildfires near to the district of l'Estaque in Marseille. French Interior Minister Dominique de Villepin said arson was to blame for starting the huge fire. Philippe Laurenson

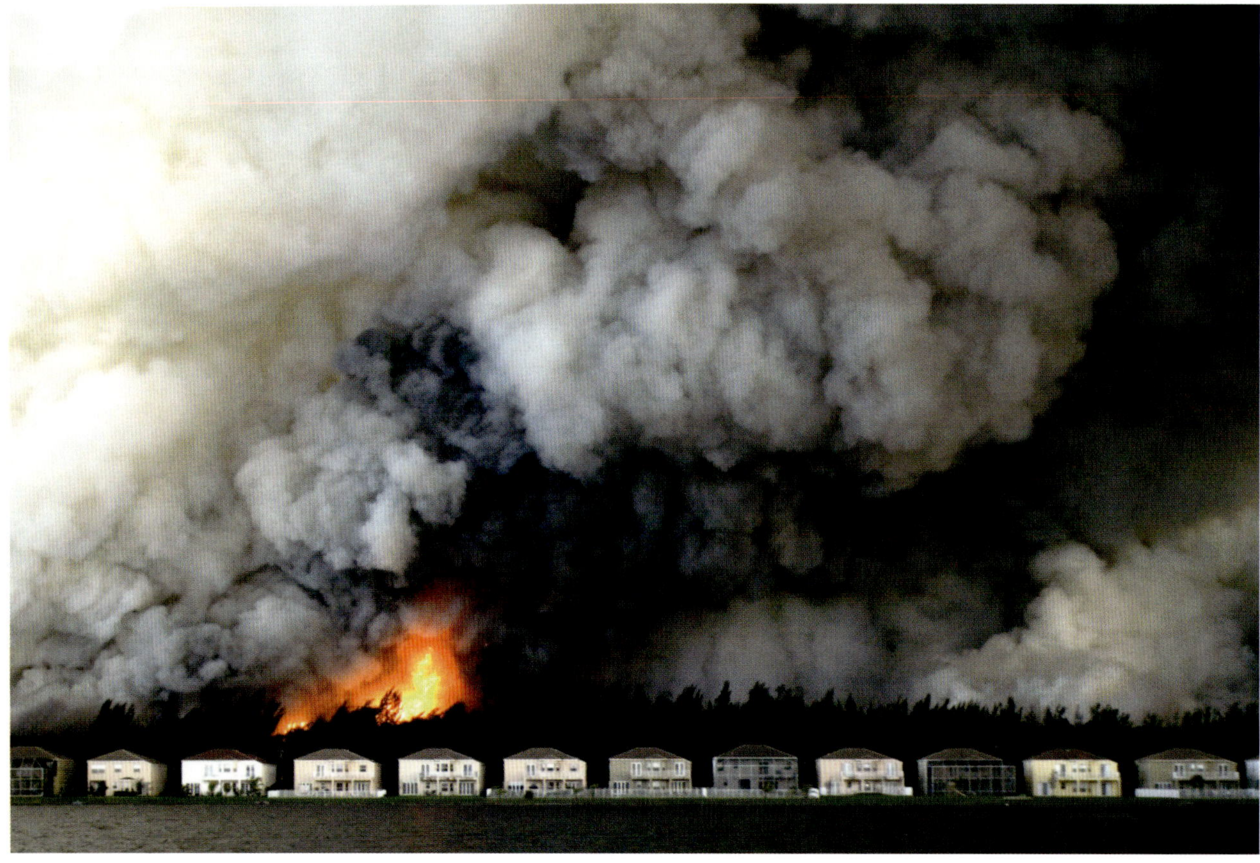

18 March 2004, FLORIDA, UNITED STATES

Homes in Sunset Lakes are threatened by the flames and smoke of a giant brush fire in Miramar, Florida. Marc Serota

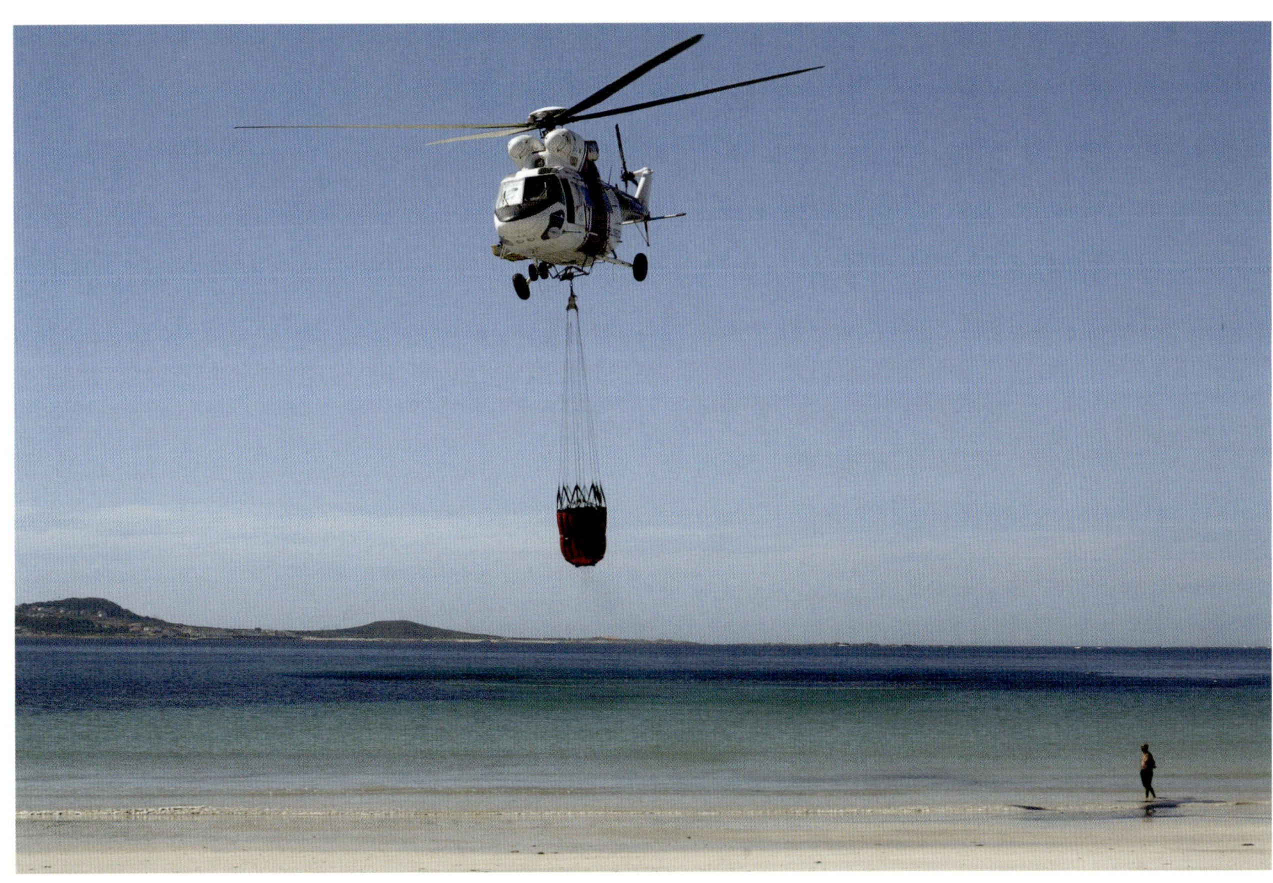

24 August 2005, GALICIA, SPAIN

A helicopter carries water over Carnota beach to drop on forest fires in Galicia, northwestern Spain. Victor Fraile

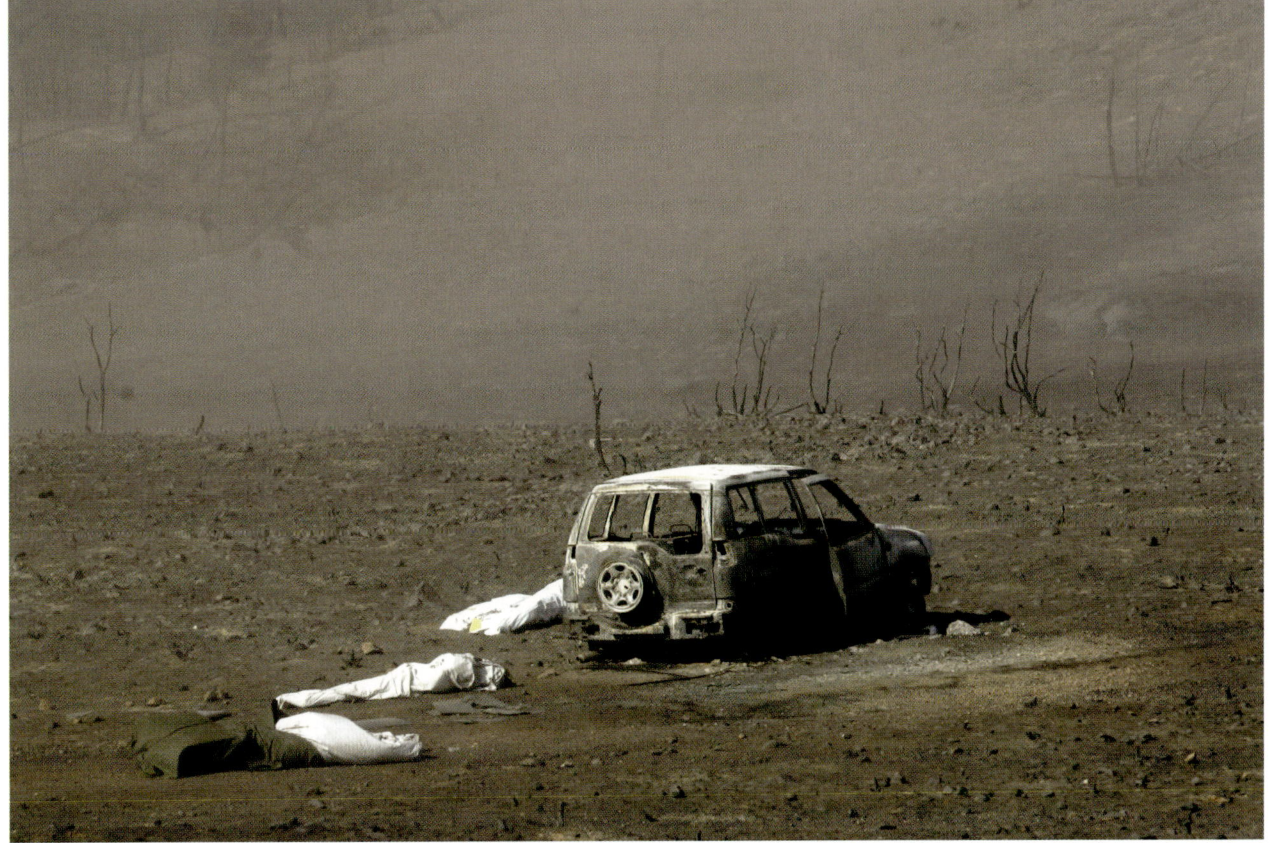

18 July 2005, SANTA MARIA DEL ESPINO, SPAIN

The covered corpses of three fire-fighters lie beside the charred chassis of a four-by-four vehicle in Spain's central village of Santa Maria del Espino, victims of a huge blaze that destroyed thousands of hectares of pine trees and brush in a nature reserve in the Guadalajara area east of Madrid. Victor Fraile

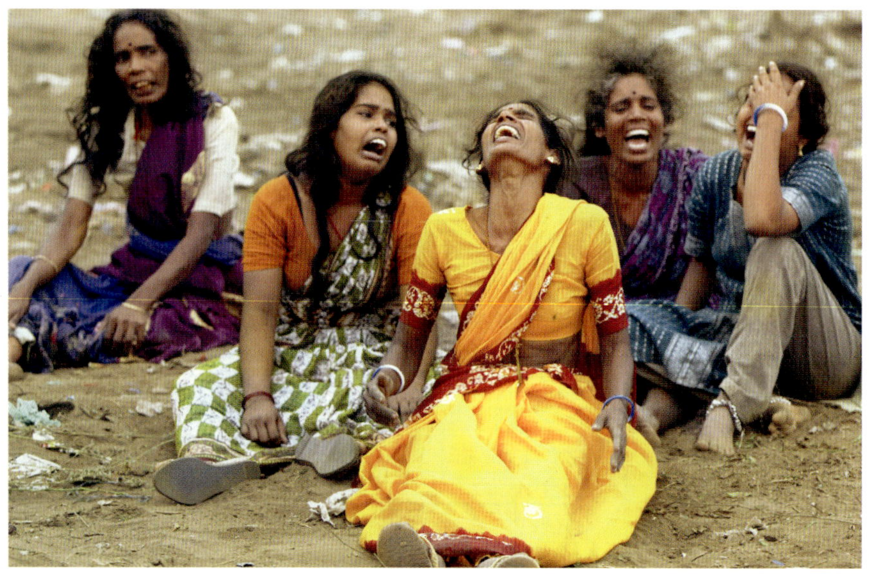

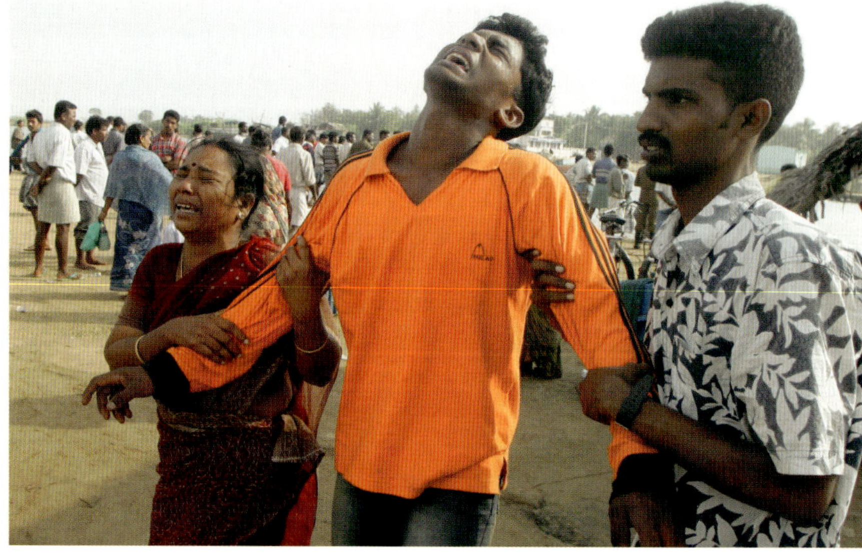

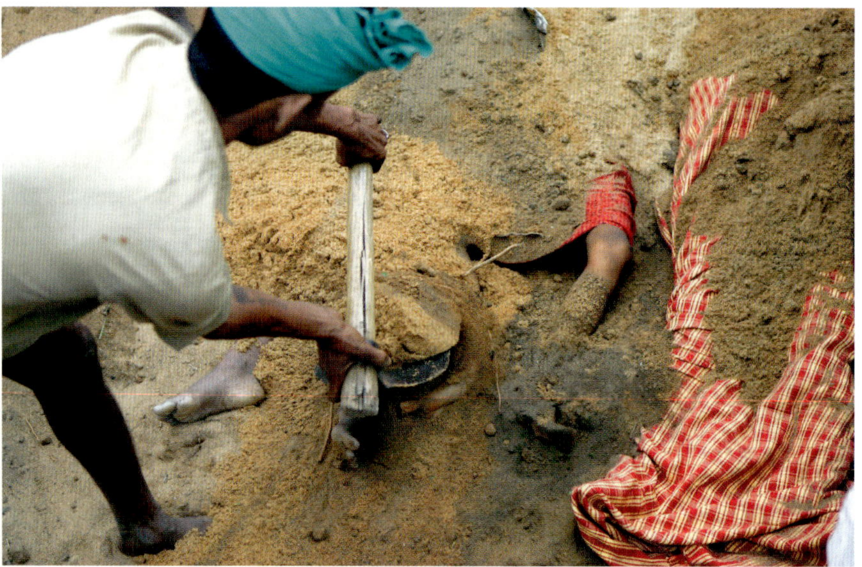

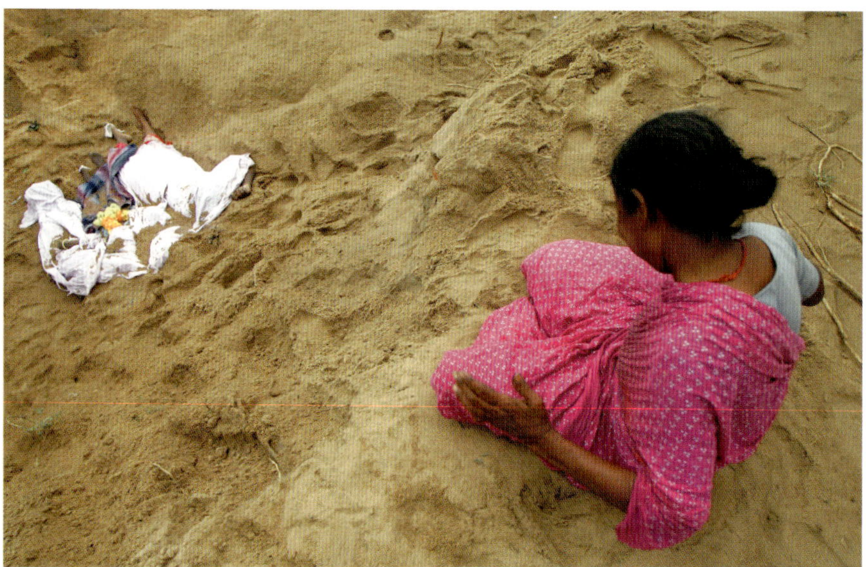

27–28 December 2004, CUDDALORE, INDIA

People mourn and bury victims of the tsunami catastrophe in Cuddalore, 180 km (112 miles) south of the Indian city of Madras. Triggered by a massive 9.15 magnitude earthquake beneath the Indian Ocean, the giant wave devastated coastal regions of Indonesia, Thailand, Sri Lanka and India on the morning of 26 December 2004. Almost 230,000 people were killed or missing. Arko Datta

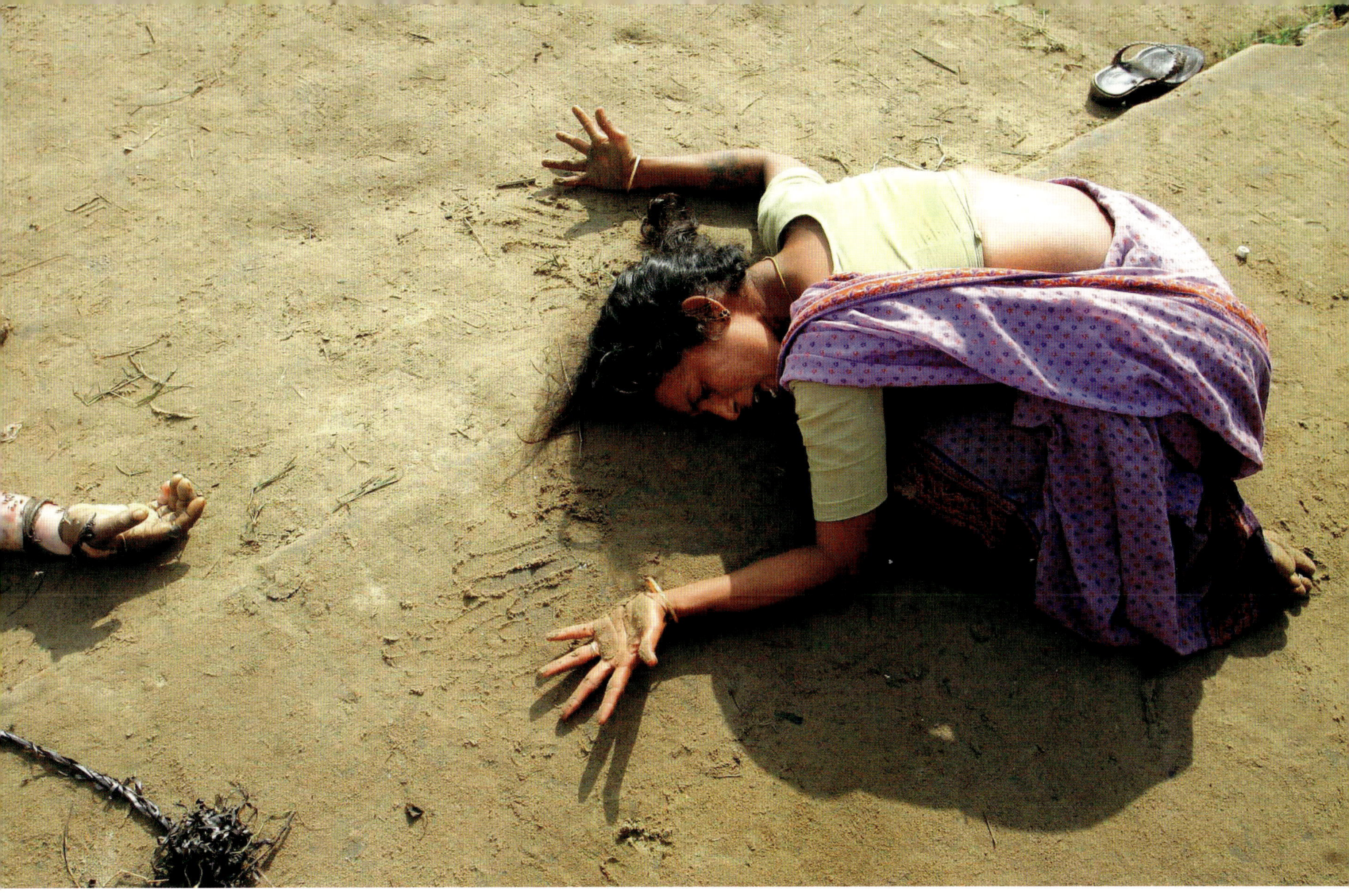

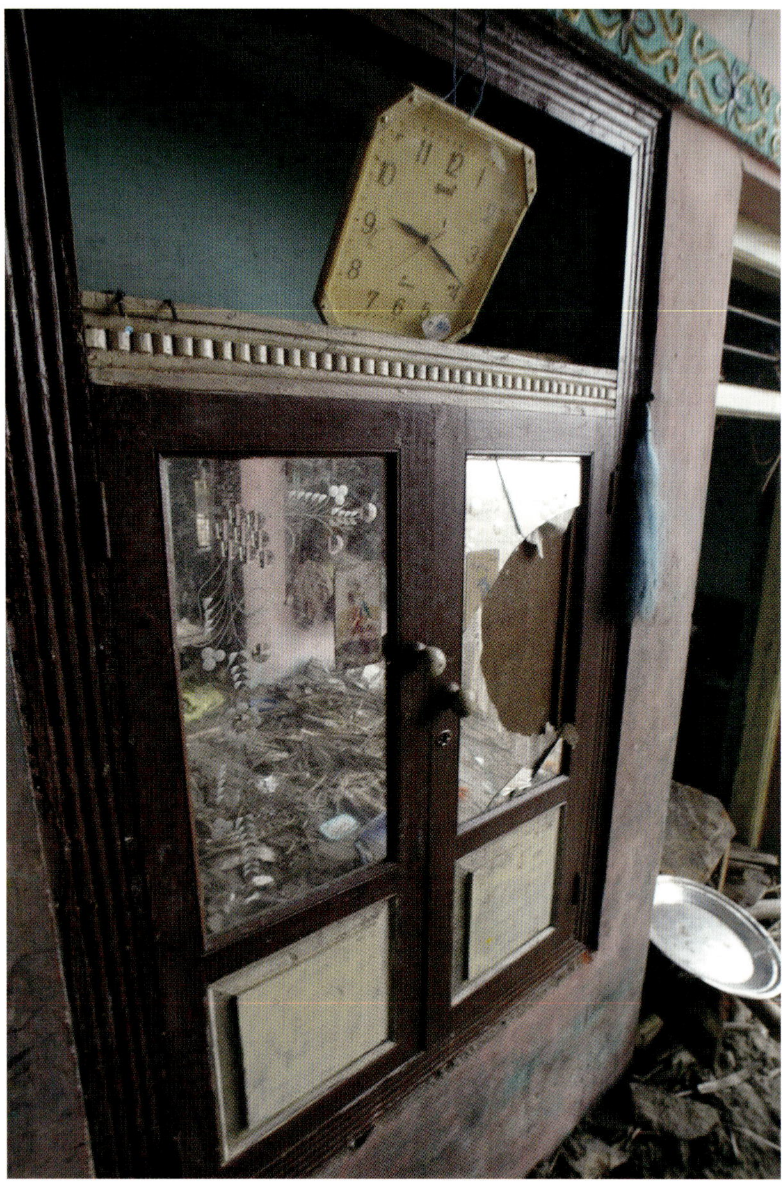

5 January 2005, NAGAPATTINAM, INDIA

A clock which stopped at the moment the tsunami struck lies atop a broken cupboard in a fishing hamlet in Nagapattinam, 350 km (219 miles) south of Madras. Arko Datta

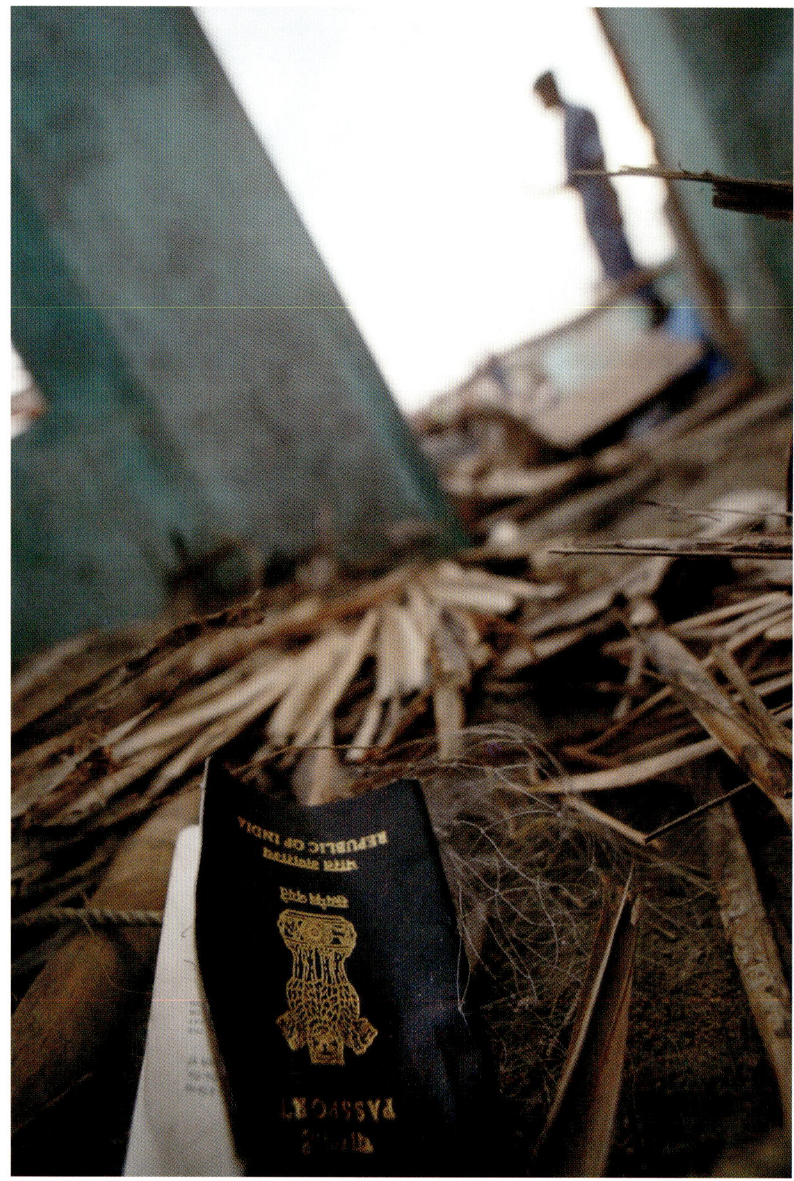

5 January 2005, NAGAPATTINAM, INDIA

An Indian passport lies amid the rubble of a tsunami-hit house as a soldier stands outside. Arko Datta

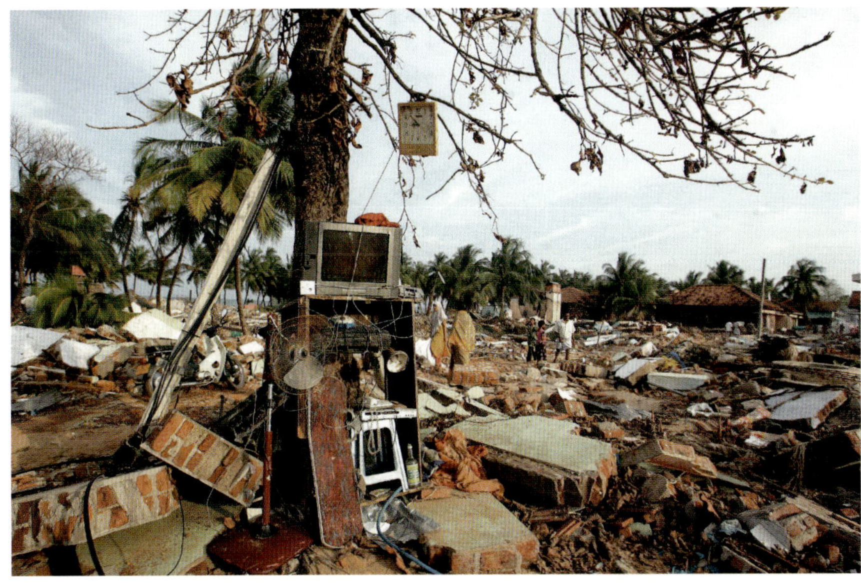

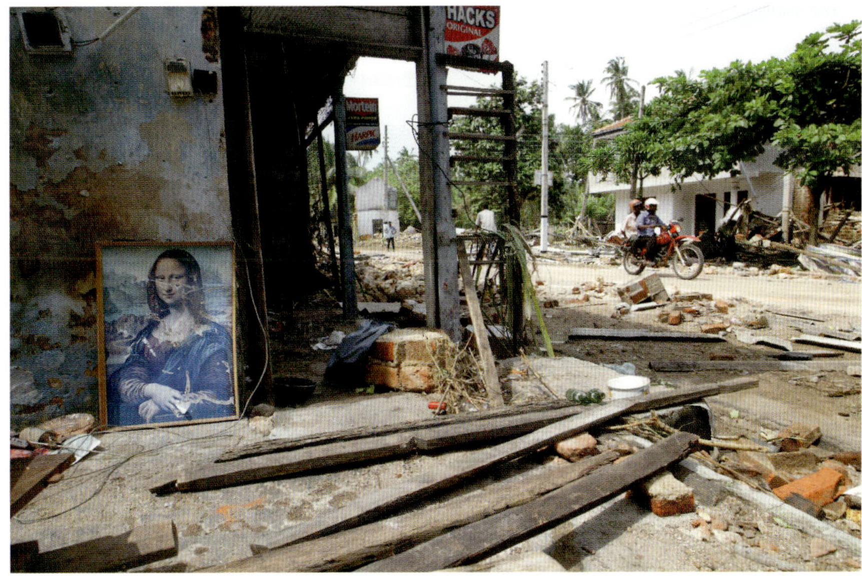

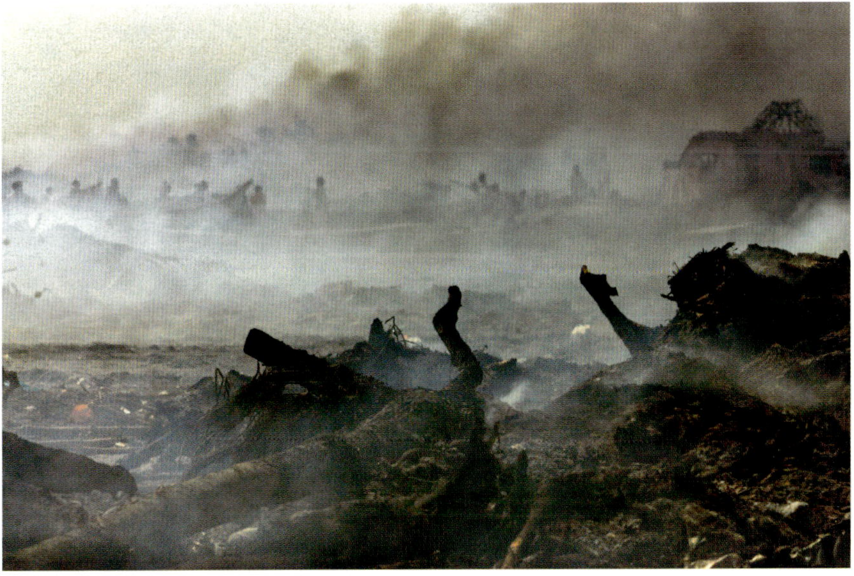

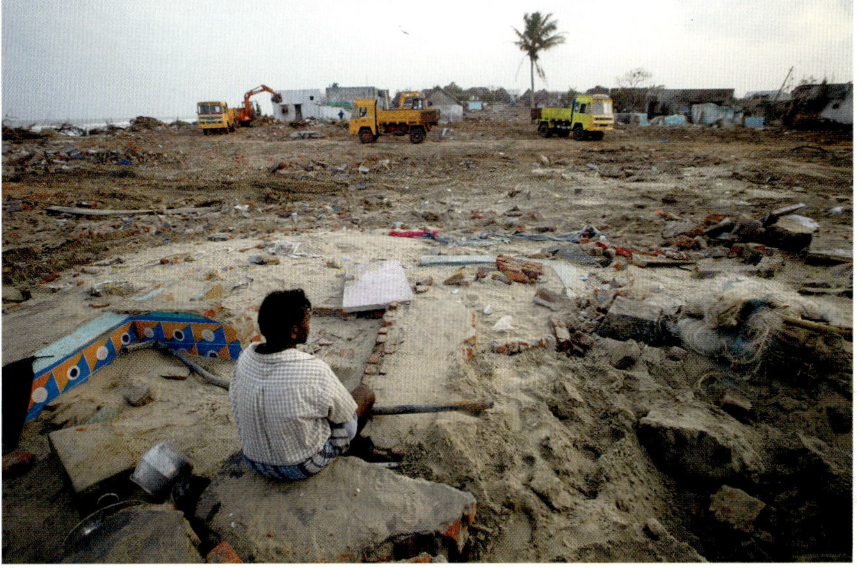

14 January 2005, KALMUNAI, SRI LANKA

Salvaged belongings are gathered by a tree in the tsunami-ravaged town of Kalmunai on Sri Lanka's east coast. Arko Datta

3 January 2005, NAGAPATTINAM, INDIA

Survivors look for their belongings amid the debris of their destroyed houses which are being burned by Indian workers. Arko Datta

28 December 2004, UNAWATUNA, SRI LANKA

Debris surrounds a shop destroyed when the tsunami struck. Thomas White

5 January 2005, NAGAPATTINAM, INDIA

A tsunami survivor watches as bulldozers clear the debris of destroyed houses. Arko Datta

29 December 2004, CUDDALORE, INDIA

A young survivor of the tsunami reaches out for her share of food and clothes donated by voluntary organizations. As the scale of the tragedy became clear, the biggest global relief effort in history was launched. Hundreds of thousands of traumatized survivors were in immediate need of food and clean water. Arko Datta

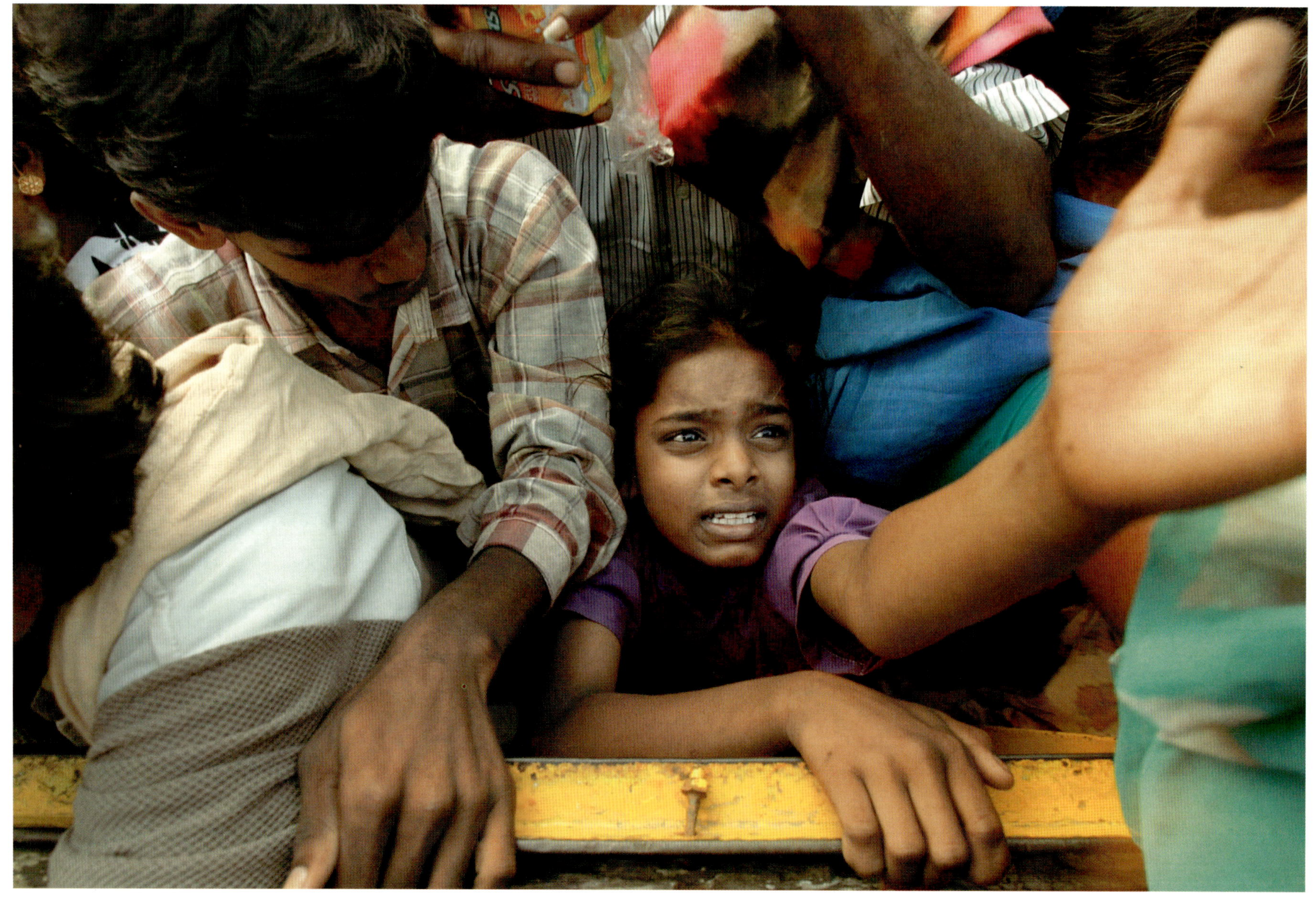

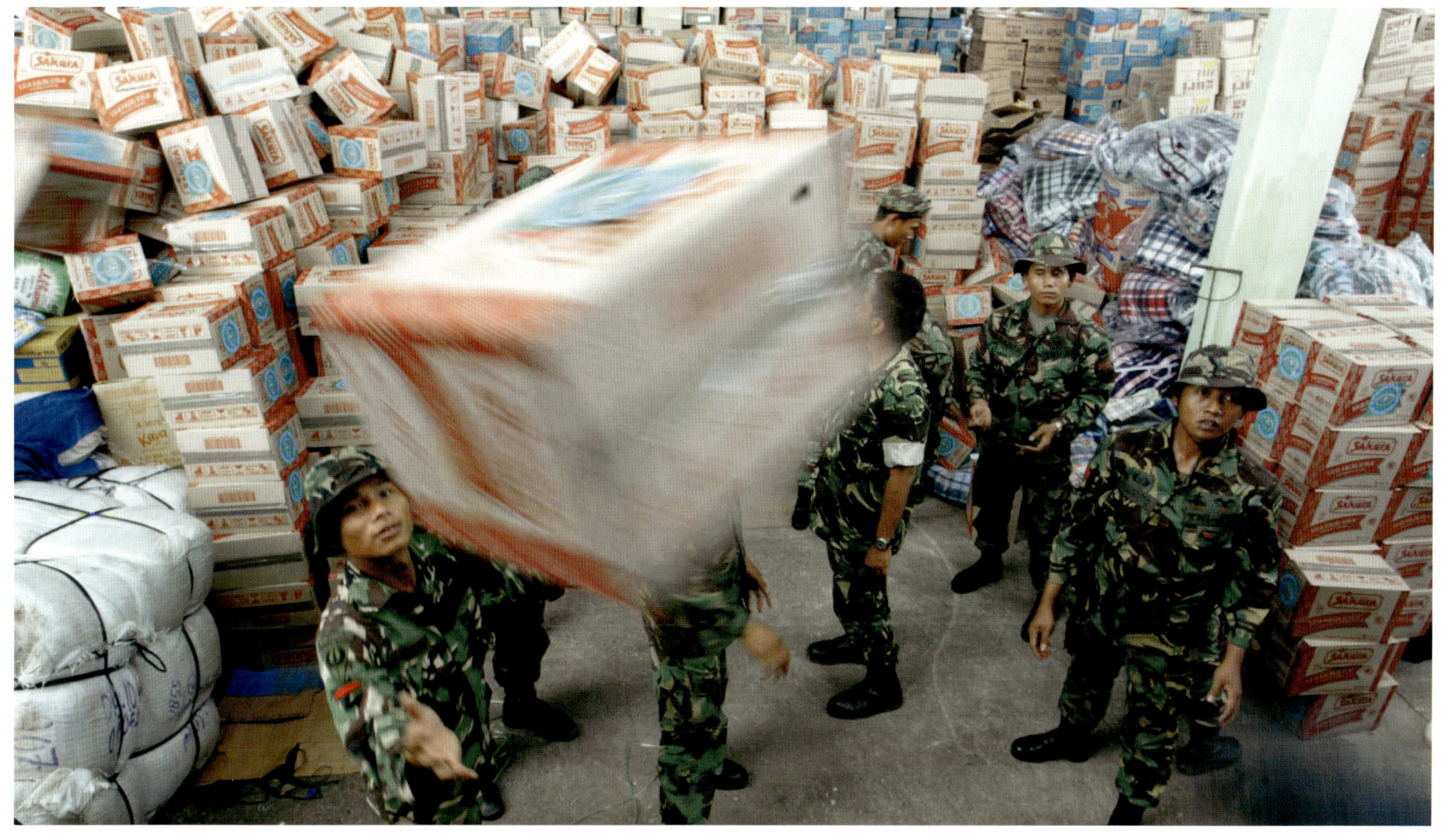

6 January 2005, BANDA ACEH, INDONESIA

Indonesian soldiers unload aid supplies at a military camp in the city of Banda Aceh on the island of Sumatra. Public and private emergency relief donations for victims of the tsunami were around U.S. $13 billion. Romeo Ranoco

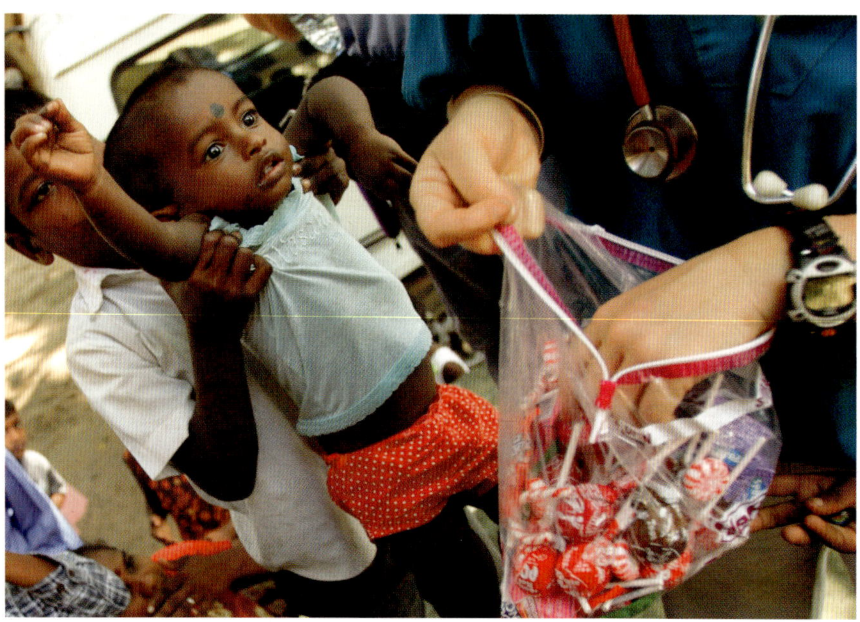

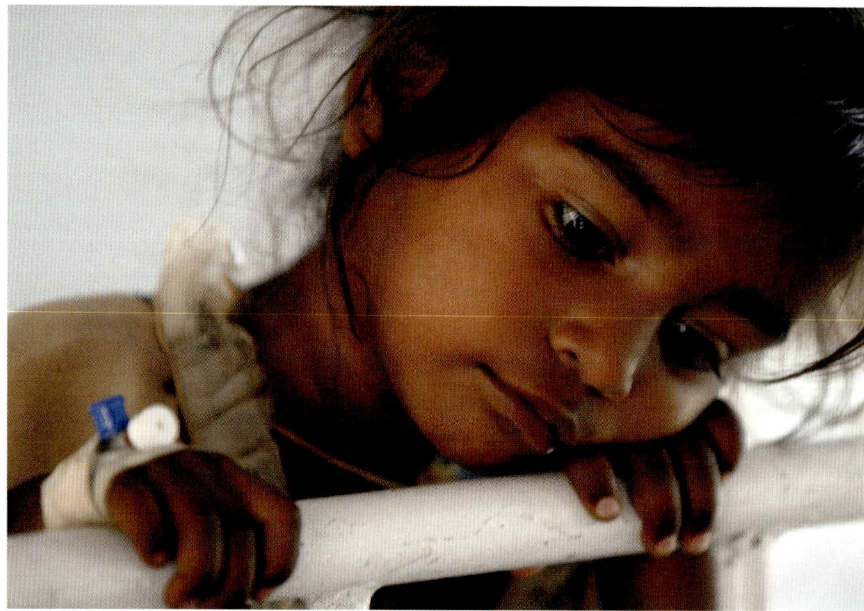

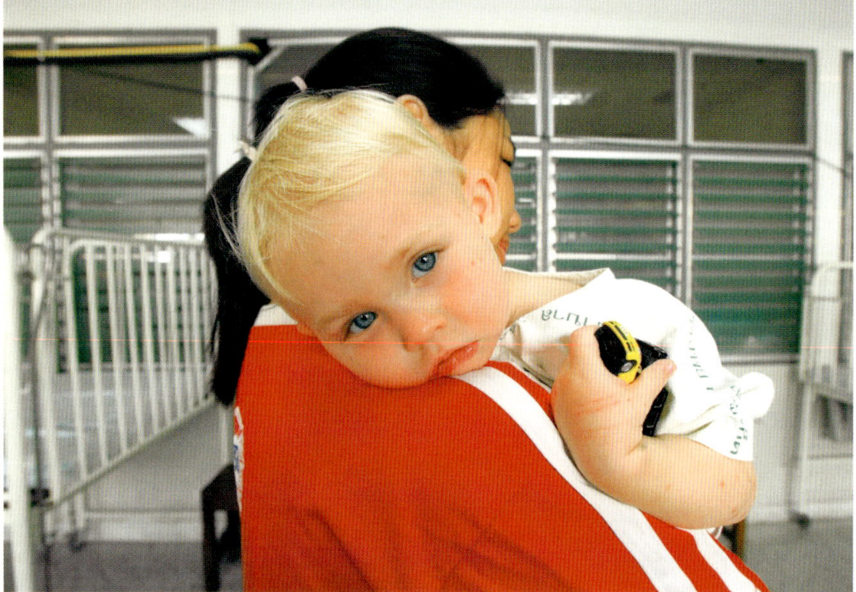

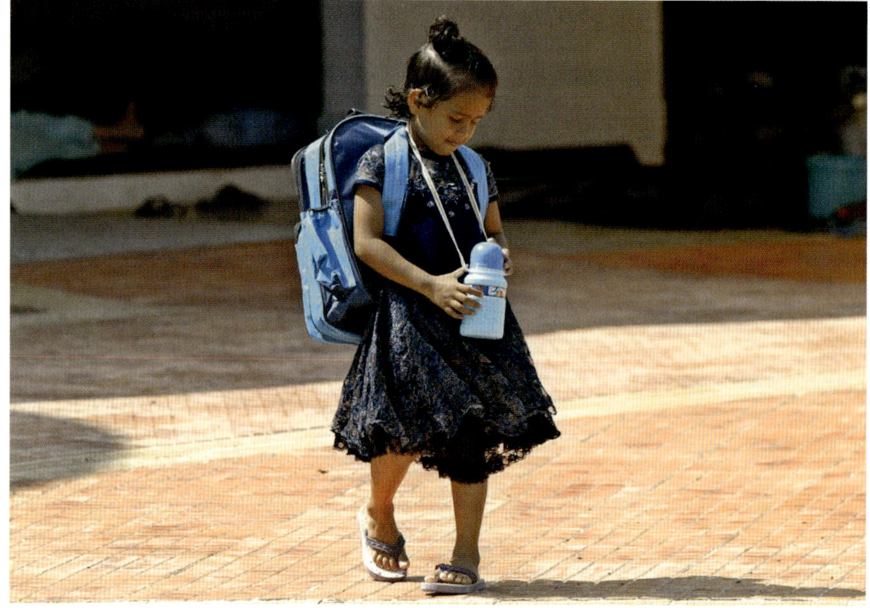

15 January 2005, KALMUNAI, SRI LANKA

A volunteer social worker gives out candies to Sri Lankan children at a makeshift shelter in the town of Kalmunai. Arko Datta

28 December 2004, PHUKET, THAILAND

One-year-old Hannes Bergman of Sweden, whose mother was killed in the tsunami, is held by a carer at a hospital in Thailand's tourist island of Phuket. Bazuki Muhammad

28 December 2004, CUDDALORE, INDIA

Kamalvathi, an Indian tsunami survivor, undergoes treatment in Cuddalore. Arko Datta

10 January 2005, PORT BLAIR, INDIA

Five-year-old Nicobarese child Saiba leaves a class at a relief camp in Port Blair, the capital of India's Andaman and Nicobar archipelago. Over 1,000 indigenous Nicobarese were evacuated to Port Blair from the devastated southern islands in the days after the tsunami. Altaf Hussain

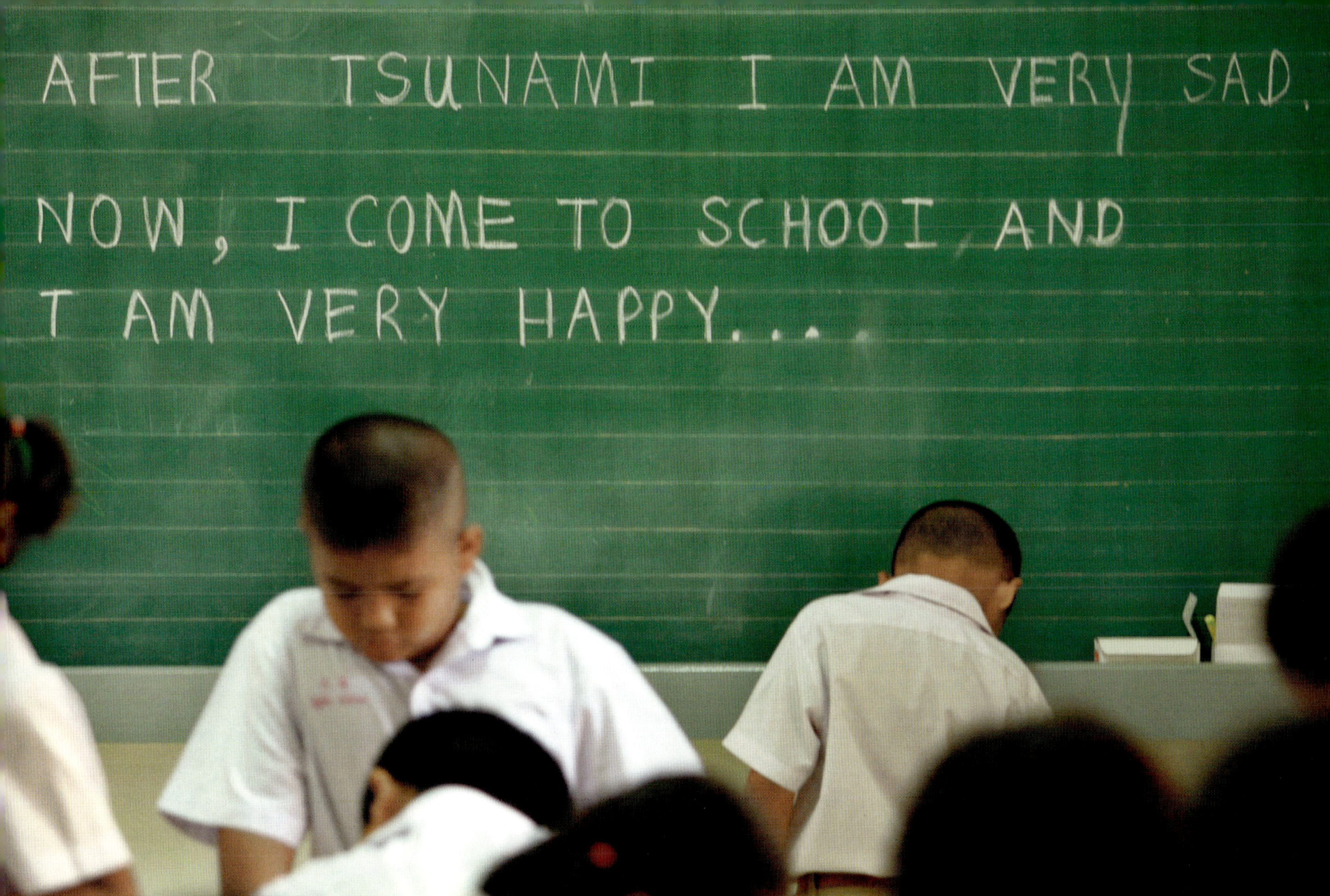

2 February 2005, PHUKET, THAILAND

Students return to school in the tsunami-damaged village of Kamala on the Thai island of Phuket. Bazuki Muhammad

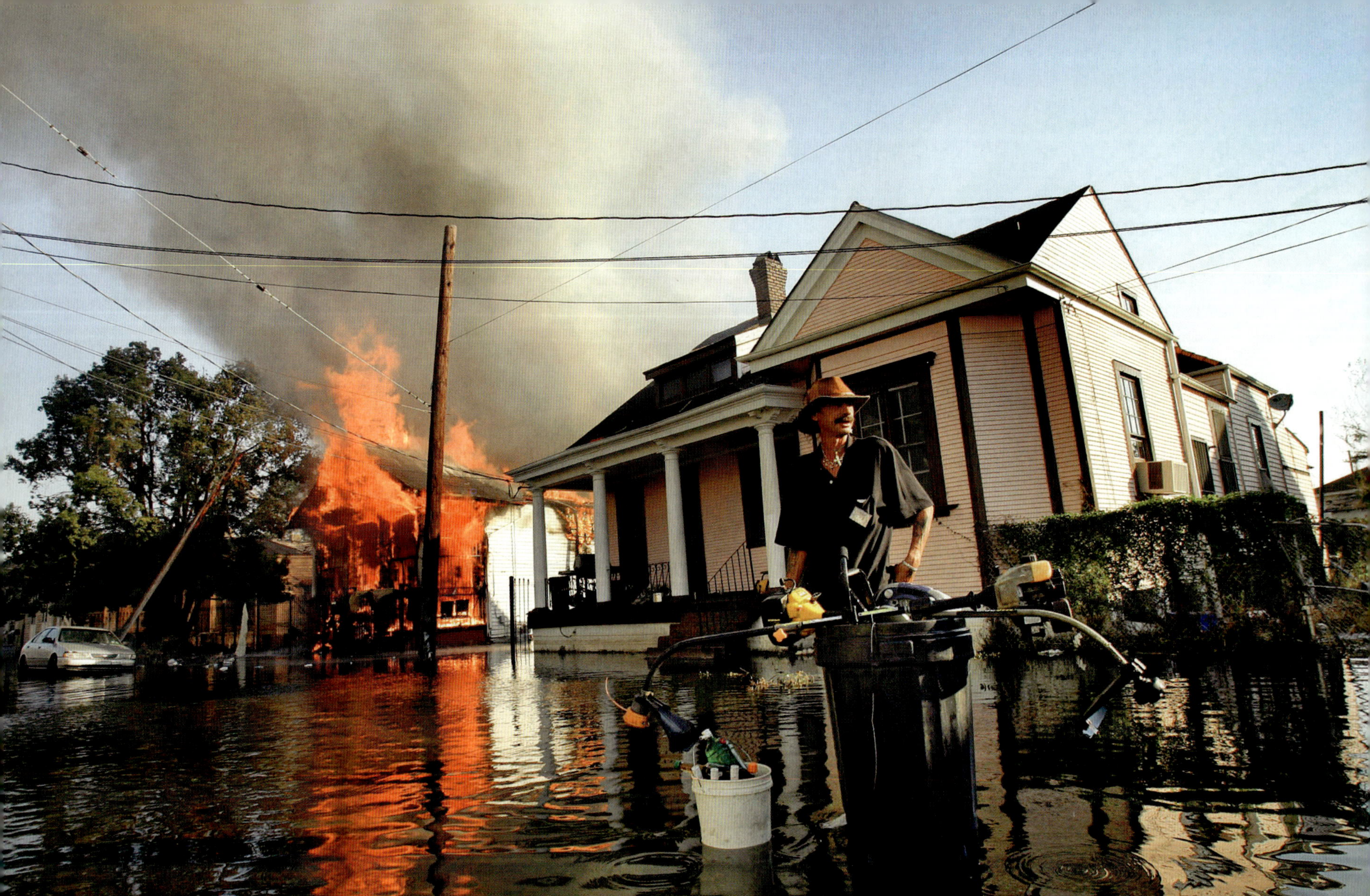

6 September 2005, NEW ORLEANS, UNITED STATES

A man stands in flood waters as fire burns down a home in the seventh ward of New Orleans in the aftermath of Hurricane Katrina, which slammed into Louisiana and Mississippi on 29 August with 224 kph (140 mph) winds and a 9-metre (30-foot) storm surge. It caused a death toll of 1,228 and at least $80 billion of damage. The flood waters that swamped New Orleans after the breaching of several of the city's levees rapidly became a toxic brew of chemicals and human waste. Shannon Stapleton

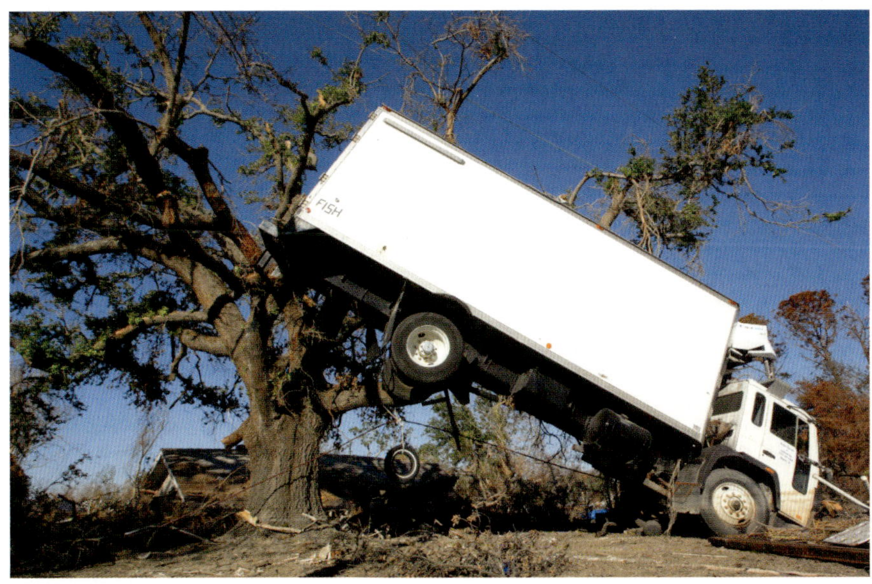

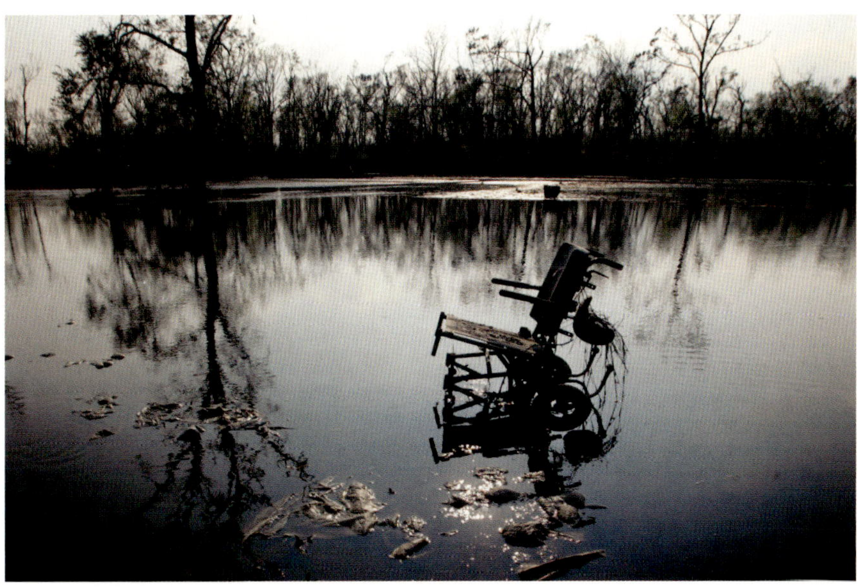

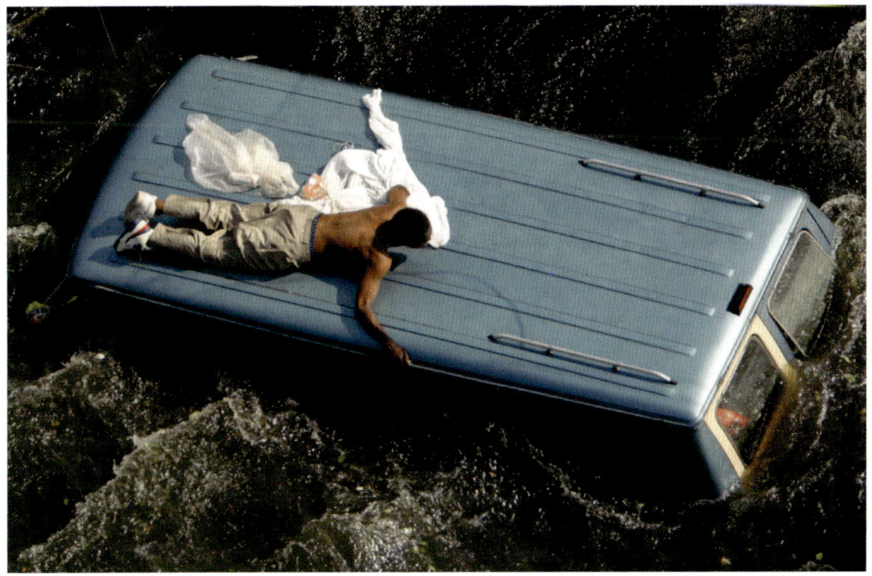

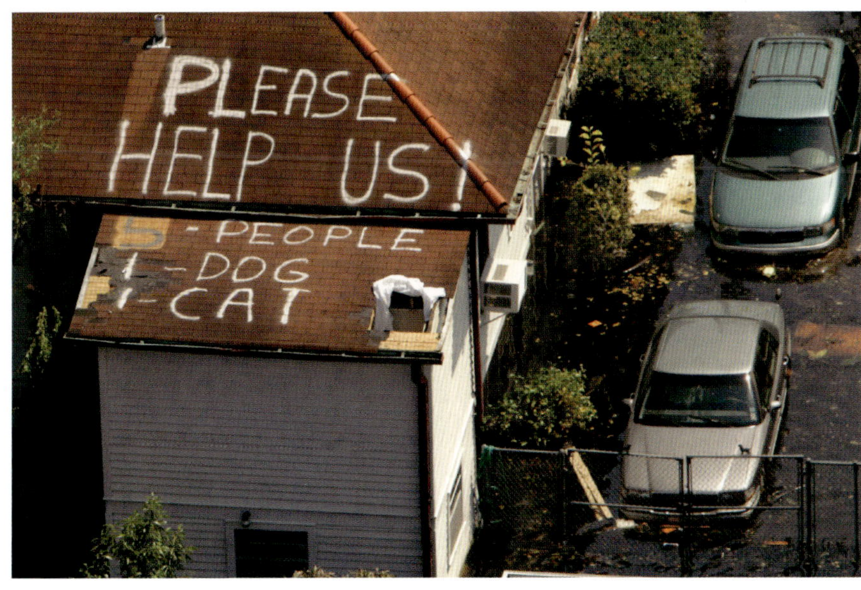

24 October 2005, EMPIRE, UNITED STATES

Hurricane Rita, which struck less than a month after Hurricane Katrina, left this truck lodged in a tree near Highway 11 north of Empire, Louisiana. Rita caused less destruction than Katrina, but nonetheless was a grave setback to recovery efforts and led to renewed flooding in parts of New Orleans. Lucas Jackson

4 September 2005, NEW ORLEANS, UNITED STATES

A man clings to the top of a vehicle as he awaits rescue by the U.S. Coast Guard from the flooded streets of New Orleans in the aftermath of Hurricane Katrina. Robert Galbraith

14 September 2005, SAINT BERNARD, UNITED STATES

A wheelchair sits outside Saint Rita's Nursing Home in Saint Bernard, Louisiana, just east of New Orleans, where 34 people died in the floodwaters from Hurricane Katrina. The owners of the nursing home were arrested and charged with 34 counts of negligent homicide. Carlos Barria

4 September 2005, NEW ORLEANS, UNITED STATES

A plea for help is seen on the roof of a flooded home in New Orleans. As the waters rose, survivors were stranded on rooftops and trapped in attics across the city. Robert Galbraith

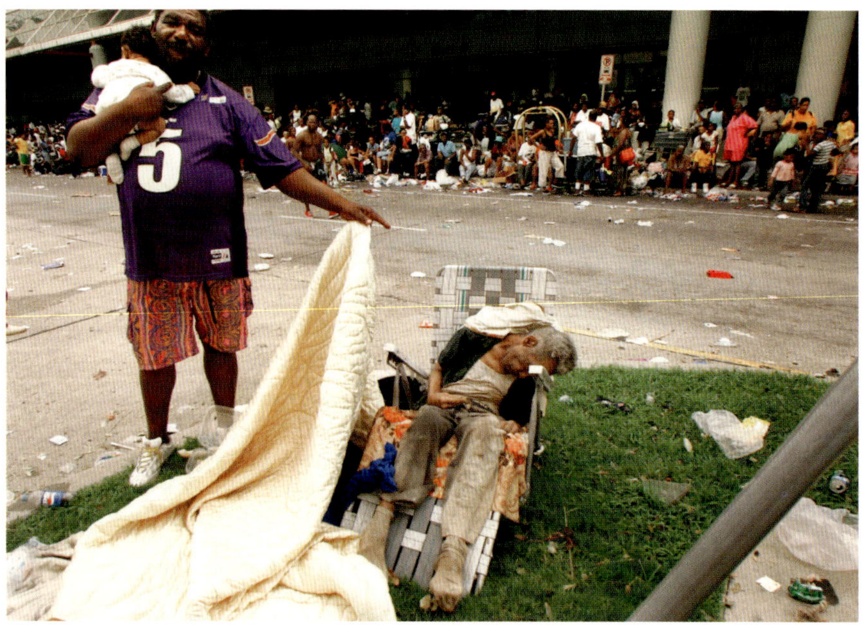

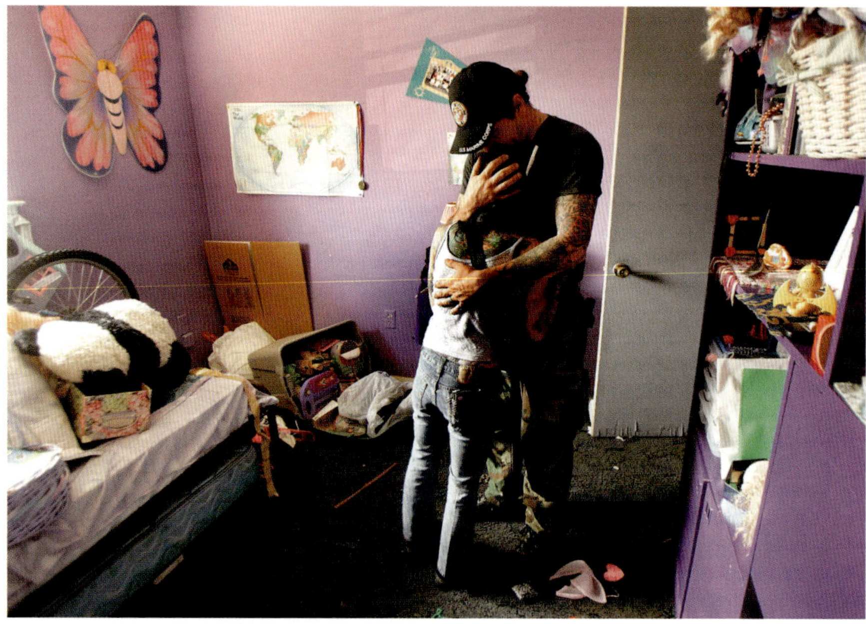

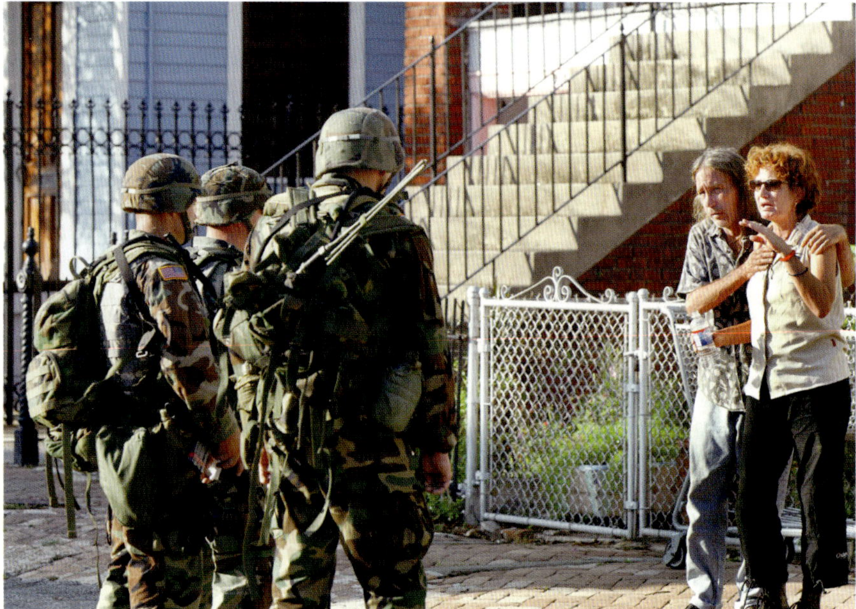

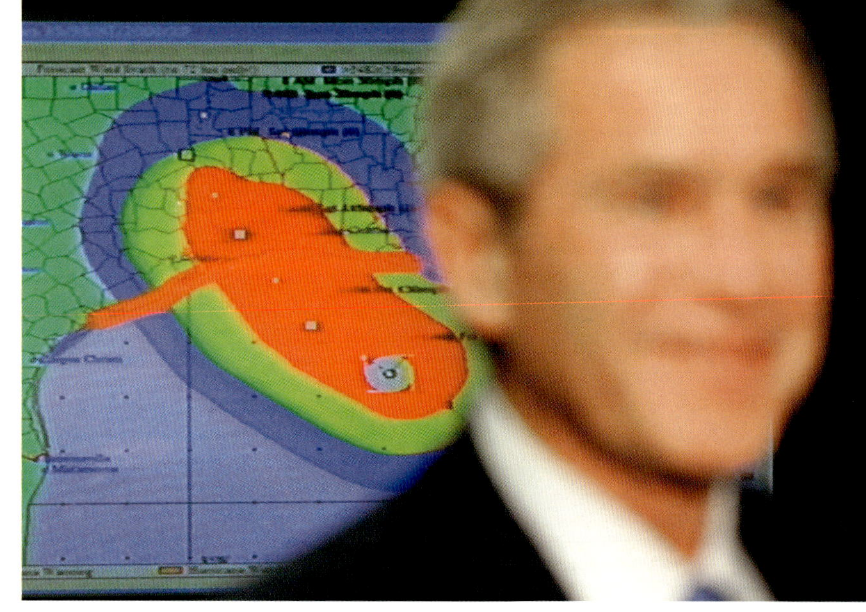

1 September 2005, NEW ORLEANS, UNITED STATES

A man holding a baby uncovers a dead body, suspected to have been sitting there for two days, outside the New Orleans Convention Center, where thousands of evacuees sought refuge in the days after Hurricane Katrina struck. Rick Wilking

7 September 2005, NEW ORLEANS, UNITED STATES

Troops from the National Guard patrol the streets of New Orleans. With three-quarters of the city underwater, basic services unavailable, and an unknown number of corpses to be collected, the authorities opted to enforce a complete evacuation. Shannon Stapleton

5 September 2005, NEW ORLEANS, UNITED STATES

Gabriel Whitfield hugs his sister-in-law Ariel Pietrello at their home in Metairie, a suburb of New Orleans. This was the first time Pietrello had been allowed back home since Hurricane Katrina ravaged the city of New Orleans. Shannon Stapleton

23 September 2005, WASHINGTON, DC, UNITED STATES

A political storm blew up over the authorities' botched response to Hurricane Katrina. Here, President George W. Bush answers a question from a reporter during a visit to Federal Emergency Management Agency (FEMA) headquarters, as a monitor tracking the progress of Hurricane Rita looms behind him. Kevin Lamarque

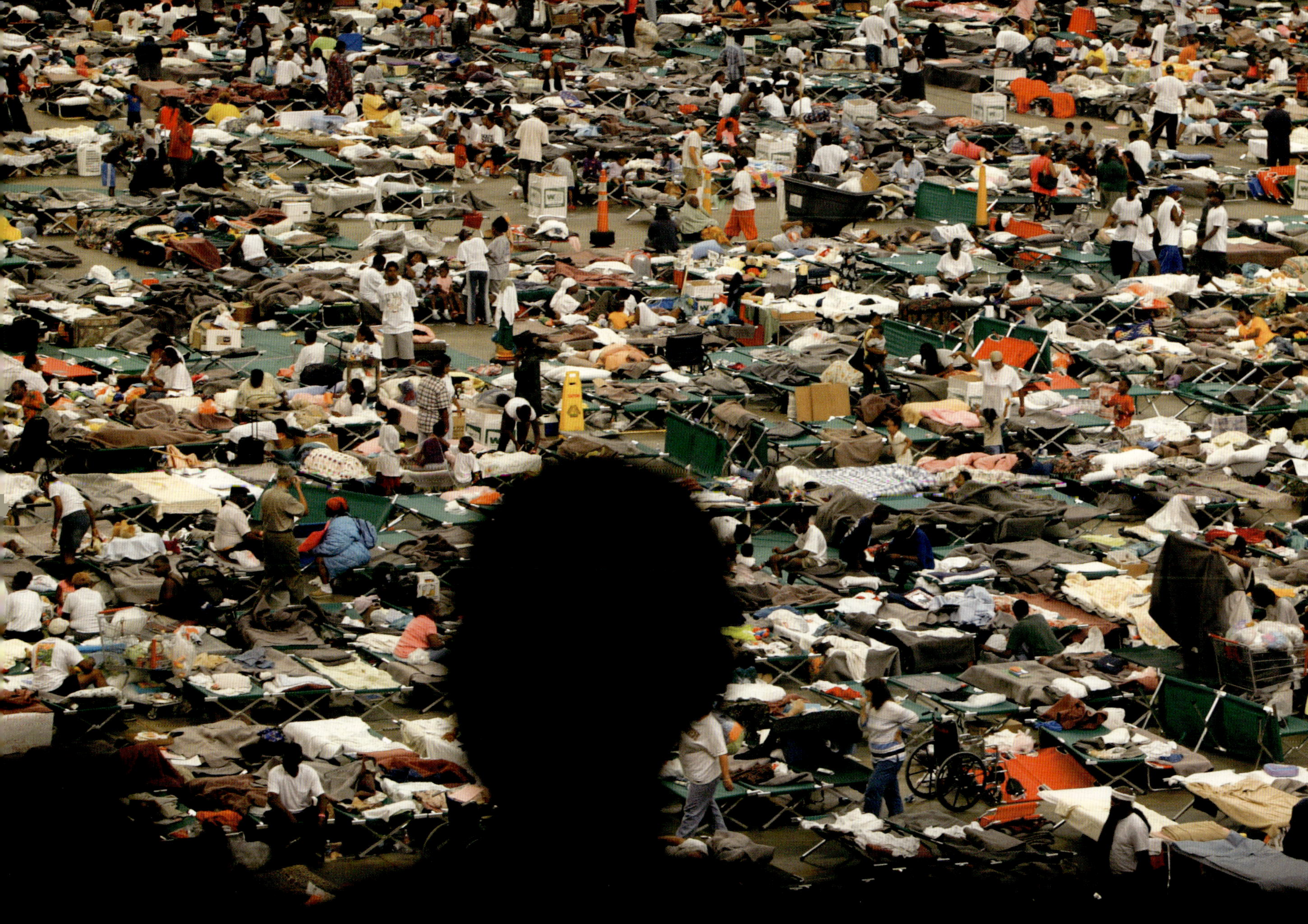

4 September 2005, HOUSTON, UNITED STATES

The Astrodome stadium in Houston, Texas, 560 km (350 miles) from New Orleans, where 16,000 Hurricane Katrina evacuees received food, shelter and medical care. Carlos Barria

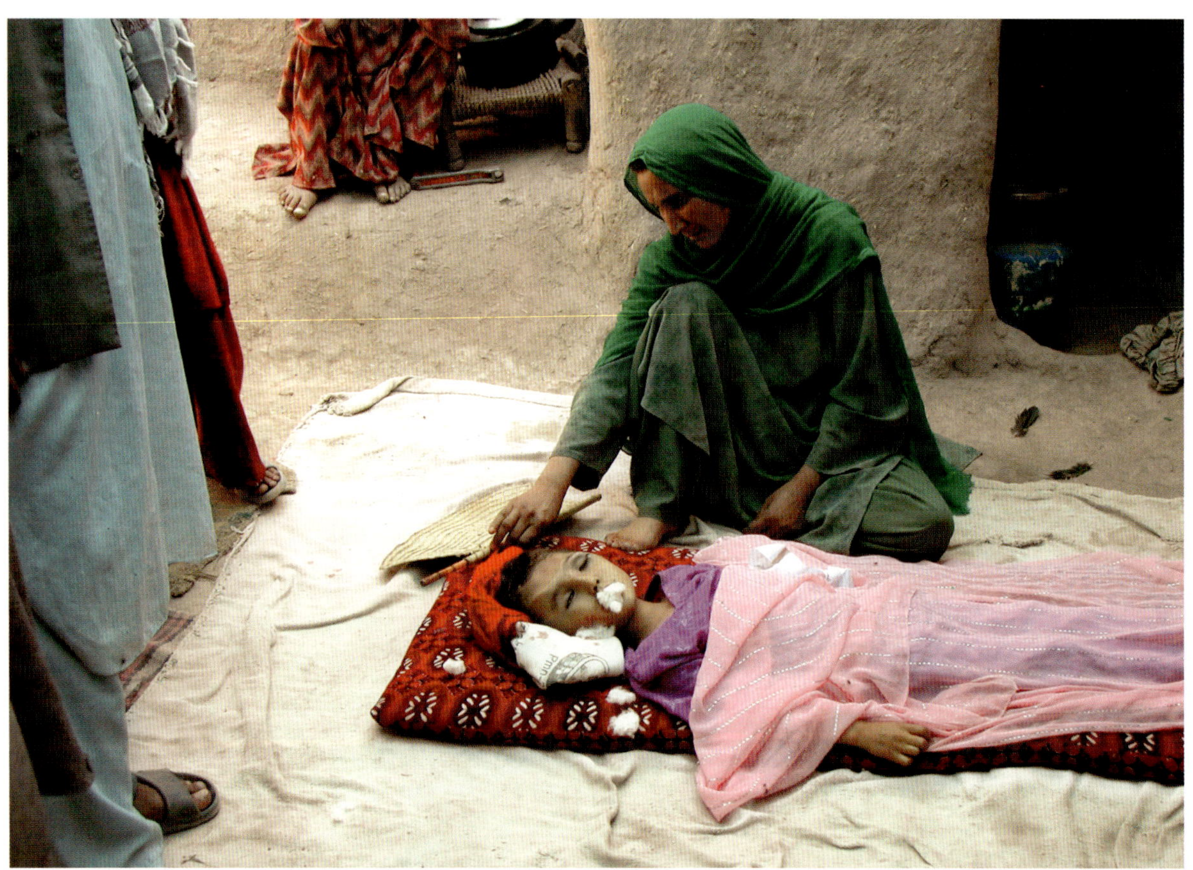

8 October 2005, NANGARHAR, AFGHANISTAN

A woman mourns her seven-year-old daughter in the eastern province of Nangarhar, Afghanistan. The earthquake that killed the child was felt across huge areas of eastern and central Afghanistan, but the destruction there was minor compared to the catastrophic death toll and damage to property in neighbouring Pakistan (see pages 50–51).

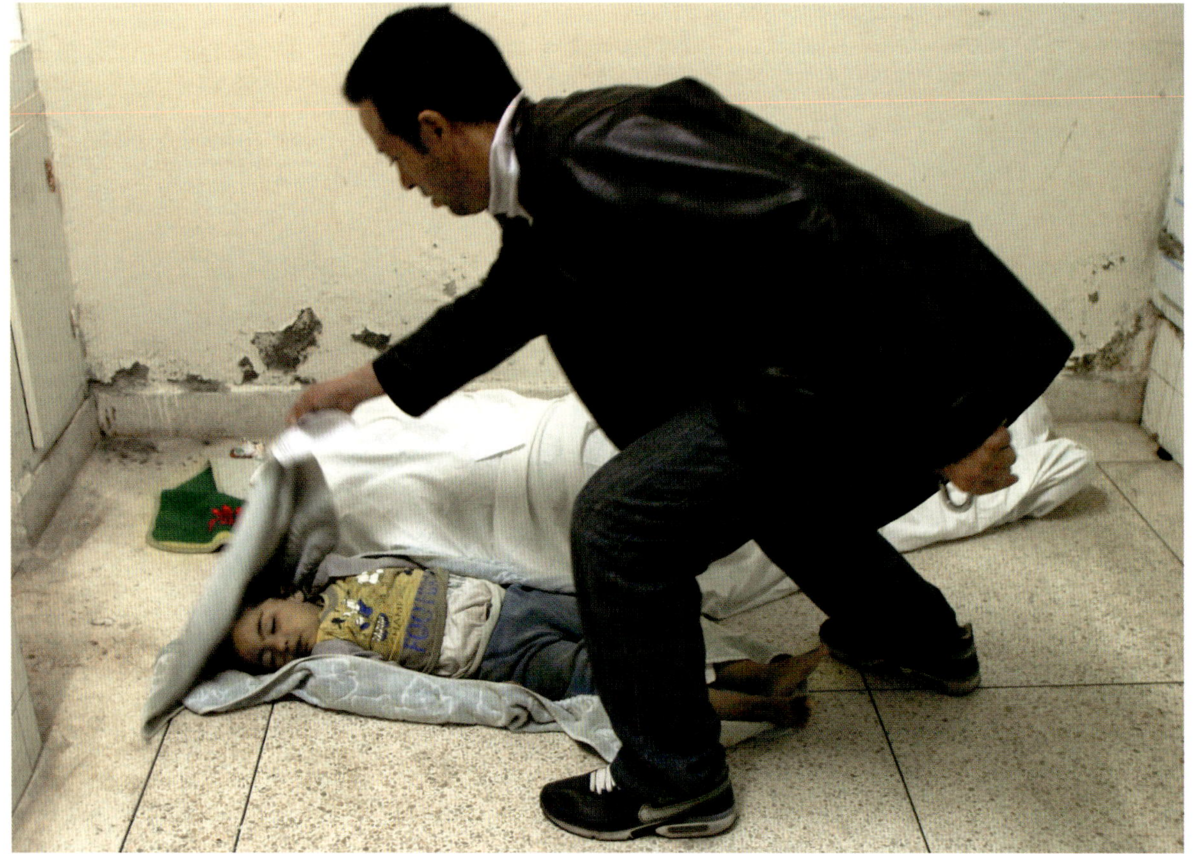

24 February 2004, AL HOCEIMA, MOROCCO

A man covers the body of a dead girl who lies beside the body of her mother at Al Hoceima's hospital, after an earthquake of magnitude 6.5 shook northern Morocco, killing over 500 people around the Mediterranean port city of Al Hoceima.

Anton Meres

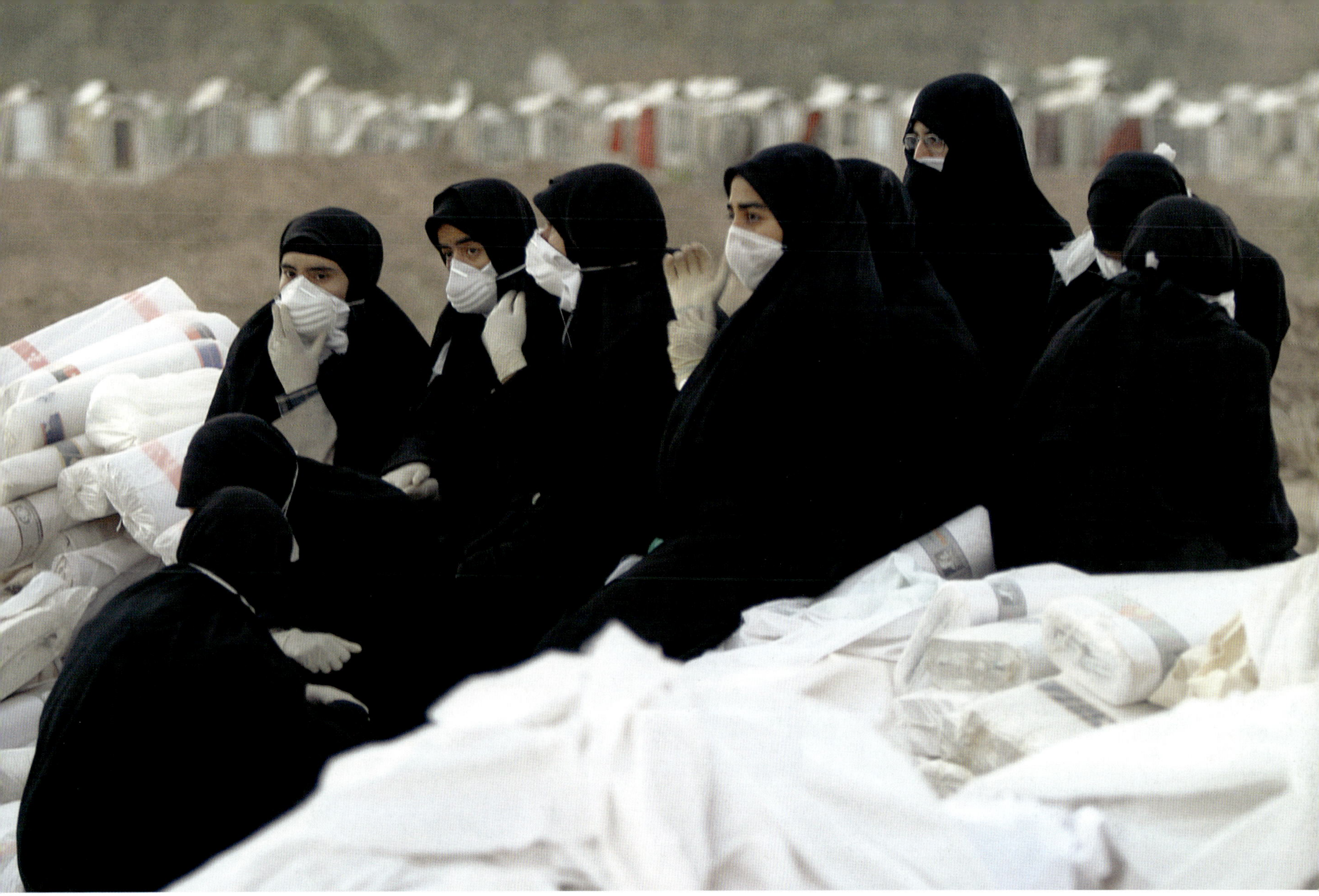

29 December 2003, BAM, IRAN

Women rest following a mass burial of the victims of the earthquake that struck Bam in southeast Iran on 26 December 2003. Over 30,000 people were killed and the ancient Silk Road city suffered extensive damage. Morteza Nikoubazl

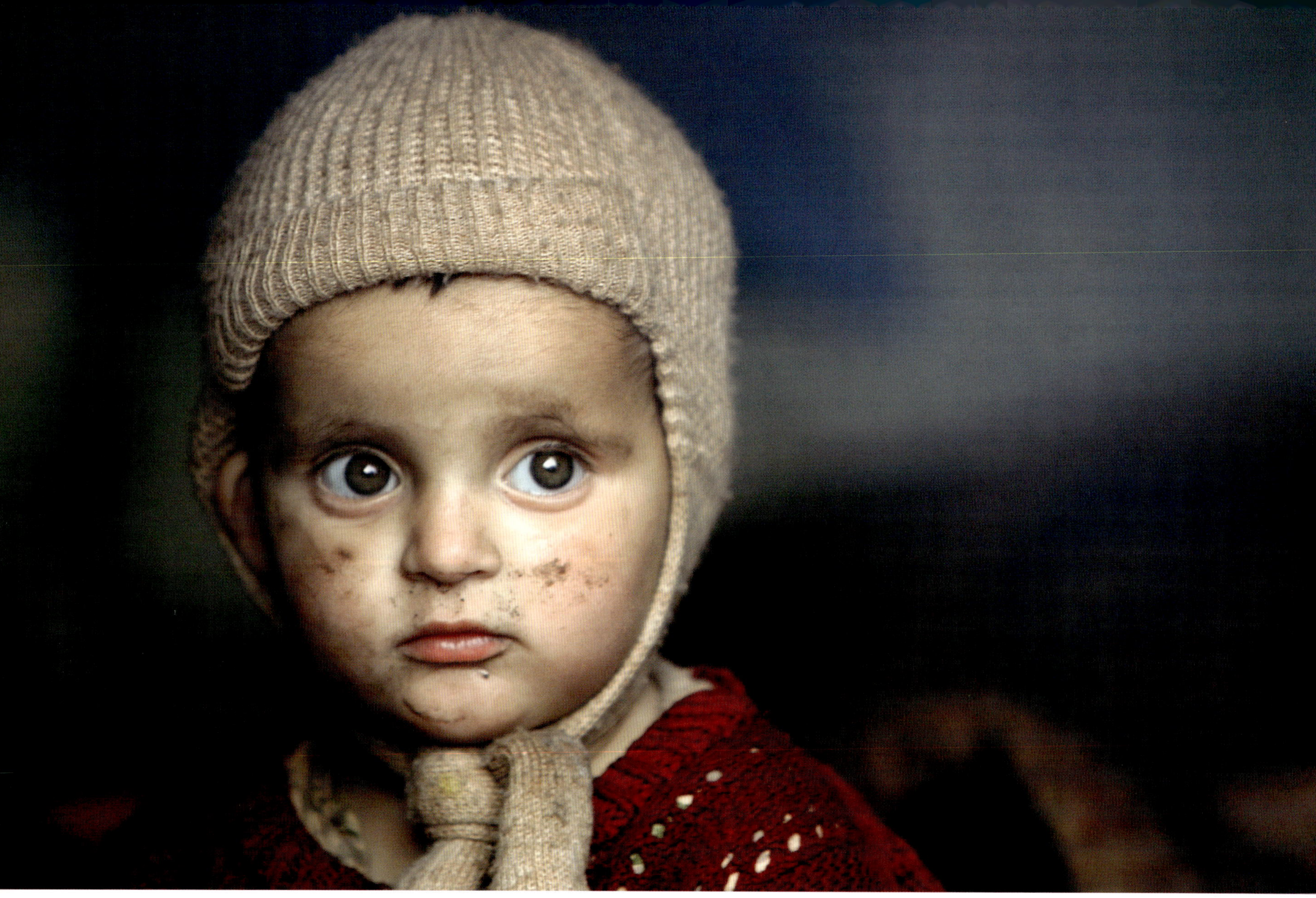

24 November 2005, MUZAFFARABAD, PAKISTAN

A young earthquake survivor sits inside a tent at a camp in the devastated city of Muzaffarabad, capital of Pakistani Kashmir. The 7.6 magnitude earthquake, which hit on 8 October 2005, was most destructive in Indian and Pakistani Kashmir and Pakistan's northwest frontier. This is an area that is both breathtakingly beautiful and difficult to access, in part because of the mountainous terrain, but also because of the tense relations between India and Pakistan over disputed Kashmir. More than 73,000 people were killed and 69,000 injured in the quake, with over 3 million left homeless. Goran Tomasevic

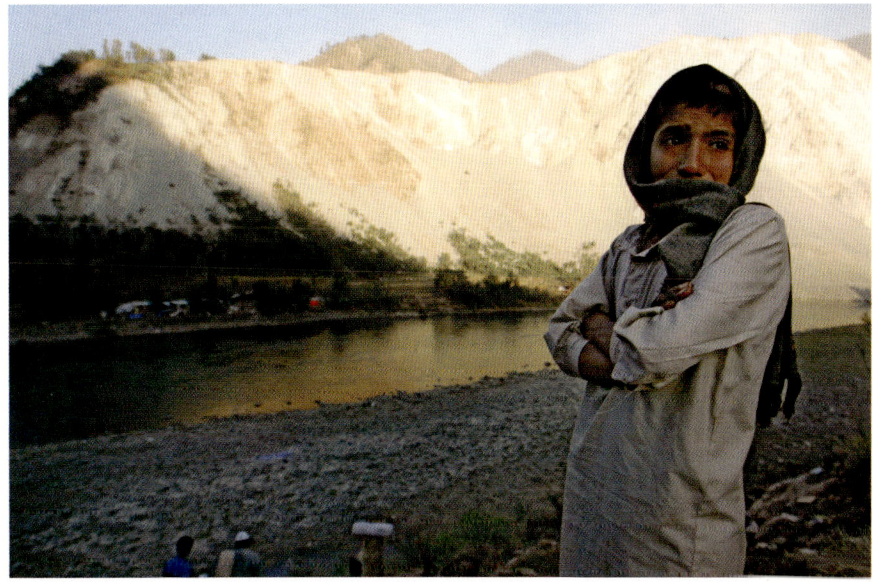

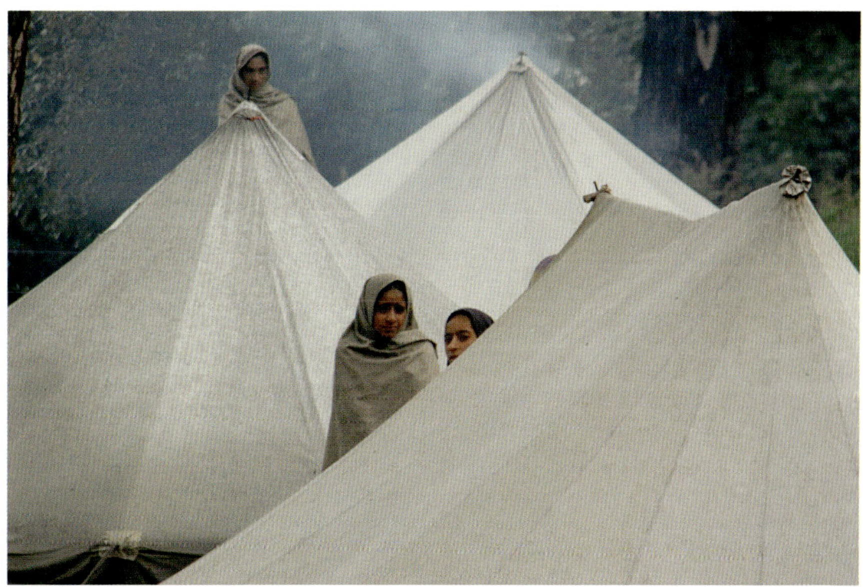

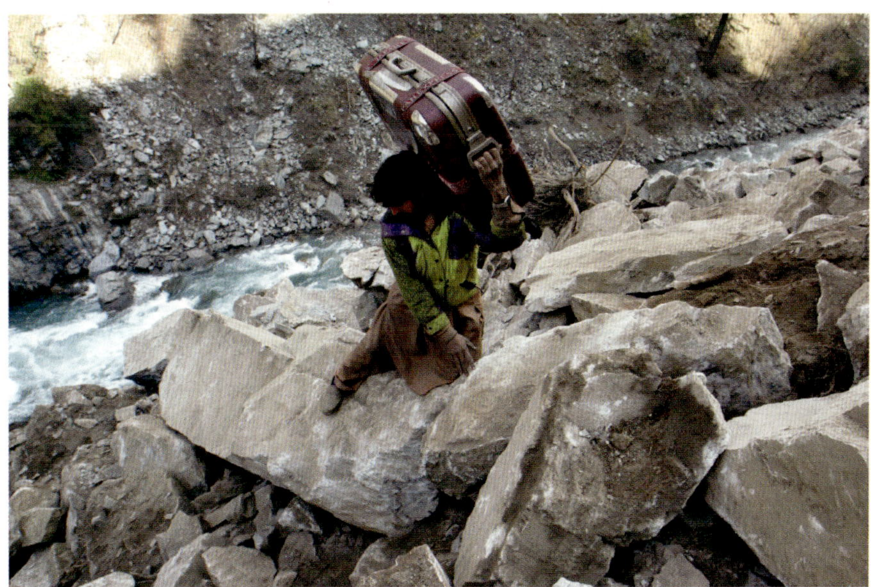

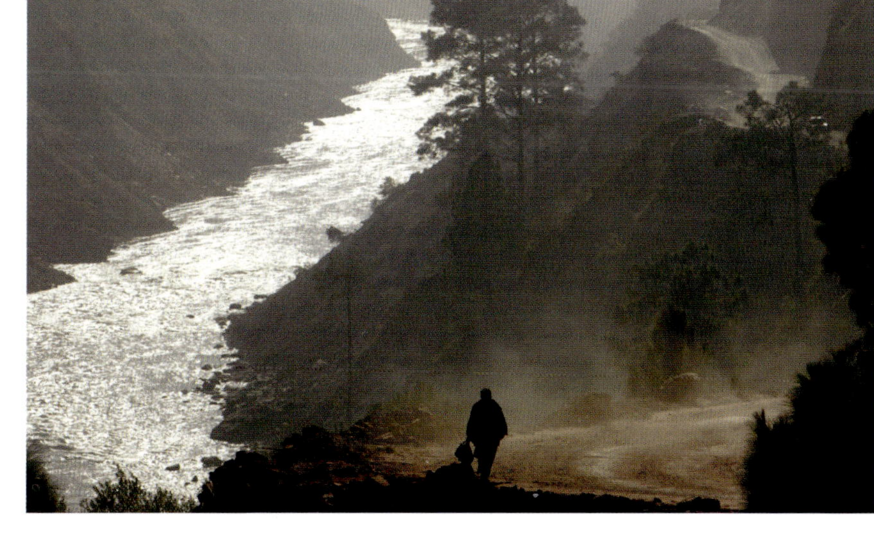

30 October 2005, NEELUM VALLEY, PAKISTAN

A Kashmiri boy waits for his father to return with supplies for the family at a village at the entrance to Neelum Valley, north of Muzaffarabad. Kimimasa Mayama

1 December 2005, FARIDABAD, PAKISTAN

An earthquake survivor climbs over a recent landslide on a road in the town of Faridabad. The first winter snowfalls in the rugged mountains prompted many thousands more survivors to leave their devastated villages and seek emergency shelter, food and medical assistance in the lowlands. Goran Tomasevic

16 October 2005, POONCH, INDIA

Earthquake survivors wait for relief materials at a relief camp in Poonch, 250 km (156 miles) northwest of the northern city of Jammu. Amit Gupta

7 December 2005, NEELUM VALLEY, PAKISTAN

An earthquake survivor walks along a road through the Neelum Valley. Damaged bridges and continuing landslides made the road dangerous to truck drivers carrying desperately needed relief supplies. Goran Tomasevic

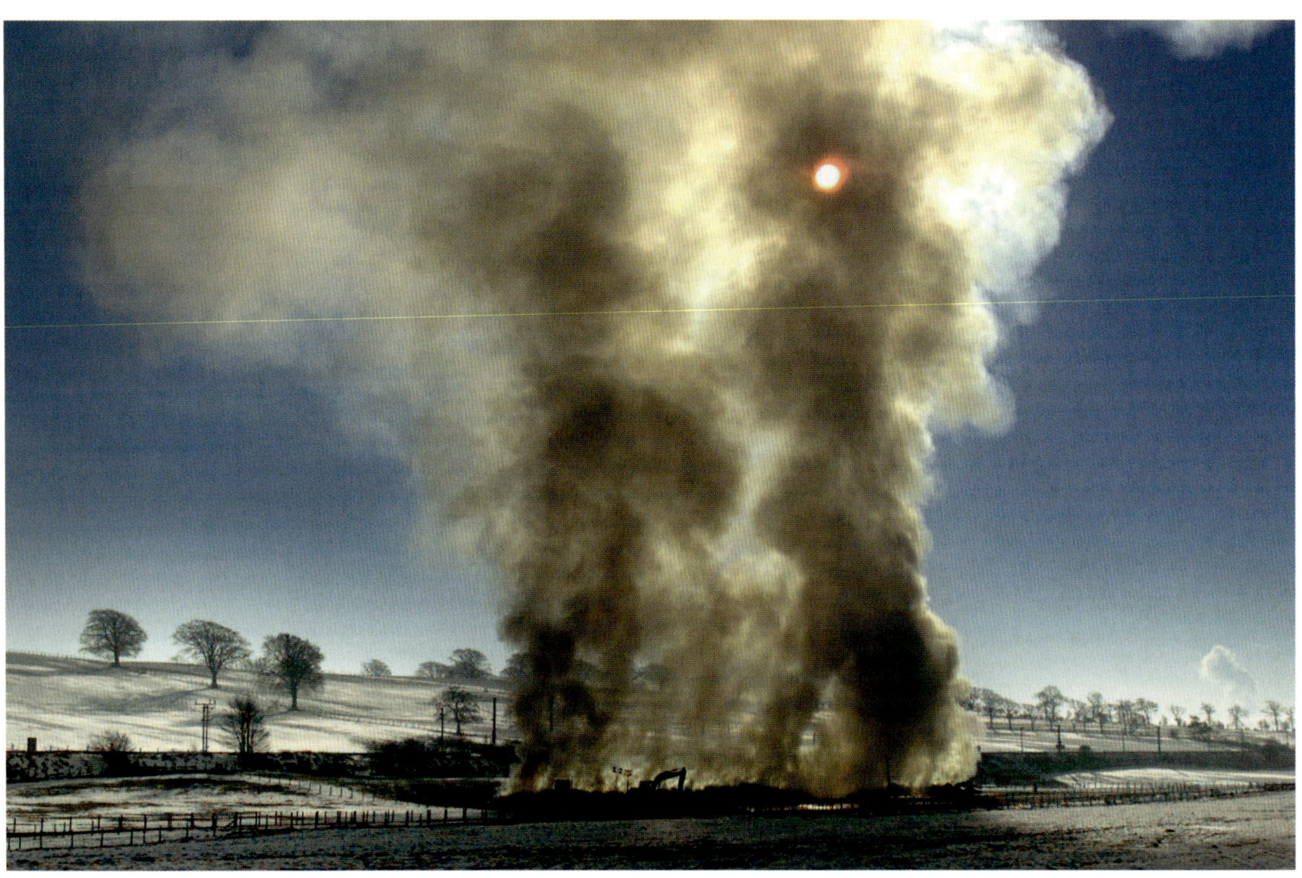

4 March 2001, LOCKERBIE, UNITED KINGDOM

Smoke fills the sky as cows and sheep are destroyed by an incinerator at Netherplace farm in Lockerbie. Outbreaks of foot-and-mouth disease occurred in livestock throughout Britain in 2001, leading to the culling of over six million animals. Jeff J. Mitchell

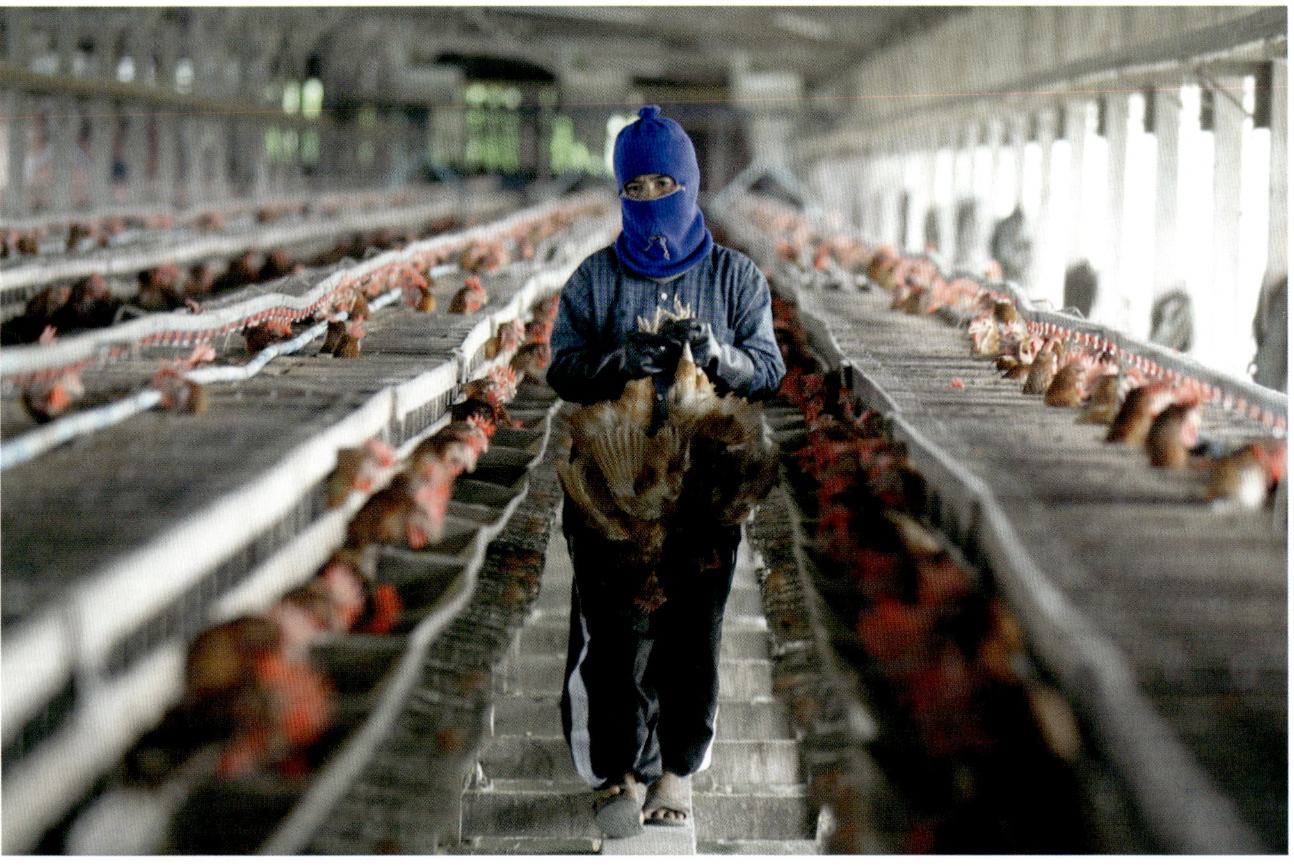

6 July 2004, AYUTTHAYA, THAILAND

Workers collect chickens to be destroyed at a farm in Ayutthaya, 80 km (50 miles) north of Bangkok, as officials investigated a possible fresh outbreak of bird flu following the death of 600 chickens within a few days at a farm near the capital. Since the H5N1 strain of bird flu first swept across Asia from late 2003, the virus has gradually moved westwards to the Middle East, Africa and Europe. Sukree Sukplang

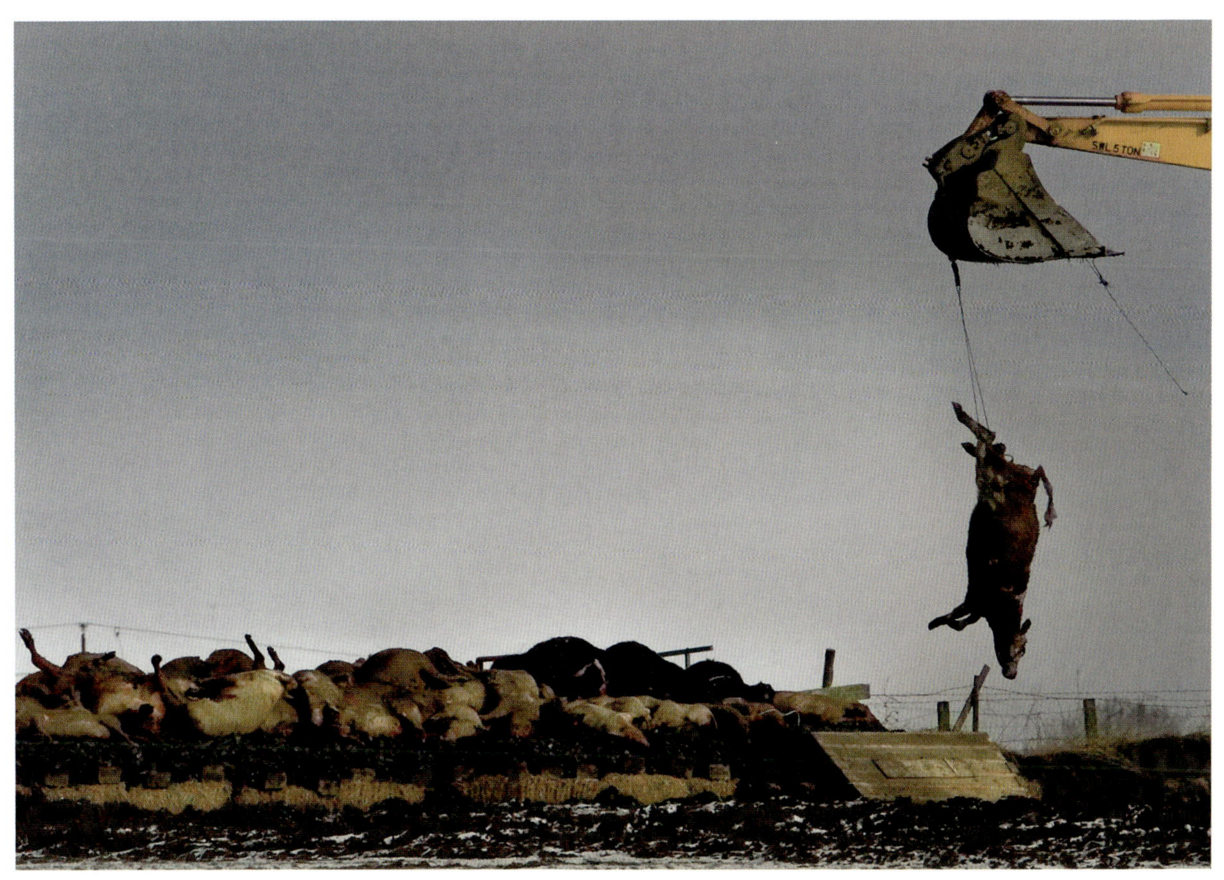

25 February 2001, HEDDON ON THE WALL, UNITED KINGDOM

Officials from Britain's Ministry of Agriculture begin to prepare slaughtered pigs and cows for the incinerator at a farm near Heddon On The Wall in northern England, after foot-and-mouth disease was discovered there. The total cost to the British economy of the 2001 foot-and-mouth outbreak is estimated at £8 billion. The impact was felt far beyond the agricultural sector. Widespread restrictions on movement in the countryside had serious consequences for the tourism industry.
Jeff J. Mitchell

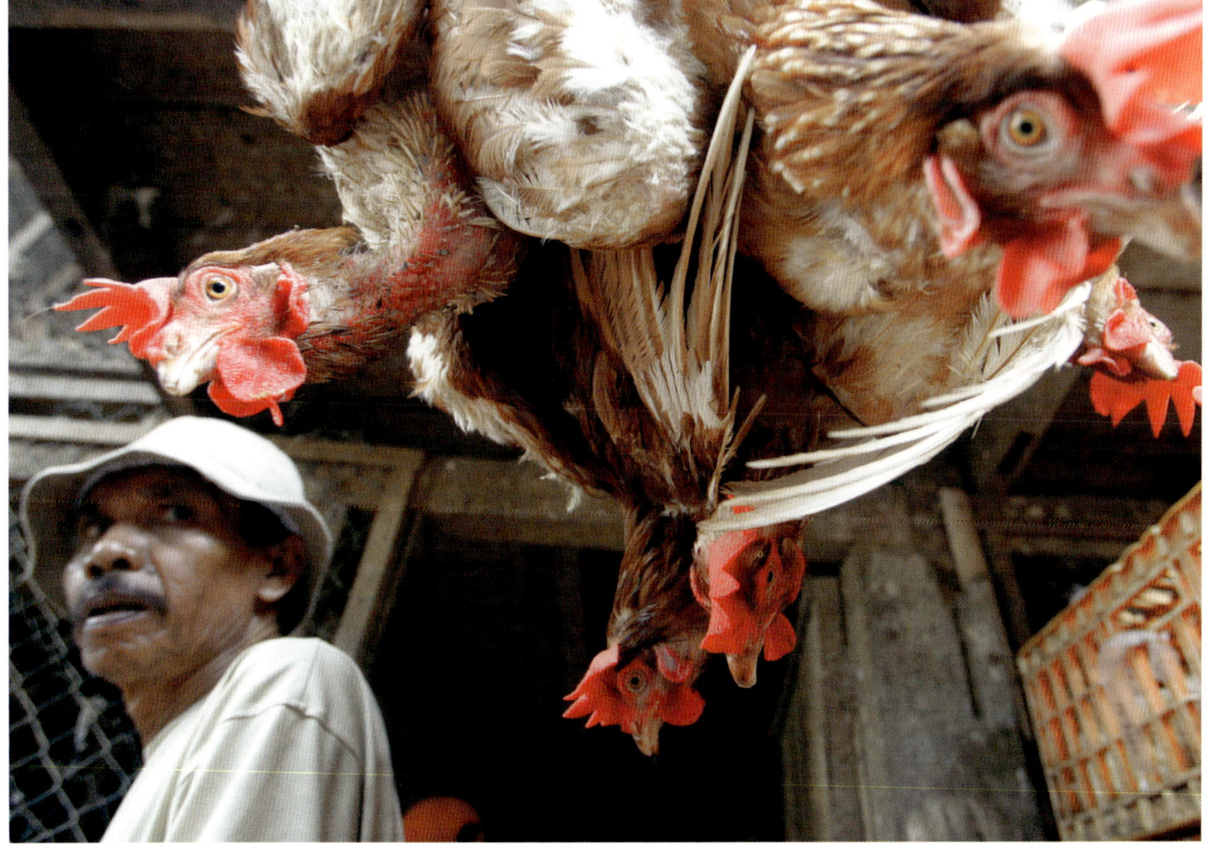

30 September 2005, JAKARTA, INDONESIA

A worker stands next to chickens before weighing them at a chicken supplier in central Jakarta. By March 2006, over 20 people in Indonesia had died from the H5N1 virus, and almost 100 worldwide, mostly through contact with infected birds. Experts fear that the virus will mutate into a form that is easily transmitted between humans, potentially triggering a global pandemic that could kill millions and cripple economies around the world. Supri

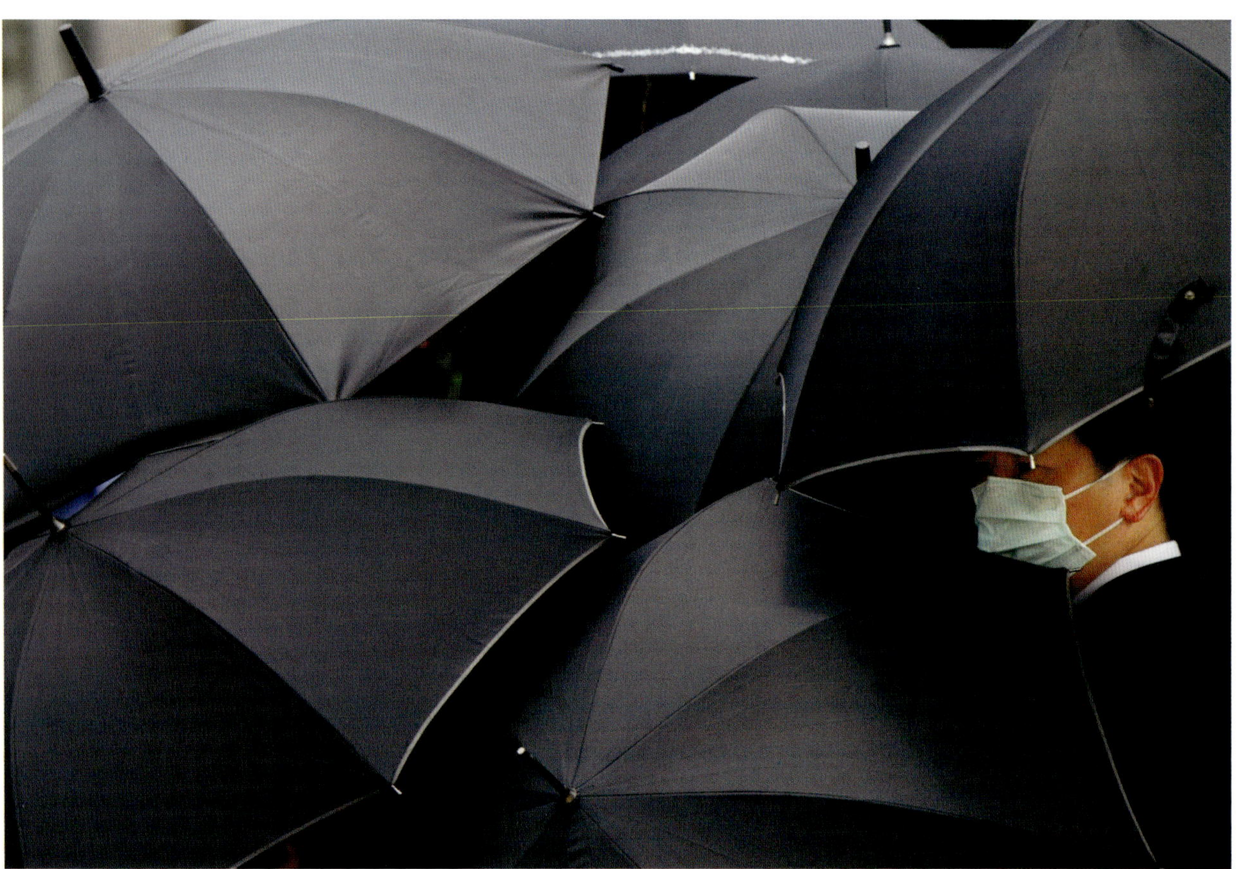

22 May 2003, HONG KONG, CHINA

A mourner wearing a mask shelters under an umbrella during the funeral of SARS doctor Tse Yuen-man in Hong Kong. The first doctor to be killed by the disease in the territory, Tse was given the highest honours at her funeral and was buried in Gallant Garden, a cemetery reserved for residents who perish in the line of duty. Severe Acute Respiratory Syndrome or SARS was the first new severe and readily transmissible disease of the twenty-first century. Between November 2002 and July 2003, a total of over 8,000 probable SARS cases and more than 774 deaths were reported in 26 countries, most of them in the Pacific Basin. Bobby Yip

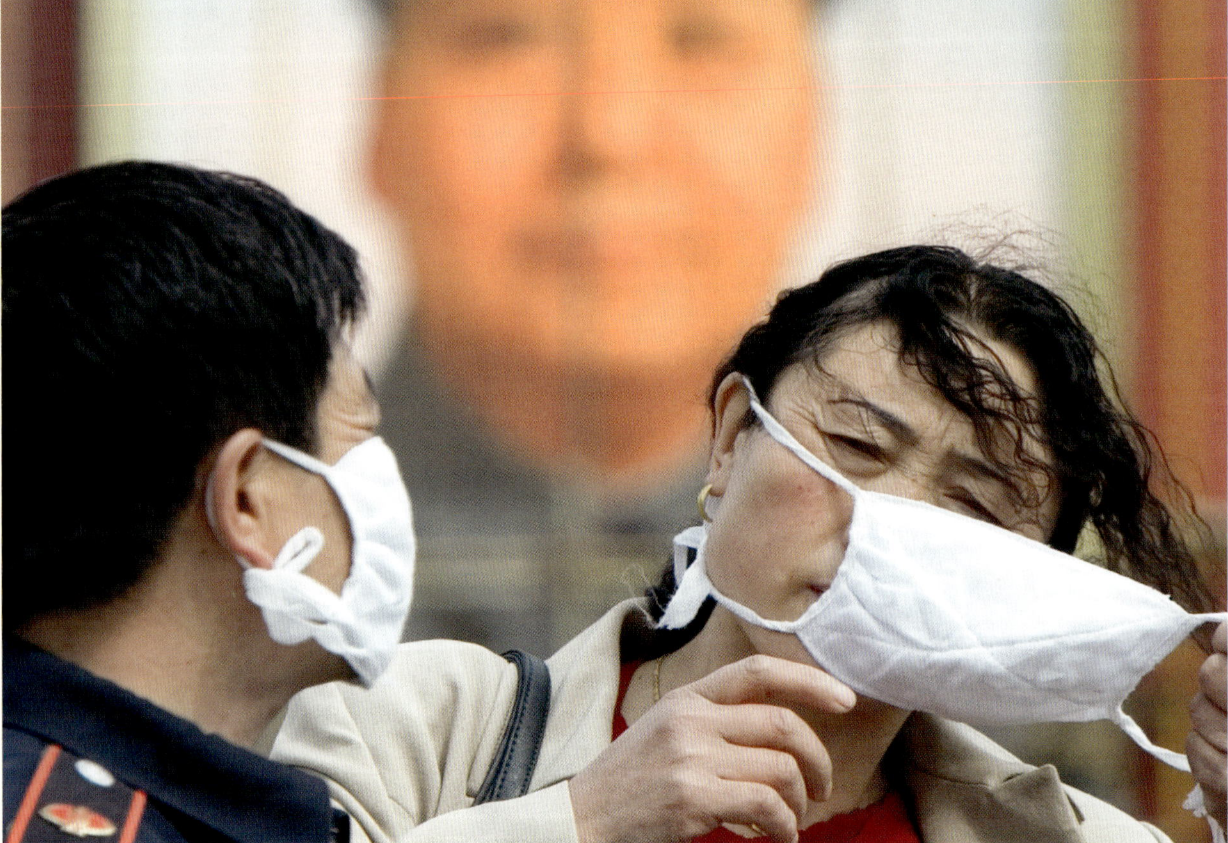

18 April 2003, BEIJING, CHINA

A Chinese couple wearing protective masks stand in front of a portrait of the late Chinese leader Mao Zedong at Tiananmen Gate in Beijing. SARS is believed to have originated in southern China in the last weeks of 2002. From there it crossed into Hong Kong, Vietnam, Singapore, Canada, Germany and beyond. Guang Niu

17 February 2004, JAKARTA, INDONESIA

An elderly Indonesian woman covers her face as a health department official sprays pesticide in a slum area in Jakarta to kill the mosquitos that transmit the dengue fever virus. The disease strikes annually during Indonesia's rainy season between October and April, but was particularly severe in 2004, with a death toll of 600 and over 52,000 reported cases across the country, double the scale of the previous year's outbreak. Dadang Tri

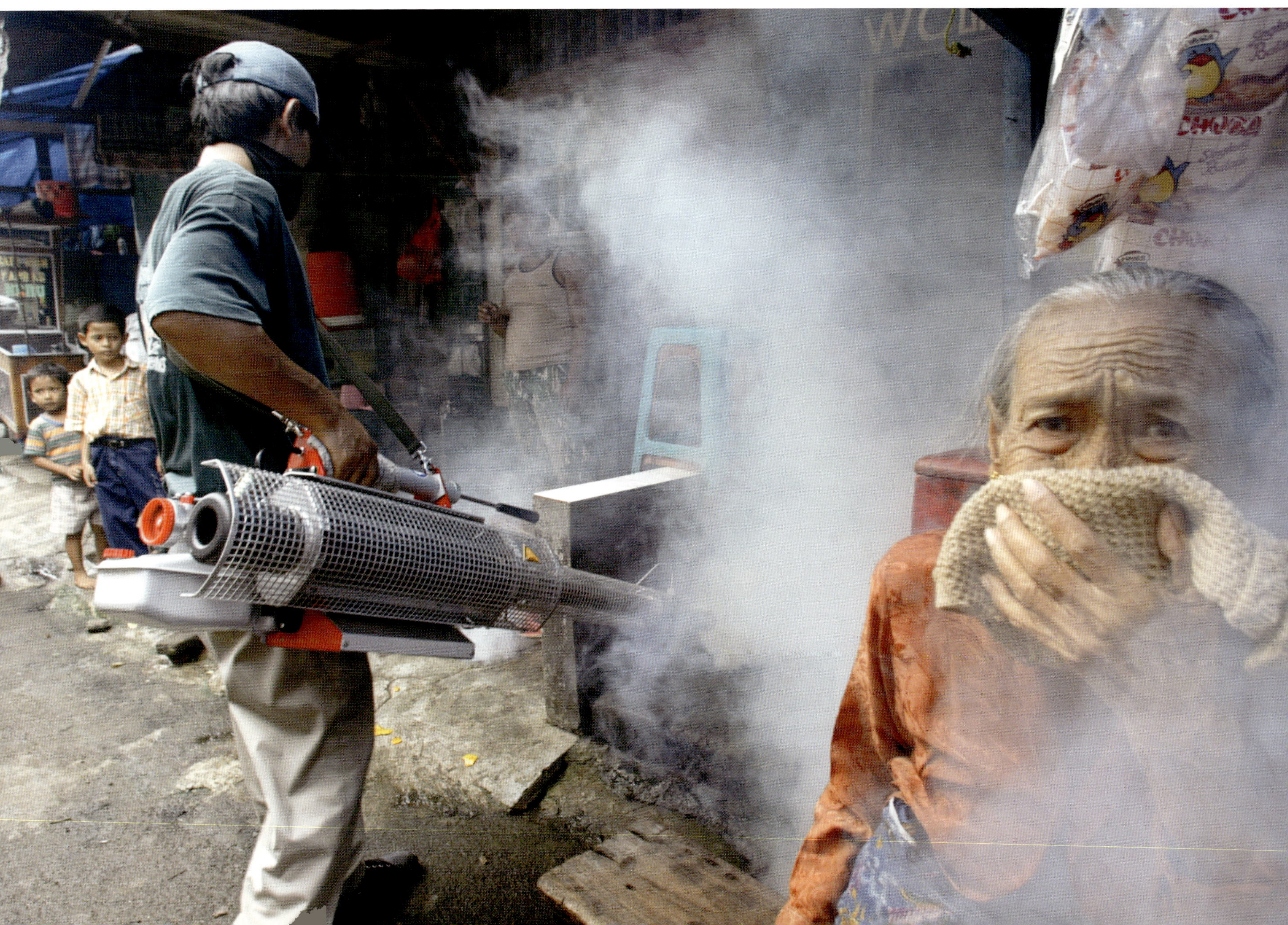

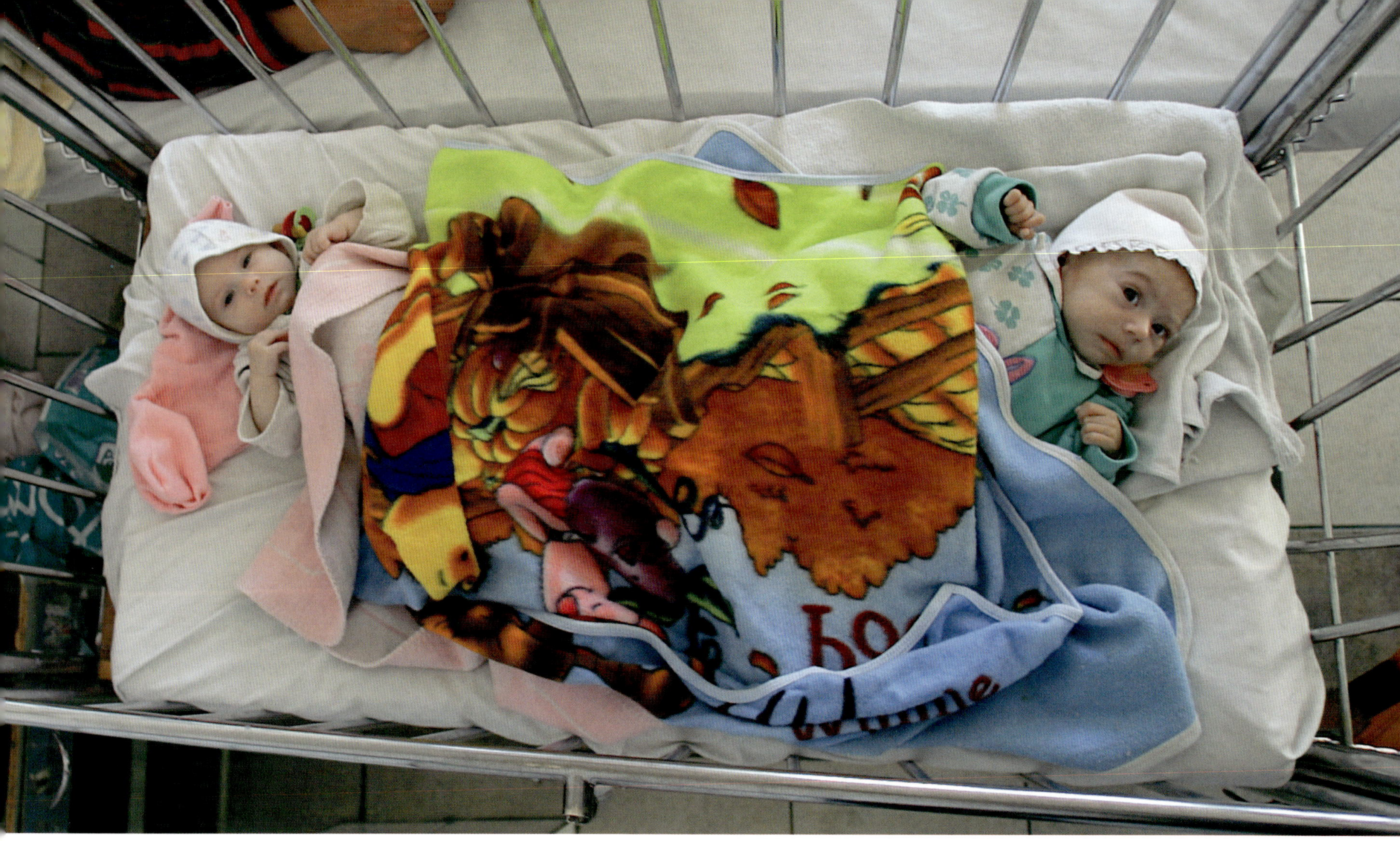

26 November 2005, CONSTANTA, ROMANIA

Two Romanian babies, said to be carrying the HIV virus, lie in a bed in a hospital in Constanta, 250 km (155 miles) east of Bucharest. Although Romania has a relatively low overall HIV/AIDS prevalence, it is the European country with the highest number of children suffering from HIV/AIDS. Most of these were infected with contaminated blood in the late 1980s and early 1990s. They are often stigmatized by their communities and denied access to mainstream education. HIV/AIDS rates among adults have continued to increase and HIV-positive children continue to be born. Bogdan Cristel

28 October 2005, PORT MORESBY, PAPUA NEW GUINEA

A nurse helps move a patient dying of HIV/AIDS in Port Moresby's General Hospital. The jungle-clad, mountainous South Pacific nation of Papua New Guinea risks succumbing to an AIDS epidemic on the scale of that in Africa. Those fighting AIDS say that belief in sorcery is widespread and infected people in remote villages are sometimes thrown into rivers to drown or dumped in graves to die, while in the capital Port Moresby the stigma of AIDS sees people abandoned at the hospital or left on the street. David Gray

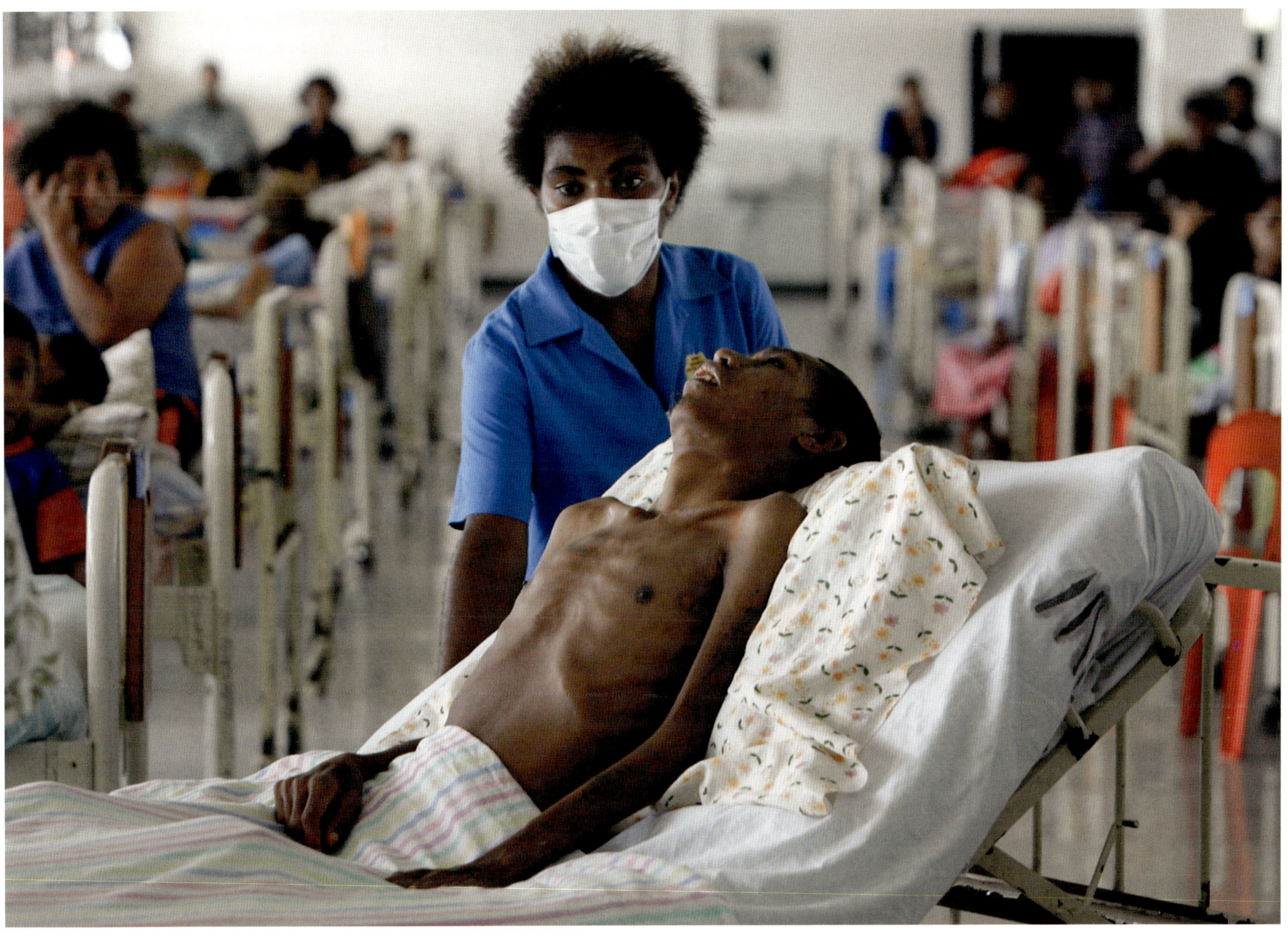

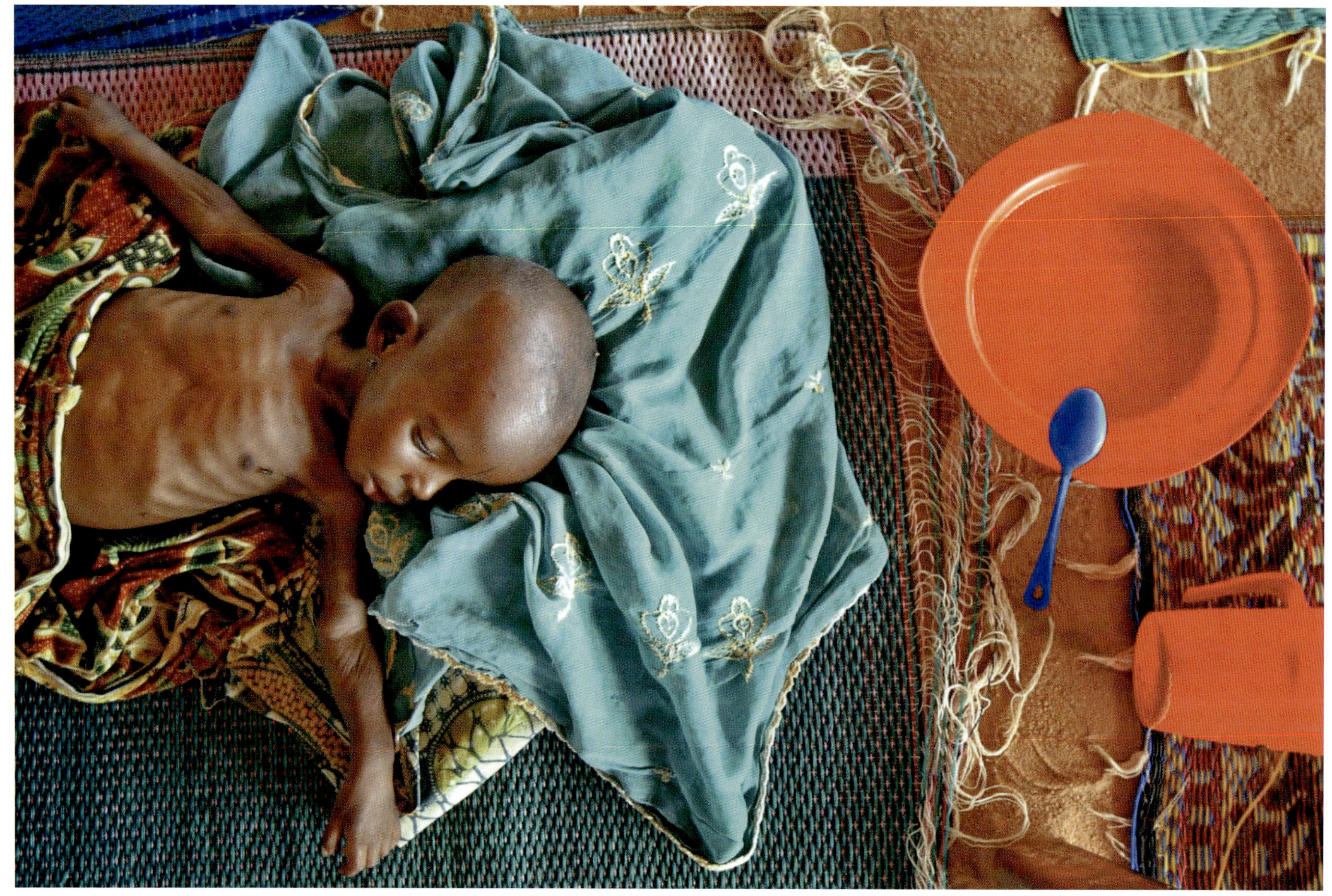

29 June 2005, MARADI, NIGER

A malnourished infant lies on the floor inside a therapeutic feeding centre run by the medical charity Médecins Sans Frontières in the town of Maradi in southern Niger. The worst drought in years left over three million people short of food in the West African country in 2005. Finbarr O'Reilly

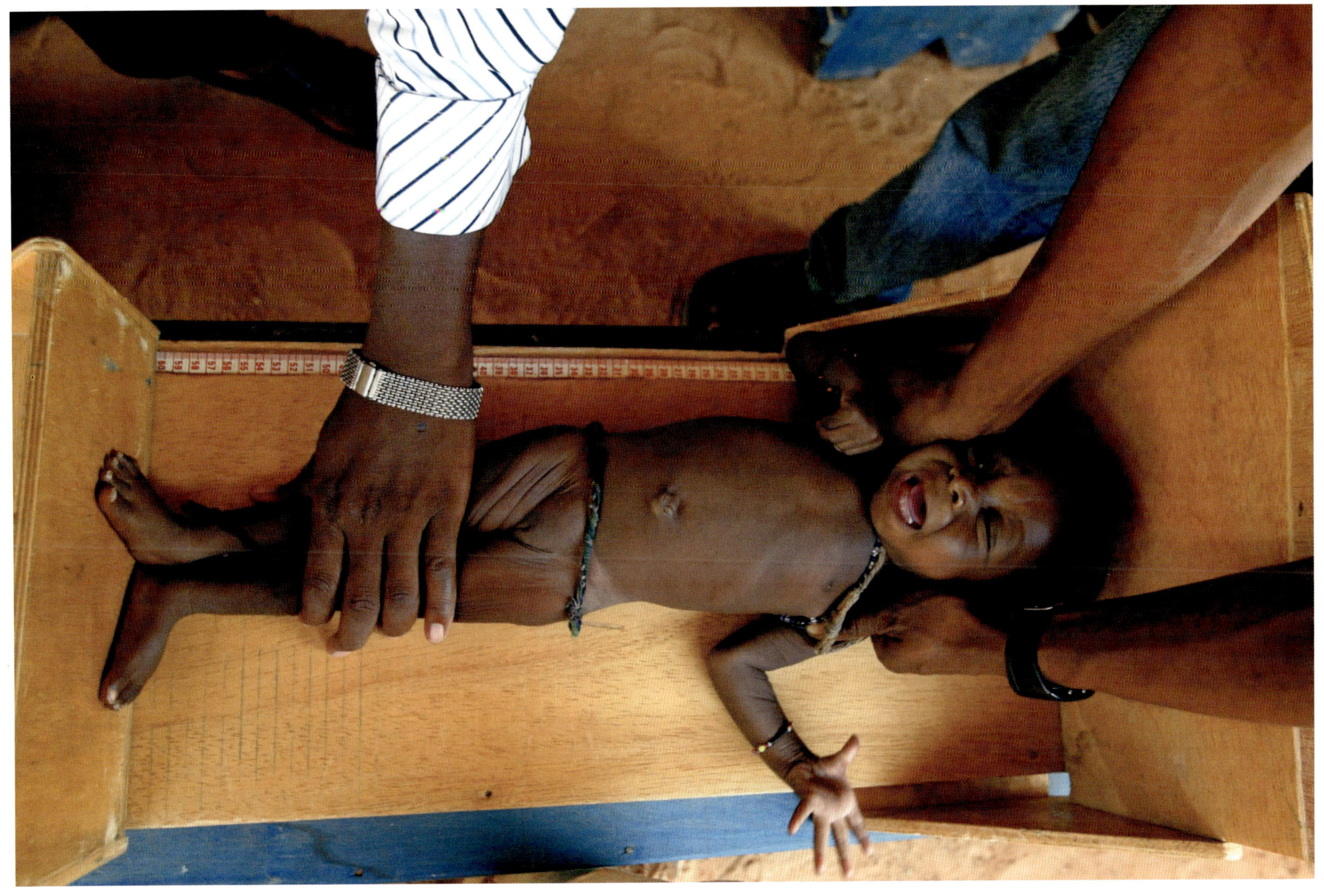

30 June 2005, GUIDAN ROUMDJI, NIGER

A malnourished infant is measured by health workers at an emergency clinic in the village of Guidan Roumdji in southern Niger. Finbarr O'Reilly

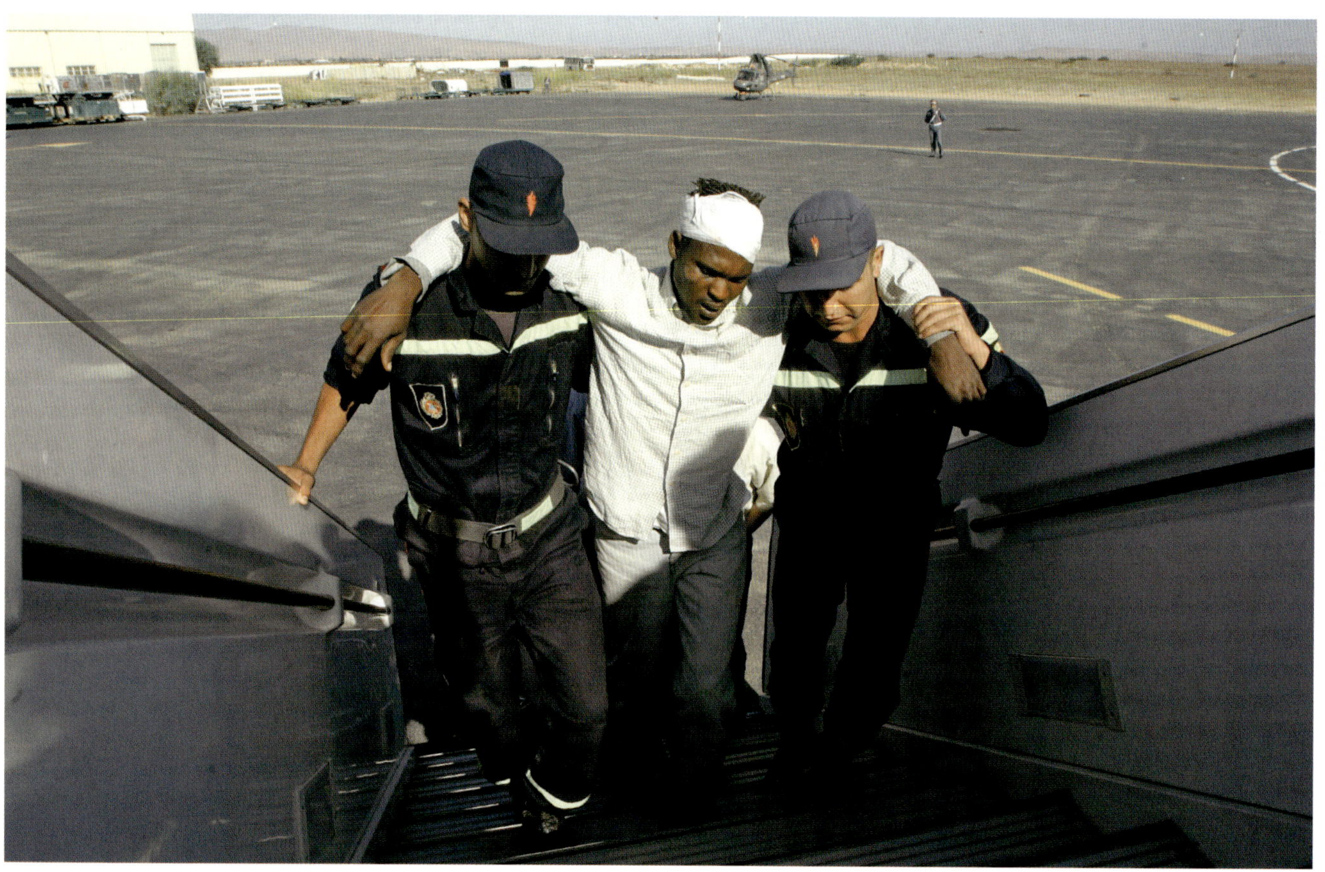

12 October 2005, OUJDA, MOROCCO

An injured African would-be migrant is helped by Moroccan officials onto a plane that will return him to Mali. Driven by poverty, war and lack of opportunity at home, many thousands of young West Africans are embarking on a desperate migration each year in pursuit of a better life in Europe.
Andrea Comas

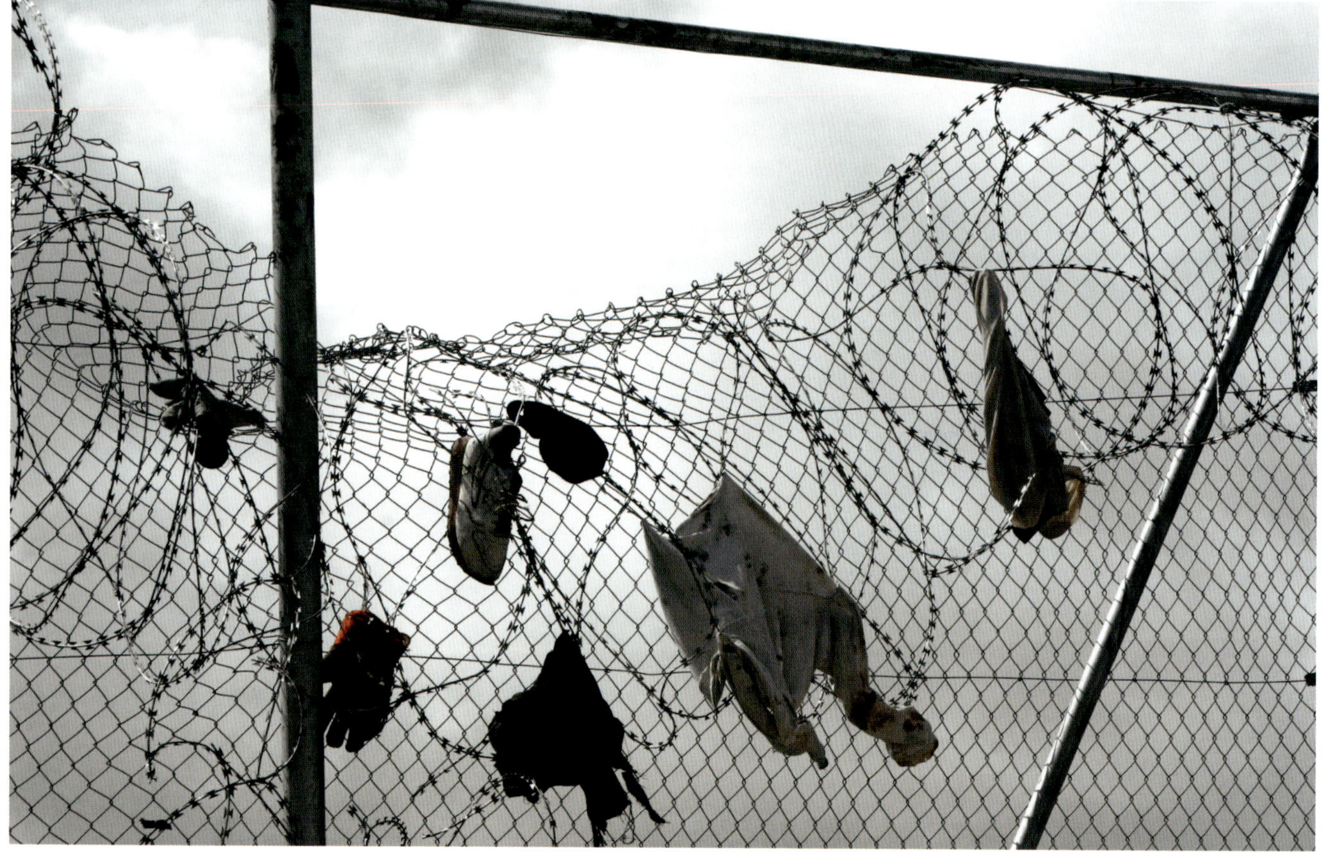

3 October 2005, MELILLA, SPAIN

Shoes and garments of African migrants are left hooked on the razor-wire fence that separates Spain's north African enclave of Melilla from Morocco. Hundreds of would-be immigrants staged a series of mass charges at the fence in an attempt to storm their way into European territory. At least 11 migrants were killed on the border fences of Spain's north African enclaves Melilla and Ceuta in October 2005. Rafael Marchante

11 October 2005, MELILLA, SPAIN

Would-be immigrants to Europe wait near the CETI (Short-stay Immigrant Centre) in Spain's north African enclave of Melilla. Andrea Comas

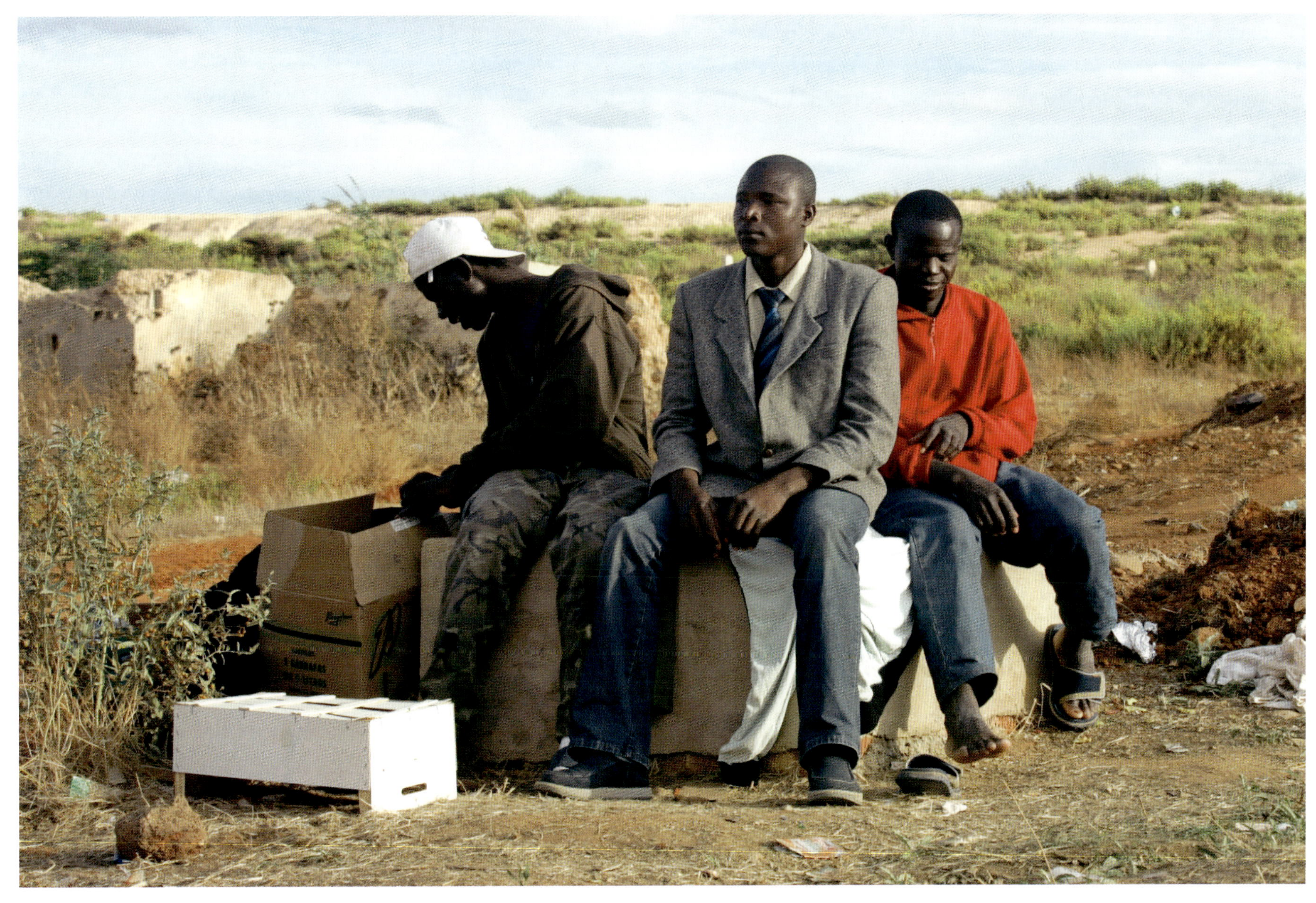

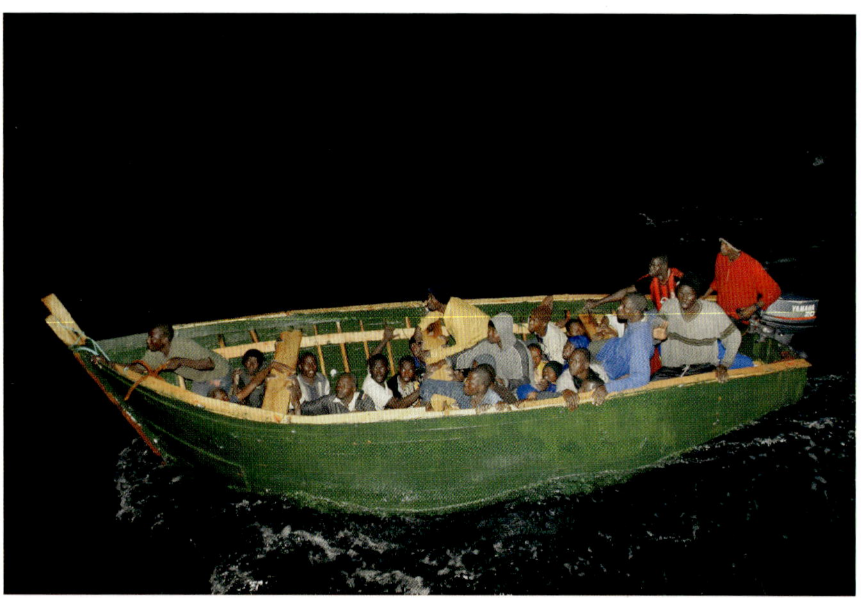

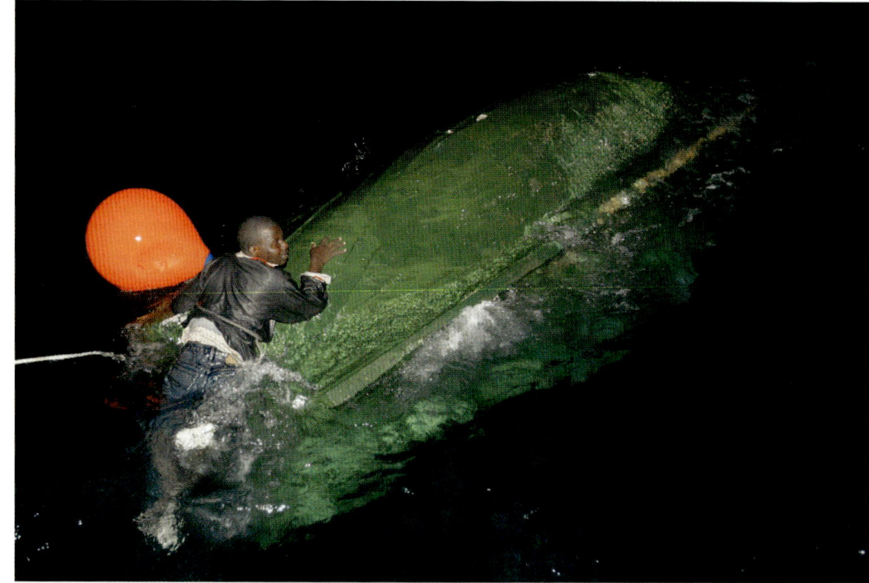

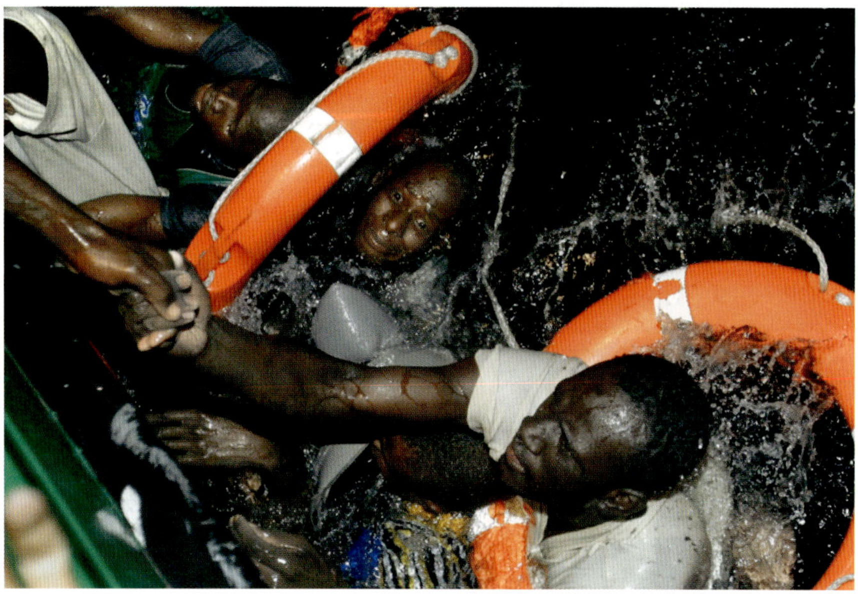

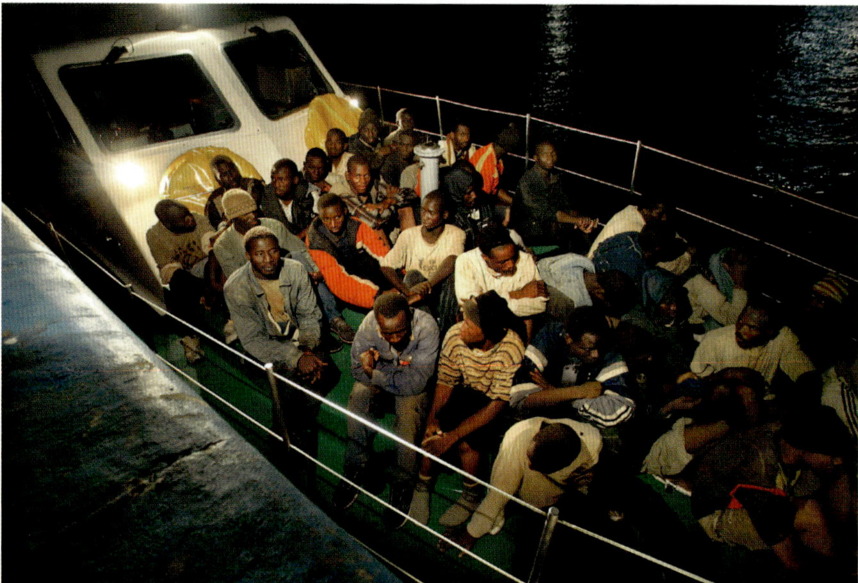

2002–2004, CANARY ISLANDS, SPAIN

This page, opposite, and overleaf Would-be immigrants to Europe are rescued by the Spanish Civil Guard. Thousands gather every year in countries on the north African coast such as Libya and Morocco, paying people-smugglers who pack them into boats and send them towards the shores of Spain and Italy, from where they hope to move on to cities across Europe. Most are fleeing poverty or drought, some war or persecution. At least 10,000 people are acknowledged to have drowned during these journeys in the past 10 years, but the actual figure is generally considered much higher. They travel in fishing boats built for 6 to 10 fishermen but which frequently carry around 50 people; up to 40 percent of these boats get into difficulties and sink or have to turn back. Many of the migrants have made arduous overland trips before taking to the water, and aid agencies report that they typically arrive dehydrated, hungry, and suffering from hypothermia. Juan Medina

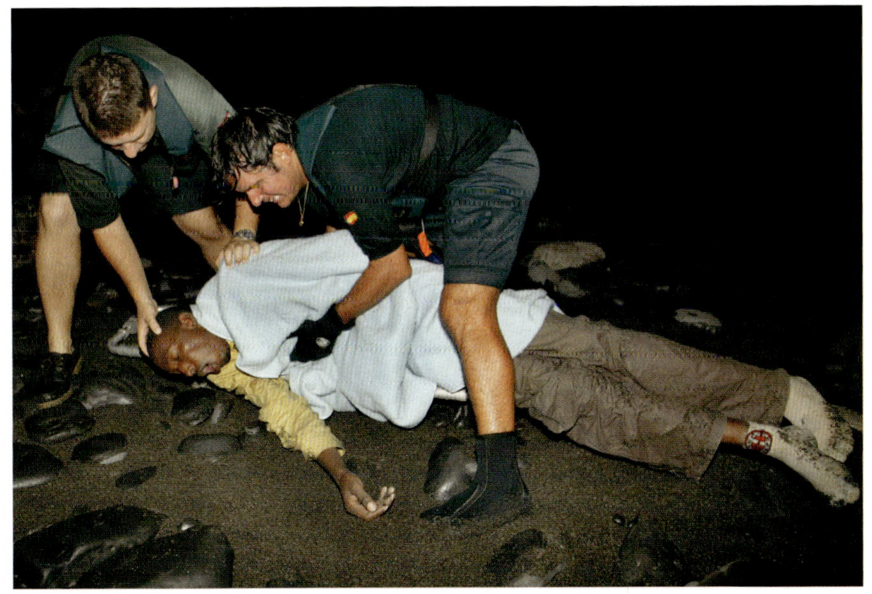

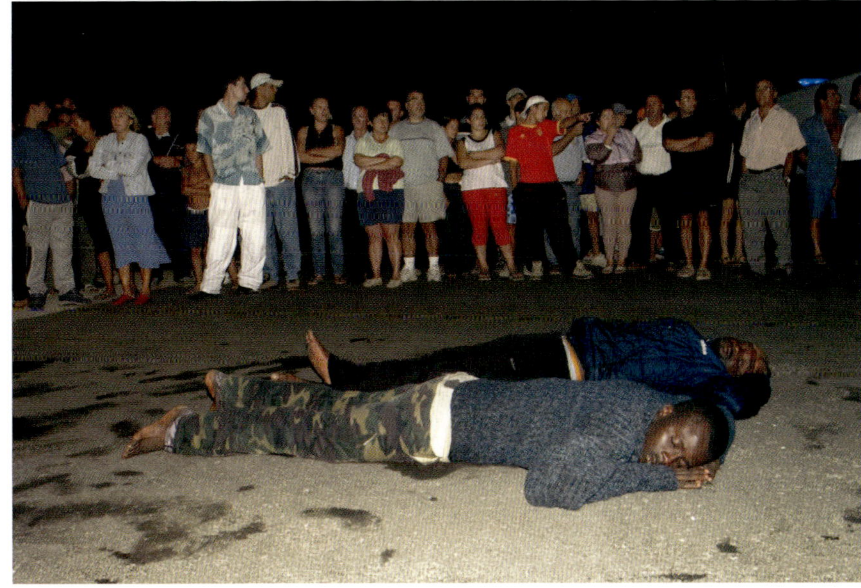

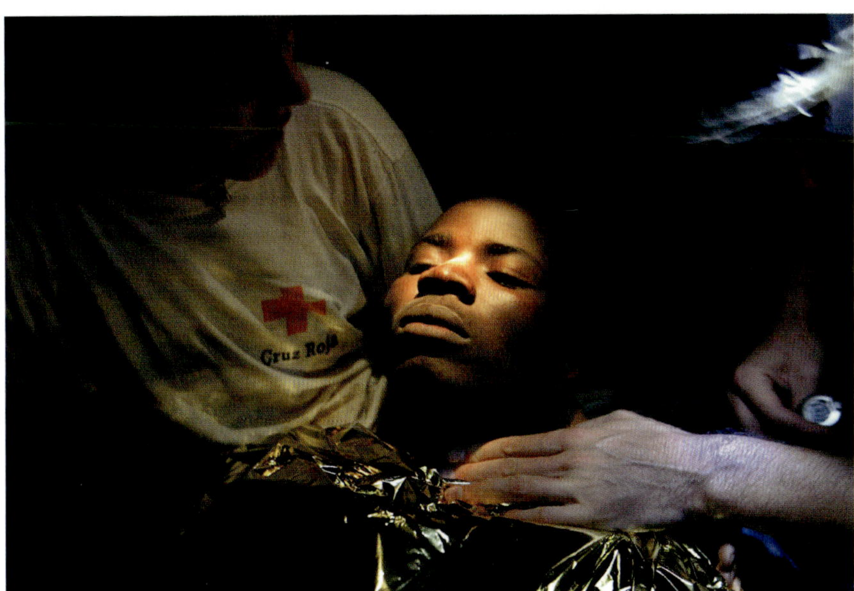

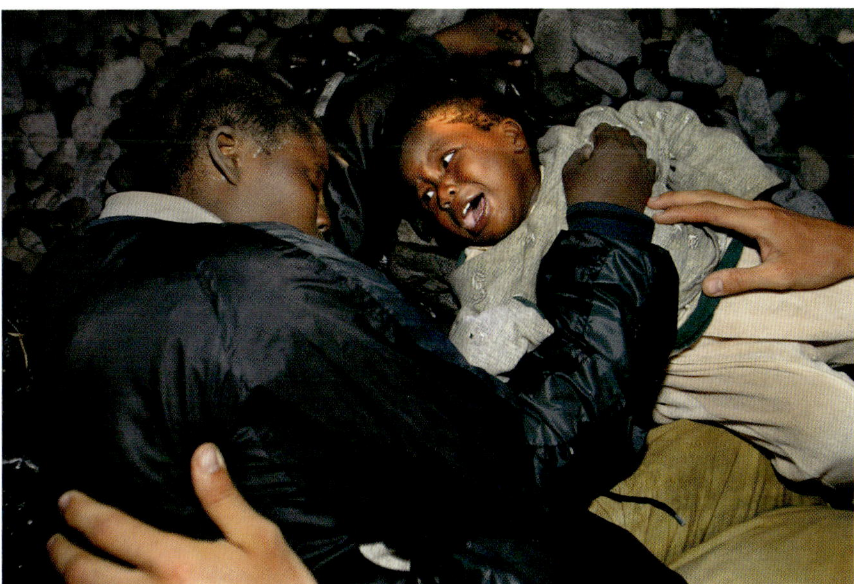

25 September 2005, MALTA

Pages 66–67 Armed Forces of Malta marines throw bottles of water to a group of around 180 illegal migrants as a rescue operation gets under way after their vessel ran into engine trouble, some 30 km (19 miles) southwest of Malta. One of the world's smallest countries, Malta says some 1,800 illegal immigrants arrived from Africa in 2005, almost all having set out from the long coastline of Libya.
Darrin Zammit Lupi

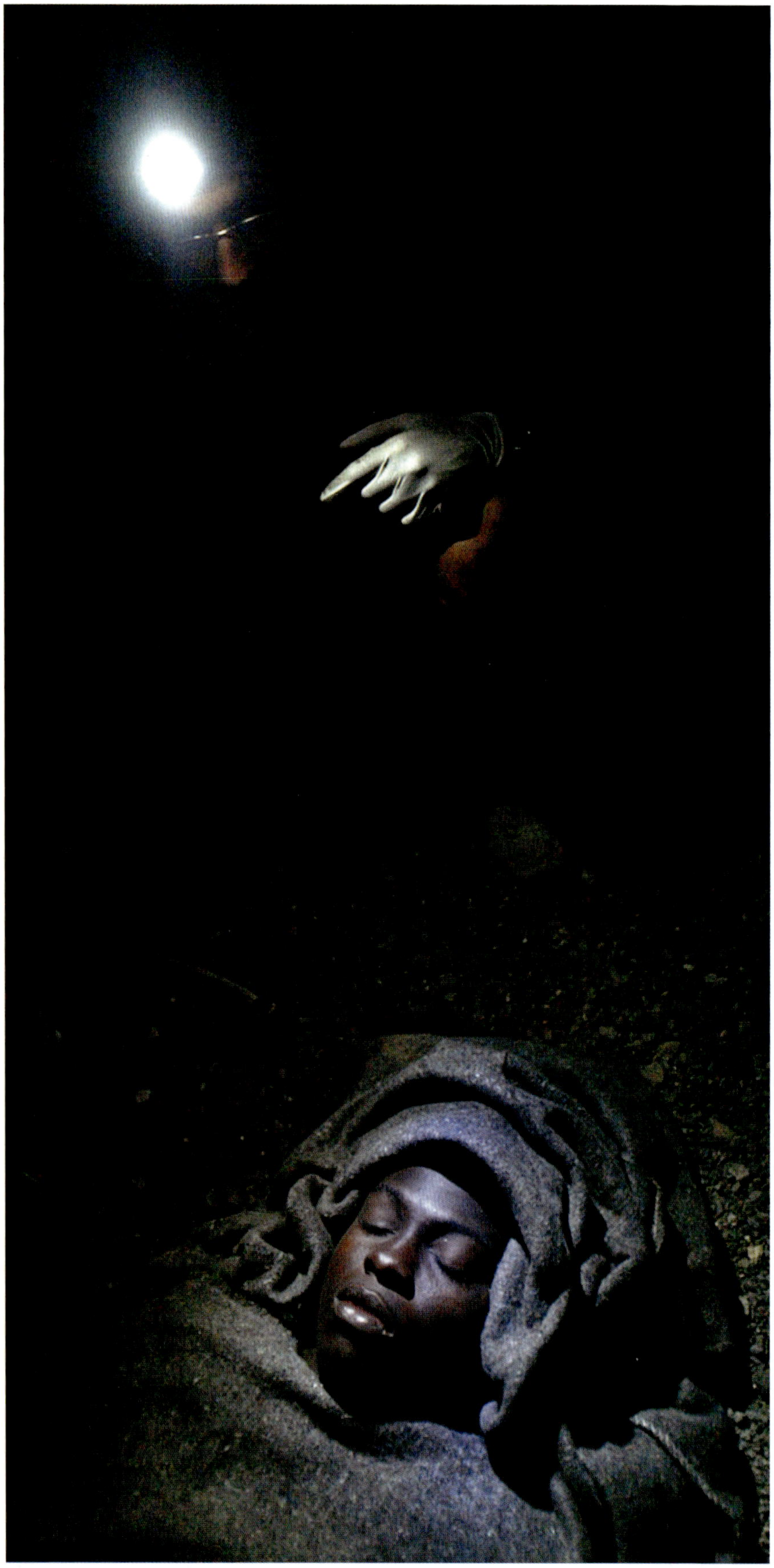

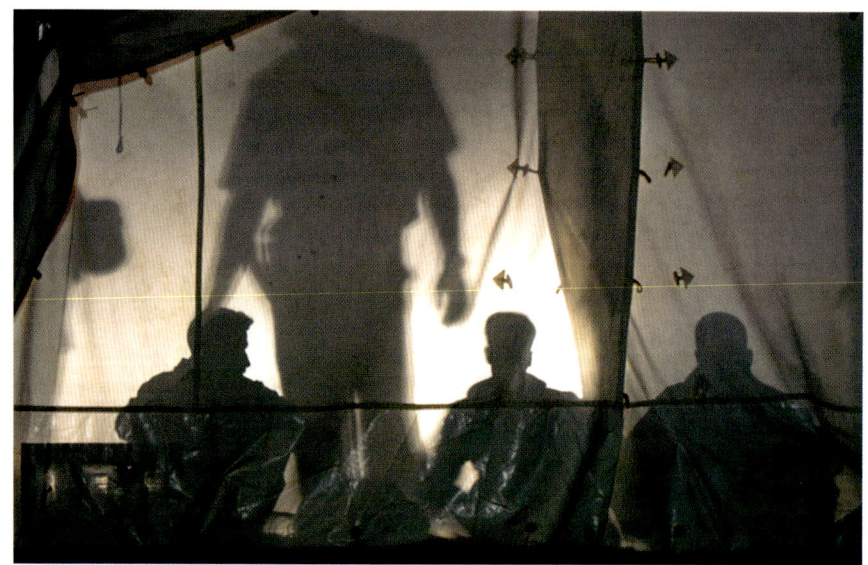

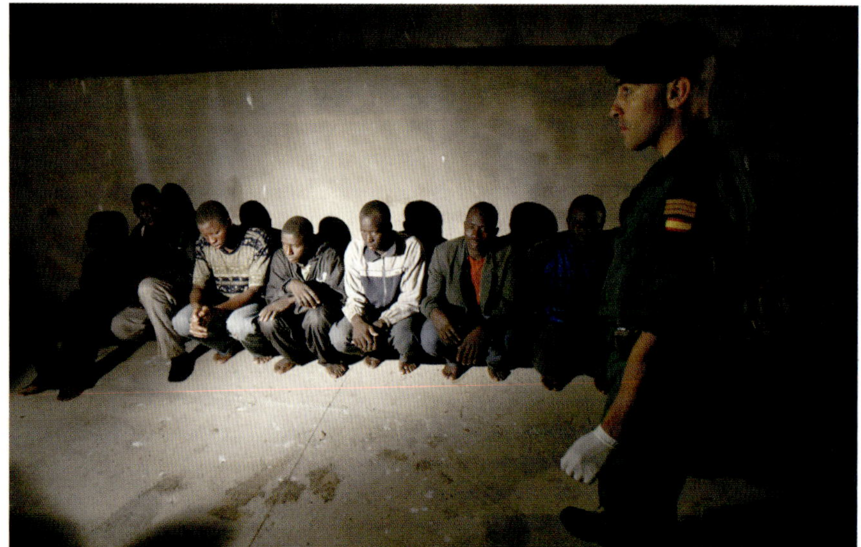

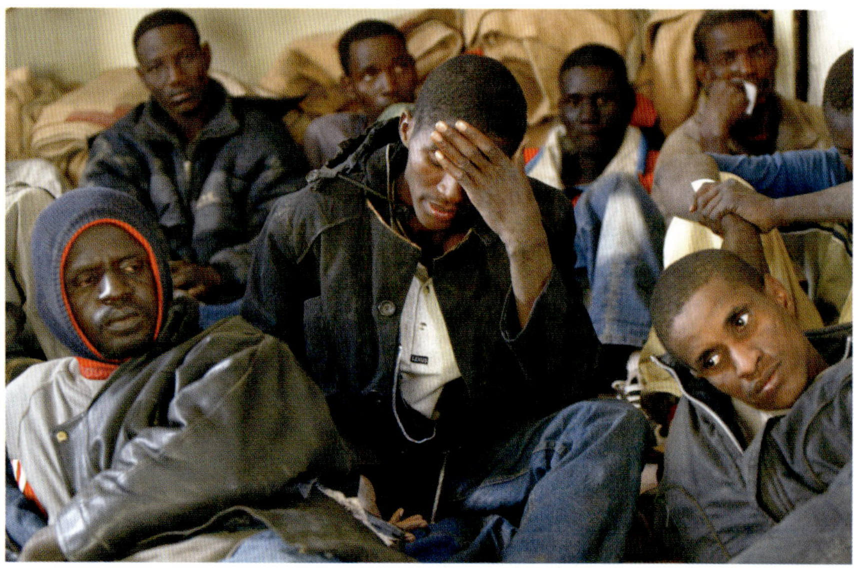

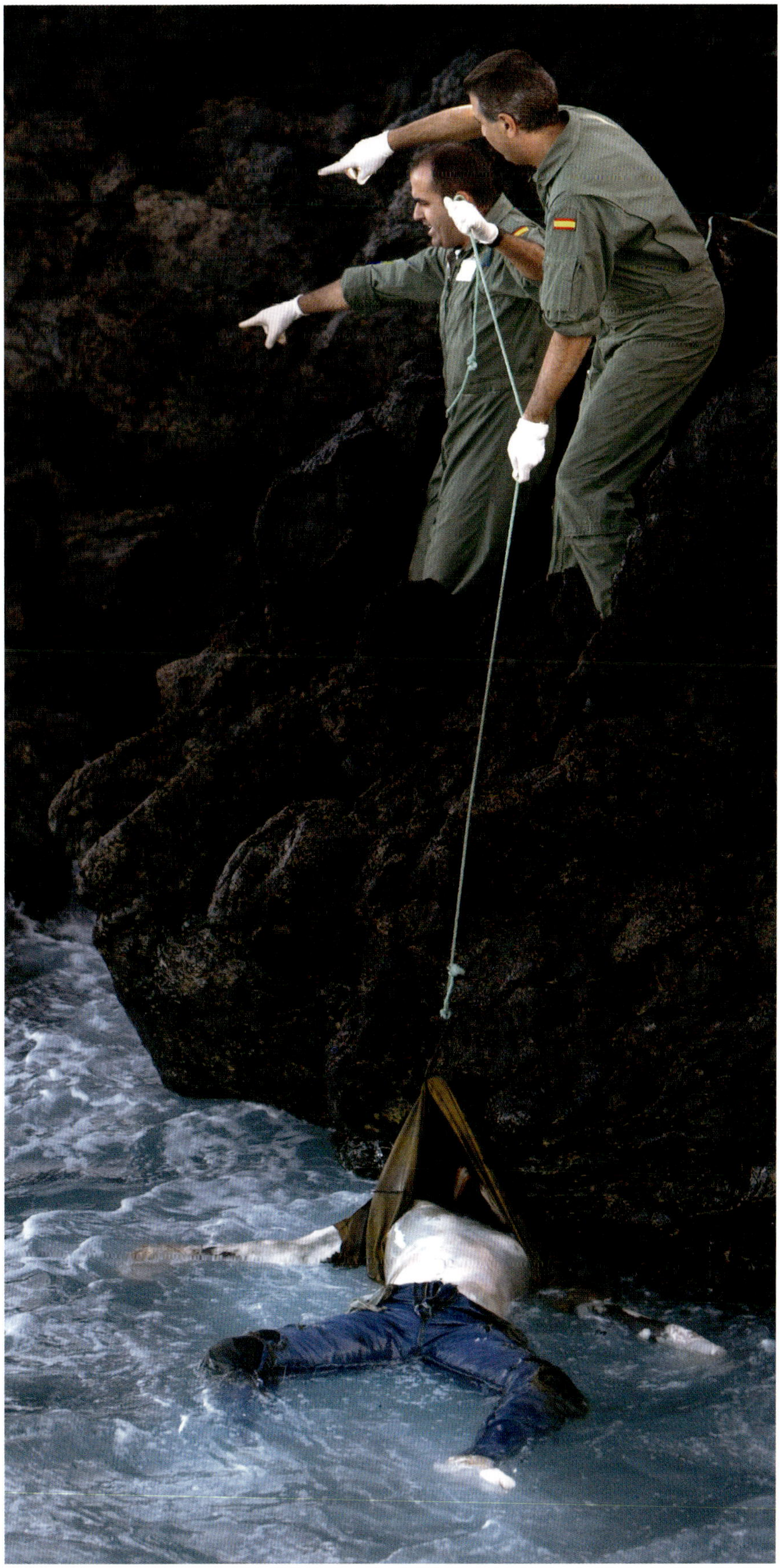

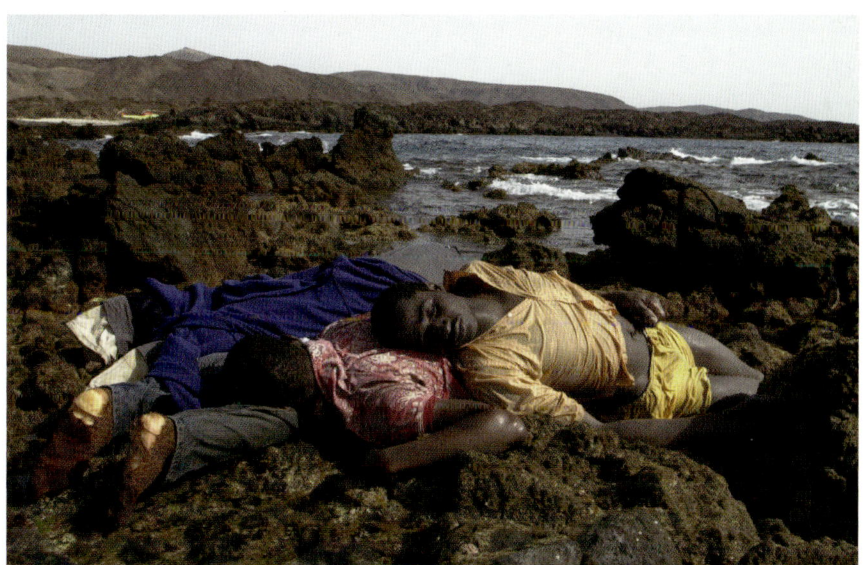

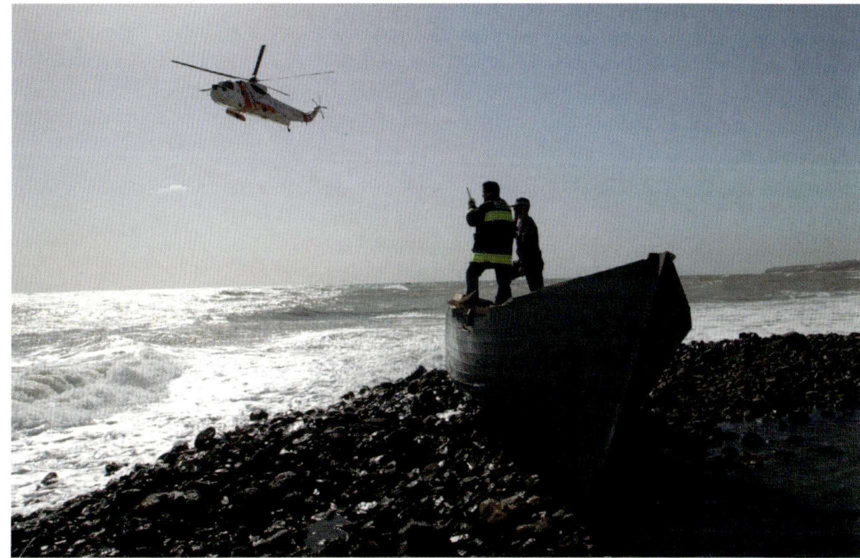

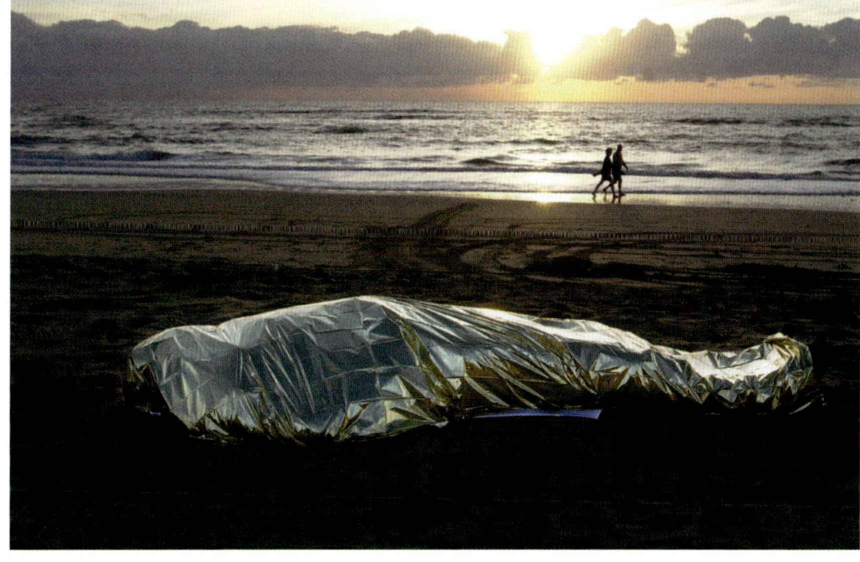

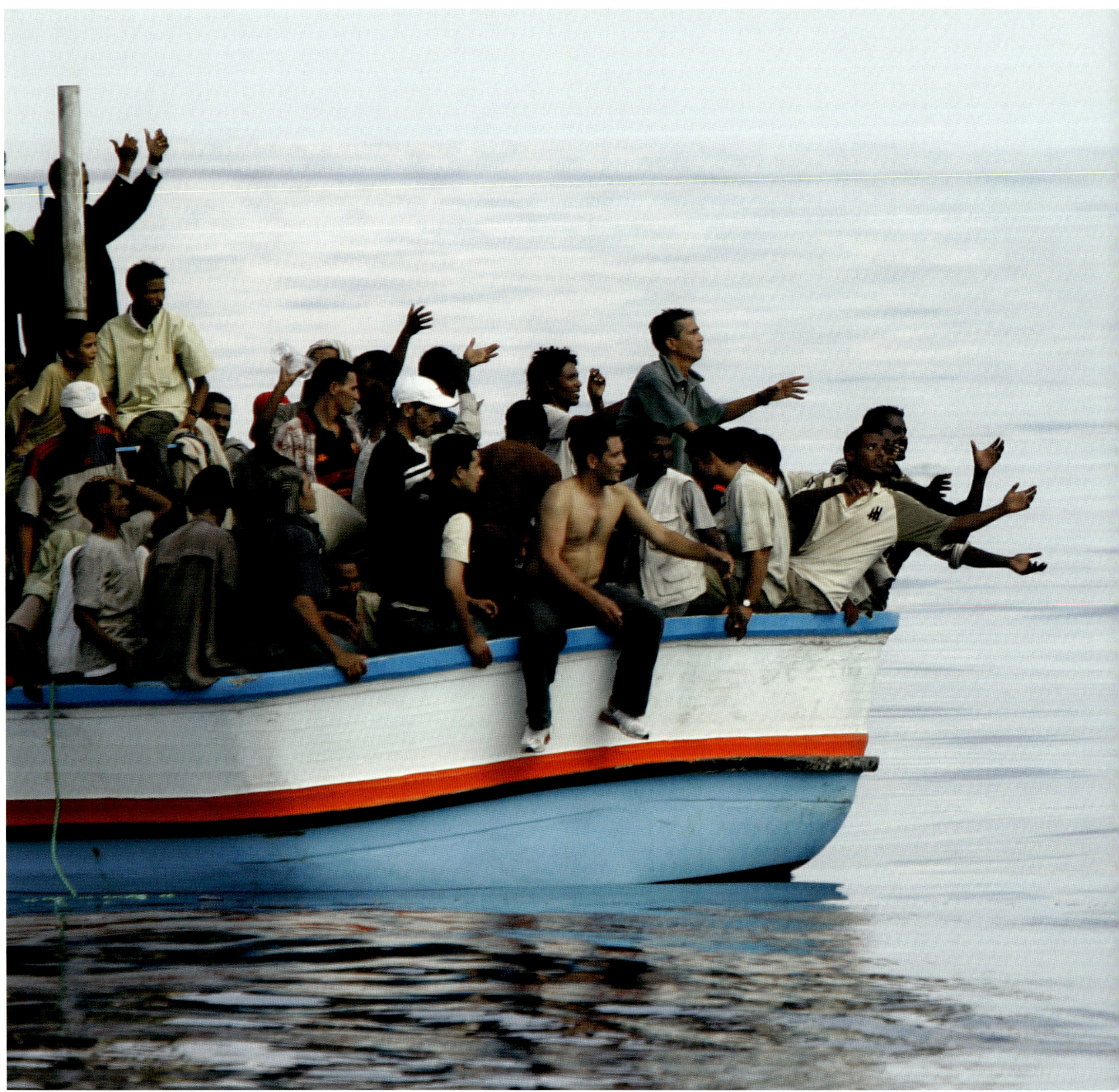

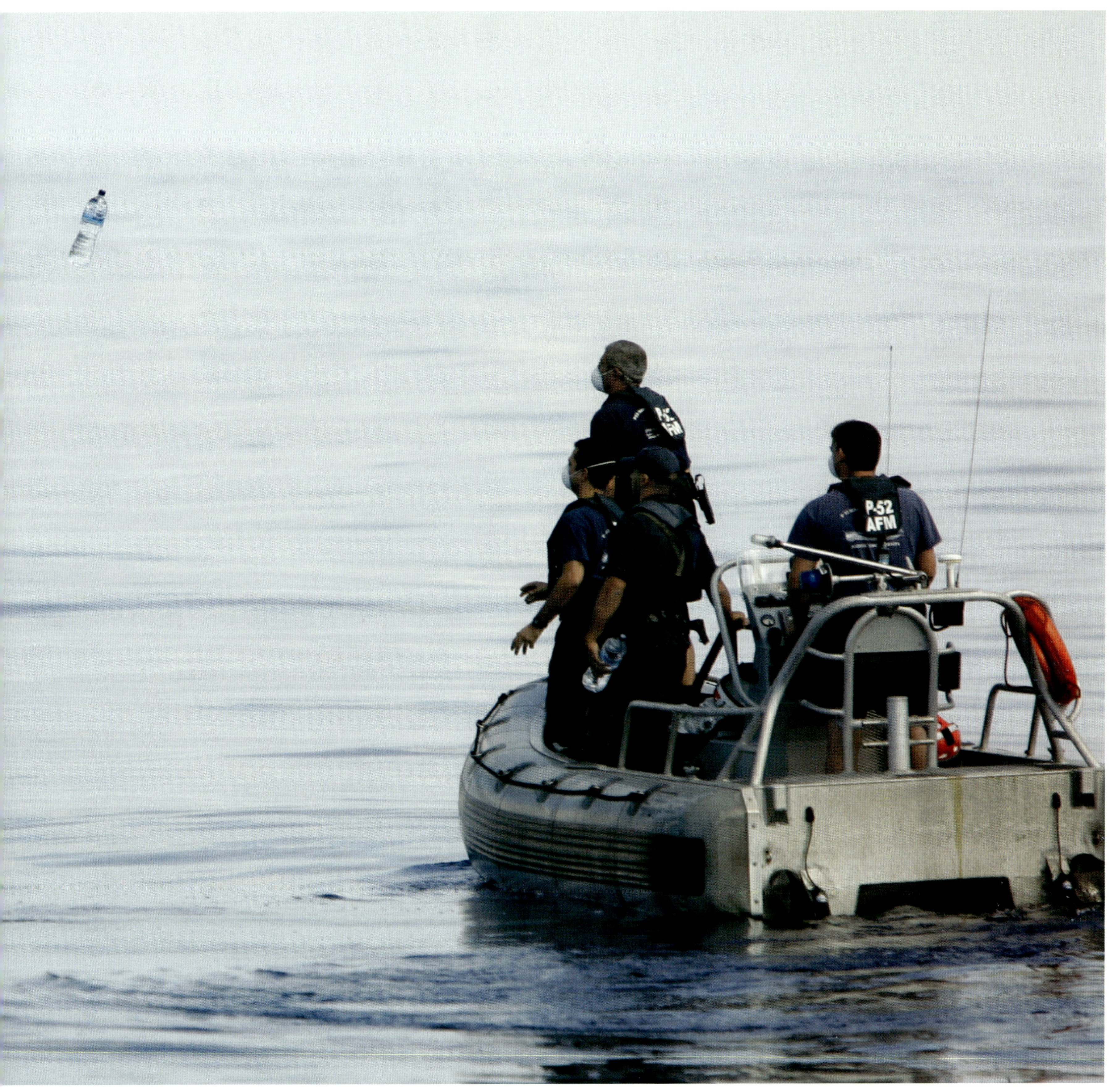
P-52
AFM

Science is powering ahead, bringing new treatments for old diseases, revolutionary materials, ever faster communications and more ingenious gadgets. Many areas of research are mired in controversy, as people question whether what is possible is also desirable. But the greatest challenges in years to come are likely to arise from global problems of rocketing population, climate change and dwindling natural resources.

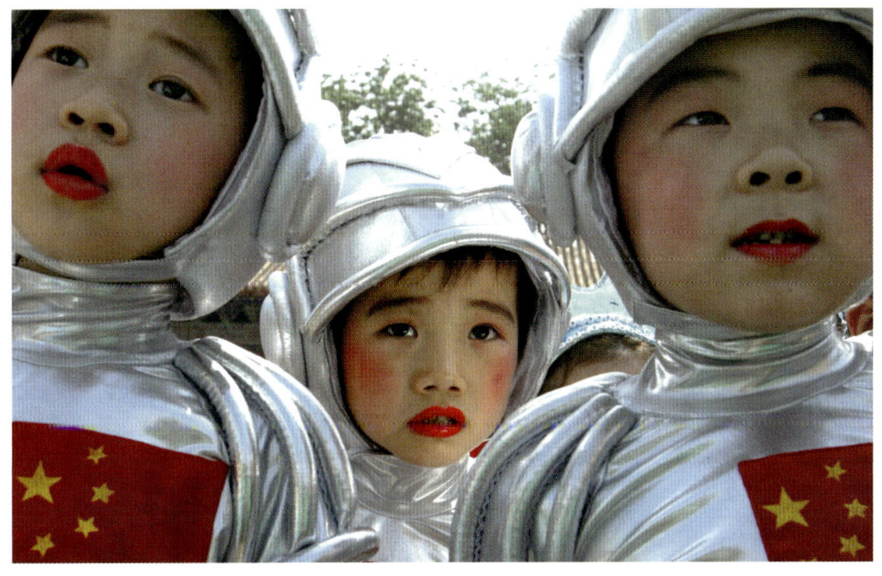

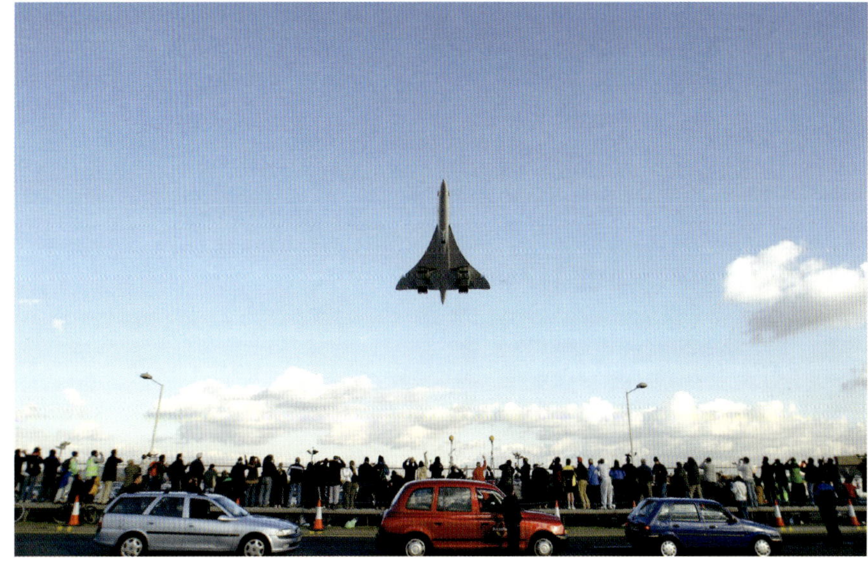

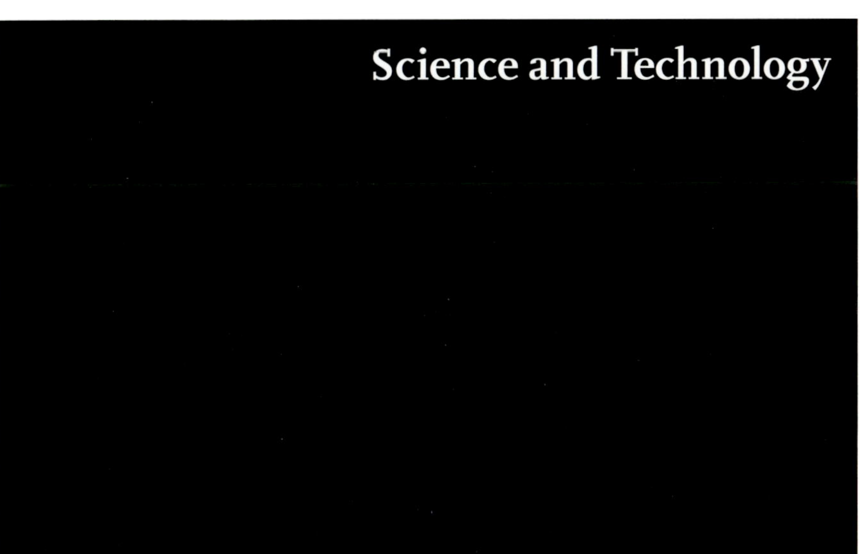

Science and Technology

Medicine / Biotechnology / Robotics
Computing / Energy / Transport
Communications / Space Exploration

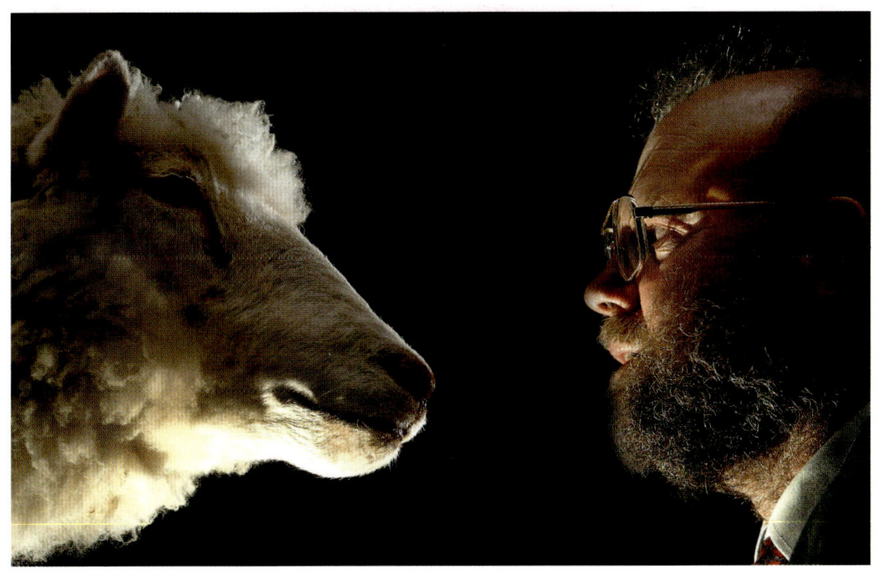

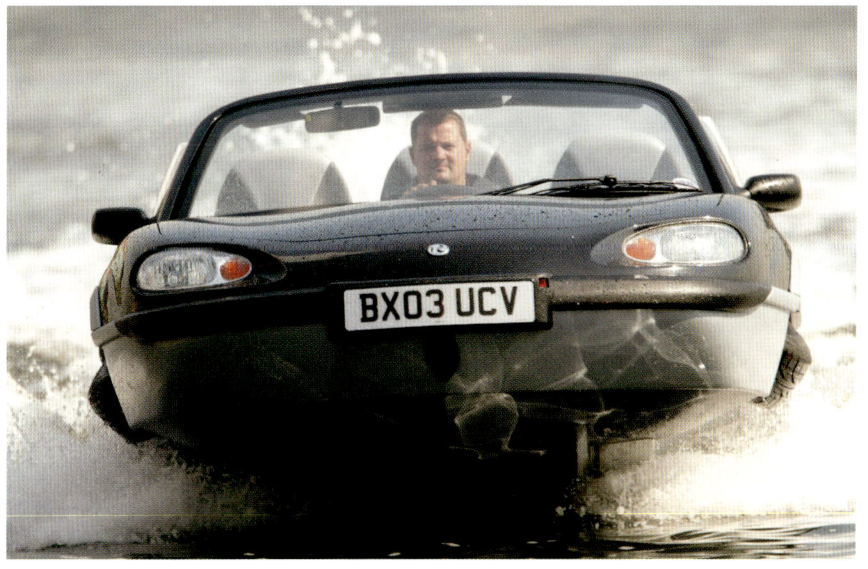

Science and Technology

Smaller, faster, smarter, cheaper. The mantra of new technology continues to lure consumers and researchers around the world in the first decade of the new century, though progress is rarely that simple. Commuters in London, home to the world's largest congestion charging system, travel no faster in their modern cars and hydrogen-fuelled buses than their grandfathers did on trams. Air travel has shrunk the globe and brought millions of people into the jet set, yet the price is noise and air pollution and the taming of the planet's last wild places.

In the years ahead the challenge will be to match accelerating technological advances in medicine, transport, energy and computing with growing economic, environmental and ethical constraints. Nowhere are the hopes higher and dilemmas greater than in healthcare. As the first of the baby boomers born after World War Two turn 60, surgeons and drug manufacturers are busy recalibrating old age. Knee replacements keep a generation of joggers on their toes, as a cocktail of blood pressure and cholesterol pills hold their heart attacks at bay. In cancer medicine, earlier detection and better treatment are starting to change the face of a disease that used to be taboo. Targeted therapies are helping patients live longer, with fewer side effects, to the extent that some experts now predict that cancer will one day become a chronic condition to be treated with daily medication.

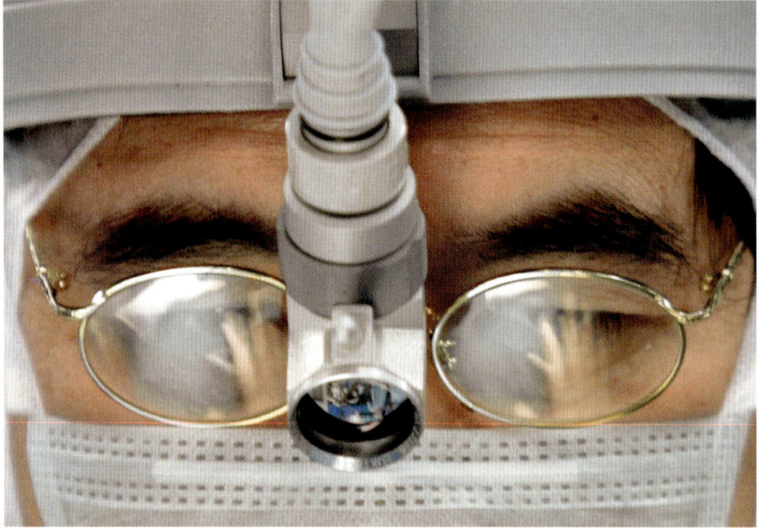

A Thai doctor performs an experimental stem cell procedure at Bangkok Heart Hospital that involves injecting the heart with cells cultivated from the patient's own blood. 19 December 2005, Chaiwat Subprasom.

The successful mapping in 2000 of the human genome – the three billion chemical pairings that make up DNA – is transforming the scientific understanding of the genetic causes of many diseases, including cancer. The result could eventually be a new era of medicines tailored to a patient's individual genetic profile, although that won't happen overnight. Applying genomic knowledge to new treatments is taking longer than originally hoped. Gene therapy, for example, which involves using a virus to carry a therapeutic gene into a patient's cells, has proved tricky to apply in practice.

The biggest prize of all could be the arrival of truly regenerative medicine unleashed by stem cells, master cells in the body that can develop into any tissue type and have the potential to treat conditions from diabetes to spinal cord injuries to Alzheimer's disease. They may finally lead to genuine cures for some of man's greatest ills. But this next frontier in bio-medicine is controversial because some people consider using stem cells from embryos, which offer the greatest potential, to be tantamount to destroying a human life. Such cells are often derived from embryos discarded after fertility treatment – another boom area of modern medicine.

> Increasingly, longevity is a privilege of the rich and a growing drag on economies in the West.

More prosaically, longer life means larger health bills. Although many treatments are clearly cost-effective (prescribing a new drug that keeps a patient out of hospital obviously makes sense), postponing death is a costly affair. Increasingly, longevity is a privilege of the rich and a growing drag on economies in the West. By the early years of the twenty-first century, U.S. carmakers were paying more in employee healthcare costs for each car rolling off the production line than the cost of sheet metal in the vehicle.

Tragically, for the majority of the world's population, modern medical miracles remain far out of reach. Millions die each year from easily treatable infections across the developing world. One African child perishes every 30 seconds of malaria, for want of a simple bed net that would keep off the mosquitoes that bear the disease. Providing the world's poorest with decent medical care will be a long haul – though it may be helped, in part, by advances in communications, allowing better monitoring and care of scattered populations.

The tumbling price of computing power, coupled with deregulation, greater bandwidth and lower connection costs around the globe, is bringing PCs and fixed and mobile telephony within reach of billions. Africa now boasts the highest rate of growth in cell phone usage of any continent, albeit off a low base, while the possibility of making telephone calls over the Internet at no charge beyond the cost of connection to the web is bringing people and businesses together across national borders.

In the industrialized world, mobile phones have become much more than devices to talk into. Nowadays, they also incorporate cameras, radios, games, video and digital music players, as well as offering Internet and email capability. As wireless coverage expands and WiFi and broadband become ubiquitous, consumers are coming to expect always-on connectivity that allows them to stay in touch at home, in the office and on the road, where their cars are increasingly guided by computerized satellite navigation technology.

A new wave of Internet entrepreneurs has emerged from the ashes of the dot-com bust of 2000, led by Google – an upstart search engine business which in 2005 overtook Time Warner to become the world's most valuable media company. Its ambitions appear boundless, ranging from mapping the planet to scanning the world's libraries. Second time around, it seems clear that e-commerce is here to stay. Cyberspace is challenging Main Street and no one any longer doubts the power of Amazon, eBay and iTunes to transform the retail world.

Computer technology is also starting to change the fabric of civil society, from experiments with electronic voting to the meteoric rise of weblogs, or blogs, that are breaking down traditional barriers between the public, media and politicians. Many governments have been keen to embrace the Internet as a way to cut down on paperwork and keep tabs on their citizens. But while some areas of e-government are straightforward – such as applying online for a driver's licence or filling out an income tax declaration – others are deeply controversial, with big concerns remaining about the risks posed by hacking and fraud.

The growing volume of data held about individuals by both governments and corporations is a concern to civil liberties groups and has opened a new front in a global debate about privacy. The game has changed, too, for law-enforcement agencies, whose surveillance techniques for tracking criminals and terrorists must now take account of roaming cell phones, internationally routed email and voice-over Internet technology.

With more than a billion of the world's population already online and hundreds of thousands joining each day, demand for better and cheaper computers is set to grow. Forty years ago Gordon Moore, co-founder of Intel, predicted the processing power of microchips would double roughly every 18 months. Moore's Law still

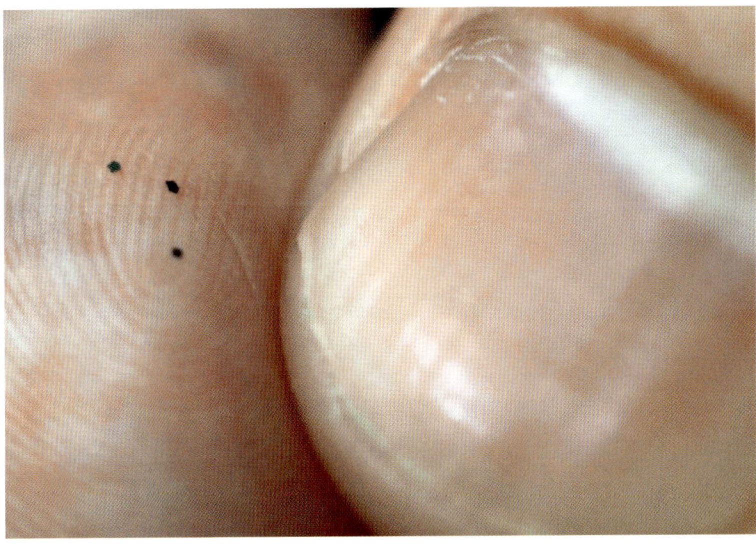

Prototype super-micro wireless automatic recognition IC chips, or 'mu-chips', created by Hitachi Ltd. These tiny microchips have a wide range of potential applications in fields including medicine, data management, and the control of counterfeit goods. Tokyo, Japan, 20 May 2003, Eriko Sugita.

holds true, but as microchips shrink in size, scientists are starting to come up against the physical limits of silicon.

Electronics is consequently one of the sectors expected to benefit from the next 'big thing' in technology, the world of the ultra-small. Nanotechnology, which involves the manipulation of materials at the molecular level, has so far given the world better sun cream, self-cleaning windows and stain-resistant clothing. But the peculiar properties of nanomaterials – including their great strength – mean they are likely to have a role as novel industrial materials, as well as in medicine and the computers of the future.

Nanotech, however, raises fears alongside hopes. Scare stories about self-replicating nanoscale robots turning the earth into a 'grey goo' may be without foundation but there are real concerns over how the release of nanoparticles will affect the environment and the human body. Similar concerns are raised by biotechnology, which likewise provides mankind with the tools to manipulate some of the fundamental properties of the physical world – for good or ill. Genetically modified crops offer the potential of higher yields combined with resistance to pests and disease, making them, some argue, the solution to hunger as the world's population continues to expand. But environmental campaigners fear that they will undermine biodiversity and will leave farmers around the globe at the mercy of a few powerful multinational corporations.

Energy companies, struggling with diminishing reserves of fossil fuels and mounting pressure to develop energy sources that do not contribute to global warming, may be among the first to jump on the nanotech bandwagon. New nanomaterials could provide the world with better methods for energy production and handling, including more efficient solar cells, hydrogen fuel cells and new hydrogen storage systems.

Hydrogen, which only produces water vapour when burned, is seen by many as the dream fuel of the future, but other alternative energy sources are also on the march around the world. The wind power industry says that by 2020 wind could provide 12 percent of the world's electricity, though many people are resisting the building of wind farms in their backyards. A more thorny debate surrounds nuclear power, whose supporters sense the pendulum is swinging their way again, 20 years after the Chernobyl disaster, as the world hunts for energy supplies that will reduce emissions of greenhouse gases. France, meanwhile, is to host the world's first prototype nuclear fusion reactor, which will seek to turn seawater into fuel by mimicking the way the sun produces energy. It is a radically different approach to conventional fission-based nuclear power and the jury is still out on whether it will be commercially viable.

After several false starts, car makers are finally coming up with alternatives to the gasoline-burning internal combustion engine. Hybrid cars – half-gas and half-electric powered – are the first manifestation of tomorrow's cleaner vehicle, although the ultimate goal for purists is a fuel-cell car powered by hydrogen produced with renewable energy sources. Getting there will not be easy. Auto and energy companies still need to figure out an efficient infrastructure for distributing hydrogen and a way of synthesizing the gas that does not involve burning fossil fuels.

Space travel for the masses, the hi-tech theme best-loved by futurologists in the twentieth century, looks like remaining science fiction for the foreseeable future. While mankind's understanding of the cosmos may be expanding as fast as the universe itself, the practicalities of reaching the stars are still daunting. The ultra-rich may get a taste of extra-planetary travel by the end of the decade, with the planned launch of the first commercial passenger spacecraft to take tourists out of this world, though they will hover in space only briefly before returning to Earth some $200,000 poorer. Landing on other worlds is another matter. President George W. Bush outlined a bold plan in the early years of twenty-first century for NASA to prepare for a manned space flight to Mars. Yet reaching the first step in the strategy – a return to the moon – is unlikely before 2020, more than 50 years after Neil Armstrong first set foot on our nearest neighbour.

Standing in the moon dust on that July day in 1969, Armstrong and his partner Edwin 'Buzz' Aldrin would have been surprised to know that only 10 more astronauts were to follow in their footsteps before the moon landings programme ended in 1972. But the truth is that the power of science has been felt most intensely not in mankind's mega projects but in people's down-to-earth daily lives, as the democratization of technology finally begins to make the 'global village' a reality.

Ben Hirschler has been with Reuters since 1987. He started as a commodities reporter in London before being assigned to Amsterdam, where he covered everything from shipping to Yugoslav peace talks in The Hague. In the mid-1990s, he was based in Johannesburg, writing about the economic challenges facing post-apartheid South Africa. Since his return to London in 1997, he has reported on emerging markets and British companies. Ben is currently European pharmaceuticals correspondent.

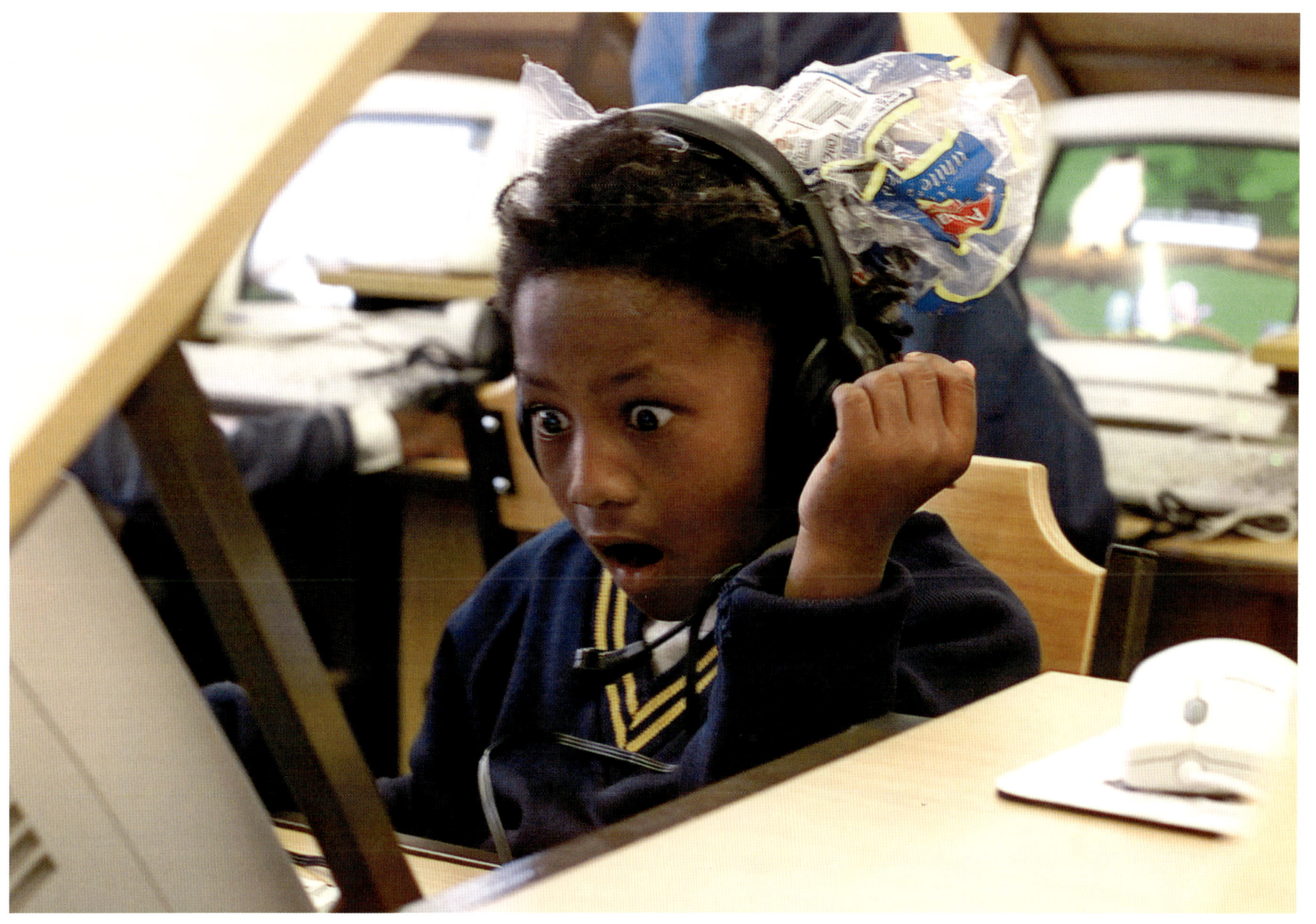

22 August 2000, CAPE TOWN, SOUTH AFRICA

Eight-year-old Jenni-Lee Mason encounters a computer for the first time at a township school in Cape Town thanks to a ground-breaking project funded by the Dutch government to teach South African children a crucial mix of computer, language and mathematics skills. Mike Hutchings

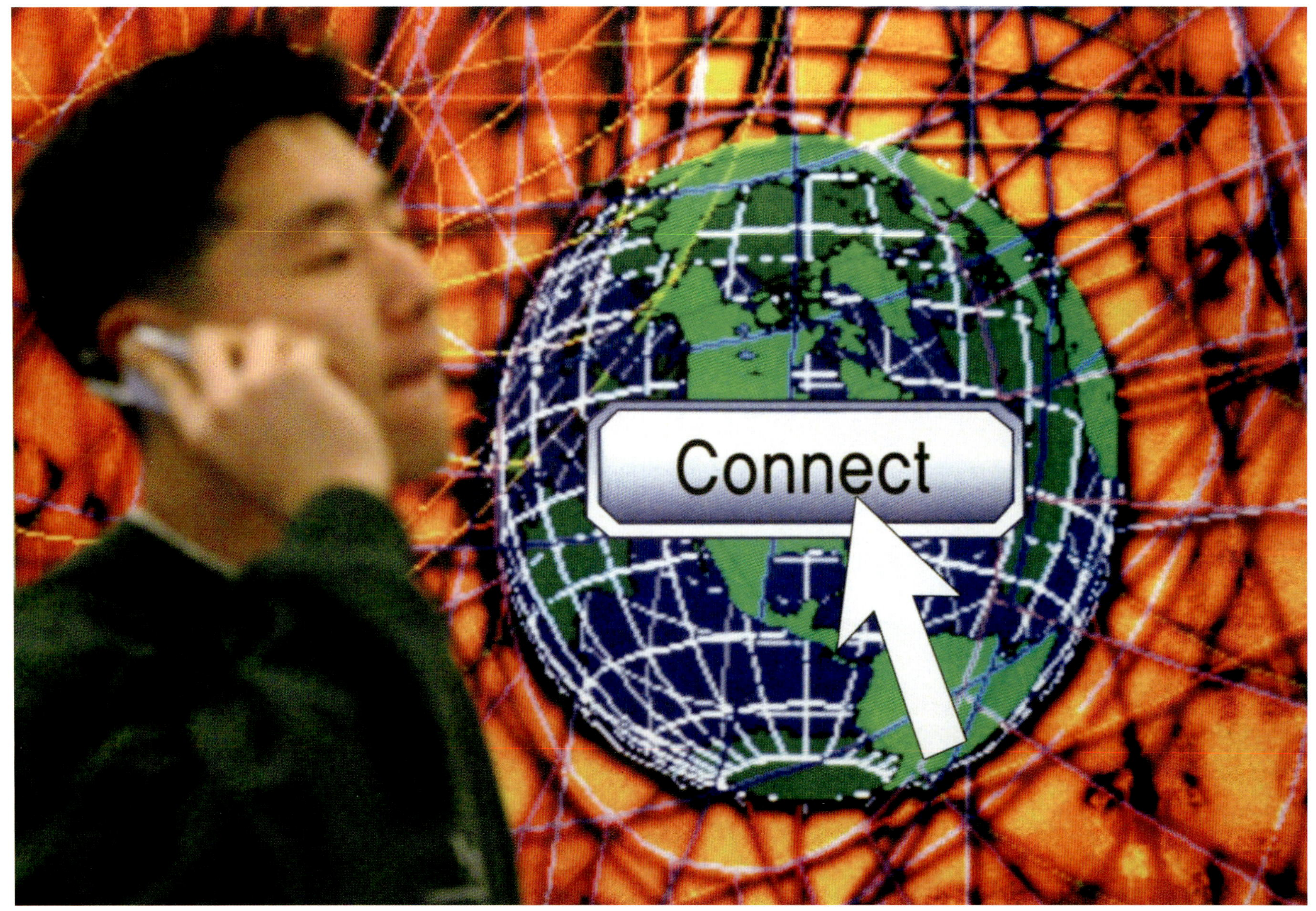

27 January 2003, SEOUL, SOUTH KOREA

A man chats on his mobile phone in front of a signboard in Seoul promoting Internet connectivity. As the most wired country in the world, South Korea was struck particularly hard by the virulent computer worm known as the 'SQL Slammer', which shut down its Internet service providers on 25 January 2003, creating chaos and nearly cutting off all web access. Kim Kyung-Hoon

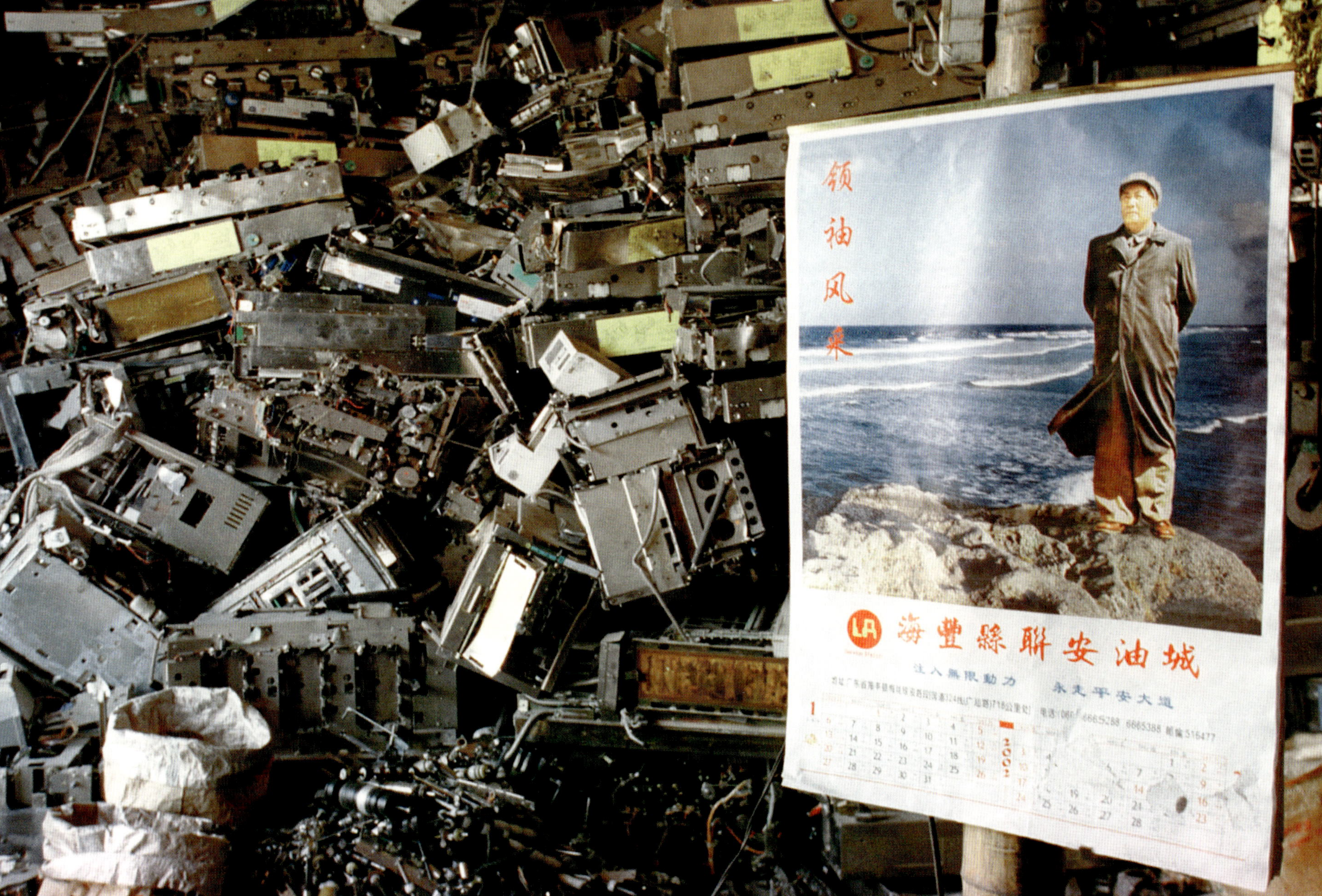

8 March 2002, GUANGDONG PROVINCE, CHINA

Computer waste is piled up inside a ramshackle hut next to a calender featuring late Chinese leader Mao Zedong at Yaocuowei village in China's southern Guangdong province. Despite the international Basel Convention which in 1994 banned export of all hazardous wastes from rich to poor countries for any reason (including recycling) electronic waste from the United States, and to a lesser extent Europe, South Korea and Japan, has ended up in China. Bobby Yip

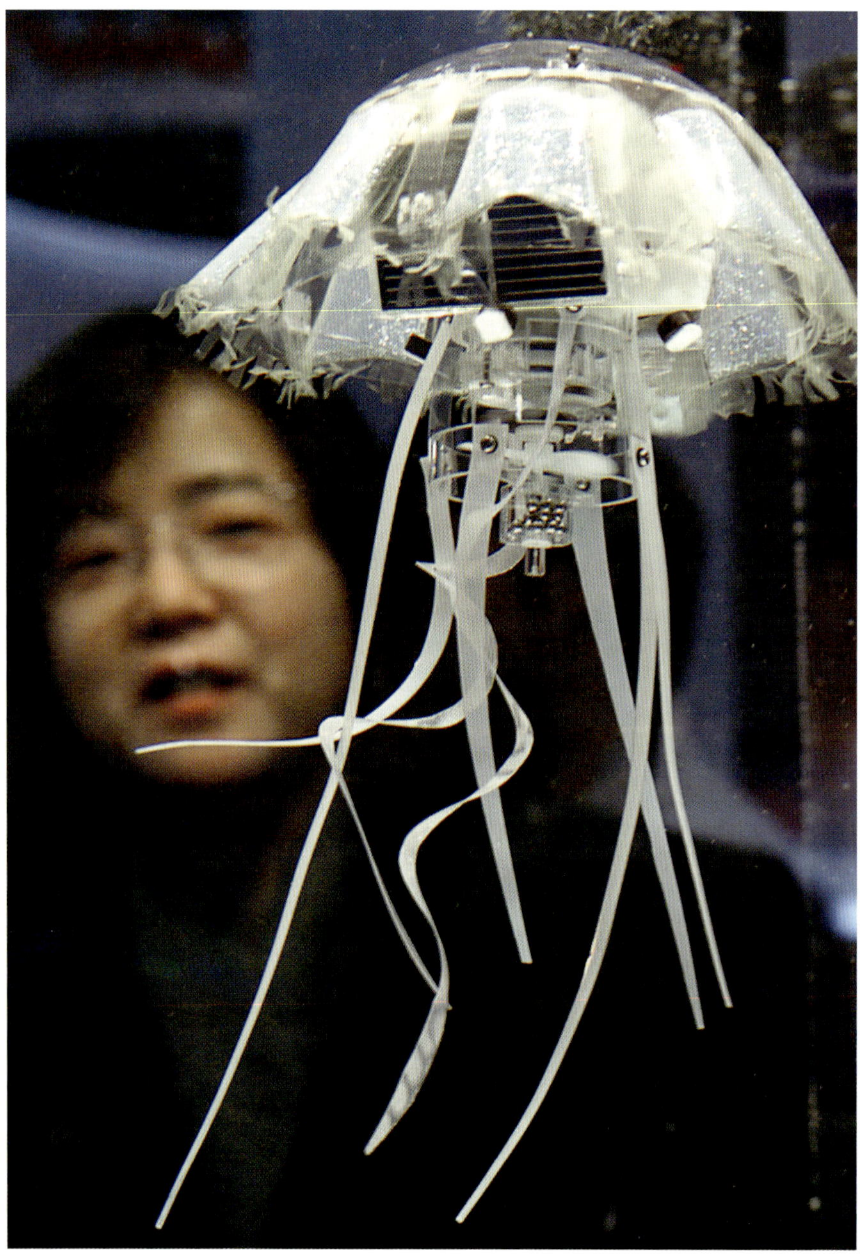

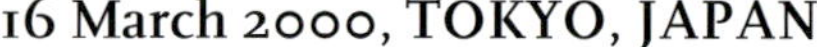

16 March 2000, TOKYO, JAPAN

An 'Aquaroid' jellyfish drifts in a water tank in the booth of Japan's leading toymaker Takara Co. Ltd at the Tokyo Toy Show in 2000. The jellyfish robot is propelled by a solar-battery-powered motor. Toshiyuki Aizawa

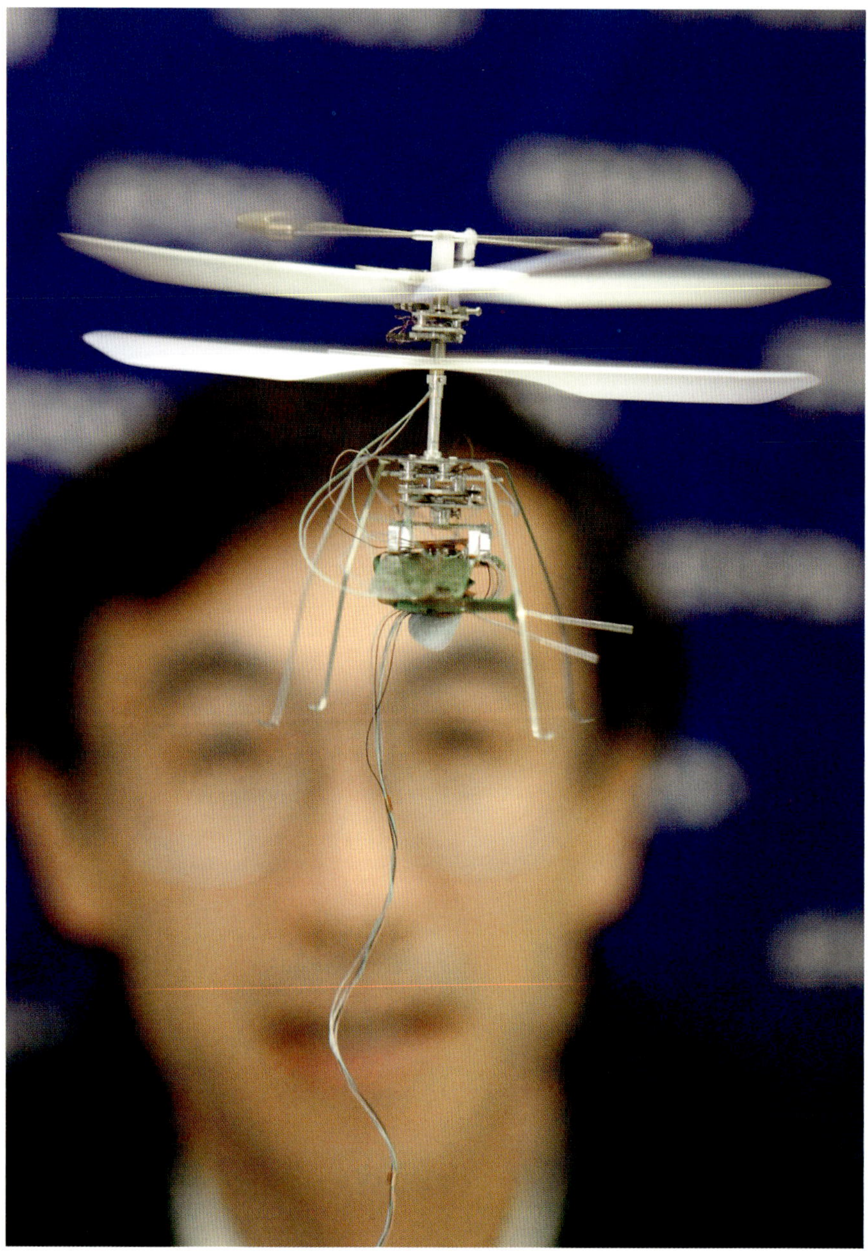

19 November 2003, TOKYO, JAPAN

The 'Micro Flying Robot' is unveiled at the 2003 International Robot Exhibition in Tokyo by its makers Seiko Epson Corp. The tiny prototype microrobot, which weighs 8.9 grammes (0.3 ounces), uses contra-rotating propellers powered by an ultra-thin, ultrasonic motor to balance in mid-air. Issei Kato

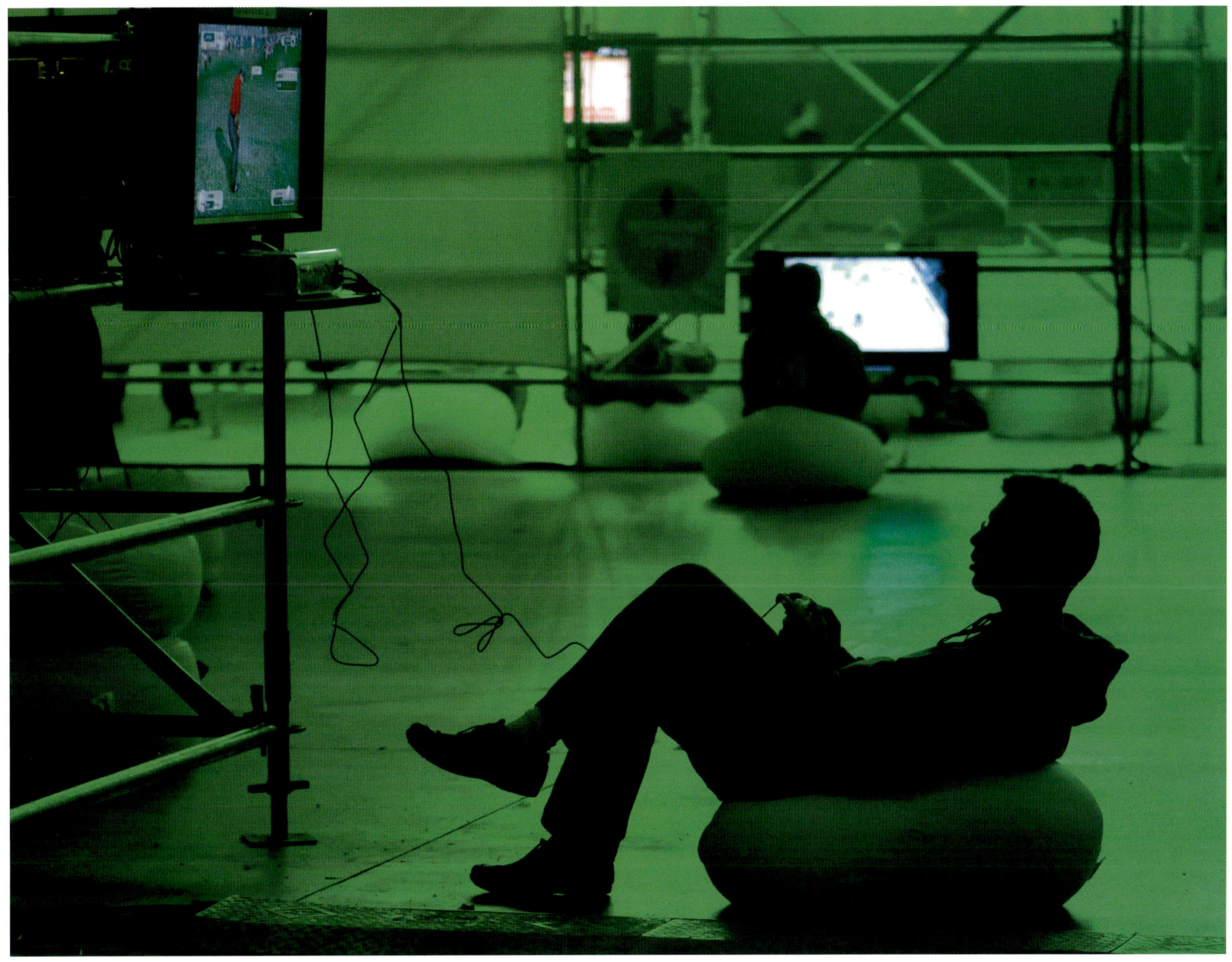

20 November 2005, PALMDALE, UNITED STATES

A gamer plays an XBox 360 during the countdown to the North American launch of Microsoft's new video game console at a party hosted in the Mojave Desert. The XBox 360 was the first of a new generation of entertainment systems designed to offer near-photo-realistic graphics, play music and video, and link up gamers over the Internet. Chris Pizzello

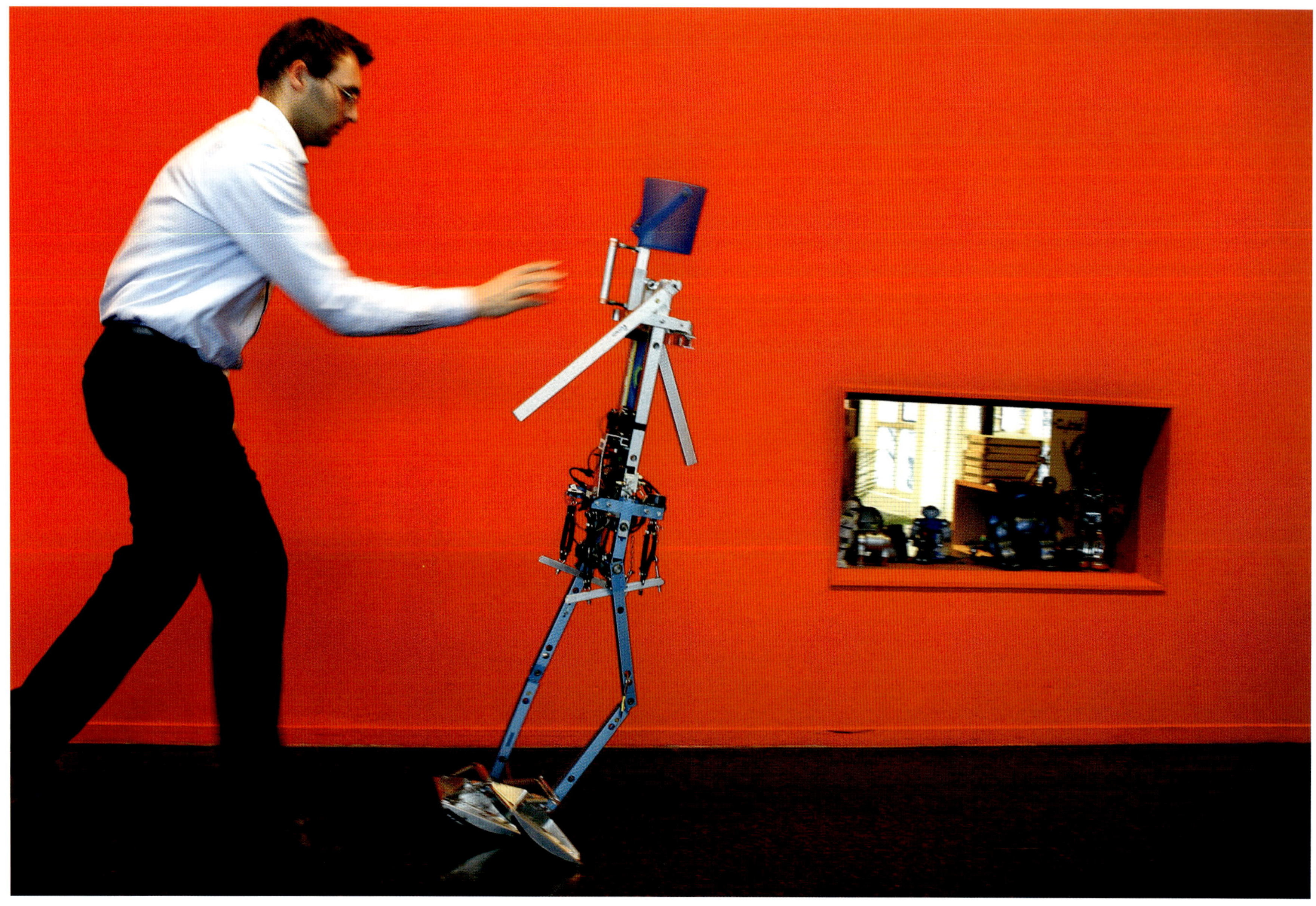

8 March 2005, DELFT, NETHERLANDS

Martijn Wisse, researcher in Bio Robotics at the Delft University of Technology, walks with the two-legged robot Denise ('The Knees') through the corridors of the university complex in Delft. Denise is one of a new generation of energy-efficient 'passive-dynamic' walking robots that mimic the human gait. Other models have been developed by teams at the Massachusetts Institute of Technology and Cornell University in the United States. Jerry Lampen

7 September 2001, LONDON, UNITED KINGDOM

Opposite above Children from the Overton Grange school participate in the 'Giant Jump' record-breaking experiment at the London Science Museum. Over a million children all over Britain took part, jumping up and down simultaneously for one minute in an attempt to produce a recordable seismic shock. Organizers estimated that they created the equivalent of a 100th of a serious earthquake. Dan Chung

4 September 2002, LONDON, UNITED KINGDOM

Opposite below A digitized version of the 700-year-old Sultan Baybar's Koran on display at the British Library, London. The unique 'Turning the Pages' technology allows visitors to turn the pages of the digital book by moving their hand across the large screen. Stephen Hird

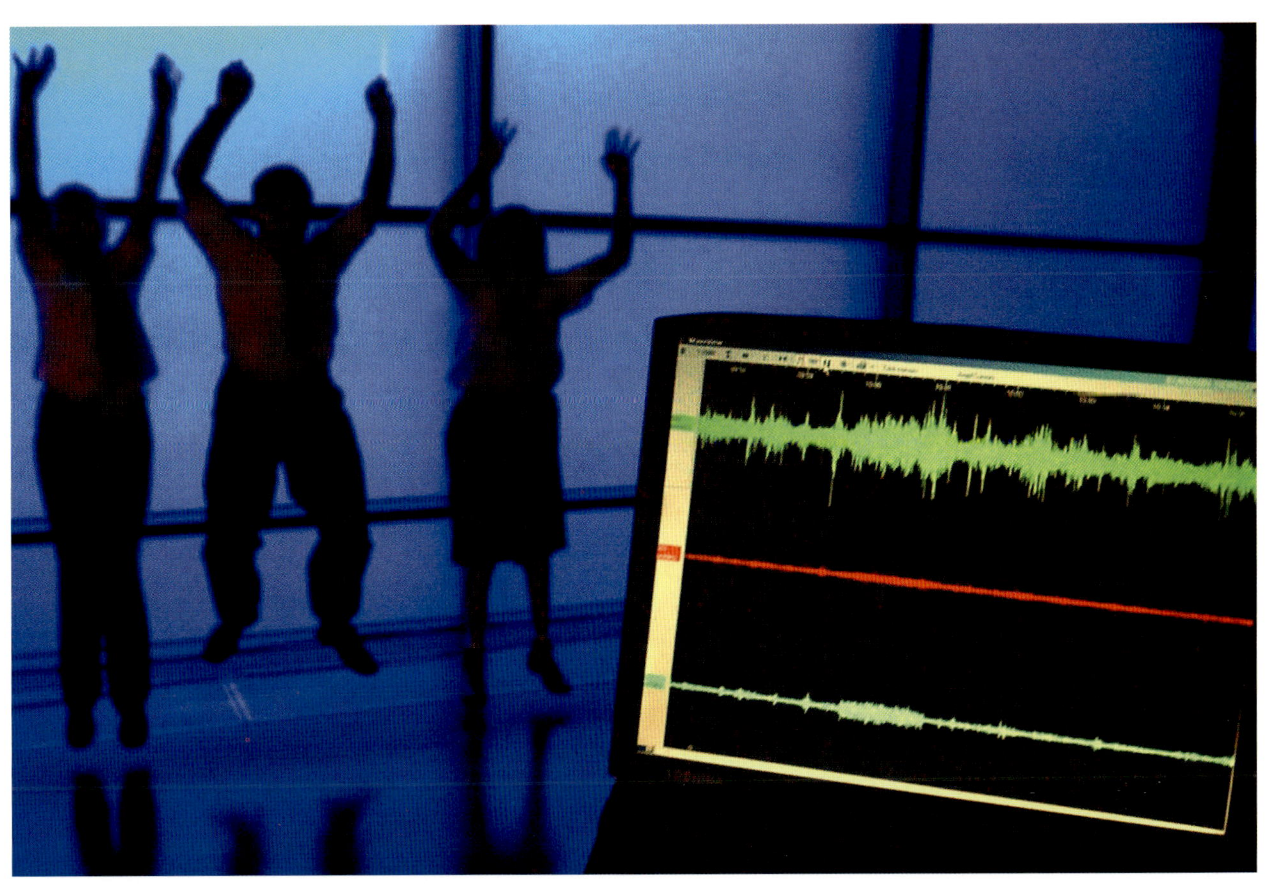

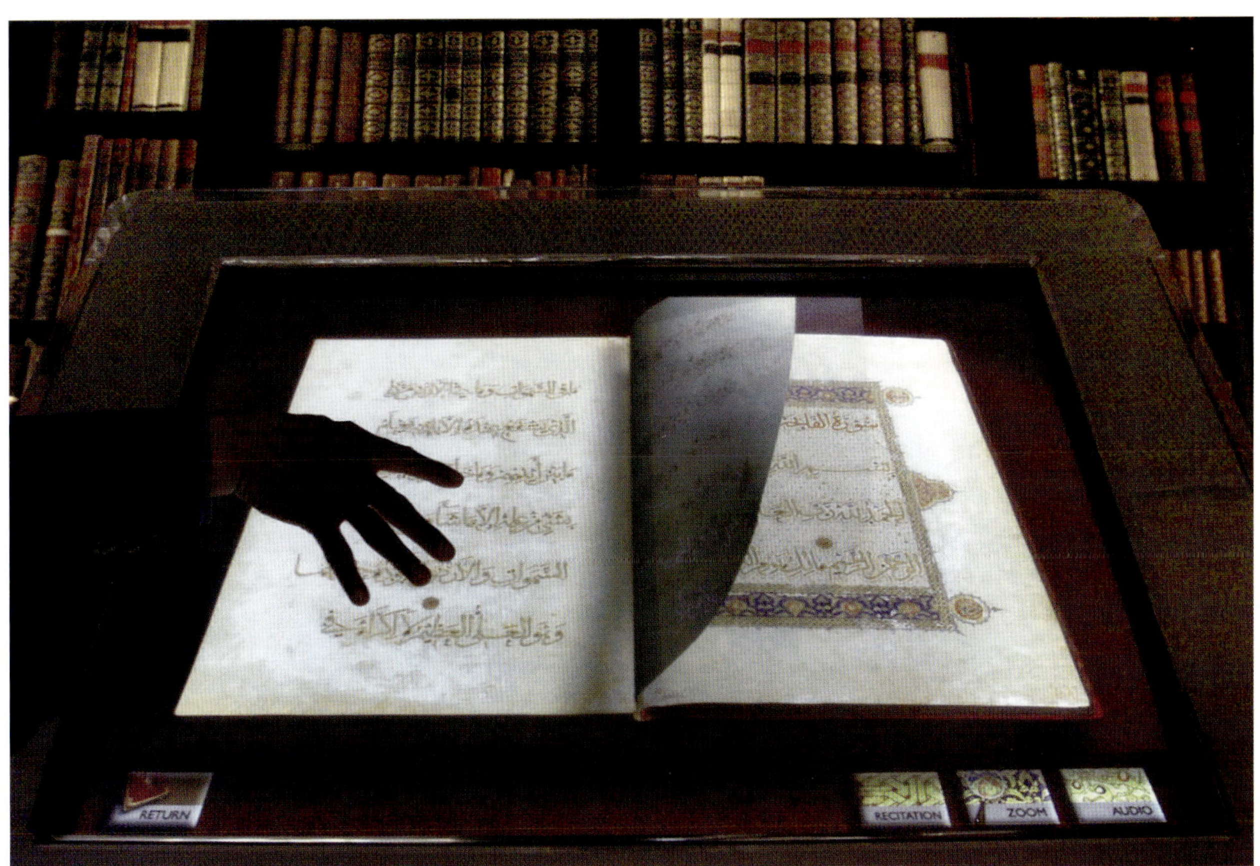
RETURN
RECITATION
ZOOM
AUDIO

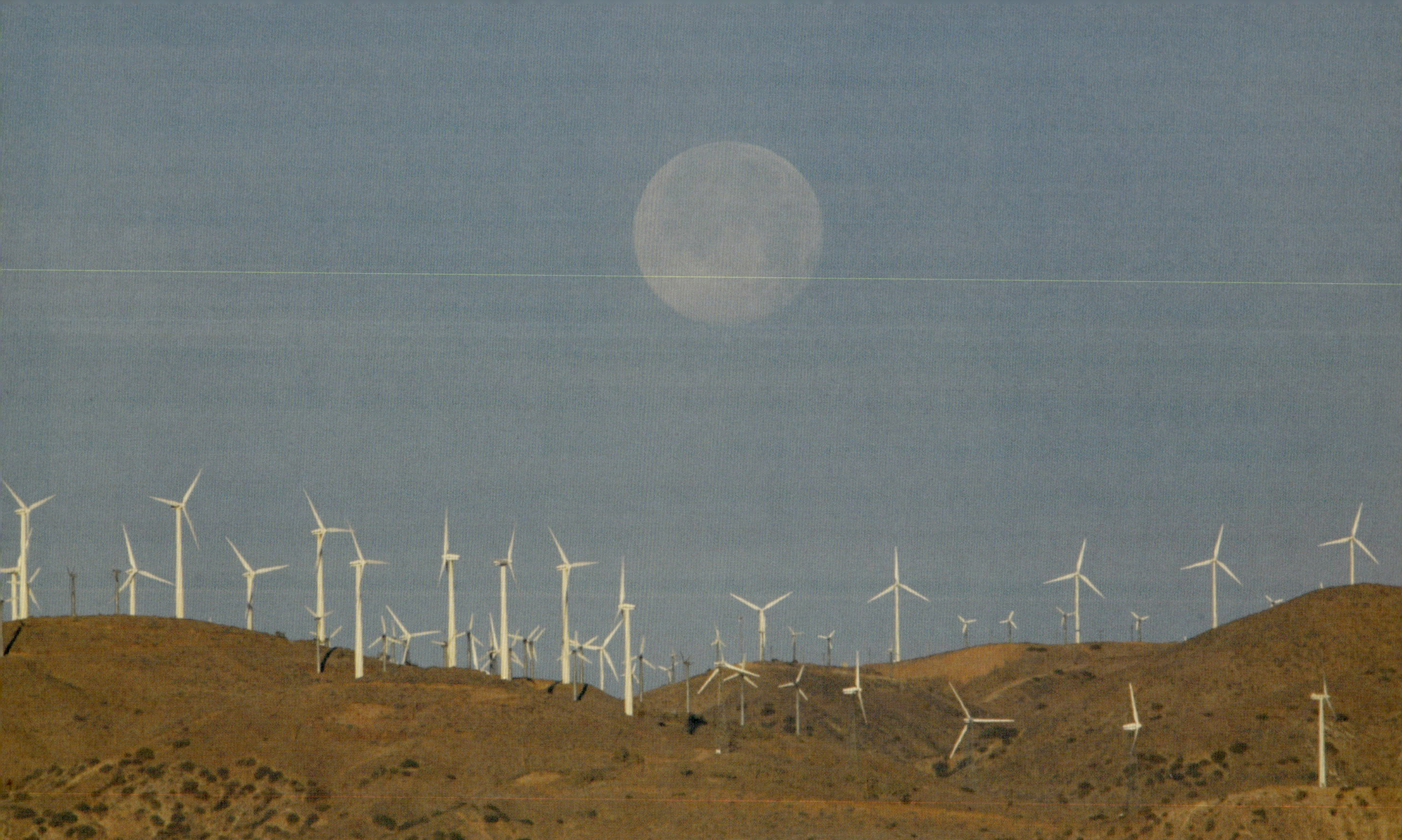

8 January 2004, MOJAVE DESERT, UNITED STATES

The full moon rises behind a wind farm in the Mojave Desert, California. California's energy plan requires power companies to generate 20 percent of electricity from natural resources by 2010. Although wind is free and wind farming produces no pollutants, it is not always the cheapest way to produce electricity. Toby Melville

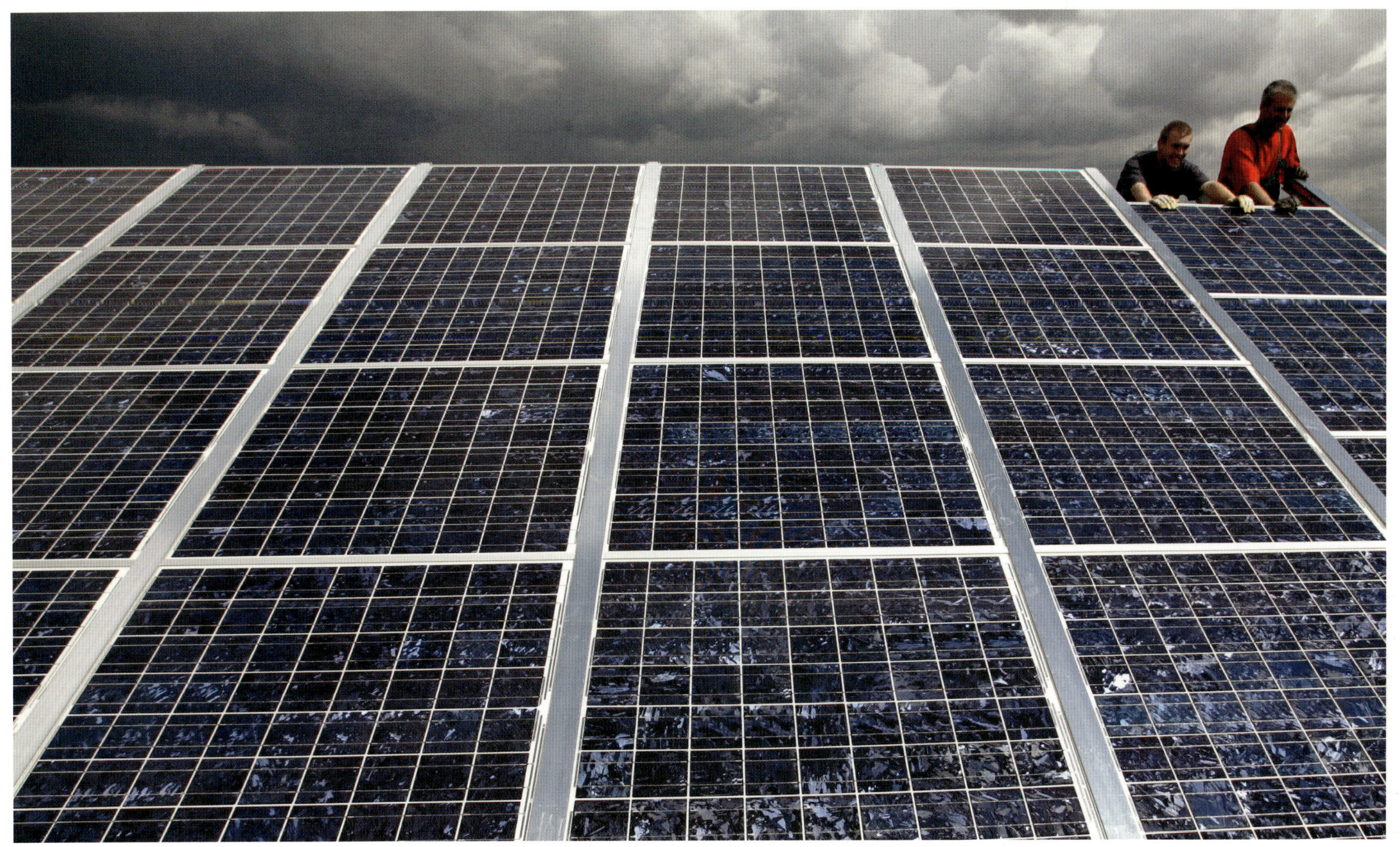

21 June 2004, GÖTTELBORN, GERMANY

Workers set up photovoltaic panels in the solar park project in Göttelborn, near the German city of Saarbrücken. The first construction phase of the park, built on the site of a decommissioned coal mine, was completed in August 2004. Eventually, the park will be the world's largest solar power plant, the size of 20 soccer pitches, consisting of 50,000 panels and with a capacity of 8 megawatts. Vincent Kessler

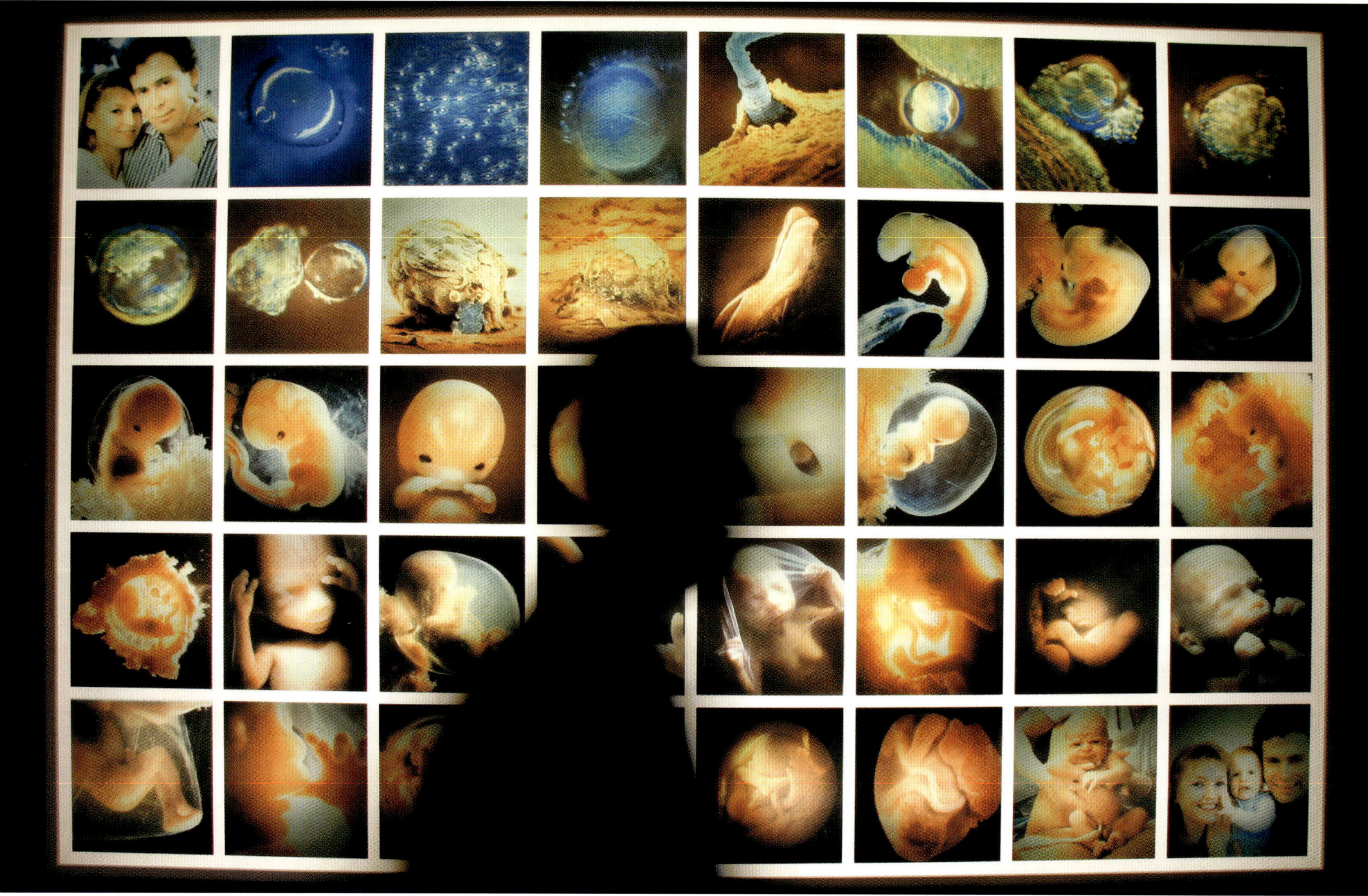

6 June 2005, ROME, ITALY

In the private clinic of controversial fertility doctor Severino Antinori, a figure is silhouetted against a panel of images showing the development of a human foetus (photographs by Lennart Nilsson from the book *A Child is Born*). Antinori made headlines in 1994 when a 62-year-old woman gave birth following fertility treatment administered by him. In 2004, a new law was passed in Italy that imposed much tougher regulations across all aspects of assisted fertility.
Alessia Pierdomenico

22 November 2000, GARCHING, GERMANY

Opposite above Samples of cows' brain tissue that are to be tested for Bovine Spongiform Encephalopathy (BSE) are examined by Petra Albrecht, an employee of Eurofins Scientific, in Garching near Munich. BSE can be passed to humans via the food chain, causing the deadly Creutzfeldt-Jacob disease. Michael Dalder

19 May 2004, HERTFORDSHIRE, UNITED KINGDOM

Opposite below Ampoules containing a medium for stem cell storage are displayed at the world's first embryonic stem cell bank. Stem cells are master cells in the body that have the capability to transform into any cell or tissue. Researchers believe they may eventually offer a revolutionary way to repair diseased and damaged body tissues. But opponents say such research is unethical because the extraction of stem cells from human embryos violates the rights of the embryo.
Peter Macdiarmid

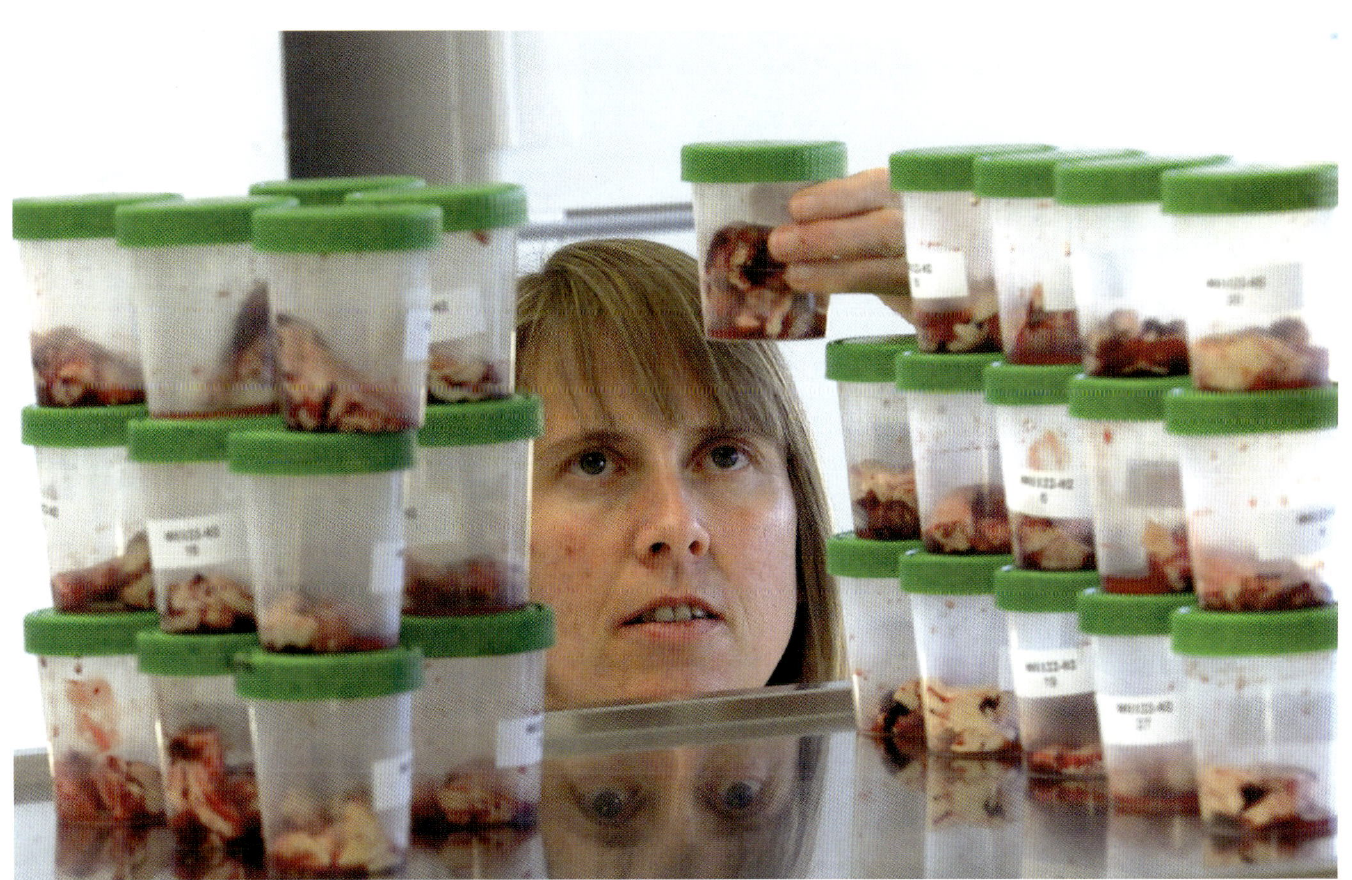

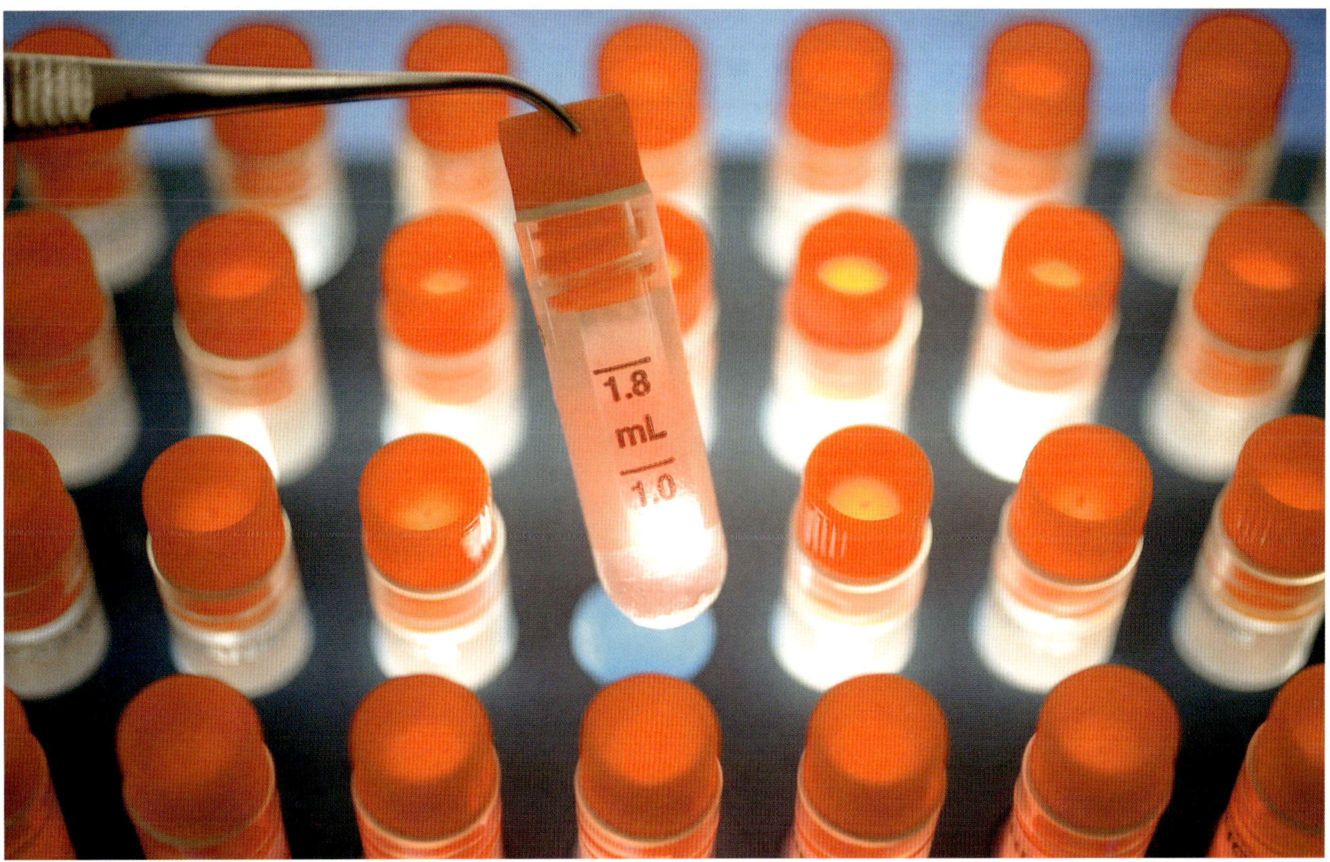
1.8
mL
1.0

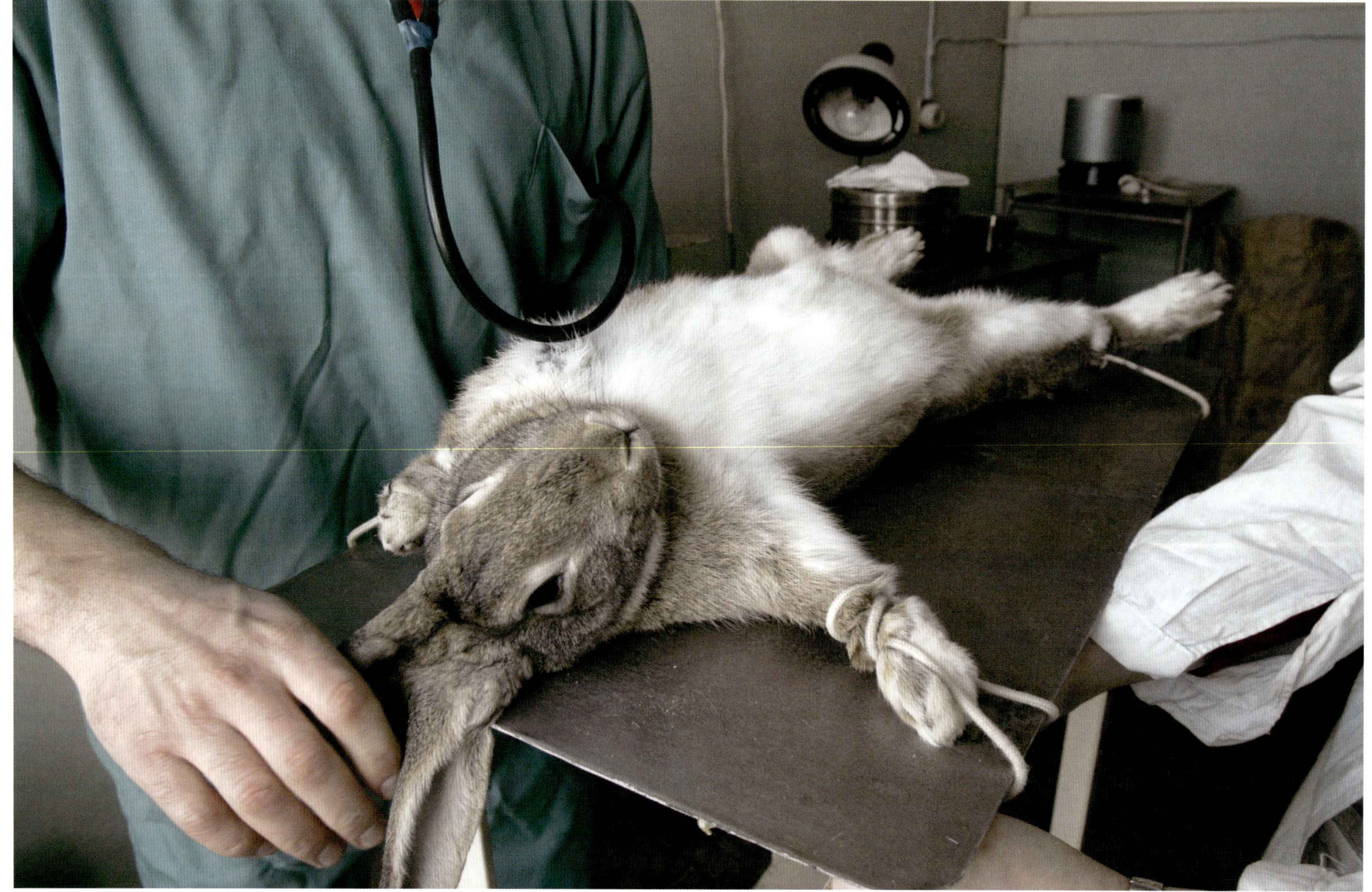

8 February 2005, MOSCOW, RUSSIA

A cloned rabbit is stretched out for tests at a biotechnology centre just outside Moscow. Many of those used in the research at the centre are clones of genetically modified rabbits which have had human genes added to their genomes. Scientists say milk from the resulting rabbits contains protein that helps treat cancer in humans. Viktor Korotayev

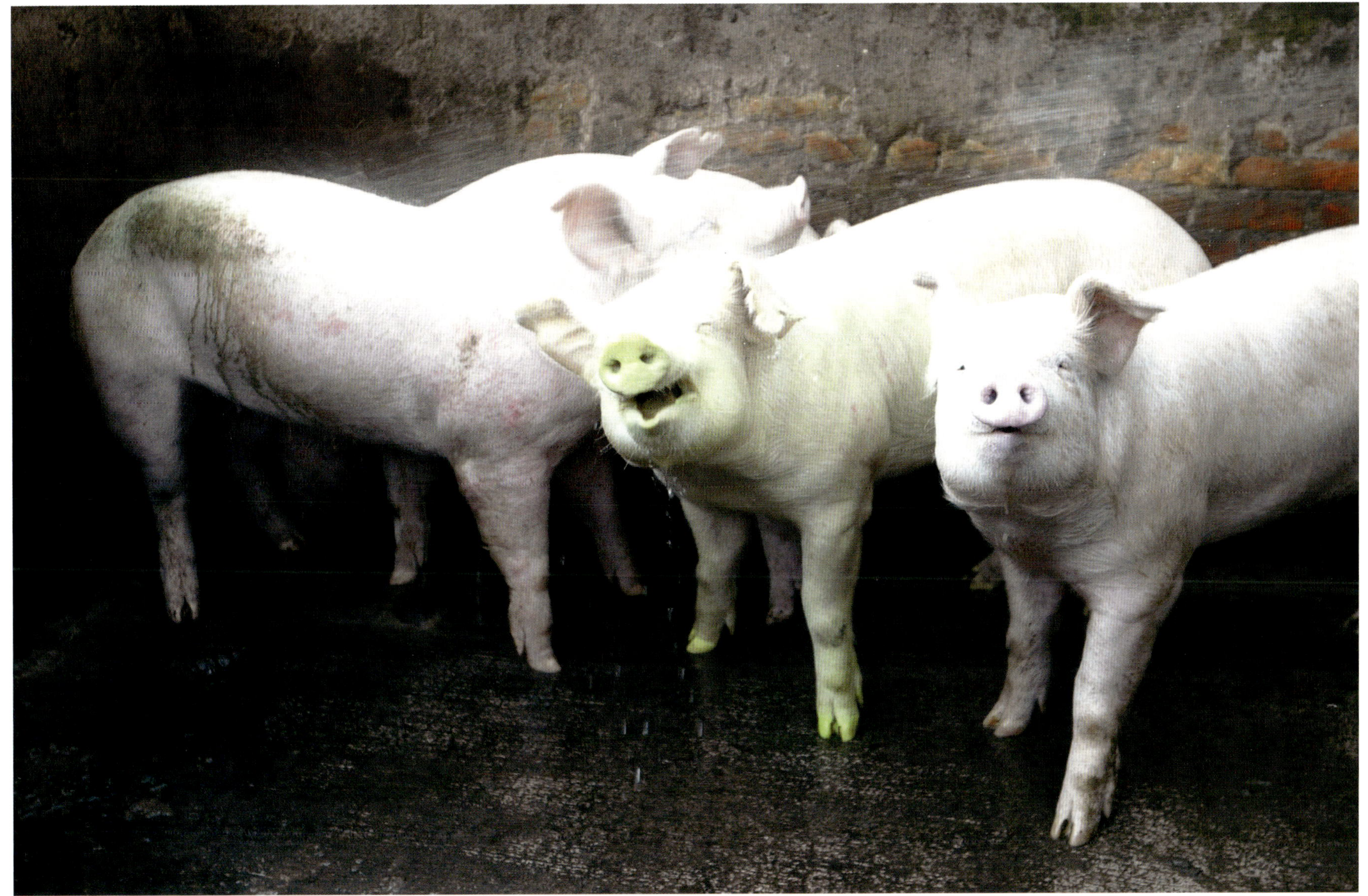

12 January 2006, TAIPEI, TAIWAN

A transgenic fluorescent green pig stands among normal pigs in Taipei. Researchers hope that the pigs, created by injecting fluorescent green protein into pig embryos, will boost stem cell research. Jay Cheng

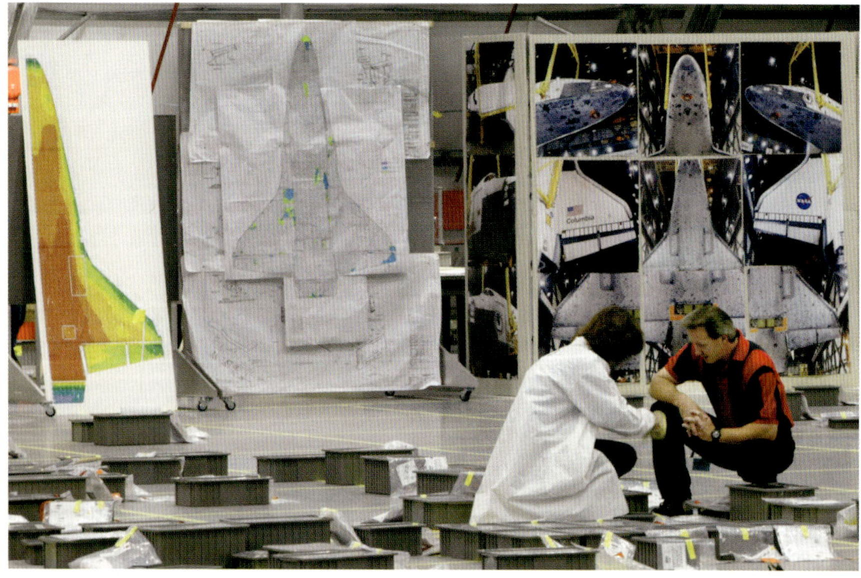

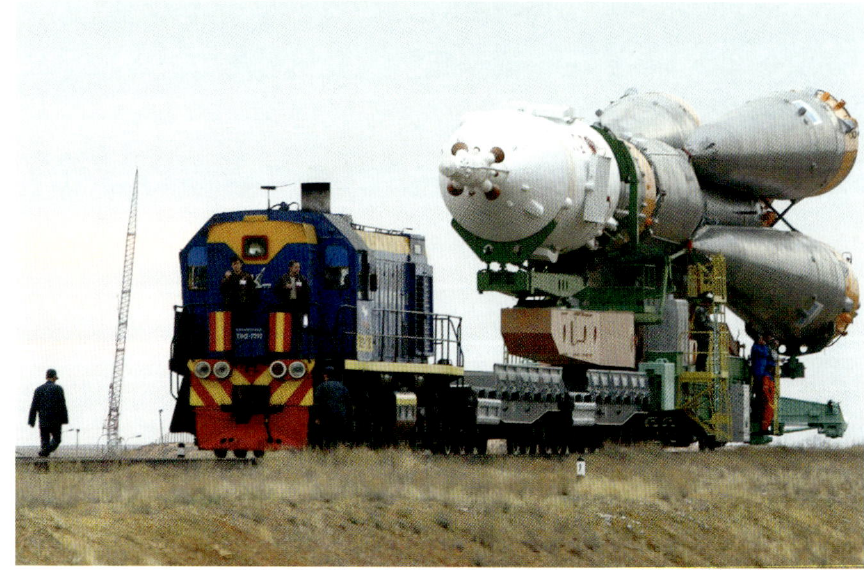

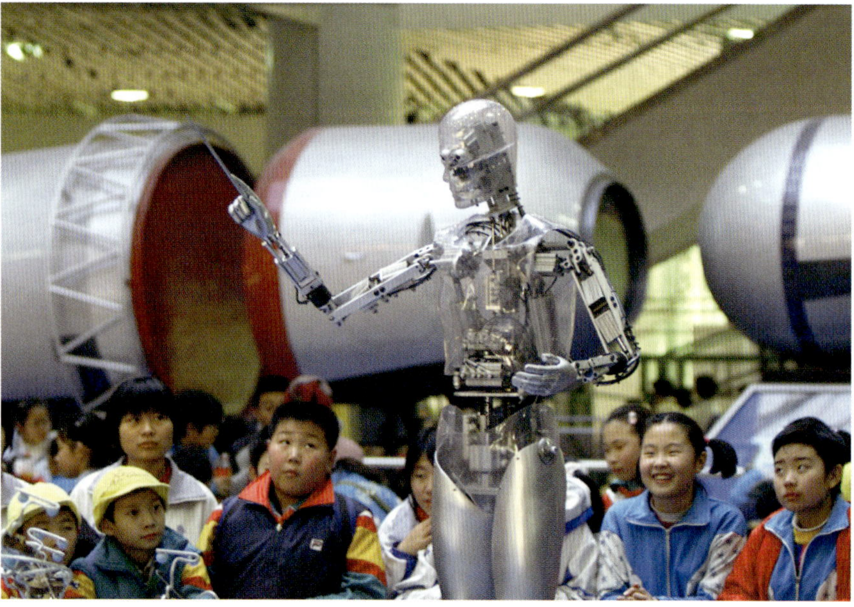

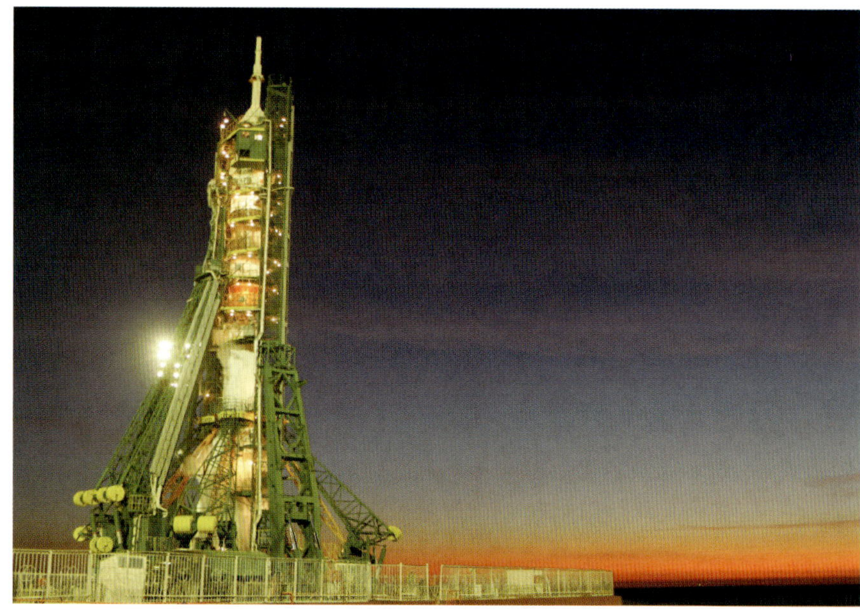

5 March 2003, CAPE CANAVERAL, UNITED STATES

Technicians at the Kennedy Space Center in Cape Canaveral, Florida, examine tile material from NASA's space shuttle Columbia, which disintegrated in the skies over Texas on 1 February 2003, killing all seven astronauts on board. Joe Skipper

22 November 2000, BEIJING, CHINA

A Chinese robot performs in front of a model of a Chinese spacecraft in Beijing. In November 2000 the Chinese government set forth ambitious targets for manned space flight, commercial satellite launches and the industrialization of space that would make China a leading player in space exploration and commerce in the coming decades. Andrew Wong

24 April 2003, BAIKONUR, KAZAKHSTAN

The Russian rocket Soyuz TMA-2 is transported to its launch pad in Baikonur, ready to carry U.S. astronaut Edward Lu and Russian Yuri Malenchenko to the International Space Station, where they were to spend six months in orbit. Baikonur is the world's biggest cosmodrome. It was built in the mid-1950s and was the top-secret centre of the Soviet space programme. Sergei Karpukhin

1 October 2005, BAIKONUR, KAZAKHSTAN

Russian spacecraft Soyuz TMA-7 prepares to launch. On board were U.S. astronaut William McArthur, Russian astronaut Valery Tokarev, and U.S. space tourist Gregory Olsen, who returned to earth 10 days later. The trip cost him a reported U.S. $20 million. Shamil Zhumatov

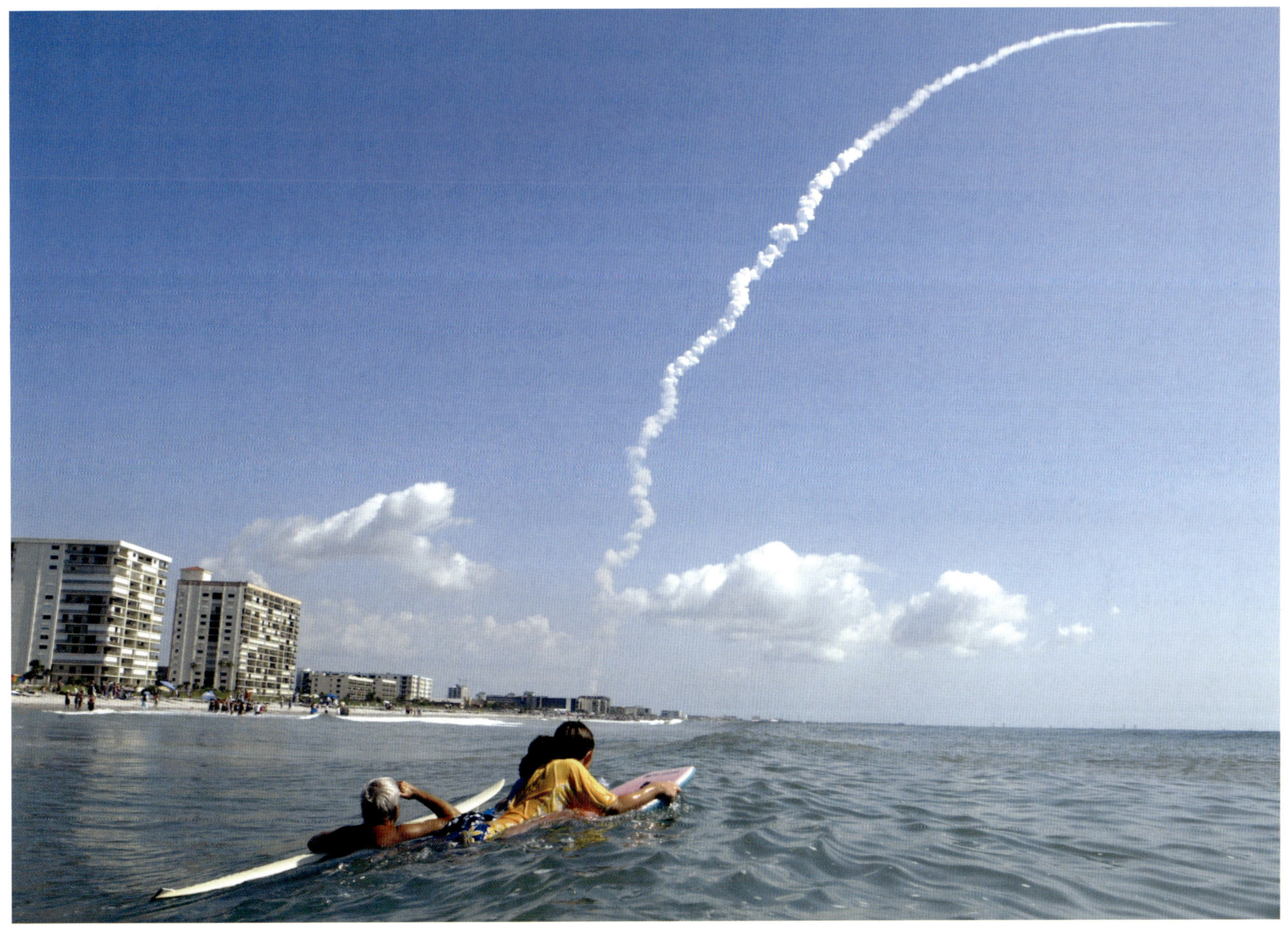

26 July 2005, CAPE CANAVERAL, UNITED STATES

The space shuttle Discovery lifts off from pad 39B at the Kennedy Space Center carrying a crew of seven astronauts bound for the International Space Station. This was the first of two successful 'Return to Flight' missions two and a half years after NASA's space shuttle Columbia broke apart as it returned to earth after a 16-day mission. Watching the take-off from Cocoa Beach are John DeBruyn and his grandsons Mark and Michael from Cheyenne, Wyoming. Marc Serota

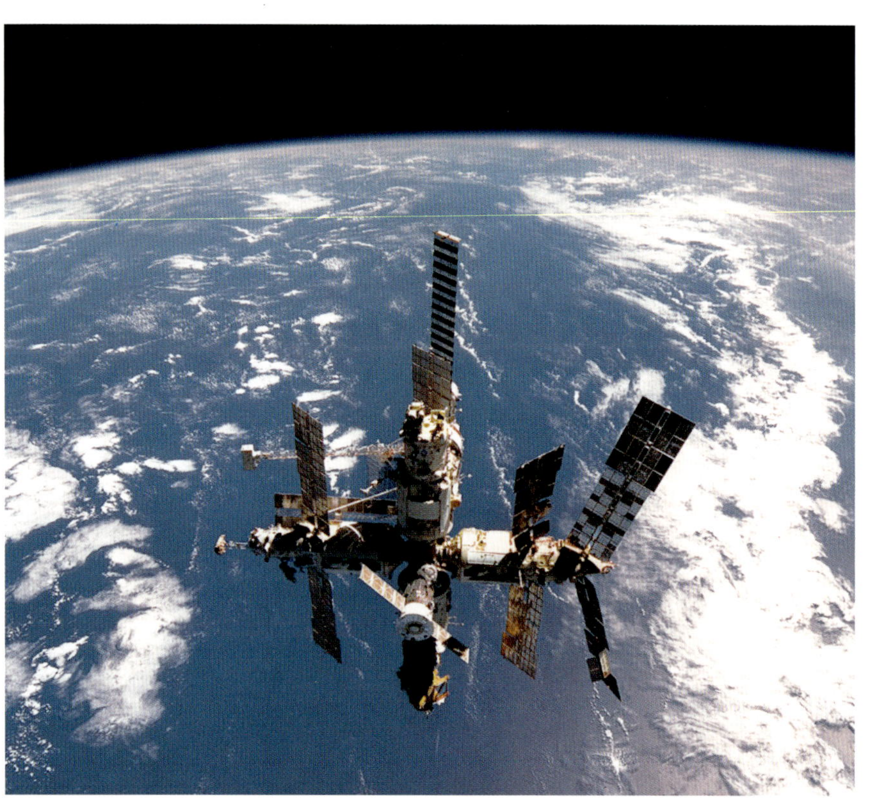

23 March 2001, SPACE

The fabled Russian space station Mir was guided back to earth in March 2001 after 15 years in orbit. Much of the structure disintegrated as it hit the earth's atmosphere, but the remainder plunged safely into the Pacific Ocean. Mir was the first inhabited long-term research station in space, visited by a total of 104 astronauts during its lifespan. This photograph shows it in orbit in June 1998. NASA

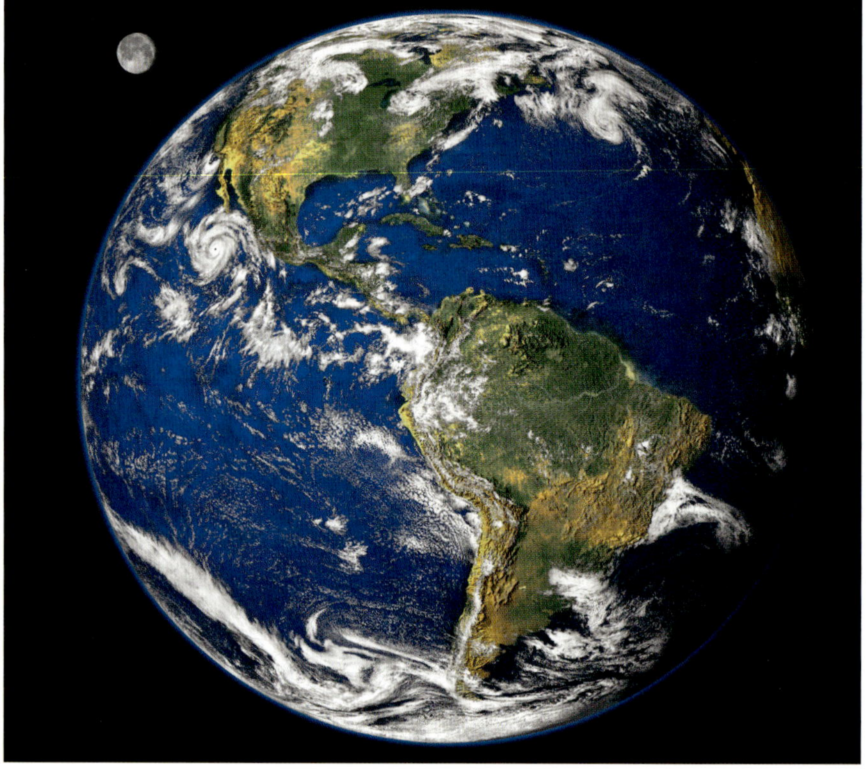

22 April 2000, SPACE

To mark Earth Day on 22 April 2000, NASA scientists released this new image of the earth, updating the famous 'Blue Marble' photograph taken by Apollo astronauts. The digital image uses data collected in 1997 from several satellites to approximate what a human could see from orbit, with the added artistic licence of having the moon in the background. The prominent storm raging off the west coast of North America is Hurricane Linda. The moon has been magnified to about twice its relative size. NASA

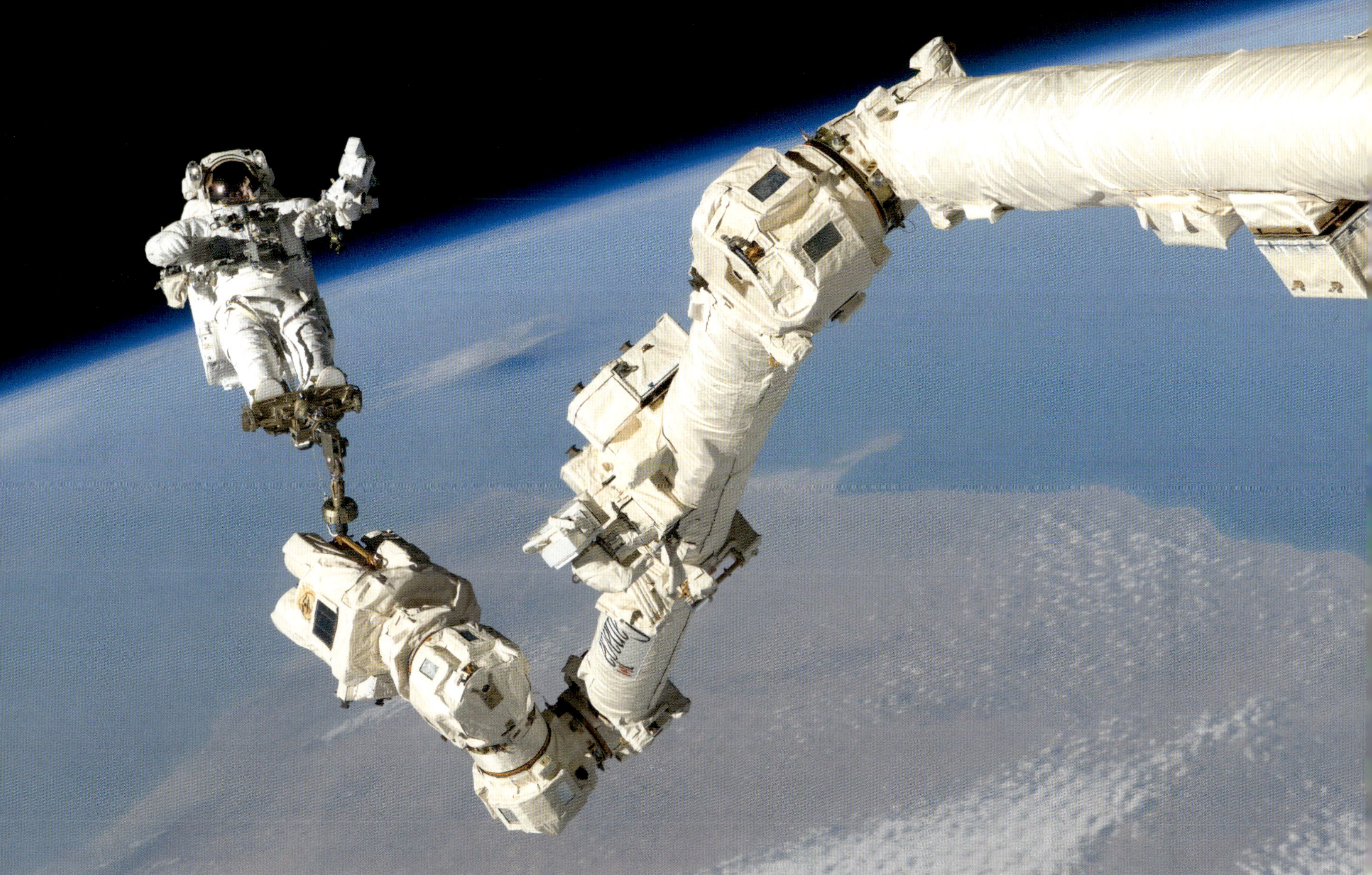

3 August 2005, SPACE

Astronaut Stephen Robinson makes the last of three spacewalks from the International Space Station during NASA's historic 'Return to Flight' STS-114 Mission. Anchored to the station's robotic arm, Robinson successfully completed a repair of the underside of the shuttle Discovery, something never previously attempted in space. NASA

15 March 2005, RAISTING, GERMANY

Following pages Telecommunication satellite dishes surround a church in the southern Bavarian village of Raisting, 40 km (25 miles) south of Munich.
Michaela Rehle

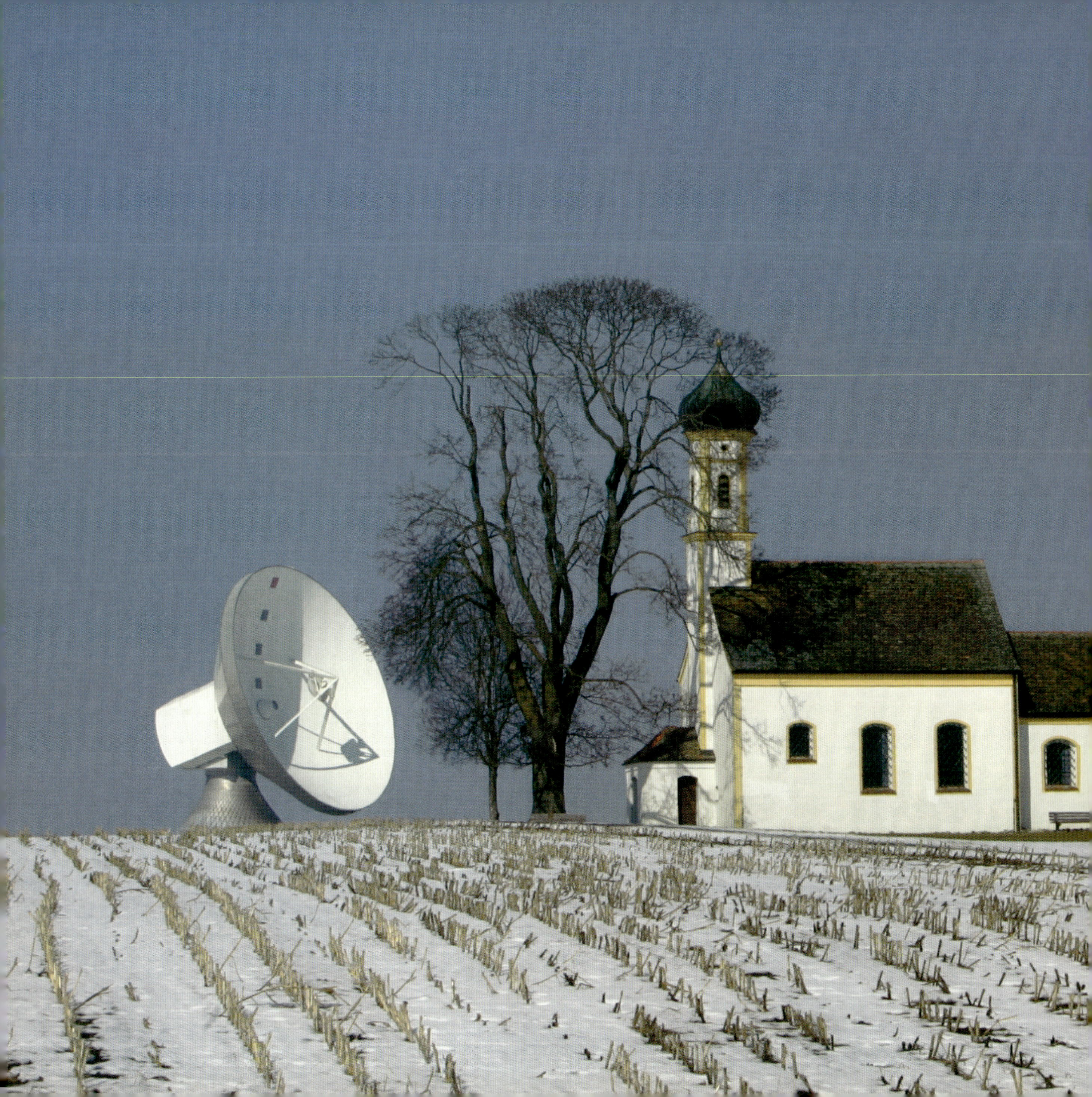

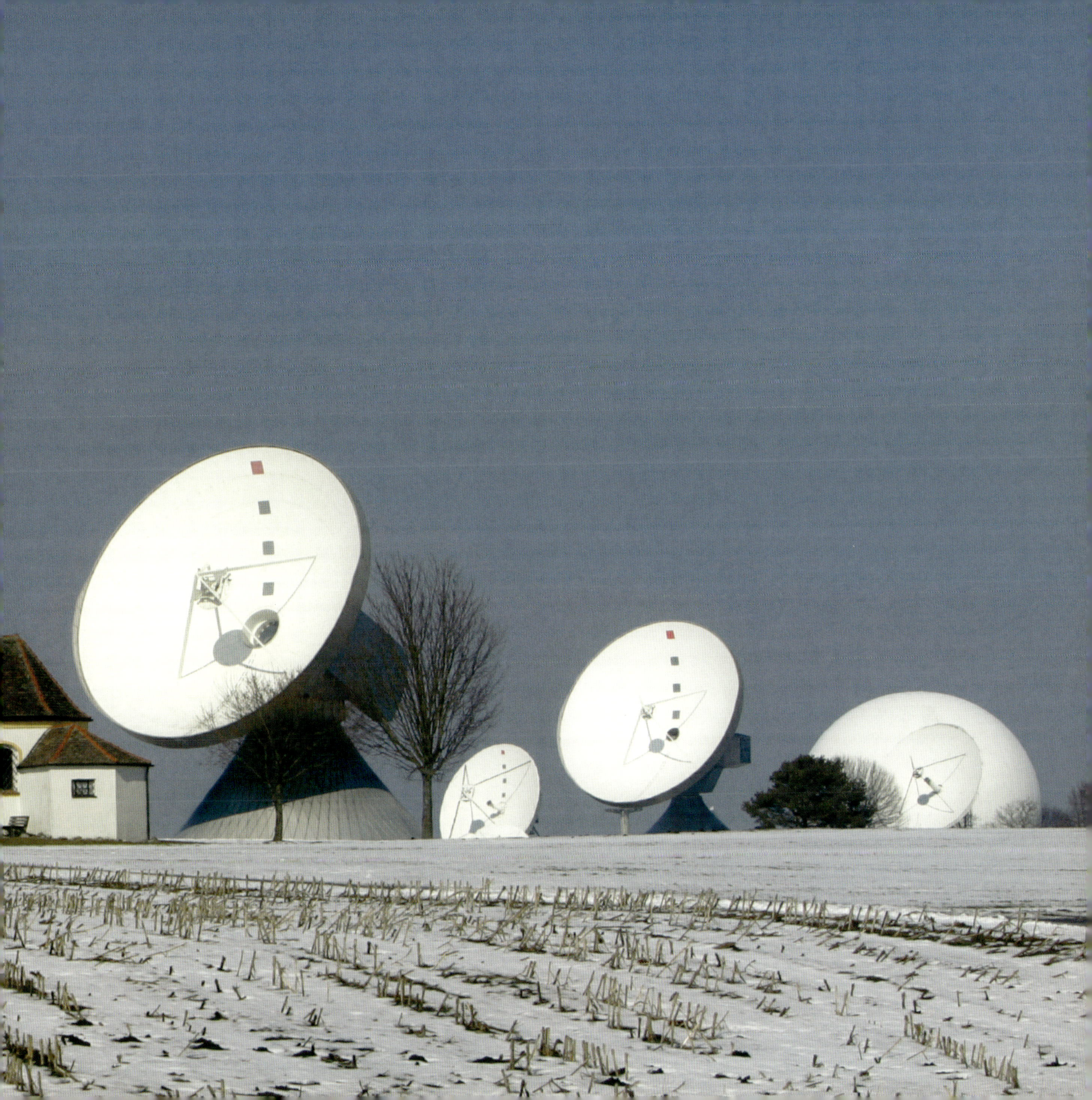

Early twentieth-century rationalists believed religion would simply fade away in time. They might be surprised to see the world today, where a multiplicity of faiths continues not only to shape the lives and identities of millions, but remains a source of bitter conflict between and within societies. Religion, in all its different expressions and moods, is still fundamental to human life across the globe.

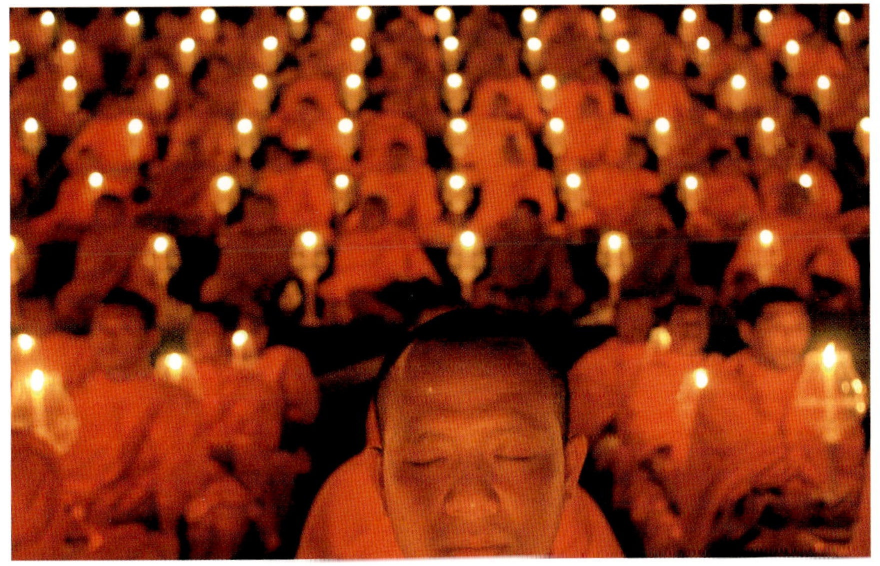

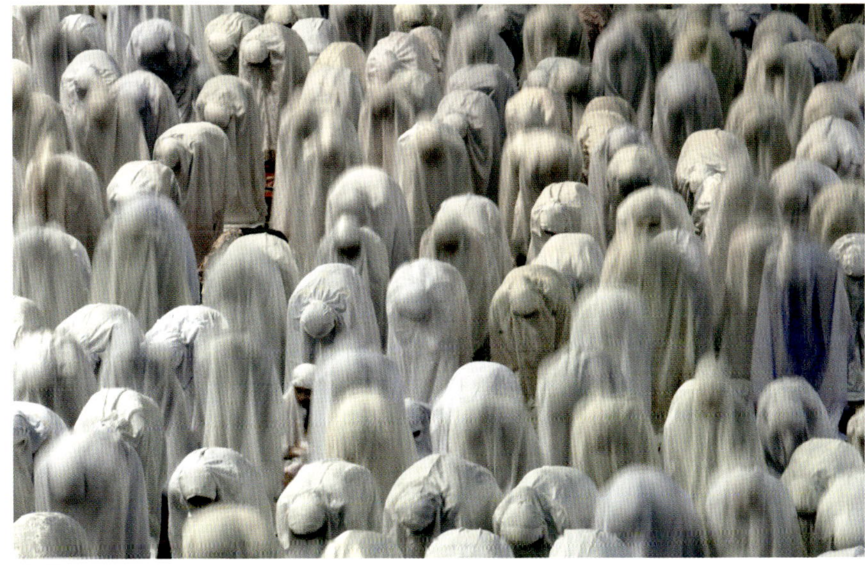

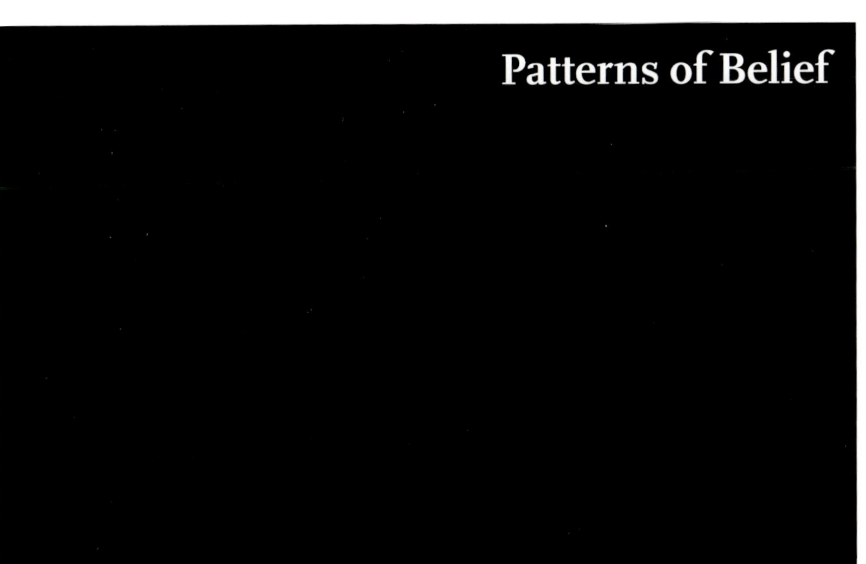

Patterns of Belief

World Faiths / Spirituality / Ritual
Identity / Memory / Tradition / Modernity
Worship / Celebration / Pilgrimage

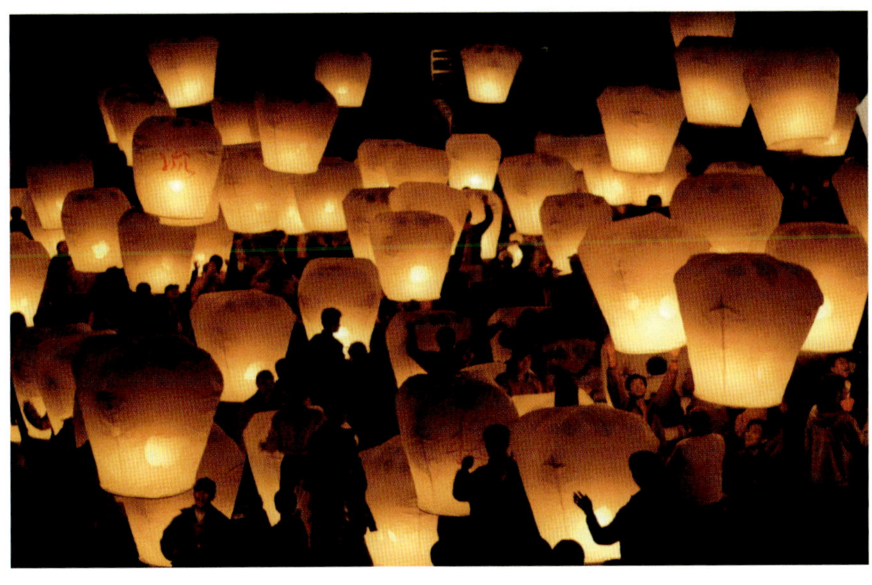

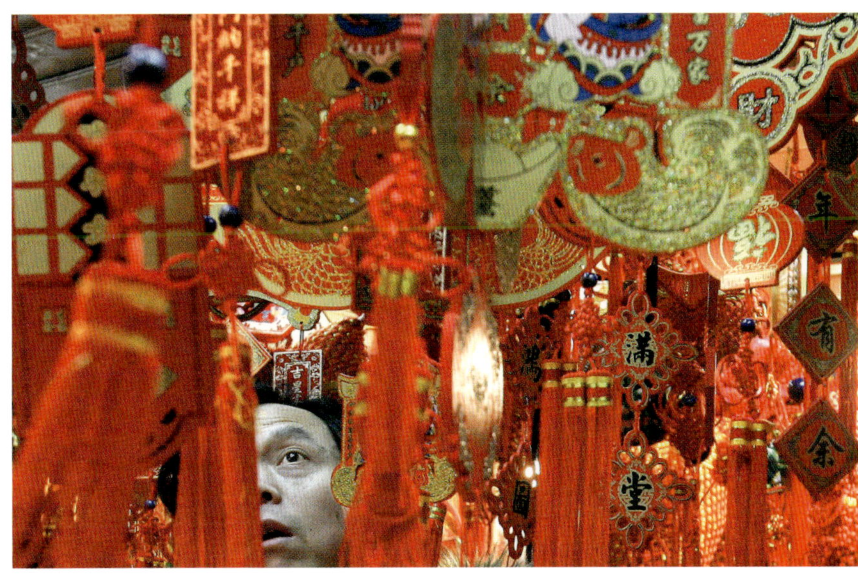

Patterns of Belief

'The twenty-first century will be religious or it will not be at all.' This forecast seemed baffling when French writer André Malraux made it in the early 1970s. The rich developed world seemed closer than ever to the day when, as intellectuals had been saying for over a century, reason and human progress would triumph and faith would fade away. In 1966, *Time* magazine asked 'Is God Dead?' on a stark black cover. Bounding ahead with each scientific discovery, humans were extending their control over so many aspects of life that the Almighty appeared to be in full retreat. He was expected to disappear from developing countries too as they followed the West on the path to prosperity.

Three decades later, religion has not only not faded away, it has roared back onto the scene with renewed vitality. Millions flock to the Muslim Haj in Mecca, the Catholic World Youth Days and the Hindu Maha Kumbh Mela in mass testimonies to belief. Disputes over issues such as abortion, cloning or the display of religious symbols rage in many countries. Religious superstars – most notably Pope John Paul II and the Dalai Lama – have inspired admiration as living symbols of integrity. Religious freedom has joined the world issues on the agenda of the United Nations.

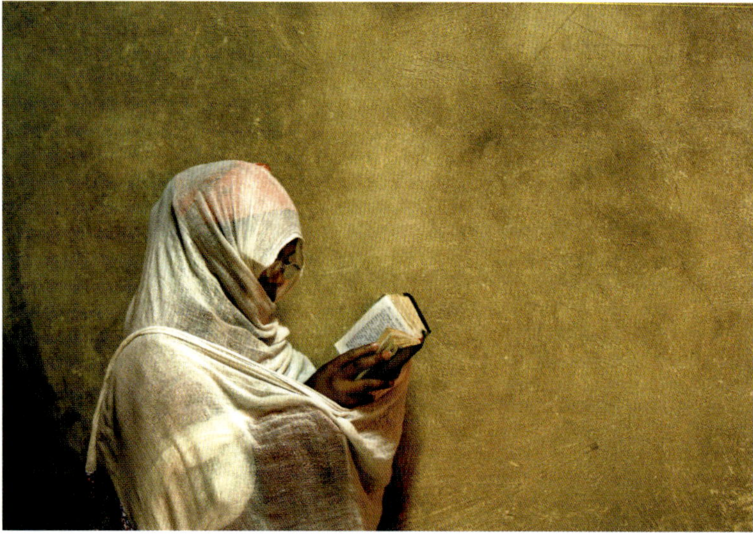

An Ethiopian woman reads from the Bible at the Holy Sepulchre Church in the Old City of Jerusalem. 8 April 2004, Jerry Lampen.

Around the world, this renewed religious vigour has appeared in myriad forms. As many Africans have turned away from their traditional animist religions, the door has been opened to aggressive missionary work by the two large monotheisms Islam and Christianity, which have competed and sometimes clashed in the search for new souls. In Latin America, struggles have emerged within Christianity, as dynamic evangelical groups have won followers from the more traditional Catholic Church with rousing church services and self-help programmes tailored to the needs of the uprooted urban poor. After seven decades of communism, the Russian Orthodox Church is reopening churches and attracting new believers. In still-communist China, rapid economic change has gone hand in hand with growing popular interest in Buddhism, Taoism, Islam and Christianity, which are tolerated within strict limits. Unofficial spiritual movements such as Falun Gong are harshly repressed.

Above all, religion made a stunning return to the world scene on September 11, 2001, when Osama bin Laden's al Qaeda militants crashed hijacked passenger airliners into New York's World Trade Center, claiming to act in God's name. Suddenly suicide bombers convinced that Paradise awaited them had brought the violence of the Middle East to the heart of the Western world. In the months and years that have followed, further bombings have hit Tunisia, Riyadh, Istanbul, Bali, Madrid and London. In U.S.-occupied Iraq, fundamentalist insurgents beheaded hostages like sacrificial lambs, to cries of 'Allahu Akbar'.

The term 'fundamentalist' has come to seem synonymous with a tiny violent minority among the world's 1.3 billion Muslims. But fundamentalism is not usually violent and Islam is not the only religion that has experienced its resurgence. The world's largest faith, Christianity (2.1 billion), has seen evangelical Christians become a political force crucial for electing George W. Bush U.S. president in 2000 and 2004. These conservative Protestants interpret the Bible literally and campaign vociferously against abortion, gay marriage and the teaching of evolution in schools. Israel's settler movement reads its scriptures as a map that entitles them to reclaim Biblical land from the Palestinians. In officially secular India, Hindu nationalists eager to reassert the rights of the country's dominant faith have won seats in national and state elections. Even gentle Buddhism has got bound up with militant nationalism in Sri Lanka.

Often branded as backward, fundamentalism is actually a modern phenomenon in which believers faced by rapid social change seek security in age-old scriptures. Fundamentalists reject modernism – the secular outlook that crowds God out of public life – but not modernity. They happily use cell phones, email and satellite television, but staunchly defend traditional moral values, finding in them the sense, certainty and community that they miss in modern everyday life. Many of today's religious extremists are city people, some with higher degrees in science and technology. Some of them retreat into tight communities, others enter the political fray to defend their interests and beliefs. Since the 1980s, a 'globalized Islam' has developed seeking to create a purer form of the faith. Both very conservative and very modern, the new faithful around the world visit Muslim websites, seek religious advice by email, and assert an Islamic identity. The vast majority is peaceful, but on the radical fringe, violent 'jihadi' militants veil their anti-Western struggle as a religious crusade, invoking Islam to inspire suicide bombers like generals used nationalist slogans to send troops to the trenches.

All this can seem quite perplexing in parts of the West, especially in Europe, where the great cathedrals are filled mostly with tourists. Human progress and divine retreat have been linked in Western thinking for over two centuries. At least since the 1789 French Revolution, successive secular ideologies have provided new ways to see the world. Scientific discoveries, social science and modern management seemed to deliver the tools to master man's destiny and made continuing secularization seem inevitable. But there was a darker side. Nationalism and imperialism in the nineteenth century and fascism and communism in the twentieth rallied or bullied whole populations into conflict with rival states, and stimulated religious and ethnic persecution. Rising tensions between the competing secular ideologies of Nazism, communism and democracy culminated in the Second World War that devastated large parts of Europe and Asia and claimed 50 million lives. The horrors of that war, especially the Holocaust of six million Jews, left many with the bitter sense that God had abandoned humankind.

Religion has not only not faded away, it has roared back onto the scene with renewed vitality.

In the post-war period, reconstructed economies again promised a bright future of longer lives, better health and plentiful consumer goods. In the developing world, national leaders replaced colonial masters and a 'green revolution' promised more abundant food. But already by the 1960s the paradigm was beginning to shift. In the West, students revolted against authority and a soulless work life they saw ahead of them. Soviet bloc economies slipped further behind the West, in a slide that ended in 1990–91 with the collapse of Moscow's empire and the end of communism as a potent ideology. Israel's victories over Muslim armies spread doubt about Arab nationalist governments and prompted a turn towards political Islam. Corruption, war and unfair trade kept poor countries from progressing. The early phases of globalization flooded poor traditional societies with Western goods and evils. In the Muslim world, the backlash was strongest in Iran, where black-robed Shi'ite clergy overthrew the pro-Western modernizer Shah Reza Pahlevi in 1979 and put Islamic issues firmly onto the world agenda. Ayatollah Ruhollah Khomeini urged Muslims across the Middle East to follow Iran's example. This challenge spurred Saudi Arabia, home to Islam's holiest places, to set out to spread its own strict Wahhabi Islam to counter the Iranian challenge.

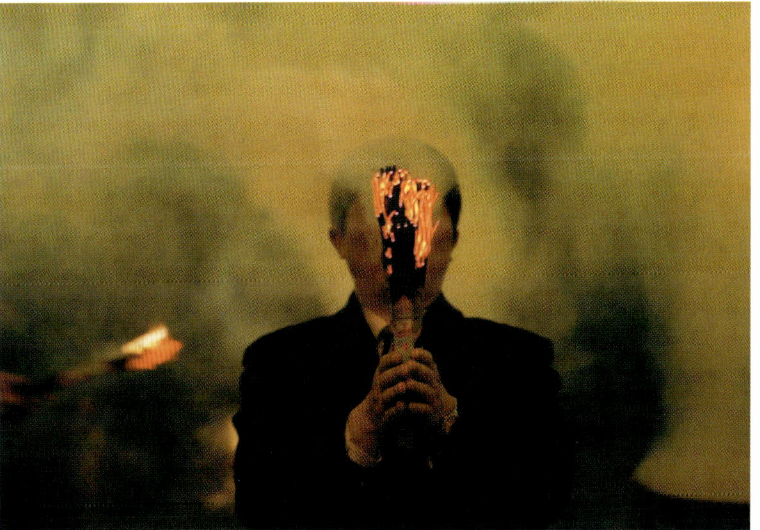

A man holds burning incense as he prays at Longhua Buddhist Temple in Shanghai, China. 1 January 2003, Guang Niu.

So the very factors that were supposed to kill off religion have in fact ended up reopening a space for the sacred in the developed world. Modern life has vastly improved standards of living but the freedoms it has brought can be frightening. Many miss a deeper meaning in the daily chase for ever more money, sex and fun. Migrants seeking work in cities and foreign countries lose their traditional identities and support networks. Instead of marching behind religious banners or national flags, the masses now flock to malls flying the United Colours of Benetton. Post-modern economic and political systems provide no higher purpose, so religion has come back to fill the 'God-shaped hole' that some people feel in their lives.

The widespread revival of religion does not, however, mean that established churches will necessarily regain their lost flocks. Fear of a wrathful God, an age-old spur to religious practice, has less place in our post-modern era. Relativism reigns: there is no fixed authority and free individuals embrace or ignore values at their will. Many people describe themselves as 'spiritual but not religious', which has led to an approach called 'believing without belonging'. Young Catholics may skip Sunday Mass but attend World Youth Days, the highly successful brainchild of Pope John Paul II. The Polish pontiff's own death and funeral in April 2005 turned into a global media event that touched far more than the world's 1.1 billion Catholics.

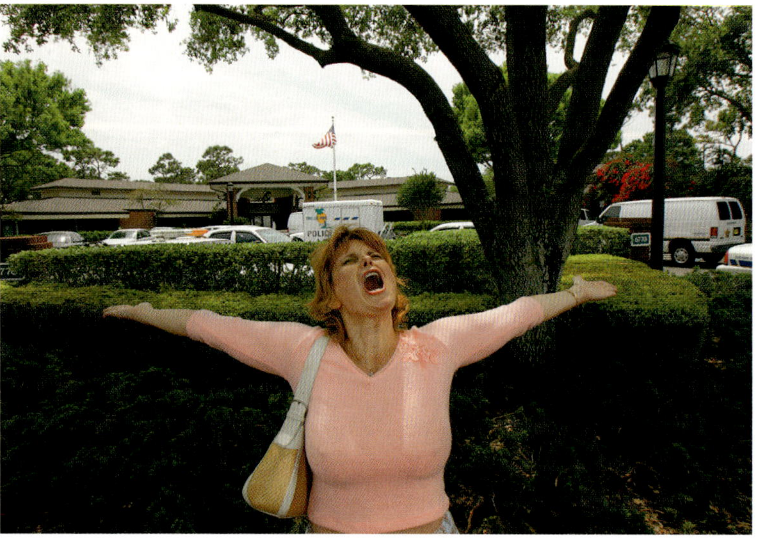

A protester screams in front of the Woodside Hospice in Pinellas Park, Florida, in response to news of the death of Terri Schiavo 13 days after a court decision to withdraw her feeding tube. The fate of the brain-damaged woman provoked a bitter legal and moral dispute in the United States over an individual's right to die. 31 March 2005, Carlos Barria.

The Internet has been one of the forces creating a level playing field. Websites about faith and spirituality are as popular as those offering pornography, gambling or stock trading. Irish Jesuits' daily prayers, ask-the-rabbi chatrooms and online fatwas from Mecca are all only a click or two away. When the Methodist Church in Britain launched an interactive church website in 2004, it got a stunning 41,000 visits in a single day.

Cults, sects and New Age spiritualities have also mushroomed in recent decades as seekers look beyond established churches. Some charismatic leaders have created large networks of followers for movements such as Transcendental Meditation or Scientology. Small-time gurus have exploited the gullible, sometimes even leading them to suicide. Fads have sprung up around mystic traditions such as Sufi Islam or Jewish Kabbalah. Even militant atheism, once a bold alternative to belief, has weakened as the power of established churches has waned. An atheist icon, British philosopher Anthony Flew, stunned his fans in 2004 when he announced he no longer ruled out the existence of a transcendental power.

Many miss a deeper meaning in the daily chase for ever more money, sex and fun.

Amid all this freelance spirituality, religion has also become an identity badge reaffirming links between individuals and communities as globalization erases borders between countries and ethnic groups. This takes us back to an original meaning of the word, related to the Latin *religare*, 'to bind together', and is giving religion a political importance that demographic trends indicate is likely to grow. Highly secularized regions such as Europe have low birthrates while the 'Global South', where religion is very much a part of life, makes up an ever greater majority of the world's population. So workers migrating to rich countries often bring conservative versions of faith which can change the religious balance in the receiving country. In the case of Muslims, this is sometimes anti-Western as well. This can cause tensions when local residents object to the newcomers' customs. In some cases, previously remote conflicts are imported. In France early in this decade, Muslim youths enraged by tough Israeli policies against Palestinians launched revenge attacks on local Jews.

Within Christianity, the Anglican Communion is near schism because its conservative Third World majority opposes liberal policies of member churches in the United States, Britain and Canada. With two-thirds of all Catholics now living in developing countries, the Vatican has little reason to enact the liberal reforms that critics in the rich West call for. In fact, Pope Benedict XVI spoke out early in his papacy against artificial insemination, abortion and

Post-modernity sees religion as one lifestyle choice among many.

gay marriage in Italy. Differences such as these could increasingly pit Christian churches against the secular societies they live in, especially as there is every reason to expect that secularizing trends will continue in rich developed countries, even the United States. The post-modern focus on individual autonomy fits well into the economic model of globalized consumerism. That this produces a religious backlash among part of the population does not contradict the trend. Post-modernity sees religion as one lifestyle choice among many. Churches may attract large flocks, but they have no broad authority over society anymore. Many believers steeped in an individualistic culture do not want to return to the orthodoxy of the past. For them, spiritual searching often trumps dogmatic certainty.

Against the growing conservatism of much established Christianity, Islam may face a different trend. Only 20 per cent of the world's Muslims now live in the Middle East, the religion's under-developed heartland. From traditionally moderate Muslims of Indonesia and Malaysia to newly Westernized generations in Europe and North America, Muslims are gradually redefining their faith. Living in freer societies, they can explore new thoughts that are taboo in the more controlled Middle East. Their debates could change Islam from within by reinterpreting its scriptures from a more individual point of view. Non-Muslims often assume this will lead towards a 'moderate Islam' and eventual secularization, but there is no guarantee that Islam in the new millennium will mimic the development of Christianity over the past two centuries.

Predicting the future is hazardous, which may explain why Malraux uttered his prediction in private but publicly denied

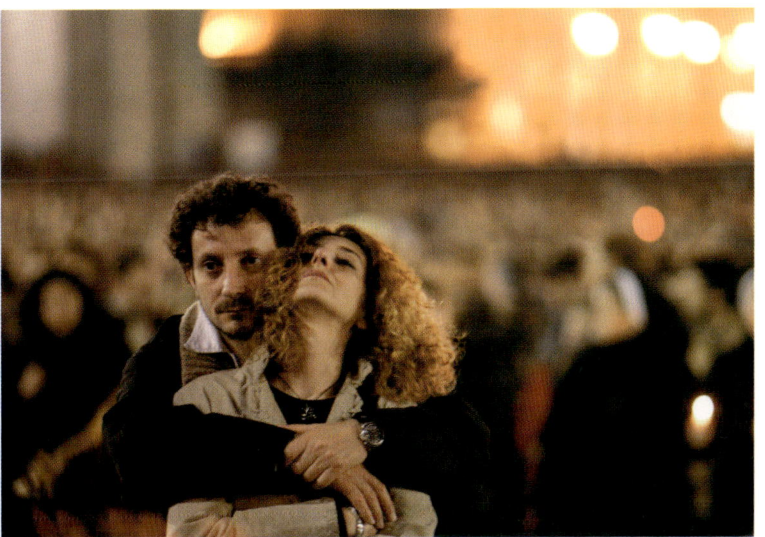

A couple embrace after hearing the news of the death of Pope John Paul II on 2 April 2005 during a vigil in St Peter's Square in the Vatican. In the following days, millions of pilgrims flocked to Rome to pay their respects and witness the funeral, which was attended by dozens of political and religious leaders from around the world. Dylan Martinez.

saying it. The lack of a written record has led to a debate among scholars about whether he actually said the twenty-first century would be religious, spiritual or mystical. As things look now, it may turn out to be all three.

Tom Heneghan has covered politics, business, war and religion in over 30 countries since joining Reuters in 1977. As Religion Editor since 2003, he has overseen worldwide religion coverage and reported on issues such as the death of Pope John Paul II and the integration of Muslims in Europe. He reported from London, Vienna, Geneva, Islamabad, Bangkok, Hong Kong and Bonn before moving to Paris in 1997. He has written *Unchained Eagle: Germany After The Wall* and chapters in several Reuters books.

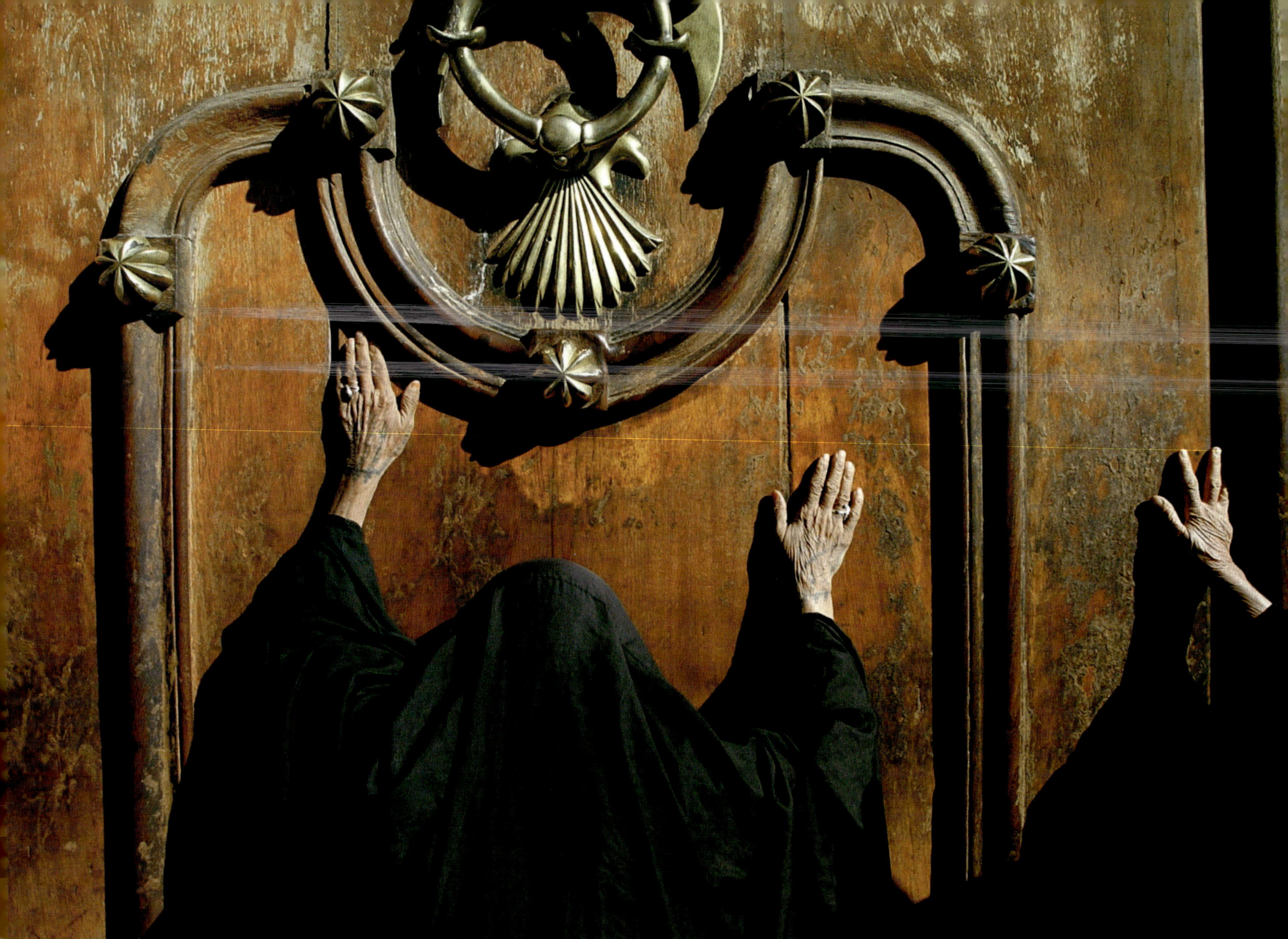

13 March 2003, AL-KAZIMIYA, IRAQ

Shi'ite Muslim women touch the door of the shrine of Imam al-Kazim in al-Kazimiya, an ancient city that is now a suburb of Baghdad, as Shi'ites mark Ashura, the day in 680 AD that Imam Hussein, the grandson of the Prophet Mohammed, was killed in a battle with a rival Muslim faction. Goran Tomasevic

5 June 2001, JERUSALEM, ISRAEL

Orthodox Jews pray at the Western Wall, Judaism's holiest site in the Old City of Jerusalem. Natalie Behring

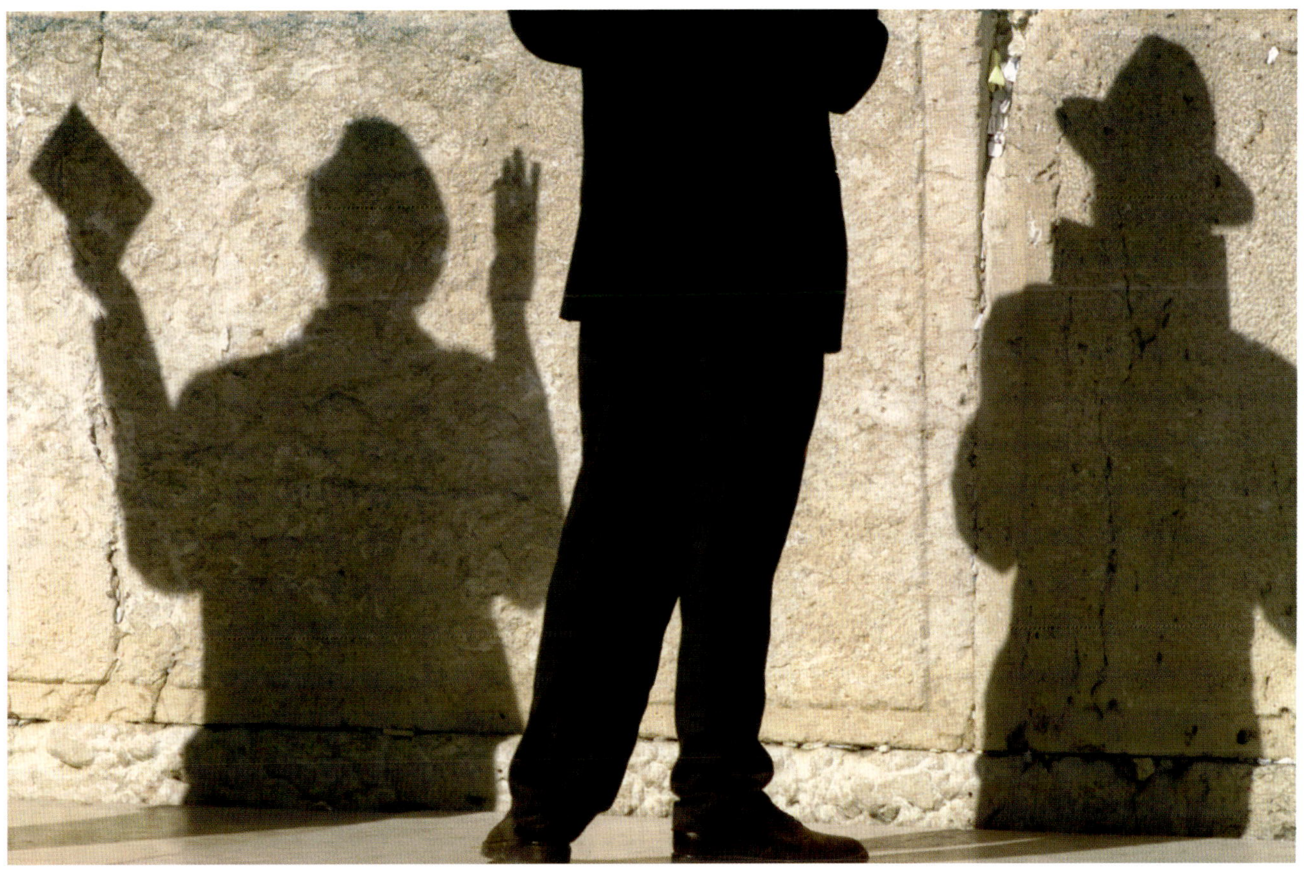

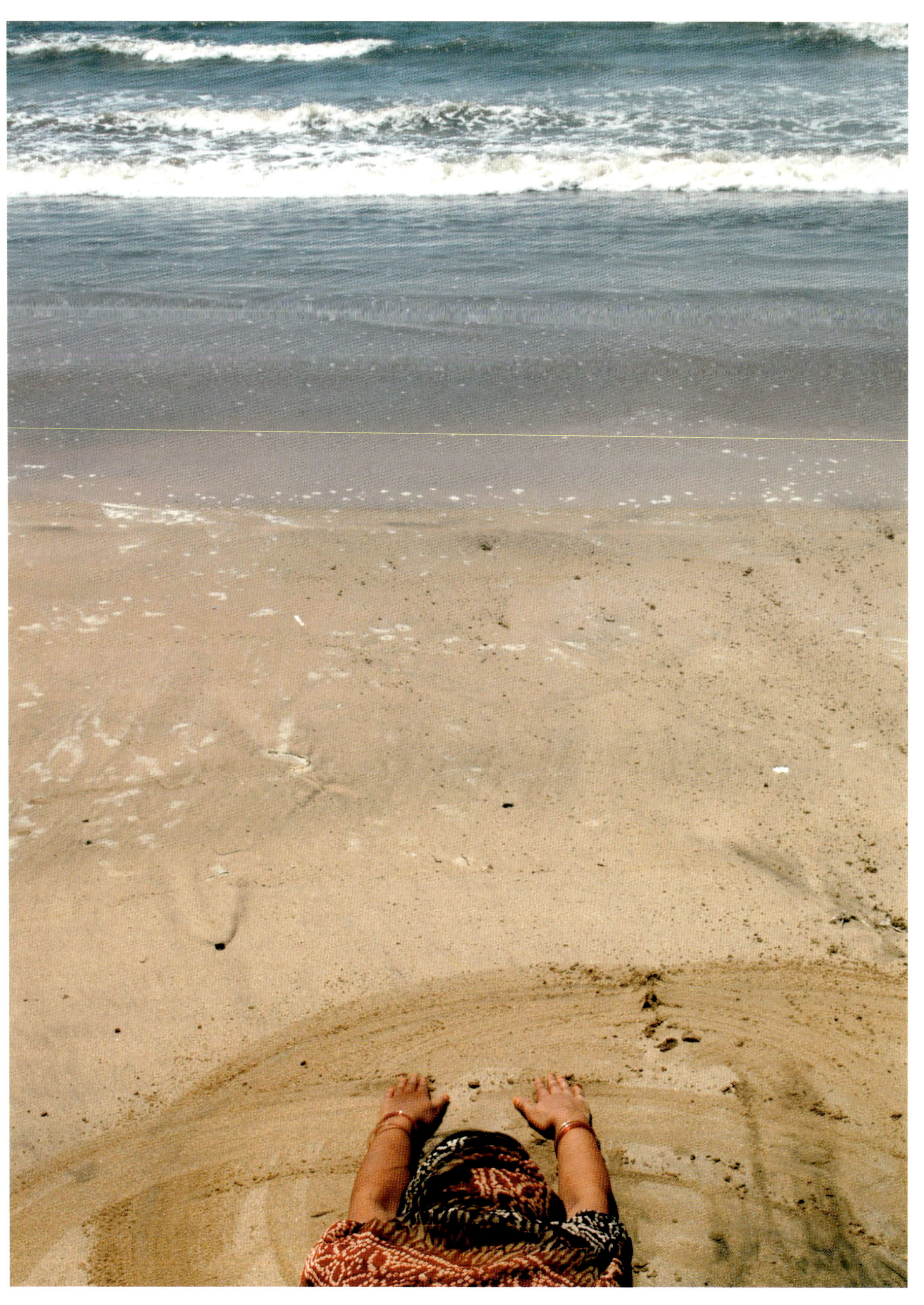

9 April 2005, MUMBAI, INDIA

This page A Hindu woman worships the earth in a ritual marking the new year in Mumbai, in the western Indian state of Maharashtra.
Adeel Halim

2 June 2005, LHASA, TIBET

Opposite A Buddhist worships outside the Jokhang Temple in Lhasa. Pilgrims circle the temple clockwise each day along Barkhor Street, either on foot or by prostrating themselves and progressing by body-lengths.
China Newsphoto

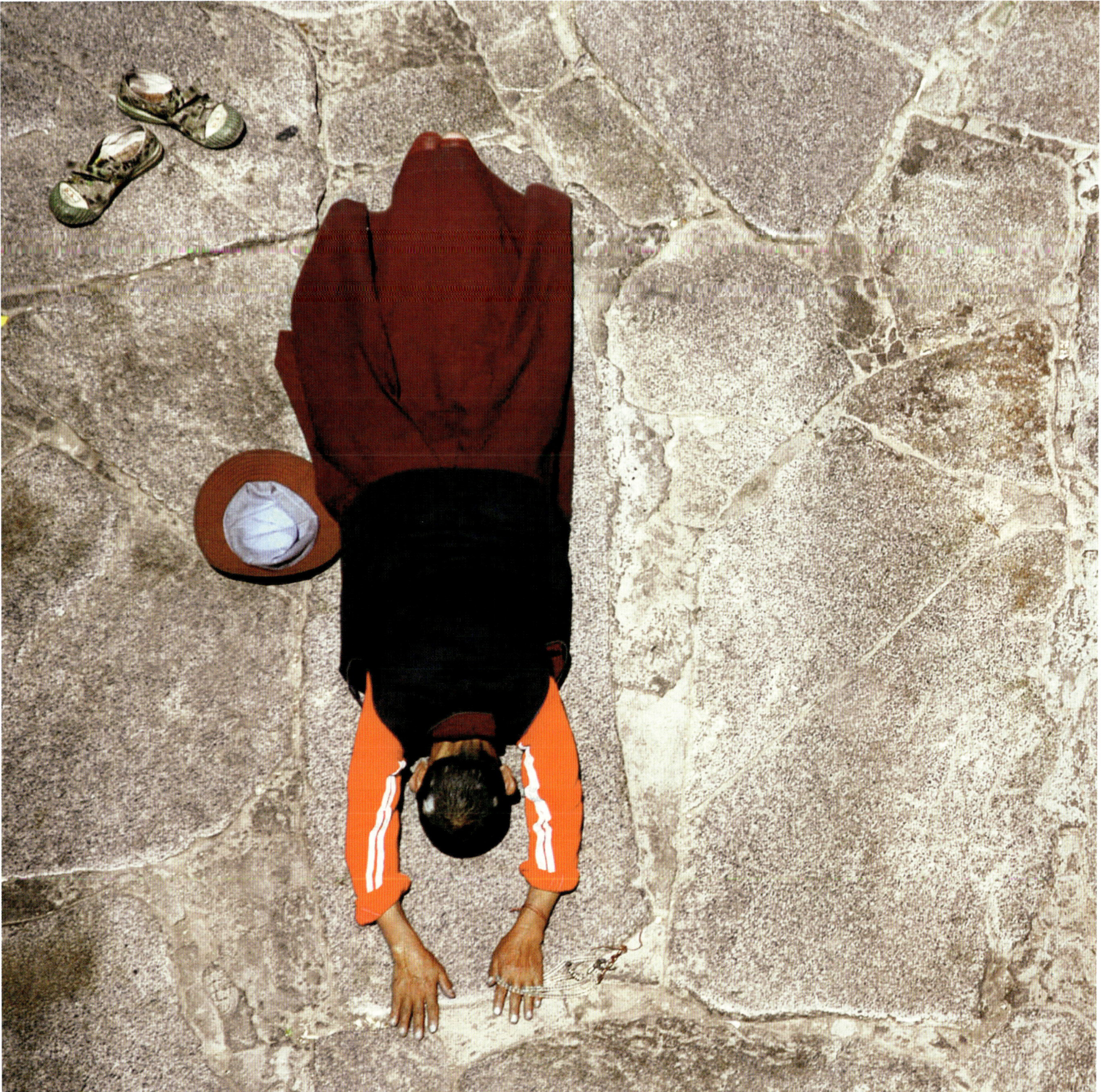

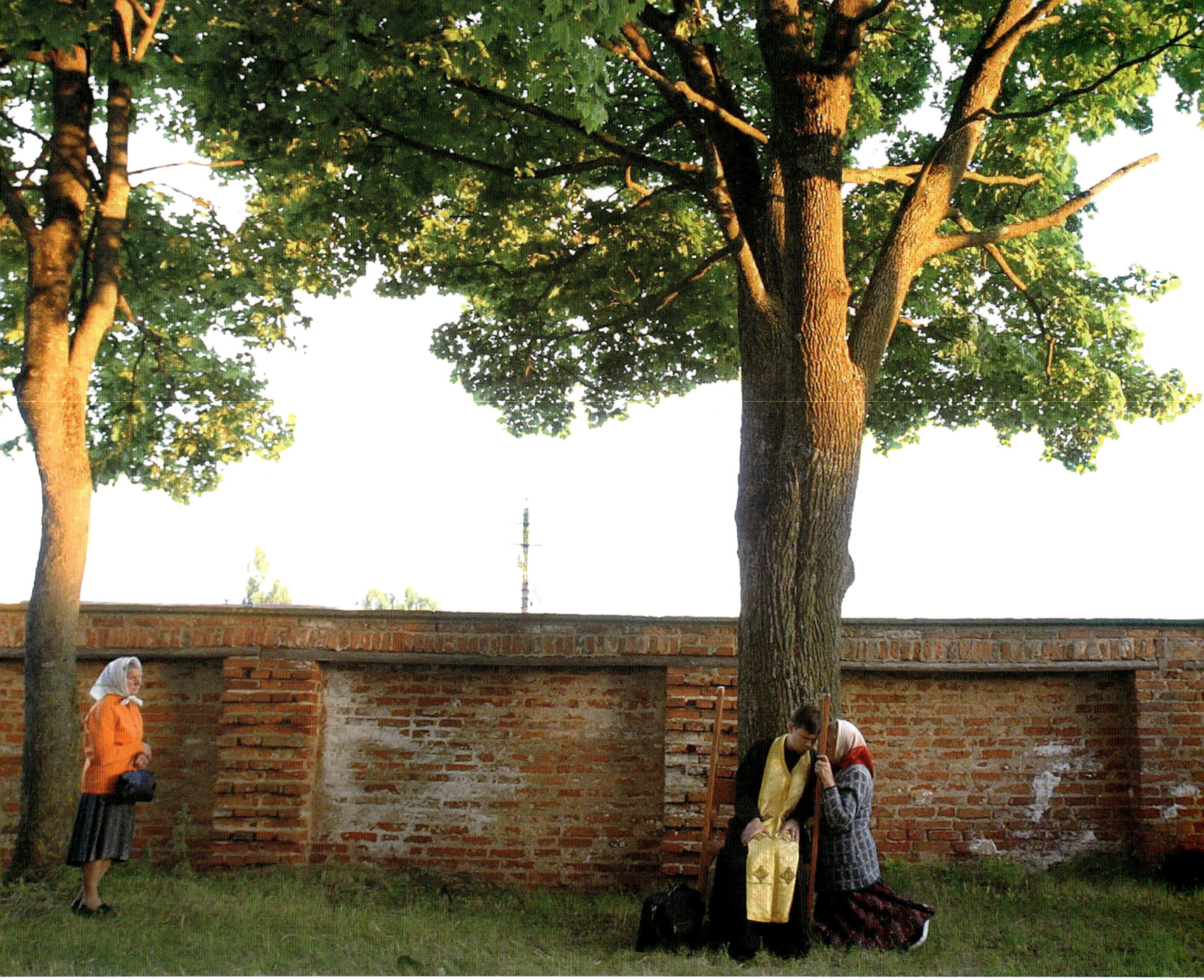

2 July 2005, BUDSLAV, BELARUS

Belarussians go to confession in the garden of a Catholic church during the Icon of Mother of God festival in the village of Budslav, some 150 km (93 miles) north of Minsk. Thousands of Catholics from Belarus and neighbouring countries take part in the annual celebration. Vasily Fedosenko

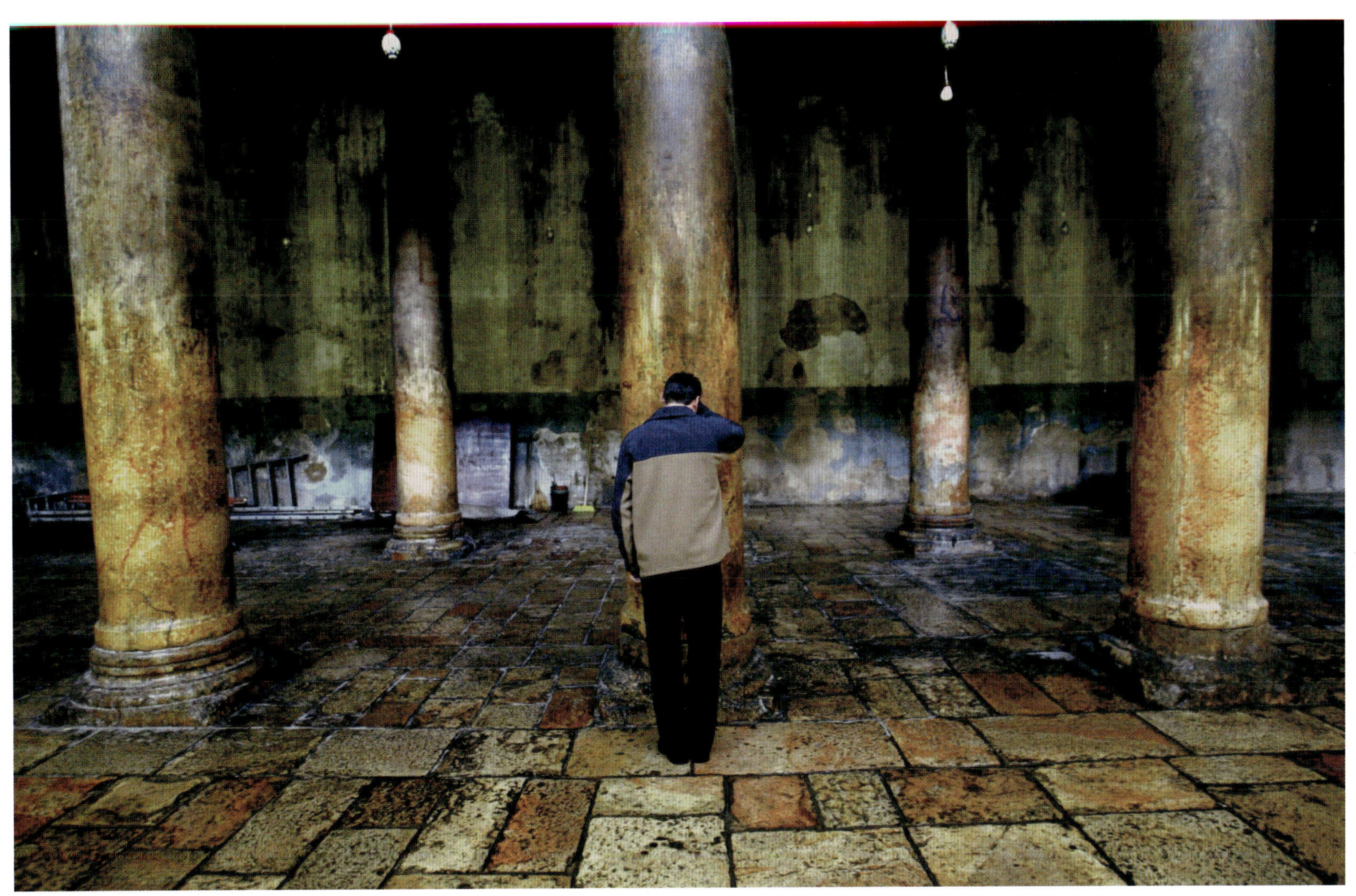

25 December 2002, BETHLEHEM, WEST BANK

A Christian pilgrim prays on Christmas day in the Church of the Nativity in Bethlehem, built on the site where the Virgin Mary is said to have given birth to Jesus. In April–May 2002, the church was subject to a 38-day siege after Palestinian gunmen took refuge there as Israeli troops entered the city. Yannis Behrakis

1 April 2005, VATICAN

A Catholic woman prays inside St Peter's Basilica at the heart of the Vatican City in Rome. Stefano Rellandini

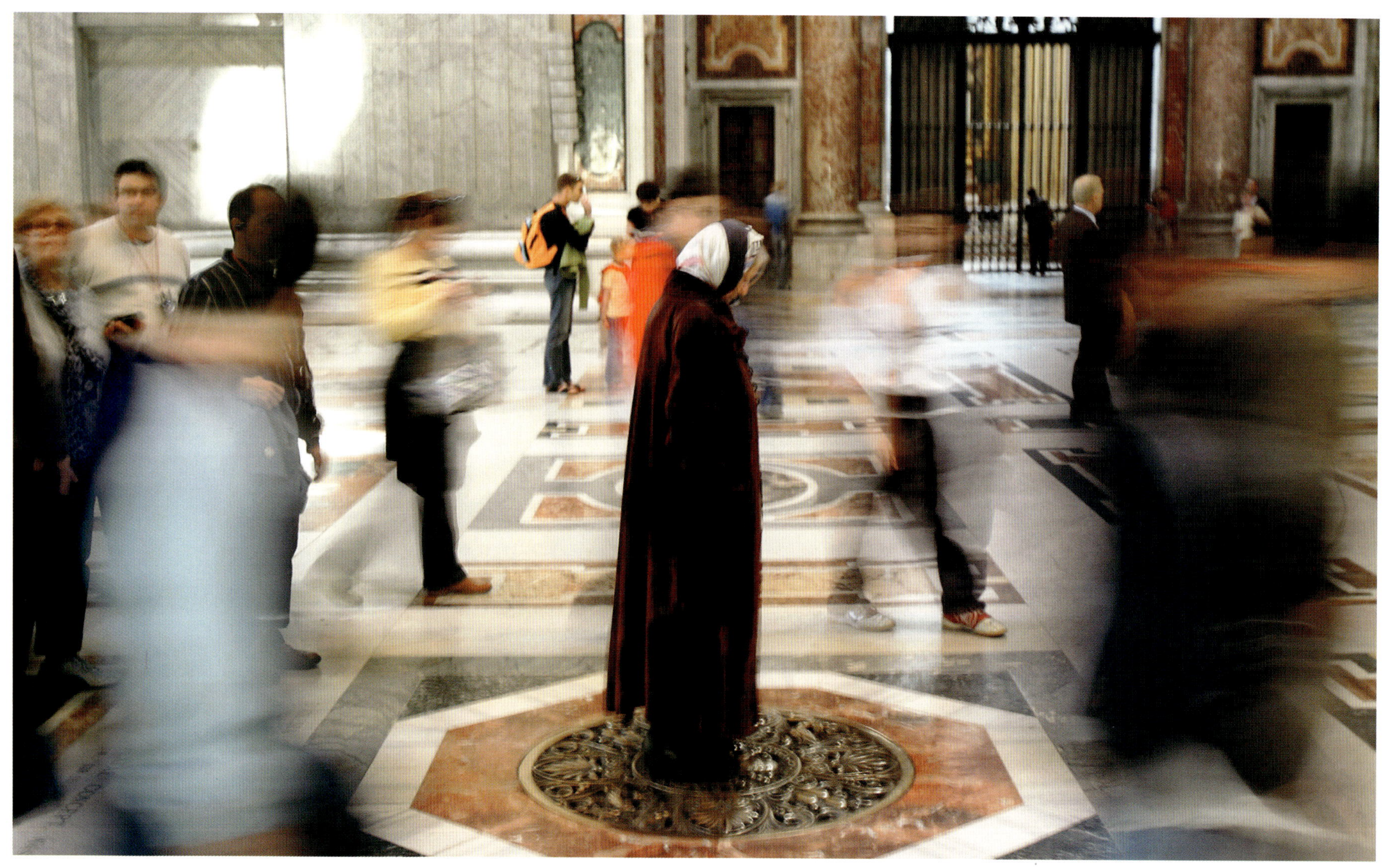

24 May 2001, TEHRAN, IRAN

A boy sits among women during morning prayers in a Tehran mosque. Damir Sagolj

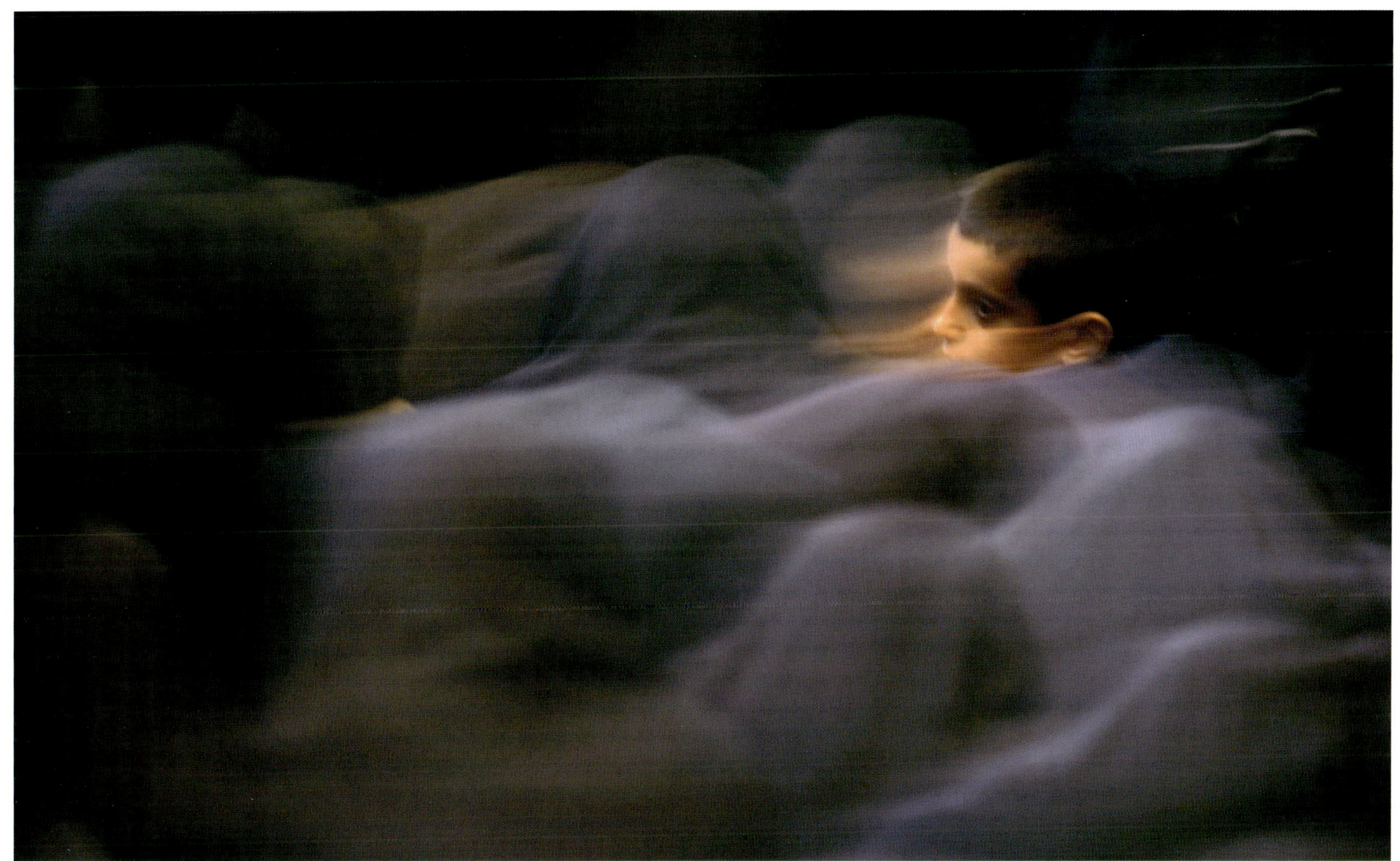

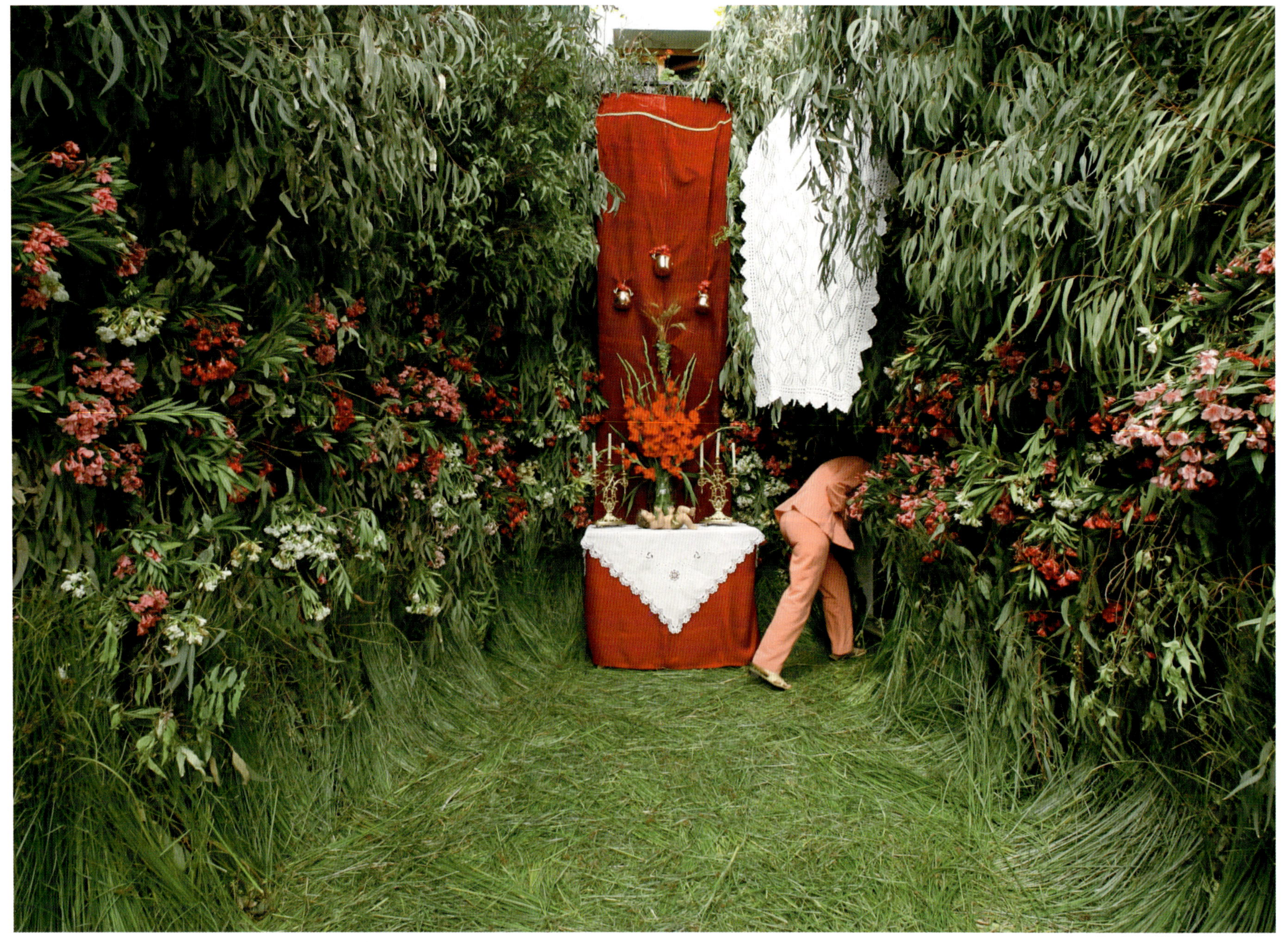

29 May 2005, ZAHARA DE LA SIERRA, SPAIN

A woman enters her house through a decorated doorway in Zahara de la Sierra, Cadiz, where villagers celebrate the festival of Corpus Christi by covering streets and the facades of houses with branches of trees and grass. Marcelo del Pozo

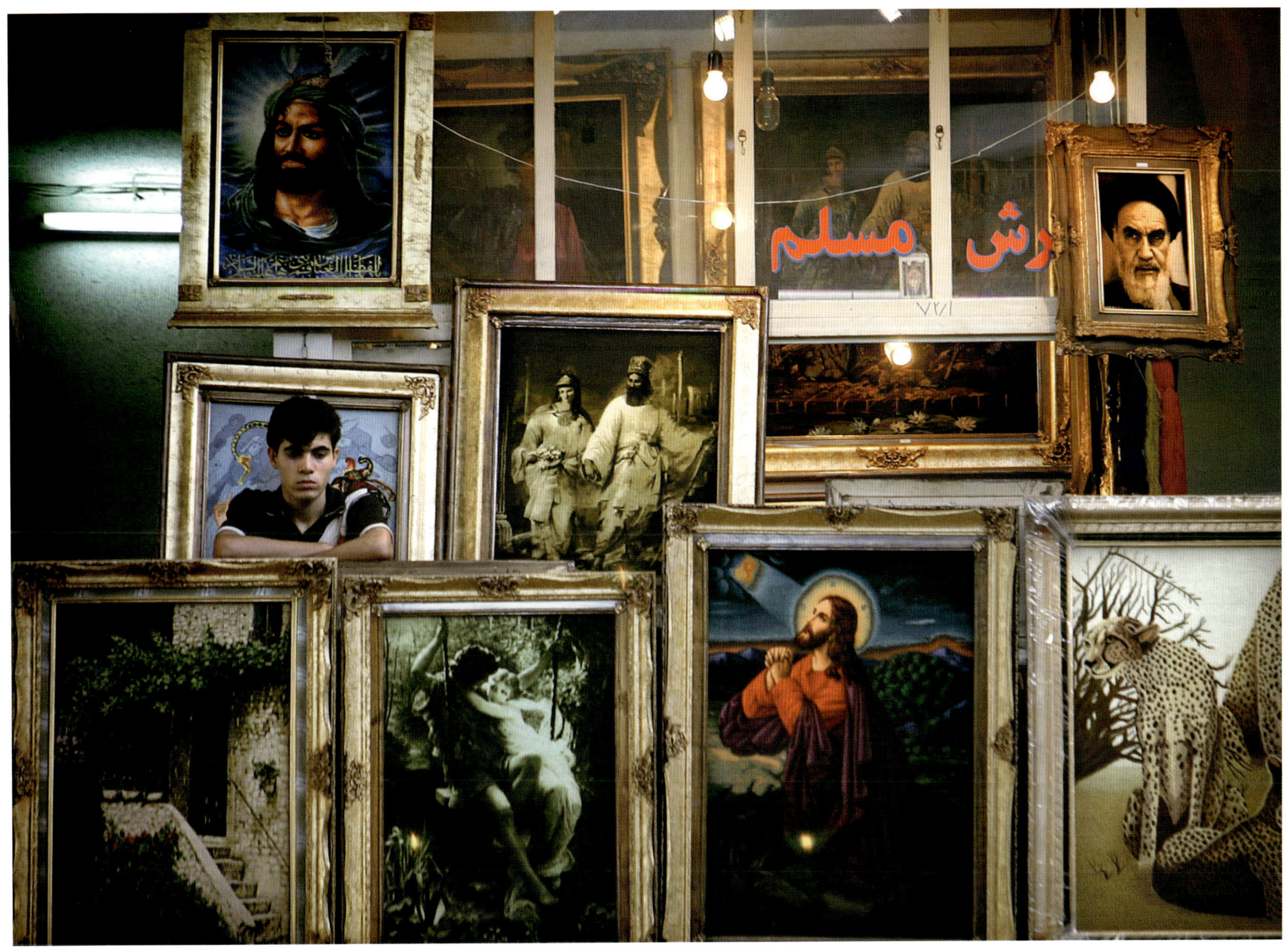

7 June 2005, TEHRAN, IRAN

Paintings on sale in Tehran's bazaar offer an eclectic array of subject-matter, both sacred and secular, Muslim and Christian. Damir Sagolj

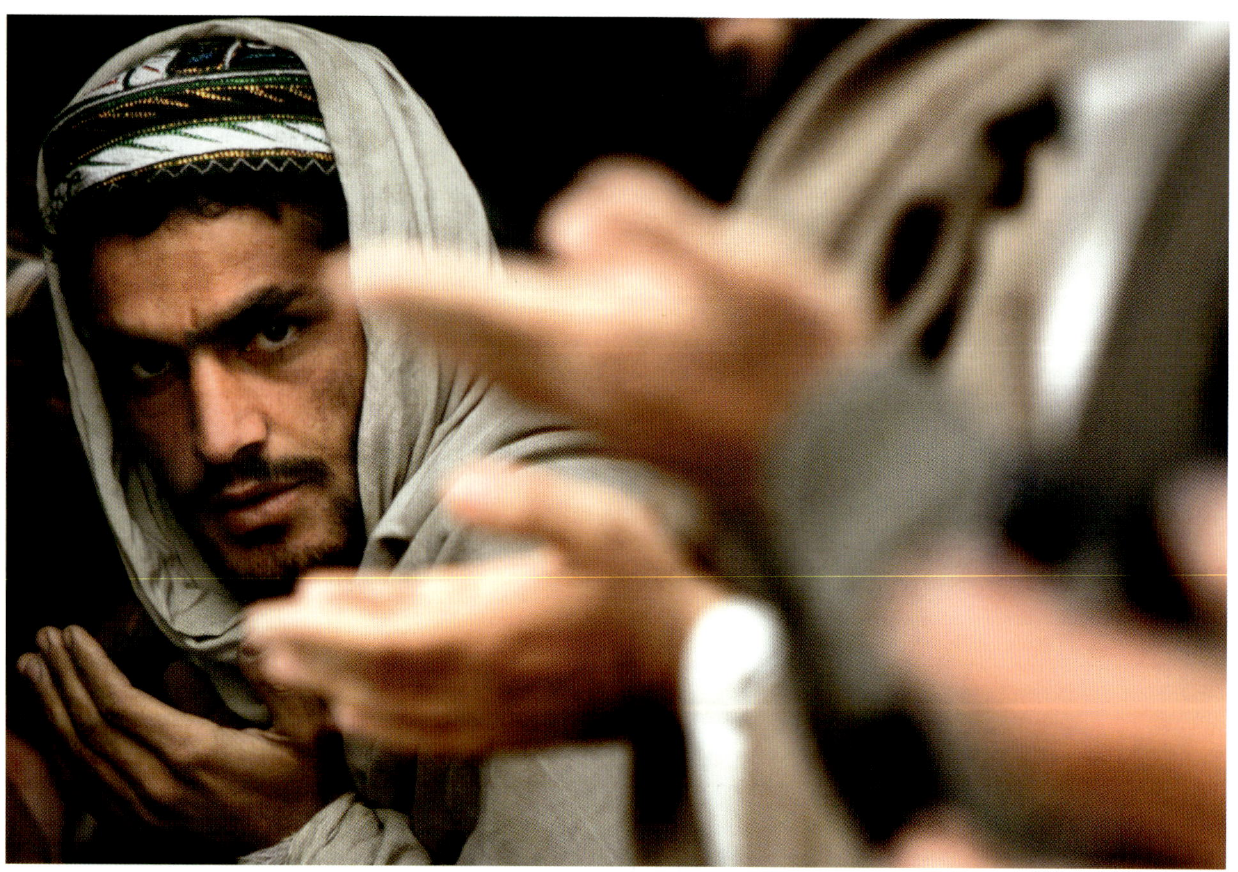

30 November 2001, KABUL, AFGHANISTAN

Friday prayers in the Pul-i-Khishti mosque in Kabul. Damir Sagolj

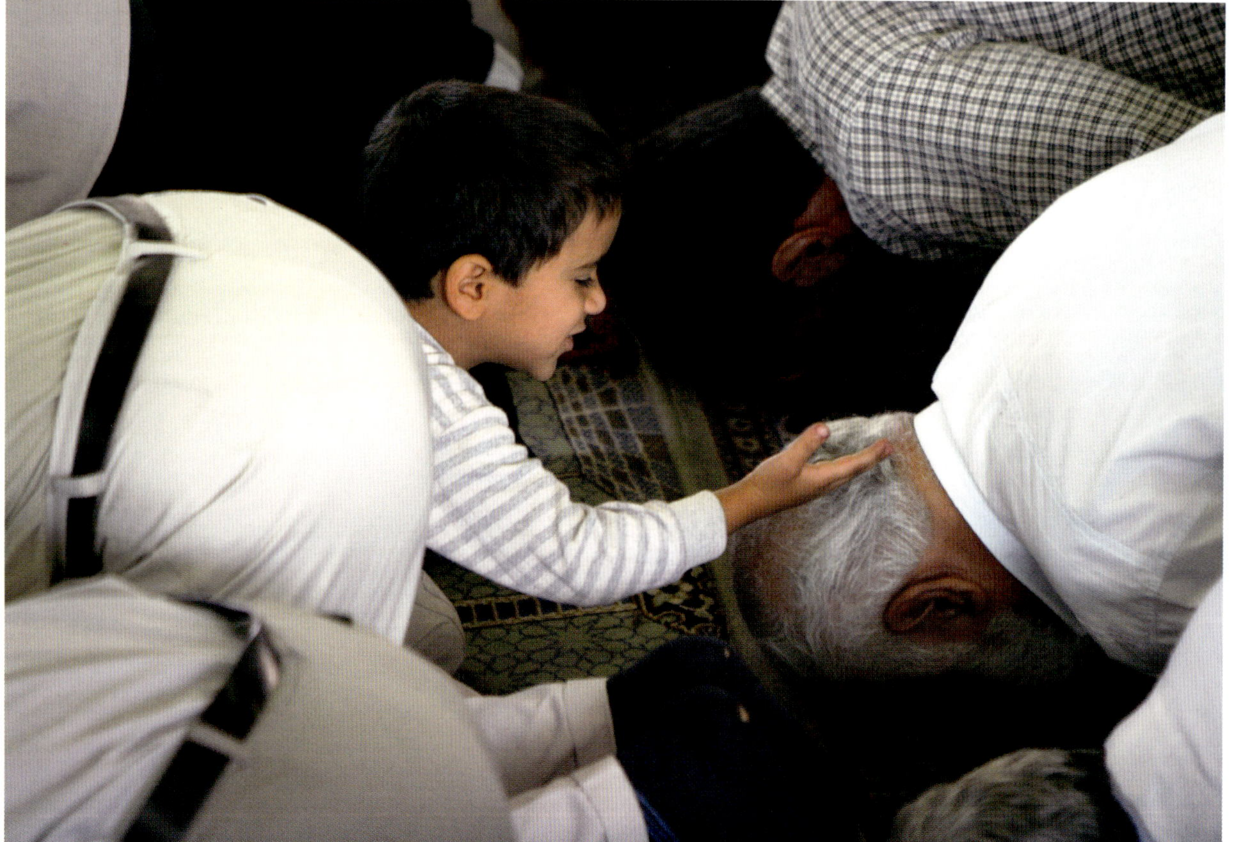

14 October 2005, TEHRAN, IRAN

A young boy among worshippers at Friday prayers in Tehran. Morteza Nikoubazl

6 September 2002, BAGHDAD, IRAQ

Al-Hanifa mosque in Baghdad just before Friday prayers. Damir Sagolj

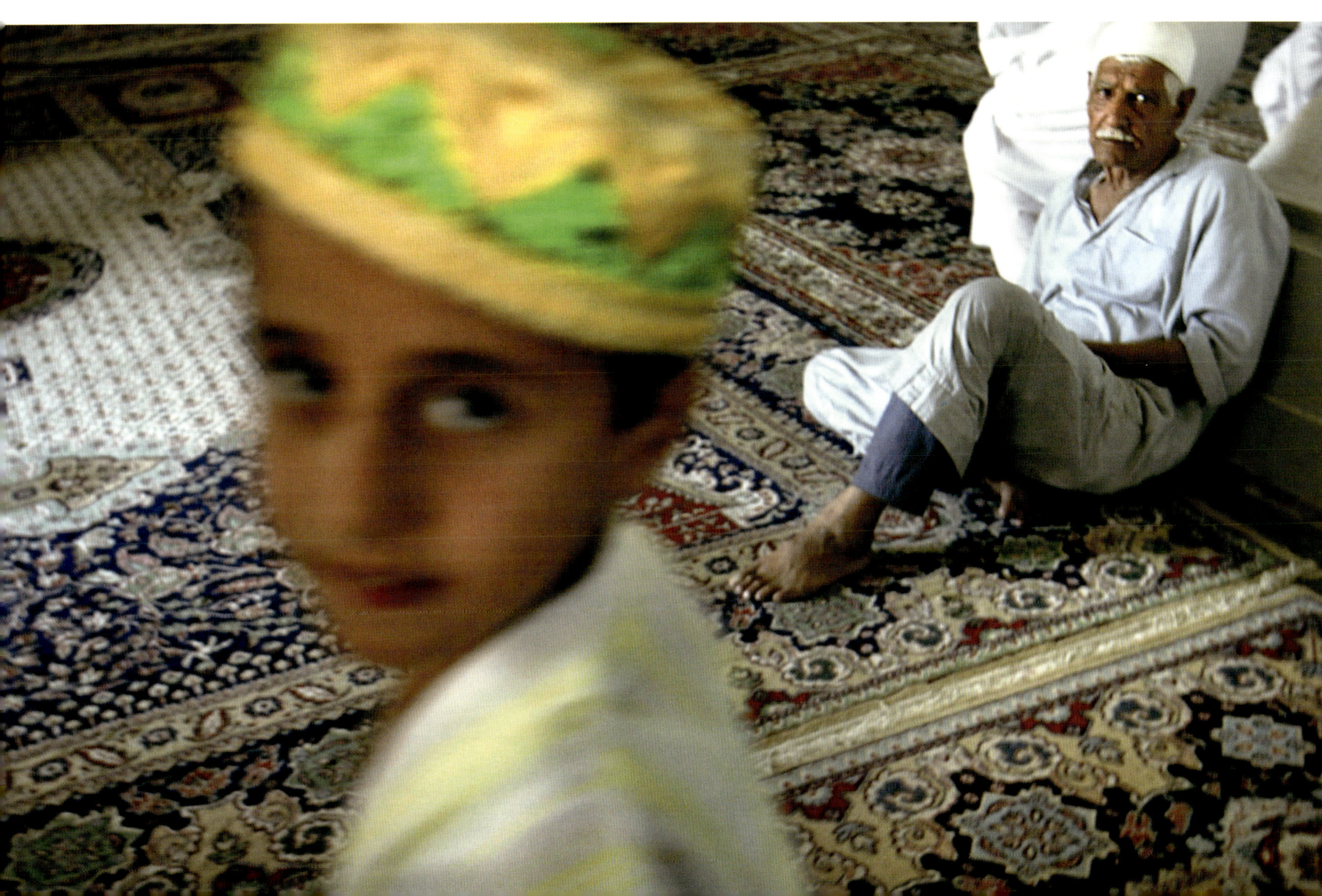

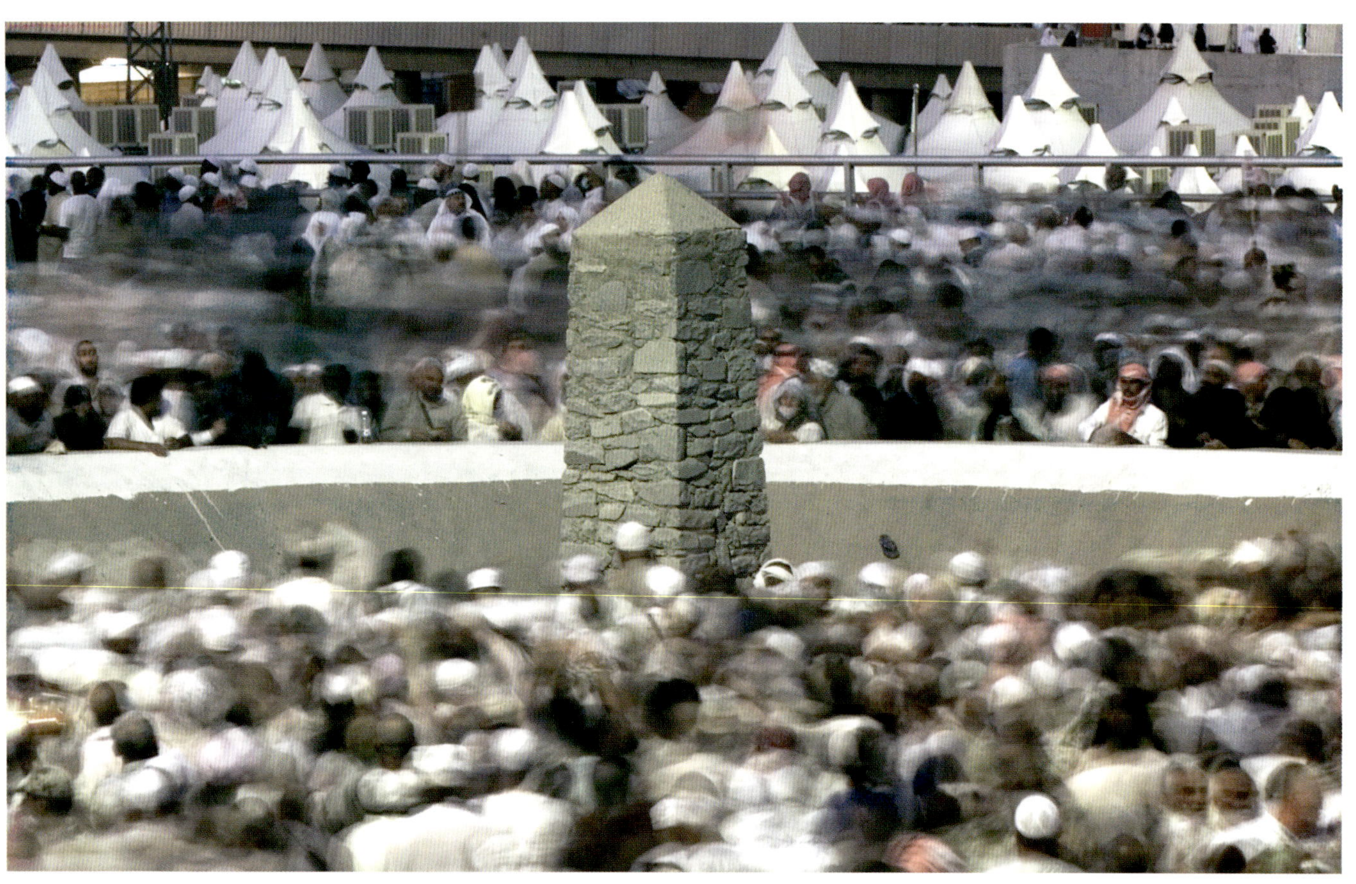

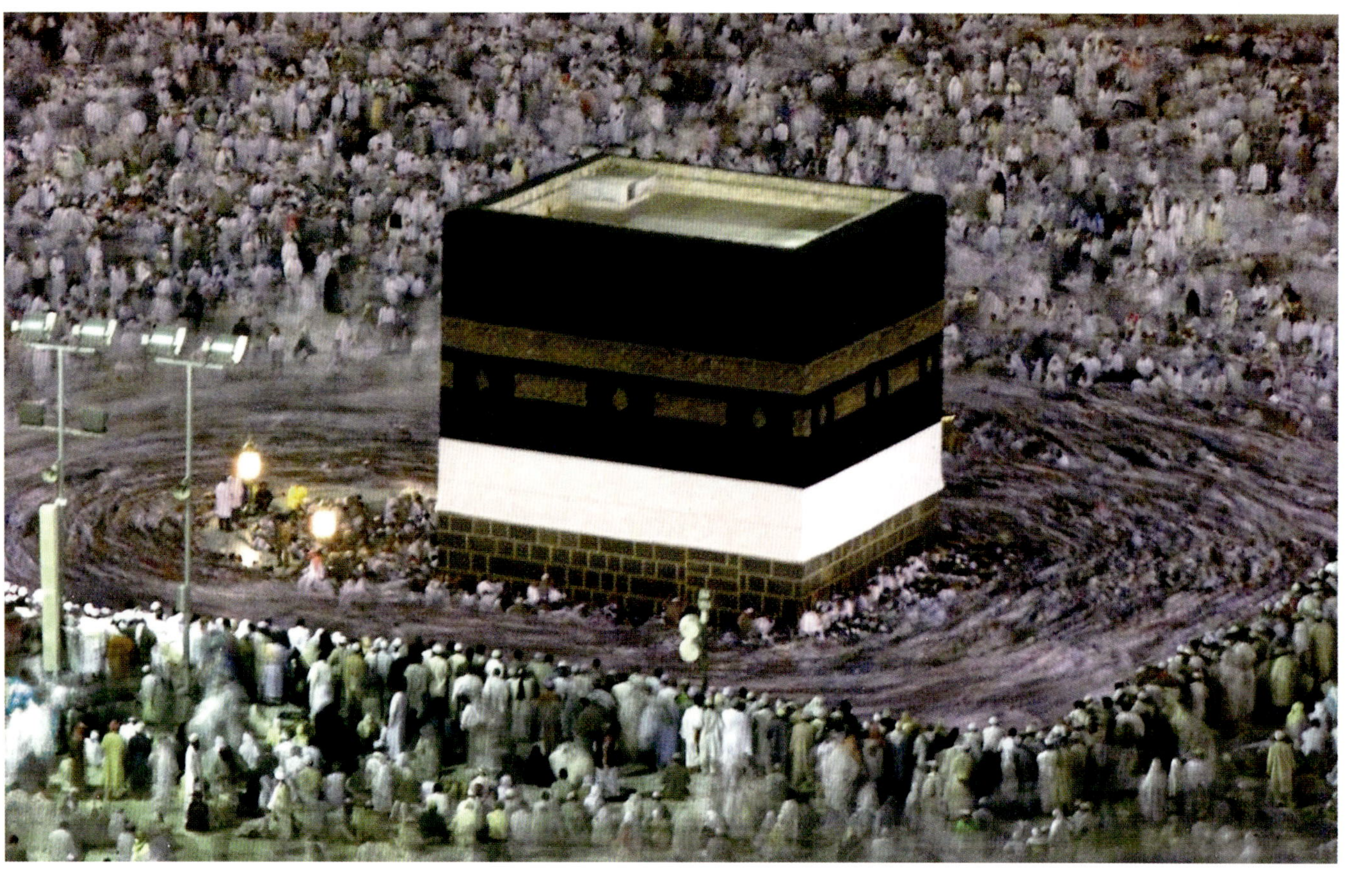

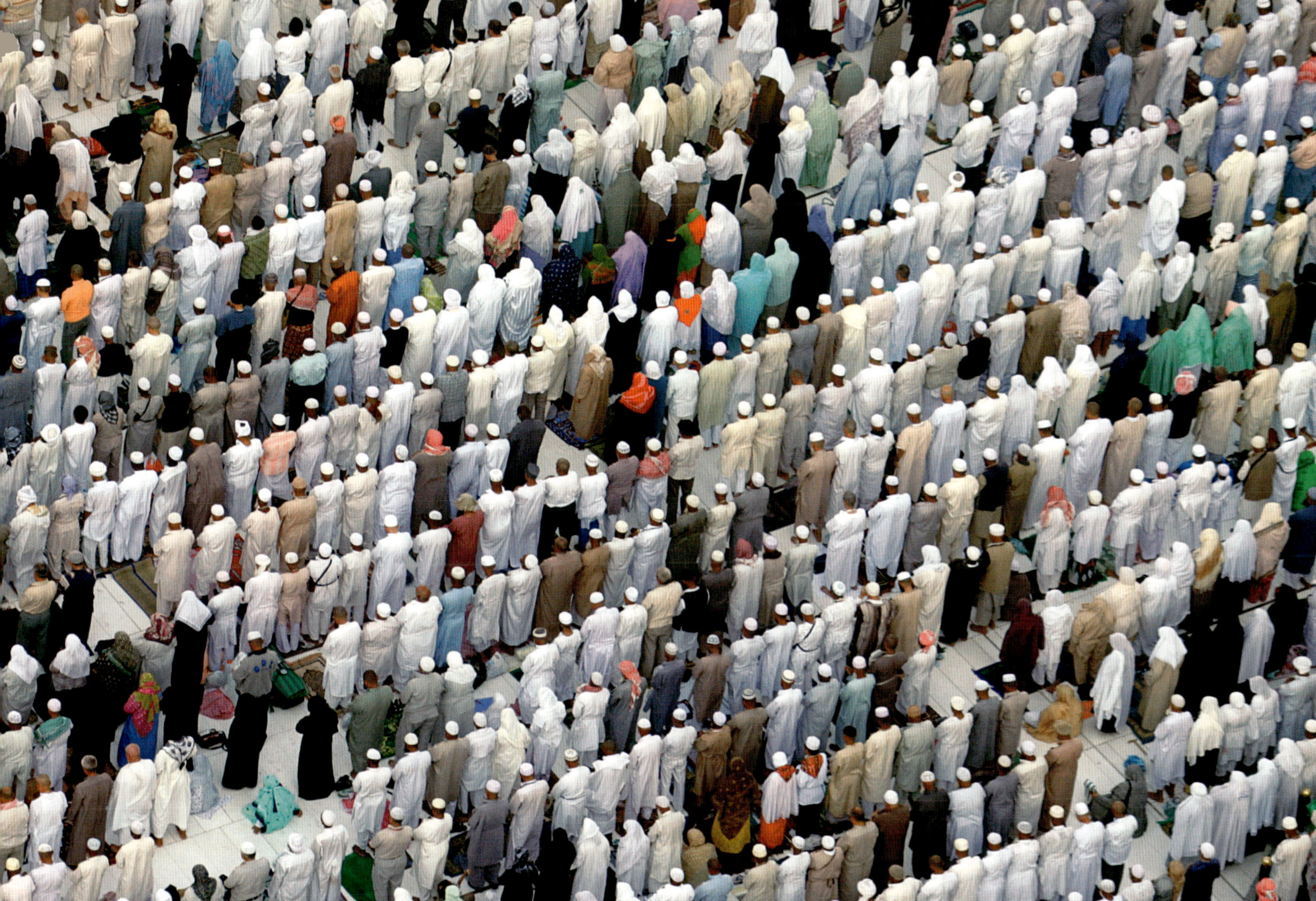

12 February 2003, MENA, SAUDI ARABIA

Opposite above Muslim pilgrims 'stone the devil' in Mena, outside of Mecca. Each pilgrim casts seven stones at the pillars symbolizing Satan to celebrate Eid al-Adha, or the Feast of Sacrifice, in the last stage of the Haj pilgrimage. Shamil Zhumatov

2 March 2001, MECCA, SAUDI ARABIA

Opposite below Hundreds of thousands of Muslim pilgrims circle the holy Kaaba, the holiest shrine in Islam and the focal point for Muslims praying from around the world. Adrees Latif

14 January 2006, MECCA, SAUDI ARABIA

Pilgrims attend prayers during the Haj in Mecca. Ali Jarekji

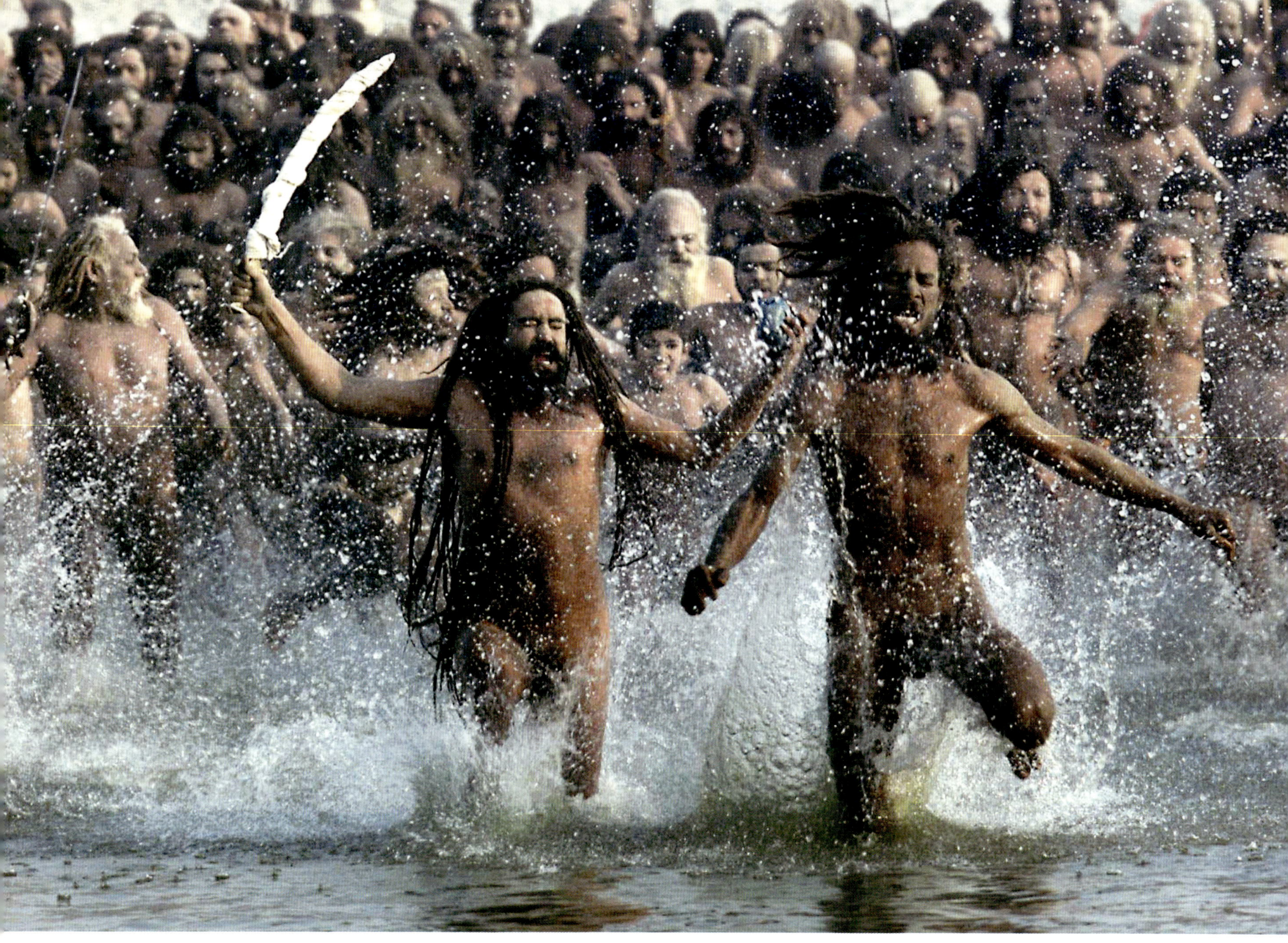

14 January 2001, ALLAHABAD, INDIA

Sadhus, Hindu holy men, run into the holy Ganges river during the Maha Kumbh Mela, or Great Pitcher Festival, in the northern Indian city of Allahabad. The 'Royal Bath' day begins about one hour before dawn, with sadhus taking turns to immerse themselves in the Ganges at the confluence point known as the 'sangam'. The organizers of the six-week festival, which takes place every 12 years, said that almost 100 million people took part. Pawel Kopczynski

25 August 2003, LHASA, TIBET

Opposite above Tibetan monks debate Buddhist philosophy at Sera Monastery in Lhasa, one of the three main monasteries in the Tibetan capital. Guang Niu

1 March 2004, TEHRAN, IRAN

Opposite below Iranian Shi'ite Muslims chant while beating themselves with iron chains inside Tehran's bazaar during the Ashura religious festival that commemorates the death of Imam Hussein, the 'leader of the martyrs' and grandson of the Prophet Mohammed. Damir Sagolj

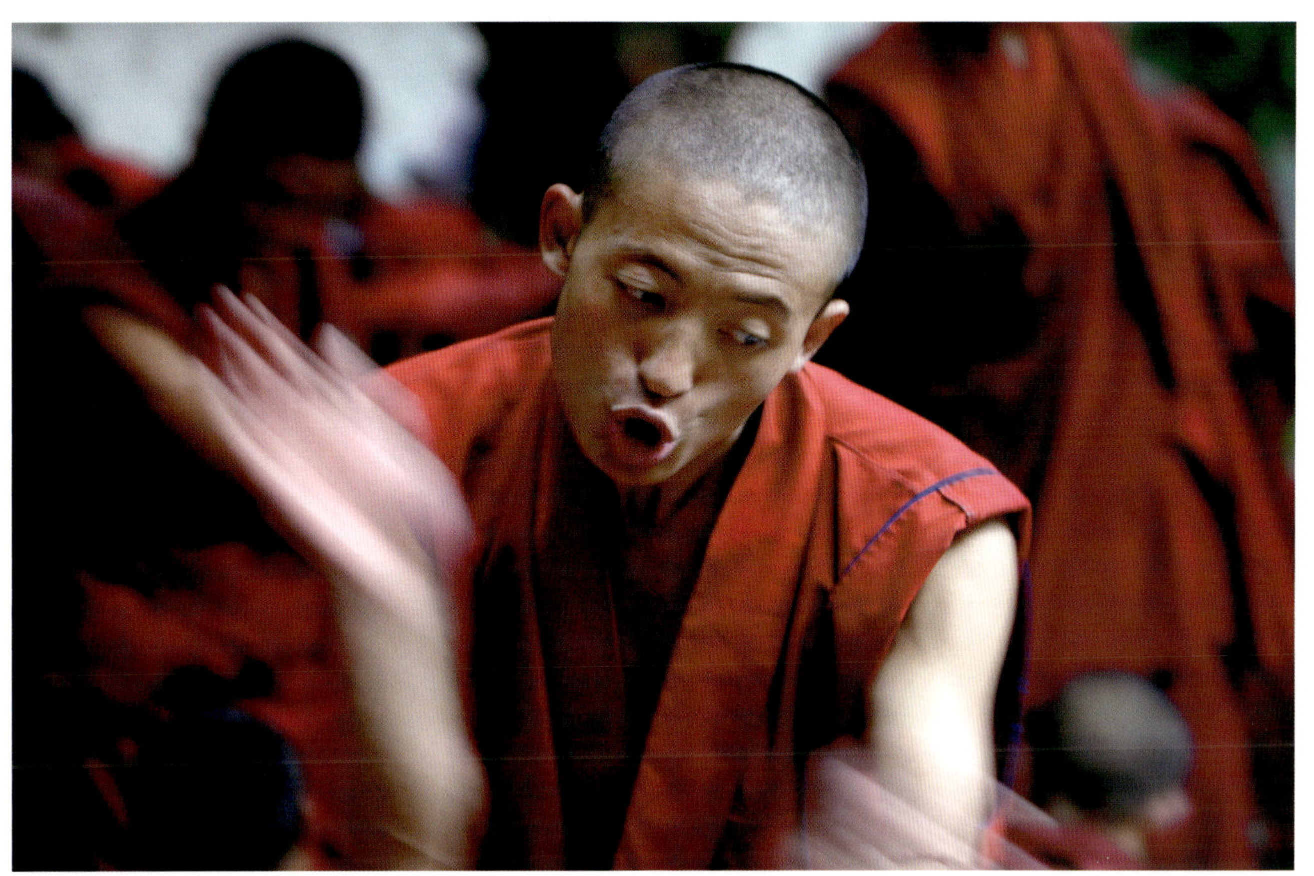

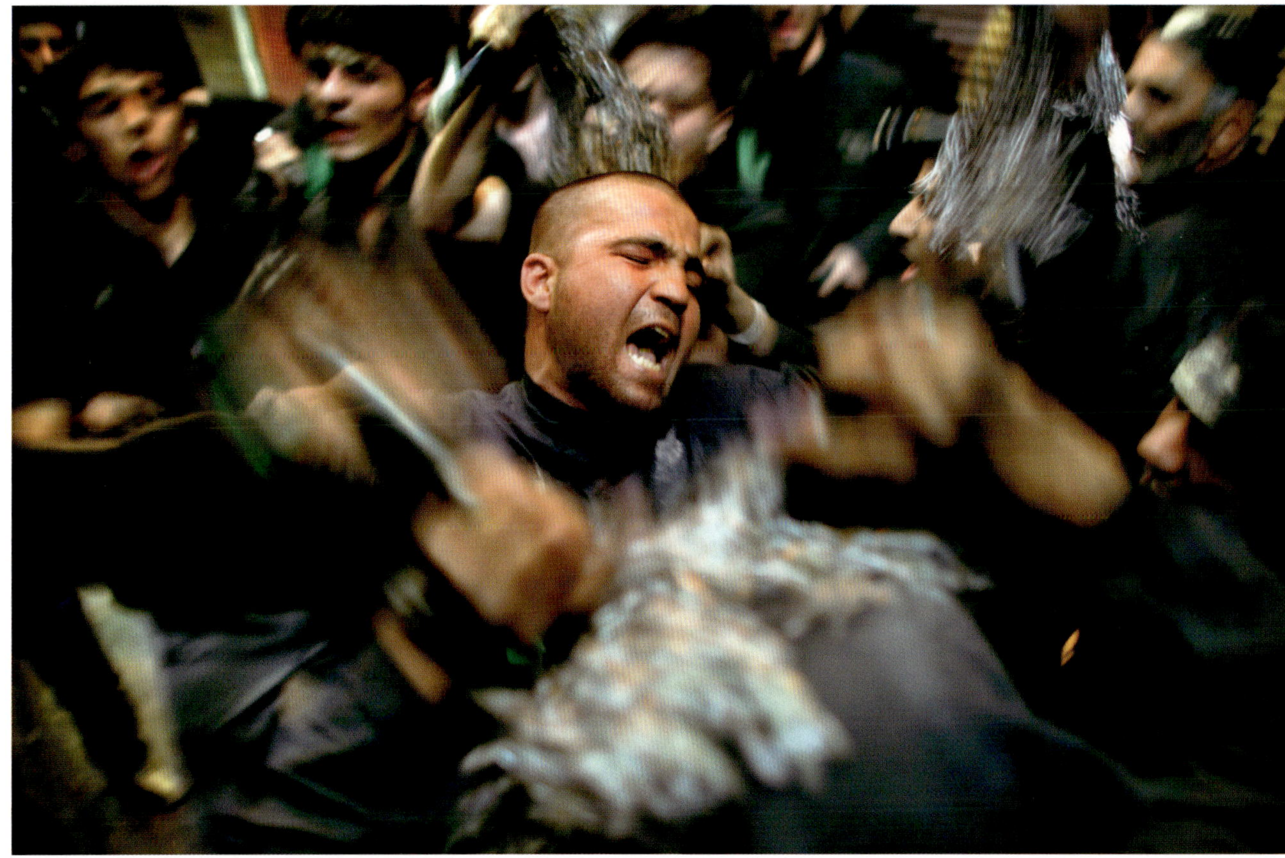

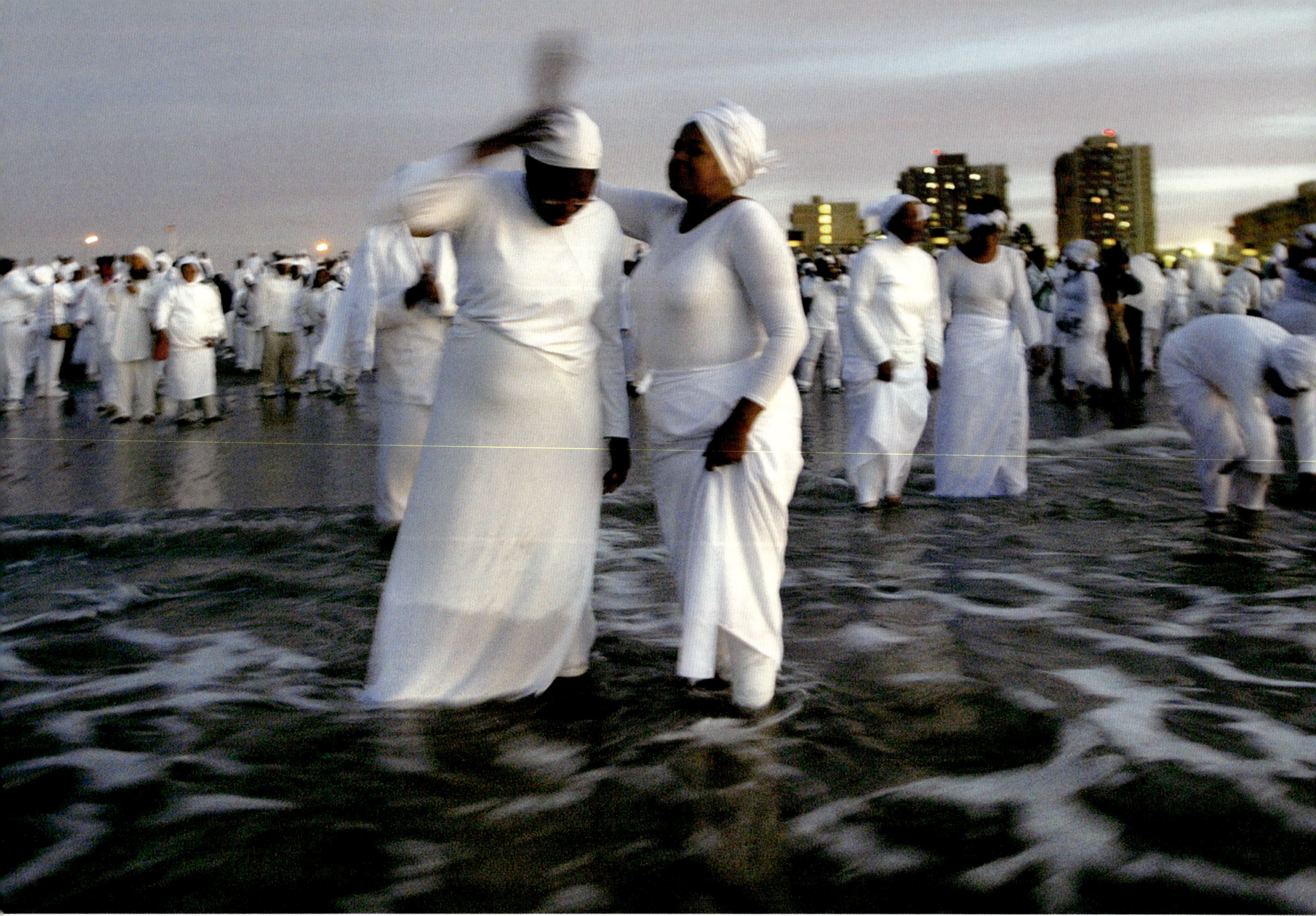

24 September 2005, NEW YORK, UNITED STATES

Women mark the eleventh commemoration of Maafa on the beaches of the Atlantic Ocean in New York. Maafa is a Kiswahili word that describes great calamity, tragedy or disaster. It was introduced into contemporary African–American scholarship by Dr Marimba Ani to refer to the Trans-Atlantic slave trade and the centuries of suffering that followed from it. Shannon Stapleton

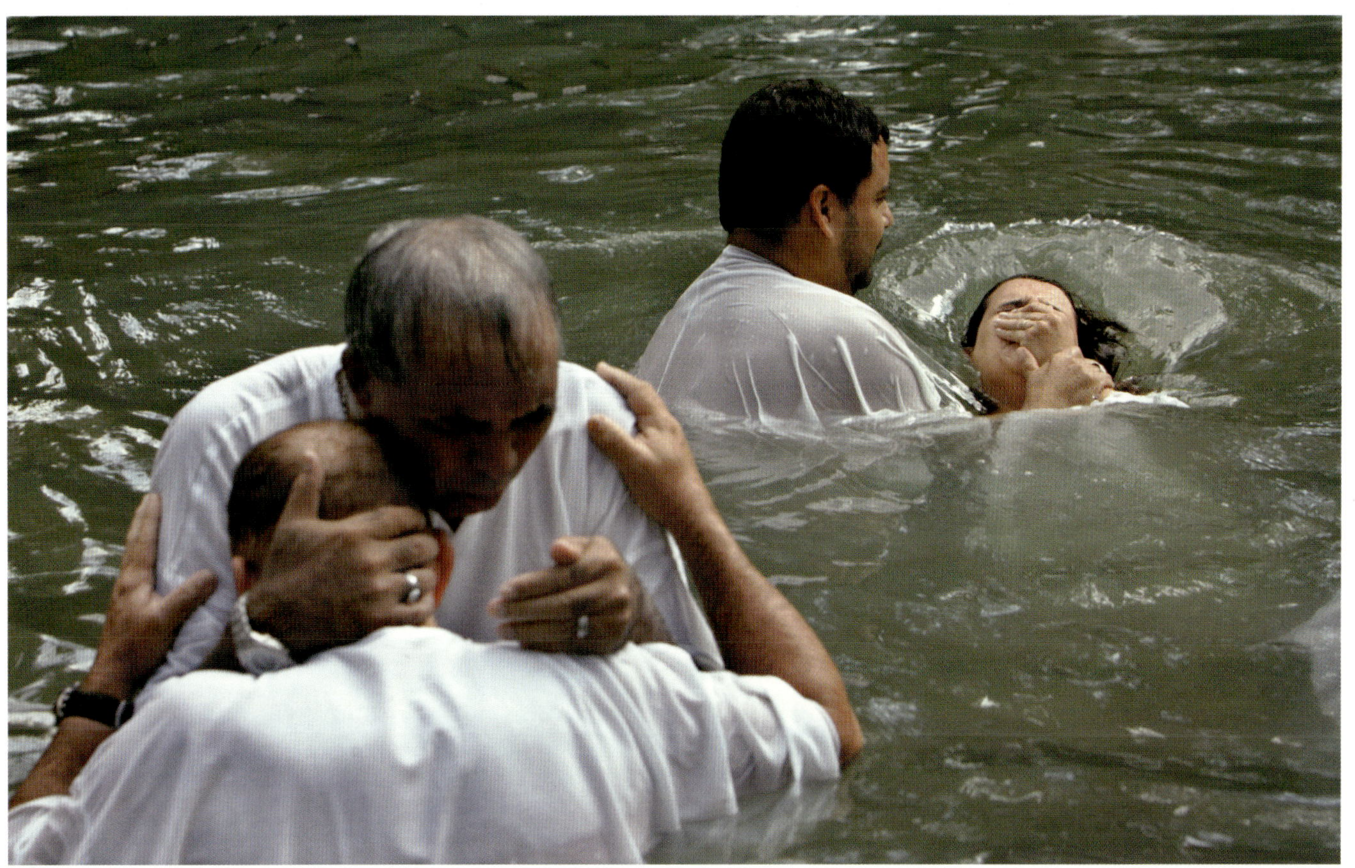

17 October 2005, RIVER JORDAN, ISRAEL

Brazilian Christians perform baptisms in the waters of the Jordan River near the Sea of Galilee. The site is one of several along the Jordan River, both in Israel and in Jordan, where it is believed Jesus Christ was baptised by John the Baptist.

Gil Cohen Magen

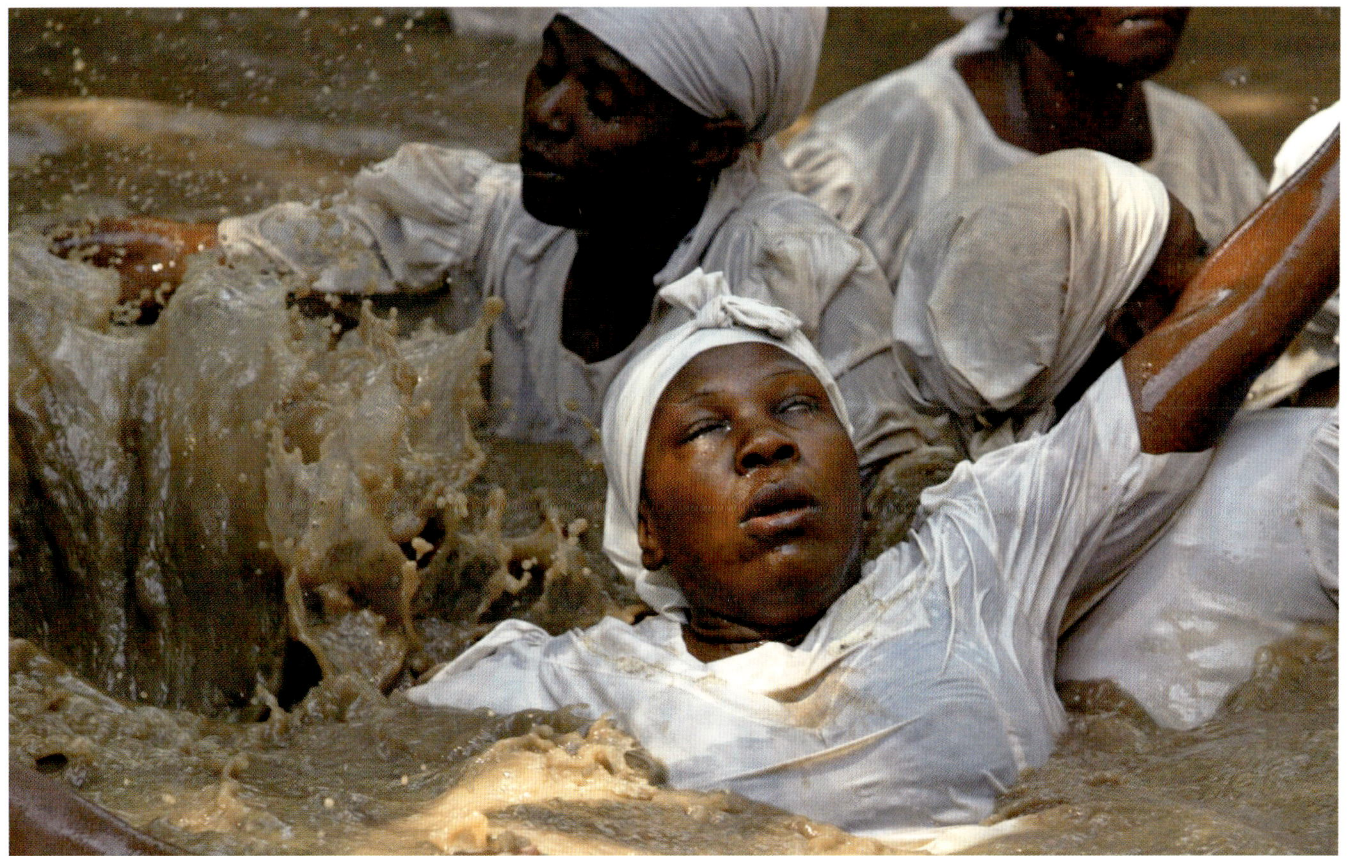

27 March 2005, SOUVENANCE, HAITI

Followers of Voodoo flail in trances in a sacred pool during a ritual at the Souvenance temple near Gonaives. The annual pilgrimage to Souvenance, coinciding with the Christian Easter week, draws Voodoo believers from all over Haiti as well as from the United States and Canada. Rituals involve dancing, singing, animal sacrifice, and offerings to the 'lwa' or spirits.

Daniel Morel

14 June 2005, SANUR, WEST BANK

An Israeli prays in the synagogue at the Sanur settlement near the West Bank city of Jenin. Sanur was one of four West Bank settlements evacuated and dismantled by Israeli forces in August 2005. Gil Cohen Magen

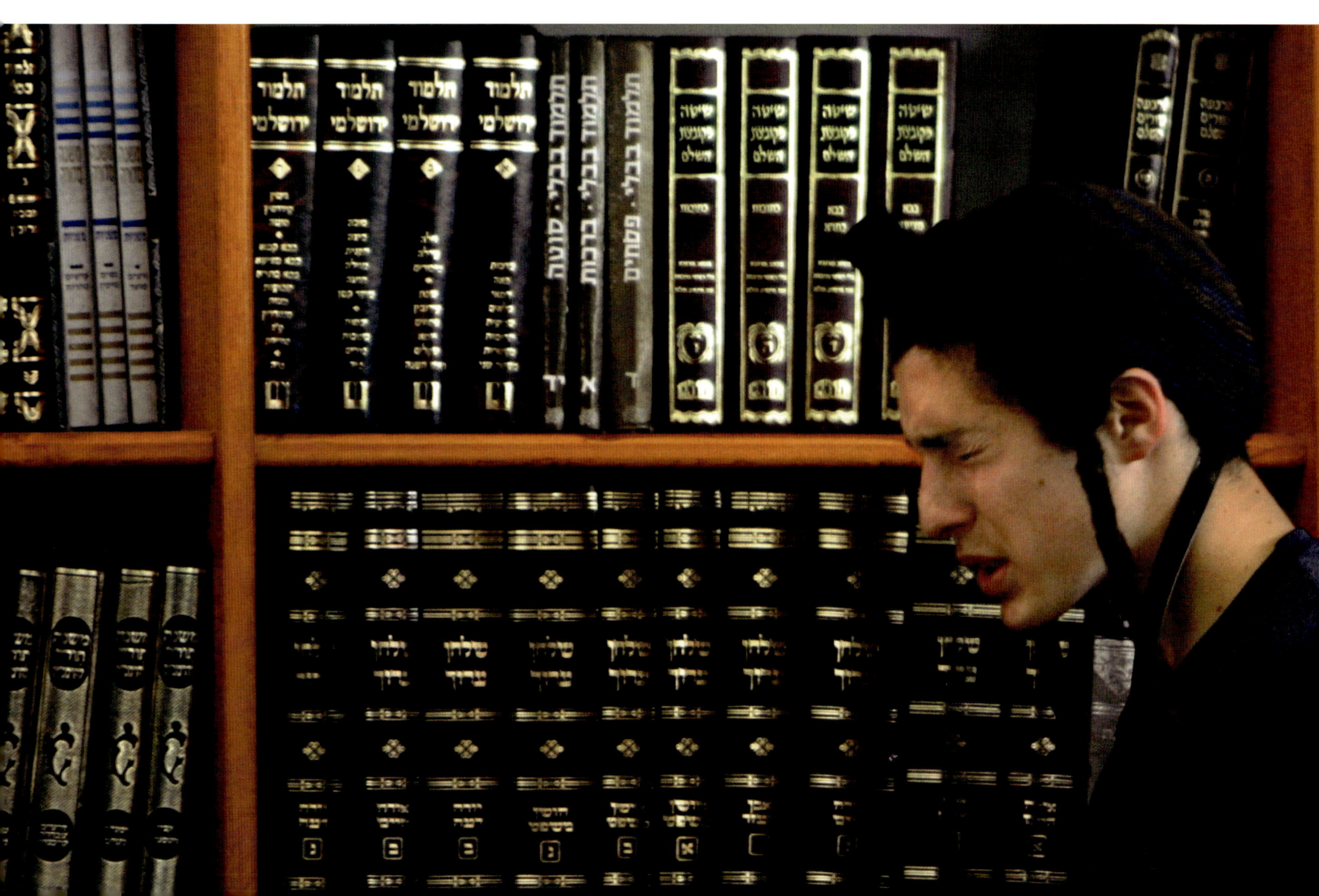

14 August 2005, KFAR DAROM, GAZA STRIP

An Israeli settler reads in a synagogue at the Jewish Gaza Strip settlement of Kfar Darom, part of the Gush Katif settlement bloc that was evacuated on the orders of the Israeli government in late summer 2005. Nir Elias

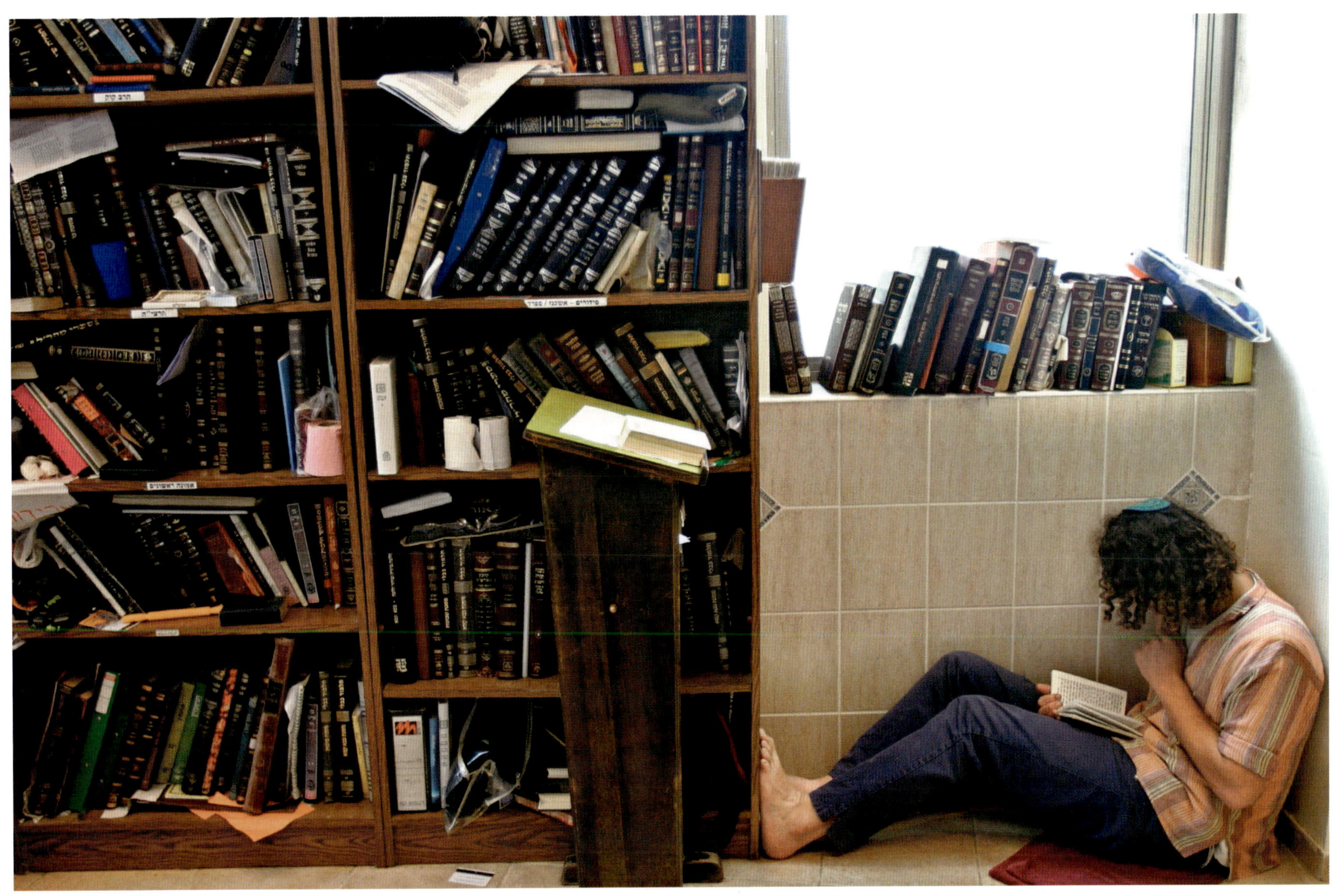

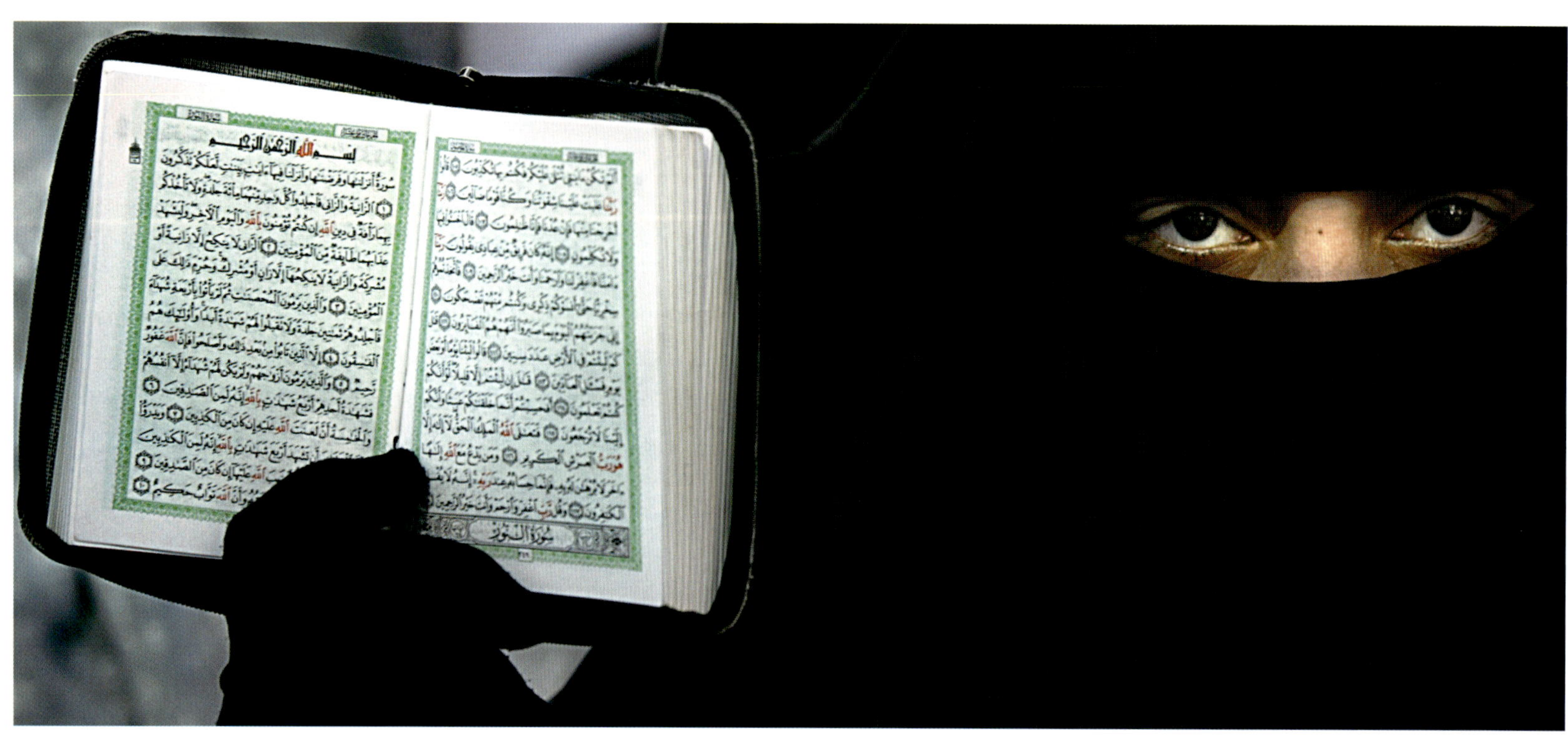

17 January 2004, GAZA CITY, GAZA STRIP

A Hamas supporter holds a copy of the Koran as she attends a demonstration in Gaza City against plans by the French government to ban the Islamic headscarf from schools. Demonstrators gathered in cities across France while Muslims in the Middle East and London also challenged the controversial proposal to ban Muslim headscarves, Jewish skullcaps and large Christian crosses from state schools. The law was passed by France's National Assembly on 10 February 2004.

Mohammed Salem

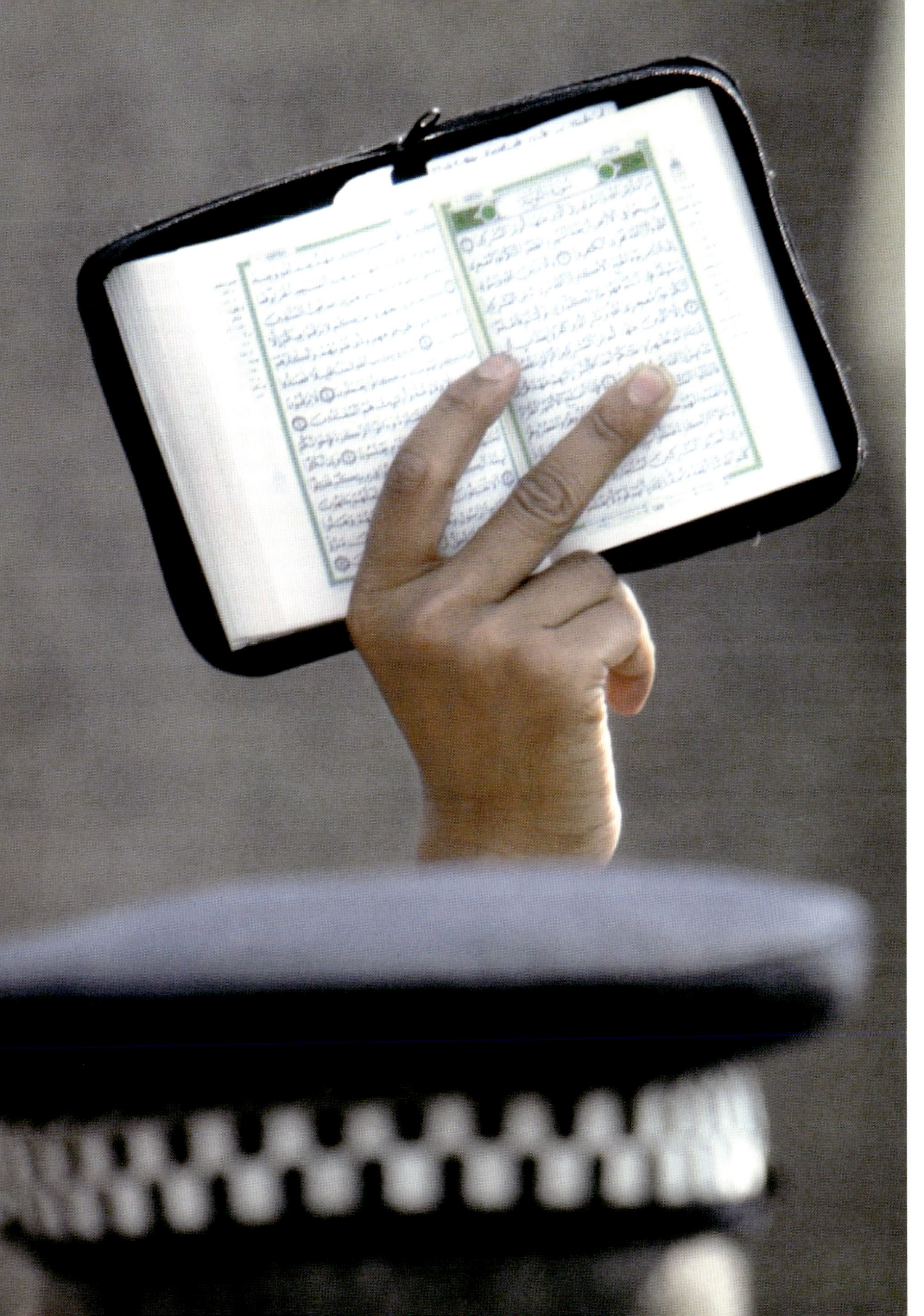

25 August 2002, LONDON, UNITED KINGDOM

A copy of the Koran is held aloft at the sixth annual Rally for Islam in London's Trafalgar Square. Ian Waldie

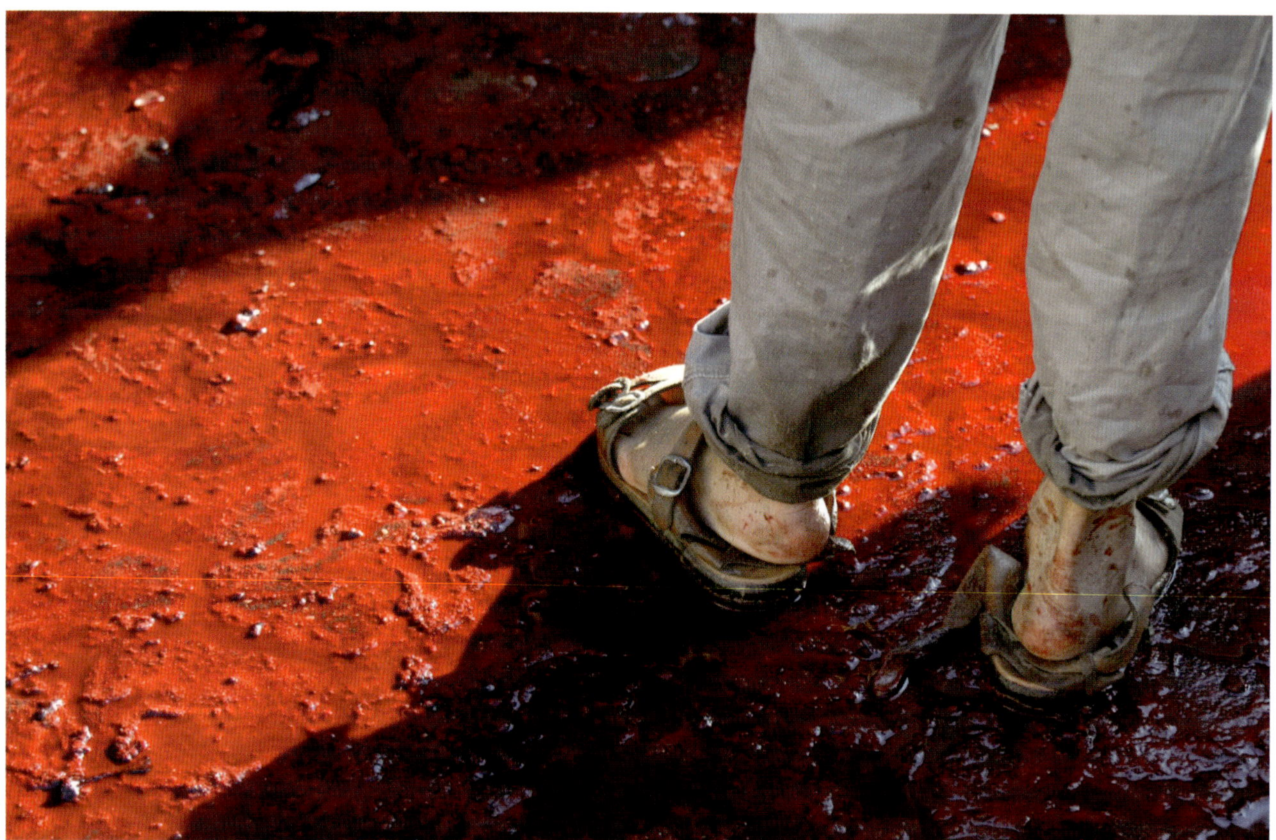

11 February 2003, GAZA CITY, GAZA STRIP

A boy watches Palestinian butchers as they slaughter a cow in Gaza City during Eid al-Adha, the Feast of Sacrifice, which commemorates Abraham's willingness to sacrifice his son in obedience to God's command. One third of the meat is distributed to the poor, one third to neighbours and relatives, and one third is kept by the person who offered the sacrifice for use within his or her own family. Radu Sigheti

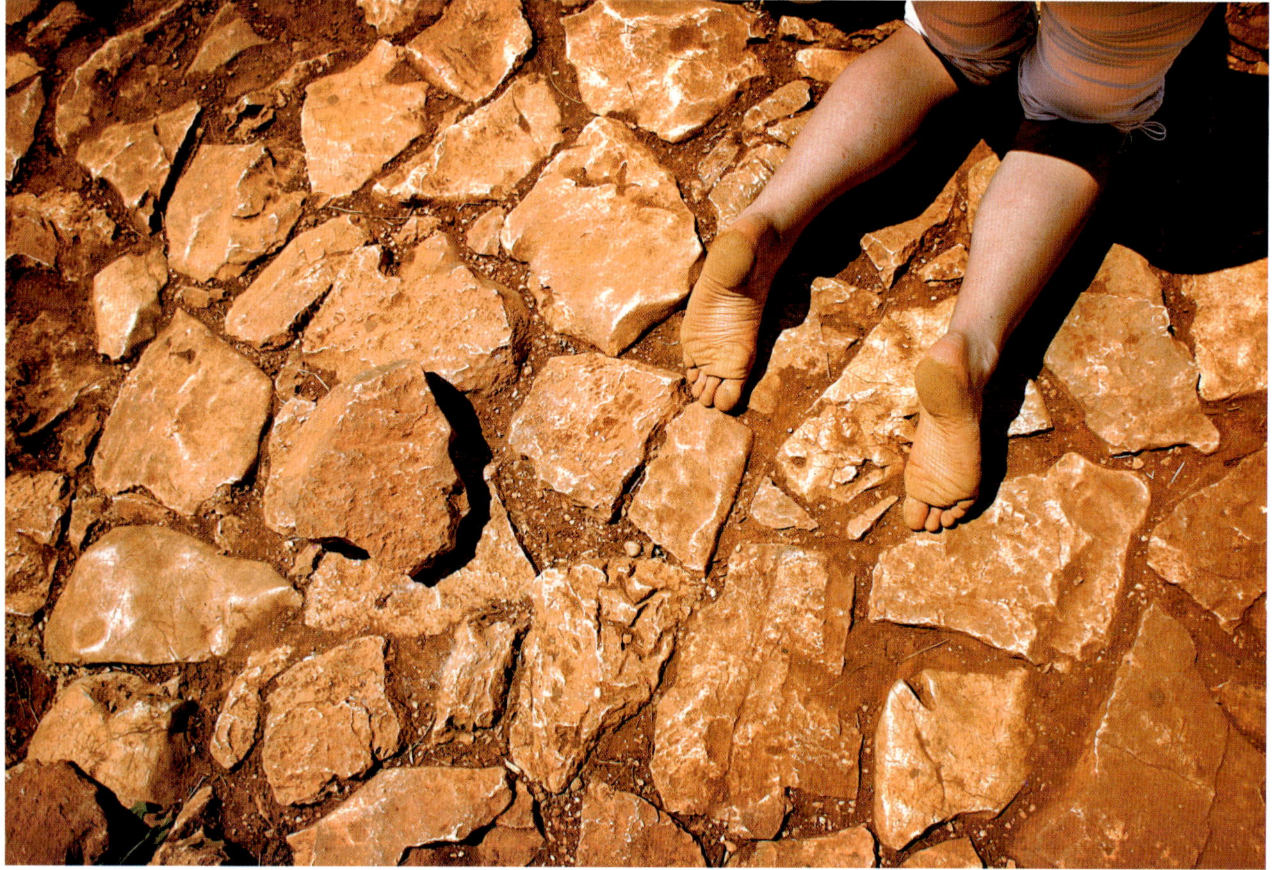

25 June 2004, MEDJUGORJE, BOSNIA

A barefoot pilgrim kneels in prayer at the site where the Virgin Mary reportedly appeared in 1981 to a group of six young people in the small Bosnian town of Medjugorje, 120 km (75 miles) south of Sarajevo. Millions of pilgrims from all over the world have visited the site. Damir Sagolj

7 October 2005, KOLKATA, INDIA

An Indian labourer walks past a reflection of an idol of Durga, the Hindu goddess of power, in Kolkata. The annual Durga Puja festival is one of the most popular in the Hindu religious calendar. Parth Sanyal

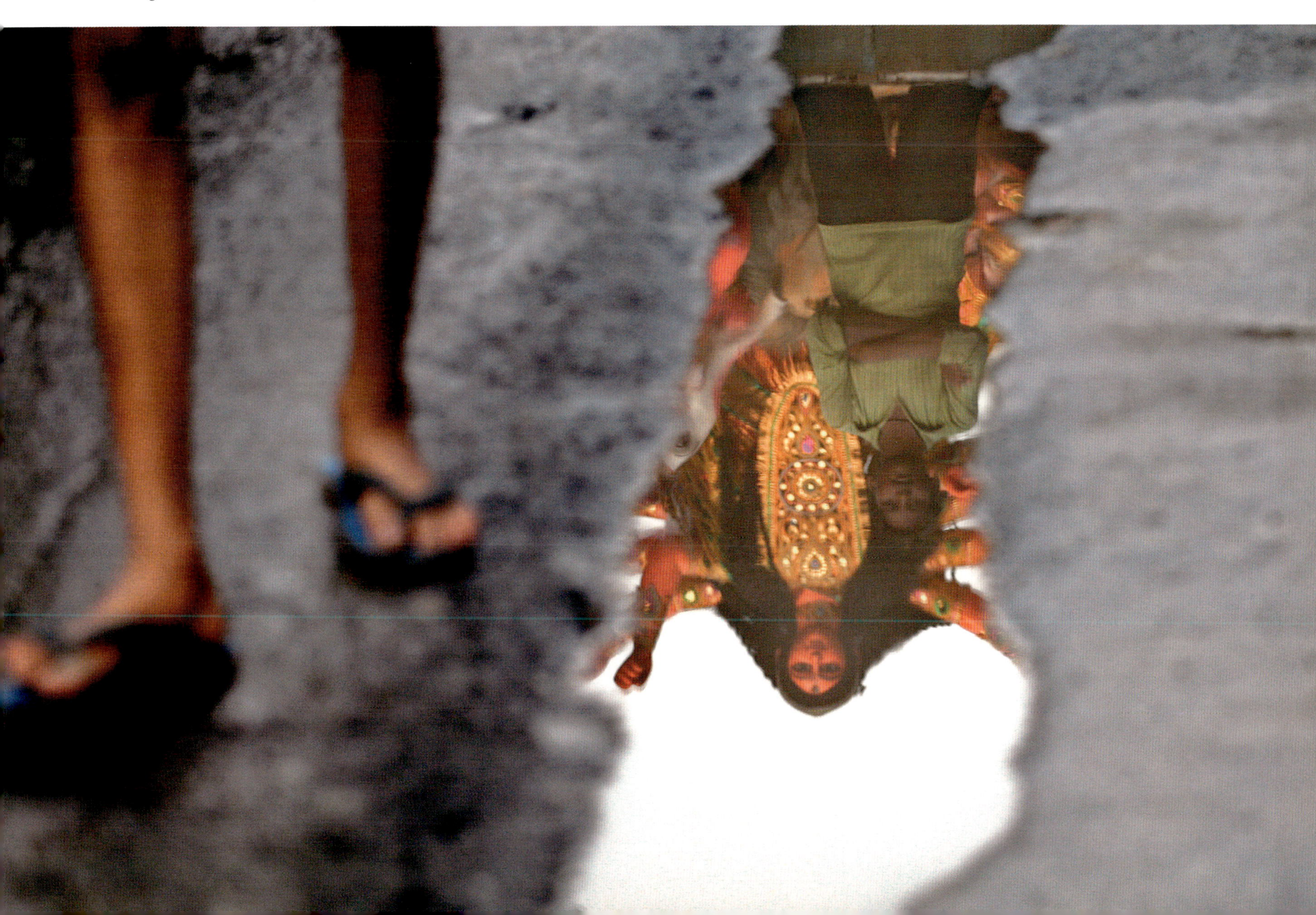

16 April 2003, SEVILLE, SPAIN

Catholic penitents walk to church for the procession of the El Baratillo brotherhood in the Andalusian capital Seville. Processions take place throughout Spain during Holy Week, drawing thousands of visitors. According to a centuries-old tradition, participants wear long robes and hoods to hide their identity from friends and neighbours as they march to do penance for their sins. Marcelo del Pozo

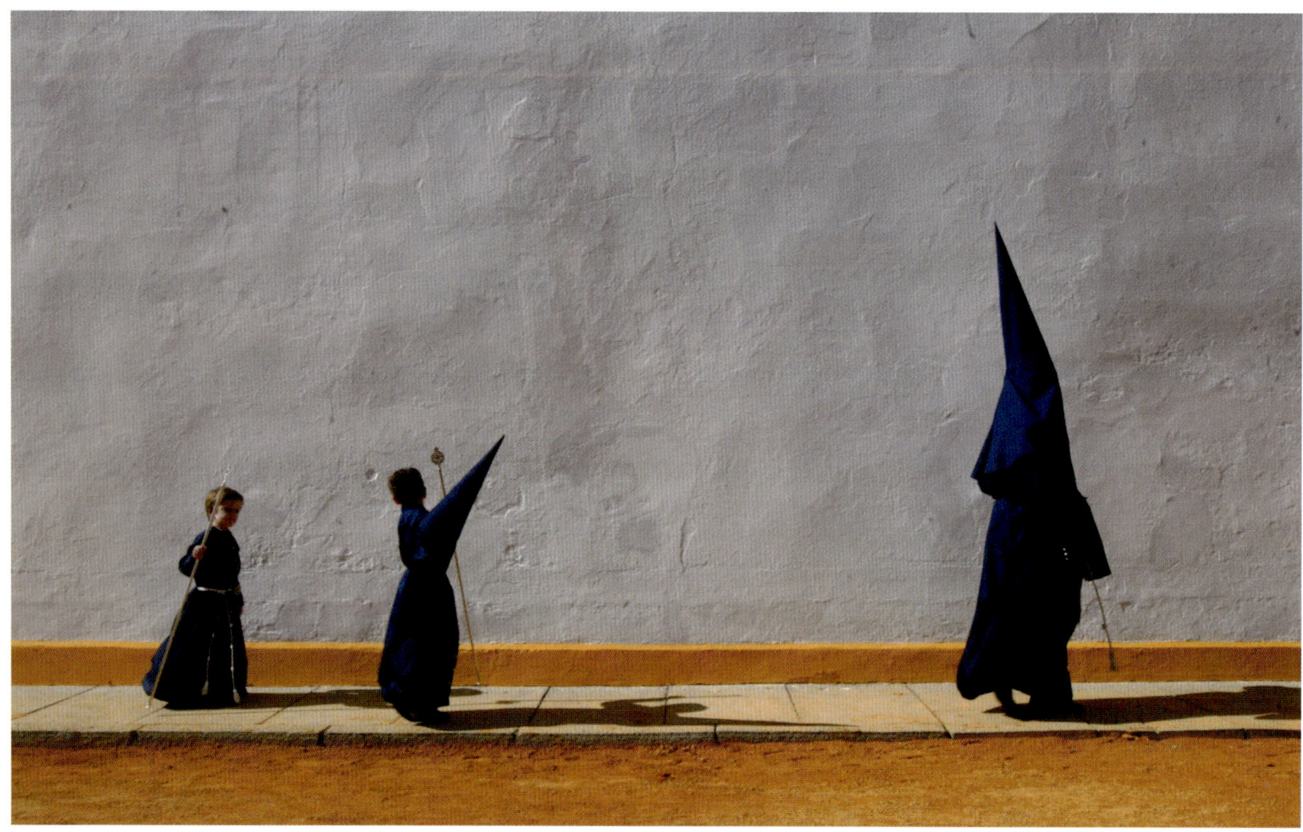

19 May 2005, ST PETERSBURG, RUSSIA

A religious procession of Russian Orthodox faithful outside the famous Church of The Saviour on the Spilt Blood in St Petersburg is reflected in the surface of a puddle. The procession marked the birthday of Russia's last Tsar Nicholas II, born in 1868, who was executed together with his family by Bolshevik revolutionaries in 1918. Alexander Demianchuk

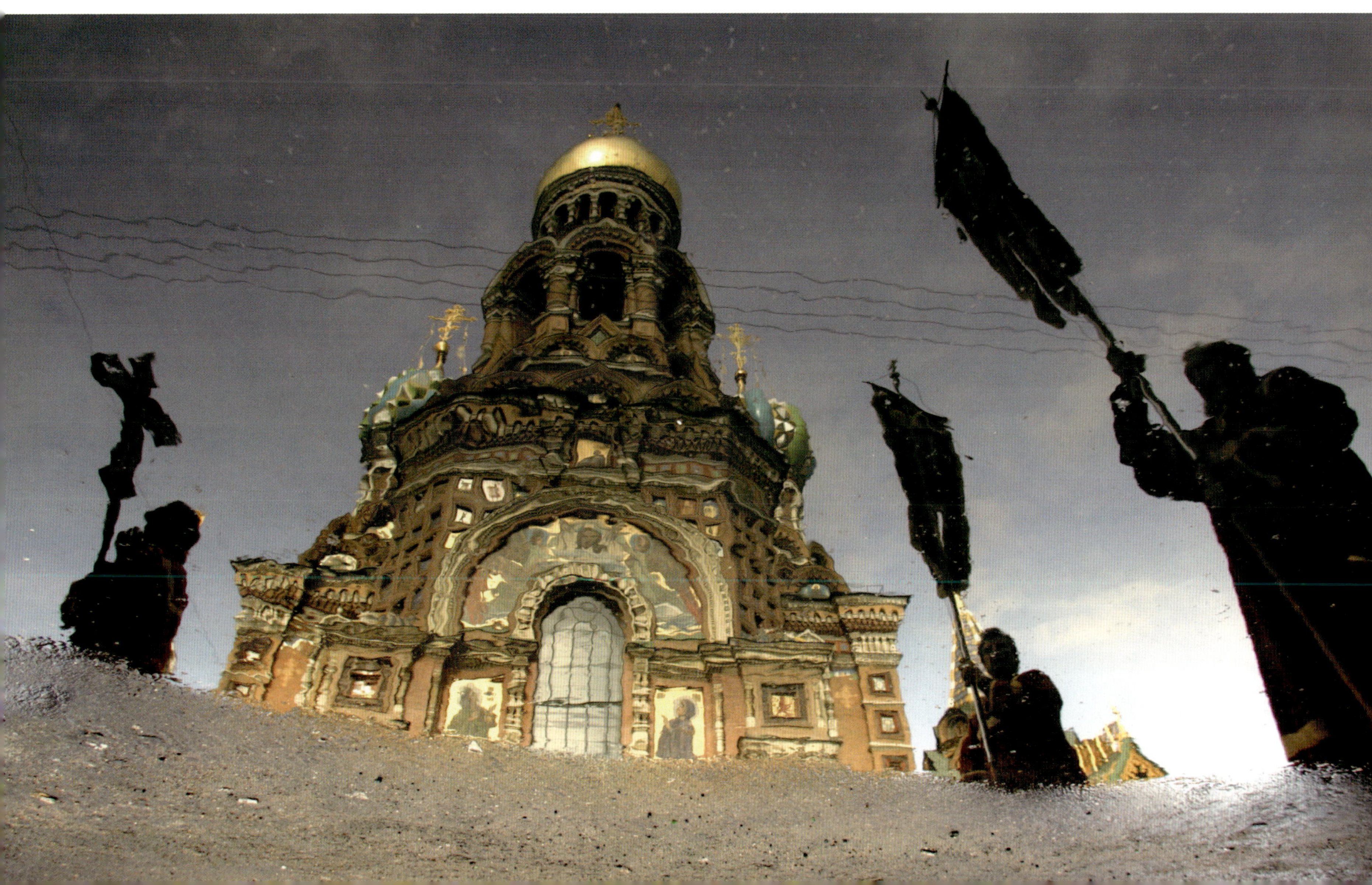

29 May 2003, BAGHDAD, IRAQ

A dervish prays during a gathering in Baghdad. Dervishes are practitioners of Sufi, a mystical order of Islam, and believe that their bodies open up to the energy of God while they are in prayer. Swaying gently at first, chanting in monotones, they slowly build up to a frenzy of prayer. Damir Sagolj

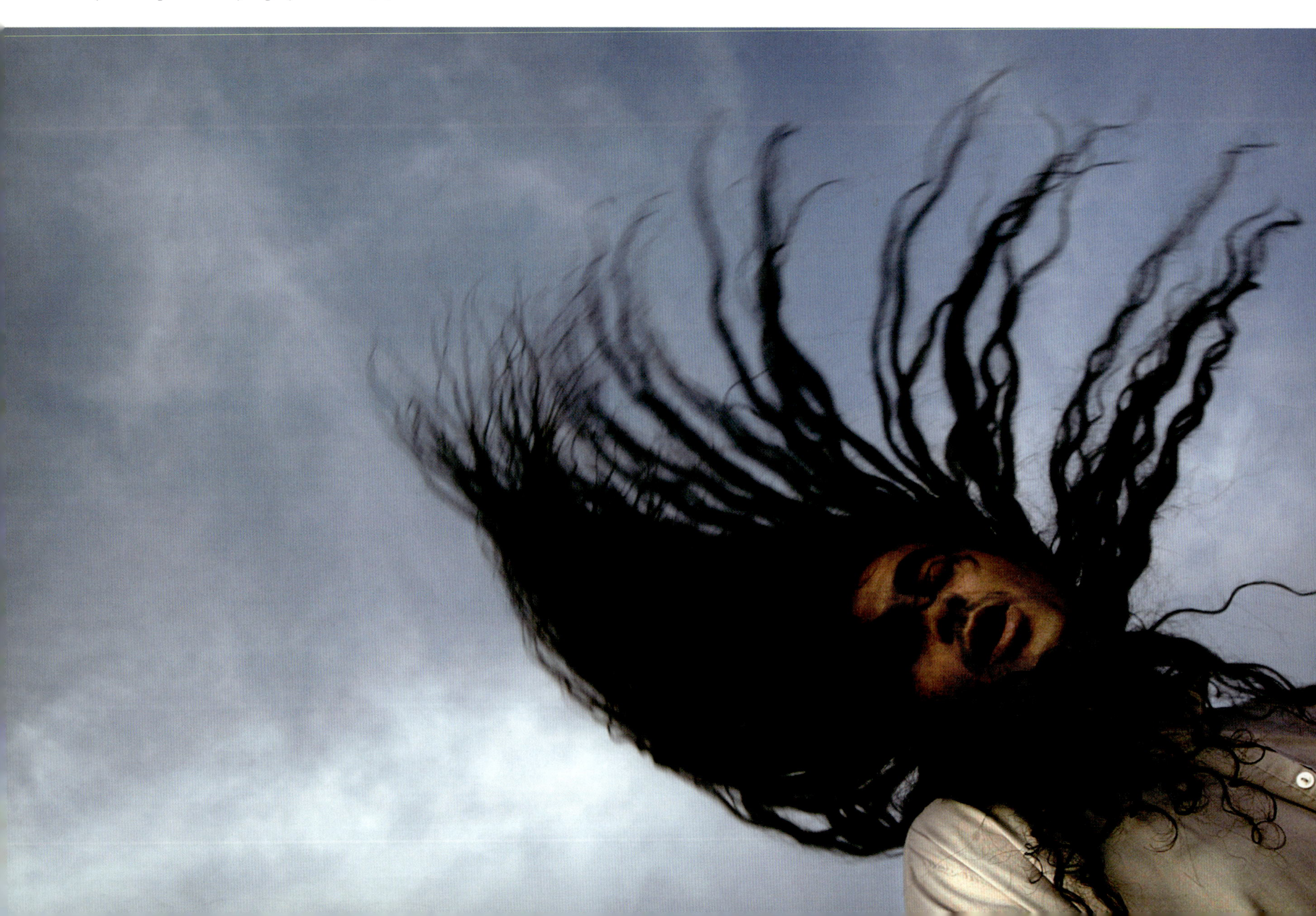

16 May 2005, BAD KÖTZTING, GERMANY

A man dressed in traditional Bavarian clothes and holding a wooden cross leads a Whit Monday horseback procession in the southern German village of Kötzting. The annual ride of Kötzting, which dates back to the year 1412, is one of the biggest religious processions on horseback in Europe. Alexandra Winkler

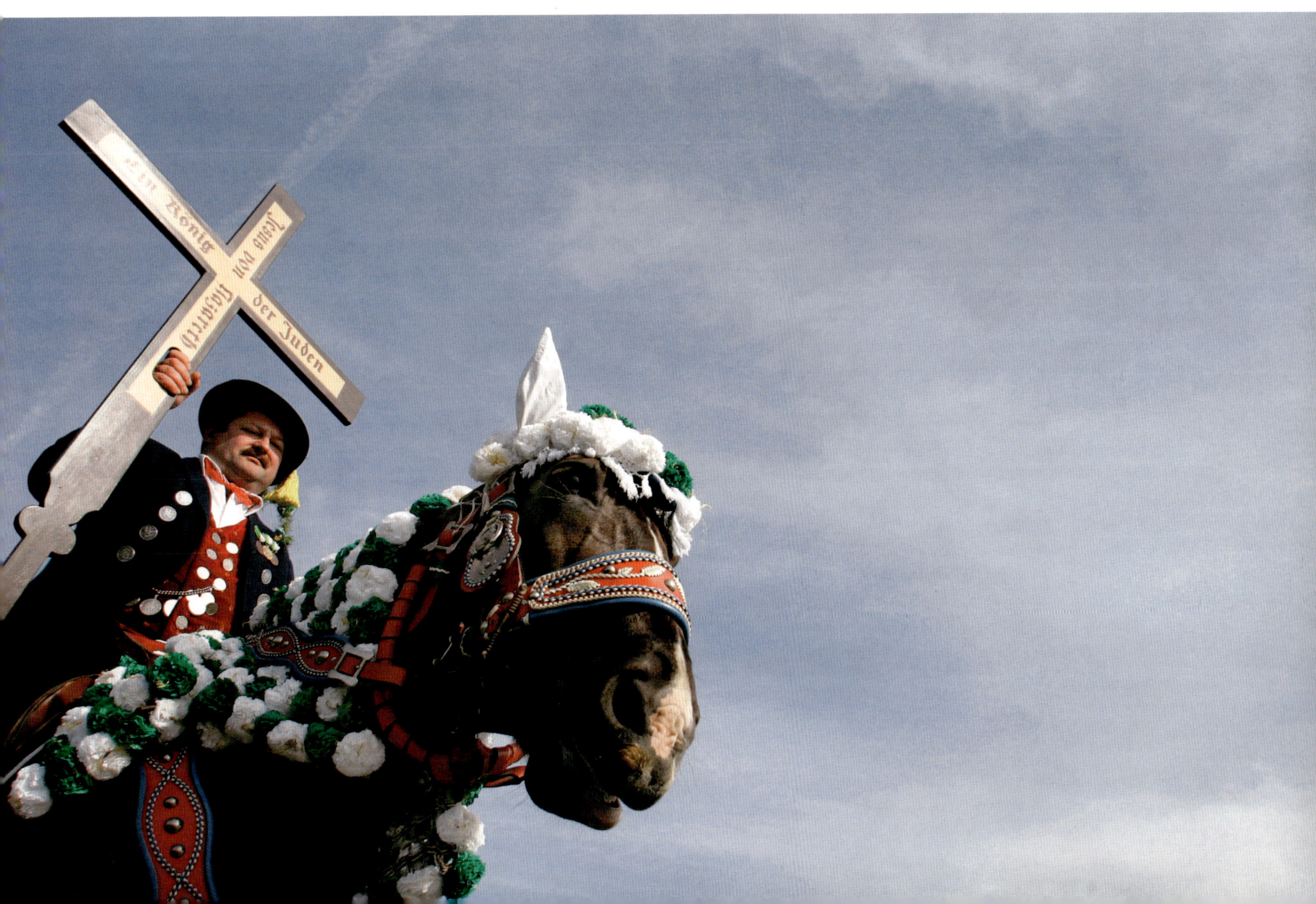

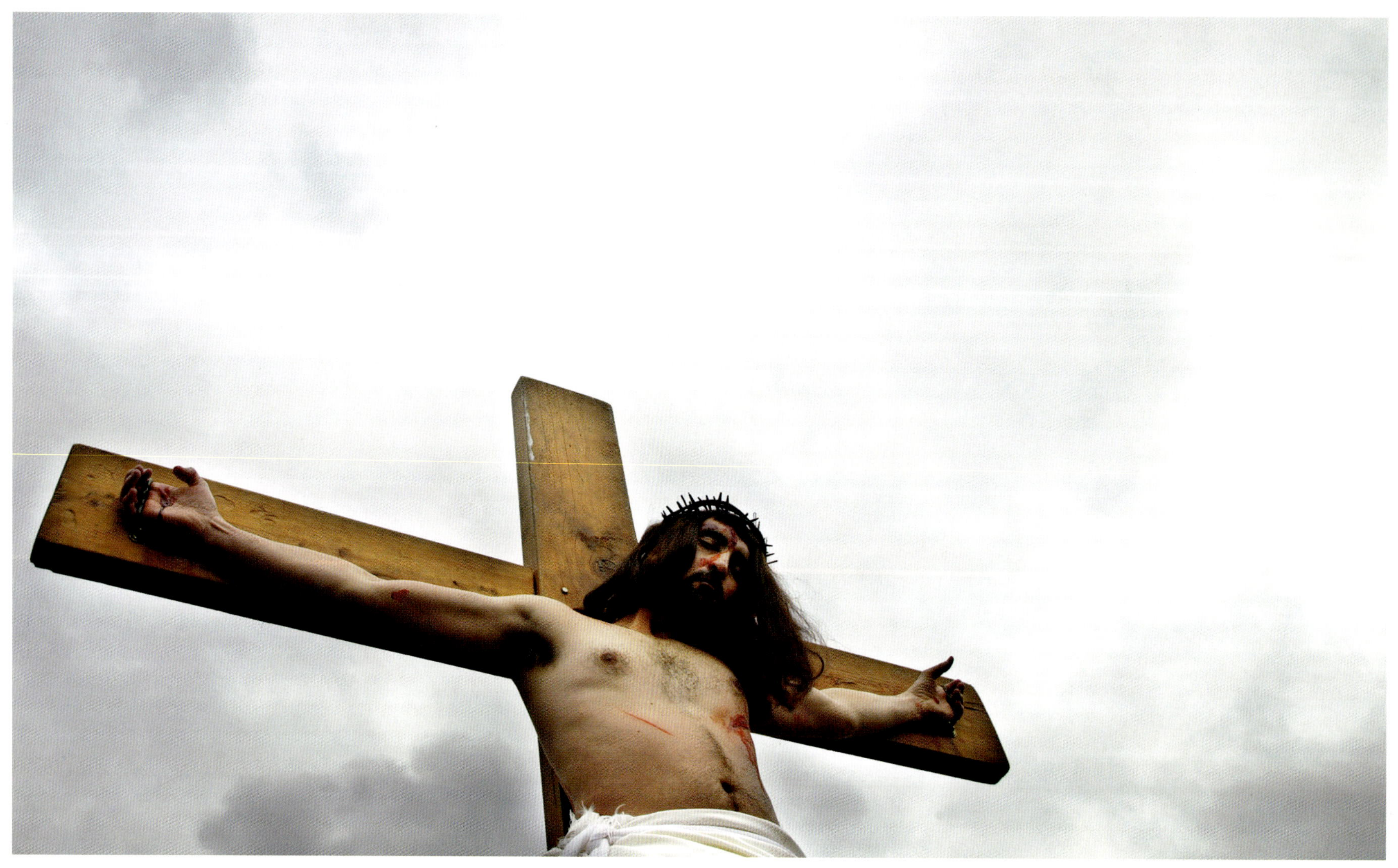

25 March 2005, CAMDEN, UNITED STATES

In Camden, New Jersey, a Christian participates in a Good Friday re-enactment of Jesus Christ's procession through the streets and his crucifixion. Shannon Stapleton

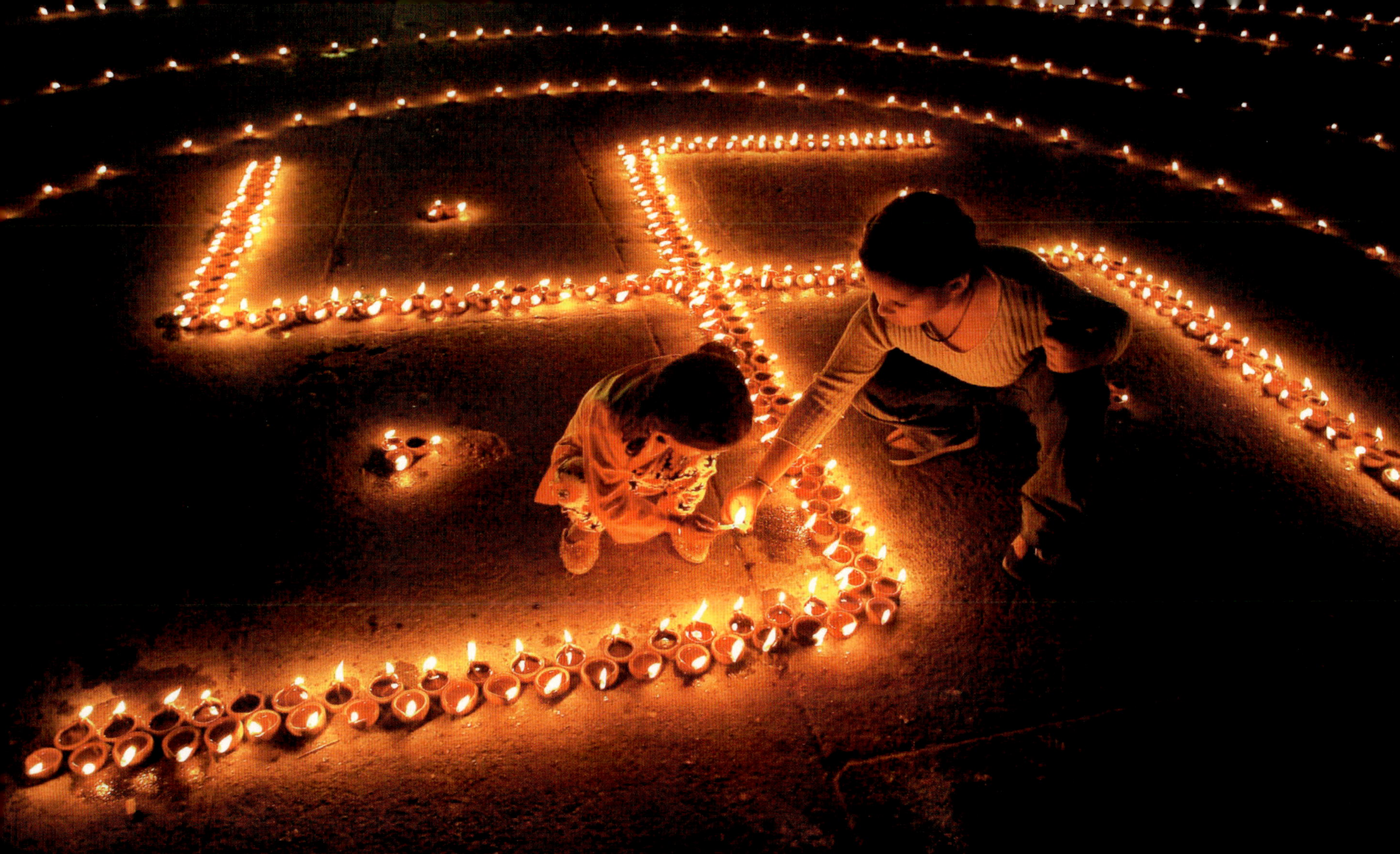

11 November 2004, CHANDIGARH, INDIA

Children light lamps in the shape of a swastika on the eve of Diwali, the Hindu festival of lights. In Hindu tradition, the swastika is a sacred symbol of good fortune and prosperity. Ajay Verma

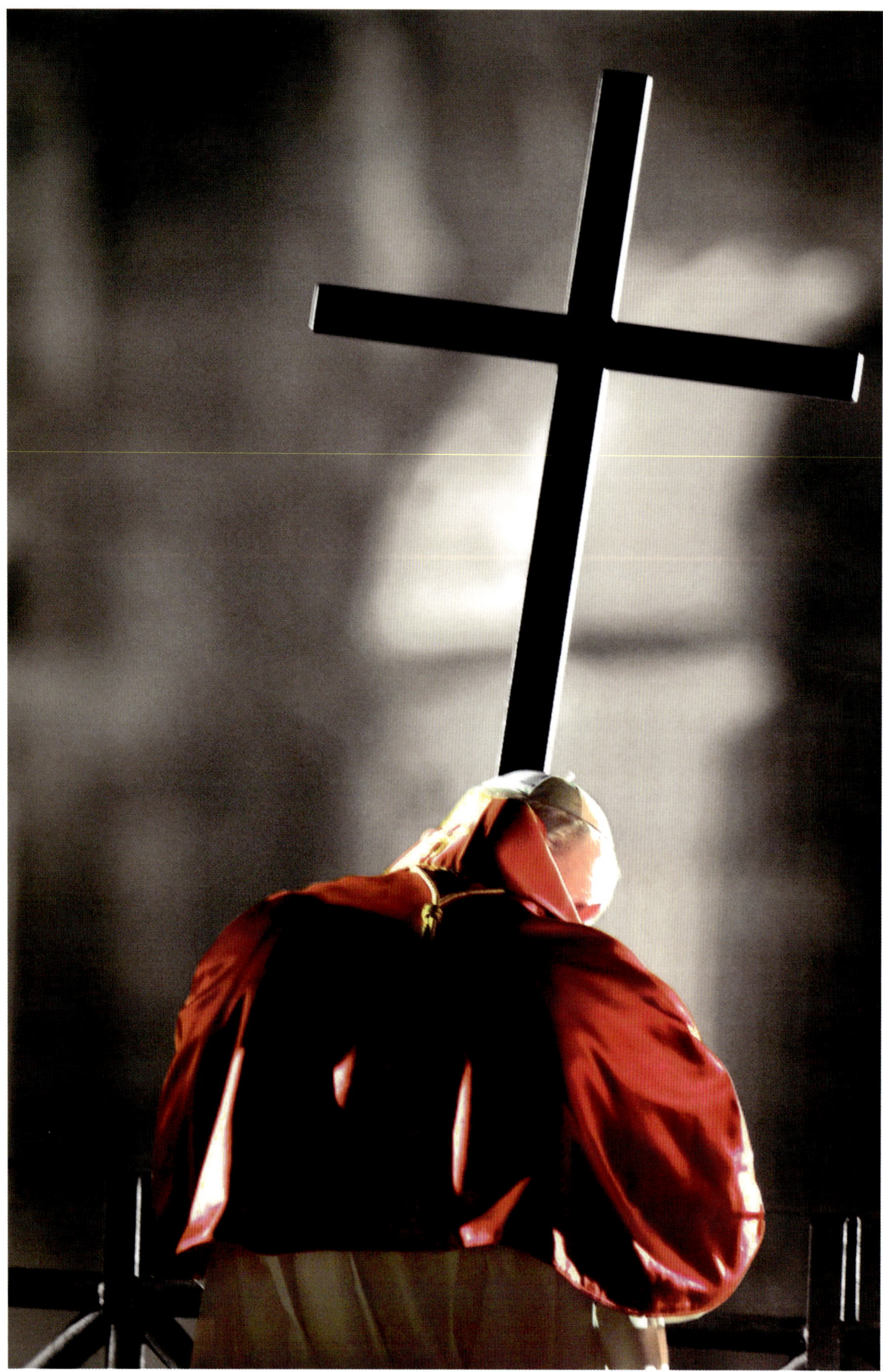

13 April 2001, ROME, ITALY

This page Pope John Paul II holds a cross at Rome's ancient Colosseum during the traditional *Via Crucis* (Way of the Cross) ceremony on Good Friday. Dylan Martinez

16 October 2003, VATICAN

Opposite above left Pope John Paul II waves to well-wishers in Paul VI Hall at the Vatican during a signing ceremony of a major document on the role of bishops that was issued on the occasion of his silver jubilee. Max Rossi

30 January 2005, VATICAN

Opposite above right Pope John Paul II with a white dove released by children from the window of his private apartment. Max Rossi

19 October 2003, VATICAN

Opposite centre left A puddle reflects St Peter's Basilica and priests as they give Holy Communion during the beatification ceremony of Mother Teresa. Catholic pilgrims, tourists and members of other religions streamed into the Vatican to see Pope John Paul II put Mother Teresa of Calcutta on the road to sainthood. Alessandro Bianchi

18 August 2002, KRAKOW, POLAND

Opposite centre right Nuns wave in welcome to Pope John Paul II as he arrives at Blonie field in Krakow to address the largest crowd that ever assembled in Poland. Jerry Lampen

13 March 2005, VATICAN

Opposite below left Pope John Paul II arrives in St Peter's Square on his return from the Gemelli hospital 18 days after he underwent throat surgery to relieve severe breathing problems. Alessandro Bianchi

7 April 2005, VATICAN

Opposite below right Mourners wait in St Peter's Square to enter the Basilica where the body of the late Pope lay in state following his death on 2 April 2005. Alessia Pierdomenico

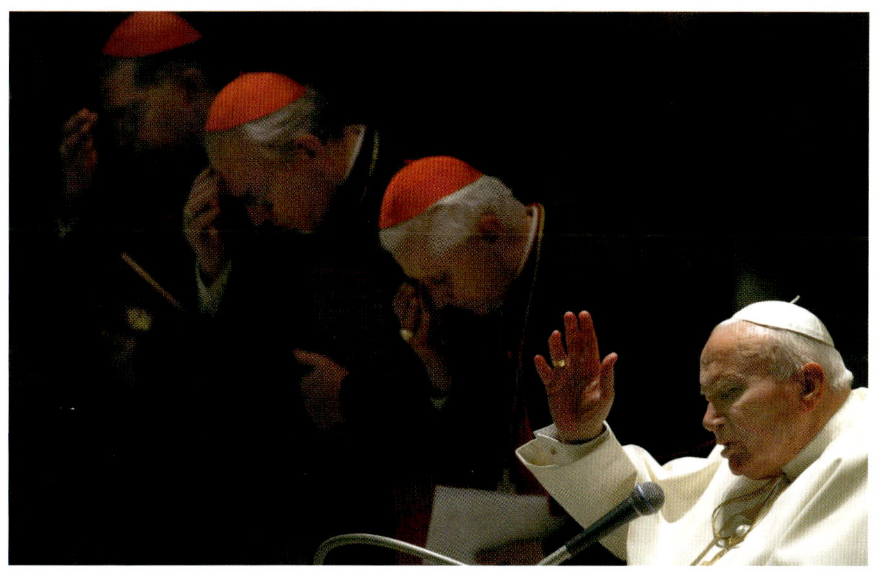
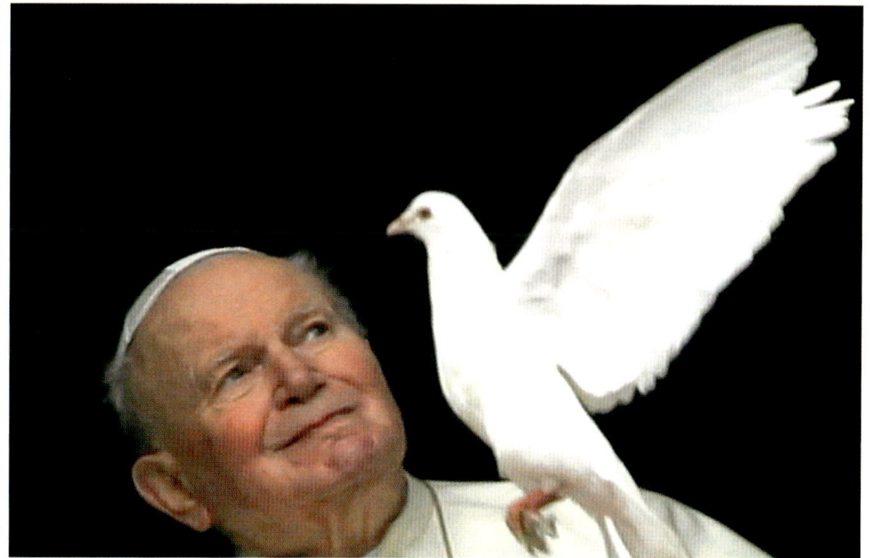
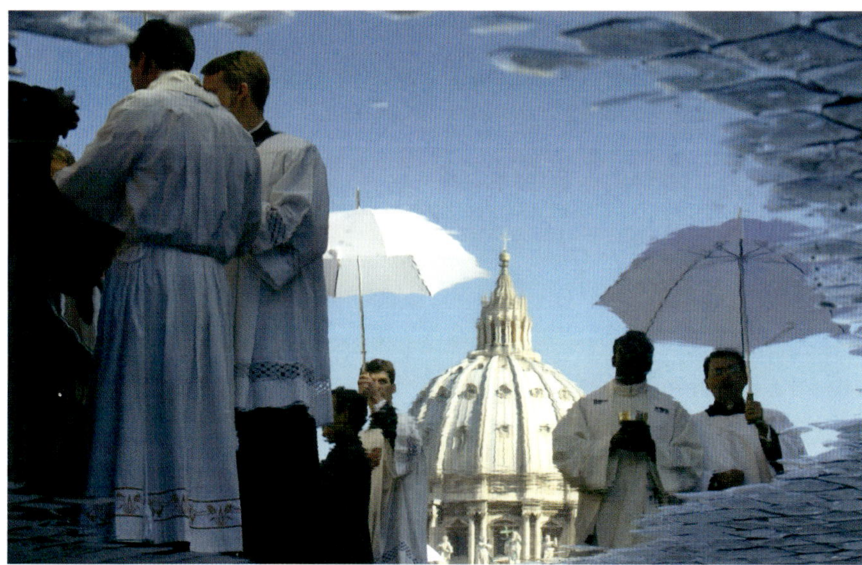
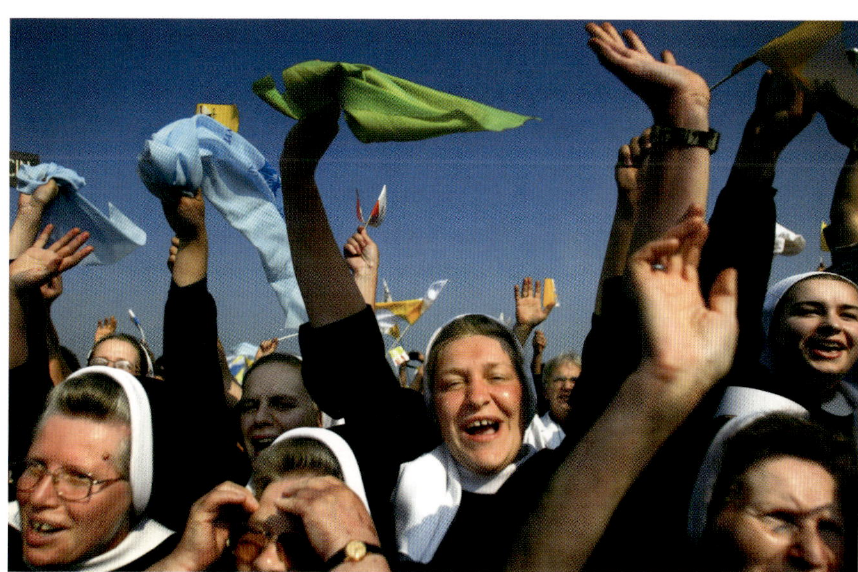
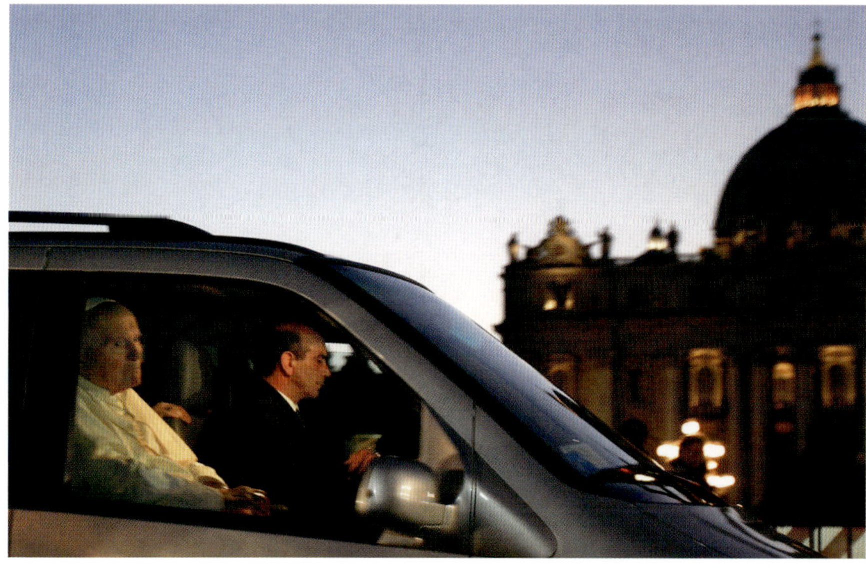
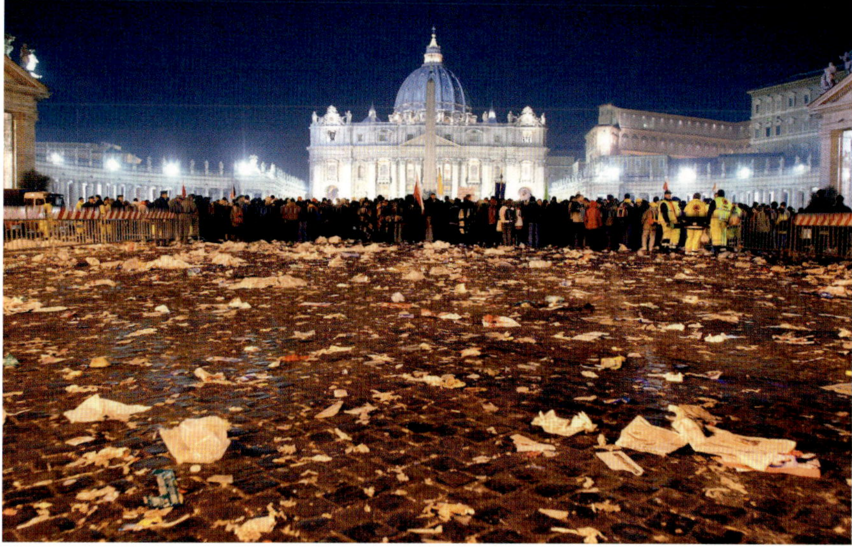

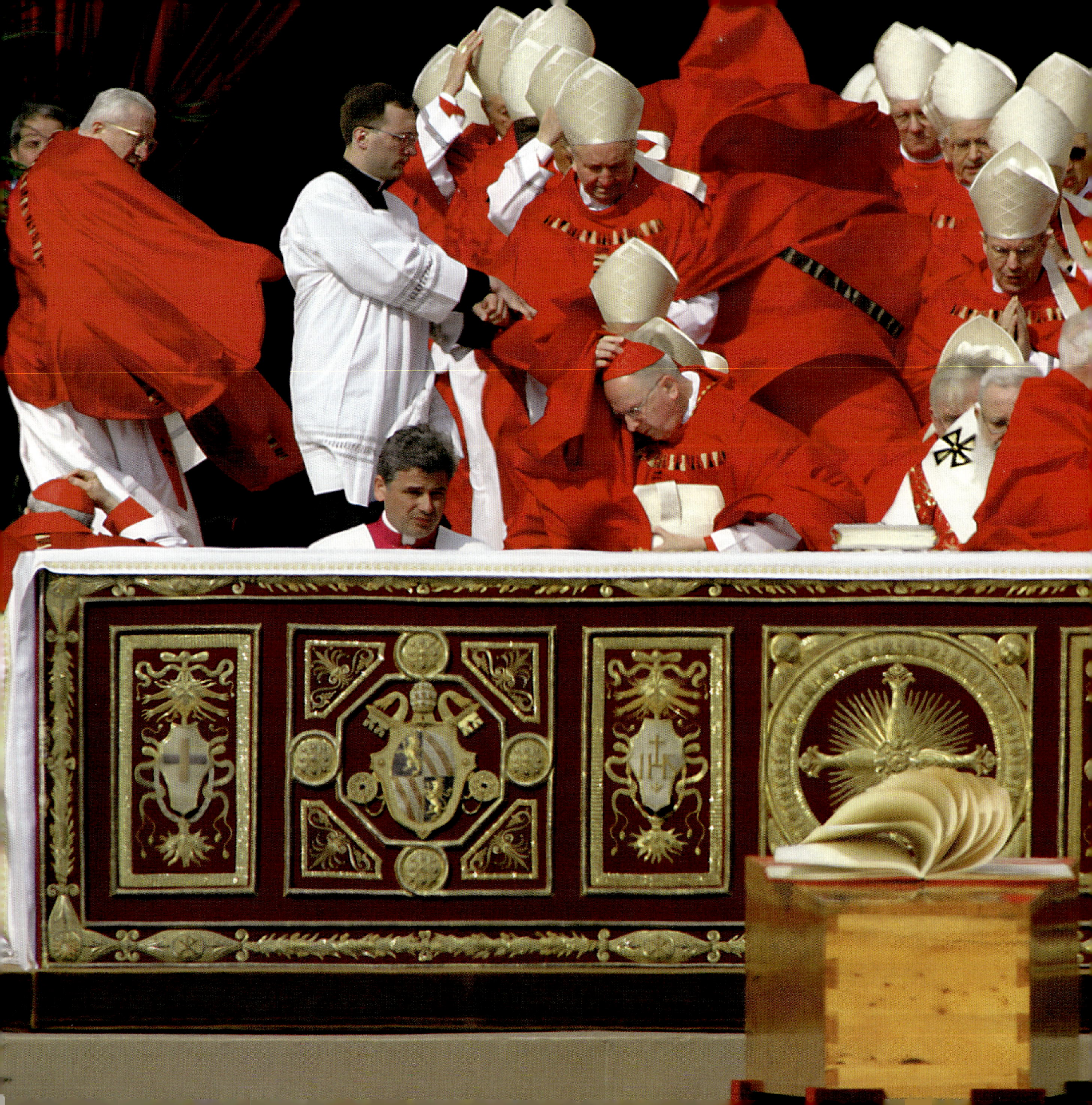

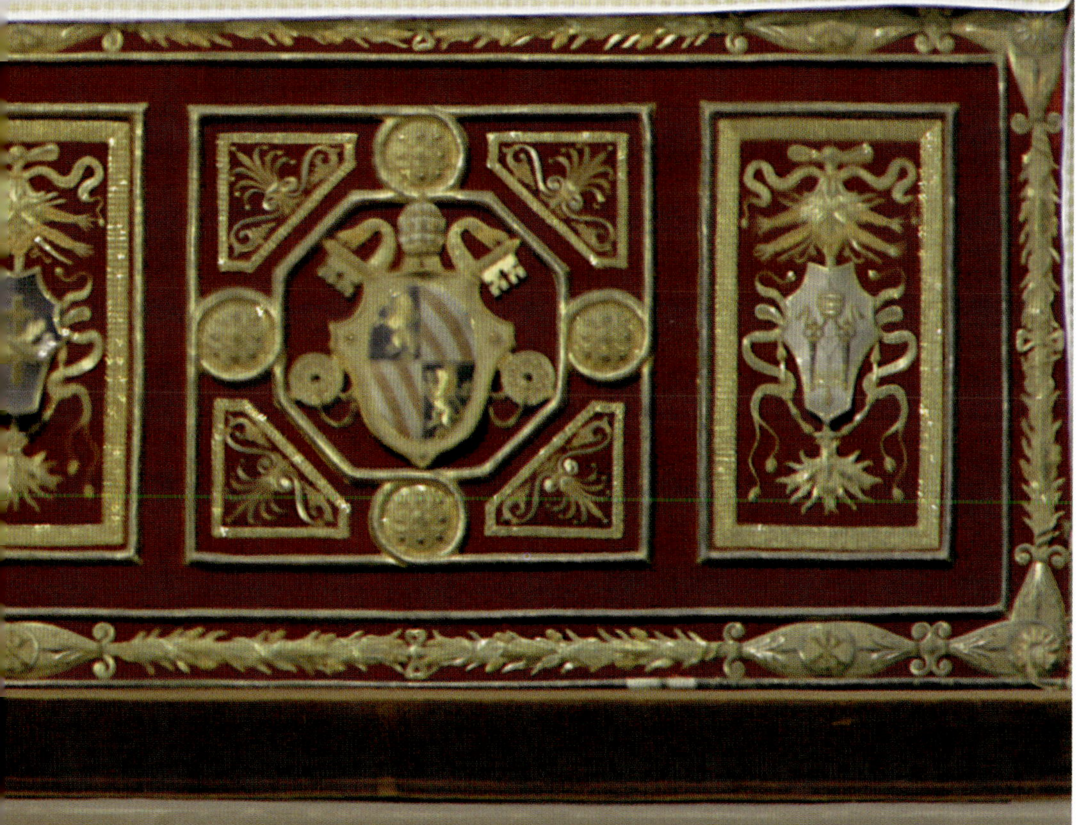

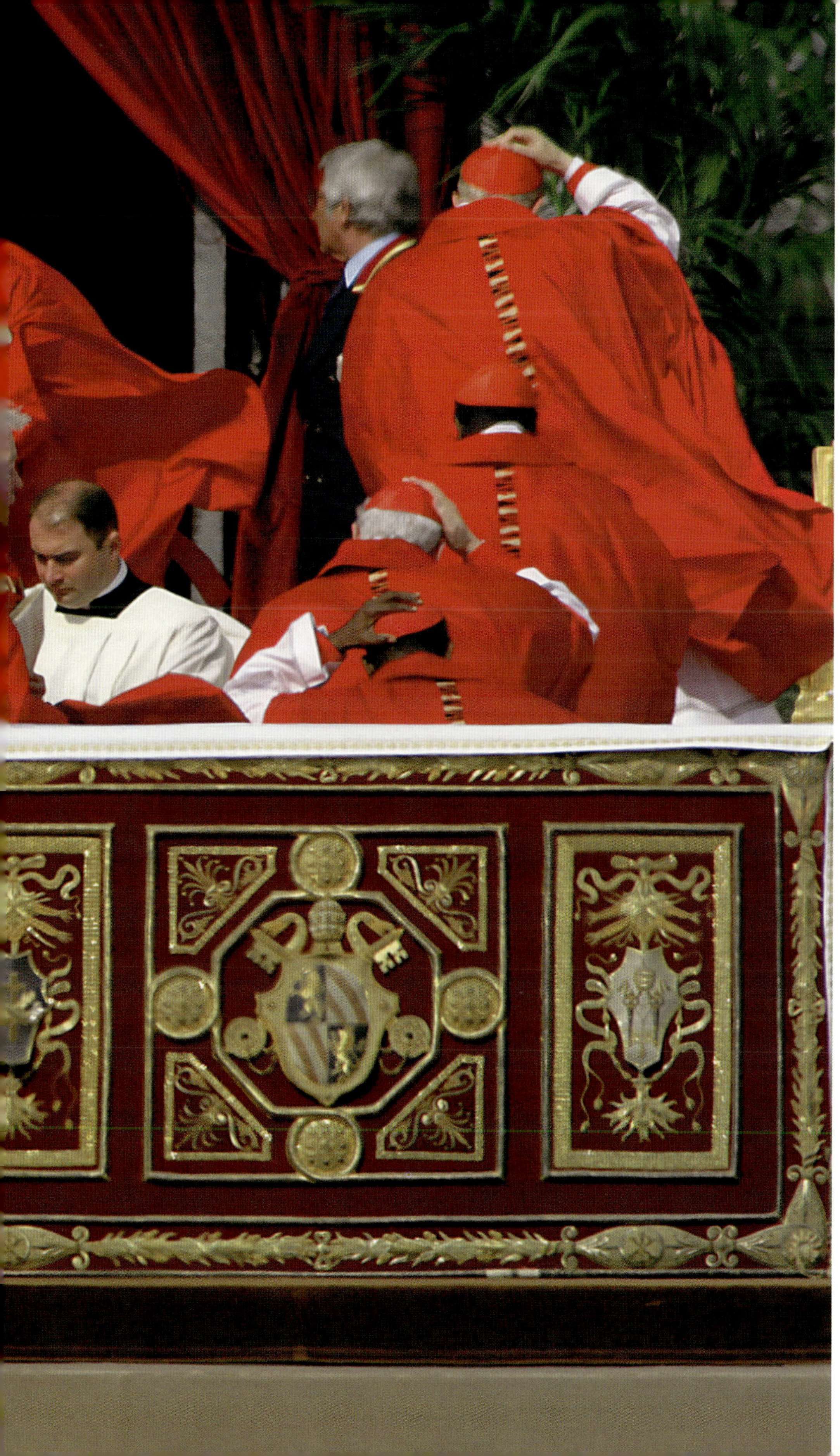

8 April 2005, VATICAN

Cardinals' vestments are blown by a gust of wind as they arrive for the funeral mass of Pope John Paul II at St Peter's Basilica in the Vatican. A multitude of humanity from Poland to Paraguay made the journey to Rome, joining the powerful of the earth to say a final goodbye to Pope John Paul. Max Rossi

7 May 2005, ROME, ITALY

Pope Benedict XVI, successor to John Paul II, waves as he arrives to lead a mass in the Basilica of St John Lateran in Rome. Max Rossi

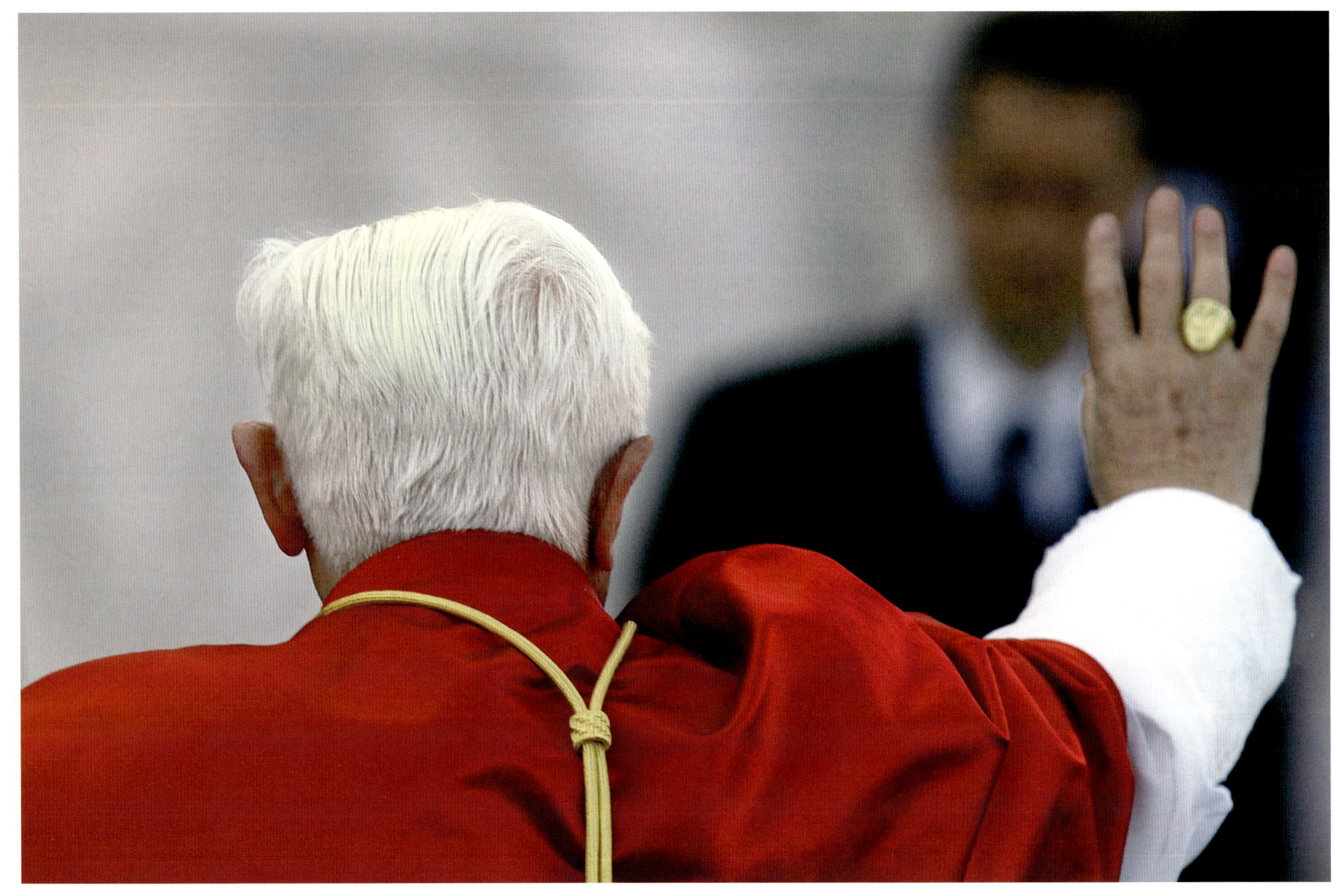

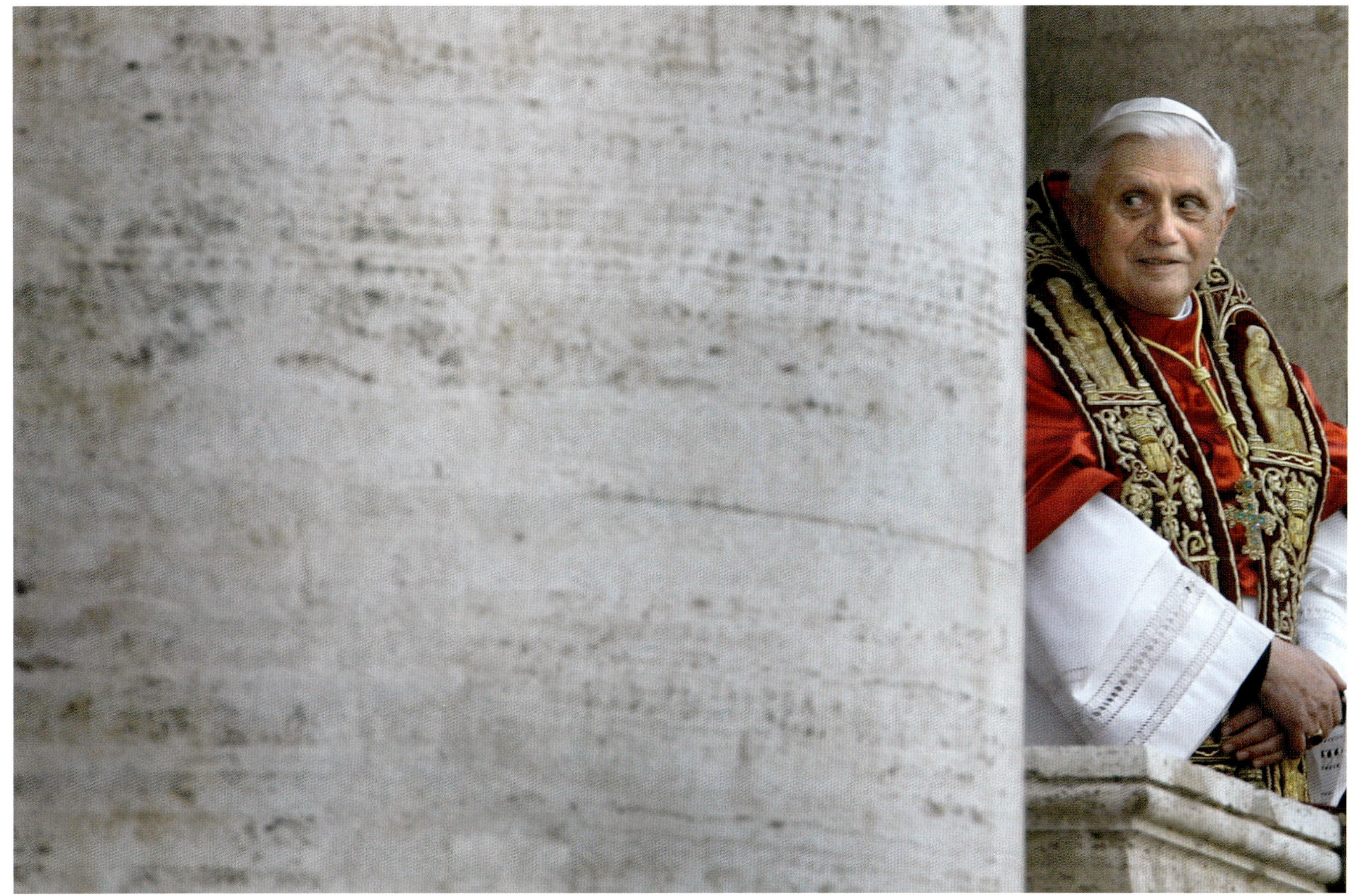

19 April 2005, VATICAN

The newly elected Pope Benedict XVI greets thousands of pilgrims from the balcony of St Peter's Basilica at the Vatican. Kai Pfaffenbach

The superpowers of the Cold War were defined by their nuclear weapons, and the resources to keep building more and better ones. The end of that era left the United States unchallenged as the world's only superpower. What will hold the key to global political power in the twenty-first century? Atom bombs again? Western-style democracy? Another ideology to command the loyalty of millions? Or just plain old hard cash?

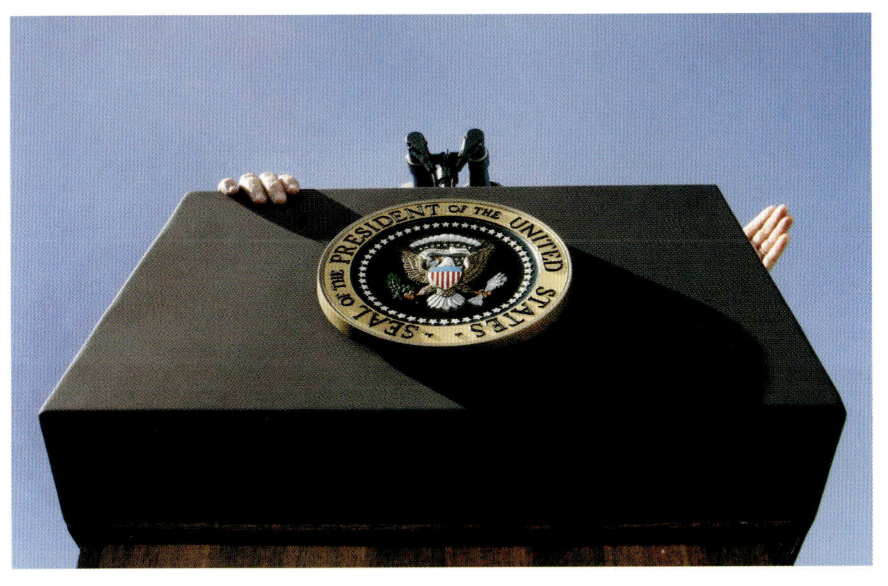

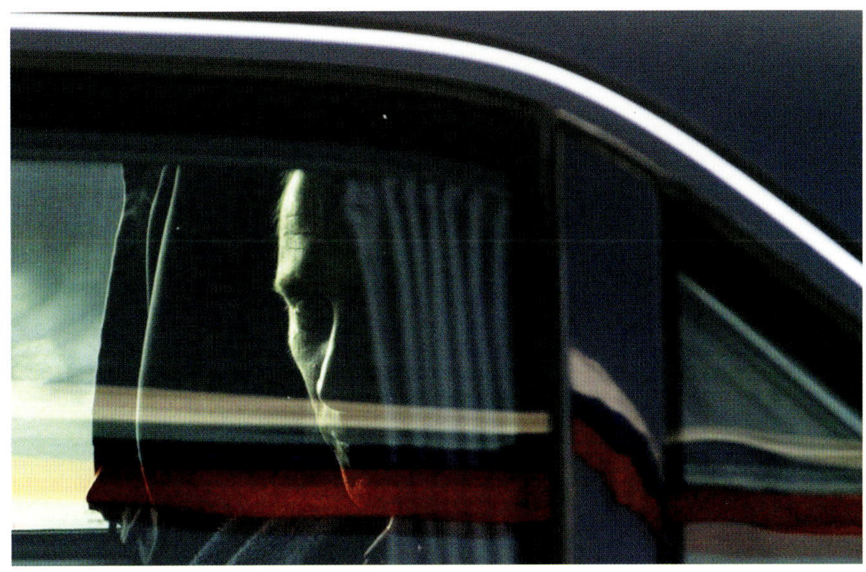

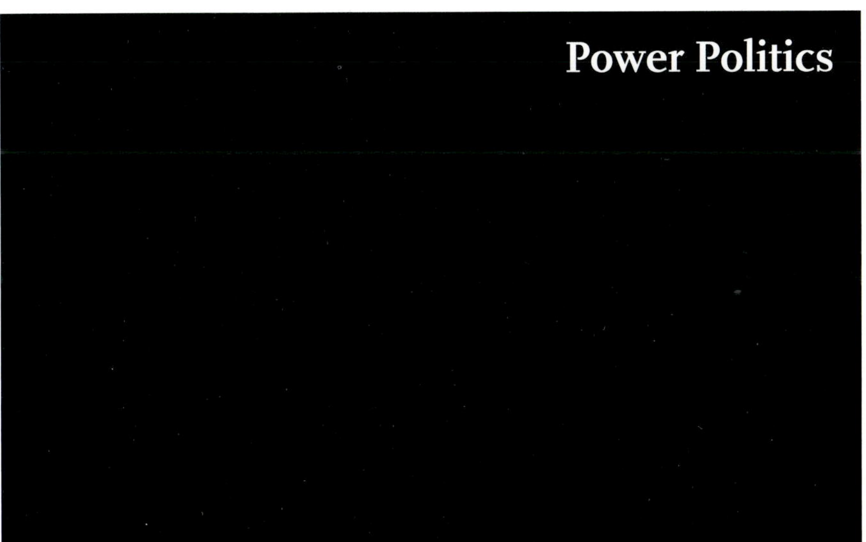

Power Politics

Democracy / Dictatorship / Diplomacy
Elections / Campaigning / Negotiation
Rights / Resistance / Revolution

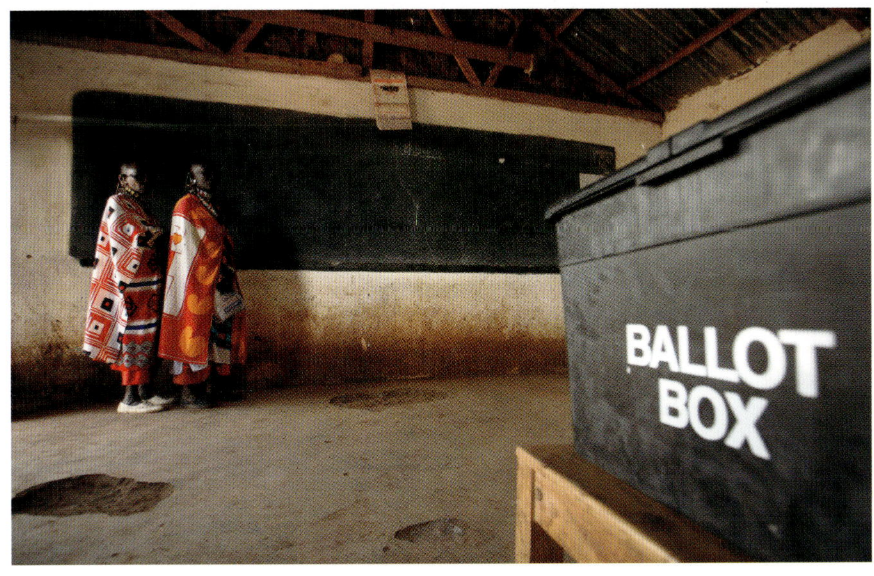

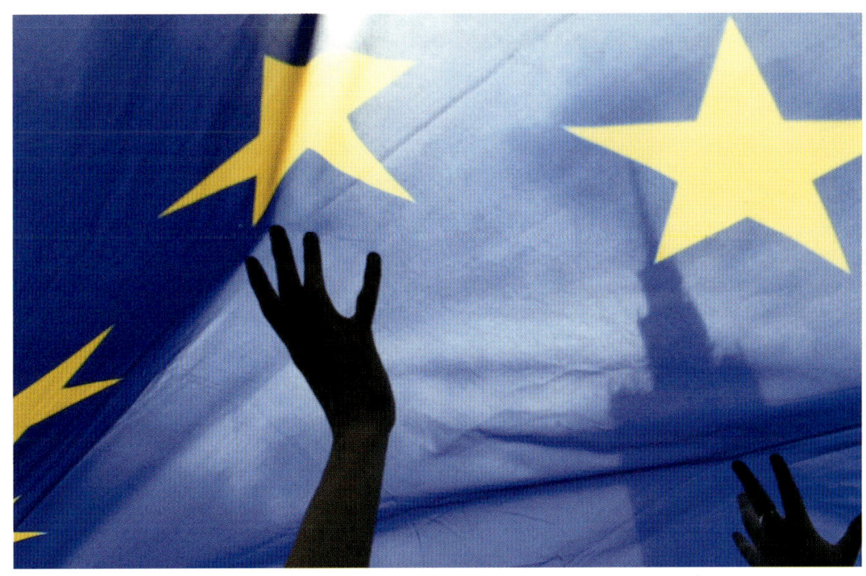

When the Soviet empire crumbled at the end of the 1980s, the American strategist Francis Fukuyama proclaimed 'the end of history': with communism discredited, ideological struggle was over and all countries would come, sooner or later, to the system of liberal democracy combined with free-market economy that the West had pioneered.

Years later, as conflicts continued to rage around the world, Fukuyama modified his views – but there was some evidence to support the theory. In the 1990s, the eastern bloc states on which Moscow had imposed communist systems after World War Two threw them off and queued up to join Western institutions like NATO and the European Union. Russia itself became a parliamentary democracy of a sort. Latin America moved uneasily in the same direction: leftist insurgencies persisted in Colombia and Peru and problems of poverty and land ownership remain unresolved, but the military dictatorships of the twentieth century faded away without the support of Cold War superpowers. In Africa too, democratic principles made headway from Mali to Mozambique, though corruption, tribalism and 'big man' politics continue to afflict the continent. Even remaining communist governments in China and Vietnam were forced to make major concessions to the capitalism they had once despised as the price of holding on to political power. Only the Arab world remained relatively impervious to the new trend, clinging on to autocratic rule by dominant elites.

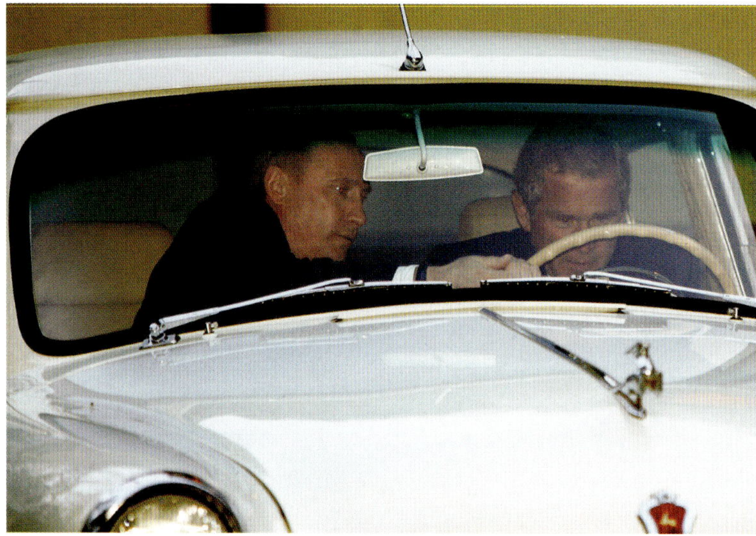

Russian President Vladimir Putin lends some assistance as U.S. President George W. Bush drives Putin's 1956 Volga after their meeting at Putin's presidential residence in Novo Ogarevo, outside Moscow. 8 May 2005, Kevin Lamarque.

In geopolitical terms, the main outcome of the end of the Cold War was to leave the United States as the sole, unchallenged superpower. Russia became a second-rank player, its once-feared military exposed as ineffectual and its huge nuclear arsenal now, somehow, irrelevant. There was general agreement that Moscow simply lost the technological war to the Americans because of its economic weakness and that, therefore, economic power must be the foundation of political power. U.S. President Bill Clinton famously wrote himself the memo 'It's the economy, stupid' as a reminder that people were primarily motivated by their bank balances.

But was that true? The U.S. economy flourished during the administration of the Democrat Clinton. Under his Republican successor George W. Bush it took a turn for the worse. Yet when American voters went to the polls in 2004 they re-elected Bush in preference to Democratic challenger John Kerry. For many voters the deciding factors were issues of national security in the aftermath of September 11, 2001, and moral values. The mood of the electorate chimed with the agenda of an ascendant religious right in the United States, which combines conservative views on social, family and sexual issues, a laissez-faire approach to business and a vigorous America-first policy in foreign affairs. This trend has disturbed some of America's long-standing friends, especially the secular powers of continental Europe.

The main outcome of the end of the Cold War was to leave the United States as the sole, unchallenged superpower.

Many governments, including some that had no love for Soviet communism, have been less than happy that there is no longer anyone to counterbalance the United States on the world stage. In particular, Arab leaders feared that U.S. predominance could enable

Washington's ally Israel to impose the settlement of its choice in the Middle East following the collapse of Israeli–Palestinian negotiations in 2000. Israel's decision to pull back unilaterally from the Gaza Strip in August 2005 while continuing to occupy the West Bank and maintain most of the Jewish settlements there did little to assuage their fears.

The international Islamic militant movement al Qaeda rose to prominence from the mid-1990s against this background. Its core was a group of highly motivated men trained in the mujahideen war against Soviet forces in Afghanistan and incensed by what they saw as a Western drive to dominate the Muslim world with the connivance of most Arab governments. Its leader was Osama bin Laden, a wealthy but ascetic Saudi driven by anger at the presence of U.S. forces on Saudi soil. Its weapon of choice was the suicide bomber. And its most spectacular action was the September 11 attacks using hijacked airliners to smash into the World Trade Center in New York and the Pentagon outside Washington, killing in all nearly 3,000 people. It was a stunning, low-budget operation of murderous audacity, beyond the wildest dreams of the former Kremlin leaders with their high-priced nuclear missile systems. Al Qaeda 'franchises' have subsequently struck in the heart of Europe, targetting transport systems in Madrid in March 2004, killing almost 200 people, and London in July 2005, killing more than 50.

Al Qaeda's leaders understood the importance of ideology in achieving their goals: that he who can command men's beliefs – persuading them that the suicide bomber is serving Islam and will travel directly to Paradise – acquires a far deadlier weapon. Whether or not they are refighting the medieval Crusades, they certainly believe that is what the Christian West is doing. Only a small number of the world's 1.6 billion Muslims support al Qaeda's actions, though more than that have at least some sympathy with its motivation. The one country – Iran – that currently has an Islamic fundamentalist government will have nothing to do with a group whose extreme brand of Sunni Islam does not accept that Shi'ites, the dominant sect in Iran, are authentic Muslims. Yet its nebulous nature is an essential part of al Qaeda's menace, out of all proportion to its actual resources. Unlike the former Soviet leadership, al Qaeda's leaders are impossible to locate or to talk to – even if there were anything to talk about.

Nevertheless, President Bush took the September 11 attacks as an act of war and responded in kind. To those who had questioned what threat confronted the United States and its mighty armed forces now that the Warsaw Pact was no more, here was the answer: terror. Within weeks, U.S.-backed forces had overthrown the Taliban rulers of Afghanistan, who had harboured al Qaeda's leadership and training camps.

It was an extension of the war on terror that led Bush and his British ally Tony Blair to invade and occupy Iraq in March 2003. The primary reason given was Iraq's supposed possession of weapons of mass destruction, but when none were found after the invasion, other justifications were advanced. The architects of the war – aides to Bush – were men testing out new ideals in the post-Cold War world. America had the might to promote its view of the new world order – so why not use it? Peace in the Middle East, they argued, would never come and the stability of its vital oil reserves never be

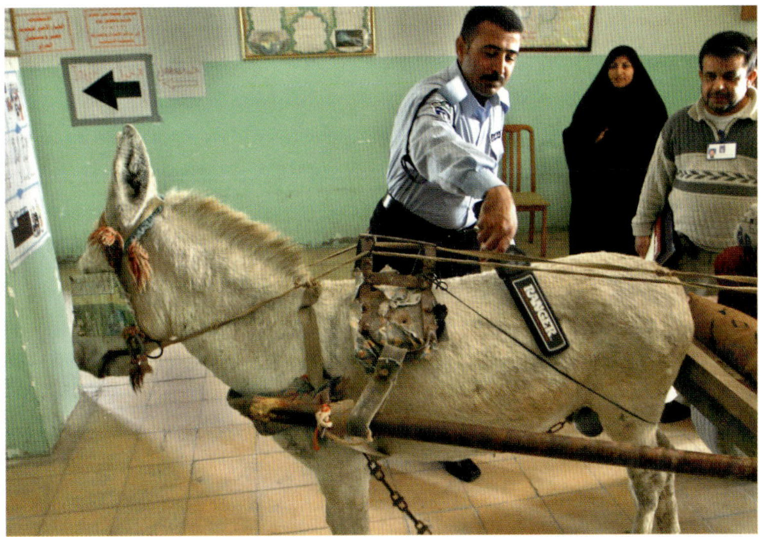

A donkey pulling a disabled man on a cart is checked by an Iraqi policeman before being allowed to enter a polling station in Basra. At least 35 people died in insurgent attacks on Iraq's historic election day. Nonetheless up to eight million Iraqis defied the threats to cast their ballots, a turnout of around 60 percent. 30 January 2005, Atef Hassan.

ensured until democracy took root in the region. And where better to start than in friendless Iraq, with its brutal dictator Saddam Hussein who had invaded two neighbouring countries and slaughtered his own people by the thousand? Taking out the Baathist regime in Baghdad, proponents reasoned, would surely send an unmistakable message to the region's two other problematic governments in Iran and Syria.

No event of recent years has divided the world community like the invasion of Iraq, which was supported by Italy, Spain, Portugal and several East European nations and opposed by France, Germany, Russia and most non-aligned states. Public opinion in much of Europe has found it hard to accept that al Qaeda outrages, however dreadful, can be compared to the former threat of nuclear annihilation. For countries such as France, the fallout from Iraq has dramatized the need to insist on the 'multipolar' nature of the twenty-first-century world following the East–West stand-off of previous decades. In other words, the United States cannot have everything its own way. The bloody insurgency that has beset U.S. attempts to install a working democracy in Iraq – more than 2,000 American servicemen have died there – has demonstrated that one thing at least has not changed since the Vietnam war: the world's most powerful army is not guaranteed victory against a ruthless guerrilla force that knows the terrain and has no fear of death.

Moreover, governments hostile to U.S. policies have by no means concluded from the experiences of Afghanistan and Iraq that they defy America at their peril. Both North Korea, which says it has nuclear weapons, and Iran, thought by the West to be somewhere along the road to developing them, have used their atomic programmes as leverage to try to wring economic and political concessions from the West. These negotiations have replaced the arcane warhead-counting of U.S.-Soviet strategic arms talks.

Interfering in other countries' internal affairs, the cardinal sin of the Cold War era, has been touted as a virtue by a new breed of Western politicians.

'Rogue states' – as Washington has dubbed them – have, nevertheless, had to reckon with a new spirit abroad in global politics. Interfering in other countries' internal affairs, the cardinal sin of the Cold War era, has been touted as a virtue by a new breed of Western politicians like Britain's Blair in cases where a government is committing atrocities against its own people. The problem has been to find an international organization to legitimize such action. The United Nations, created at the end of World War Two as the world's policeman, has for years been able to fulfil that role only in places where big-power interests were not seriously threatened, such as West Africa and Congo. Its failure explicitly to back the invasion of Iraq incurred the wrath of many in the U.S. Congress who had long seen it as a corrupt bureaucracy beholden to Third World dictatorships, although the mood at the White House was to reform rather than abandon it. NATO, the Western alliance credited with keeping the peace in Europe for half a century, has intervened in Bosnia and Kosovo and taken on peace-keeping duties in Afghanistan. Yet it too was unable to unite around the toppling of Saddam and doubts remain over its long-term role now that the Soviet threat it was built to resist has disappeared. When all else has failed, the United States has had to assemble an ad hoc 'coalition of the willing' to keep it company.

For all the apparent U.S. dominance, this has, in some ways, been the age of the small state. The number of countries with seats at the United Nations has grown steadily as the bitter experiences of the twentieth century have persuaded many that politicians of their own race and religion are the only ones they can trust to rule them. The Soviet Union split into 15 states, Yugoslavia into six and Czechoslovakia into two. Indonesia gave up East Timor. Kosovo is straining at the leash. Spheres of influence have faded. In the former Soviet Union, peaceful democratic revolutions in Georgia and Ukraine have swept to power nationalist governments less inclined to defer to Russia. Even in the Middle East, tiny Lebanon, emboldened by U.S. backing, has sought to slough off decades of Syrian domination.

The same centrifugal force has surfaced at the U.N. itself, with moves to expand the number of permanent Security Council members beyond the five original nuclear powers – the United States, Russia, Britain, France and China. Even in the European Union, hopes of ever-greater integration have stalled as voters have balked at the idea of a common constitution for the bloc, now standing at 25 states. In the core members in the west of the continent, popular disillusion has grown with the single euro currency, which general publics have blamed for inflation. And the new democracies of eastern Europe, anxious as they have been to join the rich men's club, have shown little inclination to submit to a new external master in Brussels so soon after they have freed themselves from the old one in Moscow. A general decline in voter turnout at elections in the developed world has further suggested a disconnection between the rulers and the ruled – and a realization of the limits of democracy.

Lurking in the background as the established powers tested

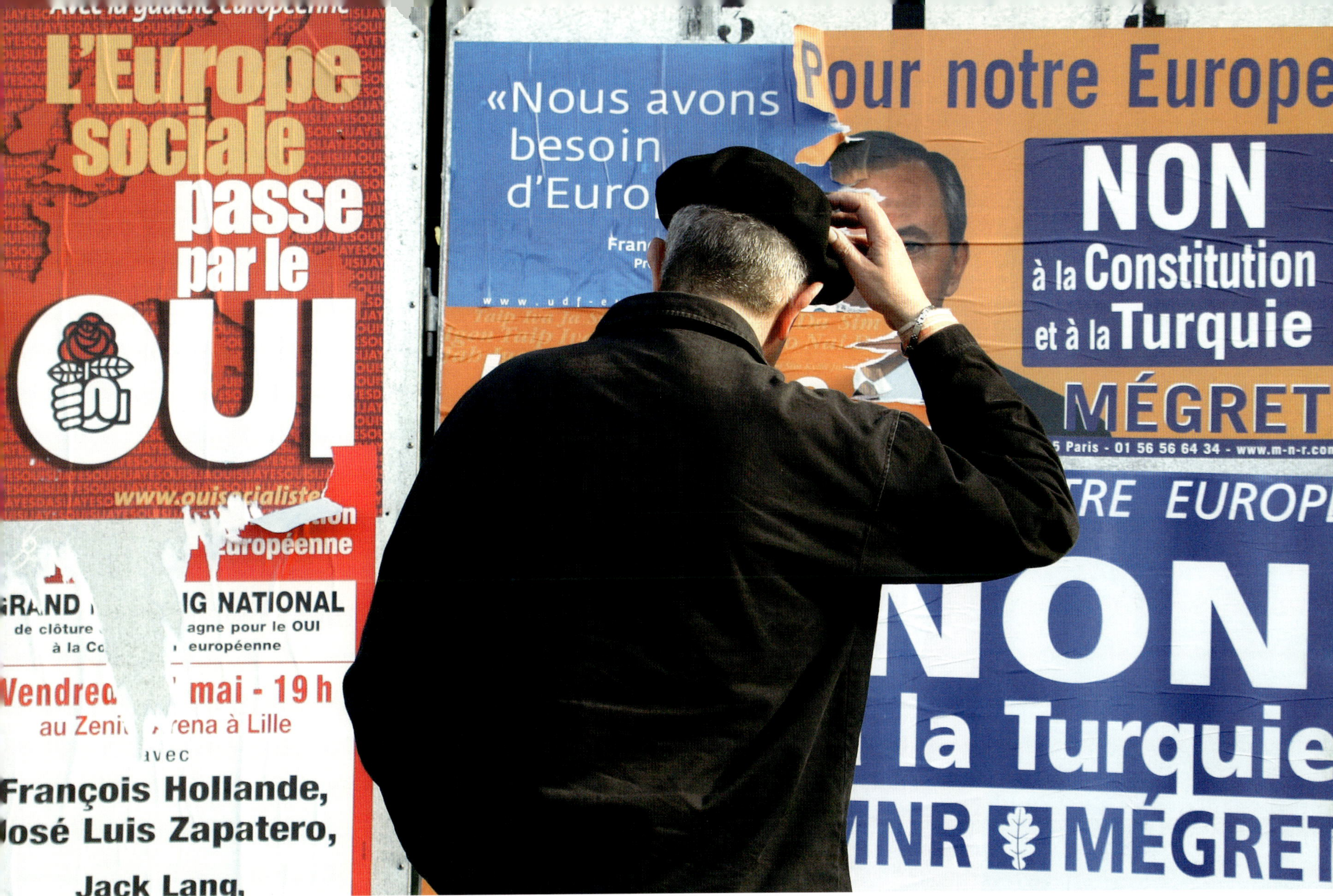

their strength at the beginning of the new millennium was the meteoric economic rise in the East of China – now growing at 9 percent annually – and India, both nuclear powers. If Washington outspent Moscow to prevail in the Cold War, could it not itself be outspent? Future decades will decide whether it is a Western-style political culture that holds the key to global power, or whether it is, after all, the economy, stupid.

Patrick Worsnip has worked for Reuters since 1971. He began as a trainee in Rome and has had successive postings as a correspondent in Moscow, Warsaw, Tehran, Beirut and, again, Rome. From 1986 to 1994 Patrick worked in London as diplomatic correspondent, covering the end of the Cold War and the fall of the Soviet bloc. He then went on to become State Department correspondent in Washington, DC, until 1998. Patrick is currently editor-in-charge on the Reuters World Desk in London.

23 May 2005, CAMBRAI, FRANCE

A resident looks at campaign posters for and against the European Union constitution in Cambrai, northern France. Designed to streamline EU leadership and make decision-making more efficient following the enlargement of the bloc, the constitution was rejected on 29 May by 55 percent of the French electorate. This resounding 'No' vote, followed by the Dutch rejection in a referendum three days later, cast the European Union into its most severe political crisis in over a decade, opening a period of uncertainty, introspection and potential paralysis.

Pascal Rossignol

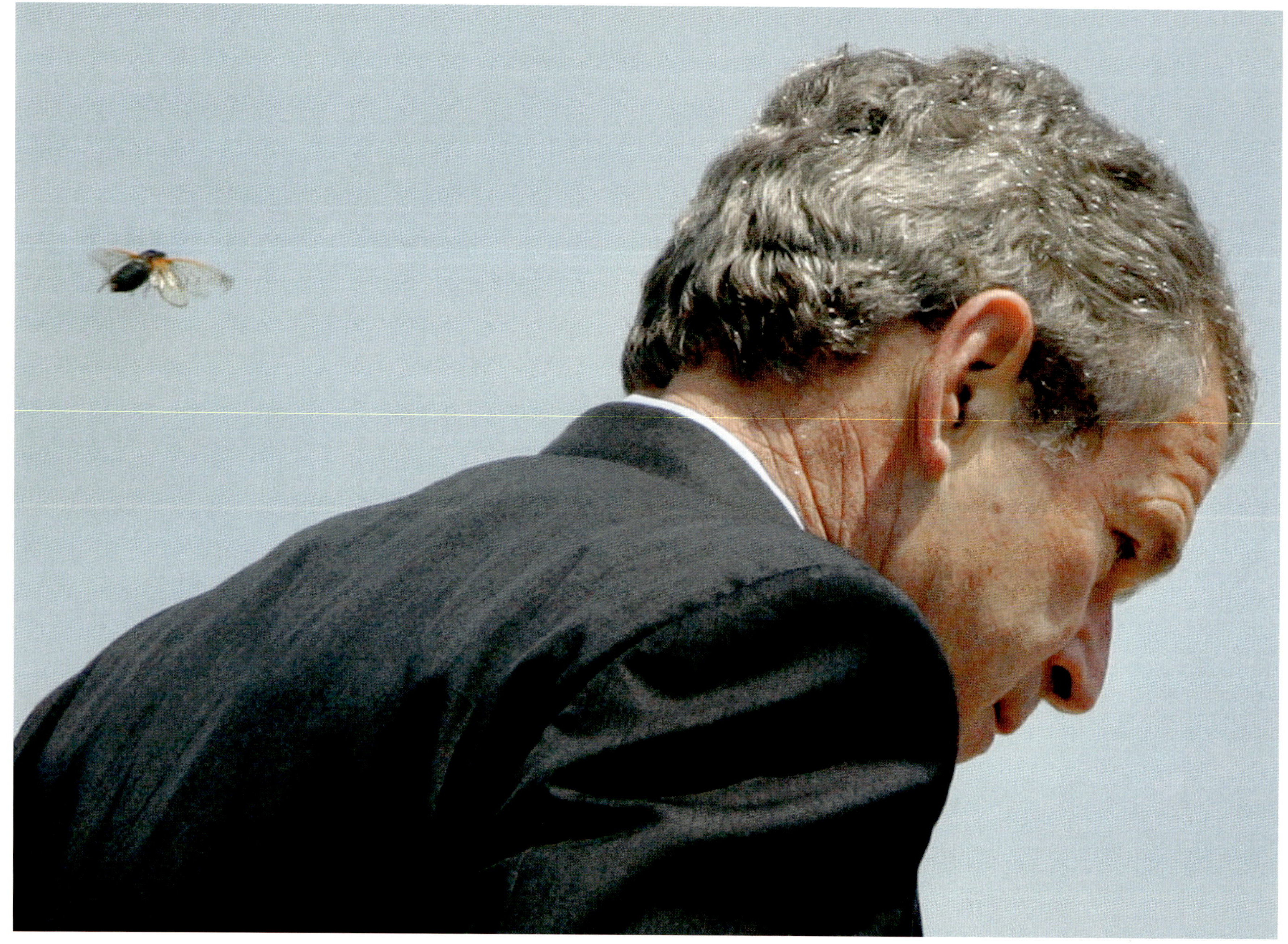

25 May 2004, WASHINGTON, DC, UNITED STATES

President George W. Bush is chased by a cicada at Andrews Air Force Base outside Washington, DC. In spring 2004 the U.S. capital was swamped by millions of the red-eyed bugs, a type of cicada known as Brood X. Its nymphs emerge from the ground en masse to mate, lay eggs and die every 17 years across the eastern United States. Larry Downing

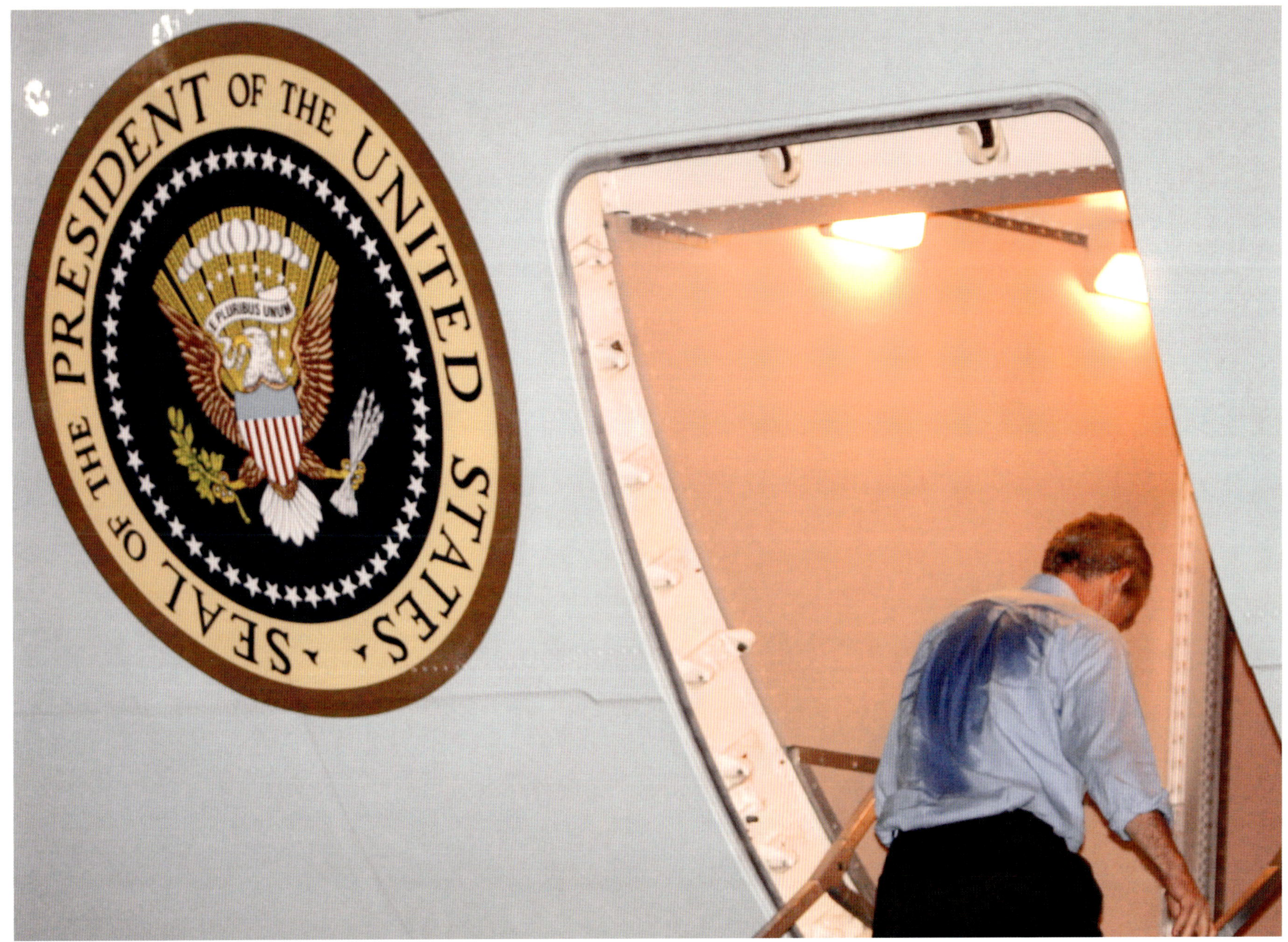

15 September 2005, NEW ORLEANS, UNITED STATES

President George W. Bush boards the presidential plane after speaking to the nation on network television from Jackson Square in New Orleans about the damage caused by Hurricane Katrina. Bush was sharply criticized for the chaotic failures of rescue attempts in the first days after Katrina smashed into the Gulf Coast, killing some 1,300 people and displacing an estimated one million in the worst natural disaster in U.S. history. Larry Downing

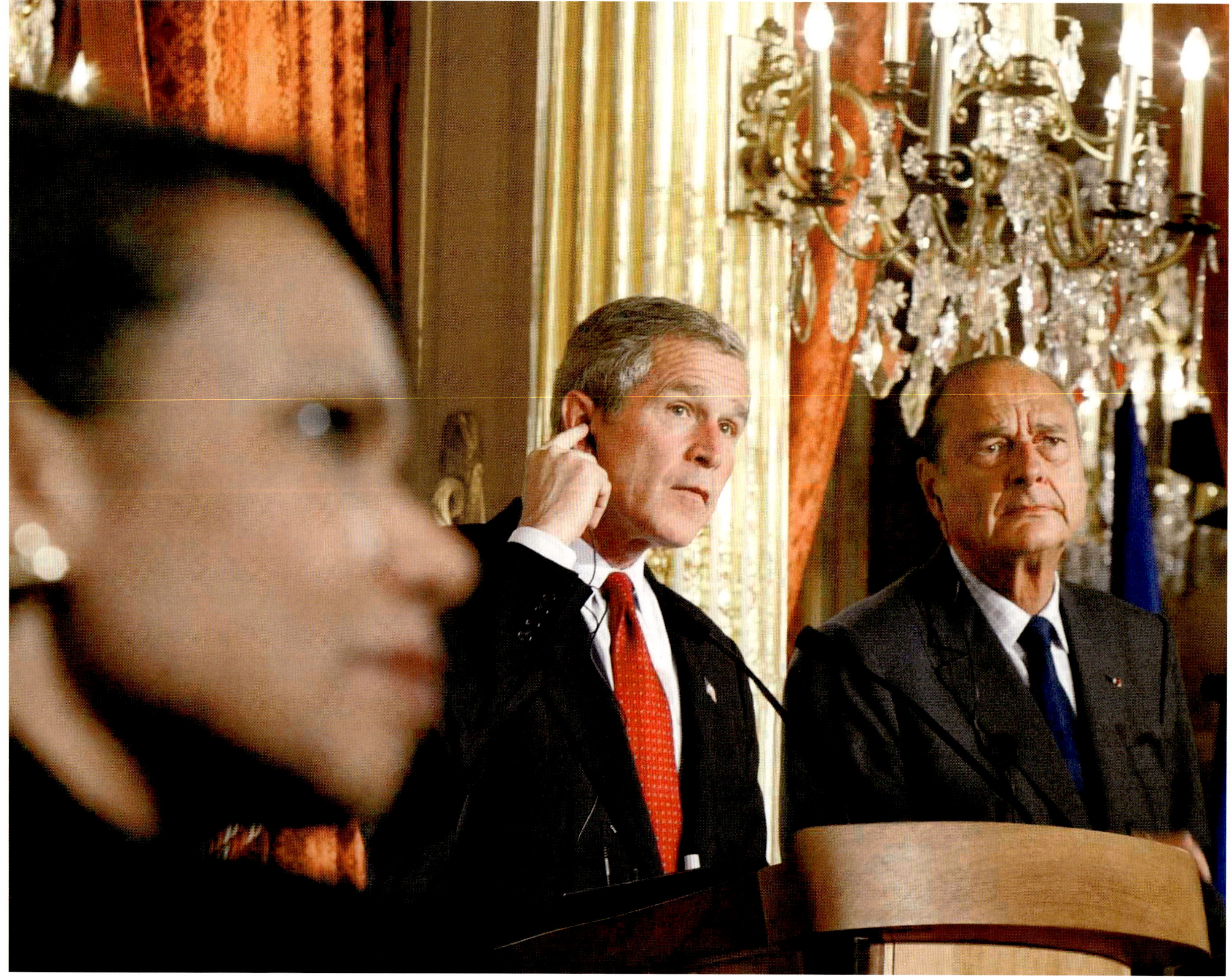

26 May 2002, PARIS, FRANCE

U.S. National Security Advisor Condoleezza Rice, President George W. Bush and French President Jacques Chirac listen to a question during a joint press conference at the Elysée Palace in Paris. Larry Downing

31 December 2000, BAGHDAD, IRAQ

Opposite Iraqi President Saddam Hussein fires shots into the air as he presides over a huge military parade. On display were sophisticated surface-to-surface and anti-aircraft missiles, artillery, and over a thousand Russian-made tanks. Saddam's government was toppled in April 2003 by the U.S.-led invasion of Iraq. Faleh Kheiber

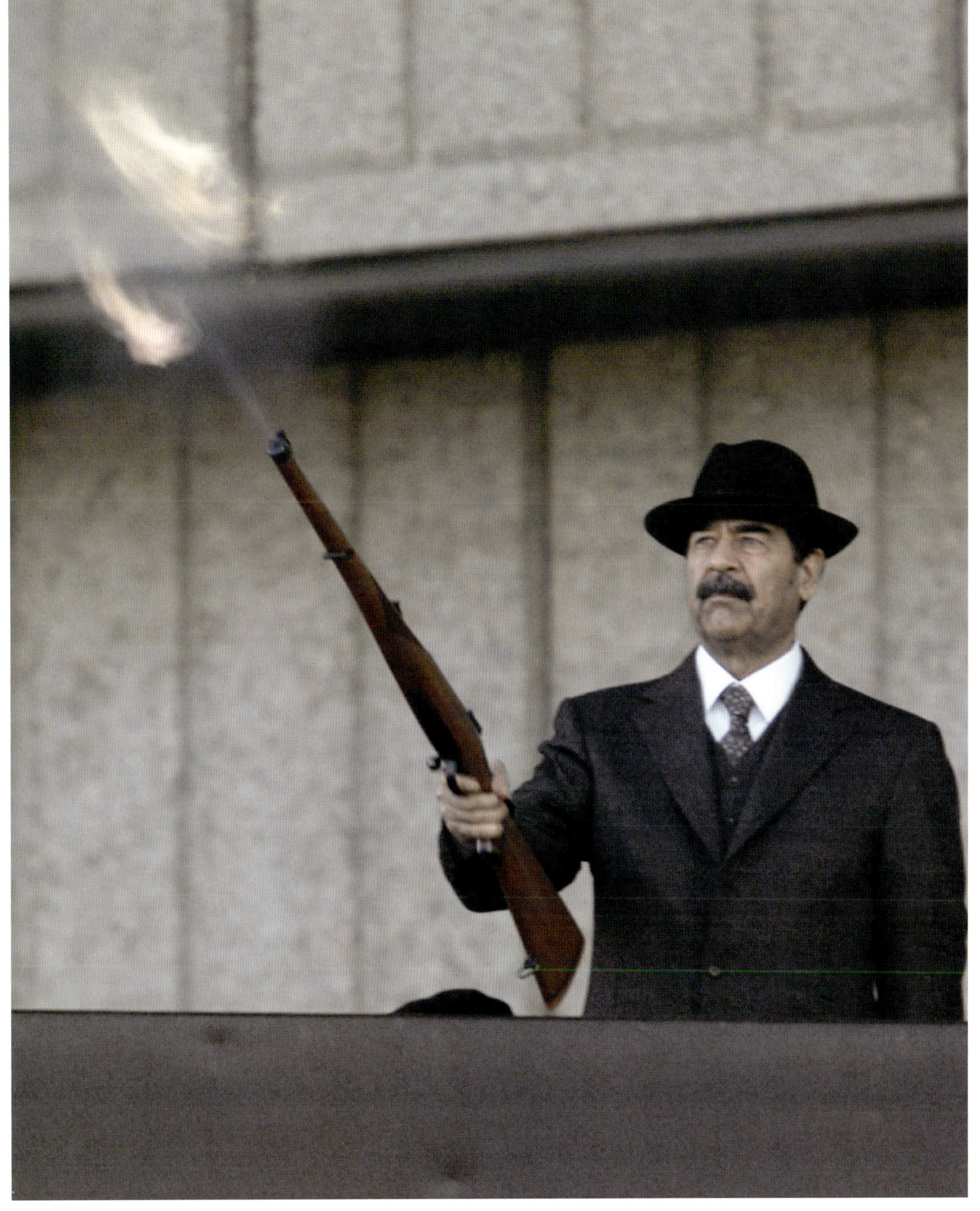

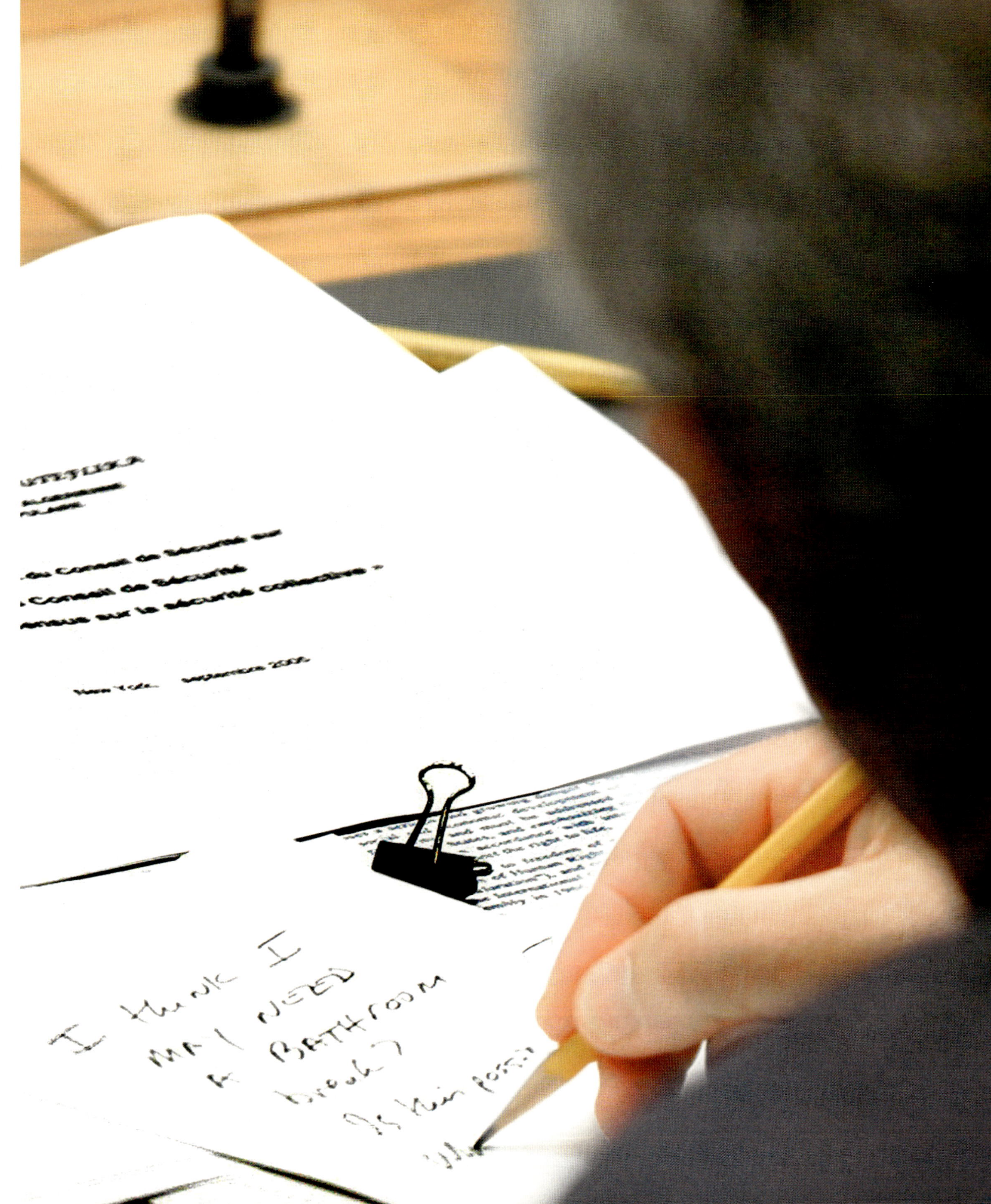
I think I
MAY NEED
A BATHROOM
break?

14 September 2005, UNITED NATIONS

Opposite U.S. President George W. Bush writes a note to Secretary of State Condoleezza Rice during a Security Council meeting at the 2005 World Summit and 60th General Assembly of the United Nations in New York.
Rick Wilking

20 July 2005, DAKAR, SENEGAL

Condoleezza Rice listens to a translation over headphones during the closing ceremony of an international trade conference in Senegal.
Finbarr O'Reilly

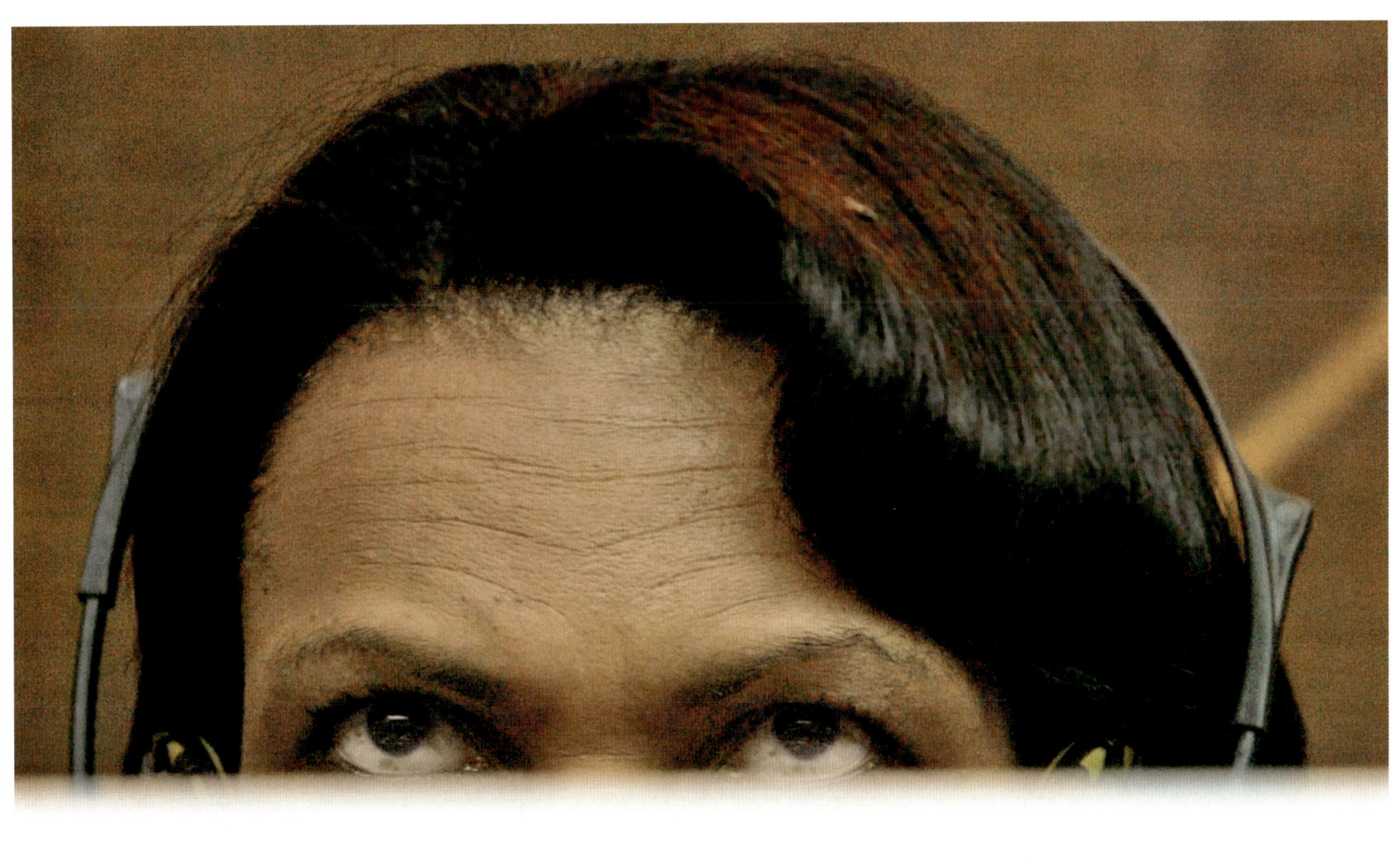

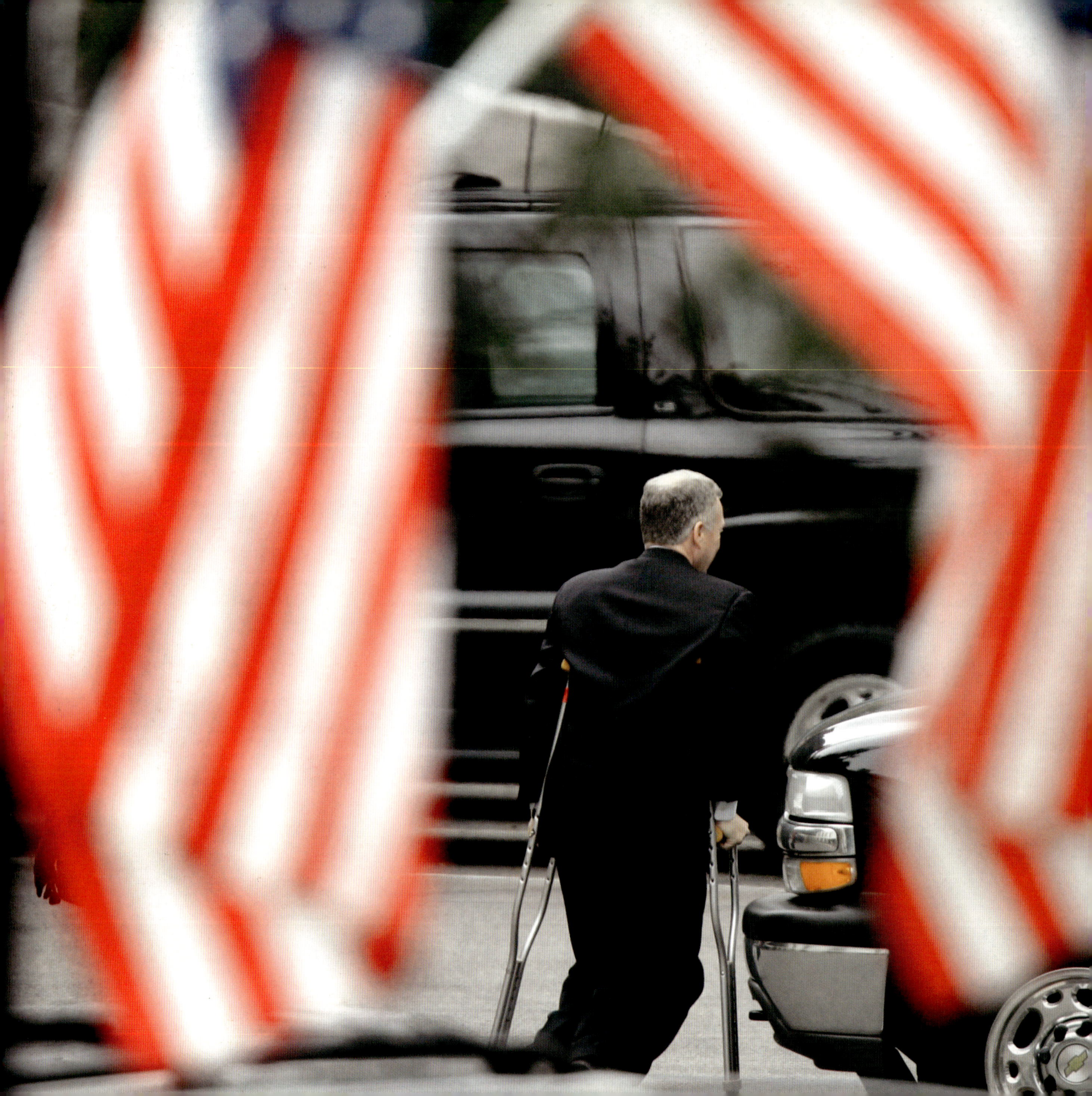

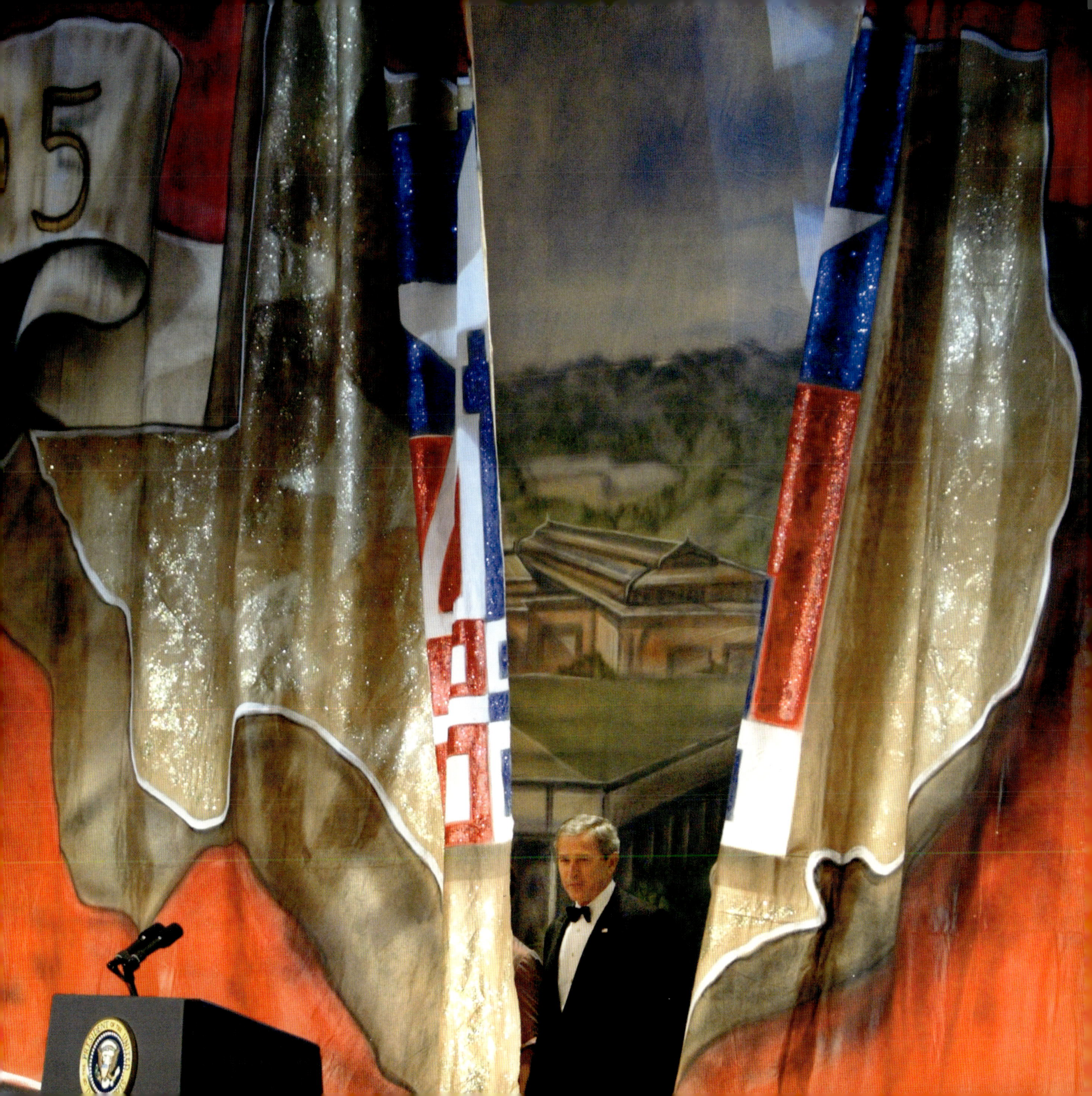

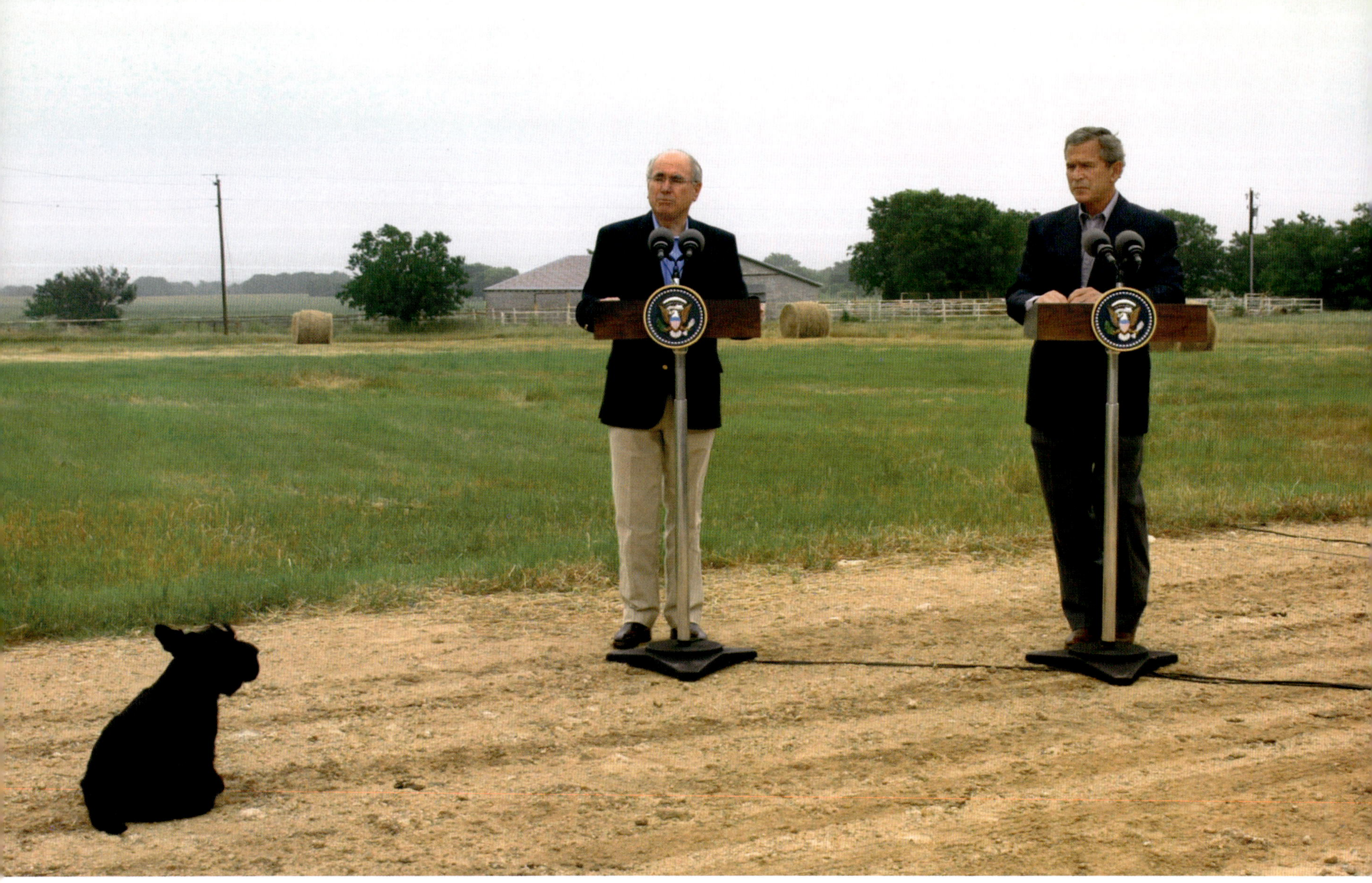

28 October 2005, WASHINGTON, DC, UNITED STATES

Previous pages (left) Top Whitehouse aide Lewis 'Scooter' Libby on the day he resigned his position as Vice President Dick Cheney's chief of staff after he was indicted for obstructing justice, perjury and lying following a two-year investigation into the leak of a covert CIA operative's identity to reporters. If convicted, he faced up to 30 years in prison. Jason Reed

19 January 2005, WASHINGTON, DC, UNITED STATES

Previous pages (right) President George W. Bush appears onstage at the 'Black Tie and Boots Inaugural Ball' in Washington DC, part of celebrations leading up to his inauguration for a second term in office. Brian Snyder

3 May 2003, CRAWFORD, UNITED STATES

Above President George W. Bush looks down at his dog Barney as he and Australian Prime Minister John Howard stage a joint press conference at the Bush ranch in Crawford, Texas. Kevin Lamarque

11 February 2005, GATESHEAD, UNITED KINGDOM

Opposite Prime Minister Tony Blair addresses his Labour Party's spring conference in Gateshead following his announcement of the first of six pledges that would form the core of his party's manifesto for the forthcoming general election. The Labour Party were to win a historic third term in office on 5 May, albeit with a significantly reduced majority. Jeff J. Mitchell

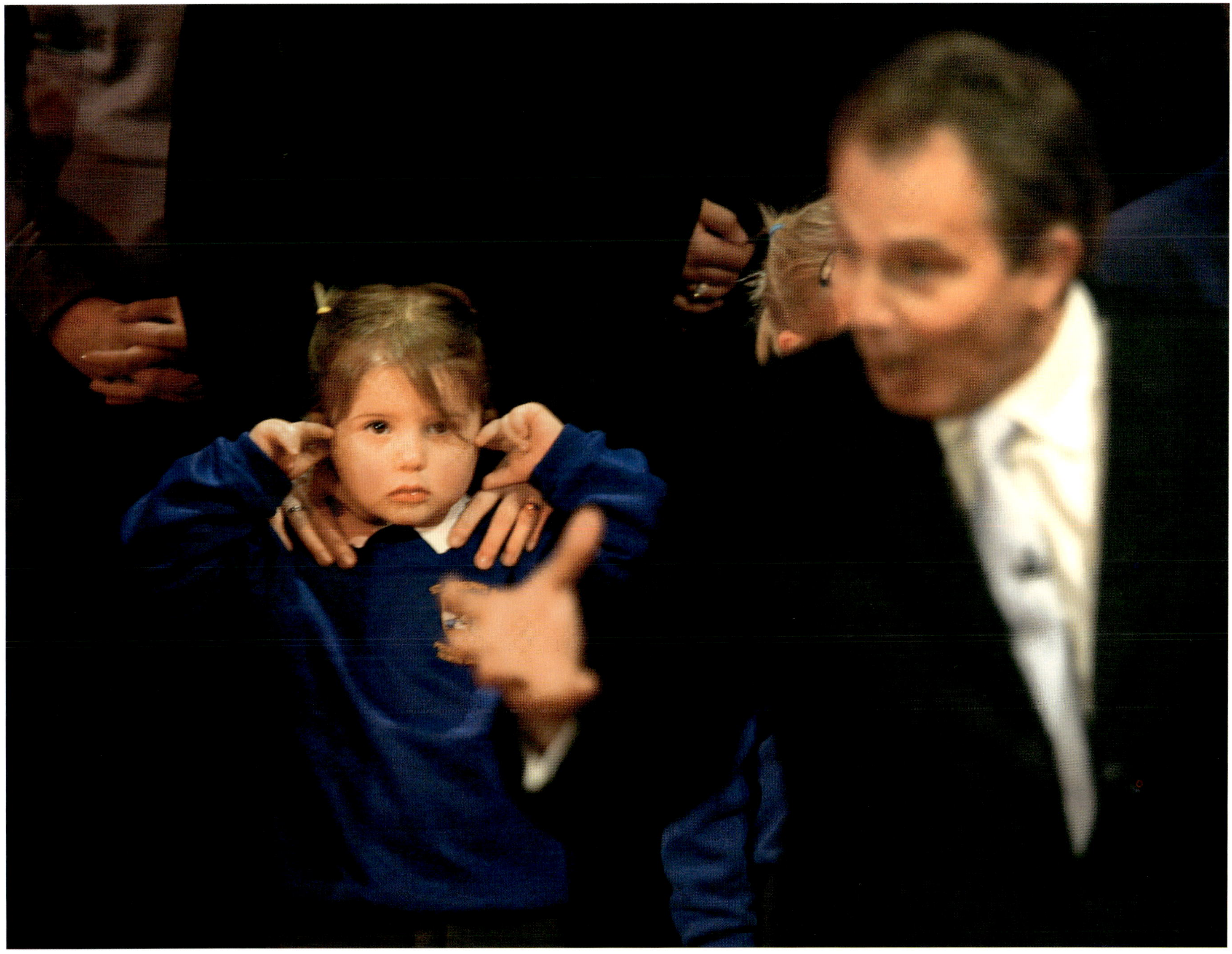

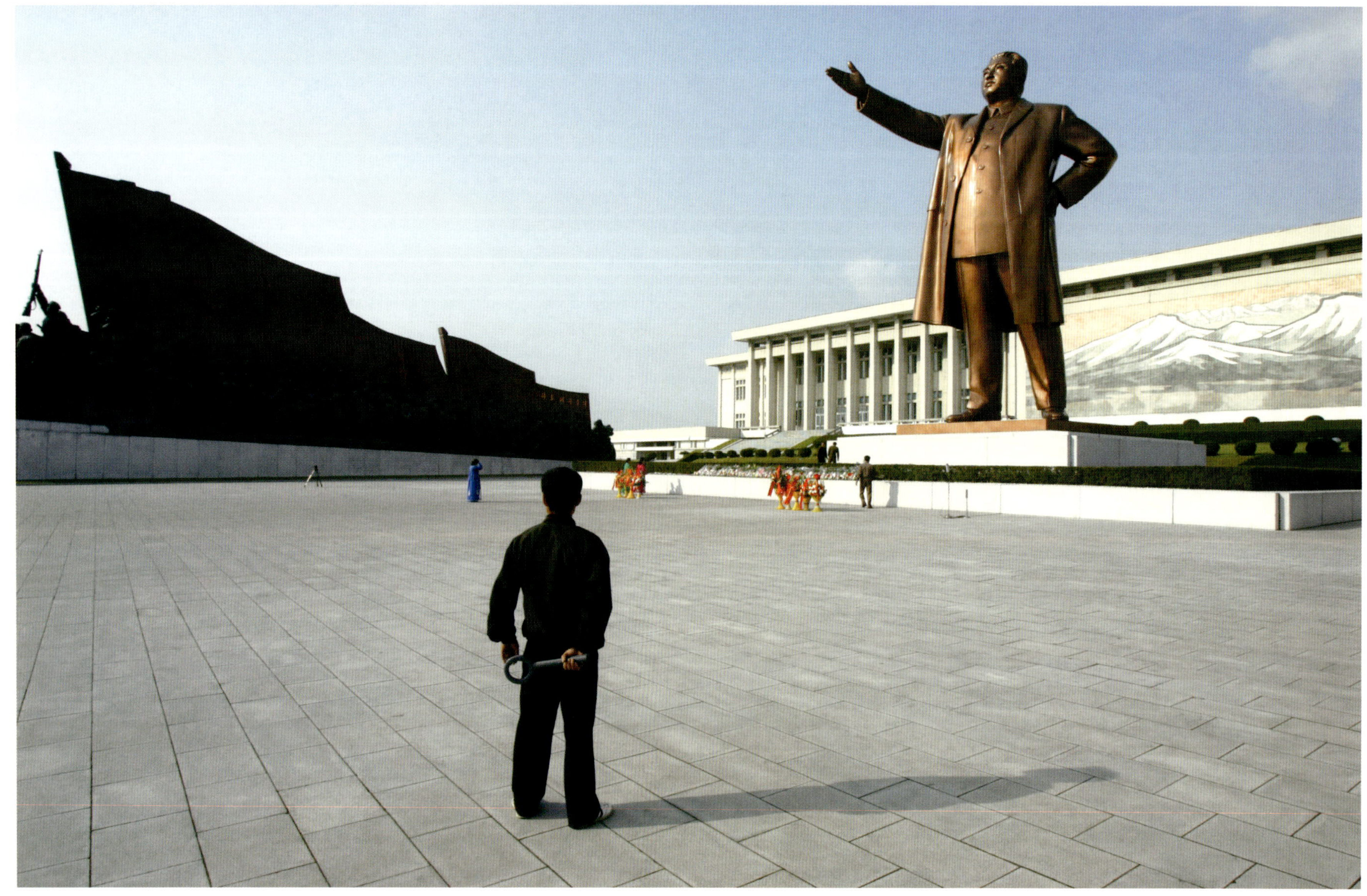

15 October 2005, PYONGYANG, NORTH KOREA

A North Korean security guard carries a metal detector in front of a giant statue of former leader Kim Il-sung in central Pyongyang. The United States accuses North Korea of covert nuclear arms development in violation of international accords, and has branded the country part of an 'axis of evil' along with Iran and pre-war Iraq. Reinhard Krause

19 October 2005, BEIJING, CHINA

U.S. Defense Secretary Donald Rumsfeld and China's Defense Minister Cao Gangchuan attend a welcoming ceremony at the Chinese Defense Ministry in Beijing. On his first visit to China since taking office in 2001 Rumsfeld urged the Chinese to be more transparent about their military activities and to open up their political system to dispel fears about their intentions and ensure future prosperity. At a joint news conference with Rumsfeld, Cao disputed U.S. assertions that China understates its military spending, saying that China's priority was to build the economy and lift 30 million people out of poverty. Jason Lee

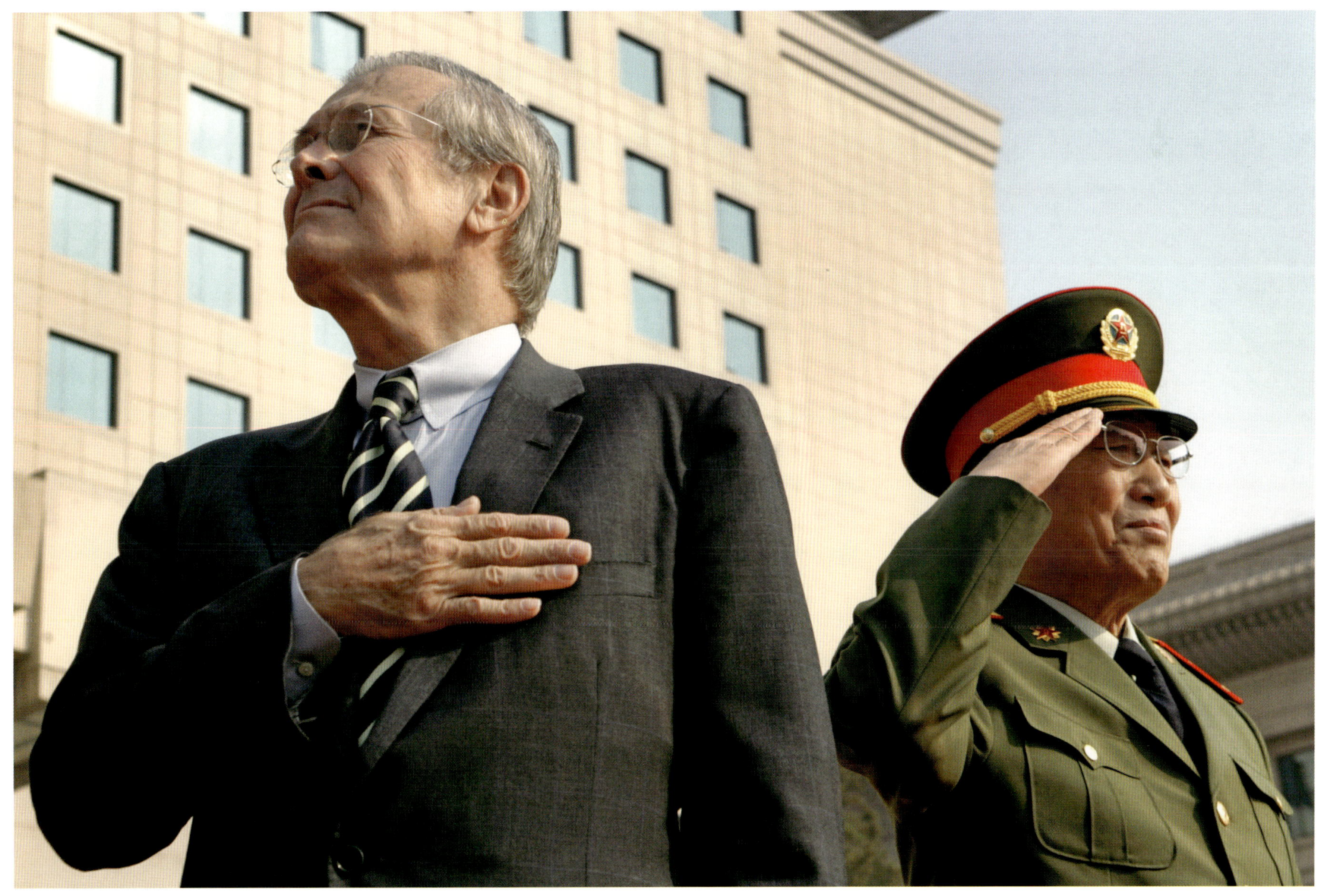

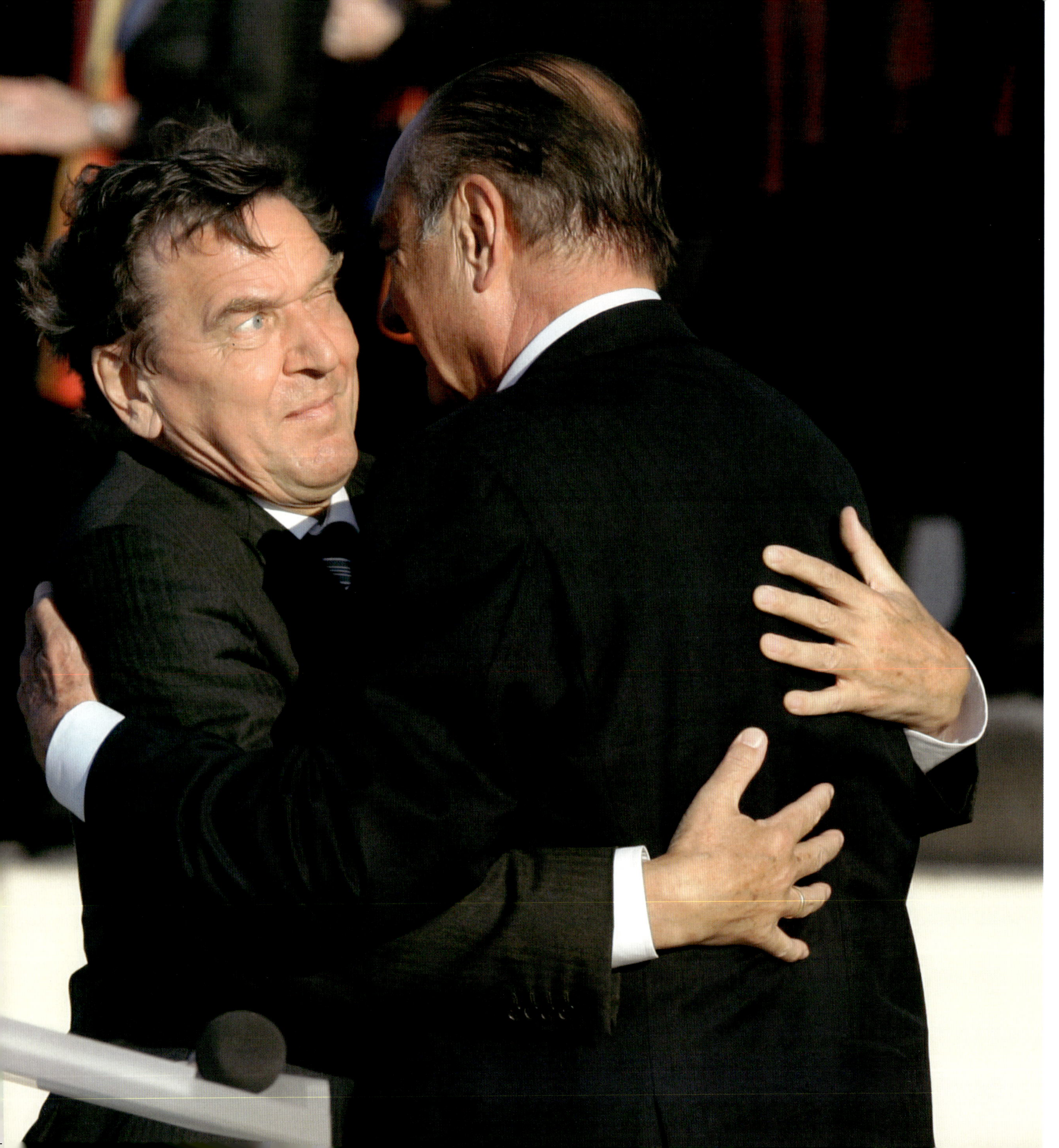

6 June 2004, CAEN, FRANCE

Opposite German Chancellor Gerhard Schröder (left) hugs French President Jacques Chirac at the end of Chirac's speech at the Memorial for Peace in Caen, Normandy, part of commemorations to mark the 60th anniversary of the D-Day landings in World War Two. German leaders joined with former enemies for the first time in a tribute to those killed on both sides. Vincent Kessler

10 November 2005, PARIS, FRANCE

President Jacques Chirac (right) speaks with Interior Minister Nicolas Sarkozy during a Franco–Spanish summit at the Elysée Palace in Paris. Philippe Wojazer

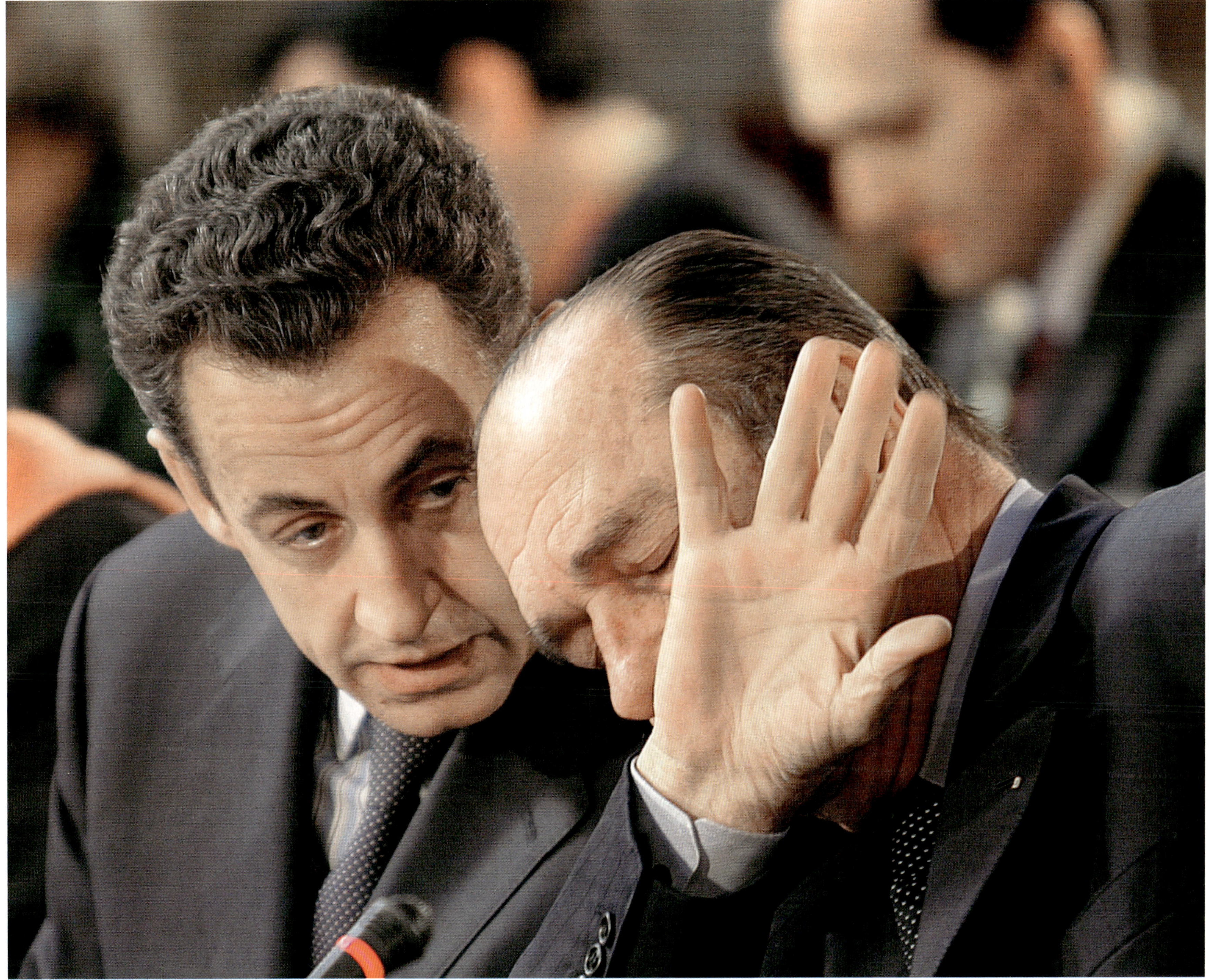

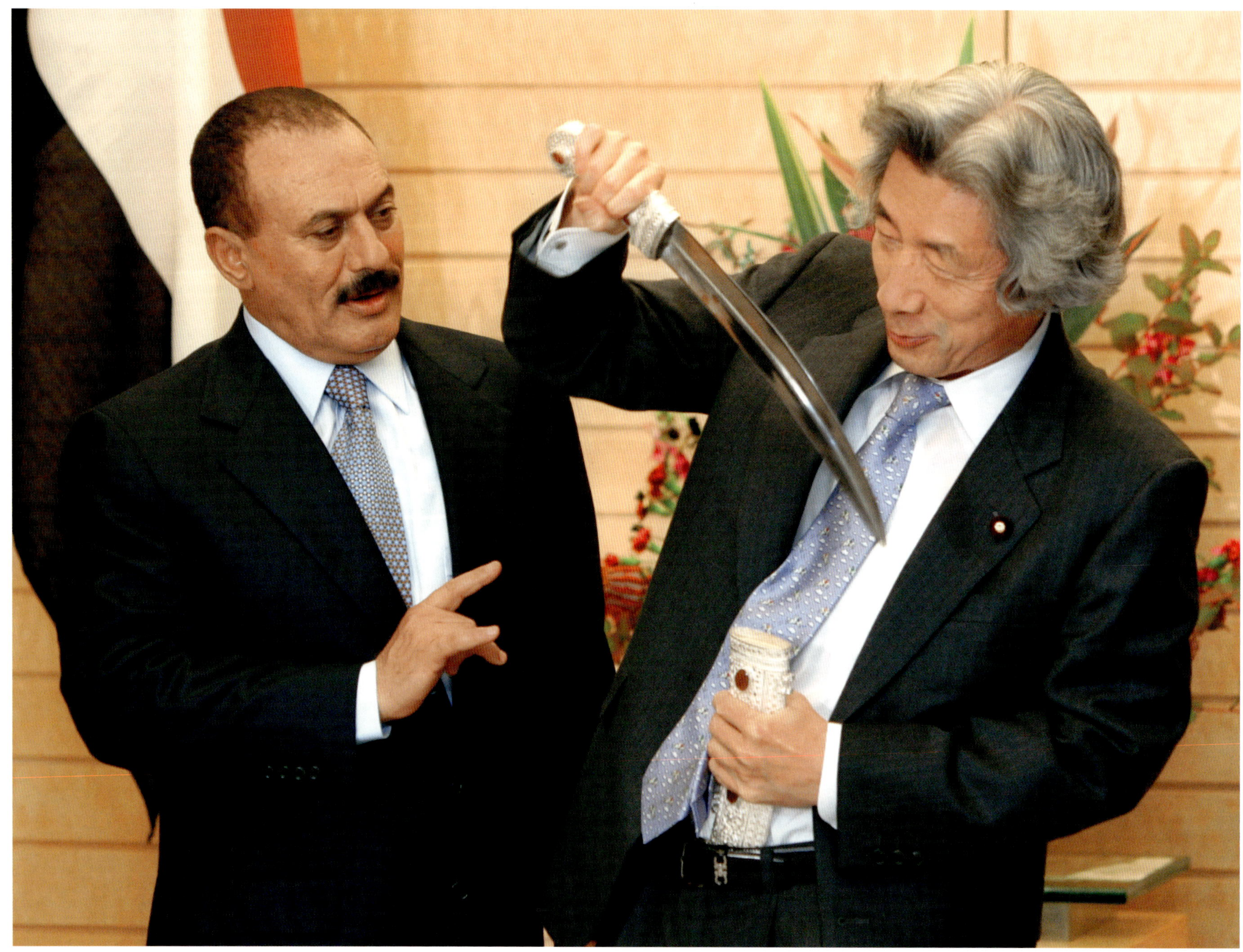

7 November 2005, TOKYO, JAPAN

Yemeni President Ali Abdullah Saleh (left) watches as Japanese Prime Minister Junichiro Koizumi whips out an Arabic *khanjar* dagger that Saleh presented as a gift during a meeting at the premier's official residence in Tokyo. Yuriko Nakao

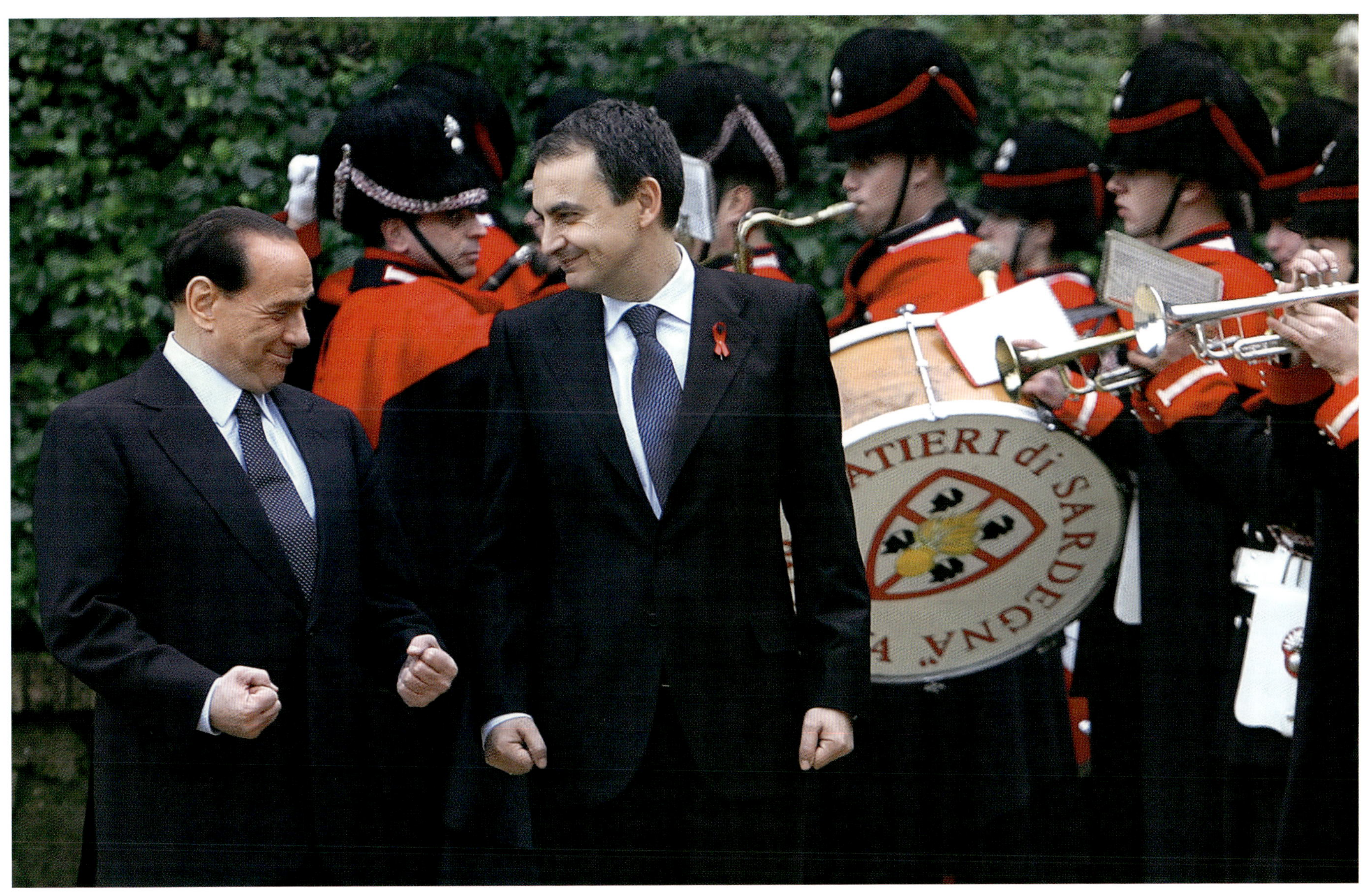

1 December 2005, ROME, ITALY

Spanish Prime Minister José Luis Rodríguez Zapatero (right) and his Italian counterpart Silvio Berlusconi listen to their national anthems during a bilateral summit between Italy and Spain held at Villa Madama in Rome. Max Rossi

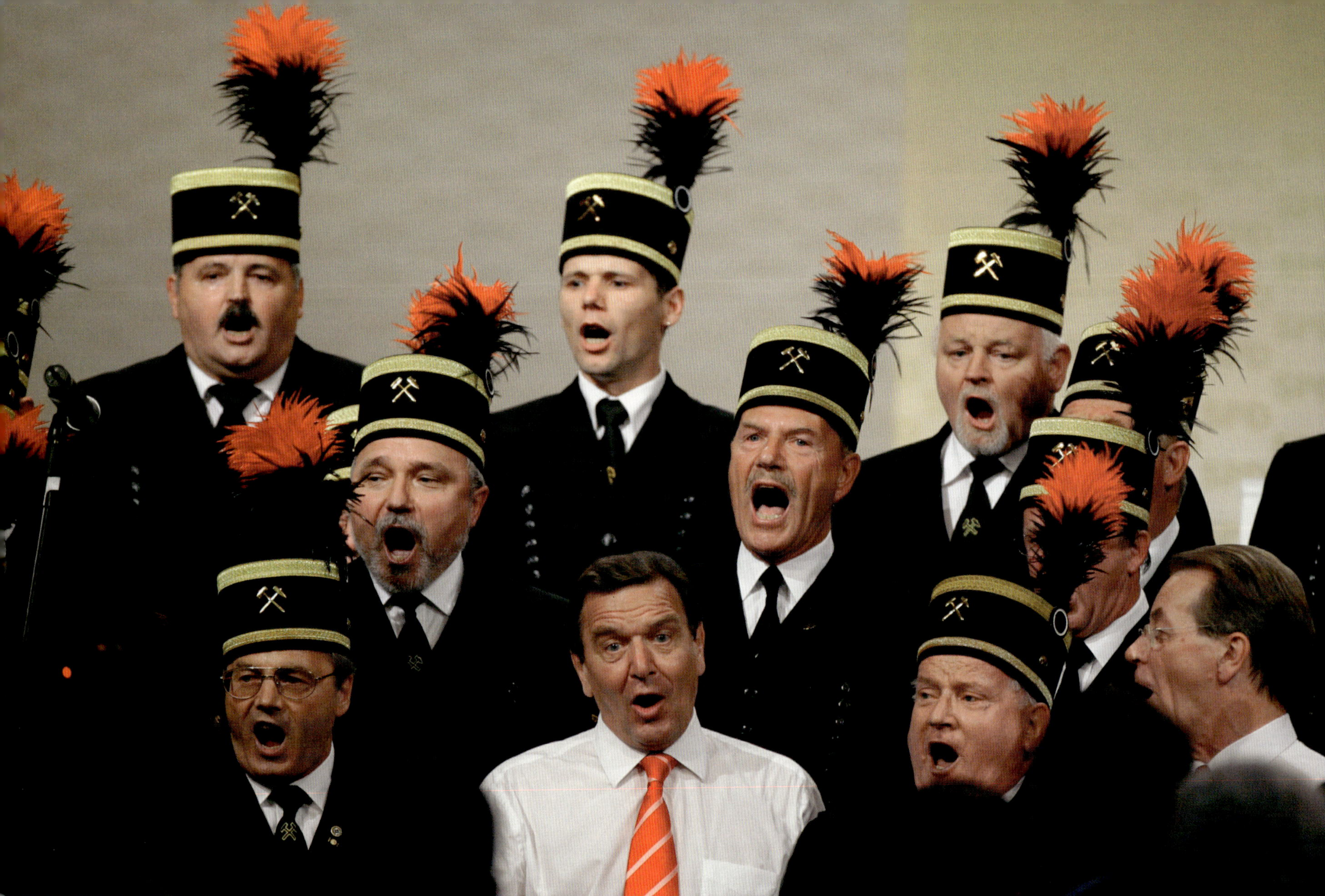

31 August 2005, BERLIN, GERMANY

Chancellor Gerhard Schröder sings with members of a coal miners' choir at the end of a Social Democrats (SPD) one-day extraordinary meeting in Berlin. High unemployment and the decline of coal mining and heavy industry in Germany's industrial heartlands caused many traditional working-class SPD voters to turn their backs on the party in 2005, despite being a major focus of Schröder's election campaigning. Arnd Wiegmann

18 September 2005, BERLIN, GERMANY

Angela Merkel, leader of the Christian Democrats (CDU), walks on stage to address supporters after results from the first exit polls in Germany's general election suggested she was on track for victory. That victory proved too narrow to permit Merkel to form a government with only her reform-minded conservative allies. After a period of political deadlock, it was announced that Merkel would become Germany's first woman chancellor at the head of a coalition government including Social Democrats, political rivals opposed to her policies of shaking up the sluggish German economy with reforms of the labour market and tax system.

Kai Pfaffenbach

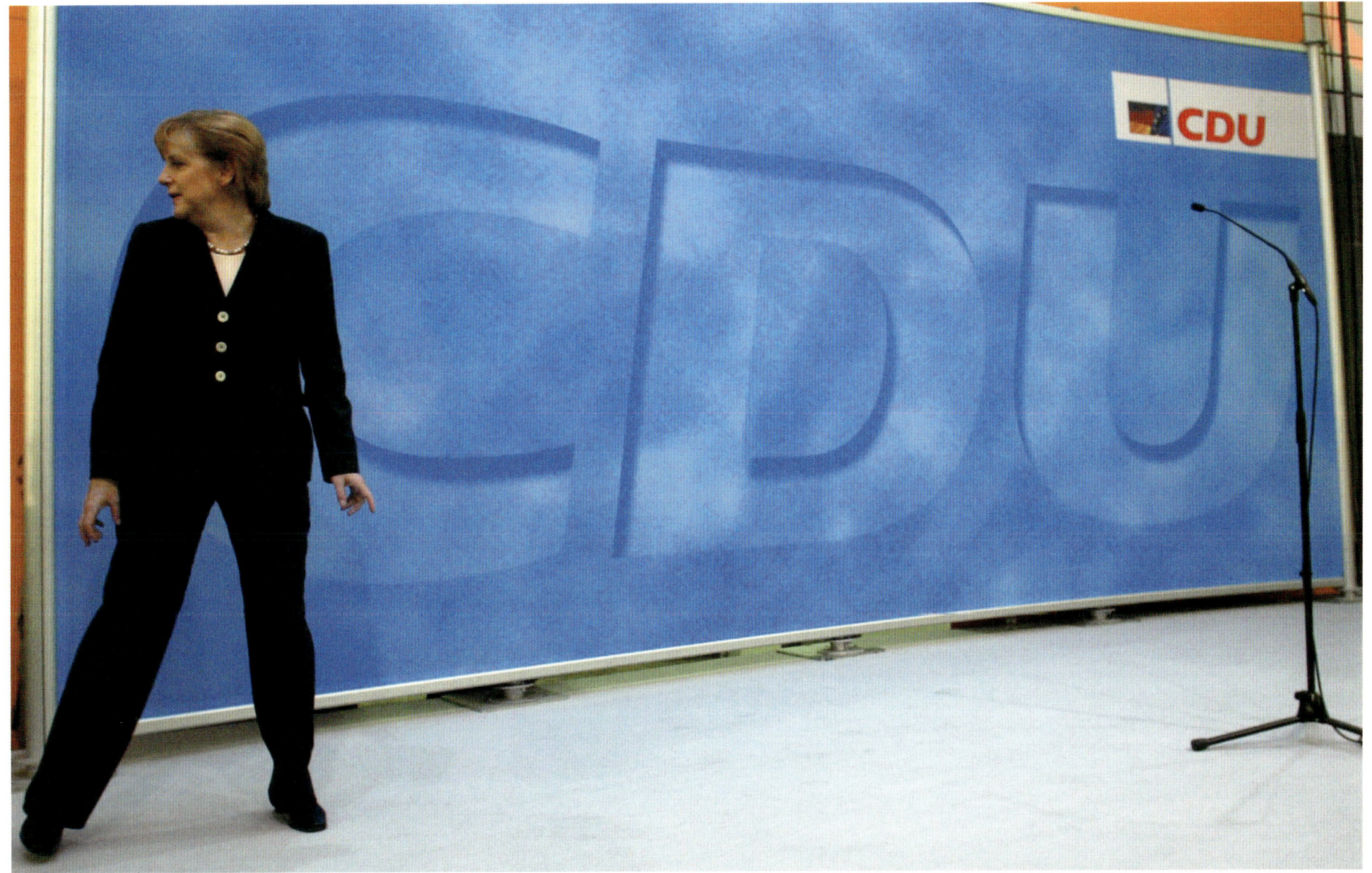

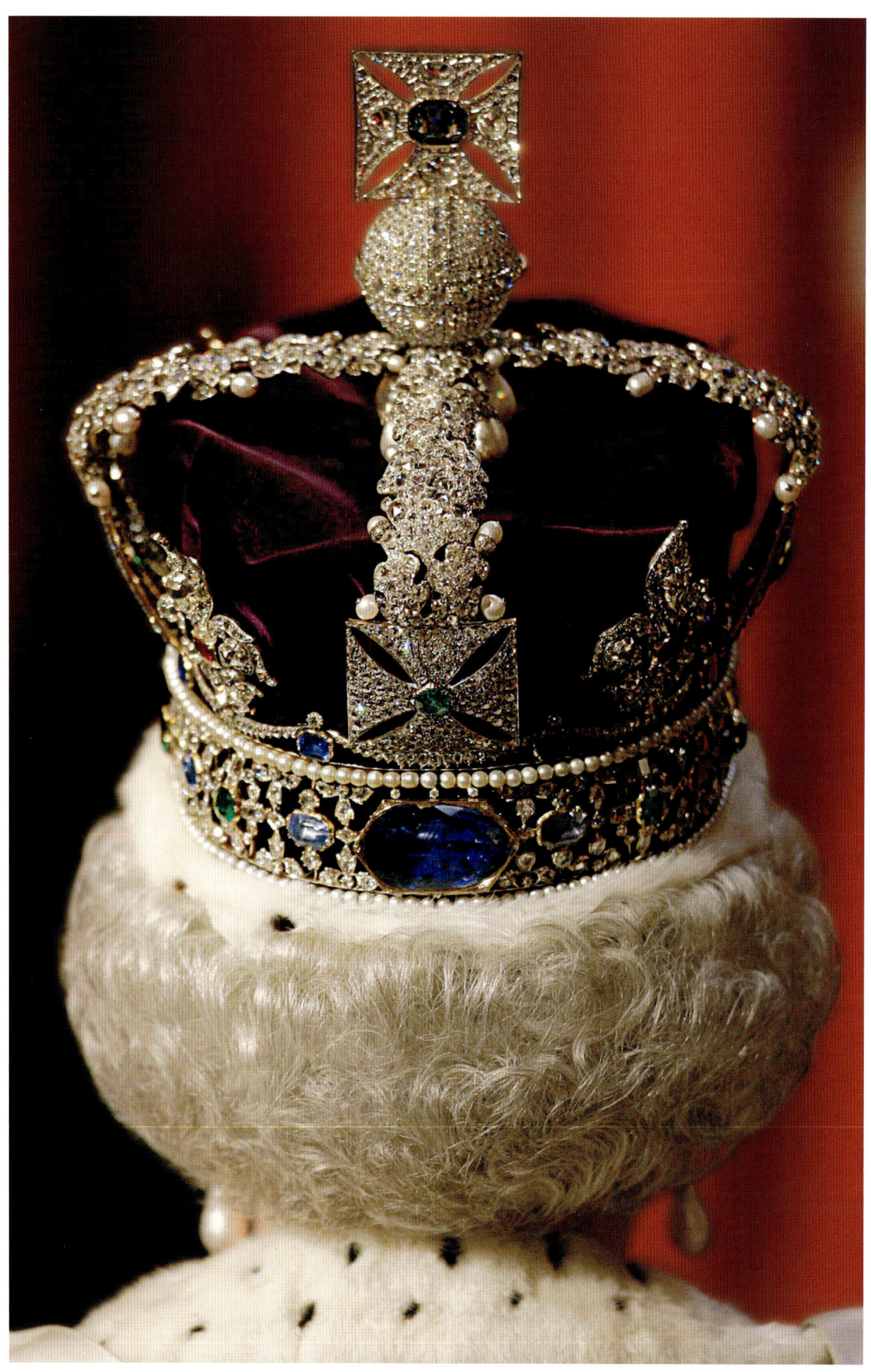

23 November 2004, LONDON, UNITED KINGDOM

Queen Elizabeth wears the State Crown as she walks through the Royal Gallery in the House of Lords at the Palace of Westminster, during the State Opening of Parliament. Russell Boyce

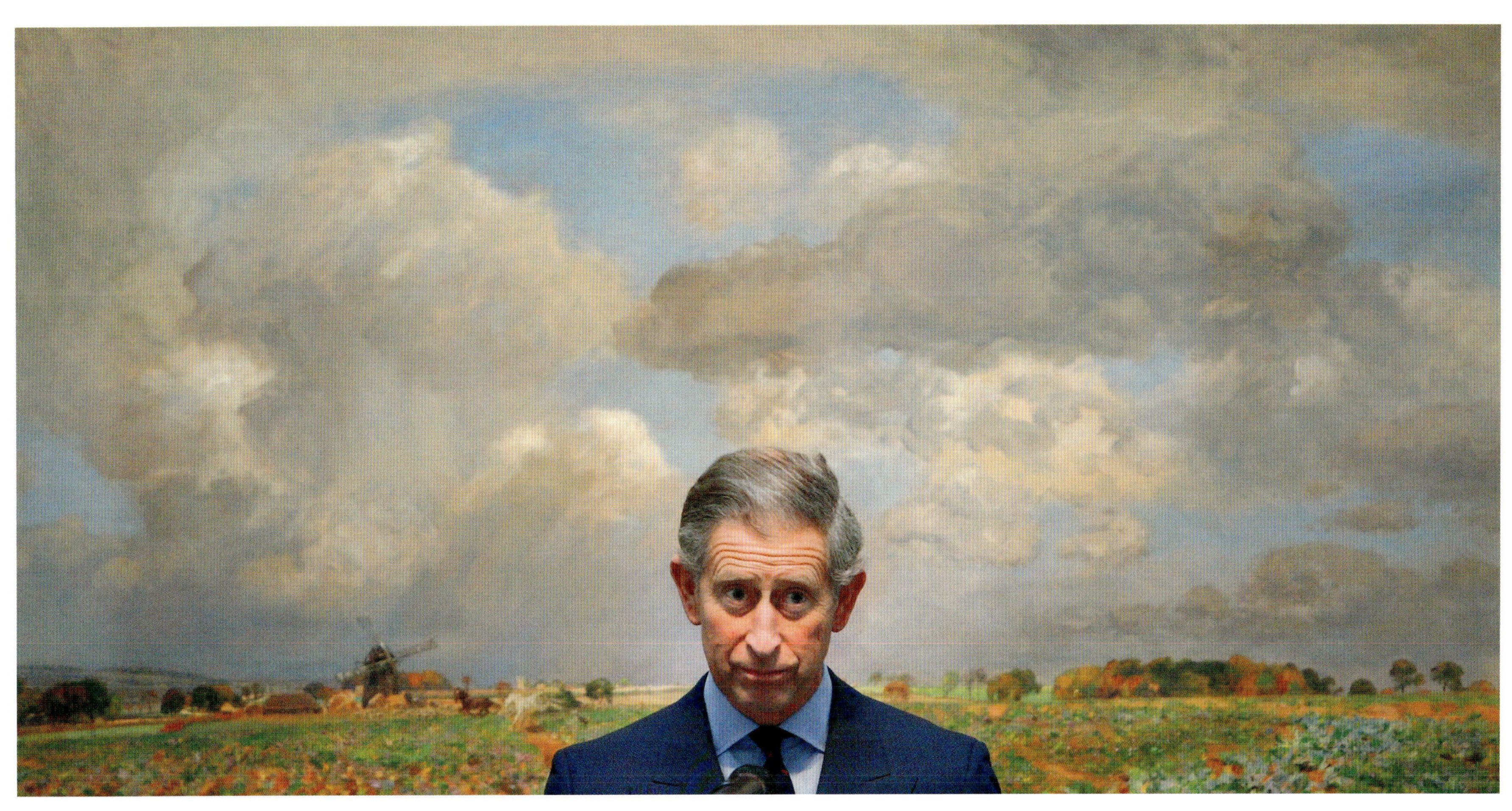

13 November 2003, LONDON, UNITED KINGDOM

The Prince of Wales launches a guide to help small, local food producers establish relationships with supermarkets and other large-scale companies at the Royal Academy of Arts in London. Peter Macdiarmid

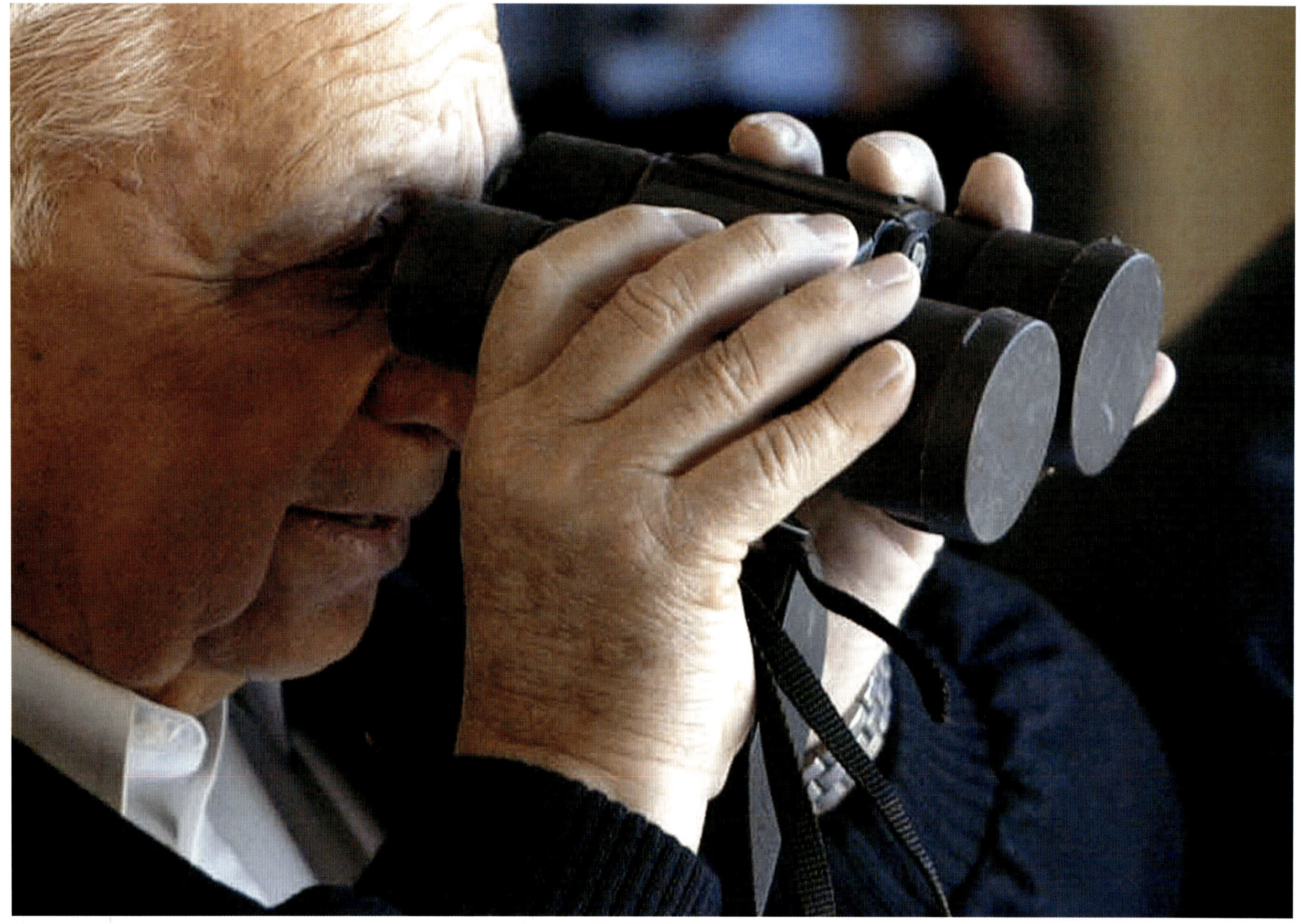

7 January 2003, TEL AVIV, ISRAEL

Prime Minister Ariel Sharon visits a military camp near Tel Aviv, where he attended a training session of an Israeli army sniper unit as part of the run-up to campaigning for a general election on 28 January 2003. Sharon's Likud party won the most seats in the Knesset in that election, but not a majority, forcing him to create a coalition government with right-wing minority parties. Nir Elias

29 October 2004, RAMALLAH, WEST BANK

Palestinian President Yasser Arafat, frail and ill, enters a helicopter to leave the compound in the West Bank city of Ramallah where he had been blockaded by Israeli forces for over two and a half years. He travelled to France, where he died in hospital on 11 November 2004. He led his people's struggle for 40 years, but died with his dream of a Palestinian state unfulfilled. He was succeeded by Mahmoud Abbas as chairman of the Palestine Liberation Organization. Ammar Awad

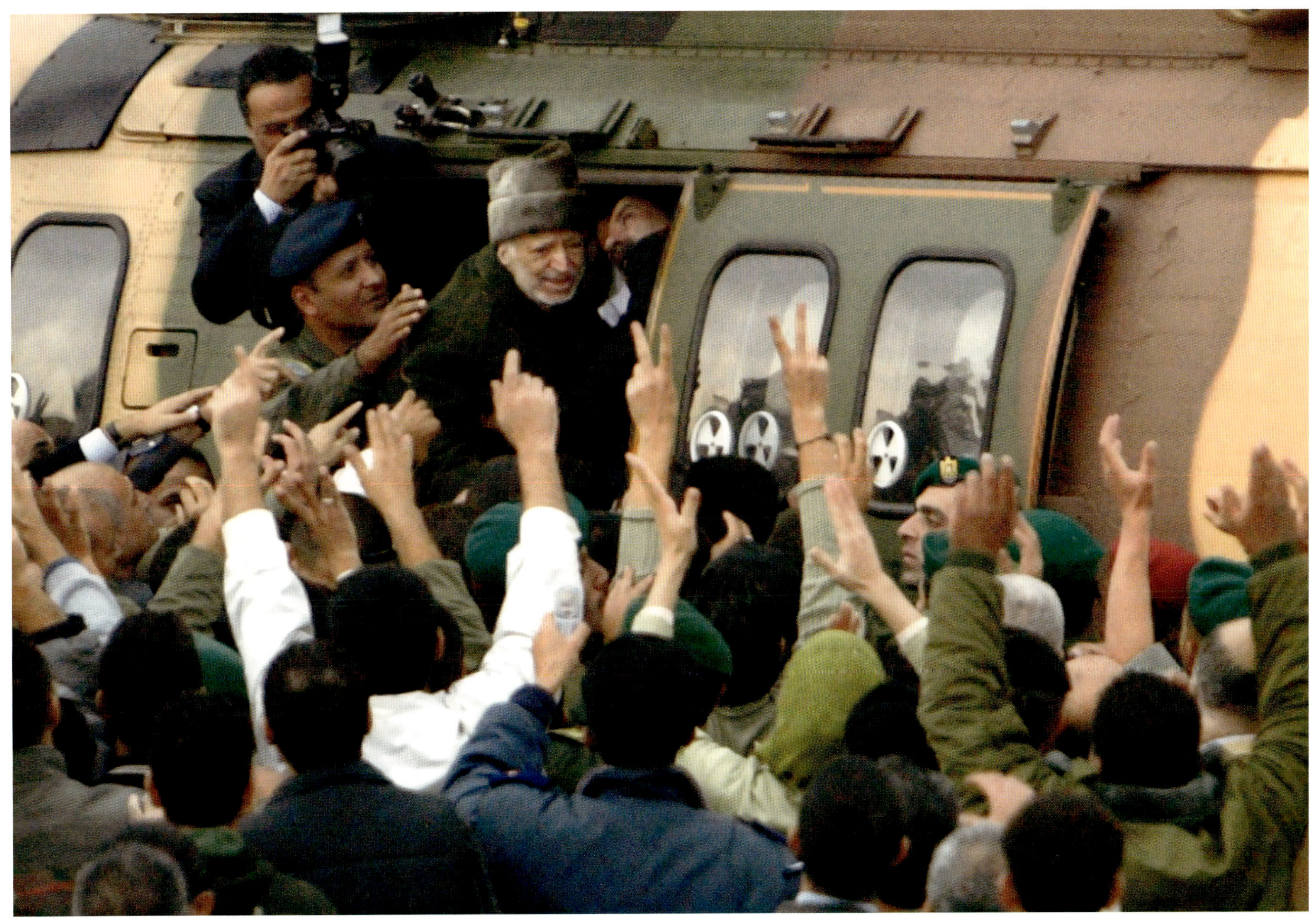

19 October 2005, BAGHDAD, IRAQ

A defiant Saddam Hussein speaks to the presiding judge in a heavily fortified courthouse in Baghdad's Green Zone. Nearly two years after he was found hiding in a hole in the ground near his hometown of Tikrit, Saddam and seven other members of his defunct Baath Party went on trial for crimes against humanity related to the torture and killing of more than 140 Iraqi Shi'ites from the village of Dujail, following a failed attempt on the former leader's life in 1982. Bob Strong

22 September 2005, TEHRAN, IRAN

Opposite above An Iranian Shahab 3 missile is driven during a military parade to commemorate the start of the 1980–88 Iran–Iraq war. To cries of 'God is Great', the Islamic regime showed off its military might and warned potential aggressors that it would vigorously repel any attack. Raheb Homavandi

24 June 2005, TEHRAN, IRAN

Opposite below Presidential candidate Mahmoud Ahmadinejad, surrounded by bodyguards, waves to supporters as he arrives at a polling centre in Tehran. The ultra-conservative Tehran mayor won a landslide victory in the election, comfortably defeating moderate cleric and former President Akbar Hashemi Rafsanjani. Damir Sagolj

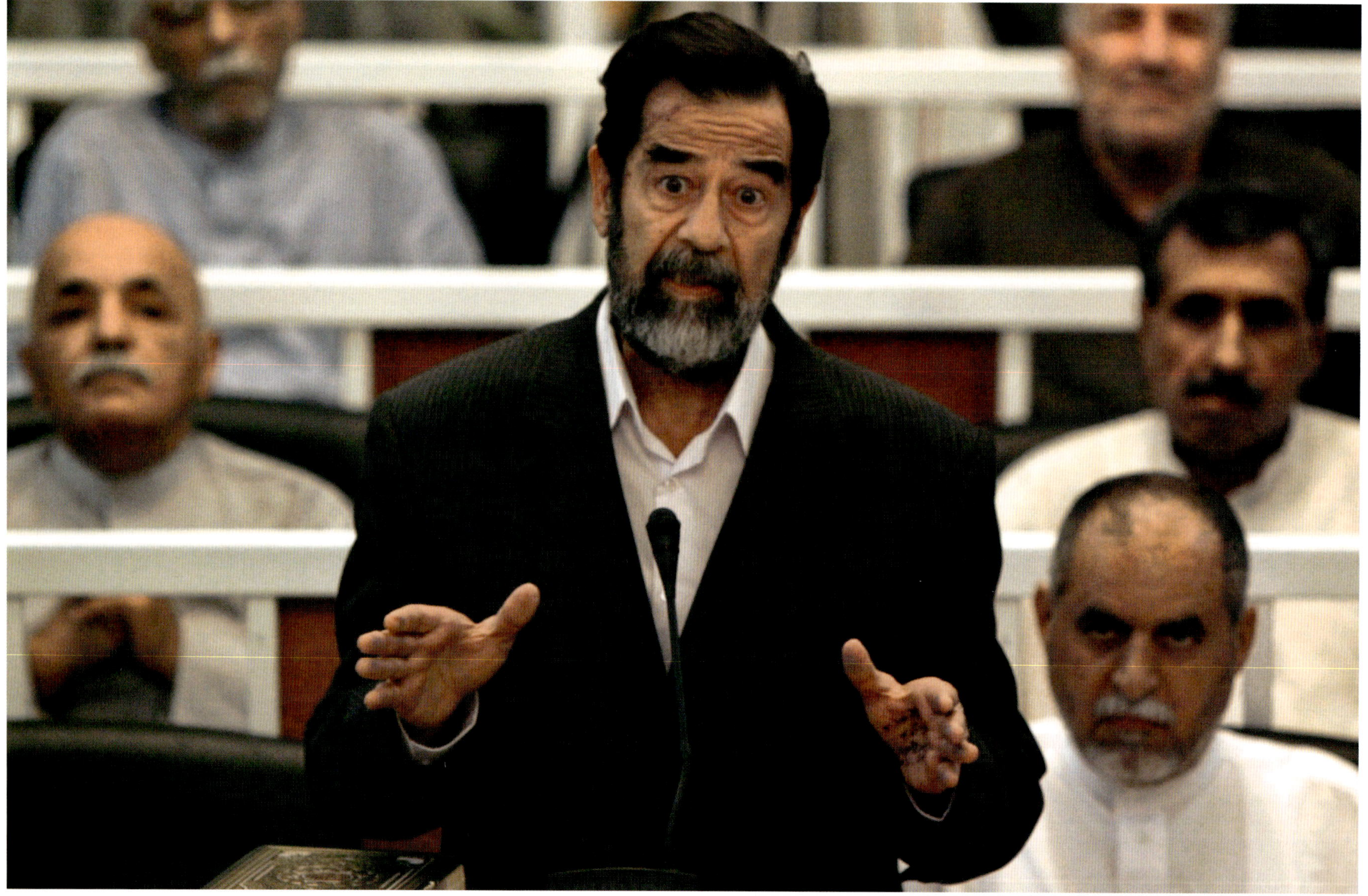

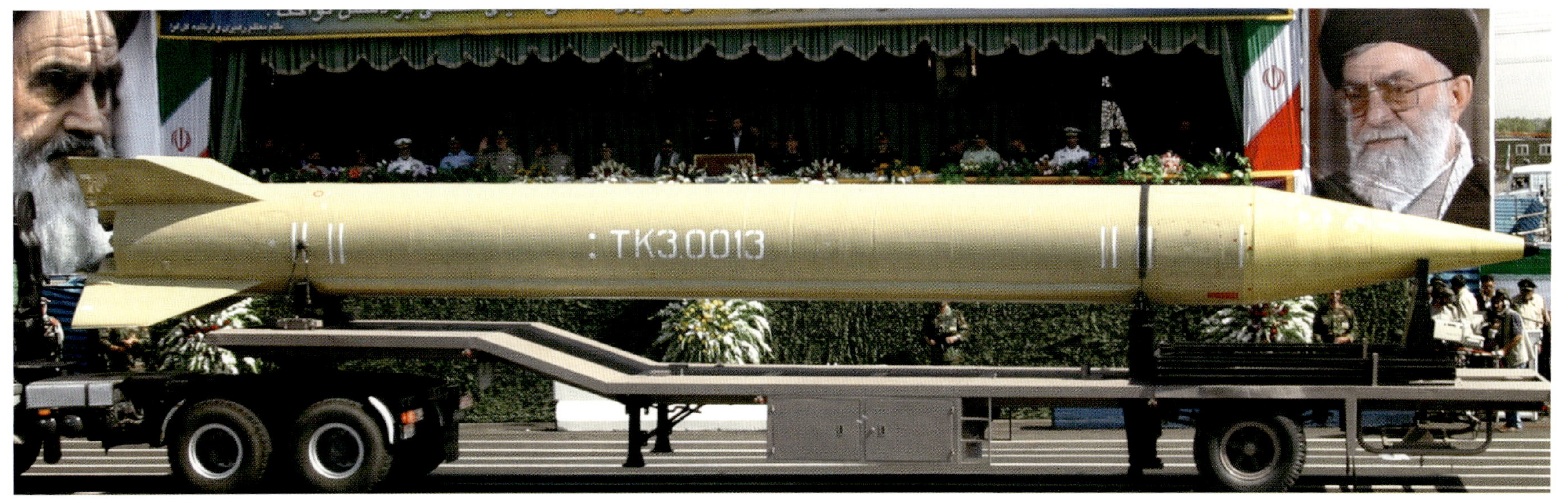
TK3.0013

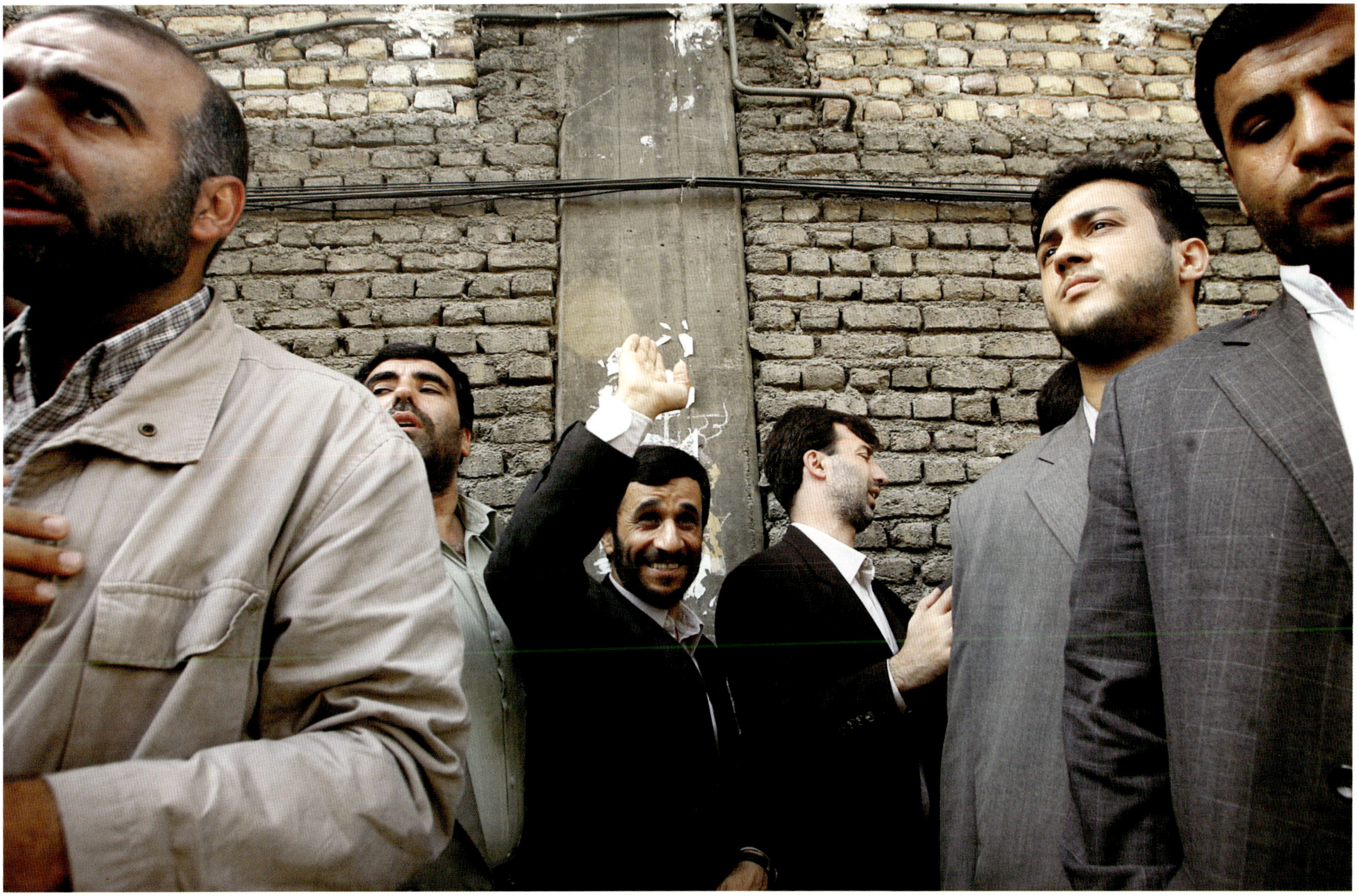

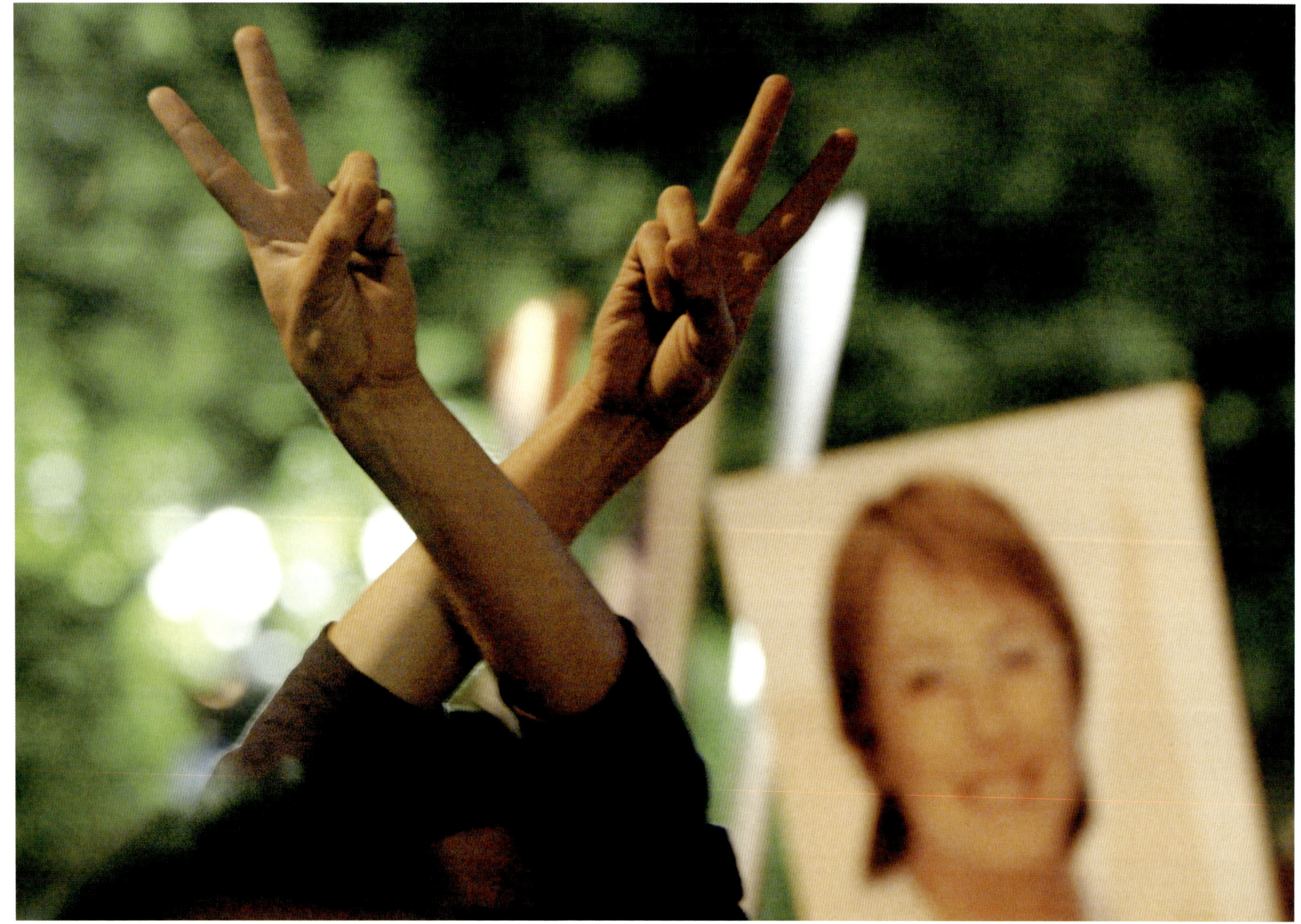

11 December 2005, SANTIAGO, CHILE

Supporters of leftist presidential candidate Michelle Bachelet of the Socialist Party celebrate her win in Chile's first-round presidential elections. She subsequently won the run-off election, defeating rightist candidate Sebastian Pinera, on 15 January 2006. Chile's first woman president is a medical doctor and former minister who was briefly imprisoned and tortured at the beginning of Augusto Pinochet's 1973–90 military dictatorship. Ivan Alvarado

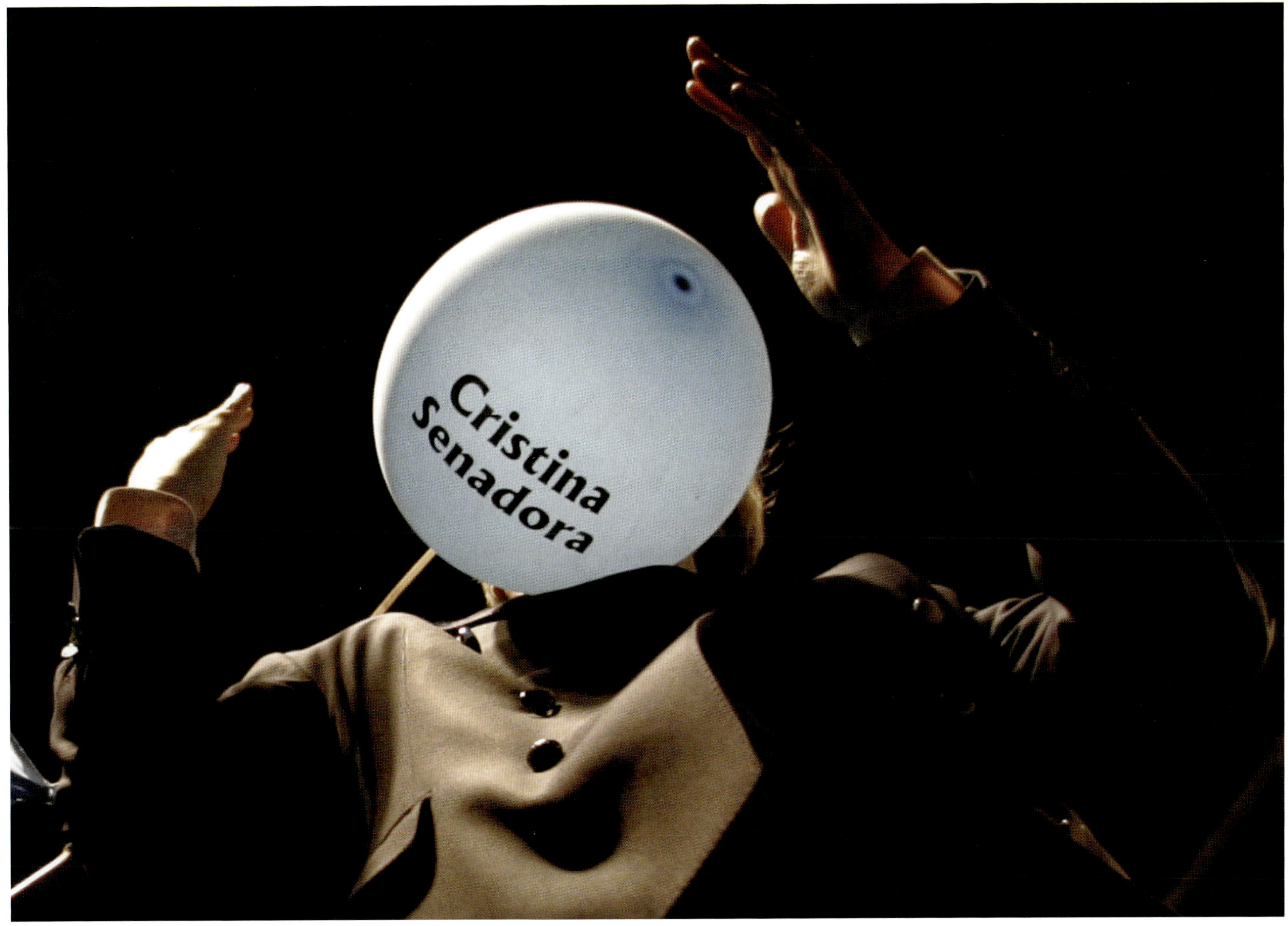

20 October 2005, BUENOS AIRES, ARGENTINA

President Néstor Kirchner tries to catch a balloon during the closing campaign rally for First Lady and senatorial candidate Cristina Fernández de Kirchner. Argentines went to the polls on 23 October 2005 to re-elect half of the Lower House and a third of the Senate. Cristina Kirchner secured a resounding victory in her bid for the Senate seat in Buenos Aires province, one of the country's most powerful and high-profile posts, winning double the votes of her opponent Hilda 'Chiche' Gonzáles de Duhalde, wife of former President Eduardo Duhalde. Across the board, the election was a victory for President Kirchner, who had billed it as a plebiscite on his government two years after taking office as an outsider with only 22 percent of the vote. Marcos Brindicci

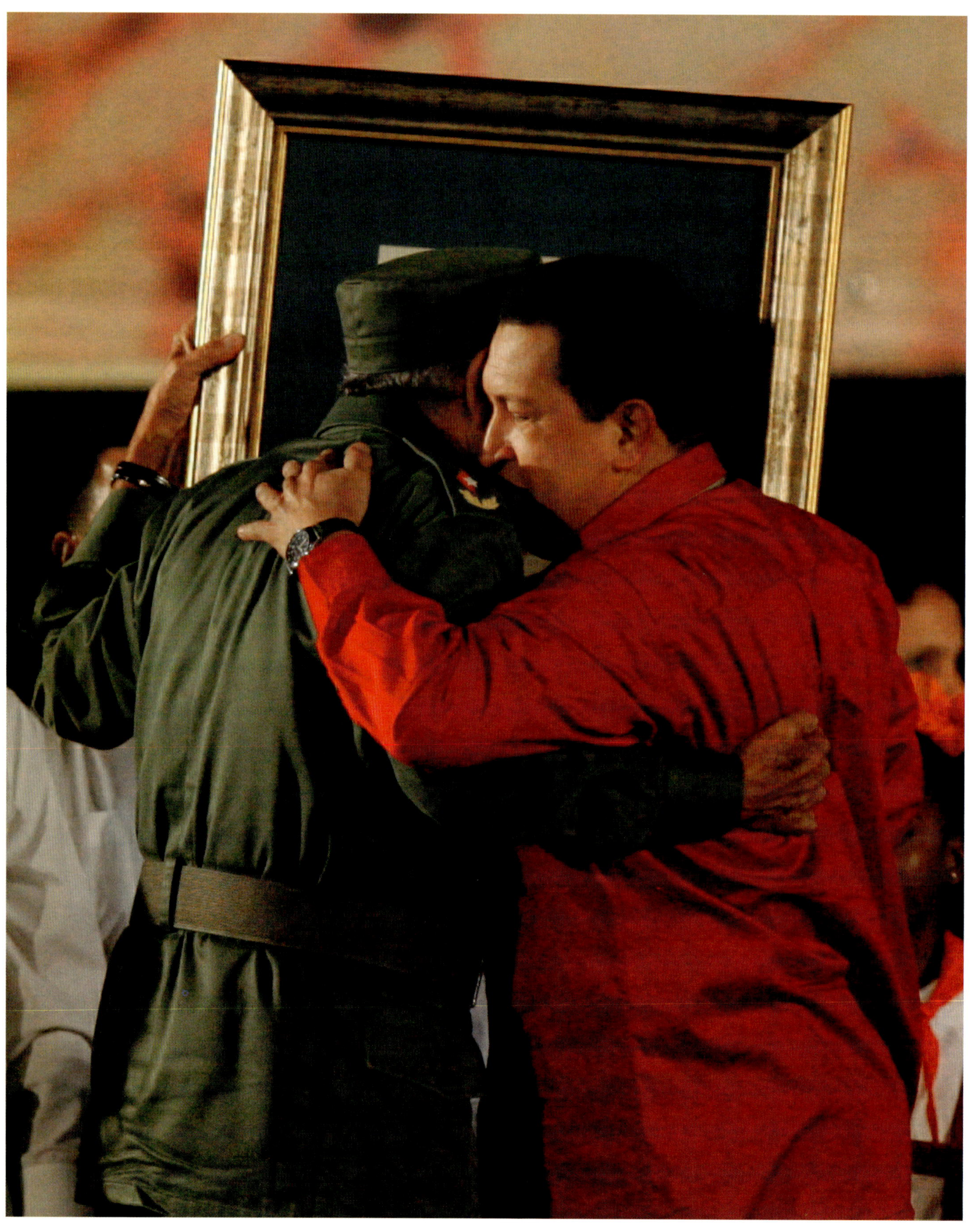

3 February 2006, HAVANA, CUBA

Cuban President Fidel Castro (left) and his Venezuelan counterpart Hugo Chávez embrace after Chávez received an international award from UNESCO in Havana. Chávez, a self-styled socialist revolutionary allied with Cuba, has clashed frequently with the United States, which he accuses of trying to topple his government in Venezuela, the world's fifth-largest oil exporter. Claudia Daut

3 January 2006, CARACAS, VENEZUELA

Opposite Bolivian President-elect Evo Morales (left) receives a replica of South American independence fighter Simón Bolívar's sword from his ally Venezuelan President Hugo Chávez. Morales and his Movement to Socialism party won 54 percent of the vote in the Bolivian election on 18 December 2005, making Morales the first Bolivian president to win an election outright since the country returned to democracy in 1982. A leftist and Aymara Indian who herded llamas as a boy, Morales' rise to power was based on his leadership of coca growers and opposition to the U.S.-funded eradication of the crop. Jorge Silva

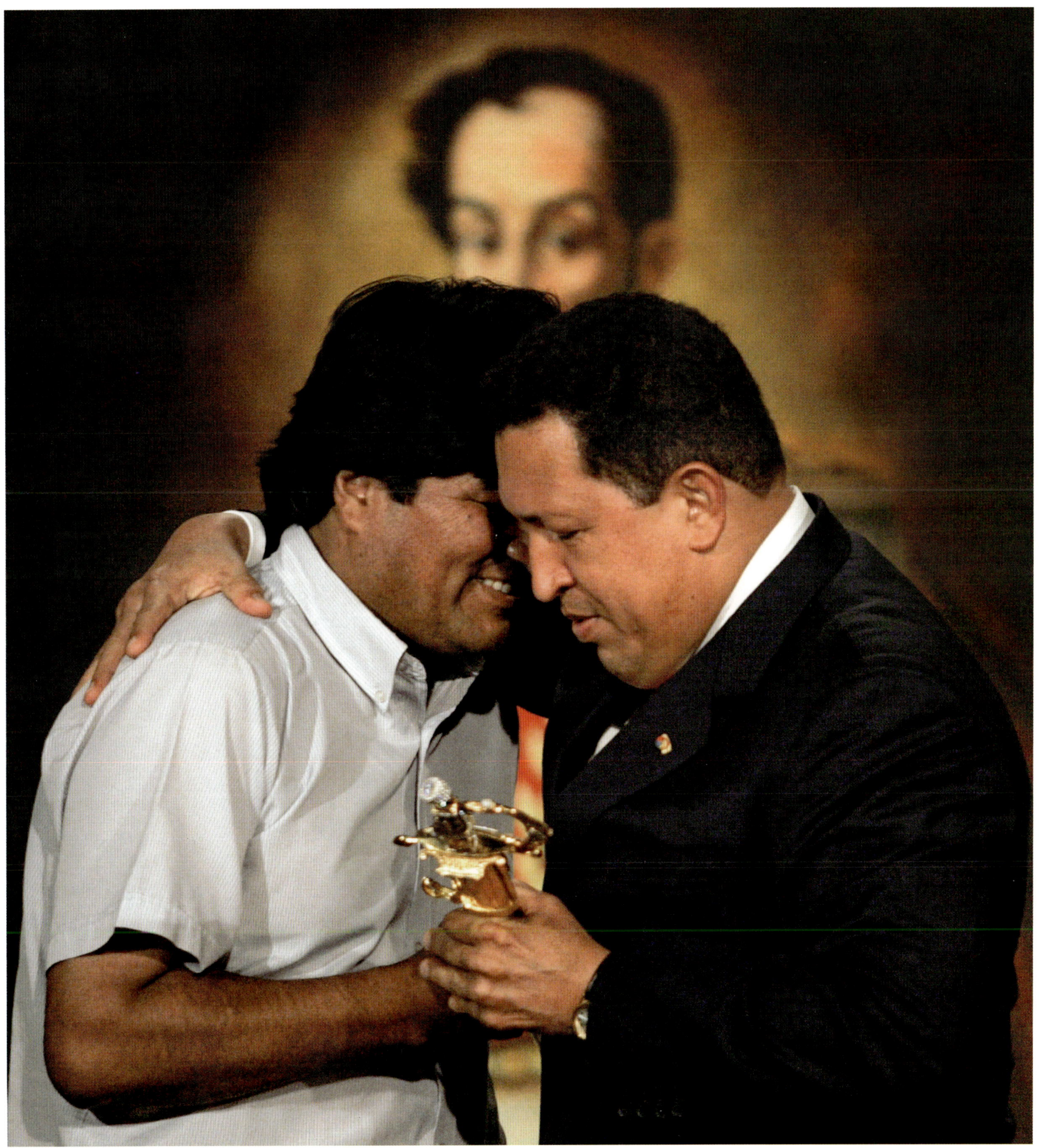

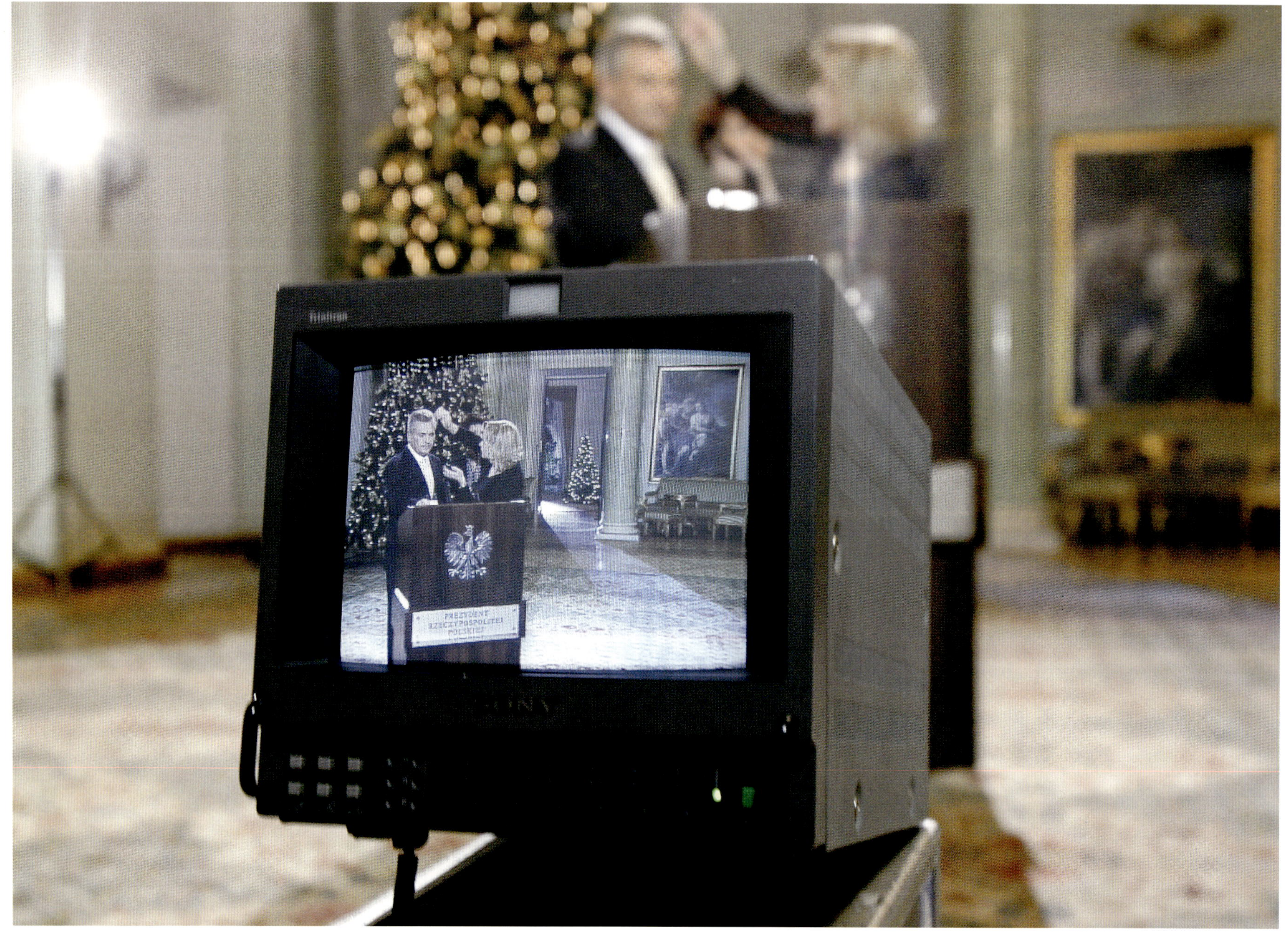

22 December 2005, WARSAW, POLAND

A make-up artist prepares Poland's outgoing President Aleksander Kwasniewski to give his televised final address to the nation at the Presidential Palace in Warsaw. After two terms of office, Kwasniewski was succeeded by veteran anti-communist activist Lech Kaczynski. Combining conservative social views with socialist economics, Kaczynski campaigned as a champion of Polish national interests willing to stand up against Brussels and Poland's big neighbours Germany and France. He called for a 'moral revolution' and a clean break from the country's post-communist past, ridding it of sleaze and ineffective government.

Peter Andrews

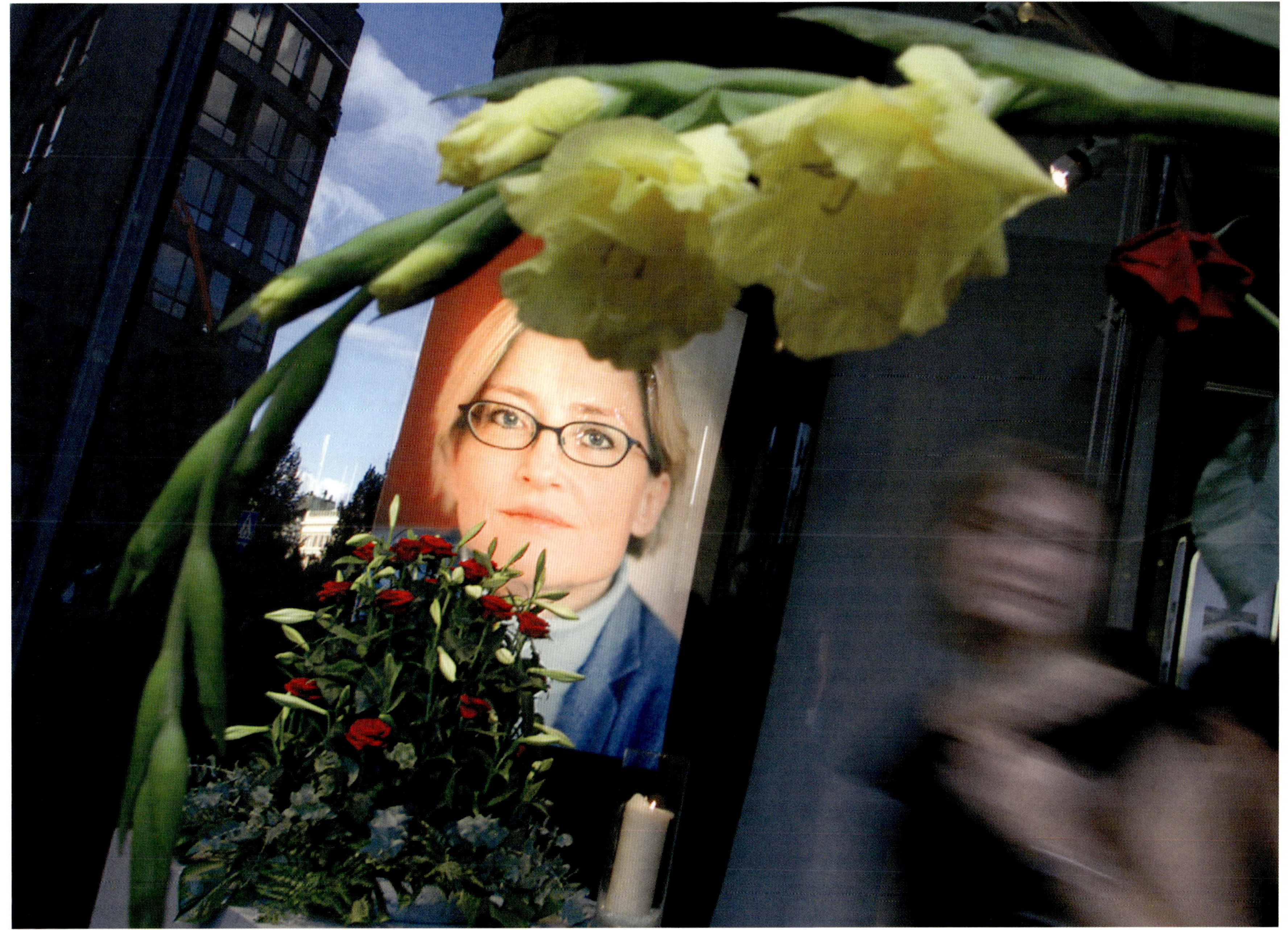

16 September 2003, STOCKHOLM, SWEDEN

A woman walks in front of a picture of murdered Swedish Foreign Minister Anna Lindh displayed in the Stockholm department store where she was fatally stabbed while out shopping without bodyguards on 10 September 2003. Tipped as Sweden's next prime minister, 46-year-old Lindh died just days before Swedes rejected joining the European single currency in a referendum. Her killer, Mijailo Mijailovic, said that 'voices' in his head were to blame for the frenzied attack. He was convicted of murder and sentenced to life imprisonment. Alexander Demianchuk

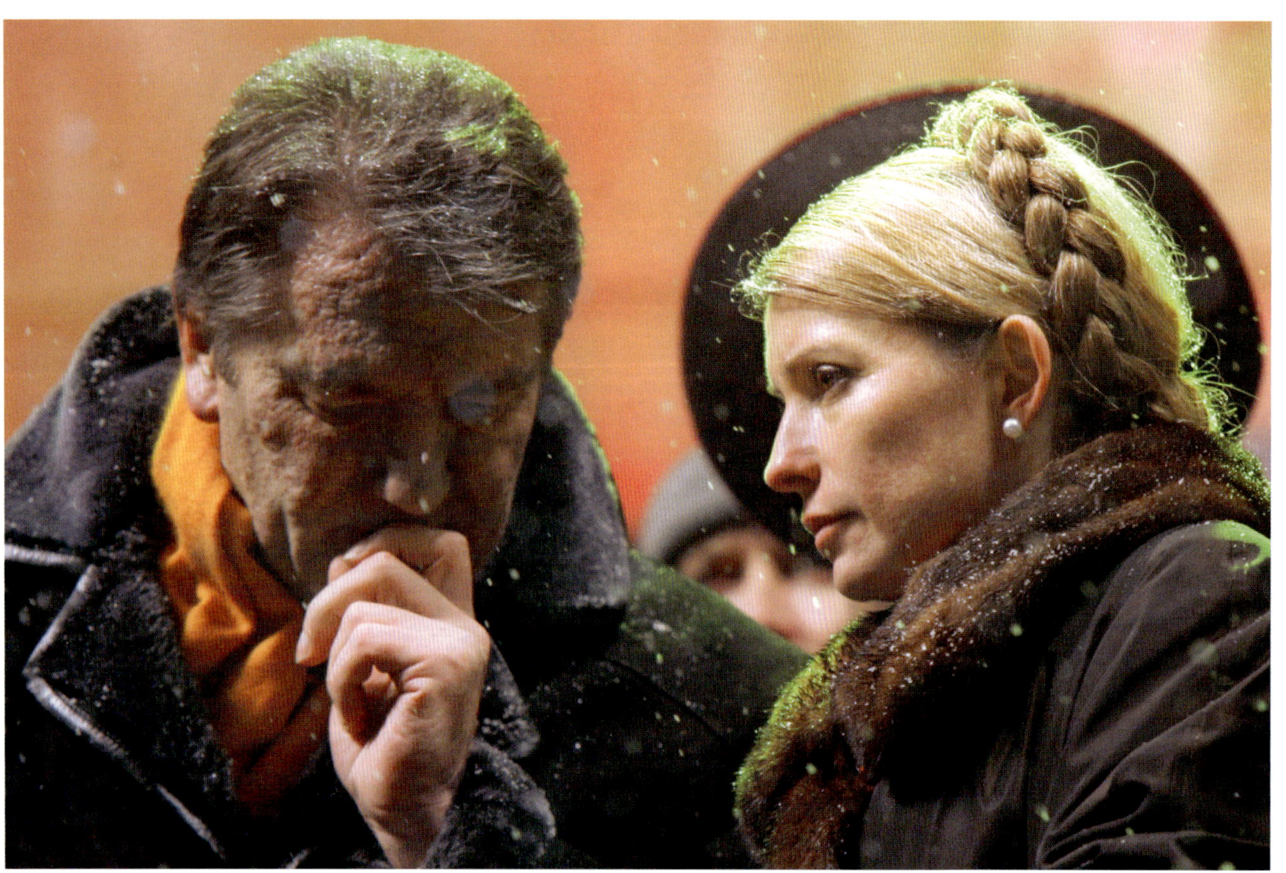

29 November 2004, KIEV, UKRAINE

Opposition leader and presidential candidate Viktor Yushchenko speaks to his aide, firebrand deputy Yulia Tymoshenko, at a rally in Kiev. After a first round of voting in the presidential election proved indecisive, a second round gave Prime Minister Viktor Yanukovich a massive lead. The opposition said the results were rigged and paralysed the capital with street protests. Tymoshenko demanded the outgoing President Leonid Kuchma sack Yanukovich and form a coalition government. Vasily Fedosenko

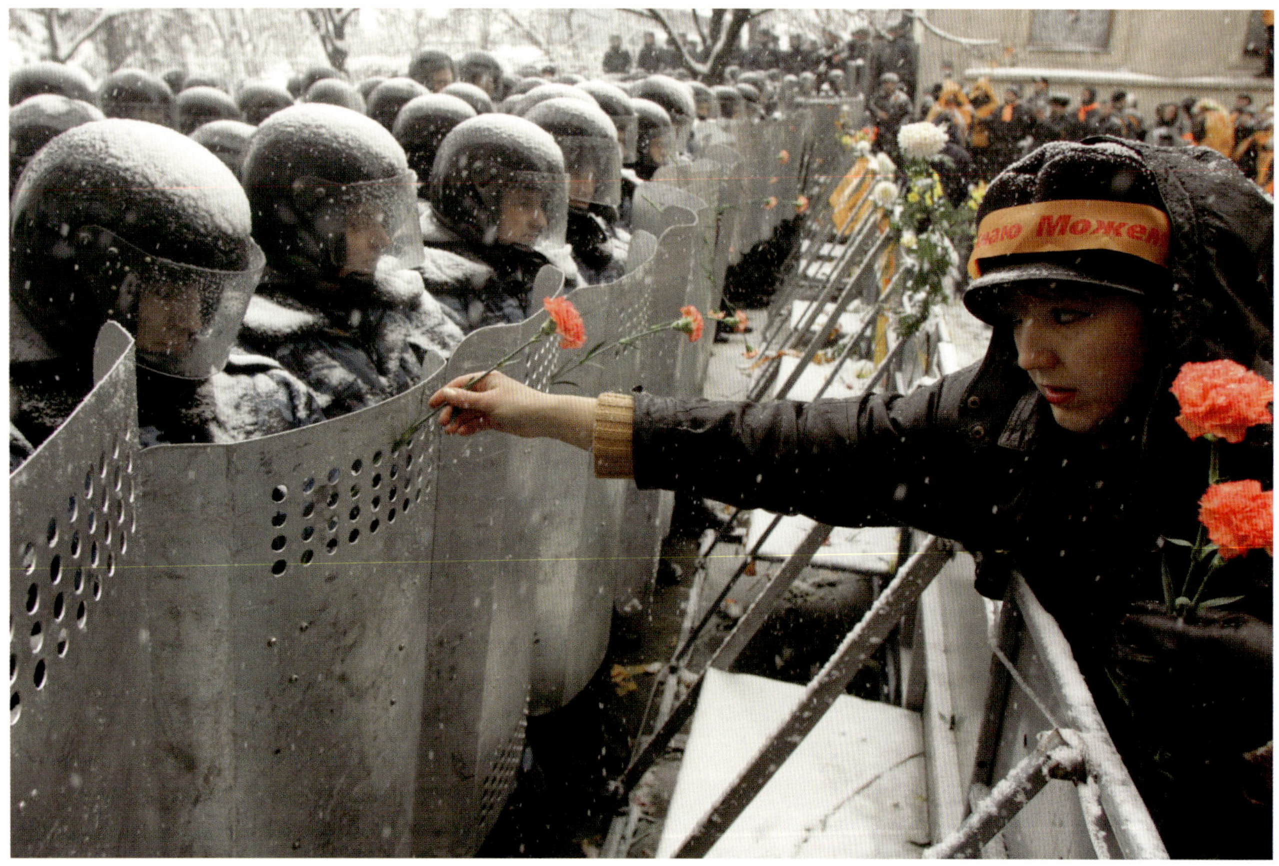

24 November 2004, KIEV, UKRAINE

A woman places carnations into the shields of anti-riot policemen standing outside the presidential office in Kiev. The historic events of these few weeks in late 2004 soon became known as the 'Orange Revolution', after the ubiquitous campaign colour of the opposition movement. Vasily Fedosenko

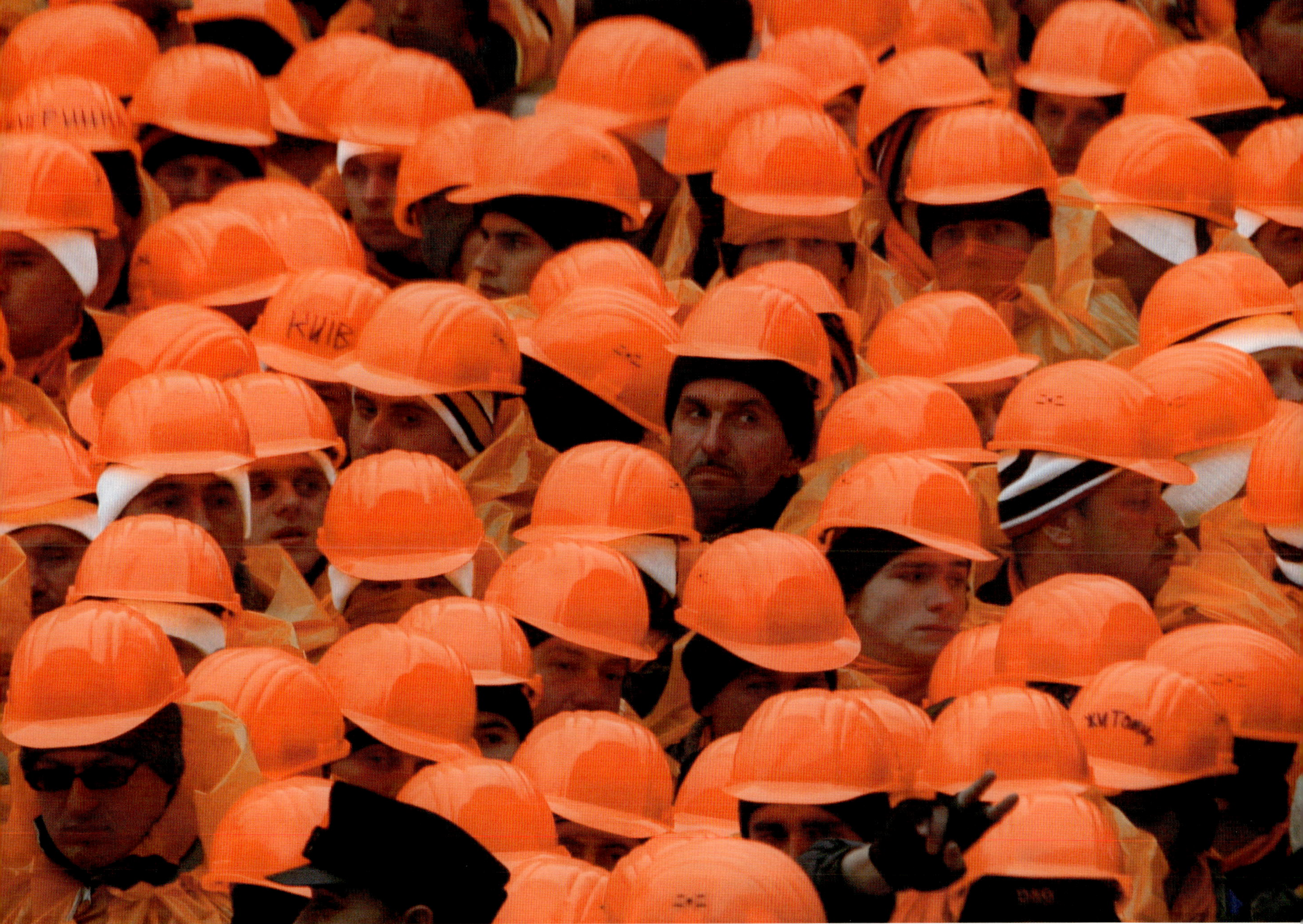

1 December 2004, KIEV, UKRAINE

Supporters of Viktor Yushchenko wearing orange helmets take part in a rally outside the government building in Kiev. On 3 December, Ukraine's Supreme Court ruled that the presidential election result was invalid and that a re-run was required, to be held on 26 December. This time Yushchenko was declared the winner, defeating Prime Minister Viktor Yanukovich with almost 52 percent of the vote. Gleb Garanich

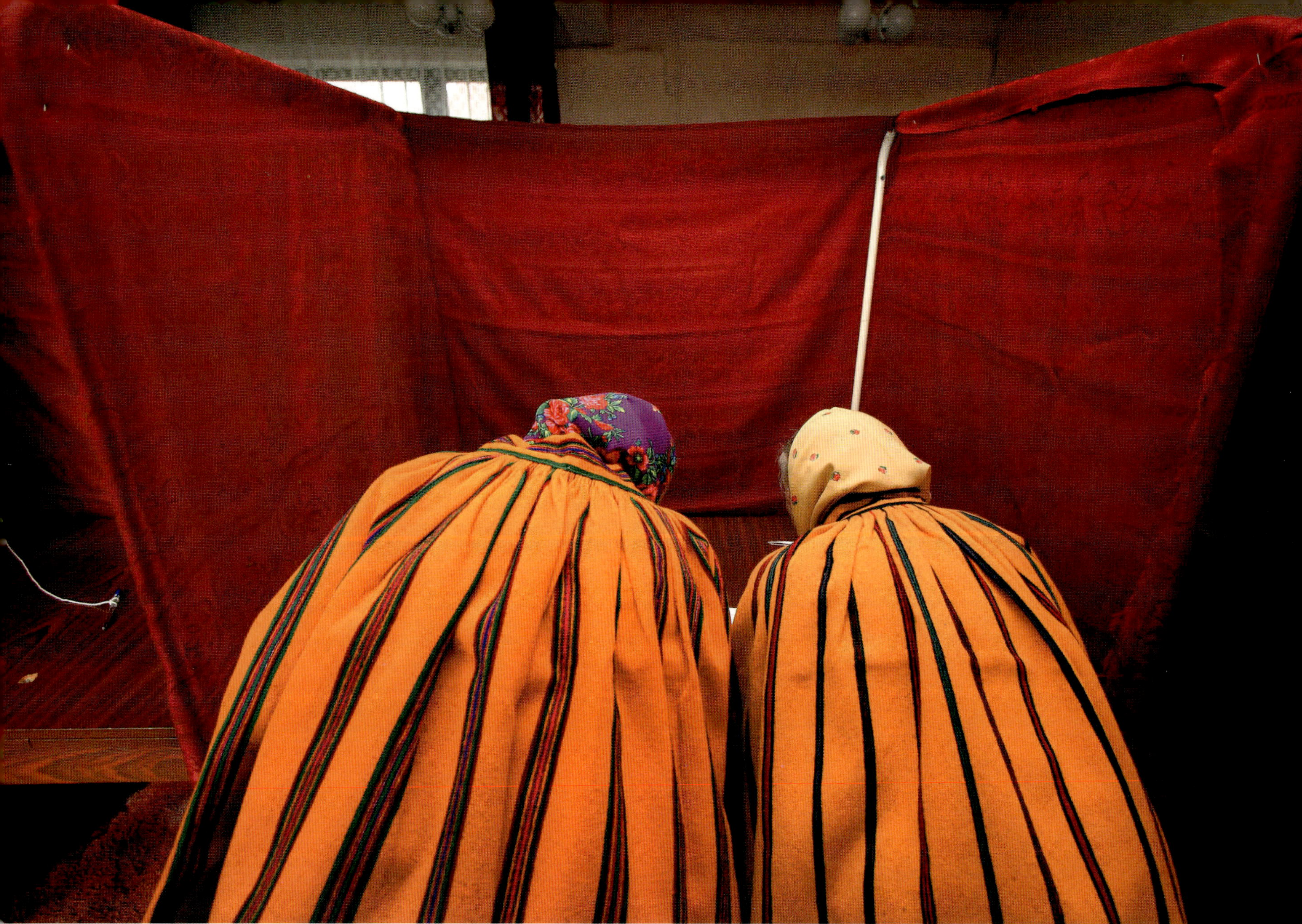

23 October 2005, GLUCHOW, POLAND

Women in traditional costume fill in their ballots during a presidential election in the village of Gluchow, central Poland. The outcome of this election gave the presidency to former anti-communist activist Lech Kaczynski, a month after the Law and Justice party led by Kaczynski's identical twin Jaroslav won general elections in Poland. Despite winning the parliamentary elections, Jaroslav Kaczynski declined to become prime minister in order to help his brother's chances of winning the presidency, saying Poles were not ready to have twins in the country's two top offices. Katarina Stoltz

18 September 2005, GUTACH, GERMANY

A woman wearing a traditional Black Forest costume casts her vote during the general election at a polling station in Gutach in southern Germany. The result of the poll was inconclusive, forcing the two biggest rivals, Angela Merkel's Conservatives (CDU) and Gerhard Schröder's Social Democrats (SPD), into a 'grand coalition'. Pascal Lauener

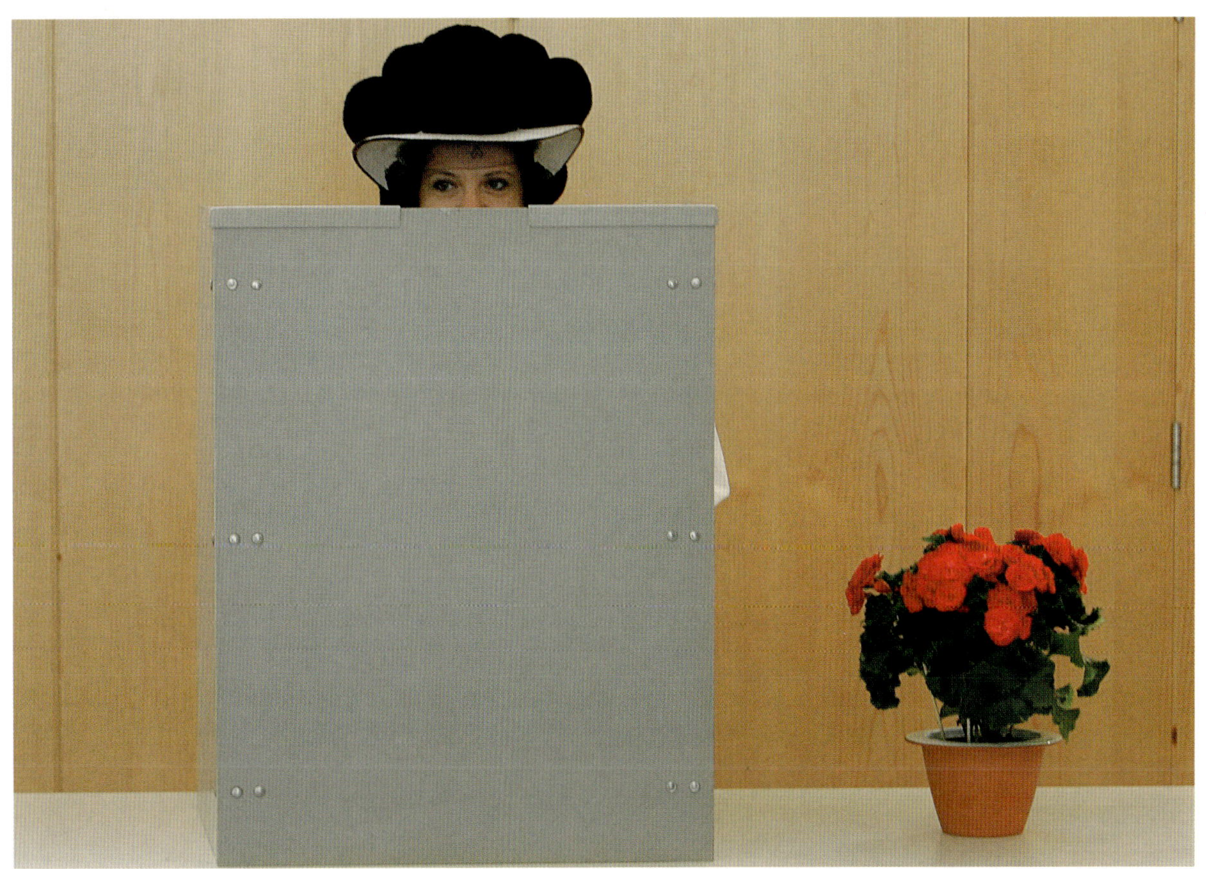

18 September 2005, KANDAHAR, AFGHANISTAN

Haji Kher Muhammed, an Afghan Kuchi nomad, inspects his inked finger before casting his ballot during elections for a national assembly and provincial councils. The Taliban had called on voters to boycott the polls. Although at least 14 people were killed in violence on election day, voting was overwhelmingly peaceful, and the opposition failed to derail the election. Each voter had an index finger dipped in indelible ink to prevent multiple voting. Adrees Latif

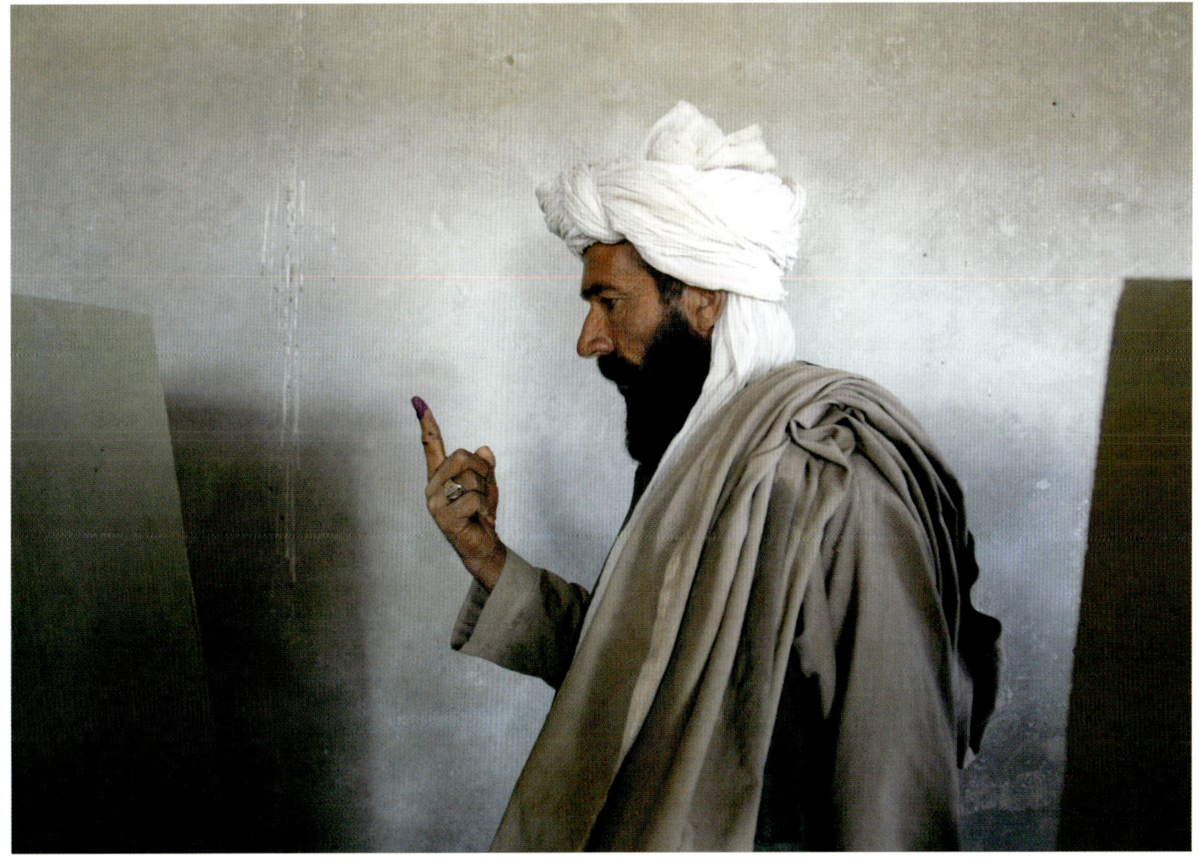

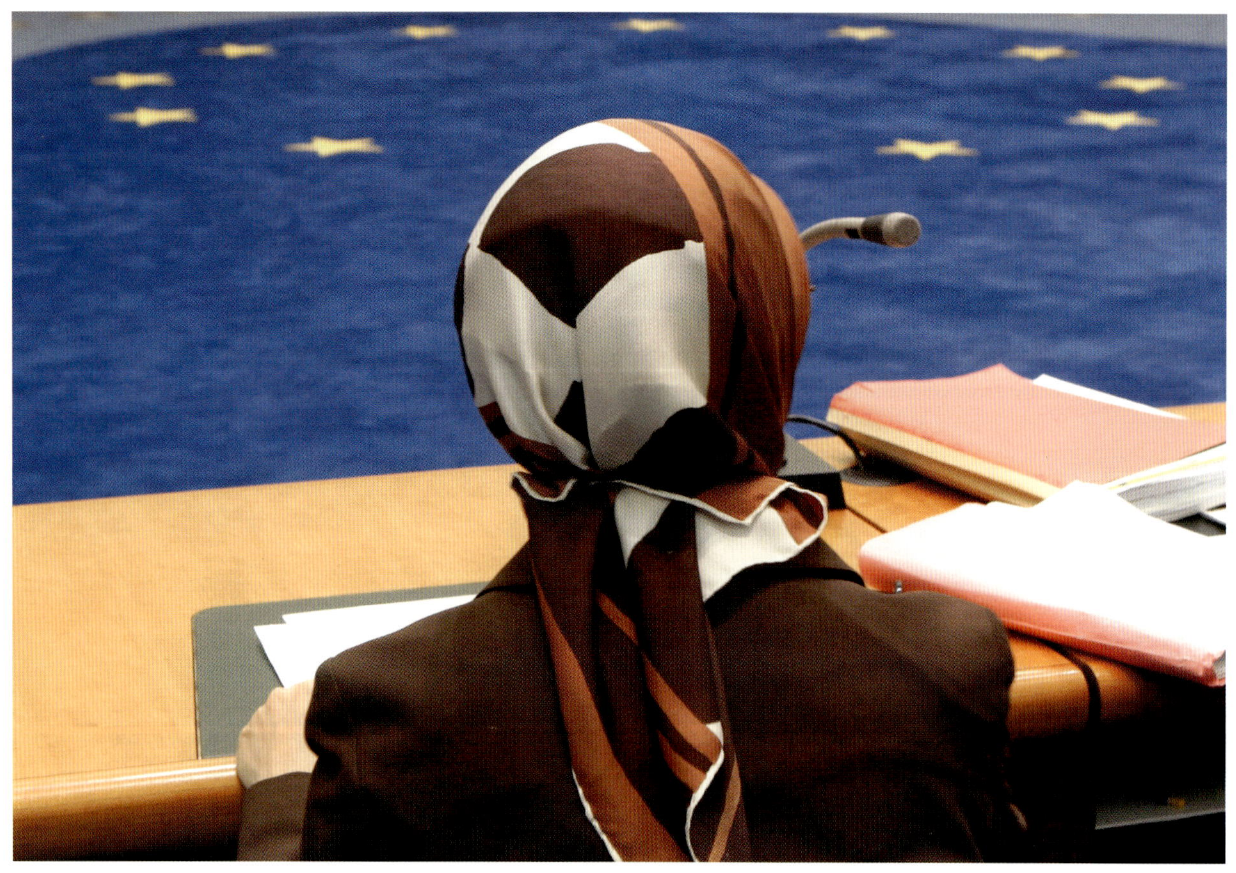

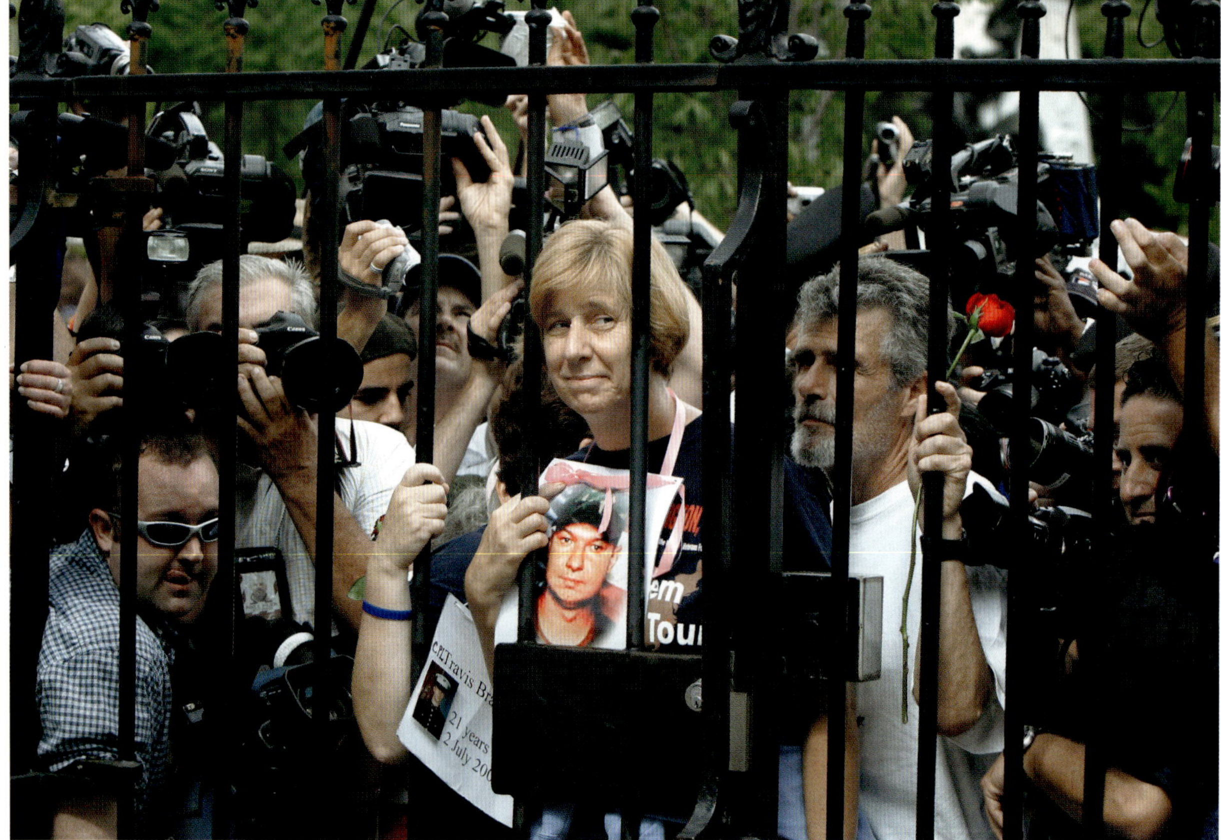

13 October 2005, STRASBOURG, FRANCE

Left Merve Safa Kavakçi awaits the hearing of her case against the Turkish parliamentary authorities at the European Court of Human Rights. Kavakçi, a member of Fazilet Partisi (the Virtue Party), was elected to the Turkish Grand National Assembly in April 1999, but was prevented from taking her oath because she wore a headscarf at the swearing-in ceremony. In 2001 the Turkish Constitutional Court dissolved Fazilet on the grounds that the party had become a 'centre of activities contrary to the principle of secularism', and Ms Kavakçi was banned from political activity for five years Vincent Kessler

26 September 2005, WASHINGTON, DC, UNITED STATES

Left below Anti-war protester Cindy Sheehan holds a portrait of her son Casey, killed in the Iraq war, as she stands at the gates of the White House to ask for a meeting with U.S. President George W. Bush. She and several dozen protesters were taken into custody after refusing to obey police orders to leave. Sheehan's vigil outside Bush's Texas ranch in August 2005 focused attention on the anti-war movement in the United States. Jason Reed

11 February 2004, ZAANDIJK, NETHERLANDS

Opposite Dutch Iranian immigrant Mehdy Kavousi protests against proposed new asylum laws in the Netherlands by sewing his lips and eyelids together. Despite protests and threatened hunger strikes, on 17 February 2004 the Dutch lower house of parliament approved plans for the mass expulsion of up to 26,000 failed asylum seekers. Paul Vreeker

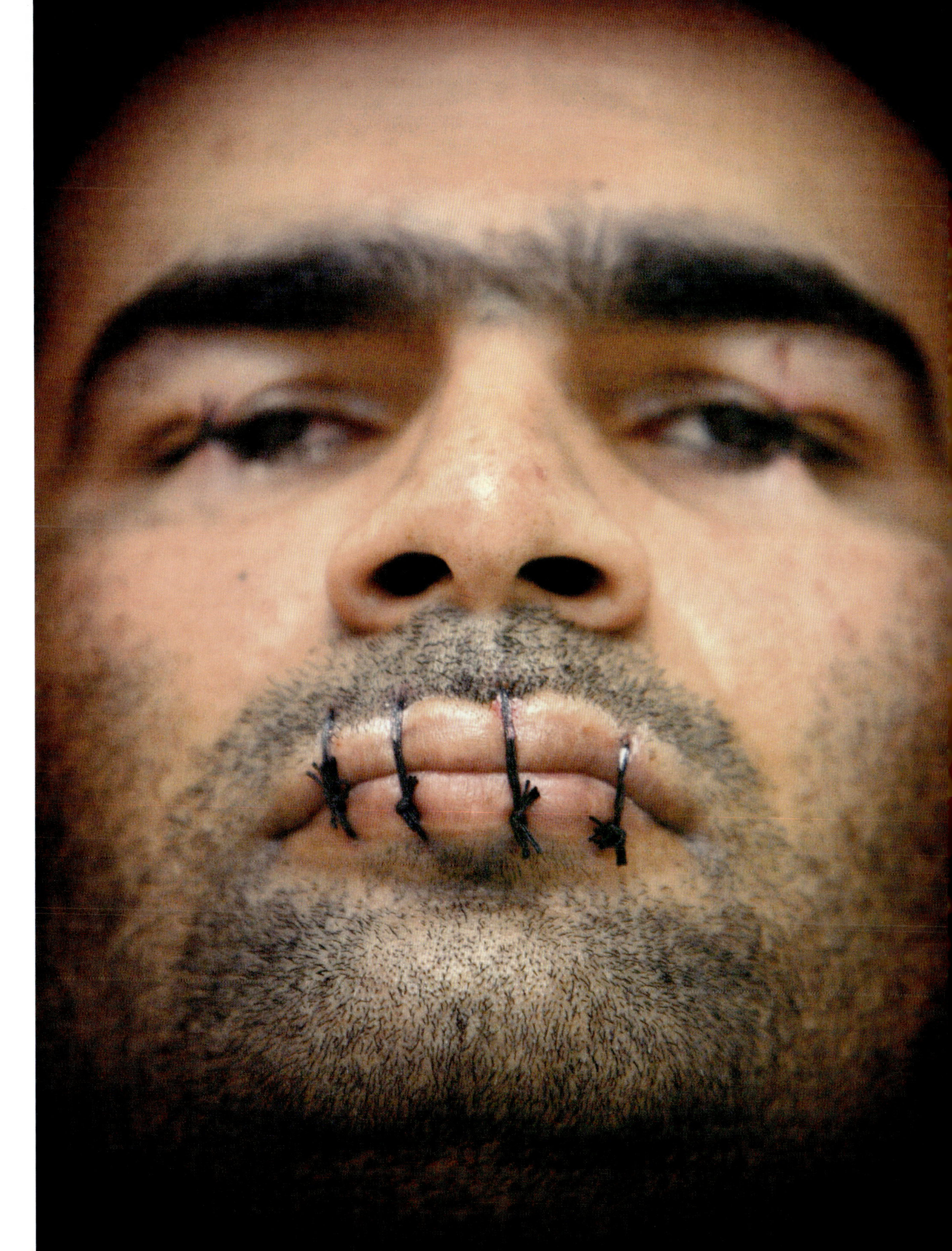

We are all potential targets in the wars of the new century – wars often fought with low-tech weapons that in the hands of determined militants can bloody even the greatest military powers. The deadliest of those weapons is the suicide bomber. The world may have avoided a nuclear holocaust in the last century, but its appetite for war in pursuit of resources, national rights and religious beliefs shows no sign of waning.

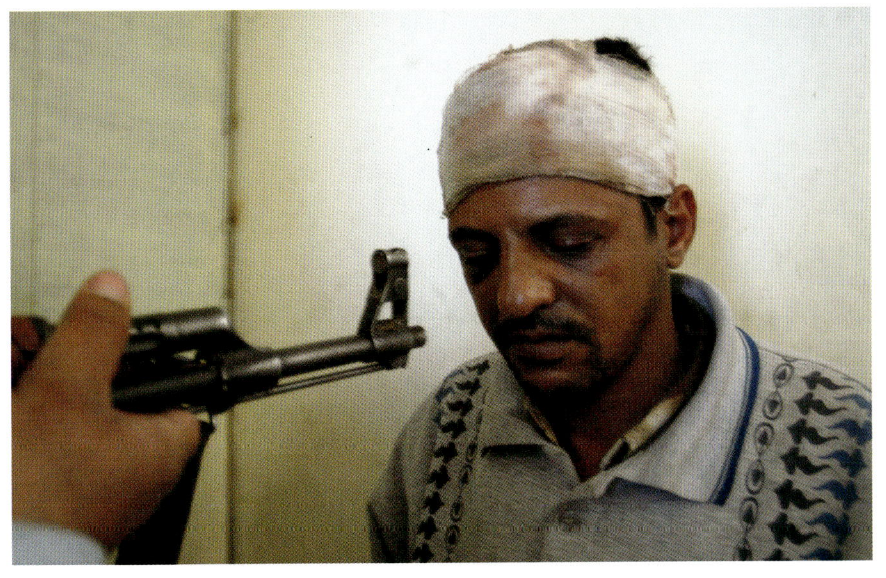

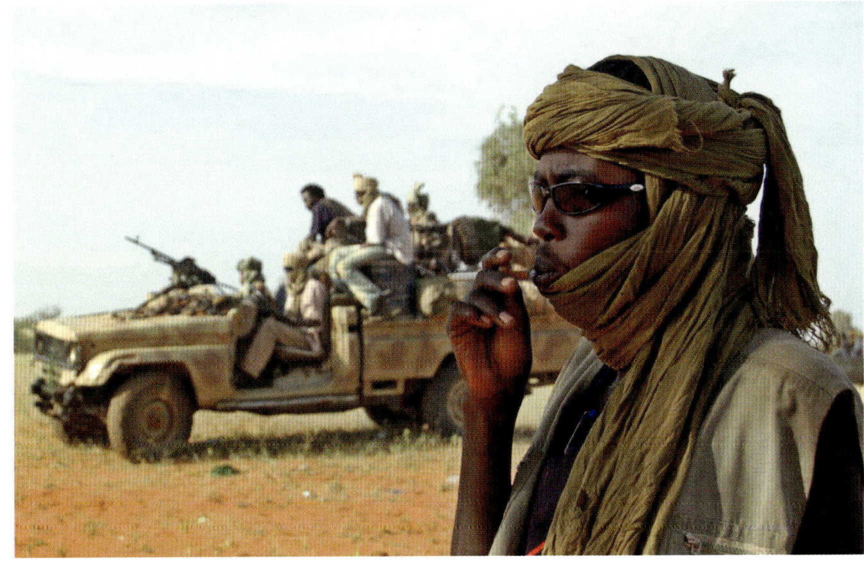

War and Conflict

Modern Warfare / Ancient Struggles
Resources / Identity / Loyalty / Defiance
Destruction / Suffering / Liberation / Hope

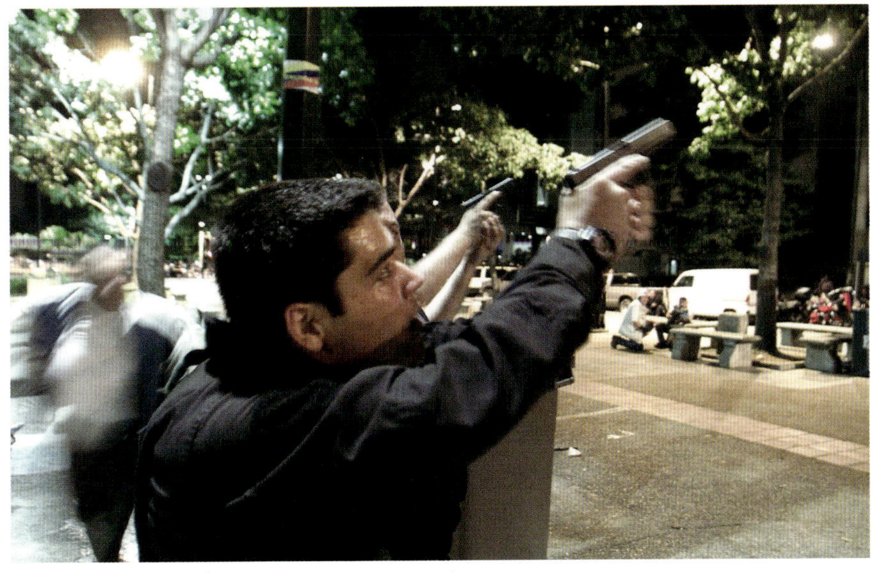

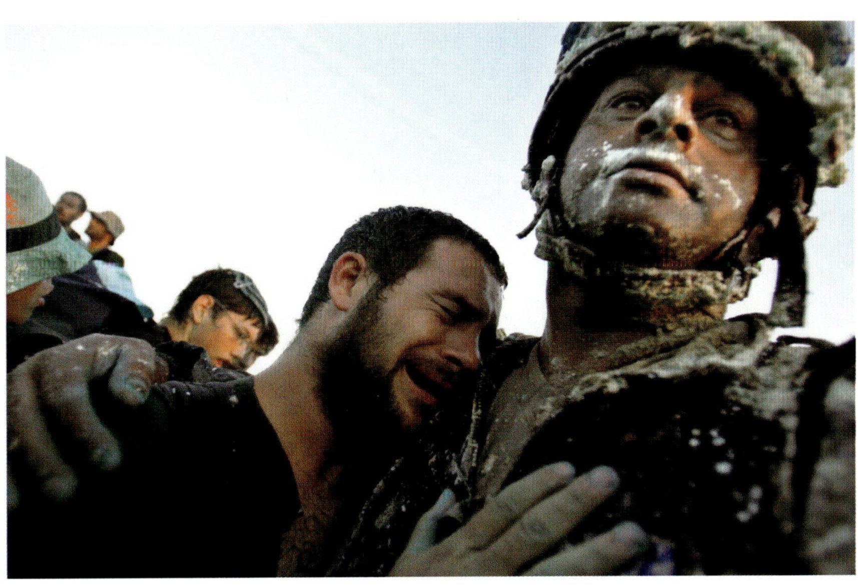

War and Conflict

'We are at war and I am a soldier,' said Mohammad Sidique Khan, a 30-year-old teaching assistant from the English city of Leeds, in a video message taped some time before he boarded a London underground train crowded with commuters and detonated a backpack full of explosives. He was one of four suicide bombers who attacked the British capital's transport system on 7 July 2005, killing 52 people.

In the U.S. city of Savannah, that same day, American soldiers wept at a memorial service for 16 special forces troops killed when Afghan rebels shot down their helicopter with a rocket-propelled grenade. In the mountains of eastern Afghanistan, U.S. forces searched for 29-year-old Petty Officer 2nd Class Matthew Axelson, missing after his Navy SEAL commando team was ambushed by the Taliban, and later found dead.

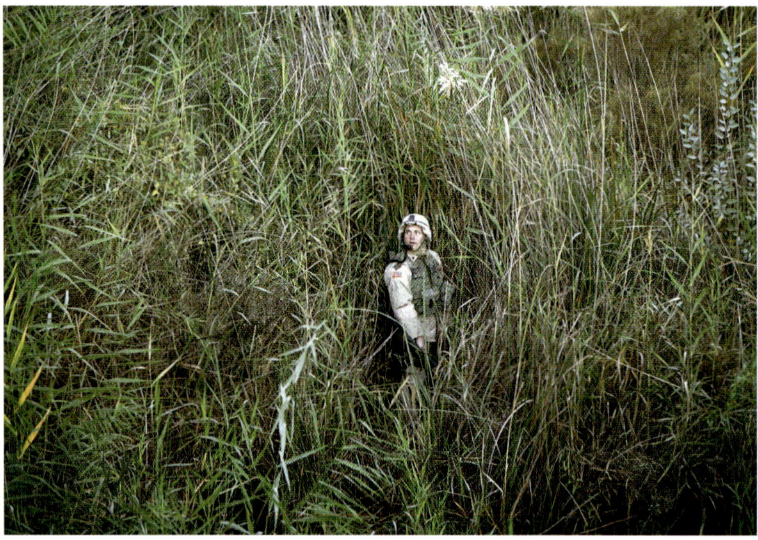

A U.S. soldier searches for Iraqi militants hiding in dense vegetation around the Diala River outside Baquba. 13 November 2003, Damir Sagolj.

Insurgents in Iraq fired more than a dozen mortar rounds towards a local government building in the northern city of Mosul, but hit a crowded marketplace instead, killing three civilians and wounding more than 50. Al Qaeda's network in Iraq announced that it had killed the Egyptian envoy to Baghdad, Ihab el-Sherif, kidnapped a few days earlier.

In the troubled Indonesian province of Aceh, ravaged by the 2004 tsunami and decades of separatist insurgency, 24-year-old Dutch aid worker Marije Mellegers was wounded when gunmen opened fire on her vehicle. NATO forces in Bosnia seized the son of Radovan Karadzic in the hope he could lead them to his father, the Bosnian Serb leader wanted on war crimes charges for orchestrating the massacre of 8,000 Muslim men and boys in Srebrenica a decade earlier. And outside the West Bank city of Nablus, Israeli troops said they killed a Palestinian militant who was trying to attack Jewish worshippers.

It was a typical day of twenty-first-century warfare.

Most of those killed that day had no idea that they were on the front lines of war. But in modern warfare, we are all on the front lines. Civilians have always suffered in wars: robbed, raped and displaced by marauding armies, massacred in ransacked cities or starved to death in sieges. But with the emergence of aerial warfare in the twentieth century, non-combatants were killed in unprecedented numbers. In World War Two, whole cities were ravaged by firebombing raids that sparked massive infernos and sucked the oxygen out of the air. Then came the nuclear strikes on Hiroshima and Nagasaki. Many of the dead were vaporized, leaving only shadows. Others died years later, blighted by radiation. For all of them, the distinction between combatants and non-combatants was irrelevant.

> The world may be changing, but it is still held prisoner by cycles of violence rooted in ancient history.

The victims of twenty-first-century war have also, overwhelmingly, been civilians. Office workers sitting at their desks at the World Trade Center in New York on a bright, sunny morning on September 11, 2001. Holidaymakers and local workers on the tropical island of Bali or in the Egyptian resort of Sharm el-Sheikh, cut down by suicide bombers as they danced in nightclubs or ate seafood on the beach. Foreign contractors, looking to earn some extra cash before retirement, kidnapped in Baghdad and decapitated, one by one, by a masked militant with a knife. Afghan villagers killed by stray U.S. bombs. And uncounted thousands of Iraqi non-combatants, killed by suicide bombers who target Shi'ite civilians to try to provoke a civil war, by insurgents who launch mortar or landmine attacks in crowded civilian areas, and by U.S. and allied troops who struggle to tell friend from foe and routinely open fire when they feel threatened. The U.S. military releases no figures on the 'collateral damage' of the war in Iraq, but most analysts estimate thousands of Iraqi civilians have been killed by American forces: shot dead at checkpoints after failing to stop quickly enough, cut down in confused firefights after roadside bomb blasts, or crushed in buildings flattened by 'precision bombs' and 'surgical strikes'. In twenty-first-century warfare, all of us are targets, whether or not we have chosen to fight.

The world may be changing, but it is still held prisoner by cycles of violence rooted in ancient history. The wars that have dominated the new century all have their roots in conflicts between Christians, Muslims and Jews that have been fought for more than a millennium. Many Muslims see the U.S. War on Terror and the military interventions in Afghanistan and Iraq as a continuation of the Crusades. Al Qaeda leader Osama bin Laden and the network's leader in Iraq, Abu Musab al-Zarqawi, portray their struggle as a Holy War against Crusaders and Zionists. Washington says it is not targeting Muslims, only terrorists. Within Iraq, battles fought 14 centuries ago that divided Muslims into Shi'ites and Sunnis still haunt the country, as sectarian violence threatens to explode into full-scale civil war. Saddam Hussein saw himself as a successor of King Nebuchadnezzar, who built an empire from his capital Babylon and conquered Jerusalem hundreds of years before the birth of Christ. And in Israel and the Palestinian territories, competing, ancient claims to holy sites still blight the prospects for peace in the Middle East.

Another age-old imperative besides religion, race and ideology is also fuelling the violence in Israel and the Palestinian territories – competition over land. Battles over territory continue to spark conflict in the twenty-first century, despite predictions that globalization and technology would gradually erase national distinctions. In southeast Turkey, the Kurds – another ethnic group without a country of their own – have been fighting an insurgency for well over a decade. Across the border in Iraq, ethnic and sectarian tensions that threaten to pull the country apart could give the Kurds the independent state they are seeking. To the north, the Chechen struggle to win independence from Moscow has turned the capital Grozny into a ruined wasteland and cost thousands of lives on both sides. A territorial dispute is also one of the likeliest flashpoints for a new nuclear conflict: Kashmir in the foothills of the Himalayas is claimed by both India and Pakistan. The two nuclear powers glower at each other across their common border, never far from war.

Elsewhere in the world, and rarely reported by most media, other wars simmer and flare. In Myanmar (formerly Burma), isolated ethnic armed groups have been fighting the military regime for decades. In Colombia, rival drugs gangs and Marxist rebels kill hundreds each year. But it is in Africa that the worst of the world's forgotten wars are being fought. In northern Uganda, the Lord's Resistance Army, a rebel group led by a former altar boy who says he gets his orders from angels, has massacred civilians, mutilated

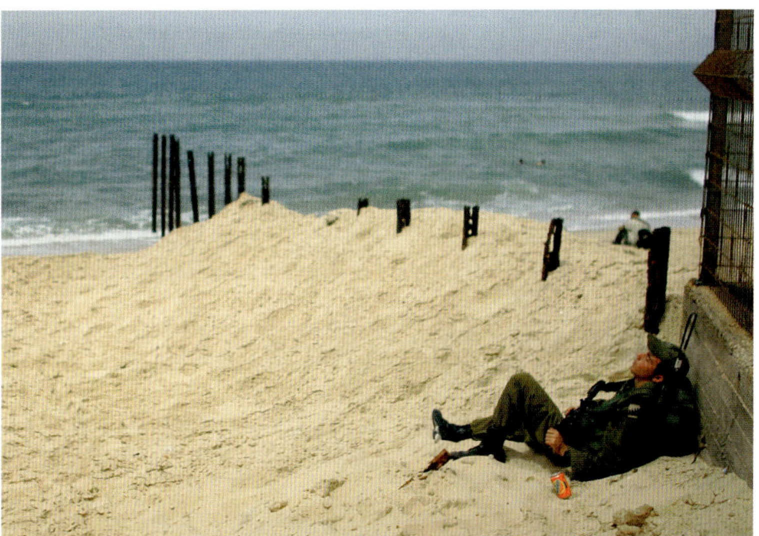

An Israeli soldier rests on a beach before a rally in Gush Katif settlement bloc against Prime Minister Ariel Sharon's plan to evacuate Jewish settlers from the Gaza Strip. 27 April 2005, Goran Tomasevic.

survivors and abducted more than 20,000 children during two decades of insurgency. Unknown numbers of women and girls have been raped. And in the Democratic Republic of the Congo, an estimated 3.8 million people have lost their lives since 1998 as a result of a brutal civil war. Aid groups say a thousand people a day are dying in the Congo due to violence, disease and malnutrition stemming from the conflict. It is a toll that dwarfs even the shocking bloodshed in Iraq.

No country can match the United States for military might. But despite its fearsome array of high-technology armaments, its Stealth bombers, unmanned Predator drones and laser-guided missiles, America's military has repeatedly been humbled by determined guerrilla fighters with only rudimentary weapons. Unbeatable in a conventional war, U.S. forces are still learning how to deal with asymmetric warfare. Guerrillas defeated the U.S. military in Vietnam, inflicted traumatic losses in Lebanon and Somalia, and have mired American forces in a violent stalemate in Iraq. Adopting hit-and-run tactics and making ingenious use of low-technology weapons, particularly roadside bombs often cobbled together from old artillery shells, insurgents have killed and wounded thousands of U.S. troops since Saddam Hussein was overthrown. In November 2003 the Reuters team based at the Sheraton Hotel in Baghdad awoke to the sound of explosions shaking the building. Insurgents had fired Russian-made Katyusha rockets at the hotel from a donkey cart. It later transpired that donkeys featured in other insurgent attacks in Baghdad that day – donkey carts were used to fire rockets at the oil ministry and a Kurdish party's headquarters, and a 'suicide' donkey was found tied to a tree strapped with a propane tank attached to explosives. 'Could you comment on the use of donkeys?,' asked a U.S. reporter at a military briefing for journalists in Baghdad. 'I mean, is this something that you're going to be looking into now?' 'Certainly,' replied Brigadier General Mark Kimmitt, spokesman for U.S. forces in Iraq. 'This is an adaptive enemy. We've said this all along.'

Of all the weapons of twenty-first-century warfare, it is the suicide bomb that has had the most impact. When human beings are not just unafraid to die, but actively want to be killed in carrying out their attacks, they are almost impossible to stop. And there is no shortage of recruits. 'Now you face people who love death just like you love life,' Zarqawi said in a taunt to President George W. Bush during the videotaped beheading of U.S. hostage Eugene Armstrong. 'Killing for the sake of God is their best wish, getting to your soldiers and allies are their happiest moments, and cutting the heads of the criminal infidels is implementing the orders of our Lord.'

For the journalists who cover conflict, and who captured the images on these pages, reporting on wars has never been more dangerous. Iraq has outstripped Vietnam and Algeria to become the deadliest war for journalists in modern history. Journalists covering wars have always risked being caught in the crossfire – that goes with the territory. But increasingly, they are being specifically targeted. No longer can a journalist expect non-combatant status to provide any protection. Trying to cover a war impartially is a fraught task – to those fighting the war, impartiality is seen as betrayal, and journalists are often despised. But without the bravery of front-line correspondents, photographers and videographers, the world would be much blinder to the realities of war.

All wars, of course, eventually come to an end – even if war itself seems to be a permanent human condition. The last century ended with the tiny territory of East Timor winning independence from Indonesia after decades of conflict that cost hundreds of thousands of lives. At a victory celebration high in the mountains above the capital Dili, emaciated Timorese guerrillas who had fought in the jungle for years wept with emotion, both over what they had won, and all that they had lost in the conflict. None of them were in any doubt that the war had been worth it – whatever the cost. In Sudan, Africa's longest civil war has ended with a peace agreement that lays the ground for power sharing between factions that for decades were enemies. And Liberia, too, is gradually emerging from a vicious civil war. The efforts of the international community to police conflict zones and resolve conflicts have often descended into farce and tragedy, but there have been successes too. And the world has also managed to prevent a global arms race from getting out of control – treaties to prevent nuclear proliferation have largely been successful, although the possible construction of atomic weapons by North Korea and alleged attempts by Iran to acquire the bomb threaten to spark new conflicts in years to come.

Humankind already has the technology to destroy itself – during the Cold War, the world looked into the abyss of a global nuclear holocaust, and world security was based on the precarious assumption that neither side would dare take a step that would lead to mutual annihilation. The Cold War may have ended but the technology survives: more countries are gaining nuclear expertise, and it is almost inevitable that militant groups will one day get their hands on a nuclear device. The wars of the twentieth century, which killed more than 150 million people and wasted so much of the world's wealth, have done nothing to diminish mankind's appetite for war in the new millennium. Technology may advance, but sadly there is no evidence to suggest that human nature will ever do the same.

Andrew Marshall has worked at Reuters since 1994. He has reported in over 20 countries, including the United Kingdom, Indonesia, Burma and Afghanistan. From 2003 to 2005, he worked as the chief correspondent in Iraq, running a team of over 100 foreign and Iraqi staff. From 2005 to 2006, Andrew was based in London, where he helped cover the 7 July suicide bomb attacks on the London transport system. He is currently Reuters Middle East bureau chief.

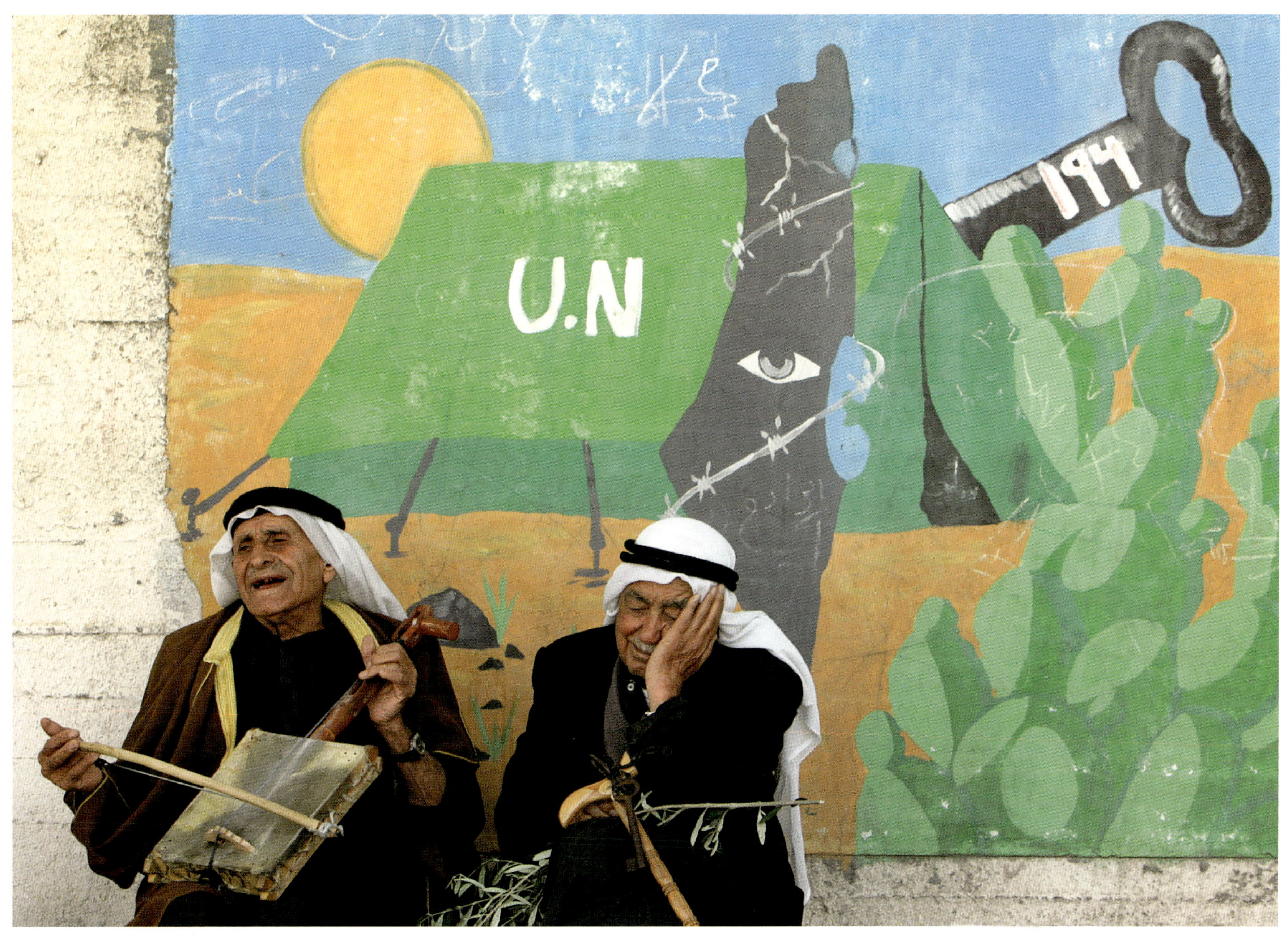

13 May 2005, BETHLEHEM, WEST BANK

Palestinian refugees Mahmud Eibed and Ahmed Alaham sit under a mural at Al-Dheishe refugee camp near the West Bank city of Bethlehem. Ammar Awad

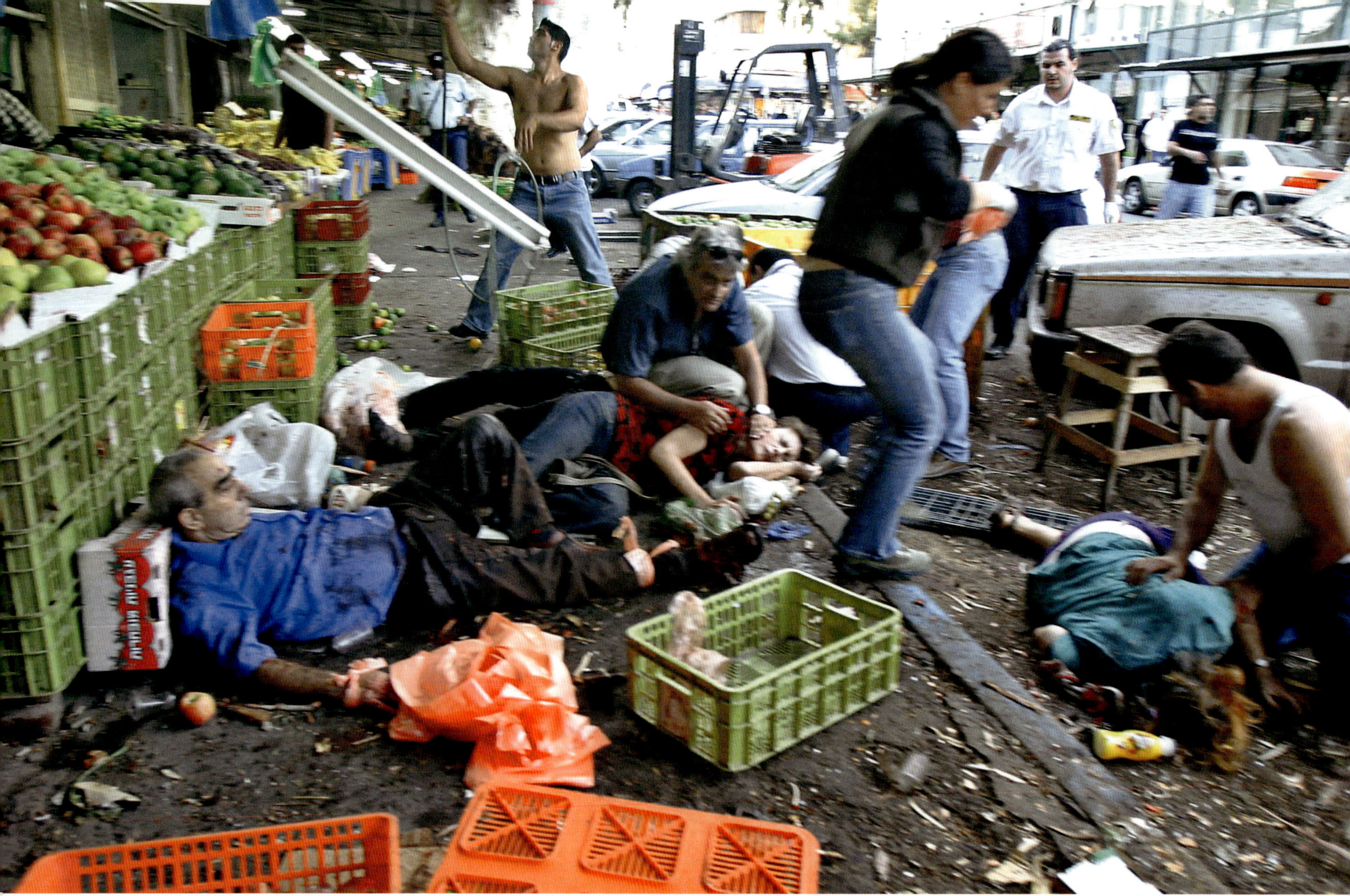

26 October 2005, HADERA, ISRAEL

Injured Israelis are helped by passers-by in the moments after a Palestinian suicide bomber blew himself up in a market in the coastal city of Hadera, killing six people and wounding 30. Islamic Jihad claimed responsibility. George Ginsberg

6 March 2003, JABALYA, GAZA STRIP

Unidentified bodies lie on a street in the Jabalya refugee camp in the northern Gaza Strip. They were victims of a raid by Israeli forces that was launched hours after a Palestinian suicide bomber killed 17 people on an Israeli bus packed with high school students in the port city of Haifa. Eleven Palestinians were killed and more than 140 injured during the nine-hour operation in Jabalya, the largest refugee camp in the Gaza Strip. Ahmed Jadallah

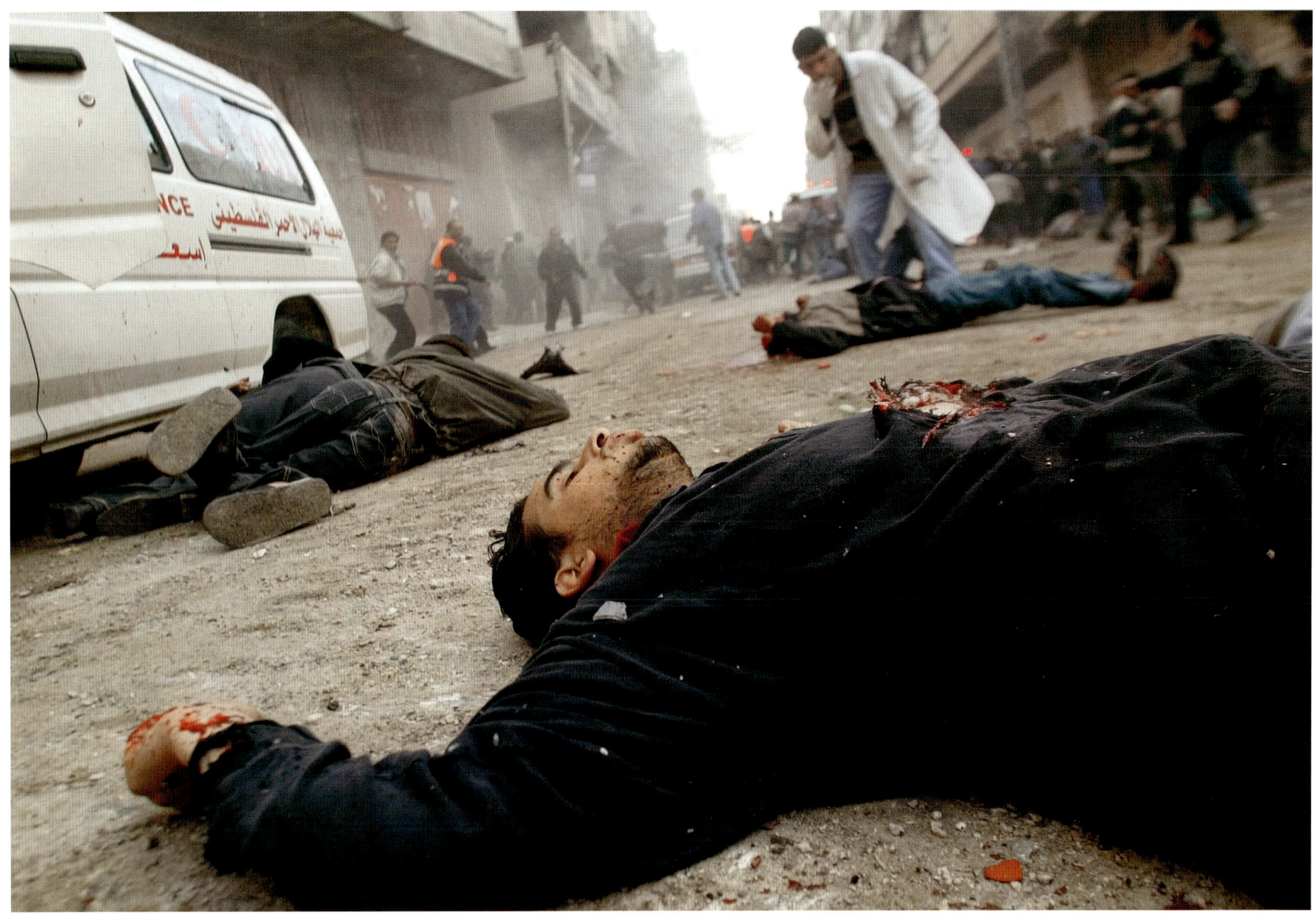

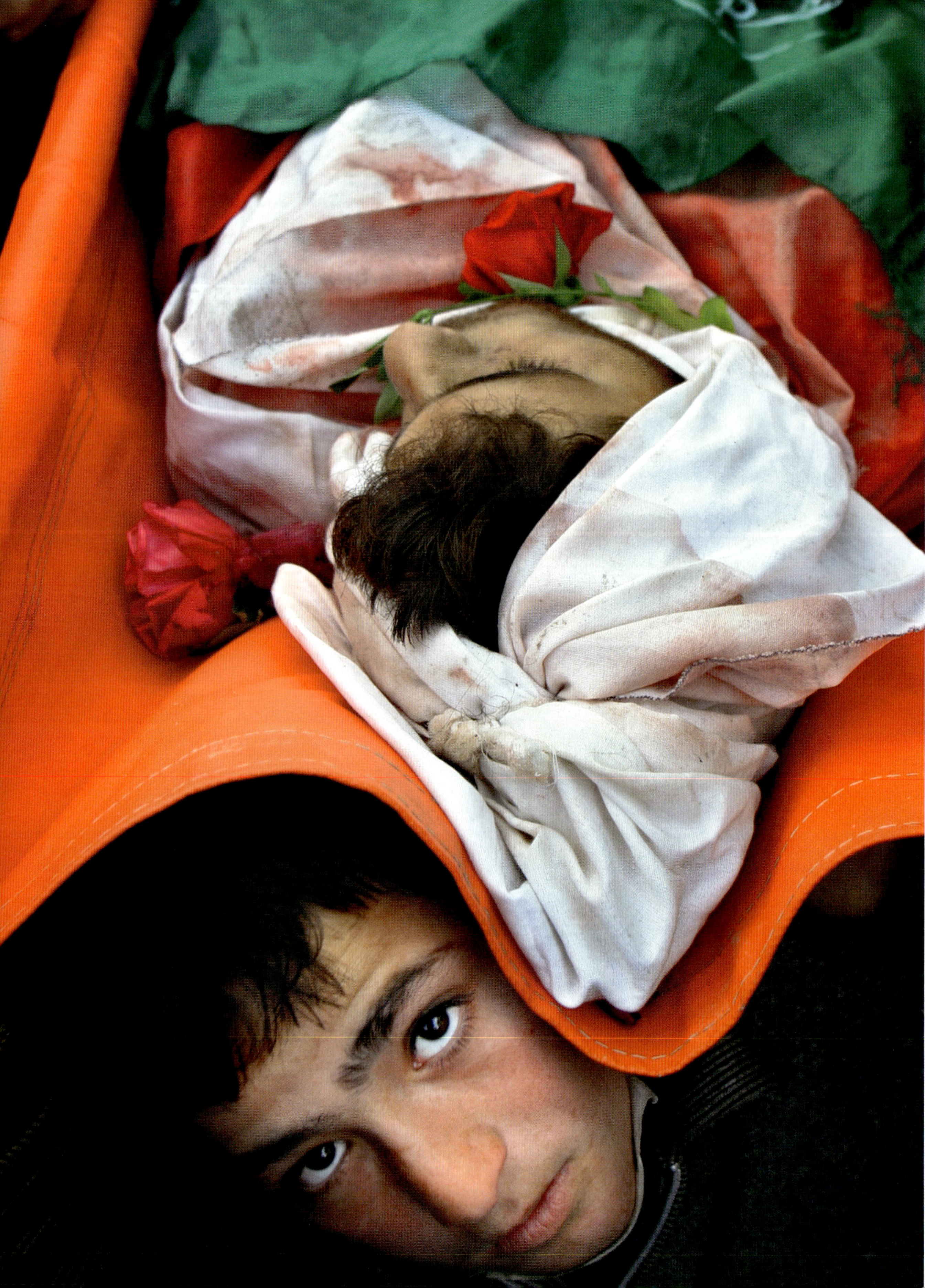

4 January 2005, BEIT LAHIYA, GAZA STRIP

Left Mohammed Kaseeh carries the body of his brother Jaber in the northern Gaza village of Beit Lahiya. Jaber was one of seven young Palestinians from two farming families who, according to witnesses and medics, were killed when an Israeli tank shell landed in the field where they had been harvesting strawberries. The Israeli army said it had been targeting militants who had crept into the strawberry patch and fired mortar bombs into a nearby Jewish settlement, wounding two people.
Mohammed Salem

5 April 2004, TULKARM, WEST BANK

Opposite A Palestinian uses a mobile phone to take a picture of the body of Rami Khalili, 20, during his funeral in the West Bank city of Tulkarm. Witnesses said that Khalili, a member of the militant Hamas group, was shot dead by Israeli troops during a rally for another Hamas militant killed on 3 April in an attack on a nearby Jewish settlement. The Israeli army said soldiers fired on a car filled with armed Palestinians that was driving near its forces in Tulkram and denied opening fire on the rally. Abed Omar Qusini

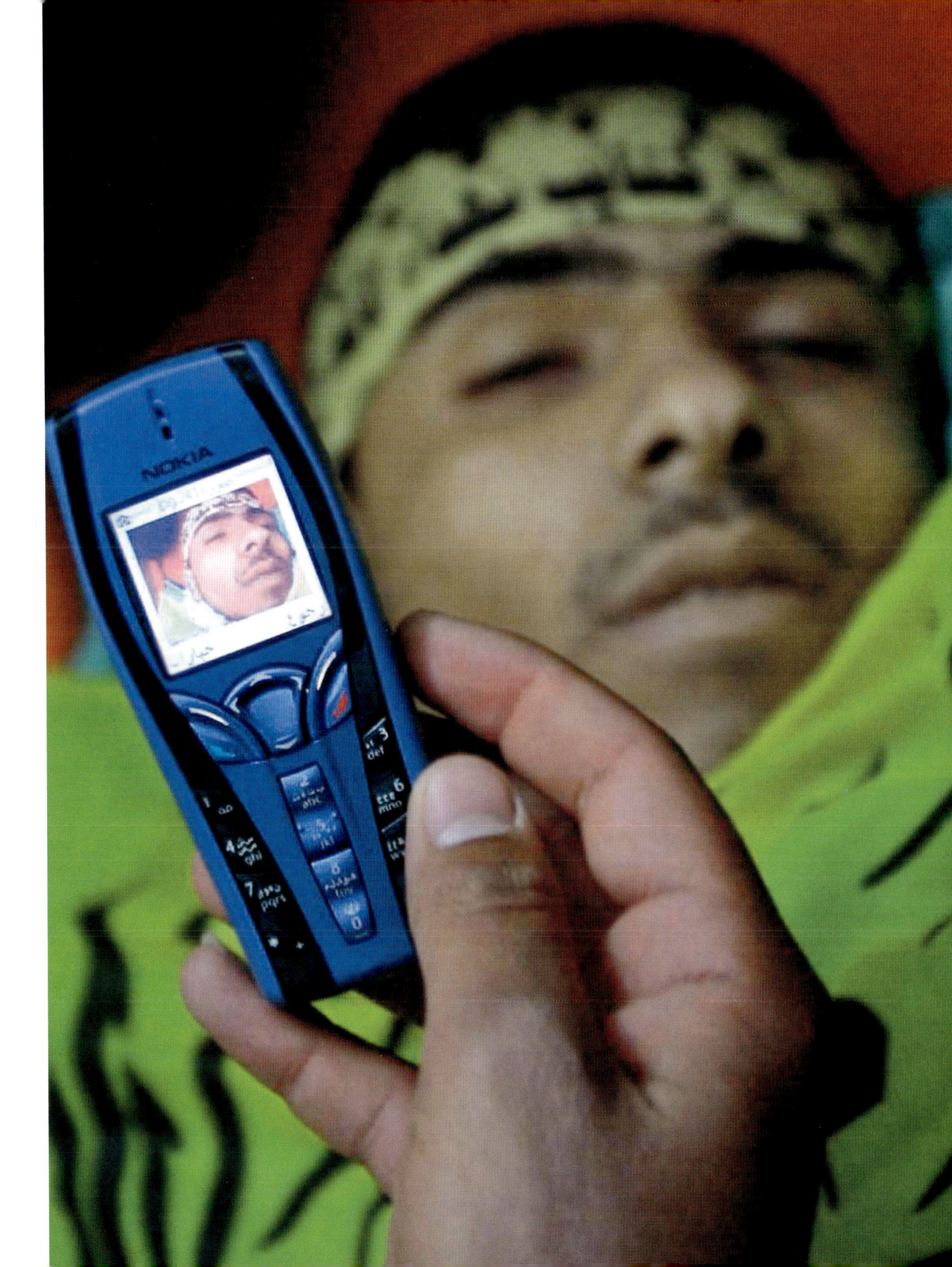
NOKIA

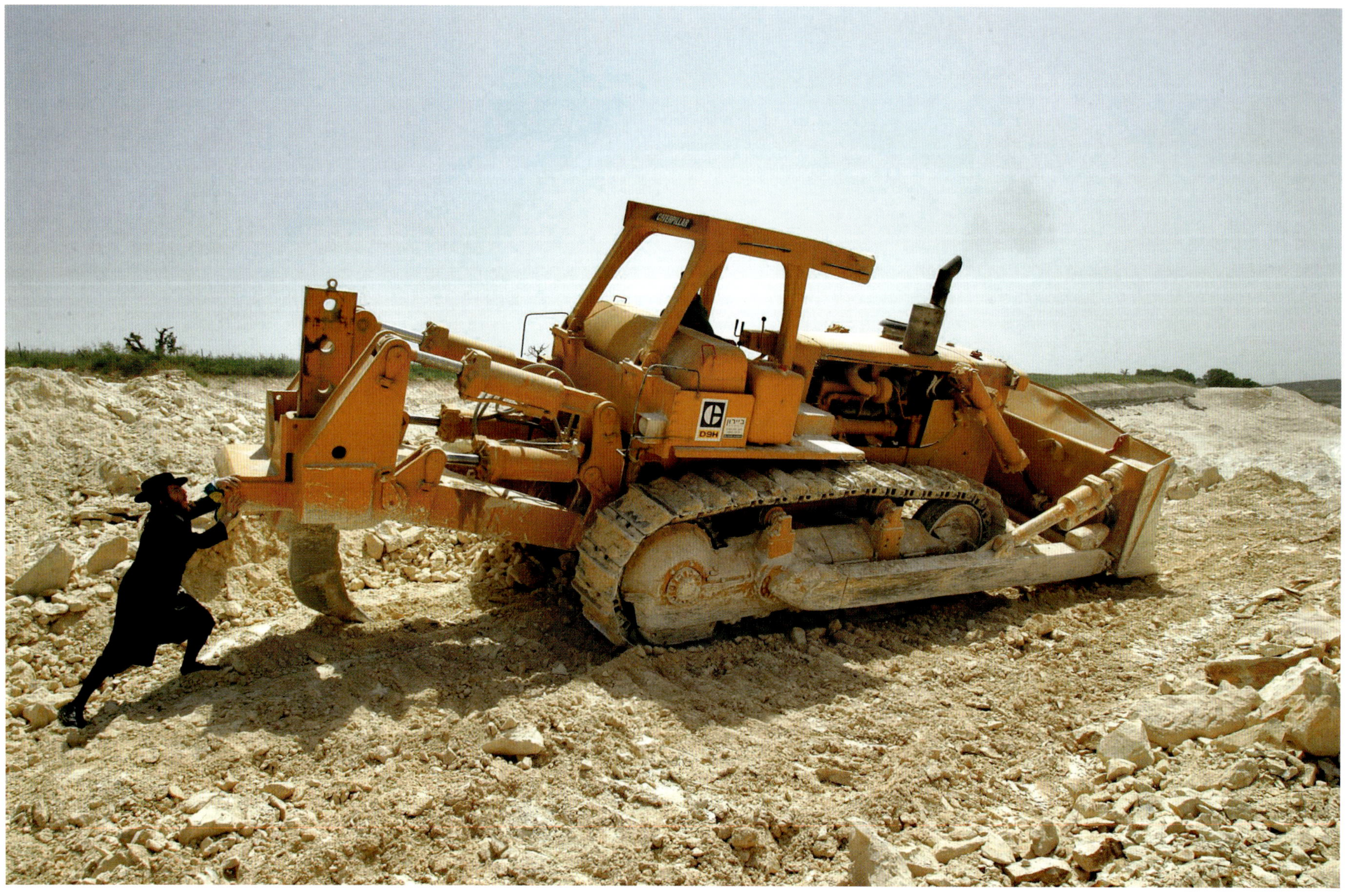

14 April 2005, REGAVIM, ISRAEL

An ultra-Orthodox Jewish protester attempts to push away a bulldozer during a demonstration against the desecration of ancient graves that were to be exhumed to allow for the construction of a new highway next to Kibbutz Regavim in northern Israel. Gil Cohen Magen

27 November 2005, SALEM, WEST BANK

Opposite An Israeli soldier looks on as an elderly Palestinian woman embraces the trunk of an olive tree in the West Bank village of Salem, near Nablus. This tree was one of at least 200 on Palestinian farms cut down and uprooted by Jewish settlers, residents and Israeli police said. Settlers from the most radical enclaves in the occupied West Bank have often attacked farms since the start of the Palestinian uprising in 2000, in which settlers have often been targeted by militants. Settlers say that the land, which Palestinians want for a state, is theirs by biblical birthright. Abed Omar Qusini

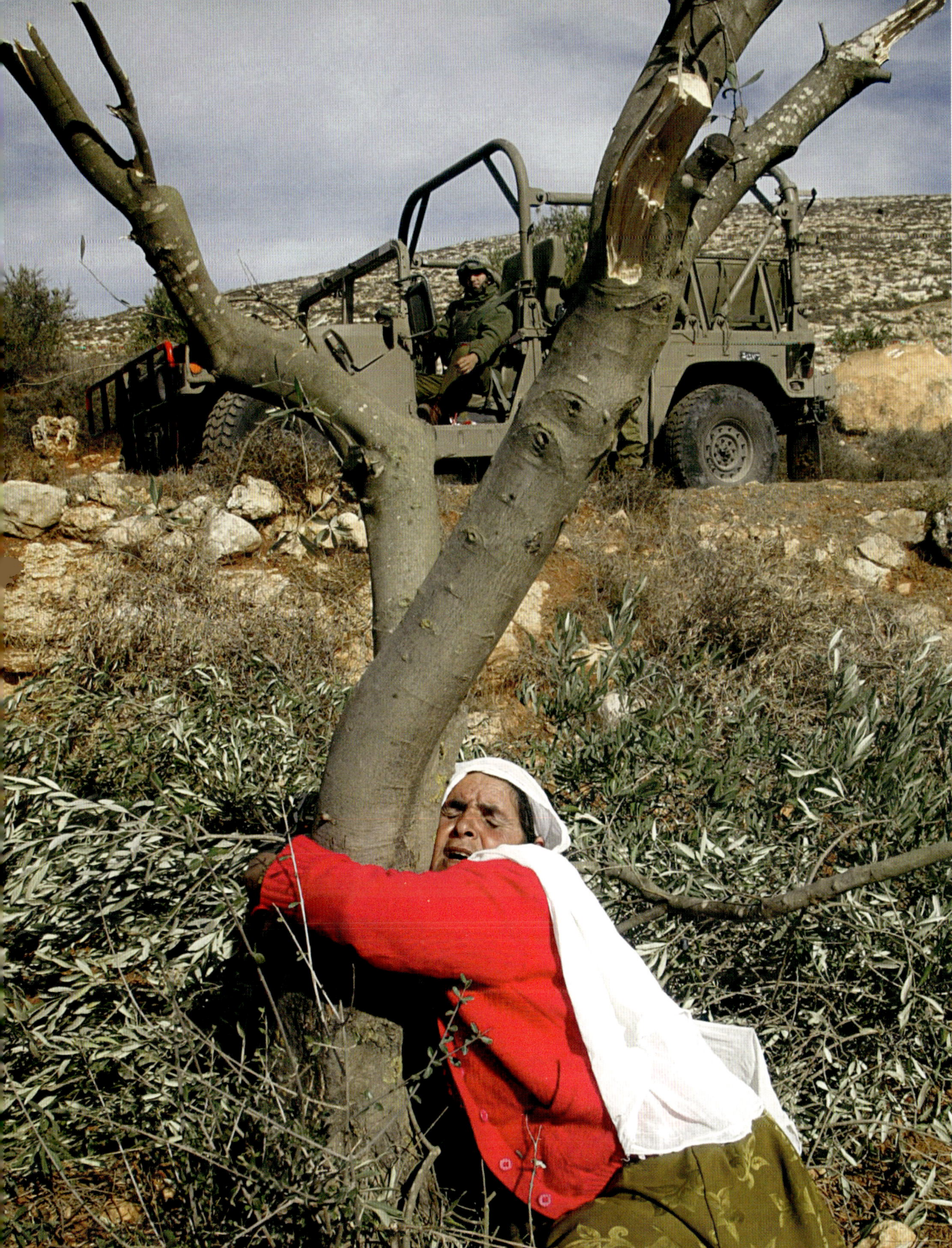

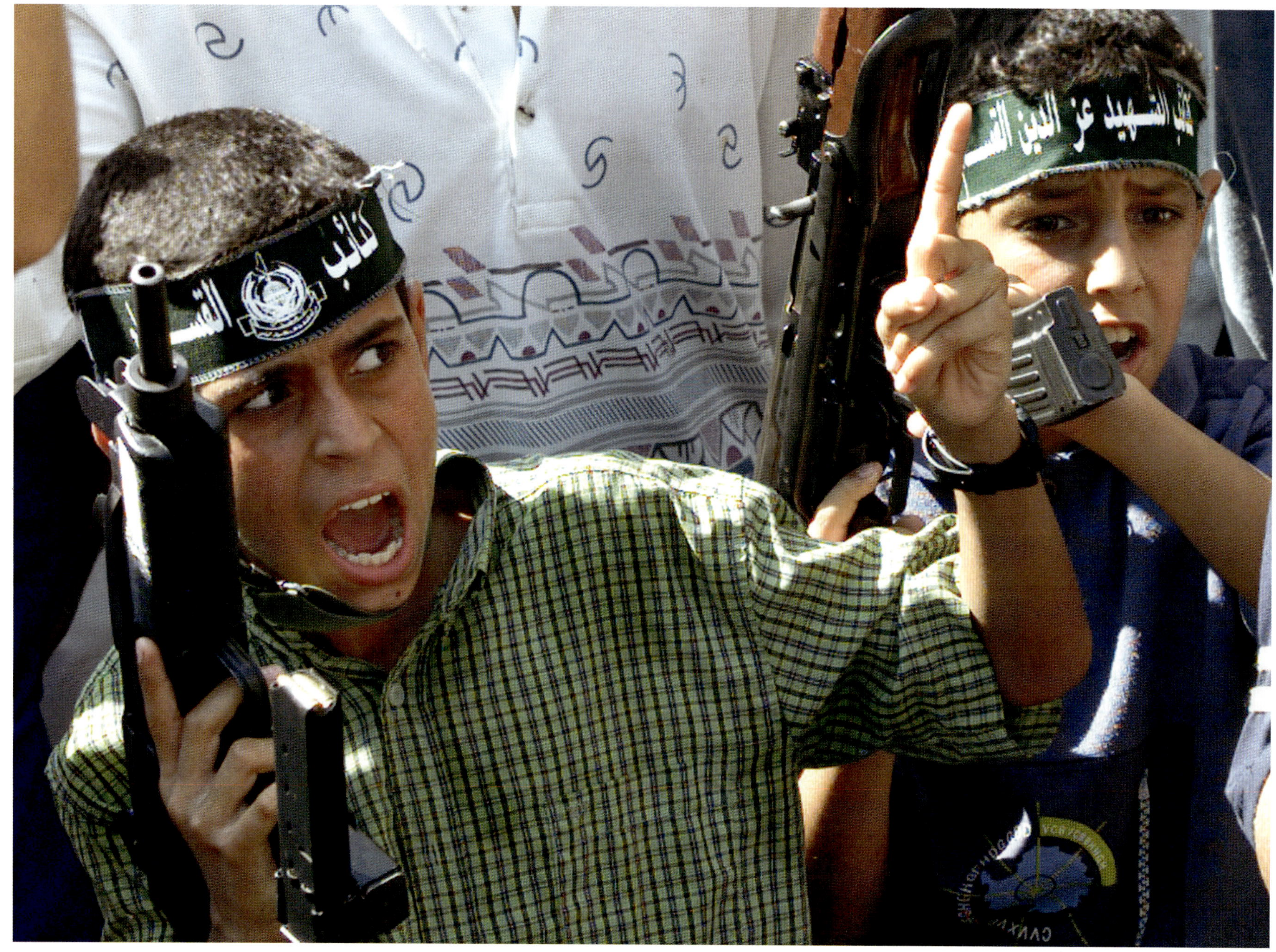

23 July 2002, GAZA CITY, GAZA STRIP

Palestinian boys march with guns during the funeral of 19 Palestinians who were killed on 22 July 2002 by an Israeli missile strike on a densely inhabited part of Gaza City. Among the dead was the target of the attack, Hamas military wing leader Sheikh Salah Shehada, blamed by Israel for scores of Israeli deaths. But the one-tonne 'smart bomb', so-called because it is guided to strike a specific target, hit a densely crowded city block. Nine of the dead were children, and 145 civilians were injured. Ahmed Jadallah

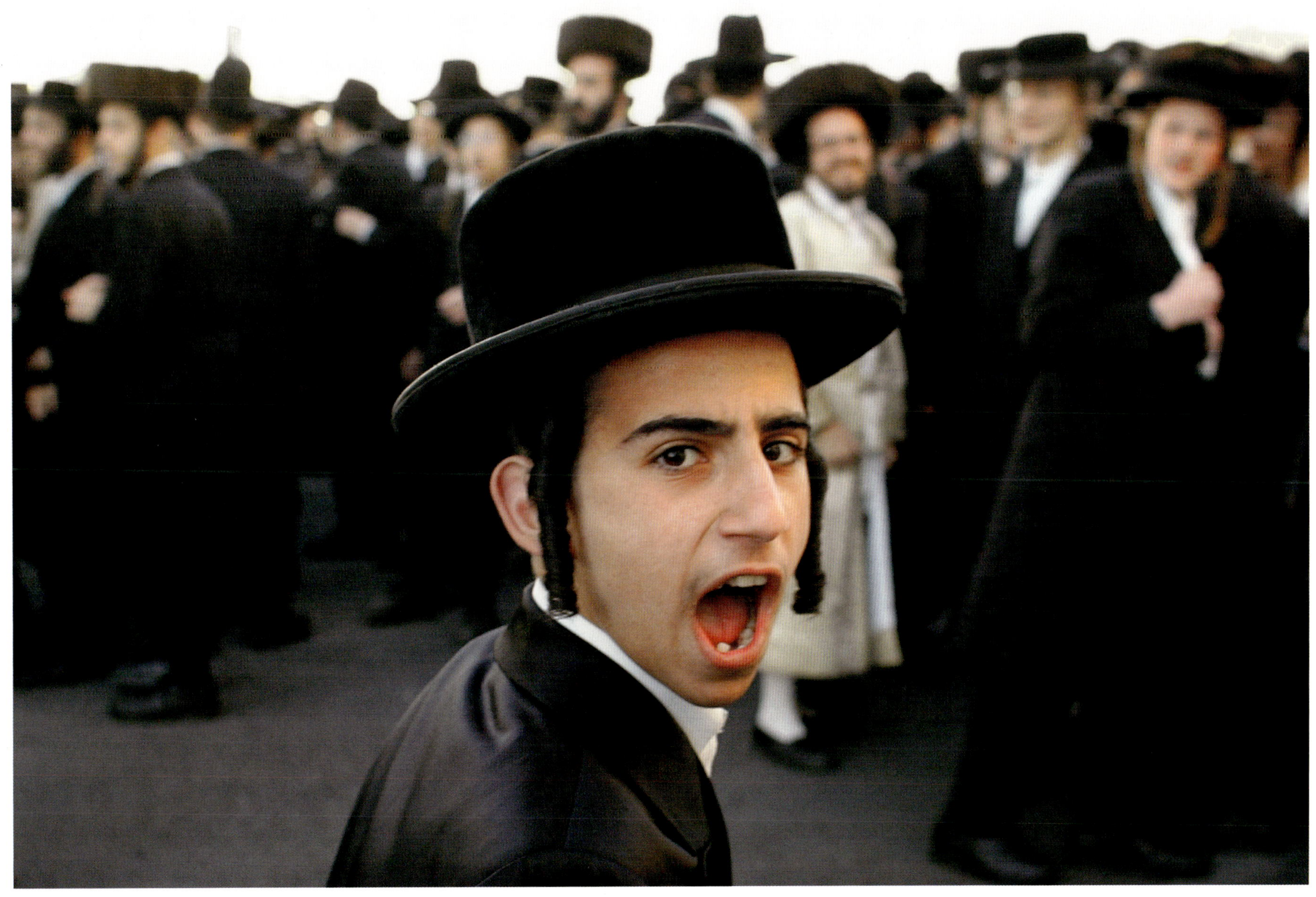

26 April 2005, JERUSALEM, ISRAEL

An ultra-Orthodox Jewish protester shouts near Israeli Prime Minister Ariel Sharon's office in Jerusalem during a demonstration against government plans to exhume ancient graves to make way for a new Israeli highway next to Kibbutz Regavim in northern Israel. Goran Tomasevic

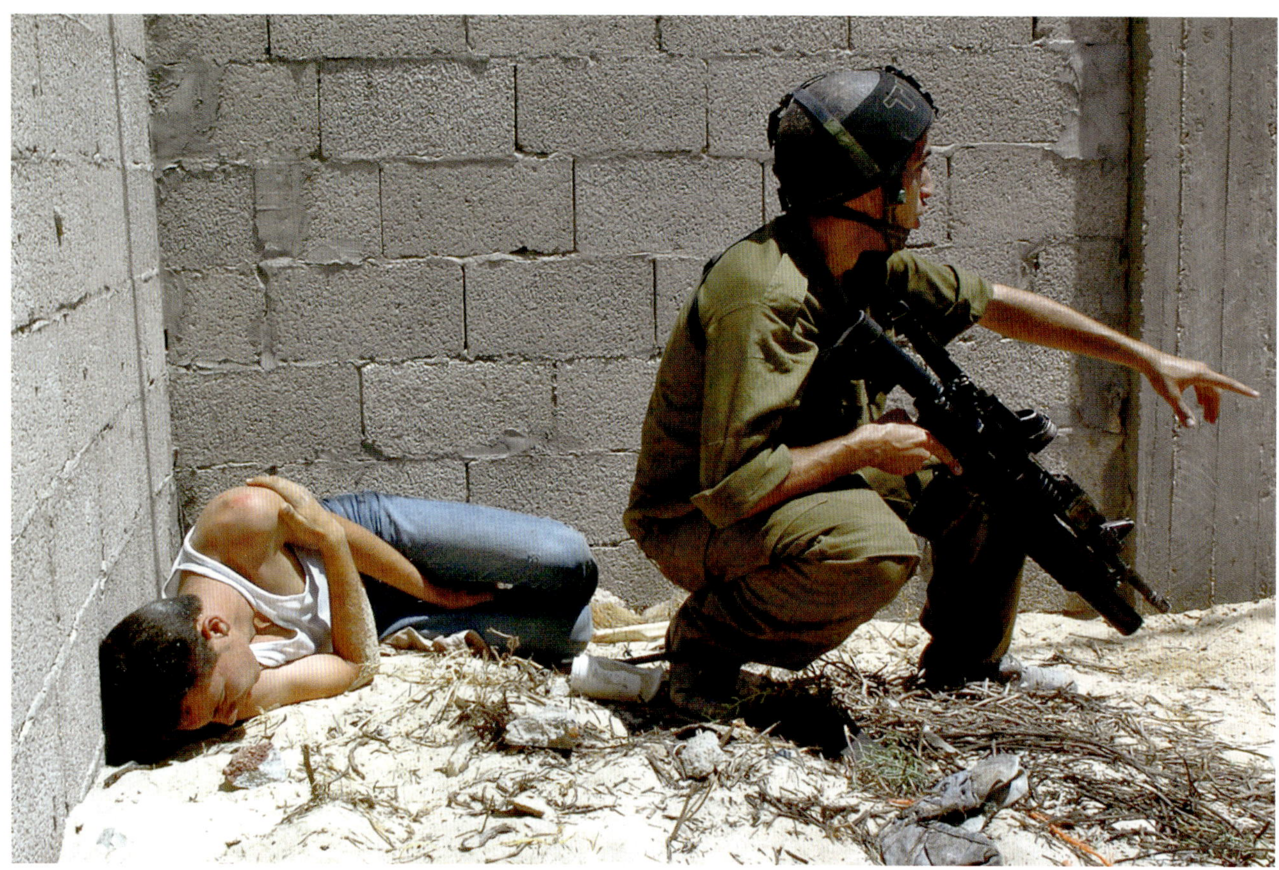

29 June 2005, SHIRAT HAYAM, GAZA STRIP

An Israeli soldier protects a wounded Palestinian man during a violent confrontation between Jewish settlers and Palestinians near Shirat Hayam settlement, part of Gush Katif settlement bloc that was scheduled for evacuation by the Israeli government in August 2005. The youth was injured in a clash with radical settlers intent on establishing a stronghold of resistance to the withdrawal in a house in a Palestinian area just outside of Gush Katif settlement. Gadi Kabalo

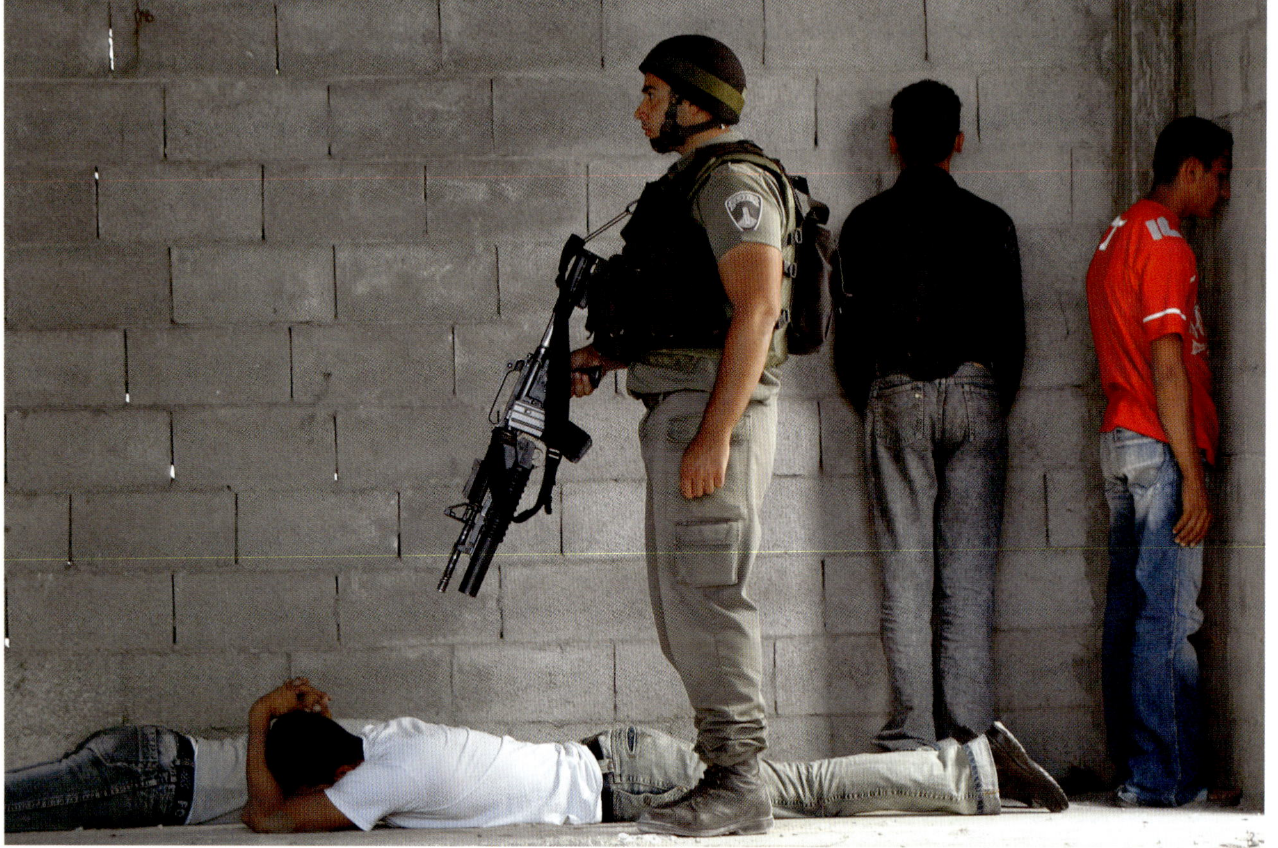

11 June 2005, HEBRON, WEST BANK

An Israeli border policeman guards detained Palestinians during a military operation in the city of Hebron.
Nayef Hashlamoun

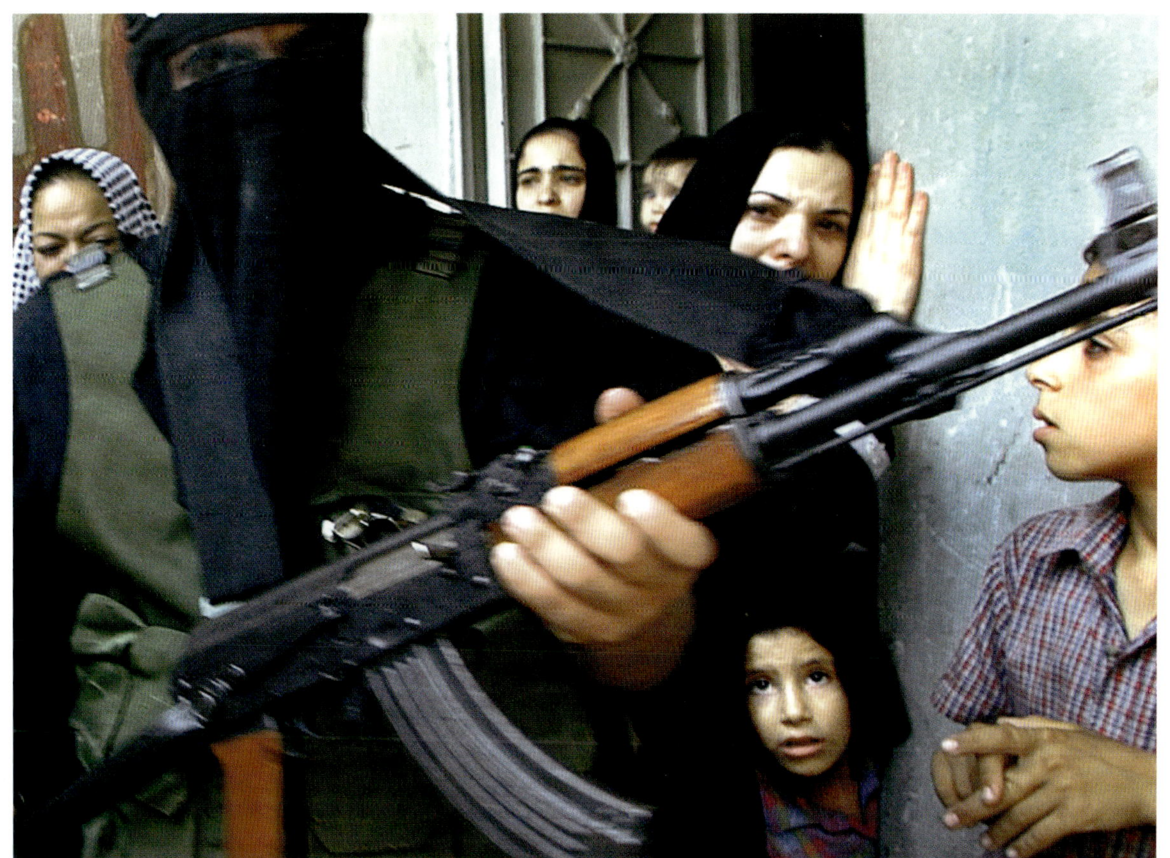

25 June 2002, GAZA STRIP

The sister of Muhammad Abu-Marasah, an 18-year-old killed by Israeli troops as he tried to attack an Israeli checkpoint, cries during his funeral in the Gaza Strip as a masked man from the military wing of Islamic Jihad passes with an AK-47 assault rifle. Ahmed Jadallah

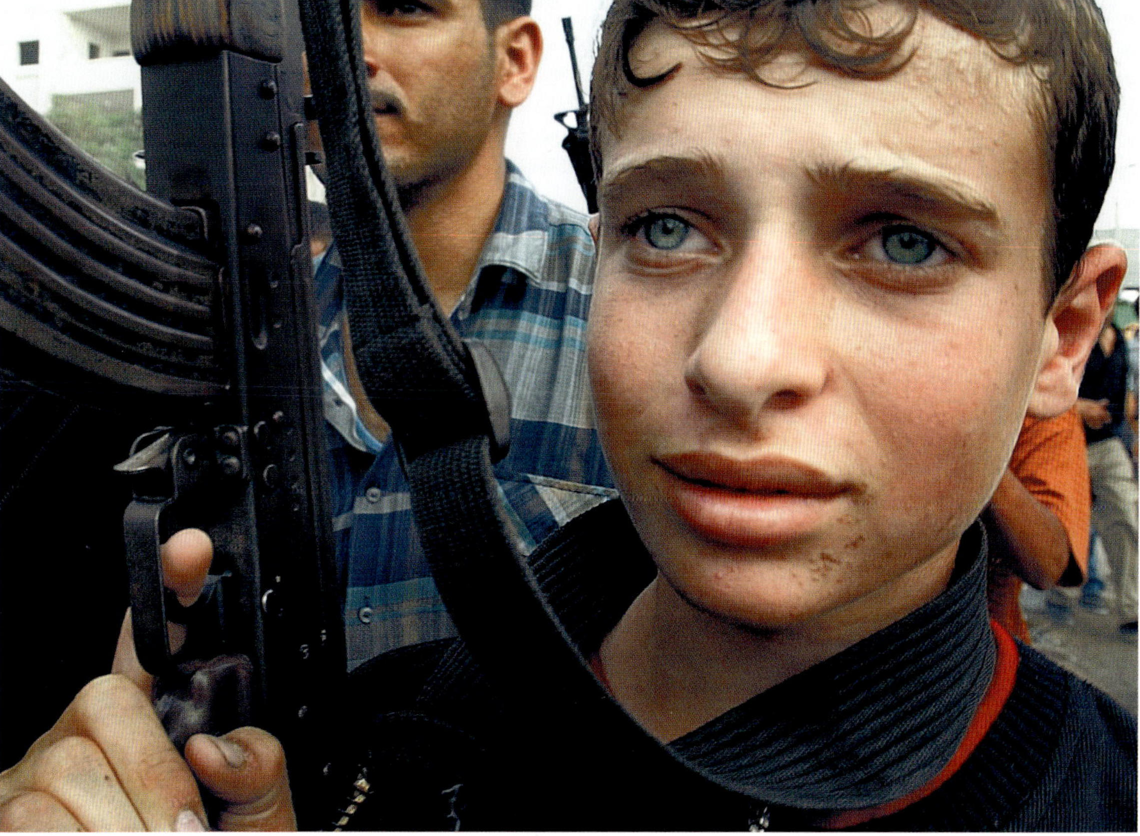

11 October 2004, JABALYA, GAZA STRIP

A Palestinian boy holds up an AK-47 rifle during the funeral of Palestinian militant Sameh al-Whade, killed during an Israeli air strike, in the Jabalya refugee camp in the northern Gaza Strip. Goran Tomasevic

26 January 2003, GAZA CITY, GAZA STRIP

Lena, the sister of Morwan Rohmi who was one of 12 Palestinians killed during an Israeli incursion into Gaza City, cries as her brother's body is brought home during his funeral. Ahmed Jadallah

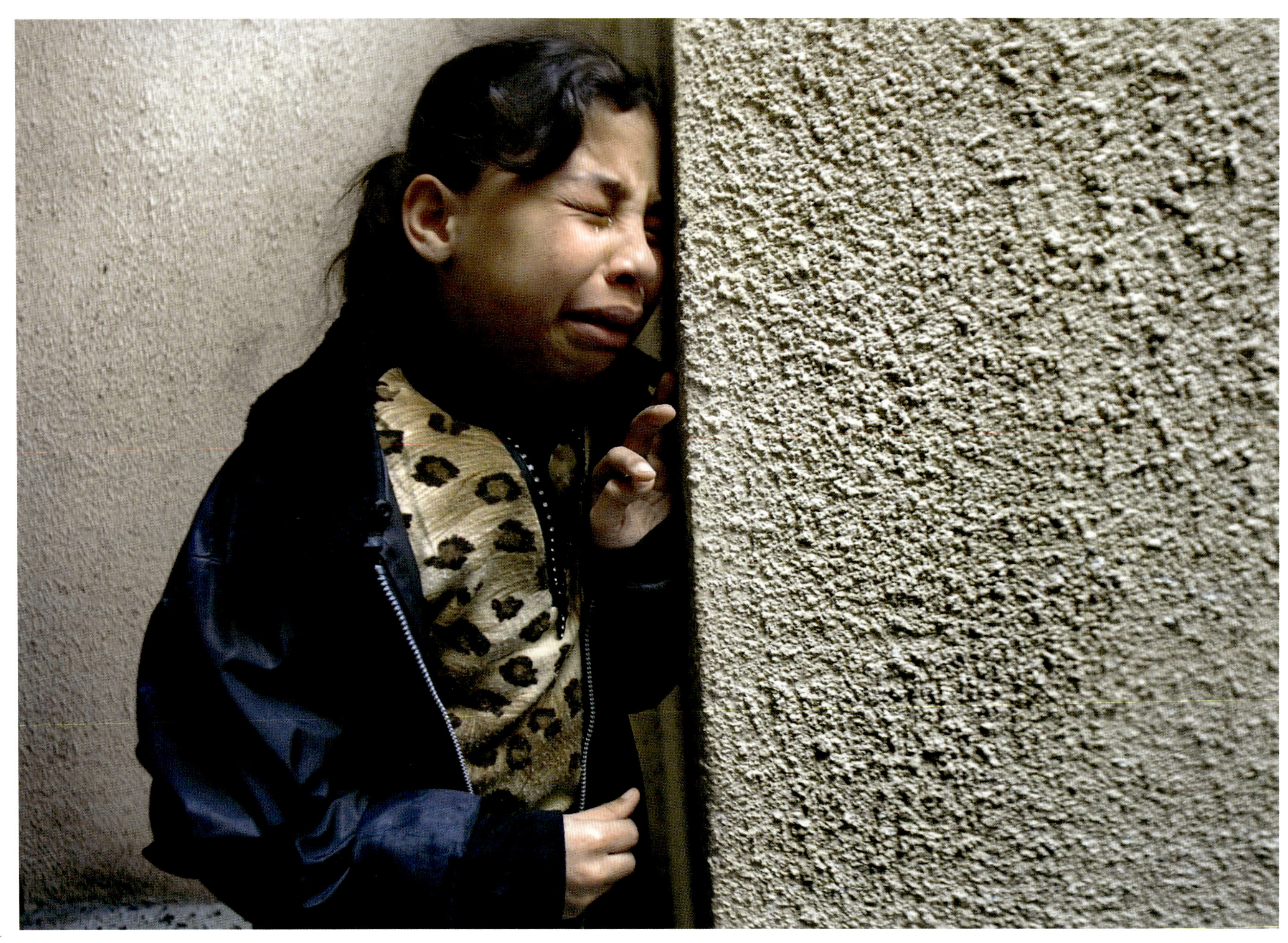

12 March 2002, JABALYA, GAZA STRIP

A Palestinian boy sits on a staircase stained with blood at a house in the Jabalya refugee camp. Family members said that the boy's father Waled Izz el Din and grandfather Abdel Rahman were killed by gunfire during violence that claimed the lives of dozens of Palestinians and Israelis in just 24 hours. Ahmed Jadallah

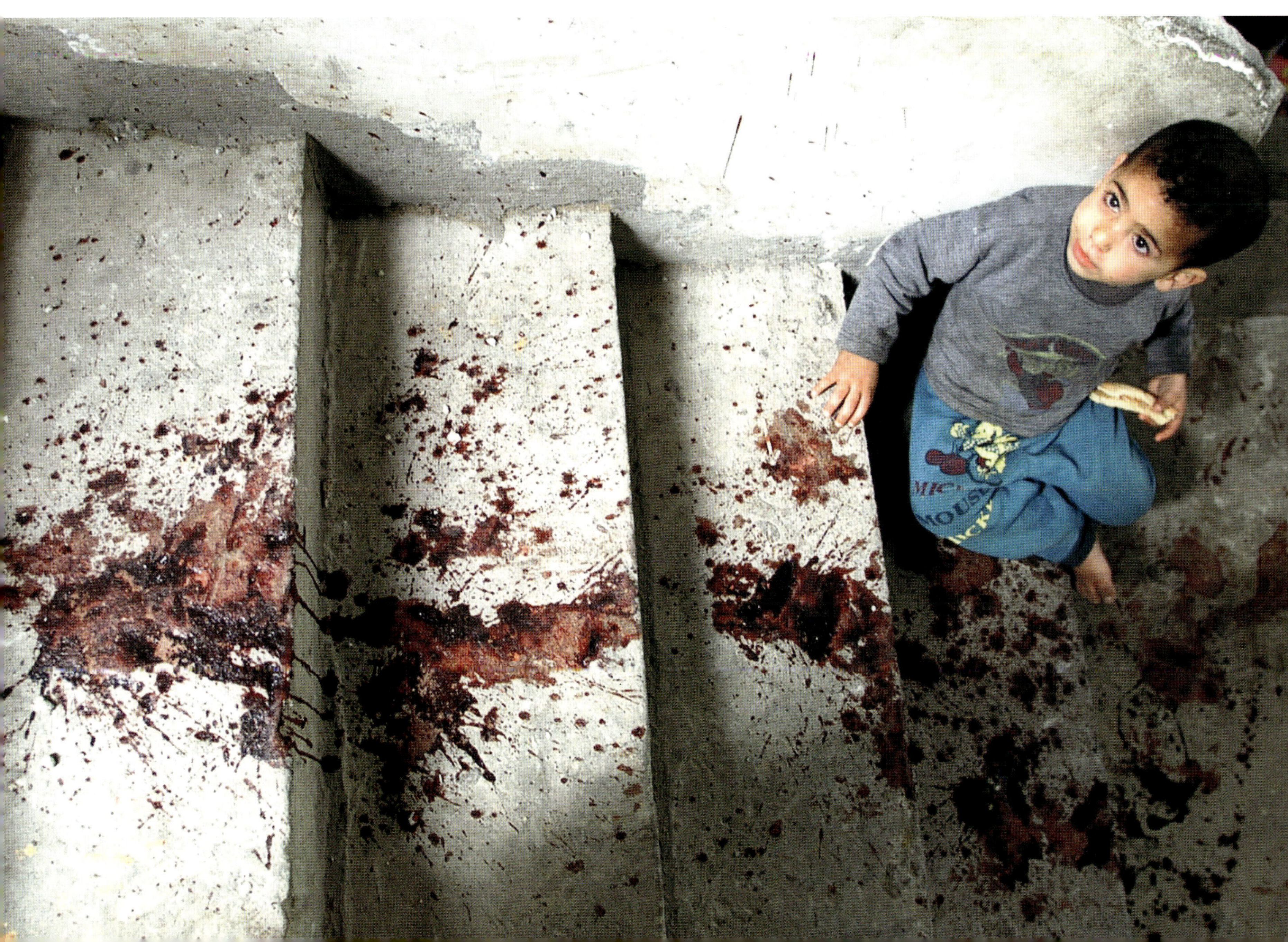

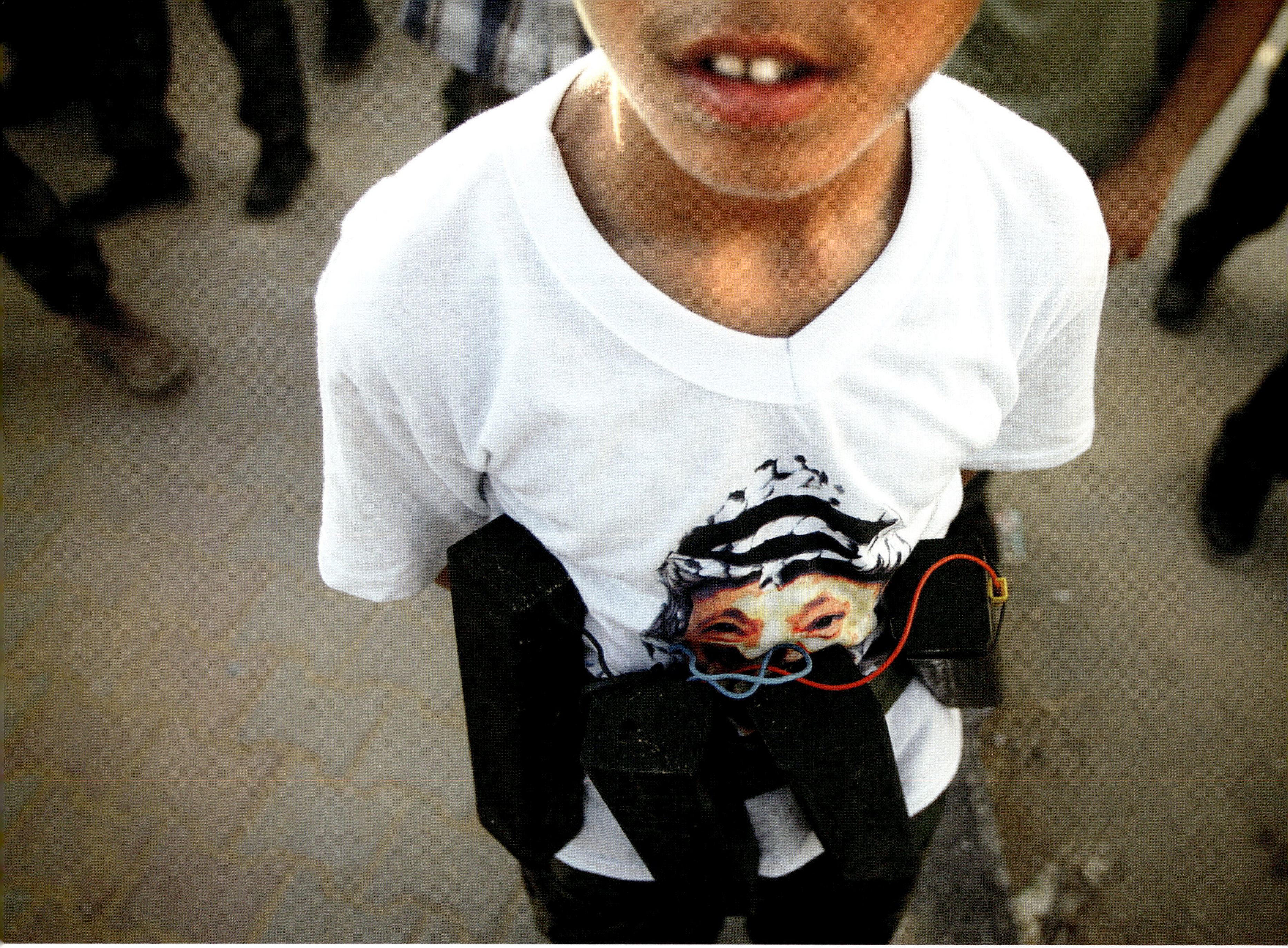

1 September 2005, GAZA CITY, GAZA STRIP

A Palestinian boy wearing a T-shirt with a picture of the late Palestinian President Yasser Arafat and a fake suicide bomber's belt attends a gathering to celebrate the Israeli evacuation of Jewish settlers from Gaza. Damir Sagolj

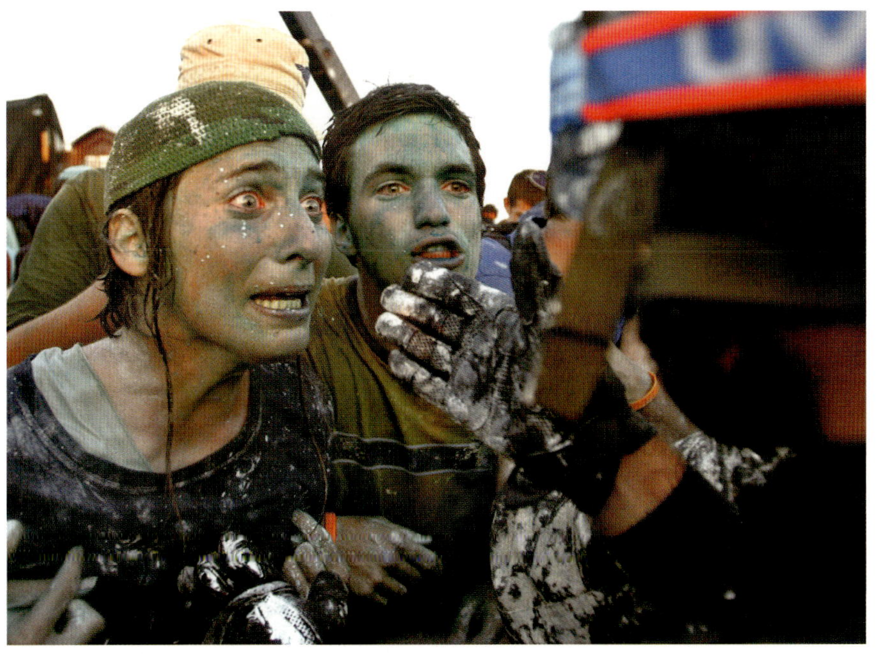

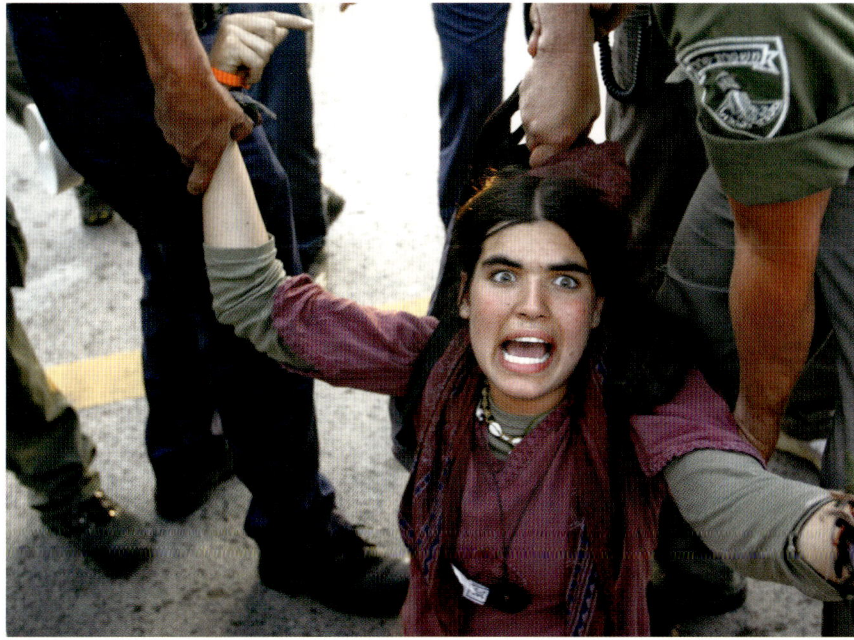

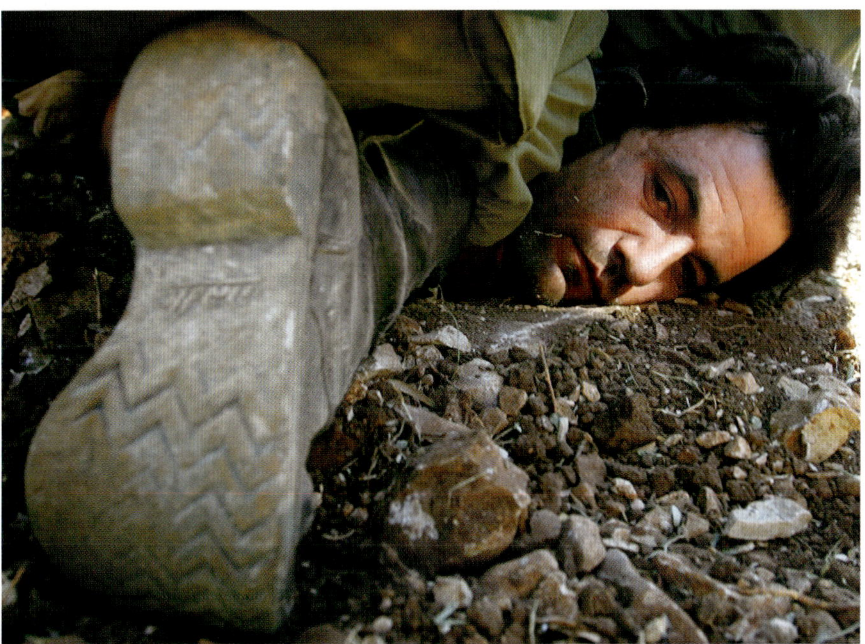

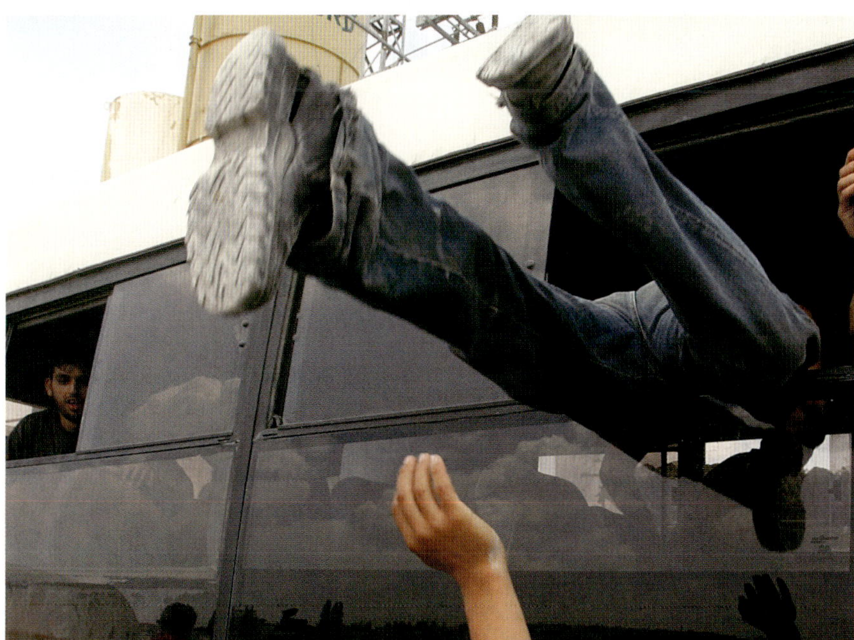

18 August 2005, KFAR DAROM, GAZA STRIP

Angry opponents of Israel's disengagement from settlements in the Gaza Strip scream at a special evacuation policeman after government forces took over the rooftop of the synagogue in Kfar Darom, in Gush Katif settlement bloc. Nir Elias

29 May 2005, RAANANA, ISRAEL

Israeli policemen try to remove a demonstrator during a protest against Israel's disengagement plan from the Gaza Strip and part of the northern West Bank. Protesters blocked a main road near the city of Raanana, north of Tel Aviv. Nir Elias

31 May 2005, BILIN, WEST BANK

An Israeli peace activist is arrested by Israeli border police after chaining himself to the ground during a joint Israeli–Palestinian protest in the West Bank village of Bilin against Israel's controversial barrier wall. Goran Tomasevic

2 June 2005, TULKARM, WEST BANK

A Palestinian jumps into a bus in his eagerness to greet a relative just released from jail, one of 400 Palestinian prisoners released by the Israeli authorities as part of a ceasefire agreement reached on 8 February 2005. Goran Tomasevic

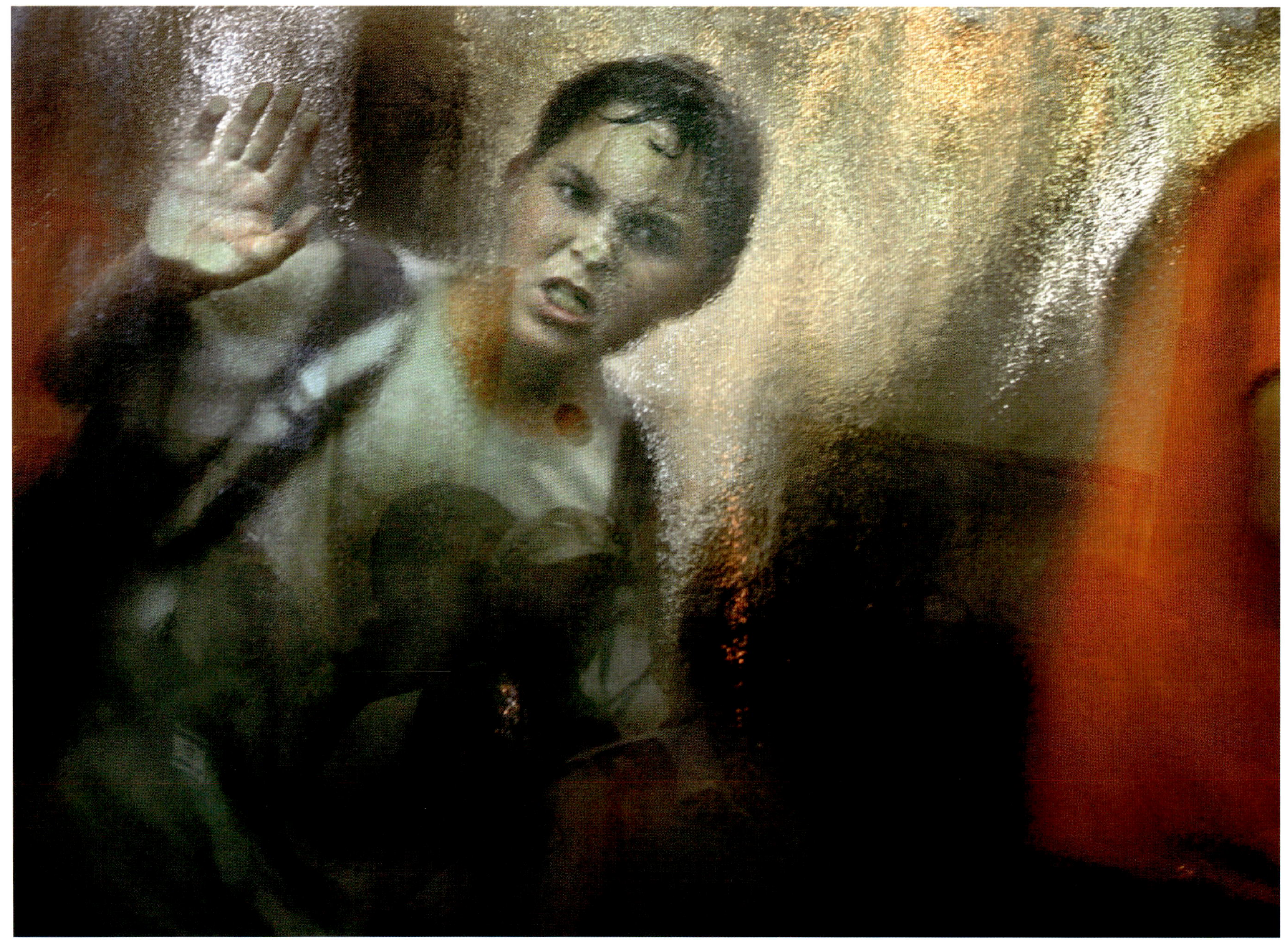

18 August 2005, NEVE DEKALIM, GAZA STRIP

An angry Jewish settler boy looks out from inside a synagogue as Israeli policemen and soldiers storm into Neve Dekalim in Gush Katif settlement bloc. Israeli troops forced their way into synagogues and dragged out screaming the last settlers and their supporters as they overcame the last bastions of resistance to the pullout from the occupied territory. Damir Sagolj

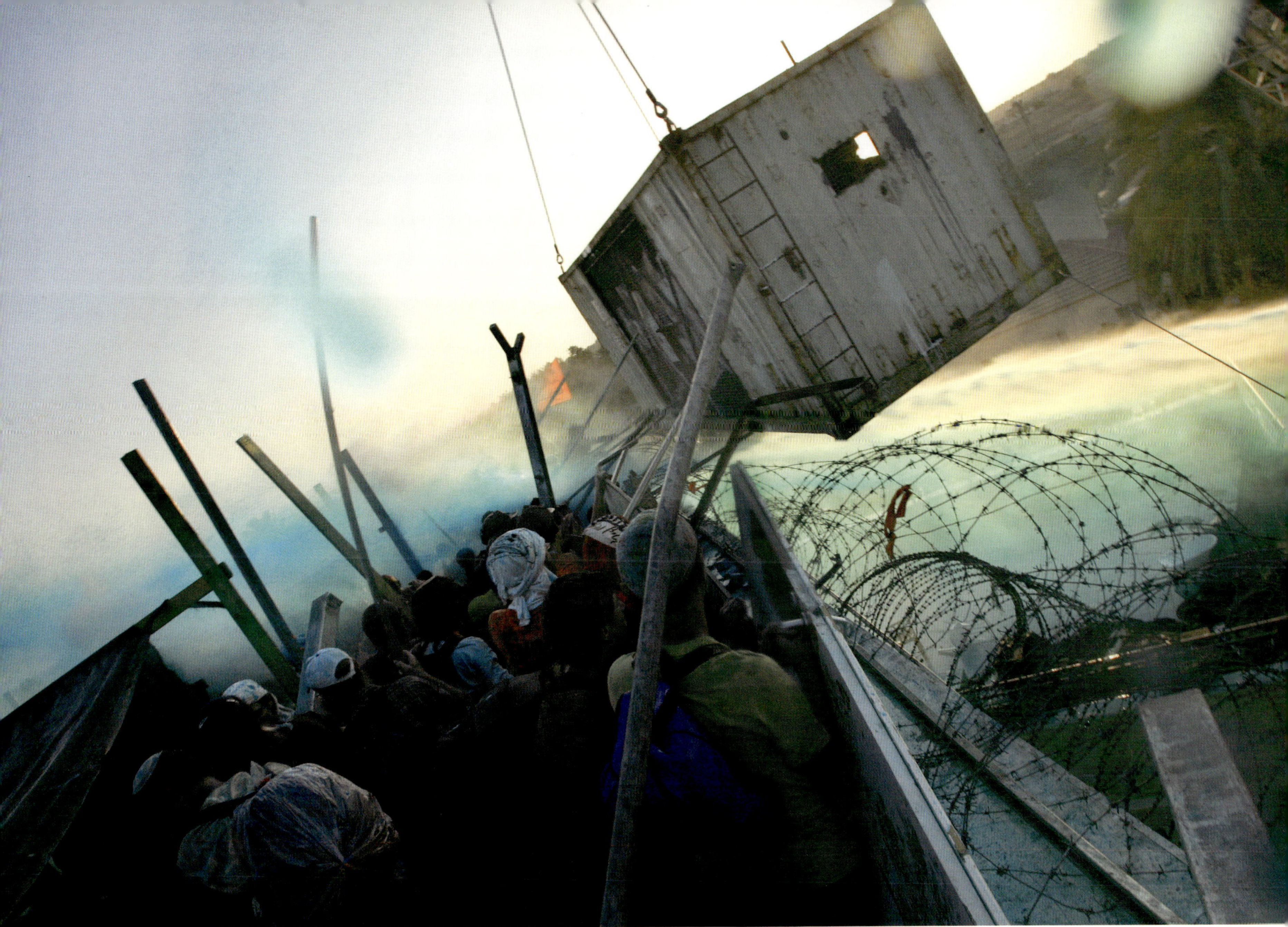

18 August 2005, KFAR DAROM, GAZA STRIP

Israeli special evacuation forces are delivered inside a container to the rooftop of a synagogue in the Jewish Gaza Strip settlement of Kfar Darom. They used cranes and water cannon against the last pockets of opposition, and eventually grappled with the remaining settlers and their supporters before forcibly carrying them away. Nir Elias

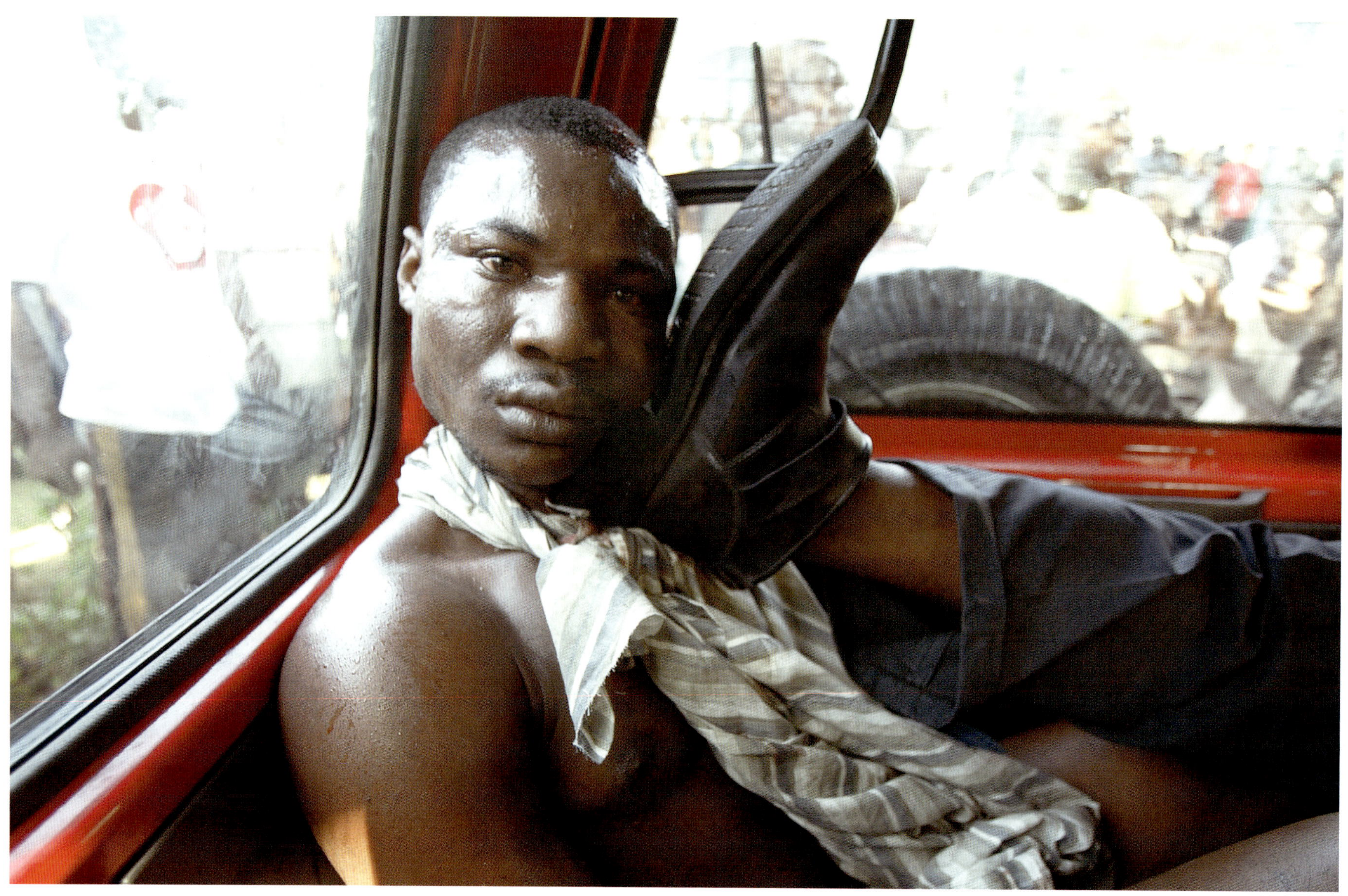

3 March 2004, PETIT GOAVE, HAITI

Three days after former Haitian President Jean-Bertrand Aristide was driven into exile, a man suspected of being a multiple assassin for his Lavalas party is detained in Petit Goave, some 50 km (30 miles) south of Port-au-Prince, where armed citizens proceeded to stone him and then burn him alive. Aristide, Haiti's first democratically elected leader, was a former priest who was once hailed as champion of Haitian democracy but was latterly accused of using thuggish tactics to stay in power. Daniel Aguilar

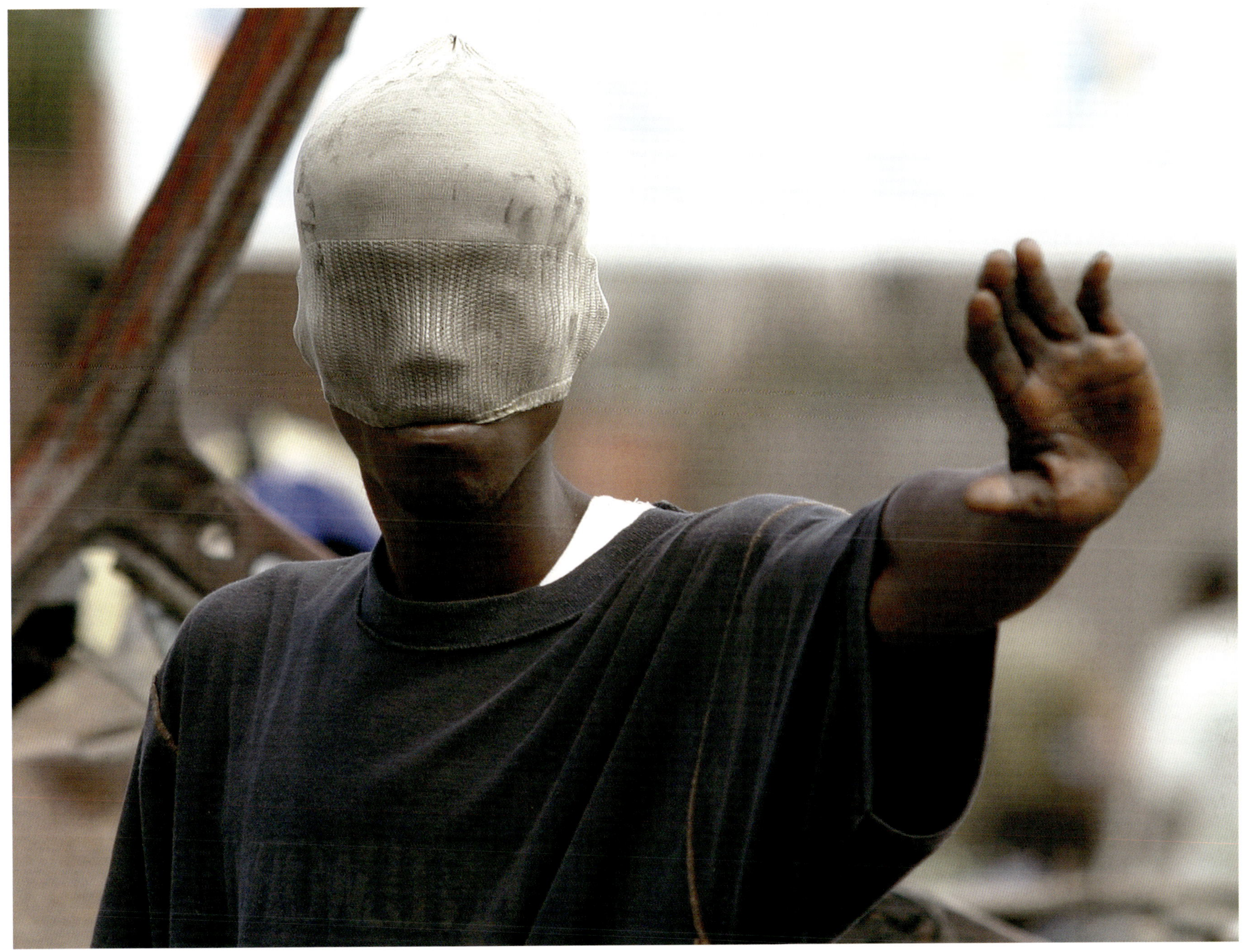

16 February 2004, GONAIVES, HAITI

A Haitian rebel stands guard at a barricade on the road into the city of Gonaives. Starting out as a street gang, the rebels were joined by ex-soldiers and paramilitaries. From 5 February 2004, they began to overrun cities in the north of the Caribbean country, eventually forcing President Jean-Bertrand Aristide to flee on 29 February. To the alarm of human rights groups, the rebel leaders included men such as former death squad leader Louis Jodel Chamblain. Daniel Aguilar

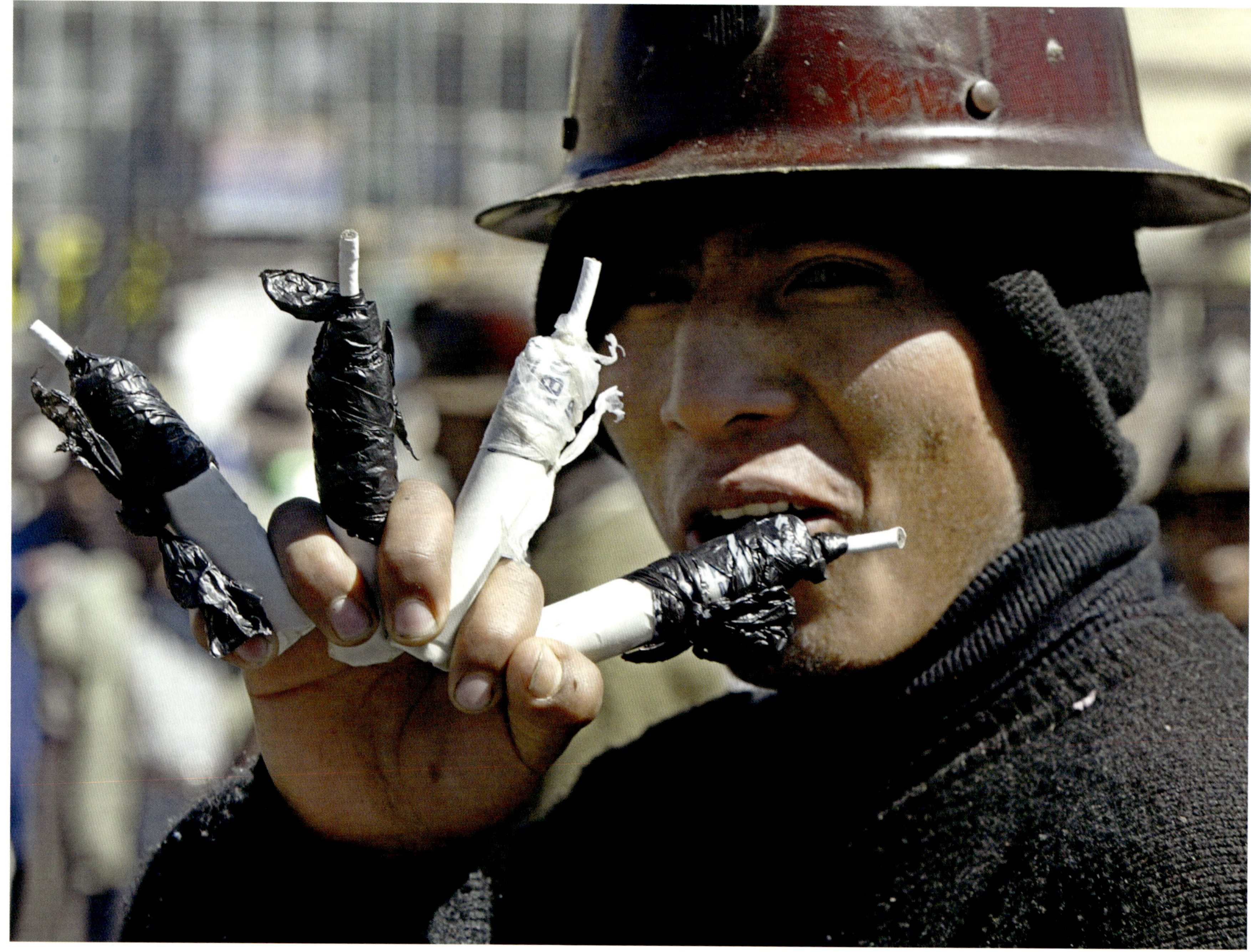

7 June 2005, LA PAZ, BOLIVIA

A worker in Caracoles mine holds dynamite sticks during a protest rally staged in La Paz by tens of thousands of Bolivian peasants and miners. The Indian-led protesters, many descended from the Incas who were enslaved in colonial silver mines, said they were seeking justice for the downtrodden majority in South America's poorest country, and demanded a new constitution and nationalization of the country's rich natural gas fields. They forced President Carlos Mesa to resign on 7 June, just 19 months after his predecessor Gonzalo Sánchez de Lozada also stepped down in an earlier wave of protests. David Mercado

1 November 2005, BUENOS AIRES, ARGENTINA

A man is caught between Argentine policemen and rioters during clashes after passengers were enraged by late-running commuter trains in Haedo, on the outskirts of Buenos Aires. The protesters set fire to trains and a train station, attacked shops, and fought pitched battles with police in some of the worst violence seen in the Argentine capital since deadly street rioting during the country's 2001–2 economic crisis. Marcos Brindicci

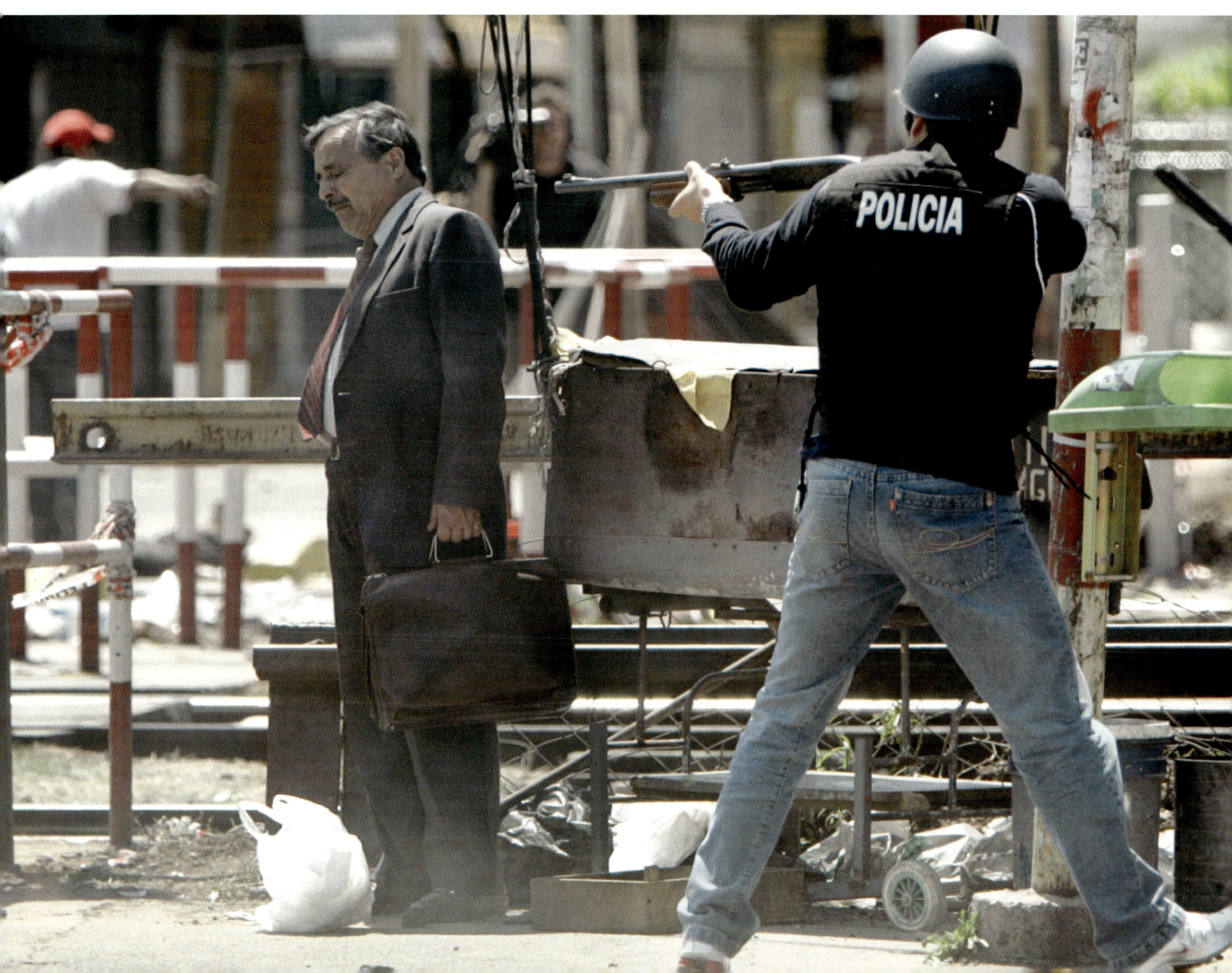

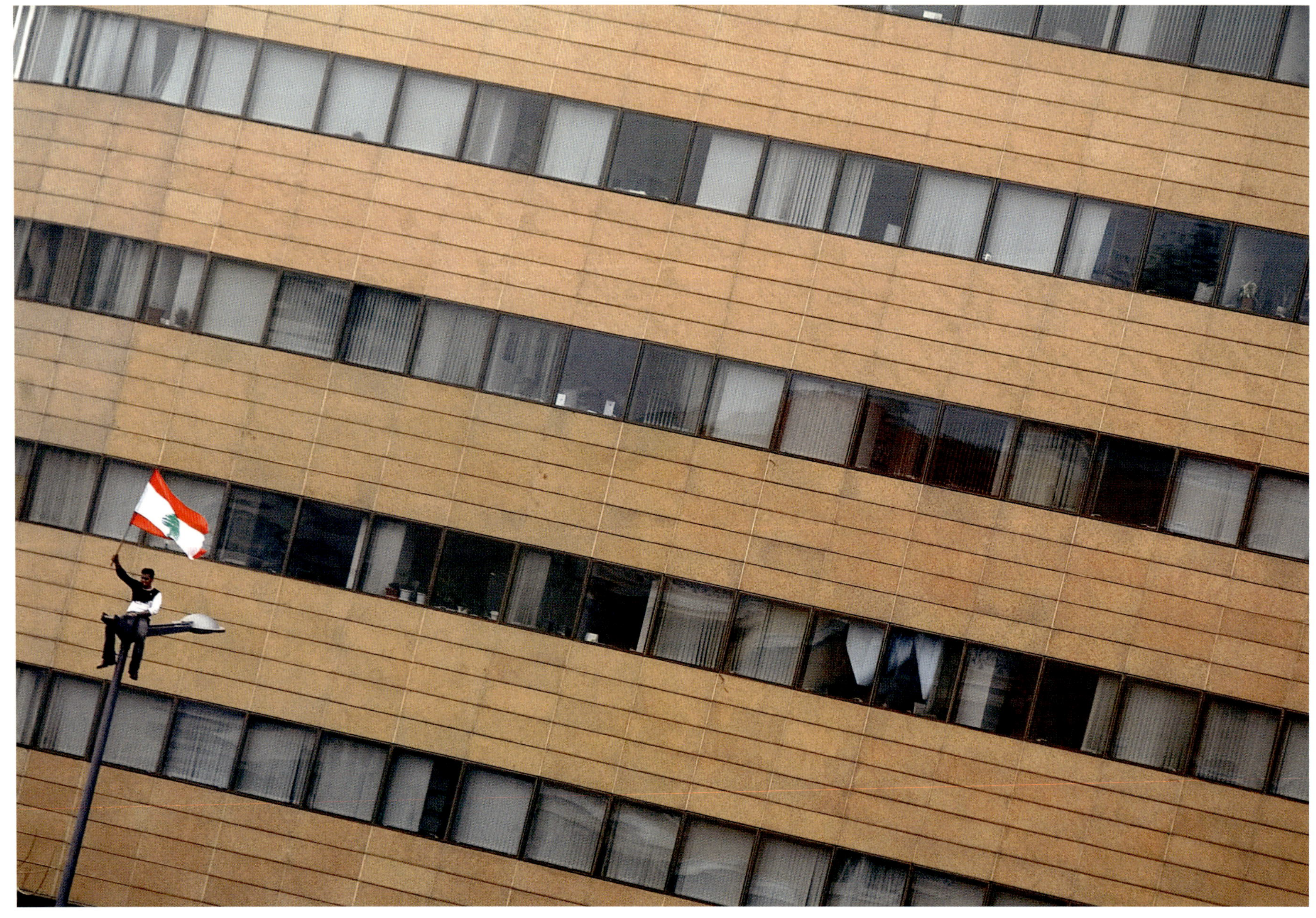

8 March 2005, BEIRUT, LEBANON

A youth waving a Lebanese flag sits on the top of a street light in front of the United Nations building during a pro-Syria rally in central Beirut. The 14 February murder of former Prime Minister Rafik al-Hariri in a car bomb (opposite) touched off daily protests against Syria, blamed by many Lebanese for his assassination. Then on 8 March, hundreds of thousands of flag-waving Lebanese turned out for a rally called by the Syria-backed Hizbollah militant group. It was the first major show of popular support for Syria in Beirut since Hariri's death, and dwarfed previous demonstrations. The rival rallies, each using the Lebanese cedar flag to show patriotism, revealed the deep rifts in Lebanon over the role of Syria, which had kept troops in the country since intervening in its civil war in June 1976.

Damir Sagolj

14 February 2005, BEIRUT, LEBANON

A man shouts for help near the site of a massive car bomb explosion on Beirut's waterfront that killed Lebanon's former Prime Minister Rafik al-Hariri. Twenty-two others died and 135 were wounded in the blast. Hariri's assassination prompted the biggest street protests in Lebanon's history and plunged the tiny country into its most serious political crisis since the end of the 1975–90 civil war.

Mohamed Azakir

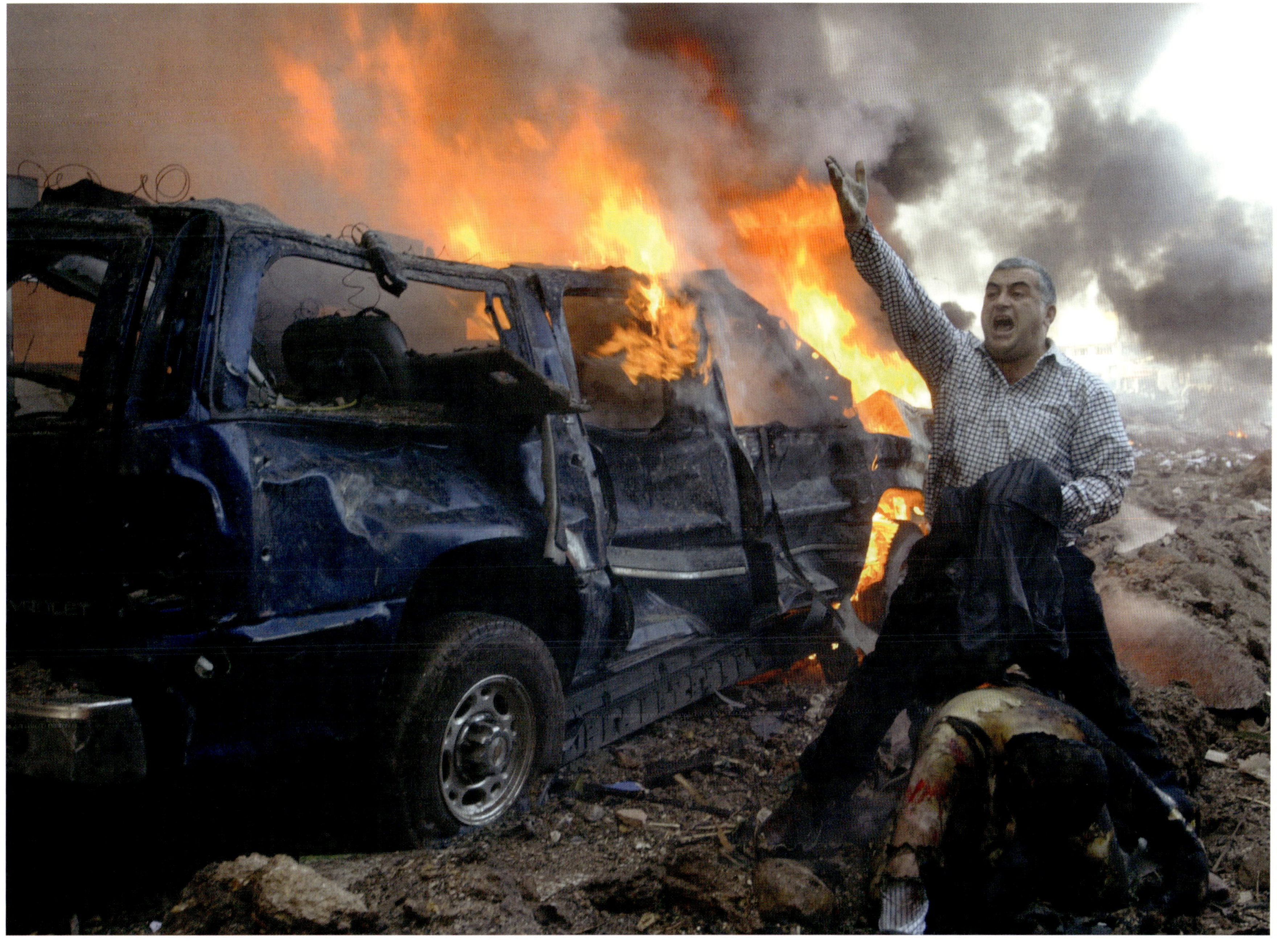

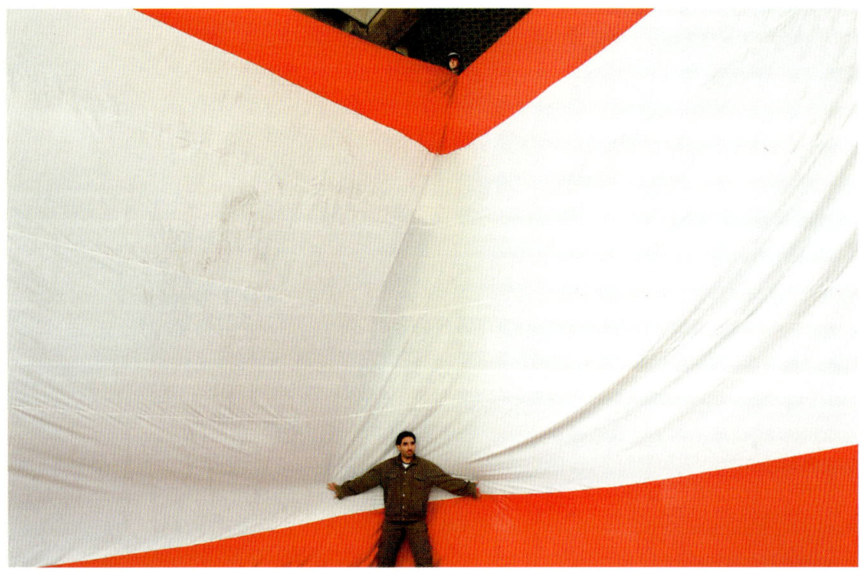

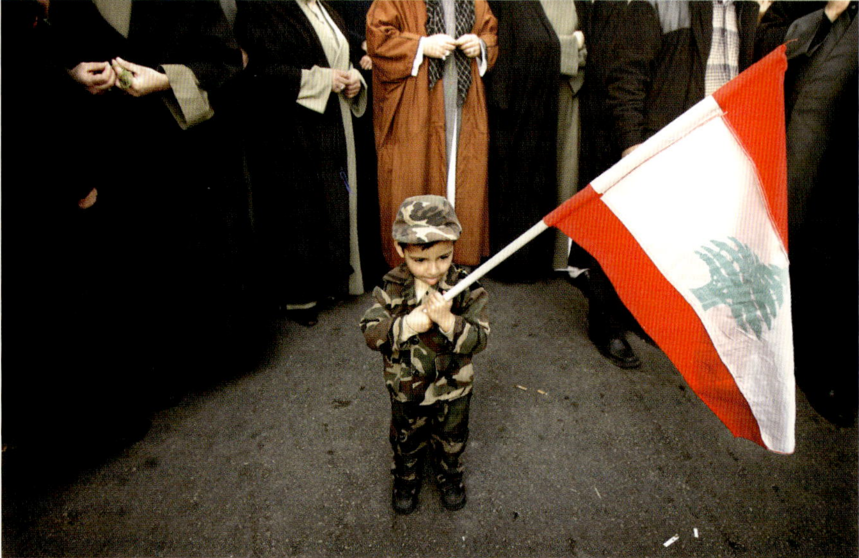

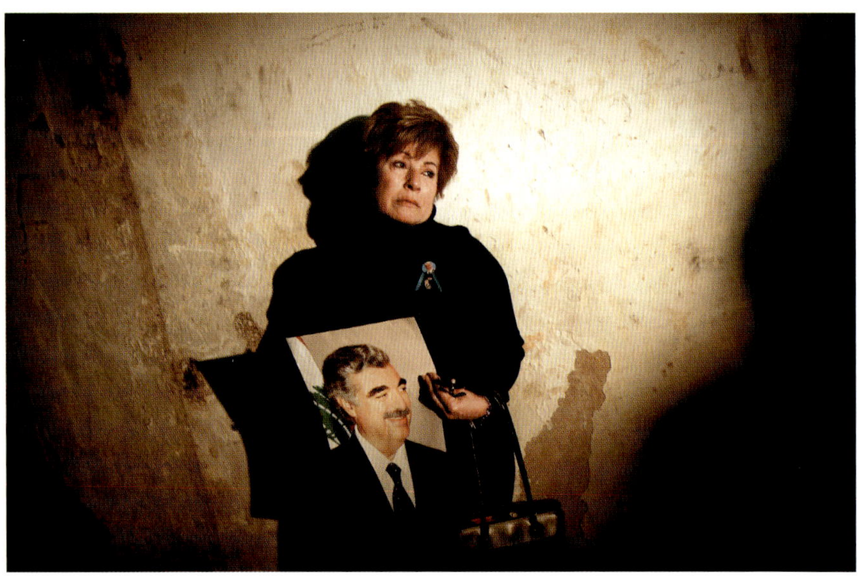

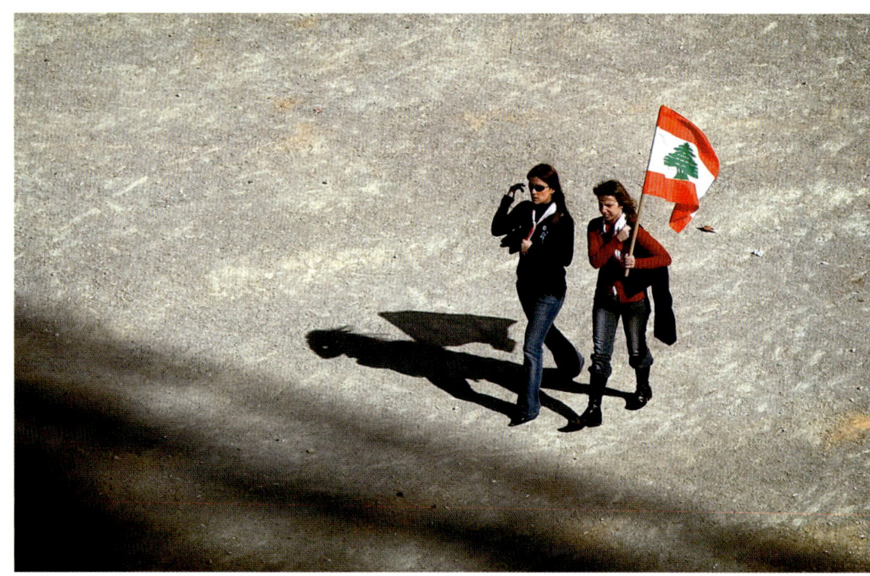

23 March 2005, KASLIK, LEBANON

A man unfolds a huge Lebanese flag at the site where a powerful bomb tore through a shopping centre in an anti-Syrian Christian heartland north of Beirut, killing three people and bringing Lebanon closer to chaos weeks before general elections. Damir Sagolj

16 March 2005, BEIRUT, LEBANON

Lebanese Jamana Tabara holds a picture of slain former Prime Minister Rafik al-Hariri as she cries inside a Syrian prison after Syrian intelligence agents pulled out of Beirut and large parts of Lebanon, a major step towards meeting U.S. and Lebanese opposition demands for Syria to release its grip on its small neighbour. Damir Sagolj

13 March 2005, NABATIYEH, LEBANON

A boy dressed in military uniform holds a Lebanese flag as he stands in front of Shi'ite Muslim clerics during a Hizbollah rally against foreign meddling in Lebanon, staged in the southern town of Nabatiyeh. Hundreds of thousands of people turned out for the rally, many carrying placards that read 'No to foreign intervention'. These were aimed not at Syria but at the United States and Israel. Damir Sagolj

26 March 2005, BEIRUT, LEBANON

Lebanese women arrive for a gathering to pay respects to former Prime Minister Rafik al-Hariri near his grave at Martyrs' Square in Beirut. At least 150,000 Lebanese turned Hariri's funeral on 16 February into an outpouring of anger against Syria. Damir Sagolj

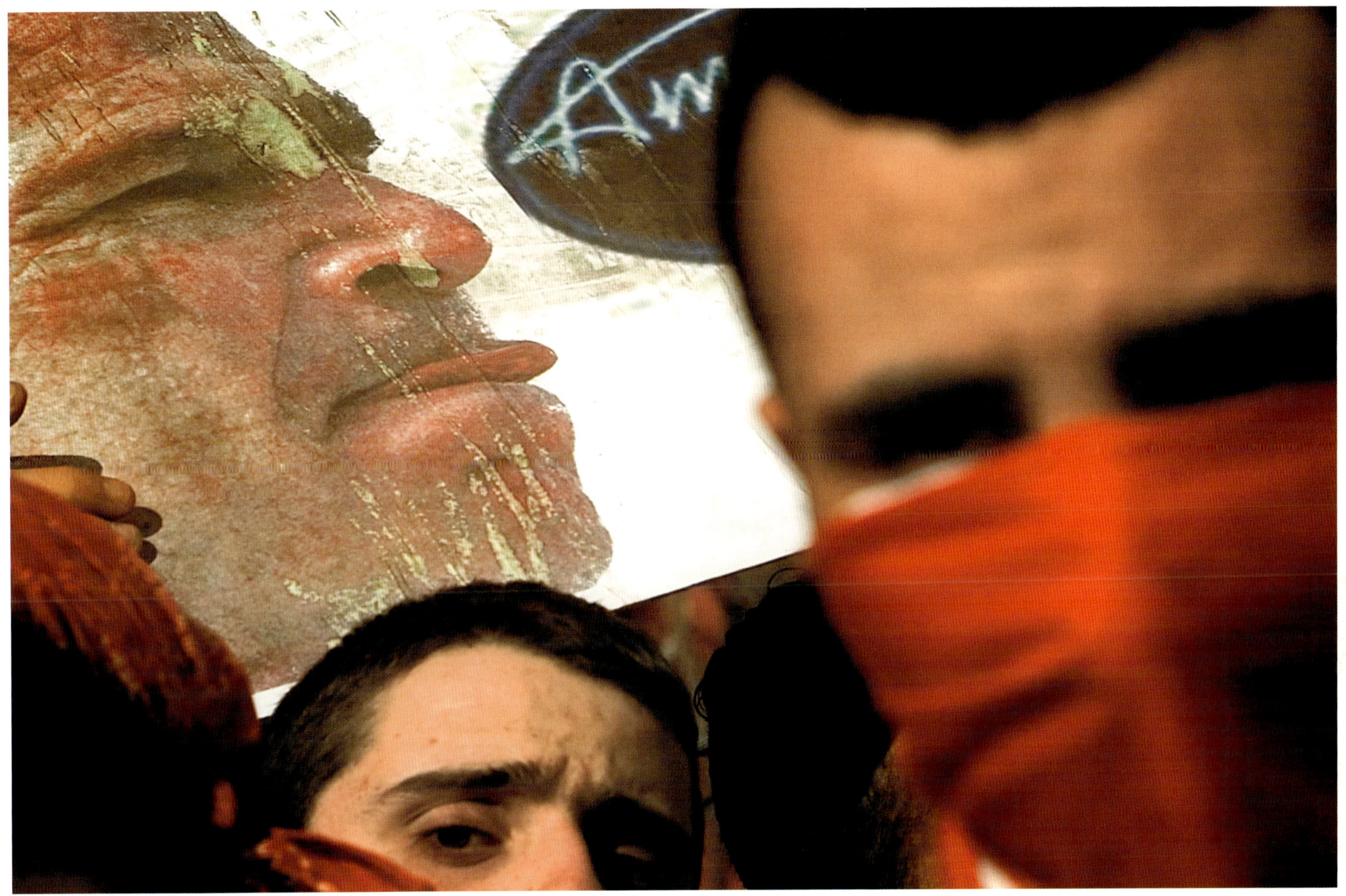

15 March 2005, BEIRUT, LEBANON

A picture of United States President George W. Bush is seen behind Lebanese students during a protest in front of the U.S. embassy near Beirut. Around 3,000 pro-Syrian students chanted 'Death to America' and burned American and Israeli flags, denouncing what they said was U.S. interference in Lebanon. Syrian President Bashar al-Assad nonetheless bowed to immense U.S.-led international pressure and agreed to withdraw all troops, intelligence agents and equipment from Lebanon. The rapid pullout was complete by 26 April 2005. Damir Sagolj

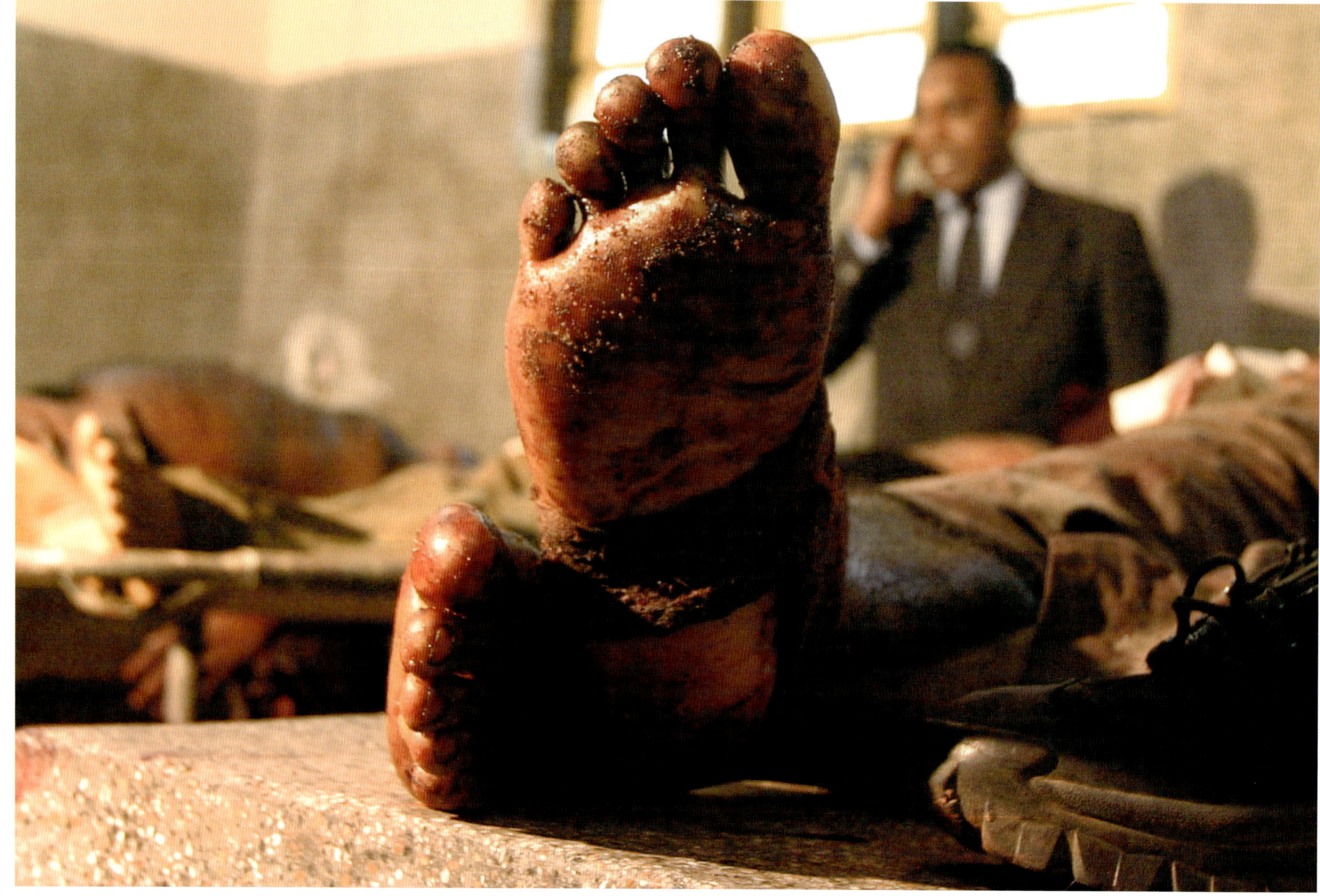

8 February 2005, POLONNARUWA, SRI LANKA

The body of E. Kousalyan, head of the Tamil Tigers' eastern political wing, lies in a hospital morgue in Polonnaruwa. Kousalyan was shot dead along with three other rebels in a government-controlled area in the restive eastern Sri Lankan district of Batticaloa. He was the most senior rebel killed since a 2002 ceasefire left in limbo the Tigers' fight for autonomy in the north and east. The incident was a setback to hopes that the humanitarian crisis caused by the December 2004 tsunami, Sri Lanka's worst natural disaster, might enable both sides to put politics aside and work together towards reconstruction and a long-elusive permanent peace.

Anuruddha Lokuhapuarachchi

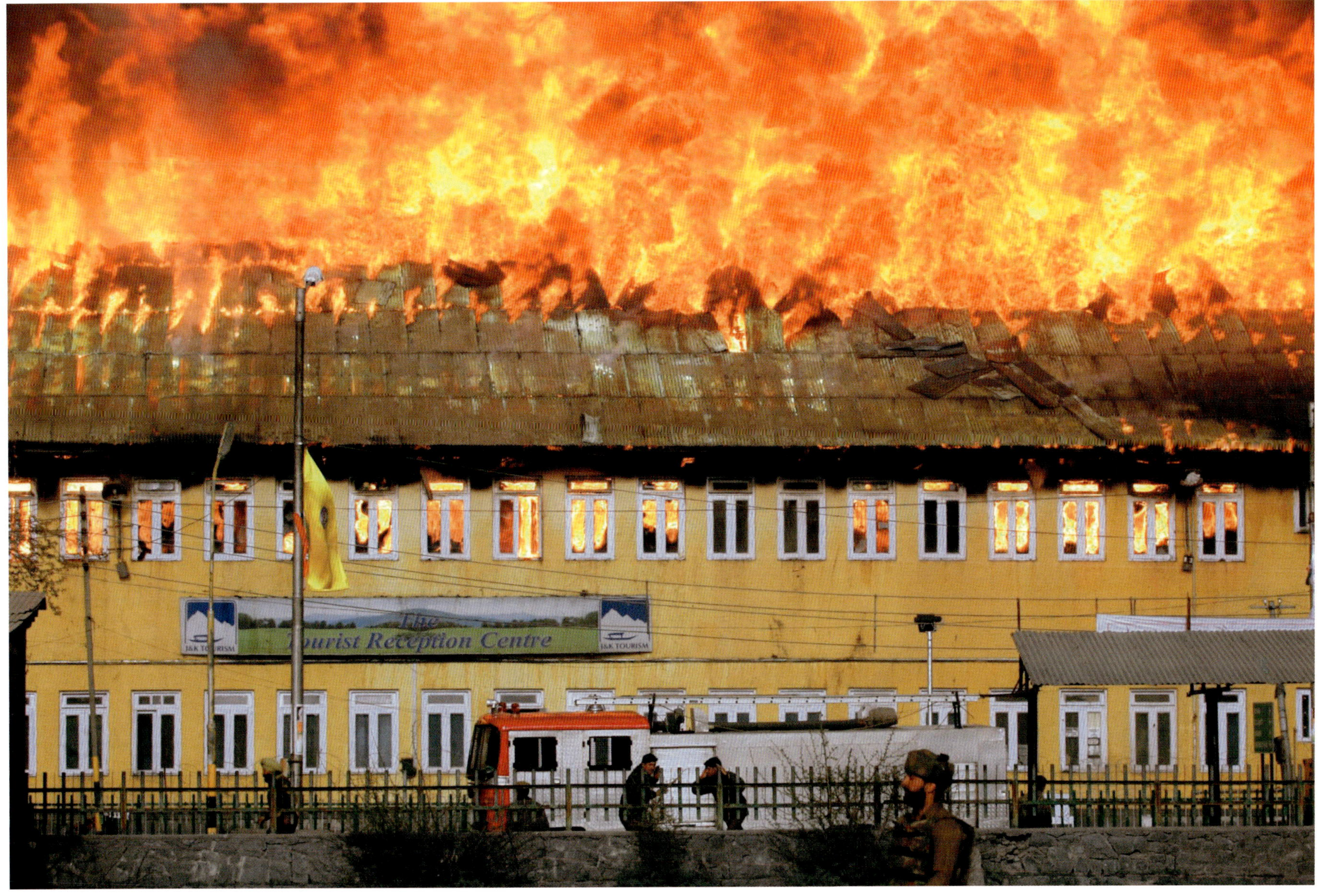

6 April 2005, SRINAGAR, INDIA

A huge blaze destroys a government building after it was stormed and torched by Islamic militant suicide attackers. The heavily guarded complex was housing passengers due to take an historic bus across divided Kashmir, the first trans-Kashmir bus in half a century and an emotional symbol of warming ties between Pakistan and India. Aside from the attackers, six people were hurt but none killed. The bus journey went ahead as planned, carrying 19 Indian Kashmiris into Pakistan-controlled Kashmir to meet relatives. Many Kashmiri families have been separated by politics and war for 60 years. Desmond Boylan

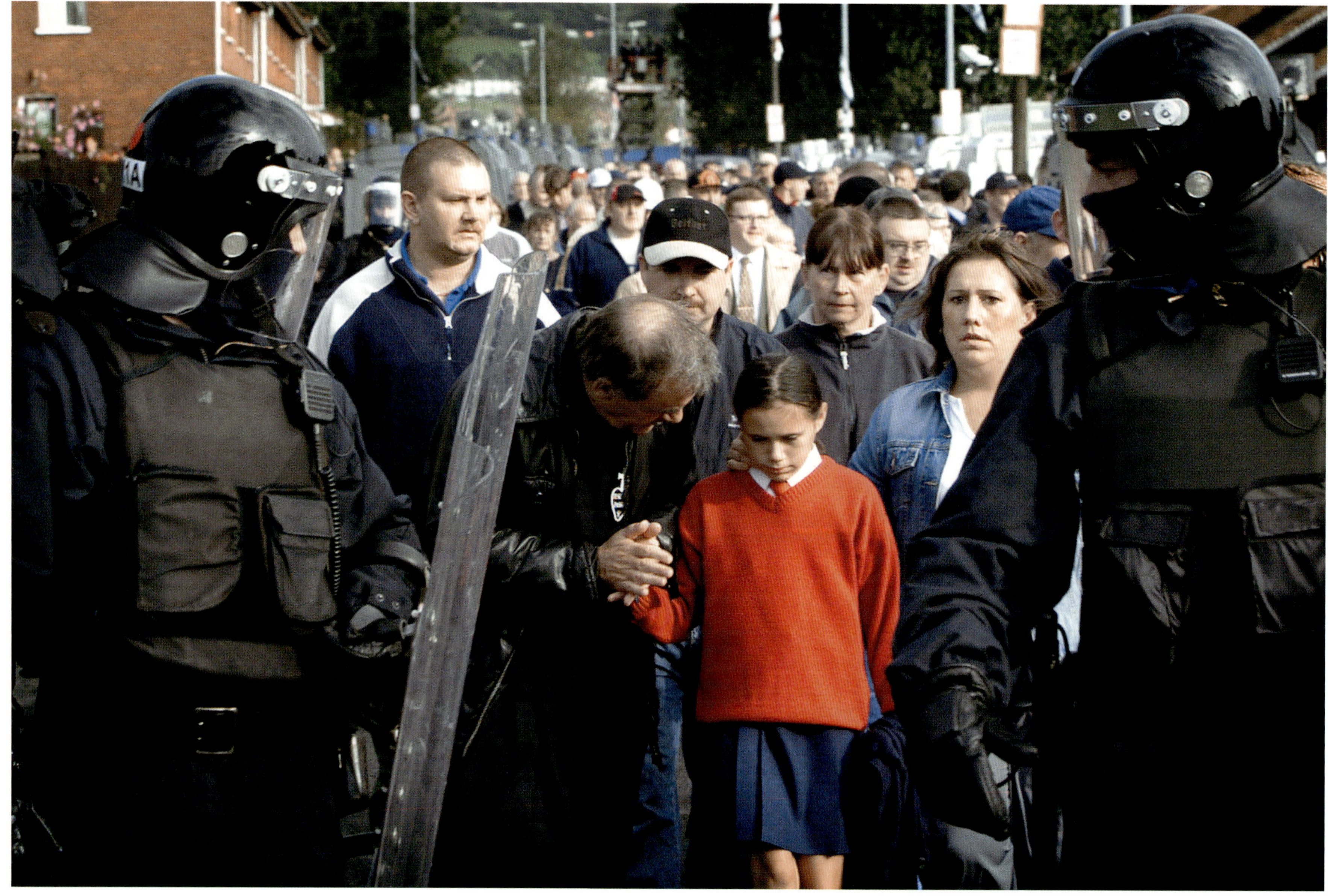

6 September 2001, BELFAST, UNITED KINGDOM

A Catholic schoolgirl is comforted by her parents as she is escorted by riot police to Holy Cross School in North Belfast. The school's front gate lies in a pocket of North Belfast where Roman Catholic and Protestant communities live in close proximity. Protestant residents blockaded the children's route to school in retaliation for what they said were frequent attacks by Roman Catholics in the previous months. Stones, bricks and verbal abuse were hurled at the children and their parents. On 5 September, two police officers were seriously hurt by a bomb thrown by a Protestant extremist just metres from the children. Paul McErlane

21 March 2004, CABRA, KOSOVO

Fourteen-year-old Kosovo Albanian Fitim Veseli cries as he looks at the flag-draped coffins of his two friends who drowned in the Ibar River. Several thousand Kosovo Albanians attended the funeral, amid heavy NATO security in case emotions sparked further ethnic violence. The unconfirmed story that the boys had drowned after jumping into the fast-flowing river to escape Serb youths who were chasing them led to an eruption of violence on 17 March that left 28 people dead and 870 injured. Hazir Reka

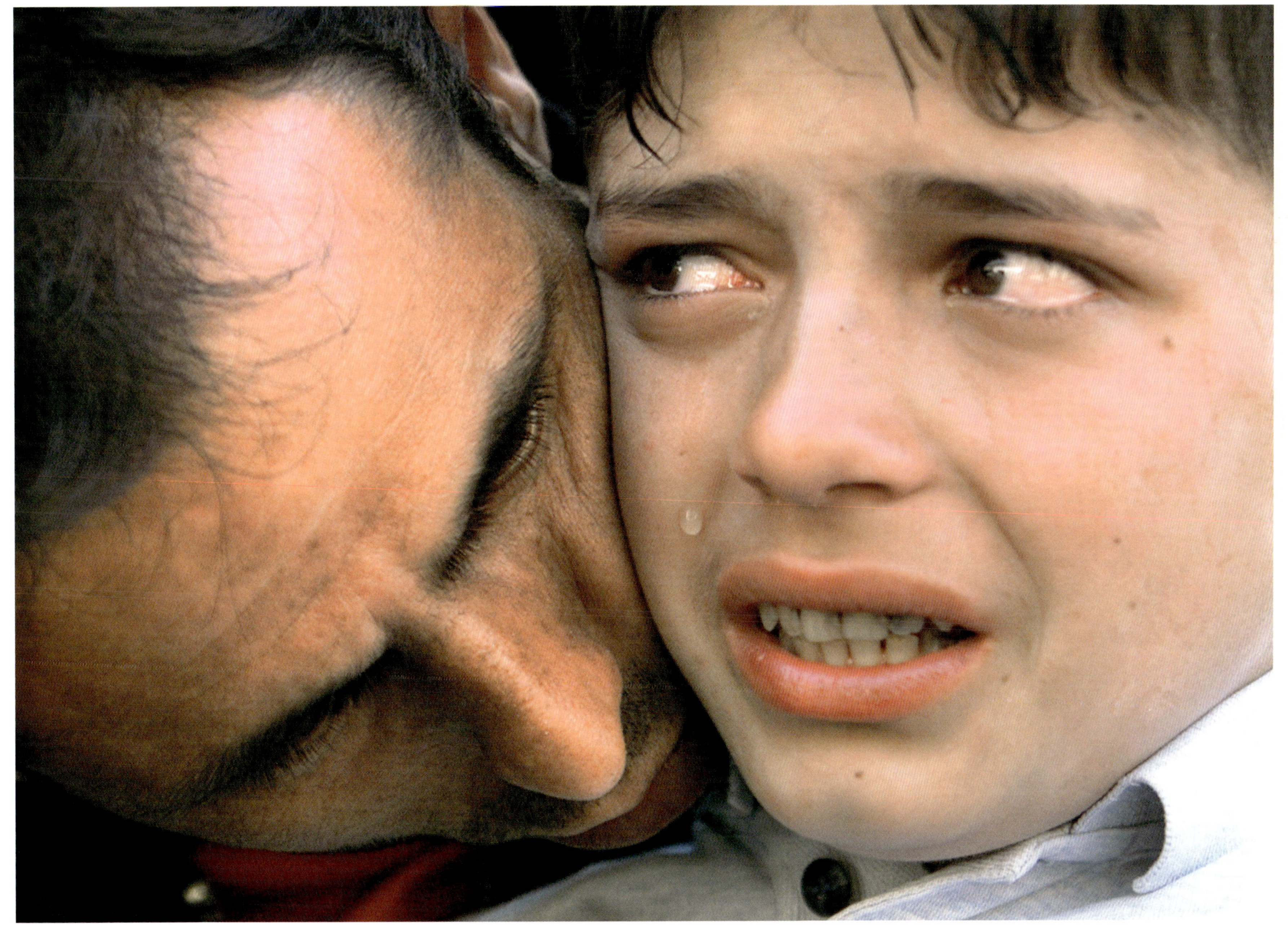

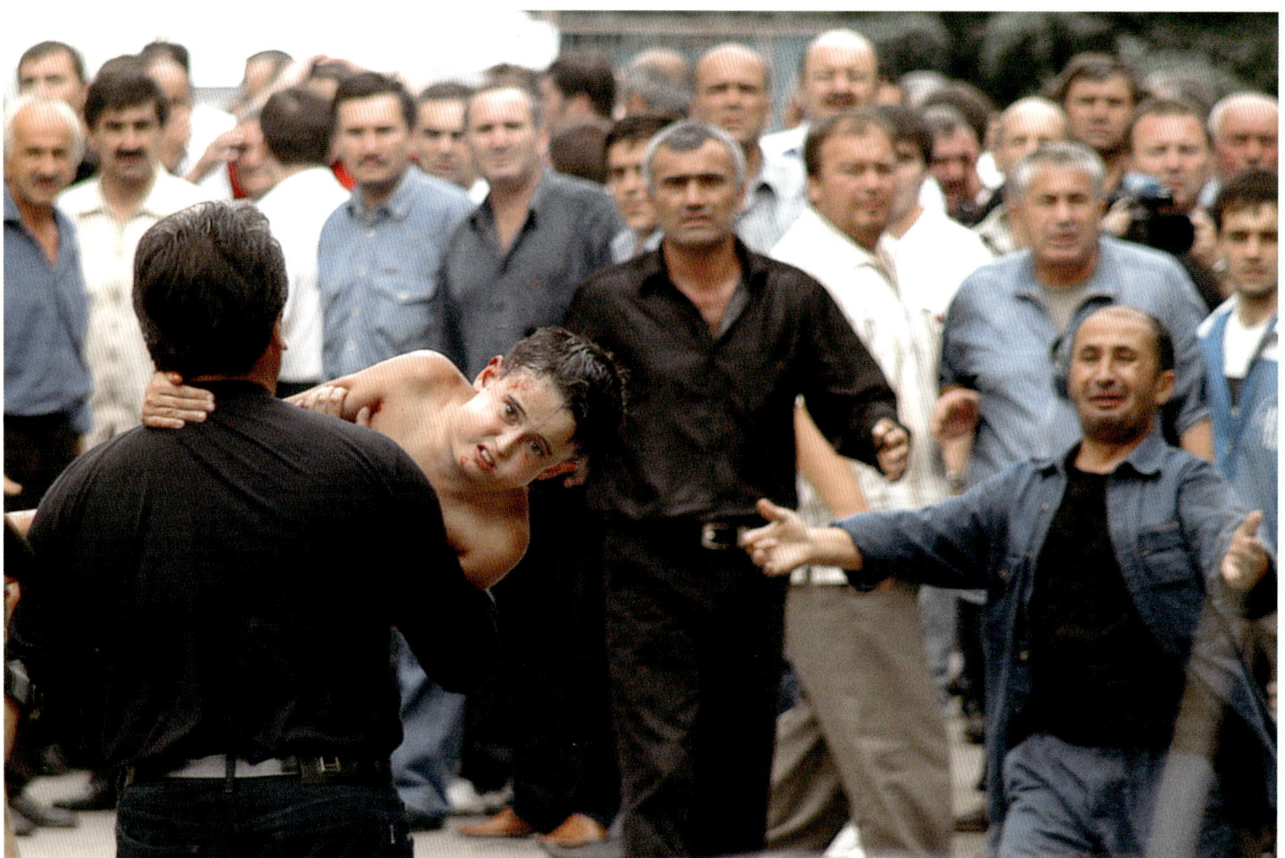

3 September 2004, BESLAN, RUSSIA

An injured boy is carried away from a school seized by heavily armed Chechen separatists in the town of Beslan in the province of North Ossetia, near Chechnya. More than 1,000 parents and children were held hostage by the gunmen in a siege that lasted 53 hours. Eduard Kornienko

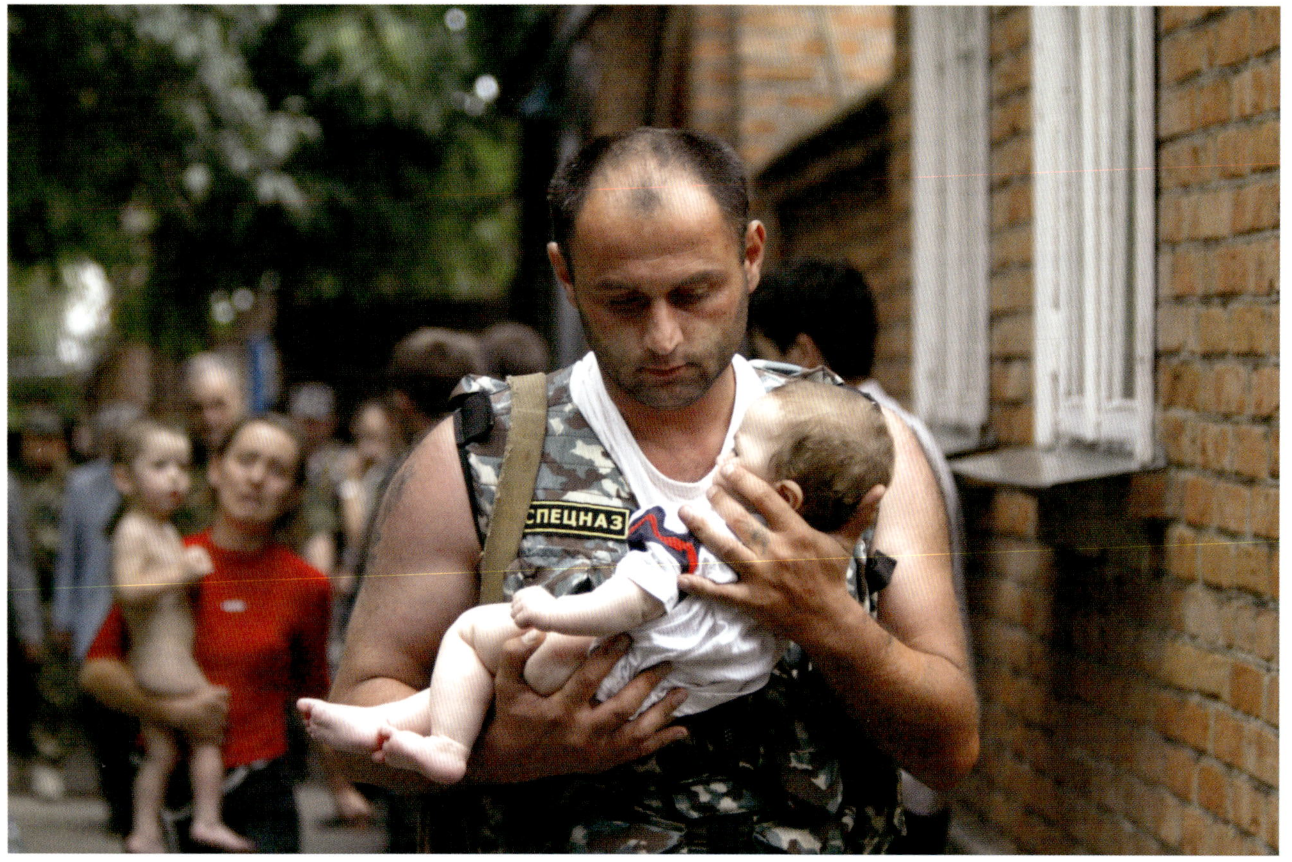

2 September 2004, BESLAN, RUSSIA

A Russian police officer carries a small child released from the school. The two-day siege ended on 3 September in a bloodbath. Russian security forces battled Chechen separatists as naked children ran out screaming amid explosions and machine-gun fire. A total of 331 people died, half of them children.
Viktor Korotayev

1 September 2005, BESLAN, RUSSIA

During a commemoration ceremony on the first anniversary of the start of the school hostage siege in Beslan, a relative grieves before a wall bearing portraits of the victims. Sergei Karpukhin

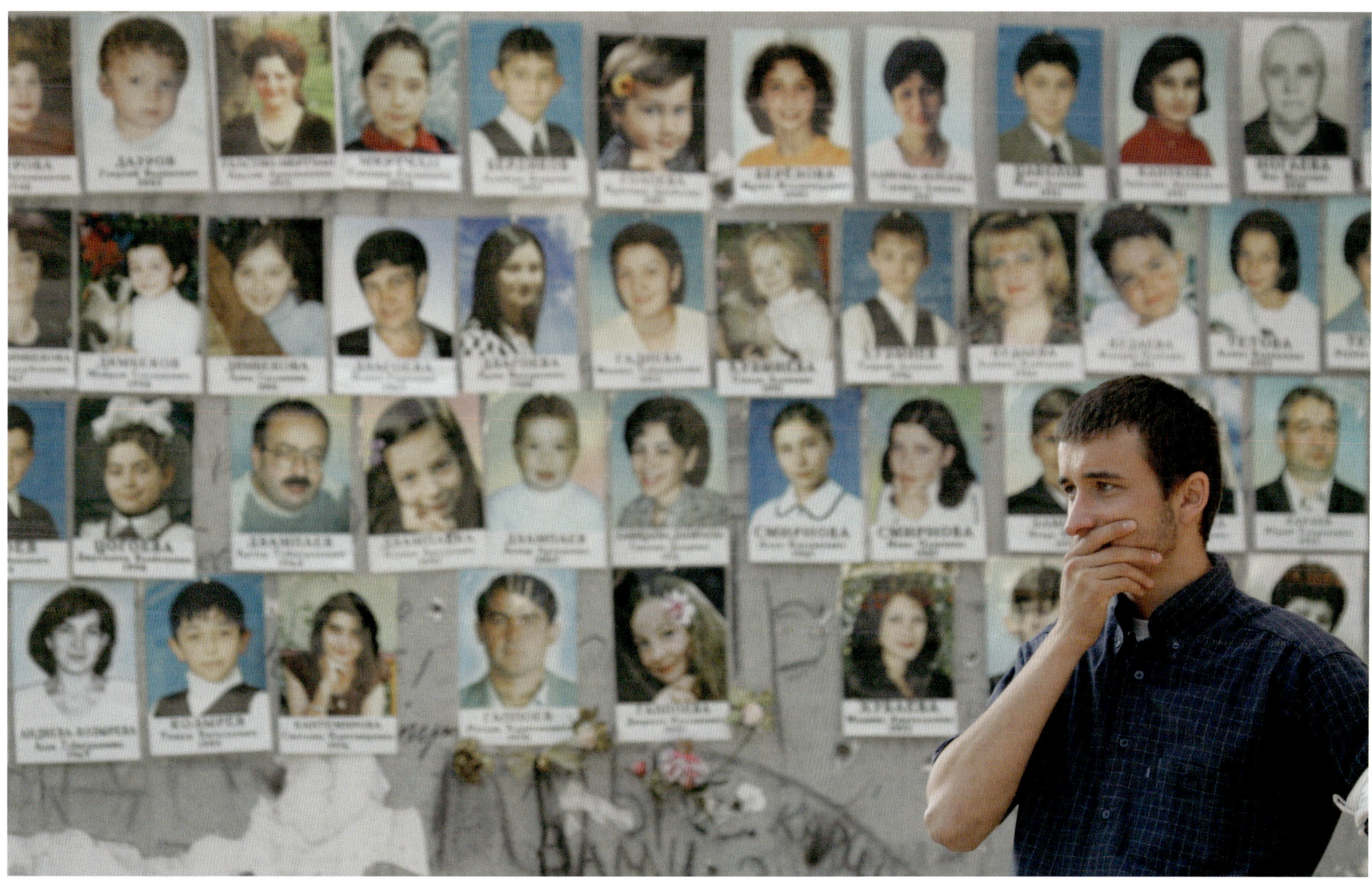

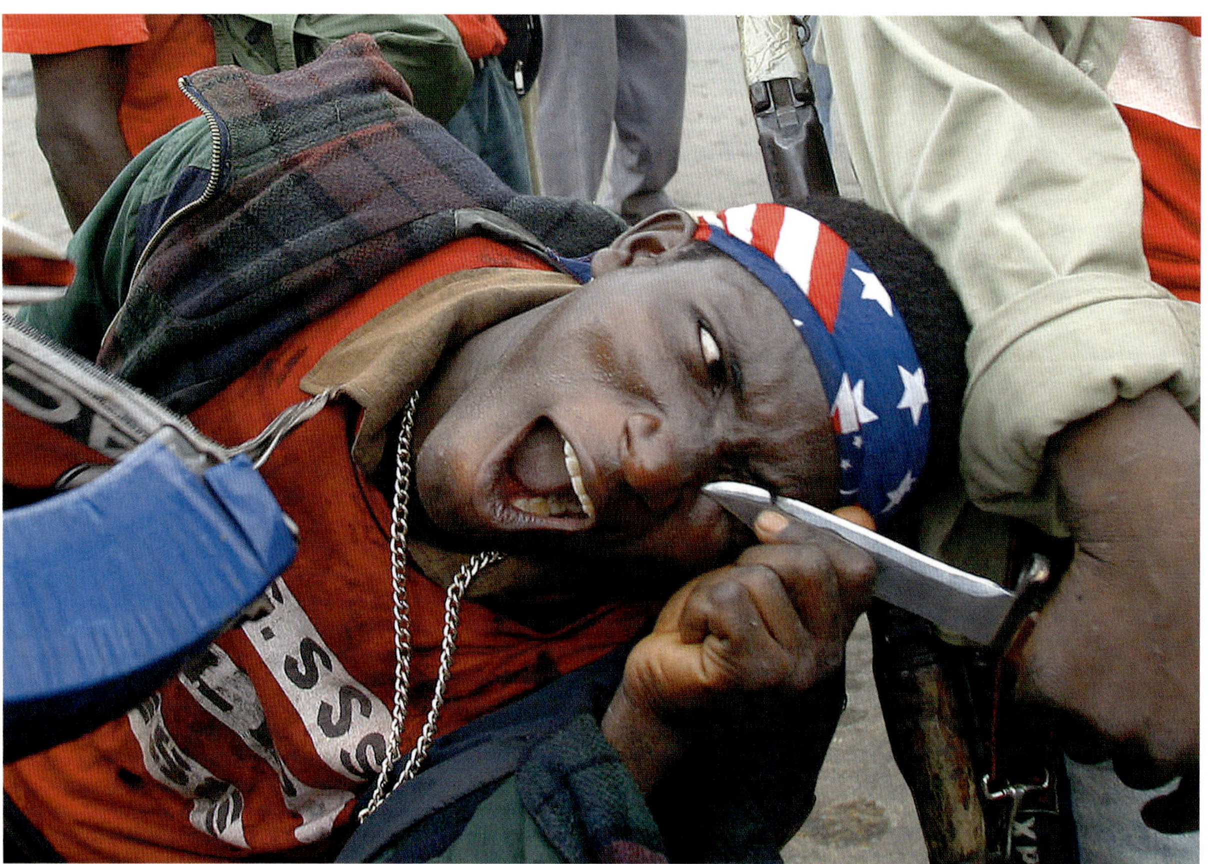

18 July 2003, MONROVIA, LIBERIA

A fighter loyal to Liberia's former President Charles Taylor shows his bravado as government forces gather in the capital Monrovia to beat off an impending rebel attack. On 11 August, having lost control of much of the city and facing pressure from the U.S. to step down, Taylor finally agreed to accept an offer of asylum in Nigeria. Monrovia was by then in the midst of a dire humanitarian crisis. But the departure of Taylor and the arrival of peacekeeping forces paved the way for a transitional government and the election of President Ellen Johnson-Sirleaf, Africa's first female elected head of state, sworn in on 16 January 2006. Taylor was brought before a U.N.-backed Special Court in Sierra Leone on 3 April 2006, charged with war crimes. He pleaded not guilty. Luc Gnago

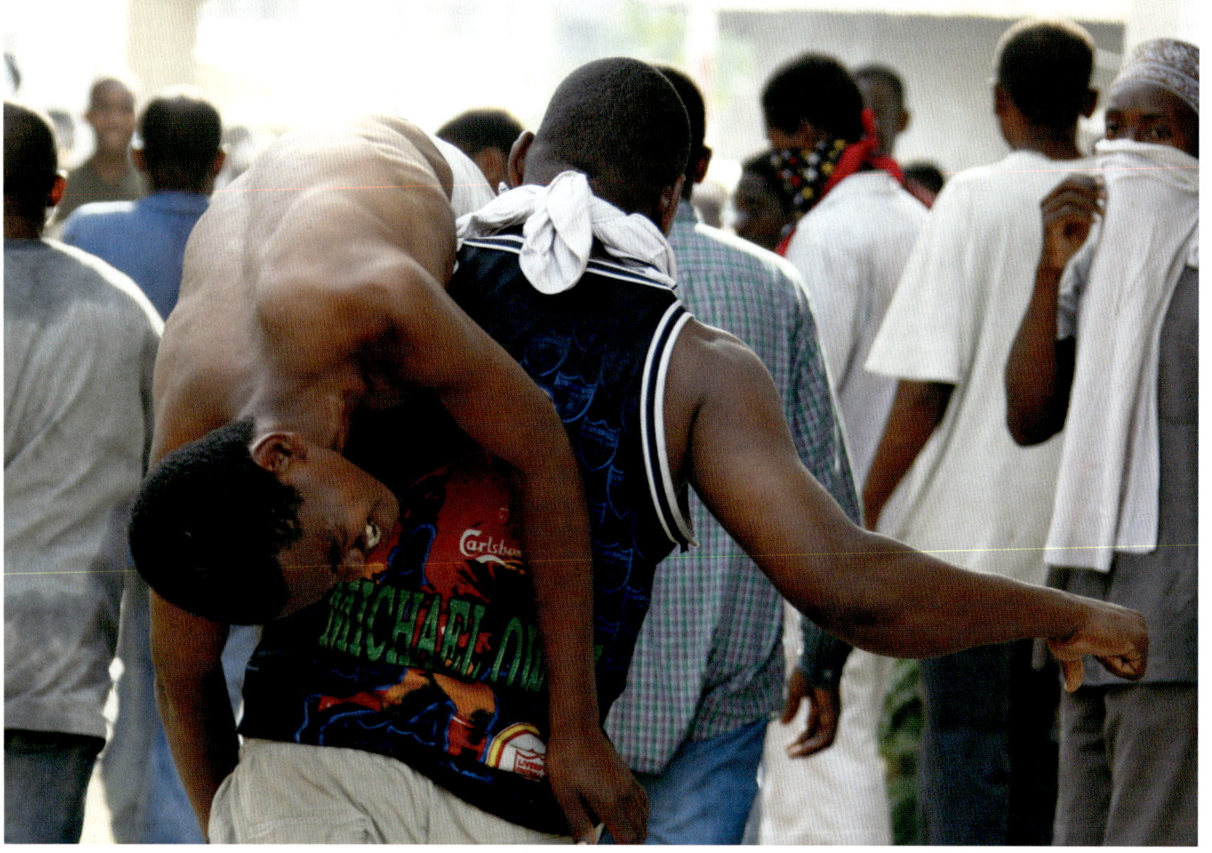

1 November 2005, ZANZIBAR, TANZANIA

An opposition Civic United Front (CUF) supporter is carried to an ambulance after clashes with security forces in Zanzibar's Stone Town. The re-election of President Amani Abeid Karume by a narrow margin was disputed by his political opponents, leading to pockets of unrest across the volatile semi-autonomous Tanzanian islands. At least one person was killed and scores wounded in the clashes between security forces and opposition supporters. CUF leader Seif Sharif Hamad has stood for president in Zanzibar and lost three times, each time accusing the ruling party of fraud and intimidation. Radu Sigheti

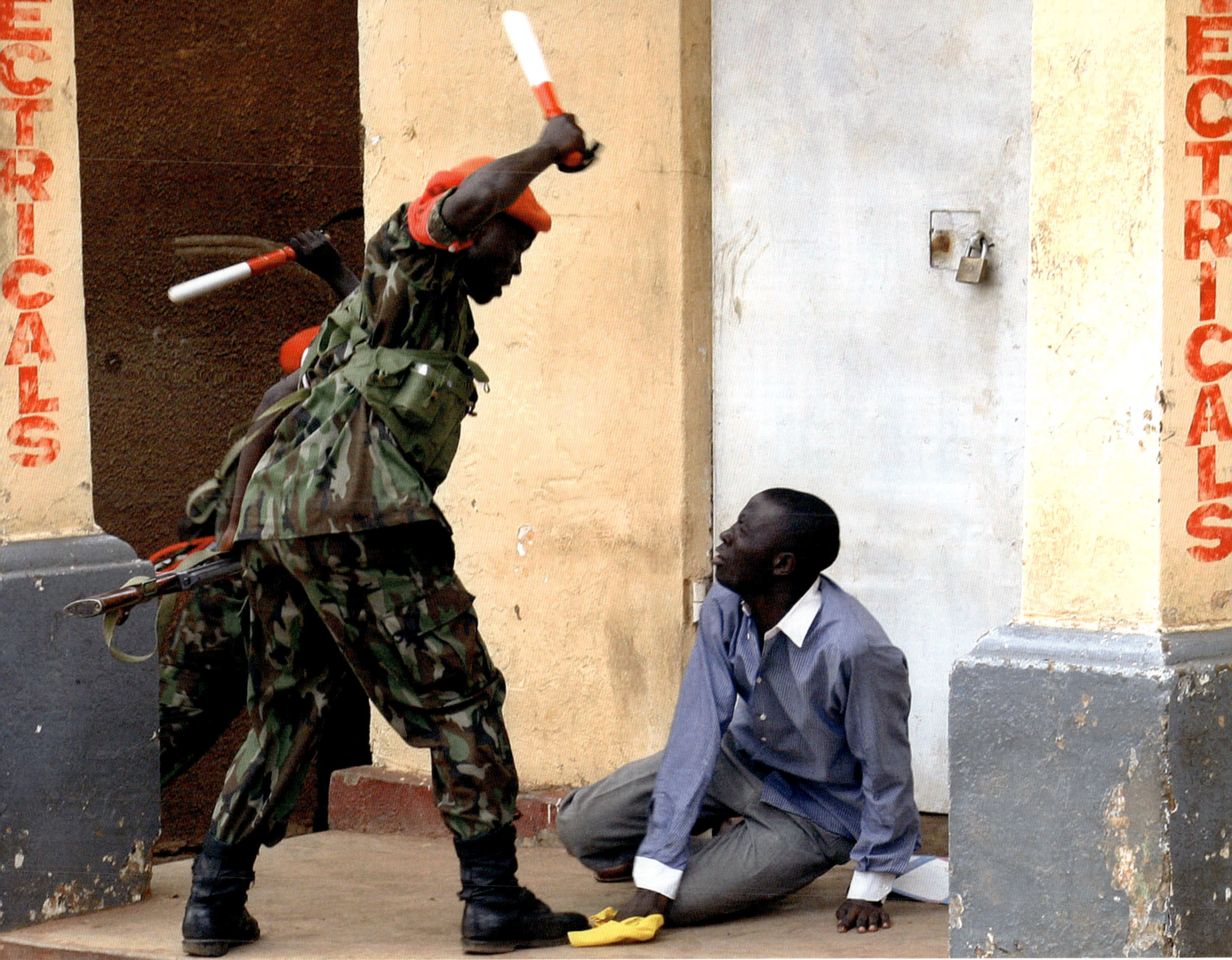

15 November 2005, KAMPALA, UGANDA

Military police disperse supporters of opposition leader Kizza Besigye during the second day of riots in Kampala. Besigye, a leading challenger to President Yoweri Museveni, was appearing in court on charges of plotting rebellion and rape – charges that his supporters believed to be politically motivated and designed to sideline him in a forthcoming presidential election. Museveni won the election, held in February 2006, extending a 20-year hold on power. James Akena

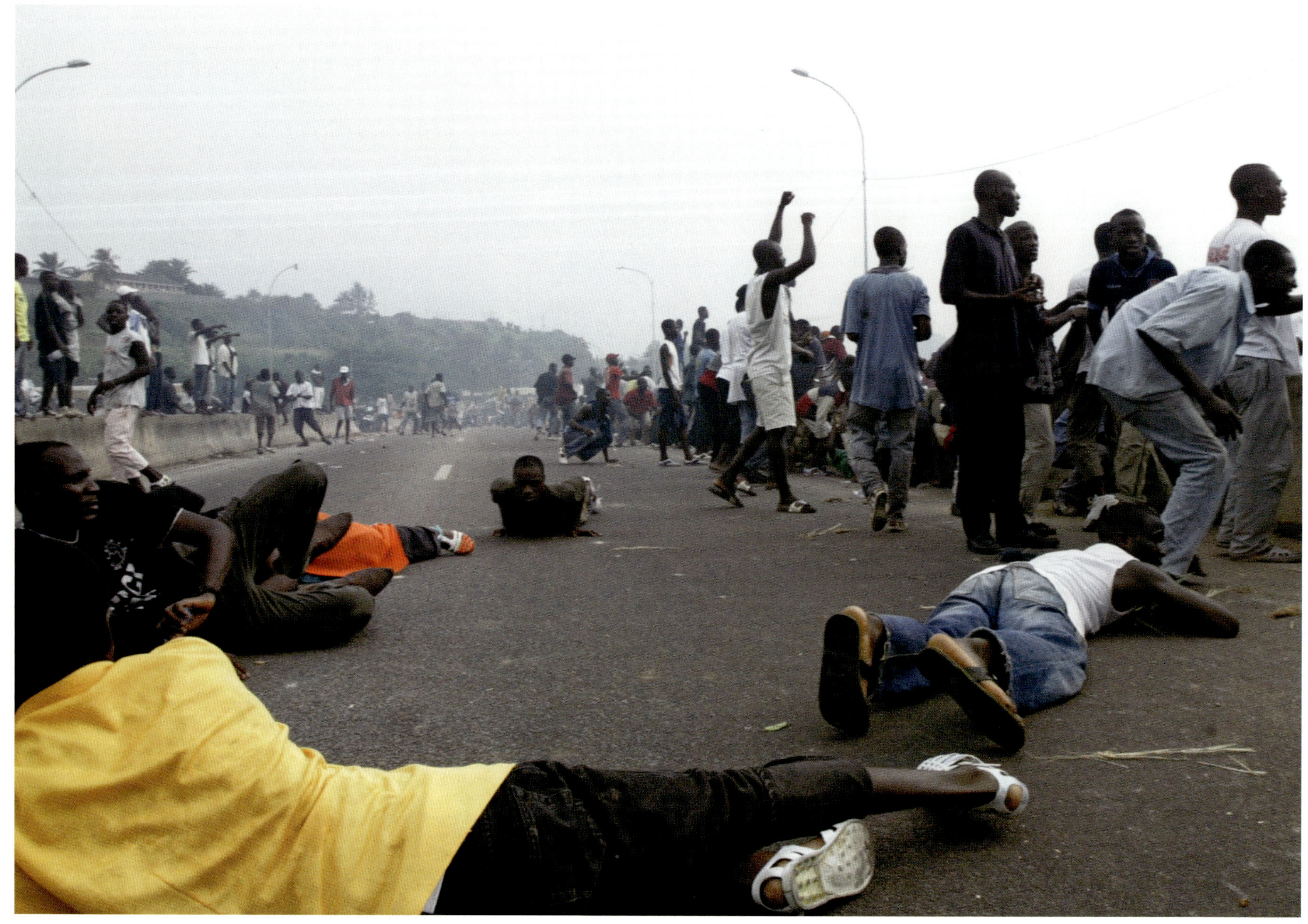

18 January 2006, ABIDJAN, IVORY COAST

Supporters of Ivorian President Laurent Gbagbo are shot at by U.N. soldiers in the Sebroko district of Abidjan. The peacekeepers opened fire to repel an attack on their base during four days of anti-U.N. riots in Abidjan and other cities in which 11 people were killed. The protesters were calling for an end to what they called foreign meddling in the West African state, which has been divided into a rebel-held north and government south since a 2002–3 civil war, which grew out of a failed coup against Gbagbo. The peacekeepers were attempting to oversee the implementation of a U.N. plan pushing for reunification and elections. Luc Gnago

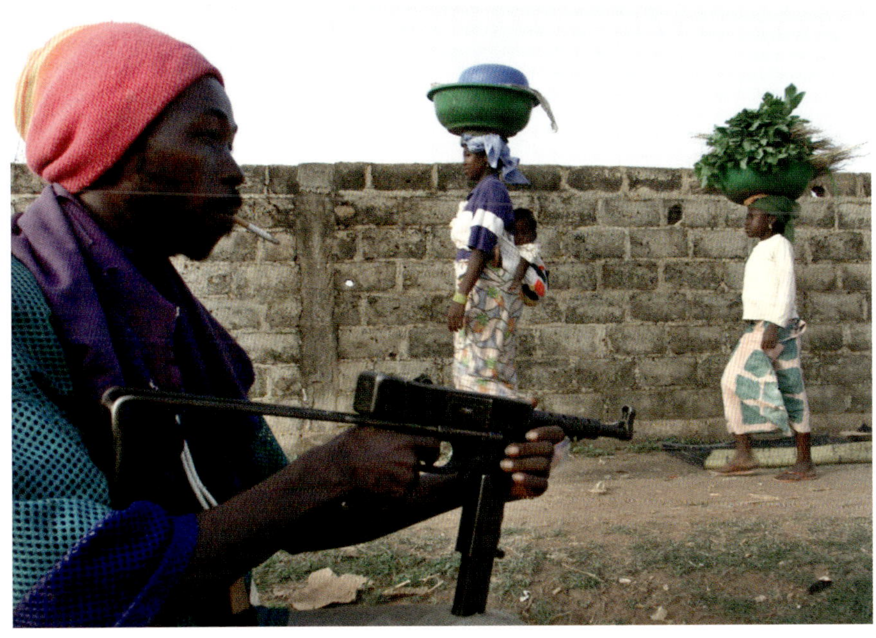

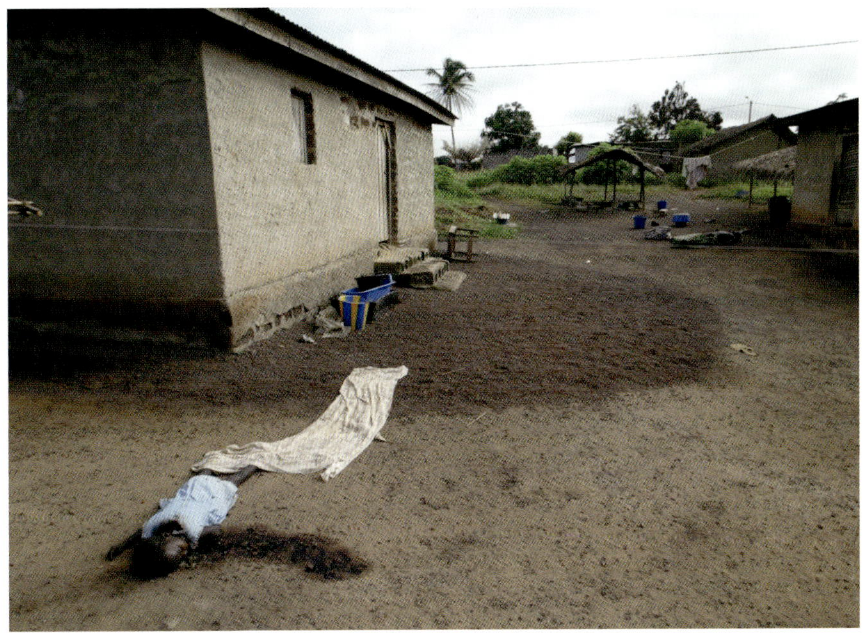

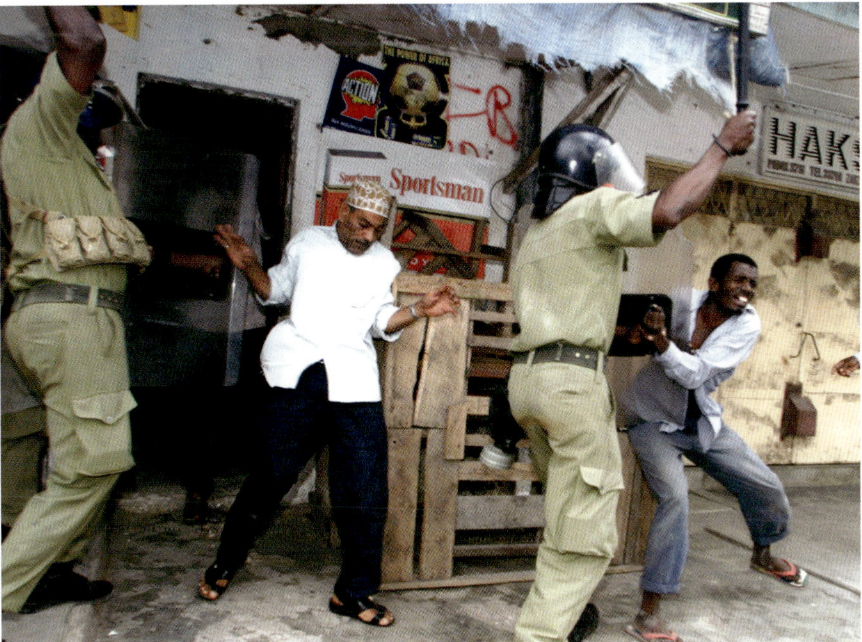

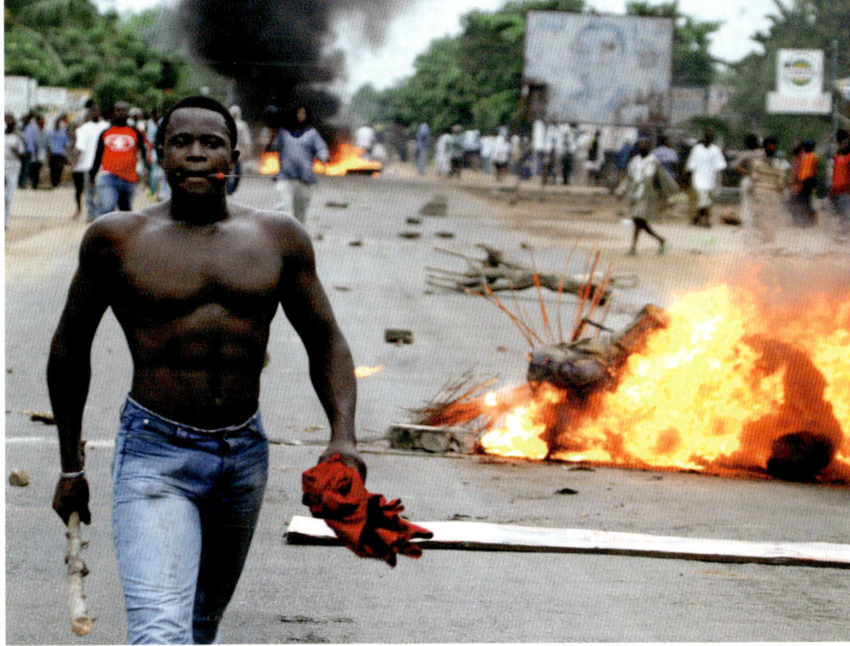

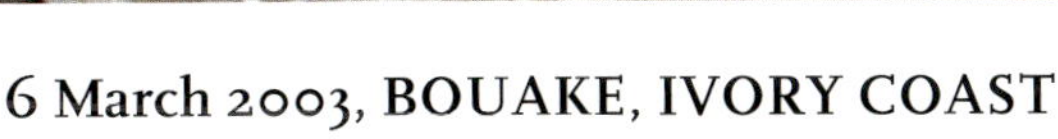

6 March 2003, BOUAKE, IVORY COAST

A rebel soldier mans a checkpoint as women traders walk by. After five months of civil war, civilians in the rebel stronghold of Bouake, the former French colony's second largest city, were struggling to survive. Luc Gnago

30 October 2000, ZANZIBAR, TANZANIA

Riot police beat suspects for allegedly throwing rocks. Violence broke out after the opposition and observers said general elections held on 29 October were not free or fair. At least 35 people were killed in weeks of protest. George Mulala

2 June 2005, DUEKOUE, IVORY COAST

Bodies of a girl and her father lie on the ground, victims of a wave of ethnic violence that led to at least 100 deaths and caused thousands to flee their homes. Luc Gnago

24 April 2005, LOME, TOGO

An opposition supporter walks in front of a roadblock of burning tyres as Togolese voters go to the polls. Togo spun into chaos after President Gnassingbe Eyadema died in February 2005 and army leaders named his son to replace him. Elections were called only in response to fierce international pressure. Finbarr O'Reilly

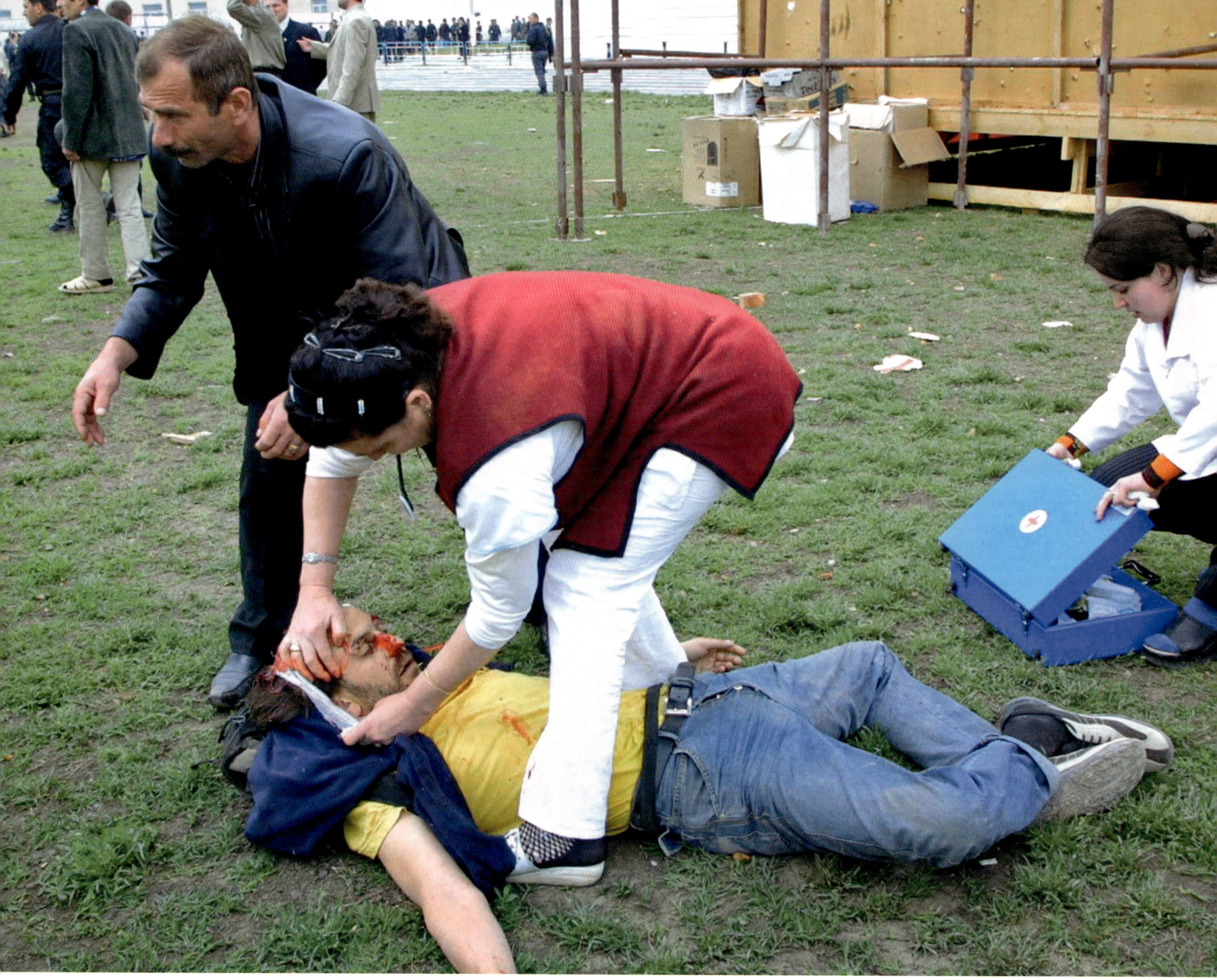

9 May 2004, GROZNY, RUSSIA

A paramedic tries to help Reuters journalist Adlan Khasanov, one of seven people killed by an explosion during celebrations in Grozny to mark the 1945 victory over Nazi Germany. The attack was directed at the Moscow-backed Chechen President Akhmad Kadyrov, who also died. Musa Sadulayev

17 June 2003, ACEH, INDONESIA

A woman mourns a relative killed by an unidentified group in Nisam village in Aceh. In May 2003 Indonesian government troops launched a fresh offensive to crush the rebels of the Free Aceh Movement, which had been fighting for independence in the gas-rich province on the island of Sumatra since 1976. The conflict killed more than 15,000 people, mainly civilians, before the devastation of the 26 December 2004 tsunami spurred the two sides to work towards a negotiated settlement. Tarmizy Harva

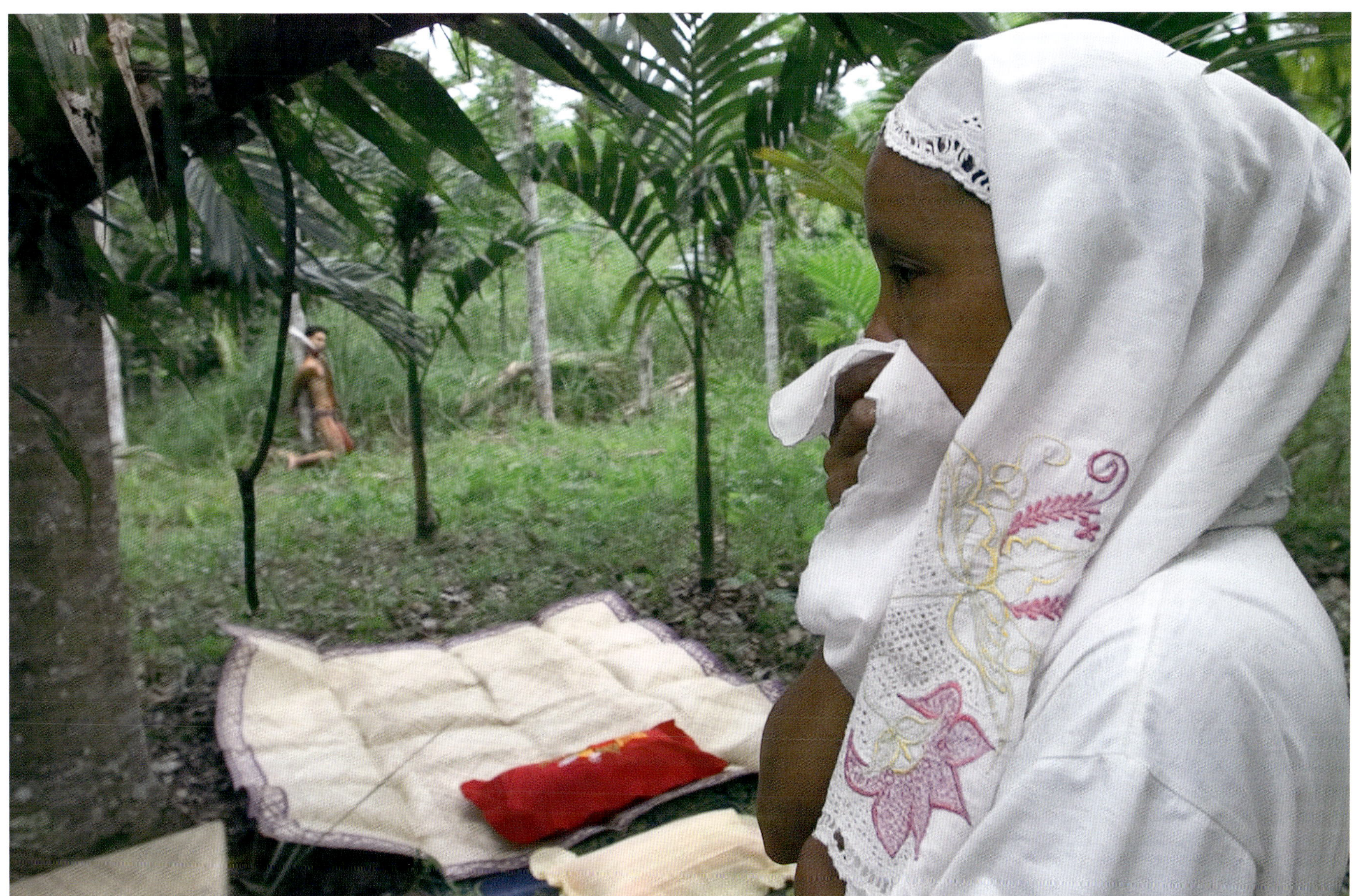

12 November 2001, RABAT, AFGHANISTAN

An opposition commander atop an observation post in the front line of Rabat, west of Bagram airport, looks at a huge bomb blast as U.S. fighter jets provide air support to advancing Northern Alliance ground troops some 25 km (15 miles) north of Kabul. Yannis Behrakis

13 November 2001, NORTH OF KABUL, AFGHANISTAN

Opposite Anti-Taliban Northern Alliance fighters pass a dead body as they ride on a T-62 tank along the motorway just 3 km (1.8 miles) north of the Afghan capital Kabul. Five weeks after the first U.S.-led air strikes against Taliban-controlled military targets, Northern Alliance forces entered Kabul, in defiance of international pressure to stay out. They later invited all Afghan factions, apart from the Taliban, to send representatives to the capital to discuss forming a new government. Yannis Behrakis

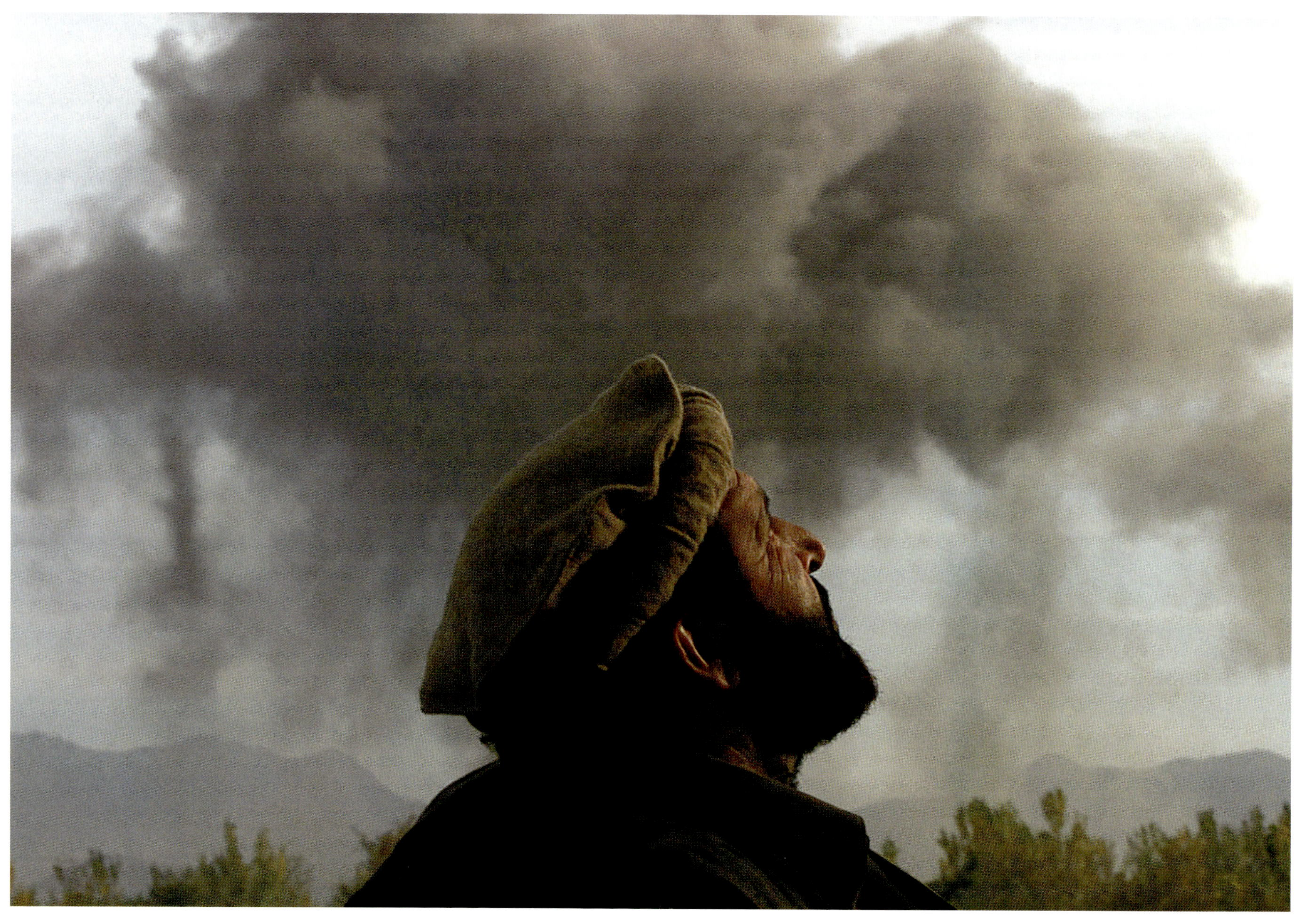

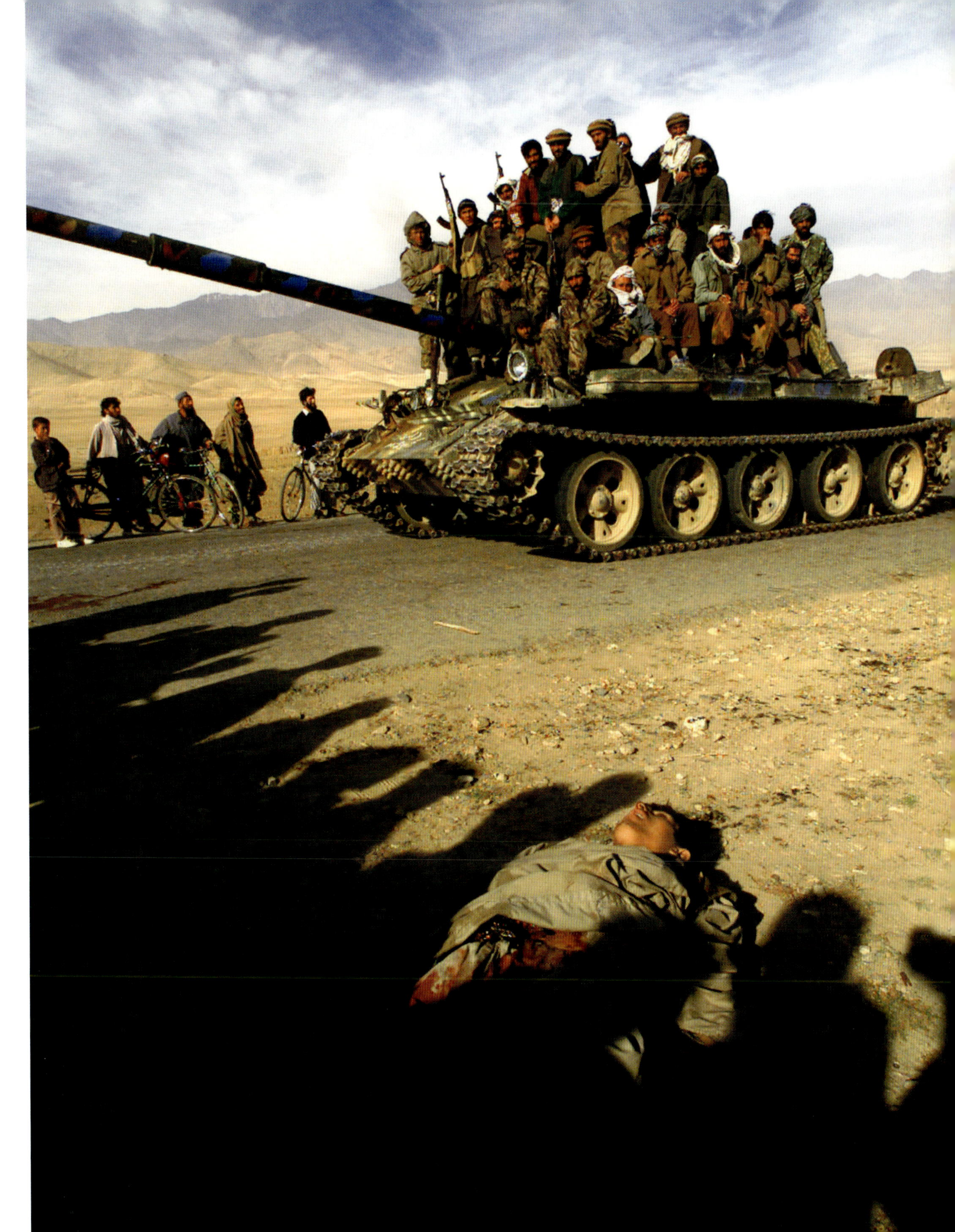

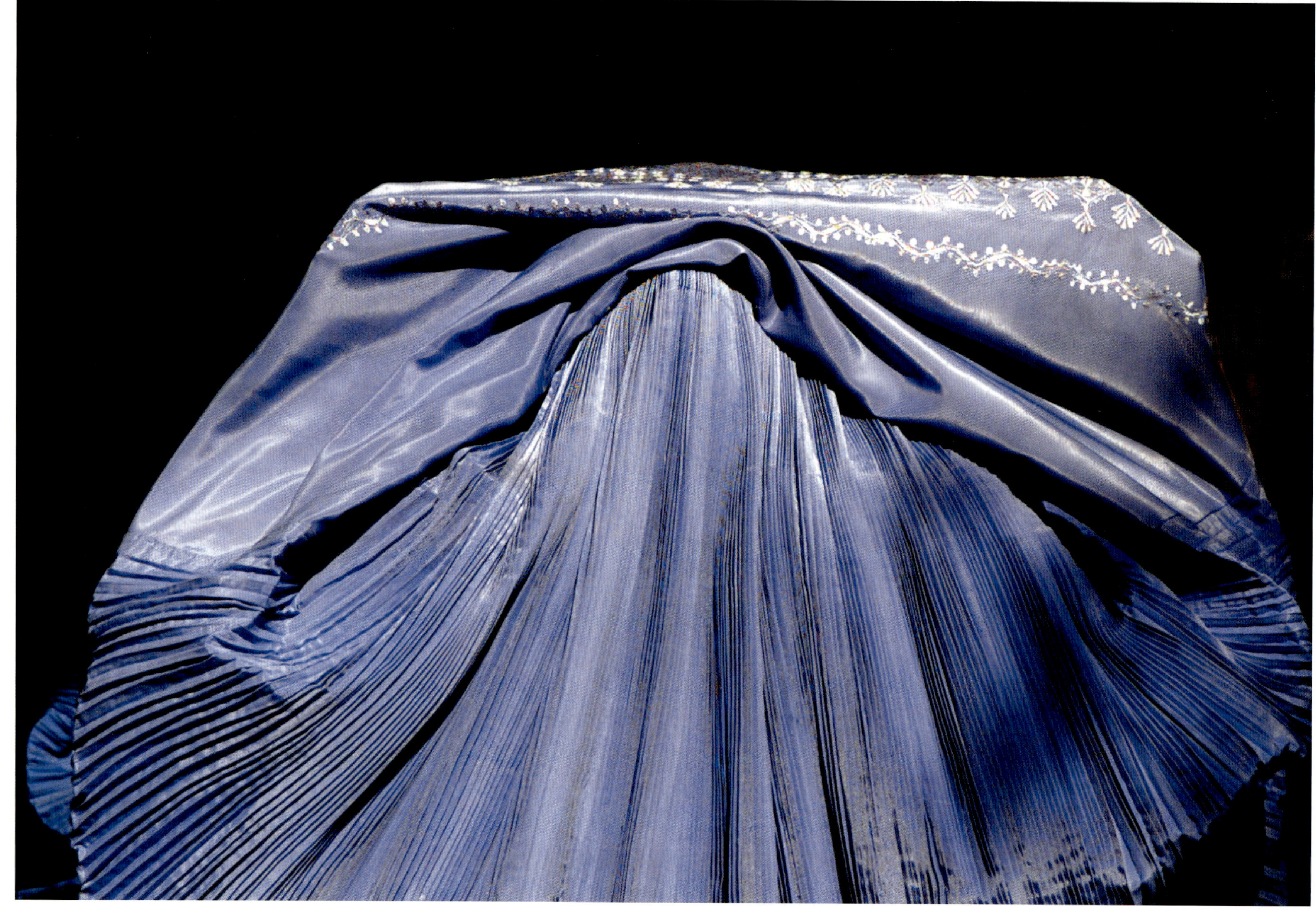

20 November 2001, KABUL, AFGHANISTAN

A woman removes her burqa as 'The General Coalition of Women' group organized a meeting of Afghan women to demonstrate for their rights. Under the strict interpretation of Islam enforced by the Taliban, women were compelled to hide behind head-to-toe burqas and forbidden to work or study. Yannis Behrakis

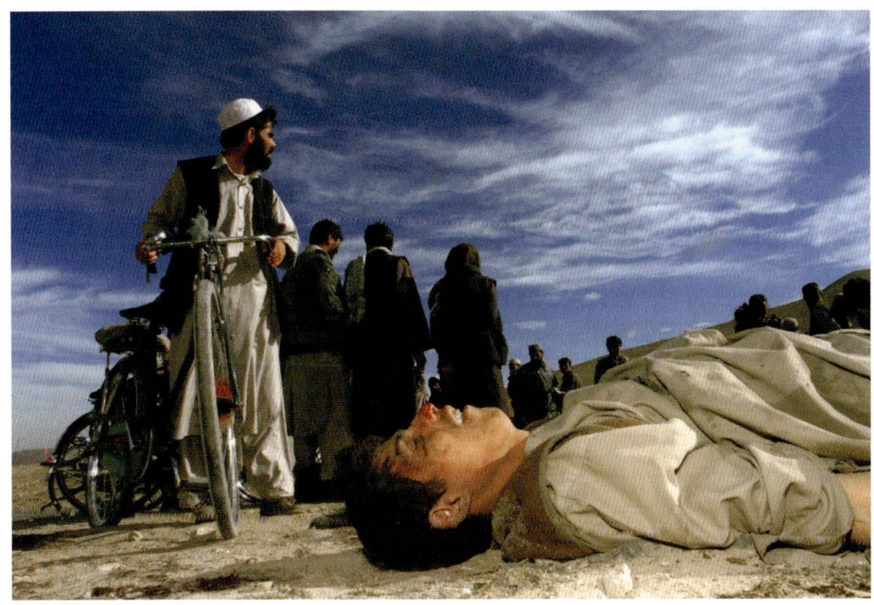

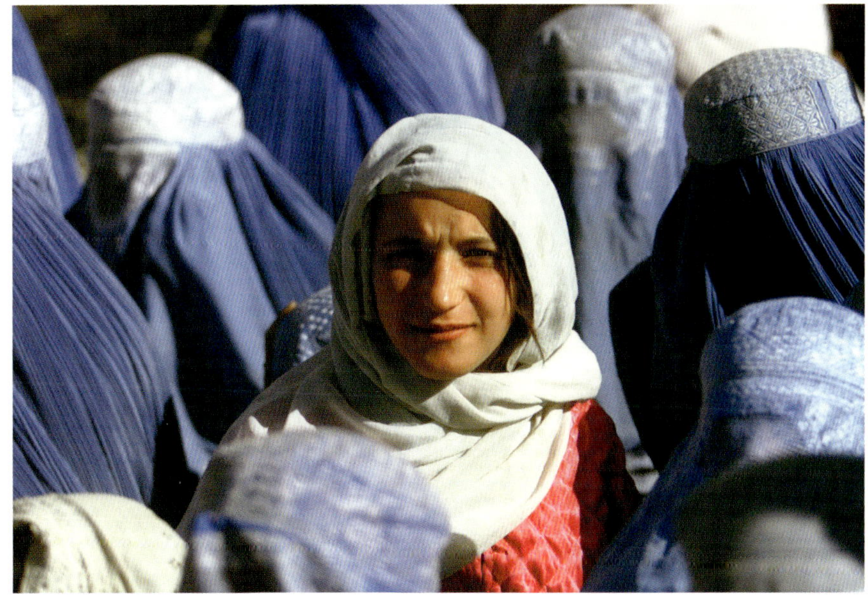

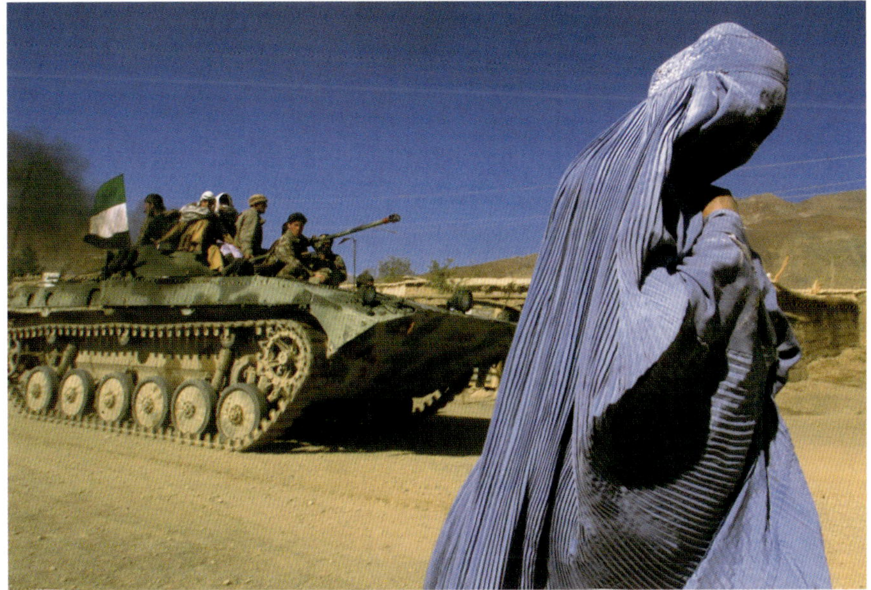

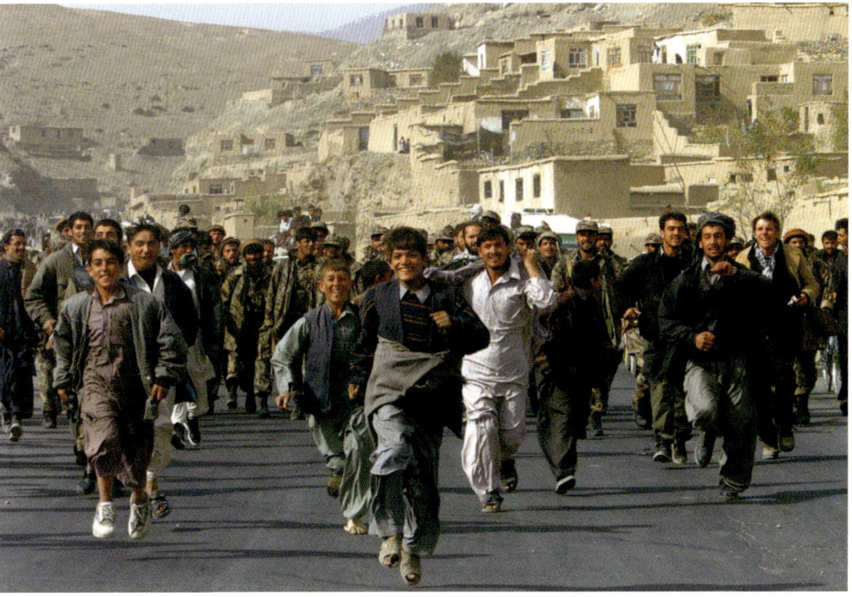

13 November 2001, KABUL, AFGHANISTAN

Afghan civilians observe dead Taliban fighters on the motorway 3 km (1.8 miles) north of Kabul. Yannis Behrakis

4 November 2001, JABAL US SERAJ, AFGHANISTAN

An Afghan woman wearing a traditional burqa walks on the side of a road as a Northern Alliance armoured personnel carrier bearing fighters and the Afghan flag drives to a new position in the outskirts of Jabal us Seraj, some 60 km (37 miles) north of Kabul. Yannis Behrakis

14 November 2001, KABUL, AFGHANISTAN

A young Afghan woman shows her face in public for the first time after five years under the Taliban and sharia law as she waits at a food distribution centre in central Kabul. Yannis Behrakis

13 November 2001, KABUL, AFGHANISTAN

Residents of Kabul celebrate and greet Northern Alliance opposition fighters as they enter the capital amid the collapse of Taliban rule. Yannis Behrakis

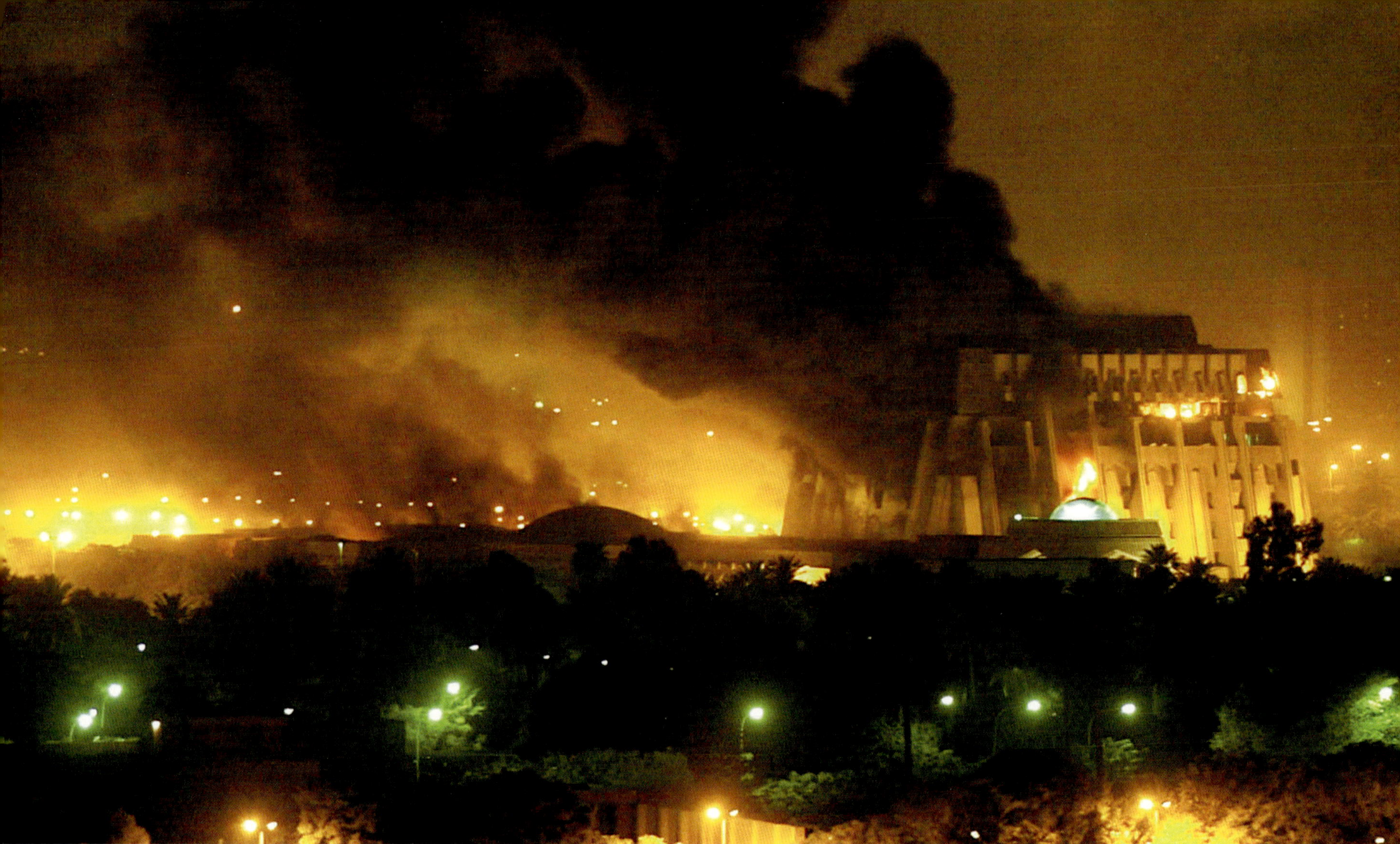

21 March 2003, BAGHDAD, IRAQ

An explosion rocks the Iraqi capital during a second night of air strikes in which U.S.-led forces unleashed a devastating blitz, triggering giant fireballs and deafening explosions and sending huge mushroom clouds above the city centre. Missiles slammed into the main palace complex of President Saddam Hussein on the bank of the Tigris River and into government buildings. Goran Tomasevic

6 November 2003, BAQUBA, IRAQ

Opposite above A U.S. soldier directs his light at an elderly Iraqi man resting in bed during a night raid in Baquba in search of members of a suspected terrorist cell planning attacks on coalition forces. Damir Sagolj

29 September 2003, TIKRIT, IRAQ

Opposite below A U.S. soldier and Iraqi policeman search a room as an Iraqi child sleeps on the bed during a joint raid in Saddam Hussein's hometown of Tikrit, about 180 km (110 miles) northwest of Baghdad, in an effort to capture Saddam loyalists. Arko Datta

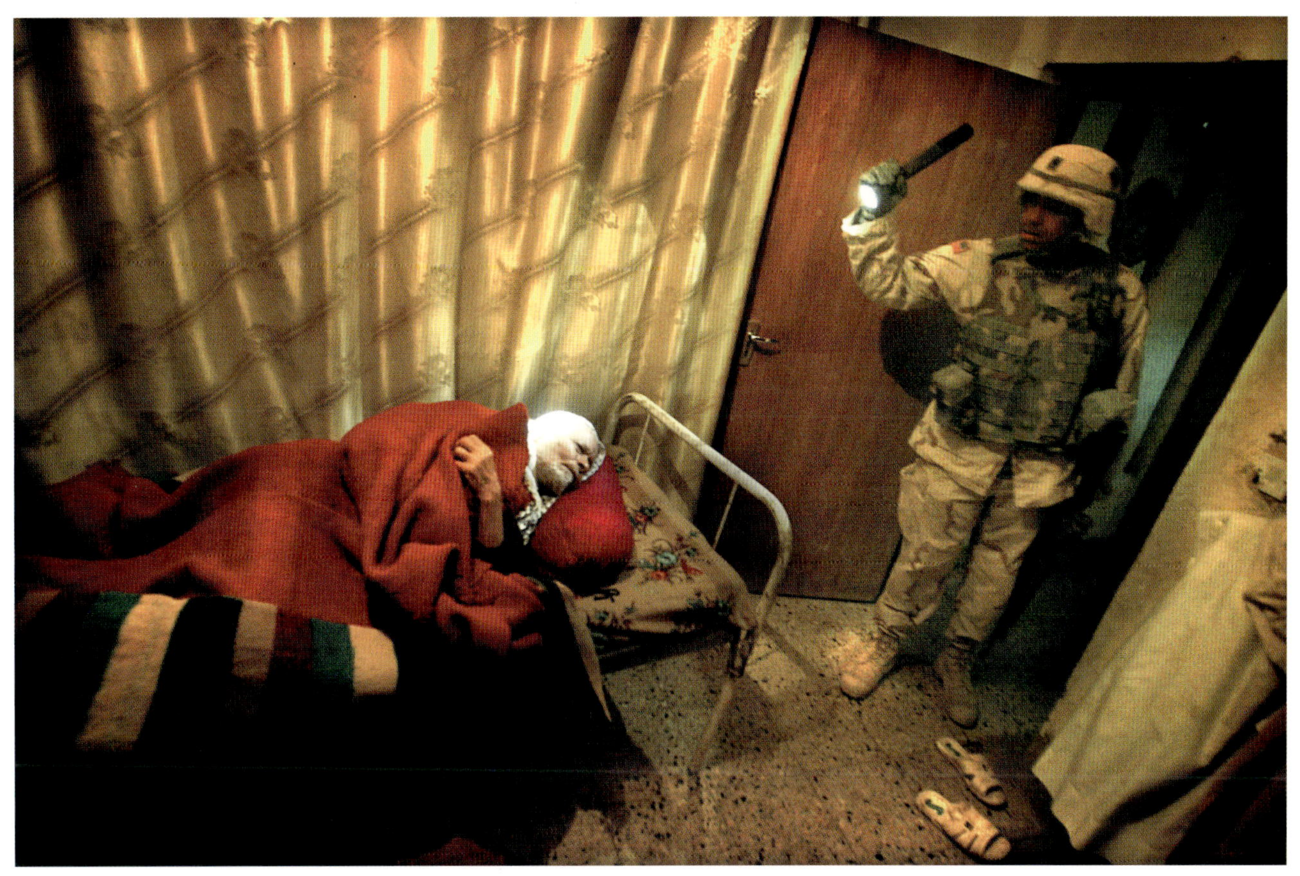

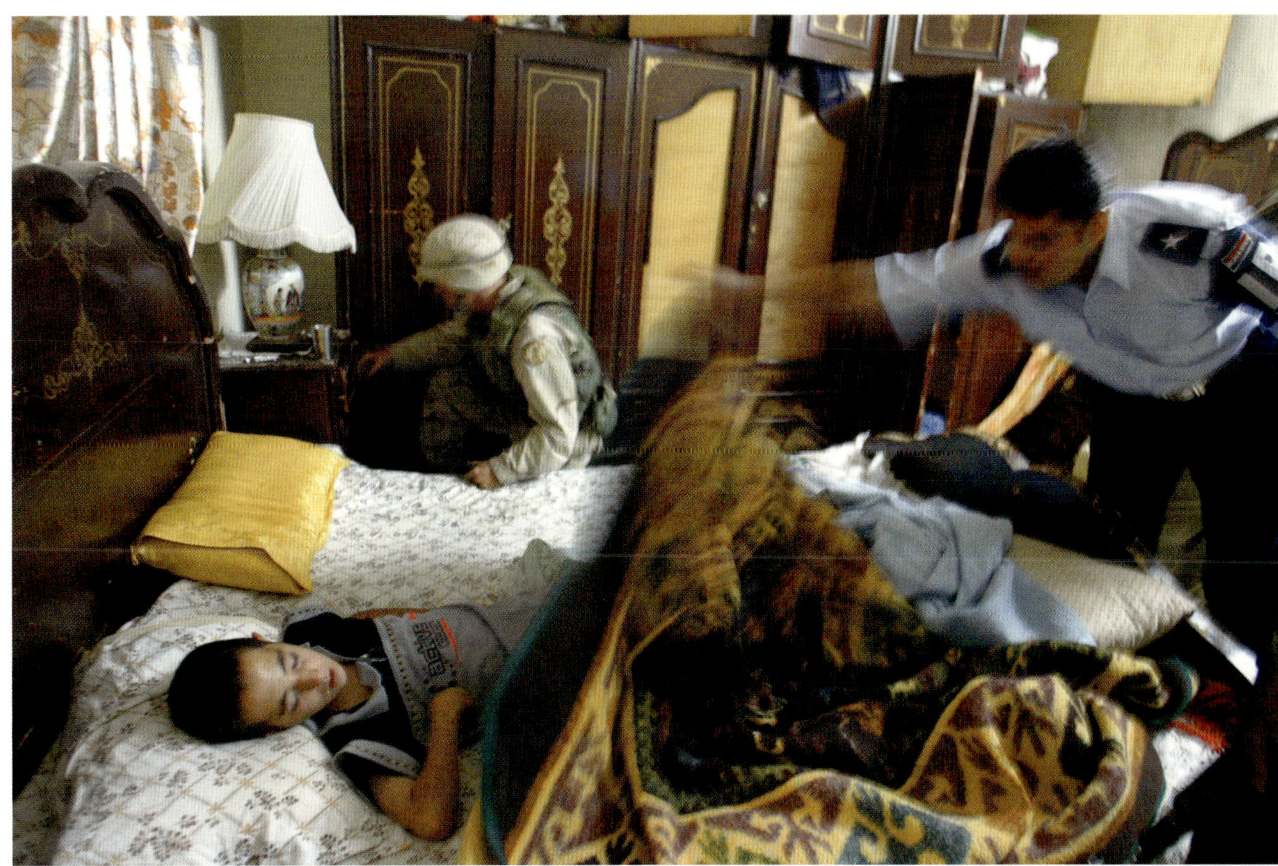

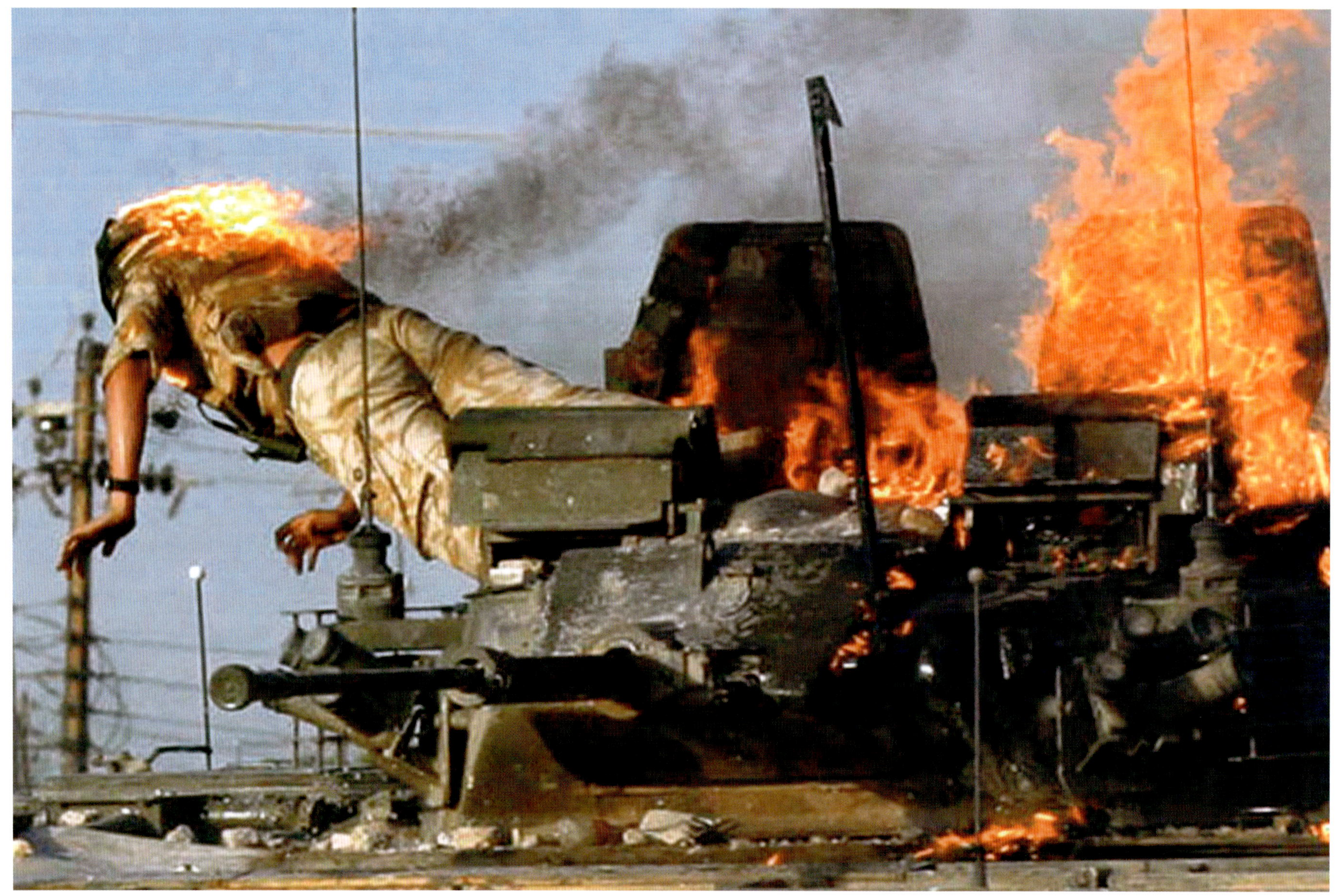

19 September 2005, BASRA, IRAQ

British soldier Sergeant George Long leaps from a burning tank that was attacked by angry crowds with petrol bombs and rocks in Basra after Iraqi authorities said they had detained two British undercover soldiers for firing on police. Long escaped with minor injuries, but inside the burning tank, 19-year-old Private Karl Hinett was severely injured, suffering 37 percent burns to his face and body.
Atef Hassan

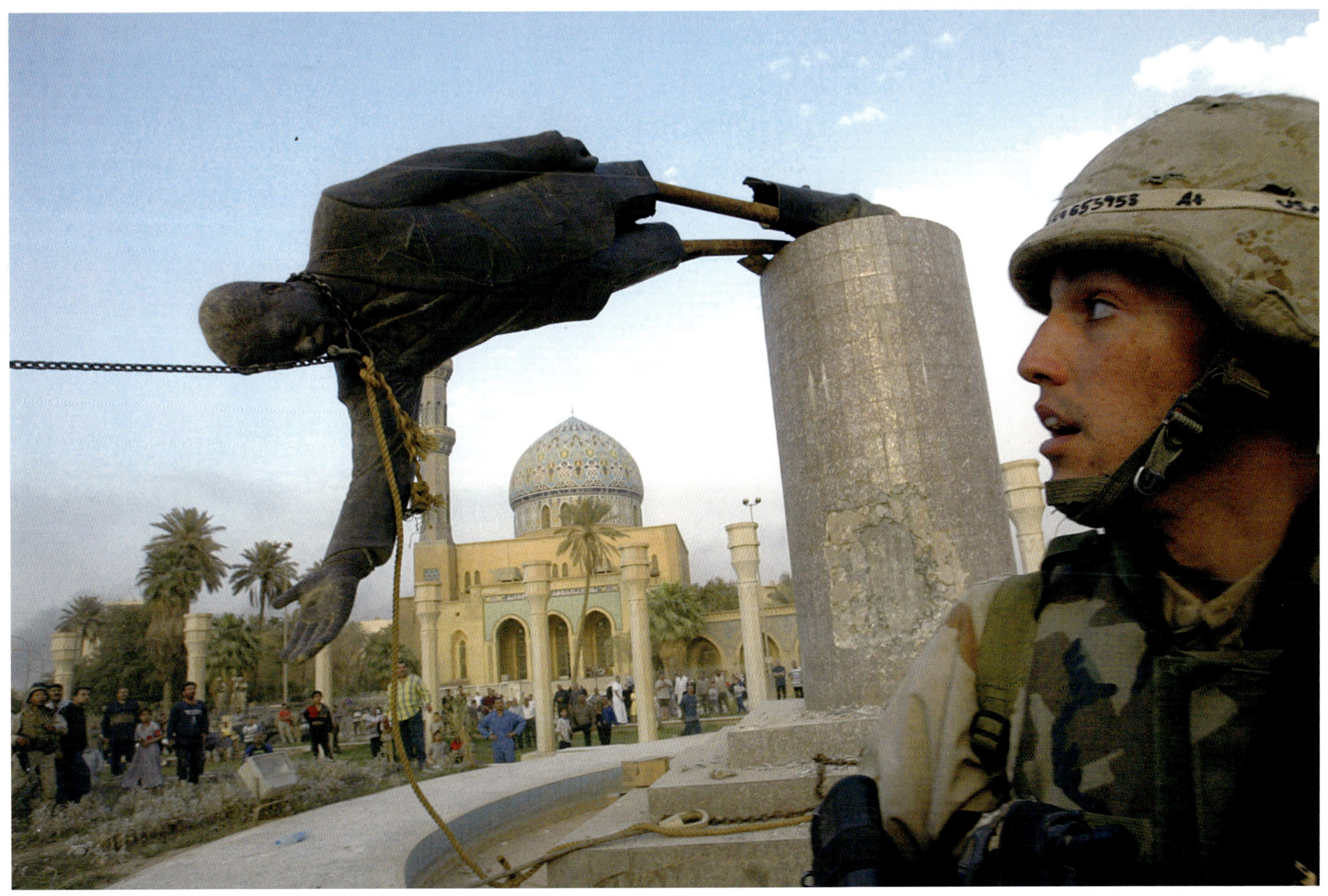

9 April 2003, BAGHDAD, IRAQ

A U.S. soldier watches as a statue of Iraq's President Saddam Hussein is toppled in a highly symbolic moment in central Baghdad on the day that U.S. forces swept into the capital and Saddam's 24-year rule crumbled. Goran Tomasevic

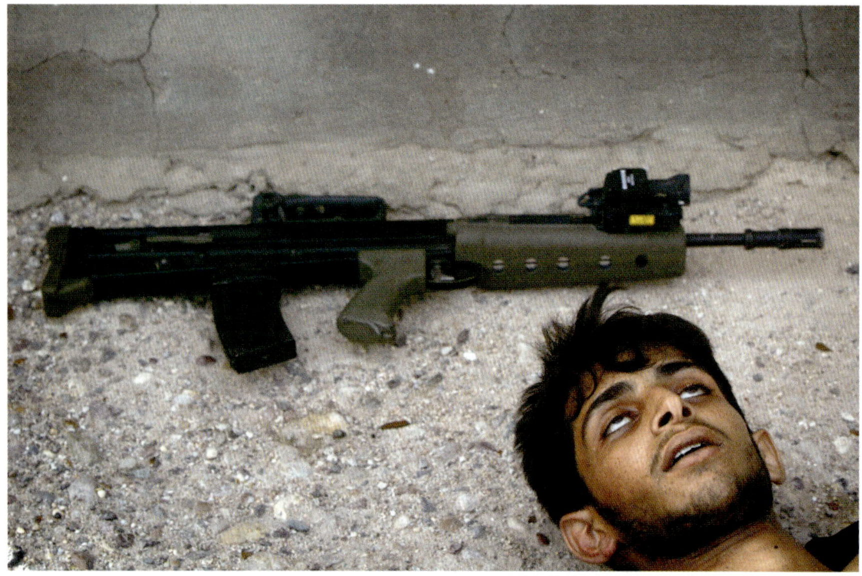

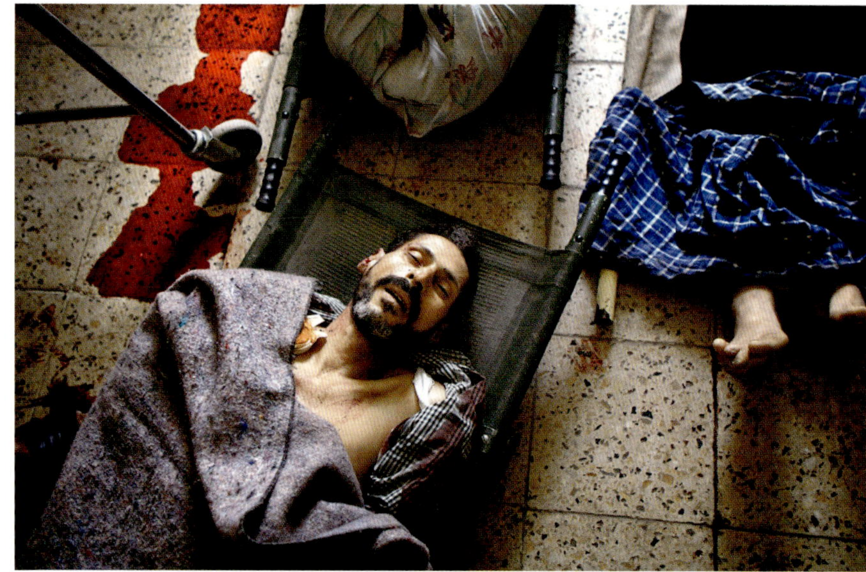

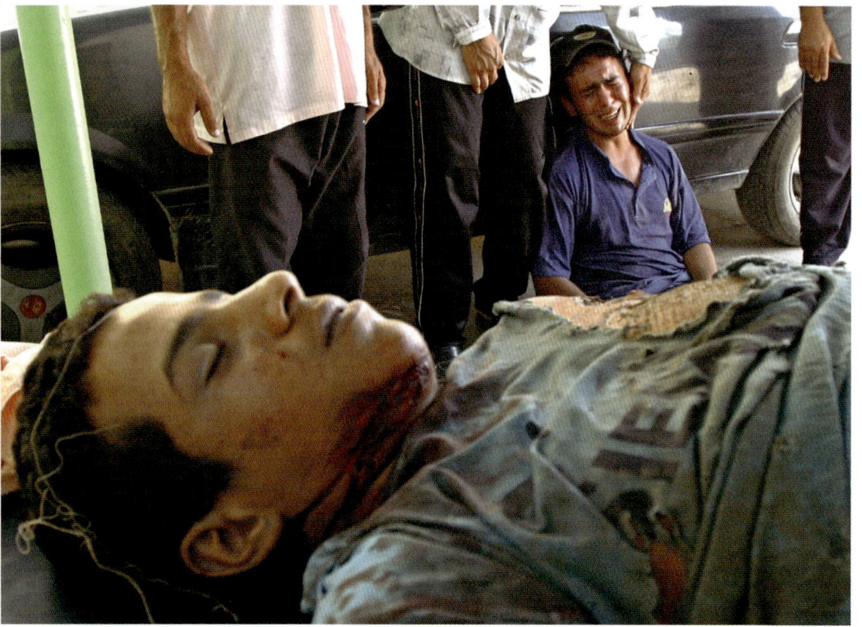

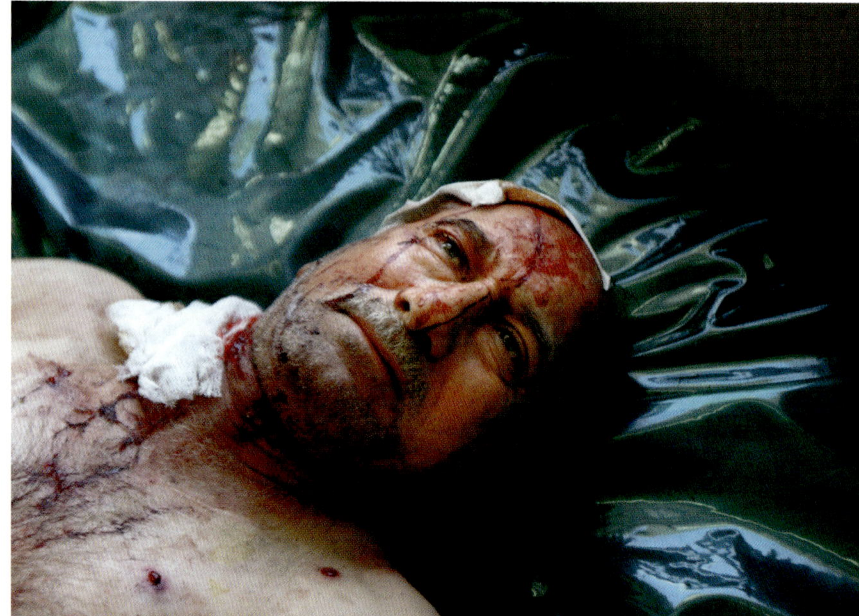

20 May 2003, BASRA, IRAQ

An Iraqi gunman who was shot by coalition soldiers after he threatened a joint police patrol with a rocket launcher is treated by British military policemen in the Hayaniya neighbourhood of Basra. Damir Sagolj

7 September 2004, BAGHDAD, IRAQ

An Iraqi boy cries next to the body of his dead brother Mudhafar Abdul Jabaar, 20, at the hospital in Baghdad's district of Sadr City, following clashes between the U.S. army and Iraqi Shi'ite militia. Namir Noor-Eldeen

9 May 2004, BAGHDAD, IRAQ

Bodies of Iraqis killed in an explosion at a busy market in the Bayaa neighbourhood of Baghdad lie inside a hospital morgue. At least seven people, including three policemen, were killed and 13 others wounded in the incident. Damir Sagolj

4 May 2005, BAGHDAD, IRAQ

An injured Iraqi man lies in hospital after a roadside bomb in Baghdad. Ali Jasim

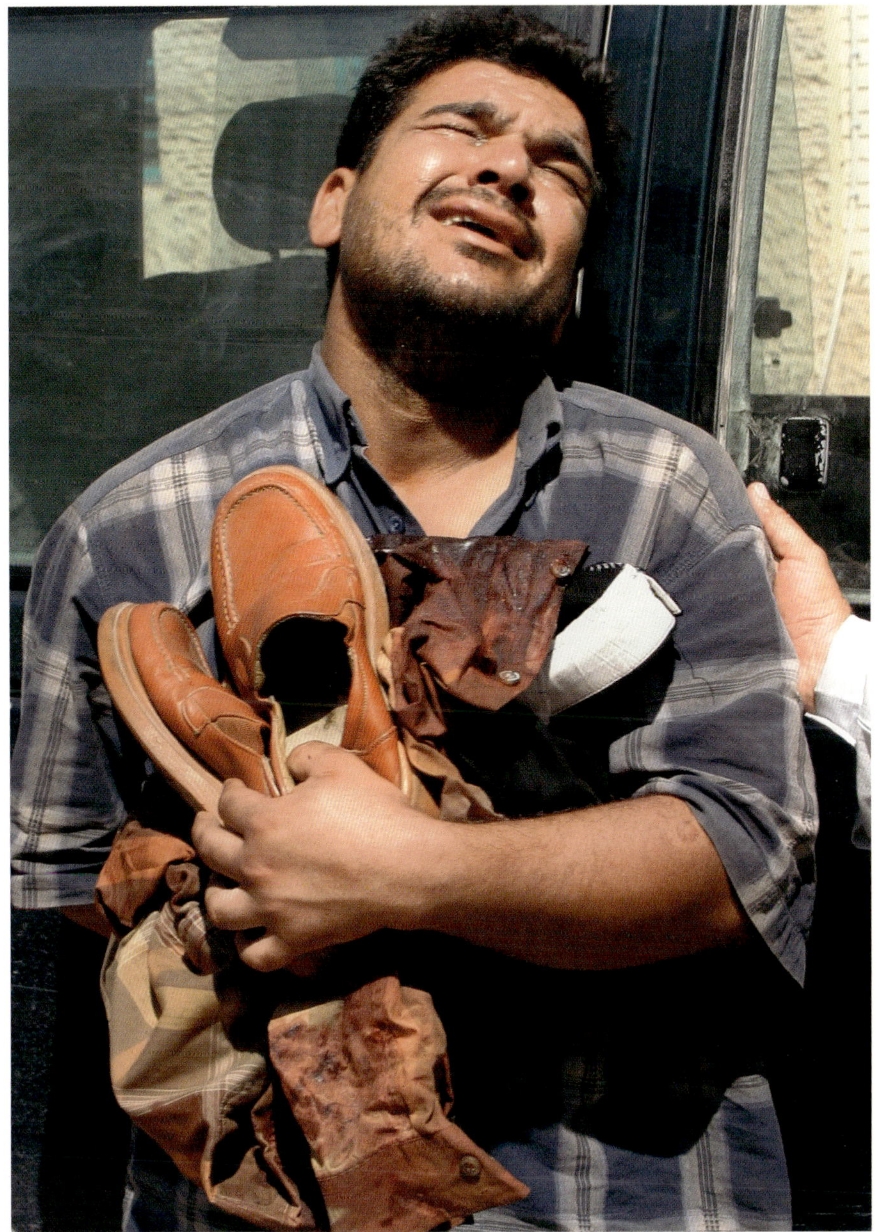

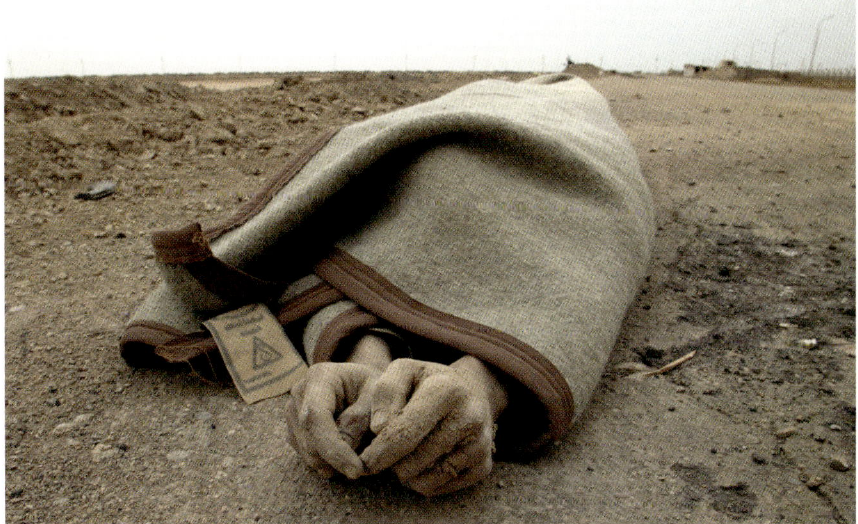

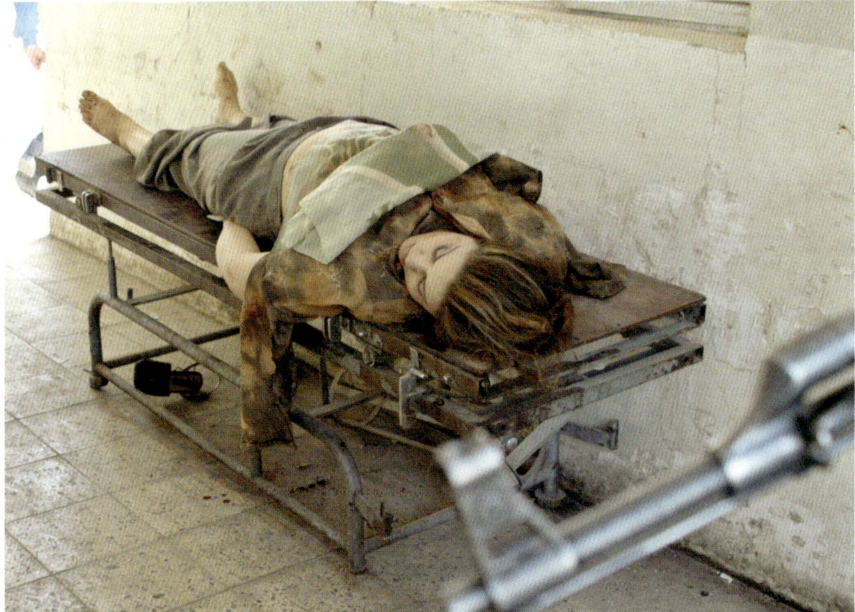

14 September 2005, BAGHDAD, IRAQ

A man clutches the bloodied clothes and shoes of a relative who was killed in a suicide car bombing in a residential part of Baghdad. Kareem Raheem

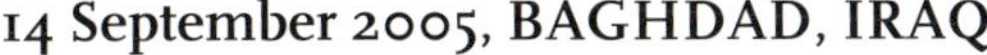

22 March 2003, AL-FAW PENINSULA, IRAQ

The body of an Iraqi soldier lies wrapped in a blanket close to his trench position following an assault by British forces on the al-Faw Peninsula in southern Iraq. Stephen Hird

23 June 2004, BAGHDAD, IRAQ

An Iraqi security officer stands guard near the body of a newlywed woman. Qais Saad Abbas was driving his new bride to work in Baghdad when a roadside bomb blew their car across the road, killing her and a boy nearby. Ali Jasim

15 October 2005, BAQUBA, IRAQ

An Iraqi man suspected of having explosives in his car is held after being arrested by the U.S. army near Baquba on the day that Iraqis went to the polls in an historic referendum to decide on a post-Saddam Hussein constitution. Intense security was in force, including a ban on all traffic in Baghdad, where voters went on foot to the city's polling stations. Jorge Silva

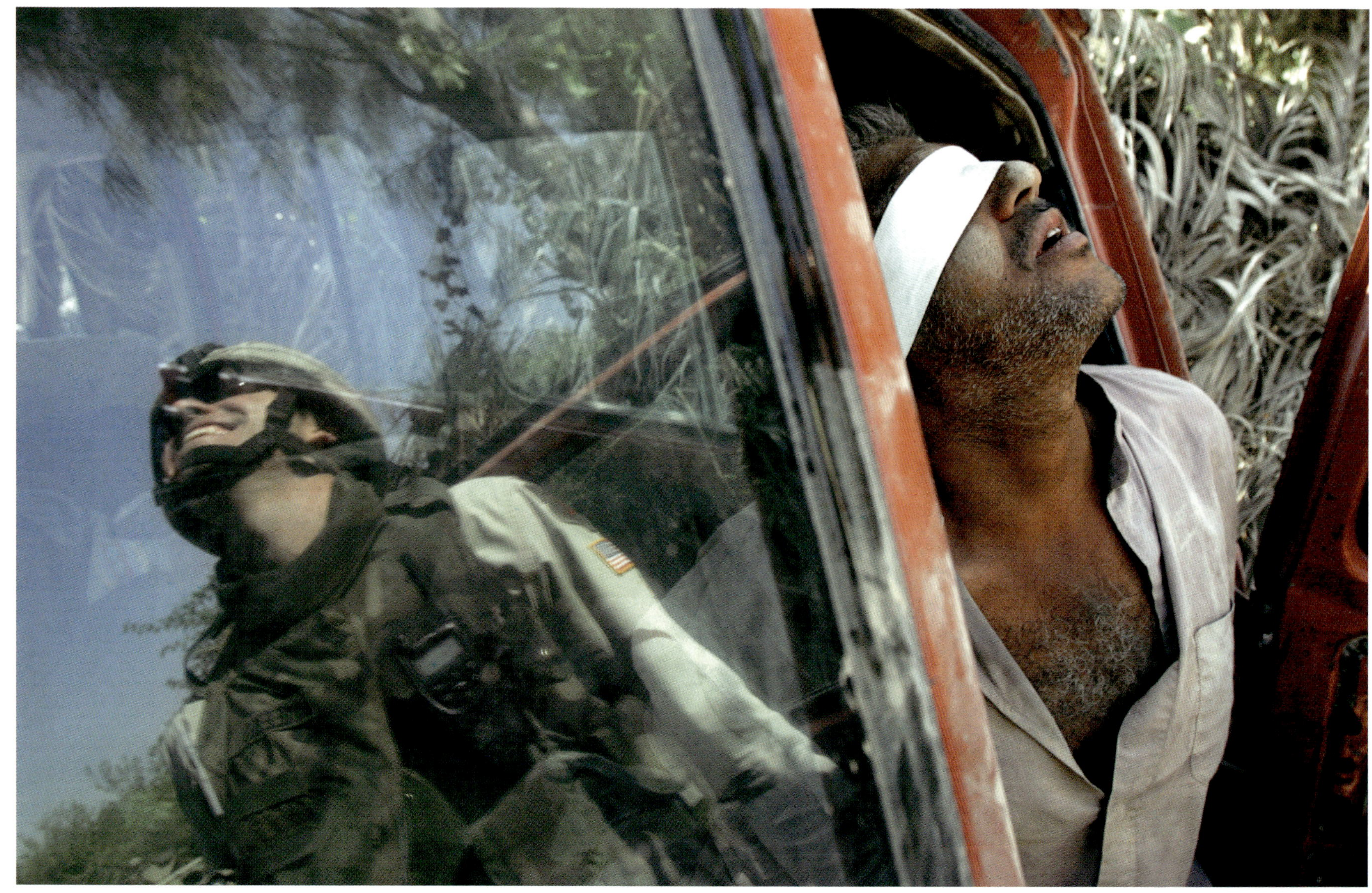

10 September 2003, TIKRIT, IRAQ

A U.S. soldier stands guard over detained Iraqis caught during an early morning raid in Tikrit. Arms and ammunition, communication devices and explosives were seized. Arko Datta

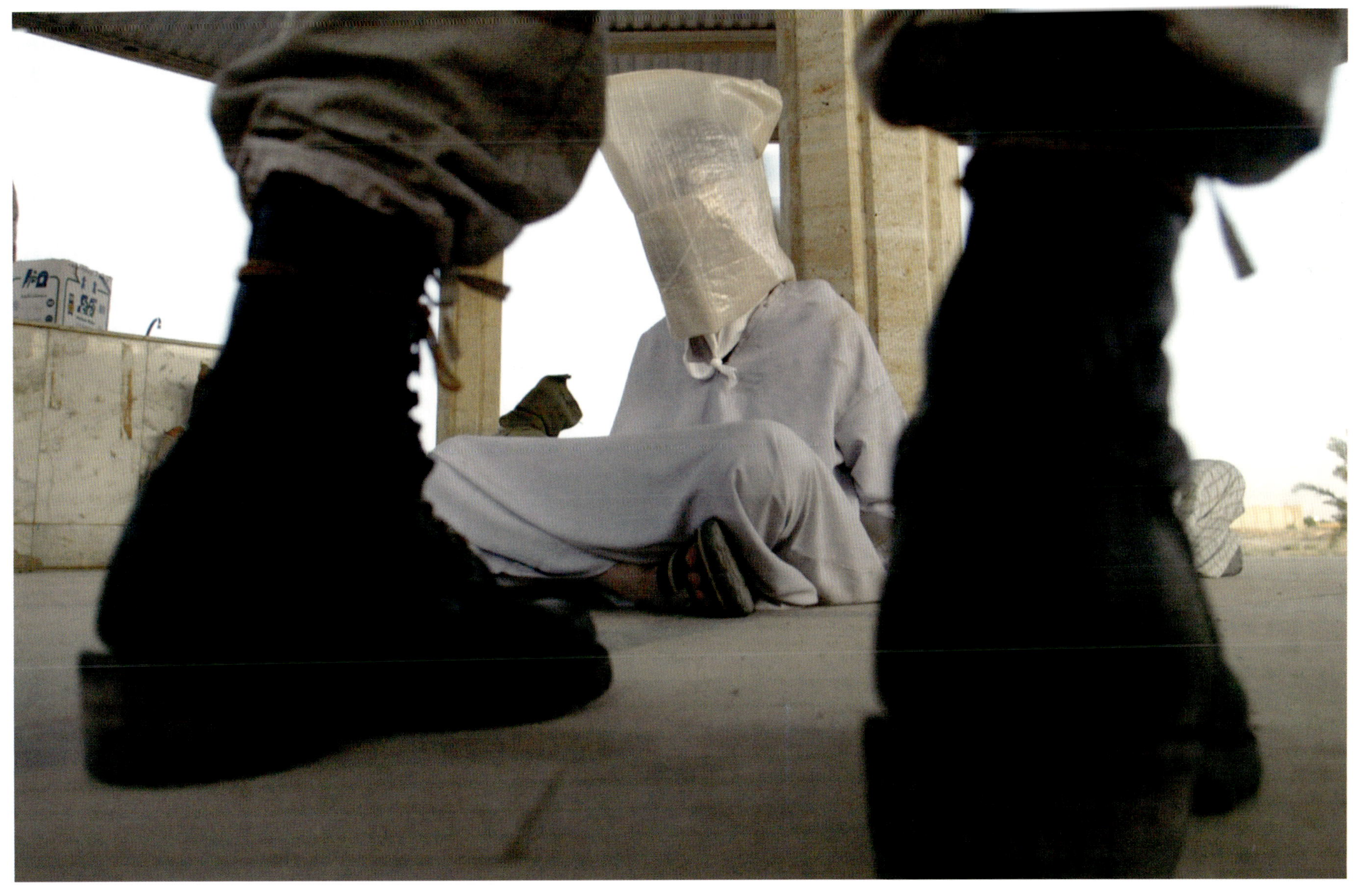

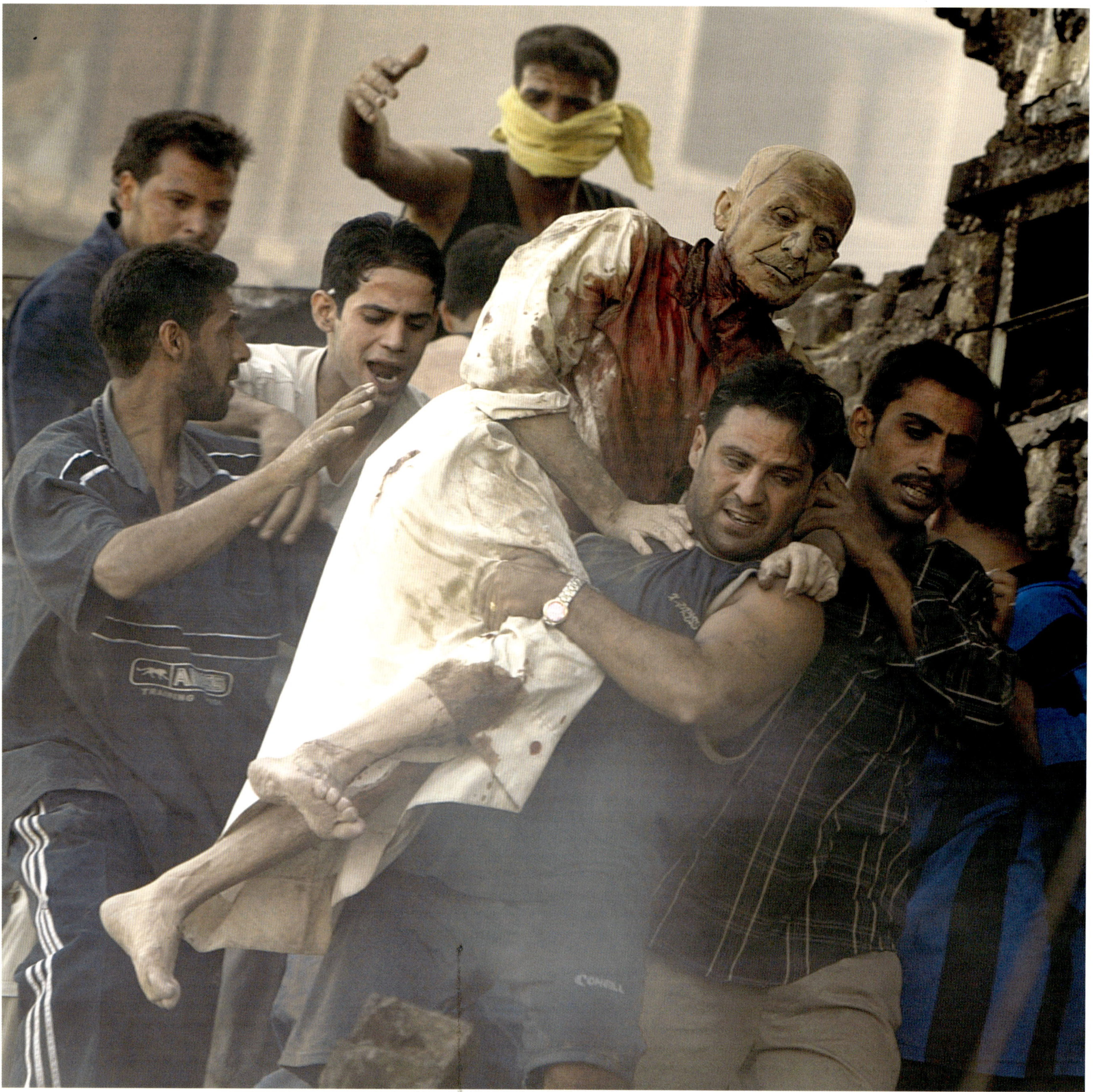

14 June 2004, BAGHDAD, IRAQ

Opposite Rescuers carry a wounded man to safety after a suicide car bomber blew himself up on a busy Baghdad street as a convoy of foreigners in civilian cars drove past, partly demolishing a nearby building. Thirteen people were killed in the incident, including five foreign contractors. Faleh Kheiber

26 June 2005, BAGHDAD, IRAQ

An Iraqi boy picks up a blood-soaked cushion from the floor of a barber's shop in a Shi'ite district of Baghdad after it was attacked by gunmen who then placed explosives in the shop and blew it up before making their escape. Three people were killed – the barber, a male customer and a nine-year-old boy. Ali Jasim

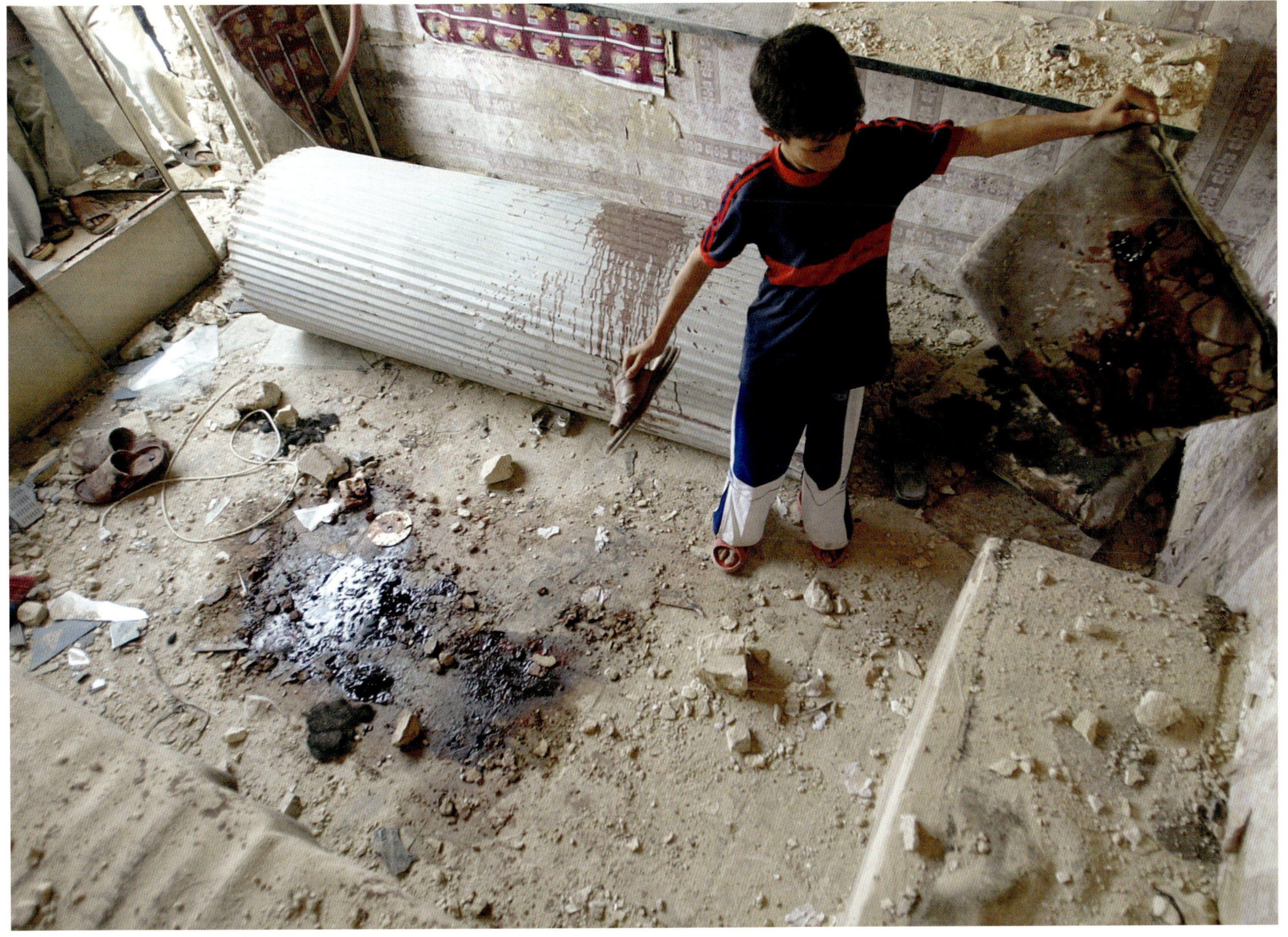

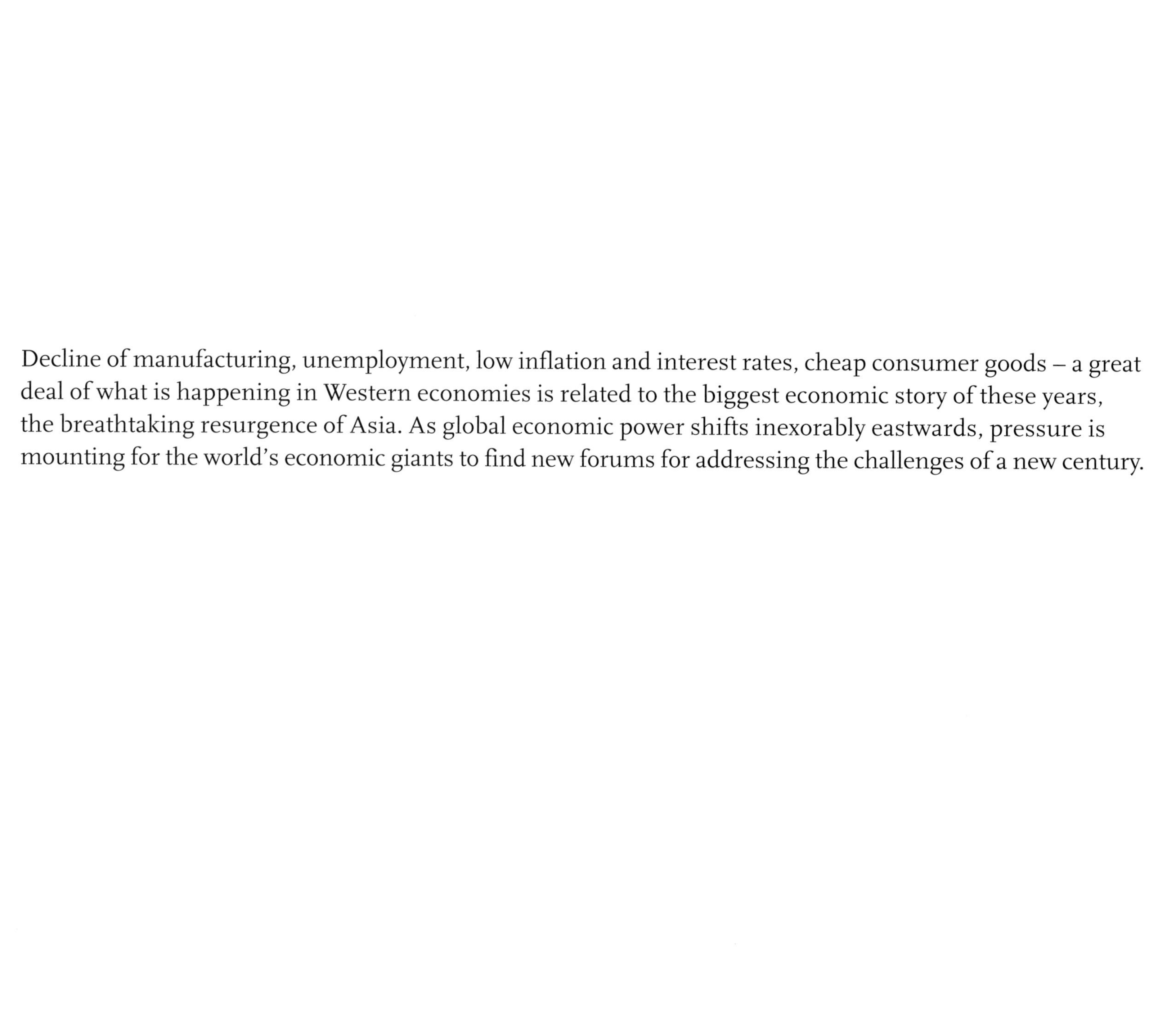

Decline of manufacturing, unemployment, low inflation and interest rates, cheap consumer goods – a great deal of what is happening in Western economies is related to the biggest economic story of these years, the breathtaking resurgence of Asia. As global economic power shifts inexorably eastwards, pressure is mounting for the world's economic giants to find new forums for addressing the challenges of a new century.

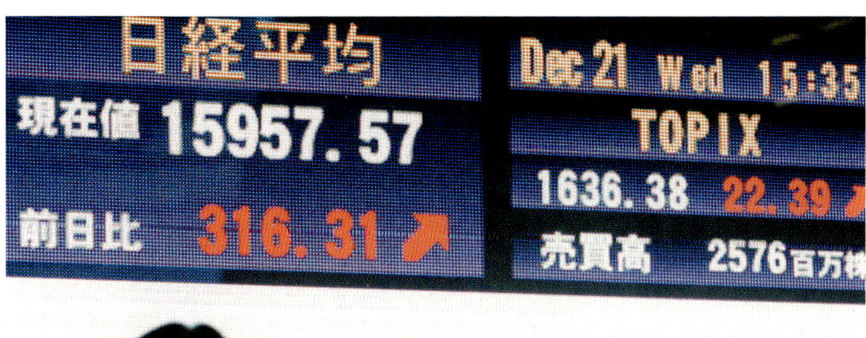

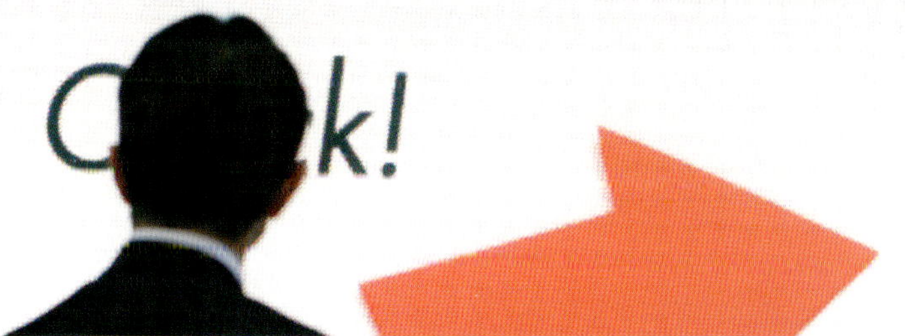

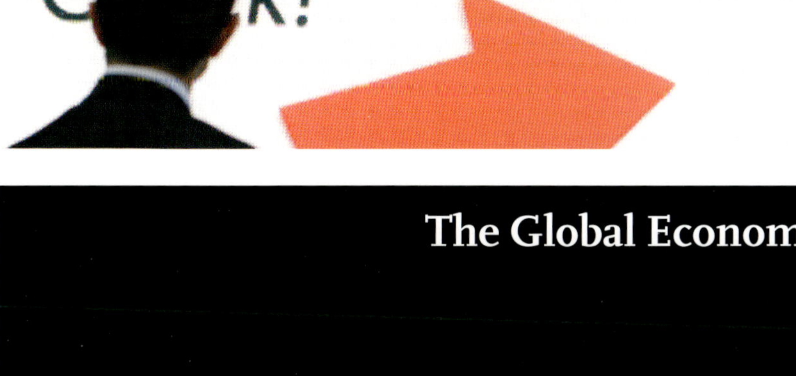

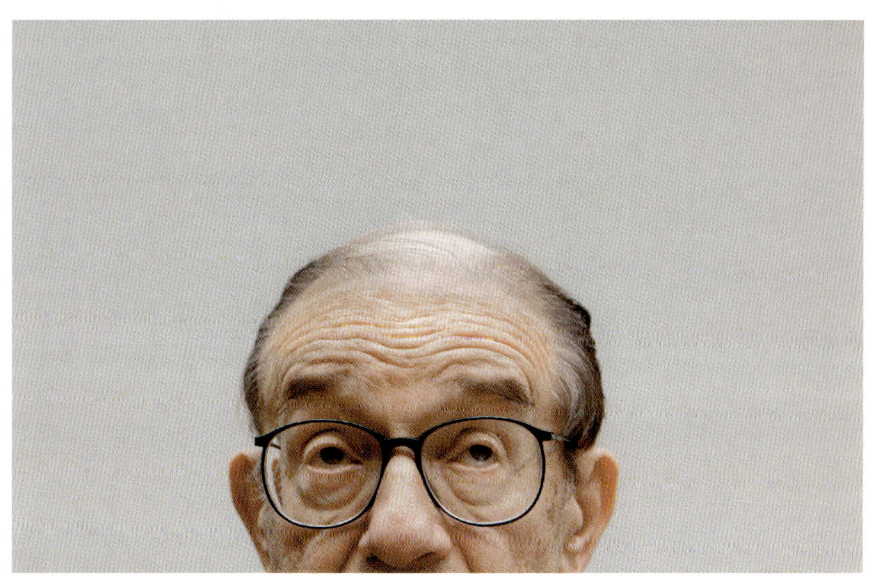

The Global Economy

Money / Trade / Growth / Opportunity
Wealth / Poverty / Energy / Resources
Manufacturing / Globalization / Protest

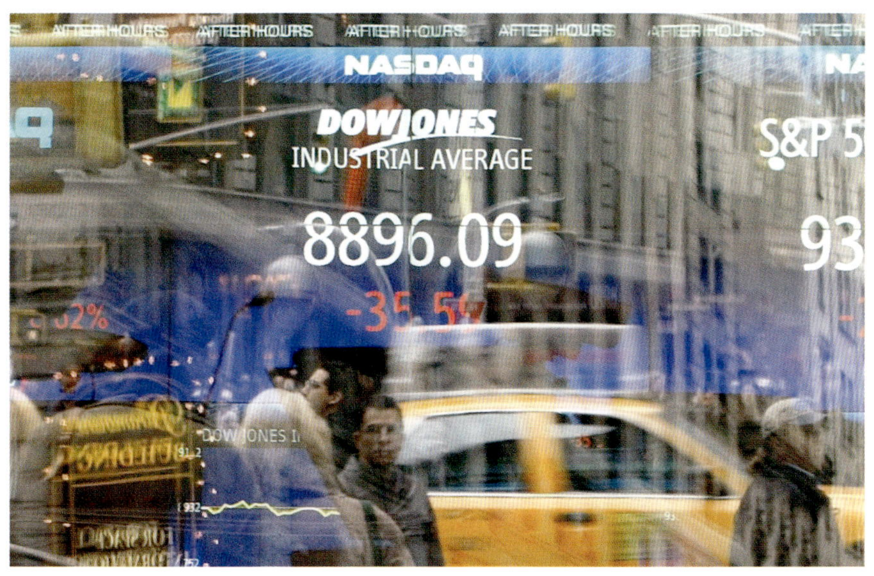

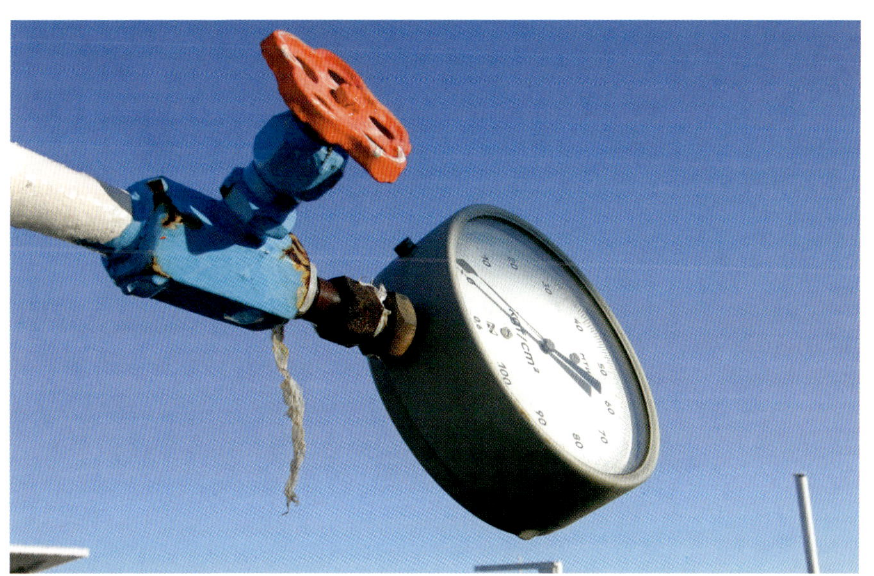

The Global Economy

Just five years into a new century, the global economy that powered giddily to the end of the last millennium has already morphed in shape and size into something barely recognizable.

For many living in North America or Europe, day-to-day life may have undergone few changes beyond those wrought by pervasive new technologies like flat-screen televisions or portable digital music players. But among the governments, businesses and households of the industrialized world, there is a distinct sense of unease that was not present as the champagne corks popped and Wall Street spiralled ever higher at the end of 1999.

A series of severe shocks over the ensuing five years has played a significant role in deflating the euphoric Western mood. The Internet-driven stock market bubble of the 1990s finally burst in 2000; mammoth corporate collapses such as Enron and WorldCom came in its wake; the September 11, 2001, attacks on the United States redrew the geopolitical map; two subsequent U.S.-led wars in Afghanistan and Iraq shrouded business planning and investment in uncertainty; and a doubling of crude oil prices in just two years squeezed consumer spending and company bottom lines the world over.

Yet despite a shallow and brief U.S. recession late in 2002, world economic growth boomed again over the next three years – registering the fastest expansion in three decades in 2004. Many now argue that the serial shocks of the first five years of the new millennium were merely distractions from more far-reaching changes to how the world works. Globalization continued apace during this period and even accelerated, despite the brickbats. In the process, the centre of world economic power shifted East. The anxiety this has created in the wealthiest Western nations stands in stark contrast to a new-found optimism and confidence in Asia – which is all the more remarkable for coming less than a decade after financial crises tore through the region's economies and seemed to threaten decades of long and painful recovery. Instead, fired by communist China's widening embrace of market economics and international trade, and the opening up of equally populous, tech-savvy India, Asia is rising again, and its trump card is an abundance of people.

The scale and origin of Asia's resurgence this century so far is breathtaking. By 2004, China was already the second-largest economy in the world behind the United States, using the International Monetary Fund's favoured method of ranking world economies – adjusting for differing prices and currency rates. If its annual growth rates of up to 10 percent over the first five years of the century were to continue for another decade, China's economy could balloon until it is 90 percent of the United States and six times the size of Germany in 2015. By the same measure, India's economy would be bigger than Japan's.

While those numbers are hotly debated, the population of these two countries is not in question – both now have more than a billion inhabitants and together make up one-third of humanity. And there's the rub for the world economy at large. The integration of China and India, catalysed by new technologies linking businesses, workers and consumers around the globe like never before, has effectively expanded the global labour force by hundreds of millions of workers.

The pool of new workers in everything from manufacturing to call centres to software design had already started to swell with the fall of the Berlin Wall in the early 1990s. By the end of the decade, some 250 million workers from the former Soviet bloc of eastern Europe and Russia – many highly educated – were drawn for the first time into the breakneck international competition that defines modern capitalism. But even that dramatic expansion has been dwarfed over the past decade by the rise of the world's two most populous countries, which have together brought up to a billion employees into the world economy. Millions of them are highly skilled and well-versed in science, engineering and computing.

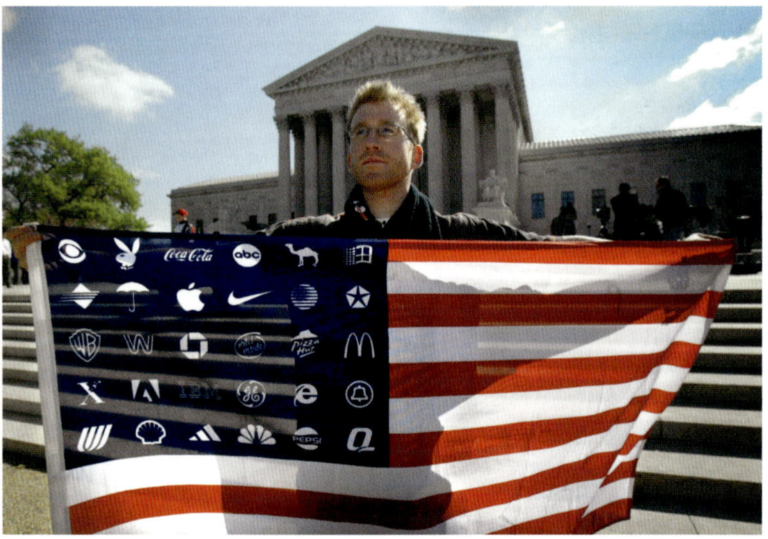

Anti-globalization protester Peter Maybarduk holds up a United States flag that substitutes corporate logos for the stars of the states outside the Supreme Court in Washington, DC. 23 April 2003, Kevin Lamarque.

As signs of this seismic event first registered, many in the West were looking elsewhere. The United States was coming to terms with the twin traumas of September 11 and its stock market crash, while 12 of the 15 countries of the European Union gazed inwards as they rolled out the notes and coins of a new single euro currency to some 300 million citizens – itself one of the biggest macroeconomic projects in recent history. Neither region seemed prepared for what was happening on the other side of the world.

The new workers who have emerged from behind the iron curtain and from the teeming cities and underused farms of China and India have been folded rapidly into the global marketplace, helped by two parallel developments. The first has a lot to do with those flat-screen TVs and digital gizmos. The revolutionary telecommunications and Internet technologies of the 1990s continued to bind the world ever closer despite the plummeting stock values of some of the leading companies. The Wall Street dot-com collapse did little to slow the spread and usage of a vast new infrastructure of Internet, cable and satellite links.

'Poverty is not socialism. To be rich is glorious.'

Former Chinese leader Deng Xiaoping

A second factor was growing sophistication of transnational corporations in linking diverse assembly lines and supply chains across dozens of countries. This accelerated the 'outsourcing' or 'offshoring' of labour-intensive parts of their operations from more costly plants in the developed nations to countries with cheaper labour costs.

The new workers of China, India and elsewhere – for now at least – are willing to toil for small fractions of the salaries demanded by comparable U.S. or European staff, whose ageing societies and generous healthcare and pension schemes make them even more relatively expensive to hire in the notional global labour force. The pension and healthcare benefits, limited working hours and strict employment rights that Western Europe's workers fought for decades to secure now appear unbearable for many domestic and international companies competing with low-cost imports and a new-found ability to tap cheaper workforces around the globe.

This new army of low-wage workers has, by providing cheaper staffing alternatives for Western multinationals and by making domestic Chinese or Indian or Vietnamese exporters super-competitive in liberalized world markets, put downward pressure on labour costs everywhere and flooded the world with cheap goods.

One result has been to underscore chronically high unemployment rates in Western Europe – joblessness that has both reflected and reinforced years of sub-par growth in Germany and elsewhere, and triggered social unrest in France. Frustration at the seemingly chronic economic malaise has bred widespread mistrust of further European integration since the EU's 2004 eastward expansion, which boosted the number of member states from 15 to 25. In the United States, too, employment gains have not matched those of previous periods of such rapid growth, and manufacturing jobs continue to decline as old industries fall by the wayside.

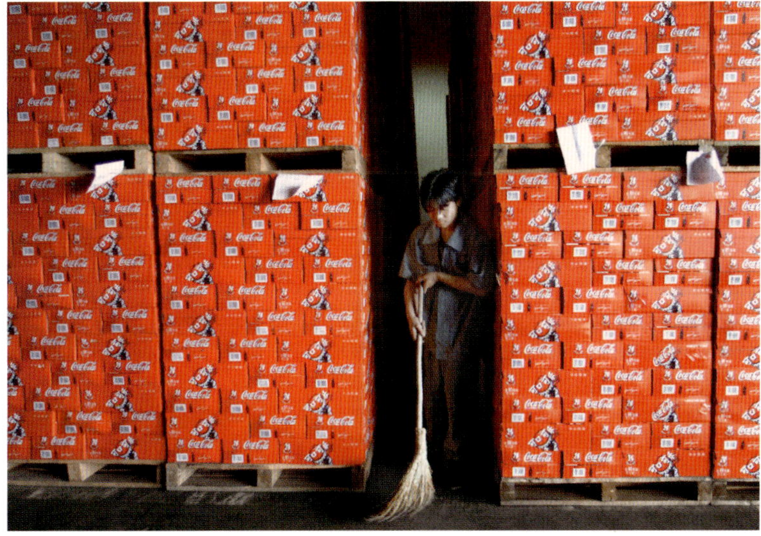

A Chinese worker sweeps the floor of a Coca-Cola warehouse in Beijing as the factory rolls out its product 24 hours a day. This Coca-Cola factory was one of the first joint ventures established in the early 1980s at the beginning of China's economic reforms. 6 July 2000, Guang Niu.

The flipside of low-cost global manufacturing has been extraordinarily and persistently low inflation. This has both increased the amount consumers in the West can buy and has allowed inflation-fighting central banks around the world to keep borrowing costs historically low for much of the past five years. The added fillip of low interest rates has been synchronized house price booms – most obviously in English-speaking countries such as the United States, Britain and Australia but also in Spain and France.

Surging exports of cheaper goods from Asia have been facilitated by the expansion of multilateral free-trade agreements and by membership of the World Trade Organization, which China joined in 2002. This has reduced tariffs, import quotas and other barriers to overseas markets.

At the same time, China and other Asian countries have bought hundreds of billions of U.S. dollars on the currency markets in recent years to prevent a falling dollar from making their exports more expensive in the United States. Much of what they have accumulated has been banked back in U.S. government bonds, effectively lowering long-term borrowing costs for the U.S. Treasury and for Americans who buy houses with loans linked to those long-term rates. This has further fuelled the house-price boom.

'This dependence on foreign oil is a matter of national security.'

U.S. President George W. Bush

The removal of restrictions on the import of Chinese textiles in 2005 rapidly triggered a political backlash in the United States and European Union as super-cheap clothes flooded Western markets and undercut domestic producers. The issue has become a touchstone for a growing chorus of protectionist voices from politicians, business and labour unions in the West. But textiles, toys and plastic goods are not the only exports from the new economic giants. Increasingly, cars, machinery and high-tech items such as computers and software are streaming from the East, and Western companies are pouring new investment into China and other low-cost countries to develop them. The trend toward locating call-centres, data hubs and consultancies in 'new economy' havens such as India's Bangalore has seen white-collar office work drift East too.

The anxiety for Western workers is obvious. But for many in Asia, the boom has helped lift millions out of poverty and raised hopes of a more prosperous future for thousands of well-educated youths who in previous generations would have faced lifelong struggle or emigration to Europe or North America.

Asia's new boom has also levied a tax on the world economy. China's brisk industrial growth and the potential for India to follow close behind mean a voracious appetite in those two nations for imported oil and other raw materials not plentiful at home. The upshot has been a doubling of world crude oil prices since the start of the decade and skyrocketing prices of other commodities such as industrial metals.

This has proved a windfall for poorer oil- and commodity-producing countries such as Russia and some Latin American nations and has led to a further transfer of wealth from the relatively rich consumers of the United States, Europe and Japan to resource-rich parts of the developing world.

But the scramble for the earth's increasingly scarce natural resources has become intense. The environmental implications are enormous as the emerging economic giants claim the right to industrialize at the same speed as the Western world did in the previous centuries. They demand that right without being fettered by new multilateral regulations and pollution standards that many in the West now feel are essential to control climate change and global warming.

Even so, there is a great deal of potential in a world economy where – geographically at least – the substantial fruits of industry and trade may at last be shared more evenly than before. Far-sighted policy-makers in the West urge greater focus on education, skills and life-long learning as a way to cope with the new worldwide competition for jobs. The emerging powers are looking at ways to consolidate their new-found prosperity by building financial and legal institutions to protect and invest their wealth and using their economic and political muscle to influence global governance at large.

But as the process of burgeoning world growth and rebalancing sets many on the road to greater prosperity, it also threatens to leave behind those too marginalized or too powerless to take part. The plight of the poorest nations – most of them in sub-Saharan Africa – may even have deepened in recent years as the rest of the world has raced away. Racked by crushing poverty, an endless cycle of violent conflicts and a plague of AIDS destroying their people and workforces, the poorest nations have also had to shoulder the burden of servicing decades-old debts to institutions such as the IMF and the World Bank.

In a campaign that peaked in 2005, pressure groups, relief organizations, celebrities and the general public in Europe and the United States demanded action be taken to relieve debt and pursue more vigorously the United Nations so-called Millennium Development Goals to tackle the most severe child mortality, healthcare and illiteracy problems.

Britain, as the 2005 chair of the Group of Eight club of industrial powers, attempted to focus the group's attention on Africa and pushed through a worldwide agreement to cancel the multilateral debts of the poorest nations. The next step is a comprehensive trade deal which would include lowering rich countries' agricultural tariffs to allow the exporters of these countries a level playing field in overseas markets.

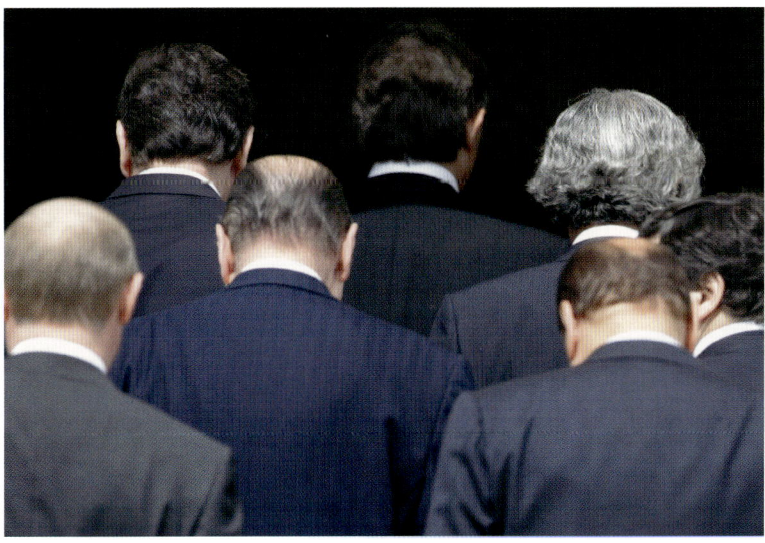

G8 leaders return to the Gleneagles Hotel following a group photo at the end of their summit in Gleneagles, Scotland. 8 July 2005, Kevin Coombs

Progress on these talks remains slow and has often teetered on the brink of unravelling entirely. But recognition of the need to do something has at least reached the top table of global economic policymaking.

As the world economy becomes more integrated and interdependent, the importance of that top table and who sits at it has become critical. Even as the economies of nation states become increasingly intertwined, they will almost certainly be forced again into stand-offs over issues such as trade imbalances and access to scarce resources. Finding consensus on how to solve some of the world's more intractable macroeconomic problems may be the most important task of the new century as businesses and workers rely more than ever on the smooth functioning of the international economy as a whole rather than the fortunes of any one region or state.

Since the mid-1970s, the closest the world has had to a global economic council has been the 'Group' of industrial powers – the number varying over the decades from five at its inception to eight now at summit gatherings. The Group of Seven forum of finance chiefs from the United States, Japan, Germany, France, Britain, Italy and Canada has remained firm as the world economy's effective steering committee, even though the addition of Russia since 1998 means the equivalent gathering of leaders is now a G8.

Over 20 years, the G7/G8 has periodically held sway over the direction of global currency markets and, as a coalition of rich nations, wields considerable power over the IMF and World Bank. Its political discussions have ranged from nuclear disarmament to Third World debt to climate change. In 2005, the G7 began inviting five emerging nations – China, India, Brazil, Russia and South Africa – to its regular gatherings and the United States has talked of a 'glide path' towards including these countries in the broader group in future. But change is slow. Even Russia's presidency of the G8 in 2006 has still not forced a formal expansion of the G7 core finance group.

Pressure for change, however, is now intense – not least because this group fails to reflect the shift of economic and financial power to the emerging giants of Asia. The G7 may accurately have represented the trans-Atlantic focus of world economic power of 20 years ago but the global economy of the twenty-first century has a distinctly trans-Pacific hue.

Michael Dolan has worked for Reuters since 1995. He started as a foreign exchange correspondent specializing in the preparations for European monetary union, and later was assigned as chief correspondent for the UK financial markets. Between 2000 and 2003, Michael was treasury news editor for Europe, the Middle East and Africa. Michael is currently economics correspondent in Washington, DC.

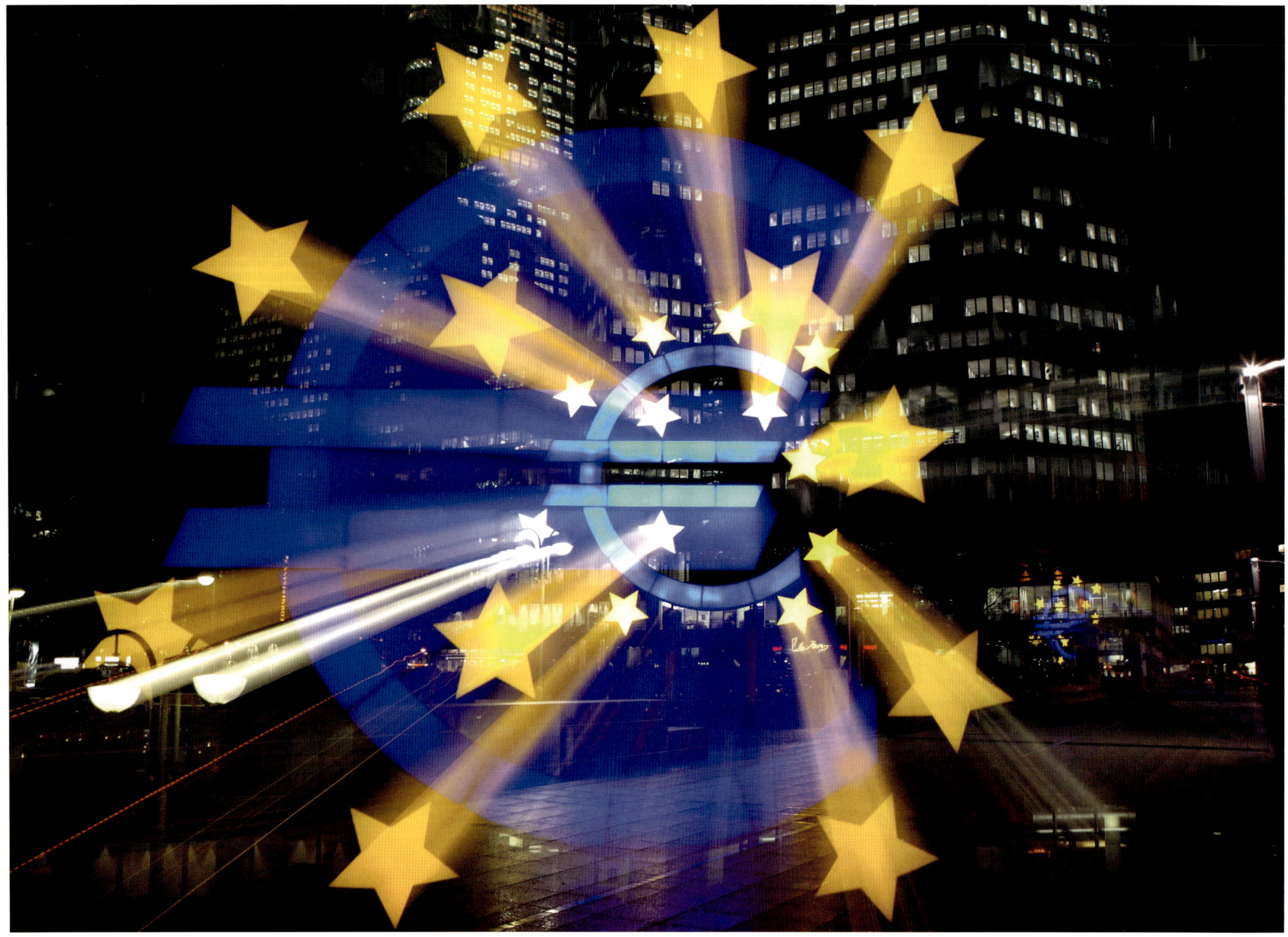

28 November 2005, FRANKFURT, GERMANY

The illuminated euro sign outside the European Central Bank's headquarters in Frankfurt. Three hundred million people in 12 countries first used the new euro notes and coins on 1 January 2002. The only EU members who chose to retain their own currencies were Sweden, Denmark and the UK. Kai Pfaffenbach

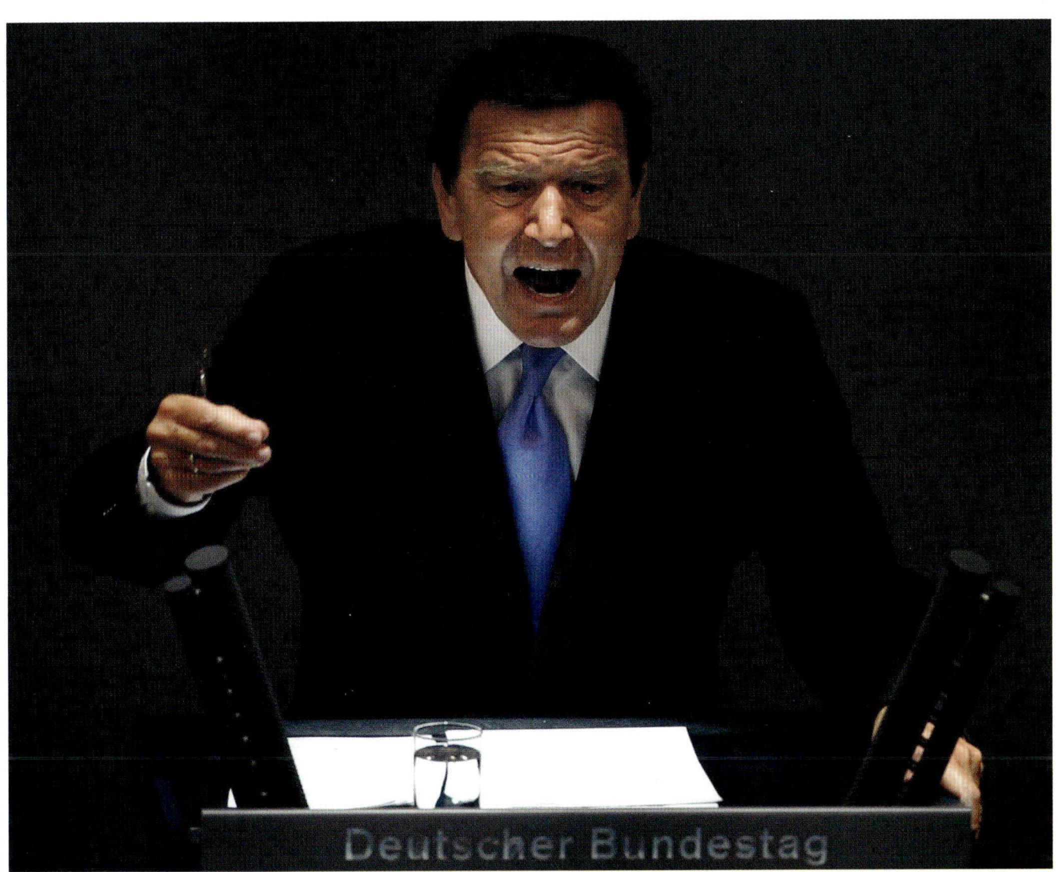

8 September 2004, BERLIN, GERMANY

Chancellor Gerhard Schröder addresses the Bundestag, the German lower house of Parliament, during a budget debate.
Kai Pfaffenbach

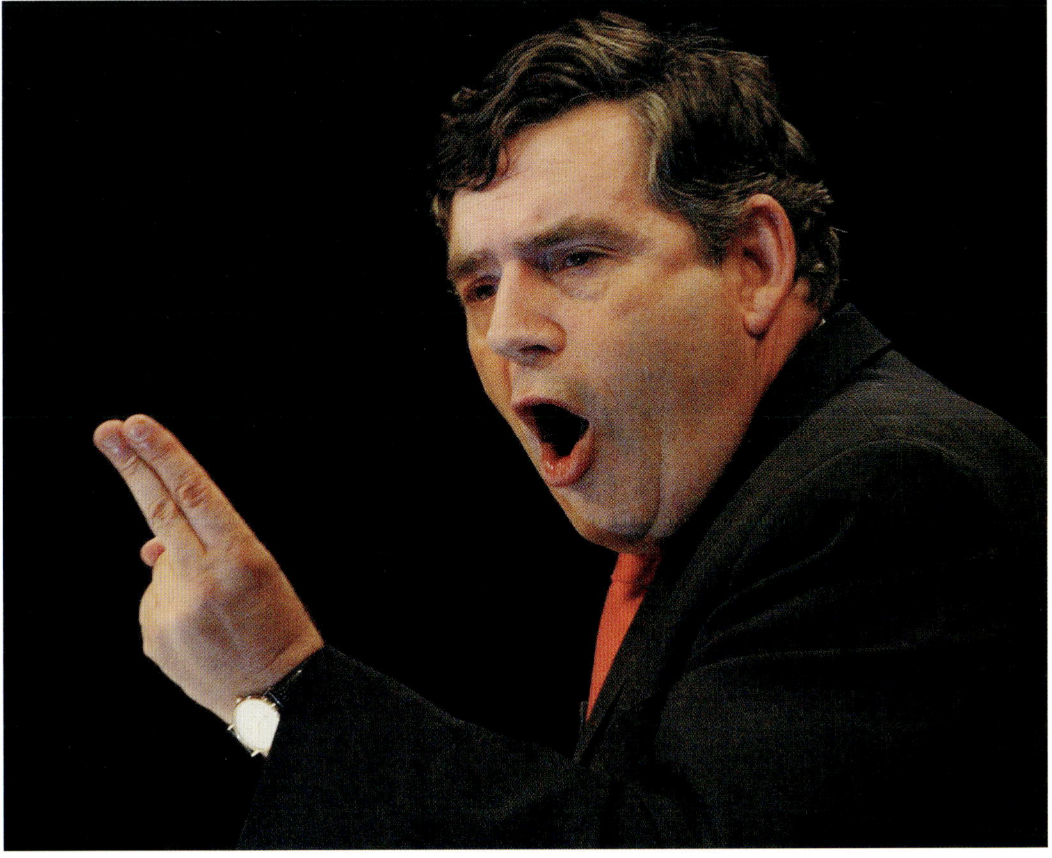

29 September 2003, BOURNEMOUTH, UNITED KINGDOM

Chancellor of the Exchequer Gordon Brown makes his keynote speech during the second day of the British Labour Party conference in Bournemouth. Toby Melville

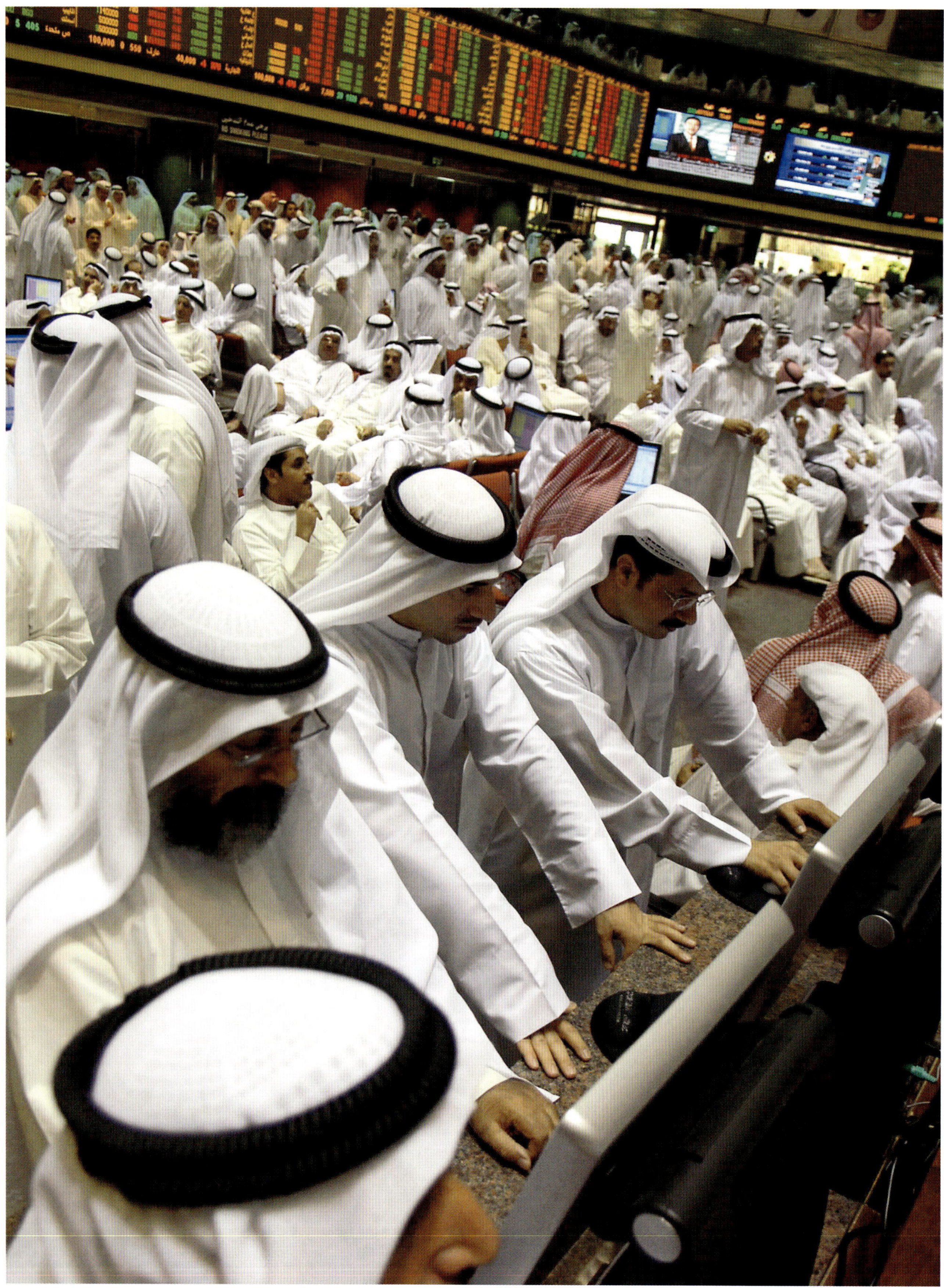

13 September 2005, KUWAIT CITY, KUWAIT

Stock traders watch computer monitors at the Kuwait Stock Exchange.

Stephanie McGehee

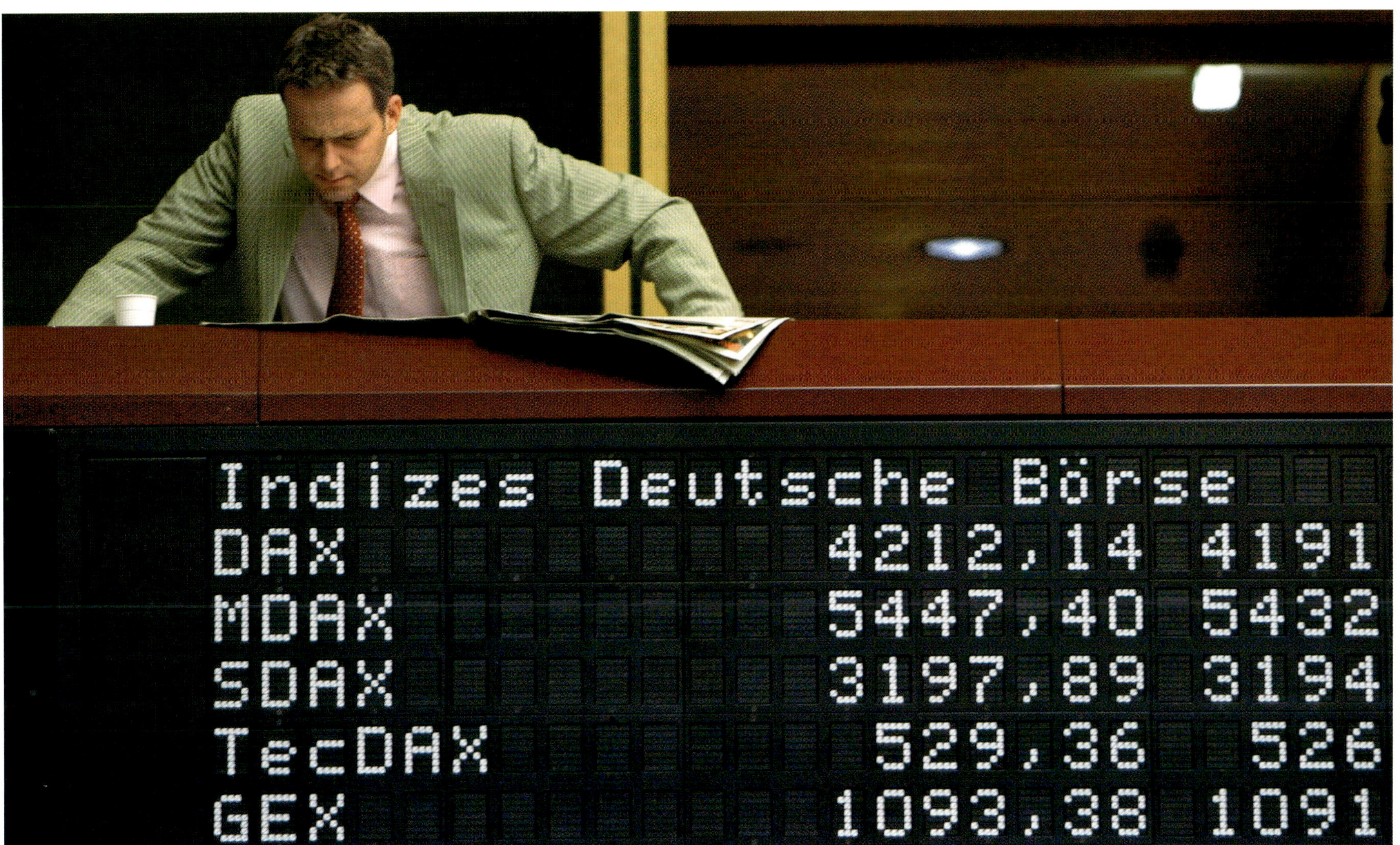

14 January 2005, FRANKFURT, GERMANY

A trader takes a break on the trading floor of Germany's stock exchange, the Deutsche Börse in Frankfurt. Kai Pfaffenbach

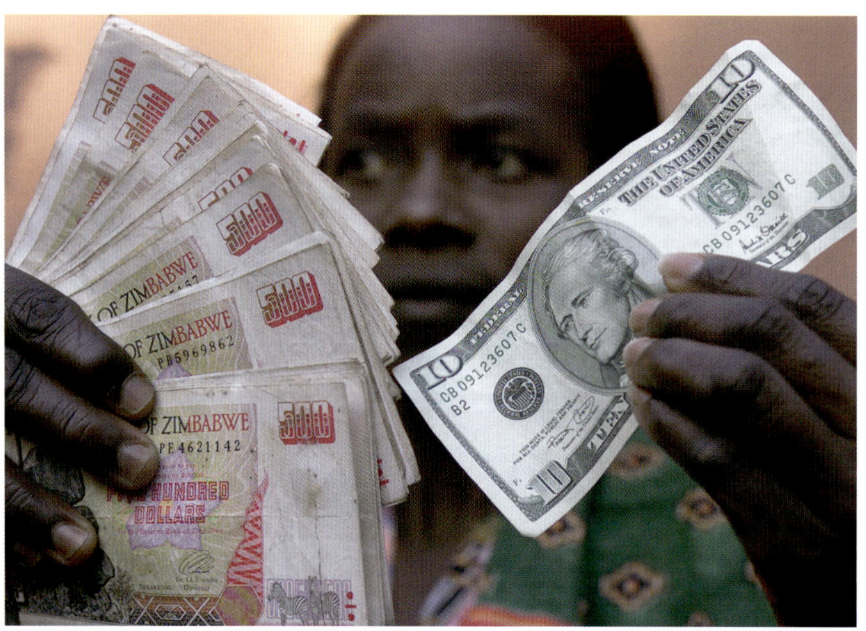

30 July 2003, HARARE, ZIMBABWE

A Zimbabwean holds a U.S. $10 bill and the black market equivalent (Z$35,000) in the country's new largest denomination of Z$500 bills. Two months later, the government introduced another new note, the Z$1,000 bill, to try to ease critical currency shortages as the country continued to battle hyperinflation. Howard Burditt

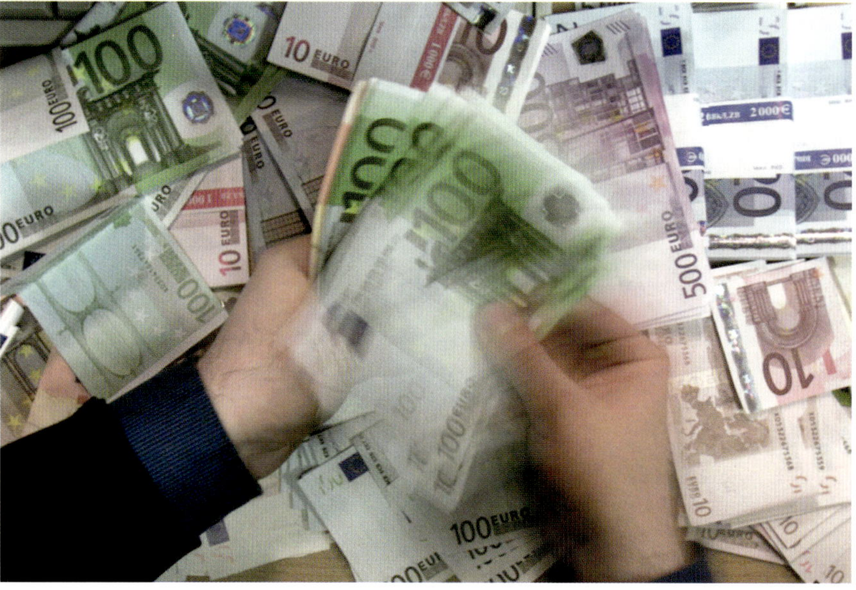

12 December 2001, LONDON, UNITED KINGDOM

A London bank worker counts out euro bank notes as the first notes arrive in Britain's high street banks, 20 days before they became legal tender across most of the rest of Europe. Britain, however, retained its sterling currency as its main tender. Russell Boyce

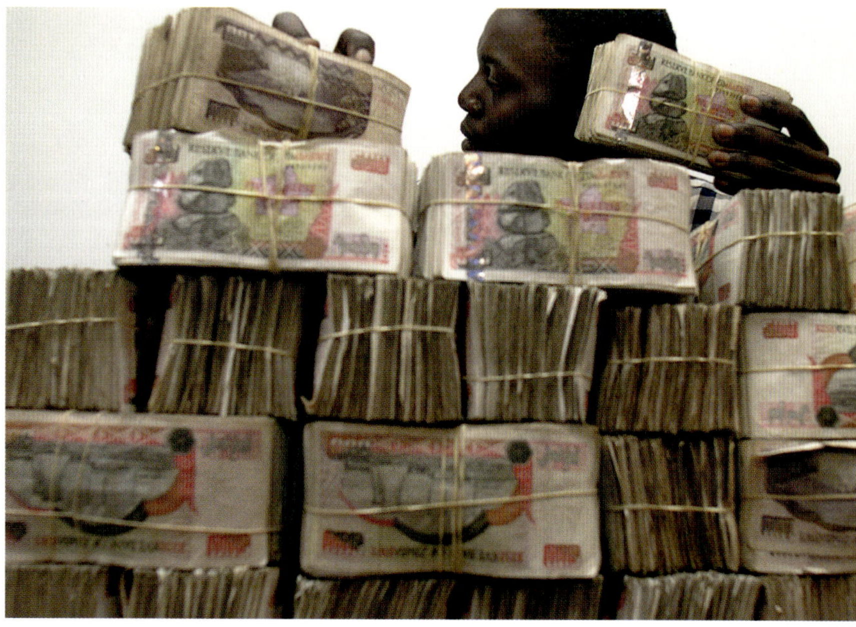

18 August 2003, HARARE, ZIMBABWE

A man piles up the black market equivalent of U.S. $1000 – approximately Z$5 million. In addition to inflation in excess of 400 percent in mid-2003, Zimbabwe was battling shortages of food and fuel, as well as unemployment of over 70 percent. By March 2006 the situation had deteriorated further, with inflation reaching a rate of over 780 percent – the highest in the world – and an estimated 4.3 million people in need of food aid. Howard Burditt

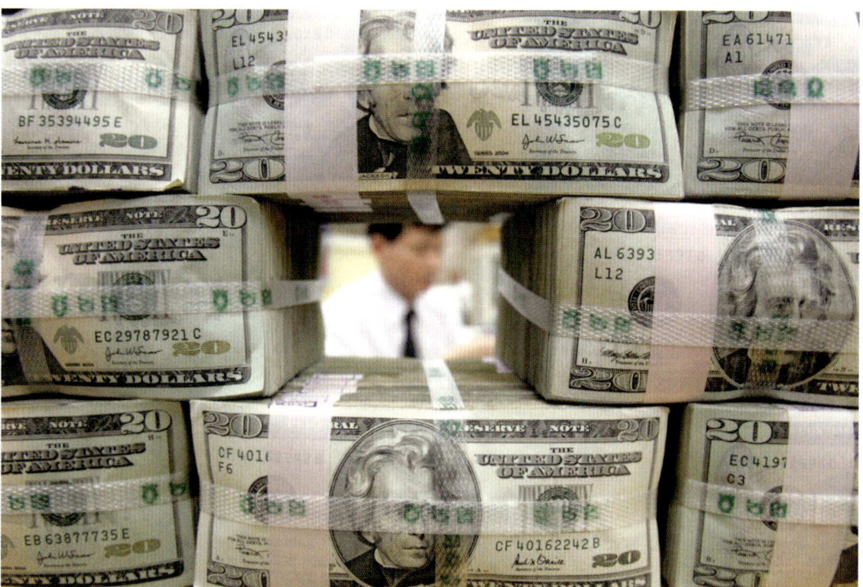

9 November 2004, SEOUL, SOUTH KOREA

A bank clerk works behind U.S. $20 bills piled at a bank in Seoul. You Sung-Ho

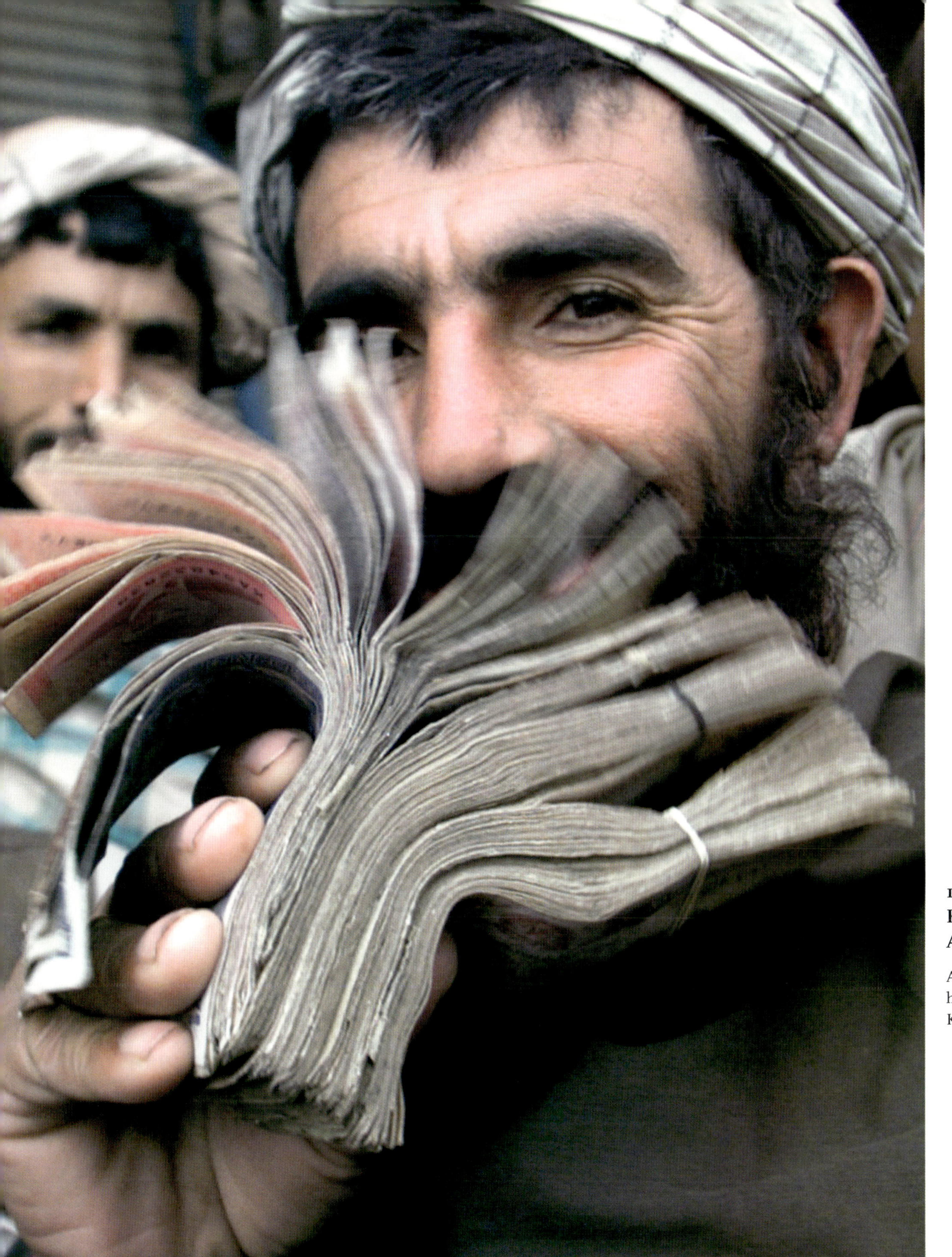

12 January 2002, KANDAHAR, AFGHANISTAN

An Afghan currency trader waves his money at a currency market in Kandahar. Zainal Abd Halim

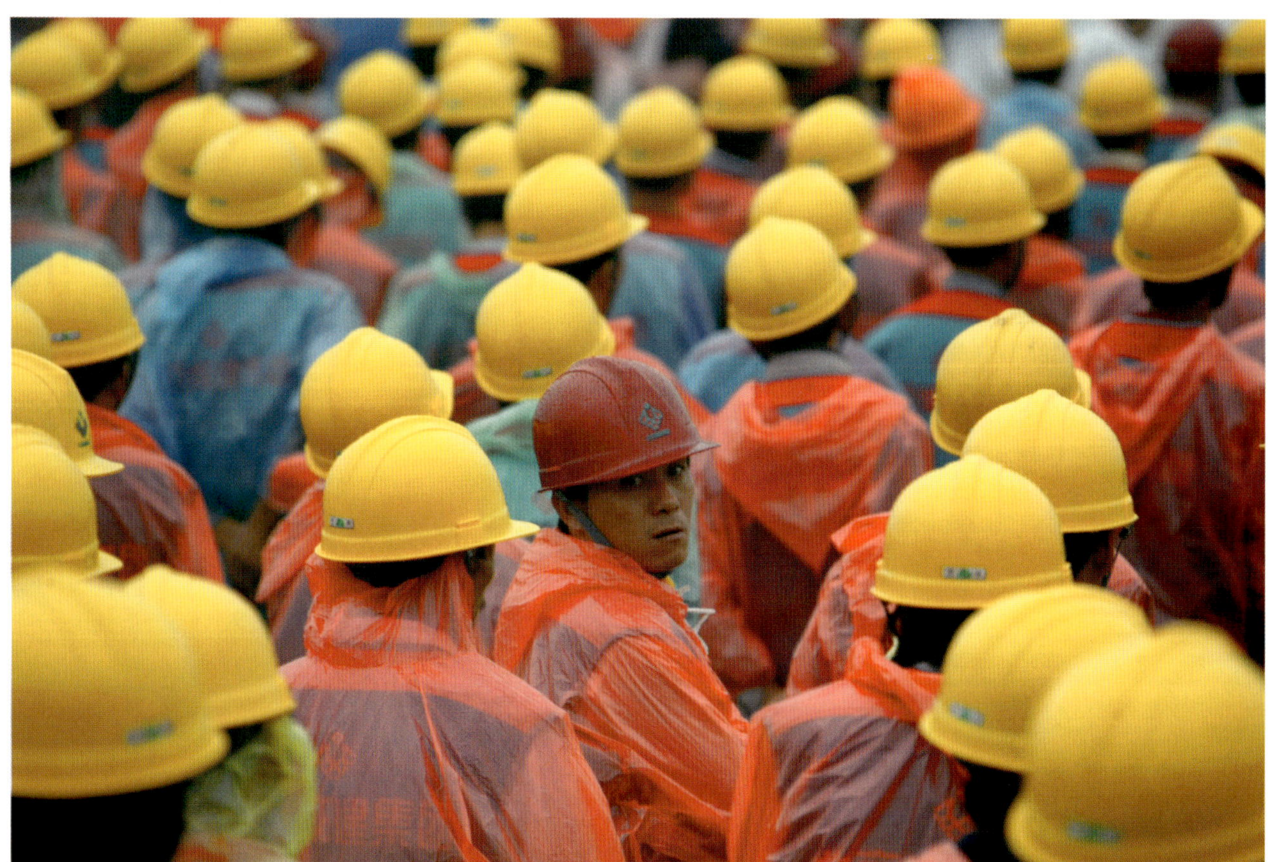

26 June 2005, BEIJING, CHINA

Construction workers attend a ceremony to mark the laying of the foundation stone for the Olympic Village in Beijing, an important component of the facilities to be built for the 2008 Olympic and Paralympic Games. By August 2008, Beijing expects to have spent a total of nearly U.S.$40 billion for the Games, most of it on building new roads and subway lines and improving the city's power grid and environment. Alfred Cheng Jin

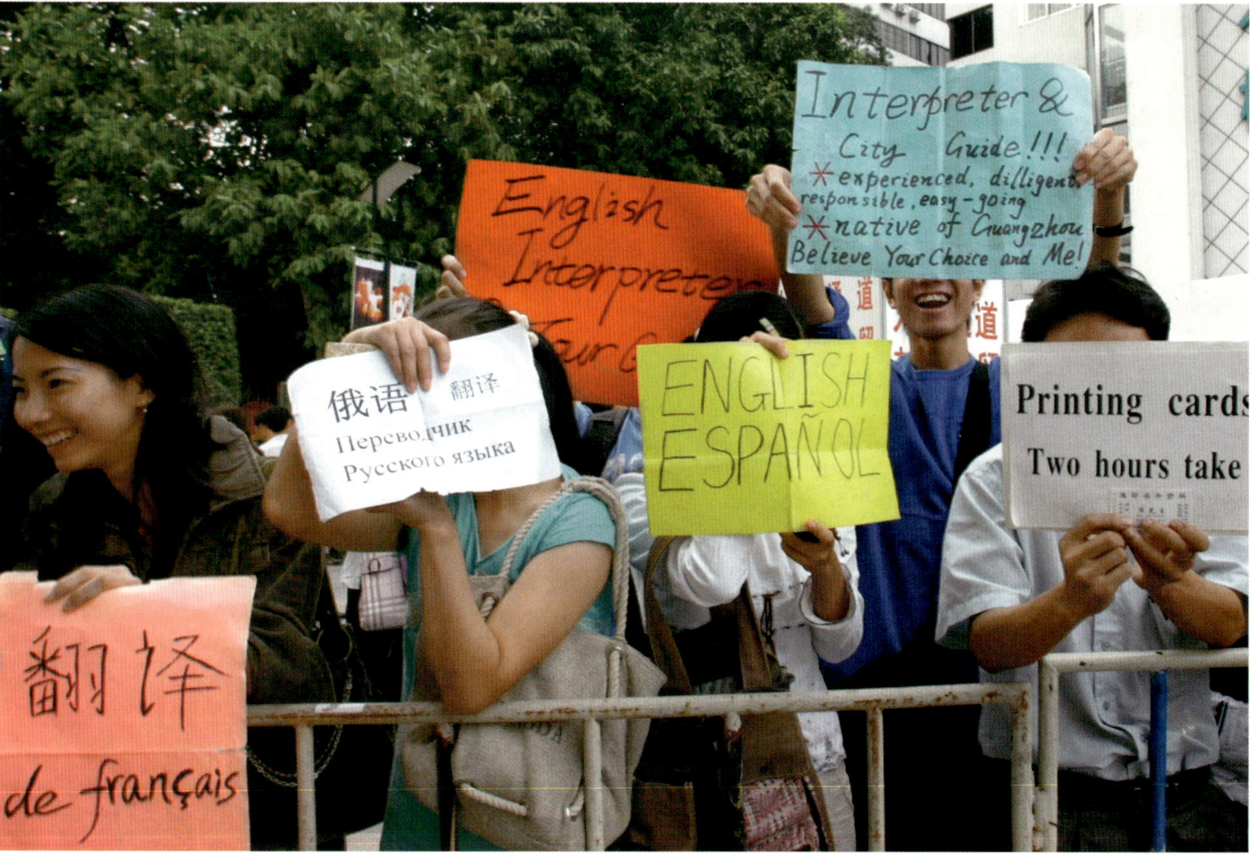

25 October 2005, GUANGZHOU, CHINA

Amateur translators offer their services to foreign visitors to the Guangzhou Export Commodities Fair, also known as the Canton Trade Fair, in southern China. The twice-yearly fair is China's biggest and most established trade show. The October 2005 session saw deals signed to the value of almost U.S. $30 billion. John Ruwitch

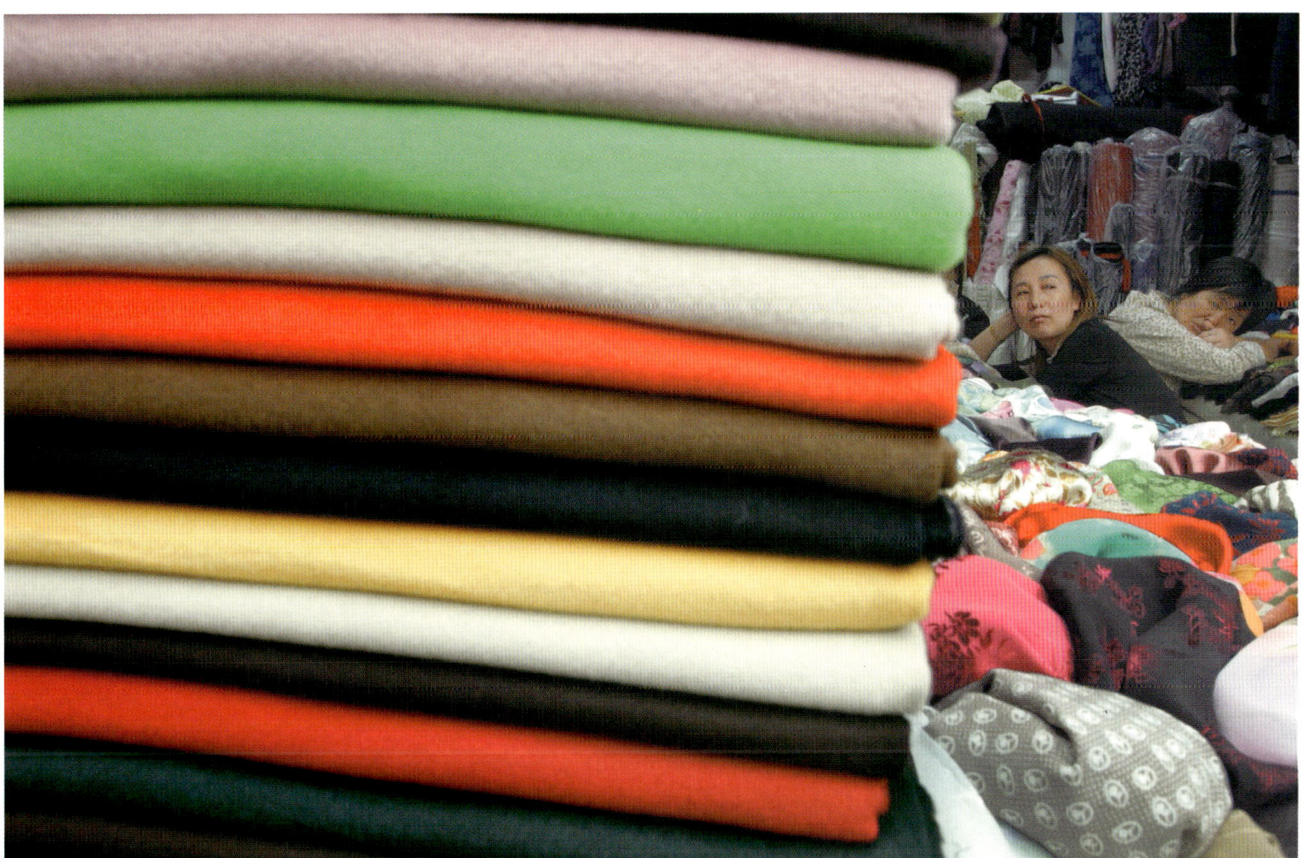

13 October 2005, SHANGHAI, CHINA

Chinese shopkeepers wait for customers at a textile market in Shanghai. Cheap labour and high-tech machinery have underpinned enormous increases in the manufacture of textiles and clothing in China. Claro Cortes IV

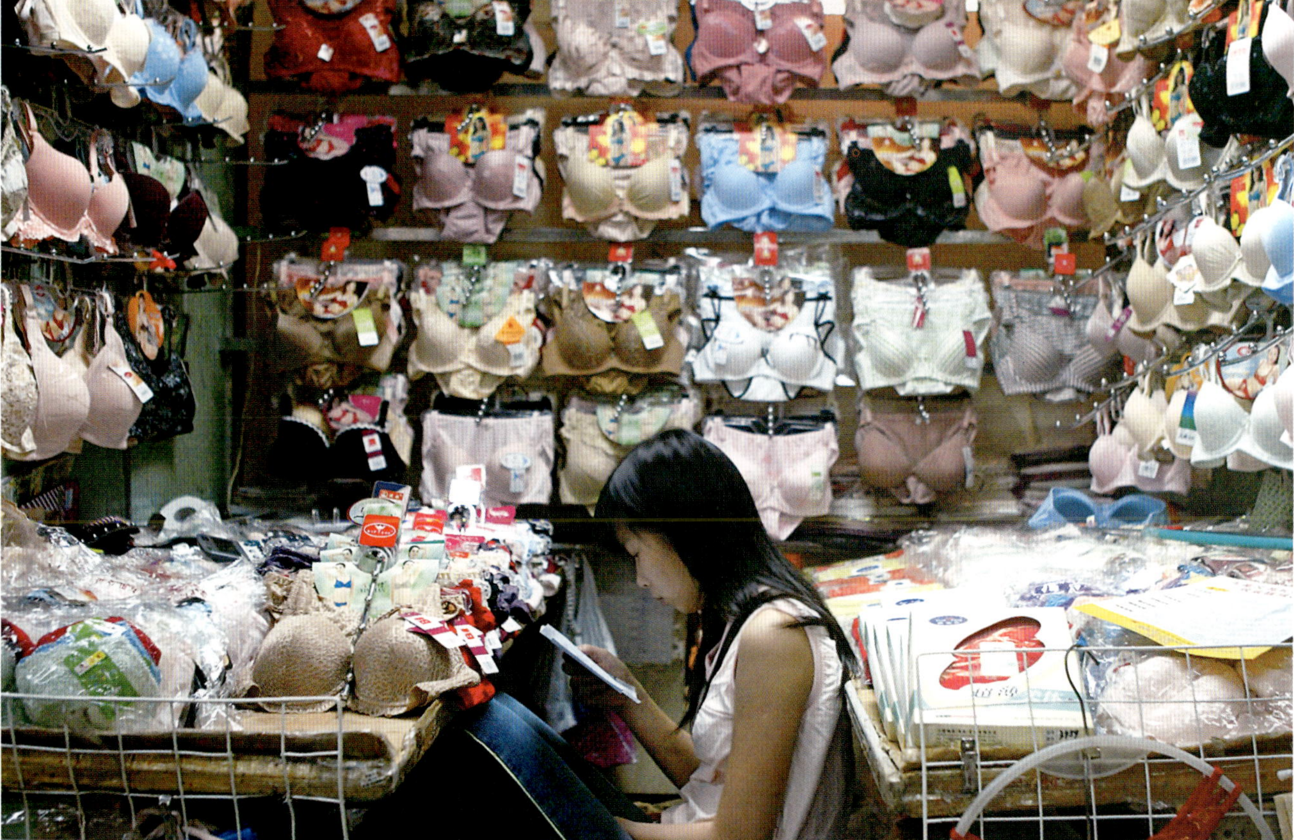

5 September 2005, SHANGHAI, CHINA

A shopkeeper reads newspapers at a Shanghai market. Following the expiry of export quotas at the start of 2005, there was a huge surge in shipments of Chinese textile goods which created a political outcry in the West. Both the U.S. and the EU reintroduced restrictions in a bid to protect their domestic industries in what became known as the 'bra wars'. Around 88 million t-shirts, bras and other items from China were impounded by EU customs in June 2005 before the new quotas were agreed. Aly Song

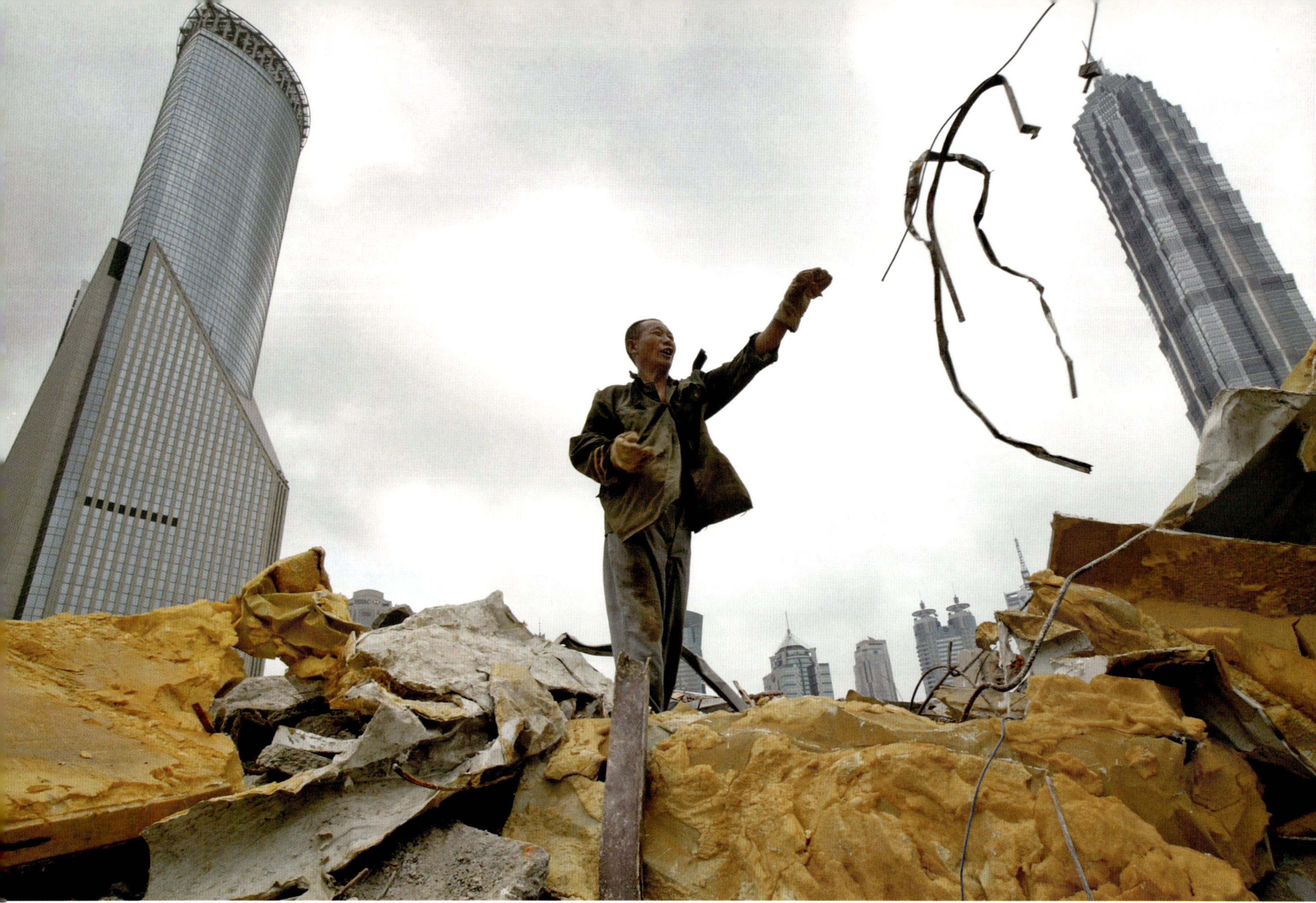

20 July 2005, SHANGHAI, CHINA

A worker collects scrap metal at a construction site in Shanghai. With 8.5 million Chinese people flocking to the cities each year, and annual growth rates of up to 10 percent over the first five years of the century, construction in China is booming. Ming Ming

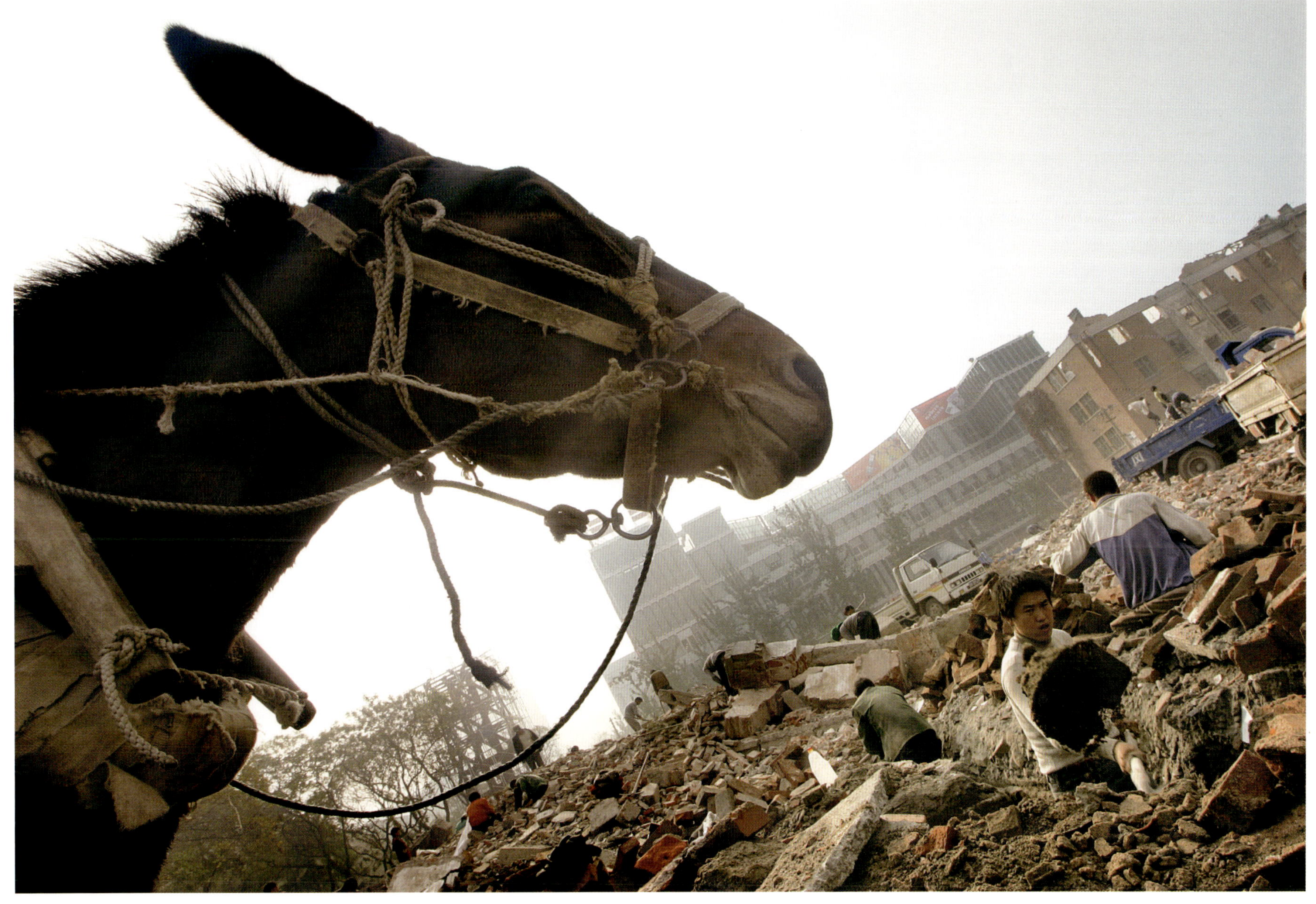

3 November 2005, BEIJING, CHINA

Chinese workers demolish old houses to make space for the construction of a new office building in Beijing's business area. Jason Lee

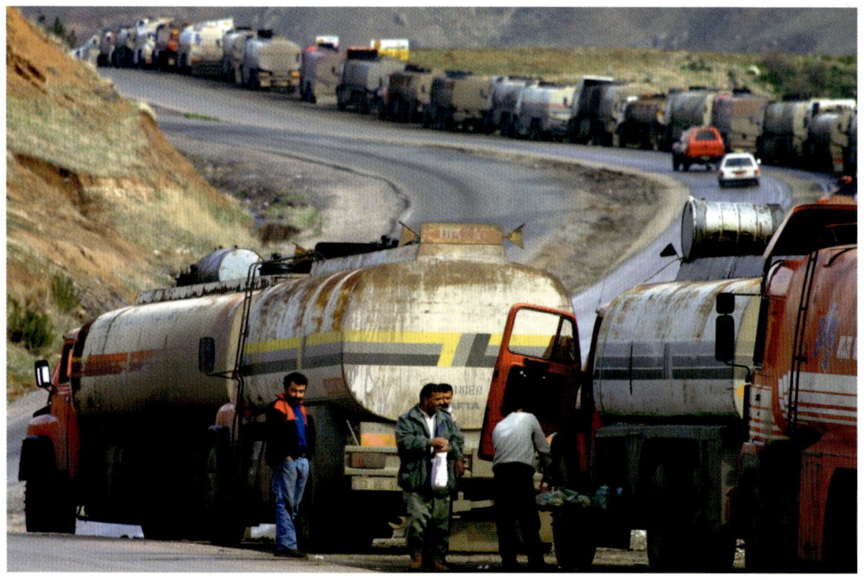

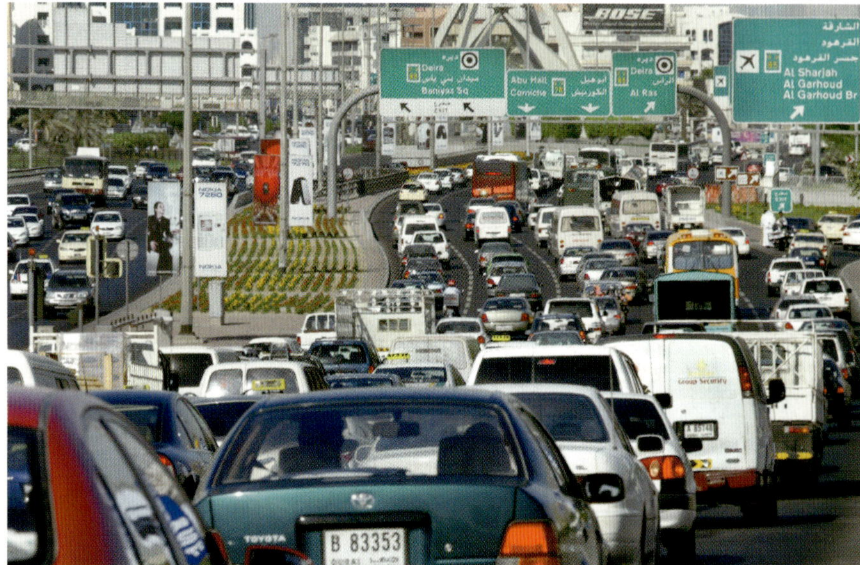

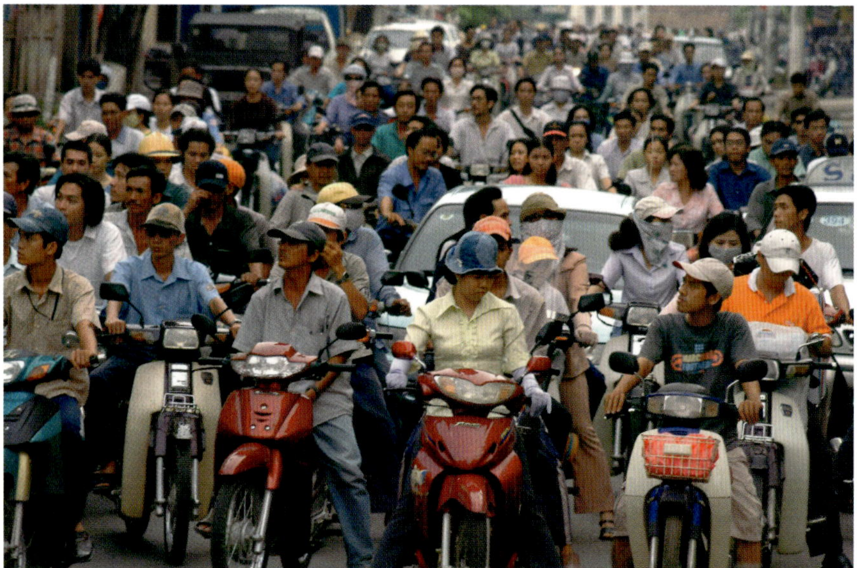

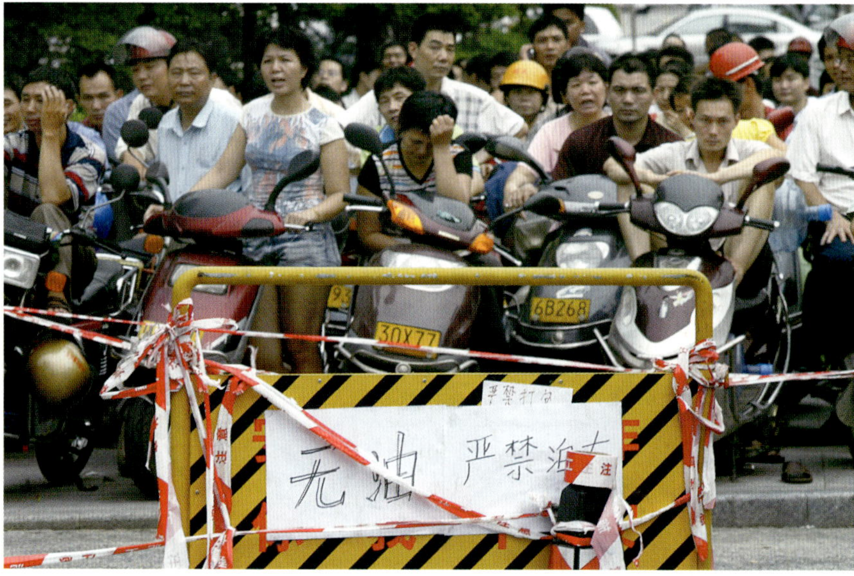

23 February 2003, MOSUL, IRAQ

Turkish truckers wait in line to carry Iraqi crude oil from the northern city of Mosul through Kurdish-held territory to Turkish refineries. Caren Firouz

5 May 2004, HO CHI MINH CITY, VIETNAM

A luxury car is surrounded by motorbike drivers at an intersection in the commercial hub of Ho Chi Minh City. While about two-thirds of Vietnamese still farm just as their ancestors did, the speed at which young entrepreneurs are garnering wealth has led to a luxury car boom.

15 October 2005, DUBAI, UNITED ARAB EMIRATES

Heavy traffic creates congestion at Makhtoum bridge in Dubai. Government officials acknowledge that traffic congestion in Dubai has grown at the same breakneck speed as the city, which is in the grip of a construction frenzy fuelled by a booming local economy. Anwar Mirza

15 August 2005, DONGGUAN, CHINA

Chinese motorists line up near a sign that reads 'no petrol' at a service station in Guangdong province, China's manufacturing heartland, where fuel shortages in 2005 led to petrol station closures, fuel rationing and hours-long queues.

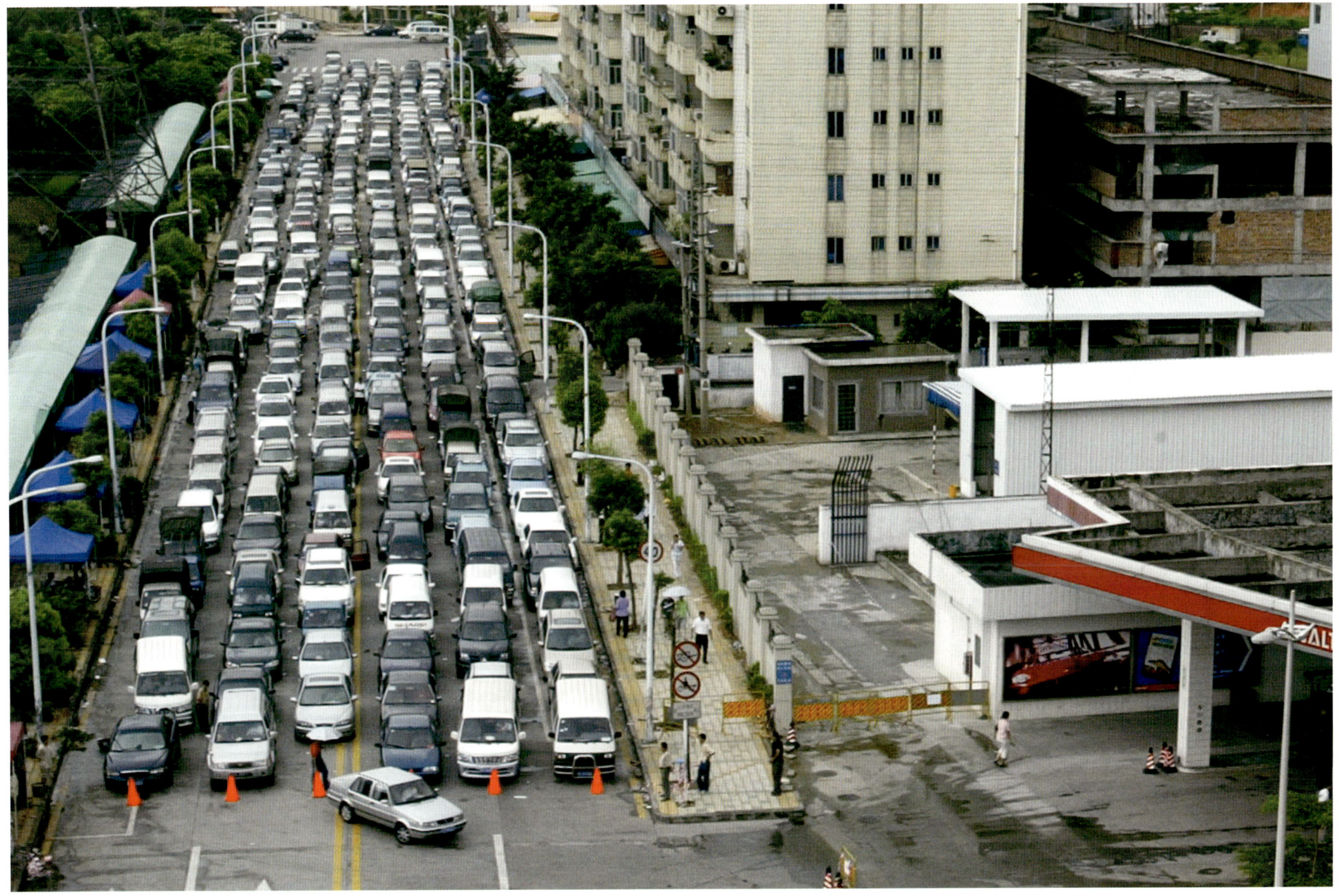

17 August 2005, DONGGUAN, CHINA

Cars queue up to buy fuel at a petrol station in Guangdong province. The fuel shortages that led to such long queues were caused in part by China's oil firms restricting supplies to the loss-making domestic market, where prices are subject to government price caps, in order to protect their balance sheets. China Newsphoto

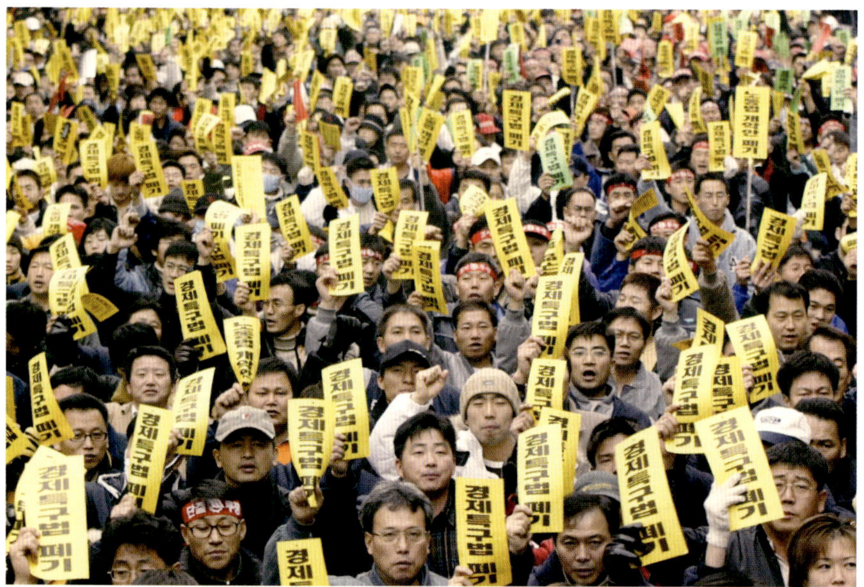

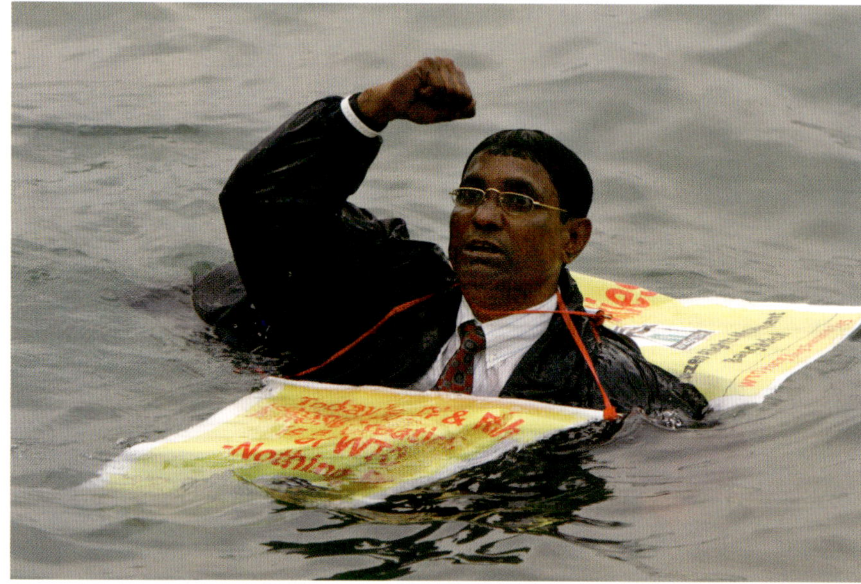

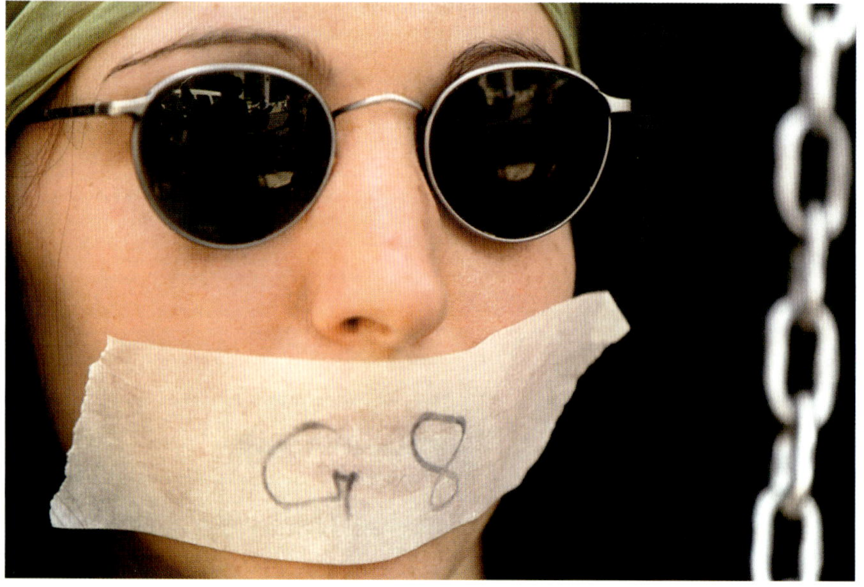

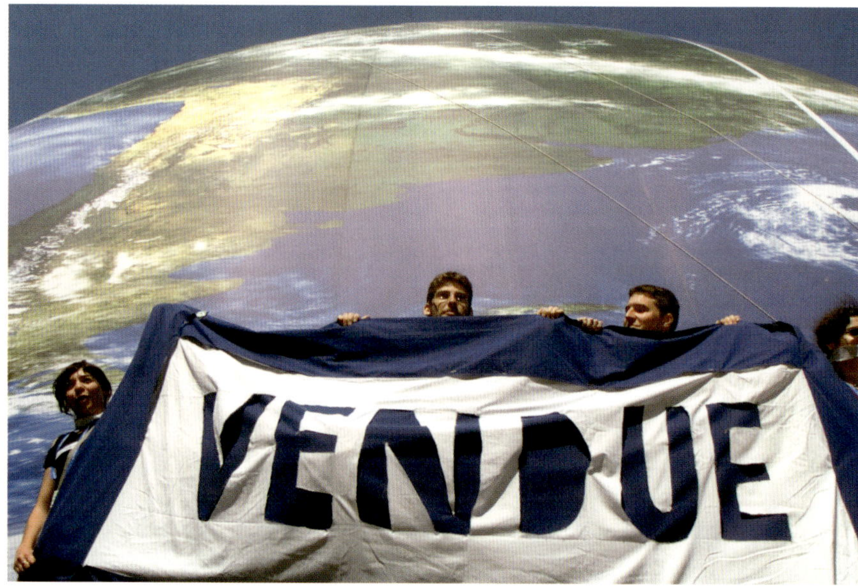

10 November 2002, SEOUL, SOUTH KOREA

South Korean protesters shout anti-government slogans at a rally in Seoul. Around 10,000 members of the Korean Confederation of Trade Unions attended the rally to protest against a proposed new law to create special economic zones which the demonstrators said would allow corporate managers to cut wages. Their signs read 'Abolition of special economic zone bill'. Kim Kyung-Hoon

29 June 2001, ATHENS, GREECE

A Greek anti-globalization protester demonstrates outside the Italian embassy in Athens, where she chained herself to the main entrance of the building ahead of the G8 summit due to be held in Genoa, Italy, the following month. Alexandros Vlachos

13 December 2005, HONG KONG, CHINA

An anti-World Trade Organization (WTO) protester floats in Victoria Harbour near the Hong Kong Convention and Exhibition Centre, the main venue of a WTO conference. Over 100 people leapt into the water after a march by 4,500 against trade liberalization. Riot police used pepper spray to hold back protesters, many of them South Korean farmers bitterly opposed to the liberalization of their country's rice market. Claro Cortes IV

3 September 2002, JOHANNESBURG, SOUTH AFRICA

French protesters demonstrate against big business during a U.N. World Summit on Sustainable Development in Johannesburg. The globe behind them is the world dome of the German car manufacturer BMW. Their sign reads 'sold'. Howard Burditt

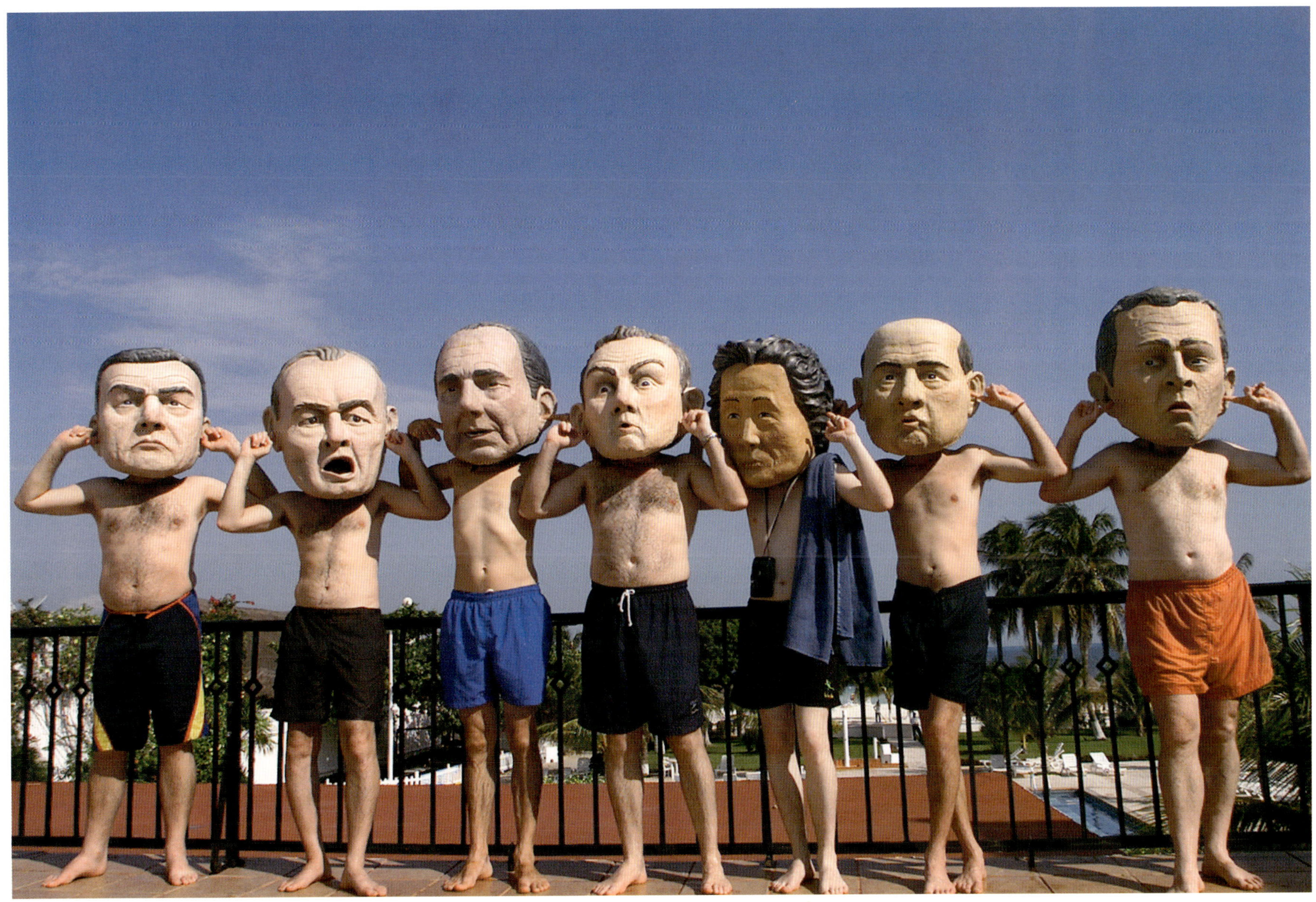

14 September 2003, CANCÚN, MEXICO

Campaigners from Oxfam lampoon leaders of the G8 countries (from left to right: Gerhard Schröder of Germany, Jean Chrétien of Canada, Jacques Chirac of France, Tony Blair of the United Kingdom, Junichiro Koizumi of Japan, Silvio Berlusconi of Italy, and George W. Bush of the United States) as the World Trade Organization meets in Cancún. Their message was that the G8 were failing to listen to voices urging them to rewrite the rules of international trade. Juan Carlos Ulate

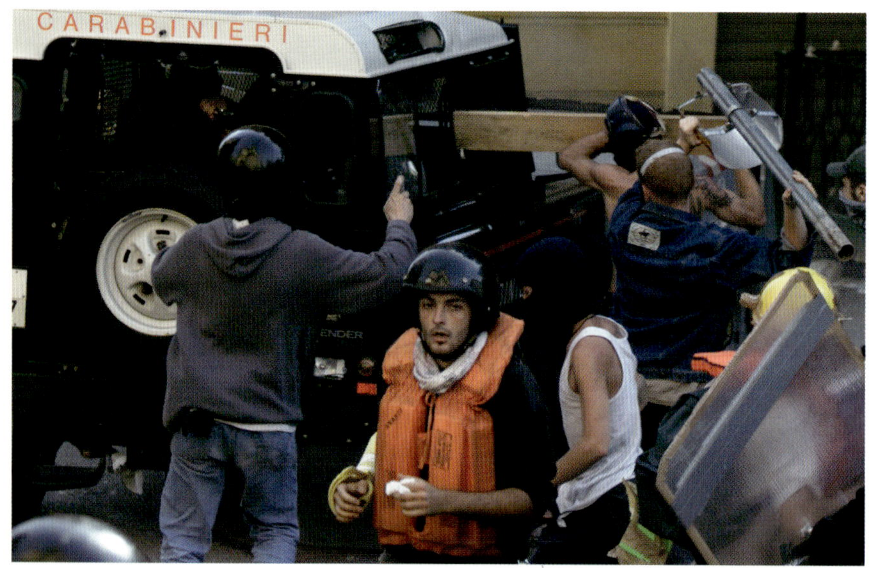
CARABINIERI

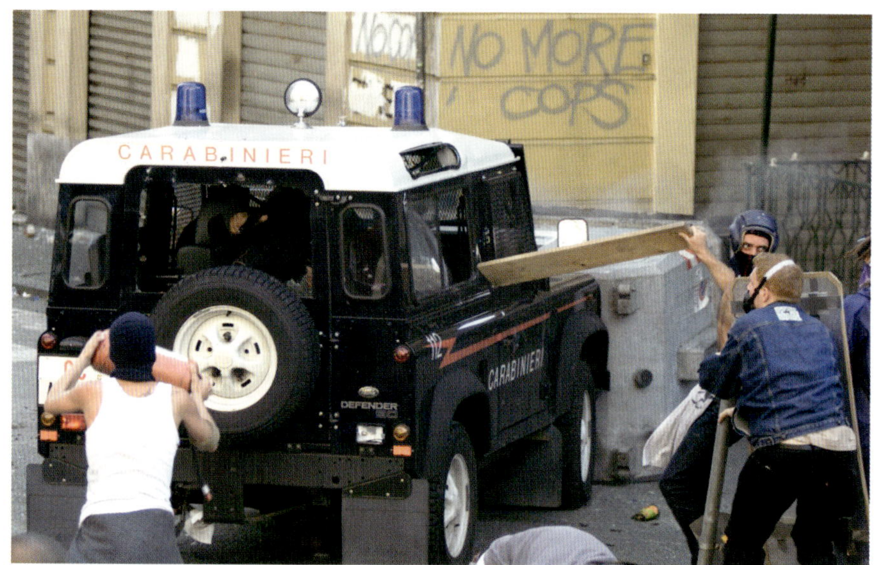
NO MORE
COPS
CARABINIERI
CARABINIERI
DEFENDER

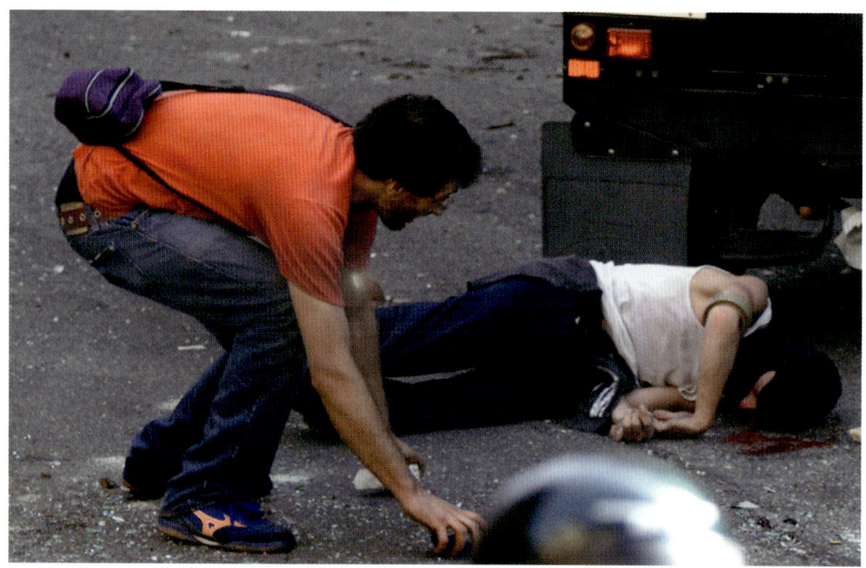

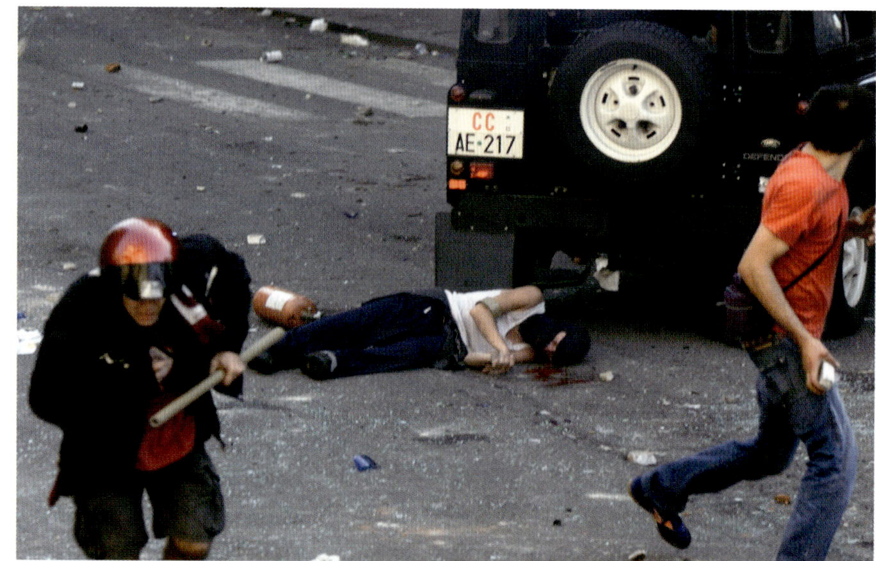
CC
AE-217

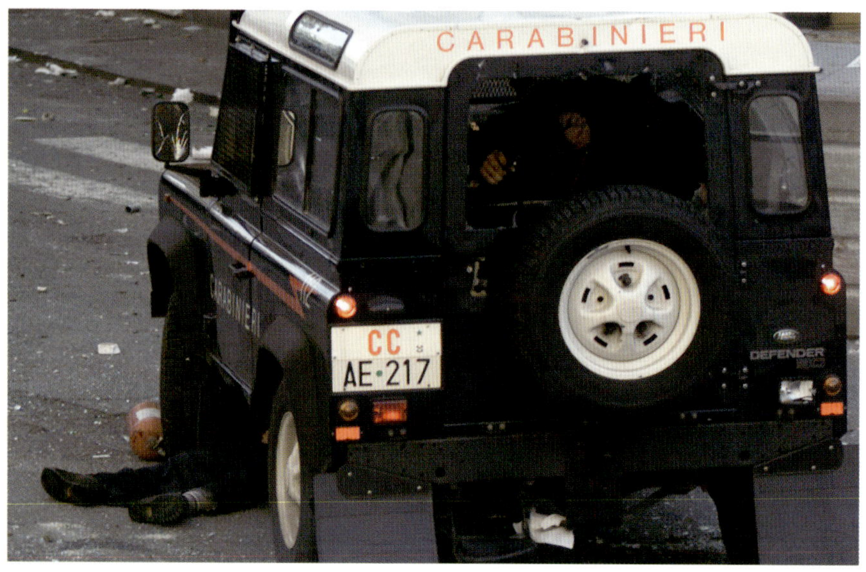
CARABINIERI
CC
AE-217
DEFENDER

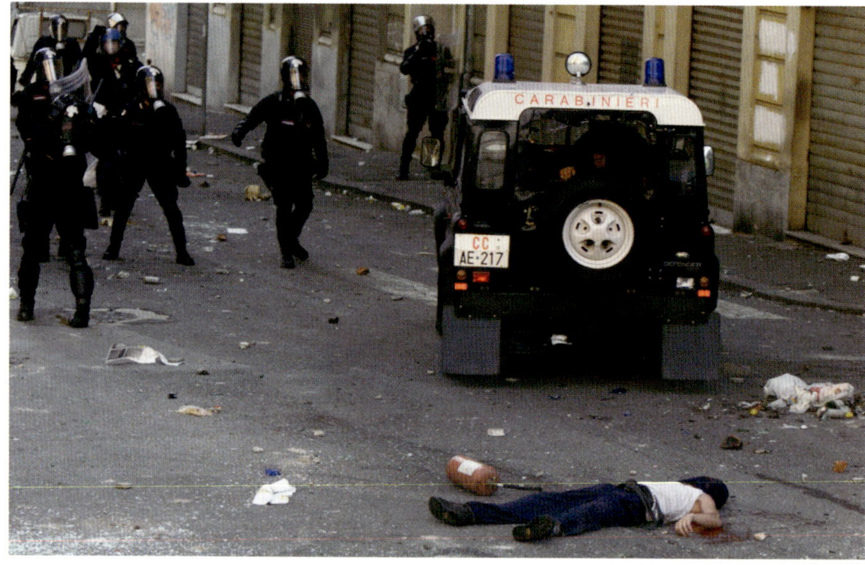
CARABINIERI
CC
AE-217

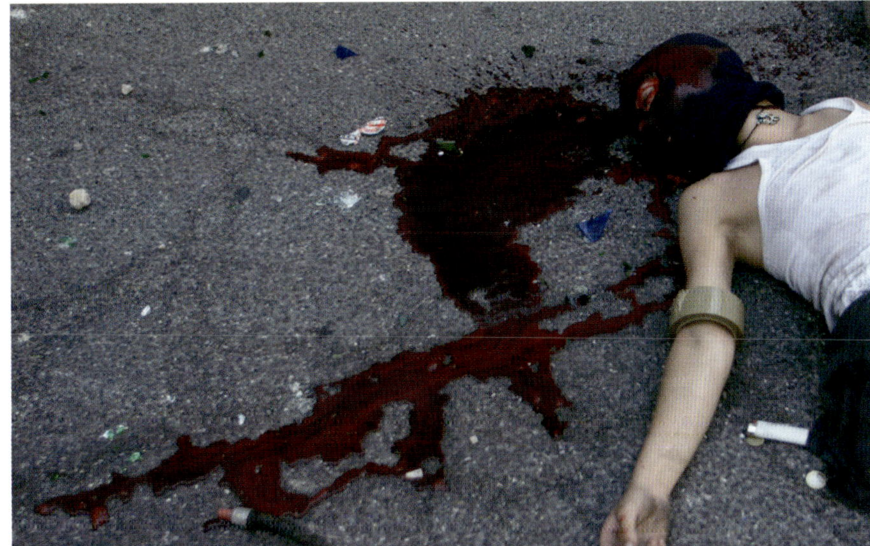

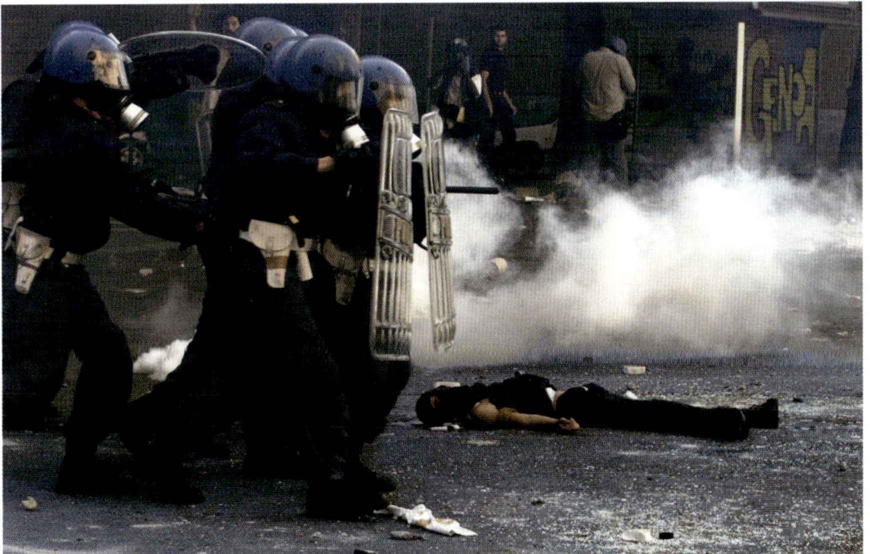

20 July 2001, GENOA, ITALY

Protests against the Group of Eight annual summit in Genoa turn into riots. Police fired live rounds, tear gas and used water cannon in an attempt to disperse thousands of anti-capitalist and anti-globalization protesters who gathered in the city. At least 300 people were injured and more than 100 arrested in the violence. Italian protester Carlo Giuliani, 23, died after being shot twice and then run over by police. The three-day summit left the ancient port of Genoa littered with burned-out cars, smashed windows and vandalized property. These events followed a series of anti-globalization riots that hit summits in cities across the world following the first major violent confrontation at the World Trade Organization summit in Seattle in 1999. Dylan Martinez, Peter Andrews (this page, bottom)

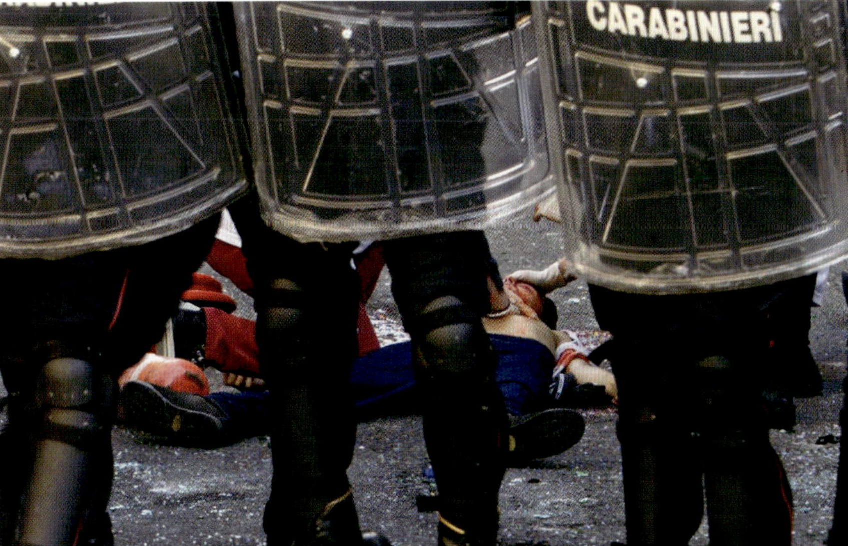

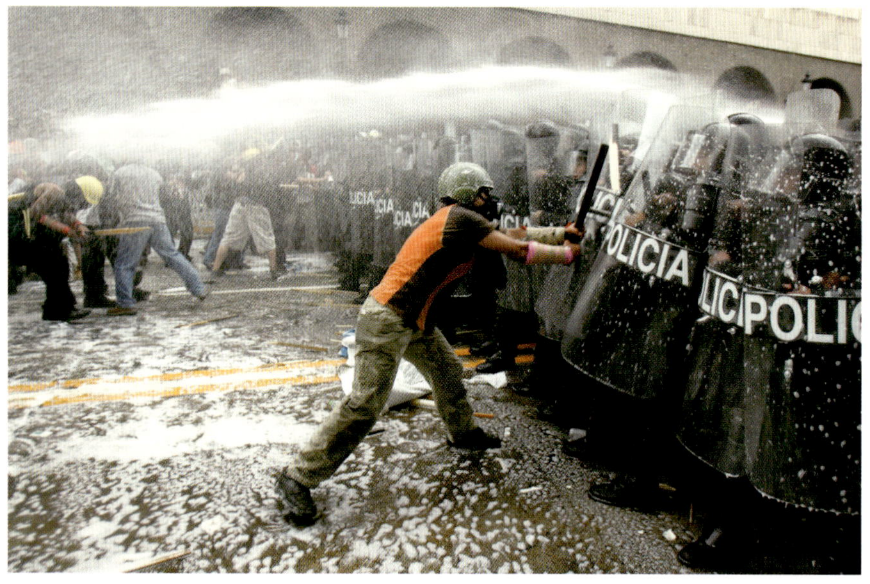

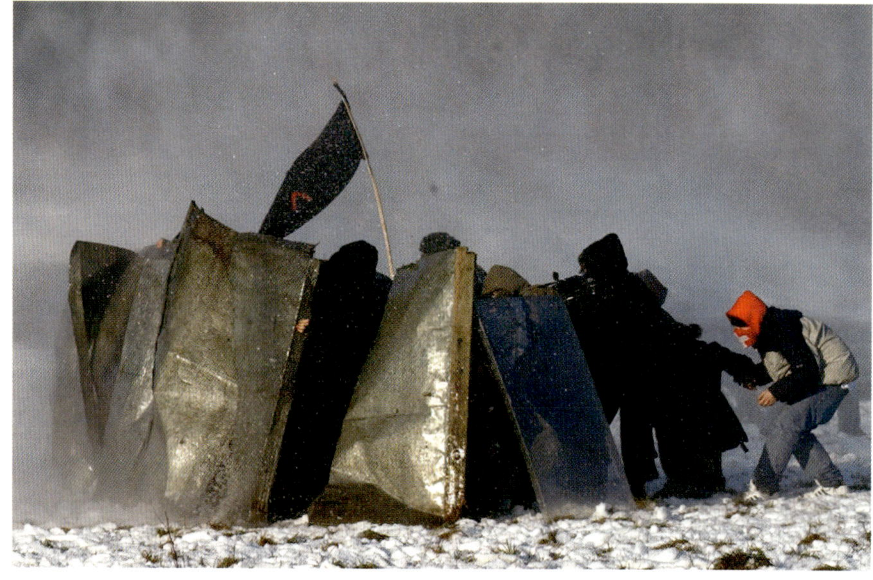

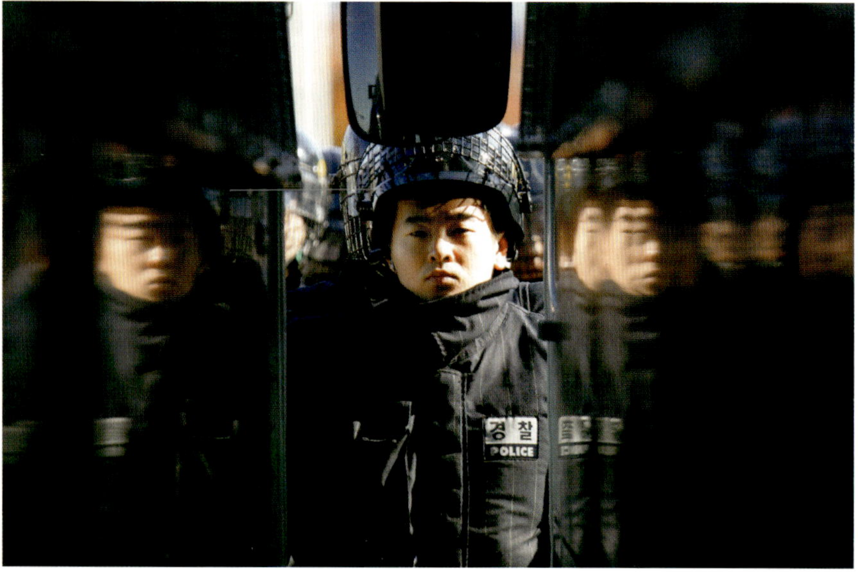

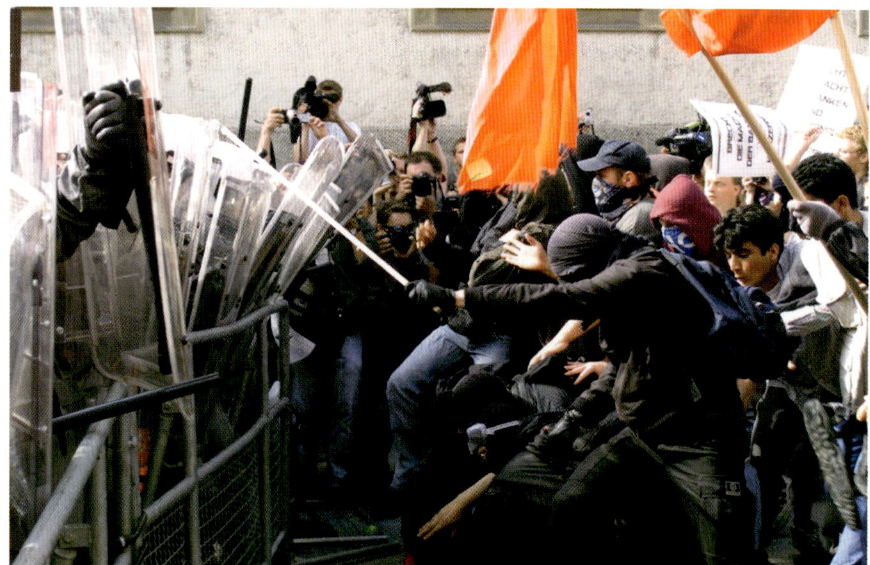

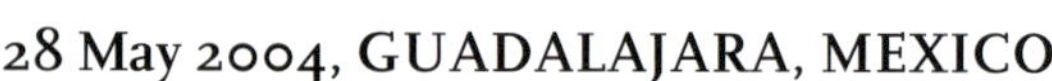

28 May 2004, GUADALAJARA, MEXICO

A protester clashes with police in Guadalajara during a demonstration against the Guadalajara summit of Latin American, Caribbean and European Union states.
Daniel Aguilar

17 November 2005, KYONGJU, SOUTH KOREA

Riot policemen stand guard at the Asia-Pacific Economic Cooperation (APEC) summit in Kyongju, where about 2,000 farmers and farm activists and 3,000 union workers took to the streets to denounce APEC, the World Trade Organization, and U.S. President George W. Bush. Reinhard Krause

25 January 2003, LANDQUART, SWITZERLAND

Anti-globalization demonstrators on their way to the World Economic Forum in Davos seek cover from a water cannon as riot police attempt to prevent an approved demonstration from escalating into violence. Hundreds of demonstrators braved a stiff security cordon to confront world leaders and denounce a threatened U.S. attack on Iraq. Denis Balibouse

1 July 2001, SALZBURG, AUSTRIA

Demonstrators clash with Austrian riot police during a protest against the World Economic Forum in Salzburg. Michael Leckel

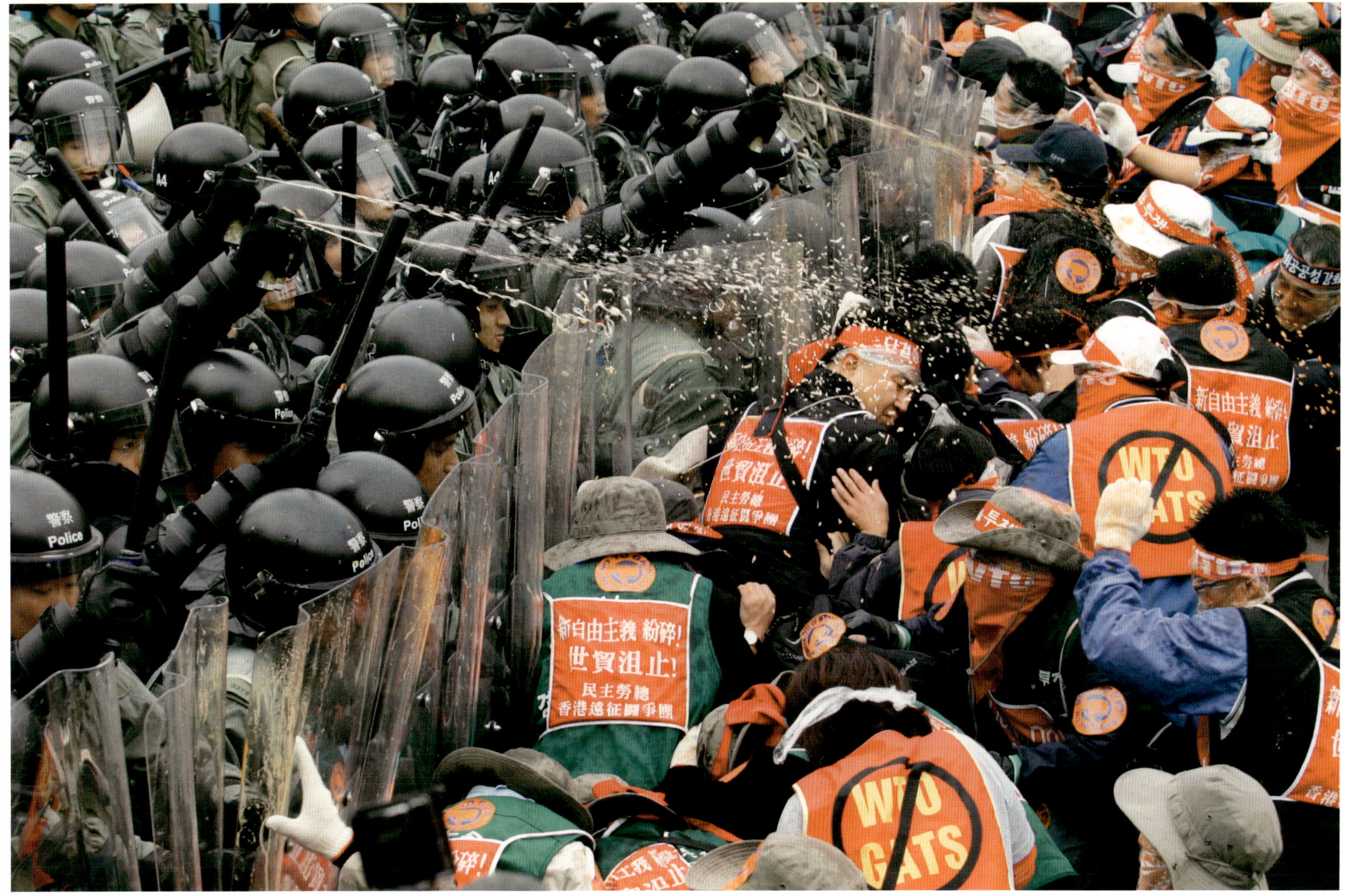

14 December 2005, HONG KONG, CHINA

Riot police use pepper spray as South Korean farmers try to break through a police barrier during an anti-globalization protest as the World Trade Organization staged a conference in Hong Kong. Bobby Yip

Our entertainment industries can now produce alternative realities more vivid than anything in the history of humankind. The celebrities they create are the demigods of our age, their deeds and misdeeds followed by millions. But ultimately the ability of people across the globe to access the same music, movies and media via the Internet may prove a unifying force beyond anything dreamed of by the founders of the United Nations.

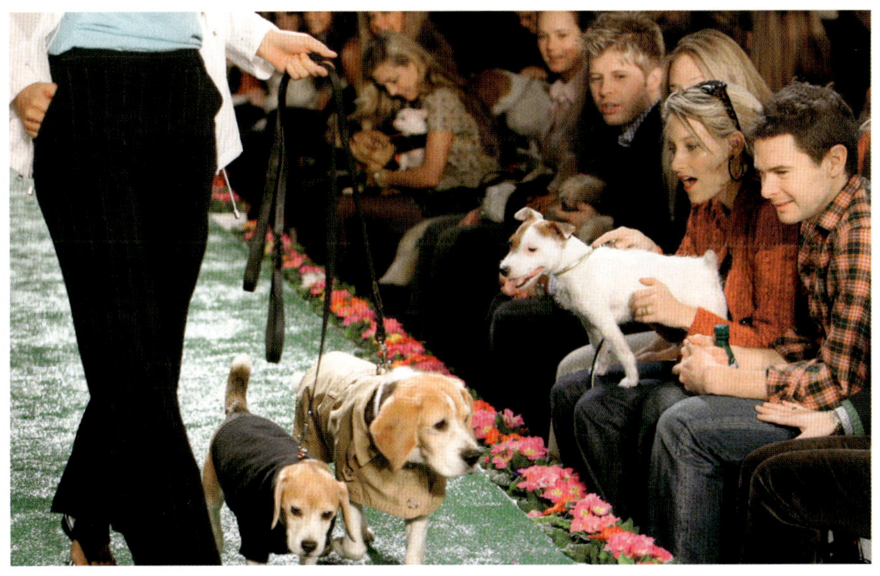

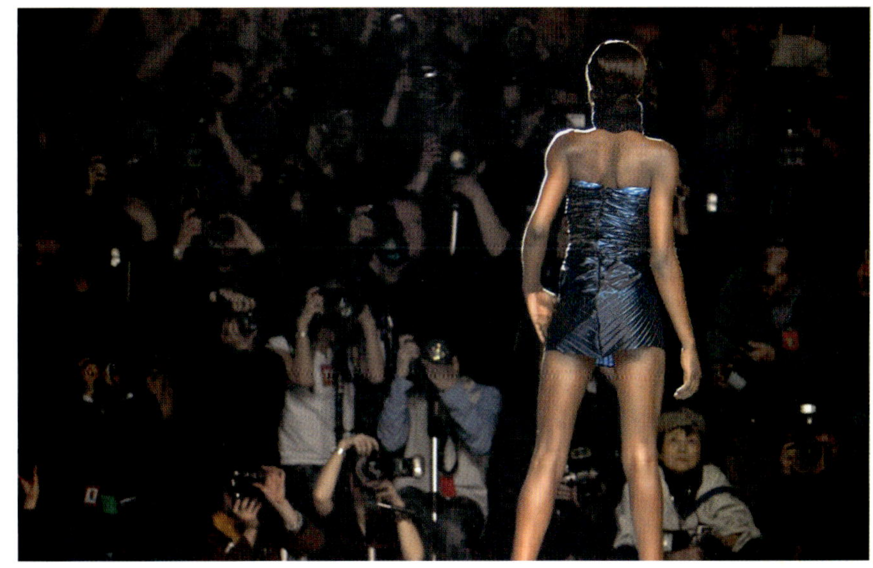

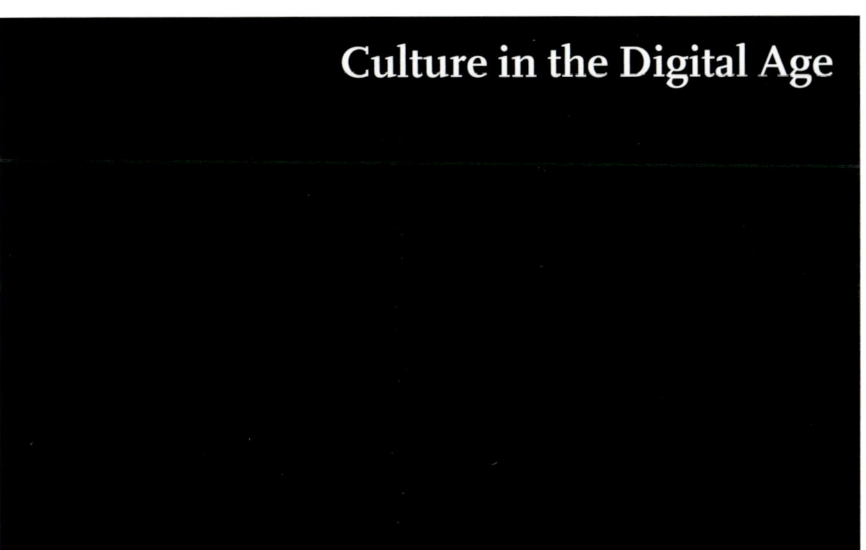

Entertainment / Celebrity / Media
Film / Fashion / Music / Politics
Performance / Art / Architecture

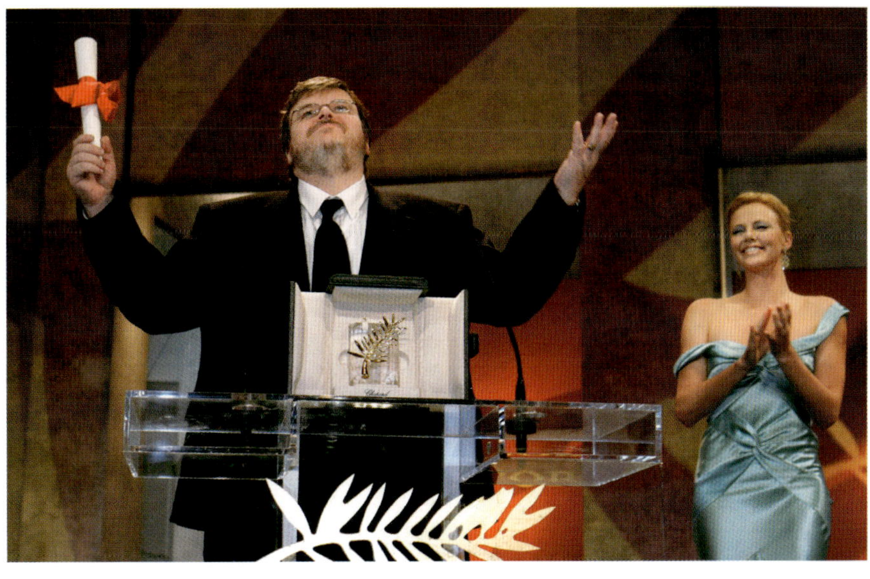

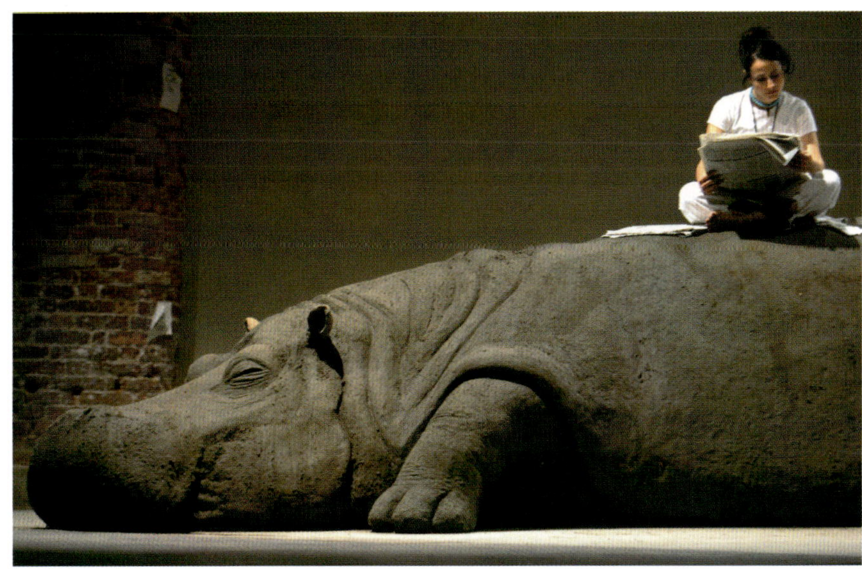

Culture in the Digital Age

When American hotel heiress Paris Hilton swept into the 2005 Cannes Film Festival, the media frenzy that greeted her said it all: an 'A'-list celebrity had arrived. Cameramen and photographers tussled for space on a creaking wooden jetty to capture her arrival by boat, then raced back across the Croisette to secure a spot at a crammed press conference in the Carlton Hotel.

The buzz was almost a match for that surrounding the biggest film launched at that year's festival, *Star Wars: Episode III – Revenge of the Sith*, the final, highly anticipated chapter in George Lucas' seminal six-part space epic. Hilton's was the kind of reception reserved for the likes of Hollywood heavyweights Tom Cruise and Nicole Kidman. And yet here was a 24-year-old party girl whose

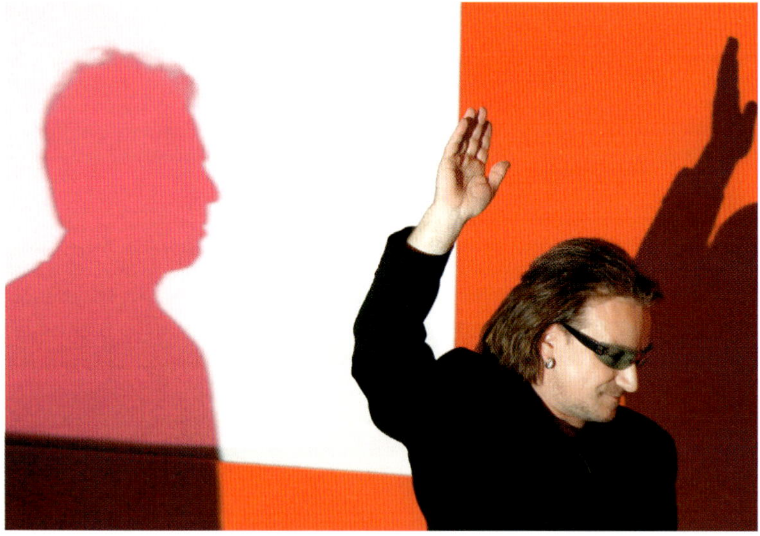

U2 frontman and campaigner Bono leaves the podium after delivering his speech to the British Labour Party conference in Brighton. The shadow of UK Prime Minister Tony Blair is visible behind him. 29 September 2004, Russell Boyce.

greatest claim to fame was having sex on a home video that found its way onto the Internet and was subsequently viewed by millions. What was Hilton in town to promote? *National Lampoon's Pledge This!*, a low-budget sorority romp not scheduled to hit cinemas until several months later.

The phrase 'famous for being famous' says much about what is happening in the world of entertainment today. The cult of celebrity is upon us. A slew of increasingly outrageous reality TV projects manufacturing instant stars of questionable talent may have left the public tired and cynical about the phenomenon. Yet the fact remains that we live in an age where fame, and with it money and influence, is easier to achieve than ever before. A passable performance on *Pop Idol*, an infamous affair, or giving birth on the set of *Big Brother* will earn you a rung on the celebrity ladder. Then it is up to you and your publicity machine to transform notoriety into celebrity as you clamber towards coveted 'A' status.

To its many critics, the cult of celebrity has dumbed down culture. To its apologists, it has made the world fairer than ever; fame, and not just 15 minutes of it, is within reach of everyone. Key to the phenomenon have been revolutionary changes in mass communications over the last 20 years. There are ever more websites, cable television channels and glossy magazines dedicated to showbusiness news, gossip and hype, which tap both technological advances and our obsession for celebrity. The more titles there are, the greater the demand for celebrity news to fill them, and so the circle continues.

The phrase 'famous for being famous' says much about what is happening in the world of entertainment today. The cult of celebrity is upon us.

Anyone watching a Hollywood starlet mobbed by photographers and fans as she exits a nightclub after a vodka cocktail too many may wonder why she would want the job. But perhaps Oscar Wilde was right: being talked about is better than not being talked about. Celebrities have to learn to take the rough with the smooth, and the media is willing to play the role of friend and foe in equal measure. On the one hand, in exchange for access and exclusivity, stories about the stars can be positive, bordering on the sycophantic: feathers are unruffled, egos lovingly massaged. At the press conference in Cannes, journalists asked Hilton to identify her top *Star Wars* characters and name her chihuahua Tinkerbell's favourite doggie designer. They were not being ironic. On the other hand, cut-throat competition among media outlets means nothing is sacred and paparazzi tactics are increasingly invasive and aggressive. Private lives, unsavoury habits, drug addiction and bad skin are all fair game in the entertainment world today.

And so genuine stars spend as much time protecting their privacy as flaunting their fame, employing ever more elaborate means to dodge press intrusion. Sobering lessons for today's aspiring celebrities abound. Britain's Princess Diana, once the most photographed woman in the world, died in a Paris car crash while being chased by paparazzi. Countless high-profile marriages fall apart in the harsh gaze of the media spotlight. Few examples are more unsettling than that of Michael Jackson, the king of pop whose every move has been reported and analysed by gossip-hungry media. He may end up being remembered as an outlandish outcast rather than a musical genius, tainted by allegations of child molestation despite his acquittal in a sensational 2005 trial.

Celebrity cynics are not hard to find, but performers are increasingly using their fame to make a serious point. One reason is the fierce debate surrounding U.S. foreign policy since the September 11 attacks of 2001. Hollywood star George Clooney has likened cinema today to that of the 1960s and 1970s, as real-life issues increasingly find their way onto the big screen. So Steven Spielberg's *Munich* explored Israel's policy of revenge after an attack by Palestinian guerrillas on its athletes at the 1972 Olympics, and questioned whether that policy created yet more enemies – a thought-provoking theme as the United States battles al Qaeda. *Paradise Now*, the Oscar-nominated film by Palestinian director Hany Abu-Assad, followed two men selected by an unnamed militant group to carry out a suicide bombing in Tel Aviv. When Michael Moore won the coveted Palme d'Or in Cannes in 2004 for his anti-Bush polemic *Fahrenheit 9/11*, it was a signal that showbusiness believed it had a role to play in the political process. But even star power has its limits: the outspoken opposition of Hollywood heavyweights failed to oust President George W. Bush from office in the 2004 presidential election.

Politics aside, artists are campaigning for other causes. Bono, U2 frontman and quintessential celebrity campaigner, wants nothing less than to end global poverty, and he has access to the corridors of power to make his case. When he lunches at the White House or shares a platform with British Prime Minister Tony Blair, it is often the politician who plays second fiddle. Fellow Irish rocker Bob Geldof pulled off two mammoth international concert events, with Live Aid in 1985 and Live 8 two decades later. Ten gigs held across four continents on 2 July 2005 combined to make Live 8 the greatest rock concert ever staged, and all to pressure rich countries to do more to help the world's poor.

But another, less positive message came out as plans for Live 8 took shape. Though African poverty was the main theme of the day, African artists were initially overlooked as Geldof focused on recruiting internationally recognized acts in order to get his point across to the widest possible audience. An additional concert organized by world music champion Peter Gabriel eventually provided a platform for the continent's musicians, but it was a show that went largely uncovered in the media as cameras zoomed in on the likes of Madonna, Paul McCartney and Elton John.

The fact is that showbusiness is dominated by the Anglo-Saxon world. While the flourishing South Korean film industry, for example, is doing roaring box office business at home, it struggles to crack the

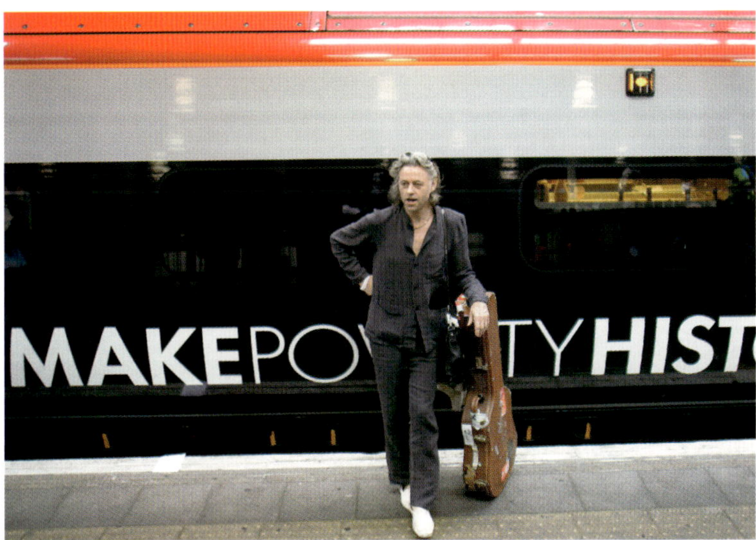

Former rock star and fellow campaigner Sir Bob Geldof prepares to depart for Edinburgh from Euston Station in London. He joined hundreds of supporters of the Make Poverty History campaign on the journey to Scotland the day before the G8 summit at Gleneagles. 5 July 2005, Stephen Hird.

lucrative markets of Europe and the United States. Bollywood, India's version of Hollywood, lives largely in a domestic bubble, although a handful of stars like Aishwarya Rai and Amitabh Bachchan are recognized beyond their shores. With a few exceptions, such as Ang Lee's *Crouching Tiger, Hidden Dragon*, Asian cinema tends to be copied by Hollywood more successfully than exported to Hollywood. Again, the number of internationally recognized celebrities from the continent is small, Ziyi Zhang of China and Malaysian-born Michelle Yeoh being the exception rather than the rule. But some critics believe that the high quality of Asian cinema, and English-speaking audiences' increasing acceptance of subtitles at the movie theatre, will gradually see it gain a significant following elsewhere.

The advent of the Internet has made fame and celebrity more accessible than ever. High art and architecture also reflect a more democratic age. When Britart wowed the art world in the early 1990s, it was shock value as much as artistic merit that mattered. And so Tracey Emin caused a stir with her unmade bed strewn with condoms, as did Damien Hirst with his dead animals suspended in tanks of formaldehyde. Some questioned whether Hirst's iconic pickled shark made in 1991 was art at all, but 14 years later it was reported that the work was sold to a U.S. buyer for a staggering £7 million. The Britart movement may have peaked in the mid-1990s, but its leading lights are still big players in the world of fine art, often more for their celebrity value than for their recent artistic output. Now in his forties, the bad boy of British art has mellowed and critics are cool to his new photorealist style, but Hirst remains one of the best known faces in the art world. In 2005, he was the first artist ever to top *ArtReview* magazine's benchmark 'Power 100' ranking, a list normally dominated by gallery owners, collectors and dealers.

If anyone demonstrates that art can be truly democratic, it is Christo and his wife Jeanne-Claude. Their 2005 installation *The Gates* was billed as the largest artwork in the world since the Sphinx. The long series of billowing fabrics suspended from over 7,500 giant frames along the pathways of Central Park in New York was free to view despite costing its creators an estimated $20 million to install.

Many of the most celebrated architectural projects of recent years have been public buildings accessible to the masses. Swiss architects Jacques Herzog and Pierre de Meuron won almost universal praise for their conversion of a huge disused power station on the banks of the River Thames in London into Tate Modern, which has become one of the most visited modern art galleries in the world since opening in May 2000. In Los Angeles-based Frank Gehry, the United States has an architect who has abandoned the straight lines of urban skylines for curves, and designed a series of revolutionary buildings to house art collections and concert halls. While he is responsible for many memorable buildings, including the Richard B. Fisher Center for the Performing Arts in New York and the Walt Disney Concert Hall in Los Angeles, Gehry's most famous project remains the Guggenheim Museum in Bilbao. Its titanium-clad curved contours are more akin to a giant sculpture than a gallery, and are as much a draw for visitors as the art works they contain. Gehry's visionary building played a large part in transforming a formerly run-down Spanish industrial port into an international cultural destination, and has inspired city planners the world over.

On an even grander scale, Britain's Norman Foster married grace with vast size in his Grand Viaduc Du Millau (see pages 2–3), the world's highest road bridge, running 280 metres (919 feet) above the French valley below. Underlining man's unceasing desire to build the biggest and the best, this project was also an expensive one, costing more than $500 million to complete.

Skyscrapers continue to grow higher, with the needle-like Burj Tower in Dubai due to overtake the Taipei 101 tower as the world's tallest building in 2008. Such structures express the rising confidence and rapid growth of the emerging economies of Asia and the Middle East. The Burj will also dwarf the new Freedom Tower that is set to replace Manhattan's destroyed World Trade Center. That highly sensitive project, by Polish-born architect Daniel Libeskind, will feature a spire that 'nods' towards the Statue of Liberty and will rise to a proposed height of 1,776 feet to match the date of the Declaration of Independence.

The digital age has opened up access to movies, music and the stars like never before. The likes of Madonna and Tom Cruise will seek to control their image as best they can despite the intense curiosity of a captivated public. Yet they cannot resist the relentless advance of technology; like other parts of the entertainment business, they must learn to harness new modes of communication or risk being left behind.

The music industry is finally beginning to reap the benefits of the Internet rather than treat it as a harbinger of commercial doom. The likes of iTunes are offering a simple, affordable and – crucially – legal way of downloading music, be it onto a laptop computer, a CD or a portable playback device. The once renegade Napster has marketed an alternative model, a rental scheme whereby users can download unlimited songs as long as they pay a regular subscription.

Artists are increasingly aware of the marketing potential of new technology, seeing the latest generation of mobile phones as another way of reaching new fans. When Robbie Williams launched his 2005 album *Intensive Care* with a concert in Berlin, it was beamed live to an estimated 100,000 phones. The debut single from Madonna's hit album *Confessions on a Dancefloor* was available first as a ringtone from selected websites. Such innovations are likely to increase as portable playback devices become video as well as audio-enabled.

The film business has yet to rise to the challenge of these new technologies. Pirated DVD copies of Hollywood films have been flooding markets for years, but given the much greater data content of a digitized movie, the industry has until now remained relatively untouched by Internet piracy and illegal downloading. The rapid expansion of computing power and high-speed broadband connections in people's homes around the world looks set to

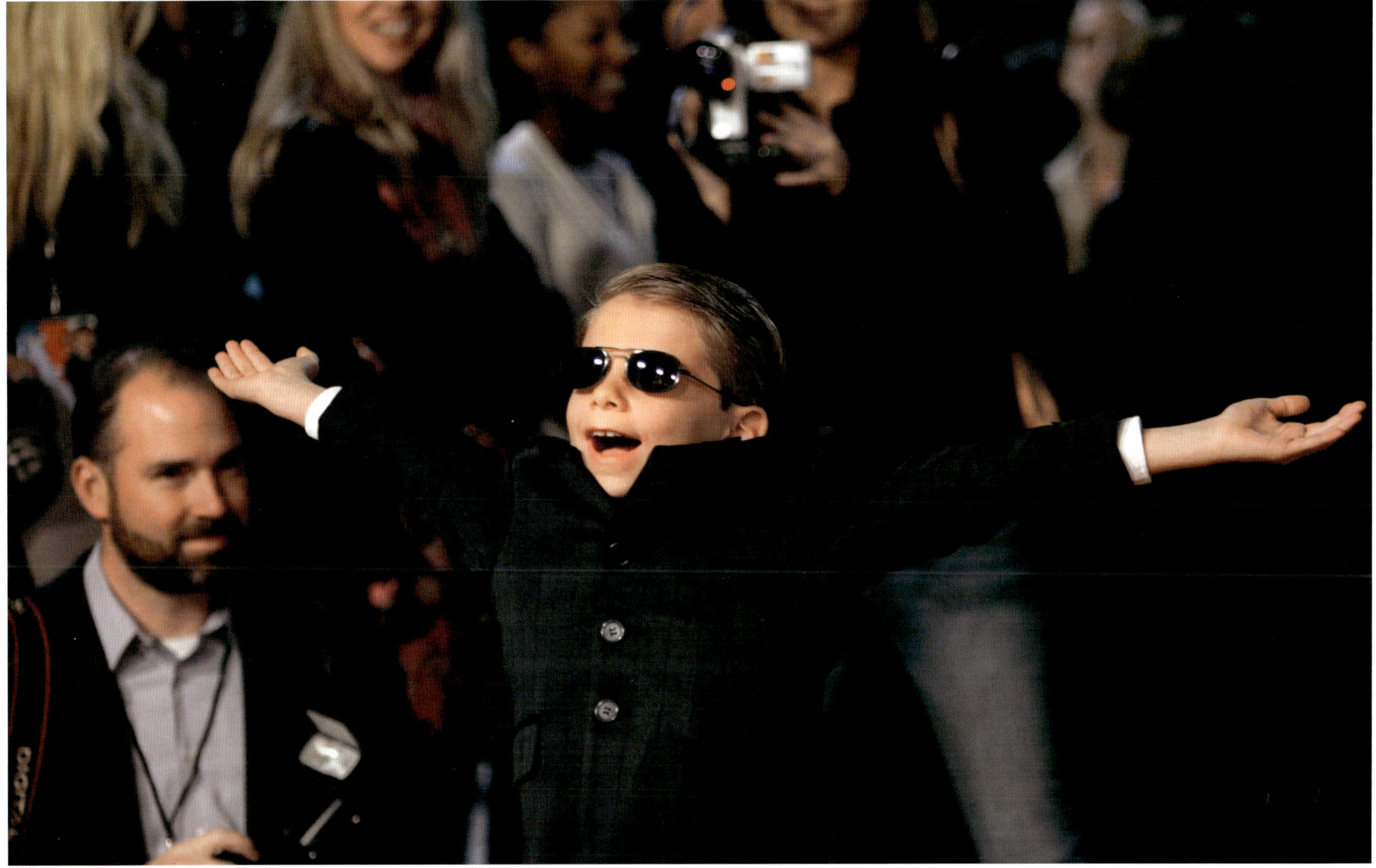

change that, and the film business is worried. Hollywood's studios say they lose around $3.5 billion every year to piracy, and fear that figure will spiral higher if swapping films via the web becomes more common.

Celebrities, be they actors, soccer idols or 'starchitects', are today's gods, to whom we look – without apparent sense of contradiction – for both inspiration and example of how not to live our lives. When life-like waxworks of England soccer captain David Beckham and his wife, one-time Spice Girl Victoria, were dressed as Mary and Joseph in a Nativity scene at Madame Tussauds in London, church groups complained bitterly. Yet the display merely told us what we already know: the adoration of celebrity has become a modern-day religion.

Just beware worshipping false idols.

14 December 2005, LOS ANGELES, UNITED STATES

Child actor Aaron Michael Drozin plays up to the gathered crowd of photographers during the Los Angeles premiere of Columbia Pictures' *Fun with Dick and Jane* at the Mann Village theatre. Mario Anzuoni

Mike Collett-White has been at Reuters since 1997. Having worked as a politics and business reporter in Moscow, he spent two years as a senior correspondent in Central Asia. After September 11, 2001, Mike worked on the front line in Afghanistan and went on to become deputy bureau chief in Pakistan and Afghanistan. He was also in Iraq covering the 2003 Gulf War and the fall of Tikrit, the last major city to succumb to U.S. forces. He is currently senior arts and entertainment correspondent based in London, where he also helped cover the suicide attacks on 7 July 2005.

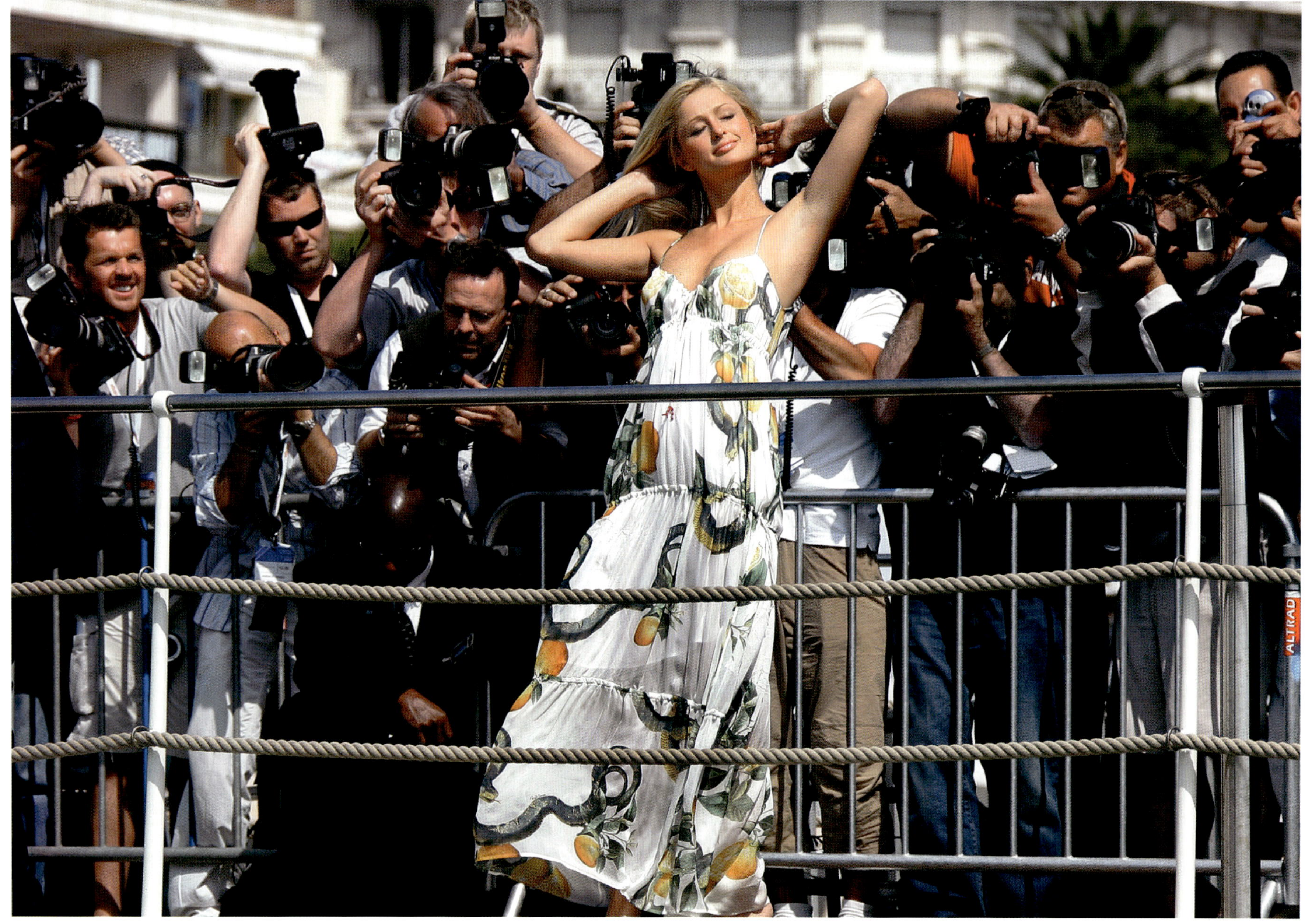

13 May 2005, CANNES, FRANCE

U.S. hotel heiress Paris Hilton poses at a photocall on the Carlton Hotel pier during the 58th Cannes Film Festival. Hilton was attending the festival to promote her film *National Lampoon's Pledge This!* Eric Gaillard

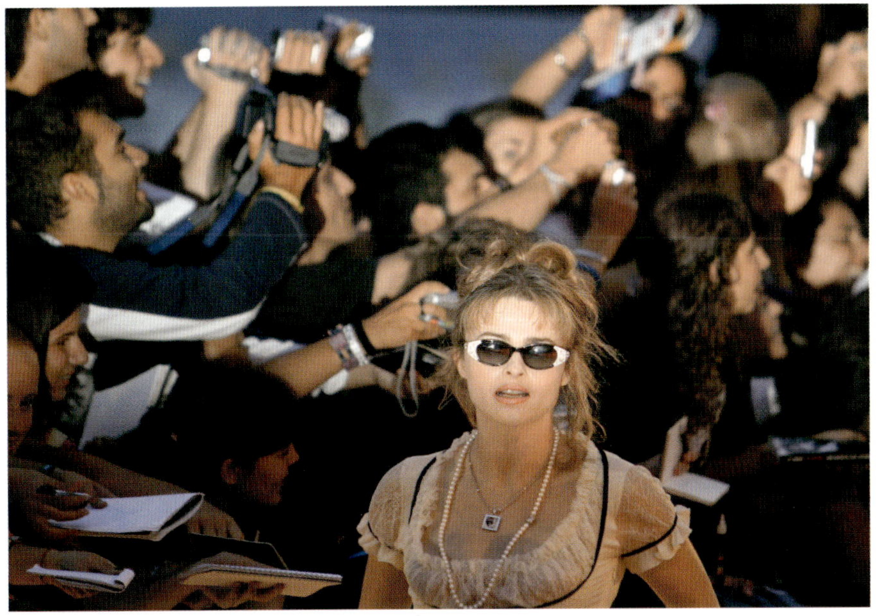

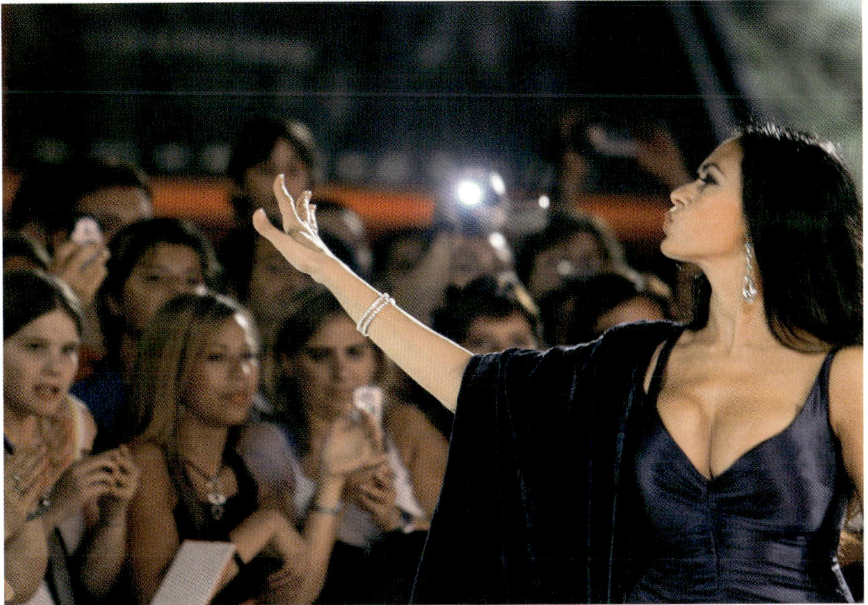

7 September 2005, VENICE, ITALY

British actress Helena Bonham Carter arrives at the Cinema Palace in Venice for the premiere of U.S. director Tim Burton's latest animation movie *Tim Burton's*

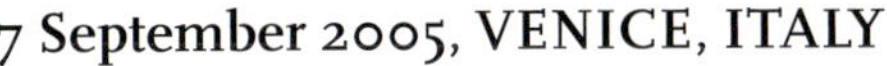

Corpse Bride at the Venice film festival. Alessia Pierdomenico

1 September 2005, VENICE, ITALY

Italian actress and producer Maria Grazia Cucinotta arrives at the Cinema Palace in Venice for the premiere of her latest movie *All the Invisible Children*. Alessia Pierdomenico

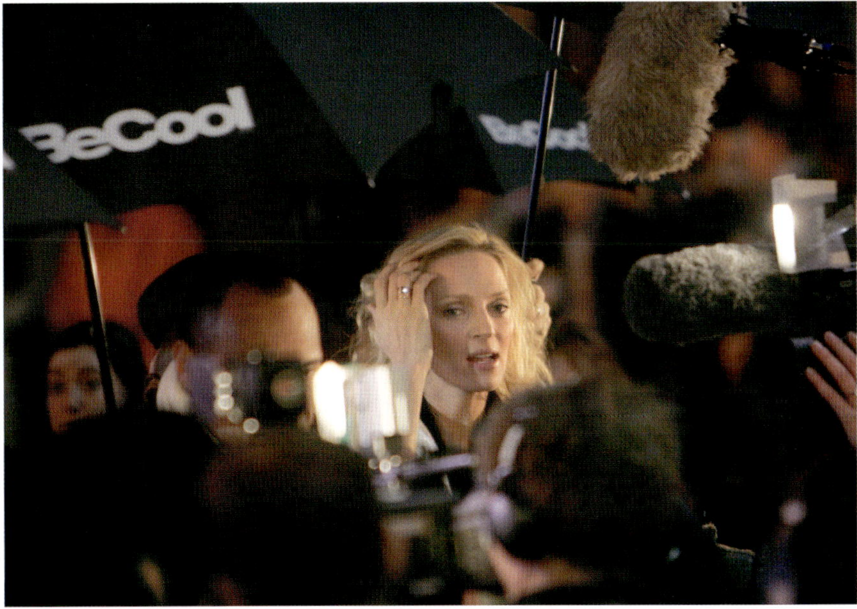

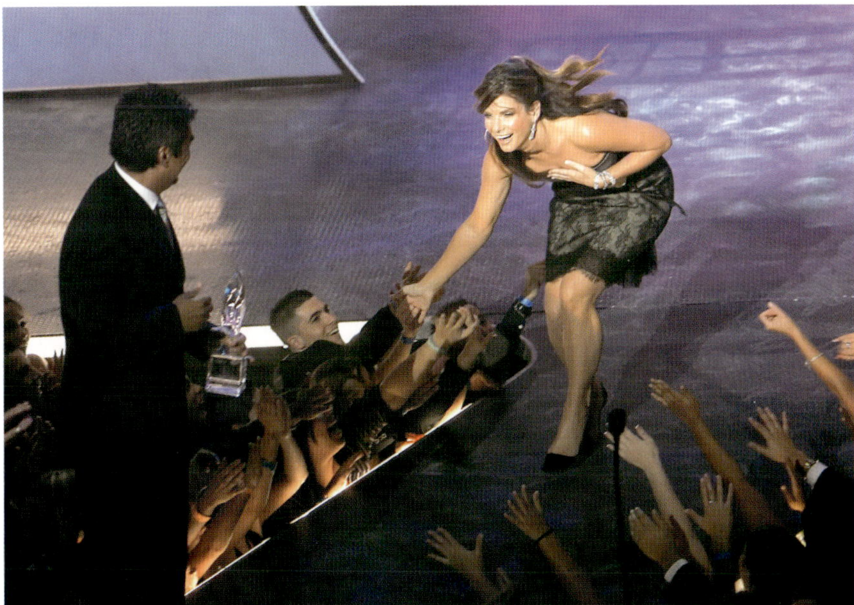

7 March 2005, LONDON, UNITED KINGDOM

U.S. actress Uma Thurman arrives at the European premiere of the film *Be Cool* at the Empire Leicester Square cinema in London. Stephen Hird

10 January 2006, LOS ANGELES, UNITED STATES

U.S. actress Sandra Bullock celebrates after accepting the award for favourite female movie star at the 32nd annual People's Choice Awards in Los Angeles. Watching at the left is comedian and presenter George Lopez. Robert Galbraith

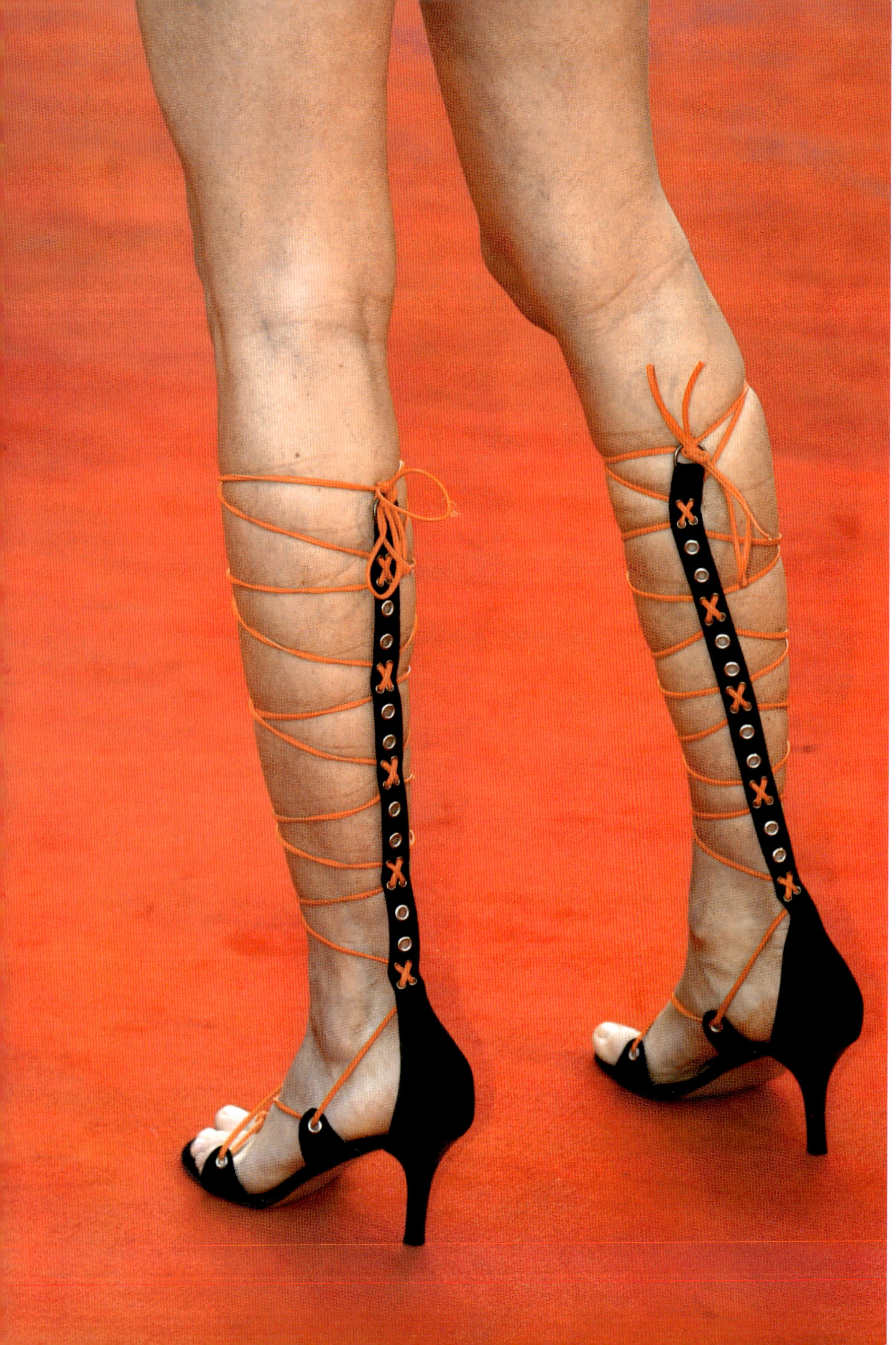

17 May 2003, CANNES, FRANCE

Former Miss France Mareva Galanter wears high-laced shoes during red-carpet arrivals at the 56th International Film Festival in Cannes. The French Riviera town hosts the most prestigious film festival in the world, with 12 days of movie premieres, deal-making and parties. Vincent Kessler

11 May 2005, CANNES, FRANCE

Workmen roll out the red carpet on the steps of the festival palace before the opening of the 58th Cannes Film Festival. Jean-Paul Pelissier

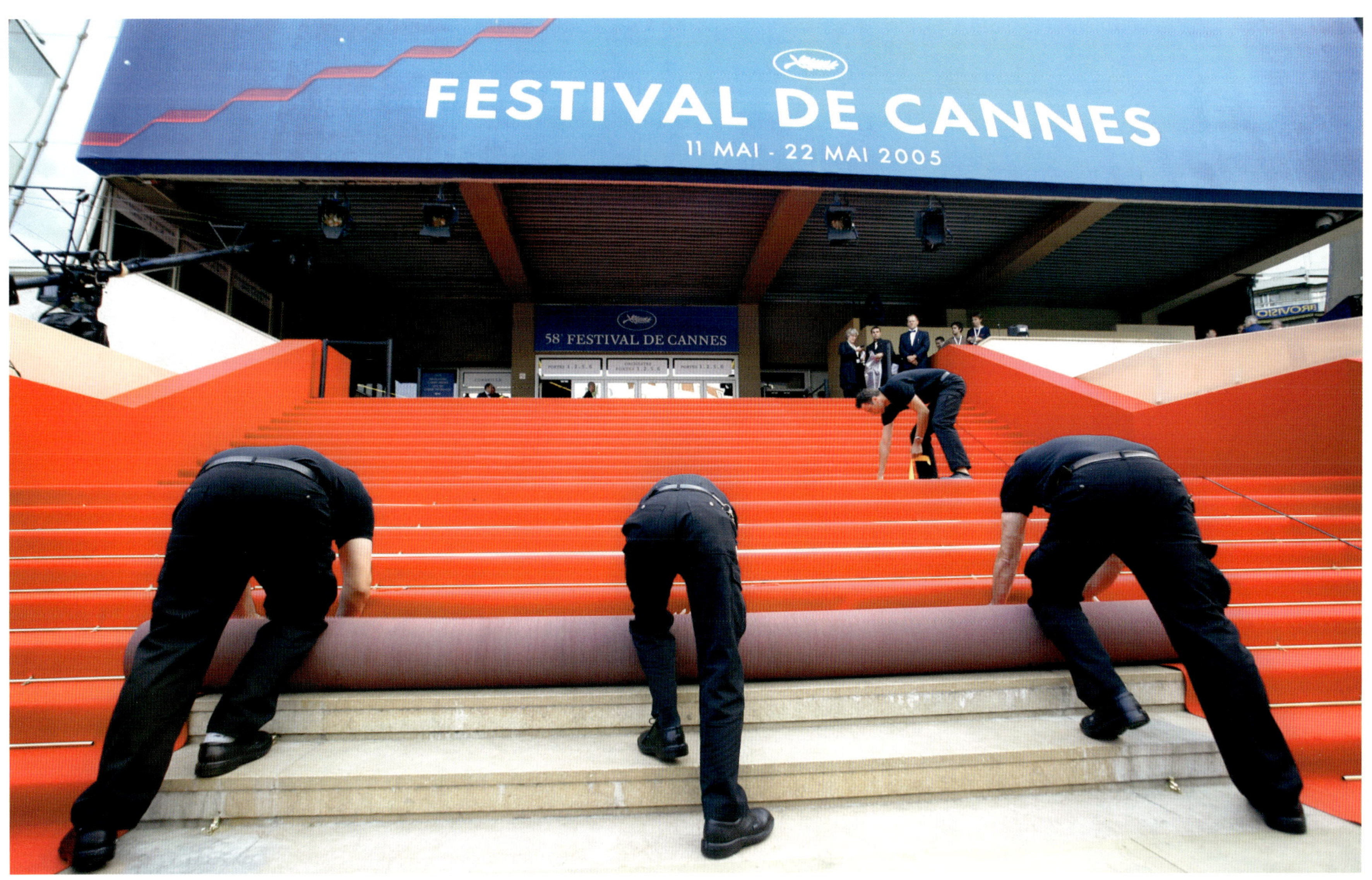

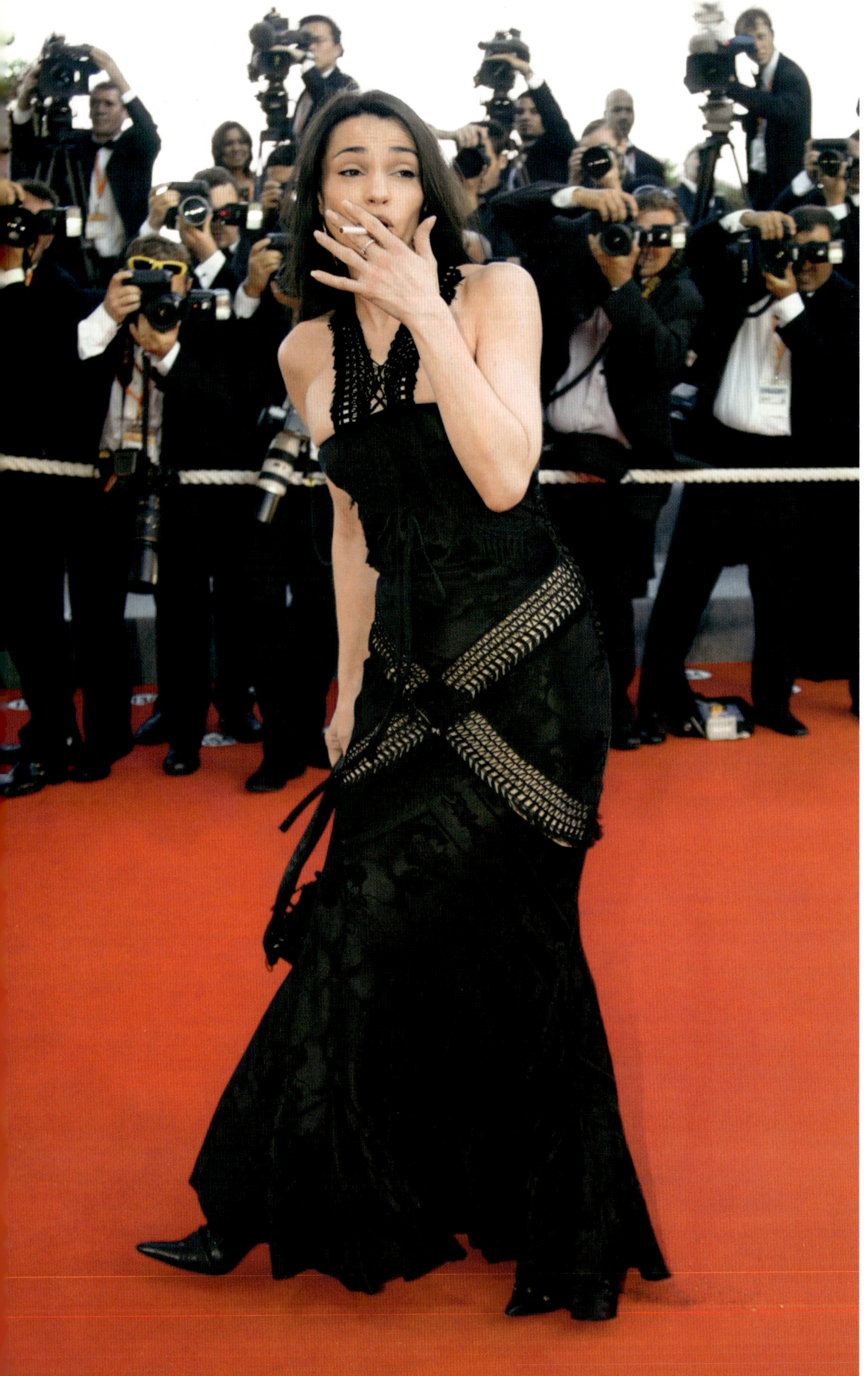

20 May 2003, CANNES, FRANCE

French actress Béatrice Dalle smokes during red-carpet arrivals for Austrian director Michael Haneke's film *Le Temps du Loup* at the 56th International Film Festival in Cannes. Eric Gaillard

18 May 2005, CANNES, FRANCE

Opposite above left Indian actress Mallika Sherawat poses during red carpet arrivals for the screening of director Robert Rodriguez and Frank Miller's film *Sin City* at the 58th International Film Festival in Cannes. Vincent Kessler

15 May 2004, CANNES, FRANCE

Opposite above right U.S. actress Cameron Diaz poses on the red carpet during arrivals for the presentation of the animated film *Shrek 2* at the 57th International Film Festival in Cannes. Vincent Kessler

15 May 2004, CANNES, FRANCE

Opposite below U.S. actor Jack Black clowns on the red carpet at the festival palace as he arrives to attend the screening of *Shrek 2* at the 57th International Film Festival in Cannes. John Schults

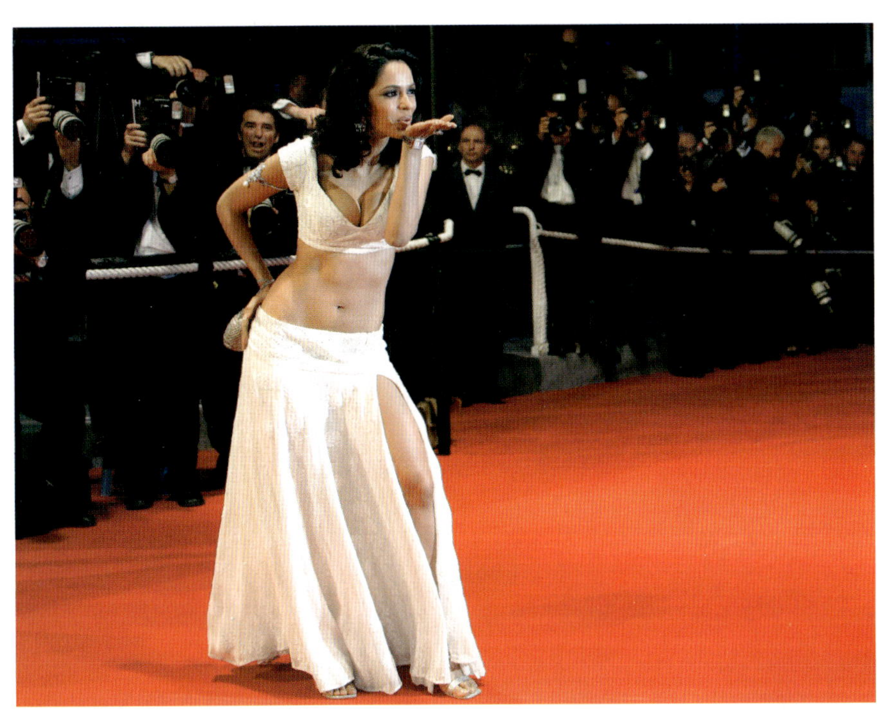

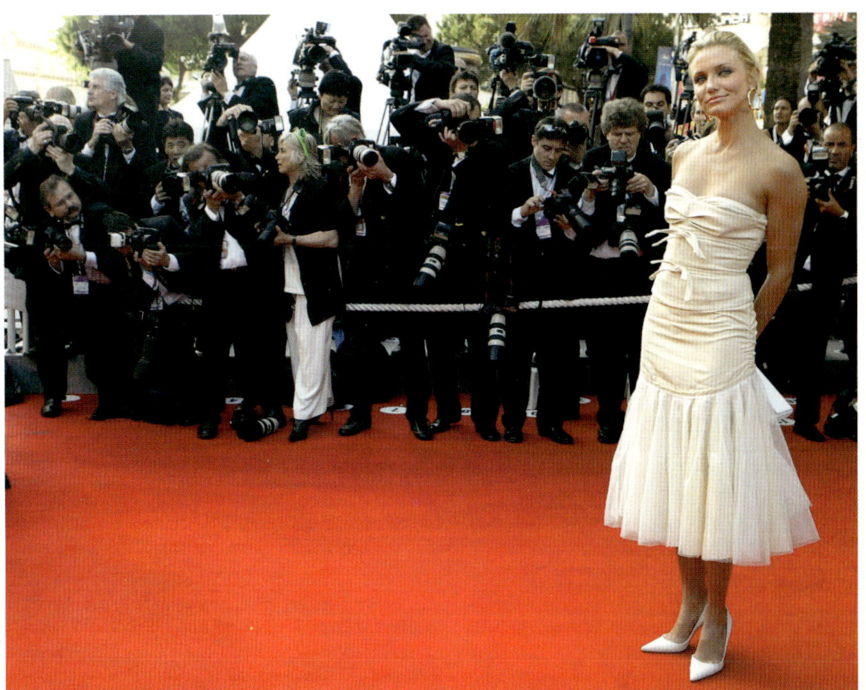

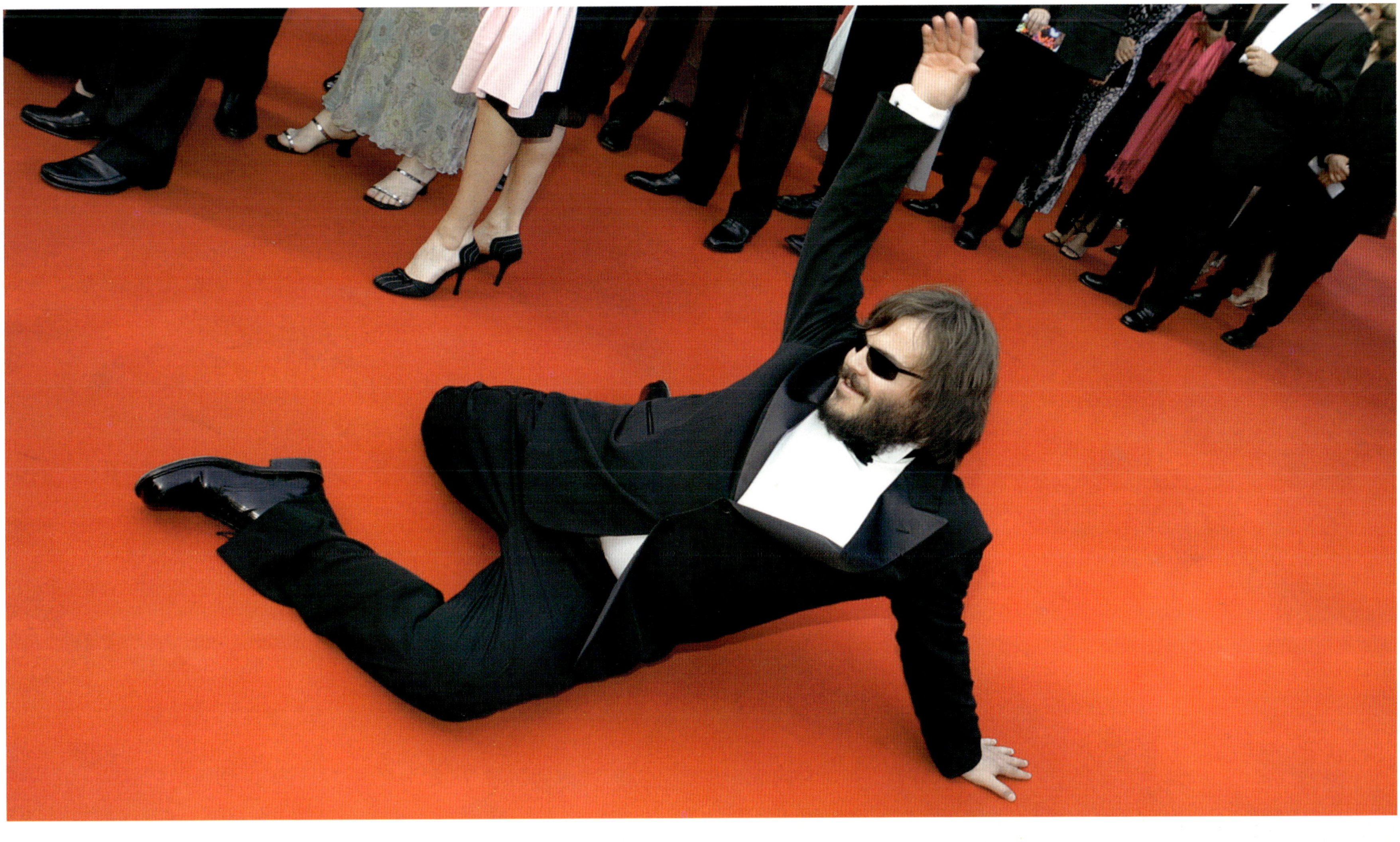

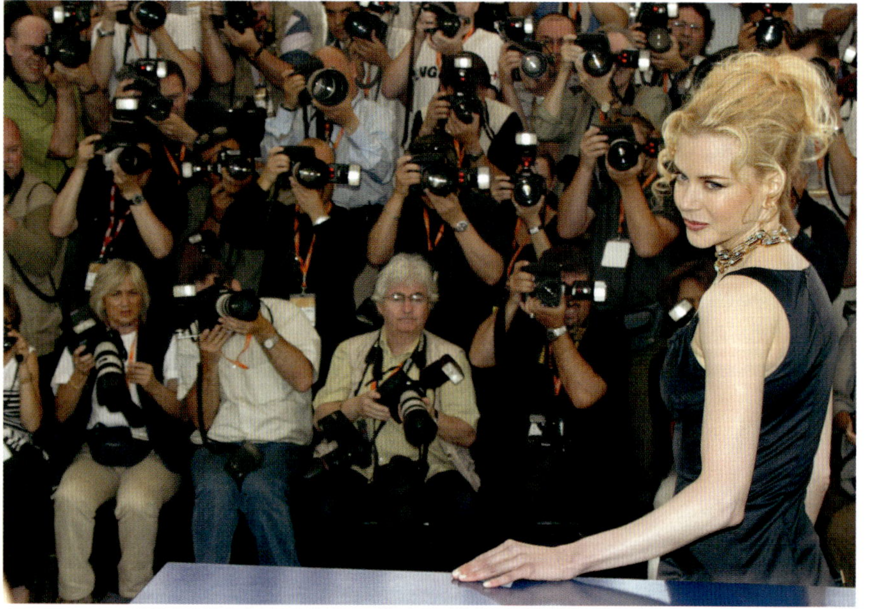

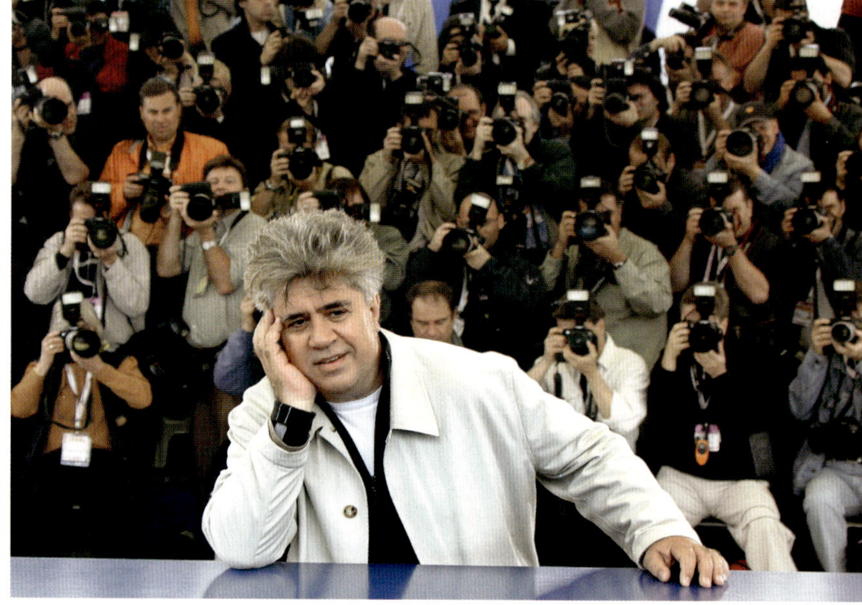

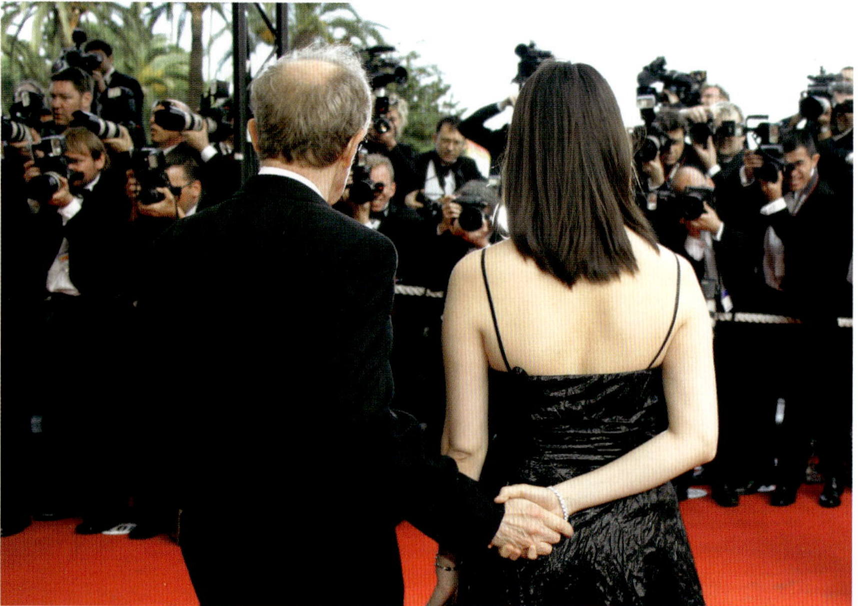

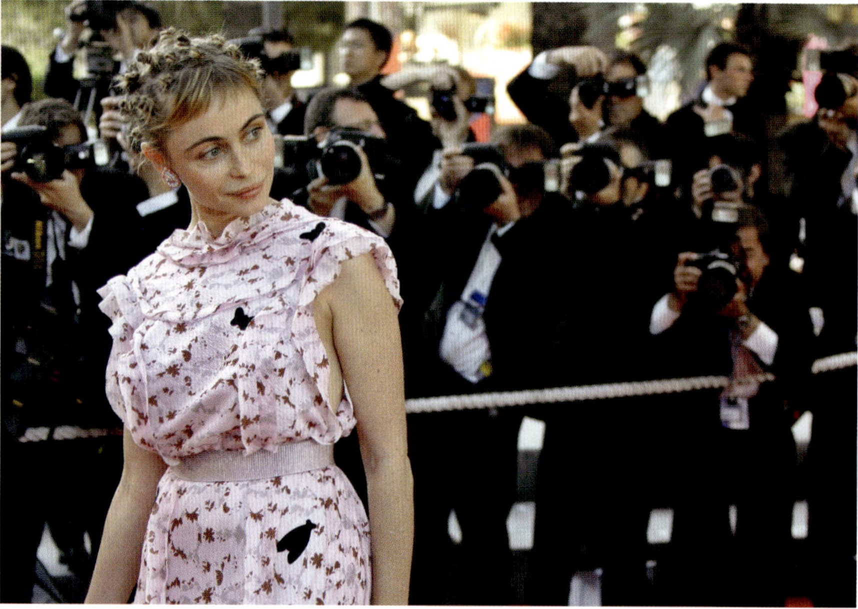

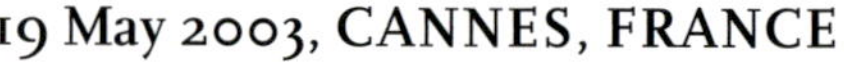

19 May 2003, CANNES, FRANCE

Australian actress Nicole Kidman poses during a photocall for Danish director Lars Von Trier's film *Dogville* at the 56th International Film Festival in Cannes. Eric Gaillard

12 May 2005, CANNES, FRANCE

U.S. director Woody Allen poses with his wife Soon-Yi Previn during red carpet arrivals for a screening of his film *Match Point* at the 58th International Film Festival in Cannes. Eric Gaillard

12 May 2004, CANNES, FRANCE

Spanish director Pedro Almodóvar poses for a photocall for his film *La Mala Educación (Bad Education)* at the 57th International Film Festival in Cannes. Eric Gaillard

18 May 2005, CANNES, FRANCE

French actress Emmanuelle Béart poses during red carpet arrivals for French directors Arnaud and Jean-Marie Larrieu's film *Peindre ou Faire l'Amour (To Paint or Make Love)* at the 58th International Film Festival in Cannes. Vincent Kessler

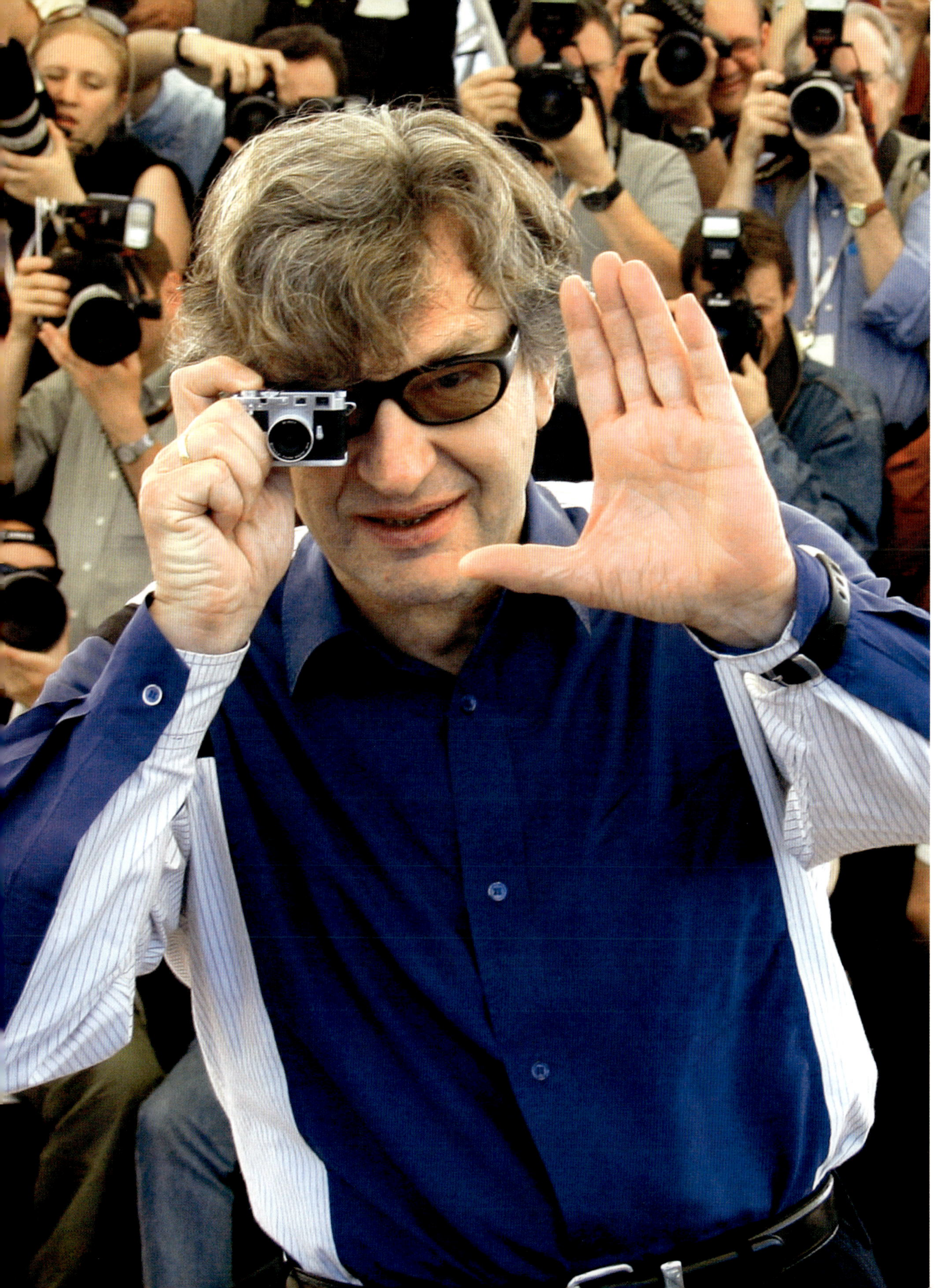

19 May 2005, CANNES, FRANCE

German director Wim Wenders poses during a photocall for his film *Don't Come Knocking* at the 58th International Film Festival in Cannes. Eric Gaillard

29 February 2004, LOS ANGELES, UNITED STATES

Charlize Theron wipes a tear as she accepts the Oscar for Best Actress at the 76th Academy Awards. She won for her role in *Monster*, directed by Patty Jenkins.

Gary Hershorn

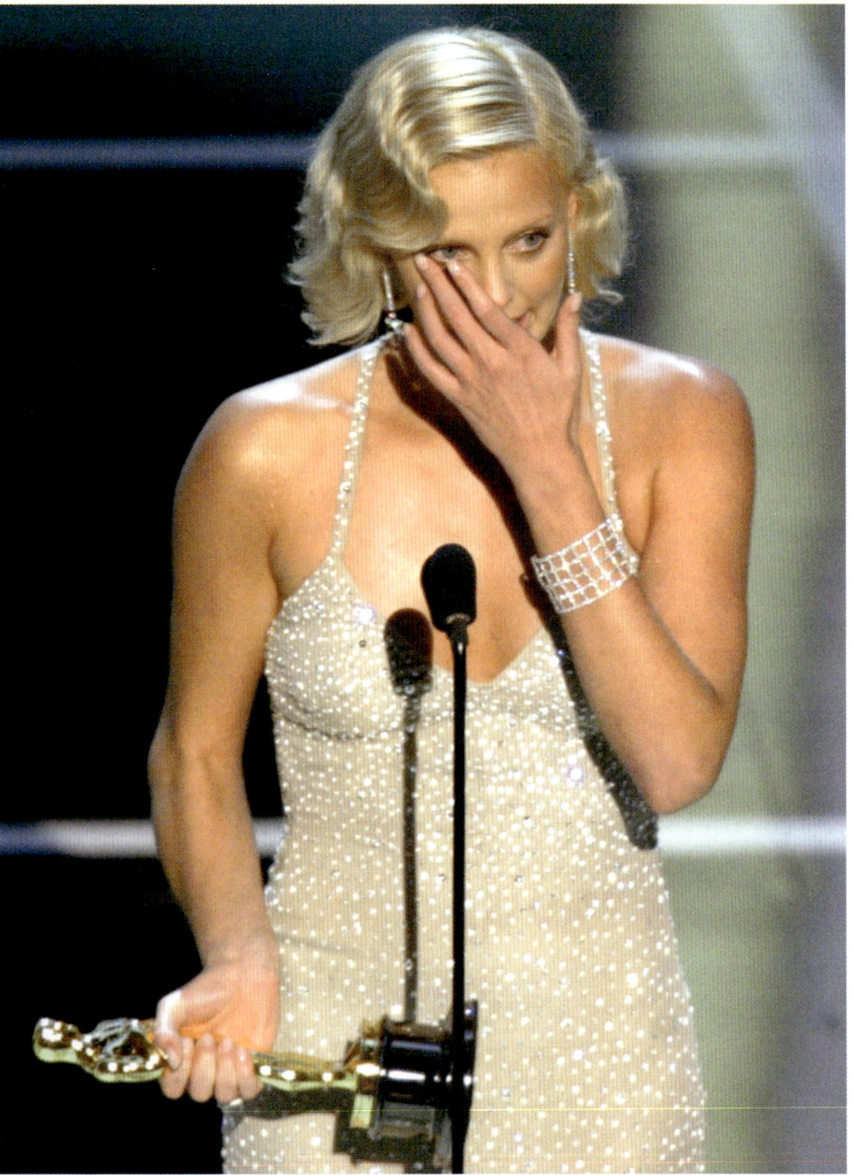

25 March 2001, LOS ANGELES, UNITED STATES

Julia Roberts accepts the Oscar for Best Actress at the 73rd Academy Awards. She won for her role in *Erin Brockovich*, directed by Steven Soderbergh.

Gary Hershorn

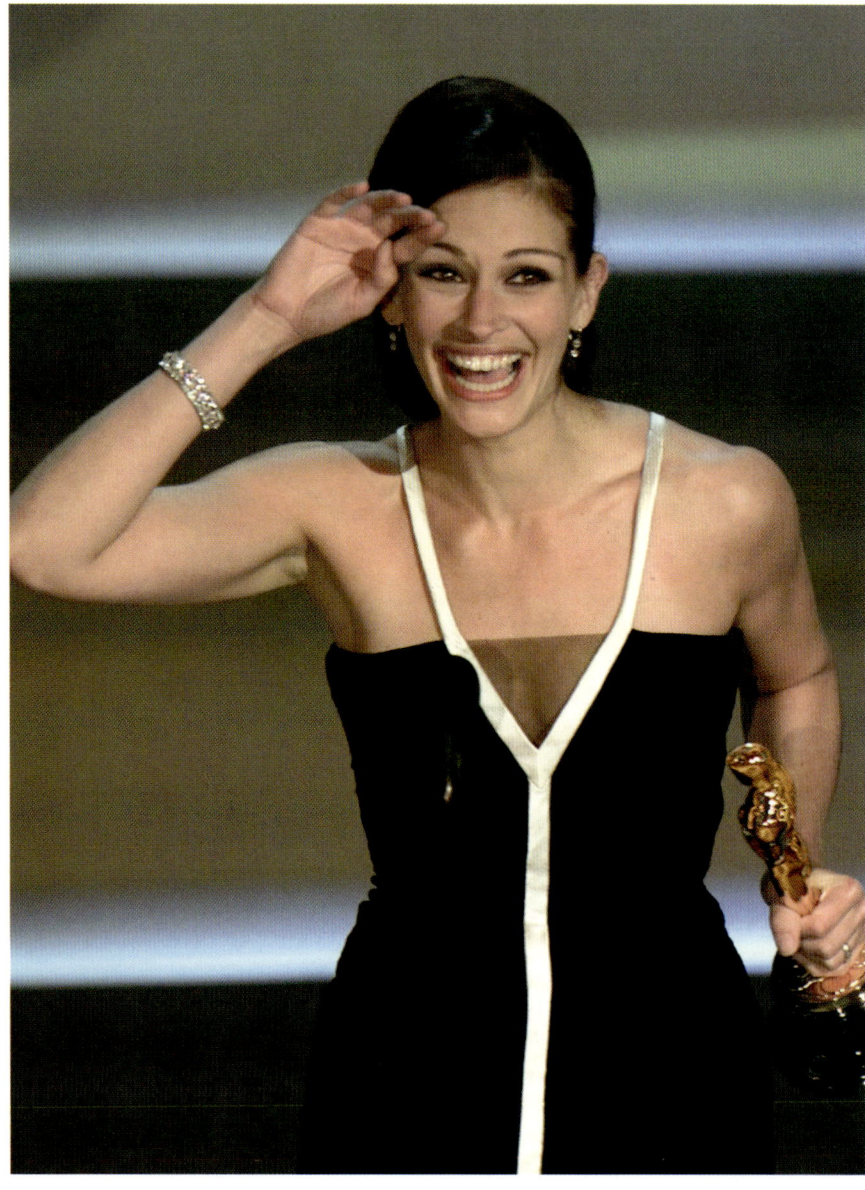

27 February 2005, LOS ANGELES, UNITED STATES

Hilary Swank accepts the Oscar for Best Actress at the 77th Academy Awards. She won for her role in *Million Dollar Baby*, directed by Clint Eastwood.
Gary Hershorn

23 March 2003, LOS ANGELES, UNITED STATES

Nicole Kidman turns away as she chokes back tears after accepting the Oscar for Best Actress at the 75th Academy Awards. She won for her role as Virginia Woolf in *The Hours*, directed by Stephen Daldry. Mike Blake

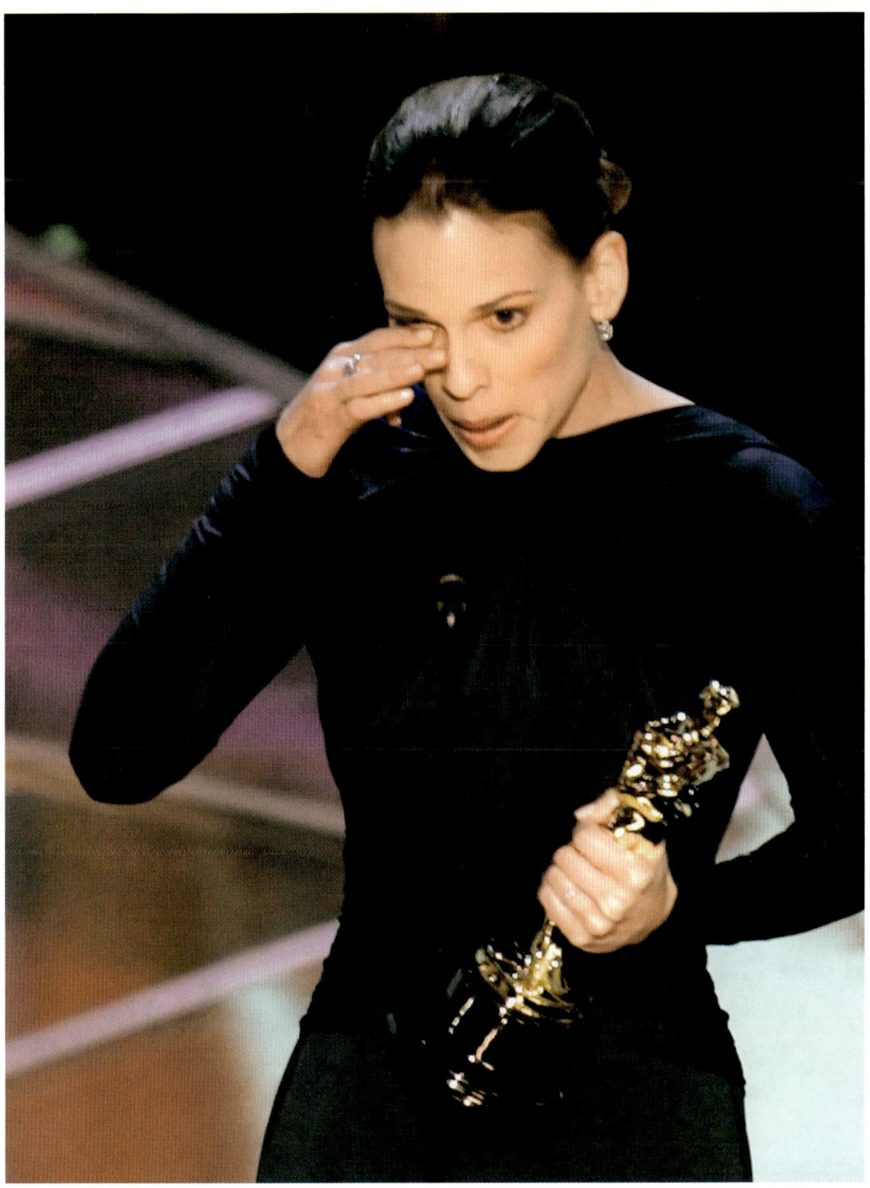

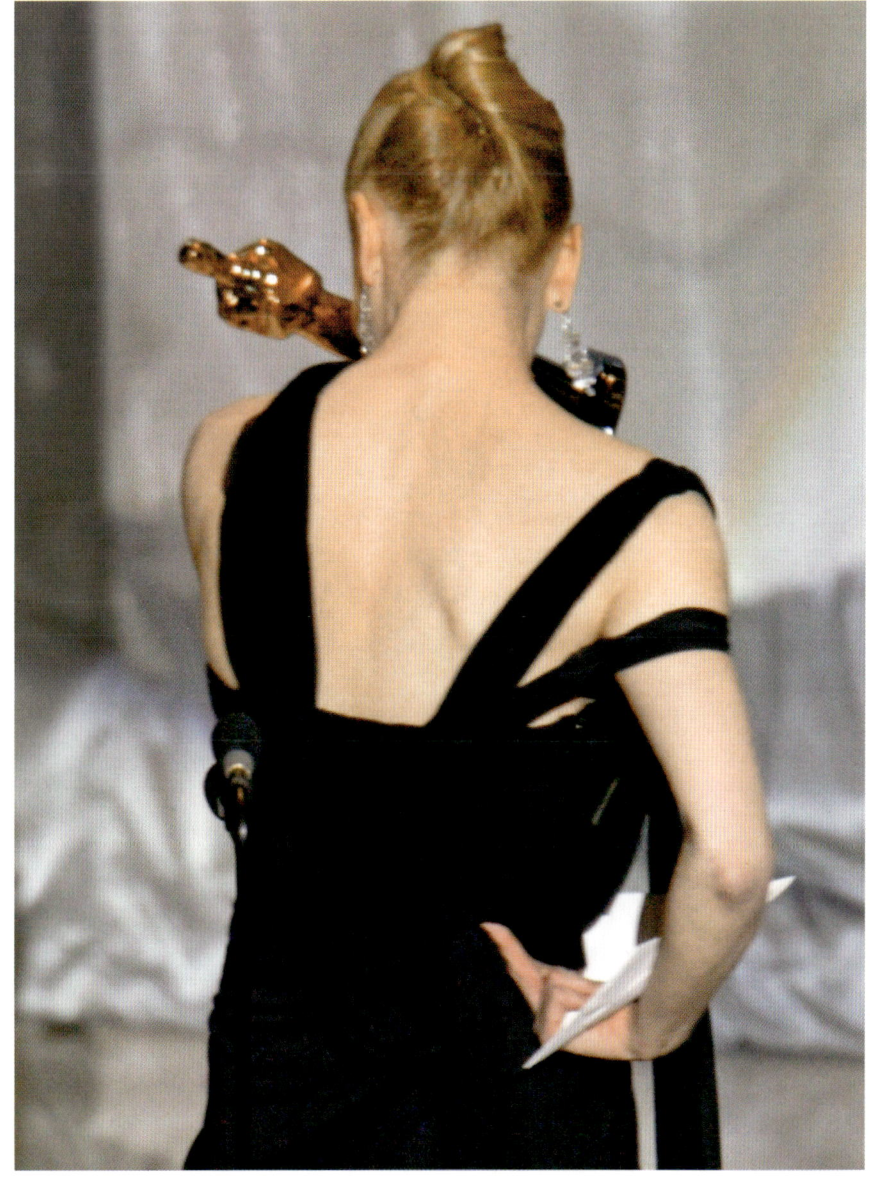

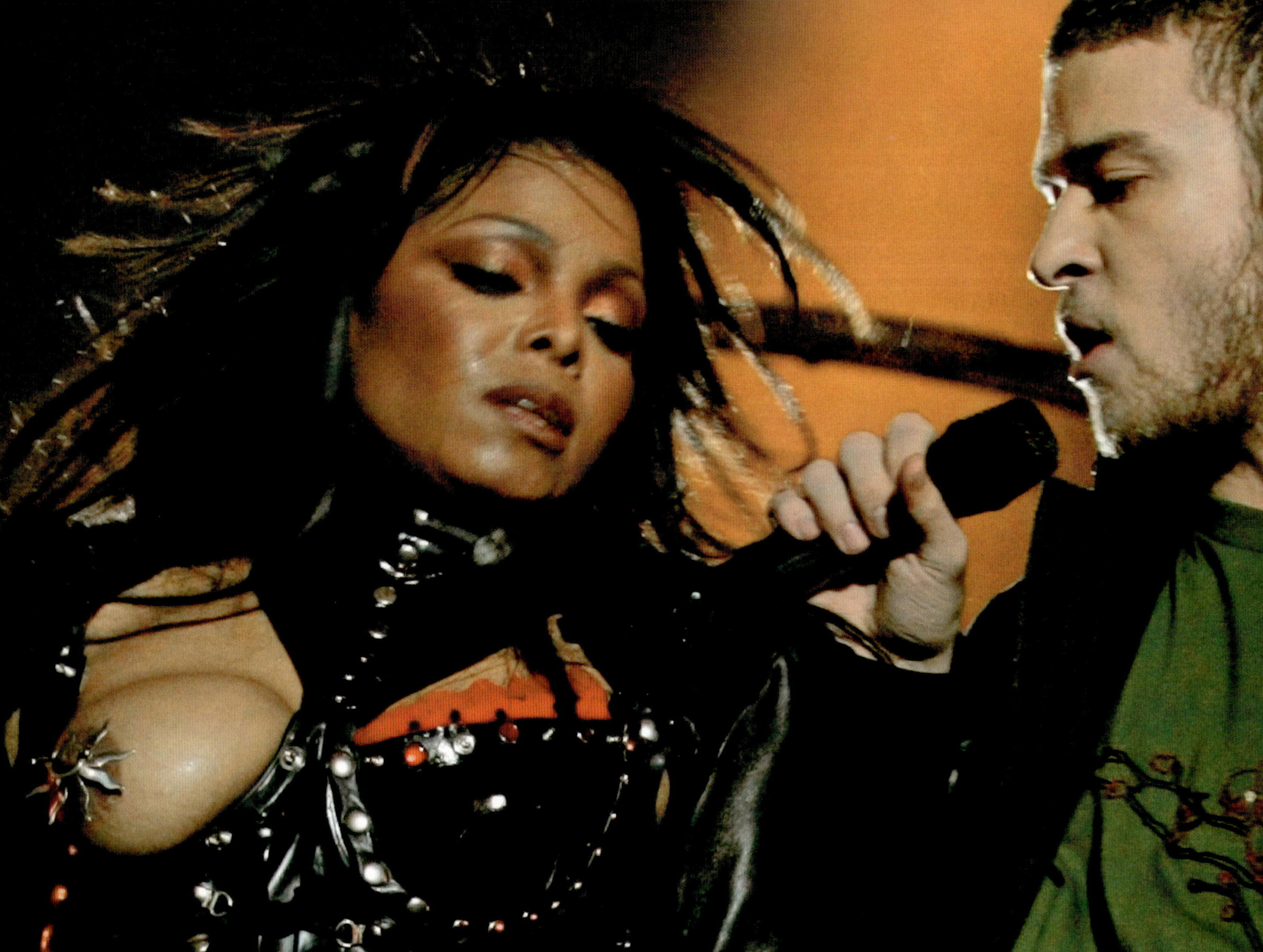

1 February 2004, HOUSTON, UNITED STATES

Janet Jackson performs with fellow singer Justin Timberlake after he ripped off one of her chest plates at the end of a half-time performance during the Super Bowl. Broadcaster CBS received a record 200,000 complaints about the incident. Both performers apologized for the flash of flesh, which they insisted was entirely unplanned. Timberlake blamed a 'wardrobe malfunction'. Win McNamee

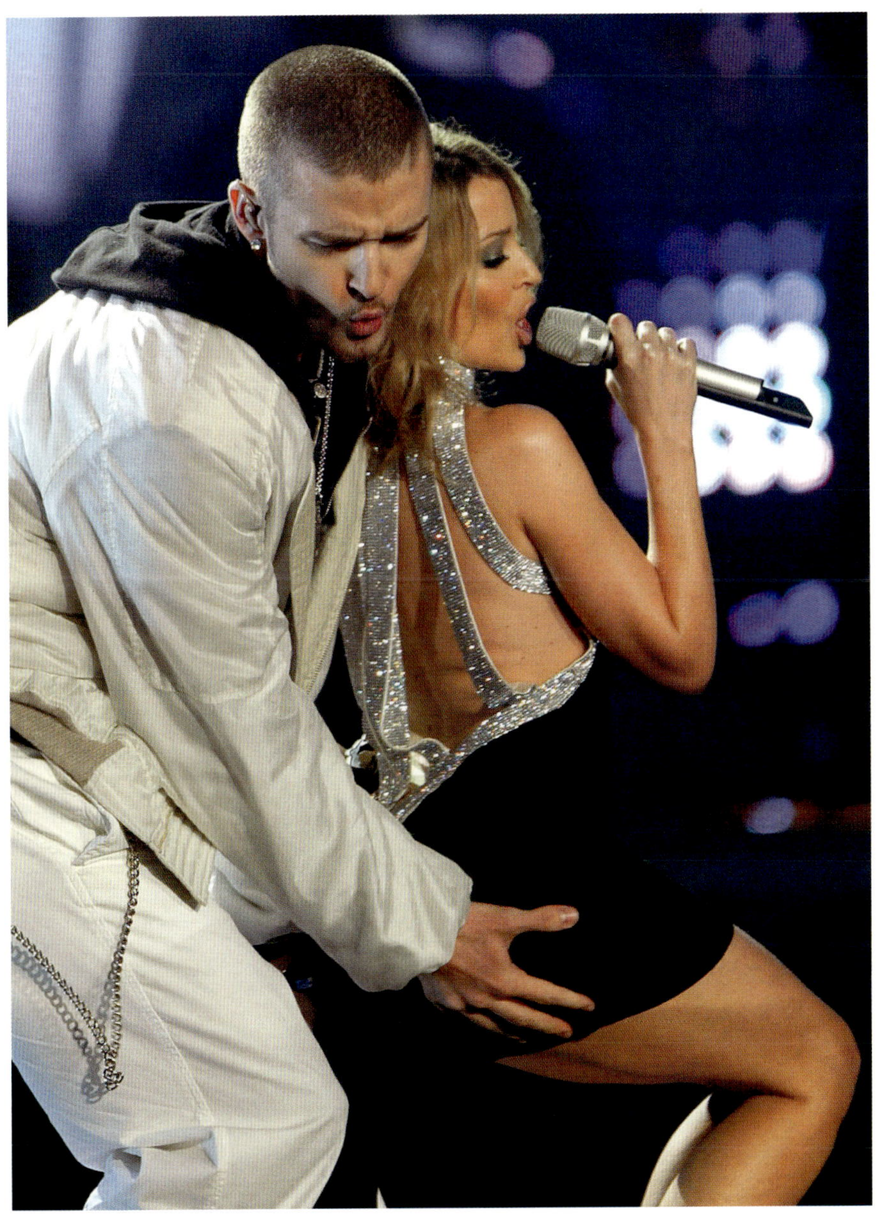

20 February 2003, LONDON, UNITED KINGDOM

Justin Timberlake and Kylie Minogue perform a duet at the 2003 Brit Awards in London. Toby Melville

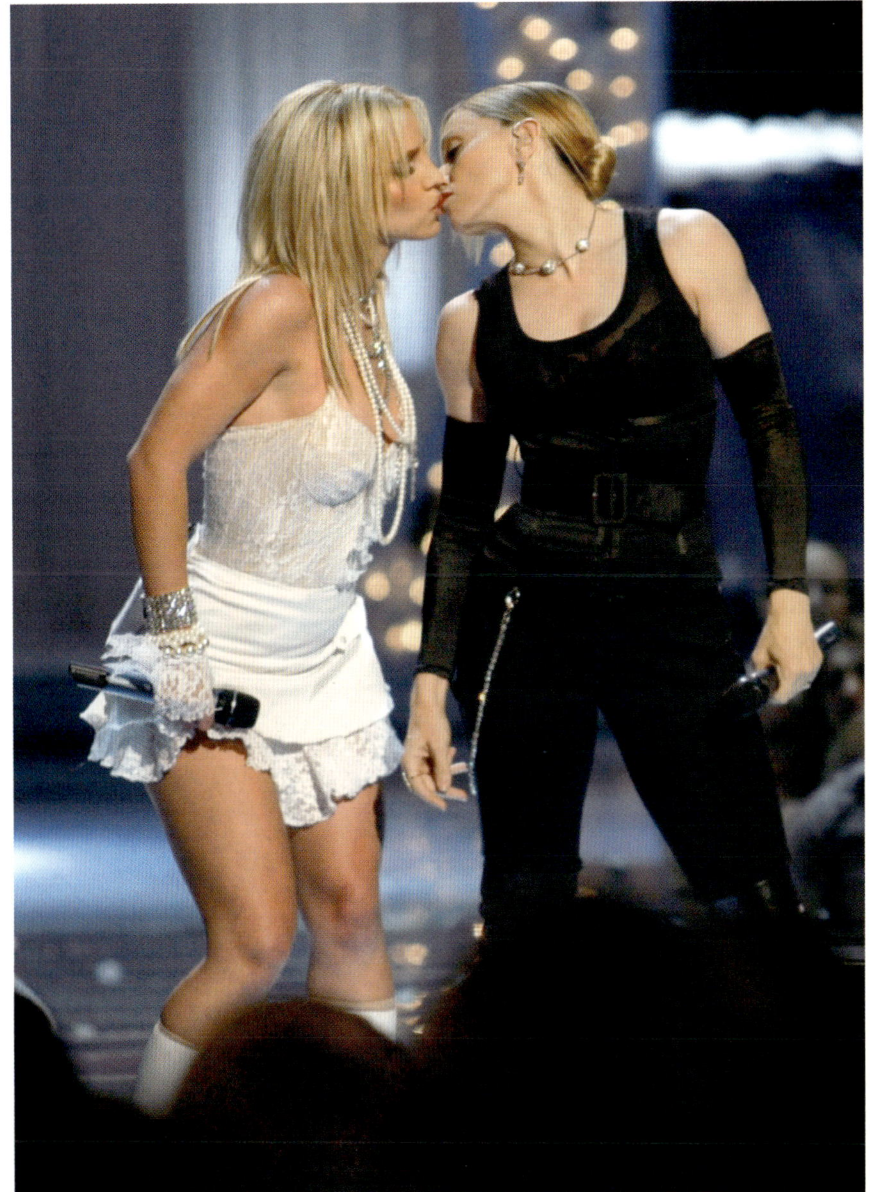

28 August 2003, NEW YORK, UNITED STATES

Madonna kisses Britney Spears during the opening of the 2003 MTV Video Music Awards at the Radio City Music Hall in New York. Win McNamee

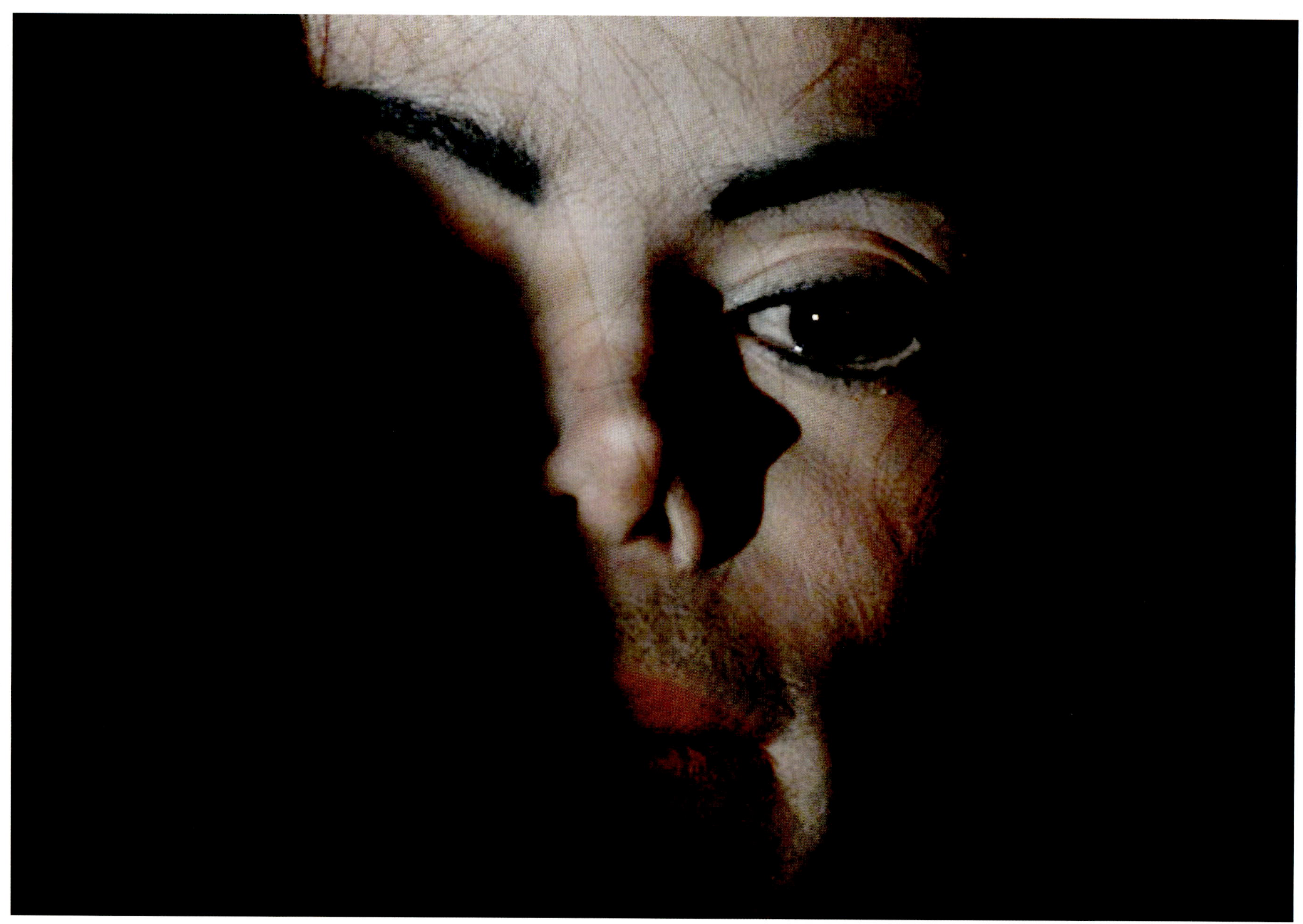

6 March 2001, OXFORD, UNITED KINGDOM

Michael Jackson arrives at the Oxford University Union to give a lecture and launch his global initiative for children, 'Heal the Kids'. Russell Boyce

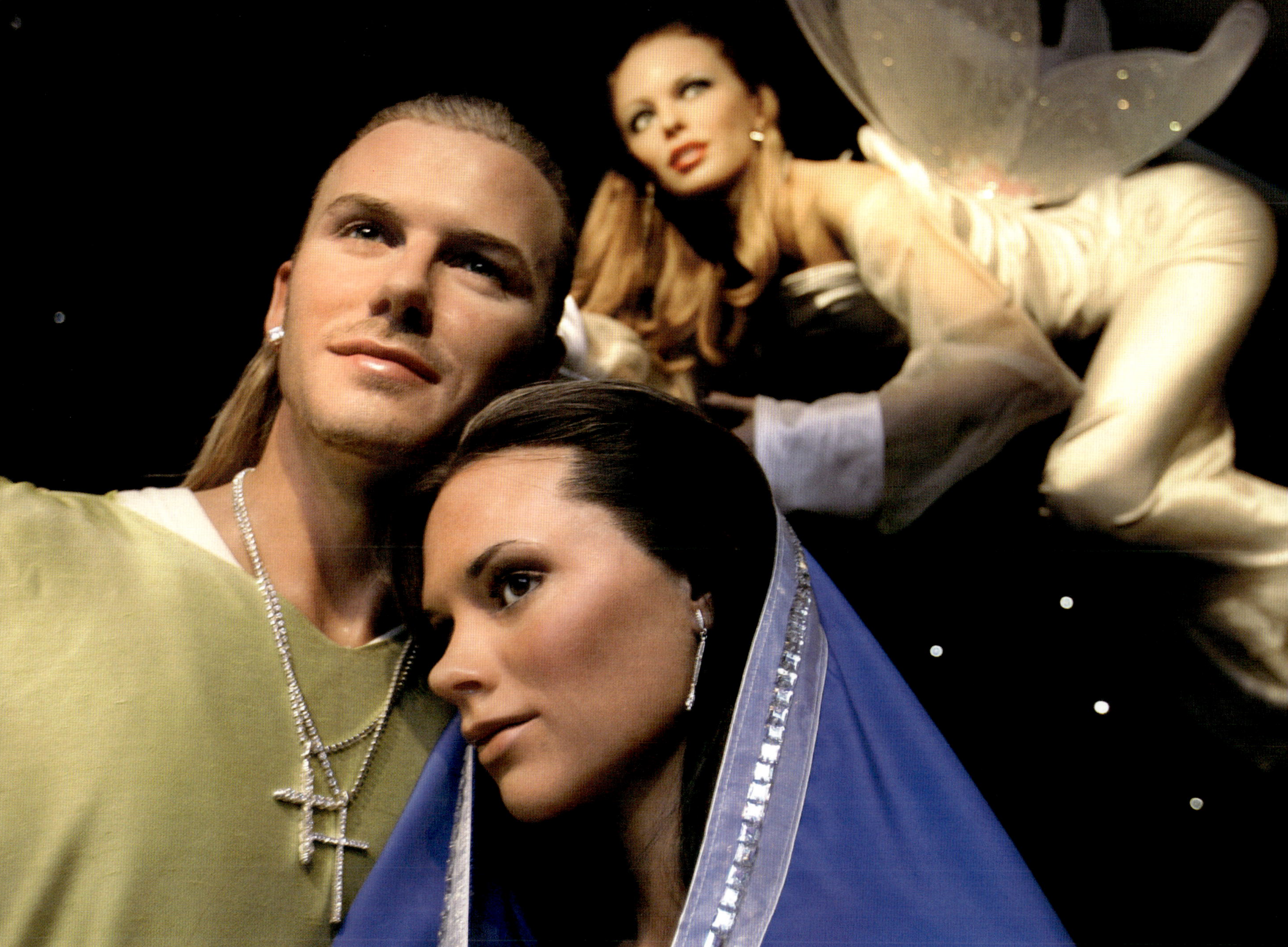

7 December 2004, LONDON, UNITED KINGDOM

Waxworks of England soccer captain David Beckham and his wife Victoria appear as Joseph and Mary, with Kylie Minogue as the angel, in a celebrity nativity scene at Madame Tussauds in London. Peter Macdiarmid

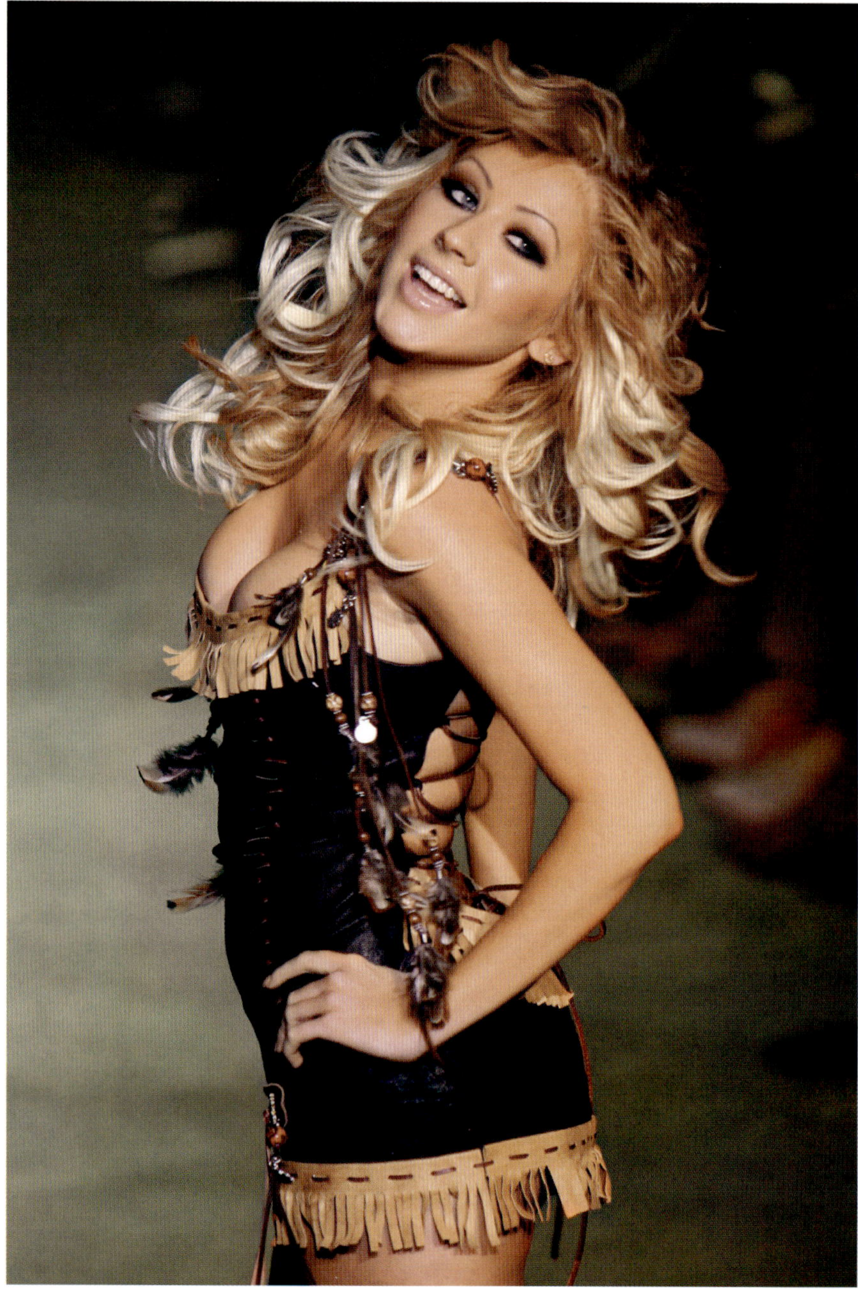

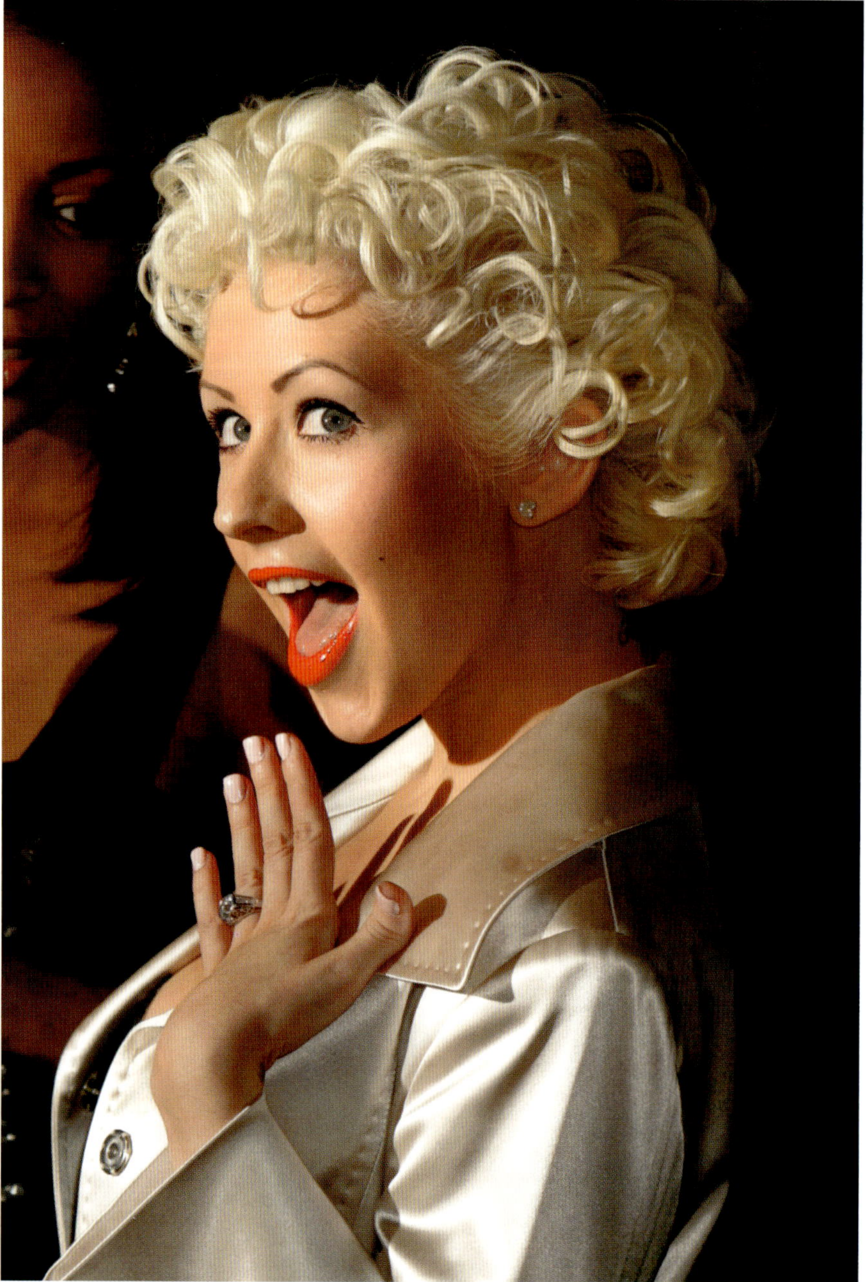

29 June 2004, MILAN, ITALY

Above U.S. singer Christina Aguilera acknowledges applause after participating in the Dsquared[2] spring/summer 2005 show during Milan Fashion Week. Daniele La Monaca

15 February 2005, BEVERLY HILLS, UNITED STATES

Above right Christina Aguilera shows off her engagement ring as she arrives at the opening of Italian fashion designer Roberto Cavalli's boutique in Beverly Hills. She had recently become engaged to music executive Jordan Bratman. Fred Prouser

Opposite, clockwise from top left

Courtney Love at the opening party of Hollywood bar and dining lounge 'ROKBAR', 30 June 2005 Mario Anzuoni. Madonna arrives for the screening of her documentary *I'm Gonna Tell You A Secret* in New York, 18 October 2005 Keith Bedford. Farrah Fawcett releases a butterfly in memory of comedian Rodney Dangerfield, 5 October 2005 Mario Anzuoni. Twin actresses Mary-Kate and Ashley Olsen in Mougins during the 58th Cannes Film Festival, 19 May 2005 Eric Gaillard. Nicole Kidman at the Sydney Opera House for the world premiere of the film *The Interpreter*, 4 April 2005 Tim Wimborne. Antonio Banderas and his wife Melanie Griffith at the premiere of *The Legend of Zorro* in Los Angeles, 16 October 2005 Mario Anzuoni

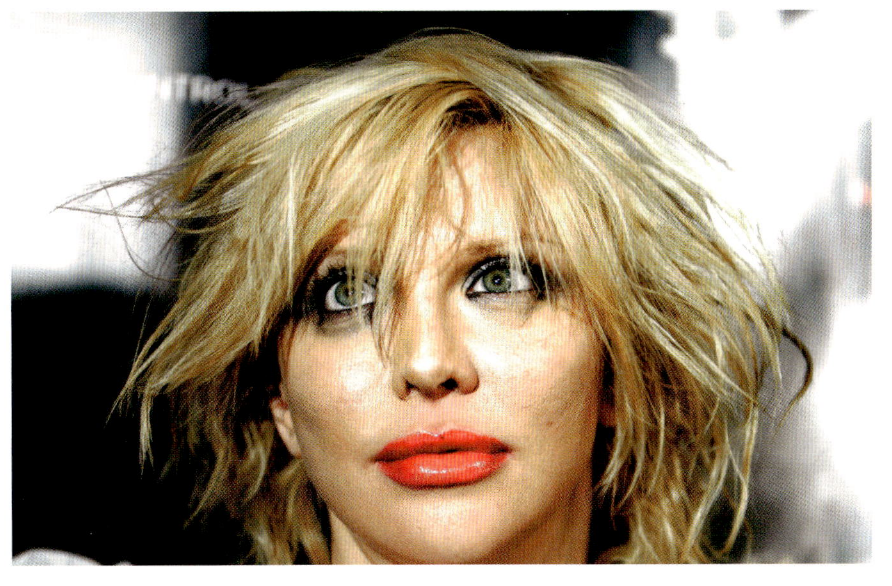
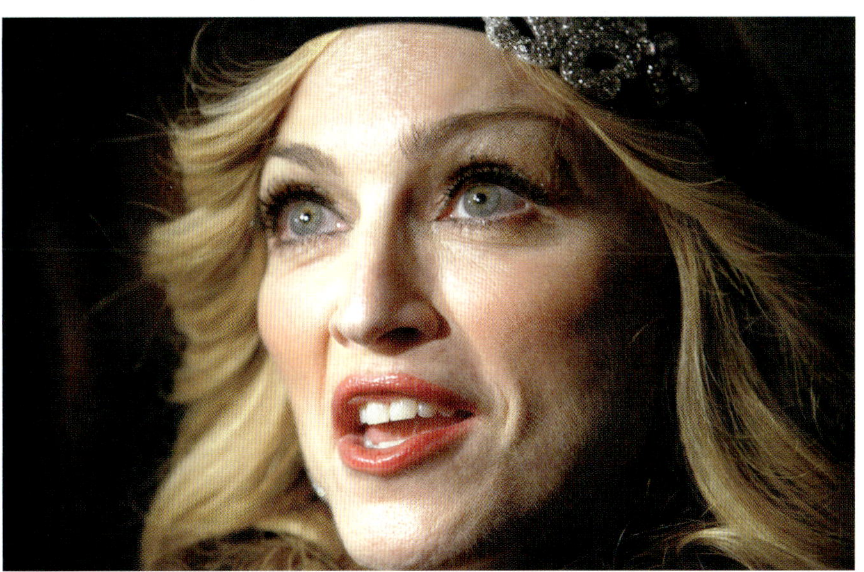
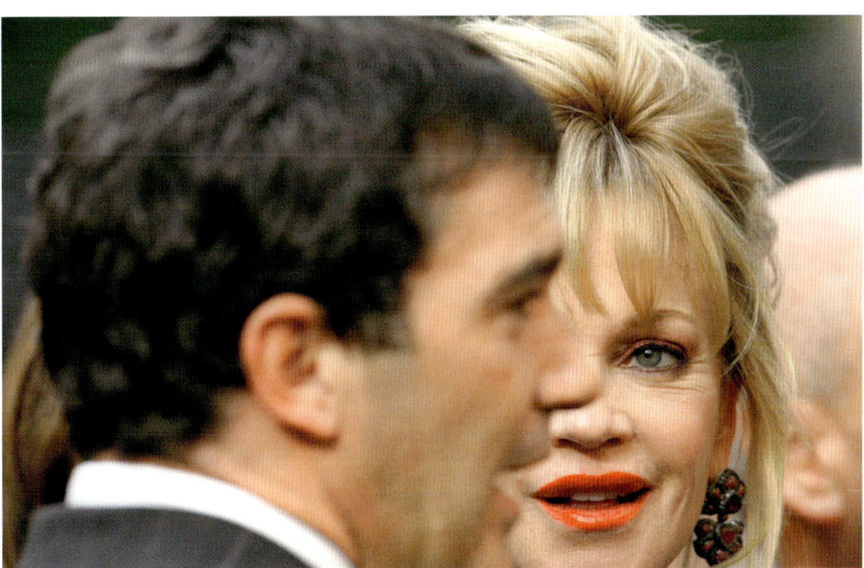
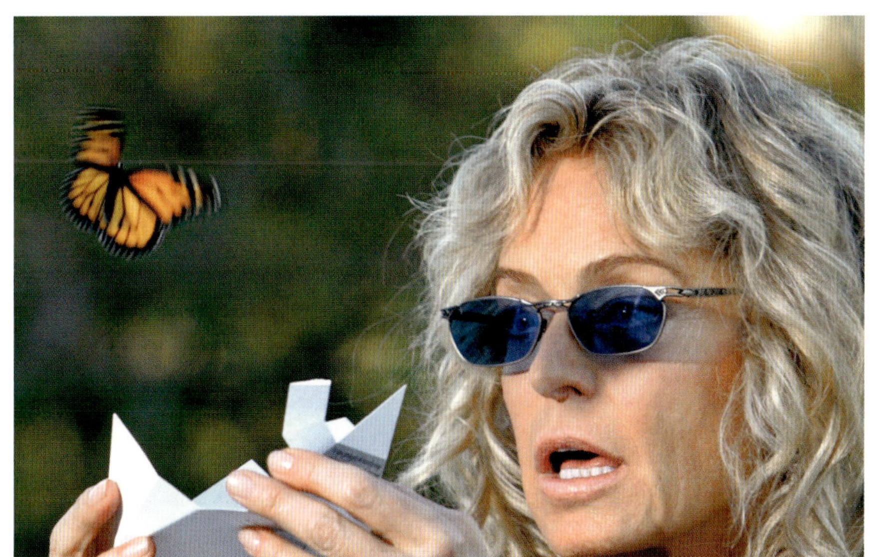
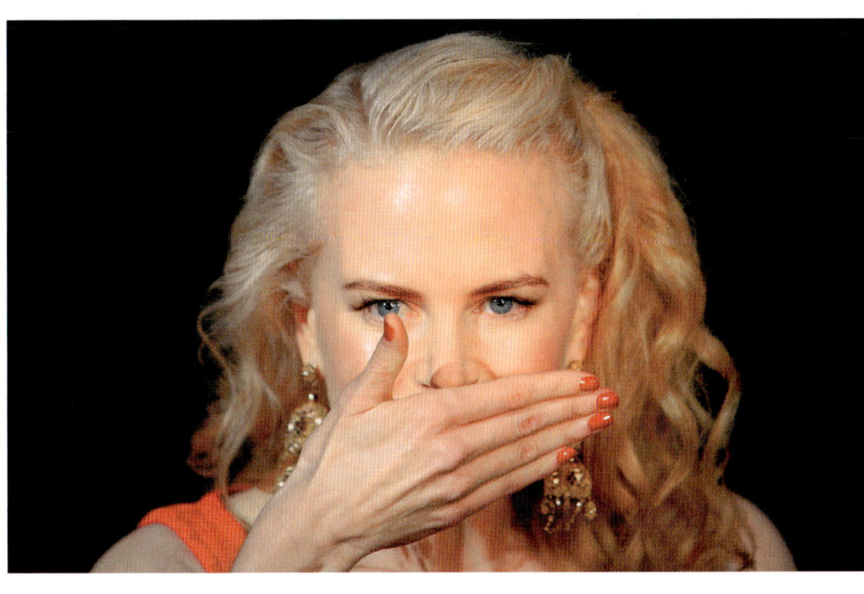
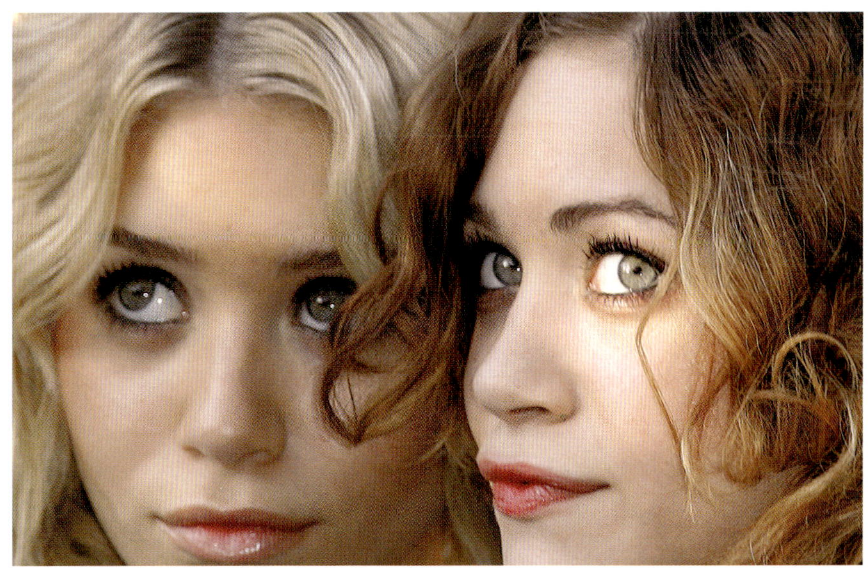

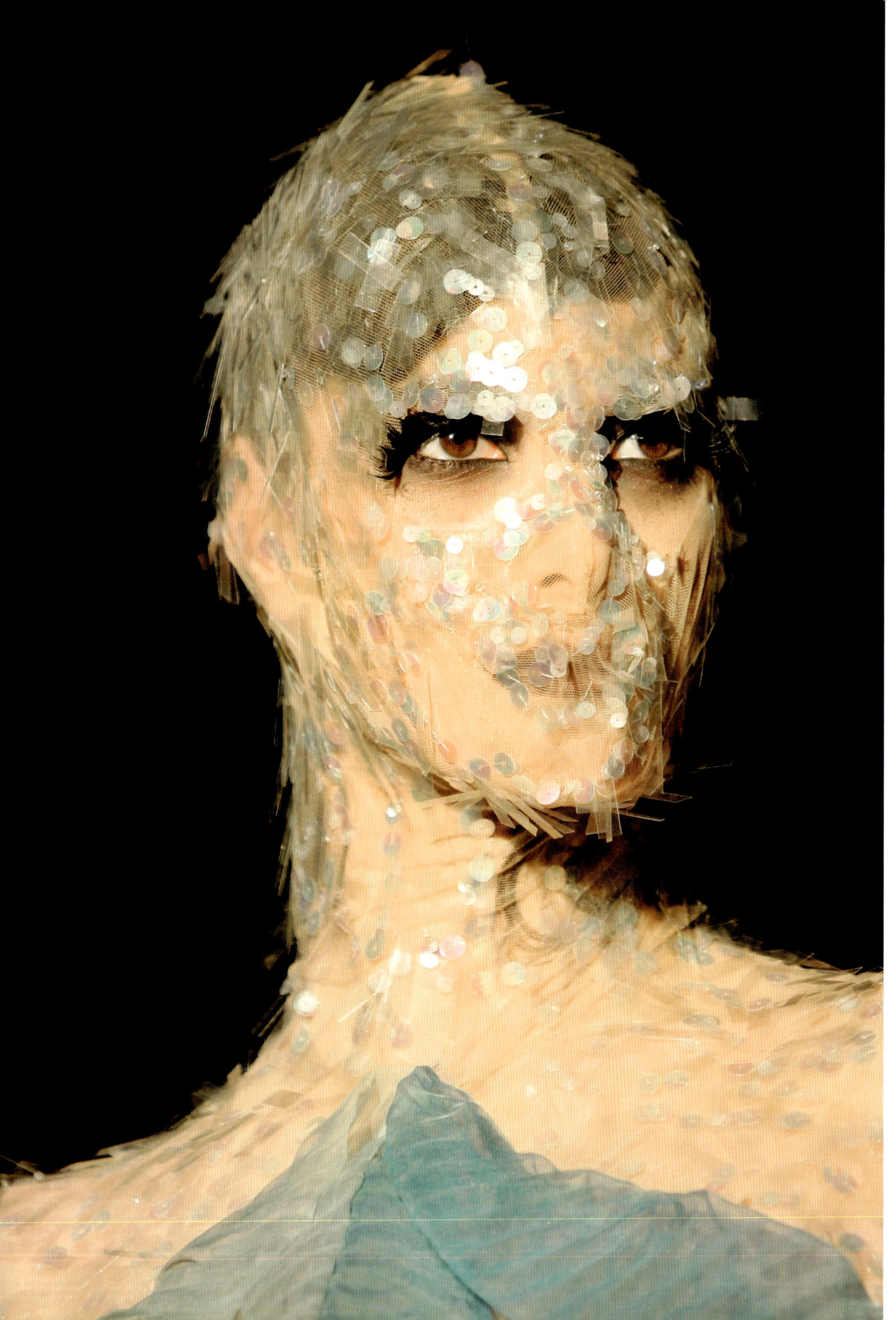

1 February 2005, ROME, ITALY

A model presents a creation from Italian fashion academy students, part of the 2005 spring/summer Haute Couture collection at Rome's Fashion Week. Max Rossi

6 October 2002, PARIS, FRANCE

Opposite A model presents a creation by British designer John Galliano, part of his ready-to-wear 2003 spring/summer collection. Philippe Wojazer

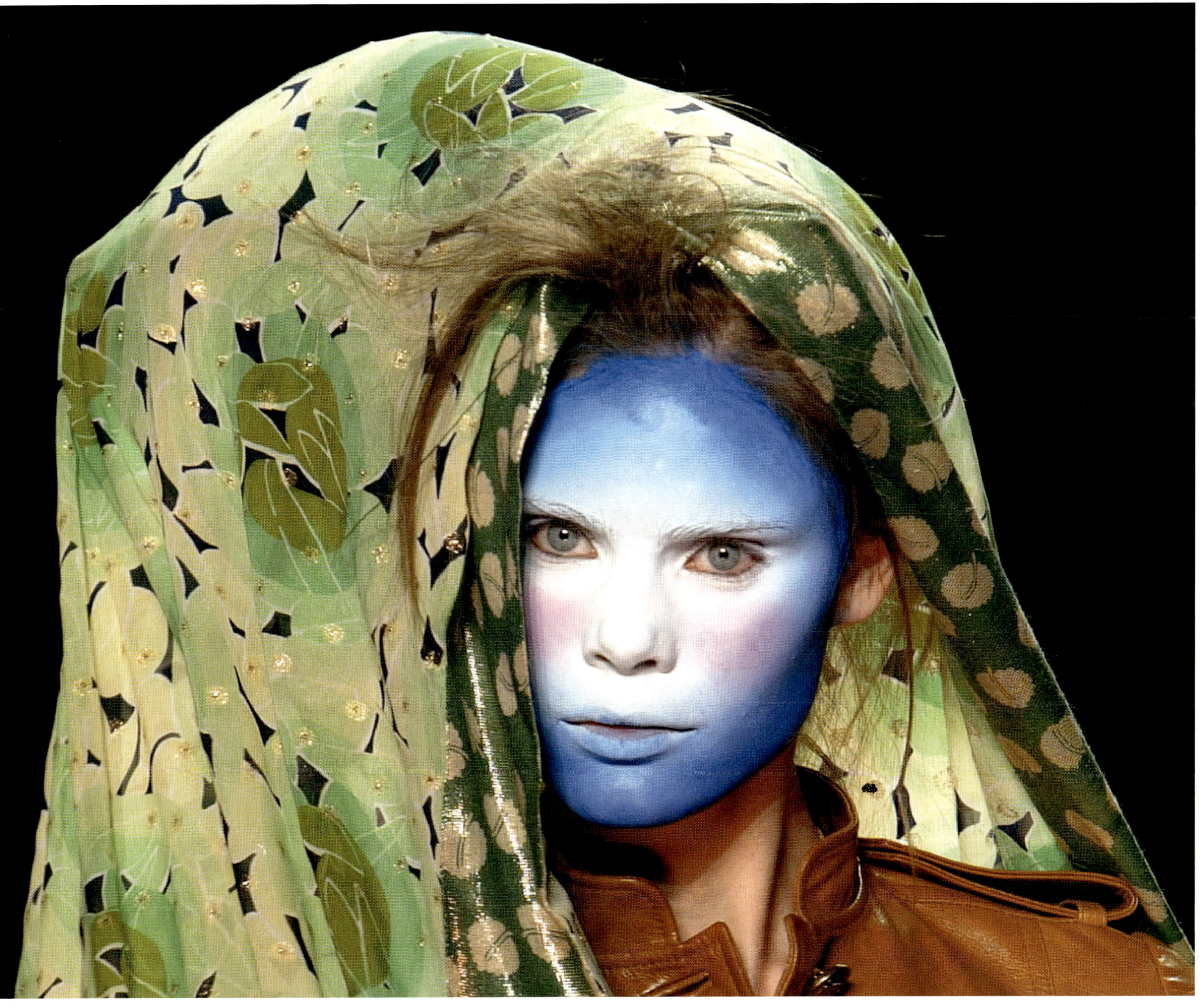

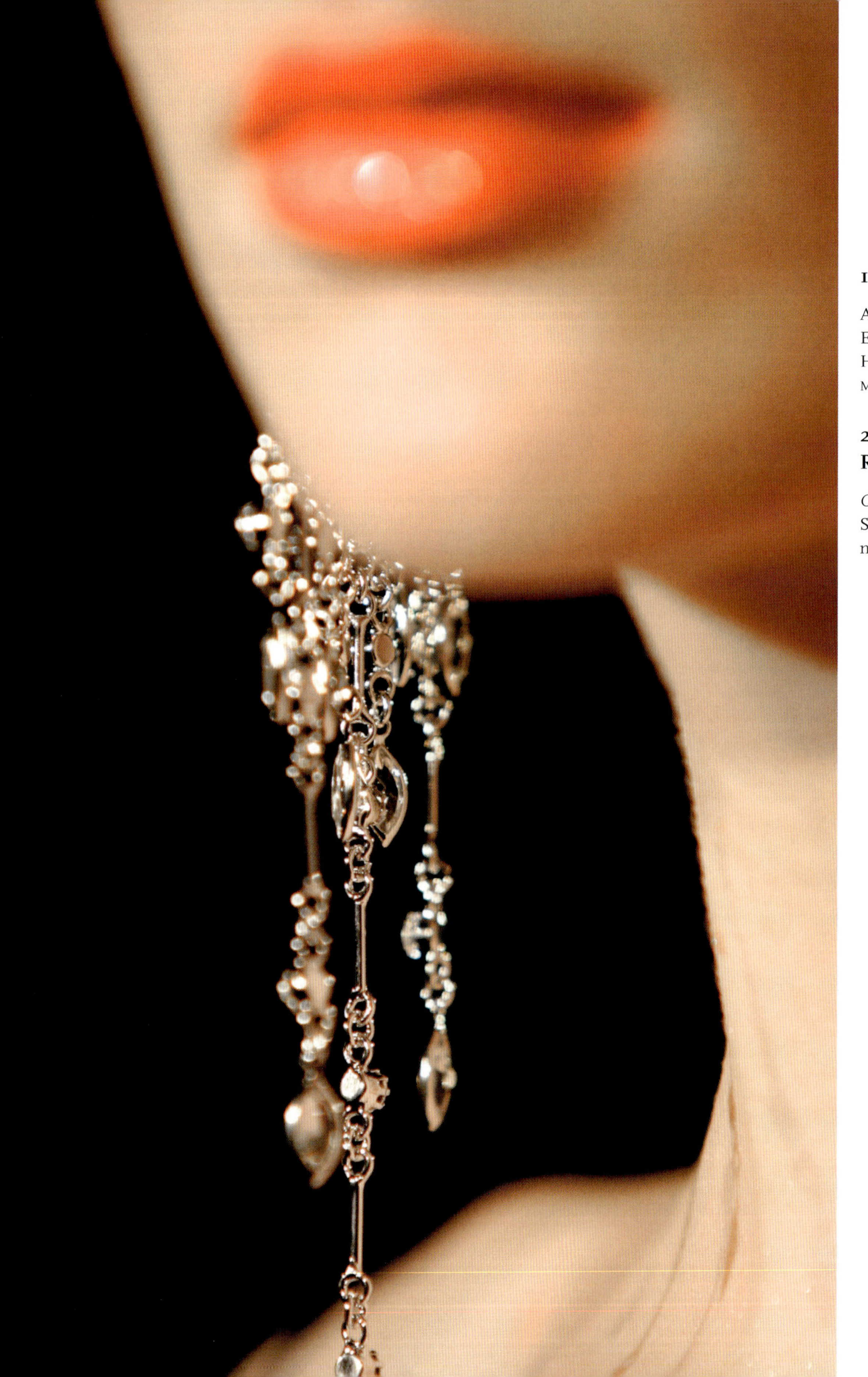

1 February 2005, ROME, ITALY

A model presents a creation from Italian designer Ettore Bilotta, part of the 2005 spring/summer Haute Couture collection at Rome's Fashion Week. Max Rossi

24 February 2005, ST PETERSBURG, RUSSIA

Opposite A Russian model performs during the St Petersburg international contest of hairdressers, nail and body art designers. Alexander Demianchuk

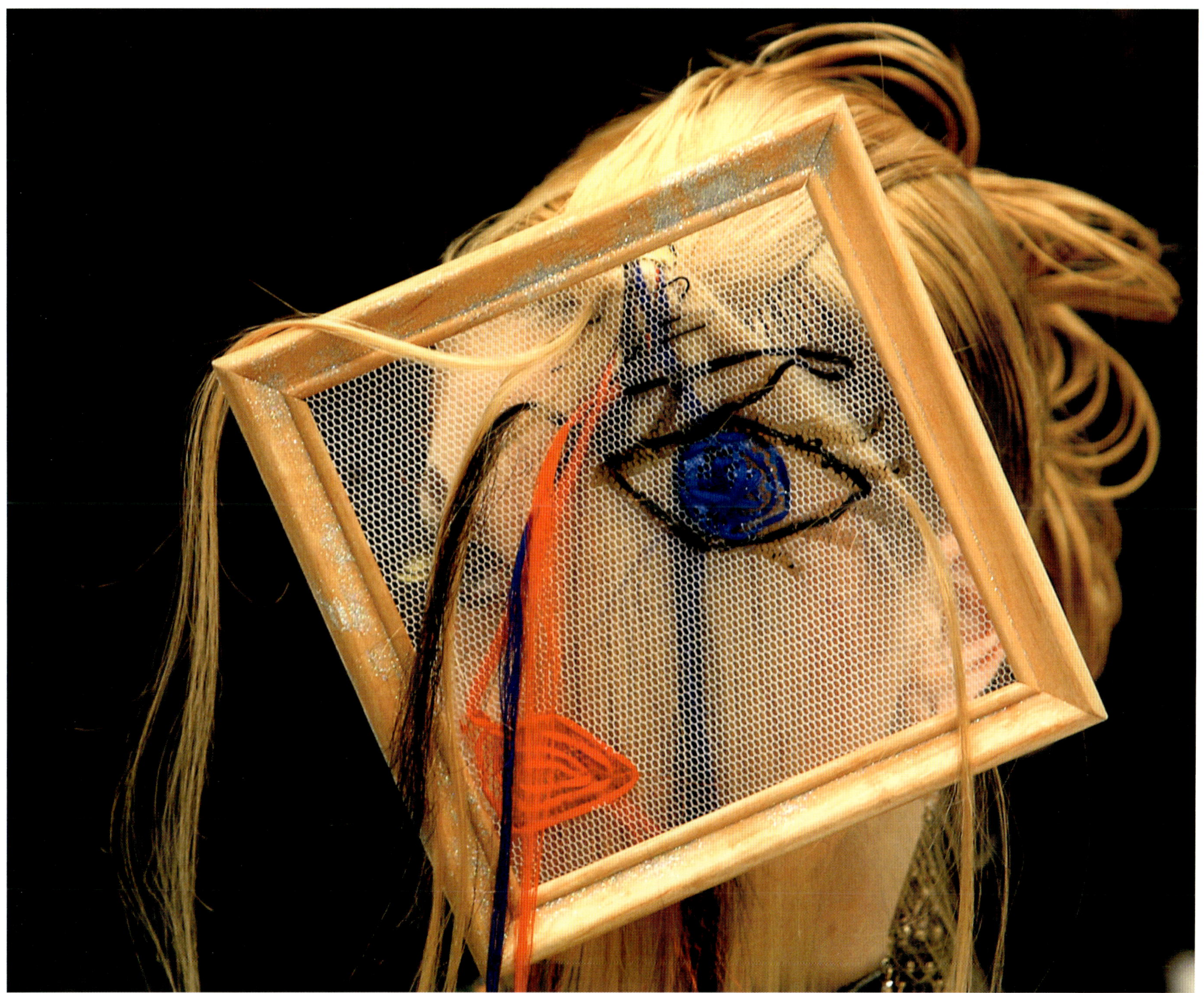

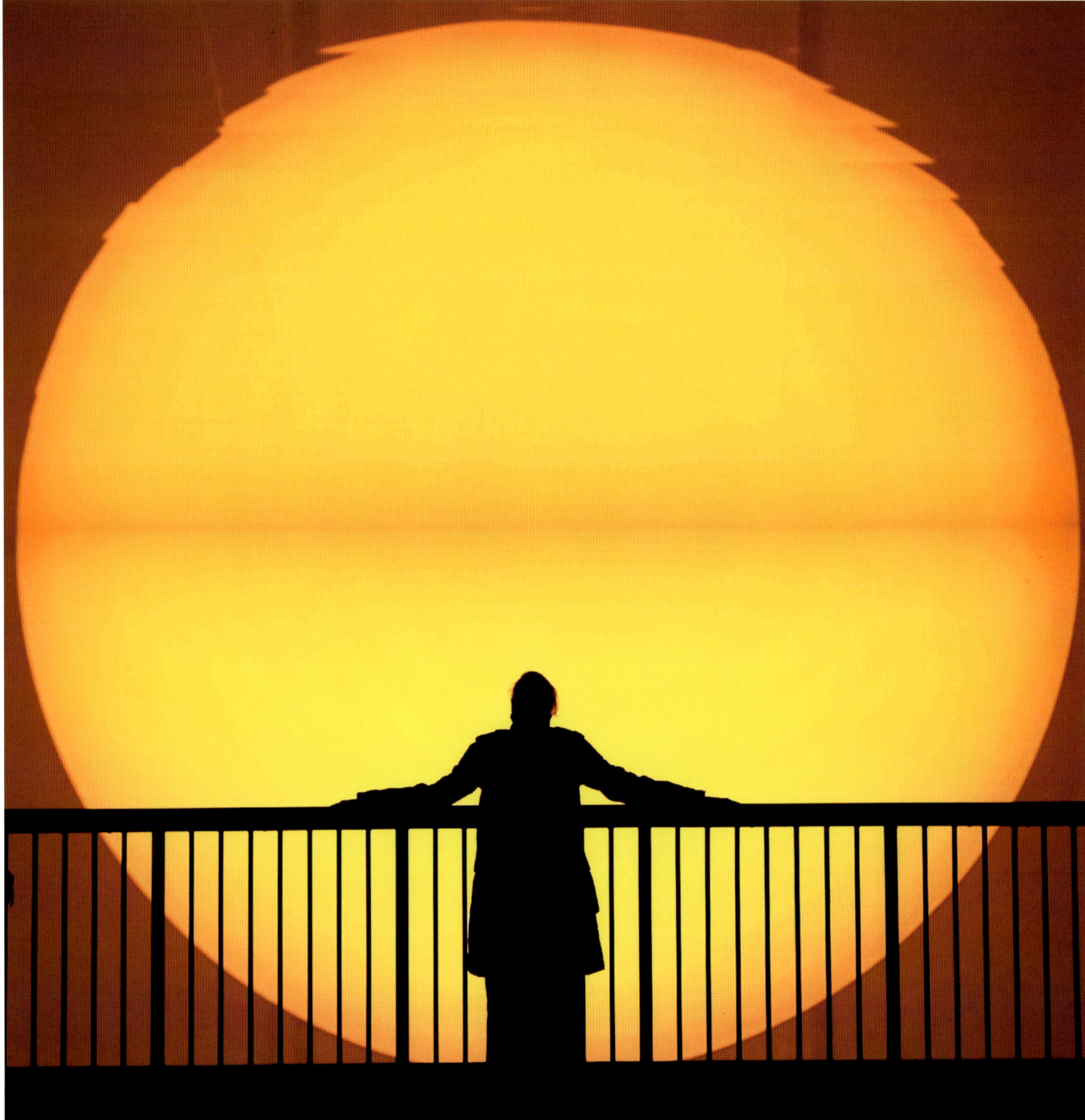

15 October 2003, LONDON, UNITED KINGDOM

Opposite A woman is silhouetted against a giant sun, part of *The Weather Project*, an installation created by Danish–Icelandic artist Olafur Eliasson for the huge Turbine Hall of London's Tate Modern art gallery. The work used mirrors, lights and fine mist to recreate the appearance and atmosphere of a setting sun on a spectacular scale. Peter Macdiarmid

2 July 2003, SYDNEY, AUSTRALIA

A visitor to 'our magic hour', an exhibition of work by Swiss artist Ugo Rondinone at the Museum of Contemporary Art in Sydney, gazes at an artwork of dizzyingly blurred concentric coloured circles. Rondinone uses painting, video, sculpture, sound and photography to create works that produce dreamlike and disorientated states in the viewer. David Gray

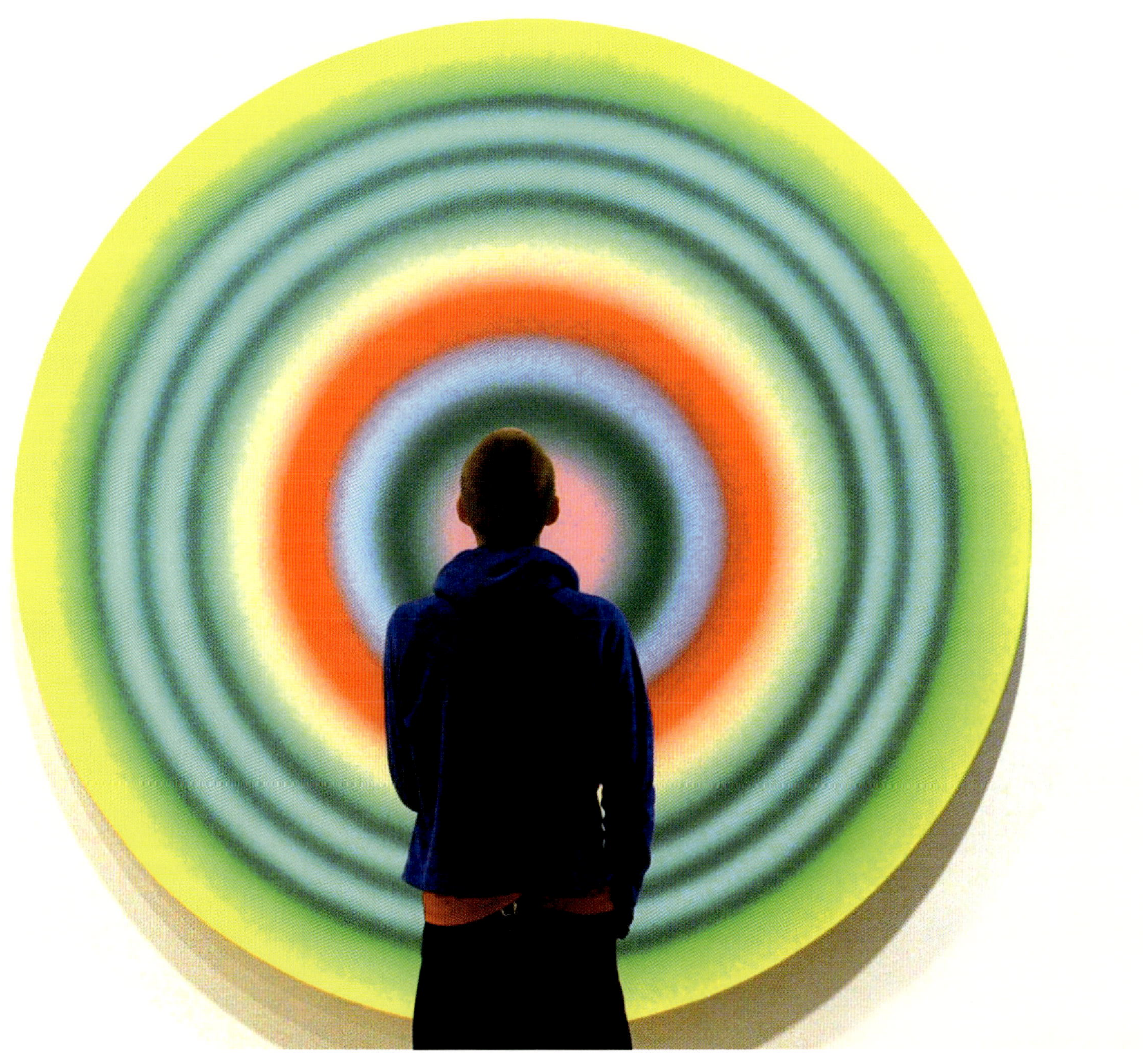

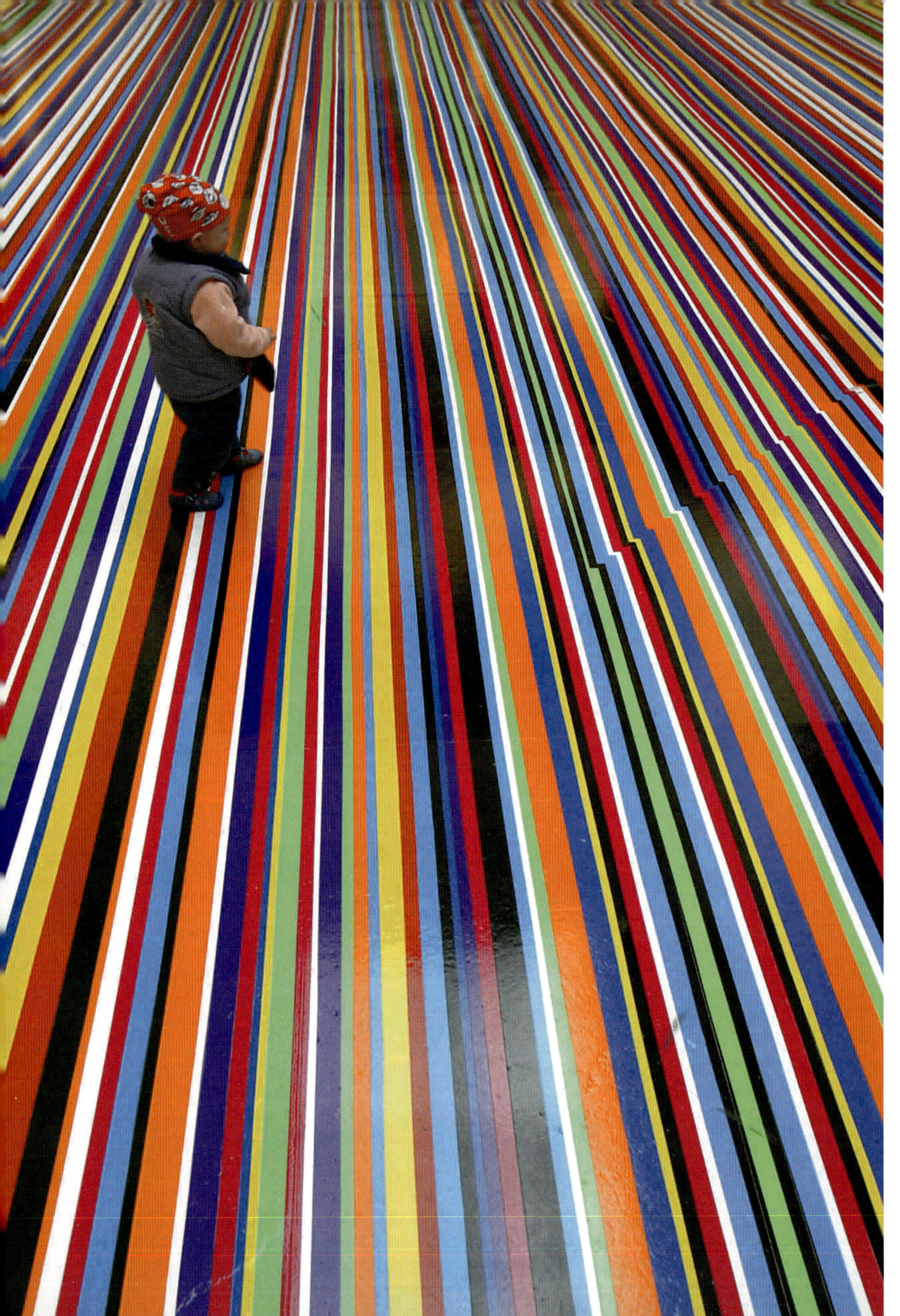

25 February 2003, LONDON, UNITED KINGDOM

A visitor walks across a striped floor by British artist Jim Lambie which formed part of 'Days Like These', the second Tate Triennial exhibition of contemporary British art at Tate Britain gallery in London. The exhibition featured the work of 23 artists, encompassing painting, sculpture, film, video, photography and sound works. Toby Melville

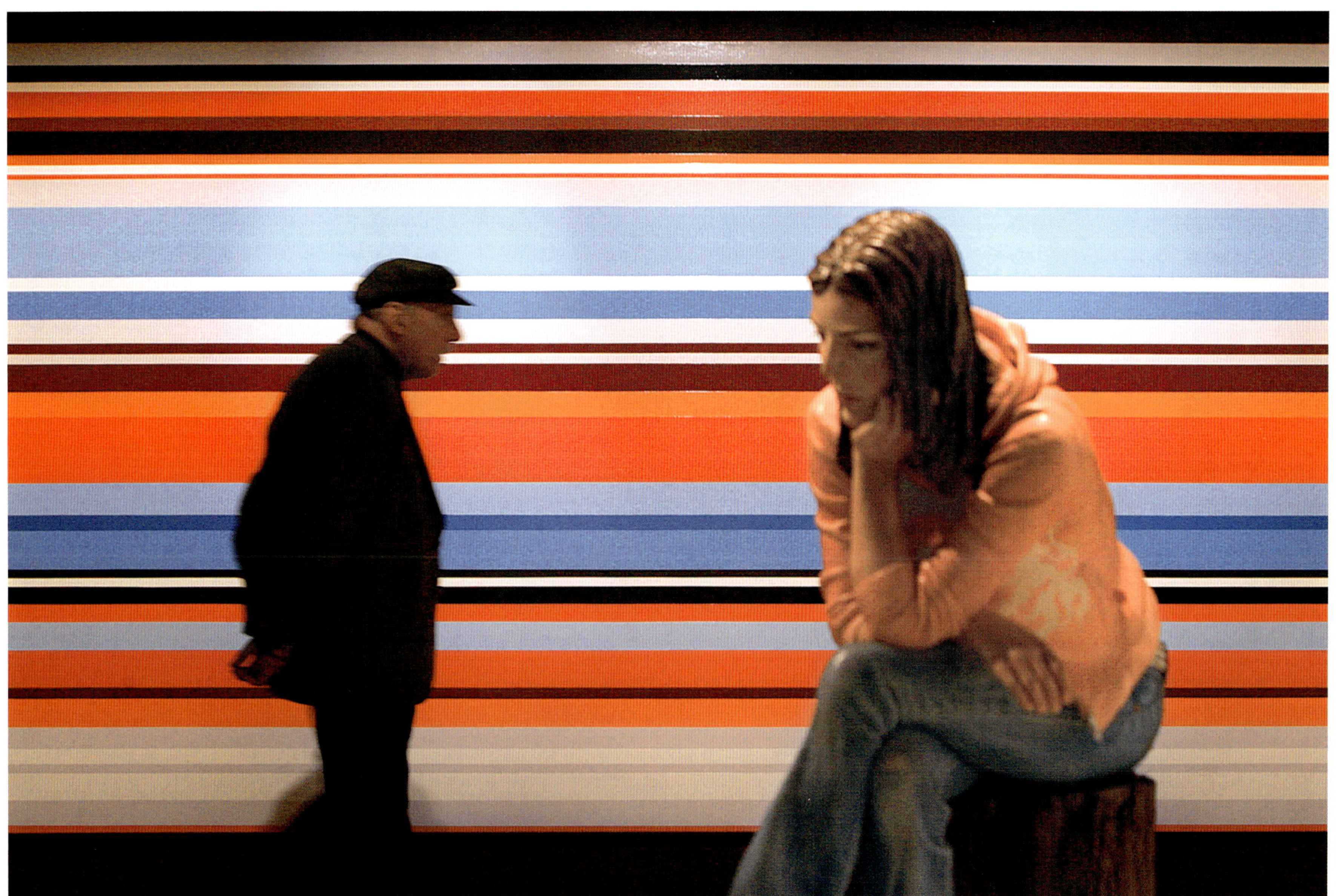

20 September 2004, SYDNEY, AUSTRALIA

A visitor to Sydney's Museum of Contemporary Art walks past a sculpture (right) by Australian artist Jan Nelson. Nelson's emotionally charged sculptures, paintings and photographs exploring angst, turmoil and the insecurities of adolescence were exhibited in a joint show with Dutch artist Liza May Post. David Gray

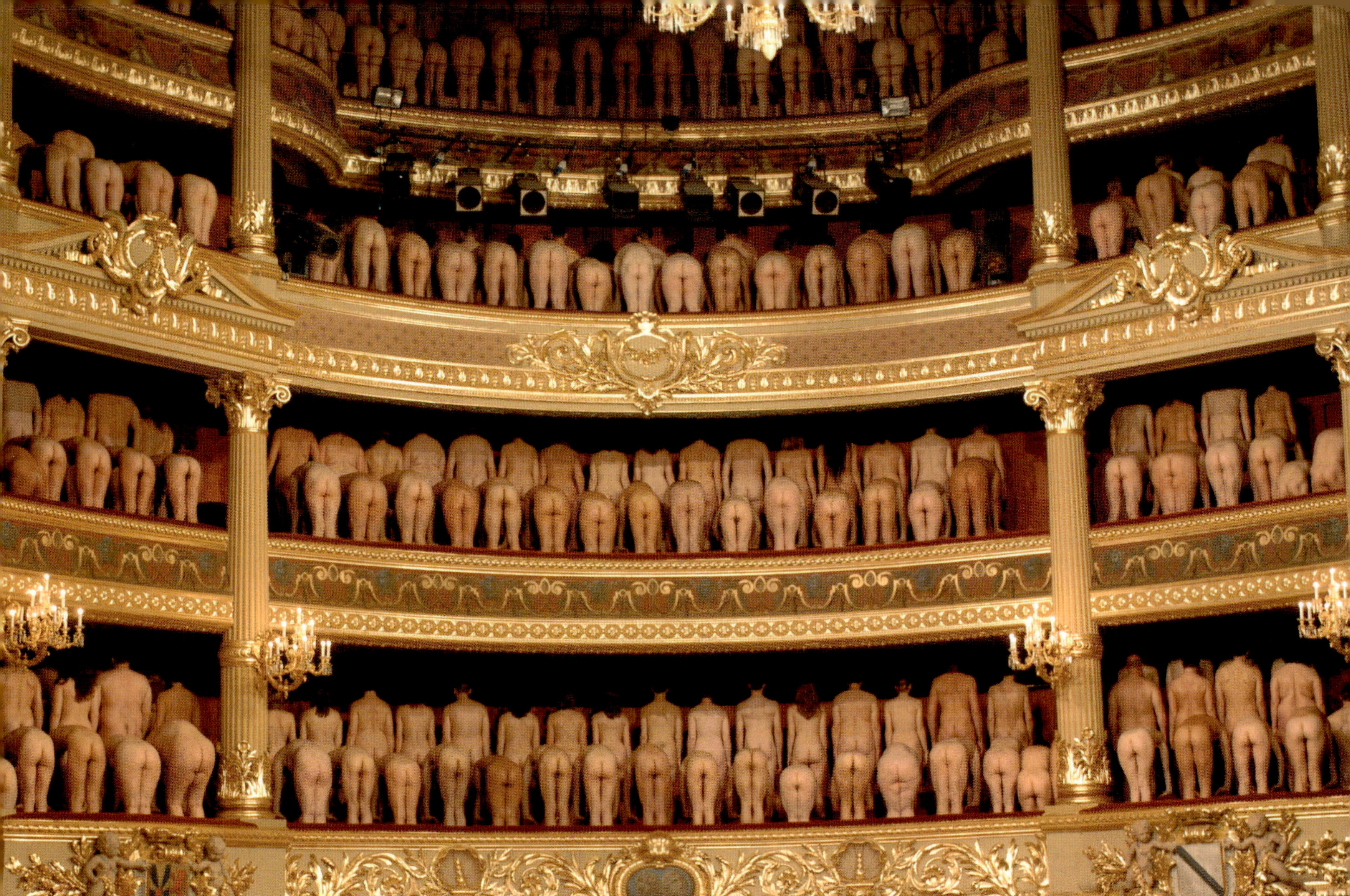

7 May 2005, BRUGES, BELGIUM

Volunteers pose naked inside Bruges' Stadschouwburg theatre during a photo session with U.S. photographer Spencer Tunick. Tunick has photographed large gatherings of nude people in locations across the world, including New York, London, São Paulo, Caracas and Vienna. Peter Maenhoudt

1 October 2004, ST PETERSBURG, RUSSIA

Young ballet dancers wait to make their first public performance in the Vaganov Academy of Russian Ballet in St Petersburg. Alexander Demianchuk

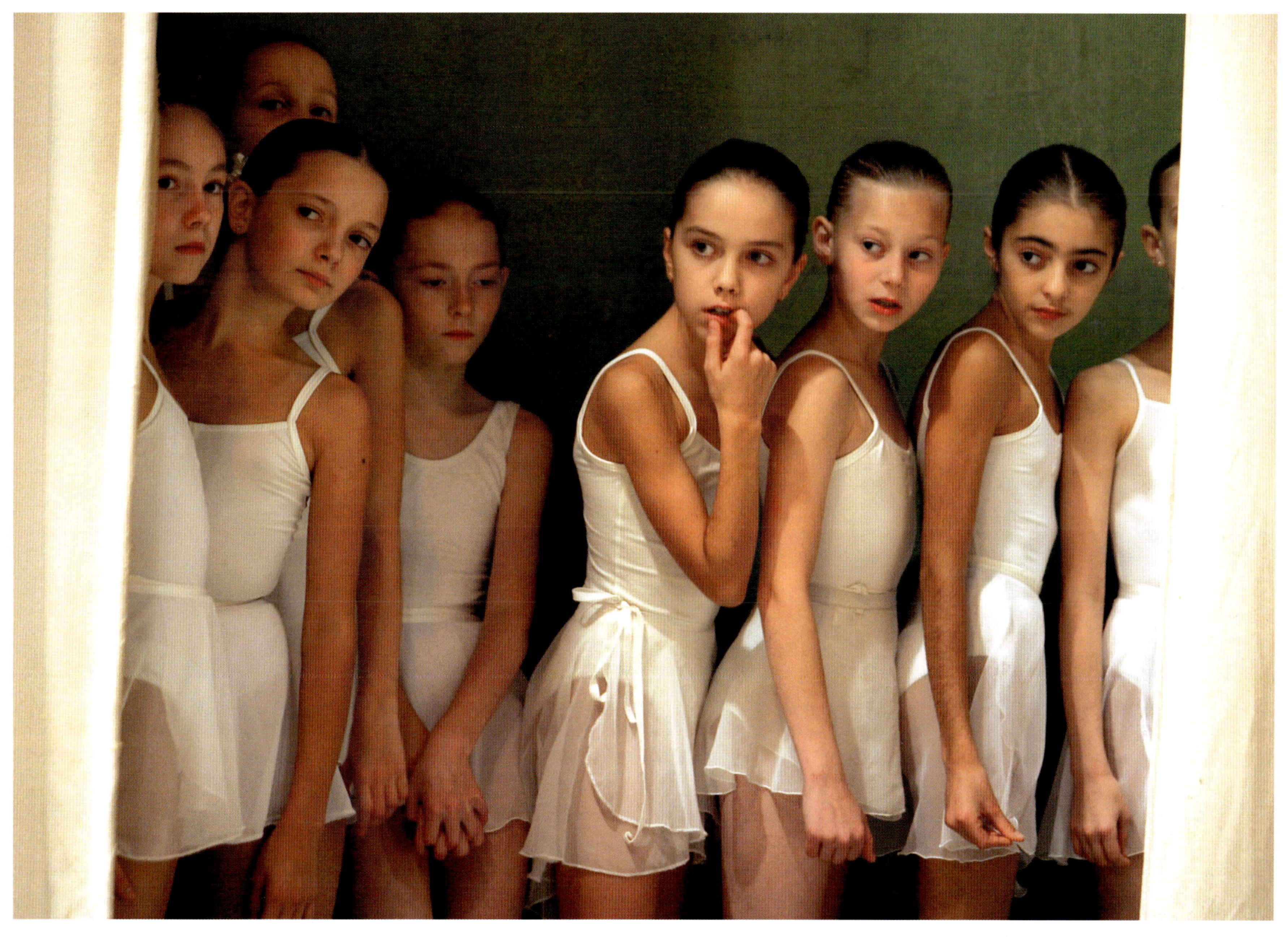

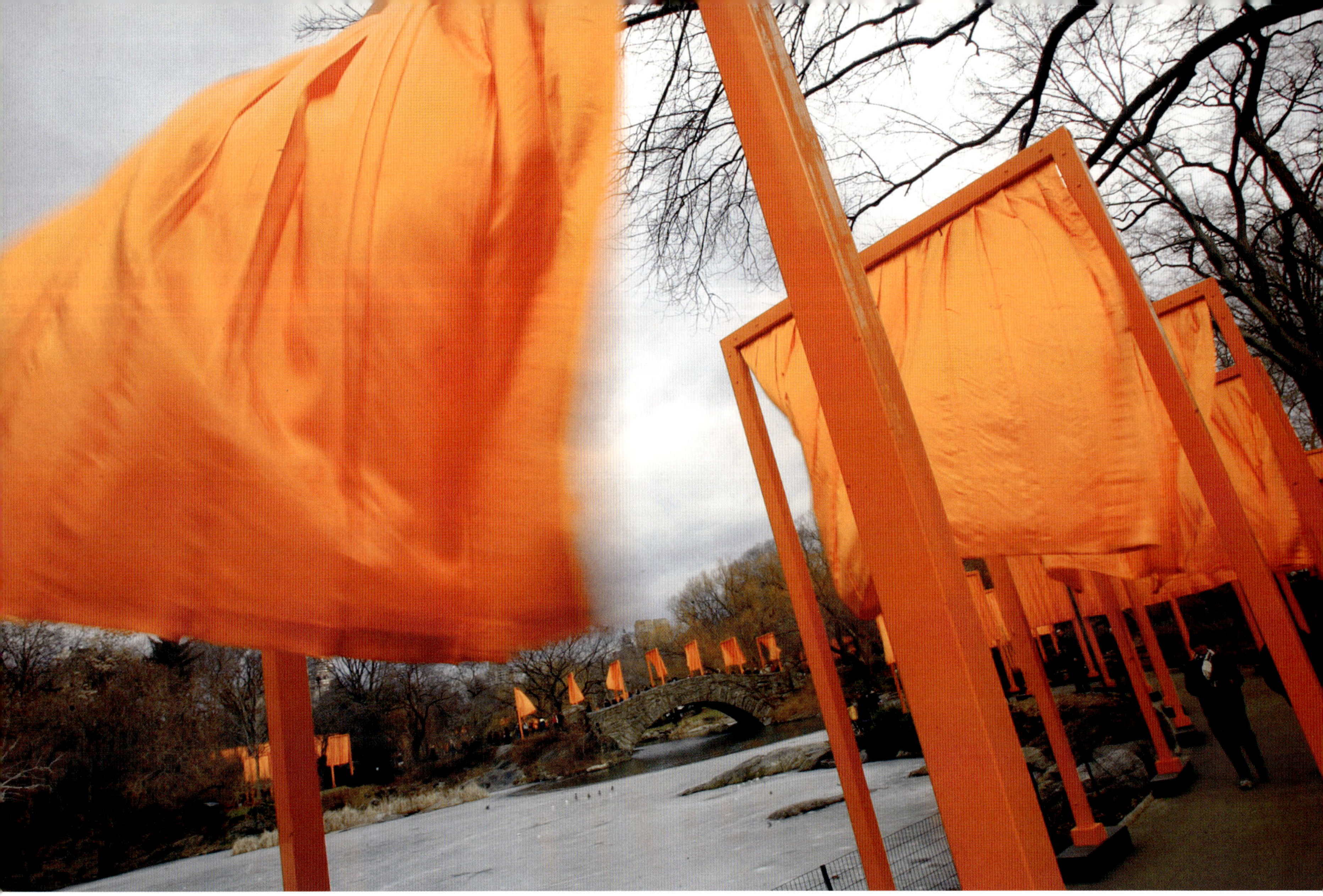

12 February 2005, NEW YORK, UNITED STATES

The Gates, a massive public art installation created by artists Christo and his wife Jeanne-Claude in New York's Central Park. The work consisted of over 7,500 giant frames from which billowing fabrics were suspended along miles of pathways for a 16-day period early in 2005. Shannon Stapleton

3 June 2005, BILBAO, SPAIN

Opposite above Visitors explore eight massive steel twisting sculptures by U.S. artist Richard Serra at the Guggenheim Museum in Bilbao, northern Spain. The works are part of Serra's *Torqued Ellipses* series. Vincent West

8 September 2004, FLORENCE, ITALY

Opposite below Visitors to the Accademia Museum in Florence look at Michelangelo's statue of David. Five hundred years after the icon of Renaissance male beauty was unveiled to the people of Florence, the town launched a year of events to celebrate Michelangelo's seminal work. It has been in the Accademia Museum since 1873, when city smog forced it to be moved indoors after hundreds of years in front of the Palazzo della Signoria. Max Rossi

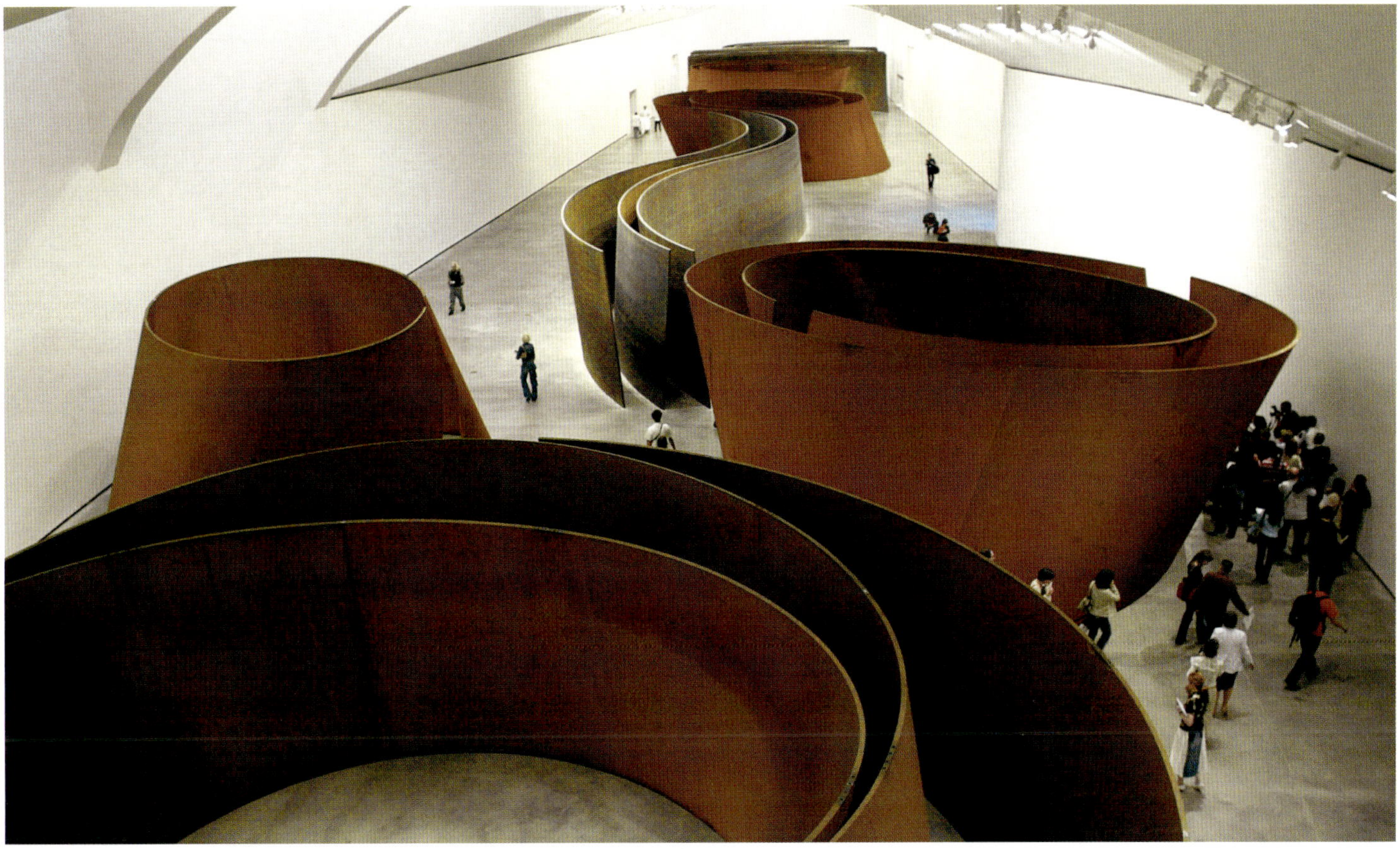

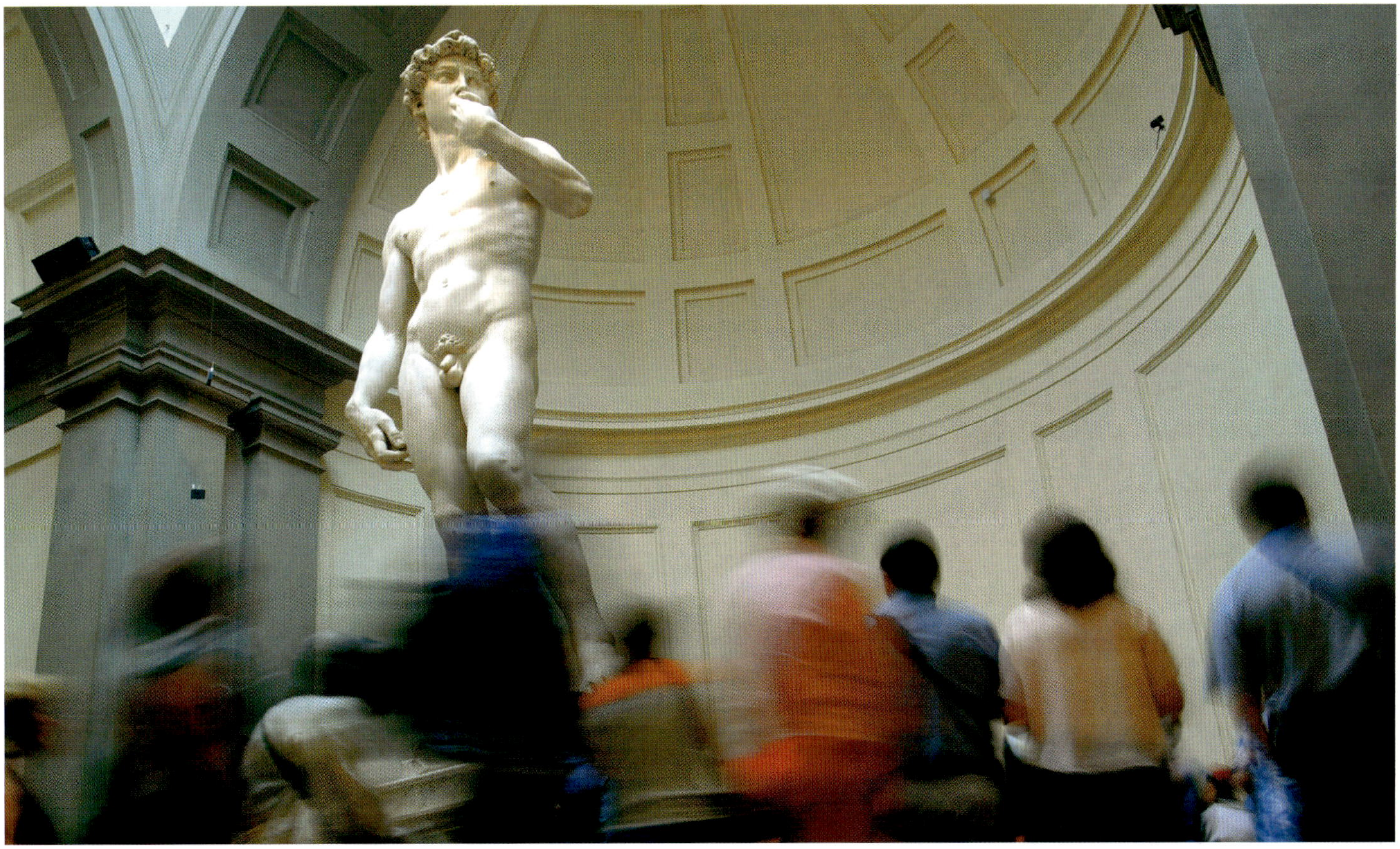

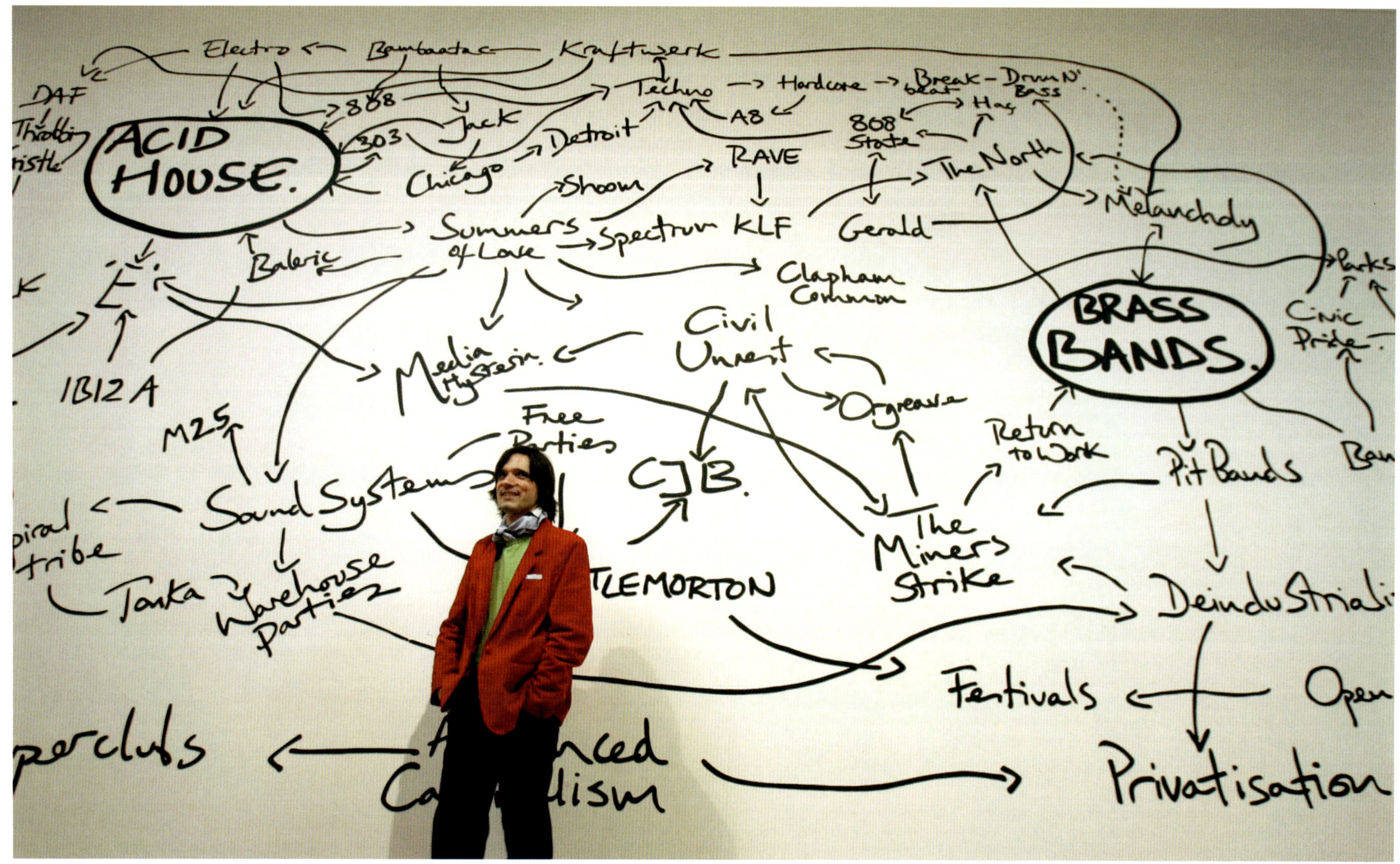

6 December 2004, LONDON, UNITED KINGDOM

British artist Jeremy Deller stands in front of his work *The History of the World* after being awarded the 2004 Turner Prize at Tate Britain gallery, London. Deller's winning entry took art lovers on a video tour of Texas, from President George W. Bush's hometown of Crawford to Waco, site of the 1993 Branch Davidian siege. The Turner Prize is one of the art world's most coveted awards, and always stirs a heated debate in Britain about what modern art is all about.
Toby Melville

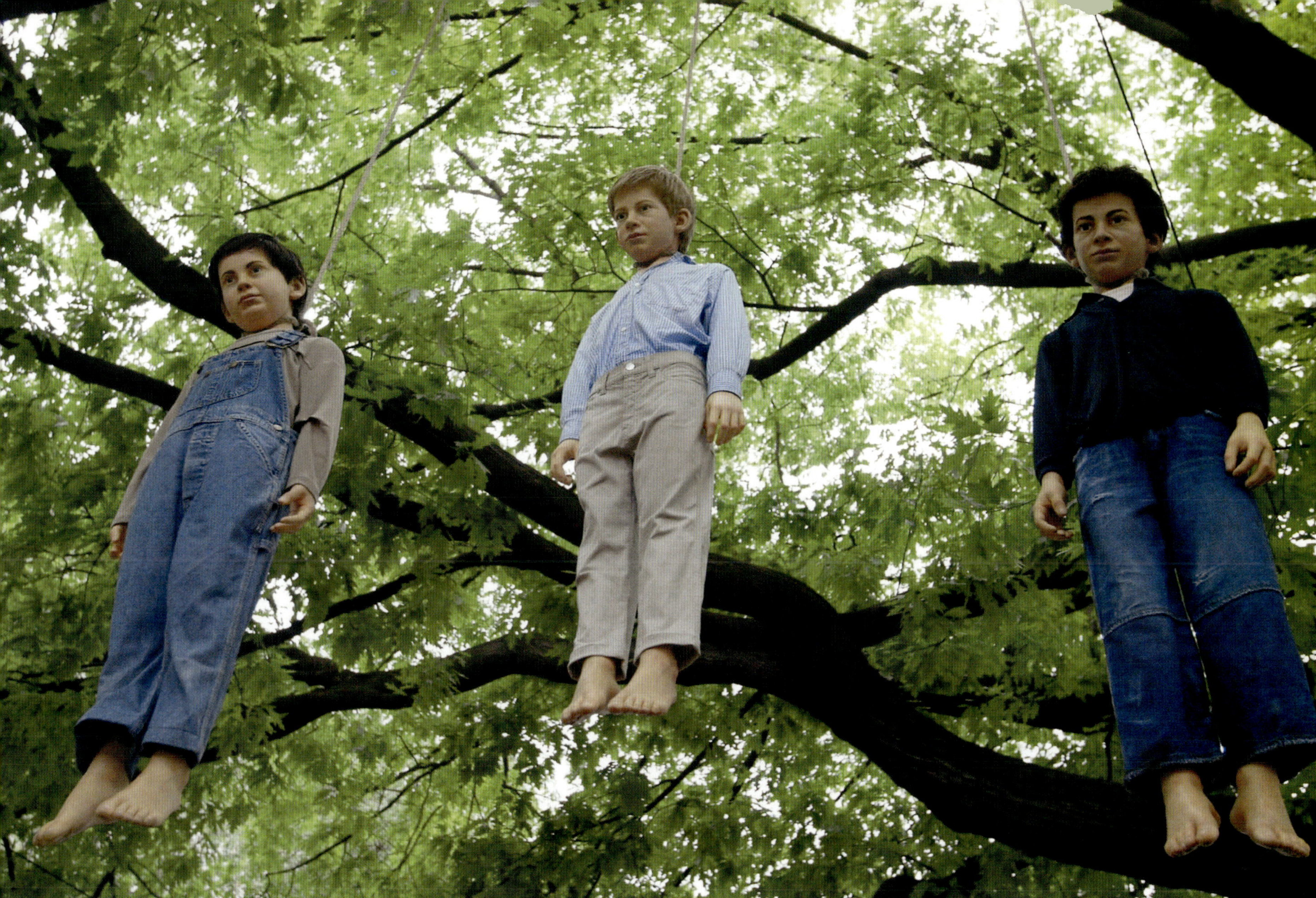

6 May 2004, MILAN, ITALY

An untitled installation of three lifesize models of hanged boys by Italian artist Maurizio Cattelan in one Milan's busiest squares. Just a day after it was unveiled – to consternation from passers-by, praise from avant-garde art critics, and front-page newspaper stories – the work was vandalized by an angry Milan resident who climbed up a tree and cut down two of the figures, then fell several metres to the ground and had to be rushed to hospital. Firemen cut down the third figure. Cattelan's past works have included a sculpture of Adolf Hitler kneeling and a likeness of Pope John Paul II felled by a meteorite. Stefano Rellandini

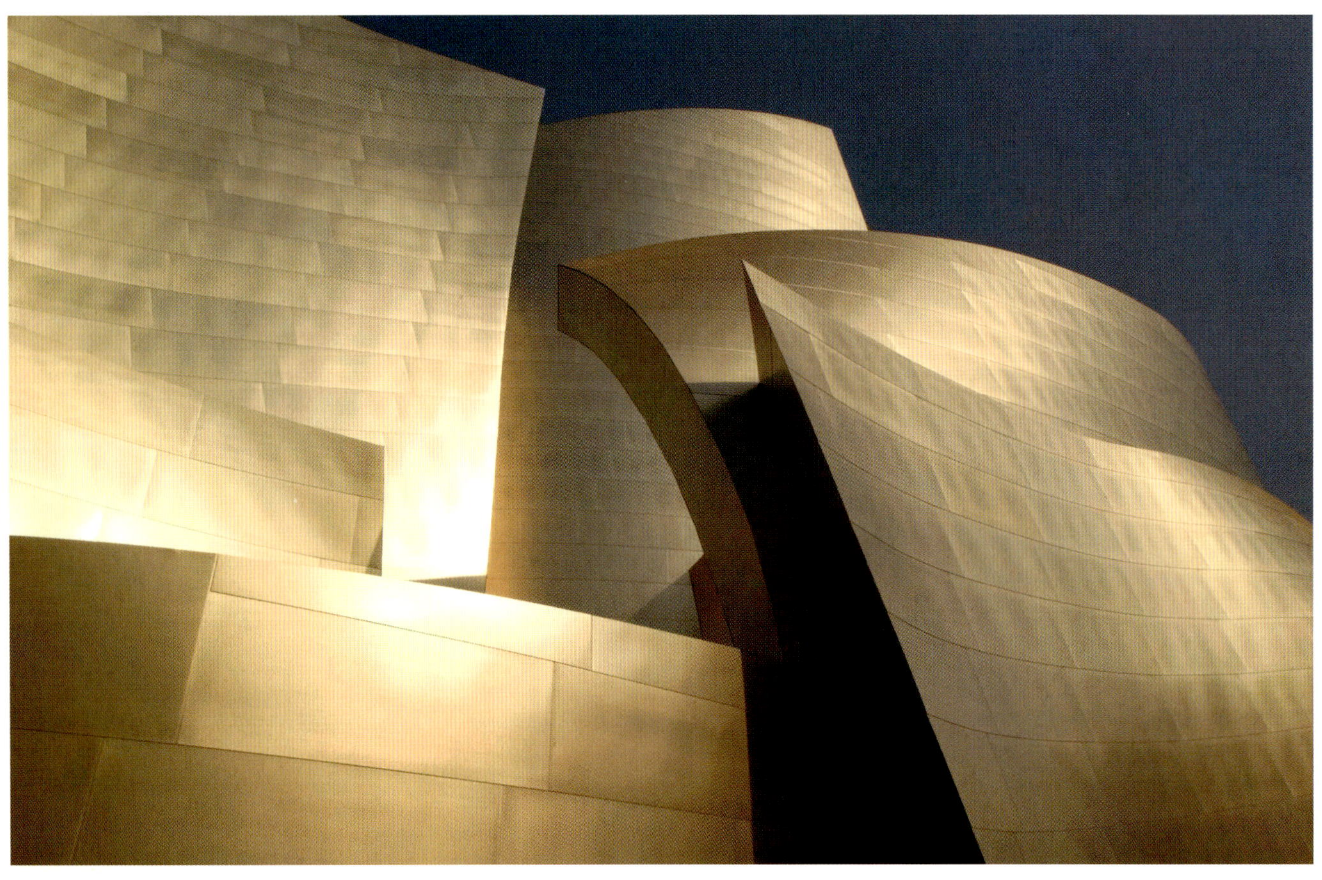

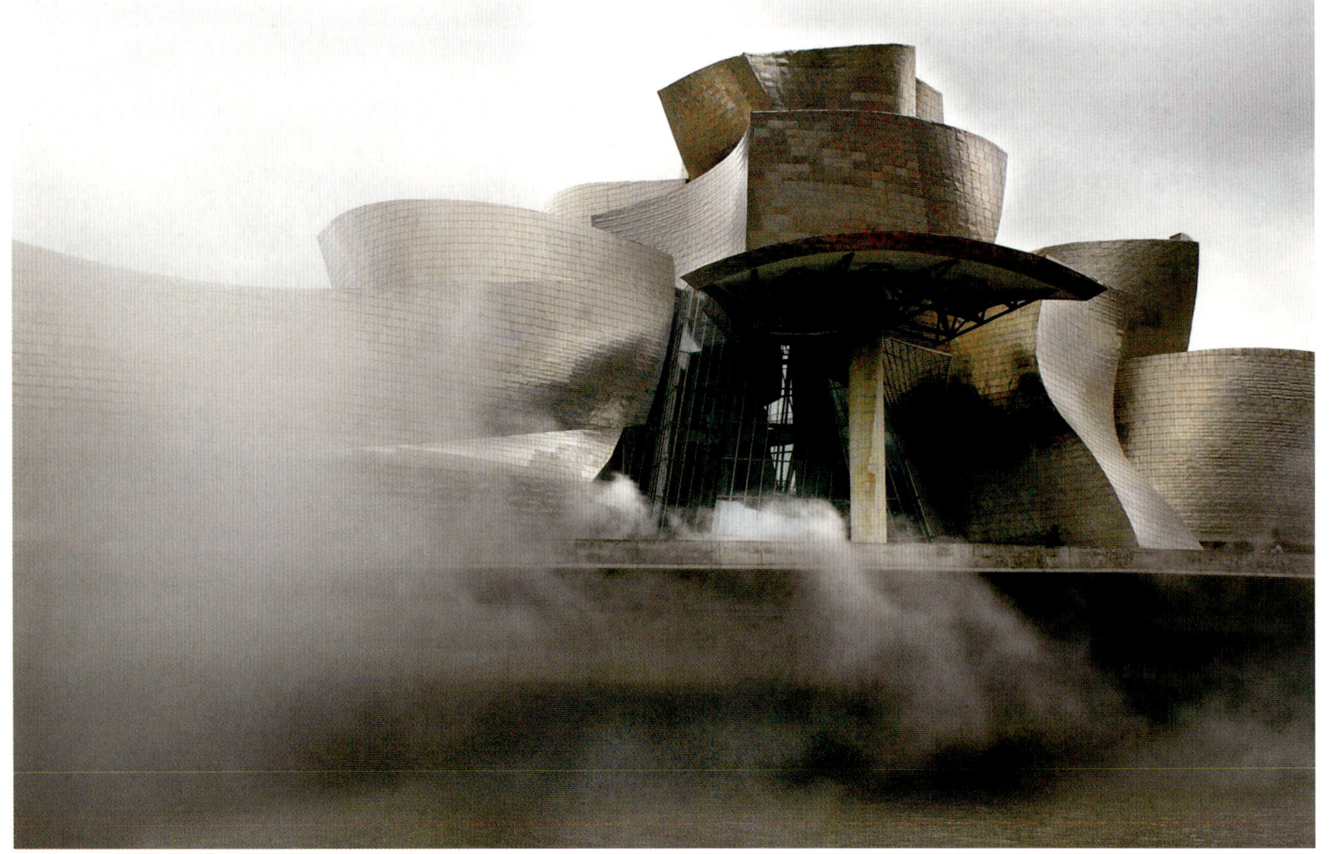

11 September 2003, LOS ANGELES, UNITED STATES

Left The stainless-steel exterior of the Walt Disney Concert Hall designed by Los Angeles-based Canadian architect Frank Gehry. The Los Angeles Philharmonic played its gala first concert on 23 October 2003 in the $274 million, 2,265-seat performance space, 16 years after the building project began. Lucy Nicholson

12 April 2005, BILBAO, SPAIN

Left below The Guggenheim Museum in Bilbao, Spain, shrouded in mist from Japanese artist Fujiko Nakaya's *Fog Sculpture #80250*. Vincent West

4 June 2004, SHANGHAI, CHINA

Opposite above A Chinese worker cleans the stand at Shanghai International Circuit. The 5.45-km (3.39-mile) circuit staged its debut Formula One race on 26 September 2004. Costing 2 billion yuan (U.S. $240 million) and designed by German Hermann Tilke, architect of Malaysia's acclaimed Sepang track, the circuit can hold more than 200,000 spectators and includes a theme park. Claro Cortes IV

30 January 2004, BERLIN, GERMANY

Opposite below Visitors explore the modern glass cupola above the main chamber of the Bundestag, the German lower house of Parliament. The cupola was designed by British architect Norman Foster as part of a U.S. $330 million Reichstag renovation. Michael Dalder

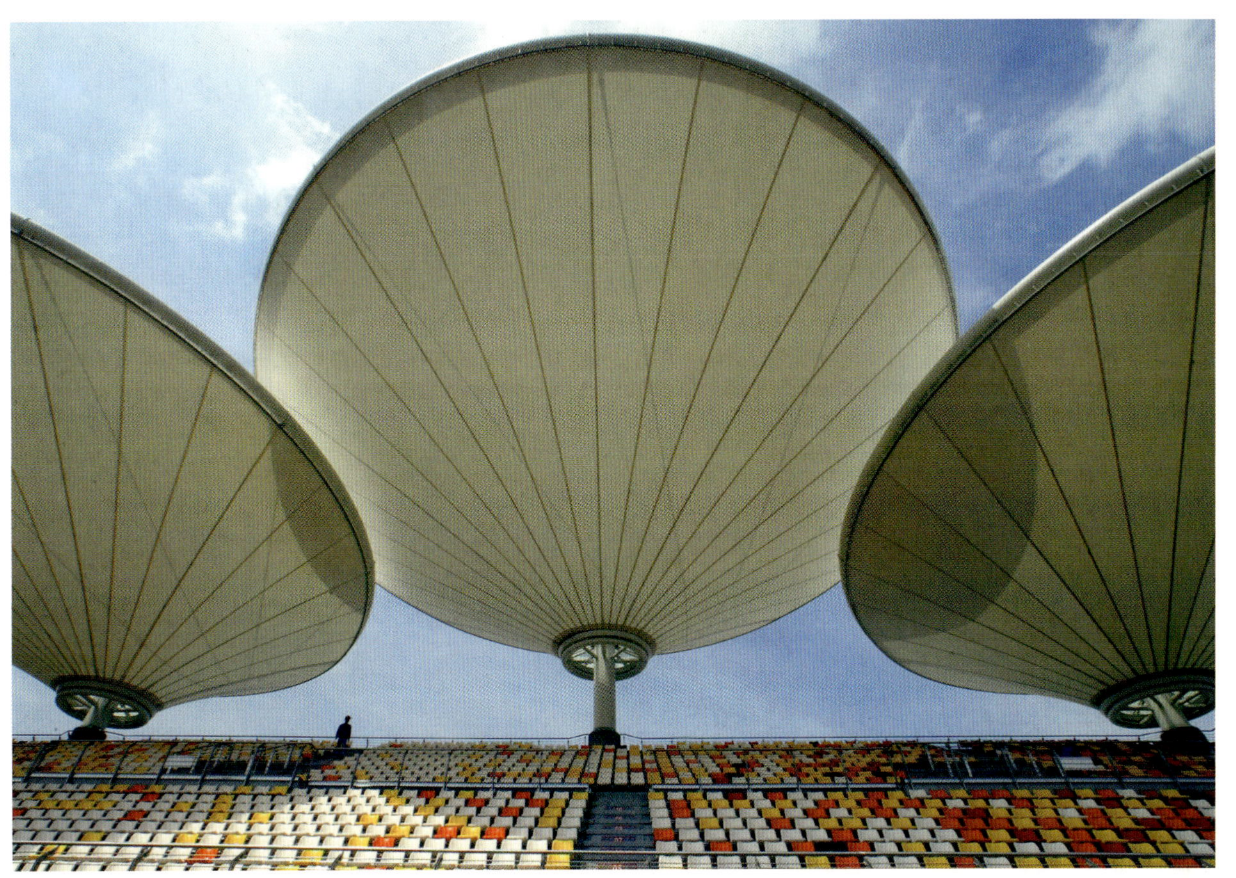

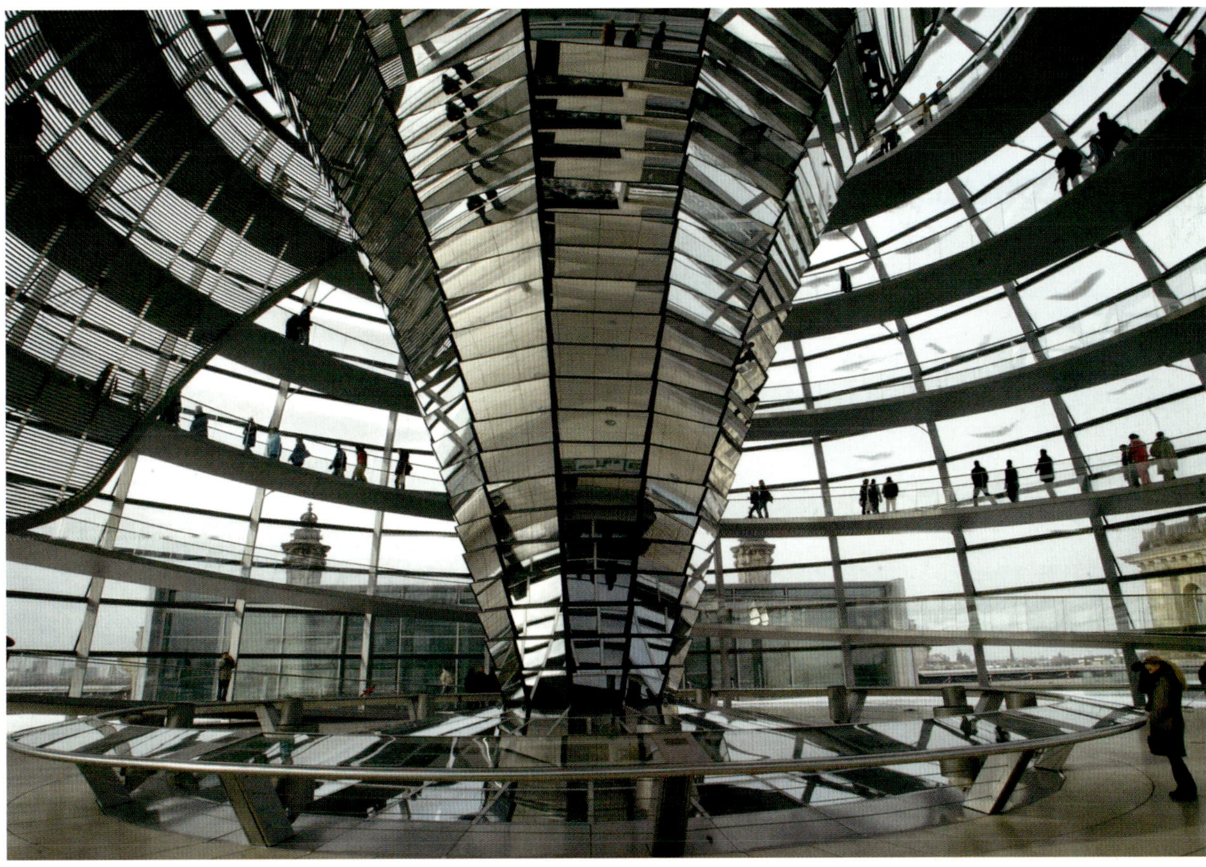

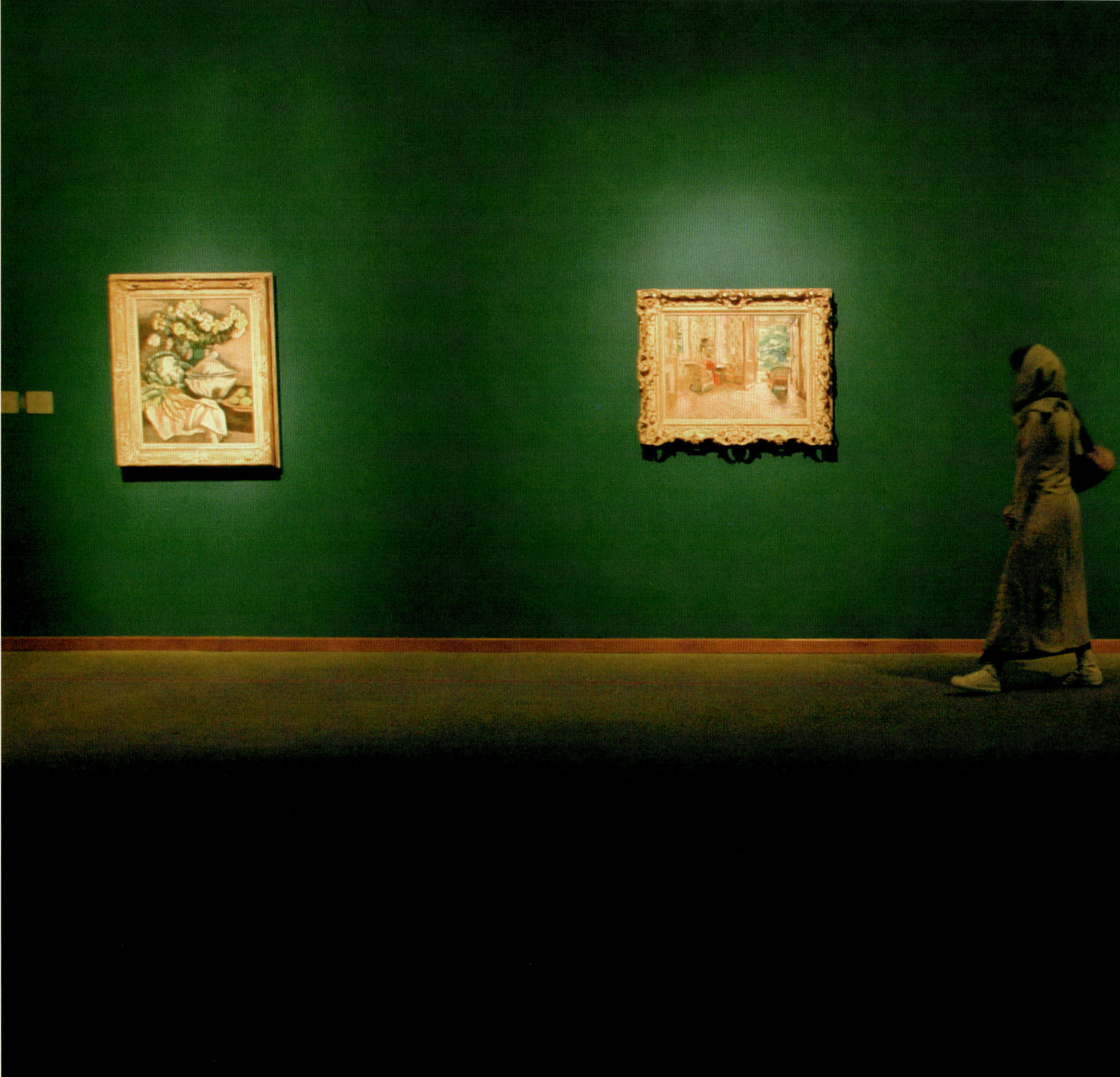

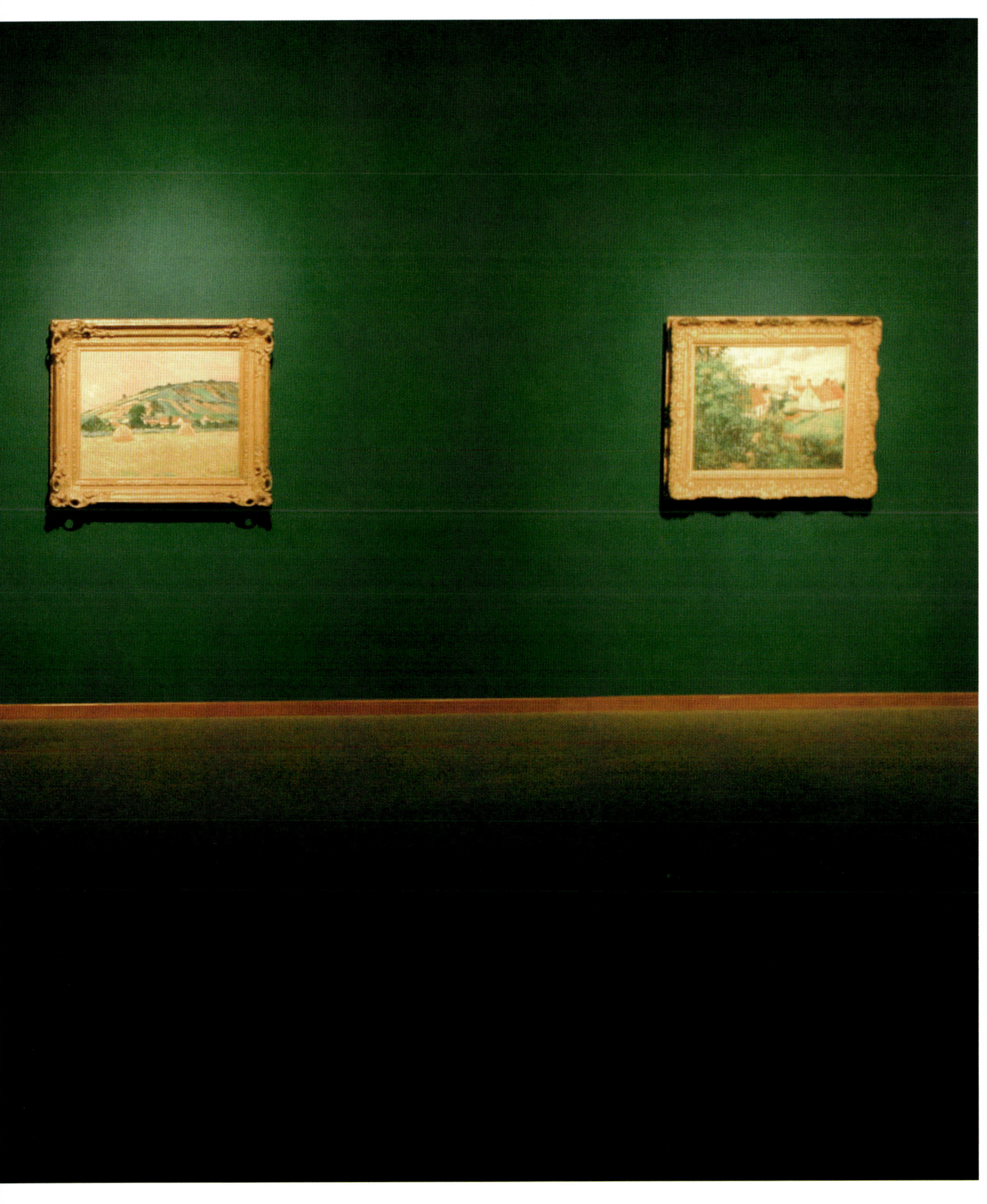

29 August 2005, TEHRAN, IRAN

A woman looks at paintings by the nineteenth-century French artist Camille Pissarro during the 'Modern Art Movement' exhibition at the Tehran Museum of Contemporary Art. The museum owns one of the most important collections of modern Western art outside of Europe and the United States, but most of it has been locked in a vault since Iran's 1979 Islamic revolution. Morteza Nikoubazl

We may share an ever more globalized culture, but there remains an extraordinary diversity in ways of living across the globe. There are also enormous inequalities. In the superabundant societies of the West, people are now spoilt for choice as never before, while across the Third World people dream of escaping a daily life that for millions is a struggle against poverty, hunger, disease and debt.

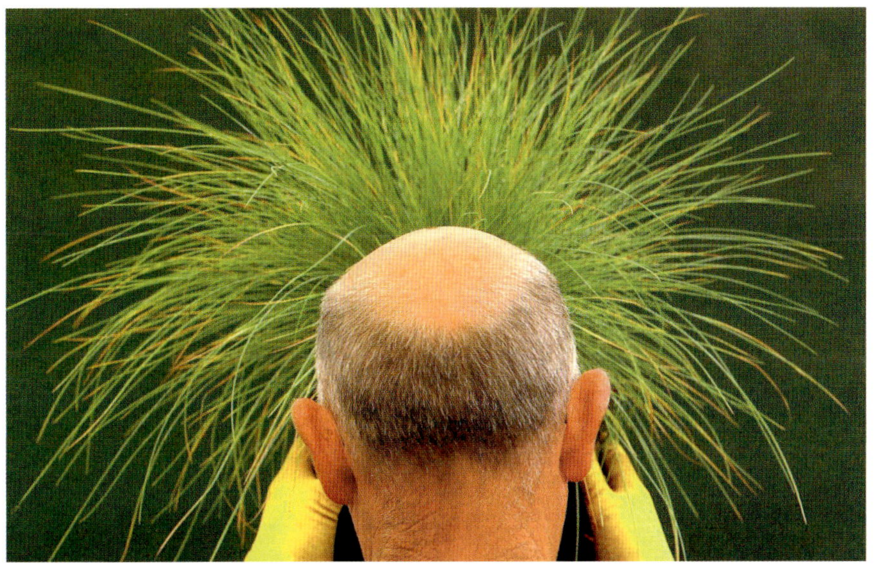

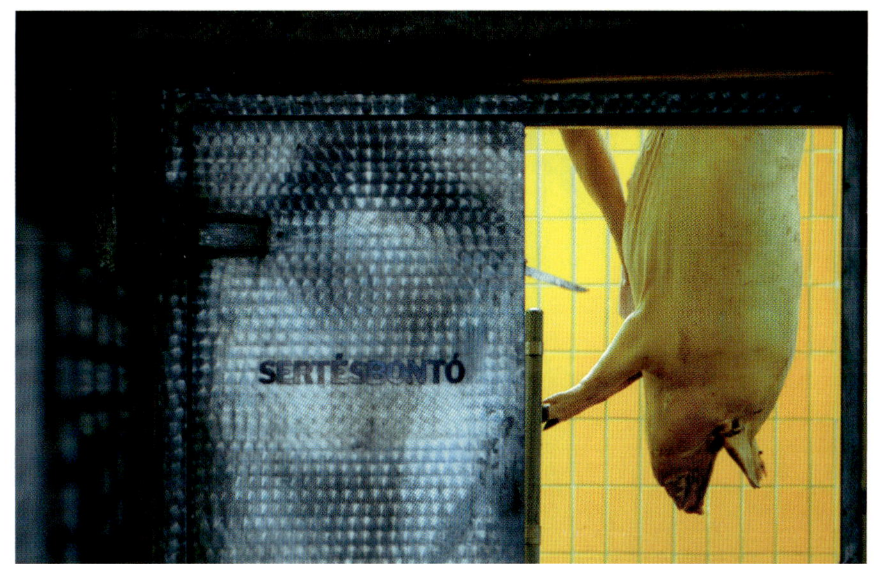

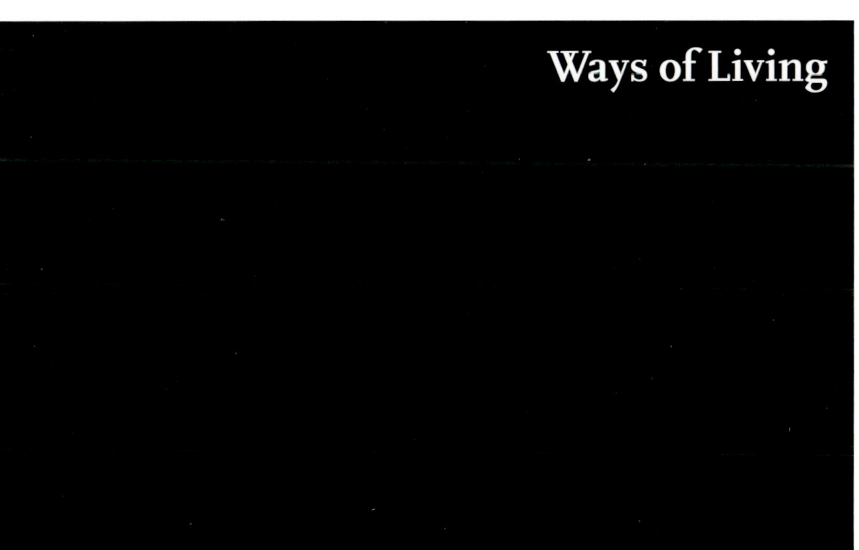

Ways of Living

People / Family / Recreation / Health
Opportunity / Poverty / Diversity / Choice
Global Contrasts / Local Connections

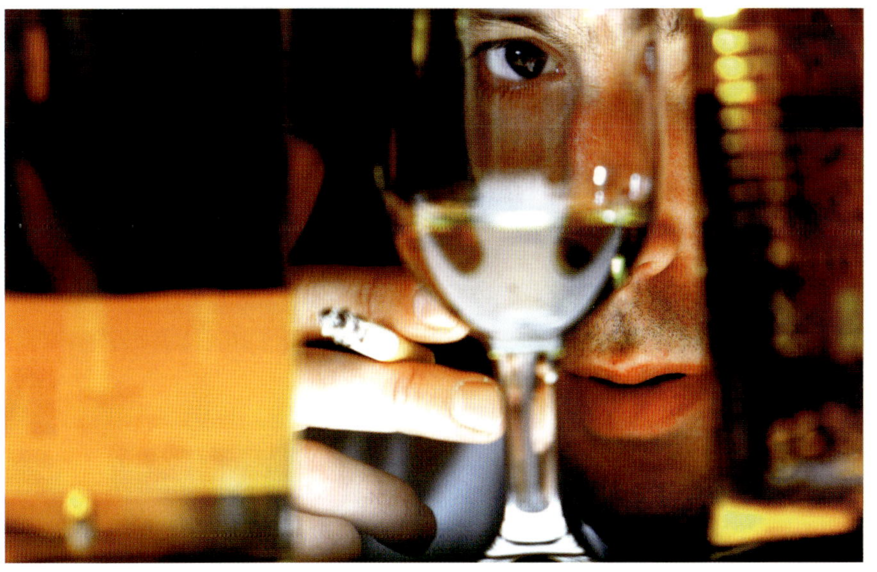

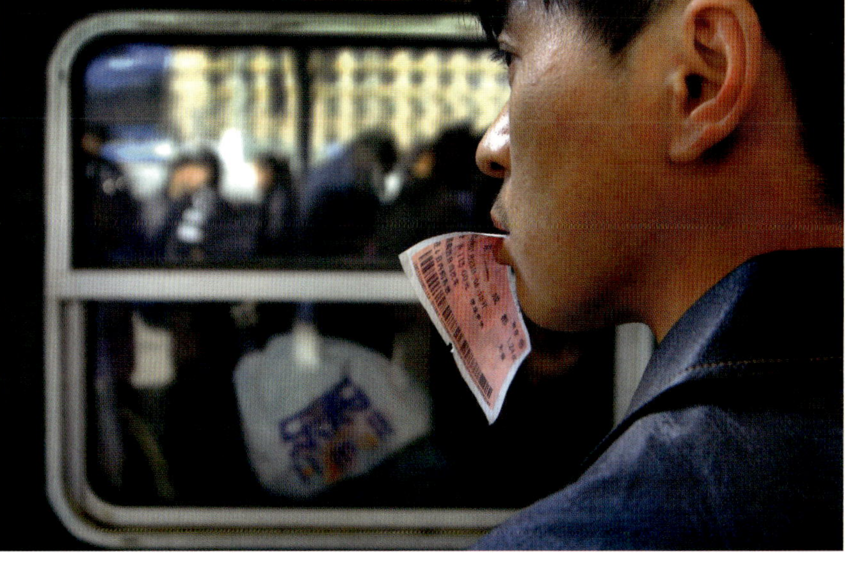

Ways of Living

The Italian car company Lamborghini opened its third Chinese dealership in 2005, evidence of growing wealth in a country for decades associated with the bicycle. Half a world away in Zimbabwe, a collapsing economy and chronic fuel shortages have pushed up the price of a bike by more than 1,800 percent in a year, taking such humble transport far beyond the reach of the impoverished majority.

For the wealthy elites of China, the world's rapidly emerging economic superpower, the decision to buy a flashy sports car for $300,000 is a lifestyle choice. For the poor in a country that was once southern Africa's breadbasket but which now is forced to import food, the luxury of such choices is more remote than ever.

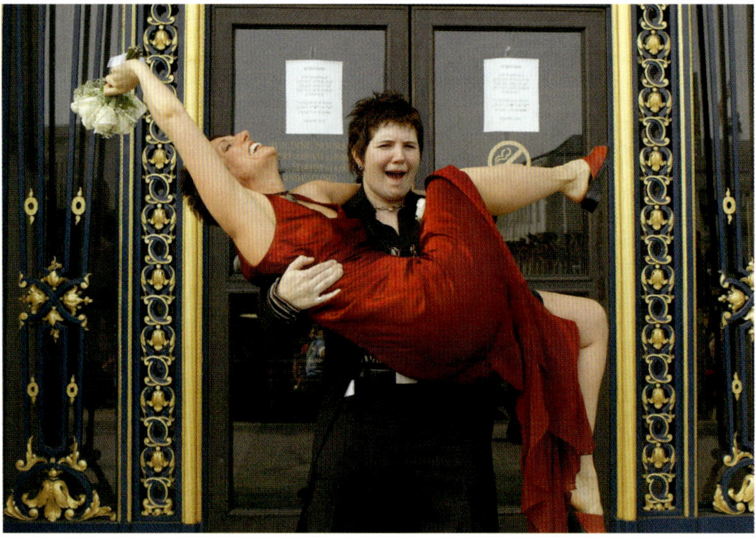

Siddiqui Ray is lifted in the air by her spouse Liz McElhinney after their marriage at City Hall in San Francisco. Hundreds of gay and lesbian couples from all across the country lined up to marry after San Francisco mayor Gavin Newsom defied state law and lifted a ban on gay marriages. 15 February 2004, Kimberly White.

It is the possibility of choice, or the lack of it, that defines much of the way we live today and illustrates the gulf between the world's rich and poor. In drought-hit villages in northern India's Rajasthan, women struggle to join a savings scheme that requires them to put aside just a few cents a month to tide them over hard times. In the United States, animal lovers will probably spend a projected $8 billion on their pets in 2007, with three-quarters of owners prepared to go into debt just to take care of a sick animal. Those in Los Angeles who feel guilty about abandoning Fido at home all day can leave him listening to DogCatRadio, an Internet station designed to keep the poor pooch company while his 'parents' are out at work.

While AIDS has cut life expectancy at birth in Zambia to just 33 years, the average U.S. citizen can now expect to live to more than 77 as medical science continues to reduce death rates from the three biggest killers: heart disease, cancer and stroke. And with the right lifestyle choices – healthy diet, regular exercise and good medical insurance – American baby boomers can live even longer than that. In Zambia, AIDS is killing 200 people a day, but in the United States, where AIDS was first reported a quarter of a century ago and billions of dollars have been spent on fighting the disease, death rates from HIV are now on the decline.

More worrying for many North Americans is a cause of death that has its roots in affluence and the choices it permits: obesity. The all-American meal of burger, fries and a giant bucket of cola may be as much of a cultural stereotype as the Chinese on their bicycles, but the effects of that sort of food are only too real. Whether they eat it because they like it or because it's cheap and available, it is the kind of diet that will eventually kill many in America and other affluent Western societies before their time.

It is the possibility of choice, or the lack of it, that defines much of the way we live today.

At the turn of the millennium the United States was spending $117 billion every year on treating obesity-related conditions – almost exactly the figure put forward by development experts as the annual sum required to meet the United Nations goal of halving poverty in Africa over the next decade. With 30 percent of its citizens now obese, the United States has become the fattest nation in history. Many Americans are literally eating themselves to death: the spread of obesity is actually projected to cause a fall in life expectancy over the next half century.

A society to which President Herbert Hoover promised 'a chicken in every pot and a car in every garage' seems to have been transformed into a culture of self-indulgence, where millions whose standard of living has never been so high devote themselves to fad diets, obsessive gym workouts, cosmetic surgery, gas-guzzling sport utility vehicles and compulsive shopping.

Luxury brands have spread across the globe. It is no longer necessary to frequent the boutiques of London's Bond Street or Rodeo Drive in Beverly Hills to keep up with what is hot. Prada suits, Gucci shoes and Louis Vuitton bags are sold in airport shopping malls and department stores around the world. In China, the number of people who can afford expensive luxury goods is growing rapidly in line with overall economic expansion and is expected to reach 250 million – not far short of the current total population of the United States – in four or five years, according to local estimates.

And if you can't afford the real thing, counterfeit copies can be bought in the street the world over, often from market stalls no more than few yards from shops selling the genuine article.

The democratization of luxury to the point where the average man or woman feels these things are theirs almost by right has been achieved more than anything by the spread of the Internet. Lifestyle choices have become more affordable as prices are driven down by a million Google searches. Online shopping has put even the most exclusive products within easy reach of anyone with a computer and a credit card. People can go to the mall to inspect the goods and mingle with their fellow man, but back home at the PC is increasingly where business is actually transacted.

Nor do people have to restrict themselves to their local mall. Cheaper air fares have democratized travel too. Europeans think nothing of flying to New York with an empty suitcase to stock up on more keenly priced Gap shirts and iPods. Holidays have become spur-of-the-moment decisions, with air fares often no more expensive than the taxi ride to the airport. Budget airlines are booming in Europe and the United States and poised to expand into Asia and Africa. One of the oldest, Ireland's Ryanair, celebrated its twentieth birthday this year with a suggestion that subsidies from airports and even income from on-board gaming could drive ticket prices down even further. 'I have a vision in the future that we will be flying everyone for free,' declared Ryanair chief Michael O'Leary.

Demand is also strong at the elite end of the scale, where a million dollars will buy a private jet and guaranteed seclusion from the likes of O'Leary's customers. The number of private jets in use around the world now stands at around 23,000 and rising.

For many thousands of the world's poor, travel is not an indulgence or a convenience, but the route to economic salvation. Early in 2004, 11 Cubans seeking a better life in the United States attempted to float their way across the Florida Straits in a green 1959 Buick. Intercepted by the U.S. Coast Guard, they were rescued and their makeshift vessel sunk, judged a hazard to shipping. Other migrants adopt less headline-grabbing strategies as they brave the waters of the Mediterranean or the deserts of Arizona to head for the promised lands of the affluent West, where they, or at least their children, may eventually earn enough money to be able to join the vacationing masses.

What such migrants leave behind is another story. As poor countries find that ever more of their brightest and most enterprising are heading for the West in search of a better life, the cost to those who stay at home, condemned to squalor, ill health and debt,

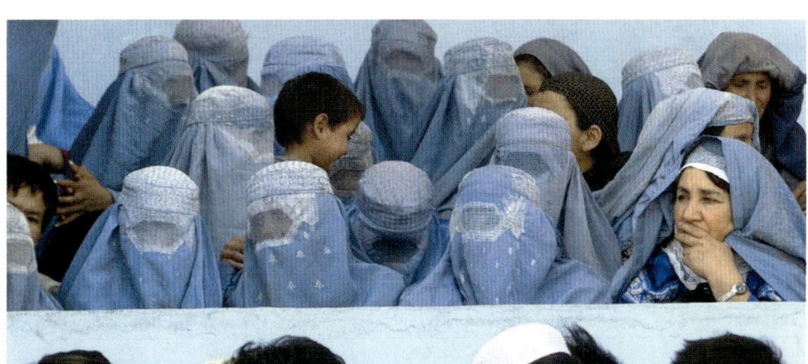

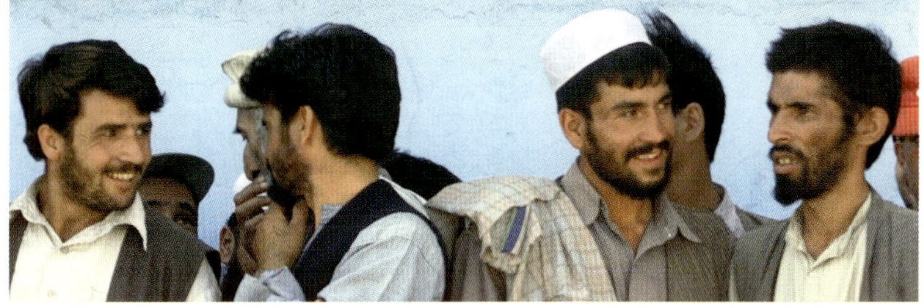

Afghan men and women await the first lottery draw in their country for 11 years. Thousands gathered at a stadium in Kabul on 15 July 2002 to attend the event, organized by the Afghan Red Crescent Society. A total of 100,000 tickets, priced at 10,000 Afghani (U.S. $0.25) per ticket, were sold, with prizes ranging from a car to bicycles, televisions and cash. Zainal Abd Halim.

becomes more onerous. Even the efforts of the international community to improve conditions can sometimes prove counter-productive. In Liberia, a country ravaged by war and poverty, United Nations agencies and international aid organizations pay much better than the country's shattered public sector, leaving still fewer doctors to run the nation's dilapidated hospitals.

The flipside of this 'brain drain' – repeated across the developing world – is seen in North America, Britain and Australia, where as many as one in four doctors is an immigrant who trained abroad. In the United States, the ageing of the post-war baby boom generation is putting the healthcare system under greater strain, which means more medical staff are needed and fewer foreign doctors will return home. Though there are now fears that the United States is missing out on the best and the brightest from abroad because of tough visa policies introduced after the attacks of September 11, 2001.

In the cultural arena, the drift towards the West remains a powerful force, even in parts of the world where the U.S. government and its allies are reviled for their policies. Television stations broadcasting to Arab audiences regularly screen U.S.-made comedies and chat shows along with newscasts from American networks. The sitcom *Friends* is popular with young people in Saudi Arabia, the country that produced 15 of the 19 hijackers responsible for September 11. The Arabic language Al Jazeera satellite news television network has taken the logical step in competing with the global broadcasters CNN and the BBC by setting up an English-language service.

In the cultural arena, the drift towards the West remains a powerful force, even in parts of the world where the U.S. government and its allies are reviled for their policies

Internet dating, which began in the United States, has spread to the Arab world. In Jordan young people often see it as a way to circumvent the more traditional attitudes of their parents towards love and marriage. Elsewhere, marriage itself is being redefined, often in the teeth of bitter opposition from religious and cultural conservatives. In 2005, Britain joined a growing list of countries and jurisdictions permitting gay civil partnerships and marriages. Among the first to solemnize their union under the new rules were Elton John and his partner David Furnish. Singer George Michael, who himself was planning to make it legal with his own partner Kenny Goss, was there on Elton's big day.

Such high-profile unions have failed to impress hardliners in America's 'red states' or in the Vatican. On the night that George W. Bush won his second term in the White House, eleven states also voted to ban gay weddings by backing local constitutional amendments defining marriage as a union between a man and woman. Pope John Paul II went further. Shortly before his death in early 2005, he denounced homosexual marriages as 'part of a new ideology of evil'. What effect the late Pope's words will have is still unclear. They did not stop South Africa's highest court ruling in late 2005 that it was unconstitutional to deny gay people the right to marry, thereby bringing to Africa a lifestyle choice previously the preserve of rich Western countries.

Western technologies, too, are rapidly being adopted and adapted to an African setting. In just one example, the number of mobile phone users in the continent is expected soon to pass 100 million as cellular networks replace landline systems that have suffered from years of under-investment and lack of maintenance. While people in the West use their mobiles to swap photos and surf the Internet, Africans without access to a traditional financial system can now get their salaries paid into cell phone bank accounts.

A successful Chinese entrepreneur can treat himself to a Lamborghini if business is looking up. In Senegal, there may be few sophisticated Italian sports cars, but fishermen heading to market can also reap the benefits of the spread of technology – by checking market prices on their cell phones.

Giles Elgood has worked for Reuters since 1980. He has reported from dozens of countries around the world, covering everything from war in Bosnia to the British royal family. Long-term assignments in Germany, Nigeria, Yugoslavia and the United States have been interspersed with shorter reporting trips to Europe, the Middle East, Africa, Asia and the Americas. After three years as an editor in Washington D.C., he is currently stationed in London as a chief sub-editor.

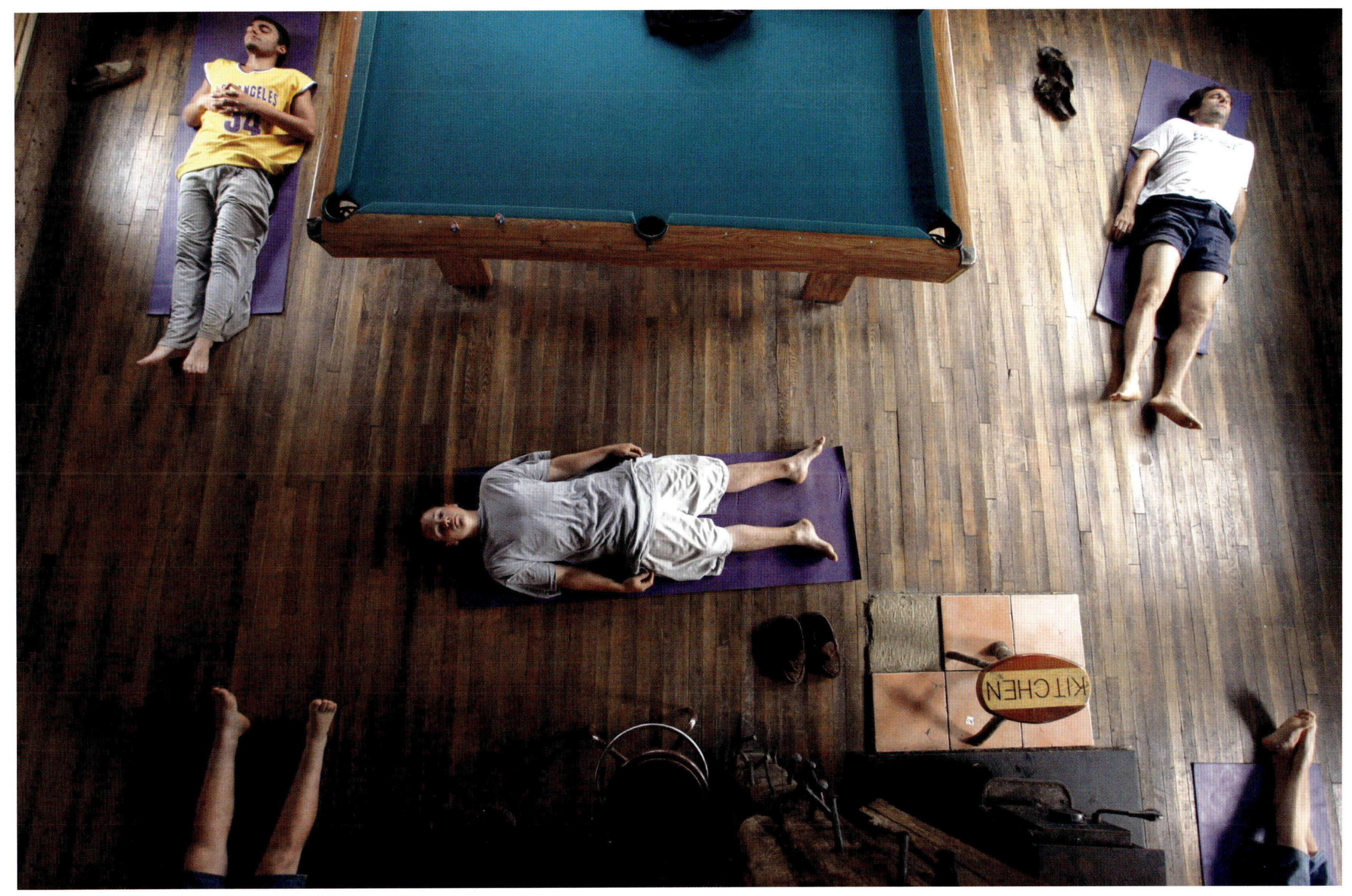

29 June 2005, PENIKESE ISLAND, UNITED STATES

Morning yoga at Penikese Island, Massachusetts, a small school for boys aged 15–18 who are in need of special services and have been in trouble with the law. Pictured here are Ricky Eaton, 16 (left), Jerry Sarro, 17, and staff member David Dersham (right). Jessica Rinaldi

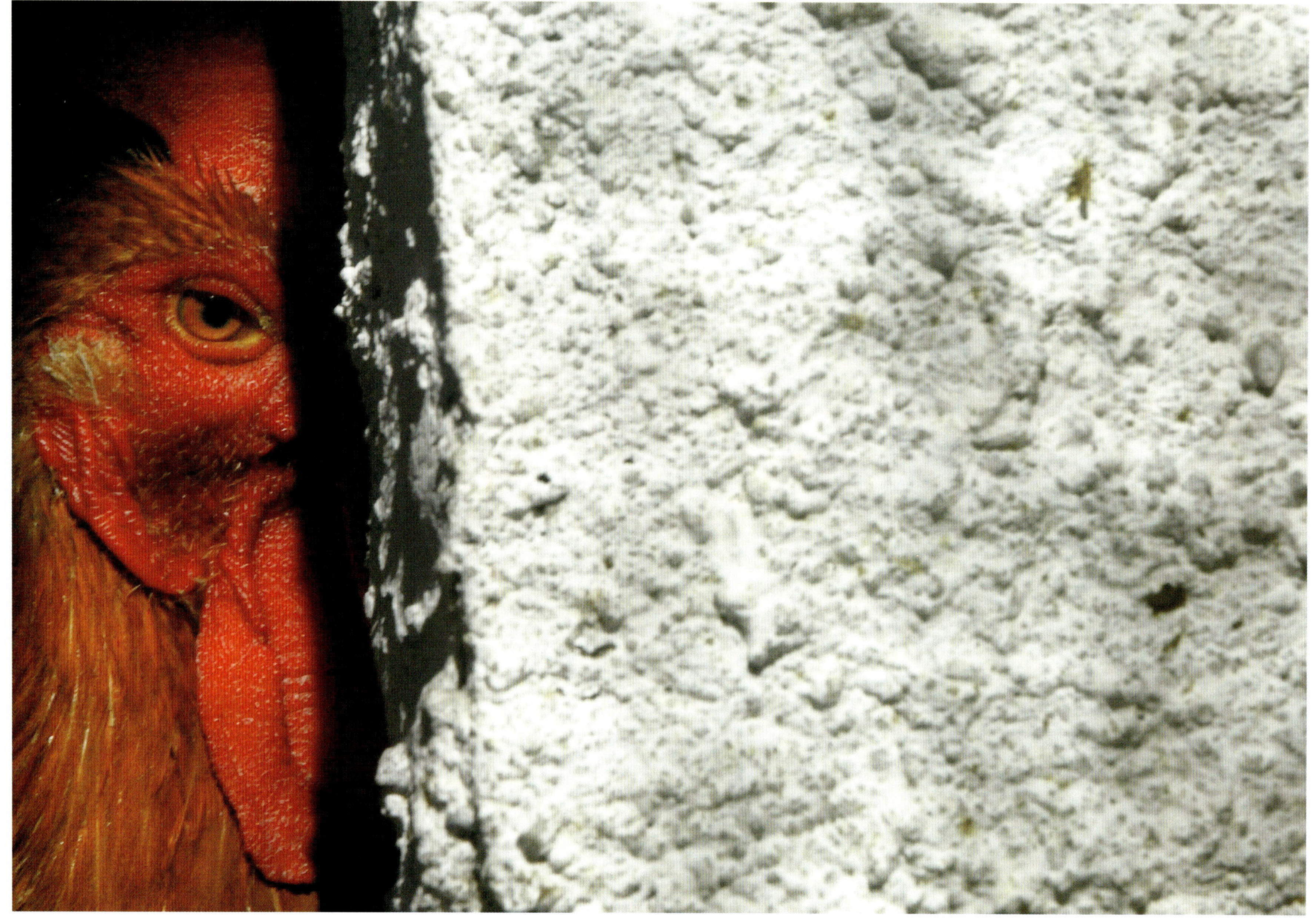

23 October 2005, MECO, PORTUGAL

A cock looks out from a poultry farm in the small Portuguese village of Meco. Food retailing in developed countries is increasingly dominated by powerful supermarket chains with huge centralized distribution networks. In emerging economies such as India and China, where millions of small convenience shops are commonplace, megastore retailers are also now rapidly expanding. Nacho Doce

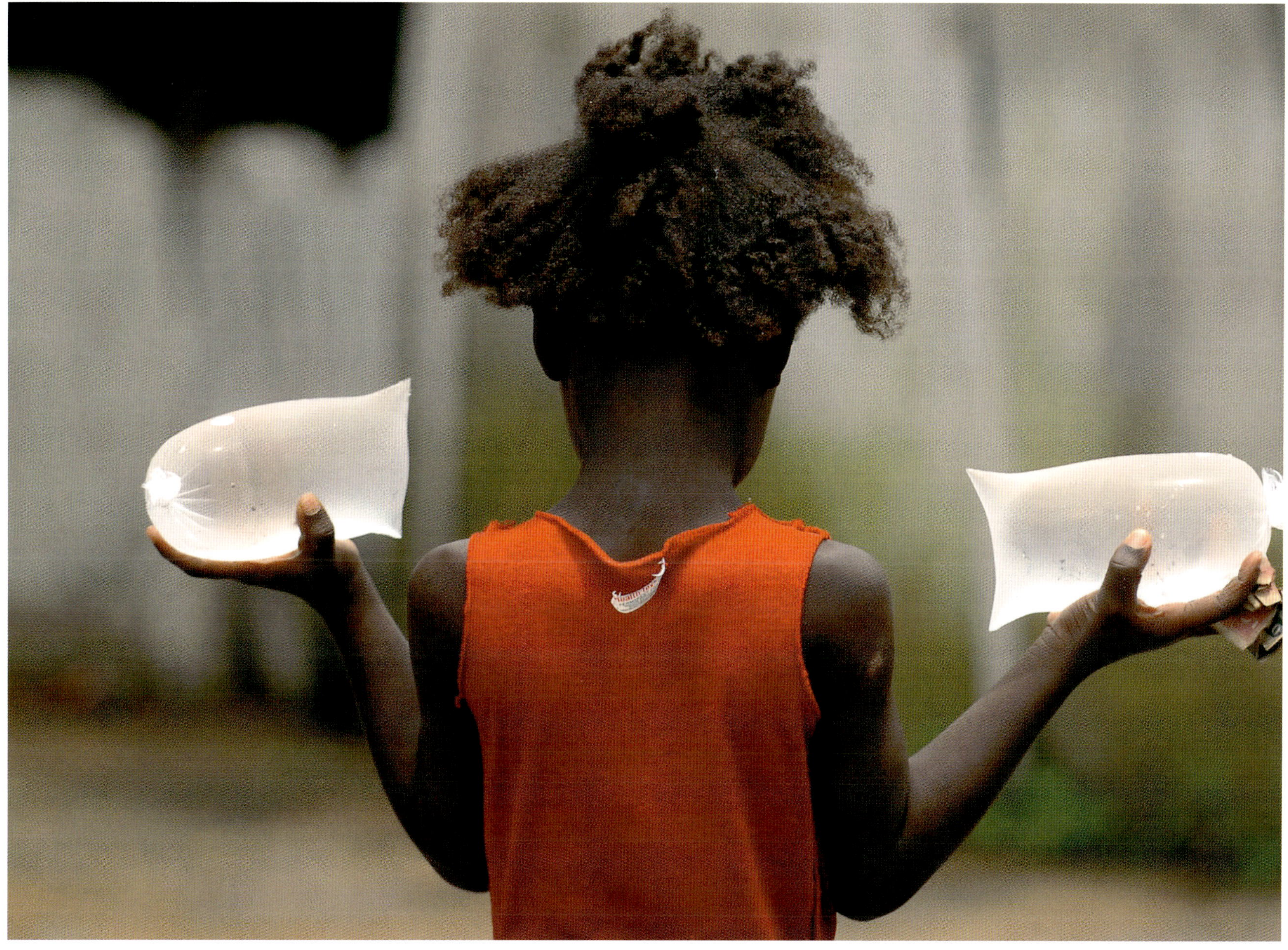

9 October 2005, MONROVIA, LIBERIA

A young girl carries bags of cold drinking water in the Liberian capital Monrovia, a city where hundreds of former child soldiers eke out a meagre living by shining shoes or pushing heavy carts stacked with jerry cans of drinking water. Jonathan Ernst

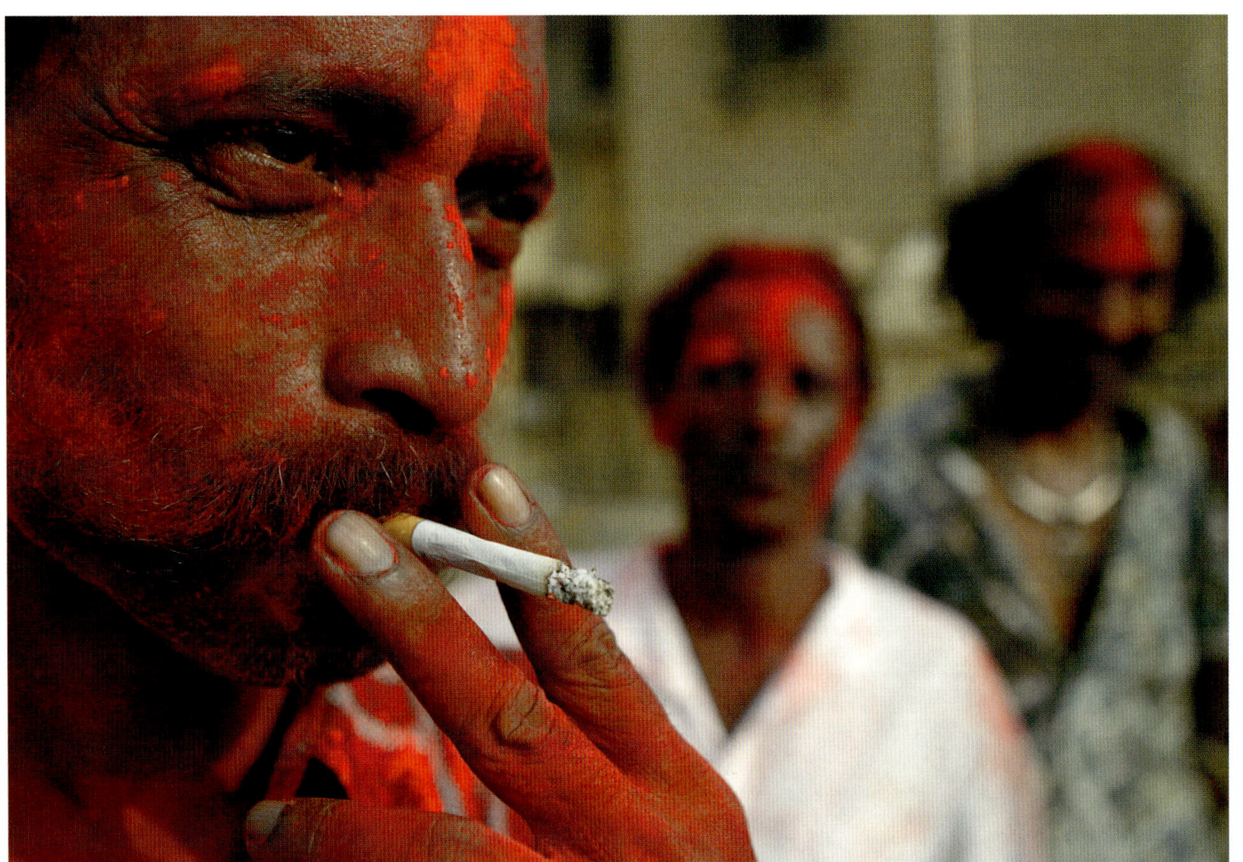

7 September 2005, MUMBAI, INDIA

An Indian reveller smokes during celebrations to mark the festival of Ganesh, Hindu deity of prosperity. India banned smoking in public places, tobacco advertising, and the sale of tobacco to minors in May 2004, after statistics showed smoking killed 2,200 people each day.

Adeel Halim

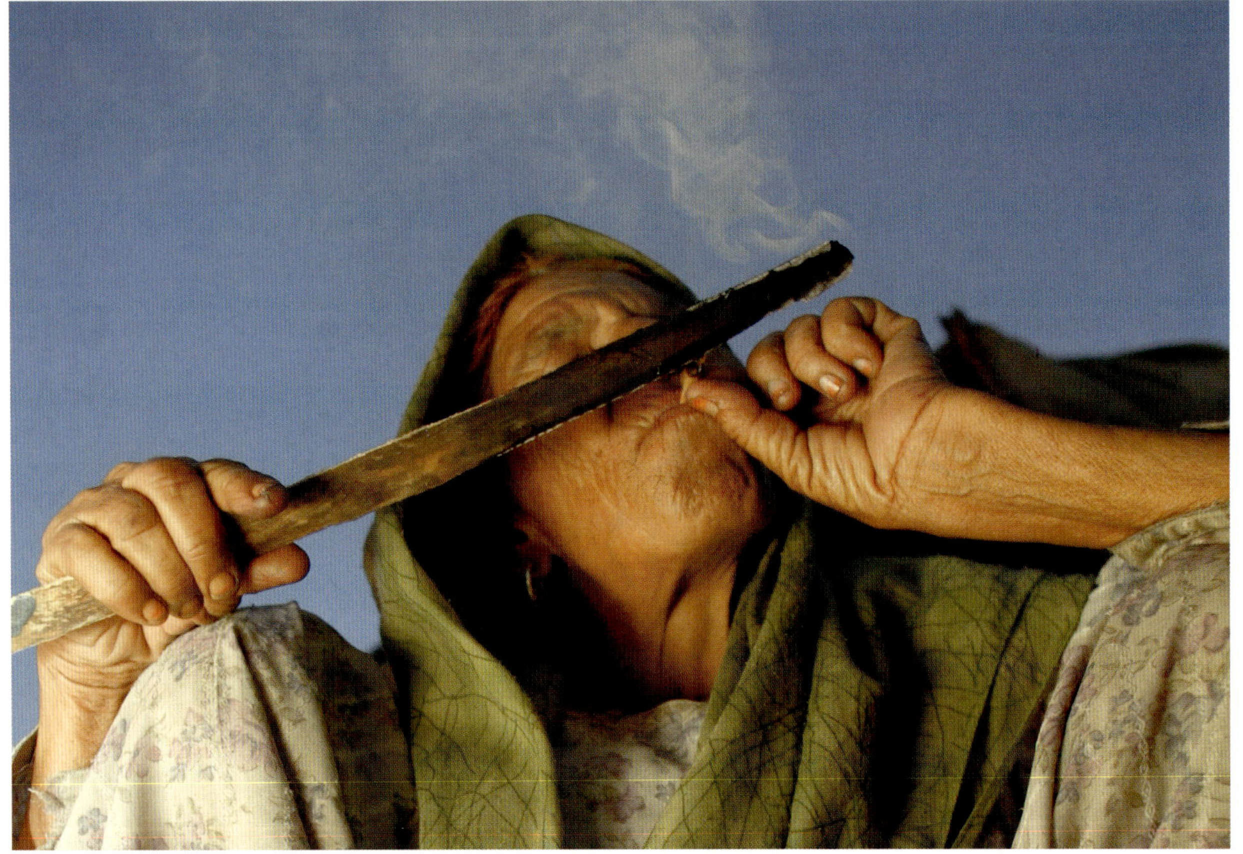

3 October 2005, SRINAGAR, INDIA

A homeless woman smokes a bidi, a single tobacco leaf rolled up and tied with a thread. Sold for next to nothing (25 for four rupees, or U.S. $0.08) and smoked by half of India's 120 million smokers, unfiltered bidis contain up to twice the nicotine of a standard cigarette.

Danish Ismail

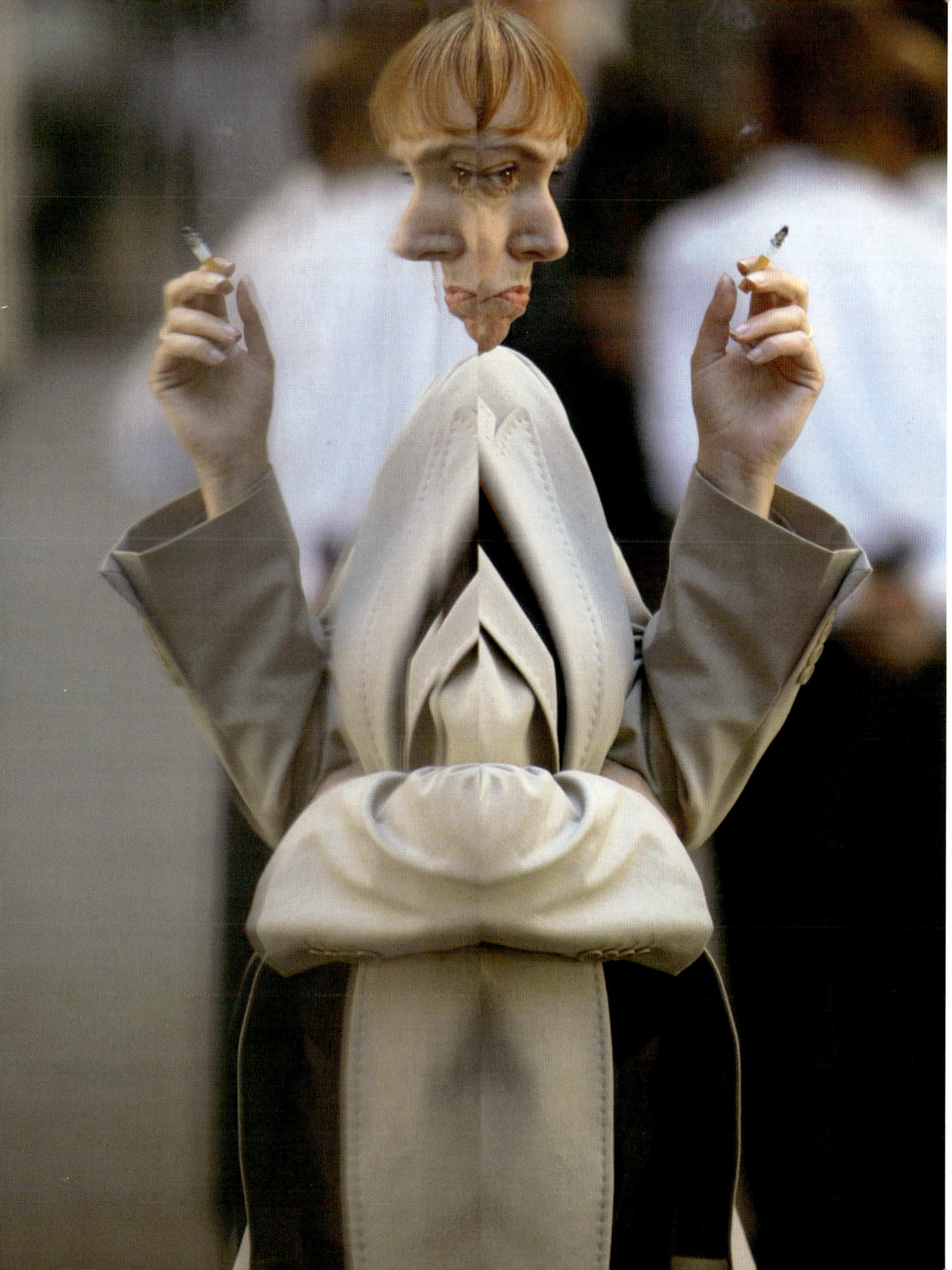

5 November 2003,
SYDNEY, AUSTRALIA

A woman smokes a cigarette in the central business district of Sydney, Australia, where smoking is banned in all office buildings and most bars and restaurants.
Will Burgess

9 July 2004, BANGKOK, THAILAND

A sex worker walks past a 'go go' bar in Bangkok's Nana Plaza. The United Nations says that 12 million people in Asia could be infected with HIV by the end of the decade as a result of low condom use, limited access to testing, gender inequality and widespread sex work and use of injected drugs. Adrees Latif

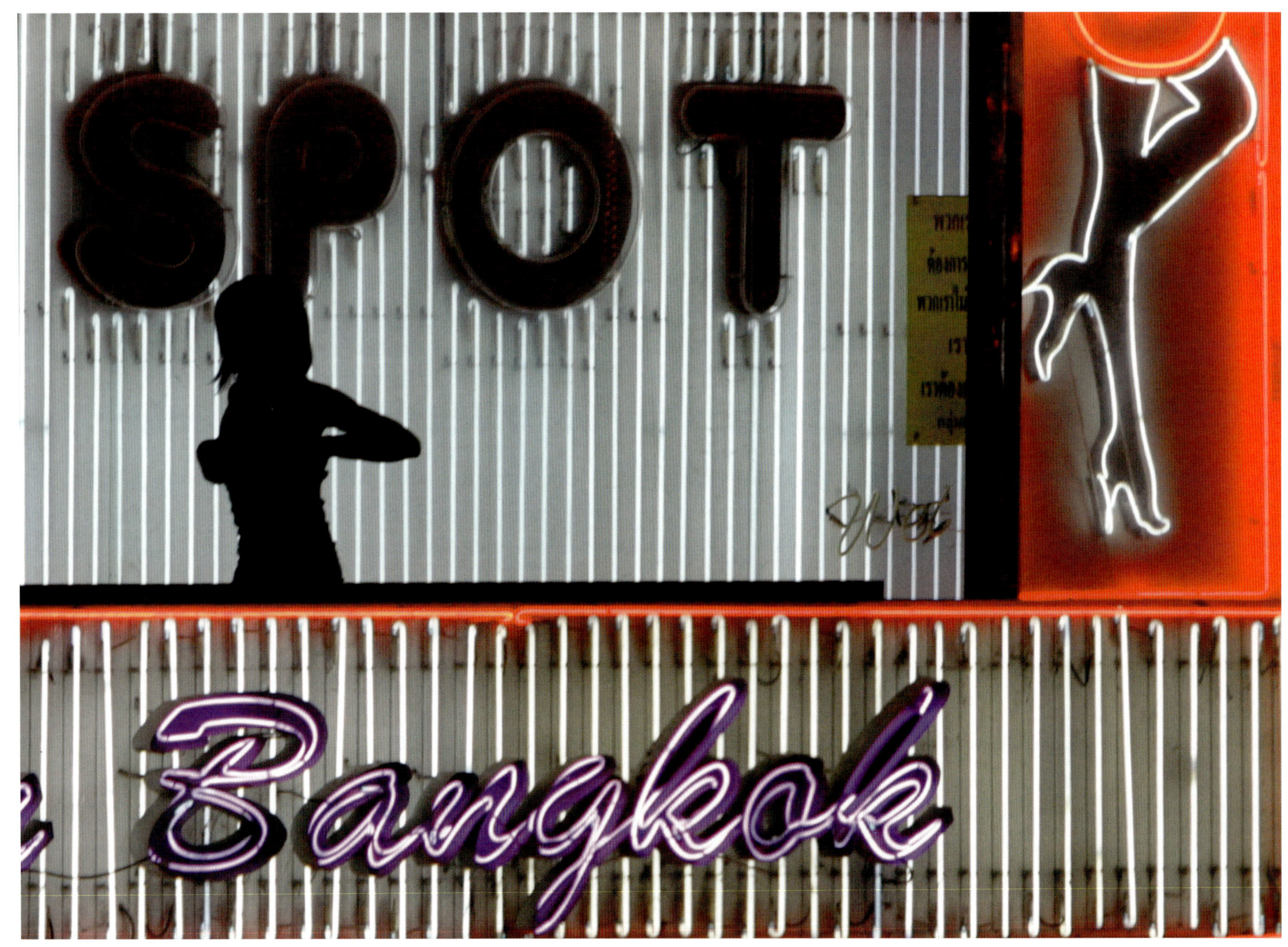

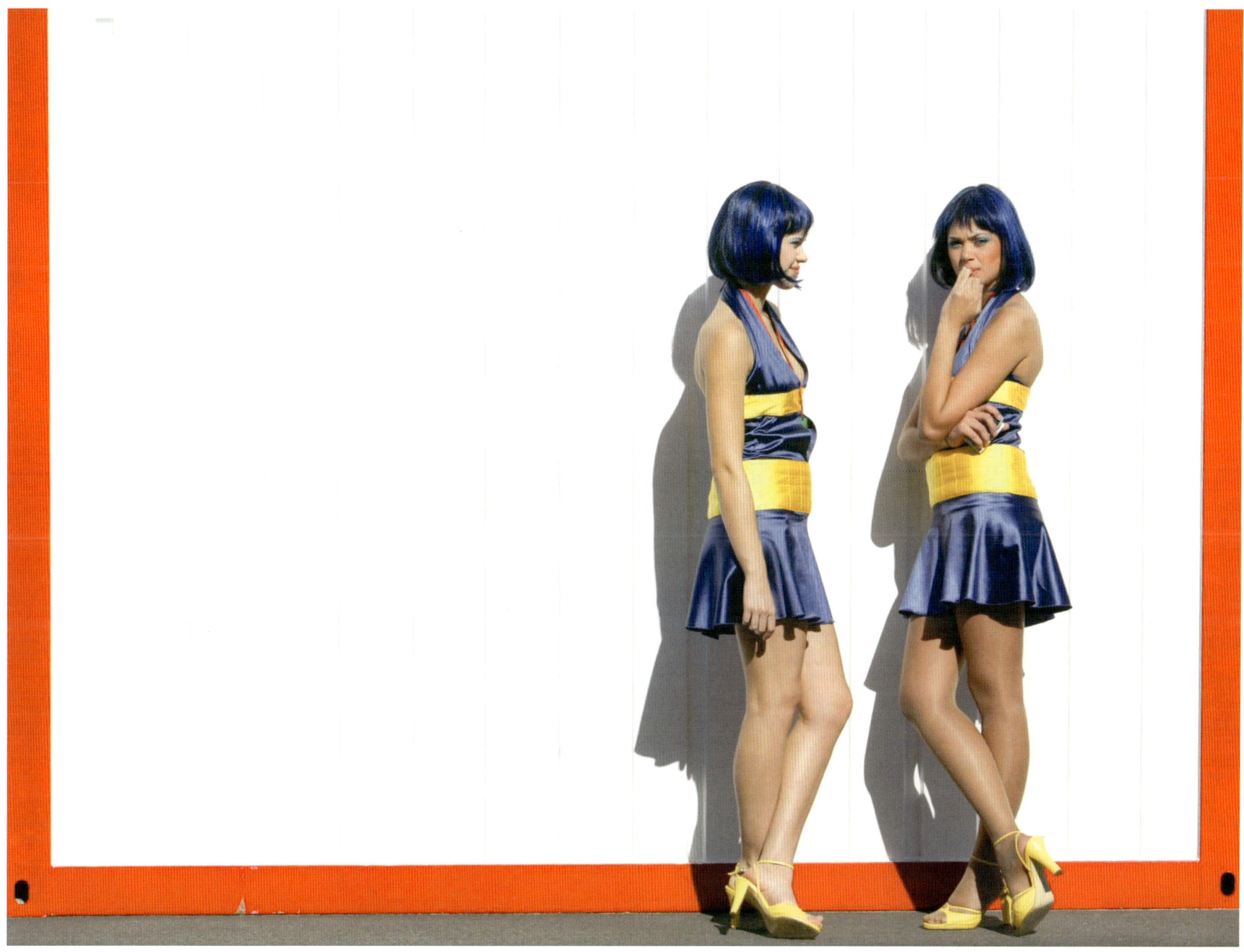

23 October 2005, ISTANBUL, TURKEY

Two grid girls rest at the paddock before the inaugural Turkish Grand Prix in Istanbul Park. With new racetracks in Malaysia, Bahrain and Shanghai, Formula One has expanded far to the east in recent years. The first Grand Prix in Istanbul extended the championship to 19 races, the longest season in the sport's history.
Umit Bektas

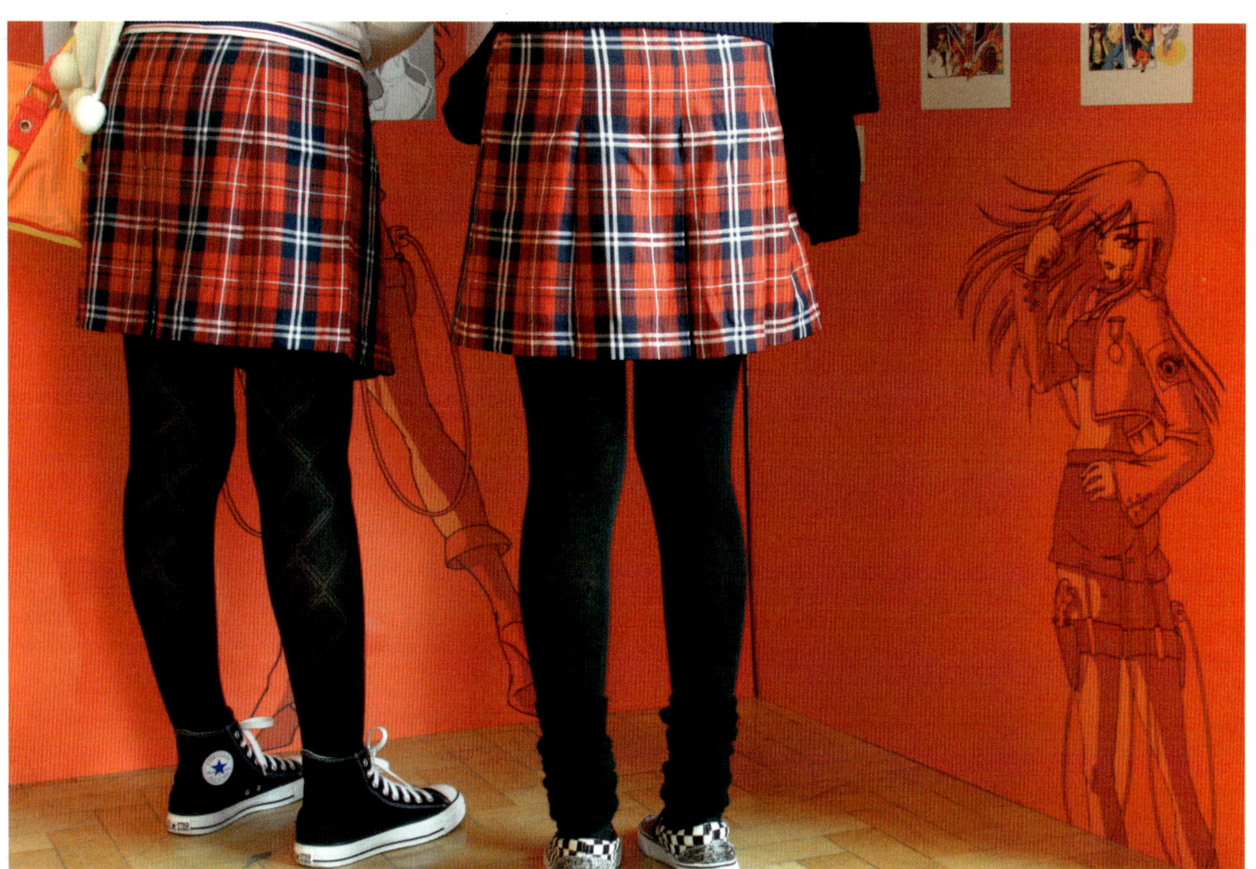

22 October 2005, LONDON, UNITED KINGDOM

Visitors view a gallery of manga characters at the International Manga and Anime Festival in London, a five-day festival of film screenings, workshops and art displays. Manga graphics and anime cartoon animations have long been hugely popular in their native Japan, and are increasingly gaining a global following. Catherine Benson

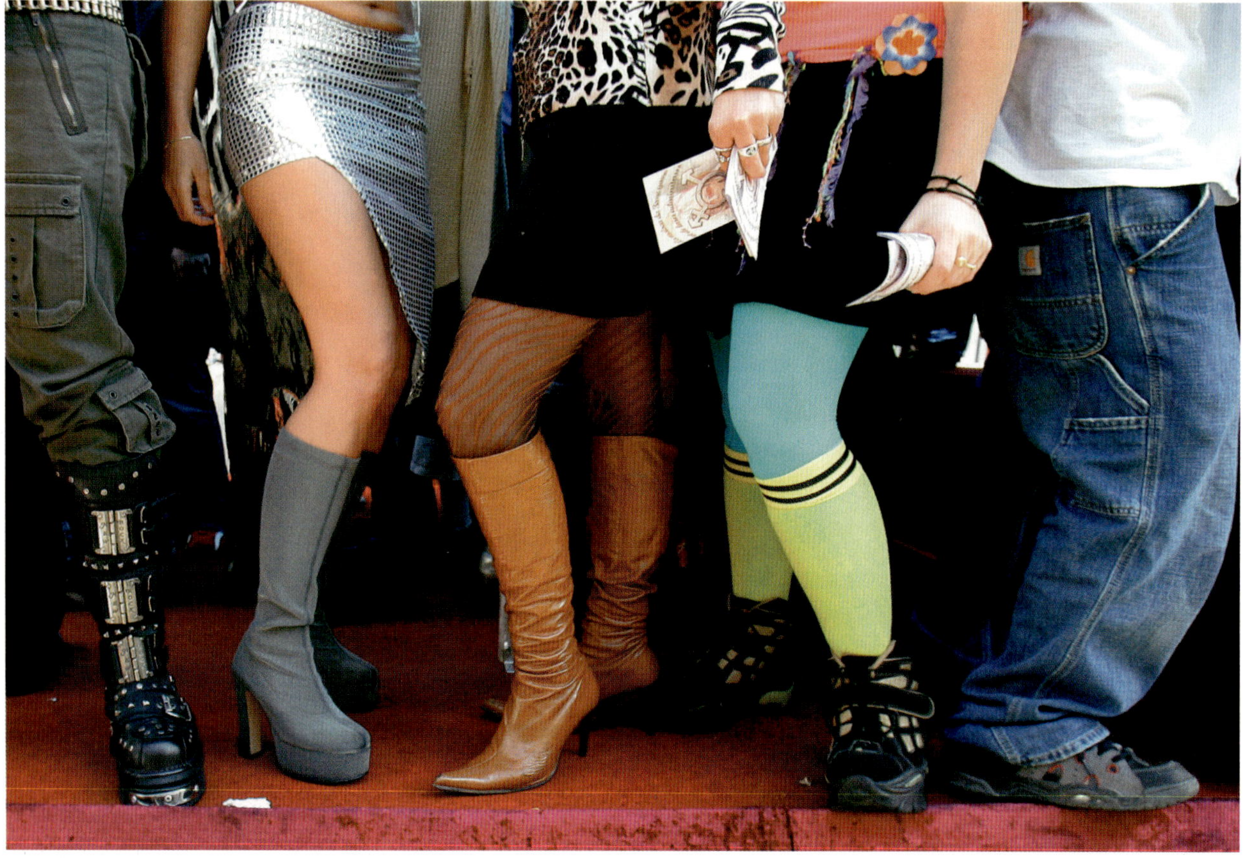

7 May 2005, BRUSSELS, BELGIUM

People dance during the traditional Gay and Lesbian Pride rally in central Brussels. In June 2003 Belgium followed the Netherlands to become the second country in the world to recognize marriages between same-sex couples. Countries that have introduced legalized partnerships or full marriage rights for same-sex couples now include Canada, Denmark, Norway, Hungary, Germany, Britain, Spain and Argentina. Yves Herman

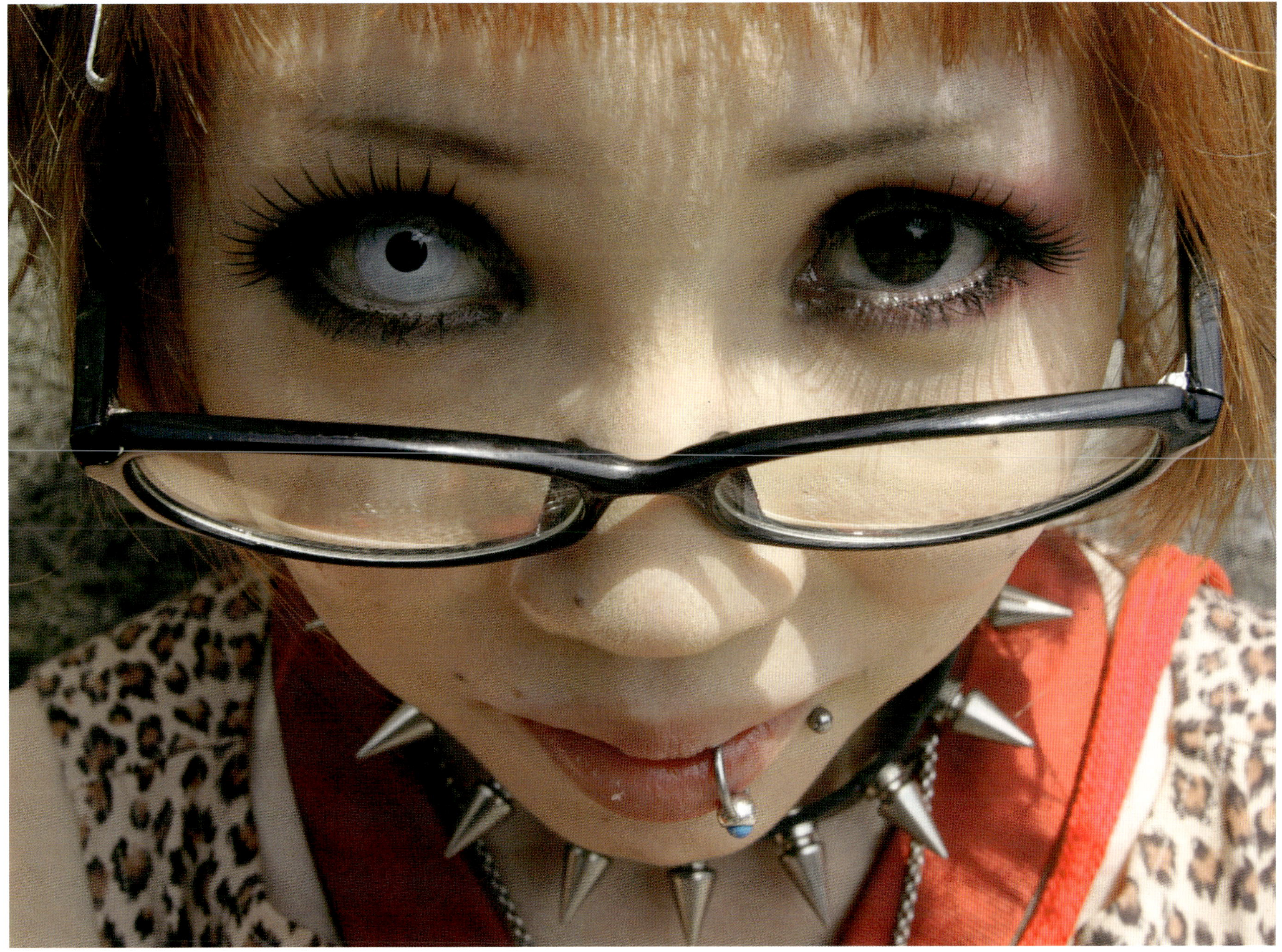

25 July 2004, TOKYO, JAPAN

A Japanese girl in punk fashion hangs out in the Tokyo shopping district of Harajuku, home of the street style often imitated by designers worldwide. Girls dressed in punk, 'Lolita' and other creative fashions often gather in the area.

Yuriko Nakao

11 July 2003, ULAN BATOR, MONGOLIA

Young Mongolian wrestlers wait for their match during Naadam Festival in the capital Ulan Bator. Naadam is the biggest national event in the Mongolian calendar, held from 11–13 July on the anniversary of the country's 1921 revolution. Claro Cortes IV

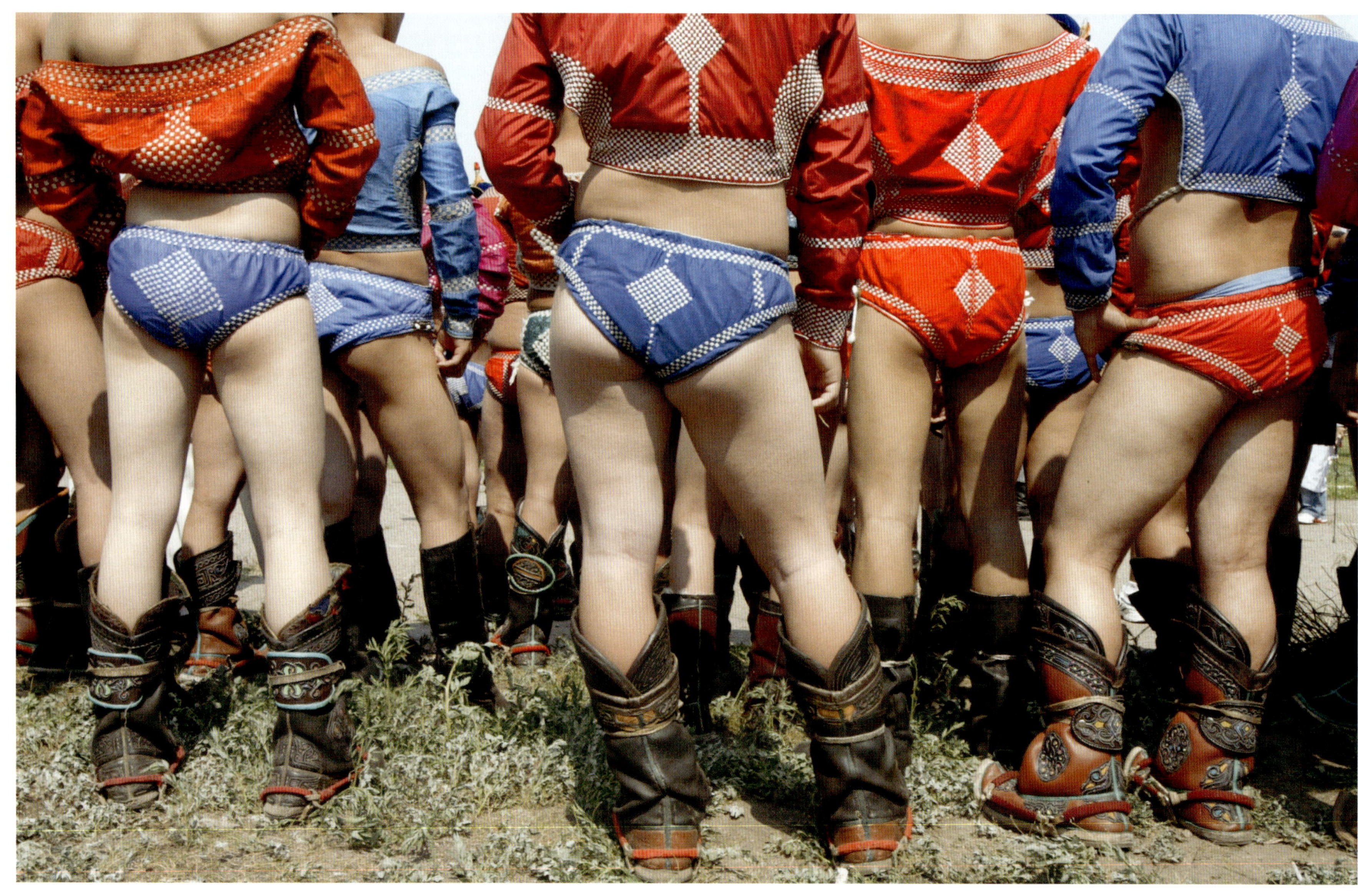

4 October 2005, BELGRADE, SERBIA

A young girl watches the Miss Serbia and Montenegro contest in Belgrade. Changing tastes and feminist protest have led the Miss World contest to fall out of favour in Britain, where the event was founded in 1951. But the annual pageant remains enormously popular elsewhere in the world, and is broadcast to global television audiences of up to two billion people. Marko Djurica

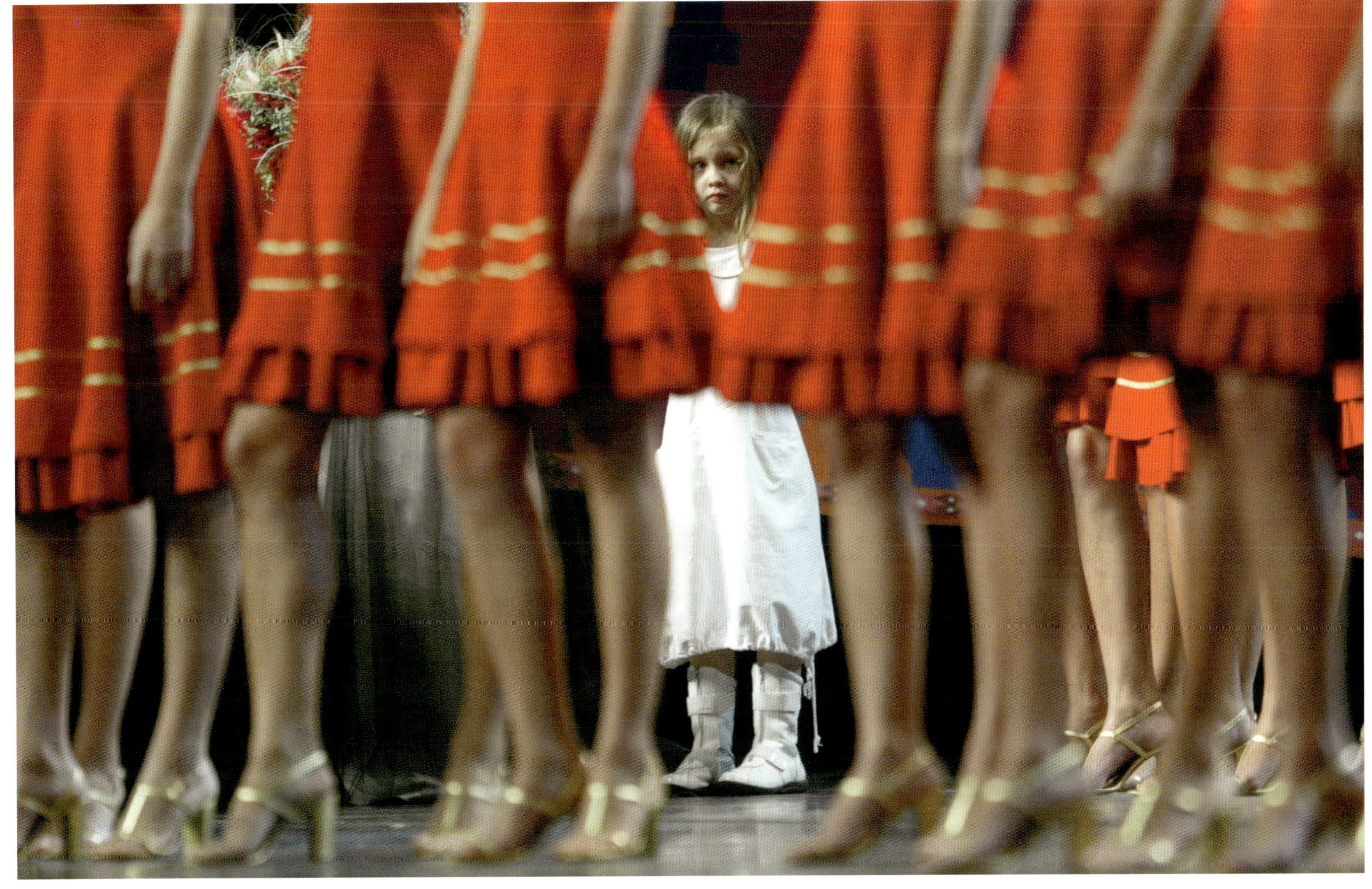

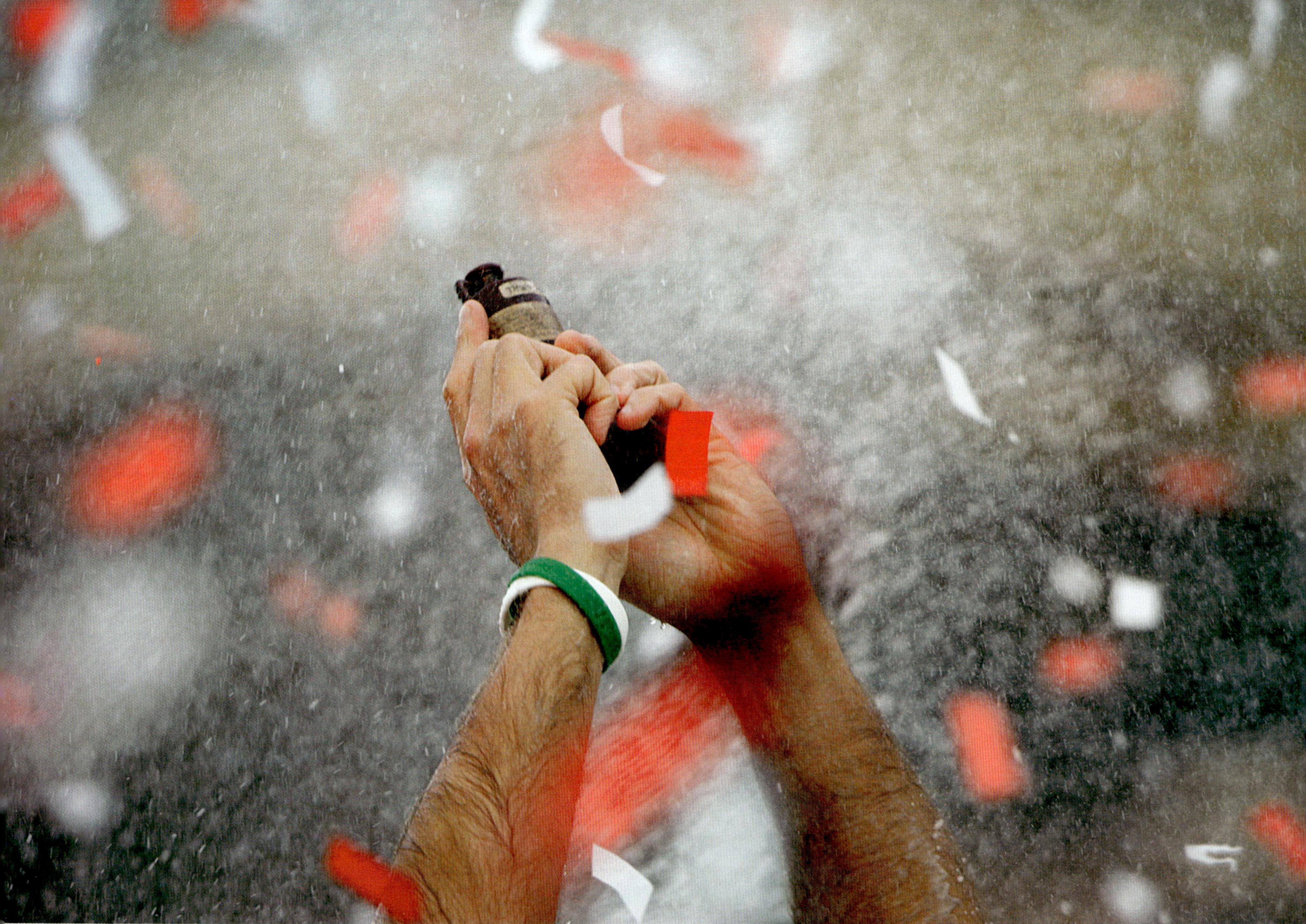

12 September 2005, LONDON, UNITED KINGDOM

England's cricket captain Michael Vaughan holds up the urn containing the Ashes after beating arch rivals Australia for the first time in almost two decades. England and Australia have competed for more than a century for the Ashes, the remnants of a bail that was burned following a famous English defeat by Australia in 1882.

Kieran Doherty

4 July 2004, LISBON, PORTUGAL

Portugal's Rui Costa (right) is consoled after his team's defeat by Greece in the final of the 2004 European Championship in Lisbon. Greece's win against the host team was one of the biggest shocks in international soccer history. Yiorgos Karahalis

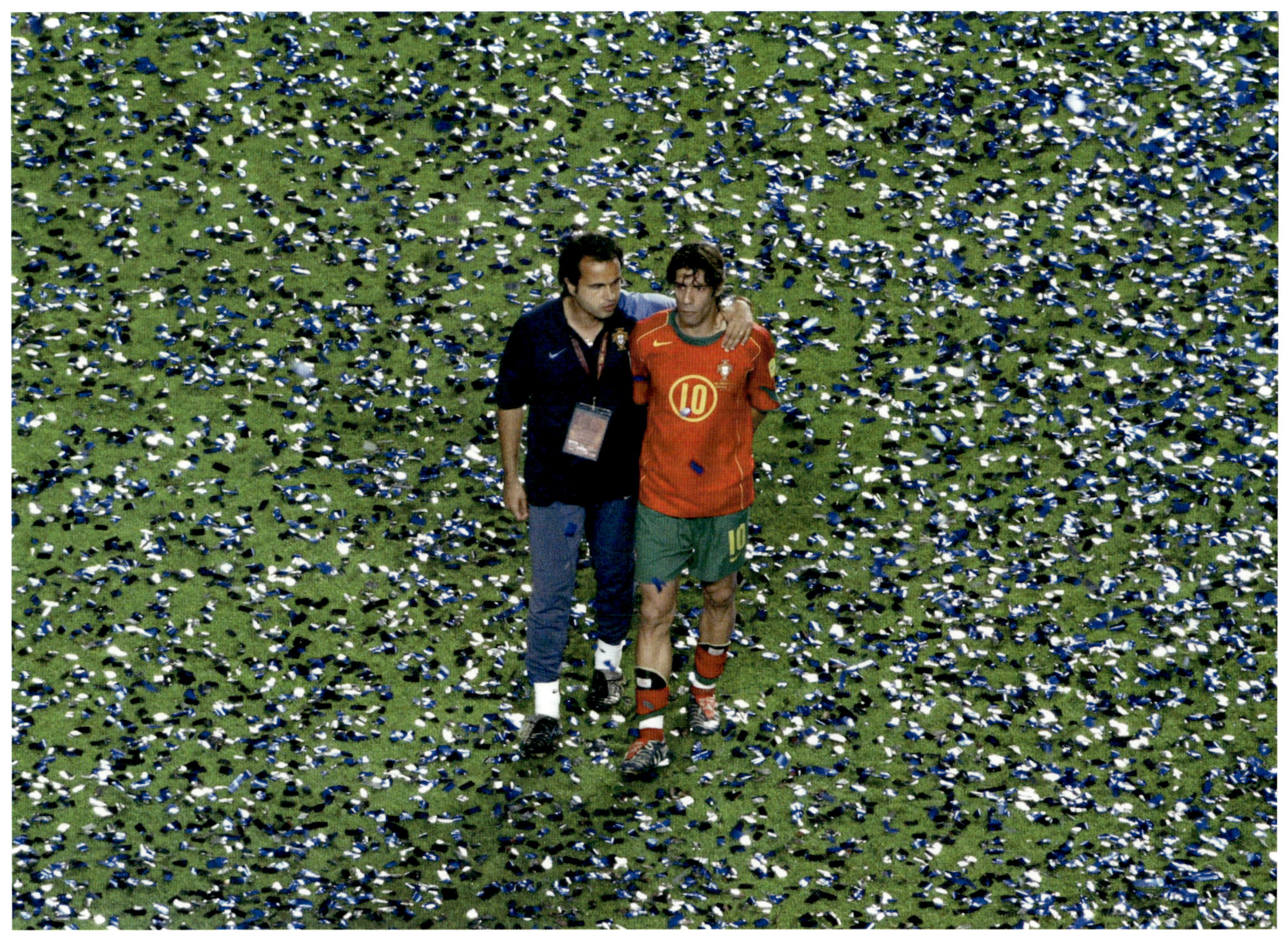

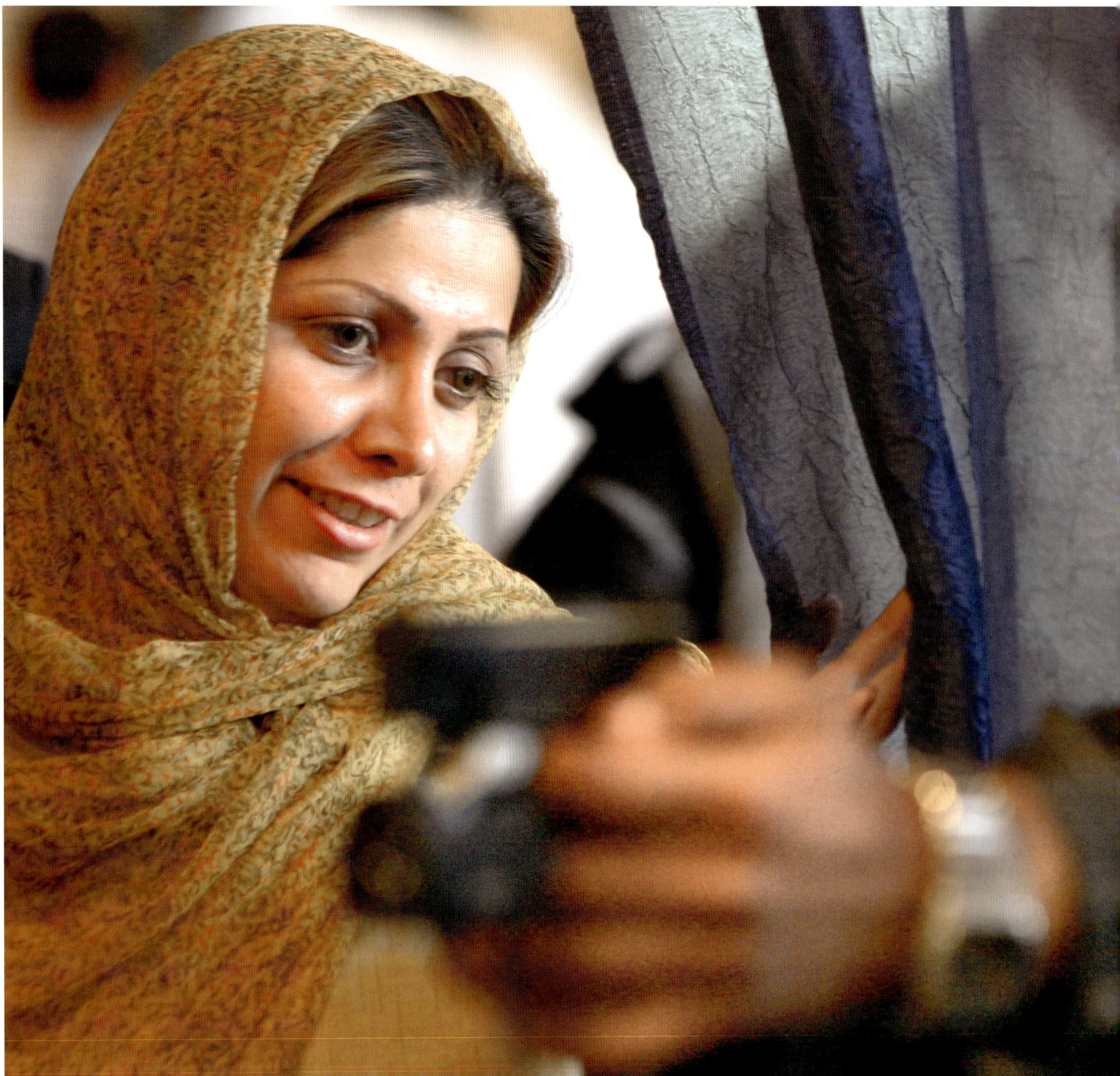

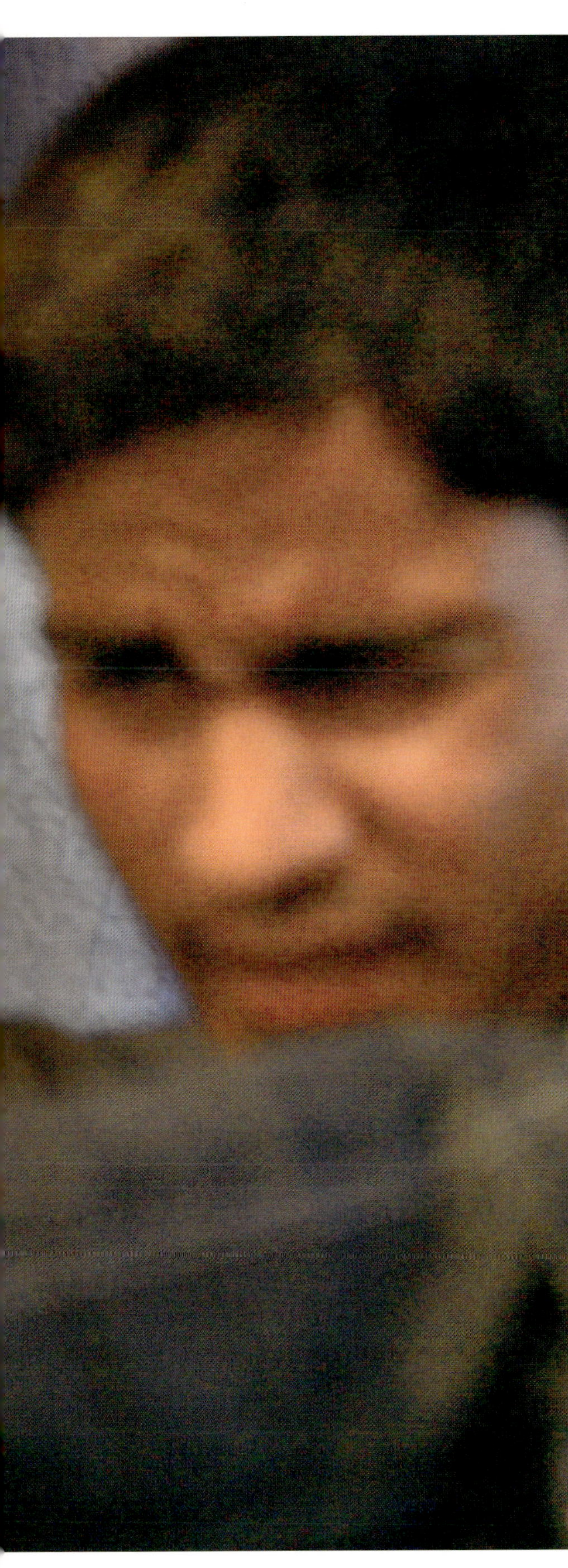

26 April 2004, TEHRAN, IRAN

An Iranian woman watches as a man practises shooting using a shooting simulator at the Fourth International Police Safety and Security Equipment Exhibition in Tehran, a trade show featuring products from 300 foreign and domestic firms. Morteza Nikoubazl

13 July 2005, PAMPLONA, SPAIN

A runner leads a bull into the ring during Pamplona's San Fermin festival. Six bulls are let loose onto the town's packed streets each morning during the week-long festival. In the evening they face the matador's sword in the town's bull ring.
Albert Gea

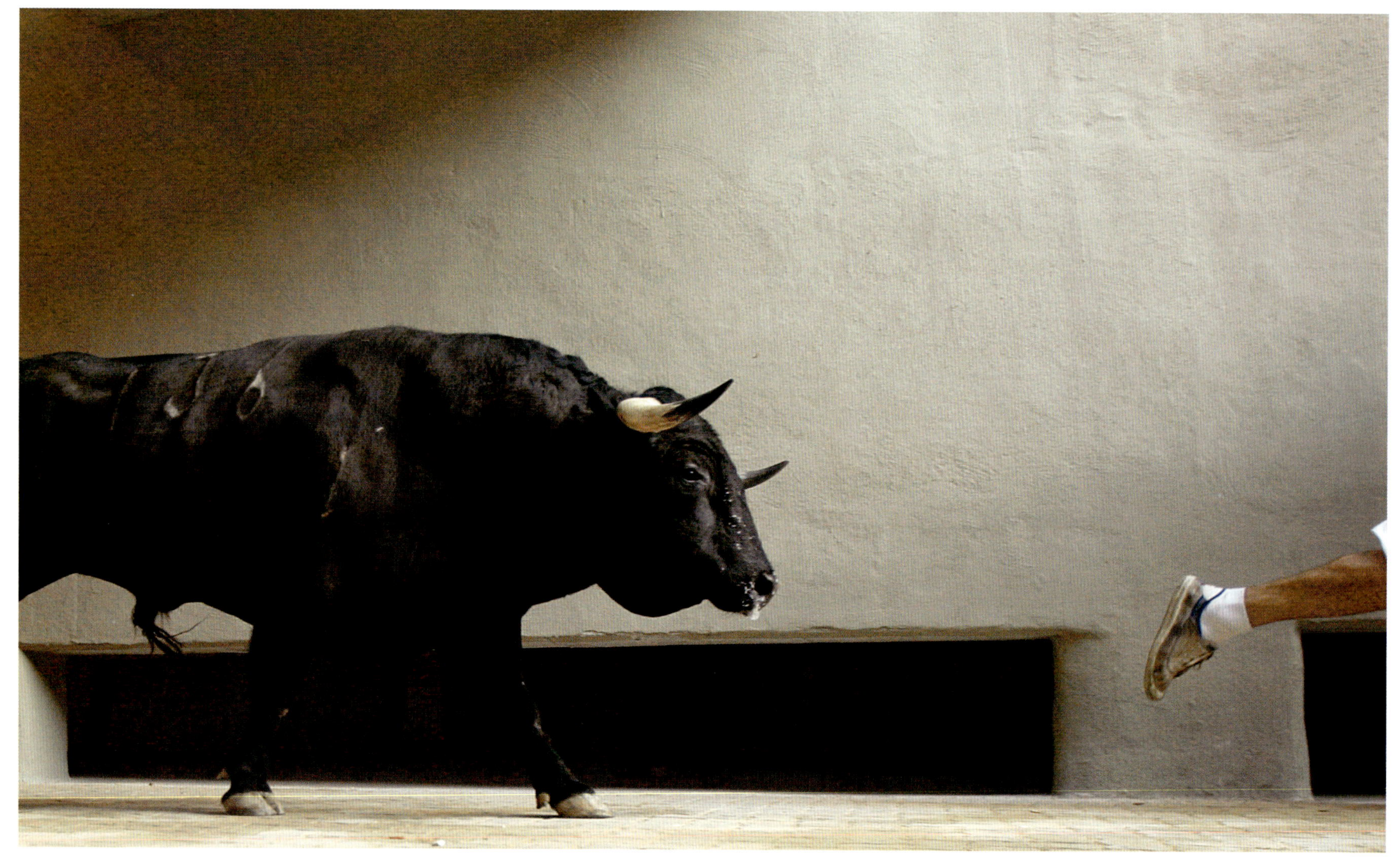

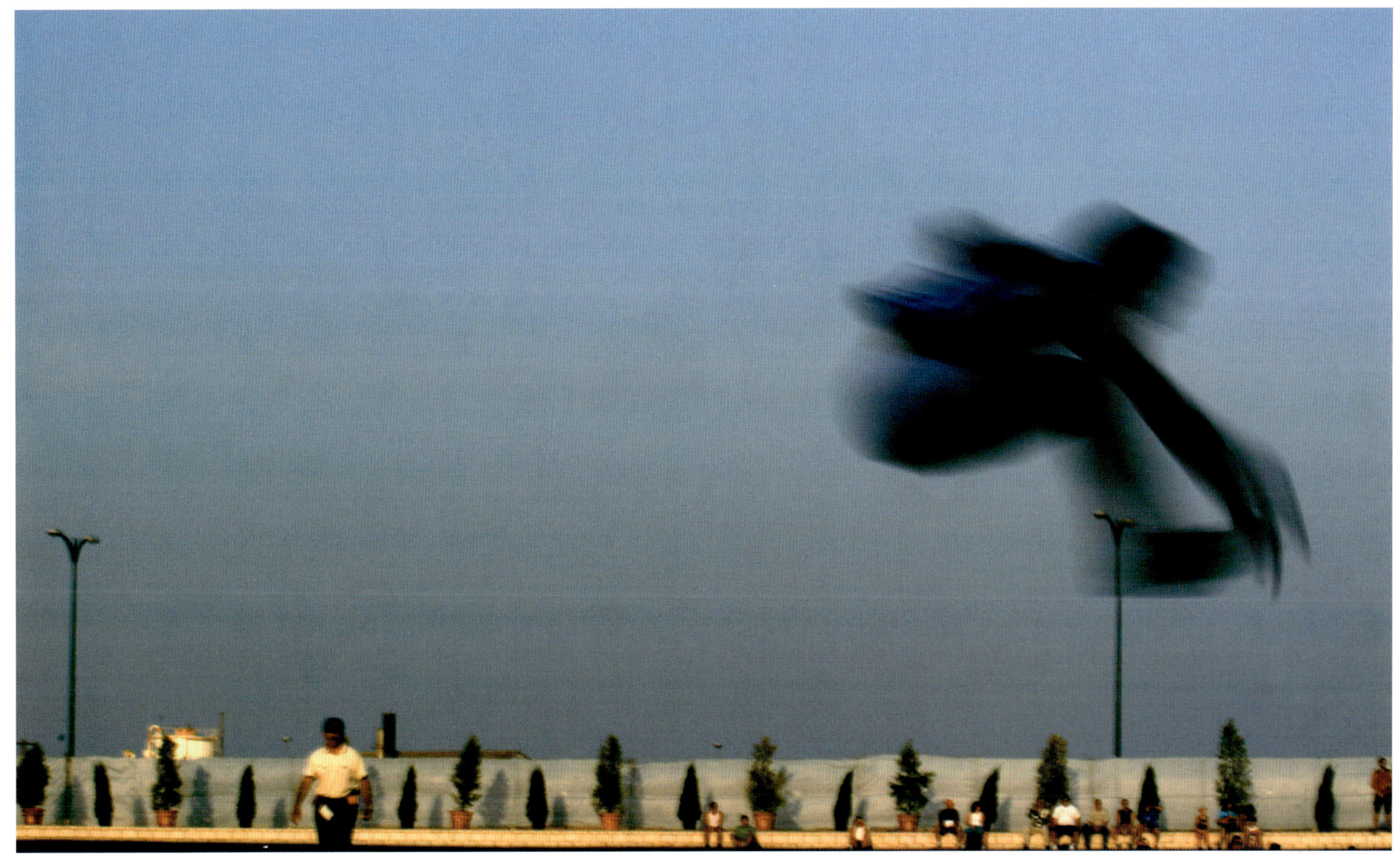

23 July 2005, MALAGA, SPAIN

Spain's Taha Bakali-Tahiri competes in the long jump event at the Spanish Athletics Championships in Malaga, southern Spain. Rafael Marchante

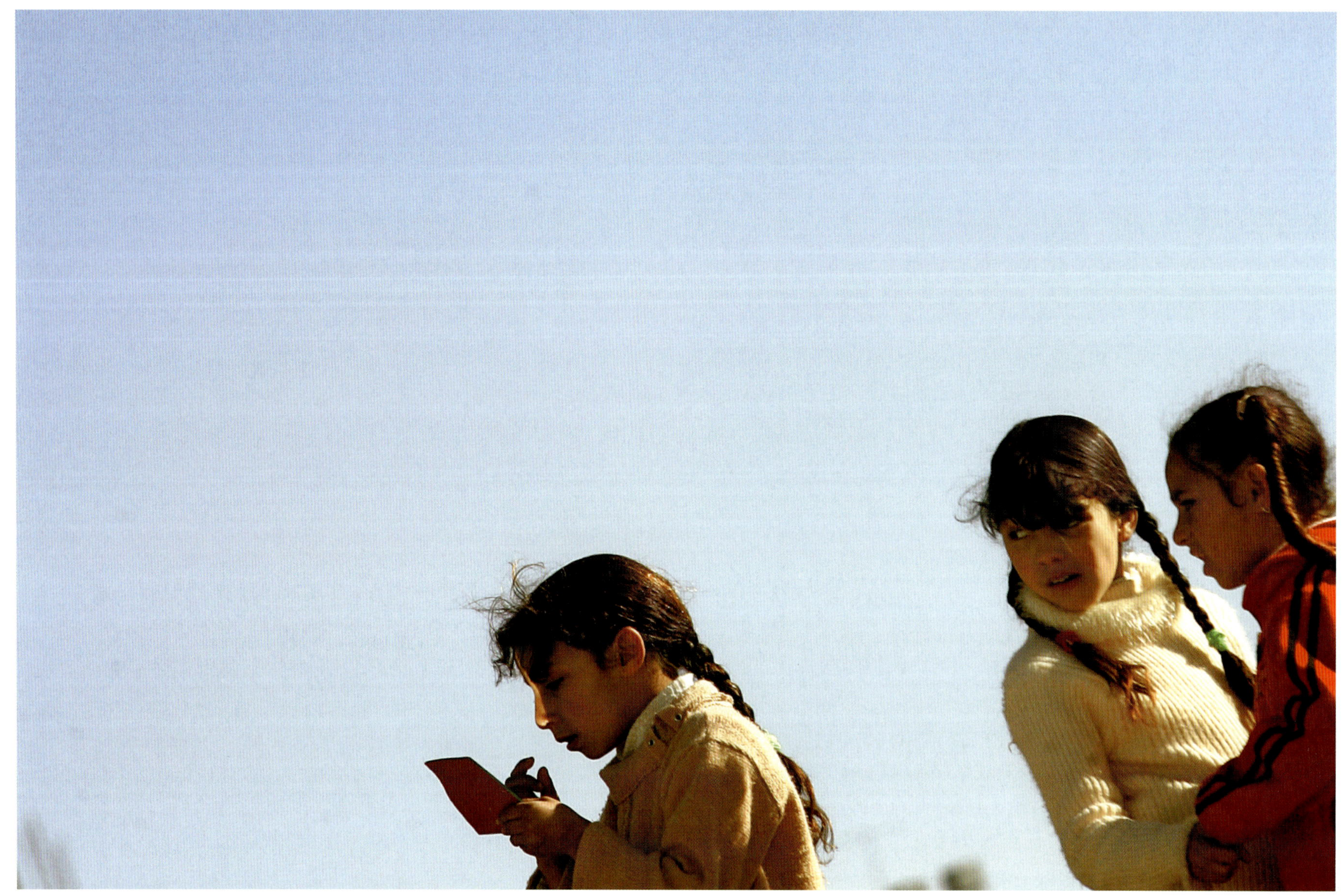

21 January 2006, HEBRON, WEST BANK

Palestinian girls check their make-up outside a polling station in Hebron.
Damir Sagolj

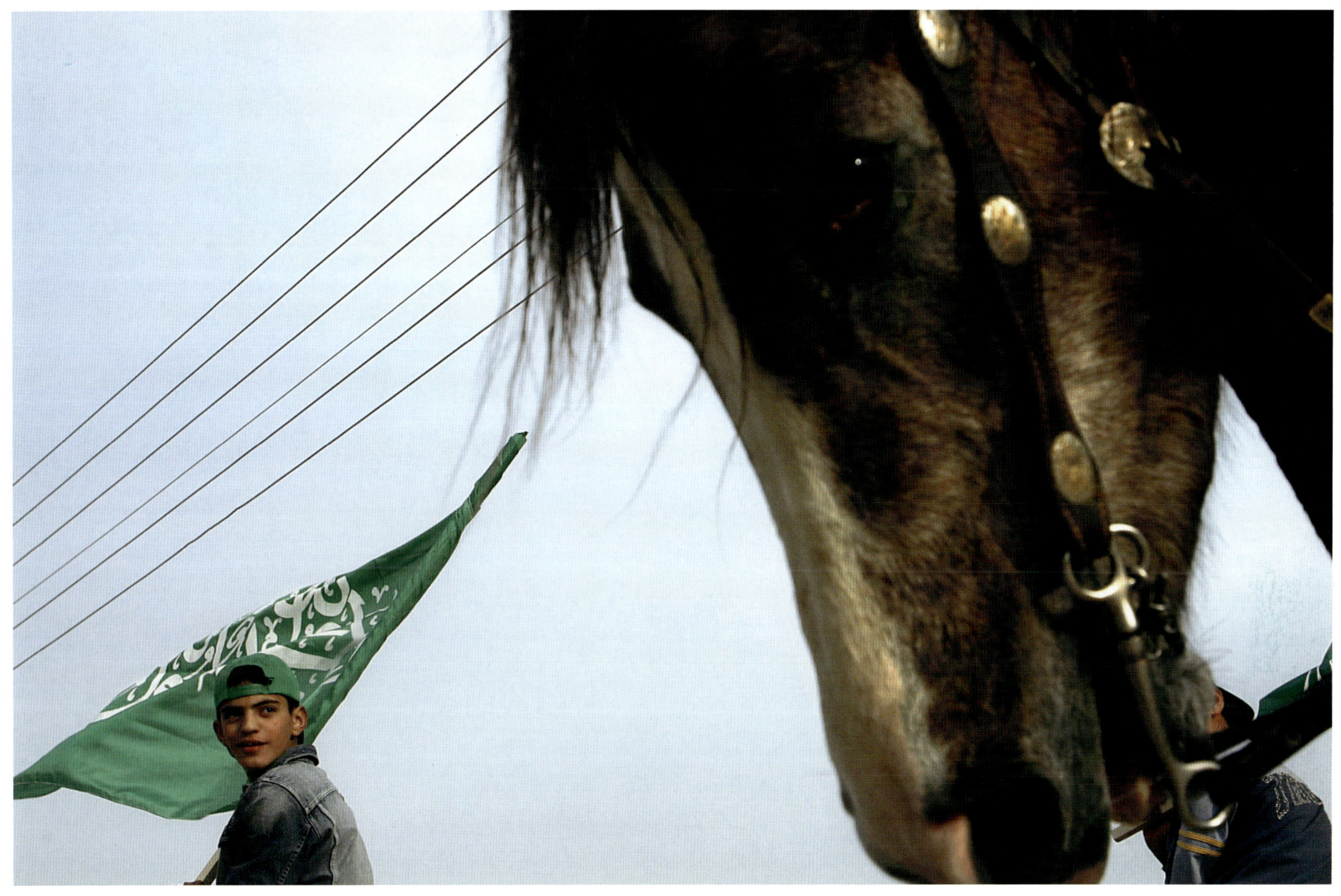

22 January 2006, ABU DIS, WEST BANK

Palestinian boys arrive on horseback for a Hamas pre-election gathering in Abu Dis, on the edge of Jerusalem. Damir Sagolj

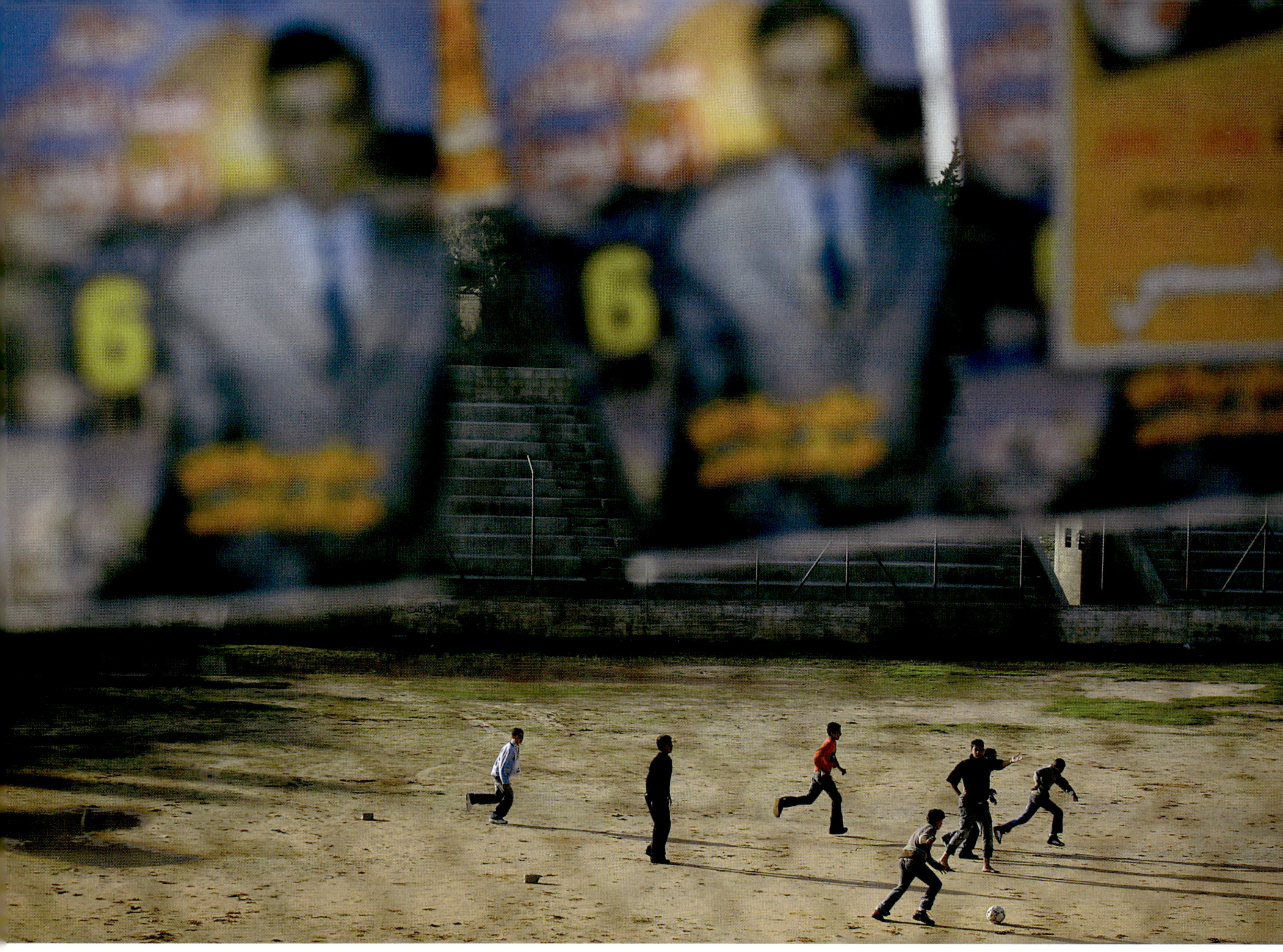

23 January 2006, DAHIET AL-BARID, WEST BANK

Palestinian youths play soccer behind election campaign posters in the village of Dahiet al-Barid, on the edge of Jerusalem. Stoyan Nenov

31 January 2006, DOJRAN, MACEDONIA

Locals drink homemade brandy and beer on the frozen Dojran lake, 170 km (106 miles) south of the Macedonian capital Skopje. Ognen Teofilovski

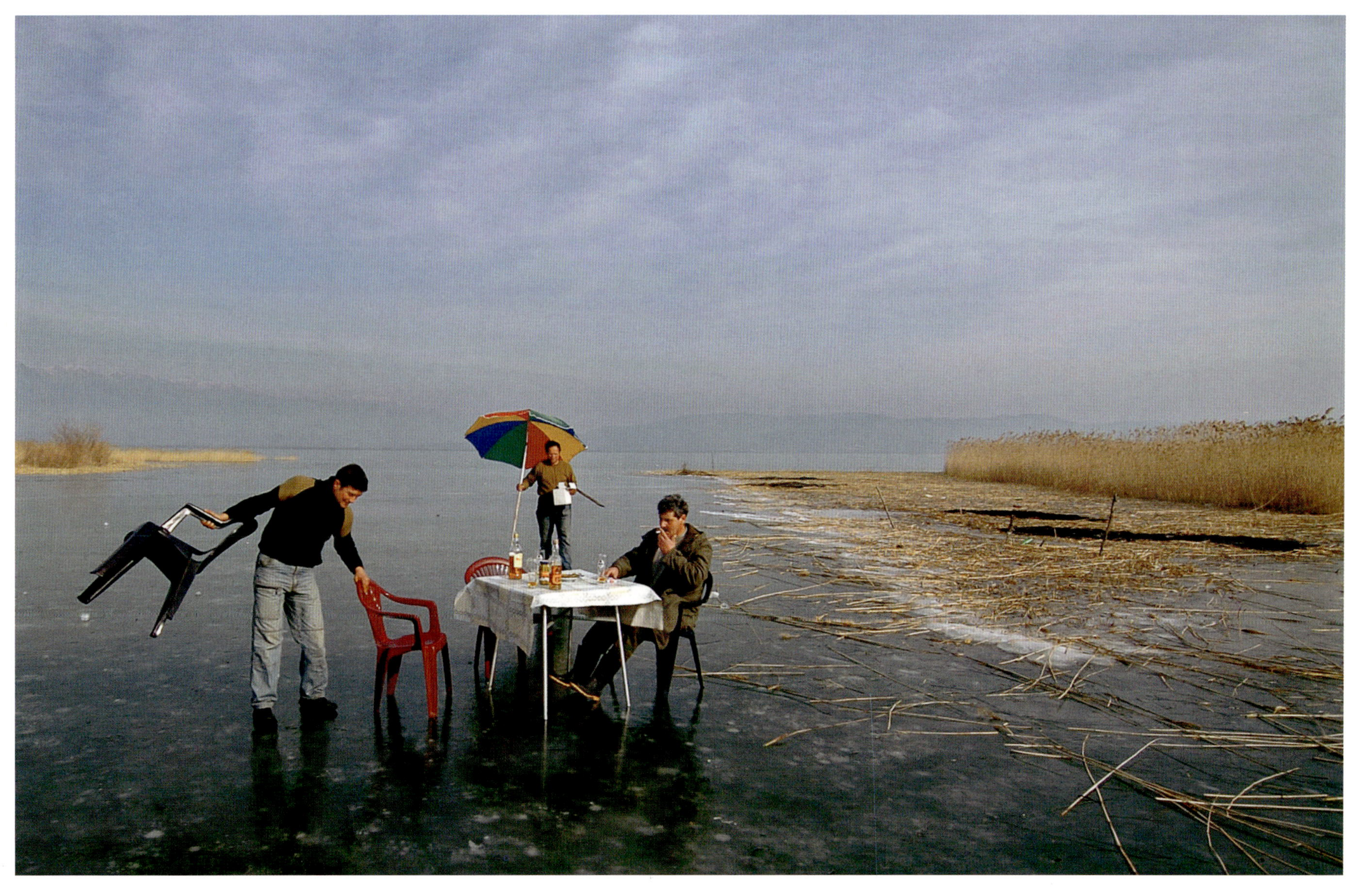

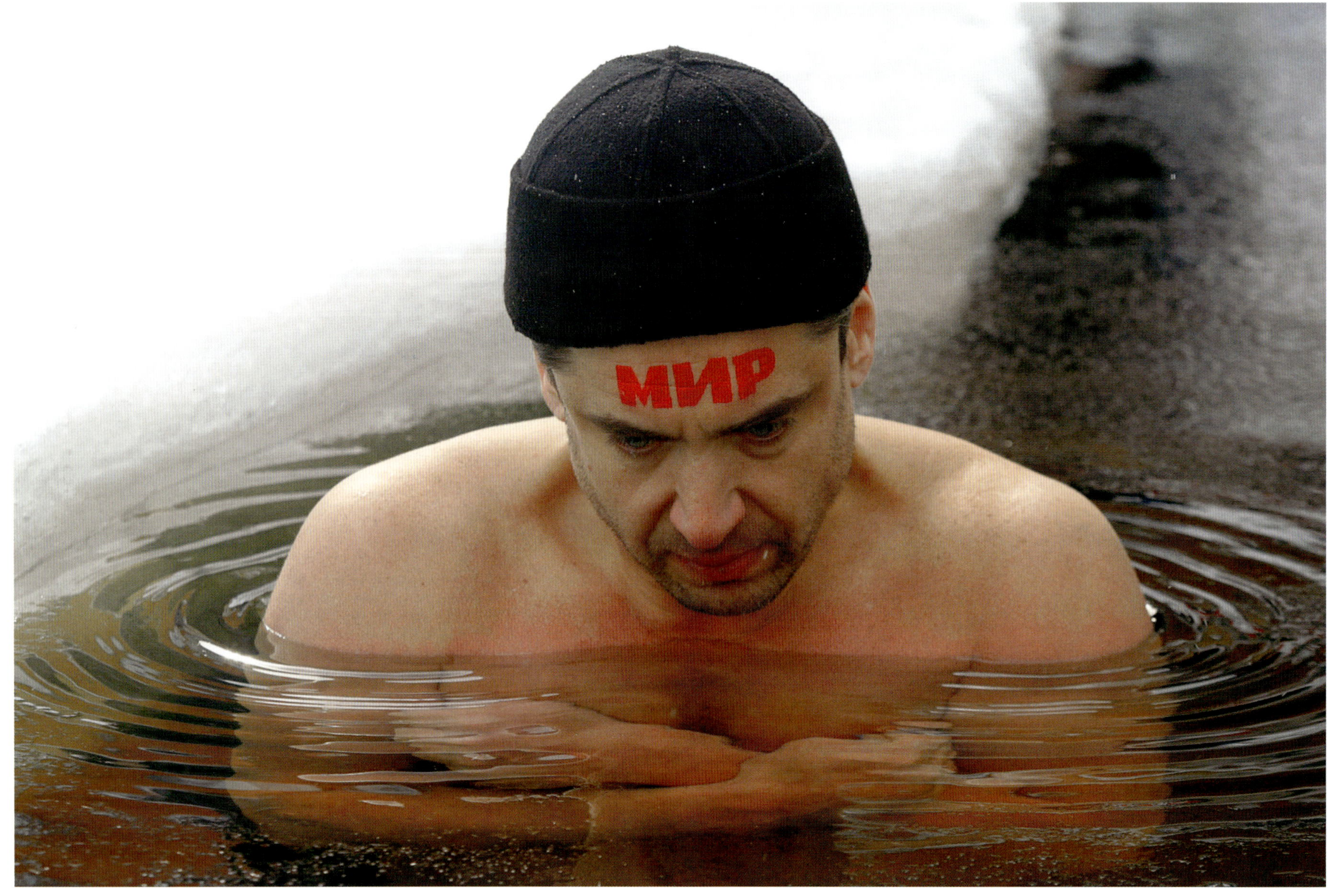

12 March 2005, MOSCOW, RUSSIA

Russian sportsman Diab Karim stands in an ice hole in Moscow River as he tries to set a record by staying in ice-cold water for 60 minutes. Karim's record attempt was dedicated to the 60th anniversary of the victory of the Soviet Union over Nazi Germany in World War Two. The text on his forehead reads 'Peace'. Sergei Karpukhin

14 May 2005, NEW YORK, UNITED STATES

A woman has a tattoo applied during the 8th Annual Tattoo Convention in New York. Shannon Stapleton

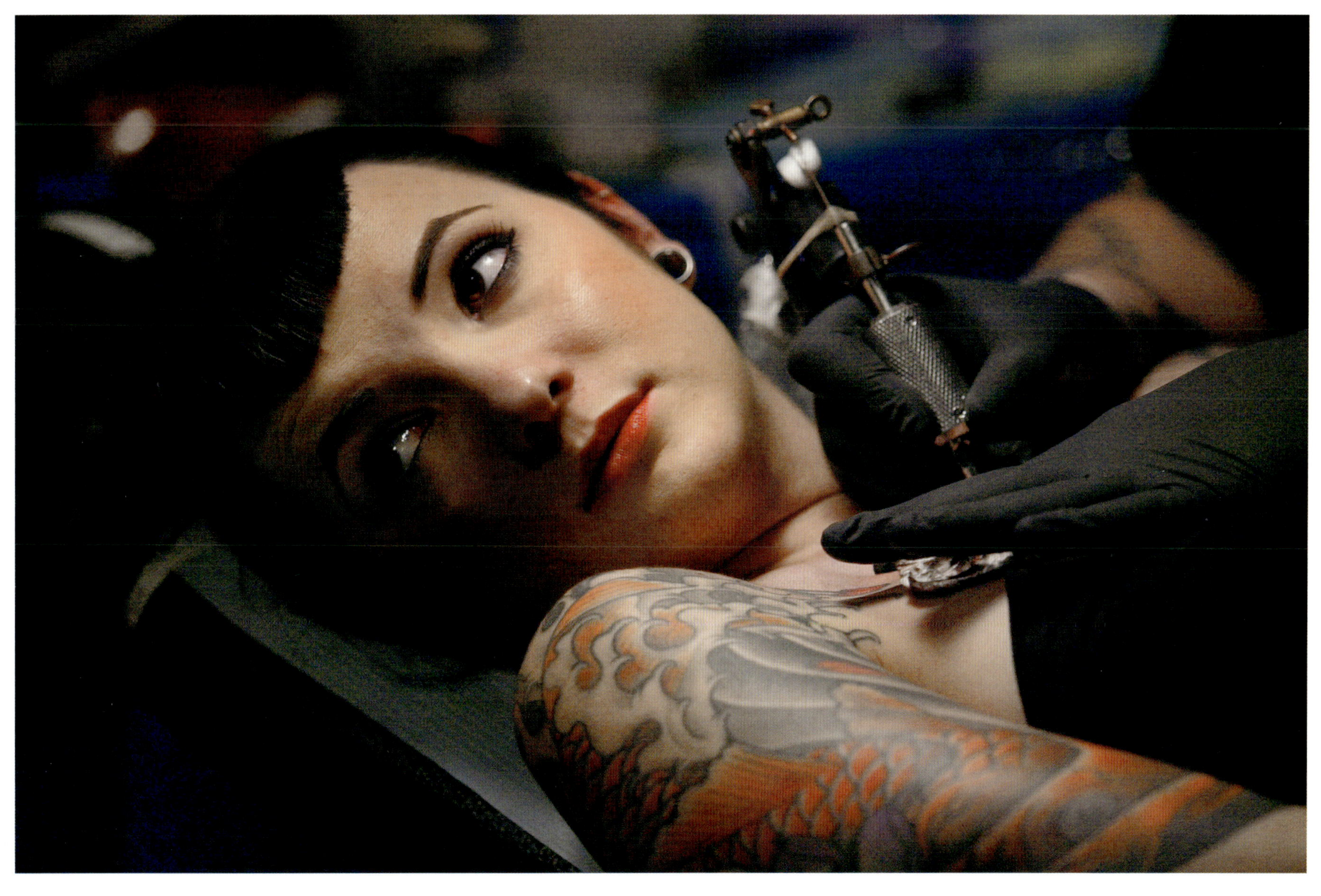

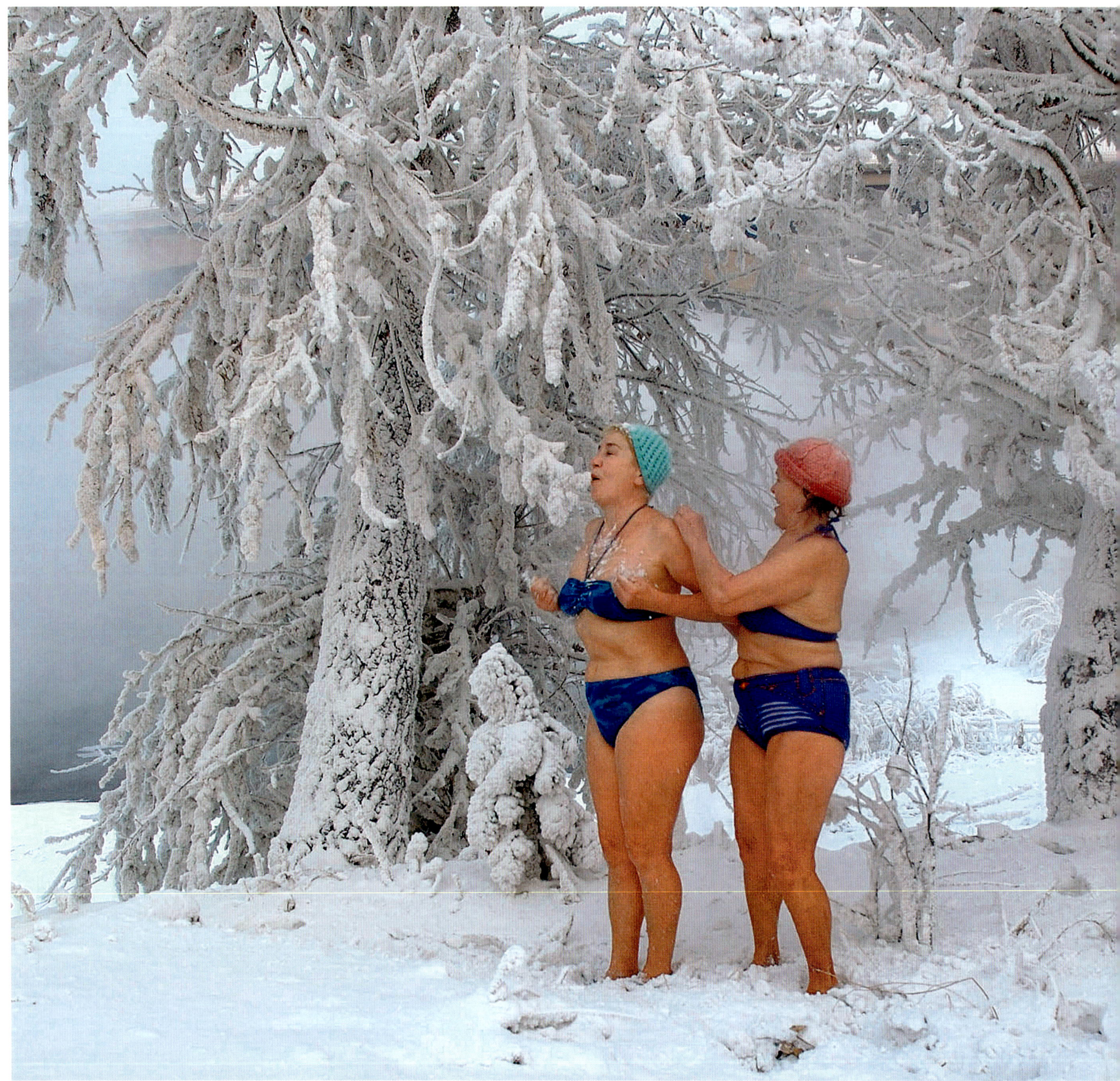

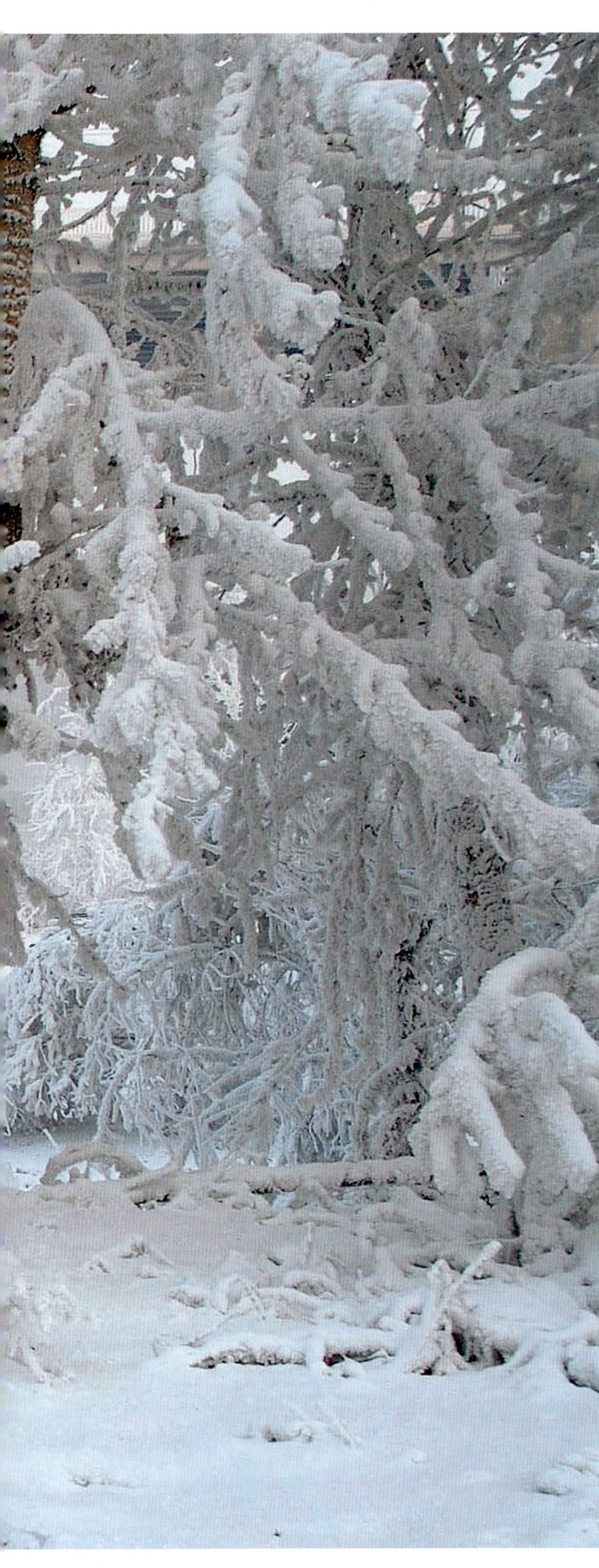

11 December 2005, KRASNOYARSK, RUSSIA

Members of a Siberian ice-bathing club rub one another with snow after enjoying a swim in the icy water of the Yenisey River in Krasnoyarsk in temperatures of around -26°C (-14.8°F). Ilya Naymushin

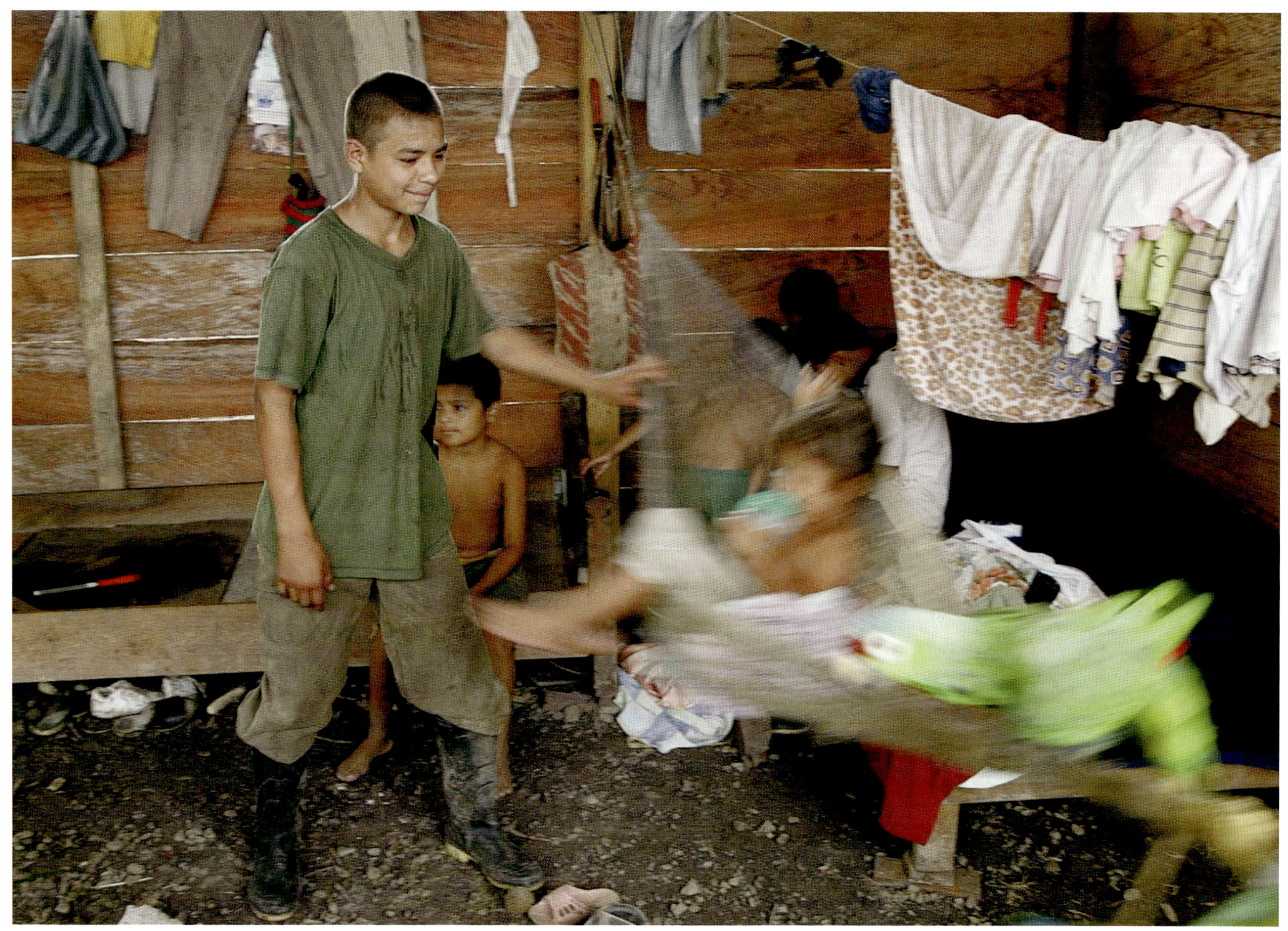

20 April 2005, SAN JOSÉ DE APARTADÓ, COLOMBIA

A Colombian boy rocks his brother on a hammock in San José de Apartadó, a town of 100 families which in 1997 declared itself a 'peace community' and neutral gun-free zone amid Colombia's guerrilla war. In February 2005 all but a handful left after an attack in which eight residents were hacked to death. Albeiro Lopera

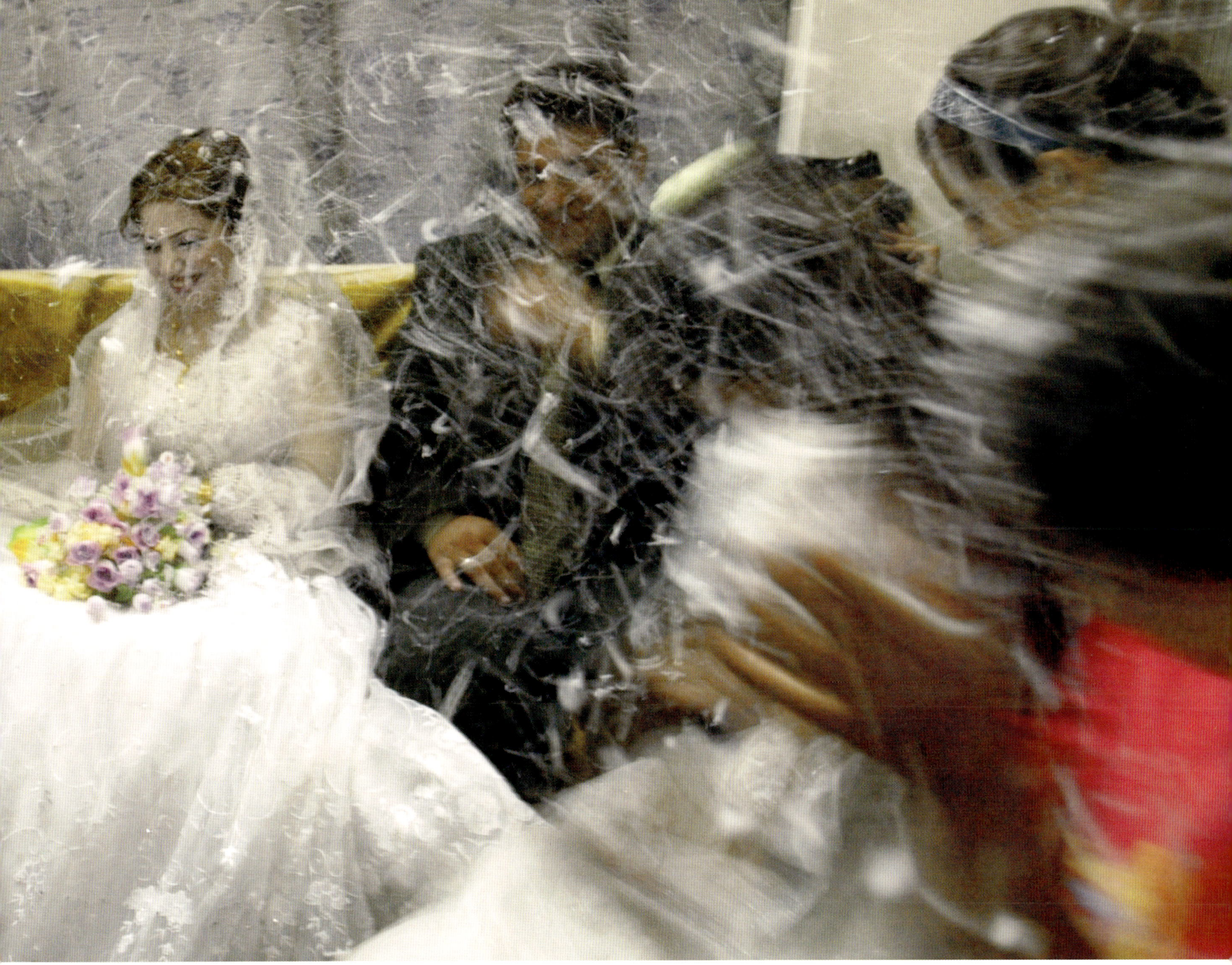

1 July 2004, BAGHDAD, IRAQ

Iraqi newlyweds Naheb Saidi, 25, and her husband Baha Turkeg, 26, are showered in foam during their wedding party in Baghdad. They married as the world watched Saddam Hussein make his first court appearance, charged with crimes against humanity. Zohra Bensemra

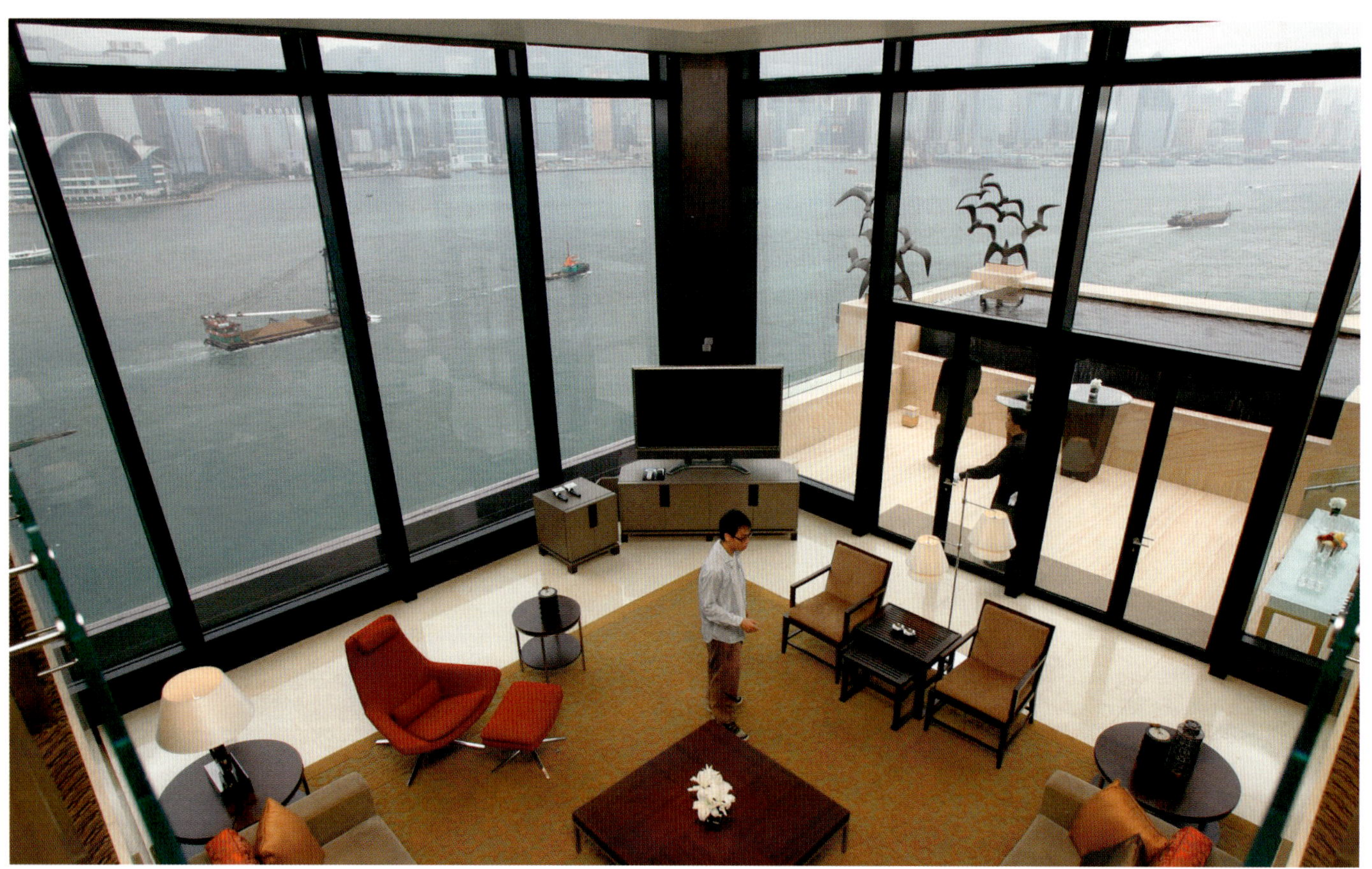

17 January 2006, HONG KONG, CHINA

The living room of the presidential suite in the InterContinental Hong Kong Hotel with a view of Victoria Harbour. The suite, covering 7,000 square feet (650 square metres) with a rooftop terrace, is the largest hotel suite in Hong Kong and charges HK $87,000 (around U.S. $11,200) plus 13% tax and service per night. Paul Yeung

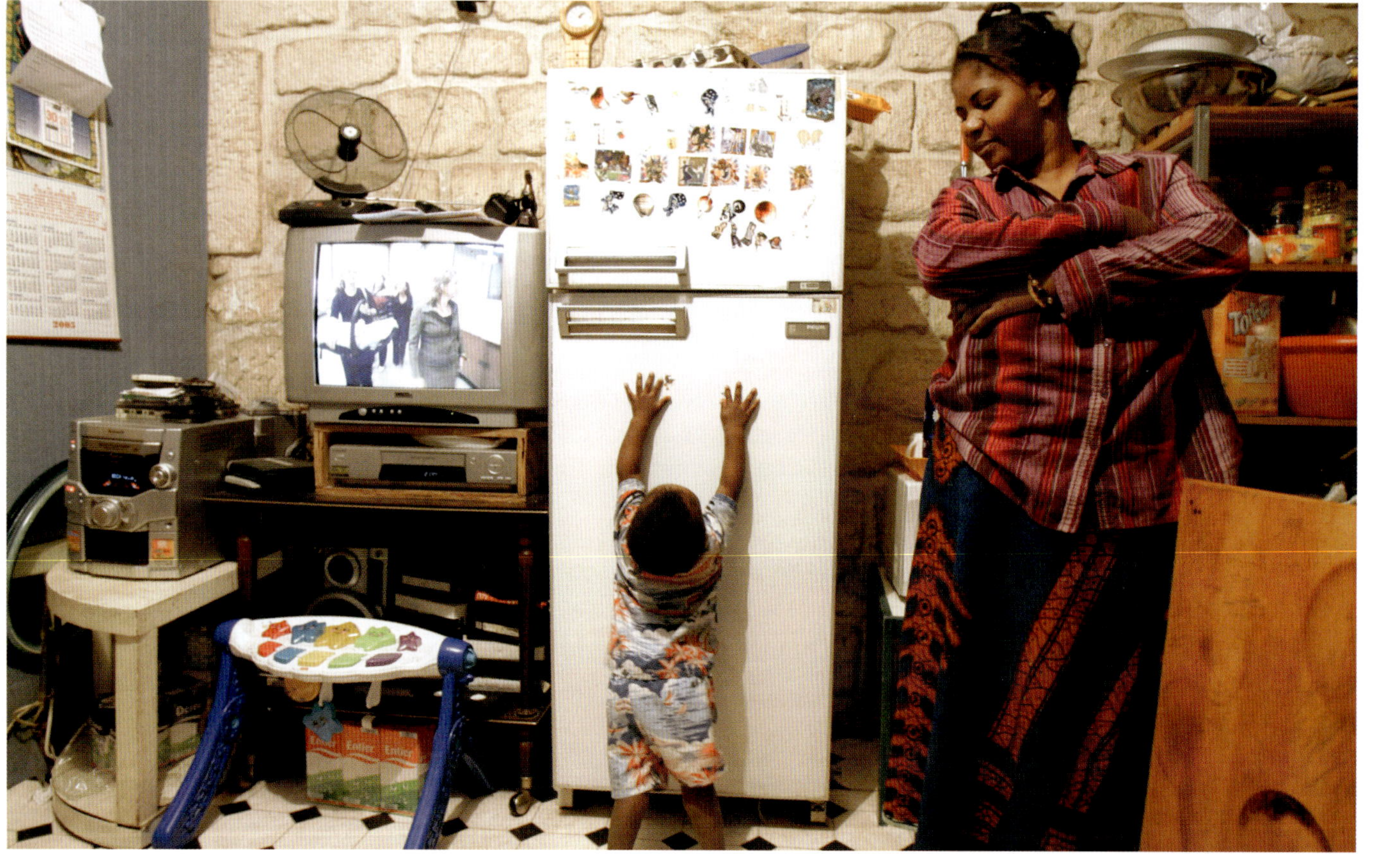

28 September 2005, PARIS, FRANCE

French mother Foffanassatou and her one-year-old son Sheriff in the kitchen of their flat in a rundown building in the 11th district of Paris. Fires in dilapidated buildings in the French capital killed almost 50 people between May and September 2005. The deaths lifted the lid on the squalid living conditions endured by thousands of families, many of them immigrants, and exposed a grave housing shortage in the capital. Franck Prevel

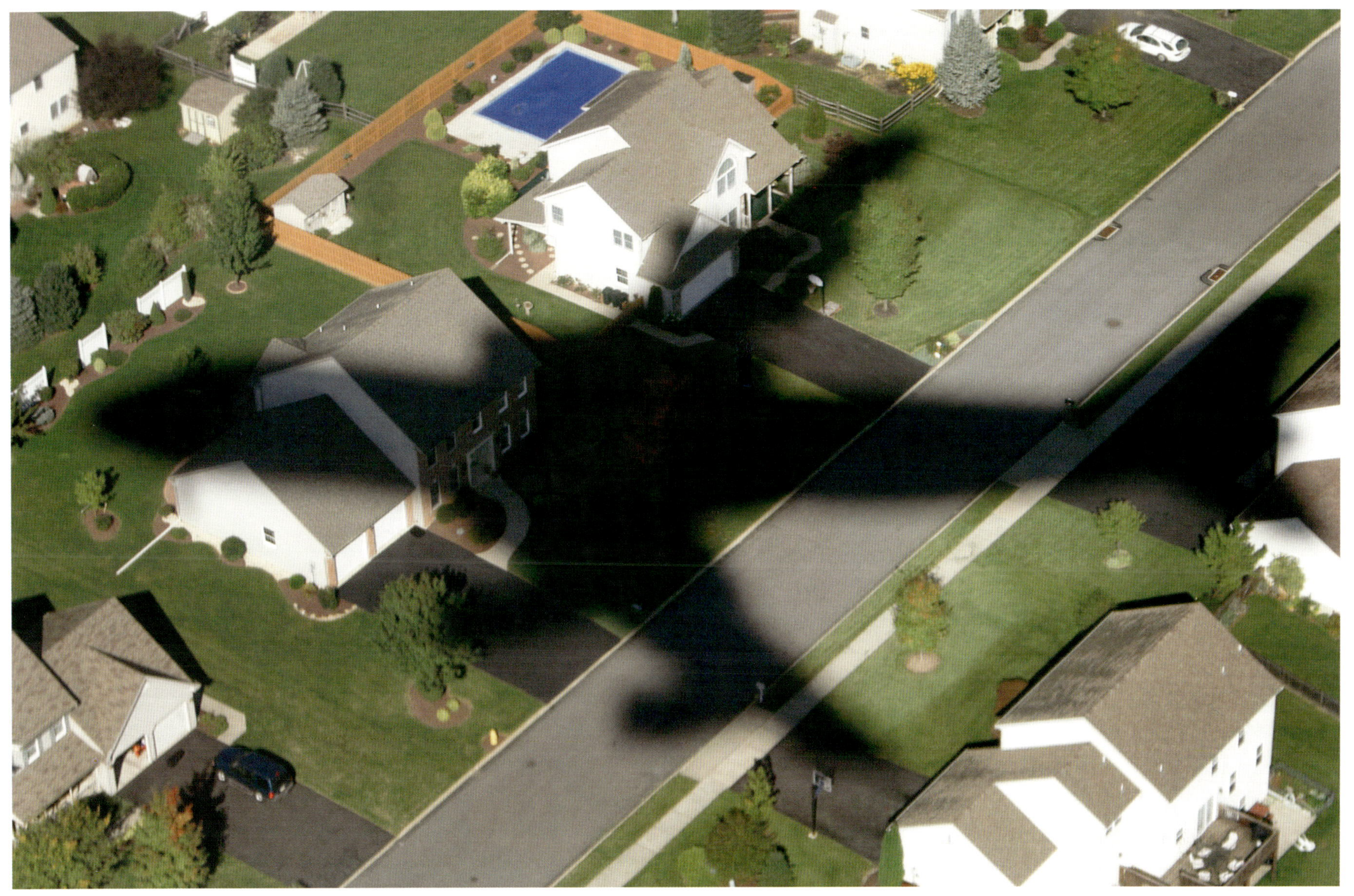

1 October 2004, ALLENTOWN, UNITED STATES

The presidential plane, Air Force One, casts its shadow over homes as it comes in to land in Allentown, Pennsylvania. Jason Reed

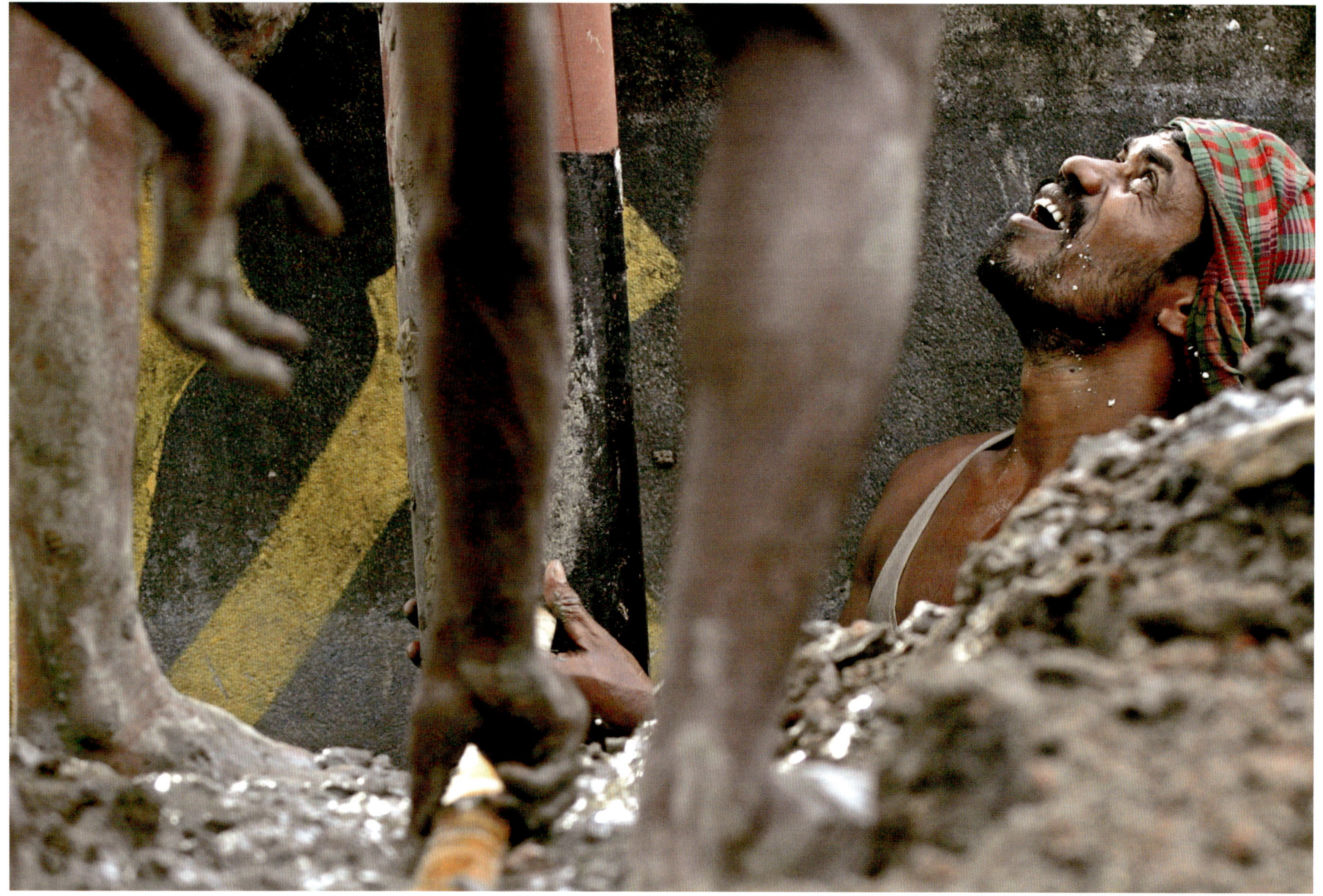

14 September 2005, KOLKATA, INDIA

Labourers work at a construction site in the eastern Indian city of Kolkata. Despite India's rapid economic expansion, as many as nine out of ten workers in South Asia still earned less than $2 per day in early 2006. Parth Sanyal

3 October 2005, ARCHER'S POST, KENYA

A Samburu woman uses a smoked glass to observe an annular solar eclipse at Archer's Post, 350 km (214 miles) north of the Kenyan capital Nairobi. An annular eclipse differs from a total eclipse in that the moon is too small to completely cover the sun. As a result, it appears surrounded by an intensely brilliant ring or annulus. Radu Sigheti

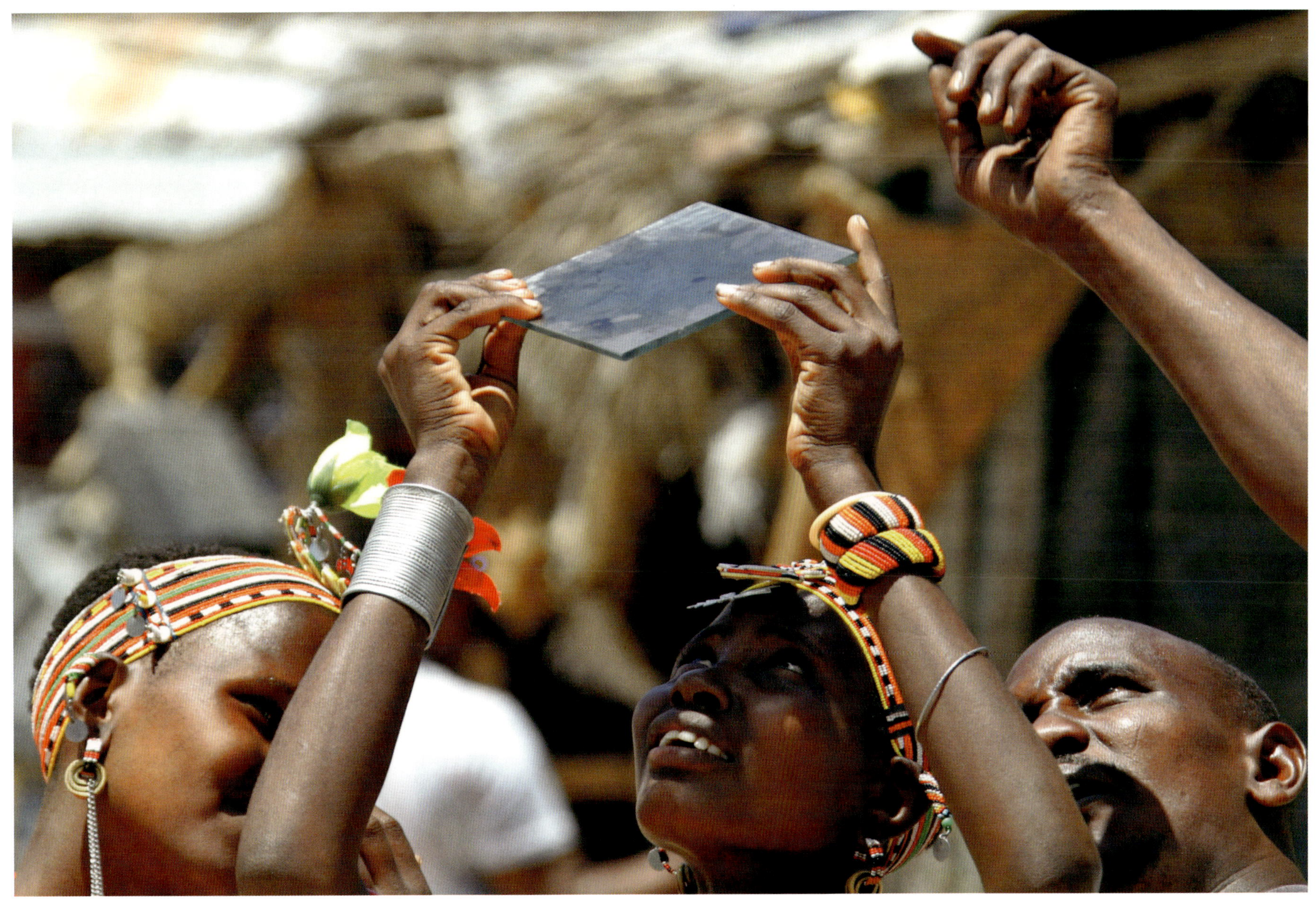

26 April 2005, HAVANA, CUBA

Ten-year-old Natalia from Ukraine receives treatment for alopecia at the Tarara Paediatric Hospital outside Havana. Since 1990, Cuba has treated 18,000 Ukrainian children free of charge for hair loss, skin disorders, cancer, leukemia and other illnesses attributed to the radioactivity unleashed by the Chernobyl nuclear reactor meltdown in 1986, years before they were born. The programme was maintained after Soviet communism collapsed, despite the deep and prolonged economic crisis Cuba has endured since losing the support of its superpower ally. Many of the children are orphans or come from poor families that cannot afford medical treatment in Ukraine. Claudia Daut

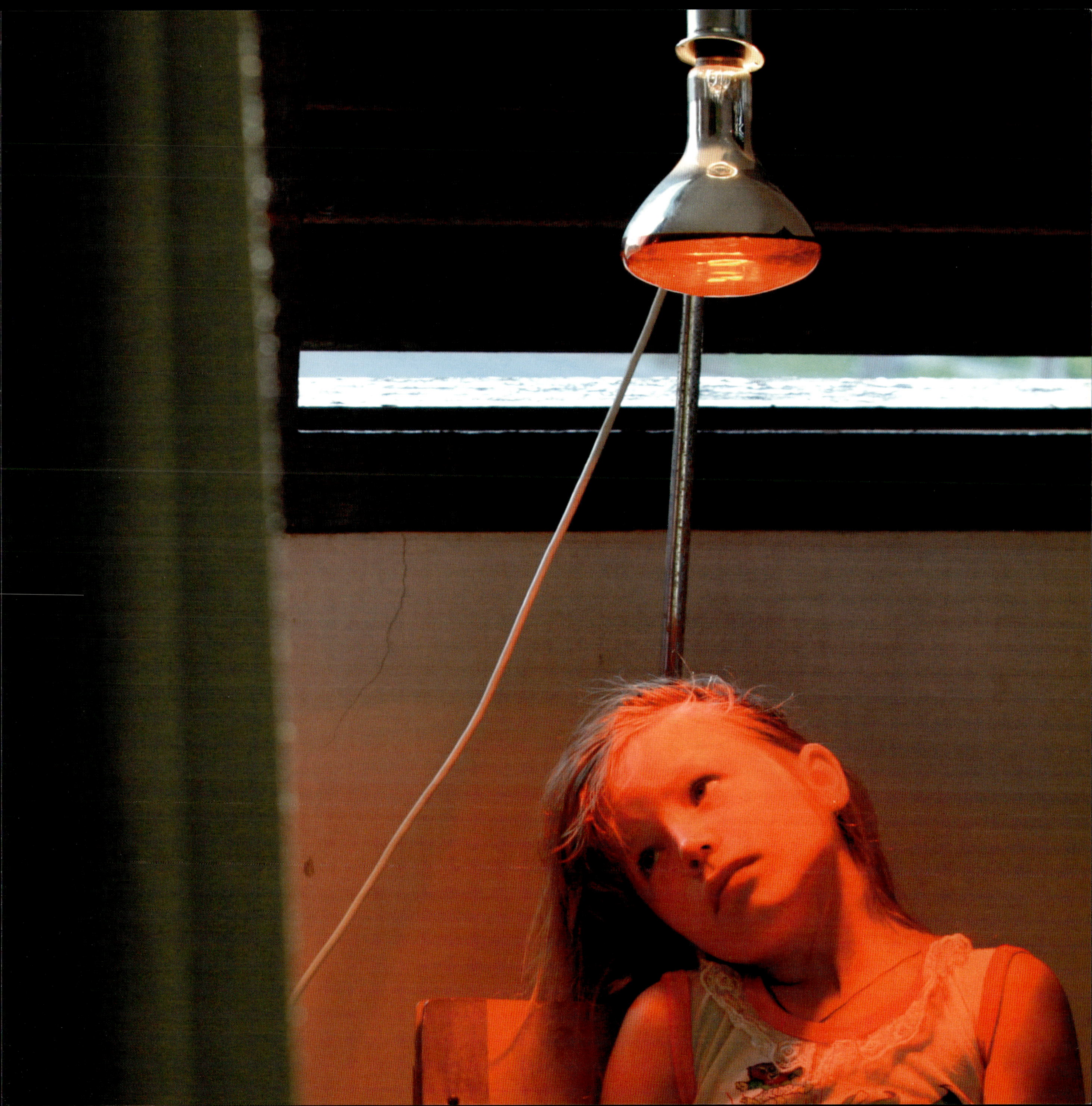

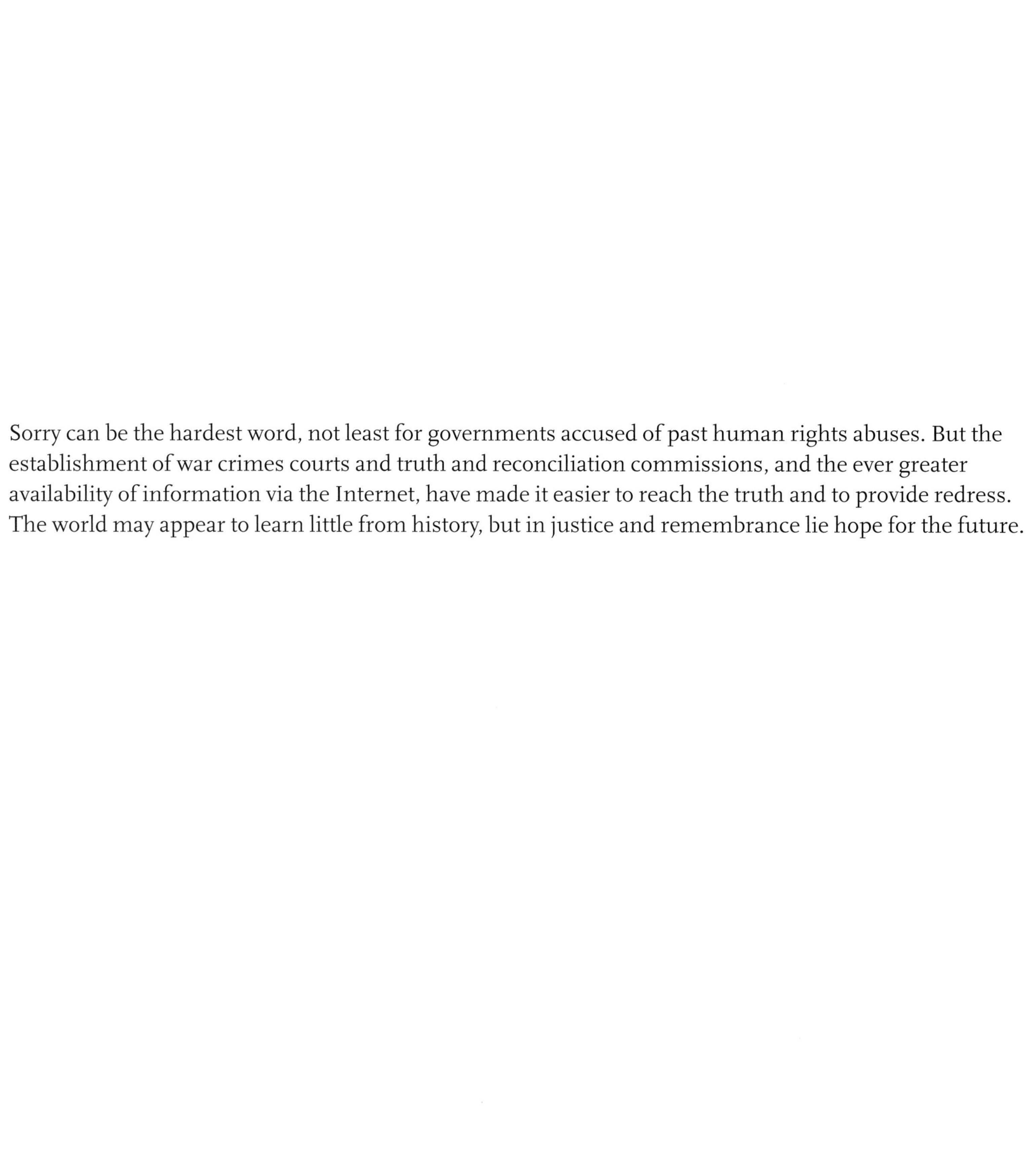

Sorry can be the hardest word, not least for governments accused of past human rights abuses. But the establishment of war crimes courts and truth and reconciliation commissions, and the ever greater availability of information via the Internet, have made it easier to reach the truth and to provide redress. The world may appear to learn little from history, but in justice and remembrance lie hope for the future.

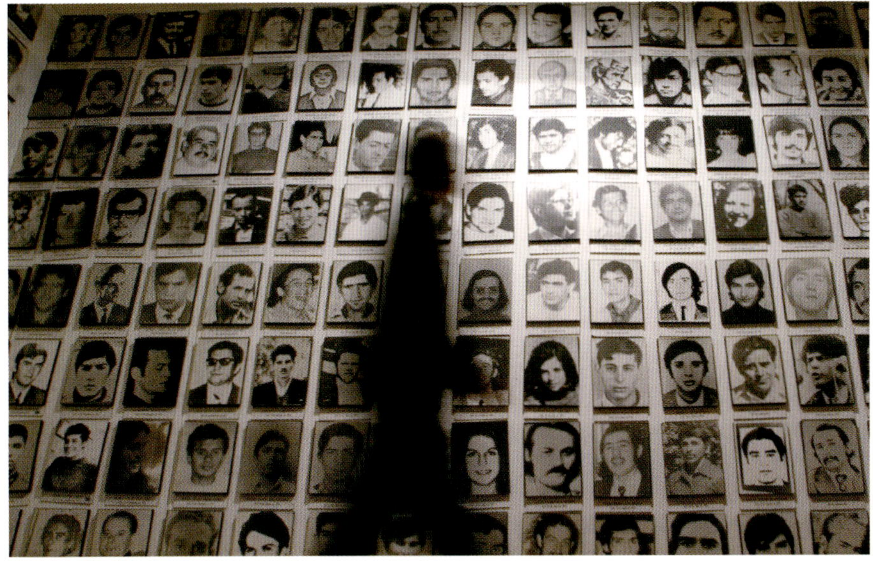

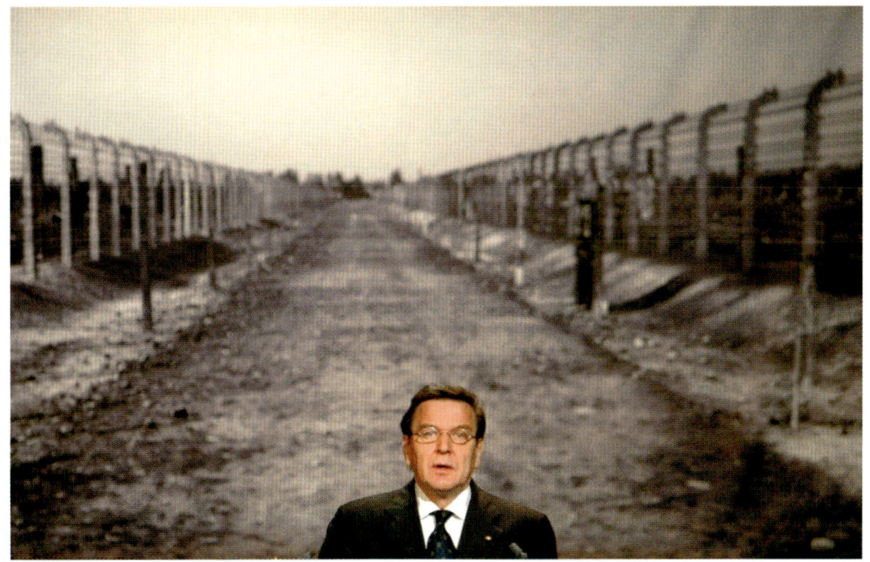

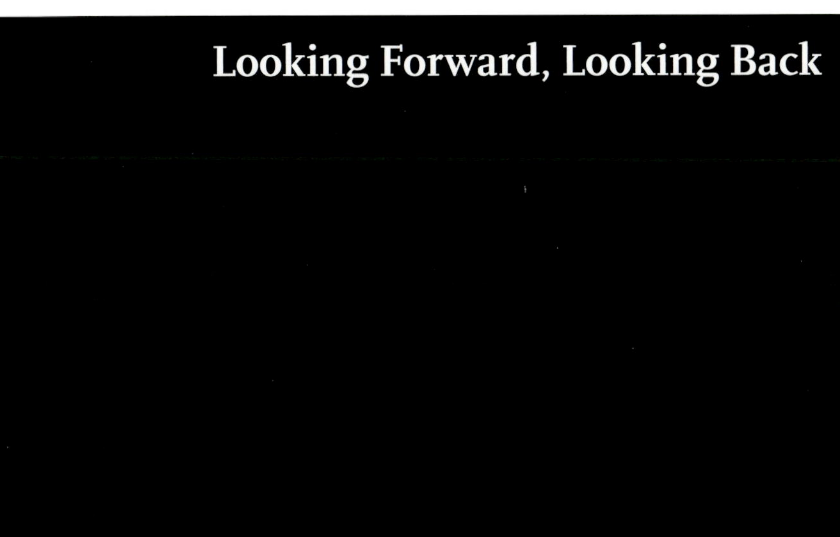

Looking Forward, Looking Back

Commemoration / Celebration / Grief
Memory / Nostalgia / Reconciliation
Truth / Justice / The Lessons of History

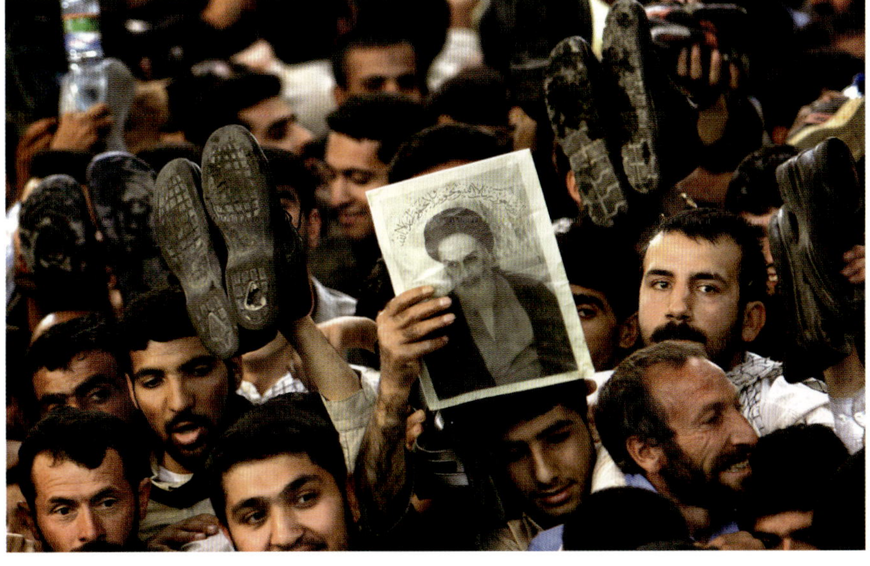

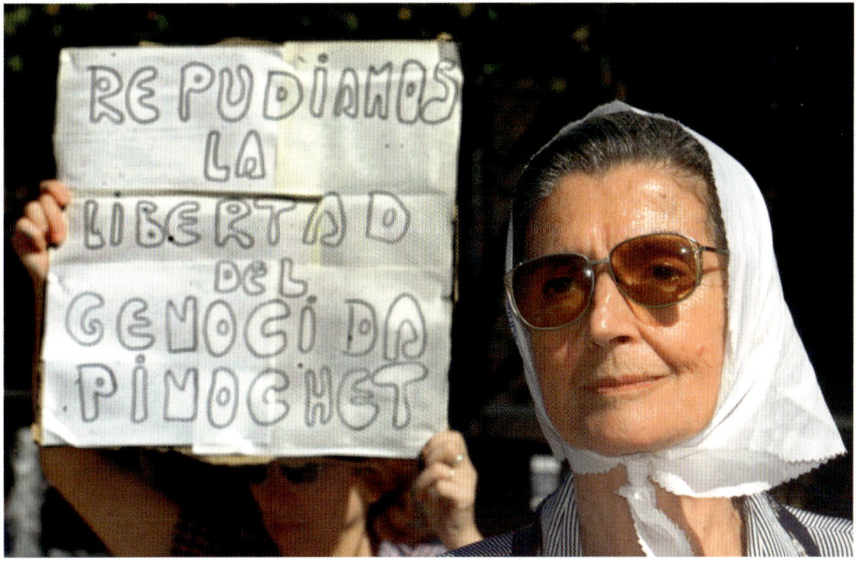

Looking Forward, Looking Back

Never forget. Nazi-hunter and concentration camp survivor Simon Wiesenthal lived by those words for six decades after World War Two. They became the epitaph of a man driven at once by a determination to ensure the six million victims of the Holocaust are remembered, and that it should never happen again.

Yet as the images in this book make all too clear, the cycle of suffering, death, violence and remembrance has continued throughout the twentieth century and beyond.

The year 2005, in which Wiesenthal died, marked the 60th anniversary of the end of World War Two, 30 years since the Vietnam War ended and 90 since the battle of Gallipoli in World War One – once believed to be the war that would end all wars.

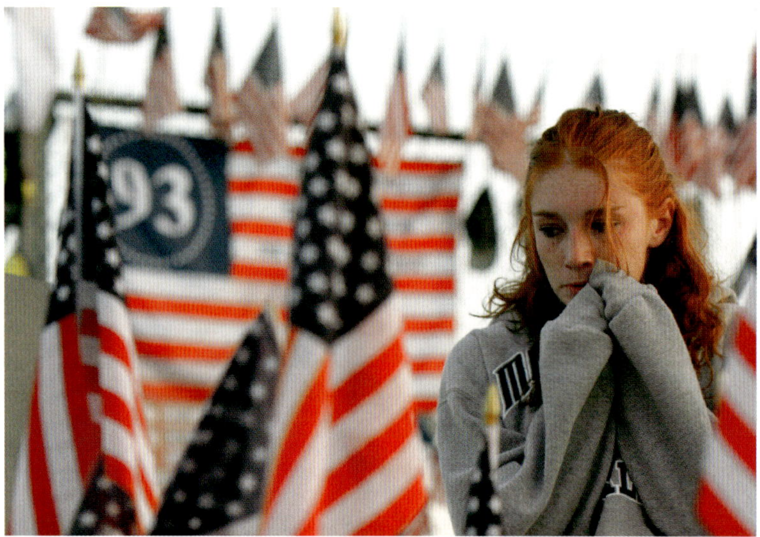

On the fourth anniversary of the September 11, 2001, attacks, Courtney Ball, 19, of Sommerville, New Jersey, cries at the Temporary Memorial at the crash site of Flight 93 just outside Shanksville, Pennsylvania. 11 September 2005, Jason Cohn.

But if the twentieth century was marked by big wars, the first years of the new century have been afflicted by large-scale attacks on civilians outside of formally declared wars – September 11, Bali, Madrid, Beslan, London.

The dawn of the twenty-first century has also been witness to horrific natural disasters, some of the worst in living memory. From the Indian Ocean tsunami to the South Asian earthquake in Kashmir to Hurricane Katrina in the United States, these catastrophes have killed hundreds of thousands, injured many times more and left millions homeless. And although recent studies show that the number and ferocity of wars, especially between nations, is falling, as is the death toll from conventional warfare, the fighting goes on in places like Iraq, Afghanistan and Africa.

Rituals of remembrance are important for healing wounds, learning lessons and moving on. But remembering can also be politically charged and fraught with blame and recrimination, especially when wrongs have not been, or cannot be, righted, or the details of precisely what happened cannot be agreed upon. Should there be an apology? Will it make any difference? Can or should today's generations, governments or institutions be held accountable for wrongs done by those who went before? These unanswered questions continue to overshadow many nations today.

Despite cooperation in a range of areas, Japan's relations with China and Korea, for example, are dogged by the past. In Japan,

> Remembering can be politically charged and fraught with blame and recrimination.

the tradition of prime ministers visiting the Yasukuni Shrine is an important part of honouring the nation's war dead. But to the Chinese and Koreans, who bitterly remember long stretches of Japanese rule, it symbolizes Tokyo's failure to acknowledge the injustices of the past, for among the 2.5 million soldiers listed on the shrine are a small number of prosecuted war criminals. 'Japan's way of atoning for its militaristic past has been a thorn deep down in the flesh of bilateral relations...and that wound is festering,' a Chinese newspaper said after Japanese Prime Minister Junichiro Koizumi visited the shrine in late 2005 on the 60th anniversary of the end of World War Two. Japan's relations with its neighbours have similarly been inflamed by school text books that critics say still whitewash Japanese aggression during World War Two. This controversy has triggered fierce street protests in China and Korea.

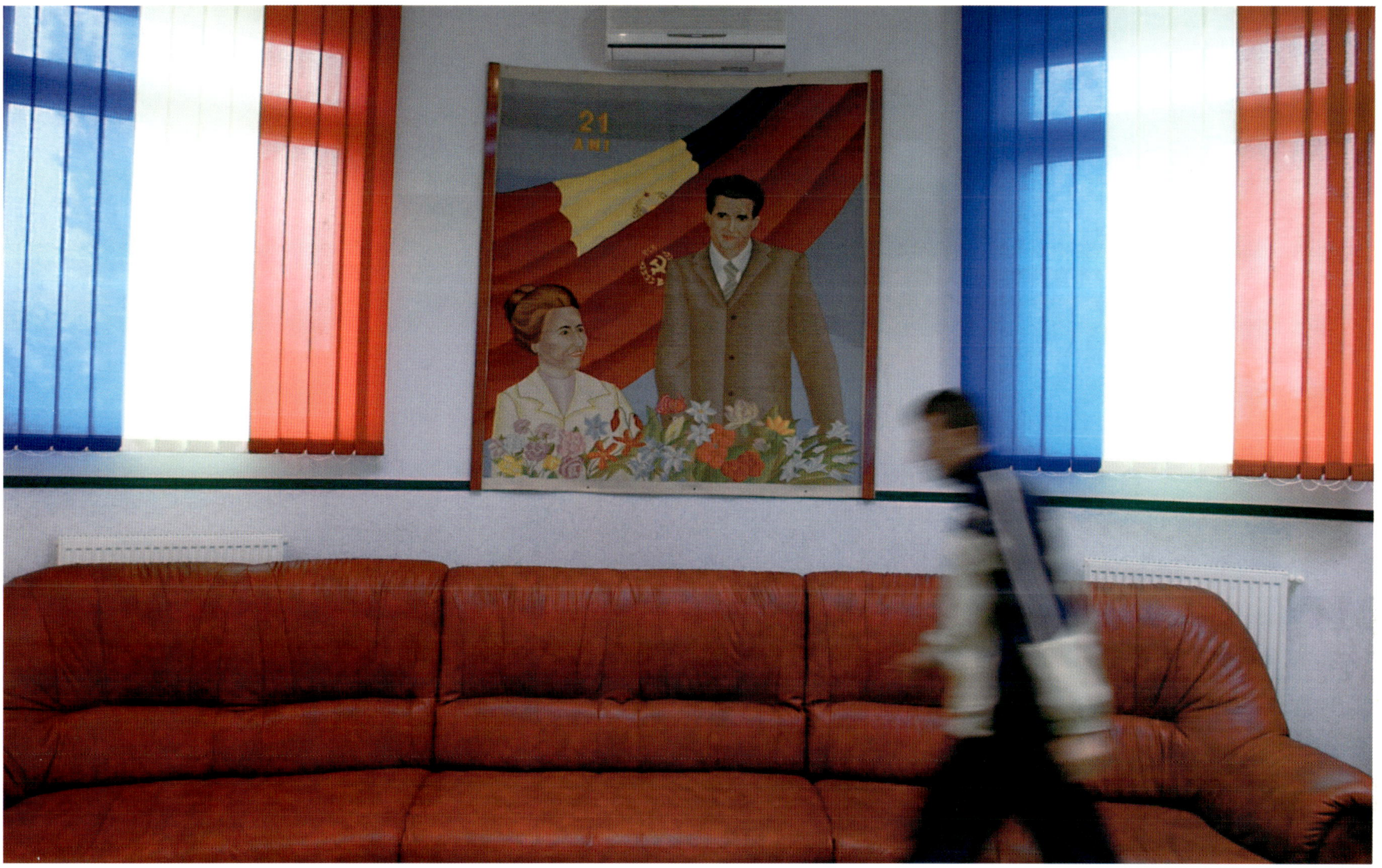

A man walks in front of a portrait of Romania's late Stalinist dictator Nicolae Ceausescu and his wife Elena in the lobby of a hotel in a private park dedicated to the country's communist past. Many in the impoverished countryside are nostalgic for Ceausescu and the social security they enjoyed during his time. 10 November 2004, Bogdan Cristel

Australia's efforts at reconciliation with its indigenous people are also haunted by differing views of the past, and in particular by a debate over whether a government in the twenty-first century should apologize for the programme of taking tens of thousands of Aboriginal children from their families and assimilating them into white society, the so-called 'Stolen Generation'. The programme, which ran from 1910 until about 1970, was described in a 1997 government inquiry as 'systematic racial discrimination and genocide'. But despite passionate calls to do so, the Australian government has refused to give a formal apology, saying that today's Australians have nothing to apologize for.

Around the world, the way the past is interpreted and remembered is continually changing. As U.S. troops pull down a statue of the once-omnipotent Saddam Hussein in Baghdad, Afghans erect a memorial to Northern Alliance commander Ahmad Shah Masood, the Lion of Panjshir, who was considered a renegade by both the Soviet and Taliban rulers of Kabul. In India, what was long called the 1857 'Mutiny' against British rule, in which local troops rose up against their British commanders, is now increasingly known as the First War of Independence, and is a theme being popularly recast in Bollywood movies.

In another poignant example, the 'Shot at Dawn' campaign has been petitioning since 1990 for posthumous pardons for more than 300 British and Commonwealth soldiers executed as deserters in World War One. It now seems clear that most of the victims, many just boys, were suffering from severe shell-shock, or what would today be recognized as post-traumatic stress disorder.

The information revolution that is still in full flow is dramatically changing the way events are captured, recorded, interpreted and studied. The first vision of the London Underground train bombings in July 2005 came from grainy videos and photographs taken deep underground on mobile phones. Likewise, the passage and impact of hurricanes and tornadoes is recorded almost instantaneously on weblogs, or blogs, by people living in the path of the devastation. Digital technology makes everyone an instant witness.

Increasingly, the Internet is also providing new, more personal ways for people to create their own ways of remembering alongside more official ceremonies and anniversaries. Whole web services are springing up to host individual memorial sites, allowing anyone to erect their own memorial in cyberspace.

Computers and the Internet give us new tools for organizing, storing and accessing information. Online, anyone can view a wealth of official records and historical documents at the click of a button from anywhere in the world, instead of sifting through paper in dusty library vaults. One effect of this has been to fuel an explosion in genealogy, the study of family history. By some accounts, genealogy is the fastest growing hobby in the Western world. Tens of millions of people are tracing their family roots across time and continents. In the United States, the National Genealogical Society estimates it is the most popular pastime after gardening.

Technology has also brought the world closer together. With 24x7 news coverage it is easier now than at any time before to shine a light on everything that is happening, no matter how distant. People in Paris, France, or Paris, Texas, were able to watch live as East Timor went up in flames in 1999, as horse-mounted tribesmen battled the sophistication of the U.S. military in Afghanistan in 2001, or as Russia's Beslan school burned in 2004. Simultaneous remembrance ceremonies have united strangers across continents for a brief moment, whether in a prayer service for the Russian children who died at the Beslan school, or the floating of lamps on the sea for victims of the tsunami or the Bali bombings.

Advances in forensics are also helping bring to account those responsible for the wrongs of the past. War crimes investigators have an amazing array of forensics tools at their hands to investigate years-old crimes from Iraq to the Balkans. Identifying those responsible for wrongs, and acknowledgment from all involved of what went wrong and how, are important steps in healing the wounds of the survivors, moving on, and ensuring past mistakes and injustices are not repeated. This is the rationale behind war crimes trials, such as those being held by the United Nations' International Criminal Tribunal for the Former Yugoslavia. Still, it is sobering to remember that the international courts set up to judge war crimes in Rwanda and the former Yugoslavia are the first since Nuremberg in 1945.

One of the most enduring characteristics of humanity is hope. 'Every area of trouble gives out a ray of hope: and the one unchangeable certainty is that nothing is certain or unchangeable,' U.S. President John F. Kennedy once said. But looking forward, are lessons ever learned? Sometimes it seems that the more things change, the more they stay the same. Nations still go to war. Militants still target civilians. The experience of the Holocaust did not prevent genocide and ethnic cleansing in Cambodia, the Balkans or Rwanda. However, the international community's failure to stop the massacre of around 800,000 Tutsis and moderate Hutus by militant Hutus in Rwanda in 1994 provoked much criticism and soul-searching, and prompted the United Nations to declare that the world must intervene to stop genocide and ethnic cleansing in future.

In the pre-dawn darkness of 25 April 1915, troops from the Australian and New Zealand Army Corp stormed ashore a small beach in western Turkey. It was the start of the Gallipoli campaign to open the Turkish Straits to Russia, a campaign that ultimately killed more than 130,000 men on all sides. It was one of the bloodiest campaigns of World War One, but one that helped shape the birth of Australia, New Zealand and Turkey. 'Those who fought here... forever changed the way we saw the world and ourselves,' Australian Prime Minister John Howard said in the 2005 Anzac Day ceremony on the Turkish beach of Anzac Cove.

There was once a debate about whether to continue to commemorate Anzac Day at all, about whether that past battle was really relevant any more. But now the annual ceremony at Anzac Cove has become an emotional pilgrimage for new generations. Thousands flock there every year. 'Visiting Gallipoli is something every Australian wants to do,' said 32-year-old Rob Walters, born almost 60 years after the landing. 'It is current with every generation.'

In an echo of Simon Wiesenthal, the traditional Anzac Day dawn ceremony always ends with the words: 'Lest We Forget.'

Terry Friel has been with Reuters since 1995. He has worked in Canberra, Jakarta and New Delhi and has also reported from East Timor, Aceh, Papua New Guinea, Afghanistan, Kashmir, Pakistan, Iraq, Sri Lanka and Nepal. His extensive coverage in India includes the tsunami disaster, the nuclear stand-off with Pakistan and the crisis in Nepal. Terry is currently chief correspondent in India.

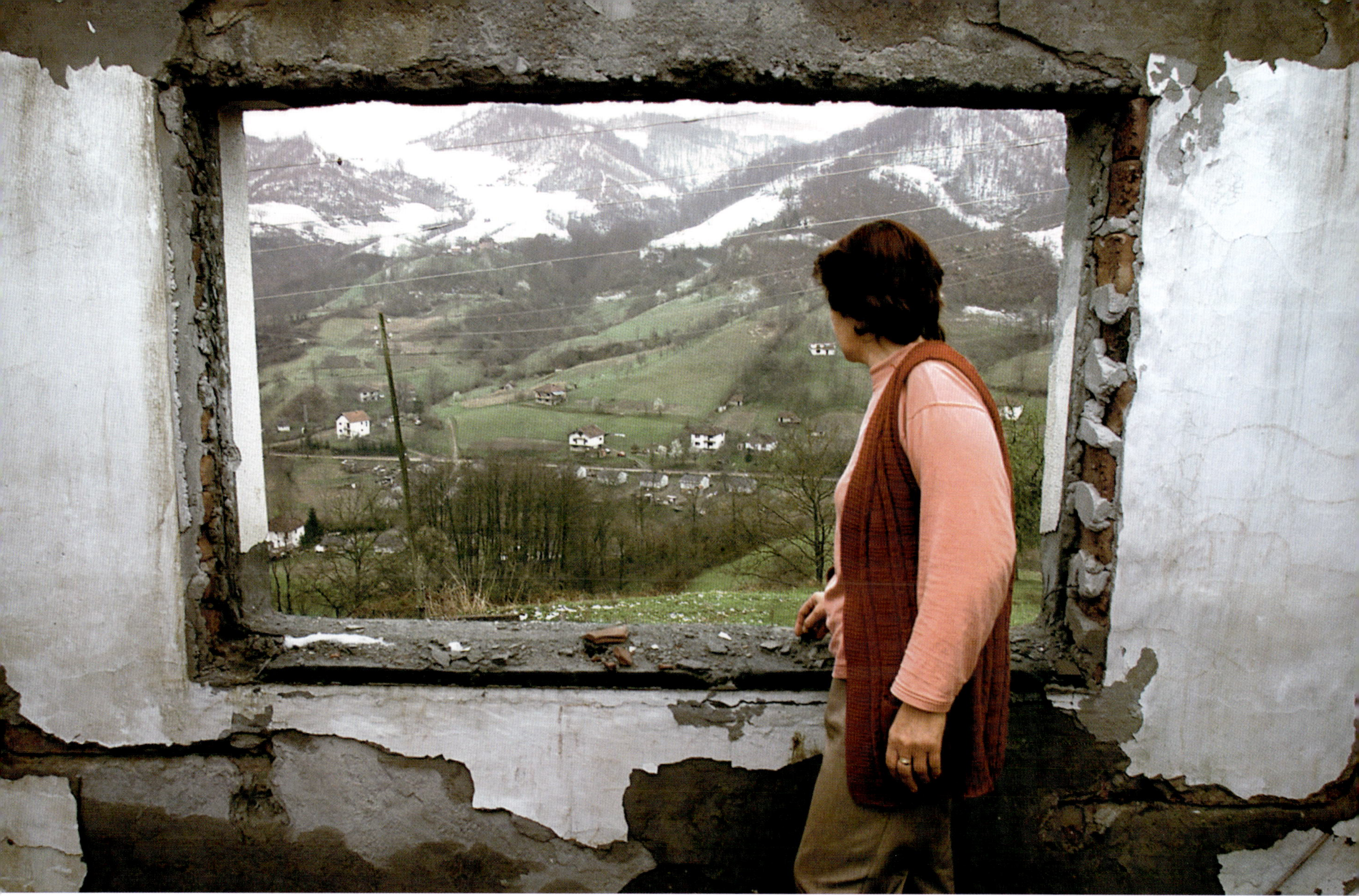

26 March 2002, GORNJI POTOCARI, BOSNIA

Nazira Efendic, a Bosnian Muslim who lost most of her relatives during the 1992–95 Bosnian war, looks through the window of her destroyed house in the village of Gornji Potocari near Srebrenica. Ten years after the war began, a group of Bosnian Muslims whose families were victims of the 1995 massacre in the U.N. 'safe area' of Srebrenica had gone back there, driven by a strong wish to return to their pre-war homes. Damir Sagolj

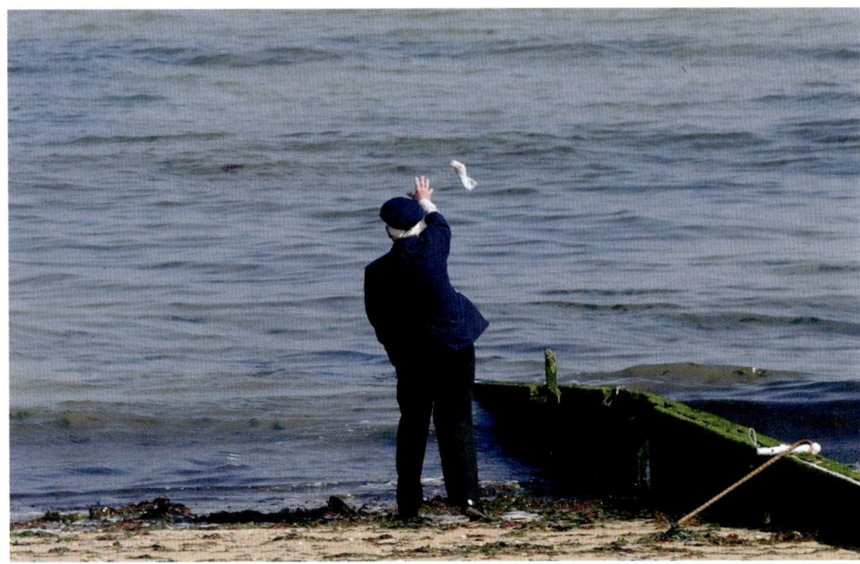

6 June 2004, NORMANDY, FRANCE

A Canadian veteran throws a memento into the waters of Juno Beach in Normandy following ceremonies marking the 60th anniversary of the D-Day landings in World War Two. Hundreds of veterans returned in 2004 to retrace their steps taken during the 1944 invasion of mainland Europe. Andy Clark

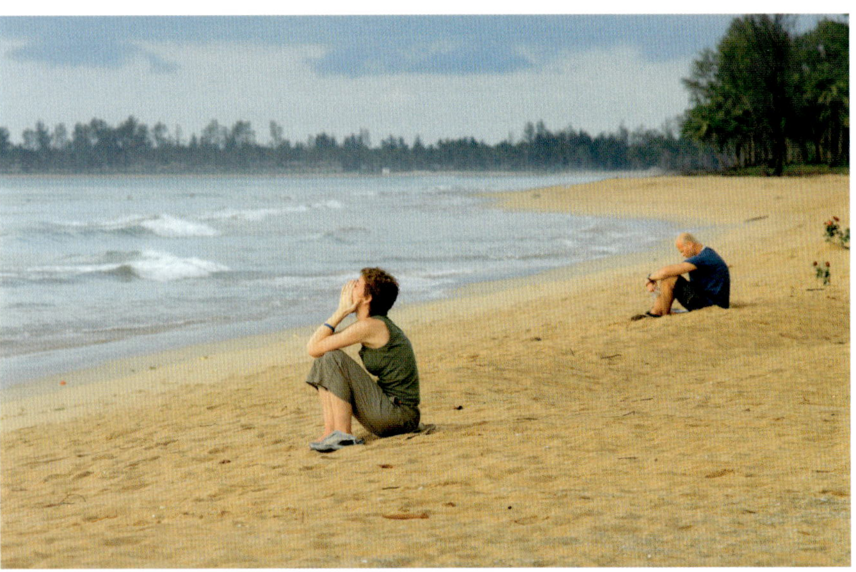

26 December 2005, KHAO LAK, THAILAND

Swedes mourn the loss of family members on the shores of the Andaman Sea in Khao Lak, about 110 km (68 miles) north of the resort island of Phuket. Locals and foreigners gathered in southern Thailand on the first anniversary of the tsunami that killed almost 230,000 people around the Indian Ocean. The Swedish death toll, at 543, was the highest of all non-Asian countries. Adrees Latif

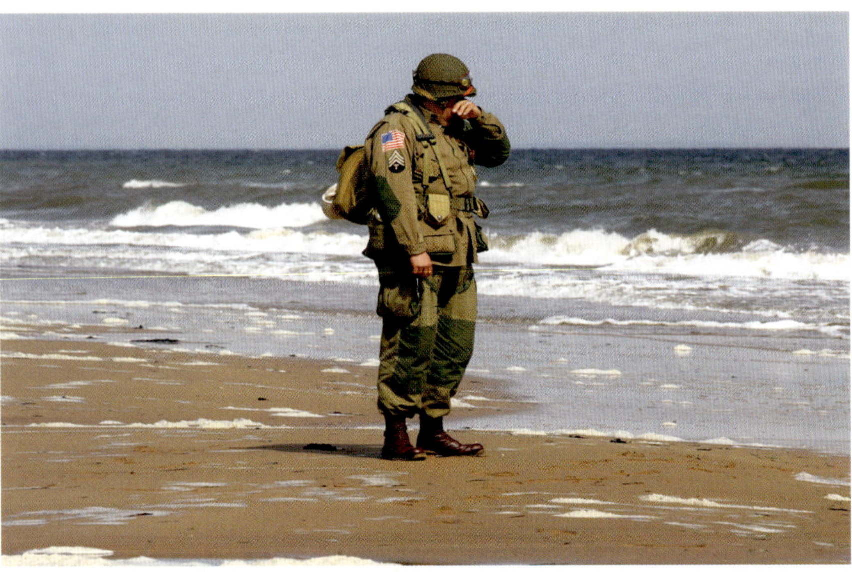

2 June 2004, NORMANDY, FRANCE

Pat Brown of Fermont, West Virginia, dressed in combat gear, wipes away tears as he stands on Omaha Beach while paying tribute to family members who took part in the Allied D-Day landings in Normandy 60 years before during World War Two. Yves Herman

25 April 2005, ANZAC COVE, TURKEY

Military personnel from Australia and New Zealand participate in a dawn ceremony at Anzac Cove on the remote Gallipoli peninsula in western Turkey. Australian Prime Minister John Howard, New Zealand Prime Minister Helen Clark, Britain's Prince Charles and other officials joined 15,000 Australians and New Zealanders, as well as Turks, to honour the Australian and New Zealand Army Corps (ANZAC) on the 90th anniversary of the start of one of the bloodiest battles of World War One. Some 4,000 Australian and New Zealand soldiers struggled ashore on this narrow beach on 25 April 1915 to launch the ill-fated Gallipoli campaign that would claim around 125,000 lives by the time it ended on 14 January 1916. Fatih Saribas

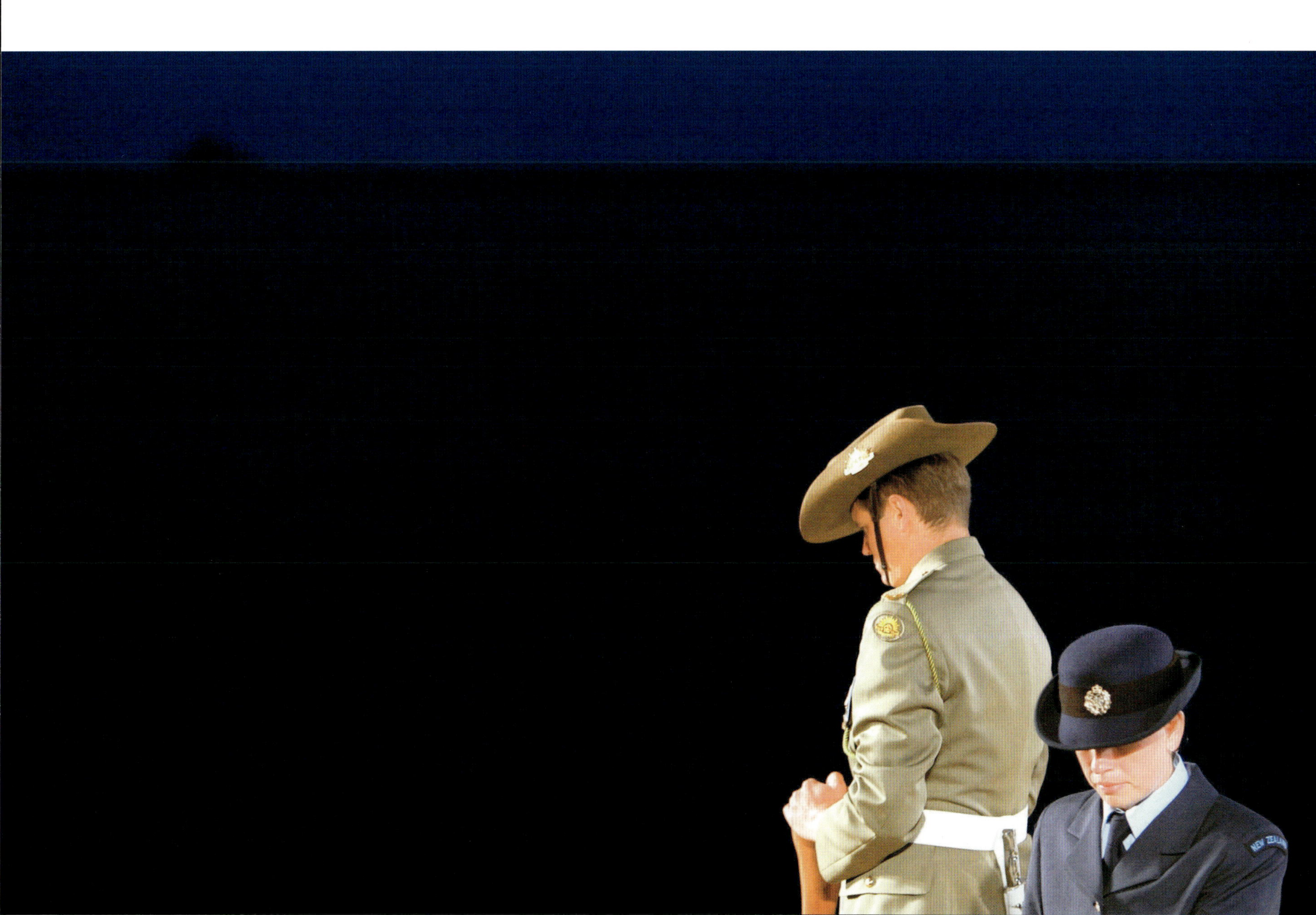

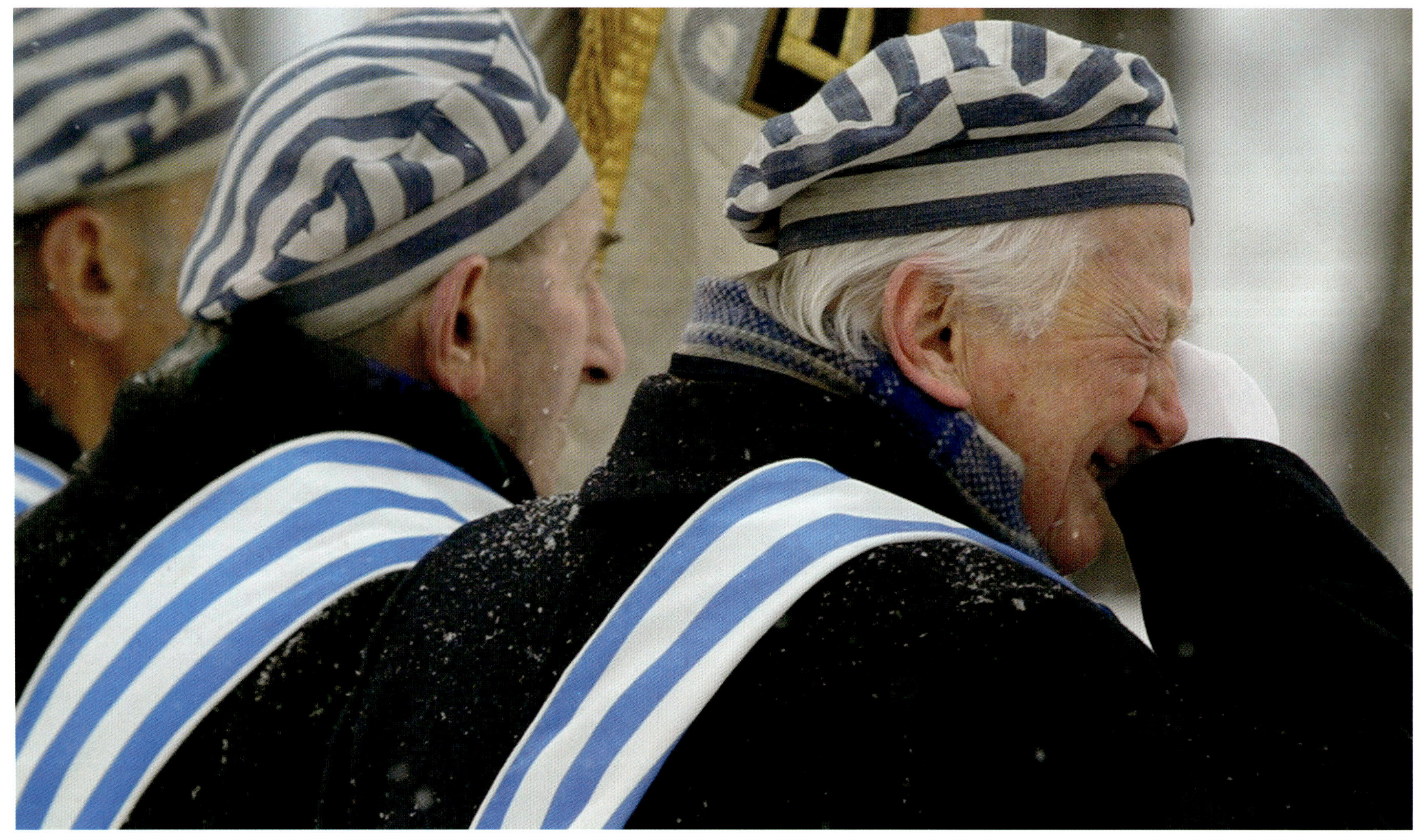

27 January 2005, OSWIECIM, POLAND

A concentration camp survivor sheds a tear during a ceremony at the former Nazi death camp of Auschwitz-Birkenau, as survivors and world leaders gathered in Poland to mark the 60th anniversary of the camp's liberation by Soviet troops and to remember the victims of the Holocaust during World War Two. Katarina Stoltz

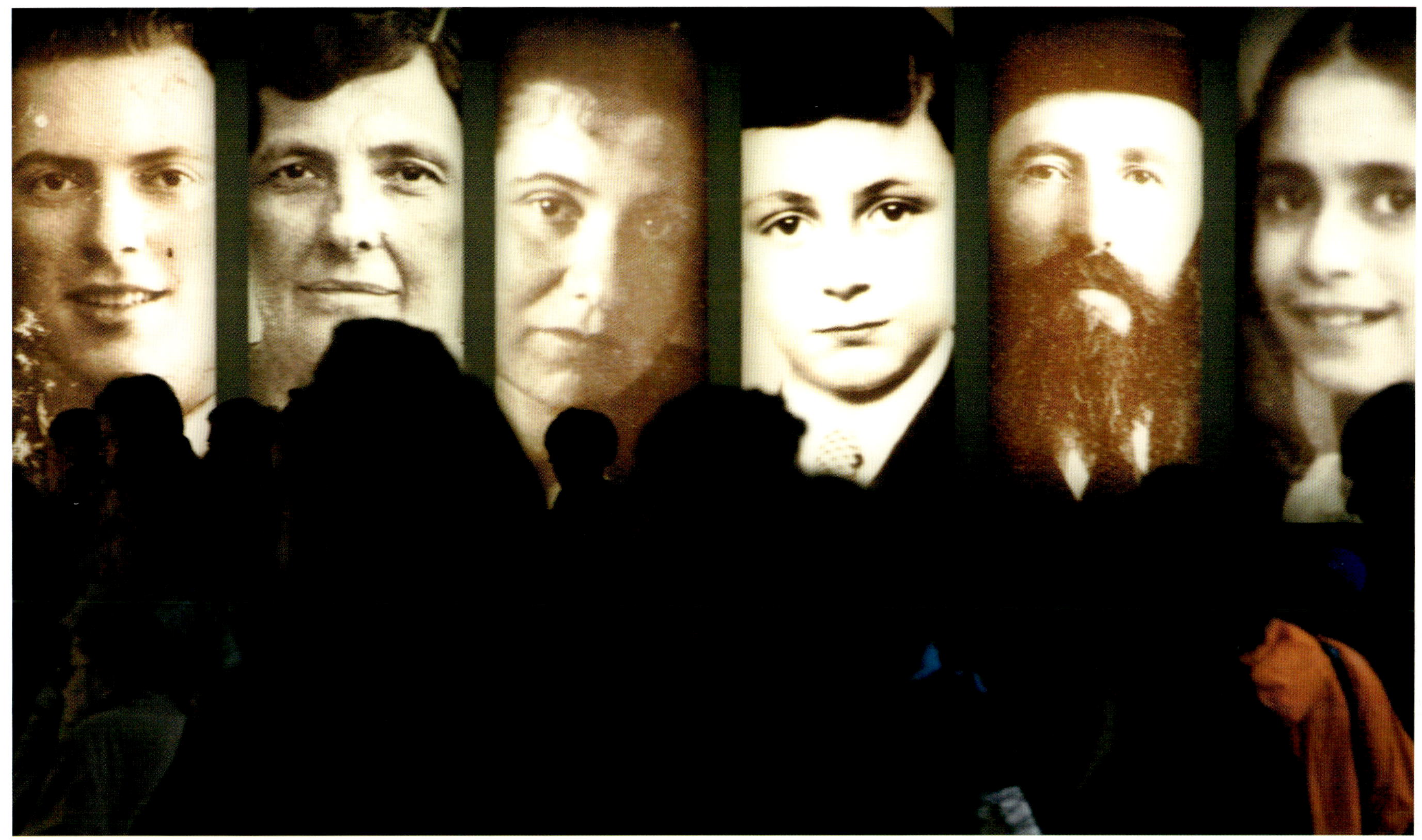

6 May 2005, BERLIN, GERMANY

Portraits of Holocaust victims are viewed by visitors to the Holocaust Memorial in Berlin, which was formally opened on 10 May 2005. Designed by U.S. architect Peter Eisenman, the memorial is made up of 2,711 charcoal-grey concrete pillars which form a tight grid. As visitors enter, the uneven ground, muffled street sounds and pillars of increasingly imposing height create a sense of disorientation and isolation that is intended to evoke something of the experiences of Jewish victims of the Nazis, as well as to encourage people to talk about the darkest chapter in German history. An underground Information Centre documents the fate of individual Jews and Jewish families during Adolf Hitler's rule from 1933 to 1945. Arnd Wiegmann

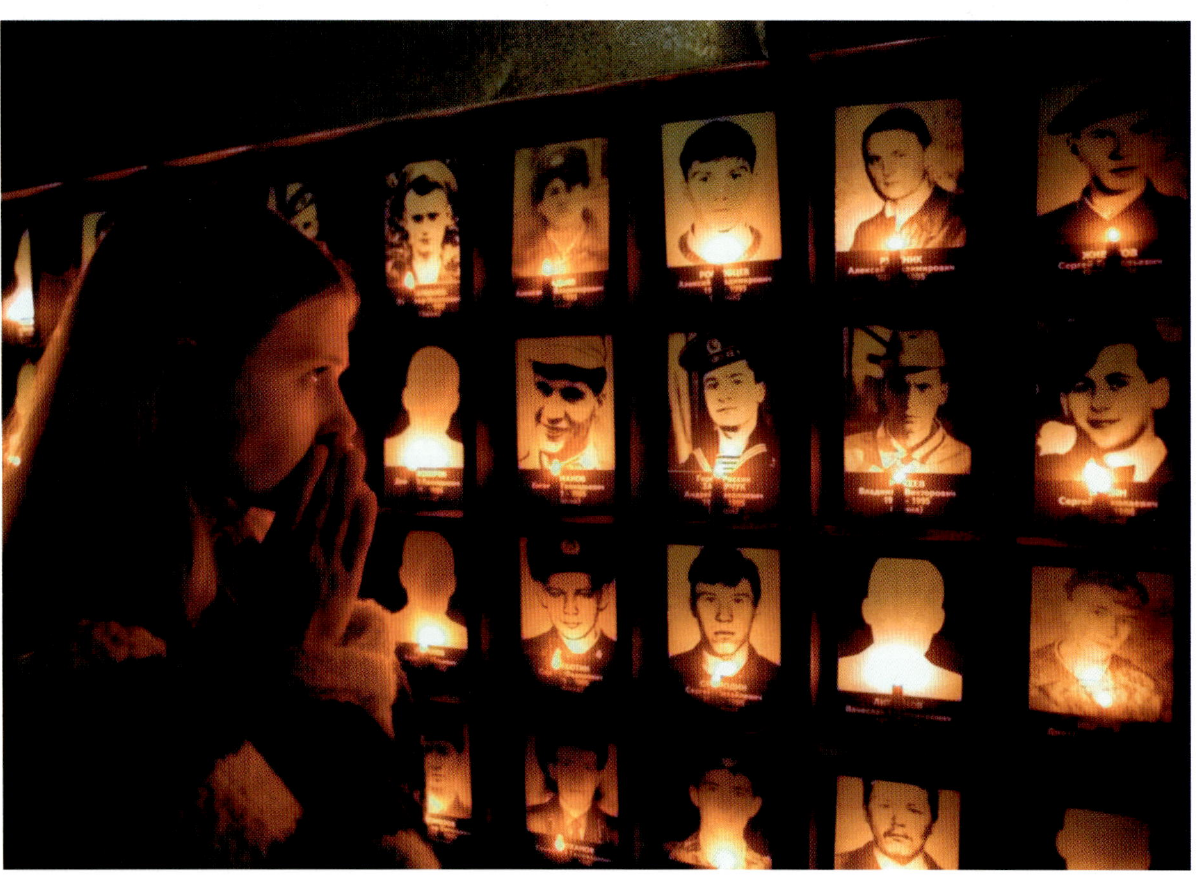

15 February 2003, KRASNOYARSK, RUSSIA

A visitor to the Krasnoyarsk Museum Centre looks at a memorial to soldiers and officers of the Krasnoyarsk region who died in Soviet military campaigns in Afghanistan and the Chechen Republic. On 15 February 2003 Russia and the former Soviet states marked the 14th anniversary of the withdrawal of Soviet forces from Afghanistan. Ilia Naymushin

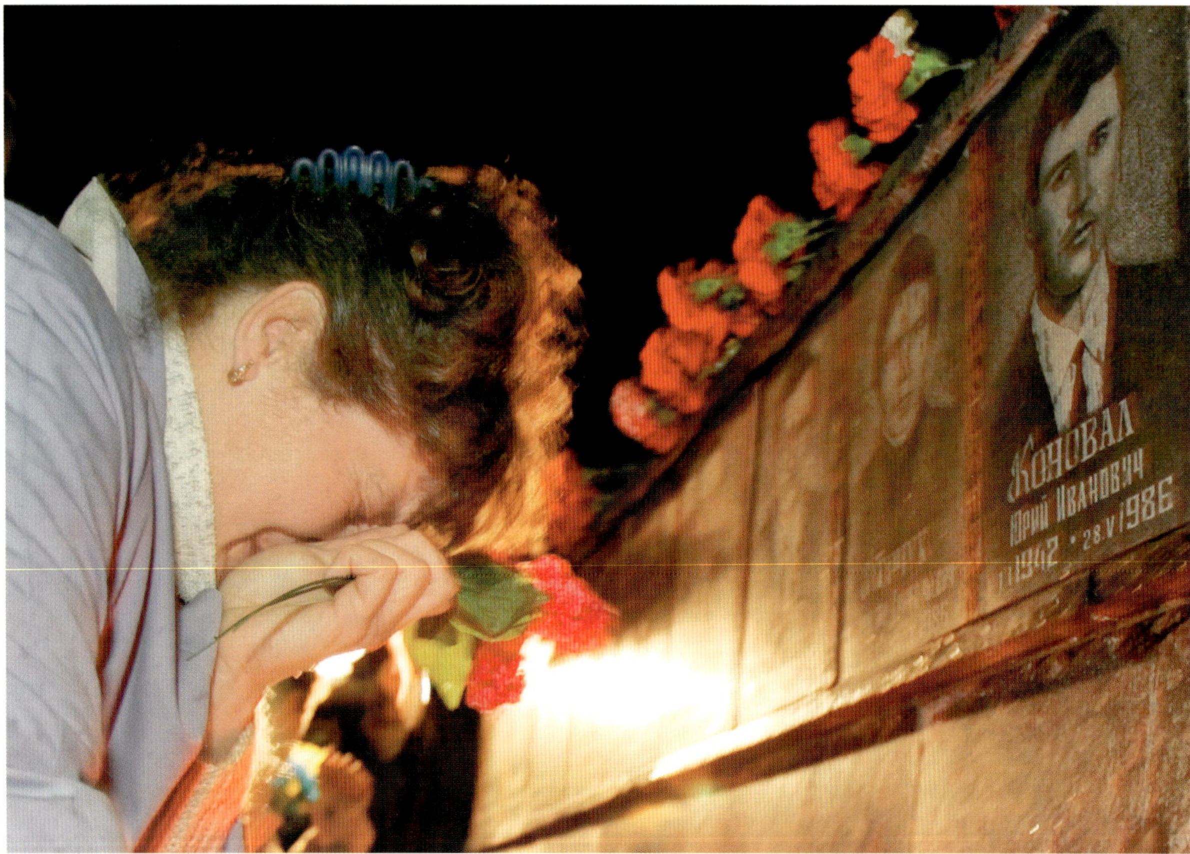

26 April 2005, SLAVUTICH, UKRAINE

A woman weeps in front of a memorial dedicated to firemen who were killed by the Chernobyl nuclear catastrophe in 1986. In 2005 Ukraine marked the 19th anniversary of the world's worst nuclear accident when Chernobyl's reactor No. 4 exploded, sending radioactive clouds across Europe and contaminating vast tracts of land in Ukraine, Belarus and Russia. Gleb Garanich

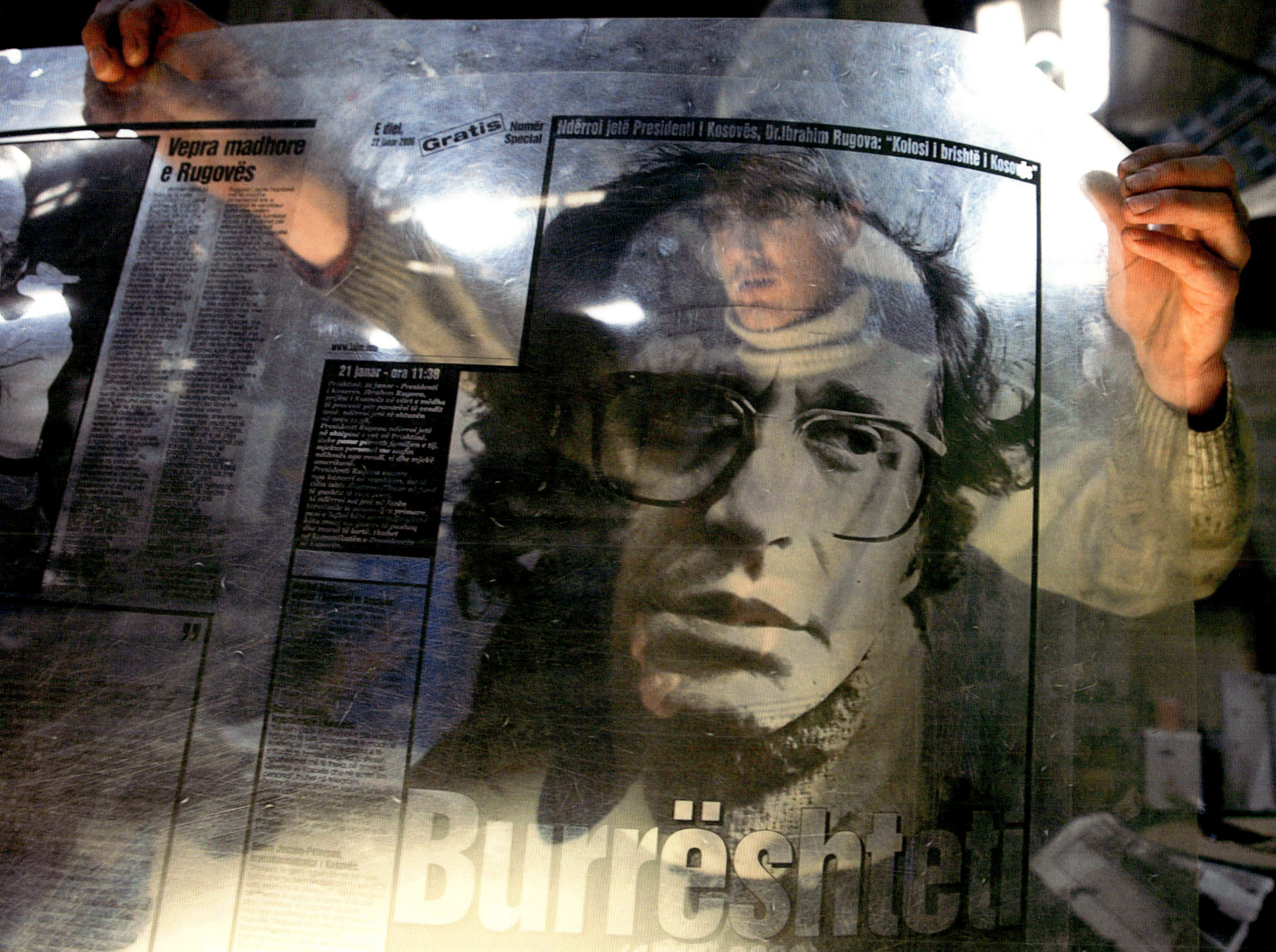

22 January 2006, PRISTINA, KOSOVO

A worker at a printing house in Pristina prepares a special tribute edition of a daily paper to former Kosovo President Ibrahim Rugova, icon of the ethnic Albanian drive to win independence from Serbia. Rugova died on 21 January 2006, aged 61. Dubbed the 'Gandhi of the Balkans' for his advocacy of non-violent resistance to Serb oppression, in the 1990s he created a parallel, underground state for Kosovo's majority ethnic Albanians, separate from Serb institutions. Hazir Reka

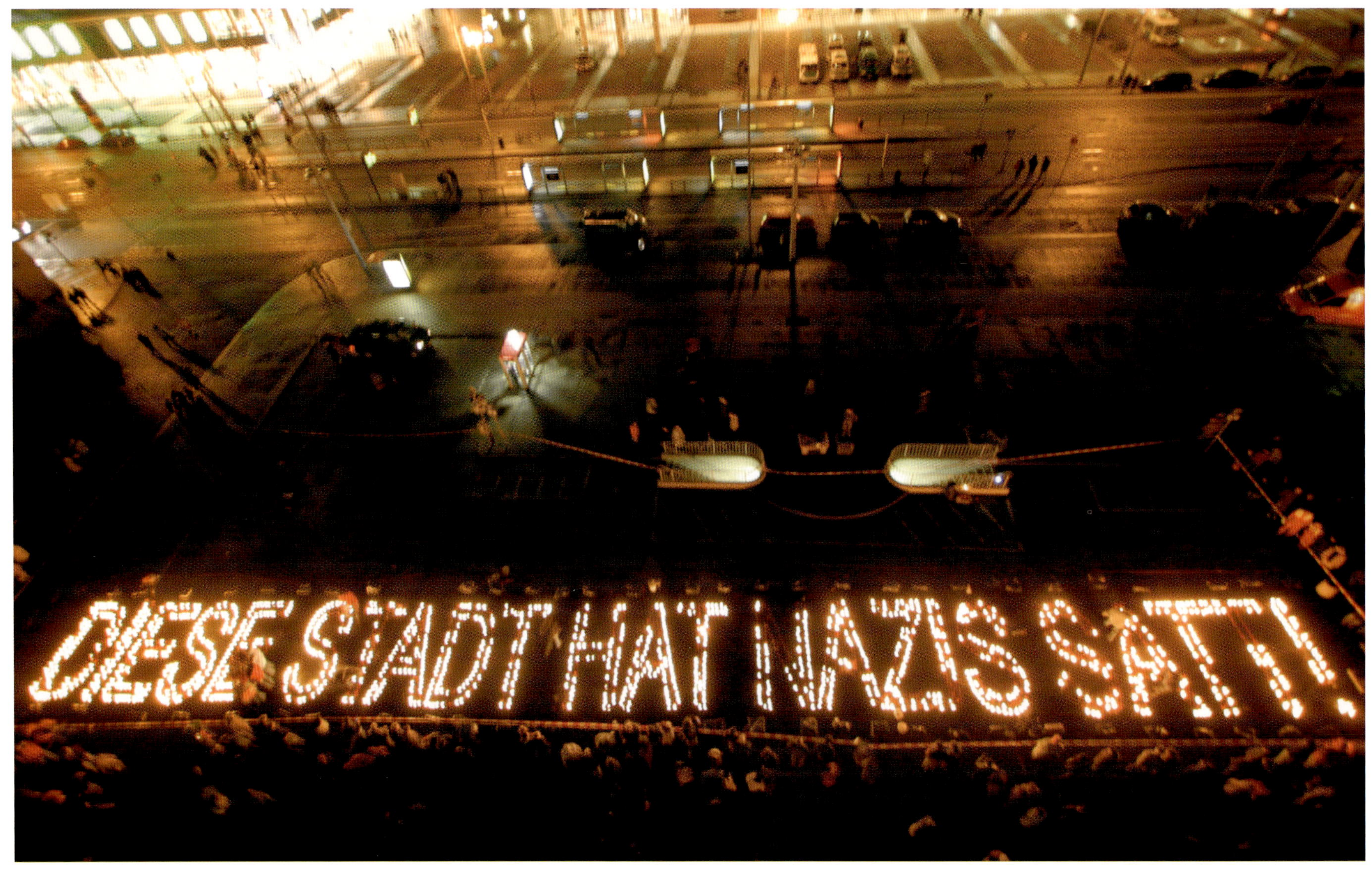

13 February 2005, DRESDEN, GERMANY

Candles compose an inscription that reads 'This town is sick of Nazis' in Dresden's Altmarkt square on the 60th anniversary of the historic city's devastation in one of the fiercest Allied bombing raids of World War Two. The death toll is officially put at around 35,000, but many survivors believe the real number was higher as bodies were reduced to ashes in the huge ensuing firestorm. The official 60th anniversary commemoration was marred by the presence of thousands of neo-Nazis, who marched on the city waving black flags and banners, ignoring Nazi atrocities and attempting to represent the bombings as evidence that Germany was a victim in World War Two. Police said around 5,000 people joined the march, making it one of the biggest far-right demonstrations since the war. Later up to 50,000 residents, wearing white roses as a symbol of reconciliation, gathered in the city's historic heart to light candles in memory of all victims of war and to reject the claims of the far right. Pawel Kopczynski

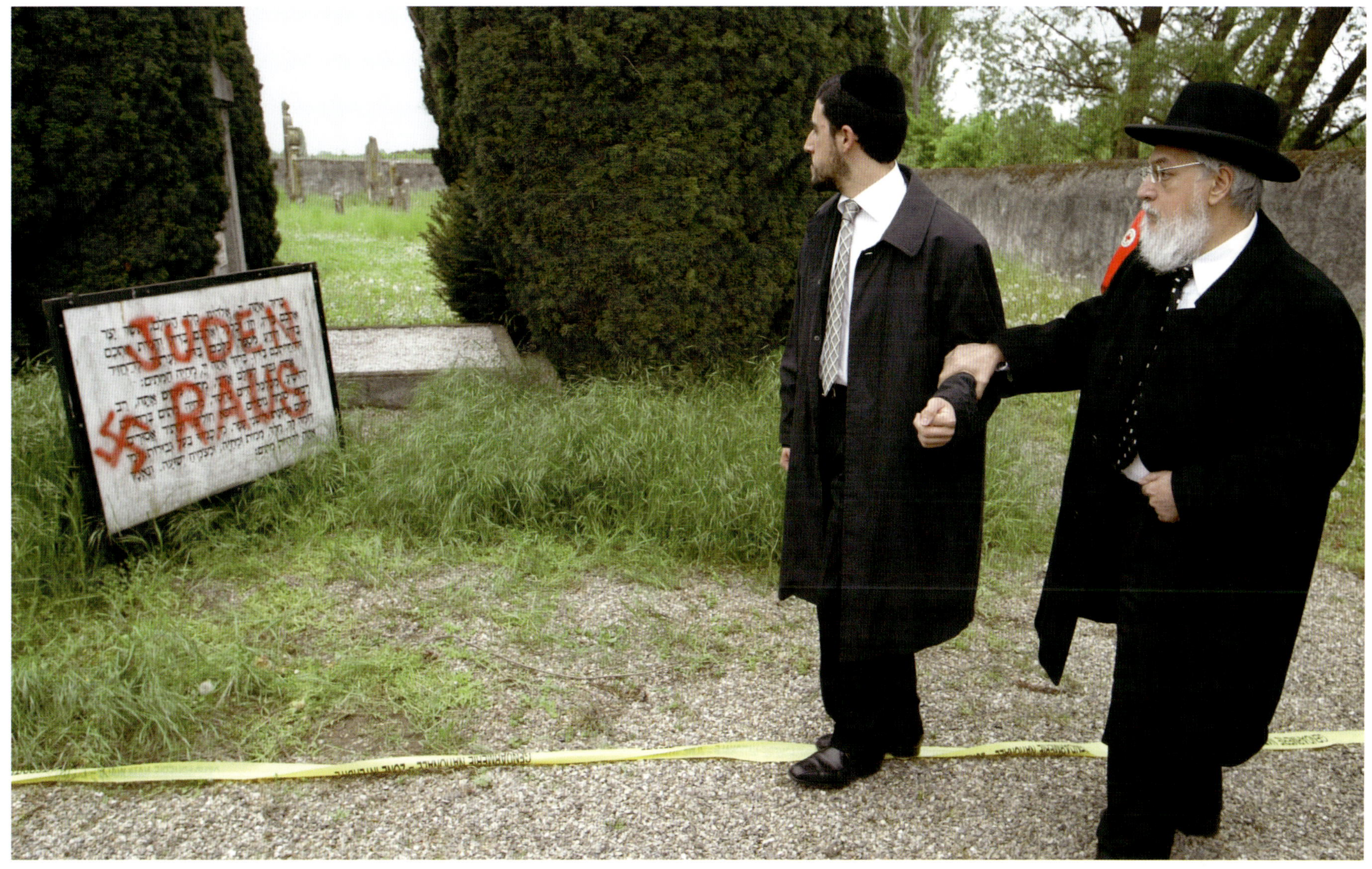

6 May 2004, HERRLISHEIM, FRANCE

The Chief Rabbi of France, Joseph Sitruk (right), is helped by a member of the Jewish community as he enters the Jewish cemetery of Herrlisheim, close to the French–German border, near a sign daubed with the slogan 'Jews out'. On 30 April 2004 some 127 graves in Herrlisheim were discovered to have been desecrated with Nazi swastikas and anti-Semitic slogans written in German. In October 2004 a French government report said that a new wave of anti-Semitism posed a threat to the fabric of French society, and proposed keeping a closer watch on racism in the media as well as schools, and the creation of a national watchdog to monitor anti-Semitism. Vincent Kessler

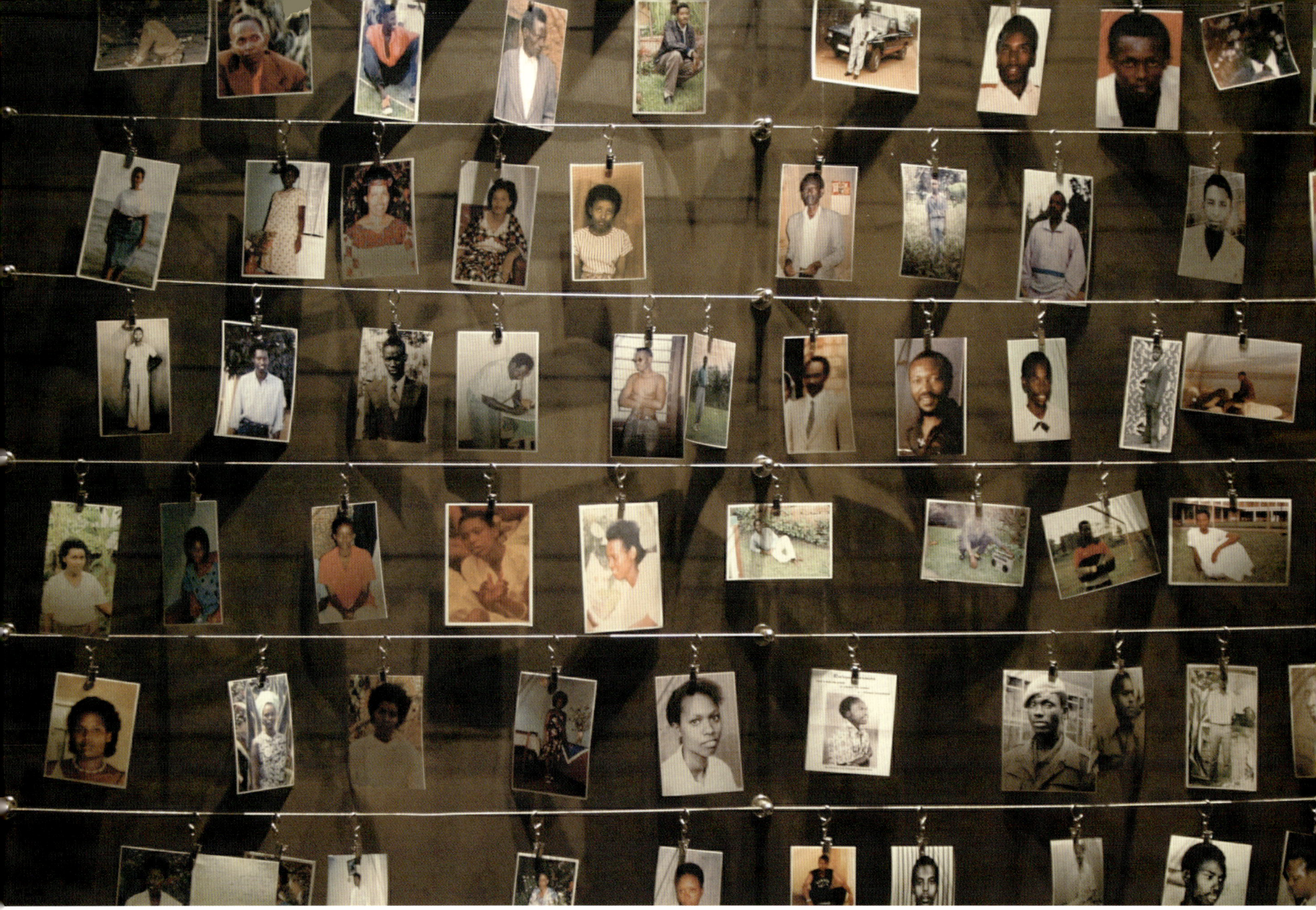

5 April 2004, KIGALI, RWANDA

Photographs of victims of Rwanda's 1994 genocide are displayed in the Gisozi memorial in Kigali, which combines a mass grave containing the remains of an estimated 250,000 people with a state-of-the-art museum with graphic displays and video presentations of the events. Ten years on, and vowing never again, Rwandans devoted a week of commemoration to the 800,000 Tutsis and politically moderate Hutus who died in the genocide. Rwandan President Paul Kagame has repeatedly criticized the outside world for failing to intervene to stop the slaughter in the tiny central African country, despite clear warnings that ethnic Hutu extremists were planning the massacres. Radu Sigheti

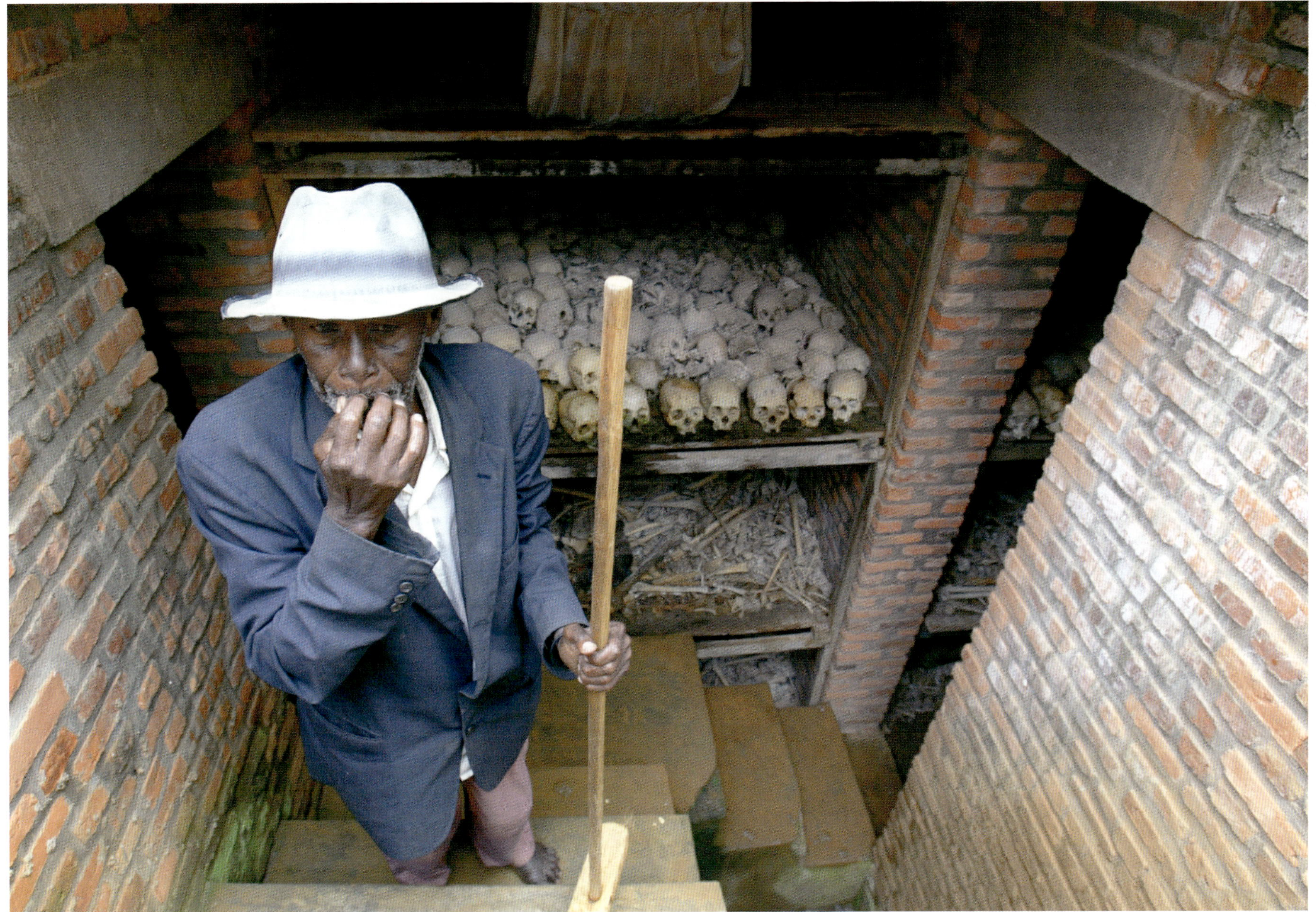

4 April 2004, NYANZA, RWANDA

A Rwandan worker weeps as he cleans a mass grave outside the church in Nyanza. The International Criminal Tribunal for Rwanda based in Tanzania was set up by the United Nations in 1995 to prosecute suspected masterminds of the genocide. But the pursuit of justice has proved slow and complex. By March 2006, only 15 cases had been completed, with 28 in progress, 8 on appeal and another 15 yet to start. Radu Sigheti

11 September 2002, NEW YORK, UNITED STATES

Workers from a construction site sing the U.S. national anthem after observing a moment of silence in honour of the victims of the World Trade Center attacks in New York, as the city marked the first anniversary of the attacks. Pascal Lauener

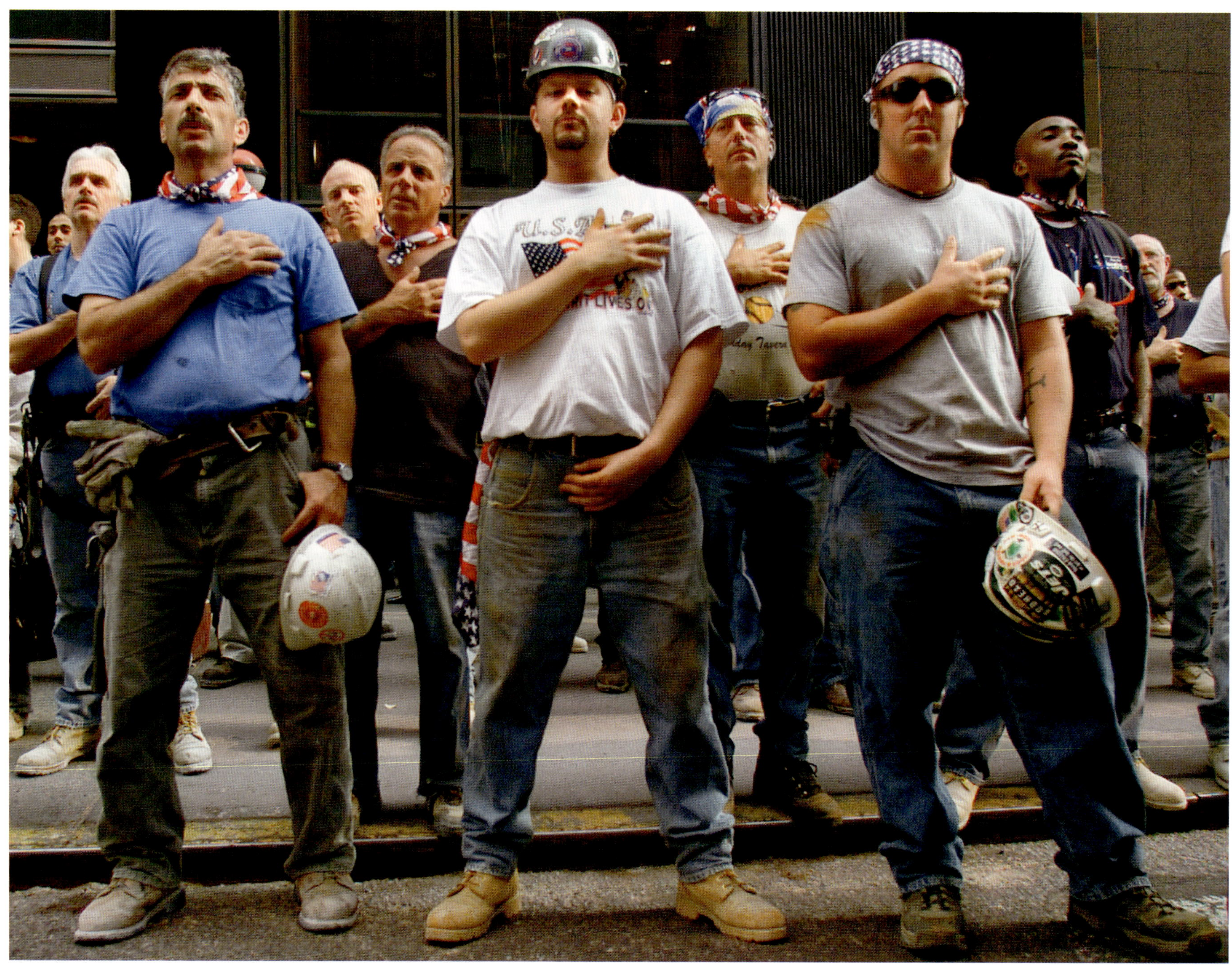

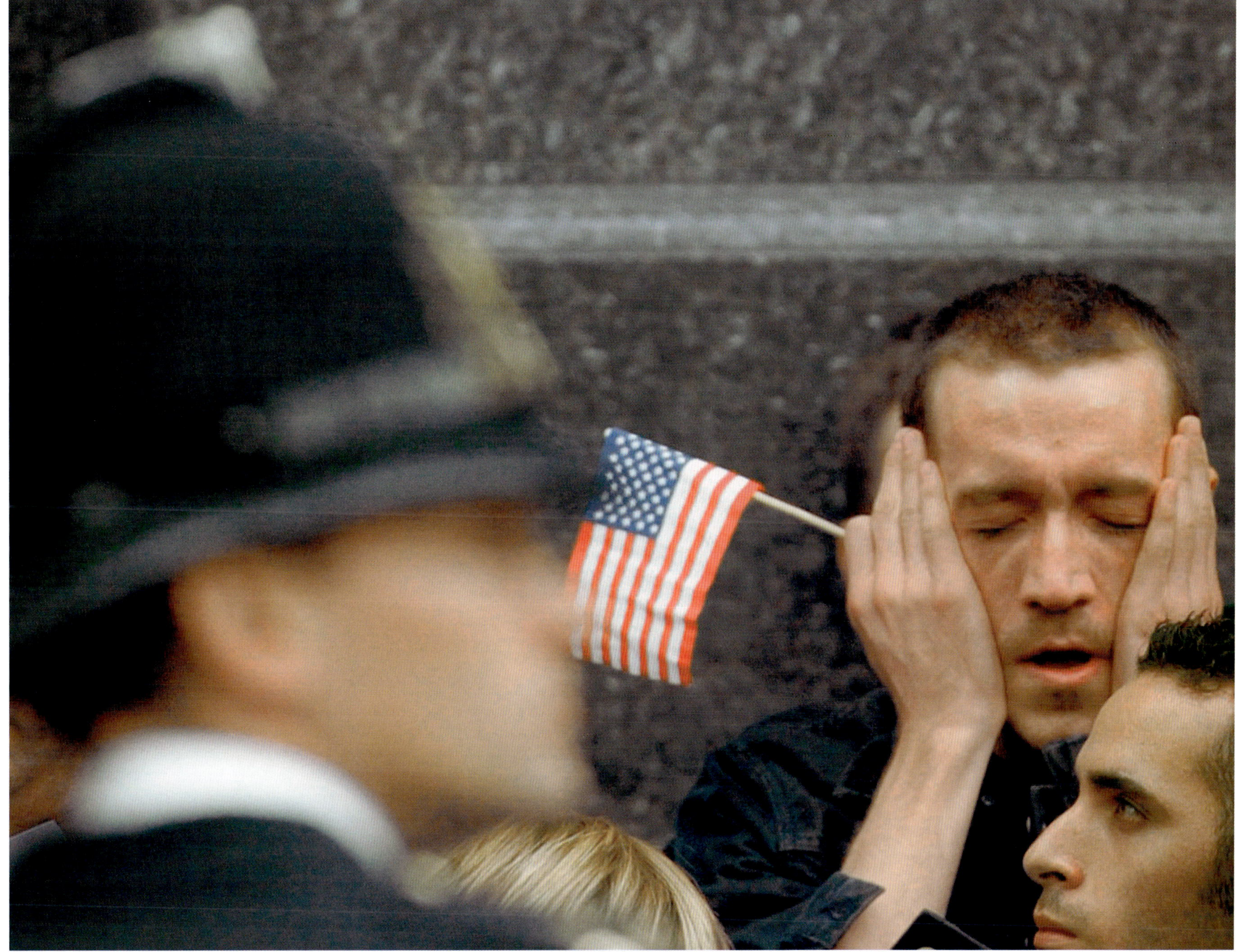

11 September 2002, LONDON, UNITED KINGDOM

Outside a remembrance service at London's St Paul's Cathedral, a man shows his emotion during a minute's silence to mark the first anniversary of the September 11 attacks on the United States. Britain's Prince Charles and Prime Minister Tony Blair were among the 2,000-strong congregation, which included friends and relatives of those who died. Dan Chung

9 April 2002, SARAJEVO, BOSNIA

Rasim Kadic, head of Bosnia's Liberal Democratic Party, stages a protest against the Israeli occupation of Palestinian towns by placing a board reading 'Ramallah' over the sign for Canton Sarajevo at the entrance to the Bosnian capital. The intention was to draw a comparison between the plight of Palestinians bombarded by Israeli tanks in the West Bank city of Ramallah and the fate of Bosnians, mostly Muslims, during the 1992–95 siege of Sarajevo, in which nearly 12,000 people were killed. Danilo Krstanovic

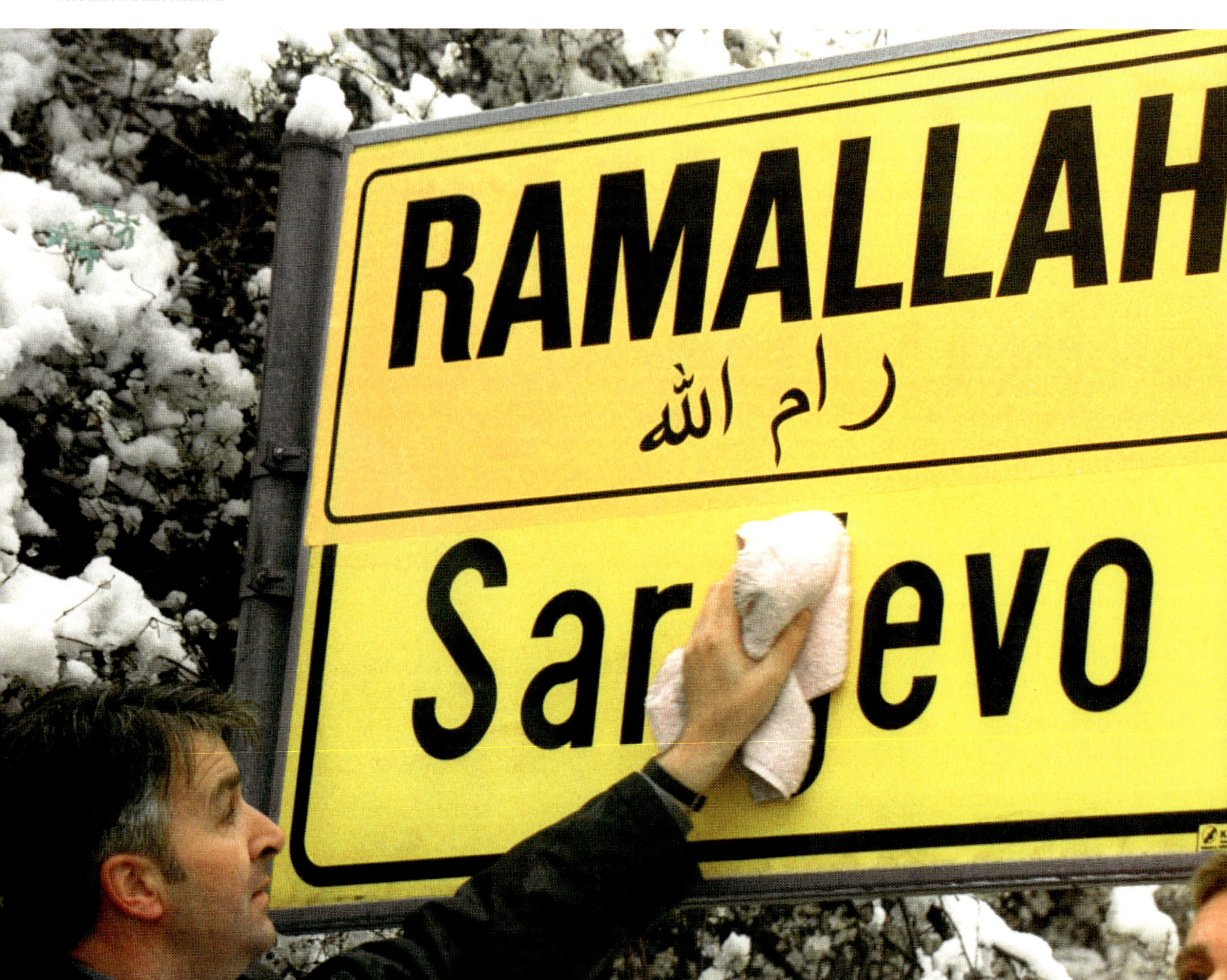

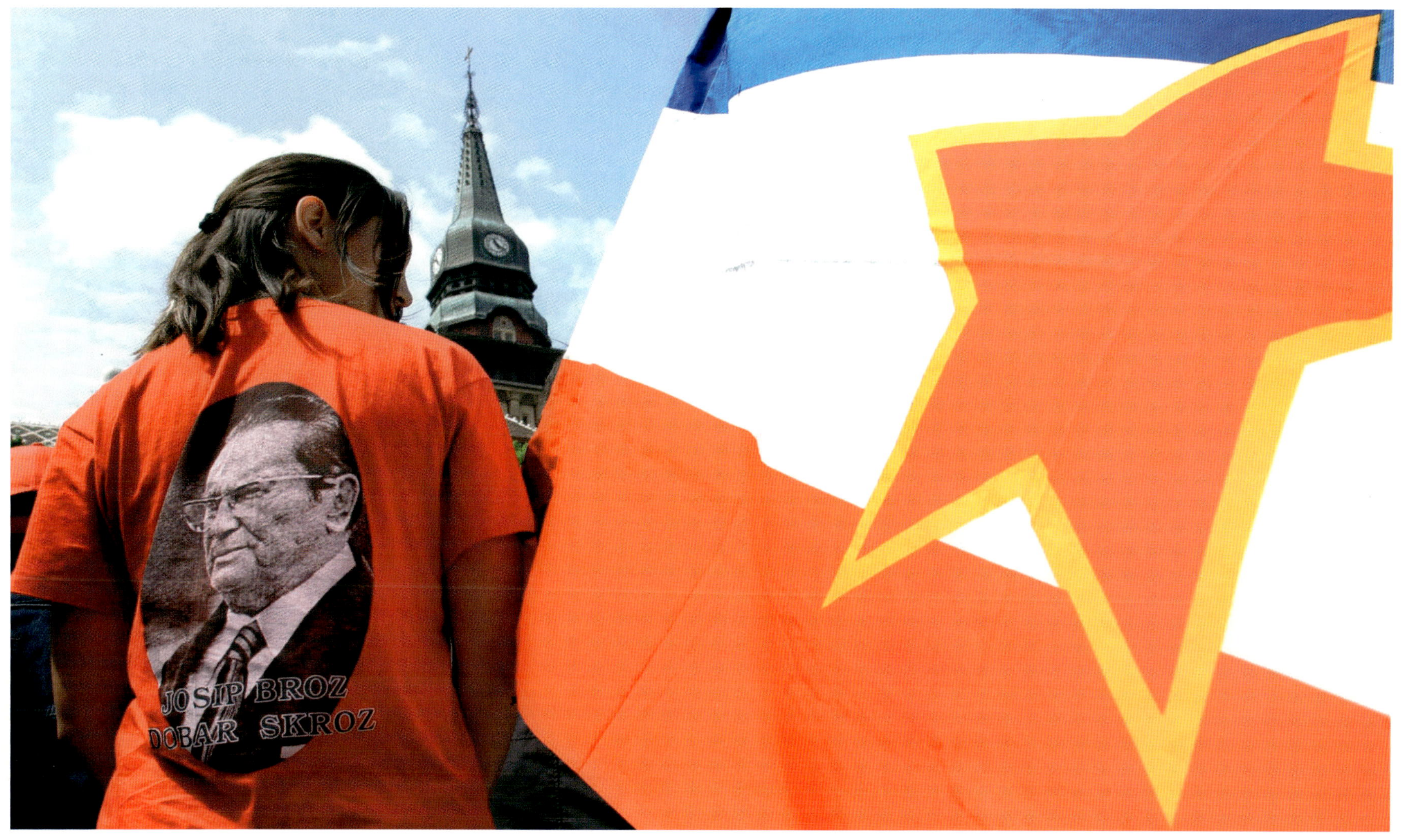

25 May 2005, SUBOTICA, SERBIA

A girl wearing a Tito T-shirt holds an old Yugoslav flag at a commemorative rally in the northern Serb town of Subotica on the occasion of the late Josip Broz Tito's birthday, an event that brought people together in nostalgia for the old Yugoslavia and affection for its leader. Tito was a half-Croatian, half-Slovenian atheist communist who ruled for almost 35 years. He became a hate figure for the ultra-religious nationalist movements that came to power in the 1990s in the former Yugoslav states. But a decade of wars and the hardship of post-communist transition have faded memories of the authoritarian character of his regime and made many long for a gentler, more innocent era. A kind of 'Tito chic' has taken off, from T-shirts, souvenir busts and personality cult websites, to bars named in his honour.

Goran Sivacki

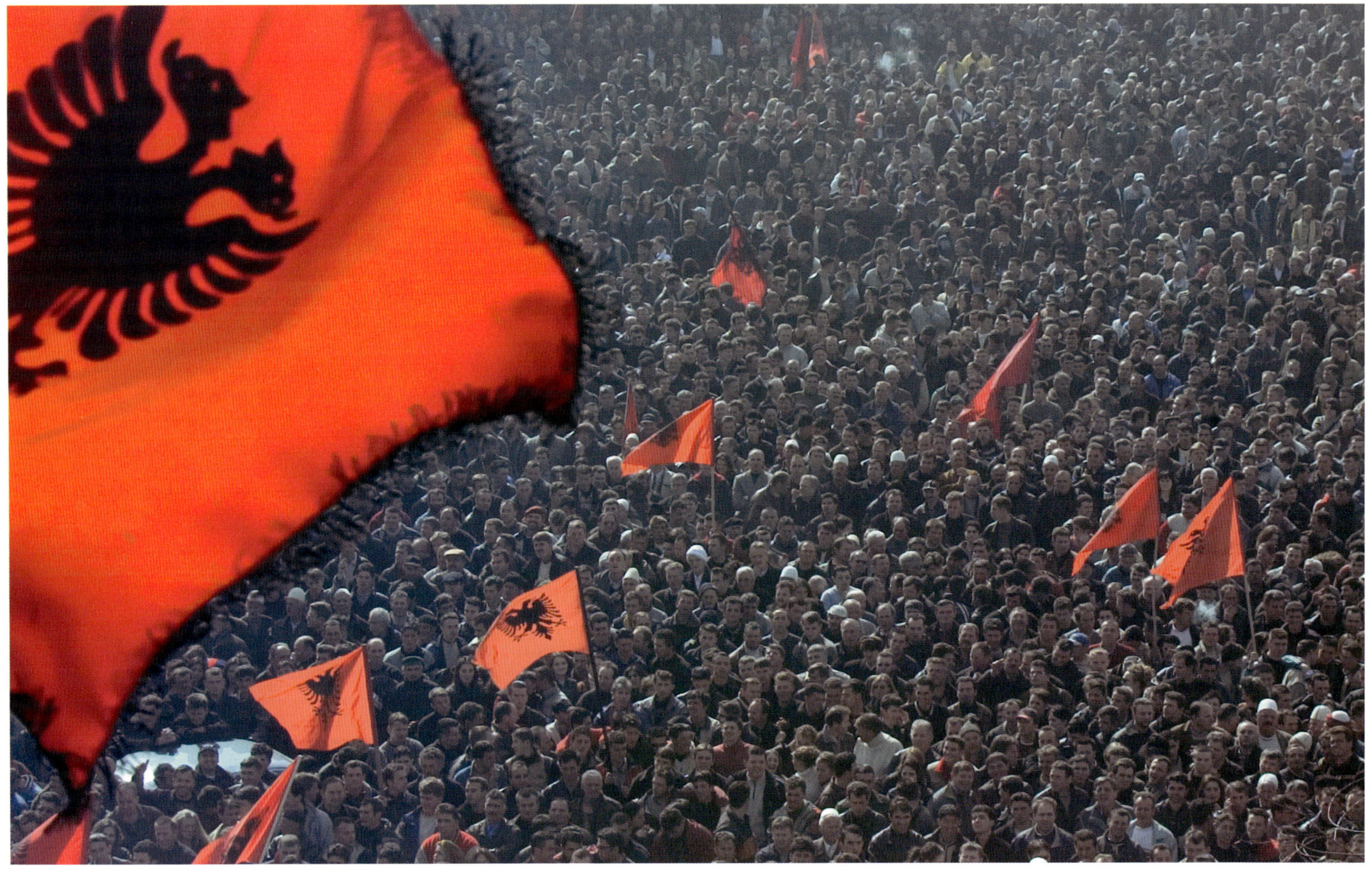

26 February 2003, PRISTINA, KOSOVO

More than 50,000 Kosovo Albanians gather in the capital Pristina to protest against the arrest of Fatmir Limaj, a former commander in the Kosovo Liberation Army (KLA). Limaj and three other ex-members of the disbanded KLA were indicted in February 2003 by the International Criminal Tribunal for the former Yugoslavia for war crimes committed during the 1998–99 fighting with Serbian forces. To Kosovo's majority Albanians, the men are seen as freedom fighters against Serb oppression. The news of Limaj's acquittal in November 2005 was greeted by triumphant celebrations in Pristina. Hazir Reka

9 March 2005, PRISTINA, KOSOVO

Following his resignation as Kosovo's prime minister, Ramush Haradinaj (left), arrives at Pristina airport accompanied by his wife for a flight to the Netherlands where he was to stand trial for war crimes. Haradinaj is the most senior Kosovo Albanian former rebel leader to be indicted by the United Nations tribunal for alleged atrocities committed during the 1998–99 separatist war against Serb forces. He is considered a hero by many Kosovo Albanians. Hazir Reka

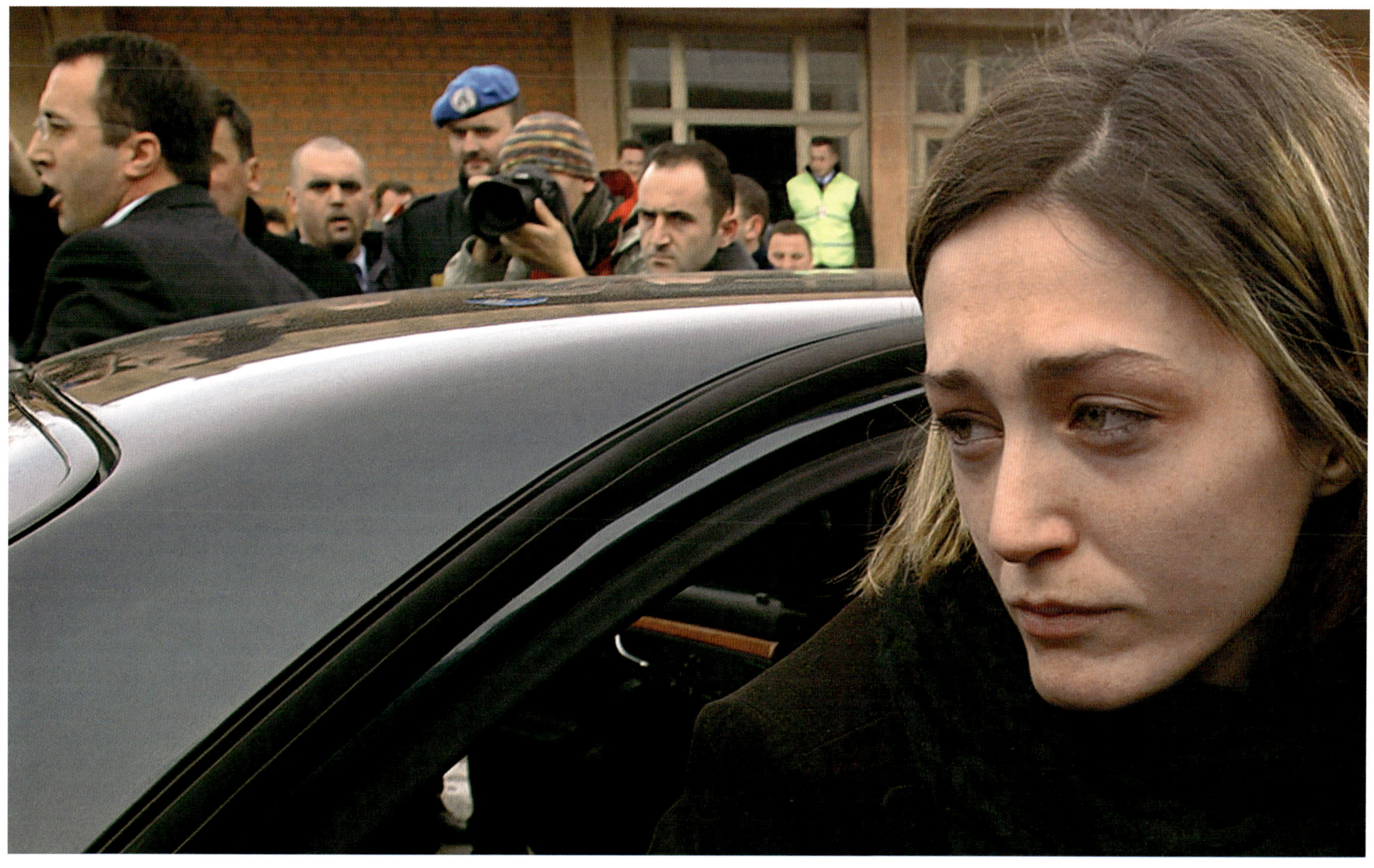

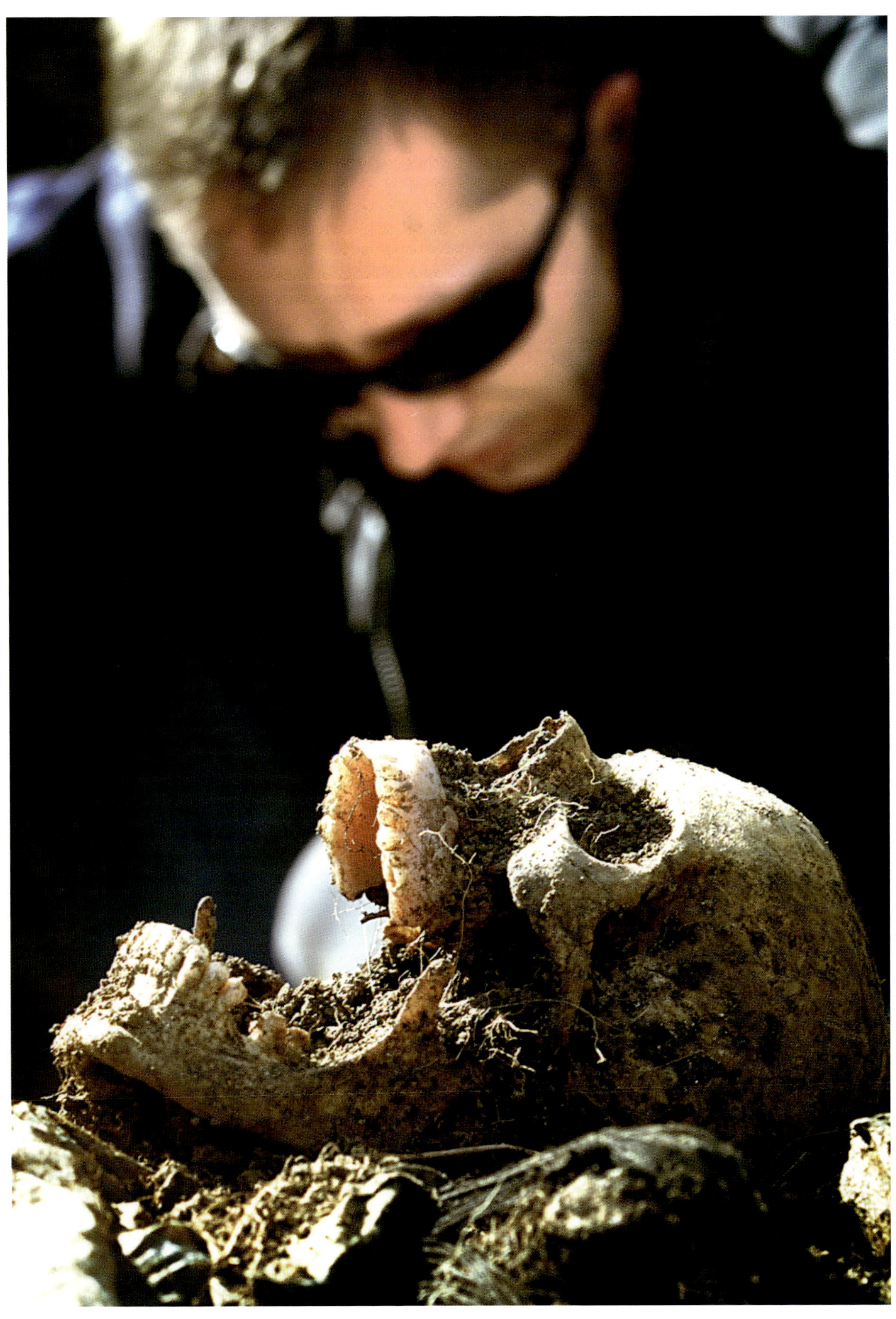

30 March 2002, SIPOVO, BOSNIA

Left An international expert searches for evidence in a mass grave near Sipovo in western Bosnia. Damir Sagolj

10 July 2005, POTOCARI, SERBIA

Opposite above Bosnian Muslim women cry over a coffin containing remains of a relative in a factory hall in Potocari, as 610 victims of the Srebrenica massacre were prepared for a mass burial ceremony on the 10th anniversary of the massacre. The dead had lain for years in hidden pits where they were flung by Bosnian Serb troops in July 1995 after the systematic slaughter of 8,000 unarmed Muslim men and boys taken from what was supposed to be a U.N.-protected 'safe area'. Their bones were painstakingly identified by DNA analysis. They were laid to rest on 11 July 2005 alongside more than 1,300 victims already buried in the Srebrenica cemetery. Damir Sagolj

6 July 2005, VISOKO, BOSNIA

Opposite below Grave markers bearing the names of Bosnian Muslim victims of the 1995 Srebrenica massacre are prepared in a morgue in the central Bosnian town of Visoko. The burial of 610 victims on 11 July 2005 raised the number of identified and reburied bodies to 2,000 – around a quarter of those believed to have died. Twenty more mass graves were still awaiting excavation. Damir Sagolj

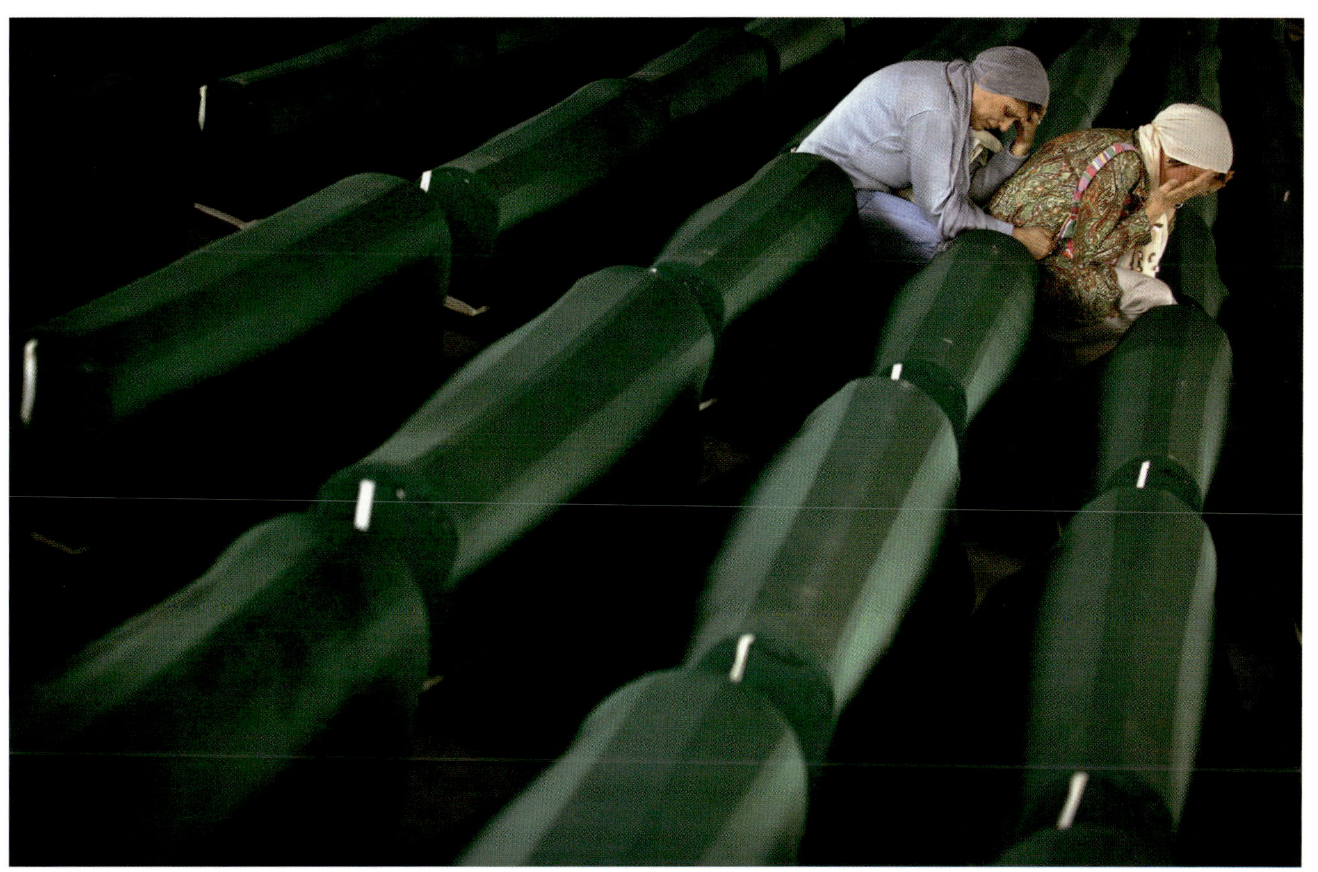

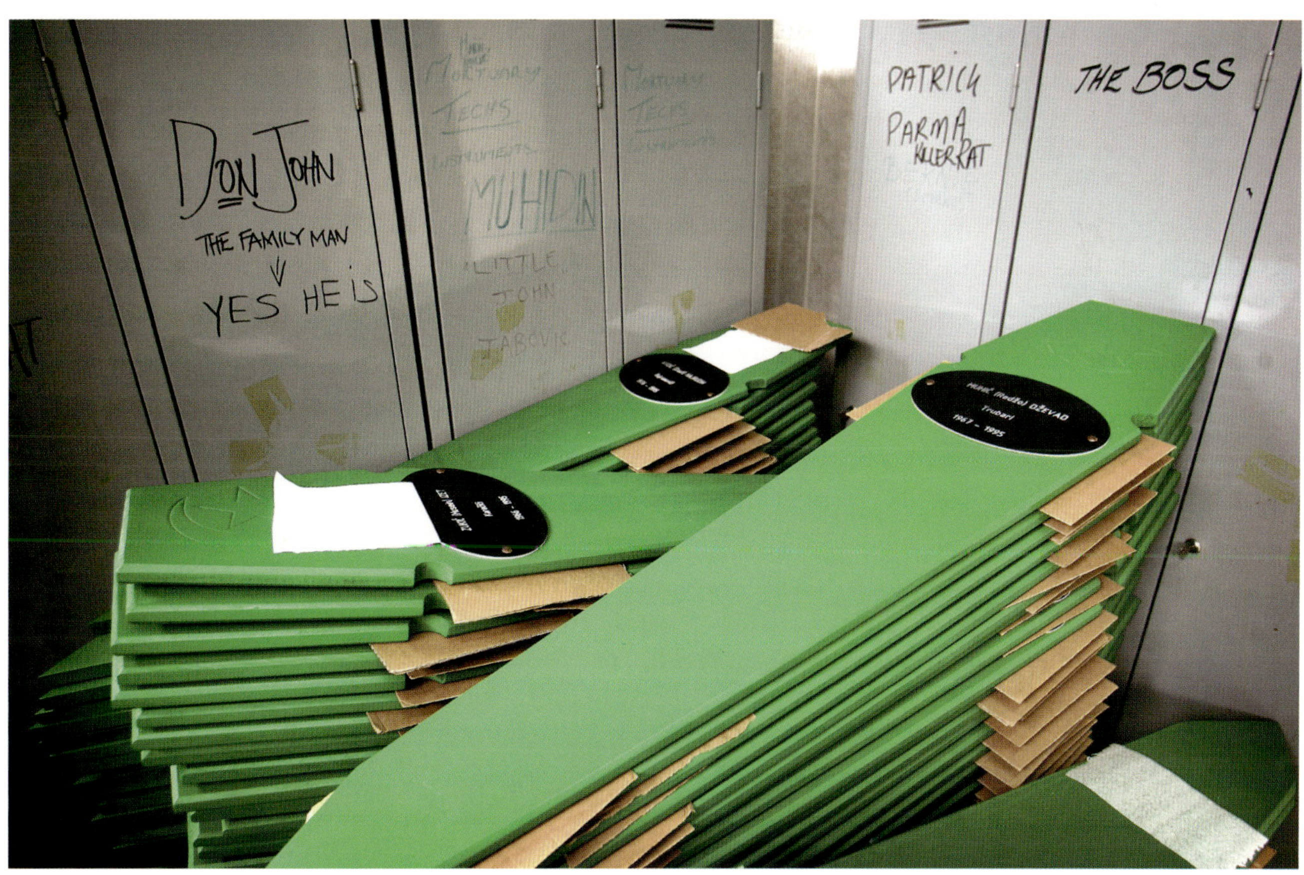
DON JOHN
THE FAMILY MAN
YES HE IS
MUHIDIN
PATRICK
PARMA
KILLER RAT
THE BOSS

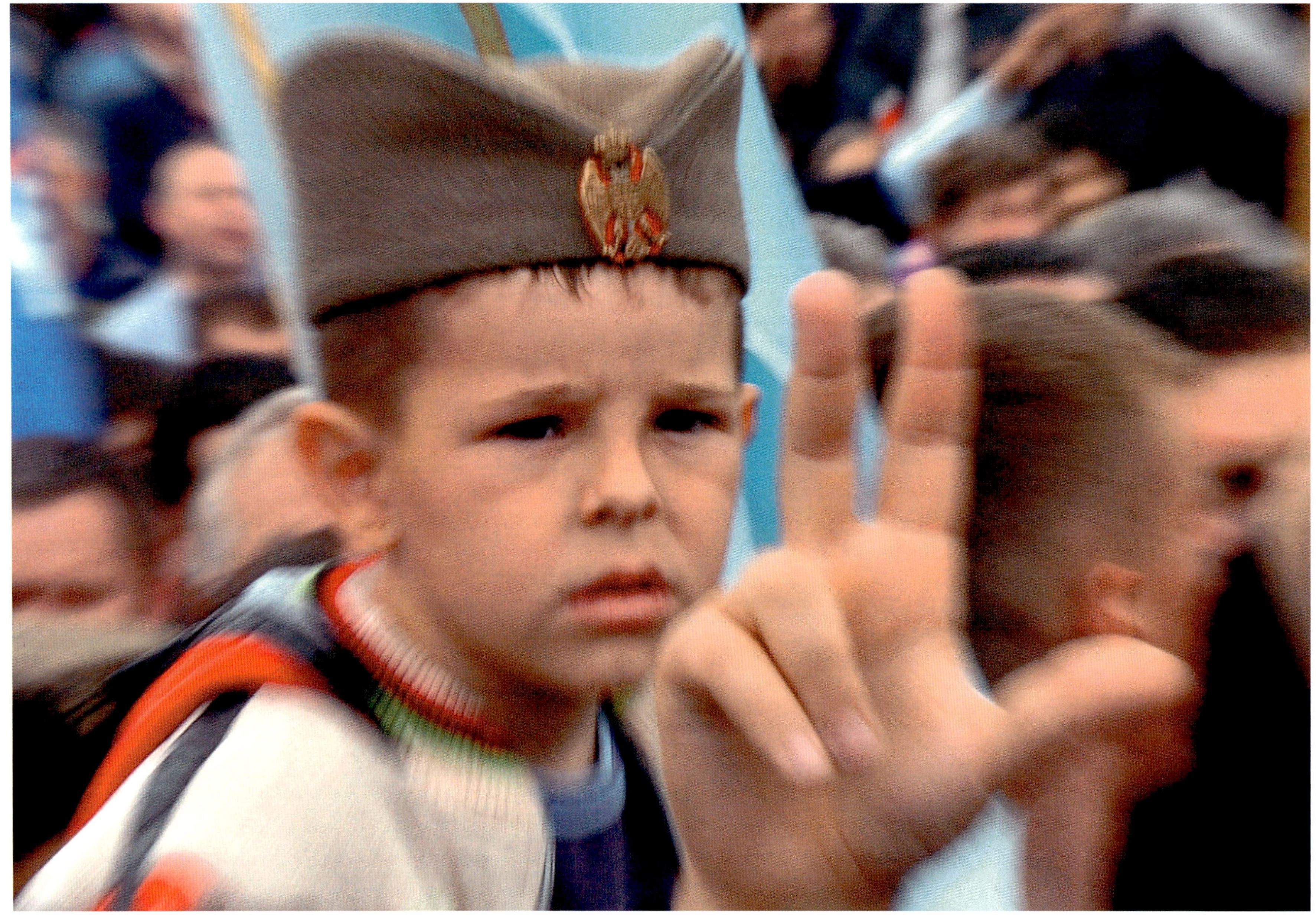

15 May 2005, RAVNA GORA, SERBIA

A young boy wearing a traditional Chetnik hat attends a rally at Ravna Gora in central Serbia. More than 20,000 supporters gathered to celebrate the role of the Chetnik Serb guerrilla movement in World War Two in a festival that was officially sponsored by the Serb government. The ultra-nationalist Chetniks are remembered by many in former Yugoslavia as backing the ruthless Nazi occupation. Although they began by fighting the Nazis, when the Allies switched their support to the communist Tito, the Chetniks changed sides and teamed up with Axis forces against their communist rivals. Milos Cvetkovic

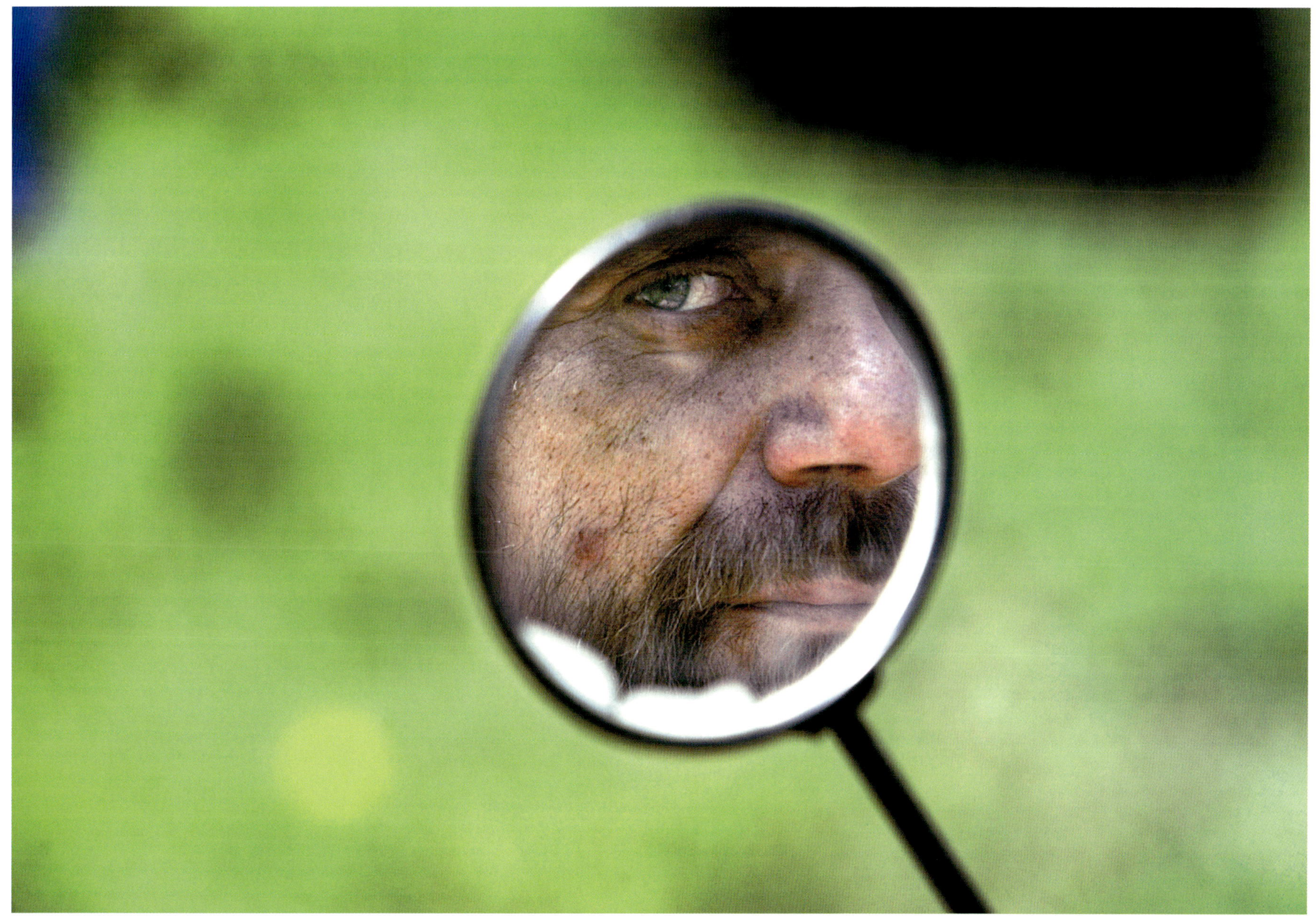

23 April 2005, PETROVO, BOSNIA

A supporter of the World War Two Chetnik guerrilla army is reflected in a wing mirror as he attends a ceremony in the central Bosnian village of Petrovo to unveil a plaque marking the 64th anniversary of the start of the Chetnik uprising, described by sympathizers as an uprising against the Nazis. For many in the Balkans, emblems such as the trademark Chetnik beard symbolize atrocities committed by Serb troops both from 1941 to 1945 and in the conflicts of the 1990s, after Yugoslavia broke up. When Croatia and Bosnia declared independence in 1991 and 1992 respectively, Serb paramilitary units used the Chetnik name and insignia as symbols of Serb pride, going on to commit some of the worst atrocities.
Damir Sagolj

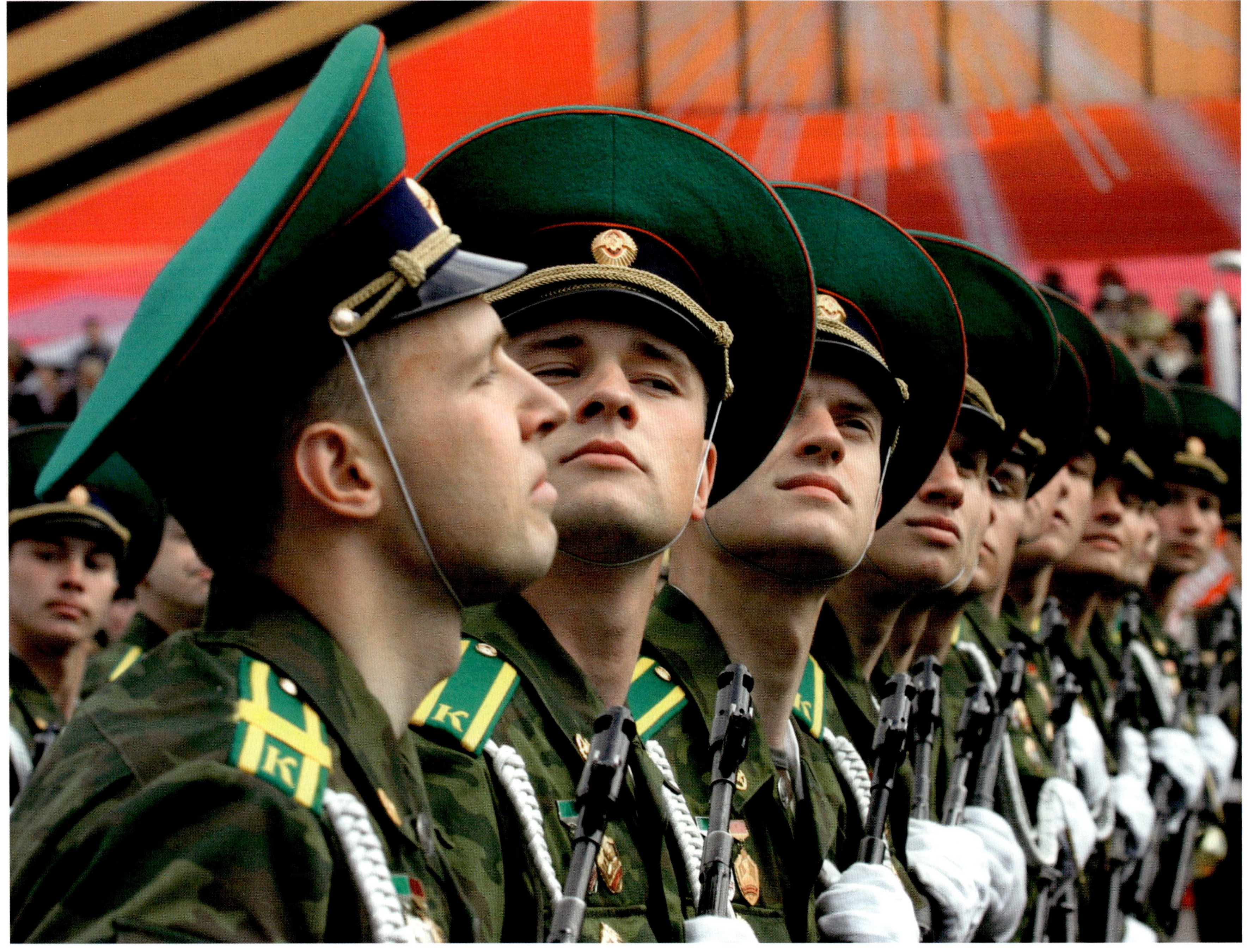

9 May 2005, MOSCOW, RUSSIA

Cadets take part in a military parade in Red Square as Russia marks the anniversary of its victory in World War Two with a display of patriotic pride and military pageantry in front of world leaders including U.S. President George W. Bush and China's Hu Jintao. The celebratory mood did not, however, quite mask political tensions between Russia and its Baltic neighbours, who say that the defeat of Nazi Germany meant for them the beginning of a second tyranny under Soviet communist rule. Russian President Vladimir Putin has refused their demand for public atonement. Grigory Dukor

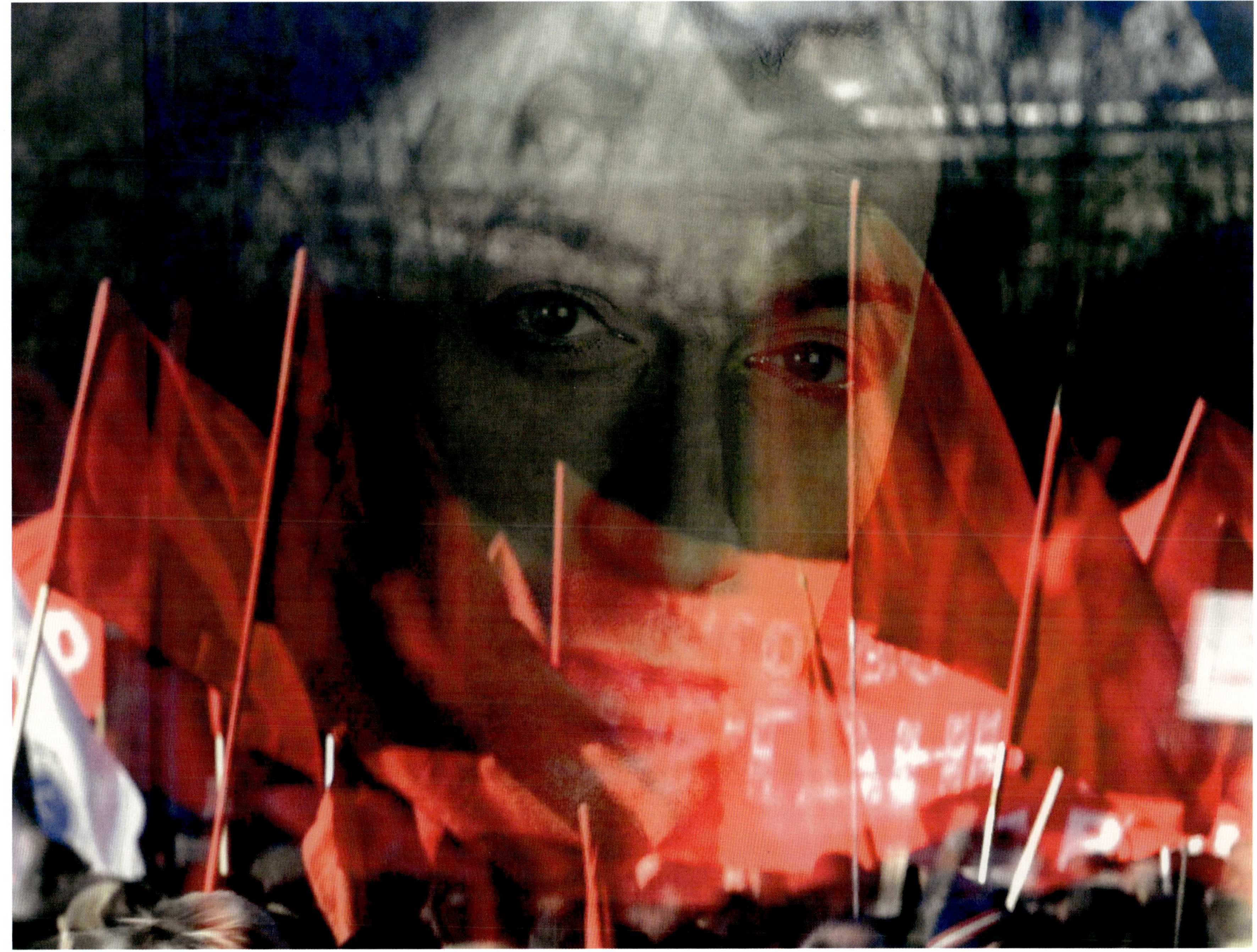

7 November 2002, MOSCOW, RUSSIA

Russian communist supporters march with flags past an advertisement in Moscow as they mark the 85th Anniversary of the 1917 Bolshevik revolution that brought Soviet state founder Vladimir Ilyich Lenin to power. The annual 7 November public holiday, renamed the Day of Reconciliation and Accord, survived for 12 years in the post-Soviet era until Russia's parliament voted in November 2004 to replace it with a holiday marking the day Moscow was liberated from Polish occupation in 1612. Viktor Korotayev

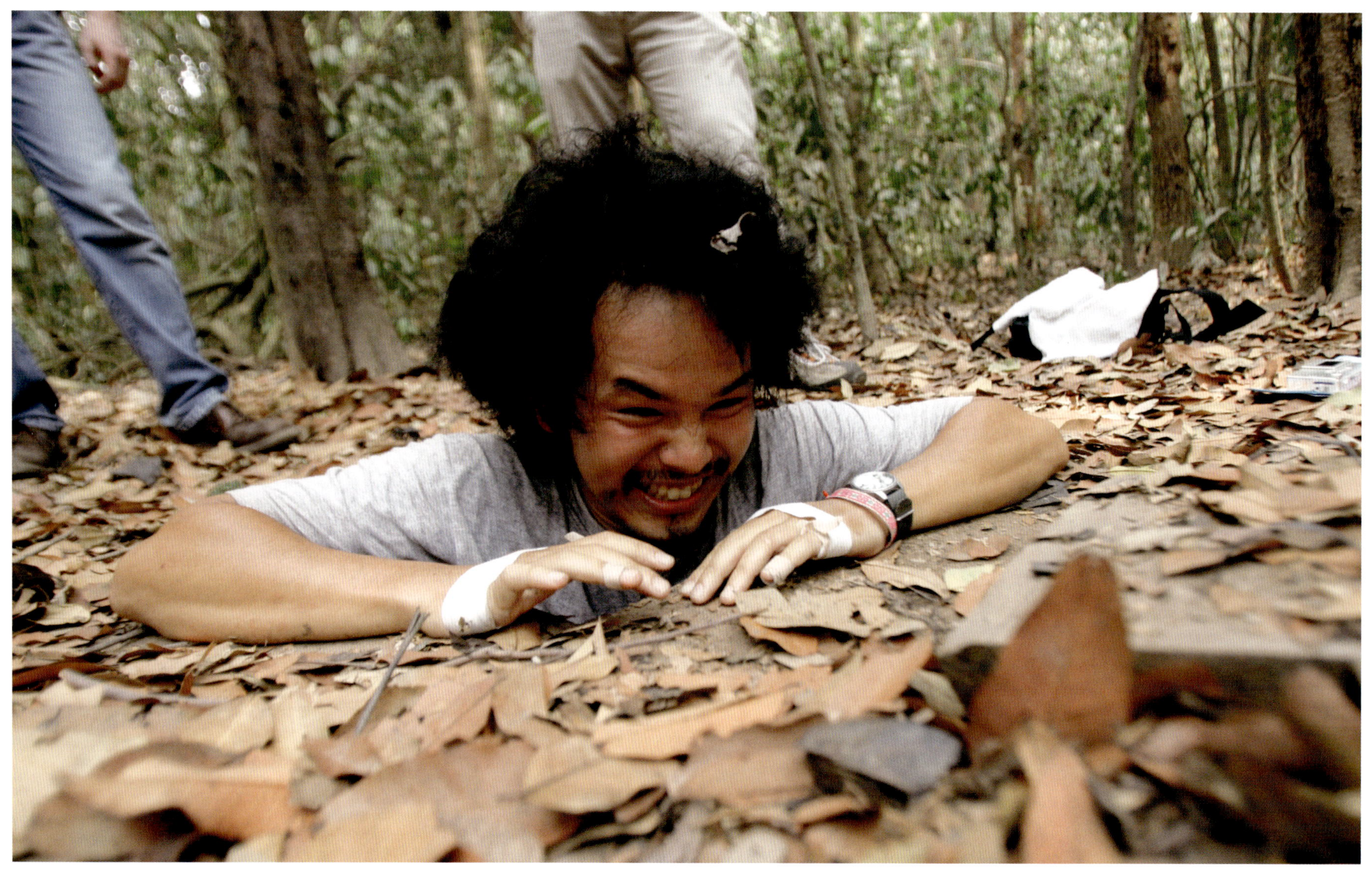

26 April 2005, CU CHI, VIETNAM

A Japanese tourist squeezes himself through a camouflaged hole in the ground during a guided tour of the Cu Chi tunnel network, about 70 km (40 miles) from Ho Chi Minh City – formerly Saigon, the capital of U.S.-backed South Vietnam. At the height of the Vietnam war, the Cu Chi network stretched for 250 km (155 miles). It included sections for living, dining, meeting and fighting, and allowed Vietcong guerrillas to communicate with far-flung units and launch surprise attacks, even within enemy bases. War tourism is now big business in Vietnam, and the Cu Chi tunnels are a major tourist attraction. Hundreds of U.S. veterans have been returning each year since relations between the two former enemies were normalized in the mid-1990s. Desmond Boylan

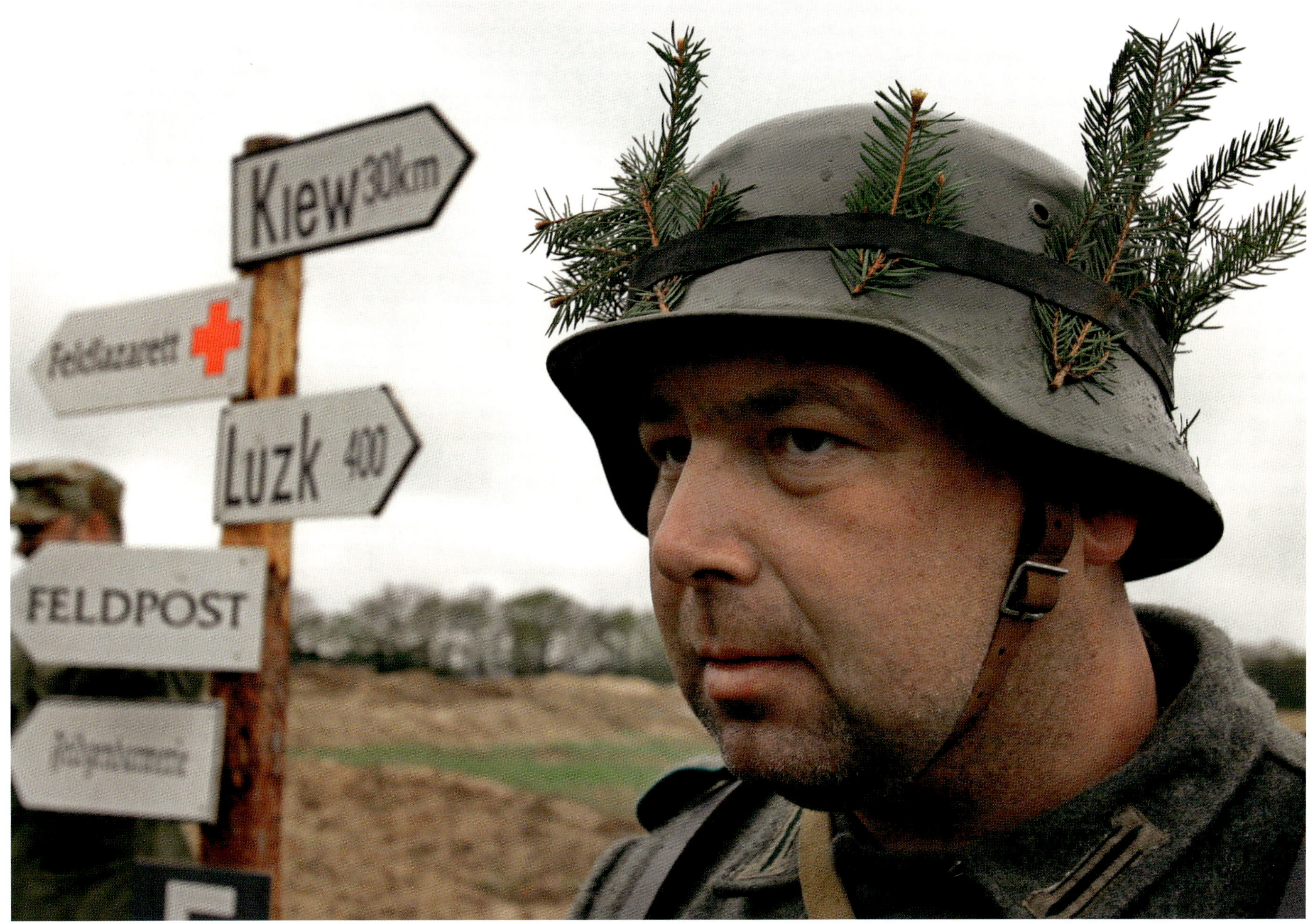

8 May 2005, NEAR KIEV, UKRAINE

A historical re-enactment of a World War Two battle that was staged near Kiev as Ukraine marked the 60th anniversary of the former Soviet Union's victory over Nazi Germany. Gleb Garanich

31 March 2004, BELFAST, UNITED KINGDOM

An actress wears 1912 period dress standing behind frosted glass during the opening of the 'Titanic At Home' exhibition in Robinson's Saloon, Belfast. Commemorating the ship which sank on its maiden voyage, 'Titanic at Home' told the story of the Titanic through the eyes of local people who helped build her or who sailed on her. Paul McErlane

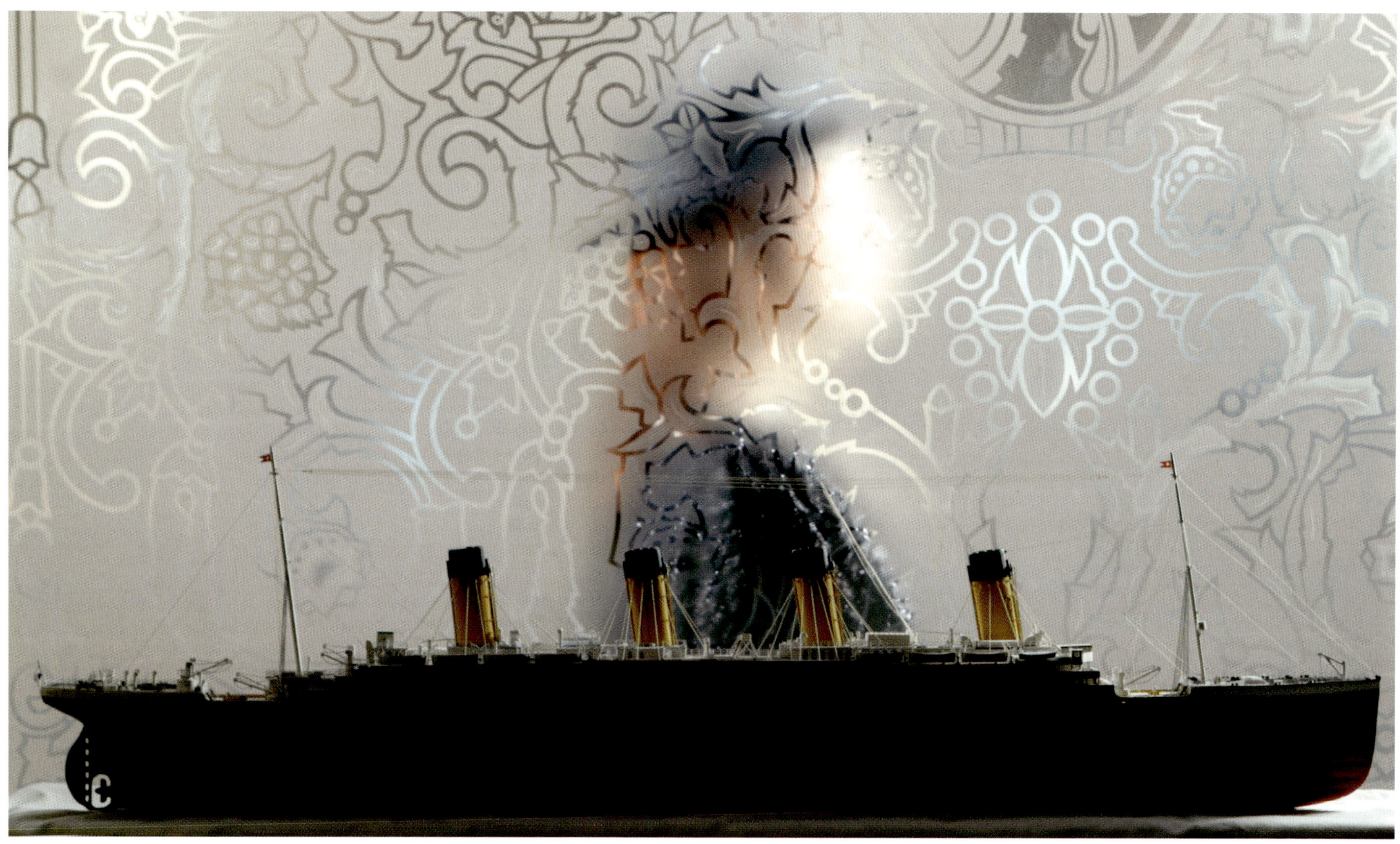

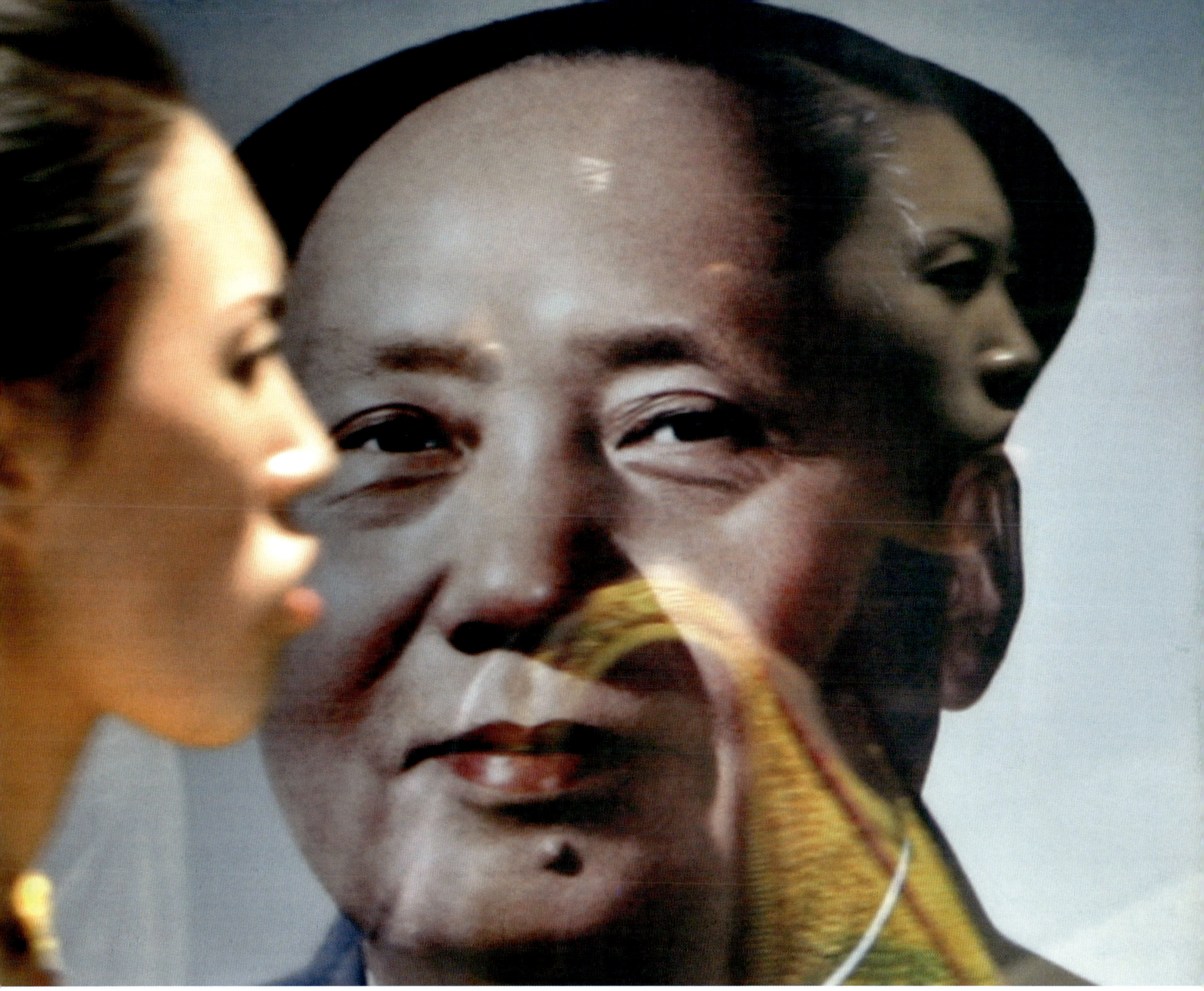

15 June 2005, BEIJING, CHINA

A Chinese woman walks past a window of a shop selling Mao Zedong memorabilia in Beijing. China is eager to boost 'red tourism' at communist heritage sites, many of them in still-poor rural areas. Jason Lee

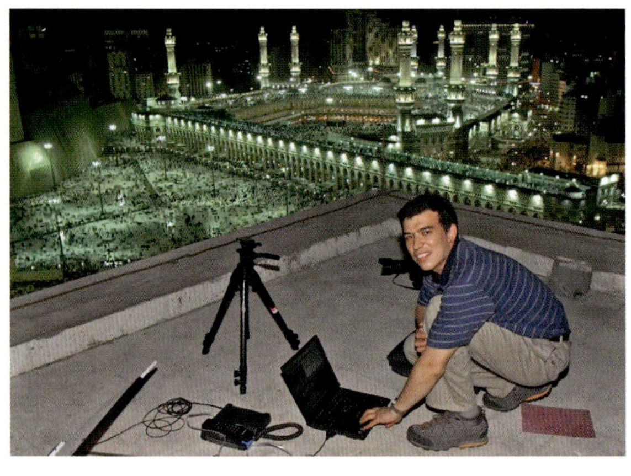
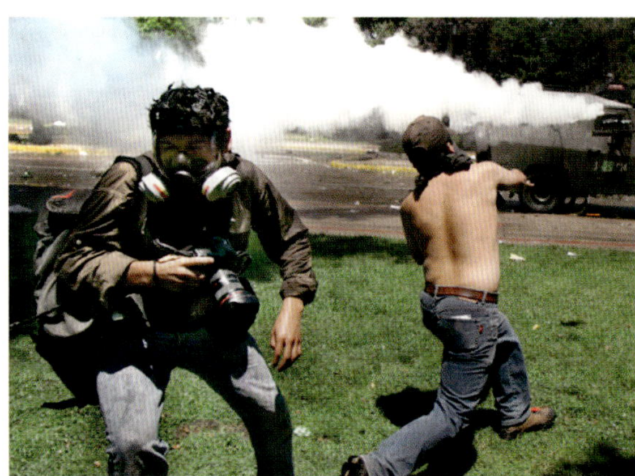
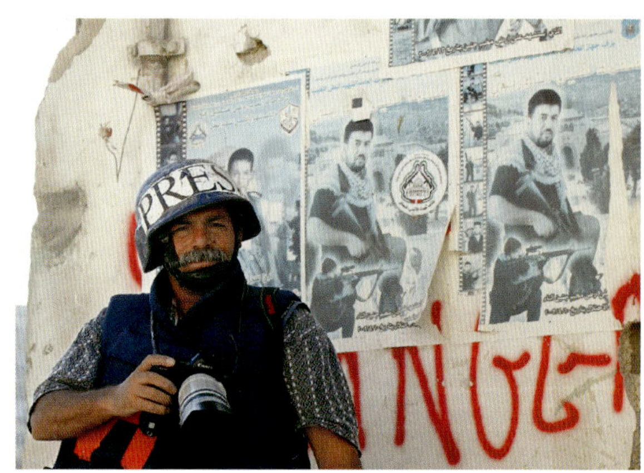
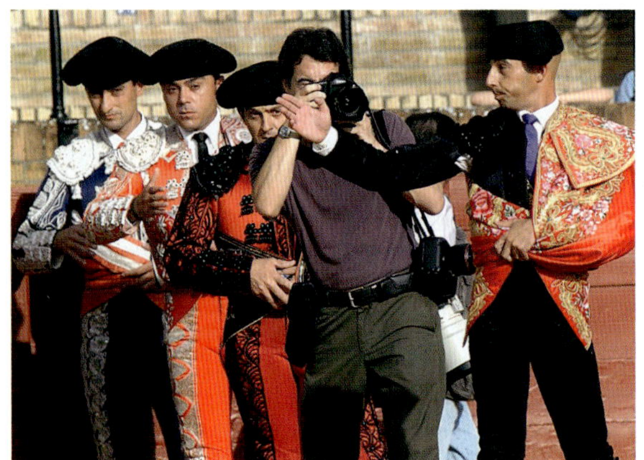
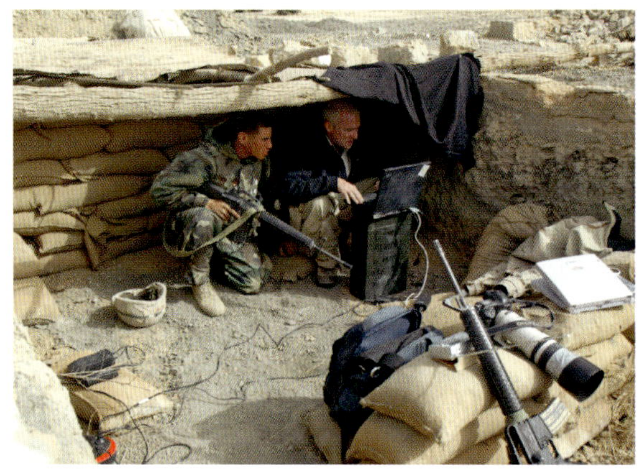
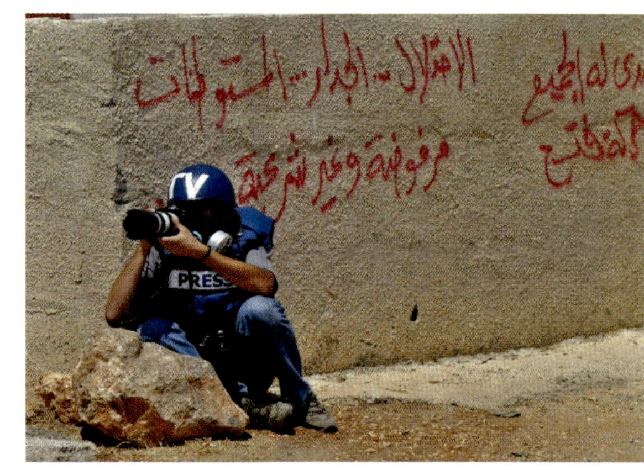
PRESS
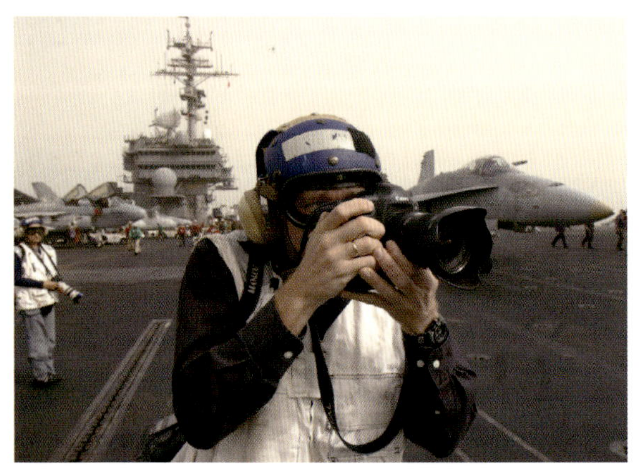
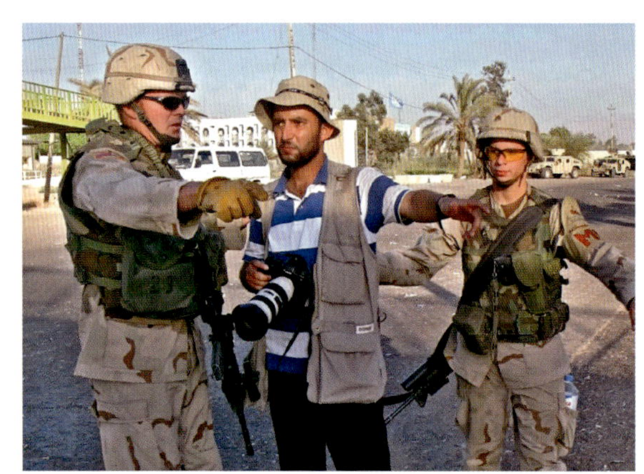
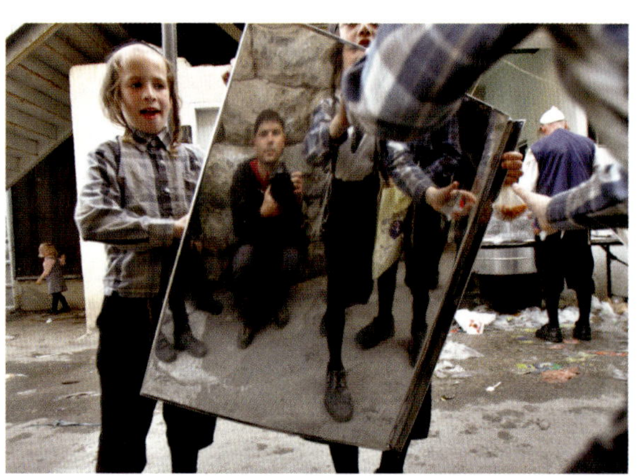
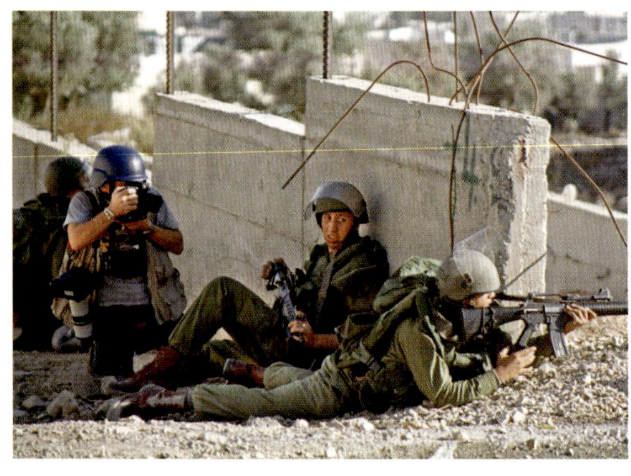
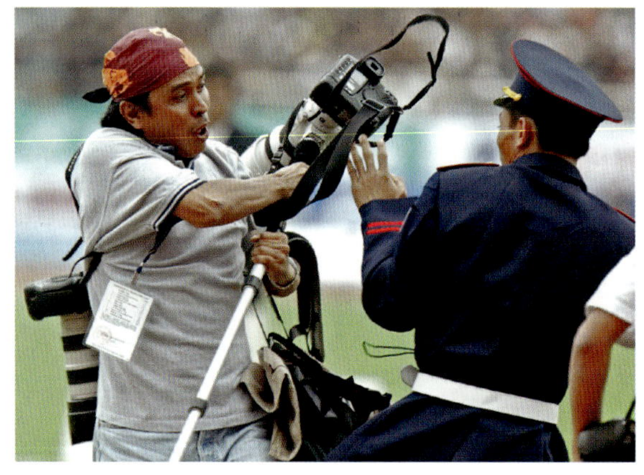
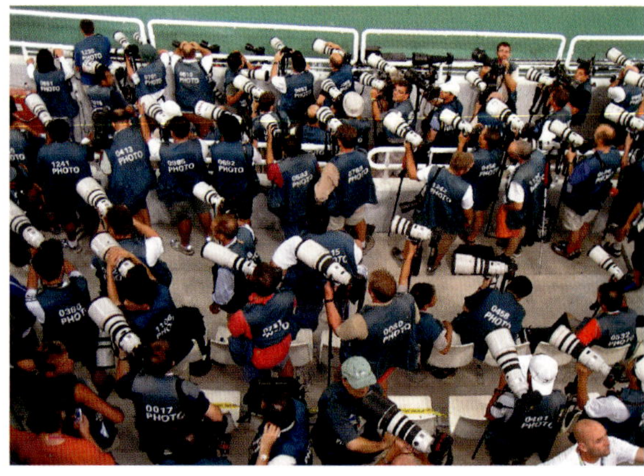

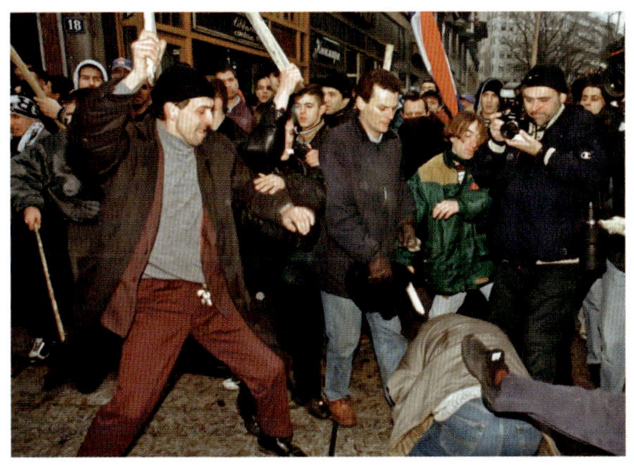

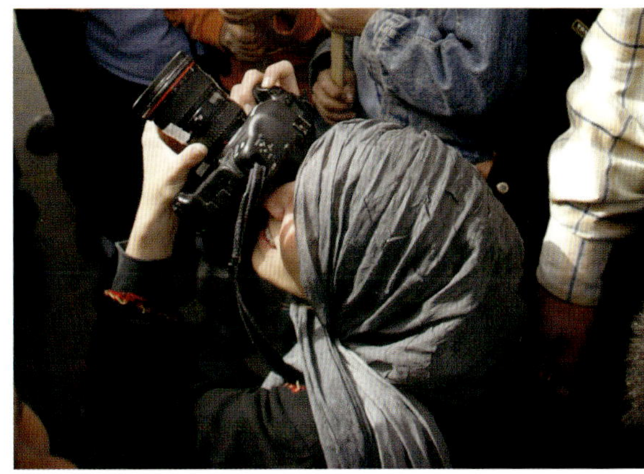

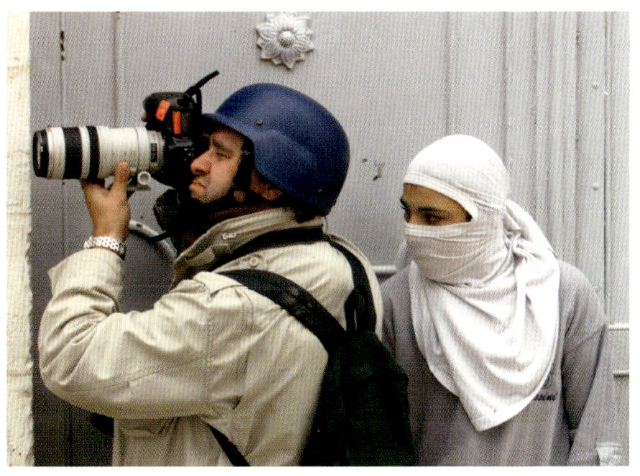

World Timeline of the Twenty-First Century

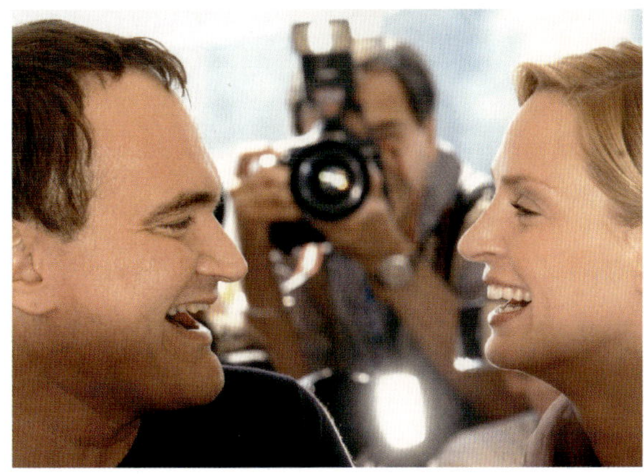

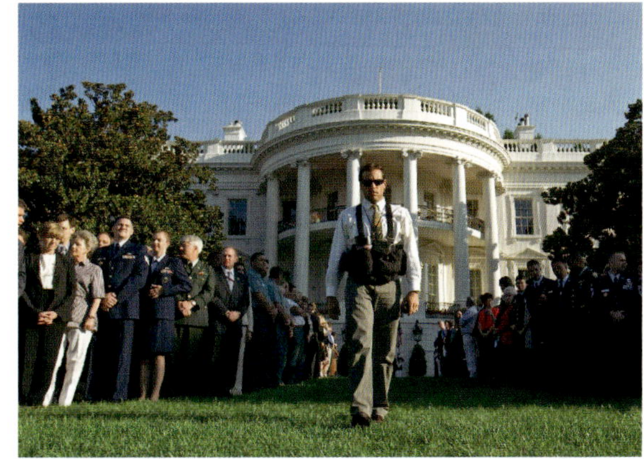

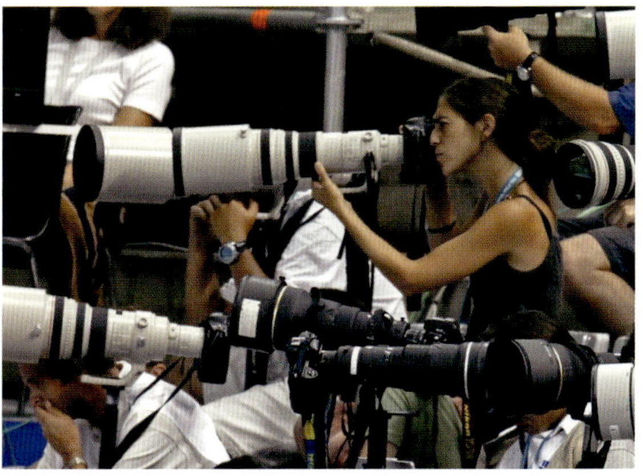

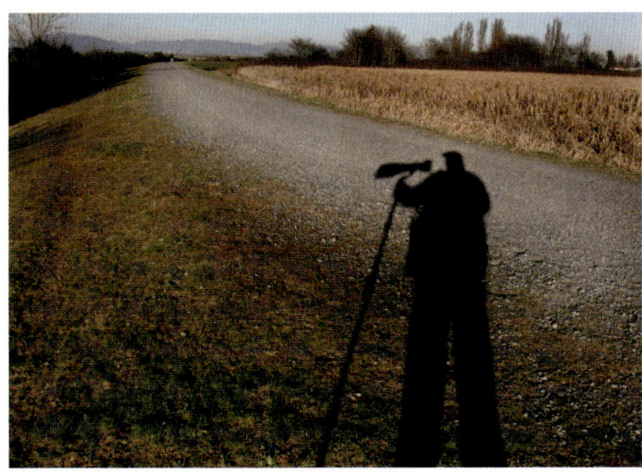

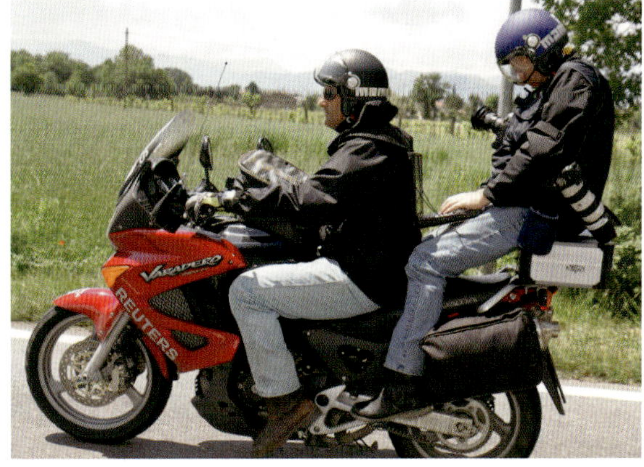

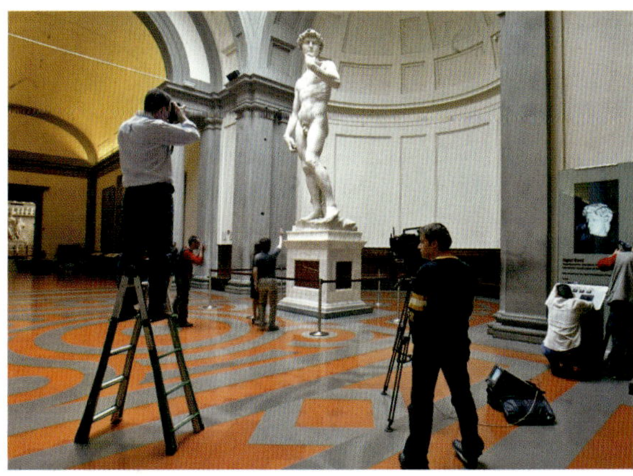

WORLD TIMELINE 2000

January

1 January WORLDWIDE
The third millennium dawns amid fireworks and revelry, but without any serious problems from the Y2K bug, which it had been feared could damage computers around the world.

10 January UNITED STATES
Internet services provider America Online Inc. says it will buy Time Warner Inc. for about $163 billion in what ranks as the largest merger deal ever.

24 January UNITED KINGDOM
Britain's EMI Group Plc and Time Warner Inc. announce the merger of their music businesses to create the world's biggest music group.

30 January KENYA
A Kenya Airways Airbus 310 en route to Nairobi with 179 passengers and crew on board slams into the sea killing 169.

23 February SPACE
The space shuttle Endeavour returns to earth having completed a mapping mission of the earth's surface.

March

12 March SPAIN
Conservative Prime Minister José María Aznar wins Spain's general election, securing the first outright majority in parliament since 1975.

14 March UNITED KINGDOM
PPL Therapeutics Plc, the British company that helped to clone Dolly the sheep, announces it has created the world's first cloned pigs. Five piglets were born on 5 March.

17 March UGANDA
Some 530 members of the obscure 'Ten Commandments of God' sect burn to death in a Ugandan church in an act of mass suicide. Around 900 cult members are eventually found dead.

11 April UNITED KINGDOM
British historian David Irving loses a libel action against a U.S. professor and her publishers who exposed him as a 'Holocaust denier'.

11 April SOUTH AFRICA
Disgraced South African captain Hansie Cronje admits receiving money from an Indian bookmaker in the worst scandal in cricketing history.

21 April UNITED NATIONS
U.N. Secretary-General Kofi Annan introduces a report for the twenty-first century, the most sweeping redefinition of the world organization's mission since its founding.

22 April CUBA/ UNITED STATES
Six-year-old castaway Elian Gonzalez is reunited with his father after being snatched from the home of his Miami relatives by U.S. agents. Enraged Cuban exiles take to the streets of Miami.

29 April IRAQ
Iraq reopens its national museum to the public for the first time since the Gulf war.

June

5 June RUSSIA
U.S. President Bill Clinton becomes the first major Western leader to address the Russian State Duma.

10 June SYRIA
President Hafez al-Assad dies in Damascus. Parliament amends the constitution to allow his son Bashar, 34, to succeed him.

19 June UNITED KINGDOM
Customs officers discover the bodies of 58 Chinese illegal immigrants crammed into a truck at the port of Dover. In April 2001 Dutch truck driver Perry Wacker is jailed for 14 years for their manslaughter.

26 June WORLDWIDE
An international team of scientists complete a working draft of the human genome, all the genes in the human body. This scientific milestone will transform the understanding of disease.

17 July GERMANY
Representatives from Germany, the U.S. and Israel sign an historic deal to pay 10 billion marks (U.S. $4.8 billion) in compensation to forced labourers under the Third Reich.

25 July FRANCE
An Air France Concorde airliner crashes after taking off from Paris bound for New York. All 109 people on board die, plus four on the ground.

28 July ITALY
L'Unità, the 76-year-old newspaper of the Italian left and once the mouthpiece of the West's largest Communist party, suspends publication due to lack of funding.

August

4 August UNITED KINGDOM
Britain's Queen Mother becomes the royal family's first centenarian, taking the nation's 100th birthday salute from the balcony of London's Buckingham Palace.

25 August ZIMBABWE
President Robert Mugabe gives notice that the government will appropriate 509 white-owned farms to resettle blacks as redress for the seizure of land by British colonialists over a century ago.

September

1 September BRAZIL
Twelve South American presidents sign a 'Declaration of Brasilia' which includes a pledge to unite South America's two main trade blocs in their first-ever summit in Brasilia.

3 September VATICAN
Despite protest from Jews and liberal Catholics, Pope John Paul II beatifies Pius IX, the nineteenth-century conservative pope accused of anti-Semitism.

7 September UNITED NATIONS
Cuban President Fidel Castro speaks for the first time with U.S. counterpart Bill Clinton; it is also believed to be the first time he has shaken the hand of a U.S. president since taking power in 1959.

28 September DENMARK
Denmark rejects the euro single currency in an historic referendum, with the anti-euro 'no' vote at 53.1% against 46.9% for 'yes'.

28 September ISRAEL/ PALESTINIAN TERRITORIES
Ariel Sharon visits the Temple Mount or al-Haram al-Sharif in East Jerusalem. Palestinians say the visit sparks their uprising or Intifada.

October

6 October YUGOSLAVIA
Opposition leader Vojislav Kostunica sweeps to power after an overnight uprising in an historic shift towards democracy after 13 turbulent years of rule by Slobodan Milosevic.

12 October YEMEN
Suicide bombers ram an explosives-laden rubber raft into U.S. destroyer Cole in the port of Aden, Yemen, killing 17 U.S. sailors. The attack is blamed on al Qaeda militants.

11 November AUSTRIA
A funicular train packed with skiers is destroyed in an Alpine tunnel blaze, killing 155 people.

13 November PHILIPPINES
Philippine President Joseph Estrada is impeached on charges of corruption by the country's House of Representatives amid scenes of pandemonium.

17 November UNITED STATES
Coca-Cola Co. agrees to pay a record $192.5 million to settle a racial bias case covering hundreds of black workers, eclipsing the previous record payout of $176.1 million.

19 November VIETNAM
U.S. President Bill Clinton ends his historic three-day visit to Vietnam. Clinton is the first serving U.S. president to visit since the end of the Vietnam war.

27 November NORWAY
Norway's King Harald opens the world's longest road tunnel in west Norway. The Laerdal Tunnel at 24.5 km (15.2 miles) beats the 16.9 km (10.5 mile) St Gotthard tunnel in Switzerland.

31 January UNITED KINGDOM
Family doctor Harold Shipman is jailed for life for murdering 15 mainly elderly patients with lethal injections of heroin. Authorities say the so-called 'Dr Death' probably killed over 250 in all.

February

4 February AUSTRIA
A coalition of conservatives and Jörg Haider's far-right Freedom Party takes office amid a storm of protest. Israel withdraws its ambassador and EU nations impose diplomatic sanctions.

4 February GERMANY
Vodafone AirTouch Plc agrees a 180 billion euro (U.S. $178.7 billion) merger with Germany's Mannesmann AG to create Europe's biggest telecoms company.

6 February FINLAND
Foreign Minister Tarja Halonen wins a presidential election to become Finland's first woman president.

26 March ISRAEL
Pope John Paul II ends a week-long pilgrimage to the Holy Land, where he has visited sacred Christian shrines in Jordan, Israel and the Palestinian territories.

26 March RUSSIA
Acting Russian President Vladimir Putin wins the presidential elections.

26 March UNITED STATES
American Beauty sweeps the board at the Academy Awards, winning Oscars for best picture, best director and best actor.

April

10 April GERMANY
Angela Merkel becomes the first woman to lead a German political party when the opposition Christian Democrats vote overwhelmingly for her at a party conference.

May

4 May WORLDWIDE
The 'Love Bug' computer virus infects computers around the world.

11 May INDIA
India welcomes its billionth citizen. The child, named Astha – Hindi for faith – is born in New Delhi.

24 May ISRAEL / LEBANON
Israel ends its 22-year occupation of south Lebanon in a rushed evacuation after the collapse of its South Lebanon Army (SLA) local militia the previous day.

29 May FIJI
Fiji's military announces it is taking over the government of the country and imposes a curfew. On 30 May they scrap the constitution which allowed an ethnic Indian to be premier.

29 June UNITED STATES
A first printing of the U.S. Declaration of Independence fetches $8.14 million in a Sotheby's online auction, breaking the record for any sale on the Internet.

July

1 July DENMARK
Queen Margrethe of Denmark and King Carl Gustaf of Sweden open the longest cable-stayed bridge in the world, marking the first time Sweden has been directly linked to Europe in 7,000 years.

3 July MEXICO
In an historic presidential ballot, opposition candidate Vicente Fox beats Francisco Labastida of the Institutional Revolutionary Party, ending its 71-year hold on power.

12 July JAPAN
Japan's Snow Brand Milk Products Co. Ltd closes all its 21 plants after more than 14,550 people fall ill with food poisoning after drinking tainted milk from its Osaka plant.

5 August ISRAEL / LEBANON
Almost 400 U.N. troops complete deployment along the Lebanese–Israeli border, following Israel's 24 May withdrawal from southern Lebanon.

7 August SPACE
International teams of astronomers in Geneva and California discover eight new planets outside our solar system, none of them ever seen by humans before.

12 August RUSSIA
The Russian navy's nuclear submarine Kursk sinks in the Barents Sea after an explosion. All 118 crew on board are killed.

14 August RUSSIA
The Russian Orthodox Church declares the last tsar, Nicholas II, and his family saints, 82 years after their murder by a Bolshevik firing squad in July 1918.

16 August UNITED KINGDOM
British Airways grounds its Concorde fleet immediately after learning the Civil Aviation Authority is to withdraw its airworthiness certificate.

8 September IRAN / ALGERIA
Iran and Algeria agree to restore full diplomatic relations after a decade of recriminations on both sides.

8 September UNITED NATIONS
The largest gathering of world leaders in history ends at a U.N. Millennium Summit. A Millennium Declaration pledges a renewed drive for peace, security and the eradication of poverty.

15 September EUROPE
Truckers in Spain, Ireland and Poland join Europe-wide protests against high petrol prices while Belgium and Britain struggle to recover from days of fuel blockades.

15 September AUSTRALIA
The Sydney Olympic Games are officially opened with the lighting of the Olympic flame by Aboriginal athlete Cathy Freeman, the world 400m champion.

15 September FRANCE / SPAIN
Spain's most wanted fugitive, Ignacio Gracia Arregui, suspected leader of the Basque guerrilla group ETA, is arrested in the French Basque town of Bidart.

15 October POLAND
Lech Walesa, the founder of Poland's Solidarity trade union, says he is withdrawing from political life after his disastrous showing in presidential elections.

18 October UNITED STATES / CUBA
The U.S. Senate overwhelmingly approves legislation allowing sales of U.S. food and medicine to Cuba, a landmark change in the four-decade-old embargo of the island.

31 October SPACE
A Soyuz TM-31 rocket blasts off to the $60 billion International Space Station carrying two Russians and an American who will become the first people to live on the station.

November

7 November UNITED STATES
Hillary Clinton beats her Republican opponent to win a U.S. Senate seat for New York. She is the only first lady ever to seek or win public office.

28 November ITALY
Italy and Spain sign an accord to create a 'Common Judicial Space' which will allow them to bypass extradition and help bring fugitive mafiosi and terrorists to justice.

December

13 December UNITED STATES
Democrat Al Gore abandons his fight for the White House after the 7 November presidential election is too close to call.

25 December CHINA
At least 309 people, including young revellers at a Christmas Day disco party, are killed when fire sweeps through a commercial centre in the city of Luoyang.

27 December GEORGIA
Georgia's Communists vote to 'rehabilitate' fellow countryman Josef Stalin, and say they believe the disgraced Soviet dictator is a role model for Russian President Vladimir Putin.

WORLD TIMELINE 2001

January

1 January NETHERLANDS
Thirteen people are killed and 180 injured in a fire in a cafe packed with teenagers celebrating the New Year in Volendam.

2 January TAIWAN / CHINA
The first Taiwanese boats in more than 50 years make legal, direct trips to the Chinese mainland, docking in the southeastern province of Fujian.

16 January DEMOCRATIC REPUBLIC OF CONGO
President Laurent Kabila is fatally shot by one of his bodyguards, plunging the war-ravaged African country into fresh uncertainty.

20 January UNITED STATES
President Bill Clinton leaves office as George W. Bush is inaugurated as the 43rd president after one of the most contentious elections in U.S. history.

12 February UNITED STATES
International scientists celebrate the publication of the sequencing of the human genetic code. The human genome, the book of life, will revolutionize research and medicine.

12 February UNITED STATES
A federal court rules that the free Internet song-swapping service Napster must stop its millions of users from exchanging copyright material.

21 February INDIA
The Maha Kumbh Mela Hindu festival winds down. Organizers say almost 100 million pilgrims have taken a sin-cleansing dip in the holy Ganges river since the festival began on 9 January.

21 February UNITED KINGDOM
Britain uncovers its first cases of foot-and-mouth disease for 20 years. The European Commission bans exports of live animals, fresh meat and milk from Britain.

March

1 April YUGOSLAVIA
Former President Slobodan Milosevic, the central figure in a decade of war in the Balkans, is arrested and jailed after a 36-hour armed stand-off with the reformists who ousted him last year.

1 April CHINA / UNITED STATES
A U.S. Navy surveillance plane makes an emergency landing on the Chinese island of Hainan after a mid-air collision with a Chinese F-8 fighter. China accuses the U.S. of ramming its aircraft.

25 April PHILIPPINES
Police arrest former President Joseph Estrada on a charge of plundering the economy, after dispersing hundreds of his supporters outside his Manila home.

May

8 May SYRIA
Pope John Paul II ends an historic visit to Syria, where he became the first pope to enter a mosque. He departs with a plea for Jews and Arabs to work for peace.

1 June ISRAEL
A Palestinian suicide bomber kills himself and 21 other people at a Tel Aviv nightclub.

4 June NEPAL
New King Dipendra dies. Rioting breaks out in Kathmandu hours after second new king, Gyanendra, younger brother of Birendra, is crowned.

7 June UNITED STATES
President George W. Bush signs into law the biggest tax cut in two decades, a sweeping $1.35 trillion bill lowering U.S. income taxes across the board.

8 June UNITED KINGDOM
Prime Minister Tony Blair wins an historic second term in power by a huge margin, prompting opposition Conservative leader William Hague to announce his resignation.

16 June ITALY
The Leaning Tower of Pisa is officially handed back to the city after 11 years of work to prevent it from toppling over.

20 July ITALY
Italian anti-globalization protester Carlo Giuliani dies after being shot by Italian paramilitary when protests against the Group of Eight annual summit in Genoa turn to violent rioting.

24 July BULGARIA
Bulgaria's parliament approves former King Simeon II as the new prime minister. Simeon Saxe-Coburg is the only ex-monarch to regain power in post-communist Europe.

August

1 August ARGENTINA
Tony Blair makes the first visit to Argentina by a British prime minister since the 1982 Falklands war and says it is time to recognize that 'the past is the past'.

2 August NETHERLANDS
Bosnian Serb General Radislav Krstic is jailed for 46 years for the murder of thousands of Muslims in the Srebrenica massacre, Europe's worst atrocity since World War Two.

9 September AFGHANISTAN
Ahmad Shah Masood, the guerrilla commander leading the fight against the ruling Taliban, is fatally wounded in a suicide bomb attack in his office in the far north of Afghanistan.

11 September UNITED STATES
Three hijacked planes crash into New York's World Trade Center twin towers and the Pentagon. A fourth plane crashes in Pennsylvania. In total 2,973 people are killed.

12 September BELGIUM
NATO invokes its mutual defence clause for the first time in its 52-year history, opening the way for a possible collective military response to the attacks of 9/11.

15 September UNITED STATES
President George W. Bush says that the United States is 'at war' after 9/11, singling out Saudi-born militant Osama bin Laden, based in Afghanistan, as a prime suspect behind the attacks.

October

12 October NORWAY
Secretary-General Kofi Annan and the United Nations win the Nobel Peace prize.

23 October UNITED KINGDOM
The Irish Republican Army says it has begun to disarm, an unprecedented step towards ending decades of bloodshed in Northern Ireland. The province's coalition government resumes business.

23 October UNITED STATES
Apple introduces its iPod, a portable digital music player that can hold an entire music collection, sparking a global fashion trend.

27 October SWEDEN
Christer Pettersson, who in 1989 was cleared by an appeal court of the 1986 assassination of Prime Minister Olof Palme, is quoted in Swedish media saying he did carry out the murder.

November

27 November SPACE
NASA announces that the Hubble Space Telescope has spied the atmosphere of a planet 150 light-years away, the first time the atmosphere of a planet outside our solar system has been directly detected.

28 November GERMANY
Germany warns the U.S. against expanding its war on terrorism in Afghanistan to countries such as Iraq and Somalia as it may trigger a wider conflict in the Middle East.

December

2 December UNITED STATES
U.S. energy trader Enron, burdened with at least $16.8 billion in debt, files for Chapter 11 bankruptcy, the biggest in U.S. history.

7 December AFGHANISTAN
Taliban rule over their last bastion of Kandahar in southern Afghanistan ends with their forces laying down arms.

20 January PHILIPPINES
Vice President Gloria Arroyo is sworn in as president of the Philippines after the Supreme Court rules that disgraced President Joseph Estrada is unfit to hold office.

31 January NETHERLANDS
Abdel Basset Al-Megrahi is jailed for life for the murder of 270 people when Pan Am flight 103 was blown up over Lockerbie, Scotland, in 1988. Britain demands compensation from Libya.

February

6 February ISRAEL
Likud leader Ariel Sharon is elected Israeli prime minister as voters reject Ehud Barak.

10 February SPACE
The International Space Station becomes the largest structure in space with the addition of the $1.4 billion science module Destiny.

13 March AFGHANISTAN
The ruling Taliban complete the destruction of two giant ancient statues of the Buddha in Bamiyan, part of a policy of destroying all statues in the country.

15 March BRAZIL
Blasts tear through a 40-storey-high offshore oil rig owned by Brazil's state oil firm Petrobas, killing 11 people. The rig, the world's biggest, sinks five days later.

23 March FIJI
Remnants of Russia's Mir space station plunge into the Pacific Ocean, after engineers end the laboratory's 15-year mission in space.

25 March UNITED STATES
Gladiator wins five Oscars, just ahead of *Crouching Tiger, Hidden Dragon* and *Traffic*, both of which net four.

April

9 May GHANA
A stampede at Accra's main soccer stadium when police fire teargas at rioting fans leaves 126 people dead. It is Africa's worst soccer disaster.

13 May ITALY
Silvio Berlusconi wins the general election at the head of a centre-right alliance that will form Italy's 59th government since 1945.

22 May AFGHANISTAN
The ruling Taliban order the country's Hindu minority to wear yellow badges to identify themselves, sparking an international chorus of condemnation.

June

1 June NEPAL
King Birendra, Queen Aishwarya and six other family members are killed by their son, Crown Prince Dipendra, who then turns the gun on himself. He is briefly declared king while in a coma.

20 June PAKISTAN
Military ruler Pervez Musharraf is formally sworn in as president, replacing Mohammad Rafiq Tarar, the figurehead president since Musharraf seized power in 1999.

29 June UNITED NATIONS
U.N. Secretary-General Kofi Annan is endorsed by the 189-member General Assembly for a second five-year term.

July

2 July UNITED STATES
The world's first self-contained mechanical heart is implanted into a patient in a seven-hour operation by University of Louisville surgeons Laman Gray and Robert Dowling.

3 July NETHERLANDS
Slobodan Milosevic makes a defiant appearance at the war crimes tribunal in The Hague, calling it an illegal body set up by his Western enemies. His refusal to enter a plea is treated as 'not guilty'.

10 August ANGOLA
Up to 252 people are killed when a train is attacked by UNITA rebels south of Luanda, one of the bloodiest incidents in the country's long-running civil war.

27 August WEST BANK
Abu Ali Mustafa, leader of the Popular Front for the Liberation of Palestine, is killed in an Israeli missile attack in Ramallah. Israel accused him of masterminding a wave of bombings.

September

2 September SOUTH AFRICA
Israel is branded a 'racist apartheid state' by non-governmental organizations meeting on the margin of the U.N. World Conference Against Racism in Durban. The U.S. and Israel pull out of the event.

7 September NIGERIA
Christian–Muslim violence flares after Muslim prayers in the city of Jos, with churches and mosques set on fire. The Red Cross says at least 500 people are killed.

1 October PHILIPPINES
Ex-President Joseph Estrada goes on trial for economic plunder. Ousted in a 'people power' revolt in January, Estrada is accused of amassing over 4 billion pesos (U.S. $78 million) while in office.

7 October AFGHANISTAN
U.S. air strikes begin against 31 military targets, with British involvement. Raids kill the 10-year-old son of Taliban leader Mullah Mohammad Omar.

7 October AFGHANISTAN
Osama bin Laden taunts U.S. President George W. Bush in a dramatic videotape, saying America will not live in peace until Palestinians do.

9 October PAKISTAN
Javed Iqbal, sentenced to be strangled, chopped into 100 pieces and dissolved in acid for the murders of dozens of children, is found dead in his cell in an apparent suicide.

10 October UNITED STATES
The White House releases a list of 22 'most wanted terrorists' as a worldwide hunt is broadened beyond Osama bin Laden, whom President George W. Bush has already said he wants 'dead or alive'.

9 November GERMANY
The first synagogue built in the former East Germany since the Nazi era is dedicated in Dresden 63 years after its predecessor was burnt down during the Kristallnacht rampage against Jews.

12 November UNITED STATES
An American Airlines Airbus A-300-600 crashes into the New York borough of Queens, sparking initial fears of another attack. At least 265 people are killed in the accident.

13 November AFGHANISTAN
Opposition fighters capture Kabul in defiance of international pressure to stay out. The Northern Alliance later invite all factions apart from the Taliban to Kabul to discuss forming a new government.

21 November UNITED STATES
A 94-year-old woman from Connecticut becomes the fifth person in the U.S. to die from inhaling anthrax in a baffling case that revives fears of bioterrorism following the 9/11 attacks.

22 November VATICAN
In his first message sent to the world directly over the Internet, Pope John Paul II apologizes to victims of sexual abuse by priests and other clergy.

11 December CHINA
China becomes a member of the World Trade Organization.

13 December INDIA
Armed men open fire in India's parliament complex. Fourteen people are killed, including the five gunmen, in an unprecedented attack on the seat of power in the world's biggest democracy.

20 December ARGENTINA
The economy minister quits after 27 people die in unrest triggered by his austerity measures. Fernando de la Rua later steps down as president, as does the new president just days later.

22 December AFGHANISTAN
A six-month interim administration is sworn in, led by Hamid Karzai, a tribal leader of the Pashtun, Afghanistan's largest ethnic group.

29 December PERU
More than 300 people are killed when a fire roars through a crowded shopping area in the Peruvian capital Lima. The blaze started with an explosion at a shop selling fireworks for New Year parties.

WORLD TIMELINE 2002

January

1 January EUROPEAN UNION
300 million people in 12 countries first use the new currency the euro. Only EU members Sweden, Denmark and Britain retain their own national currencies.

5 January NEPAL
Pakistan President Pervez Musharraf shakes hands with Indian Prime Minister Atal Behari Vajpayee at a summit, despite India's refusal to hold peace talks to end the countries' massive military build-up.

21 January EGYPT
Senior Jewish, Muslim and Christian religious leaders from the Holy Land call for a ceasefire and a return to peace talks during the first interfaith conference of its kind in Alexandria.

22 January RUSSIA
Russia abruptly pulls the plug on the country's only nationwide independent television station, giving the Kremlin a monopoly of the airwaves for the first time since the Soviet era.

12 February NETHERLANDS
The trial of Slobodan Milosevic opens in The Hague. He is charged with crimes against humanity in Croatia and Kosovo and genocide in the 1992–95 Bosnian war.

20 February EGYPT
An inferno engulfs a packed passenger train heading from Cairo to Luxor, killing 361 people and injuring 60 in Egypt's worst rail disaster.

22 February PAKISTAN
U.S. and Pakistani officials announce that journalist Daniel Pearl, kidnapped while trying to contact Islamic radical groups, was murdered by his captors, who recorded his death on videotape.

23 February ANGOLA
Jonas Savimbi is confirmed dead by his UNITA rebel movement after television networks show his bullet-riddled body. He was killed by government troops the previous day.

March

19 March ZIMBABWE
Zimbabwe is suspended from the Commonwealth for one year following President Robert Mugabe's controversial victory in elections.

24 March UNITED STATES
For the first time two black actors win Oscars for best actor and best actress: Denzel Washington for *Training Day* and Halle Berry for *Monster's Ball*. *A Beautiful Mind* wins best picture.

27 March ISRAEL
A suicide bomber blows himself up in the lobby of the seaside Park Hotel in the resort town of Netanya, killing 28 people and wounding more than 100. Hamas claims responsibility.

30 March UNITED KINGDOM
Queen Elizabeth the Queen Mother dies at the age of 101. Thousands of mourners line the streets of London for her funeral on 9 April.

April

1 May WORLDWIDE
Nationalists, anarchists, pacifists and environmentalists join traditional May Day marches across the world. In France more than a million take to the streets to protest against Jean-Marie Le Pen.

3 May EUROPE
Foreign ministers and representatives from the Council of Europe, a human rights watchdog, sign a document pledging the total abolition of the death penalty, even in times of war.

5 May FRANCE
France says 'No' to extreme-right leader Jean-Marie Le Pen in a presidential election that sweeps conservative incumbent Jacques Chirac to victory with more than 80% of the vote.

6 May MYANMAR
National League for Democracy leader Aung San Suu Kyi is freed after 19 months of house arrest. She tells supporters she will continue to fight for democracy in the military-ruled country.

6 May NETHERLANDS
Dutch anti-immigrant politician Pim Fortuyn is shot dead in Hilversum, days before a national election.

June

15 June UNITED STATES
A federal jury finds accounting firm Andersen guilty of obstructing justice in the investigation of its client, Enron Corp.

30 June JAPAN
Brazil wins the 2002 World Cup final, beating Germany 2–0.

July

1 July NETHERLANDS
The new International Criminal Court, the first permanent world tribunal set up to prosecute individuals for war crimes, officially comes into being.

19 August POLAND
Pope John Paul II, wrapping up an emotional homecoming that has revived him and his fellow Poles, asks for the physical and spiritual strength to continue his pontificate 'to the end'.

September

3 September UNITED STATES
Internet song-swap service Napster folds after a U.S. bankruptcy court blocks its final sale to German media group Bertelsmann AG.

4 September SOUTH AFRICA
Some 103 world leaders end the U.N. Earth Summit in acrimony with jeers for U.S. Secretary of State Colin Powell and criticism that the summit would do little to help the poor or the planet.

19 September IVORY COAST
Government troops kill Ivory Coast's former military ruler Robert Guei during what authorities say was a vain but bloody attempt by the one-time strongman to seize power again.

16 October EGYPT
The Alexandria Library, one of the world's first and most celebrated centres of learning, reopens after a 1,600-year hiatus and is hailed as a message of peace between civilizations.

24 October UNITED STATES
Police arrest two men in possession of a rifle later confirmed as the weapon used to kill 10 people and wound three in the Washington, DC, area in a shooting spree that began on 2 October.

26 October RUSSIA
Special forces storm a Moscow theatre to end a three-day siege by Chechen rebels. Of 750 hostages, 129 are killed, 127 of them poisoned by a gas released by the rescuers to overcome the rebels.

28 October JORDAN
Senior U.S. diplomat Lawrence Foley is assassinated in Jordan outside his Amman home, the first Western diplomat to be killed there.

31 October UNITED KINGDOM
George Carey steps down as Archbishop of Canterbury after more than 11 tumultuous years in the job. Archbishop of Wales Rowan Williams succeeds him.

18 November IRAQ
U.N. chief weapons inspector Hans Blix and his team fly into the Iraqi capital Baghdad to resume their search for weapons of mass destruction after a four-year absence.

19 November SPAIN
The Prestige, a tanker carrying over 65,000 tonnes of fuel oil, sinks off the coast of northwestern Spain, blackening the rugged coastline of Galicia with thousands of tonnes of spilled oil.

22 November NIGERIA
Nigeria decides to abandon the Miss World contest following a third day of Muslim–Christian fury in Kaduna. At least 215 people die in the rioting over the pageant.

25 November NETHERLANDS
North Korea, Iran, India, Pakistan, China and Israel are among the countries that choose not to sign an International Code of Conduct against Ballistic Missile Proliferation.

28 November KENYA
Suicide bombers blow up the Mombasa Paradise hotel popular with Israelis, killing 15 and wounding 80. In a second attack, missiles narrowly miss an Israeli Arkia Boeing 757 as it departs Mombasa.

29 January AFGHANISTAN
Afghanistan's old national flag is hoisted over Kabul for the first time since the 1978 communist takeover that marked the beginning of 23 years of invasion and bloodshed.

31 January IRELAND
Ireland's Roman Catholic church agrees to pay 128 million euros (U.S. $110 million) in compensation to people abused while in children's homes run by religious orders.

February

6 February UNITED KINGDOM
Queen Elizabeth marks 50 years on the throne with a visit to a new cancer treatment centre. Her father King George VI died after battling the disease.

9 February UNITED STATES
The Winter Olympics open in Salt Lake City.

2 March RUSSIA
Pope John Paul II pays Moscow a virtual visit, joining his flock through a live satellite broadcast, despite opposition from the Russian Orthodox Church, which dubs it an 'invasion'.

3 March SWITZERLAND
Swiss voters abandon centuries of political isolationism and narrowly agree that their staunchly neutral country should join the United Nations.

6 March INDIA
More than 800 people die in a week of communal violence, including 58 Hindus burned alive when a suspected Muslim mob torch a train, triggering the wave of revenge killings.

9 March FRANCE
The Mont Blanc Alpine tunnel reopens to car traffic after a fire in 1999 that killed 39 people. Protesters vow to try to block heavy goods vehicles from using it again.

14 March NETHERLANDS
Abdel Basset al-Megrahi loses his appeal against his murder conviction for the 1988 Lockerbie mid-air bombing. Five Scottish appeals judges uphold the conviction.

1 April NETHERLANDS
Euthanasia becomes legal in the Netherlands a year after parliament voted to make it the first country to permit mercy killing.

4 April ANGOLA
Angola's army and UNITA rebels sign a formal ceasefire in the capital Luanda to end the 27-year war in which around 1 million people have died.

24 April VATICAN
A landmark meeting aimed at restoring credibility in the scandal-ridden American Church ends with an ambiguously worded statement that differentiates between serial child abuse and one-off cases.

26 April GERMANY
A 19-year-old student, bent on revenge for being expelled, shoots dead 12 teachers, two pupils, a secretary, a police officer and himself, at the Gutenberg high school in the town of Erfurt.

May

10 May WEST BANK
A siege of Bethlehem's Church of the Nativity, one of Christianity's holiest sites, ends after 38 days. It began after Palestinian gunmen took refuge there as Israeli troops entered the city on 2 April.

13 May UNITED STATES
President George W. Bush announces an agreement with Russia on a treaty to sharply cut the two countries' nuclear arsenals from about 6,000 to 1,700–2,200 deployed strategic warheads.

20 May EAST TIMOR
East Timor declares its independence shortly after midnight as U.N. Secretary-General Kofi Annan transfers power from the U.N. mission that has run East Timor since 1999.

24 May FINLAND
Finland decides to build the first new nuclear reactor in Western Europe in more than a decade to meet rising energy demands despite bitter opposition from environmentalists.

25 May TAIWAN
A China Airlines Boeing 747-200 on a flight from Taipei to Hong Kong crashes into the Taiwan Strait near Penghu island. All 225 people on board are killed.

16 July UNITED KINGDOM
In an unprecedented statement, the IRA offers 'sincere apologies and condolences' to families of victims of three decades of conflict during its campaign against British rule in Northern Ireland.

21 July UNITED STATES
WorldCom Inc., the second biggest U.S. long-distance telecoms group, buckles under a $3.85 billion accounting scandal and files for bankruptcy protection in the largest ever U.S. insolvency.

August

4 August SPAIN
ETA leaders Francisco 'Pakito' Mugica and Jose Maria 'Fiti' Arregui are each sentenced to 743-year prison terms for an accumulated series of offences.

7 August BRAZIL
The International Monetary Fund throws a $30 billion cash lifeline to Brazil, the fund's biggest bailout ever, seeking to shore up the economy.

24 September UNITED KINGDOM
Britain publishes a dossier on Iraq's weapons programme which says Saddam Hussein could launch a weapon of mass destruction at just 45 minutes' notice.

25 September INDIA
Indian commandos storm Akshardham Temple in western Gujarat, ending a siege and killing two gunmen who massacred 28 and wounded more than 70 the night before.

October

5 October DEMOCRATIC REPUBLIC OF CONGO
The last of 21,666 Rwandan troops leave the Democratic Republic of Congo, lifting hopes of peace in the resource-rich but troubled Great Lakes region.

12 October INDONESIA
Bombs explode in the Kuta Beach nightclub district of Bali, killing 202 and injuring 300. The banned Islamic group Jemaah Islamiyah, linked to al Qaeda, admits responsibility.

November

5 November UNITED STATES
Republicans recapture control of the Senate in the midterm election as well as retaining control of the House of Representatives.

8 November FRANCE
Former President Valéry Giscard d'Estaing, head of the Convention on the Future of Europe, says that Turkey is not a European country and its entry would be 'the end of the EU'.

14 November UNITED STATES
The U.S. Treasury says more than $56 million in funds connected to the Taliban and Osama bin Laden's al Qaeda network have been blocked worldwide since 9/11.

16 November CHINA
The first known case of atypical pneumonia appears in the southern province of Guangdong. The mystery disease is later identified as Severe Acute Respiratory Syndrome (SARS).

December

7 December IRAQ
Iraq hands U.N. inspectors a dossier on its military programmes, denying it has any banned weapons.

9 December UNITED STATES
United Airlines files for bankruptcy in the largest such case ever in the global airline industry after high costs leave the world's second biggest carrier with too much debt and little cash.

13 December DENMARK
The European Union seals an historic deal to admit 10 mostly former communist East European states to the bloc in May 2004.

23 December ITALY
Italy's royal family, reviled by many Italians after World War Two for collaborating with fascist dictator Benito Mussolini, return home for a short visit, ending 56 years in exile.

WORLD TIMELINE 2003

January

1 January BRAZIL
Luiz Inacio Lula da Silva becomes Brazil's first working-class president.

26 January CHINA/TAIWAN
The first Taiwanese commercial flight to China for more than 50 years arrives in Shanghai.

27 January UNITED NATIONS
Arms inspector Hans Blix tells the U.N. Security Council that Iraq has not given enough information about its weapons programmes, but that does not lead him to conclude Iraq possesses banned arms.

February

19 February LEBANON
Syrian troops begin pulling out of north Lebanon, the first step in the planned withdrawal of some 4,000 soldiers from the country Syrian forces entered in the 1970s.

March

2 March NEW ZEALAND
Alinghi, representing landlocked Switzerland, becomes the first European team to win sailing's America's Cup, world sport's oldest trophy.

2 March ALGERIA
Half a million Algerians give French President Jacques Chirac a rousing welcome at the start of the first full state visit by a French president since Algeria won independence from France in 1962.

12 March SERBIA AND MONTENEGRO
Serbian Prime Minister Zoran Djindjic is assassinated in front of the main government building in Belgrade.

23 March UNITED STATES
Movie musical *Chicago* wins the Oscar for best film at the Academy Awards. Director Roman Polanski and actor Adrien Brody also win best director and best actor for *The Pianist*.

April

9 April IRAQ
Saddam Hussein's rule crumbles as U.S. forces sweep into the heart of Baghdad, taking control of the capital and toppling a huge statue of the man who ruled over the country for 24 years.

24 April UNITED STATES
Thirty-four men file sexual abuse lawsuits totalling $1.85 billion against the Roman Catholic diocese on New York's Long Island.

May

21 May ALGERIA
An earthquake of 6.7 magnitude strikes Algiers and nearby towns to the east, killing at least 2,250.

21 May SWITZERLAND
The 192 member countries of the World Health Organization adopt the world's first anti-smoking treaty aimed at breaking the habit that kills nearly 5 million people a year.

30 May MYANMAR
Nobel peace laureate Aung San Suu Kyi is detained with other opposition leaders after clashes between supporters and opponents of her National League for Democracy in which four people die.

31 May NORTH ATLANTIC
The moon blots out the sun over the North Atlantic around dawn in the region's biggest eclipse since 1954.

June

20 July UNITED KINGDOM
The BBC confirms that scientist David Kelly, whose body was found two days earlier, was the source for its report that the British government exaggerated intelligence to justify war in Iraq.

22 July IRAQ
U.S. troops storm a house in Mosul and kill Saddam Hussein's sons Uday and Qusay, numbers two and three on the U.S.'s most-wanted list after Saddam.

29 July CHINA
China announces that its last 12 SARS patients have recovered, marking an apparent end to the scourge in China. The virus killed more than 340 people in the country.

30 July MEXICO
The world's last 'Love Bug' Volkswagen Beetle rolls off the production line, ending the long history of a car that was originally Adolf Hitler's idea.

August

27 August SPACE
Mars passes just 55.76 million km (34.65 million miles) from earth, the closest such encounter since the Stone Age.

29 August IRAQ
A car bomb kills at least 83 Iraqis, including top Shi'ite Muslim leader Ayatollah Mohammed Baqer al-Hakim, in an apparent assassination at the Imam Ali mosque in Najaf.

29 August FRANCE
France says the August heatwave, when temperatures soared above 40°C (104°F), claimed more than 11,400 lives.

September

1 September NETHERLANDS
The Netherlands becomes the world's first country to make cannabis available as a prescription drug for those suffering from HIV/AIDS, cancer and multiple sclerosis.

October

4 October VATICAN
Pope John Paul II tells the Archbishop of Canterbury that allowing openly homosexual clergy in the Anglican communion is a 'serious difficulty' on the path to Christian unity.

7 October UNITED STATES
Austrian-born Hollywood actor Arnold Schwarzenegger becomes governor of California, ousting unpopular Democrat Gray Davis, who was forced to seek re-election by a million-signature petition.

15 October CHINA
China becomes the third nation to put man in space, sending an astronaut on a 21-hour odyssey around the earth.

17 October TAIWAN
The Taipei 101 office block reaches its full height of 508 metres (1,667 feet), succeeding Malaysia's Petronas Towers as the world's tallest building.

9 November SAUDI ARABIA
Eighteen people are killed and 120 injured when suspected al Qaeda suicide bombers attack the guarded 200-villa Muhaya complex in the Saudi Arabian capital, Riyadh.

20 November TURKEY
Suicide bombers kill 32 people in Istanbul's second attack in a week. The earlier attack killed 30. Al Qaeda later claim responsibility.

23 November GEORGIA
After relentless pressure by the opposition, who accuse him of rigging parliamentary elections, President Eduard Shevardnadze quits in what becomes known as the 'Rose Revolution'.

24 November ITALY/ISRAEL
Italian Deputy Prime Minister Gianfranco Fini denounces Italy's fascist past during a visit to Israel to symbolically cut his National Alliance party's links to fascism.

December

1 February SPACE
The space shuttle Columbia breaks up over Texas on re-entering the earth's atmosphere at end of an almost 16-day flight, killing all seven astronauts on board.

4 February YUGOSLAVIA
The Yugoslav parliament endorses the creation of a loose union of Serbia and Montenegro in a session that officially buries the bloodied federation.

15 February WORLDWIDE
In the biggest wave of demonstrations since the Vietnam war, more than 6 million people take to the streets in 600 towns and cities to protest against any war in Iraq.

18 February SOUTH KOREA
At least 182 people are killed and 300 are missing after flames and smoke engulf two crowded subway trains in the city of Taegu.

19 February IRAN
An Iranian military plane crashes near Kerman in southeastern Iran. Iran says all 276 on board were killed.

16 March PORTUGAL
U.S. President George W. Bush meets the leaders of Spain and Britain to plot final diplomatic moves to try to win U.N. backing for war against Iraq.

17 March UNITED STATES
In a 13-minute White House speech, President George W. Bush orders Saddam Hussein to leave Iraq with his sons by 4:15 a.m. (01:15 GMT) on 20 March or face the might of the U.S. military.

19 March UNITED NATIONS
At a U.N. Security Council session France and Germany say it is illegal for the Bush administration to depose Saddam Hussein. Russia also maintains there is no proof Iraq poses a threat to the U.S.

20 March IRAQ
The U.S. launches war against Iraq, targeting the leadership with selective strikes on Baghdad using more than 3,000 bombs and missiles. Iraq fires Scud missiles at Kuwait.

21 March SOUTH AFRICA
In the final report of the Truth and Reconciliation Commission, Archbishop Desmond Tutu criticizes white South Africans and big business for ignoring their role in apartheid.

1 May IRAQ
U.S. President George W. Bush says the major fighting in Iraq is over.

6 May IRAQ / UNITED STATES
U.S. President George W. Bush names former State Department counterterrorism chief L. Paul Bremer as the top civil administrator for Iraq, supplanting Jay Garner.

12 May SAUDI ARABIA
Suicide bombers shoot their way into housing compounds for expatriates in Saudi capital Riyadh as residents sleep. The death toll is 35, including nine Americans.

14 May ITALY
After nearly four decades of planning and debate, work finally begins on underwater barriers to try to protect Venice from flooding.

16 May MOROCCO
Suicide bombers set off at least five blasts in Morocco's biggest city, Casablanca. Forty-five people are killed including 12 bombers.

1 June RUSSIA
The Moscow Treaty, also called the Strategic Offensive Reductions Treaty or SORT, is signed by President Vladimir Putin and President George W. Bush to slash deployed nuclear warheads.

4 June UNITED STATES
The House of Representatives approves a ban on 'partial birth' abortions, the first time a specific form of abortion has been outlawed since the 1973 Roe versus Wade ruling that legalized abortion.

July

4 July JAPAN
Japan's lower house of parliament gives the go-ahead for the nation's biggest foreign troop deployment since World War Two, allowing soldiers to help rebuild Iraq.

16 July SÃO TOMÉ AND PRINCIPE
The government of São Tomé and Principe is toppled in a military coup while the president of the potentially oil-rich African island state is out of the country.

11 August AFGHANISTAN
NATO takes command of Kabul's peacekeeping force, its first operation outside Europe in its 54-year history.

14 August IRAN
Iran gives the green light to a larger scale nuclear programme despite international concern it may be building an atomic bomb.

14 August UNITED STATES / CANADA
Power goes out across much of the northeastern U.S. and parts of Canada, creating a huge blackout across major cities including New York, Detroit, Boston, Cleveland and Ottawa.

15 August UNITED NATIONS
Libya accepts responsibility for the 1988 bombing of Pan Am 103 over Lockerbie, Scotland. On 22 August it hands over $2.7 billion to compensate victims' families.

19 August IRAQ
A massive truck bomb destroys the U.N. headquarters in Baghdad. Among the 22 killed is Sergio Vieira de Mello, the top U.N. envoy to Iraq.

6 September WEST BANK
Palestinian Prime Minister Mahmoud Abbas resigns after a power struggle with President Yasser Arafat, dealing a serious blow to the U.S.-backed roadmap to peace.

9 September ARGENTINA
Argentina defaults on a $3 billion debt to the International Monetary Fund, the biggest single missed payment in the IMF's history.

10 September SWEDEN
Swedish Foreign Minister Anna Lindh is stabbed in Stockholm and dies the next day.

16 September SWEDEN
Former U.N. chief weapons inspector Hans Blix says he believes Iraq destroyed its weapons of mass destruction 10 years ago.

25 September FRANCE
The biggest and most expensive cruise ship ever, the Queen Mary II, sets sail days after a deal between France and the EU saves its makers, Alstom, from bankruptcy.

21 October UNITED KINGDOM
John de Chastelain, the retired Canadian general charged with overseeing guerrilla disarmament, confirms the Irish Republican Army has 'decommissioned' weapons.

23 October UNITED STATES
After talks with former President Bill Clinton's foundation, four companies agree to supply drugs to millions of HIV and AIDS sufferers in Africa and the Caribbean at about half the current price.

25 October RUSSIA
Mikhail Khodorkovsky, Russia's wealthiest man and head of oil giant YUKOS, is arrested in Siberia and charged with massive fraud and tax-evasion offences.

November

2 November UNITED STATES
The Reverend Canon V. Gene Robinson is consecrated as the first openly gay bishop of the U.S. Episcopal Church, a move that threatens to tear apart the worldwide Anglican community.

13 December IRAQ
U.S. troops find Saddam Hussein in a hole in the ground behind a shepherd's hut near Tikrit late in the evening. 'We got him ... The tyrant is a prisoner,' said Iraq's U.S. governor Paul Bremer.

13 December ZIMBABWE
Zimbabwe informs the Commonwealth it is withdrawing from the 54-nation group in response to its extended suspension.

16 December TAIWAN
Vice President Annette Lu says Chinese missiles directed at Taiwan are a form of 'state terrorism'. Taiwan's parliament passes resolutions calling for removal of nearly 500 missiles aimed at the island.

19 December ITALY
Italy's biggest food firm, Parmalat, reveals a 4 billion-euro (U.S. $4.9 billion) hole in its accounts in a statement that wipes out two-thirds of its already battered share price.

26 December IRAN
A major earthquake of 6.8 magnitude strikes the historic city of Bam, 970 km (600 miles) southeast of Tehran, killing over 30,000 people.

WORLD TIMELINE 2004

January

3 January SPACE
The U.S. lander carrying the Spirit rover, a robotic explorer designed to search for signs of life on Mars, arrives safely after seven months of space travel. A second rover, Opportunity, lands on 24 January.

4 January AFGHANISTAN
Rival Afghan factions attending the Loya Jirga agree on a national constitution, paving the way for the first free elections after nearly a quarter-century of war.

22 January CUBA
Patriarch Bartholomew, spiritual leader of Orthodox Christians, visits Cuba to open the first church to be built since the 1959 revolution. It is also the first visit to Latin America by a Patriarch.

27 January WORLD
MyDoom is the latest worm to infect computers over the Internet, becoming the fastest-spreading attack since the twin attacks by the Blaster worm and SoBig virus in 2003.

4 February PAKISTAN
Pakistan's top nuclear scientist Abdul Qadeer Khan accepts full responsibility for leaking weapons secrets and equipment to Iran, Libya and North Korea.

10 February FRANCE
Deputies in France's National Assembly vote to ban Muslim headscarves, Jewish skullcaps and large Christian crosses from state schools.

18 February IRAN
Runaway train wagons laden with a lethal cocktail of fuel and fertilizers blow up in northeast Iran, killing almost 320 people and injuring up to 450.

26 February MACEDONIA
Macedonian President Boris Trajkovski is killed when his twin-engined Beechcraft 200 Super King Airplane crashes into Bosnian mountains in thick fog.

29 February HAITI
President Jean-Bertrand Aristide leaves Haiti after an armed revolt and Chief Justice Boniface Alexandre is sworn in as president.

22 March GAZA
Israeli helicopters kill Hamas leader Sheikh Ahmed Yassin. Seven others die in the Gaza City missile strike. About 200,000 mourners attend a funeral procession for Yassin later that day.

April

2 April UNITED NATIONS / SUDAN
U.N. emergency relief coordinator Jan Egeland says Arab 'Janjaweed' militias are conducting an organized campaign of ethnic cleansing to drive black Africans from Sudan's Darfur region.

3 April SPAIN
The suspected Tunisian ringleader of the Madrid bombings, Serhane ben Abdelmajid Farkhet, blows himself up with up to six accomplices after police corner them in a Madrid apartment.

14 April IRAQ
Fabrizio Quattrocchi, one of four Italians being held hostage in Iraq, is killed. Quattrocchi is the first reported foreign hostage killed in Iraq.

1 May EUROPEAN UNION
Ten new members, mainly former communist countries in eastern Europe, join the European Union, bringing the membership to 25.

4 May ITALY
Prime Minister Silvio Berlusconi's government becomes Italy's longest-serving administration since World War Two, having survived 1,060 days.

5 May UNITED STATES
Picasso's *Boy With the Pipe* sets a world record for the most expensive painting sold at auction when it fetches $104,168,000 at Sotheby's in New York.

6 May LIBYA
A Libyan court sentences six Bulgarian medics and a Palestinian doctor to death by firing squad for deliberately infecting hundreds of Libyan children with the deadly HIV virus.

9 May RUSSIA
Chechnya's Moscow-backed President Akhmad Kadyrov is killed when a bomb blast tears through a packed stadium. At least five others are killed and 50 wounded. Five people are arrested.

June

6 June FRANCE
German Chancellor Gerhard Schröder visits Normandy on the 60th anniversary of the D-Day landings, joining Germany's former enemies for the first time in a tribute to those killed on both sides.

28 June IRAQ
Prime Minister Iyad Allawi and President Ghazi al-Yawar are formally sworn in at a ceremony two days earlier than announced marking the U.S. handover of sovereignty to an interim Iraqi government.

28 June UNITED STATES / LIBYA
The United States formally restores its diplomatic ties with Libya, after 24 years.

30 June SPACE
NASA's Cassini spacecraft slips through Saturn's rings and into orbit to make the most detailed study ever of the sixth planet from the sun.

August

1 August PARAGUAY
Fire sweeps through a supermarket on Asuncion's outskirts, killing at least 364 people. Officials believe the blaze was caused by faulty maintenance of a chimney.

3 August UNITED STATES
The Statue of Liberty reopens to visitors for the first time since the 9/11 attacks after security and safety improvements paid for by more than $30 million in donations.

13 August GREECE
The Olympics open in Athens with a pageant to welcome home the Games, weaving ancient tradition and modern technology.

22 August NORWAY
Armed robbers steal a version of *The Scream* and another masterpiece by Norwegian artist Edvard Munch in a bold daytime raid on an Oslo museum packed with terrified tourists.

21 September UNITED STATES
Cigarette makers lied and tried to confuse the public about the dangers of smoking for 50 years, the U.S. government says as its $280 billion case against the industry goes to trial.

October

15 October ZIMBABWE
The High Court acquits opposition leader Morgan Tsvangirai of plotting to assassinate President Robert Mugabe and seize power, saying the state failed to prove its case beyond reasonable doubt.

15 October ITALY
Italy's top court upholds the verdict of two previous trials that had cleared former Prime Minister Giulio Andreotti of charges that he had links to the Mafia, ending a judicial saga that began in 1993.

November

December

3 December UKRAINE
The Supreme Court rules that a disputed presidential election won by the country's prime minister was invalid and that a re-run is required.

7 December ITALY
Italy's famed La Scala Milan opera house re-opens after a three-year renovation.

10 December VIETNAM
A United Airlines plane lands in Vietnam's Ho Chi Minh City, the first commercial American airliner to fly to the country since the Vietnam war.

11 December UKRAINE
Austrian doctors say that Ukrainian opposition leader Viktor Yushchenko was poisoned by dioxin during the presidential election campaign.

28 January UNITED KINGDOM
Lord Hutton's inquiry clears Prime Minister Tony Blair of any blame for the suicide of scientist David Kelly, exposed as the source of a BBC report that Blair exaggerated the case for war in Iraq.

February

1 February IRAQ
More than 110 people are killed and 133 wounded when two suicide bombers blow themselves up in Arbil at the offices of the two main Kurdish factions in northern Iraq.

1 February AUSTRALIA
The first passenger train to travel from the southern coast of Australia to the north coast sets off from Adelaide on its 2,979 km (1,861 mile) journey to Darwin. It arrives two days later.

1 February SAUDI ARABIA
At least 251 Muslim pilgrims are trampled to death at the climax of the Haj, after pilgrims flock to Jamarat Bridge in Mena.

29 February UNITED STATES
The Lord of the Rings: The Return of the King wins a record-equalling 11 Academy Awards, including one for best film.

March

2 March IRAQ
Bombers kill 171 people in twin attacks in Baghdad and the Shi'ite holy city of Kerbala as Iraq's majority Shi'ites mark their holiest day, Ashura.

11 March SPAIN
Simultaneous bomb explosions in packed Madrid rush-hour trains kill 191 people and wound over 1,800. Islamist militants later claim responsibility for the attacks in the name of al Qaeda.

14 March SPAIN
Spaniards throw out their centre-right government in a spectacular election upset triggered by the bomb attacks in Madrid. Jose Luis Rodriguez Zapatero becomes prime minister.

21 April ISRAEL
Nuclear whistleblower Mordechai Vanunu leaves prison after 18 years, saying he is proud of revealing secrets that exposed the Jewish state as an atomic power.

22 April NORTH KOREA
A train laden with explosives blows up at a station near the centre of Ryongchon. At least 161 people are killed and hundreds are injured. Nearly 2,000 homes are destroyed.

24 April CYPRUS
Greek Cypriots defy international pressure and vote against a U.N.-backed plan to end partition and usher a united Cyprus into the European Union. Turkish Cypriots accept it.

28 April UNITED STATES
CBS television broadcasts images taken at Abu Ghraib prison in late 2003 that show American troops abusing Iraqi inmates, inflaming Arab rage.

May

13 May INDIA
Indian Prime Minister Atal Behari Vajpayee hands his resignation to the president after a shock loss to the opposition Congress party in a national election.

17 May IRAQ
Governing Council leader Abdul Zahra Othman Mohammad, a Shi'ite Muslim also known as Izzedin Salim, is killed by a suicide car bomb as his convoy waits to enter coalition headquarters in Baghdad.

17 May UNITED STATES
Massachusetts becomes the first U.S. state to allow same-sex marriage, an election-year milestone fuelling legal and political battles nationwide.

19 May EUROPEAN UNION
The EU ends its controversial ban on genetically modified foods as its executive body authorizes imports of a biotech maize, the first new EU approval of GM foods in five years.

30 May SAUDI ARABIA
Saudi commandos free 41 foreign hostages held at the Oasis housing complex by suspected al Qaeda militants. Some 22 civilians are killed. The leader of the militant group is arrested.

July

9 July NETHERLANDS
The International Court of Justice rules that the barrier wall Israel is building in the West Bank breaches international law and is not justified by security concerns. Israel later vows to continue building.

14 July UNITED KINGDOM
A report by Lord Butler concludes that Britain's pre-war intelligence on Iraqi armaments contained serious flaws, and that Saddam Hussein probably had no banned weapons ready for use.

22 July UNITED STATES
The commission investigating 9/11 says U.S. leaders and intelligence agencies failed to grasp the gravity of the threat posed by radical Islamists, and suffered from a collective 'failure of imagination'.

31 July GERMANY
Berlin's refurbished Olympic Stadium is reopened. Germans hope the arena, built for the 1936 Olympics, will shed the association of its Nazi past.

24 August RUSSIA
Bombs on two passenger planes cause them to crash almost simultaneously, killing all 90 people on board. The Islambouli Brigades, an Islamist group, claim responsibility three days later.

26 August IRAQ
Ayatollah Ali al-Sistani, Iraq's most revered Shi'ite leader, agrees a deal with rebel cleric Moqtada al-Sadr to end a three-week uprising by Sadr's militiamen in Najaf.

September

3 September RUSSIA
331 people, half of them children, die during the bloody end to a hostage-taking at a school in Beslan in southern Russia. Chechen warlord Shamil Basayev later claims responsibility.

15 September UNITED KINGDOM
Six pro-hunting demonstrators burst onto the floor of parliament to disrupt a debate on a ban on hunting with dogs. Lawmakers vote in favour of the ban after the debate is resumed.

2 November NETHERLANDS
Controversial filmmaker and journalist Theo van Gogh, who made a film about violence against women in Islamic societies, is murdered in Amsterdam by Islamist militant Mohammed Bouyeri.

3 November UNITED STATES
Presidential challenger Democratic Senator John Kerry concedes the race for the White House to President George W. Bush. The Republicans expand their hold on the U.S. Congress.

4 November RUSSIA
President Vladimir Putin approves Russia's ratification of the Kyoto Protocol on global warming. Russia's ratification makes the protocol, so far backed by 126 states, internationally binding.

8 November IRAQ
U.S. troops launch a full-scale offensive on Falluja. Eight days later, Iraq's minister of state for national security says over 1,600 insurgents have been killed in the offensive and 1,052 captured.

11 November FRANCE
Yasser Arafat dies in a Paris hospital, aged 75. Mahmoud Abbas succeeds him as chairman of the Palestine Liberation Organization.

13 December CHILE
A Chilean judge formally charges former dictator Augusto Pinochet with homicide and kidnapping in one of many pending cases related to human rights abuses committed during his 17-year rule.

14 December FRANCE
President Jacques Chirac inaugurates the Millau Viaduct, the world's highest bridge, taller than the Eiffel Tower and longer than the Champs Elysées.

26 December ASIA
A magnitude 9.15 earthquake – the biggest in four decades – triggers a tsunami that leaves almost 230,000 people dead or missing across a dozen Indian Ocean nations.

28 December UKRAINE
Viktor Yushchenko is declared winner of the 26 December re-run of the presidential election.

31 December TAIWAN
Taipei opens the world's tallest building, a 101-storey tower built to withstand major tremors and storms on the earthquake- and typhoon-prone island.

WORLD TIMELINE 2005

January

9 January WEST BANK
Palestinians elect former Prime Minister Mahmoud Abbas to succeed Yasser Arafat as president.

9 January SUDAN
First Vice President Ali Osman Mohamed Taha and John Garang of the Sudan People's Liberation Movement sign a peace accord in Nairobi, ending a 21-year conflict.

25 January UNITED STATES
Microsoft Chairman Bill Gates announces that the Bill and Melinda Gates Foundation will donate $750 million to pay for wider vaccination programmes in developing countries.

27 January POLAND
World leaders and survivors remember the horror of the Holocaust at a ceremony in Auschwitz-Birkenau on the 60th anniversary of the liberation of the Nazi death camp.

16 February WORLDWIDE
The Kyoto Protocol on curbing human emissions of heat-trapping gases by 2012 comes into force, but is rejected as an economic straitjacket by the U.S., the world's top polluter.

23 February ALGERIA
President Abdelaziz Bouteflika acknowledges for the first time that 150,000 people have died in more than a decade of an Islamic holy war or 'jihad' in Algeria.

27 February UNITED STATES
The film *Million Dollar Baby* wins four Oscars, including best film and best director for Hollywood legend Clint Eastwood.

28 February IRAQ
A suicide car bomb attack in Hilla, south of Baghdad, kills 125 people and wounds 130. It is postwar Iraq's worst single blast. Al Qaeda's wing in Iraq later claims responsibility.

March

6 April MONACO
Prince Rainier, who turned one of the world's smallest states from a faded gambling centre into a billionaires' haven, dies. His son Prince Albert succeeds him.

9 April UNITED KINGDOM
Heir to the throne Prince Charles weds longtime lover Camilla Parker Bowles. The newly titled Duchess of Cornwall goes from 'commoner' to second most senior royal woman after Queen Elizabeth.

18 April INDIA
Declaring their peace process irreversible, India and Pakistan agree to open up the heavily militarized frontier dividing Kashmir, capping a visit to New Delhi by Pakistani President Pervez Musharraf.

19 April VATICAN
German Cardinal Joseph Ratzinger is elected Pope and chooses to call himself Pope Benedict XVI.

26 April LEBANON
Syria withdraws its last soldiers and intelligence agents from Lebanon, ending a 29-year military presence in its small neighbour.

13 June UNITED STATES
Pop singer Michael Jackson is found not guilty of molesting a 13-year-old boy in 2003 and is cleared of all charges in a dramatic trial that had threatened to send him to prison for nearly two decades.

15 June ANTARCTICA
A 45-nation Antarctic Treaty meeting agrees that the Antarctic's environment will be protected by new rules forcing polluters to clean up or pay up for any contamination.

16 June EUROPEAN UNION
Despite French and Dutch 'No' votes, EU leaders agree to try to keep the new EU constitution alive by extending the ratification deadline until at least mid-2007, after French and Dutch elections.

24 June IRAN
Ultra-conservative Tehran mayor Mahmoud Ahmadinejad sweeps to victory in presidential elections and vows to turn Iran into a strong and exemplary Islamic state.

July

24 July FRANCE
Lance Armstrong announces his retirement from cycling after winning the Tour de France for a record seventh time.

26 July UNITED STATES
The U.S. space shuttle Discovery blasts off from its launchpad at Cape Canaveral in Florida in NASA's first shuttle mission since Columbia was destroyed in 2003.

28 July UNITED KINGDOM
The Irish Republican Army formally ends its 30-year armed campaign against British rule in Northern Ireland.

August

1 August SUDAN
Sudan confirms that southern leader and Vice President John Garang, a key figure in a January peace deal hailed as a rare African success story, has died in a helicopter accident.

31 August IRAQ
More than 1,000 Shi'ite Muslims die in a stampede over a bridge near the Kadhimiya mosque in the old district of north Baghdad, provoked by rumours of a suicide bomber.

September

9 September EGYPT
President Hosni Mubarak wins a fifth six-year term in office with 88.6% of votes cast in the country's first multi-candidate presidential election.

14 September UNITED NATIONS
The U.N. marks its 60th anniversary with one of the largest summits in history. Some 150 monarchs, presidents and prime ministers converge on the Manhattan headquarters.

26 September UNITED STATES
Lyndie England, the U.S. soldier pictured holding a leash to a naked Iraqi inmate in Abu Ghraib prison, prompting global outrage, is found guilty of abuse and sentenced to three years in prison.

19 October IRAQ
A defiant Saddam Hussein goes on trial for crimes against humanity over the killing of 148 Shi'ite Muslims more than two decades ago. He pleads 'not guilty'.

20 October LEBANON
A U.N. report on the murder of former Prime Minister Rafik al-Hariri says high-level Syrian officials and their Lebanese allies were involved, with suspicion cast even on President Emile Lahoud.

25 October IRAQ
Iraqis have ratified their new constitution with 79% of voters backing the charter and 21% opposed to it, according to results from the 15 October referendum.

26 October IRAN
President Mahmoud Ahmadinejad says Israel should be 'wiped off the map'. In December he expresses doubt that the Holocaust occurred and suggests that Israel should be moved to Europe.

27 October FRANCE
The death of two teenagers of African origin while apparently fleeing police triggers weeks of riots across France. Hundreds of youths fight with police throughout the suburbs of Paris.

21 November UNITED NATIONS
The Joint U.N. Programme on HIV/AIDS says 4.9 million people were infected by HIV globally in 2005, the highest ever jump, taking the number living with the virus to 40.3 million.

22 November GERMANY
Angela Merkel takes office as Germany's first woman chancellor, ending months of political uncertainty.

26 November SPACE
A Japanese space probe Hayabusa – Japanese for 'falcon' – lands on the surface of an asteroid and collects rock samples that could give clues to the origin of the solar system.

December

2 December UNITED STATES
North Carolina double murderer Kenneth Lee Boyd becomes the 1,000th prisoner executed in the U.S. since the reinstatement of capital punishment in 1976.

30 January IRAQ
At least nine suicide bombers strike on Iraq's election day, killing at least 35 countrywide. Up to 8 million Iraqis brave the insurgent attacks to cast their ballots, a turnout of around 60%.

February

1 February NEPAL
King Gyanendra sacks the government and assumes power for the next three years, saying the leadership has failed to hold elections or to restore peace. Later a state of emergency is declared.

8 February EGYPT
Israel and the Palestinians announce a ceasefire at a summit in Egypt to try to halt more than four years of violence.

14 February LEBANON
A huge car bomb kills Lebanon's former Prime Minister Rafik al-Hariri. Another 22 people are killed and 135 wounded in the blast.

24 March KYRGYZSTAN
The opposition declares itself in power after seizing key buildings. President Askar Akayev leaves the country following days of violent protests. He accuses the opposition of an 'anti-constitutional coup'.

31 March UNITED STATES
Terri Schiavo, the brain-damaged Florida woman whose fate sparked a highly politicized family feud, dies. A state court had ordered her feeding tube to be removed.

April

2 April VATICAN
Pope John Paul II, who headed the Roman Catholic Church for 26 years and played a crucial role in the fall of communism in Europe, dies. He was 84 years old.

2 April ZIMBABWE
President Robert Mugabe's party wins a parliamentary election with the two-thirds majority needed to pass constitutional changes. The opposition and Western governments declare the poll a fraud.

May

5 May UNITED KINGDOM
Prime Minister Tony Blair survives opposition over Britain's involvement in the Iraq war to secure a third election victory for his Labour Party, though with a significantly reduced majority.

31 May UNITED STATES
Former FBI No. 2 Mark Felt is named as 'Deep Throat', the legendary source who leaked Watergate scandal secrets to the *Washington Post* and helped bring down President Richard Nixon.

31 May RUSSIA
A court finds Mikhail Khodorkovsky, once Russia's richest man and former head of oil giant YUKOS, guilty of fraud and tax evasion. He is sentenced to nine years in prison, later reduced to eight.

June

2 July WORLDWIDE
In the global event Live 8, a galaxy of stars rock the world in a series of concerts to demand that the Group of Eight richest nations agree to cancel much of Africa's debt and boost aid.

7 July UNITED KINGDOM
Four suicide bombers attack London's transport system, killing 52 people, as G8 leaders meet in Scotland. In September al Qaeda says it carried out the attack to strike at 'British arrogance'.

18 July UNITED KINGDOM/ UNITED STATES
The sixth Harry Potter volume sells over 8.9 million copies in its first 24 hours on sale in the U.S. and Britain, making it the fastest-selling book in history.

21 July UNITED KINGDOM
Further attempted attacks occur on three London underground stations and one bus. All four bombs fail to explode and four suspects are later arrested.

23 July EGYPT
Two car bombs and a suitcase bomb rip through hotels and shopping areas in the Egyptian resort of Sharm el-Sheikh, killing 67 and wounding more than 200.

12 August SRI LANKA
Foreign Minister Lakshman Kadirgamar, a hardliner in dealing with the island's Tamil Tiger rebels, is assassinated in an attack blamed on separatist rebels.

15 August GAZA
Israeli Prime Minister Ariel Sharon begins his promised pullout from Gaza.

16 August VENEZUELA
A West Caribbean Airways MD-80 aircraft crashes in the mountains near Venezuela's border with Colombia. All 160 passengers and crew are killed.

19 August BURUNDI
Former Hutu rebel leader Pierre Nkurunziza wins the presidency in a legislative vote under a peace plan to end a 12-year civil war that has killed 300,000 people.

29 August UNITED STATES
Hurricane Katrina slams into Louisiana and Mississippi with 224 kph (140 mph) winds and a 9-metre (30-foot) storm surge. It causes a death toll of 1,228 and at least $80 billion of damage.

October

1 October INDONESIA
Three suicide bombers strike restaurants at Jimbaran Beach and Kuta Beach on the holiday island of Bali, killing 20 people and wounding around 150.

8 October GUATEMALA
Hurricane Stan sweeps across Guatemala and El Salvador, killing more than 1,000 in mudslides and floods.

8 October PAKISTAN
More than 73,000 people are killed by a quake measuring 7.6 magnitude that strikes 100 km (60 miles) northeast of Islamabad. It also rocks Indian Kashmir, killing 1,309 people there.

12 October SYRIA
Interior Minister Ghazi Kanaan commits suicide three weeks after being questioned by a U.N. team probing the killing of former Lebanese Prime Minister Rafik al-Hariri.

29 October INDIA
Three bombs tear through New Delhi markets ahead of the biggest Hindu and Muslim festivals of the year, killing 66. The Islami Inqilabi Mahaz (Islamic Revolutionary Group) claims responsibility.

November

9 November JORDAN
Three suicide bombers attack three hotels in the Jordanian capital Amman, killing 57 people including wedding guests. Iraq's al Qaeda later claims responsibility.

10 November ISRAEL
Shimon Peres is ousted as Labour Party leader by Amir Peretz, who vows to quit Ariel Sharon's ruling coalition. On 21 November Sharon quits his Likud party to lead new centrist party, Kadima.

15 November JAPAN
Princess Sayako, only daughter of Emperor Akihito, weds a commoner in a private ceremony at a Tokyo hotel, losing her privileged status as a member of the imperial family.

15 December IRAQ
Iraqis go to the polls to elect a new parliament. The results released in January 2006 give the Shi'ite Islamist Alliance 128 seats, 10 short of a majority in the 275-seat chamber.

18 December ISRAEL
Prime Minister Ariel Sharon suffers a minor stroke. He returns to work two days later but suffers a massive stroke in early January 2006.

19 December UNITED KINGDOM
A lesbian couple in Northern Ireland become the first to take advantage of a new British civil partnership law. Two days later pop singer Elton John 'weds' his long-term partner David Furnish.

19 December AFGHANISTAN
President Hamid Karzai inaugurates his country's first parliament in decades.

19 December ITALY
Bank of Italy Governor Antonio Fazio resigns, finally succumbing to intense pressure after becoming mired in a bank takeover scandal.

Additional Photo Credits

Opening pages

Pages 2–3

The Millau Viaduct, which crosses the valley of the River Tarn. The 280m (919 ft) high structure designed by British architect Norman Foster is the highest bridge in the world. 9 December 2004, Millau, France. Jean-Philippe Arles

Introduction

Page 6 top row, left to right

French musician Jean Michel Jarre stages a New Year's Eve concert in front of the 4,500-year-old Giza pyramids. 1 January 2000, Cairo, Egypt. Aladin Abdel Naby

A 'Peace' dove is released by the Palestinian Authority in front of the Church of the Nativity, traditional birthplace of Jesus Christ. 1 January 2000, Bethlehem, West Bank. Evelyn Hockstein

Fireworks explode over the temple of the Parthenon during a light and sound show created by German director Gert Hof. 1 January 2000, Athens, Greece. Yiorgos Karahalis

Fireworks explode over the Peace Tower and Canada's Parliament buildings. 1 January 2000, Ottawa, Canada. Jim Young

Page 6 middle row, left to right

A firework display lights up Britain's Houses of Parliament. 1 January 2000, London, United Kingdom. Dylan Martinez

Revellers Blauri Graterol and James Karabelas kiss as fireworks and confetti explode overhead. 1 January 2000, New York, United States. Jim Bourg

Poles celebrate as fireworks explode over the National Theatre. 1 January 2000, Warsaw, Poland. Pawel Kopczynski

Fireworks light up the sky over the cupola of St Peter's Basilica. 1 January 2000, Vatican. Paolo Cocco

Page 6 bottom row, left to right

Fireworks light up the sky behind the Compania church. 31 December 1999, Quito, Ecuador. Guillermo Granja

Fireworks burst from the Eiffel Tower. 1 January 2000, Paris, France. Charles Platiau

Fireworks explode above the Washington Monument. 1 January 2000, Washington, DC, United States. Molly Riley

Fireworks explode over the National Theatre. 1 January 2000, Sarajevo, Bosnia. Danilo Krstanovic

Big Issues

Page 11 clockwise from top left

A Haitian holds a woman who has fallen into a flooded street during a storm. 23 October 2005, Port-au-Prince, Haiti. Eduardo Munoz

A door remains standing after a house was flattened by an earthquake in Qiongkuer Qiake township. 26 February 2003, Xinjiang, China. Claro Cortes IV

The body of a drowned African immigrant lies in the water on the rocky coast in Fuerteventura, one of the Spanish Canary Islands. 1 August 2003, Fuerteventura, Spain. Juan Medina

Mourners gather at Laigh Kirk in Paisley for the funeral of Helen Jones, who died in the London bombings on 7 July 2005. 25 July 2005, Scotland, United Kingdom. Jeff J. Mitchell

Science and Technology

Page 69 clockwise from top left

Chinese children dressed in space suits wait to perform during celebrations marking International Children's Day in Beijing. 1 June 2004, Beijing, China. Guang Niu

The last British Airways passenger Concorde flight lands at London's Heathrow airport from New York. 24 October 2003, London, United Kingdom. Jonathan Bainbridge

The Gibbs Aquada, the world's first high-speed amphibian vehicle, is demonstrated at its unveiling on the River Thames. 3 September 2003, London, United Kingdom. Stephen Hird

Dr Ian Wilmut, leader of the team that created Dolly the sheep – the world's first mammal cloned from an adult cell – faces her preserved body displayed at the National Museum of Scotland. 9 April 2003, Edinburgh, United Kingdom. Jeff J. Mitchell

Patterns of Belief

Page 93 clockwise from top left

Buddhist monks recite prayers during a multi-faith candlelit vigil for victims of the tsunami. 19 January 2005, Takua Pa, Thailand. Bazuki Muhammad

Muslim women pray on the eve of the holy month of Ramadan in Istiqlal mosque. 26 October 2003, Jakarta, Indonesia. Supri

A shopper checks out Lunar New Year decorations. 6 February 2005, Shanghai, China. Claro Cortes IV

Taiwanese release sky lanterns to celebrate the traditional Chinese Lantern Festival on the first full moon of the Lunar New Year. 5 February 2004, Taipei, Taiwan. Simon Kwong

Power Politics

Page 135 clockwise from top left

U.S. President George W. Bush speaks from a podium while campaigning in Columbia, Missouri. 7 September 2004, Columbia, United States. Larry Downing

Russian President Vladimir Putin leaves Berlin's Tegel airport on a visit to Germany for talks with German Chancellor Gerhard Schröder. 9 February 2003, Berlin, Germany. Alexandra Winkler

People wave a European Union flag during a parade to celebrate European unity and support Ukraine's EU ambitions ahead of a Council of Europe Heads of State and Government Summit. 15 May 2005, Warsaw, Poland. Katarina Stoltz

Two Maasai women wait to cast their ballots at a polling station. 21 November 2005, Kiserian, Kenya. Radu Sigheti

War and Conflict

Page 177 clockwise from top left

An Iraqi policeman points his gun towards a suspected kidnapper just arrested in Baghdad. 26 February 2005, Iraq. Ali Jasim

A young guerrilla soldier from Sudan's western Darfur region smokes a cigarette as he stands guard during the rebel Sudan Liberation Army unity conference. 29 October 2005, Haskanita, Sudan. Opheera McDoom

Emanuel (left), an opponent of Israel's disengagement from Gaza, embraces a policeman after the authorities overcame the last bastions of resistance to withdrawal from the Jewish settlement of Kfar Darom in Gush Katif settlement bloc. 18 August 2005, Kfar Darom, Gaza Strip. Nir Elias

Policemen fire at alleged snipers in a plaza in Caracas as military officers opposed to leftist President Hugo Chávez stage a protest. 6 December 2002, Caracas, Venezuela. Daniel Aguilar

The Global Economy

Page 233 clockwise from top left

A man looks at a stock quotation board showing the Nikkei share average. 21 December 2005, Tokyo, Japan. Toru Hanai

Chairman of the Federal Reserve Alan Greenspan listens to a question while testifying before the U.S. House Financial Services Committee on Capitol Hill. 17 February 2005, Washington, DC, United States. Larry Downing

A gauge on a Ukrainian main gas pipeline in the village of Boyarka near the capital Kiev. 1 January 2006, Boyarka, Ukraine. Gleb Garanich

New York pedestrians reflected in the NASDAQ building window in Times Square. 30November 2002, New York, United States. Shannon Stapleton

Culture in the Digital Age

Page 257 clockwise from top left

A beagle (right) wears an Isaac Mizrahi Signature Trench Coat on the runway at Target's 'Doggie Show' during presentations of Fall 2005 collections. 11 February 2005, New York, United States. Peter Morgan

A model wears designs by Spanish-born designer Rafael Lopez at his Autumn/Winter 2003 women's range show at London Fashion Week. 19 February 2003, London, United Kingdom. Toby Melville

A performer reads a newspaper on the back of a mud sculpture of a hippopotamus, an installation by Puerto Rico-based artists Jennifer Allora and Guillermo Calzadilla at the Venice arts Biennale. 8 June 2005, Venice, Italy. Chris Helgren

U.S. director Michael Moore is awarded the Palme d'Or at the 57th Cannes Film Festival for his documentary film *Fahrenheit 9/11* as South African actress Charlize Theron applauds. 22 May 2004, Cannes, France. John Schults

Ways of Living

Page 297 clockwise from top left

A worker at London's Chelsea Flower Show examines a grass plant during preparation for the annual show. 21 May 2004, London, United Kingdom. Peter Macdiarmid

A Mangalica long-haired pig is processed at a slaughterhouse in western Hungary. The pig was heading for extinction in the 1990s until it was rediscovered by Spanish Serrano ham producers. 25 September 2004, Szombathely, Hungary. Laszlo Balogh

A Chinese migrant worker, ticket in his mouth, waits to board a train in Nanjing. 23 January 2006, Jiangsu Province, China.

A Scots smoker eyes his whisky glass hours ahead of a budget in which Britain's Chancellor of the Exchequer Gordon Brown raised, as expected, duty on cigarettes and alcohol. 21 March 2000, Glasgow, United Kingdom. Jeff J. Mitchell

Looking Forward, Looking Back

Page 335 clockwise from top left

A visitor to the Salvador Allende museum in Santiago walks past photos of prisoners who disappeared under the government of dictator General Augusto Pinochet. 10 September 2003, Santiago, Chile. Carlos Barria

German Chancellor Gerhard Schröder stands in front of a picture showing a street in the former Nazi concentration camp of Auschwitz as he gave an address during a ceremony to commemorate the 60th anniversary of the camp's liberation. 25 January 2005, Berlin, Germany. Arnd Wiegmann

Members of the Argentine human rights group Mothers of Plaza de Mayo stage a protest walk on the day that former Chilean leader General Augusto Pinochet flew back to Chile after Britain decided not to proceed with an extradition case on the basis of medical reports that declared him unfit to stand trial. The sign reads, 'We repudiate the freeing of genocidal Pinochet'. 2 March 2000, Buenos Aires, Argentina. Enrique Marcarian

Iranians struggle to get closer during supreme leader Ayatollah Ali Khamenei's address. Hundreds of thousands gathered at the mausoleum of late leader Ayatollah Ruhollah Khomeini to mark the 16th anniversary of his death. 4 June 2005, Tehran, Iran. Damir Sagolj

Acknowledgments

Picture Editor

Ayperi Karabuda Ecer started at Sipa in 1984 as International Editor, later becoming Bureau Chief in New York. In 1991 Ayperi joined Magnum in Paris as Editor-in-Chief. She has taught three times at the annual Joop Swart Masterclass at World Press Photo, sharing her experience of the editorial photographic world. Ayperi joined Reuters in 2002 as Director of Development of Photography, based in Paris. She is of Swedish–Turkish nationality.

World Timeline of the Twenty-First Century

David Cutler is Senior Researcher at Reuters London Editorial Reference Unit. Born in Glasgow, he qualified in Information Science and started his career at London's Imperial War Museum. In 1980, he joined the BBC as a researcher offering back-up to programme makers and joined Reuters eight years later. The Reference unit provides research and information for journalists and bureaux around the world.

Alison Williams is a senior sub editor on Reuters' World Desk in London and works editing political and general news copy from the Middle East, Africa and Europe. Williams joined Reuters in 2001, having worked in British regional newspapers since 1995.

Additional thanks to Vincent Baby, Paul Barker, Catherine Benson, Valerie Bezzina, Vicki Bradin, Claire Chapman, Spiritas Cho, Leslie D'Souza, Maya Ecer, Nelson Graves, Angela Kearney, Sean Maguire, Peter Millership, Simon Newman, Gary Regenstrief, Musa Sadulayev (AP), Victoria Simpson, Alexia Singh, Akio Suga, Thomas Szlukovenyi, Aldrina Thirunagaran, Sara Veness, Heather Vickers, Stephen Weeks, Dennis Yeo, Kimitsu Yogachi, Deborah Zabarenko and Aisha Zia

Contributing Photographers

This book features images by 227 Reuters photographers of almost 70 different nationalities on rotating locations around the world. The country that follows each name represents the photographer's nationality.

Abed Omar Qusini, Palestinian Territories
Adeel Halim, India
Adnan Abidi, India
Adrees Latif, United States
Ahmed Jadallah, Palestinian Territories
Ajay Verma, India
Aladin Abdel Naby, Egypt
Albeiro Lopera, Colombia
Albert Gea, Spain
Alessandro Bianchi, Italy
Alessia Pierdomenico, Italy
Alexander Demianchuk, Ukraine
Alexander Vlachos, Greece
Alexandra Winkler, Germany
Alfred Cheng Jin, China
Ali Jarekji, Syria
Ali Jasim, Iraq
Altaf Hussain, India
Aly Song, China
Amit Dave, India
Amit Gupta, India
Ammar Awad, Israel
Andrea Comas, Spain
Andrew Wong, Britain
Andy Clark, Canada
Anton Meres, Spain
Anuruddha Lokuhapuarachchi, Sri Lanka
Anwar Mirza, Pakistan
Arko Datta, India
Arnd Wiegmann, Germany
Asim Tanveer, Pakistan
Atef Hassan, Iraq
Athar Hussain, Pakistan
Bazuki Muhammad, Malaysia
Bob Strong, United States
Bobby Yip, Japan
Bogdan Cristel, Romania
Brad Rickerby, United States
Brian Snyder, United States
Caren Firouz, Iran
Carlos Barria, Argentina
Carlos Duarte, Guatemala
Catherine Benson, Britain
Chaiwat Subprasom, Thailand
Charles Platiau, France
Chip East, United States
Chris Helgren, Canada
Chris Pizzello, United States
Chris Watt, Britain
Claro Cortes IV, Philippines
Claudia Daut, Germany
Dadang Tri, Indonesia
Damir Sagolj, Bosnia
Dan Chung, Britain
Daniel Aguilar, Mexico
Daniel Morel, United States
Daniele La Monaca, Italy
Danilo Krstanovic, Bosnia
Danish Ismail, India
Darrin Zammit Lupi, Malta
David Gray, Australia
David Mercado, Bolivia
Davor Kovacevic, Croatia
Denis Balibouse, Switzerland
Desmond Boylan, Ireland
Dylan Martinez, Britain
Eduard Kornienko, Russia
Eduardo Munoz, Colombia
Enrique Marcarian, Argentina
Eric Gaillard, France
Eriko Sugita, Japan
Evelyn Hockstein, Israel
Faisal Mahmood, Pakistan
Faleh Kheiber, Iraq
Fatih Saribas, Turkey
Finbarr O'Reilly, Canada
Franck Prevel, France
Francois Lenoir, Belgium
Fred Prouser, United States
Gadi Kabalo, Israel
Gary Hershorn, Canada
George Mulala, Kenya
Gil Cohen Magen, Israel
Gleb Garanich, Russia
Goran Sivacki, Serbia
Goran Tomasevic, Serbia
Grigory Dukor, Russia
Guang Niu, China
Guillermo Granja, Ecuador
Hazir Reka, Kosovo
Howard Burditt, Zimbabwe
Ian Waldie, Australia
Ilia Naymushin, Russia
Issei Kato, Japan
Ivan Alvarado, Colombia
James Akena, Uganda
Jason Cohn, United States
Jason Lee, China
Jason Reed, Australia
Jay Cheng, Taiwan
Jean-Paul Pelissier, France
Jean-Philippe Arles, France
Jeff Christensen, United States
Jeff J. Mitchell, Britain
Jerry Lampen, Netherlands
Jessica Rinaldi, United States
Jim Bourg, United States
Jim Young, Canada
Joe Skipper, United States
John Ruwitch, United States
John Schults, United States
Jonathan Bainbridge, Britain
Jonathan Ernst, United States
Jorge Silva, Mexico
Juan Carlos Ulate, Costa Rica
Juan Medina, Argentina
Kai Pfaffenbach, Germany
Kareem Raheem, Iraq
Katarina Stoltz, Sweden
Keith Bedford, United States
Kevin Coombs, Britain
Kevin Lamarque, United States
Kieran Doherty, Britain
Kim Kyung-Hoon, South Korea
Kimberly White, United States
Kimimasa Mayama, Japan
Larry Downing, United States
Laszlo Balogh, Hungary
Luc Gnago, Ivory Coast
Lucas Jackson, United States
Lucy Nicholson, Britain
Luis Galdamez, El Salvador
Marc Serota, United States
Marcelo del Pozo, Spain
Marcos Brindicci, Argentina
Mario Anzuoni, Italy
Marko Djurica, Serbia
Matko Biljak, Croatia
Max Rossi, Italy
Mian Khursheed, Pakistan
Michael Dalder, Germany
Michael Leckel, Austria
Michaela Rehle, Germany
Miguel Vidal, Spain
Mihai Barbu, Romania
Mike Blake, Canada
Mike Hutchings, Britain
Milos Cvetkovic, Serbia
Ming Ming, China
Mohamed Azakir, Lebanon
Mohammed Salem, Palestinian Territories
Mohsin Raza, Pakistan
Molly Riley, United States
Morteza Nikoubazl, Iran
Nacho Doce, Spain
Namir Noor-Eldeen, Iraq
Natalie Behring, United States
Nayef Hashlamoun, Palestinian Territories
Nir Elias, Israel
Ognen Teofilovski, Macedonia
Opheera McDoom, Britain, Guyana
Paolo Cocco, Italy
Parth Sanyal, India
Pascal Lauener, Switzerland
Pascal Rossignol, France
Paul Mcerlane, Ireland
Paul Vreeker, Netherlands
Paul Yeung, Hong Kong, China
Pawel Kopczynski, Poland
Peter Andrews, Poland
Peter Macdiarmid, Britain
Peter Maenhoudt, Belgium
Peter Morgan, United States
Philip Massie, South Africa
Philippe Laurenson, France
Philippe Wojazer, France
Pierre Holtz, France
Radu Sigheti, Romania
Rafael Marchante, Spain
Rafiqur Rahman, Bangladesh
Raheb Homavandi, Iran
Ray Stubblebine, United States
Reinhard Krause, Germany
Rick Wilking, United States
Robert Galbraith, United States
Romeo Ranoco, Philippines
Russell Boyce, Britain
Sean Adair, United States
Sergei Karpukhin, Russia
Shamil Zhumatov, Kazakhstan
Shannon Stapleton, United States
Shaun Best, Canada
Simon Kwong, Taiwan
Stefano Rellandini, Italy
Stephanie Mcgehee, United States
Stephen Hird, Britain
Stoyan Nenov, Bulgaria
Sukree Sukplang, Thailand
Supri, Indonesia
Susana Vera, Spain
Tarmizy Harva, Indonesia
Thierry Roge, Belgium
Thomas White, Britain
Tim Wimborne, Australia
Toby Melville, Britain
Tony Gentile, Italy
Toru Hanai, Japan
Toshiyuki Aizawa, Japan
Umit Bektas, Turkey
Vasily Fedosenko, Belarus
Victor Fraile, Spain
Viktor Korotayev, Russia
Vincent Kessler, France
Vincent West, Britain
Vladimir Pirogov, Kyrgyzstan
Will Burgess, Australia
Win Mcnamee, United States
Yang Xi, China
Yannis Behrakis, Greece
Yiorgos Karahalis, Greece
You Sung-Ho, South Korea
Yuriko Nakao, Japan
Yves Herman, Belgium
Zahid Hussein, Pakistan
Zainal Abd Halim, Malaysia
Zohra Bensemra, Algeria

Index